ENCYCLOPEDIA OF
ASSOCIATIONS®

AN ASSOCIATIONS UNLIMITED REFERENCE

ISSN 0071-0202

ENCYCLOPEDIA OF
ASSOCIATIONS®

AN ASSOCIATIONS UNLIMITED REFERENCE

A Guide to More Than 25,000 National and International Organizations, Including: Trade, Business, and Commercial; Environmental and Agricultural; Legal, Governmental, Public Administration, and Military; Engineering, Technological, and Natural and Social Sciences; Educational; Cultural; Social Welfare; Health and Medical; Public Affairs; Fraternal, Nationality, and Ethnic; Religious; Veterans', Hereditary, and Patriotic; Hobby and Avocational; Athletic and Sports; Labor Unions, Associations, and Federations; Chambers of Commerce and Trade and Tourism; Greek Letter and Related Organizations; Fan Clubs.

50th
EDITION

VOLUME 3
SUPPLEMENT

An Inter-Edition Issue Reporting New Associations and Projects and Important Changes for Groups Listed in Volume 1, National Organizations of the U.S.

Tara E. Atterberry, Project Editor

GALE
CENGAGE Learning™

Detroit • New York • San Francisco • New Haven, Conn • Waterville, Maine • London

Encyclopedia of Associations, 50th Edition,
Volume 3: Supplement

Product Management: Michele LaMeau

Project Editor: Tara E. Atterberry

Composition and Electronic Capture: Gary
Oudersluys

Manufacturing: Rita Wimberley

For product information and technology assistance, contact us at
Gale Customer Support, 1-800-877-4253.
For permission to use material from this text or product,
submit all requests online at **www.cengage.com/permissions.**
Further permissions questions can be emailed to
permissionrequest@cengage.com

Gale
27500 Drake Rd.
Farmington Hills, MI 48331-3535

ISBN-13: 978-1-4144-4662-2
ISBN-10: 1-4144-4662-4

ISSN 0071-0202

Printed in the United States of America
1 2 3 4 5   15 14 13 12 11

FD285

Contents

The *Supplement,* Volume 3, is published between editions of the *Encyclopedia of Associations: National (EA)* and lists new or newly discovered associations, as well as important new changes to current *EA* listings.

Hundreds of New Listings and Thousands of Important Changes

Each year, hundreds of new associations form and others undergo changes that directly affect the user's ability to contact them. The *Supplement* provides information on 500 new and 3000 existing associations in one convenient volume. Importantly, half of all updated entries were for sections identified as "priority" by *EA* customers.

Preparation of the *Supplement*

Information for new and updated entries was compiled or confirmed through written correspondence, through the association's recently updated web site, by telephone or through e-mail.

Content and Arrangement of the *Supplement*

New and updated entries are interfiled within the mainbody of the *Supplement* and are numbered sequentially. For additional information about the format of the new entries and details about the types of associations included, see the "User's Guide" in Volume 1 of the main edition of the *Encyclopedia of Associations.*

Updated entries consist of the complete heading information, with changes to one or more of the following:

- Organization name and/or status
- Address
- Telephone number
- Fax number
- Toll-free number
- E-mail address
- Executive officer or association contact
- Website

The new information is highlighted in boldface type for easy identification. Changes in the organization name or status are explained in a brief textual note. An example of an updated entry follows this introduction.

Available in Electronic Formats

Licensing. National Organizations of the U.S. is available for licensing. The complete database is provided in a fielded format and is deliverable on such media as disk or CD-ROM. For more information, contact Gale's Business Development Group at 1-800-877-GALE, or visit our web site at http://gale.cengage.com/bizdev.

Online. The complete *Encyclopedia of Associations (EA)* series (including associations listed in the international and regional, state and local editions) is also accessible as File 114 through Dialog and as File ENASSC through LexisNexis. For more information, contact Dialog, 2250 Perimeter Park Dr., Ste. 300, Morrisville, NC 27560; phone: (919) 804-6400; toll-free: 1-800-3-DIALOG; or LexisNexis, PO Box 933, Dayton, OH 45401-0933; phone: (937) 865-6800; toll-free: 800-227-9597.

The Directory is also available online as part of the Gale Directory Library. For more information, call 1-800-877-GALE.

Associations Unlimited. Associations Unlimited is a modular approach to the *Encyclopedia of Associations* database, allowing customers to select the pieces of the series that they want to purchase. The four modules include each of the *EA* series (national, international, and regional) as well as one module featuring U.S. government data on more than 450,000 nonprofit organizations.

Associations Unlimited is available on a subscription basis through InfoTrac, Gale's online information resource that features an easy-to-use end-user interface, powerful search capabilities, and ease of access through the World-Wide Web. For more information, call 800-877-GALE.

Acknowledgments

The editors are grateful to the large number of organization officials in the United States and abroad who generously responded to our requests for updated information, provided additional data by telephone, fax, or email and helped in the shaping of this edition with their comments and suggestions throughout the year.

Special thanks go to Jeannine M. James for her research contributions. Appreciation is also extended to the American Society of Association Executives for its ongoing support.

Comments and Suggestions Welcome

Matters pertaining to specific listings in *EA,* as well as suggestions for new listings, should be directed to Tara Atterberry, Editor, *Encyclopedia of Associations.*

Please write or call:

Encyclopedia of Associations
Gale
27500 Drake Rd.
Farmington Hills, MI 48331-3535

Phone: (248) 699-4253
Toll-free: 800-347-GALE
Fax: (248) 699-8075

Descriptive Listings

Entries in *EA* are arranged into 18 subject sections, as outlined on the Contents page. Within each section, organizations are arranged in alphabetical order according to the assigned principal subject keyword that appears as a subhead above the organization names. An alphabetical list of keywords used throughout *EA* follows the "Abbreviations" list. Within each keyword, entries are listed alphabetically by organization name.

Access to entries is facilitated by the alphabetical *Name and Keyword Index.* An explanation of this index follows the discussion of the sample entry.

Sample Entry

The number preceding each portion of the sample entry designates an item of information that might be included in an entry. Each numbered item in the sample entry is explained in the "Description of Numbered Elements" that follows the sample.

▌1▐ **Storytelling**

▌2▐ 3348 ▪ ▌3▐ Association of Eclectic Storytellers ▌4▐ (AES) ▌5▐ (6325)
▌6▐ 123 Amanda Ave.
PO Box 1992
Eldridge, NY 13201
▌7▐ Ph: (315)555-9500
▌8▐ Free: (800)555-2000
Fax: (315)555-9505
Telex: 123456
▌9▐ E-mail: harmersway@aes.org
▌10▐ Website: http://www.aes.org
▌11▐ Contact: Grant Smith, Pres.

Description of Numbered Elements

▌1▐ **Keyword.** In each of the sections, keywords are given as subheadings and listed alphabetically. Organizations are listed in alphabetical order under their principal keyword subheading. Since the listings are arranged by keyword, the user will find organizations having similar interests grouped together within each keyword subheading.

▌2▐ **Entry Number.** Entries are numbered sequentially and the entry number (rather than the page number) is used in the Name and Keyword Index to refer to the organization. To facilitate location of the entries in the text, the first entry number on each left-hand page and the last entry number on each right-hand page are provided at the top outer corners of the pages.

▌3▐ **Organization Name.** The formal name is given; "The" and "Inc." are omitted in most listings, unless they are an integral part of the acronym used by the association.

▌4▐ **Acronym.** Indicates the short form or abbreviation of the organization's name, usually composed of the initial letter or syllable of each word in it.

▌5▐ **Former Entry Number.** This is the entry number for the association in Volume 1 in the previous edition of the *Encyclopedia of Associations.* Use this number when consulting Volume 1 for additional descriptive information about an entry.

▌6▐ **Address.** The address is generally that of the permanent national headquarters, or of the chief official for groups that have no permanent office.

▌7▐ **Telephone Numbers.** These are listed when furnished by the organization.

▌8▐ **Toll-free, Fax, and Telex.** These are listed when furnished by the organization.

▌9▐ **E-mail.** This is listed when furnished by the organization.

▌10▐ **Website.** The primary internet web address for the organization or contact person listed.

▌11▐ **Chief Official and Title.** The name of a full-time executive, an elected officer, or other contact person designated by the association is provided.

Name and Keyword Index

The alphabetical Name and Keyword index provides quick access to the numbered listings in this *Supplement.* Please note that each reference refers to the entry number, rather than the page on which the entry is listed. Also, a star ★ before an entry number in the index signifies that the reference is not listed separately, but is mentioned within the text of another entry. Alphabetization rules ignore articles, prepositions, and conjunctions.

All associations listed in the *Supplement* are referenced in the index by:

- Complete name

- Principal keywords (see list following this User's Guide)

- Other important words in the organization name

- Former and alternate names (denoted with a star)

A collection of references in the Name & Keyword index would appear in this way:

❚1❚ Amer. Soc. of Earth Sciences **[6359]**, 123 Salina St., Syracuse, NY 13201 (315)222-950
❚2❚ Earth Sciences, Amer. Soc. of **[6359]**
❚3❚ Earth Sciences Soc., USA **[★6359]**
❚4❚ Geology
  Amer. Soc. of Earth Sciences **[6359]**

Description of Numbered Index References

❚1❚ Each association's primary reference includes the mailing address and telephone number of the group.

❚2❚ Associations are alphabetized by important words in the name. These references aid in locating organizations whose correct name is unknown to the user.

❚3❚ Any reference with a ★ preceding the entry number indicates that the organization is not listed separately, but is mentioned within the description of another entry. These references would include the organization's former or alternate name as well as names of important committees, projects, or programs.

❚4❚ Associations appear alphabetically by primary (see keyword list in this volume) and added keywords. These references allow the user to access all organizations within a particular field of interest.

Geographic Abbreviations

United States and U.S. Territories

AK	Alaska
AL	Alabama
AR	Arkansas
AZ	Arizona
CA	California
CO	Colorado
CT	Connecticut
DC	District of Columbia
DE	Delaware
FL	Florida
GA	Georgia
GU	Guam
HI	Hawaii
IA	Iowa
ID	Idaho
IL	Illinois
IN	Indiana
KS	Kansas
KY	Kentucky
LA	Louisiana
MA	Massachusetts
MD	Maryland
ME	Maine
MI	Michigan
MN	Minnesota
MO	Missouri
MS	Mississippi
MT	Montana
NC	North Carolina
ND	North Dakota
NE	Nebraska
NH	New Hampshire
NJ	New Jersey
NM	New Mexico
NV	Nevada
NY	New York
OH	Ohio
OK	Oklahoma
OR	Oregon
PA	Pennsylvania
PR	Puerto Rico
RI	Rhode Island
SC	South Carolina
SD	South Dakota
TN	Tennessee
TX	Texas
UT	Utah
VA	Virginia
VI	Virgin Islands
VT	Vermont
WA	Washington
WI	Wisconsin
WV	West Virginia
WY	Wyoming

Table of Abbreviations Used in Addresses and the Index

Acad	Academy
AFB	Air Force Base
Amer	American
APO	Army Post Office
Apt	Apartment
Assn	Association
Ave	Avenue
Bd	Board
Bldg	Building
Blvd	Boulevard
Br	Branch
Bur	Bureau
c/o	Care of
Co	Company
Coll	College
Comm	Committee
Commn	Commission
Conf	Conference
Confed	Confederation
Cong	Congress
Corp	Corporation
Coun	Council
Ct	Court
Dept	Department
Div	Division
Dr	Drive
E	East
Expy	Expressway
Fed	Federation
Fl	Floor
Found	Foundation
FPO	Fleet Post Office
Ft	Fort
Fwy	Freeway
Govt	Government
GPO	General Post Office
Hwy	Highway
Inc	Incorporated
Inst	Institute
Intl	International
Ln	Lane
Ltd	Limited
Mfrs	Manufacturers
Mgt	Management
Mt	Mount
N	North
Natl	National
NE	Northeast
No	Number
NW	Northwest
Pkwy	Parkway
Pl	Place
PO	Post Office
Prof	Professor
Rd	Road
RD	Rural Delivery
RFD	Rural Free Delivery
Rm	Room
RR	Rural Route
Rte	Route
S	South
SE	Southeast
Sect	Section
Soc	Society

Sq	Square	Subcommn	Subcommission	UN	United Nations
St	Saint, Street	SW	Southwest	Univ	University
Sta	Station	Terr	Terrace, Territory	U.S.	United States
Ste	Sainte, Suite	Tpke	Turnpike	U.S.A.	United States of America
Subcomm	Subcommittee	T.V.	Television	W	West

Keyword List

Following is a list of keywords used in EA. The section(s) in which each keyword appears are listed after each keyword. Within each keyword, entries are arranged alphabetically by organization name.

Accountants

1 ■ American Society of Women Accountants (ASWA) (10)
1760 Old Meadow Rd., Ste.500
McLean, VA 22102
Ph: (703)506-3265
Free: (800)326-2163
Fax: (703)506-3266
E-mail: aswa@aswa.org
URL: http://www.aswa.org
Contact: **Lee K. Lowery, Exec. Dir.**

2 ■ American Woman's Society of Certified Public Accountants (AWSCPA) (11)
136 S Keowee St.
Dayton, OH 45402
Ph: (937)222-1872
Free: (800)297-2721
Fax: (937)222-5794
E-mail: info@awscpa.org
URL: http://www.awscpa.org
Contact: **Wendy S. Lewis, Pres.**

3 ■ Association of Chartered Accountants in the United States (ACAUS) (14)
1050 Winter St., Ste.1000
Waltham, MA 02451
Ph: (508)395-0224
E-mail: admin@acaus.org
URL: http://www.acaus.org
Contact: **Lindi Jarvis, Pres.**

4 ■ Association of Insolvency and Restructuring Advisors (AIRA) (14)
221 Stewart Ave., Ste.207
Medford, OR 97501
Ph: (541)858-1665
Fax: (541)858-9187
E-mail: **aira@aira.org**
URL: http://www.airacira.org
Contact: Grant W. Newton CIRA, Exec. Dir.

5 ■ DFK International/USA (DFK/USA)
1025 Thomas Jefferson St. NW, Ste.500 E
Washington, DC 20007
Ph: (202)452-8100
Fax: (202)833-3636
E-mail: exec@dfkusa.com
URL: http://www.dfkusa.com
Contact: Jay Hauck, Exec. Dir.

6 ■ Institute of Internal Auditors (IIA) (35)
247 Maitland Ave.
Altamonte Springs, FL 32701-4907
Ph: (407)937-1100
Fax: (407)937-1101
E-mail: custserv@theiia.org
URL: http://www.theiia.org
Contact: **Gunther Meggeneder CIA, Chm.**

7 ■ International Federation of Accountants (IFAC) (36)
545 5th Ave., 14th Fl.
New York, NY 10017
Ph: (212)286-9344
Fax: (212)286-9570
E-mail: **communications@ifac.org**
URL: http://www.ifac.org
Contact: **Goran Tidstrom, Pres.**

8 ■ International Society of Filipinos in Finance and Accounting (ISFFA)
801 S Grand Ave., Ste.400
Los Angeles, CA 90017
Free: (800)375-2689
E-mail: **csoneil@gmail.com**
URL: http://www.isyfa.org
Contact: Carmelita O'Neil, Pres./Exec. Dir.
Status Note: Formerly International Society of Young Filipino Accountants.

9 ■ National Society of Accountants for Cooperatives (NSAC) (48)
136 S Keowee St.
Dayton, OH 45402
Ph: (937)222-6707
Fax: (937)222-5794
E-mail: info@nsacoop.org
URL: http://www.nsacoop.org
Contact: **Russell D. Watson, Pres.**

10 ■ Professional Association of Small Business Accountants (PASBA)
6405 Metcalf Ave., Ste.503
Shawnee Mission, KS 66202
Free: (866)296-0001
Fax: (913)432-1812
E-mail: director@pasba.org
URL: **http://www.smallbizaccountants.com**
Contact: **Jen Trabon, Exec. Dir.**

11 ■ Society of Depreciation Professionals (SDP) (60)
347 5th Ave., Ste.703
New York, NY 10016
Ph: (646)417-6378
E-mail: **admin@depr.org**
URL: http://www.depr.org
Contact: **Rob Pierce CDP, Pres.**

Administrative Services

12 ■ Association for Financial Technology (AFT) (68)
34 N High St.
New Albany, OH 43054
Ph: (614)895-1208
Fax: (614)895-3466
E-mail: aft@aftweb.com
URL: http://www.aftweb.com
Contact: James R. Bannister, Exec. Dir.

13 ■ Association of Healthcare Administrative Professionals (AHCAP) (69)
455 S 4th St., Ste.650
Louisville, KY 40202
Ph: (502)574-9040 (502)574-9029
Free: (888)320-0808
Fax: (502)589-3602
E-mail: ahcap@hqtrs.com
URL: http://www.ahcap.org
Contact: **Monica Harper, Exec. Dir.**

14 ■ Black Data Processing Associates (BDPA) (70)
9500 Arena Dr., Ste.350
Largo, MD 20774
Ph: **(301)584-3135**
Free: (800)727-BDPA
Fax: **(301)560-8300**
E-mail: **office@bdpa.org**
URL: http://www.bdpa.org
Contact: **Yvette Graham, Natl. Pres.**

15 ■ International Virtual Assistants Association (IVAA) (75)
375 N Stephanie St., Ste.1411
Henderson, NV 89014
Ph: **(702)583-4970**
Free: (888)259-2487
E-mail: president@ivaa.org
URL: http://www.ivaa.org
Contact: **Doreen DeJesus, Pres.**

16 ■ Office Business Center Association International (OBCAI) (74)
2030 Main St., Ste.1300
Irvine, CA 92614
Ph: (949)260-9023
Free: (800)237-4741
Fax: (949)260-9021
E-mail: **rmeyers@obcal.org**
URL: **http://www.obcai.com**
Contact: Richard Meyers, Exec. Dir.

17 ■ Society of Corporate Secretaries and Governance Professionals (73)
521 5th Ave.
New York, NY 10175
Ph: (212)681-2000
Fax: (212)681-2005
E-mail: research@governanceprofessionals.org
URL: http://www.governanceprofessionals.org
Contact: **Kenneth A. Bertsch, Pres./CEO**

Advertising

18 ■ Advertising Club of New York (ACNY) (62)
235 Park Ave. S, 6th Fl.
New York, NY 10003-1450
Ph: (212)533-8080
Fax: (212)533-1929

E-mail: gina@theadvertisingclub.org
URL: http://www.theadvertisingclub.org
Contact: **Gina Grillo, Pres./CEO**

19 ■ Antique Advertising Association of America (AAAA)
13915 David Rd.
Woodstock, IL 60098
E-mail: twgeneral@comcast.net
URL: http://www.pastimes.org
Contact: Margaret Szlachta, Contact

20 ■ Mobile Marketing Association (MMA)
(110)
8 W 38th St., Ste.200
New York, NY 10018
Ph: **(646)257-4515**
E-mail: mma@mmaglobal.com
URL: http://mmaglobal.com
Contact: **Greg Stuart Stuart, CEO**

21 ■ National Agri-Marketing Association (NAMA) (2565)
11020 King St., Ste.205
Overland Park, KS 66210
Ph: (913)491-6500
Fax: (913)491-6502
E-mail: agrimktg@nama.org
URL: http://www.nama.org
Contact: **Jenny Pickett, Exec. VP/CEO**

22 ■ Point-of-Purchase Advertising International (POPAI) (112)
1600 Duke St., Ste.610
Alexandria, VA 22314
Ph: (703)373-8800
Fax: (703)373-8801
URL: http://www.popai.com
Contact: **Mr. Chris Young, Chm.**

23 ■ Retail Advertising and Marketing Association (RAMA) (116)
325 7th St. NW, Ste.1100
Washington, DC 20004-2818
Ph: (202)661-3052
Fax: (202)737-2849
E-mail: **gattim@nrf.com**
URL: http://www.rama-nrf.org
Contact: **Mike Gatti, Exec. Dir.**

Advertising Auditors

24 ■ Publishers Information Bureau (PIB)
(126)
810 7th Ave., 24th Fl.
New York, NY 10019
Ph: (212)872-3700 **(212)872-3722**
E-mail: **pib@magazine.org**
URL: http://www.magazine.org
Contact: Wayne Eadie, Pres.

Aerospace

25 ■ Air Transport Association of America (ATA) (120)
1301 Pennsylvania Ave. NW, Ste.1100
Washington, DC 20004-7017
Ph: (202)626-4000
E-mail: ata@airlines.org
URL: http://www.airlines.org
Contact: **Nicholas E. Calio, Pres./CEO**

26 ■ Aviation Distributors and Manufacturers Association (ADMA) (139)
100 N 20th St., 4th Fl.
Philadelphia, PA 19103-1443
Ph: (215)564-3484
Fax: **(215)564-2175**
E-mail: **mtaft@fernley.com**
URL: http://www.adma.org
Contact: Meg Taft, Exec. Dir.

27 ■ Aviation Industry CBT Committee (AICC) (141)
PO Box 4067
Federal Way, WA 98063
Ph: (253)218-1408
Fax: (253)218-1408
E-mail: **chairman@aicc.org**
URL: http://www.aicc.org
Contact: **Herbert Schwarz, Chm.**

28 ■ Flight Safety Foundation (FSF) (147)
801 N Fairfax St., Ste.400
Alexandria, VA 22314
Ph: (703)739-6700
Fax: (703)739-6708
E-mail: **wahdan@flightsafety.org**
URL: http://flightsafety.org
Contact: **William R. Voss, Pres./CEO**

29 ■ Helicopter Foundation International (HFI) (148)
1635 Prince St.
Alexandria, VA 22314-2818
Ph: (703)683-4646 (703)360-1521
Fax: (703)341-6454
URL: http://www.helicopterfoundation.org
Contact: **Edward F. Dicampli, Corporate Sec.**

30 ■ International Association of Space Entrepreneurs (IASE)
16 First Ave.
Nyack, NY 10960
E-mail: **gsohnlein@spaceentrepreneurs.org**
URL: **http://spaceentrepreneurs.ning.com**
Contact: Guillermo Sohnlein, Founder/Chm.

31 ■ International Society of Transport Aircraft Trading (ISTAT) (154)
401 N Michigan Ave., Ste.2200
Chicago, IL 60611
Ph: (312)321-5169
Fax: (312)673-6579
E-mail: **istat@istat.org**
URL: http://www.istat.org
Contact: **Joe Ozimek, Pres.**

32 ■ National Aeronautic Association (NAA)
(155)
1 Reagan Natl. Airport
Hangar 7, Ste.202
Washington, DC 20001-6015
Ph: (703)416-4888
Fax: (703)416-4877
E-mail: **jgaffney@naa.aero**
URL: http://www.naa.aero
Contact: Jonathan Gaffney, Pres.

33 ■ National Aircraft Resale Association (NARA) (188)
PO Box 3860
Grapevine, TX 76099
Ph: **(402)475-2611**
Free: **(866)284-4744**
Fax: **(866)447-1777**
E-mail: **dsurpless@nara-dealers.com**
URL: http://www.nara-dealers.com
Contact: **Steve Gade, Chair**

34 ■ Organization of Black Airline Pilots (OBAP) (161)
1 Westbrook Corporate Center
Westchester, IL 60154
Ph: (703)753-2047
Free: (800)JET-OBAP
Fax: (703)753-1251
E-mail: nationaloffice@obap.org
URL: http://www.obap.org
Contact: **Cheryl Chew, Exec. Dir.**

35 ■ Pilatus Owners and Pilots Association (POPA)
6890 E Sunrise Dr., Ste.120-114
Tucson, AZ 85702
Ph: (520)299-7485
Free: (877)745-1694

Fax: (520)844-6161
E-mail: popapc12@aol.com
URL: http://www.pilatusowners.com
Contact: Bob MacLean, Pres.

36 ■ Professional Aviation Maintenance Association (PAMA) (164)
400 N Washington St., Ste.300
Alexandria, VA 22314
Ph: (703)778-4647
Fax: (703)683-5480
E-mail: hq@pama.org
URL: http://www.pama.org
Contact: **Clark Gordon, Chm.**

37 ■ Regional Airline Association (RAA) (166)
2025 M St. NW, Ste.800
Washington, DC 20036-3309
Ph: (202)367-1170
Fax: (202)367-2170
E-mail: raa@raa.org
URL: http://www.raa.org
Contact: **Jim Rankin, Chm.**

38 ■ United States Pilots Association (USPA)
(168)
1652 Indian Point Rd.
Branson, MO 65616
Ph: **(417)338-2225**
E-mail: jan@uspilots.org
URL: http://www.uspilots.org
Contact: Jan Hoynacki, Exec. Dir.

Agents

39 ■ North American Performing Arts Managers and Agents (NAPAMA) (175)
459 Columbus Ave., No. 133
New York, NY 10024
Ph: (718)797-4577
Fax: (718)797-4576
E-mail: conal@napama.org
URL: http://www.napama.org
Contact: **Robert Baird, Pres.**

Agricultural Equipment

40 ■ Farm Equipment Manufacturers Association (FEMA) (179)
1000 Executive Pkwy., Ste.100
St. Louis, MO 63141-6369
Ph: (314)878-2304
Fax: **(314)732-1480**
E-mail: vernon@farmequip.org
URL: http://www.farmequip.org
Contact: **John Malinowski, Pres.**

41 ■ North American Equipment Dealers Association (NAEDA) (185)
1195 Smizer Mill Rd.
Fenton, MO 63026-3480
Ph: (636)349-5000
Fax: (636)349-5443
E-mail: **naeda@naeda.com**
URL: http://www.naeda.com
Contact: Paul E. Kindinger, Pres./CEO

Alcoholic Beverages

42 ■ Fermenters International Trade Association (FITA) (200)
c/o Dee Roberson, Sec.-Treas.
PO Box 1373
Valrico, FL 33595
Ph: (813)685-4261
Fax: (813)681-5625
E-mail: droberson1@verizon.net
URL: http://www.fermentersinternational.org
Contact: **John Pastor, Pres.**

43 ■ United States Sommelier Association (USSA) (211)
1111 Lincoln Rd., Ste.400-9
Miami Beach, FL 33139
Ph: (954)437-0449
E-mail: info@ussommelier.com
URL: http://www.ussommelier.com
Contact: Rick Garced DVS, Pres./CEO

44 ■ Wine and Spirits Shippers Association (WSSA) (201)
11800 Sunrise Valley Dr., Ste.425
Reston, VA 20191
Ph: (703)860-2300
Free: (800)368-3167
E-mail: info@wssa.com
URL: http://www.wssa.com
Contact: Louis Healey, Pres.

Apparel

45 ■ Custom Tailors and Designers Association of America (CTDA) (231)
42732 Ridgeway Dr.
Broadlands, VA 20148
Free: (888)248-2832
Fax: (866)661-1240
E-mail: info@ctda.com
URL: http://www.ctda.com
Contact: **David Eisele, Pres.**

46 ■ World Shoe Association (WSA) (255)
15821 Ventura Blvd., Ste.415
Encino, CA 91436-2974
Ph: (818)379-9400
Fax: (818)379-9410
E-mail: **operations@wsashow.com**
URL: http://www.wsashow.com
Contact: **Elyse Kroll, Chair**

Appliances

47 ■ Appliance Parts Distributors Association (APDA) (246)
3621 N Oakley Ave.
Chicago, IL 60618
Ph: **(773)230-9851**
Fax: **(888)308-1423**
E-mail: ro@apda.com
URL: http://www.apda.com
Contact: Kirk Coburn, Pres.

48 ■ National Appliance Parts Suppliers Association (NAPSA) (260)
4015 W Marshall Ave.
Longview, TX 75604
E-mail: **board11@napsaweb.org**
URL: http://www.napsaweb.org
Contact: Jim Bossman, Pres.

Appraisers

49 ■ American Society of Agricultural Appraisers (ASAA)
PO Box 186
Twin Falls, ID 83303-0186
Ph: **(208)733-1122**
Free: (800)488-7570
Fax: (208)733-2326
E-mail: ag@amagappraisers.com
URL: http://www.amagappraisers.com
Contact: Jay Proost, Exec. Dir.

50 ■ Association of Appraiser Regulatory Officials (AARO)
13200 Strickland Rd., Ste.114-264
Raleigh, NC 27613
Ph: (919)235-4544 **(919)870-4854**
Fax: (919)870-5392

E-mail: **milneallen@charter.com**
URL: http://www.aaro.net
Contact: **Ami Milne-Allen, Pres.**

51 ■ Independent Automotive Damage Appraisers Association (IADA) (312)
PO Box 12291
Columbus, GA 31917-2291
Free: (800)369-4232
Fax: (888)IADA-NOW
E-mail: admin@iada.org
URL: http://www.iada.org
Contact: **Rob White, Pres.**

52 ■ International Society of Appraisers (ISA) (264)
303 W Madison St., Ste.2650
Chicago, IL 60606
Ph: (312)981-6778
Fax: **(312)265-2908**
E-mail: isa@isa-appraisers.org
URL: http://www.isa-appraisers.org
Contact: Judith M. Martin, Pres.

53 ■ National Association of Real Estate Appraisers (NAREA) (285)
PO Box 879
Palm Springs, CA 92263
Ph: (760)327-5284
Free: **(877)815-4172**
Fax: (760)327-5631
E-mail: support@assoc-hdqts.org
URL: http://www.narea-assoc.org
Contact: Dave Ehrnstein, Contact

Aquaculture

54 ■ International Professional Pond Contractors Association (IPPCA)
4045 N Arnold Mill Rd.
Woodstock, GA 30188
Ph: (770)592-9790
Free: (866)484-7722
Fax: (770)924-9589
E-mail: info@ippca.com
URL: http://www.ippca.com
Contact: **John Olson, Pres.**

Architecture

55 ■ Association of Licensed Architects (ALA) (286)
22159 N Pepper Rd., Ste.2N
Barrington, IL 60010
Ph: (847)382-0630
Fax: (847)382-8380
E-mail: **ala@alatoday.org**
URL: http://www.licensedarchitect.org
Contact: **Jeffrey Budgell, Pres.**

56 ■ Graham Foundation (290)
4 W Burton Pl.
Chicago, IL 60610-1416
Ph: (312)787-4071
E-mail: info@grahamfoundation.org
URL: http://www.grahamfoundation.org
Contact: **Linda Searl, Pres.**

Archives

57 ■ Academy of Certified Archivists (ACA) (275)
1450 Western Ave., Ste.101
Albany, NY 12203
Ph: **(518)694-8471**
Fax: (518)463-8656
E-mail: **mphdean@lib.siu.edu**
URL: http://www.certifiedarchivists.org
Contact: **Pam Hackbart-Dean CA, Pres.**

Art

58 ■ Association of Science Fiction and Fantasy Artists (ASFA) (291)
PO Box 65011
Phoenix, AZ 85082-5011
E-mail: secretary@asfa-art.org
URL: http://www.asfa-art.org
Contact: **Mitchell Bentley, Pres.**

59 ■ Fine Art Dealers Association (FADA)
PO Box D-1
Carmel, CA 93921
Ph: (310)455-6117
E-mail: **janeglassman@fada.com**
URL: http://www.fada.com
Contact: Ms. Betina Tasende, Pres.

60 ■ Private Art Dealers Association (PADA)
PO Box 872
Lenox Hill Sta.
New York, NY 10021
Ph: (212)572-0772
E-mail: pada99@msn.com
URL: http://www.pada.net
Contact: **Robert Simon, Pres.**

Associations

61 ■ Alliance for Nonprofit Management (296)
731 Market St., Ste.200
San Francisco, CA 94103
Ph: **(415)704-5058**
Fax: **(415)541-7708**
E-mail: info@allianceonline.org
URL: http://www.allianceonline.org
Contact: Jeanne Bell, Chair

62 ■ Association Media and Publishing (303)
1760 Old Meadow Rd., Ste.500
McLean, VA 22102
Ph: (703)506-3285
Fax: (703)506-3266
E-mail: **info@associationmediaandpublishing.org**
URL: **http://associationmediaandpublishing.org**
Contact: Amy E. Lestition, Exec. Dir.

63 ■ National Council of Nonprofits (NCN) (302)
1101 Vermont Ave. NW, Ste.1002
Washington, DC 20005
Ph: (202)962-0322
Free: (800)201-0779
Fax: (202)962-0321
E-mail: **tdelaney@councilofnonprofits.org**
URL: http://www.councilofnonprofits.org
Contact: Tim Delaney, Pres./CEO
Status Note: Formerly National Council of Nonprofit Associations.

Auctions

64 ■ Industrial Auctioneers Association (IAA)
3213 Ayr Ln.
Dresher, PA 19025
Ph: (215)366-5450
Free: (800)805-8359
Fax: (215)657-1964
E-mail: info@industrialauctioneers.org
URL: http://www.industrialauctioneers.org
Contact: **Terrance Jacobs, Pres.**

Audiovisual

65 ■ Association for Information Media and Equipment (AIME) (345)
PO Box 9844
Cedar Rapids, IA 52409-9844
Ph: (319)654-0608

Fax: (319)654-0609
URL: http://www.aime.org
Contact: **Betty Gorsegner Ehlinger, Exec. Dir.**

Automatic Identification

**66 ■ Association for Automatic Identification
and Mobility North America (AIM NA) (334)**
1 Landmark N
20399 Rte., Ste.203
Cranberry Township, PA 16066
Ph: **(724)742-4473**
Fax: **(724)742-4476**
E-mail: info@aim-na.org
URL: http://www.aim-na.org
Contact: Chuck Evanhoe, Pres.

67 ■ GS1 US (317)
Princeton Pike Corporate Center
1009 Lenox Dr., Ste.202
Lawrenceville, NJ 08648
Ph: (609)620-0200 (937)435-3870
Free: (866)280-4013
Fax: (609)620-1200
E-mail: info@gs1us.org
URL: **http://www.gs1us.org**
Contact: Robert W. Carpenter, Pres./CEO

**68 ■ International RFID Business Association
(RFIDba)**
5 W 37th St., 5th Ave., 9th Fl.
New York, NY 10018
Ph: (610)357-0990
E-mail: **info@rfidba.org**
URL: http://www.rfidba.org
Contact: Harry P. Pappas, Founder/Pres./CEO

Automotive Industries

**69 ■ American Salvage Pool Association
(ASPA) (327)**
PMB 709
2900 Delk Rd., Ste.700
Marietta, GA 30067
Ph: (678)560-6678
Fax: (678)560-9112
E-mail: natalie@aspa.com
URL: http://www.aspa.com
Contact: Natalie Nardone CMP, Exec. Dir.

**70 ■ Automotive Aftermarket Industry
Association | Heavy Duty Distribution
Association (HDDA) (339)**
7101 Wisconsin Ave., Ste.1300
Bethesda, MD 20814
Ph: (301)654-6664
Fax: (301)654-3299
E-mail: **aaia@aftermarket.org**
URL: http://www.aftermarket.org/Segments/hdda.
   aspx
Contact: **David W. Scheer, Chm.**

**71 ■ Automotive Communications Council
(ACC) (325)**
7101 Wisconsin Ave., Ste.1300
Bethesda, MD 20814
Ph: (240)333-1089
Fax: (301)654-3299
E-mail: acc@aftermarket.org
URL: http://www.acc-online.org
Contact: **Tony Molla, Pres.**

72 ■ Automotive Hall of Fame (AHF) (363)
21400 Oakwood Blvd.
Dearborn, MI 48124
Ph: (313)240-4000
Fax: (313)240-8641
E-mail: **bchapin@thedrivingspirit.org**
URL: http://www.automotivehalloffame.org
Contact: **William R. Chapin, Pres.**

**73 ■ Automotive Industry Action Group
(AIAG) (344)**
26200 Lahser Rd., Ste.200
Southfield, MI 48033-7100
Ph: (248)358-3003 (248)358-3570
Fax: (248)358-3253
E-mail: order_inquiry@aiag.org
URL: http://www.aiag.org
Contact: **John Batchik, Chm.**

**74 ■ Automotive Trade Association
Executives (ATAE) (330)**
8400 Westpark Dr.
McLean, VA 22102
Ph: (703)821-7072
Fax: (703)556-8581
URL: http://www.atae.info
Contact: **Stephen Smith, Chm.**

**75 ■ Automotive Training Managers Council
(ATMC) (351)**
101 Blue Seal Dr. SE, Ste.101
Leesburg, VA 20175
Ph: (703)669-6670
E-mail: info@atmc.org
URL: http://www.atmc.org
Contact: **Stefan Baier, Chm.**

76 ■ Global Automakers (341)
1050 K St. NW, Ste.650
Washington, DC 20001
Ph: **(202)650-5555 (202)650-5548**
E-mail: **info@globalautomakers.org**
URL: http://www.globalautomakers.org
Contact: Michael J. Stanton, Pres./CEO
Status Note: Formerly Association of International
Automobile Manufacturers.

**77 ■ Heavy Duty Manufacturers Association |
Heavy-Duty Business Forum** (HDBF) (338)
10 Lab. Dr.
PO Box 13966
Research Triangle Park, NC 27709-3966
Ph: **(919)549-4800**
Fax: (919)549-4824
E-mail: info@hdma.org
URL: http://www.hdma.org/Main-Menu/HDMA-
   Councils/HDBF
Contact: Tim Kraus, Pres./COO

**78 ■ National Auto Body Council (NABC)
(348)**
191 Clarksville Rd.
Princeton Junction, NJ 08550
Free: (888)667-7433
Fax: (609)799-7032
E-mail: info@autobodycouncil.org
URL: http://www.autobodycouncil.org
Contact: **Cynthia Prisco, Mgr.**

**79 ■ Overseas Automotive Council (OAC)
(349)**
PO Box 13966
Research Triangle Park, NC 27709-3966
Ph: **(919)406-8846**
Fax: (919)549-4824
E-mail: **jdenton@mema.org**
URL: **http://www.aftermarketsuppliers.org/
   Councils/OAC**
Contact: **John Brunke, Chm.**

Automotive Manufacturers

**80 ■ Auto International Association (AIA)
(371)**
7101 Wisconsin Ave., Ste.1300
Bethesda, MD 20814
Ph: (301)654-6664 (240)333-1050
Fax: (301)654-3299
E-mail: **aia@aftermarket.org**
URL: **http://aftermarket.org/Segments/AIA**
Contact: **Stephen Bearden, Chm.**

**81 ■ Automotive Aftermarket Suppliers
Association | Brake Manufacturers Council**
(BMC) (381)
PO Box 13966
Research Triangle Park, NC 27709-3966
Ph: **(919)549-4800**
Fax: (919)549-4824
E-mail: **media@mema.org**
URL: **http://www.aftermarketsuppliers.org/
   Councils/Brake-Manufacturers-Council-BMC**
Contact: Rick Jamieson, Chm.

**82 ■ Automotive Engine Rebuilders
Association (AERA) (375)**
500 Coventry Ln., Ste.180
Crystal Lake, IL 60014-7592
Ph: **(815)526-7600**
Free: (888)326-2372
Fax: **(815)526-7601**
E-mail: **info@aera.org**
URL: http://www.aera.org
Contact: John Goodman, Pres.

**83 ■ Automotive Occupant Restraints
Council (AORC) (389)**
1081 Dove Run Rd., Ste.403
Lexington, KY 40502
Ph: (859)269-4240
Fax: (859)269-4241
E-mail: info@aorc.org
URL: http://www.aorc.org
Contact: **Douglas P. Campbell, Pres.**

84 ■ Battery Council International (BCI) (394)
401 N Michigan Ave., 24th Fl.
Chicago, IL 60611-4267
Ph: (312)644-6610
Fax: (312)527-6640
E-mail: info@batterycouncil.org
URL: http://www.batterycouncil.org
Contact: **John Craig, Pres.**

85 ■ Electrical Rebuilder's Association (ERA)
PO Box 906
Union, MO 63084
Ph: (636)584-7400
Fax: (636)584-7401
E-mail: **office@electricalrebuilders.org**
URL: http://www.electricalrebuilders.org
Contact: **Henry Henke, Pres.**

86 ■ Equipment and Tool Institute (ETI) (368)
134 W Univ. Dr., Ste.205
Rochester, MI 48307
Ph: (248)656-5080 (248)656-5085
Fax: (603)971-2375
E-mail: **jessiek@etools.org**
URL: http://www.etools.org
Contact: Mike Cable, Pres.

**87 ■ Filter Manufacturers Council (FMC)
(384)**
PO Box 13966
Research Triangle Park, NC 27709-3966
Ph: (919)549-4800 **(919)406-8846**
Free: (800)993-4583
Fax: (919)406-1306
E-mail: jdenton@mema.org
URL: **http://www.aftermarketsuppliers.org/
   Councils/Filter-Manufacturers-Council**
Contact: Jeremy Denton, Contact

**88 ■ Heavy Duty Representatives
Association (HDRA) (401)**
160 Symphony Way
Elgin, IL 60120
Ph: (847)760-0067
E-mail: **bill.wade@wade-partners.com**
URL: http://hdra.org
Contact: Larry Rosenthal, Pres.

89 ■ National Truck Equipment Association (NTEA) (412)
37400 Hills Tech Dr.
Farmington Hills, MI 48331-3414
Ph: (248)489-7090
Free: (800)441-NTEA
Fax: (248)489-8590
E-mail: info@ntea.com
URL: http://www.ntea.com
Contact: **Jim Carney, Exec. Dir.**

90 ■ PGI
The Terminus Bldg.
3280 Peachtree Rd. NW
Atlanta, GA 30305
Free: (866)548-3203
E-mail: **publicrelations@pgi.com**
URL: http://www.pgi.com/us/en
Contact: Boland T. Jones, Chm./CEO

91 ■ Specialty Equipment Market Association (SEMA) (382)
1575 S Valley Vista Dr.
Diamond Bar, CA 91765
Ph: (909)396-0289
Fax: **(909)860-0184**
E-mail: member@sema.org
URL: http://www.sema.org
Contact: Christopher J. Kersting CAE, Pres./CEO

92 ■ Spring Research Institute (SRI) (384)
422 Kings Way
Naples, FL 34104
Ph: (317)439-4811 **(239)643-7769**
E-mail: johndthomson@att.net
URL: http://www.springresearch.org
Contact: John D. Thomson, Pres.

93 ■ Truck Trailer Manufacturers Association (TTMA) (422)
1020 Princess St.
Alexandria, VA 22314-2247
Ph: (703)549-3010
E-mail: ttma@erols.com
URL: http://www.ttmanet.org
Contact: **Jeff Sims, Pres.**

Automotive Services

94 ■ Automotive Maintenance and Repair Association (AMRA) (393)
201 Park Washington Ct.
Falls Church, VA 22046
Ph: (703)532-2027
Fax: (202)318-0378
E-mail: amra@amra.org
URL: **http://www.amra.org**
Contact: Mr. Barry E. Soltz, Pres.

95 ■ Automotive Parts Remanufacturers Association (APRA) (388)
4215 Lafayette Center Dr., Ste.3
Chantilly, VA 20151-1243
Ph: (703)968-2772
Fax: (703)968-2878
E-mail: **gager@buyreman.com**
URL: http://www.bigrshow.com
Contact: William C. Gager, Pres.

96 ■ Gasoline and Automotive Service Dealers Association (GASDA) (410)
372 Doughty Blvd., Ste.2C
Inwood, NY 11096
Ph: (516)371-6201
Fax: (516)371-1579
E-mail: **gasda@nysassrs.com**
URL: http://www.nysassrs.com/gasda/gasd-amainpage.htm
Contact: **Ralph Bombardiere, Exec. Dir.**

97 ■ Inter-Industry Conference on Auto Collision Repair (414)
5125 Trillium Blvd.
Hoffman Estates, IL 60192-3600
Ph: (847)590-1198
Free: (800)422-7872
Fax: (800)590-1215
E-mail: john.edelen@i-car.com
URL: http://www.i-car.com
Contact: **Elise Quadrozzi, Chair**

98 ■ Service Specialists Association (SSA) (412)
160 Symphony Way, Ste.2
Elgin, IL 60120
Ph: (847)760-0067
E-mail: **rbrothers@wade-partners.com**
URL: http://www.truckservice.org
Contact: **Rick Sheehan, Pres.**

99 ■ Truck-Frame and Axle Repair Association (TARA) (454)
c/o Ken Dias
364 W 12th St.
Erie, PA 16501
Free: (877)735-1687
Fax: **(877)735-1688**
E-mail: **leafspg@aol.com**
URL: http://www.taraassociation.com
Contact: Bill Hinchcliffe, Pres.

100 ■ Used Truck Association (UTA) (416)
325 Country Club Dr., Ste.A
Stockbridge, GA 30281
Free: (877)438-7882
E-mail: contact@uta.org
URL: http://www.uta.org
Contact: **Rick Clark, Pres.**

Aviation

101 ■ Airline Passenger Experience Association (APEX) (425)
355 Lexington Ave., 15th Fl.
New York, NY 10017
Ph: (212)297-2177
Fax: (212)370-9047
E-mail: info@waea.org
URL: http://apex.aero
Contact: Patrick Brannelly, Pres.
Status Note: Formerly World Airline Entertainment Association.

102 ■ Black Pilots of America (BPA) (430)
PO Box 7463
Pine Bluff, AR 71611
Ph: (504)214-7346
E-mail: president@bpapilots.org
URL: http://www.bpapilots.org
Contact: **John W. Hicks Jr., Pres.**

103 ■ International Aviation Womens Association (IAWA) (437)
PO Box 1088
Edgewater, MD 21037
Ph: (410)571-1990
E-mail: **info@iawa.org**
URL: http://www.iawa.org
Contact: Katherine Staton, Pres.

Awards

104 ■ Awards and Recognition Association (ARA) (426)
4700 W Lake Ave.
Glenview, IL 60025
Ph: (847)375-4800 (901)385-0400
Free: (800)344-2148
Fax: (847)375-6480
E-mail: info@ara.org
URL: http://www.ara.org
Contact: **Guy Barone, Pres.**

Baking

105 ■ Bread Bakers Guild of America (450)
670 W Napa St., Ste.B
Sonoma, CA 95476
Ph: (707)935-1468
Fax: (707)935-1672
E-mail: info@bbga.org
URL: http://www.bbga.org
Contact: **Solveig Tofte, Chair**

106 ■ Independent Bakers Association (IBA) (448)
PO Box 3731
Washington, DC 20007
Ph: (202)333-8190
Fax: (202)337-3809
E-mail: **independentbaker@yahoo.com**
URL: http://www.independentbaker.net/independent-bakersassociation
Contact: Nicholas A. Pyle, Pres.

107 ■ Retail Bakers of America (RBA) (439)
202 Village Cir., Ste.1
Slidell, LA 70458
Ph: **(985)643-6504**
Free: (800)638-0924
Fax: **(985)643-6929**
E-mail: info@rbanet.com
URL: http://www.retailbakersofamerica.org
Contact: **Rick Boone, Pres.**

Banking

108 ■ American Council of State Savings Supervisors (ACSSS) (444)
1129 20th St. NW, 9th Fl.
Washington, DC 20036-3403
Ph: (202)728-5757 (225)925-4675
Fax: (225)925-4548
E-mail: sseymour@ofi.state.la.us
URL: http://www.acsss.org
Contact: Ed Smith, Exec. Dir.

109 ■ Arab Bankers Association of North America (ABANA)
150 W 28th St., Ste.801
New York, NY 10001
Ph: (212)599-3030
Fax: (212)599-3131
E-mail: info@arabbankers.org
URL: http://www.arabbankers.org
Contact: Ms. Susan Peters, Exec. Dir.

110 ■ Electronic Transactions Association (ETA) (468)
1101 16th St. NW
Washington, DC 20036
Ph: (202)828-2635
Free: (800)695-5509
Fax: (202)828-2639
E-mail: **info@electran.org**
URL: http://www.electran.org
Contact: **Richard B. Pylant, Pres.**

111 ■ Hellenic American Bankers Association (HABA)
PO Box 7244
New York, NY 10150-7201
Ph: (212)421-1057
E-mail: administrator@haba.org
URL: http://www.haba.org
Contact: **Georgia Mouzakis Tavlarios, Pres.**

112 ■ National Association of Affordable Housing Lenders (NAAHL) (484)
1667 K St., Ste.210
Washington, DC 20006
Ph: (202)293-9850
Fax: (202)293-9852
E-mail: **naahl@naahl.org**
URL: http://www.naahl.org
Contact: Judith Kennedy, Pres./CEO

113 ■ National Association of Mortgage Processors (NAMP)
1250 Connecticut Ave. NW, Ste.200
Washington, DC 20036
Ph: (202)261-6505
Free: (800)977-1197
Fax: (202)318-0655
E-mail: **contact@mortgageprocessor.org**
URL: http://www.mortgageprocessor.org
Contact: Bonnie Wilt-Hild, Contact

114 ■ National Investment Banking Association (NIBA)
PO Box 6625
Athens, GA 30604
Ph: (706)208-9620
Fax: **(706)993-3342**
E-mail: emily@nibanet.org
URL: http://www.nibanet.org
Contact: Emily Foshee, Exec. Dir.

115 ■ Retirement Industry Trust Association (RITA) (497)
820 Jorie Blvd., Ste.420
Oak Brook, IL 60523-2284
Ph: (941)724-0900
Fax: (941)866-7321
E-mail: **mmohr@ritaus.org**
URL: http://www.ritaus.org
Contact: Mary Mohr, Exec. Dir.

Batteries

116 ■ National Alliance for Advanced Technology Batteries (NAATBatt)
122 S Michigan Ave., Ste.1700
Chicago, IL 60603
Ph: **(312)588-0477**
E-mail: **jgreenberger@naatbatt.org**
URL: http://naatbatt.org
Contact: Jim Greenberger, Exec. Dir.

Biotechnology

117 ■ Organization of Regulatory and Clinical Associates (ORCA) (506)
PO Box 3490
Redmond, WA 98073
Ph: (206)464-0825
E-mail: info@orcanw.org
URL: http://www.orcanw.org
Contact: **Allene Dodge, Pres.**

Blacksmiths

118 ■ American Farrier's Association (AFA) (532)
4059 Iron Works Pkwy., Ste.1
Lexington, KY 40511
Ph: (859)233-7411
Fax: (859)231-7862
E-mail: info@americanfarriers.org
URL: http://www.americanfarriers.org
Contact: **Buck McClendon CJF, Pres.**

119 ■ Artist-Blacksmith's Association of North America (ABANA) (508)
259 Muddy Fork Rd.
Jonesborough, TN 37659
Ph: **(423)913-1022**
Fax: **(423)913-1023**
E-mail: abana@abana.org
URL: http://www.abana.org
Contact: **Peyton Anderson, Pres.**

Boating

120 ■ States Organization for Boating Access (SOBA) (512)
231 S LaSalle St., Ste.2050
Chicago, IL 60604
Ph: (312)946-6283
Fax: (312)946-0388
E-mail: info@sobaus.org
URL: http://www.sobaus.org
Contact: **James Adams, Pres.**

Bowling

121 ■ International Bowling Pro Shop and Instructors Association (IBPSIA) (500)
PO Box 6574
Arlington, TX 76005-6574
Ph: (817)649-0079
Free: (800)659-9444
Fax: (817)633-2940
E-mail: bill@ibpsia.com
URL: http://www.ibpsia.com
Contact: Bill Supper, Exec. Dir.

Bridal Services

122 ■ Association of Bridal Consultants (ABC) (502)
56 Danbury Rd., Ste.11
New Milford, CT 06776
Ph: (860)355-7000
Fax: (860)354-1404
E-mail: **info@bridalassn.com**
URL: http://www.bridalassn.com
Contact: David M. Wood III, Pres.

123 ■ Bridal Show Producers International (BSPI)
17730 W Center Rd., Ste.110-311
Omaha, NE 68130
Ph: **(402)330-8900**
Fax: **(402)939-0582**
E-mail: info@bridalfair.com
URL: http://www.bspishows.com
Contact: Bruce Thiebauth, Dir.

124 ■ Wedding Industry Professionals Association (WIPA)
8912 E Pinnacle Peak Rd., Ste.F9-111
Scottsdale, AZ 85255
Ph: **(480)626-1657**
Fax: **(480)513-3207**
E-mail: **corinne@wipausa.org**
URL: http://www.wipausa.org
Contact: Joyce Scardina Becker CMP, Pres.

Broadcasting

125 ■ Alliance for Women in Media (AWM) (516)
1760 Old Meadow Rd., Ste.500
McLean, VA 22102
Ph: (703)506-3290
Fax: (703)506-3266
E-mail: **efuller@allwomeninmedia.org**
URL: http://www.awrt.org
Contact: **Erin M. Fuller, Pres.**
Status Note: Formerly American Women in Radio and Television.

126 ■ Association of Public Television Stations (APTS) (546)
2100 Crystal Dr., Ste.700
Arlington, VA 22202
Ph: (202)654-4200
Fax: (202)654-4236
E-mail: **pbutler@apts.org**
URL: http://www.apts.org
Contact: **Patrick Butler, Pres./CEO**

127 ■ CTAM - Cable and Telecommunications Association for Marketing (547)
201 N Union St., Ste.440
Alexandria, VA 22314
Ph: (703)549-4200
Fax: **(703)684-1167**
E-mail: info@ctam.com
URL: http://www.ctam.com
Contact: Char Beales, Pres./CEO

128 ■ MRFAC (549)
899-A Harrison St. SE
Leesburg, VA 20175
Ph: **(703)669-0320**
Free: (800)262-9206
Fax: **(703)669-0322**
E-mail: jpakla@mrfac.com
URL: http://www.mrfac.com
Contact: Tom Fagan, Pres.

129 ■ National Association of Black Owned Broadcasters (NABOB) (567)
1201 Connecticut Ave. NW, Ste.200
Washington, DC 20036
Ph: (202)463-8970
Fax: (202)429-0657
E-mail: **nabobinfo@nabob.org**
URL: http://www.nabob.org
Contact: Bennie L. Turner, Pres.

130 ■ National Translator Association (NTA) (576)
5611 Kendall Ct., Ste.2
Arvada, CO 80002
Ph: (303)465-5742 (303)378-8209
Fax: (303)465-4067
E-mail: **bap@baplaw.com**
URL: http://www.tvfmtranslators.com
Contact: Byron St. Clair, Pres.

Building Industries

131 ■ Affordable Housing Investors Council (AHIC)
c/o Toni Sylvester, Exec. Admin.
PO Box 986
Irmo, SC 29063
Ph: (803)781-1638
Free: (800)246-7277
Fax: (803)732-0135
E-mail: info@ahic.org
URL: http://www.ahic.org
Contact: **Leila Ahmadifar, Pres.**

132 ■ Affordable Housing Tax Credit Coalition (AHTCC) (586)
401 9th St. NW, Ste.900
Washington, DC 20004
Ph: **(202)585-8162**
Fax: **(202)585-8080**
E-mail: info@taxcreditcoalition.org
URL: http://taxcreditcoalition.org
Contact: Victoria E. Spielman, Exec. Dir.

133 ■ Alliance for Sustainable Built Environments (ASBE)
5150 N Port Washington Rd., Ste.260
Milwaukee, WI 53217
Free: (866)913-9473
Fax: (414)332-6998
E-mail: info@greenerfacilities.org
URL: http://www.greenerfacilities.org
Contact: Craig Zurawski, Exec. Dir.
Founded: 2003. **Description:** Represents building industry manufacturers who practice and are recognized for leadership in sustainability. Promotes sustainable building products and services to building owners and operators. Delivers high performance sustainable solutions for the built environment.

134 ■ American Fiberboard Association (AFA) (551)
1935 S Plum Grove Rd., No. 283
Palatine, IL 60067
Ph: (847)934-8394
Fax: (847)934-8394
E-mail: afa@fiberboard.org
URL: http://www.fiberboard.org
Contact: Louis Wagner, Exec. Dir.

135 ■ Asphalt Emulsion Manufacturers Association (AEMA) (577)
3 Church Cir.
PMB 250
Annapolis, MD 21401
Ph: (410)267-0023
Fax: (410)267-7546
E-mail: krissoff@aema.org
URL: http://www.aema.org
Contact: **Bucky Brooks, Pres.**

136 ■ Associated Air Balance Council (AABC) (592)
1518 K St. NW
Washington, DC 20005
Ph: (202)737-0202
Fax: (202)638-4833
E-mail: info@aabc.com
URL: http://www.aabc.com
Contact: **Michael T. Renovich, Pres.**

137 ■ Associated Construction Distributors International (ACD) (593)
1605 SE Delaware Ave., Ste.B
Ankeny, IA 50021
Ph: (515)964-1335
Fax: (515)964-7668
E-mail: acdi@acdi.net
URL: http://www.acdi.net
Contact: Tom Goetz, Exec. VP

138 ■ Association for Better Insulation (ABI)
3906 Auburn Hills Dr.
Greensboro, NC 27407
Ph: (603)768-3984
Fax: (270)721-0022
E-mail: service@betterinsulation.com
URL: http://www.betterinsulation.com
Contact: **Douglas Colby, Dir.**

139 ■ Association of Millwork Distributors (AMD) (645)
10047 Robert Trent Jones Pkwy.
New Port Richey, FL 34655-4649
Ph: (727)372-3665
Free: (800)786-7274
Fax: (727)372-2879
E-mail: **mail@amdweb.com**
URL: http://www.amdweb.com
Contact: Rosalie Leone, CEO

140 ■ Association of Synthetic Grass Installers (ASGi)
17487 Penn Valley Dr., Ste.B103
Penn Valley, CA 95946
Ph: (530)432-5851
Free: (888)705-8880
Fax: (530)432-1098
E-mail: admin@asgi.us
URL: http://www.asgi.us
Contact: Annie Costa, Exec. Dir.
Founded: 2007. **Membership Dues:** associate (agency, association, individual), $98 (annual) ● general, $248 (annual). **Multinational. Description:** Represents synthetic grass suppliers, manufacturers, installers, designers, architects, planners, consumables and synthetic grass market partners. Promotes the use of artificial grass and synthetic turf. Aims to demonstrate best business practices and excellence in the artificial grass industry.

141 ■ Building Commissioning Association (BCA)
100 SW Main St., Ste.1600
Portland, OR 97204
Free: (877)666-2292
Fax: (503)227-8954
E-mail: info@bcxa.org
URL: http://www.bcxa.org
Contact: Edward Faircloth, Pres.

142 ■ Ceramic Tile Distributors Association (CTDA) (605)
800 Roosevelt Rd., Bldg. C, Ste.312
Glen Ellyn, IL 60137
Ph: (630)545-9415
Free: (800)938-CTDA
Fax: (630)790-3095
E-mail: info@ctdahome.org
URL: http://www.ctdahome.org
Contact: **Ryan Calkins, Pres.**

143 ■ Construction Employers Association (CEA) (598)
c/o Michael Walton, Sec.
1646 N California Blvd., Ste.500
Walnut Creek, CA 94596-4148
Ph: (925)930-8184 (925)930-0014
Fax: (925)930-9014
E-mail: mwwalton@cea-ca.org
URL: http://www.cea-ca.org
Contact: **Patrick Callahan, Pres.**

144 ■ Cool Metal Roofing Coalition
680 Andersen Dr.
Pittsburgh, PA 15220
Ph: (412)922-2772
Fax: (412)922-3213
E-mail: gcrawford@steel.org
URL: http://www.coolmetalroofing.org
Contact: Gregory L. Crawford, Exec. Dir.
Founded: 2002. **Description:** Represents architects, building owners, specifiers, codes and standards officials and stakeholders. Educates the building industry about the benefits of cool metal roofing. Fosters better public understanding of the business and environmental rationale for specifying cool metal roofing systems.

145 ■ Elevator U (EU)
751 N Olcott Ave.
Harwood Heights, IL 60706
E-mail: jimmie.anicich@asu.edu
URL: http://www.elevatoru.org
Contact: Jim Anicich, Pres.
Membership Dues: professional, industry, affiliate, associate, $100 (annual). **Description:** Fosters excellence in the design, construction and maintenance of all forms of vertical transportation. Facilitates the exchange of knowledge and technical expertise to properly build and maintain vertical transportation that is safe, durable and efficient.

146 ■ Green Builder Coalition
PO Box 7507
Gurnee, IL 60031
E-mail: info@greenbuildercoalition.org
URL: http://www.greenbuildercoalition.org
Contact: Ron Jones, Chm./Founder
Founded: 2010. **Membership Dues:** charter, $300 (annual). **Description:** Represents building professionals in architecture, design, materials manufacturing, remodeling, energy rating, academia, engineering and government. Aims to achieve balance and harmony between the built and natural environments by providing a platform for those devoted to sustainable living.

147 ■ International Cast Polymer Association (ICPA) (616)
1010 N Glebe Rd., Ste.450
Arlington, VA 22201
Ph: **(703)525-0320**
Fax: (703)525-0743

E-mail: **icpa@icpa-hq.org**
URL: http://www.icpa-hq.org
Contact: **Jamie Myers, Pres.**

148 ■ International Society for Concrete Pavements (ISCP)
7085 Highland Creek Dr.
Bridgeville, PA 15017
Ph: **(412)221-8450**
Fax: **(412)221-0409**
E-mail: **president@concretepavements.org**
URL: http://www.concretepavements.org
Contact: **Mark B. Snyder PhD, Pres.**

149 ■ Leading Builders of America (LBA)
1455 Pennsylvania Ave. NW, Ste.400
Washington, DC 20004
Ph: (202)621-1815
E-mail: info@leadingbuildersofamerica.org
URL: http://www.leadingbuildersofamerica.org
Contact: Kenneth T. Gear, Contact
Founded: 2009. **Multinational. Description:** Represents the interests of building companies in North America. Aims to preserve home affordability for American families. Addresses issues of home affordability and engages in dialogue with policymakers.

150 ■ Materials and Methods Standards Association (MMSA) (620)
4125 LaPalma Ave., No. 250
Anaheim, CA 92807
URL: http://www.mmsa.ws
Contact: **Jim Whitfield, Pres.**

151 ■ Moulding and Millwork Producers Association (MMPA) (100)
507 1st St.
Woodland, CA 95695
Ph: (530)661-9591
Free: (800)550-7889
Fax: (530)661-9586
E-mail: info@wmmpa.com
URL: http://wmmpa.com
Contact: Kellie A. Schroeder, Exec. VP/CEO
Status Note: Formerly Wood Moulding and Millwork Producers Association.

152 ■ National Association of Construction Contractors Cooperation (NACCC)
7447 Holmes Rd., Ste.300
Kansas City, MO 64131
Ph: (816)442-8680
Fax: (816)444-3226
E-mail: info@nacccusa.org
URL: http://www.nacccusa.org
Contact: Mr. Umberto Anastasio, Chm.
Founded: 2000. **Description:** Aims to redevelop America's urban core and impoverished rural communities. Develops and implements programs to meet the needs of micro-small business owners.

153 ■ National Association of the Remodeling Industry (NARI) (636)
780 Lee St., Ste.200
Des Plaines, IL 60016
Ph: (847)298-9200
Free: (800)611-NARI
Fax: (847)298-9225
E-mail: info@nari.org
URL: http://www.nari.org
Contact: **Michael S. Hydeck, Pres.**

154 ■ National Council of Acoustical Consultants (NCAC) (631)
9100 Purdue Rd., Ste.200
Indianapolis, IN 46268
Ph: (317)328-0642
Fax: (317)328-4629
E-mail: info@ncac.com
URL: http://www.ncac.com
Contact: **Bennett Brooks, Pres.**

155 ■ National Roof Certification and Inspection Association (NRCIA)
2232 E Wilson Ave.
Orange, CA 92867
Free: (888)687-7663
Fax: (866)210-7464
E-mail: info@nrcia.com
URL: http://www.nrcia.com
Contact: Les Watrous, Exec. Dir.
Founded: 1995. **Description:** Provides roof certification and inspection services. Trains roofers who will specialize in prevention rather than repair.

156 ■ National Sunroom Association (NSA) (653)
1300 Sumner Ave.
Cleveland, OH 44115-2851
Ph: (216)241-7333 (330)468-0700
Fax: (216)241-0105
E-mail: info@nationalsunroom.org
URL: http://www.nationalsunroom.org
Contact: **Lyndon B. Johnson, Pres.**

157 ■ National Wood Flooring Association (NWFA) (640)
111 Chesterfield Indus. Blvd.
Chesterfield, MO 63005
Free: (800)422-4556
Fax: (636)519-9664
E-mail: **info@nwfa.org**
URL: http://www.nofma.org
Contact: **Ed Korczak, CEO**

158 ■ North American Building Material Distribution Association (NBMDA) (644)
401 N Michigan Ave.
Chicago, IL 60611
Ph: (312)321-6845
Free: (888)747-7862
Fax: (312)644-0310
E-mail: info@nbmda.org
URL: http://www.nbmda.org
Contact: **Brian Schell, Pres.**

159 ■ Preservation Trades Network (PTN)
PO Box 151
Burbank, OH 44214-0151
Ph: **(330)465-1504**
Free: (866)853-9335
Fax: (866)853-9336
E-mail: info@ptn.org
URL: http://www.iptw.org
Contact: Rudy R. Christian, Exec. Dir.

160 ■ Scaffold Industry Association (SIA) (657)
400 Admiral Blvd.
Kansas City, MO 64106
Ph: (816)595-4860
Fax: (816)472-7765
E-mail: **srs@edgeintl.com**
URL: http://www.scaffold.org
Contact: **Steve Smith, Pres.**

161 ■ Structural Insulated Panel Association (SIPA) (641)
PO Box 1699
Gig Harbor, WA 98335
Ph: (253)858-7472
Fax: (253)858-0272
E-mail: info@sips.org
URL: http://www.sips.org
Contact: **Terry Dieken, Pres.**

Business

162 ■ American Business Women's Association (ABWA) (680)
PO Box 8728
Kansas City, MO 64114-0728
Free: (800)228-0007
Fax: **(913)732-5100**

E-mail: **abwa@abwa.org**
URL: http://www.abwa.org
Contact: **Lynn Drowne, Natl. Pres.**

163 ■ Association for Enterprise Information (AFEI) (687)
2111 Wilson Blvd., Ste.400
Arlington, VA 22201
Ph: (703)247-9474 (703)247-2597
Fax: (703)522-3192
E-mail: dchesebrough@afei.org
URL: http://www.afei.org
Contact: **Margaret E. Myers PhD, Chair**

164 ■ Association of Moroccan Professionals in America (AMPA)
5301 Pooks Hill Rd.
Bethesda, MD 20814
Fax: (801)996-6334
E-mail: jaridati@amp-usa.org
URL: http://www.amp-usa.org
Contact: Karim Sijlmassi, Pres.

165 ■ Canadian-American Business Council (CABC) (675)
1900 K St. NW, Ste.100
Washington, DC 20006
Ph: (202)496-7906
Fax: (202)496-7756
E-mail: **erigby@mckennalong.com**
URL: http://www.canambusco.org
Contact: Ms. Emma Rigby, Deputy Dir.

166 ■ Institute of Certified Business Counselors (ICBC) (714)
18831 Willamette Dr.
West Linn, OR 97068
Free: (877)422-2674
Fax: **(503)635-1340**
E-mail: **membership@i-cbc.org**
URL: http://www.i-cbc.org
Contact: David Finsterwald, Contact

167 ■ International Downtown Association (IDA) (718)
1025 Thomas Jefferson St. NW, Ste.500W
Washington, DC 20007
Ph: (202)393-6801
Fax: (202)393-6869
E-mail: question@ida-downtown.org
URL: http://www.ida-downtown.org
Contact: **Jim Cloar, Interim Pres.**

168 ■ International Executive Service Corps (IESC) (728)
1900 M St. NW, Ste.500
Washington, DC 20036
Ph: (202)589-2600
Fax: (202)326-0289
E-mail: iesc@iesc.org
URL: http://www.iesc.org
Contact: **Thomas Miller, Pres./CEO**

169 ■ International Ombudsman Association (IOA) (722)
390 Amwell Rd., Ste.403
Hillsborough, NJ 08844
Ph: (908)359-0246
Fax: (908)842-0376
E-mail: info@ombudsassociation.org
URL: http://www.ombudsassociation.org
Contact: **Tom Kosakowski, Pres.**

170 ■ Italian American Alliance for Business and Technology (IAABT) (2277)
74 W Long Lake Rd., Ste.204
Bloomfield Hills, MI 48304
Ph: (248)227-6143
E-mail: info@iaabt.org
URL: http://iaabt.org
Contact: Massimo Denipoti, Pres.

171 ■ Mountains and Plains Independent Booksellers Association (MPIBA)
8020 Springshire Dr.
Park City, UT 84098
Ph: **(435)649-6079**
Free: (800)752-0249
Fax: **(435)649-6105**
E-mail: info@mountainsplains.org
URL: http://www.mountainsplains.org
Contact: **Laura Ayrey, Exec. Dir.**

172 ■ National Association for Female Executives (NAFE) (737)
PO Box 3052
Langhorne, PA 19047
Free: (800)927-6233
E-mail: **roxanne.natale@nafe.com**
URL: http://www.nafe.com
Contact: Dr. Betty Spence, Pres.

173 ■ National Society of Hispanic MBAs (NSHMBA) (742)
1303 Walnut Hill Ln., Ste.100
Irving, TX 75038
Ph: (214)596-9338 (214)524-7532
Free: (877)467-4622
Fax: (214)596-9325
E-mail: saramos@nshmba.org
URL: http://www.nshmba.org
Contact: **Manny Gonzalez, CEO**

174 ■ Representative of German Industry and Trade (RGIT) (755)
1776 I St. NW, Ste.1000
Washington, DC 20006
Ph: (202)659-4777
Fax: (202)659-4779
E-mail: info@rgit-usa.com
URL: http://www.rgit-usa.com
Contact: **Dr. Thomas Zielke, Pres.**

175 ■ Singapore America Business Association (SABA)
3 Twin Dolphin Dr., Ste.150
Redwood City, CA 94065
Ph: (650)260-3388
Fax: **(415)252-1160**
E-mail: **sabausainfo@gmail.com**
URL: http://www.saba-usa.org
Contact: **Chek Tan, CEO**

176 ■ United States Council for International Business (USCIB) (766)
1212 Avenue of the Americas
New York, NY 10036
Ph: (212)354-4480 **(212)703-5046**
Fax: (212)575-0327
E-mail: membership@uscib.org
URL: http://www.uscib.org
Contact: Mr. Peter M. Robinson, Pres./CEO

177 ■ United States-Indonesia Society (USINDO)
1625 Massachusetts Ave. NW, Ste.550
Washington, DC 20036-2260
Ph: (202)232-1400
Fax: (202)232-7300
E-mail: **usindo@usindo.org**
URL: http://www.usindo.org
Contact: David Merrill, Pres.

178 ■ U.S.-Ukraine Business Council (USUBC)
1300 I St. NW, Ste.720 W
Washington, DC 20005
Ph: (202)429-0551 (240)505-9494
Fax: (202)223-1224
E-mail: mwilliams@usubc.org
URL: http://www.usubc.org
Contact: Mr. Morgan Williams, Pres./CEO
Founded: 1995. **Membership Dues:** regular, $5,000 (annual) ● regular small business, $2,500 (annual) ● associate, $1,250 (annual). **Multinational. Description:** Promotes strong, friendly bilateral ties between United States and Ukraine. Advances United States

and Ukraine business relations and partnerships by facilitating regular interactions between its members and senior Ukrainian government and business leaders.

179 ■ US-Ireland Alliance
2800 Clarendon Blvd., Ste.502 W
Arlington, VA 22201
Ph: **(202)643-8742**
E-mail: vargo@us-irelandalliance.org
URL: http://www.us-irelandalliance.org
Contact: Trina Vargo, Pres.

Celtic

180 ■ North American Celtic Buyers Association (NACBA)
27 Addison Ave.
Rutherford, NJ 07070
Ph: (201)842-9922
Fax: (201)804-9143
E-mail: info@celticbuyers.com
URL: http://www.celticbuyers.com
Contact: **Fran Siefert, Pres.**

Chefs

181 ■ United States Personal Chef Association (USPCA)
5728 Major Blvd., Ste.750
Orlando, FL 32819
Ph: (505)994-6372
Free: (800)995-2138
Fax: (505)994-6399
E-mail: customerservice@uspca.com
URL: http://www.uspca.com

Chemicals

182 ■ American Chemistry Council (ACC) (795)
700 2nd St. NE
Washington, DC 20002
Ph: **(202)249-7000**
Fax: **(202)249-6100**
URL: http://www.americanchemistry.com
Contact: Calvin M. Dooley, Pres./CEO

183 ■ American Cleaning Institute (ACI) (810)
1331 L St. NW, Ste.650
Washington, DC 20005
Ph: (202)347-2900
Fax: (202)347-4110
E-mail: **info@cleaninginstitute.org**
URL: http://www.cleaninginstitute.org
Contact: Brian Sansoni, VP, Communication and Membership
Status Note: Formerly Soap and Detergent Association.

184 ■ Halogenated Solvents Industry Alliance (HSIA) (806)
1530 Wilson Blvd., Ste.690
Arlington, VA 22209
Ph: **(703)875-0683**
Fax: **(703)875-0675**
E-mail: info@hsia.org
URL: http://www.hsia.org

185 ■ Institute for Polyacrylate Absorbents (IPA) (807)
1850 M St. NW, Ste.700
Washington, DC 20036-5810
Ph: **(202)721-4154**
Fax: (202)296-8120
E-mail: **helmest@socma.com**
URL: **http://www.socma.org**
Contact: **Tucker C. Helmes PhD, Exec. Dir.**

186 ■ Methacrylate Producers Association (MPA) (750)
17260 Vannes Ct.
Hamilton, VA 20158
Ph: (540)751-2093
Fax: (540)751-2094
E-mail: **e.hunt@comcast.net**
URL: http://www.mpausa.org

187 ■ Pine Chemicals Association (PCA) (813)
3350 Riverwood Pkwy. SE, Ste.1900
Atlanta, GA 30339
Ph: (770)984-5340
Fax: **(404)890-5665**
URL: http://www.pinechemicals.org
Contact: **Gary Reed, Chm./CEO**

188 ■ SB Latex Council (SBLC) (771)
1250 Connecticut Ave. NW, Ste.700
Washington, DC 20036
Ph: (202)419-1500
Fax: **(202)637-9178**
E-mail: info@regnet.com
URL: http://www.regnet.com/sblc
Contact: Robert J. Fensterheim, Exec. Dir.

189 ■ Society for Chemical Hazard Communication (SCHC)
PO Box 1392
Annandale, VA 22003-9392
Ph: (703)658-9246
Fax: (703)658-9247
E-mail: schc-admin@schc.org
URL: http://www.schc.org
Contact: **Lori Chaplin, Admin.**

Child Care

190 ■ Association of Premier Nanny Agencies (APNA)
c/o Ginger Swift
400 S Colorado Blvd., Ste.300
Denver, CO 80246
E-mail: daryl@spnannies.com
URL: http://www.theapna.org
Contact: **Daryl Camarillo, Pres.**

Coal

191 ■ American Coke and Coal Chemicals Institute (ACCCI) (834)
1140 Connecticut Ave. NW, Ste.705
Washington, DC 20036
Ph: (202)452-7198
Fax: (202)463-6573
E-mail: information@accci.org
URL: http://www.accci.org
Contact: **Robert Mason, Chm.**

Coatings

192 ■ Aluminum Anodizers Council (AAC) (837)
1000 N Rand Rd., No. 214
Wauconda, IL 60084
Ph: (847)526-2010
Fax: (847)526-3993
E-mail: mail@anodizing.org
URL: http://www.anodizing.org
Contact: **R. Todd Hamilton, Chm.**

Color

193 ■ Color Marketing Group (CMG) (840)
1908 Mt. Vernon Ave.
Alexandria, VA 22301
Ph: (703)329-8500 (703)647-4729
Fax: **(703)548-2212**

E-mail: **sgriffis@colormarketing.org**
URL: http://www.colormarketing.org
Contact: **Sharon Griffis, Exec. Dir.**

Comics

194 ■ Comics Professional Retailers Organization (ComicsPRO)
PO Box 75446
Colorado Springs, CO 80970
Free: (877)574-8618
Fax: **(877)574-8618**
E-mail: info@comicspro.org
URL: http://www.comicspro.org
Contact: Joe Field, Pres.

Communications

195 ■ 911 Industry Alliance (9IA)
c/o Reid French, Vice Chm.
1611 N Kent St., Ste.802
Arlington, VA 22209
Ph: **(202)737-6001**
E-mail: **reid.french@911alliance.org**
URL: http://www.911alliance.org
Contact: Kevin Murray, Chm.

196 ■ MultiService Forum (MSF)
48377 Fremont Blvd., Ste.117
Fremont, CA 94538
Ph: (510)492-4050 (510)492-4051
Fax: (510)492-4001
E-mail: info@msforum.org
URL: http://www.msforum.org
Contact: **Alysia Johnson, Exec. Dir.**

197 ■ Society for Technical Communication (STC) (883)
9401 Lee Hwy., Ste.300
Fairfax, VA 22031
Ph: (703)522-4114
Fax: (703)522-2075
E-mail: stc@stc.org
URL: http://www.stc.org
Contact: **Dr. Hillary Hart, Pres.**

Concrete

198 ■ International Concrete Repair Institute (ICRI) (899)
10600 W Higgins Rd., Ste.607
Rosemont, IL 60018
Ph: (847)827-0830
Fax: (847)827-0832
E-mail: kelly.page@icri.org
URL: http://www.icri.org
Contact: **Don Ford, Pres.**

199 ■ National Concrete Masonry Association (NCMA) (901)
13750 Sunrise Valley Dr.
Herndon, VA 20171-4662
Ph: (703)713-1900
Fax: (703)713-1910
E-mail: **rthomas@ncma.org**
URL: http://www.ncma.org
Contact: Robert D. Thomas, Pres.

200 ■ National Precast Concrete Association (NPCA) (902)
1320 City Center Dr., Ste.200
Carmel, IN 46032
Ph: (317)571-9500
Free: (800)366-7731
Fax: (317)571-0041
E-mail: npca@precast.org
URL: http://www.precast.org
Contact: **Dan Houk, Chm.**

201 ■ Precast/Prestressed Concrete Institute (PCI) (869)
200 W Adams St., No. 2100
Chicago, IL 60606
Ph: (312)786-0300 (312)360-3204
Fax: **(312)621-1114**
E-mail: info@pci.org
URL: http://www.pci.org
Contact: James G. Toscas, Pres.

Construction

202 ■ American Construction Inspectors Association (ACIA) (909)
530 S Lake Ave., No. 431
Pasadena, CA 91101
Ph: (626)797-2242
Fax: (626)797-2214
E-mail: office@acia.com
URL: http://www.acia.com
Contact: **Dennis Dooley RCI, Pres.**

203 ■ American Fence Association (AFA) (910)
800 Roosevelt Rd., Bldg. C-312
Glen Ellyn, IL 60137
Ph: (630)942-6598
Free: (800)822-4342
Fax: (630)790-3095
E-mail: **rod@southernfence.com**
URL: http://www.americanfenceassociation.com
Contact: **Rod Wilson, Pres.**

204 ■ Equipment Managers Council of America (EMCA)
PO Box 794
South Amboy, NJ 08879-0794
Ph: (610)360-1736
Fax: **(610)966-2304**
E-mail: mike.emca@gmail.com
URL: http://www.emca.org
Contact: **Mike Eder, Pres.**

205 ■ Firestop Contractors International Association (FCIA) (916)
4415 W Harrison St., No. 436
Hillside, IL 60162
Ph: (708)202-1108
Fax: (708)449-0837
E-mail: info@fcia.org
URL: http://www.fcia.org
Contact: **Bob Hasting, Pres.**

206 ■ National Association of Black Women in Construction (NABWIC)
1910 NW 105 Ave.
Pembroke Pines, FL 33026
E-mail: info@nabwic.org
URL: http://nabwic.org
Contact: Gladys Keith, Contact
Membership Dues: student, $35 (annual) ● individual, government employee, $100 (annual) ● corporate, $1,000 (annual) ● corporate benefactor, $1,500 (annual) ● corporate sponsor, $2,000 (annual) ● corporate contributor, $5,000 (annual) ● life, $7,500. **Description:** Promotes the advancement of black women in the construction industry. Supports aspiring construction executives. Provides advocacy, mentorship and professional development for its members.

207 ■ Quartzite Rock Association (QRA) (916)
PO Box 661
Sioux Falls, SD 57101
Ph: (605)339-1520
E-mail: **qra@lgeverist.com**
URL: http://www.quartzite.com

Consulting

208 ■ American Association of Insurance Management Consultants (AAIMCo) (926)
Texas Insurance Consulting
8980 Lakes at 610 Dr., Ste.100
Houston, TX 77054
Ph: (713)664-6424 **(614)261-0552**
E-mail: thomas.braniff@aaimco.com
URL: http://www.aaimco.com
Contact: Mr. Thomas M. Braniff, Pres.

209 ■ American Society of Theatre Consultants (ASTC) (874)
c/o Edgar L. Lustig, Sec./CFO
12226 Mentz Hill Rd.
St. Louis, MO 63128
Ph: (314)843-9218
Fax: (314)843-4955
E-mail: elustig@swbell.net
URL: http://www.theatreconsultants.org
Contact: **Jim Read, Pres.**

210 ■ Association of Professional Consultants (APC) (933)
PO Box 51193
Irvine, CA 92619-1193
Free: (800)745-5050
E-mail: apc@consultapc.org
URL: http://www.consultapc.org
Contact: **Shannon Barnes, Pres.**

211 ■ Association of Professional Material Handling Consultants (APMHC) (931)
8720 Red Oak Blvd., Ste.201
Charlotte, NC 28217-3992
Ph: (704)676-1184 (704)676-1190
Free: (800)345-1815
Fax: (704)676-1199
E-mail: **rniemeyer@mhia.org**
URL: http://www.mhia.org/about/societies/apmhc
Contact: **Ray Niemeyer, Exec. Dir.**

212 ■ Professional and Technical Consultants Association (PATCA) (939)
PO Box 2261
Santa Clara, CA 95055
Ph: (408)971-5902
Free: (800)74-PATCA
Fax: (866)746-1053
E-mail: info@patca.org
URL: http://www.patca.org
Contact: **Jerry W. Rice, Pres.**

Containers

213 ■ Recycled Paperboard Technical Association (RPTA) (911)
PO Box 5774
Elgin, IL 60121-5774
Ph: (847)622-2544
Fax: (847)622-2546
E-mail: rpta@rpta.org
URL: http://www.rpta.org
Contact: **Deborah White, Exec. Dir.**

Contractors

214 ■ ADSC: The International Association of Foundation Drilling (925)
8445 Freeport Pkwy., Ste.325
Irving, TX 75063
Ph: **(469)359-6000**
Fax: **(469)359-6000**
E-mail: adsc@adsc-iafd.com
URL: http://www.adsc-iafd.com
Contact: Michael D. Moore, Exec. Dir.

215 ■ American Society of Concrete Contractors (ASCC) (973)
2025 S Brentwood Blvd., Ste.105
St. Louis, MO 63144
Ph: (314)962-0210
Free: (866)788-2722
Fax: (314)968-4367
E-mail: questions@ascconline.org
URL: http://www.ascconline.org
Contact: **Mr. Clay Fischer, Pres.**

216 ■ American Subcontractors Association (ASA) (991)
1004 Duke St.
Alexandria, VA 22314-3588
Ph: (703)684-3450
Free: (888)374-3133
Fax: (703)836-3482
E-mail: asaoffice@asa-hq.com
URL: http://www.asaonline.com
Contact: **Timmy McLaughlin, Pres.**

217 ■ Associated Builders and Contractors (ABC) (953)
4250 N Fairfax Dr., 9th Fl.
Arlington, VA 22203-1607
Ph: (703)812-2000
Fax: (703)812-8201
E-mail: gotquestions@abc.org
URL: http://www.abc.org
Contact: **Michael D. Bellaman, Pres./CEO**

218 ■ Associated Builders and Contractors I National Electrical Contractors Council (NECC) (967)
4250 N Fairfax Dr., 9th Fl.
Arlington, VA 22203-1607
Ph: (703)812-2000 (703)812-2006
Fax: (703)812-8201
E-mail: electrical@abc.org
URL: http://www.abc.org/Business_Development/
    Resources/Electrical_Contractors.aspx
Contact: **Michael D. Bellaman, Pres./CEO**

219 ■ Ceilings and Interior Systems Construction Association (CISCA) (980)
405 Illinois Ave., Unit 2B
St. Charles, IL 60174
Ph: (630)584-1919
Fax: (866)560-8537
E-mail: cisca@cisca.org
URL: http://www.cisca.org
Contact: **Bill Shannon, Pres.**

220 ■ Construction Financial Management Association (CFMA) (1000)
100 Village Blvd., Ste.200
Princeton, NJ 08540
Ph: (609)452-8000
Fax: (609)452-0474
E-mail: **jburkett@cafcoconstruction.com**
URL: http://www.cfma.org
Contact: **Joseph Burkett, Chm.**

221 ■ Joint Industry Board of the Electrical Industry (JIBEI) (977)
158-11 Harry Van Arsdale Jr. Ave.
Flushing, NY 11365
Ph: (718)591-2000
Fax: **(718)380-7741**
URL: http://www.jibei.org
Contact: Dr. Gerald Finkel, Chm.

222 ■ National Association of Small Business Contractors (NASBC)
1200 G St. NW, Ste.800
Washington, DC 20005
Free: (888)861-9290
E-mail: **support@nasbc.org**
URL: http://www.nasbc.org
Contact: Cris Young, Pres.

223 ■ National Association of State Contractors Licensing Agencies (NASCLA) (1012)
23309 N 17th Dr., Bldg. 1, Unit 10
Phoenix, AZ 85027
Ph: (623)587-9354
Fax: (623)587-9625
E-mail: info@nascla.org
URL: http://www.nascla.org
Contact: **Keith Warren, Pres.**

224 ■ National Association of Women in Construction (NAWIC) (962)
327 S Adams St.
Fort Worth, TX 76104
Ph: (817)877-5551
Free: (800)552-3506
Fax: (817)877-0324
E-mail: nawic@nawic.org
URL: http://www.nawic.org
Contact: **Debra M. Gregoire, Pres.**

225 ■ National Demolition Association (1031)
16 N Franklin St., Ste.203
Doylestown, PA 18901-3536
Ph: (215)348-4949
Free: (800)541-2412
Fax: (215)348-8422
E-mail: **drachel@rachelcontracting.com**
URL: http://www.demolitionassociation.com
Contact: **Don Rachel, Pres.**

226 ■ National Frame Builders Association (NFBA) (969)
4700 W Lake Ave.
Glenview, IL 60025
Free: (800)557-6957
Fax: (847)375-6495
E-mail: nfba@nfba.org
URL: http://www.nfba.org
Contact: **Anne Cordes, Interim Exec. Dir.**

227 ■ National Utility Contractors Association (NUCA) (977)
11350 Random Hills Rd.
Arlington, VA 22203-1627
Ph: (703)358-9300
Free: (800)662-6822
Fax: (703)358-9307
E-mail: bill@nuca.com
URL: http://www.nuca.com
Contact: Bill Hillman, CEO

228 ■ National Utility Locating Contractors Association (NULCA)
1501 Shirkey Ave.
Richmond, MO 64085
E-mail: **executivedirector@nulca.org**
URL: http://www.nulca.org
Contact: **Vincent Marchese III, Pres.**

229 ■ Power and Communication Contractors Association (PCCA) (1031)
1908 Mt. Vernon Ave.
Alexandria, VA 22314
Ph: (703)212-7734
Free: (800)542-7222
Fax: (703)548-3733
E-mail: info@pccaweb.org
URL: http://www.pccaweb.org
Contact: **Tommy Muse, Pres.-Elect**

230 ■ Professional Construction Estimators Association of America (PCEA) (1048)
PO Box 680336
Charlotte, NC 28216
Ph: (704)489-1494 (704)987-9978
Free: (877)521-7232
Fax: (704)489-1495
E-mail: pcea@pcea.org
URL: http://www.pcea.org
Contact: **Randall Williams, Pres.**

231 ■ Professional Women in Construction (PWC) (994)
315 E 56th St.
New York, NY 10022-3730
Ph: **(212)486-4712**
Fax: (212)486-0228
E-mail: pwc@pwcusa.org
URL: http://www.pwcusa.org
Contact: Lenore Janis, Pres./Co-Founder

232 ■ Tilt-Up Concrete Association (TCA) (987)
PO Box 204
Mount Vernon, IA 52314
Ph: (319)895-6911
Fax: (320)213-5555
E-mail: info@tilt-up.org
URL: http://www.tilt-up.org
Contact: **Ed McGuire, Pres.**

233 ■ Women Construction Owners and Executives U.S.A. (WCOE USA) (1033)
1004 Duke St.
Alexandria, VA 22314
Free: (800)788-3548
Fax: (202)330-5151
E-mail: info@wcoeusa.org
URL: http://www.wcoeusa.org
Contact: **Rosana Privitera Biondo, Pres.**

Cooperatives

234 ■ National Cooperative Business Association (NCBA) (1073)
1401 New York Ave. NW, Ste.1100
Washington, DC 20005
Ph: (202)638-6222
Fax: (202)638-1374
E-mail: **info@ncba.coop**
URL: http://www.ncba.coop
Contact: Paul Hazen, Pres./CEO

235 ■ National Cooperative Grocers Association (NCGA)
14 S Linn St.
Iowa City, IA 52240
Ph: (319)466-9029
Fax: **(866)872-1225**
URL: http://www.ncga.coop
Contact: Robynn Shrader, CEO

Corporate Responsibility

236 ■ CEO Netweavers
PO Box 700393
Dallas, TX 75370
E-mail: info@ceonetweavers.org
URL: http://www.ceonetweavers.org
Contact: **Tom Lyons, CEO**

237 ■ Corporate Responsibility Officers Association (CROA)
343 Thornall St., Ste.515
Edison, NJ 08837-2209
Ph: (732)476-6160
Fax: (732)476-6155
E-mail: jay.whitehead@sharedxpertise.com
URL: http://www.croassociation.org
Contact: **Richard Crespin, Exec. Dir.**

238 ■ Corporate Social Responsibility Association (CSRA)
155 E Boardwalk Dr., No. 544
Fort Collins, CO 80525
Ph: **(303)944-4225**
Fax: **(303)496-0437**
E-mail: jhall@csrassn.com
URL: http://csrassn.com
Contact: John Hall, Exec. Dir.

Cosmetology

239 ■ Allied Health Association (AHA)
5420 S Quebec St., Ste.102
Englewood, CO 80111
Free: (800)444-7546
Fax: (303)662-9845
E-mail: **contact@alliedhealth.net**
URL: http://www.alliedhealth.net

240 ■ National - Interstate Council of State Boards of Cosmetology (NIC) (5511)
7622 Briarwood Cir.
Little Rock, AR 72205
Ph: (501)227-8262
Fax: (501)227-8212
E-mail: dnorton@nictesting.org
URL: http://www.nictesting.org
Contact: **Kay Kendrick, Pres.**

241 ■ Professional Beauty Association I Nail Manufacturers Council (NMC) (1046)
15825 N 71st St., Ste.100
Scottsdale, AZ 85254
Ph: (480)281-0424
Free: (800)468-2274
Fax: (480)905-0708
E-mail: **info@probeauty.org**
URL: http://www.probeauty.org/about/committees/nmc
Contact: Bruce Selan, Chm.

242 ■ Society of Permanent Cosmetic Professionals (SPCP) (1032)
69 N Broadway
Des Plaines, IL 60016
Ph: (847)635-1330
Fax: (847)635-1326
E-mail: **facialdesigns@charter.net**
URL: http://www.spcp.org
Contact: **Marilyn Rustand CPCP, Pres.**

Cotton

243 ■ Cotton Council International (CCI) (1056)
1521 New Hampshire Ave. NW
Washington, DC 20036
Ph: (202)745-7805
Fax: (202)483-4040
E-mail: cottonusa@cotton.org
URL: http://www.cottonusa.org
Contact: **Wallace L. Darneille, Chm.**

244 ■ National Cotton Council of America (NCC) (1061)
PO Box 2995
Cordova, TN 38088-2995
Ph: (901)274-9030
Fax: (901)725-0510
URL: http://www.cotton.org
Contact: **Charles H. Parker, Chm.**

Credit

245 ■ International Association of Credit Portfolio Managers (IACPM)
360 Madison Ave., 17th Fl.
New York, NY 10017-7111
Ph: (646)289-5430
Fax: (646)289-5429
E-mail: **dara@iacpm.org**
URL: http://www.iacpm.org
Contact: Som-lok Leung, Exec. Dir.

246 ■ Printing Industry Credit Executives (PICE) (1069)
1100 Main St.
Buffalo, NY 14209
Free: (800)226-0722
Fax: (716)878-0479

E-mail: agcisupport@abc-amega.com
URL: http://www.pice.com
Contact: **Pat Rydzik, Pres.**

Credit Unions

247 ■ Association of Credit Union Internal Auditors (ACUIA) (1072)
815 King St., Ste.308
Alexandria, VA 22314
Ph: **(703)535-5757**
Fax: **(703)683-0295**
E-mail: acuia@acuia.org
URL: http://www.acuia.org
Contact: Samuel Capuano CBA, Chm.

248 ■ National Association of Credit Union Services Organizations (NACUSO) (1046)
3419 Via Lido
PMB 135
Newport Beach, CA 92663
Ph: (949)645-5296
Free: (888)462-2870
Fax: (949)645-5297
E-mail: info@nacuso.org
URL: http://www.nacuso.org
Contact: **Jack M. Antonini, Pres./CEO**

249 ■ National Association of Federal Credit Unions (NAFCU) (1032)
3138 10th St. N
Arlington, VA 22201-2149
Ph: (703)522-4770
Free: (800)336-4644
Fax: (703)524-1082
URL: http://www.nafcu.org
Contact: **Michael N. Lussier, Pres./CEO**

250 ■ World Council of Credit Unions (WOCCU) (1105)
5710 Mineral Point Rd.
Madison, WI 53705-4454
Ph: (608)395-2000
Fax: (608)395-2001
E-mail: mail@woccu.org
URL: http://www.woccu.org
Contact: Teresa Clegg, Contact

Dairy Products

251 ■ American Cheese Society (ACS) (1095)
2696 S Colorado Blvd., Ste.570
Denver, CO 80222-5954
Ph: (720)328-2788
Fax: **(720)328-2786**
E-mail: info@cheesesociety.org
URL: http://www.cheesesociety.org
Contact: Nora Weiser, Exec. Dir.

252 ■ National Yogurt Association (NYA) (1049)
2000 Corporate Ridge, Ste.1000
McLean, VA 22102
Ph: (703)821-0770
E-mail: lsarasin@affi.com
URL: http://www.aboutyogurt.com
Contact: **Kraig Naasz, Pres.**

Design

253 ■ American Association of Human Design Practitioners (HDP) (1151)
PO Box 195
Ranchos de Taos, NM 87557-0195
URL: http://www.humandesignsystem.net
Contact: Zeno Dickson, Pres.

254 ■ Universal Design Alliance (UDA) (1118)
3651-E Peachtree Pkwy., Ste.311
Suwanee, GA 30024
Ph: **(813)368-7420**

Fax: **(813)661-5839**
E-mail: info@universaldesign.org
URL: http://www.universaldesign.org
Contact: Mike Schilling, Pres.

Disposable Products

255 ■ Foodservice and Packaging Institute (FPI) (1119)
201 Park Washington Ct.
Falls Church, VA 22046
Ph: (703)538-3552 **(703)538-3551**
Fax: (703)241-5603
E-mail: fpi@fpi.org
URL: http://www.fpi.org
Contact: **Lynn Dyer, Pres.**

256 ■ Manufacturers Representatives of America (MRA) (1075)
1111 Jupiter Rd., Ste.204D
Plano, TX 75074
Ph: **(972)422-0428**
Fax: **(972)422-7351**
E-mail: assnhqtrs@aol.com
URL: http://www.mra-reps.com
Contact: **Eric Rud, Pres.**

Do It Yourself Aids

257 ■ Home Improvement Research Institute (HIRI) (1076)
3922 Coconut Palm Dr., 3rd Fl.
Tampa, FL 33619
Ph: (813)627-6750 **(813)627-6976**
Fax: (813)627-7063
E-mail: aangel@hiri.org
URL: http://www.hiri.org
Contact: Angie Angel, Admin. Coor.

Domestic Services

258 ■ Vacation Rental Housekeeping Professionals (VRHP)
5380 Gulf of Mexico Dr., Ste.105
Longboat Key, FL 34228
Ph: (850)303-1358
Free: **(866)457-2582**
Fax: **(800)741-6988**
E-mail: webmaster@vrhp.org
URL: **http://www.vrhp.org**
Contact: Stephen Craig, Dir.

Door

259 ■ American Association of Automatic Door Manufacturers (AAADM) (1124)
1300 Sumner Ave.
Cleveland, OH 44115-2851
Ph: (216)241-7333
Fax: (216)241-12100
E-mail: **info@aaadm.com**
URL: http://www.aaadm.com
Contact: John H. Addington, Exec. Dir.

260 ■ Institutional Locksmiths' Association (ILA) (1125)
PO Box 9560
Naperville, IL 60567-9560
E-mail: **jack@ilanational.org**
URL: http://www.ilanational.org
Contact: Jack Walder CJIL, Pres.

E-Commerce

261 ■ Merchant Risk Council (MRC)
2400 N 45th St., Ste.15
Seattle, WA 98103
Ph: (206)364-2789

Fax: (206)367-1115
E-mail: info@merchantriskcouncil.org
URL: http://www.merchantriskcouncil.org
Contact: **Greg Goeckner, Exec. Dir.**

262 ■ WECAI Network
PO Box 550856
Fort Lauderdale, FL 33355-0856
Ph: (954)625-6606
Free: **(877)947-3337**
E-mail: info@wecai.org
URL: http://www.wecai.org
Contact: Heidi Richards Mooney MS, Founder/CEO

Economic Development

263 ■ Enterprise for a Sustainable World (ESW)
1609 Shadford Rd.
Ann Arbor, MI 48104
Ph: (734)369-8060
URL: http://www.e4sw.org
Contact: Stuart L. Hart, Founder/Pres.
Founded: 2006. **Multinational. Description:** Works with companies to develop and nurture the capabilities necessary for sustainable enterprise. Provides consulting and education that facilitates effective clean technology, base of the pyramid and green leap initiatives by firms.

264 ■ New America Alliance (NÁA) (1131)
8150 N Central Expy., Ste.1625
Dallas, TX 75206
Ph: (214)466-6410 (214)466-6412
Fax: (214)466-6415
E-mail: **info@naaonline.org**
URL: http://www.naaonline.org
Contact: **Maria del Pilar Avila, CEO**

265 ■ Rising Tide Capital
348 Martin Luther King Dr.
Jersey City, NJ 07305
Ph: **(201)432-4316**
E-mail: info@risingtidecapital.org
URL: http://risingtidecapital.org
Contact: Doug Forrester, Chm.

Economics

266 ■ Association of Specialized and Professional Accreditors (ASPA) (1085)
3304 N Broadway St., No. 214
Chicago, IL 60657
Ph: **(773)857-7900**
Fax: **(773)857-7901**
E-mail: aspa@aspa-usa.org
URL: http://www.aspa-usa.org
Contact: **Joseph Vibert, Exec. Dir.**

267 ■ International Society for Ecological Economics (ISEE) (1137)
c/o Anne C. Aitken, Managing Dir.
15 River St., No. 204
Boston, MA 02108
E-mail: secretariat@ecoeco.org
URL: http://www.ecoeco.org
Contact: John Gowdy, Pres.

Elections

268 ■ National Association of State Election Directors (NASED) (1139)
12543 Westella Dr., Ste.100
Houston, TX 77077-3929
Ph: (281)752-6200
Fax: (281)293-0453
E-mail: services@nased.org
URL: http://www.nased.org
Contact: **Kathy Scheele, Pres.**

Electrical

269 ■ Electrical Equipment Representatives Association (EERA) (1144)
638 W 39th St.
Kansas City, MO 64111
Ph: (816)561-5323
Fax: (816)561-1249
E-mail: info2005@eera.org
URL: http://www.eera.org
Contact: **Scott Whitehead, Pres.**

270 ■ Energy Telecommunications and Electrical Association (ENTELEC) (1149)
5005 Royal Ln., Ste.116
Irving, TX 75063
Free: (888)503-8700
Fax: (972)915-6040
E-mail: amanda@entelec.org
URL: http://www.entelec.org
Contact: **Joel Prochaska, Pres.**

271 ■ International Association of Electrical Inspectors (IAEI) (1147)
PO Box 830848
Richardson, TX 75083-0848
Ph: (972)235-1455
Free: (800)786-4234
Fax: (972)235-6858
E-mail: iaei@iaei.org
URL: http://www.iaei.org
Contact: **Chuck Mello, Intl. Pres.**

272 ■ National Rural Electric Cooperative Association (NRECA) (1155)
4301 Wilson Blvd.
Arlington, VA 22203
Ph: (703)907-5500 (703)907-5732
Fax: (703)907-5517
E-mail: **michael.lynch@nreca.coop**
URL: **http://www.nreca.coop/Pages/default.aspx**
Contact: **Glenn English, CEO**

273 ■ North American Electric Reliability Corporation (NERC) (1099)
116-390 Village Blvd.
Princeton, NJ 08540-5721
Ph: (609)452-8060
Fax: (609)452-9550
E-mail: **kimberly.mielcarek@nerc.net**
URL: http://www.nerc.com
Contact: Gerry W. Cauley, Pres./CEO

274 ■ Professional Electrical Apparatus Recyclers League (PEARL) (1159)
4255 S Buckley Rd., No. 118
Aurora, CO 80013
Free: (877)AT-PEARL
Fax: (888)996-3296
E-mail: pearl@pearl1.org
URL: http://www.pearl1.org
Contact: **Brian Corekin, Pres.**

275 ■ Women's International Network of Utility Professionals (WiNUP) (1164)
PO Box 817
Fergus Falls, MN 56538-0817
Ph: (218)731-1659
Fax: (320)284-2299
E-mail: drexler@runestone.net
URL: **http://myetech.info**
Contact: **Vikki Michalski, Pres.**

Electronics

276 ■ ALMA - The International Loudspeaker Association (1168)
55 Littleton Rd., 13B
Ayer, MA 01432
Ph: (617)314-6977
Fax: (617)848-9935

E-mail: management@almainternational.org
URL: http://www.almainternational.org
Contact: Stu Lumsden, Pres.

277 ■ Asian America MultiTechnology Association (AAMA) (1166)
3 W 37th Ave., Ste.19
San Mateo, CA 94403-4470
Ph: (650)350-1124
E-mail: aama@aamasv.com
URL: http://www.aamasv.com
Contact: **Ben Park, Exec. Dir.**

278 ■ Association for High Technology Distribution (AHTD) (1205)
N19 W24400 Riverwood Dr.
Waukesha, WI 53188
Ph: (262)696-3645
Fax: **(262)696-3646**
E-mail: **ahtd@ahtd.org**
URL: **http://www.ahtdmembers.org**
Contact: Timothy York, Pres.

279 ■ Digital Living Network Alliance (DLNA)
400 Kruse Way Pl.
Bldg. 2, Ste.250
Lake Oswego, OR 97035
Ph: **(503)908-1115**
Fax: **(503)908-1125**
E-mail: admin@dlna.org
URL: http://www.dlna.org
Contact: Nidhish Parikh, Pres.

280 ■ Electronic Industry Citizenship Coalition (EICC)
c/o Carrie Hoffman, Dir. of Communications
1155 15th St. NW, Ste.500
Washington, DC 20005
Ph: (202)962-0167
Fax: (202)530-0659
E-mail: **bbruno@eicc.info**
URL: http://www.eicc.info
Contact: John Gabriel, Chm.

281 ■ Electronics Representatives Association (ERA) (1175)
111 N Canal St., Ste.885
Chicago, IL 60606
Ph: **(312)559-3050**
Free: (800)776-7377
Fax: **(312)559-4566**
E-mail: info@era.org
URL: http://www.era.org
Contact: **Robert Walsh, Chm.**

282 ■ International Society of Certified Electronics Technicians (ISCET) (1129)
3608 Pershing Ave.
Fort Worth, TX 76107-4527
Ph: (817)921-9101 **(817)921-9061**
Free: (800)946-0201
Fax: (817)921-3741
E-mail: info@iscet.org
URL: http://www.iscet.org
Contact: Mack Blakely, Exec. Dir.

283 ■ IPC - Association Connecting Electronics Industries (1203)
3000 Lakeside Dr., 309 S
Bannockburn, IL 60015
Ph: (847)615-7100
Fax: (847)615-7105
E-mail: **dmcguirk@ipc.org**
URL: http://www.ipc.org
Contact: Dennis P. McGuirk, Pres./CEO

284 ■ JEDEC (1183)
3103 N 10th St., Ste.240-S
Arlington, VA 22201-2107
Ph: (703)907-7540 **(703)907-7560**
Fax: (703)907-7583
E-mail: emilyd@jedec.org
URL: http://www.jedec.org
Contact: Ms. Emily Desjardins, Dir.

285 ■ National Electronics Service Dealers Association (NESDA) (1224)
3608 Pershing Ave.
Fort Worth, TX 76107-4527
Ph: (817)921-9061
Free: (800)797-9197
Fax: (817)921-3741
E-mail: info@nesda.com
URL: http://www.nesda.com
Contact: **Mack Blakely, Exec. Dir.**

286 ■ National Systems Contractors Association (NSCA) (1207)
3950 River Ridge Dr. NE
Cedar Rapids, IA 52402
Ph: (319)366-6722
Free: (800)446-6722
Fax: (319)366-4164
E-mail: nsca@nsca.org
URL: http://www.nsca.org
Contact: **Ron Pusey, Pres.**

287 ■ North America Chinese Clean-tech and Semiconductor Association (NACSA) (1187)
PO Box 61086
Sunnyvale, CA 94088-1086
E-mail: info@nacsa.com
URL: http://www.nacsa.com
Contact: **Renxin Xia, Chm.**

288 ■ North American Retail Dealers Association (NARDA) (1188)
222 S Riverside Plz., Ste.2100
Chicago, IL 60606
Ph: (312)648-0649
Free: (800)621-0298
Fax: **(312)648-1212**
E-mail: nardasvc@narda.com
URL: http://www.narda.com
Contact: Otto Papasadero, Interim Exec. Dir.

289 ■ Professional Audio Manufacturers Alliance (PAMA)
11242 Waples Mill Rd., Ste.200
Fairfax, VA 22030
Ph: (703)279-9938 **(703)279-9939**
Fax: **(703)278-8082**
E-mail: duffywilbert@pamalliance.org
URL: http://www.pamalliance.org
Contact: Duffy J. Wilbert, Exec. Dir.

290 ■ Variable Electronic Components Institute (VECI) (1132)
PO Box 1070
Vista, CA 92085-1070
Ph: (760)631-0178
Fax: **(760)631-0178**
E-mail: **veci2@cox.net**
URL: http://www.veci-vrci.com
Contact: Stanley Kukawka, Exec. Dir.

Employee Benefits

291 ■ Employers Council on Flexible Compensation (ECFC) (1201)
927 15th St. NW, Ste.1000
Washington, DC 20005
Ph: (202)659-4300
Fax: (877)747-3539
E-mail: **david@ecfc.org**
URL: http://www.ecfc.org
Contact: Mr. Dennis Triplett, Chm.

292 ■ International Foundation of Employee Benefit Plans (IFEBP) (1204)
PO Box 69
Brookfield, WI 53008-0069
Ph: (262)786-6700 (262)786-6710
Free: (888)334-3327
Fax: (262)786-8670
E-mail: membership@ifebp.org
URL: http://www.ifebp.org
Contact: **John J. Simmons, Pres./Chm.**

293 ■ International Society of Certified Employee Benefit Specialists (ISCEBS) (1149)
PO Box 209
Brookfield, WI 53008-0209
Ph: (262)786-8771
Fax: (262)786-8650
E-mail: iscebs@iscebs.org
URL: http://www.iscebs.org
Contact: **Steven E. Grieb, Pres.**

294 ■ National Association of Benefits and Work Incentive Specialists (NABWIS)
12009 Shallot St.
Orlando, FL 32837
Ph: **(407)859-7767**
Fax: **(407)240-6592**
E-mail: **nabwis@gmail.com**
URL: http://www.ilr.cornell.edu/edi/nabwis
Contact: Thomas P. Golden, Pres.

Employee Ownership

295 ■ National Center for Employee Ownership (NCEO) (160)
1736 Franklin St., 8th Fl.
Oakland, CA 94612
Ph: (510)208-1300
Fax: (510)272-9510
E-mail: **customerservice@nceo.org**
URL: http://www.nceo.org
Contact: **Loren Rodgers, Exec. Dir.**

Employment

296 ■ Green Collar Association
PO Box 2093
Washington, DC 20013
Free: (866)262-5735
URL: http://www.greencollar.org
Contact: Michael Dayan PhD, Contact

Members: 85,000. **Multinational. Description:** Represents the workforce, educational community and corporations. Promotes the creation and growth of green collar jobs through education and training. Provides a clearinghouse for exchanging best practices, tools and ideas in the green economy.

297 ■ Industrial Foundation of America (IFA) (1225)
179 Enterprise Pkwy., Ste.102
Boerne, TX 78006
Ph: (830)249-7899
Free: (800)592-1433
Fax: (800)628-2397
E-mail: ifasmith@gvtc.com
URL: http://www.ifa-america.com
Contact: Bill Smith, Exec. Dir.

298 ■ National Association of Professional Employer Organizations (NAPEO) (1233)
707 N St. Asaph St.
Alexandria, VA 22314
Ph: (703)836-0466
Fax: (703)836-0976
E-mail: info@napeo.org
URL: http://www.napeo.org
Contact: **Brian Fayak, Pres.**

299 ■ WorldatWork (1185)
14040 N Northsight Blvd.
Scottsdale, AZ 85260
Ph: (480)951-9191 (480)922-2020
Free: (877)951-9191
Fax: (480)483-8352
E-mail: customerrelations@worldatwork.org
URL: http://www.worldatwork.org
Contact: **David Smith CCP, Chm.**

Energy

300 ■ Domestic Energy Producers Alliance (DEPA)
PO Box 18359
Oklahoma City, OK 73154
Ph: (405)424-1699
URL: http://www.depausa.org
Contact: Harold Hamm, Chm.

Description: Represents small businessmen and women of the energy industry. Promotes the survival of United States crude oil and natural gas exploration and production. Fights to preserve the economic activity and tax revenues generated by onshore drilling and production activities within the United States.

301 ■ Energy Efficiency Business Coalition (EEBC)
5500 E Yale St., Ste.360
Denver, CO 80222
Ph: (720)445-3728
E-mail: shane@eebco.org
URL: http://energyefficiencybusinesses.org
Contact: Shane Flansburg, Exec. Dir.

Founded: 2007. **Membership Dues:** manufacturer, association, $3,000 (annual) ● distibutor, $1,500 (annual) ● independent manufacturer's representative, DSM implementor, $1,000 (annual) ● contractor/engineer, $250 (annual). **Description:** Provides a voice to businesses involved in the manufacturing, distribution, installation and sales and marketing of energy efficiency technologies. Increases the business potential of the energy efficiency industry. Collaborates with utilities, municipalities and government organizations to assure energy efficiency programs.

302 ■ Energy Information Standards Alliance (EIS Alliance)
65 Washington St., Ste.170
Santa Clara, CA 95050
Ph: (650)938-6945
Fax: (408)253-9938
E-mail: info@eisalliance.org
URL: http://www.eisalliance.org
Contact: David Bunzel, Exec. Dir.

Founded: 2009. **Description:** Represents companies that provide products and services in the areas of energy management systems and smart grid technologies. Serves as an energy consumer's voice for the use of energy management systems. Provides information on how energy management systems and smart grid technologies can help modernize the electricity system.

303 ■ Leadership for Energy Automated Processing (LEAP)
c/o Mary Dortenzio, Treas.
Glencore
301 Tresser Blvd.
Stamford, CT 06901
Ph: (203)846-1300
E-mail: info@energyleap.org
URL: http://energyleap.org
Contact: Don Steiner, Exec. Dir.

Founded: 2006. **Multinational. Description:** Promotes efficient and reliable transaction processing within the energy industry through voluntary automation and standardization. Works to increase accuracy and timeliness, consistency, efficiency and manage risk and regulatory credibility of energy trades.

304 ■ Retail Energy Supply Association (RESA)
PO Box 6089
Harrisburg, PA 17112
Ph: (717)566-5405
Fax: (717)566-4933
E-mail: **tmccormick@resausa.org**
URL: http://www.resausa.org
Contact: Tracy McCormick, Exec. Dir.

305 ■ TopTen USA
1620 St. NW, Ste.210
Washington, DC 20006
E-mail: norm@toptenusa.org
URL: http://www.toptenusa.org
Contact: Norman L. Dean, Exec. Dir./Pres.

Description: Promotes various ways of conserving energy through the use of energy-efficient products. Identifies and publicizes top energy-efficient products on the market. Encourages manufacturing innovations in making more energy-efficient products.

Engines

306 ■ Engine Manufacturers Association (EMA) (1166)
333 W Wacker Dr., Ste.810
Chicago, IL 60606
Ph: (312)929-1970
Fax: (312)929-1975
E-mail: **ema@emamail.org**
URL: http://www.enginemanufacturers.org
Contact: Jed R. Mandel, Pres.

307 ■ Outdoor Power Equipment Aftermarket Association (OPEAA) (1253)
341 S Patrick St.
Alexandria, VA 22314
Ph: (703)549-7608
Fax: (703)549-7609
E-mail: opeaa@opeaa.org
URL: http://www.opeaa.org
Contact: **Mike Watts, Pres.**

Entertainment

308 ■ Amusement and Music Operators Association (AMOA) (1179)
600 Spring Hill Ring Rd., Ste.111
West Dundee, IL 60118
Ph: (847)428-7699
Free: (800)937-2662
Fax: (847)428-7719
E-mail: **jackamoa@aol.com**
URL: http://www.amoa.com/joomla
Contact: Jack Kelleher, Exec. VP

309 ■ International Association of Amusement Parks and Attractions (IAAPA) (1265)
1448 Duke St.
Alexandria, VA 22314
Ph: (703)836-4800
Fax: **(703)836-6742**
E-mail: **ccleary@iaapa.org**
URL: http://www.iaapa.org
Contact: **Chip Cleary, Pres./CEO**

310 ■ International Entertainment Buyers Association (IEBA)
9 Music Sq. W
Nashville, TN 37203
Ph: (615)251-9000
Fax: **(615)866-0116**
E-mail: info@ieba.org
URL: http://www.ieba.org
Contact: Tiffany Davis, Exec. Dir.

311 ■ National Association of Black Female Executives in Music and Entertainment (NABFEME)
59 Maiden Ln., 27th Fl.
New York, NY 10038
Ph: **(212)424-9568**
Fax: (212)397-4273
E-mail: **nabfeme@gmail.com**
URL: http://www.nabfeme.org
Contact: Johnnie Walker, Chair/Founder

312 ■ National Association of Casino Party Operators (NACPO) (1277)
PO Box 5626
South San Francisco, CA 94083
Free: (888)922-0777
E-mail: **info@casinoparties.com**
URL: http://www.nactpo.com
Contact: Mike Miller, Dir.

313 ■ National Association of Theatre Owners (NATO) (1295)
750 1st St. NE, Ste.1130
Washington, DC 20002
Ph: (202)962-0054
Fax: (202)962-0370
E-mail: nato@natodc.com
URL: http://www.natoonline.org
Contact: **Tony Kerasotes, Chm.**

314 ■ Organization of Black Screenwriters (OBS) (1287)
3010 Wilshire Blvd., No. 269
Los Angeles, CA 90010
Ph: (323)735-2050 (310)844-8755
E-mail: jwilliams@obswriter.com
URL: http://www.obswriter.com
Contact: Jennifer Williams, Pres.

315 ■ Outdoor Amusement Business Association (OABA) (171)
1035 S Semoran Blvd., Ste.1045A
Winter Park, FL 32792
Ph: (407)681-9444
Free: (800)517-OABA
Fax: (407)681-9445
E-mail: **oaba@oaba.org**
URL: http://www.oaba.org
Contact: Robert W. Johnson, Pres.

Environmental Health

316 ■ Responsible Purchasing Network (RPN)
1201 Martin Luther King Jr. Way
Oakland, CA 94612
Free: (866)776-1330
E-mail: info@responsiblepurchasing.org
URL: http://www.responsiblepurchasing.org
Contact: Phillip Kobernick, Mgr.
Founded: 2005. **Membership Dues:** federal agency, $450 (annual) ● state agency, municipal agency, educational institution (based on population), $225-$450 (annual) ● non-profit organization, $160 (annual) ● business (based on annual sales), $315-$1,350 (annual). **Description:** Represents an international network of buyers dedicated to socially responsible and environmentally sustainable purchasing. Develops effective purchasing tools, educates the market and uses its collective purchasing power to maximize environmental stewardship, protect human health and support local and global sustainability.

Exhibitors

317 ■ International Sport Show Producers Association (ISSPA) (1304)
PO Box 480084
Denver, CO 80248-0084
Ph: (303)892-6966 **(303)892-6800**
Free: (800)457-2434
Fax: (303)892-6322
E-mail: dhathorne@iei-expos.com
URL: http://www.sportshow.org
Contact: Debbie Hathorne, Exec. Sec.

Farriers

318 ■ Guild of Professional Farriers (1314)
PO Box 4541
Midway, KY 40347
URL: http://www.guildfarriers.org
Contact: **Russ Vanderlei RJF, Pres.**

Film Industry

319 ■ Academy of Motion Picture Arts and Sciences (AMPAS) (1326)
8949 Wilshire Blvd.
Beverly Hills, CA 90211
Ph: (310)247-3000
Fax: (310)859-9619
E-mail: **contact@oscars.org**
URL: http://www.oscars.org
Contact: Bruce Davis, Exec. Dir.

320 ■ Alliance of Motion Picture and Television Producers (AMPTP) (1233)
15301 Ventura Blvd., Bldg. E
Sherman Oaks, CA 91403
Ph: (818)995-3600 **(818)935-5938**
E-mail: amptp@tw.amptp.org
URL: http://www.amptp.org/index.html
Contact: Carol Lombardini, Pres.

321 ■ Association of Cinema and Video Laboratories (ACVL) (1320)
c/o Peter Bulcke, Treas.
1833 Centinela Ave.
Santa Monica, CA 90404
Ph: (310)828-1098
Fax: (310)828-9737
E-mail: **treasurer@acvl.org**
URL: http://www.acvl.org
Contact: **Kevin Dillon, Pres.**

322 ■ Independent Film and Television Alliance (IFTA) (1235)
10850 Wilshire Blvd., 9th Fl.
Los Angeles, CA 90024-4321
Ph: (310)446-1000 **(310)446-1020**
Fax: (310)446-1600
E-mail: rburt@ifta-online.org
URL: http://www.ifta-online.org
Contact: Lloyd Kaufman, Chm.

323 ■ International Cinema Technology Association (ICTA) (3811)
770 Broadway, 7th Fl.
New York, NY 10003-9522
Ph: **(212)493-4097 (212)257-6428**
Fax: **(212)257-6428**
E-mail: **edith.malijan@filmexpos.com**
URL: **http://www.internationalcinematechnolog-yassociation.com**
Contact: Robert H. Sunshine, Exec. Dir.

324 ■ Media Communications Association International (MCA-I) (1339)
PO Box 5135
Madison, WI 53705-0135
Free: (888)899-6224
Fax: (888)862-8150
E-mail: **loiswei@aol.com**
URL: http://www.mca-i.org
Contact: **Don Glass, Pres.-Elect**

Finance

325 ■ American Finance Association (AFA) (1352)
Univ. of California
Haas School of Bus.
Berkeley, CA 94720-1900
Free: (800)835-6770
Fax: (781)388-8232
E-mail: pyle@haas.berkeley.edu
URL: http://www.afajof.org
Contact: **Raghuram Rajan, Pres.**

326 ■ Asian Financial Society (AFS) (232)
32 Broadway, Ste.1701
New York, NY 10004
Ph: **(646)580-5066**
E-mail: afswww@yahoo.com
URL: http://asianfinancialsociety.org
Contact: **Tracy Wan, Pres.**

327 ■ Association for Financial Professionals (AFP) (1383)
4520 E West Hwy., Ste.750
Bethesda, MD 20814
Ph: (301)907-2862
Fax: (301)907-2864
E-mail: afp@afponline.org
URL: http://www.afponline.org
Contact: **Michael Connolly, Chm.**

328 ■ Business Products Credit Association (BPCA)
607 Westridge Dr.
O'Fallon, MO 63366
Ph: (636)294-5775
Free: **(888)514-2722**
Fax: (636)272-2973
E-mail: service@bpca.org
URL: http://www.bpca.org

329 ■ Clearpoint Financial Solutions
8000 Franklin Farms Dr.
Richmond, VA 23229-5004
Free: (877)422-9040
Fax: **(804)526-8271**
E-mail: **customer.service@clearpointccs.org**
URL: http://www.clearpointfinancialsolutions.org
Contact: **Christopher J. Honenberger, Pres./CEO**

330 ■ Community Financial Services Association (CFSA) (1293)
515 King St., Ste.300
Alexandria, VA 22314
Free: **(888)572-9329**
Fax: (703)684-1219
E-mail: **info@cfsaa.com**
URL: **http://cfsaa.com**
Contact: **Lynn DeVault, Dir.**

331 ■ Credit Professionals International (CPI) (1358)
10726 Manchester Rd., Ste.210
St. Louis, MO 63122
Ph: (314)821-9393
Fax: (314)821-7171
E-mail: creditpro@creditprofessionals.org
URL: http://www.creditprofessionals.org
Contact: **Billie Plasker PCS, Pres.**

332 ■ Emerging Markets Private Equity Association (EMPEA) (1368)
1077 30th St. NW, Ste.100
Washington, DC 20007
Ph: (202)333-8171
Fax: (202)333-3162
E-mail: info@empea.net
URL: http://www.empea.net
Contact: Sarah E. Alexander, Pres./CEO

333 ■ Forius Business Credit Resources (181)
8441 Wayzata Blvd., Ste.270
Golden Valley, MN 55426
Free: (800)279-6226
E-mail: info@forius.com
URL: http://www.forius.com
Contact: **Bennett Krenik CCE, Chm.**

334 ■ International Consortium on Governmental Financial Management (ICGFM) (1378)
PO Box 1077
St. Michaels, MD 21663
Ph: **(410)745-8570**
Fax: **(410)745-8569**
E-mail: icgfm@icgfm.org
URL: http://www.icgfm.org
Contact: **Linda Fealing, Pres.**

335 ■ International Factoring Association (IFA) (1380)
2665 Shell Beach Rd., Ste.3
Pismo Beach, CA 93449-1778
Ph: **(805)773-0011**
Free: **(800)563-1895**

Fax: (805)773-0021
E-mail: info@factoring.org
URL: http://www.factoring.org
Contact: **Paul Cattone, Advisory Bd.**

336 ■ Middle East Investment Initiative (MEII)
500 Eighth St. NW
Washington, DC 20004
Ph: (202)741-6283
Fax: (202)898-2590
E-mail: vicky.wolf@meiinitiative.org
URL: http://www.meiinitiative.org
Contact: **Ziad Asali, Pres.**

337 ■ National Association of Corporate Treasurers (NACT) (1387)
12100 Sunset Hills Rd., Ste.130
Reston, VA 20190
Ph: (703)437-4377
Fax: (703)435-4390
E-mail: nact@nact.org
URL: http://www.nact.org
Contact: **Scott Morrison, Chm.**

338 ■ National Association of Financial and Estate Planning (NAFEP) (1314)
515 E 4500 S, No. G-200
Salt Lake City, UT 84107
Free: **(800)454-2649**
Fax: **(877)890-0929**
URL: http://www.nafep.com
Contact: **Scott Janko, Pres.**

339 ■ National Association of State and Local Equity Funds (NASLEF)
1970 Broadway, Ste.250
Oakland, CA 94612
Ph: **(510)444-1101**
Fax: **(510)444-1191**
E-mail: info@naslef.org
URL: http://www.naslef.org
Contact: **Dana Boole, Pres.**

340 ■ National Rural Utilities Cooperative Finance Corporation (NRUCFC) (1441)
2201 Cooperative Way
Herndon, VA 20171
Ph: (703)709-6700
Free: (800)424-2954
URL: **http://www.nrucfc.coop**
Contact: Sheldon C. Petersen, CEO

341 ■ Native American Finance Officers Association (NAFOA) (1390)
PO Box 50637
Phoenix, AZ 85076-0637
Ph: (602)330-9208 (602)466-8697
Fax: **(201)447-0945**
E-mail: **william@nafoa.org**
URL: http://www.nafoa.org
Contact: **William Lomax, Pres.**

342 ■ Network Branded Prepaid Card Association (NBPCA) (1443)
110 Chestnut Ridge Rd., Ste.111
Montvale, NJ 07645-1706
Ph: (201)746-0725
E-mail: **kathy@nbpca.org**
URL: http://www.nbpca.com
Contact: Rod Boyer, Pres.

343 ■ Society of Cost Estimating and Analysis (SCEA) (1402)
527 Maple Ave. E, Ste.301
Vienna, VA 22180
Ph: (703)938-5090
Fax: (703)938-5091
E-mail: scea@sceaonline.org
URL: http://www.sceaonline.net
Contact: **Erin Whittaker, Exec. Dir.**

344 ■ Society of Insurance Financial Management (SIFM) (51)
PO Box 9001
Mount Vernon, NY 10552
Ph: (914)966-3180
Fax: (914)966-3264
E-mail: sifm@cinn.com
URL: http://www.sifm.org
Contact: **Edward J. Majkowski, Pres.**

345 ■ Women in Housing and Finance (WHF) (1407)
400 N Washington St., Ste.300
Alexandria, VA 22314
Ph: (703)683-4742
Fax: (703)683-0018
E-mail: whf@whfdc.org
URL: http://www.whfdc.org
Contact: **Rhonda Daniels, Pres.**

Financial Planning

346 ■ American Association of Daily Money Managers (AADMM) (1403)
174 Crestview Dr.
Bellefonte, PA 16823
Free: (877)326-5991
Fax: (814)355-2452
E-mail: info@aadmm.com
URL: http://www.aadmm.com
Contact: **Pete Conklin, Pres.**

347 ■ Association of Divorce Financial Planners (ADFP)
514 Fourth St.
East Northport, NY 11731
Ph: (631)754-6125
Free: (888)838-7773
E-mail: **adfp@divorceandfinance.org**
URL: http://www.divorceandfinance.org
Contact: Lili A. Vasileff CFP, Pres.

348 ■ Fixed Income Analysts Society (FIASI)
244 Fifth Ave., Ste.L230
New York, NY 10001
Ph: (212)726-8100
Fax: **(212)591-6534**
E-mail: fiasi@fiasi.org
URL: http://www.fiasi.org
Contact: Ms. Lauren Nauser, Exec. Dir.

349 ■ National Association of Christian Financial Consultants (NACFC) (1413)
1055 Maitland Center Commons Blvd.
Maitland, FL 32751
Ph: (407)644-9793
Free: (877)966-2232
E-mail: info@nacfc.org
URL: http://www.nacfc.org
Contact: **Charlie Nelson, Exec. Dir.**

350 ■ National Association of Estate Planners and Councils (NAEPC) (1421)
1120 Chester Ave., Ste.470
Cleveland, OH 44114
Free: (866)226-2224
Fax: (216)696-2582
E-mail: admin@naepc.org
URL: http://www.naepc.org
Contact: **Joseph V. Falanga, Pres.**

Fire Protection

351 ■ Alliance for Fire and Smoke Containment and Control (AFSCC)
4 Brookhollow Rd. SW
Rome, GA 30165-6509
Ph: (706)291-9355
Fax: (706)291-9355
E-mail: **info@gocryer.com**
URL: http://afscc.org
Contact: **Rick Kabele, Exec. Dir.**

352 ■ National Fireproofing Contractors Association (NFCA) (1423)
PO Box 1571
Westford, MA 01886
Free: (866)250-4111
Fax: (978)250-9788
E-mail: nfca@nfca-online.com
URL: http://nfca-online.org
Contact: **Mike Nehnevajsa, Pres.**

Fishing Industries

353 ■ American Albacore Fishing Association (AAFA)
4364 Bonita Rd.
Box 311
Bonita, CA 91902
Ph: (619)941-2307
Free: (866)851-3918
Fax: (619)863-5046
E-mail: nataliewebster@americanalbacore.com
URL: http://www.americanalbacore.com
Contact: Bobby Blocker, Sec.

354 ■ At-sea Processors Association (APA) (1430)
PO Box 32817
Juneau, AK 99803
Ph: (907)523-0970 (206)285-5139
Fax: **(907)523-0798**
E-mail: smadsen@atsea.org
URL: http://www.atsea.org
Contact: Stephanie Madsen, Exec. Dir.

355 ■ International Seafood Sustainability Association (ISSA)
PO Box 11110
McLean, VA 22102
Ph: (703)752-8897
E-mail: mcrispino@iss-association.org
URL: http://www.iss-association.org
Contact: Susan Jackson, Pres.
Membership Dues: processor/trader, $300,000 (annual). **Multinational. Description:** Represents tuna processors and marketers who follow the conservation measures implemented by the International Seafood Sustainability Foundation (ISSF). Promotes science-based initiatives for the long-term conservation and sustainable use of tuna stocks.

Flag

356 ■ Flag Manufacturers Association of America (FMAA)
994 Old Eagle School Rd., Ste.1019
Wayne, PA 19087
Ph: (610)971-4850 **(610)376-2400**
Fax: (610)971-4859
E-mail: info@fmaa.usa.com
URL: http://www.fmaa-usa.com
Contact: Sandy Van Lieu, Chair

Florists

357 ■ American Institute of Floral Designers (AIFD) (1310)
720 Light St.
Baltimore, MD 21230
Ph: (410)752-3318
Fax: (410)752-8295
E-mail: aifd@assnhqtrs.com
URL: http://www.aifd.org
Contact: **Sharon McGukin AIFD, Pres.**

358 ■ Holiday and Decorative Association (HDA) (1362)
PO Box 420244
Dallas, TX 75342-0244
Ph: (214)742-2747
Fax: (214)742-2648

E-mail: hda@hdanow.org
URL: http://www.hdanow.org
Contact: Ronald D. Poling CAE, Pres.
Status Note: Formerly American Floral Industry Association.

Food

359 ■ American Spice Trade Association (ASTA) (1455)
2025 M St. NW, Ste.800
Washington, DC 20036
Ph: (202)367-1127
Fax: (202)367-2127
E-mail: info@astaspice.org
URL: http://www.astaspice.org
Contact: **Donna Tainter, Pres.**

360 ■ American Wholesale Marketers Association (AWMA) (1323)
2750 Prosperity Ave., Ste.530
Fairfax, VA 22031
Ph: (703)208-3358
Free: (800)482-2962
Fax: (703)573-5738
E-mail: info@awmanet.org
URL: http://www.awmanet.org
Contact: **Bill Marshall, Pres.**

361 ■ Flavor and Extract Manufacturers Association of the United States (FEMA) (1466)
1620 I St. NW, Ste.925
Washington, DC 20006
Ph: (202)293-5800
Fax: (202)463-8998
E-mail: **jcox@vertosolutions.net**
URL: http://www.femaflavor.org
Contact: **Ed R. Hays, Pres.**

362 ■ Food Trade Sustainability Leadership Association (FTSLA)
PO Box 51267
Eugene, OR 97405
Ph: (541)852-0745
E-mail: info@ftsla.org
URL: http://www.ftsla.org
Contact: **Nate Schlachter, Exec. Dir.**

363 ■ Institute for Food Safety and Health (IFSH) (1491)
6502 S Archer Rd.
Summit, IL 60501-1957
Ph: (708)563-1576 (708)563-8267
Fax: (708)563-1873
E-mail: nnoka@iit.edu
URL: http://www.iit.edu/ifsh
Contact: Dr. Robert Brackett, VP/Dir.
Status Note: Formerly National Center for Food Safety and Technology.

364 ■ International Food and Agribusiness Management Association (IAMA) (1475)
PO Box 14145
College Station, TX 77841-4145
Ph: (979)845-2118
Fax: **(979)862-1487**
E-mail: iama@ifama.org
URL: http://www.ifama.org
Contact: Paul Jasper, Pres.

365 ■ International Maple Syrup Institute (IMSI) (1486)
387 County Rd.
Woodstock, CT 06281
Ph: **(860)974-1235**
Fax: (802)868-5445
E-mail: **r.norman@snet.net**
URL: http://www.internationalmaplesyrupinstitute.com
Contact: **Richard Norman, Pres.**

366 ■ National Barbecue Association (NBBQA) (1497)
455 S Fourth St., Ste.650
Louisville, KY 40202
Free: (888)909-2121
Fax: (502)589-3602
E-mail: nbbqa@hqtrs.com
URL: http://www.nbbqa.org
Contact: **Kell Phelps, Pres.**

367 ■ National Frozen Pizza Institute (NFPI) (193)
2000 Corporate Ridge, Ste.1000
McLean, VA 22102
Ph: (703)821-0770
Fax: (703)821-1350
URL: http://www.affi.com/index.asp?sid=28
Contact: **Lucas Darnell, Exec. Dir./Sec.**

368 ■ National Frozen and Refrigerated Foods Association (NFRA) (1381)
PO Box 6069
Harrisburg, PA 17112
Ph: (717)657-8601
Fax: (717)657-9862
E-mail: info@nfraweb.org
URL: http://www.nfraweb.org
Contact: **H.V. Shaw Jr., Pres./CEO**

369 ■ Peanut and Tree Nut Processors Association (PTNPA) (1428)
PO Box 2660
Alexandria, VA 22301
Ph: (301)365-2521
Fax: (301)365-7705
E-mail: **jhodges@ptnpa.org**
URL: http://www.ptnpa.org
Contact: **Jeannie Hodges, Exec. Dir.**

370 ■ Pickle Packers International (PPI) (1506)
1620 I St. NW, Ste.925
Washington, DC 20006
Ph: (202)331-2456
Fax: **(202)463-8998**
E-mail: **bbursiek@vertosolutions.net**
URL: http://ilovepickles.org

371 ■ Retail Confectioners International (RCI) (1515)
2053 S Waverly, Ste.C
Springfield, MO 65804
Ph: (417)883-2775
Free: (800)545-5381
Fax: (417)883-1108
E-mail: **info@retailconfectioners.org**
URL: http://www.retailconfectioners.org
Contact: Kelly Brinkmann, Exec. Dir.

372 ■ UniPro Foodservice (1543)
2500 Cumberland Pkwy., Ste.600
Atlanta, GA 30339
Ph: (770)952-0871
Fax: (770)952-0872
E-mail: info@uniprofoodservice.com
URL: http://www.uniprofoodservice.com
Contact: **Joe Natcher, Chm.**

373 ■ United States Beet Sugar Association (USBSA) (1405)
1156 15th St. NW, Ste.1019
Washington, DC 20005
Ph: (202)296-4820
Free: **(800)872-0127**
Fax: (202)331-2065
E-mail: beetsugar@aol.com
URL: http://www.beetsugar.org
Contact: James Johnson, Pres.

Food Service

374 ■ International Food Service Executive's Association (IFSEA) (1533)
4955 Miller St., Ste.107
Wheat Ridge, CO 80033
Free: (800)893-5499
Fax: **(303)420-9579**
E-mail: hq@ifsea.com
URL: http://www.ifsea.com
Contact: **Barbara Sadler, Chair**

375 ■ Multicultural Foodservice and Hospitality Alliance (MFHA) (1475)
1144 Narragansett Blvd.
Providence, RI 02905
Ph: (401)461-6342 **(401)461-6357**
Fax: (401)461-9004
E-mail: info@mfha.net
URL: http://www.mfha.net
Contact: Gerry Fernandez, Pres.

376 ■ National Independent Concessionaires Association (NICA)
PO Box 89429
Tampa, FL 33689
Ph: (727)346-9302
Fax: (727)346-9312
E-mail: **rudyseastcoast@aol.com**
URL: http://www.nicainc.org
Contact: **Russ Harrison CCE, Chair**

377 ■ Restaurant Marketing and Delivery Association (RMDA)
4921 Boone Ave. N
New Hope, MN 55428
E-mail: **ron.patel@justdinein.com**
URL: http://www.rmda.info
Contact: **Ron Patel, Pres.**

378 ■ Society for Foodservice Management (SFM) (1541)
15000 Commerce Pkwy., Ste.C
Mount Laurel, NJ 08054
Ph: (856)380-6829
Fax: (856)439-0525
E-mail: sfm@ahint.com
URL: http://www.sfm-online.org
Contact: **Carol Bracken-Tilley, Pres.**

Footwear

379 ■ Footwear Distributors and Retailers of America (FDRA) (1549)
1319 F St. NW, Ste.700
Washington, DC 20004-1121
Ph: (202)737-5660
Fax: (202)645-0789
E-mail: info@fdra.org
URL: http://www.fdra.org
Contact: **Matt Rubel, Chm.**

380 ■ National Shoe Retailers Association (NSRA) (1435)
3037 W Ina Rd.
Tucson, AZ 85741
Free: (800)673-8446
E-mail: info@nsra.org
URL: http://www.nsra.org
Contact: Alan Miklofsky, Chm.

381 ■ Pedorthic Footwear Association (PFA) (1488)
2025 M St. NW, Ste.800
Washington, DC 20036
Ph: (202)367-1145
Free: (800)673-8447
Fax: (202)367-2145
E-mail: info@pedorthics.org
URL: http://www.pedorthics.org
Contact: **Kristi Hayes, Pres.**

382 ■ Shoe Service Institute of America (SSIA) (1489)
305 Huntsman Ct.
Bel Air, MD 21015
Ph: (410)569-3425
Fax: (410)569-8333
E-mail: don@shoeglue.com
URL: http://www.ssia.info
Contact: Donald Rinaldi, Pres.

383 ■ Two/Ten Footwear Foundation (1550)
1466 Main St.
Waltham, MA 02451-1623
Ph: (781)736-1522 (781)736-1502
Free: (800)346-3210
E-mail: info@twoten.org
URL: http://www.twoten.org
Contact: Peggy Meill, Pres.

Forest Industries

384 ■ American Loggers Council (ALC)
PO Box 966
Hemphill, TX 75948
Ph: (409)625-0206
Fax: (409)625-0207
E-mail: loggersweb@americanloggers.org
URL: http://www.americanloggers.org
Contact: Matt Jensen, Pres.

385 ■ Pacific Lumber Exporters Association (PLEA) (1568)
2633 NW Raleigh St., No. 39
Portland, OR 97210
Ph: (503)598-3325
Fax: (503)670-9663
E-mail: info@lumber-exporters.org
URL: http://lumber-exporters.org
Contact: Mike Parr, Pres.

Forest Products

386 ■ American Walnut Manufacturers Association (AWMA) (204)
1007 N 725 W
West Lafayette, IN 47906-9431
E-mail: jackson@purdue.edu
URL: http://www.walnutassociation.org
Contact: Liz Jackson, Exec. Dir.

387 ■ Cork Institute of America (1496)
715 Fountain Ave.
Lancaster, PA 17601
Ph: (717)295-3400
Fax: (717)295-3414
E-mail: info@corkinstitute.com
URL: http://www.corkinstitute.com

388 ■ National Hardwood Lumber Association (NHLA) (1604)
PO Box 34518
Memphis, TN 38184-0518
Ph: (901)377-1818
Free: (800)933-0318
Fax: (901)399-7581
E-mail: membership@nhla.com
URL: http://www.nhla.com
Contact: Mark Barford, Exec. Dir.

389 ■ Wood I-Joist Manufacturers Association (WIJMA)
PO Box 1088
Roseburg, OR 97470
Ph: (541)784-2817
Fax: (541)784-2593
E-mail: davea@rfpco.com
URL: http://i-joist.org
Contact: Dave Anderson, Pres.
Multinational. Description: Represents major producers engaged in the manufacture of prefabricated wood I-joists and structural composite lumber (SCL). Provides technical assistance and information to residential and commercial construction industries. Seeks to engage in activities that enhance and increase the use of prefabricated wood I-joists and structural composite lumber in the construction industry.

Franchising

390 ■ National Franchisee Association (NFA) (1620)
1701 Barrett Lakes Blvd. NW, Ste.180
Kennesaw, GA 30144
Ph: (678)797-5160
Fax: (678)797-5170
E-mail: amyk@namgllc.com
URL: http://www.nfabk.org
Contact: Amy Kuhn, Gen. Admin.

Fuel

391 ■ Advanced Biofuels Association (ABFA)
2099 Pennsylvania Ave. NW Ste.100
Washington, DC 20006
Ph: (202)469-5140
E-mail: michael.mcadams@hklaw.com
URL: http://www.advancedbiofuelsassociation.com
Contact: Michael J. McAdams, Pres.
Description: Promotes the advancement of biofuels industry to strengthen energy and economic security. Engages the federal and state governments to secure a level playing field for innovative biofuels technologies. Serves as the voice of the advanced biofuels industry.

392 ■ Global Biofuels Alliance
1540 E Lake Rd.
Erie, PA 16511
Ph: (814)528-9067
E-mail: info@globalbiofuels.org
URL: http://www.globalbiofuels.org
Contact: Brad Davis, Pres./Exec. Dir.
Founded: 2010. **Multinational. Description:** Aims to advance the sustainable growth of the biofuel industry. Supports increased production, distribution and use of environmentally sound biofuels in markets worldwide. Seeks to address crucial issues pertinent to the biofuel industry.

Fundraising

393 ■ Direct Marketing Fundraisers Association (DMFA) (1627)
PO Box 1038
New York, NY 10028
Ph: (646)675-7314
Fax: (201)266-4006
E-mail: info@dmfa.org
URL: http://www.dmfa.org
Contact: Bryan Terpstra, Pres.

394 ■ Giving Institute (GI) (1658)
303 W Madison St., Ste.2650
Chicago, IL 60606
Ph: (312)981-6794
Fax: (312)265-2908
E-mail: info@givinginstitute.org
URL: http://www.givinginstitute.org
Contact: Mr. Thomas W. Mesaros, Chm.

Furniture

395 ■ Futon Association International (FAI) (1696)
10705-7 Rocket Blvd.
Orlando, FL 32824
Ph: (407)447-1706
Free: (800)327-3262
Fax: (866)595-1355
E-mail: info@futon.org
URL: http://www.futon.org/aboutfutons.php3
Contact: Tammy Weaver, Contact

396 ■ High Point Market Authority (1701)
164 S Main St., Ste.700
High Point, NC 27260
Ph: (336)869-1000
Free: (800)874-6492
E-mail: bcasey@highpointmarket.org
URL: http://www.highpointmarket.org
Contact: Kevin O'Connor, Pres.

397 ■ Sustainable Furnishings Council (SFC)
PO Box 205
Chapel Hill, NC 27514
Ph: (919)967-1137
E-mail: susan@sustainablefurnishings.org
URL: http://www.sustainablefurniturecouncil.org
Contact: Susan Inglis, Exec. Dir.

Gifts

398 ■ National Specialty Gift Association (NSGA) (1665)
7238 Bucks Ford Dr.
Riverview, FL 33578
Ph: (813)374-1777
E-mail: nsga@giftprofessionals.com
URL: http://www.nsgaonline.com/nsga

Glass

399 ■ Glass Association of North America (GANA) (219)
800 SW Jackson St., Ste.1500
Topeka, KS 66612-1200
Ph: (785)271-0208
Fax: (785)271-0166
E-mail: gana@glasswebsite.com
URL: http://www.glasswebsite.com
Contact: William M. Yanek, Exec. VP

400 ■ National Glass Association (NGA) (1706)
1945 Old Gallows Rd., Ste.750
Vienna, VA 22182
Ph: (703)442-4890
Free: (866)DIAL-NGA
Fax: (703)442-0630
E-mail: pjames@glass.org
URL: http://www.glass.org
Contact: Steven R. Burnett, Chm.

Government Contracts

401 ■ Coalition for Government Procurement (CGP) (1680)
1990 M St. NW, Ste.450
Washington, DC 20036
Ph: (202)331-0975 (202)315-1051
Fax: (202)822-9788
E-mail: rwaldron@thecgp.org
URL: http://netforum.avectra.com/eWeb/StartPage.aspx?Site=CGP
Contact: Roger Waldron, Pres.

Grain

402 ■ American Association of Grain Inspection and Weighing Agencies (AAGIWA) (1686)
PO Box 26426
Kansas City, MO 64196
Ph: (816)569-4020
Fax: (816)221-8189
E-mail: info@aagiwa.org
URL: http://www.aagiwa.org
Contact: Larry Kitchen, Pres.

403 ■ Transportation, Elevator and Grain Merchants Association (TEGMA) (1726)
PO Box 26426
Kansas City, MO 64196
Ph: (816)569-4020
Fax: (816)221-8189
E-mail: bob.petersen@tegma.org
URL: http://www.tegma.org
Contact: Robert R. Petersen, Pres.

Graphic Arts

404 ■ California Society of Printmakers (CSP) (1703)
PO Box 194202
San Francisco, CA 94119
E-mail: info@caprintmakers.org
URL: http://www.caprintmakers.org
Contact: Mark Welschmeyer, Pres.

405 ■ Graphic Arts Education and Research Foundation (GAERF) (1698)
1899 Preston White Dr.
Reston, VA 20191
Ph: (703)264-7200
Free: (866)381-9839
Fax: (703)620-3165
E-mail: gaerf@npes.org
URL: http://www.gaerf.org
Contact: Stephen L. Johnson, Chm.

406 ■ Gravure Association of America (GAA) (1713)
PO Box 25617
Rochester, NY 14625
Ph: (201)523-6042
Fax: (201)523-6048
E-mail: gaa@gaa.org
URL: http://www.gaa.org
Contact: Bill Martin, Pres./CEO

407 ■ IDEAlliance - International Digital Enterprise Alliance (1715)
1421 Prince St., Ste.230
Alexandria, VA 22314-2805
Ph: (703)837-1070 (703)837-1066
Fax: (703)837-1072
E-mail: dsteinhardt@idealliance.org
URL: http://www.idealliance.org
Contact: David J. Steinhardt, Pres./CEO

408 ■ National Association of Litho Clubs (NALC) (1723)
3268 N 147th Ln.
Goodyear, AZ 85395
Ph: (650)339-4007
E-mail: dreyfus@sbcglobal.net
URL: http://www.graphicarts.org
Contact: Raymond Siegel, Pres.

409 ■ National Association for Printing Leadership (NAPL) (1753)
75 W Century Rd., Ste.100
Paramus, NJ 07652-1408
Ph: (201)634-9600
Free: (800)642-6275
Fax: (201)634-0324
E-mail: jtruncale@napl.org
URL: http://www.napl.org
Contact: Joseph P. Truncale CAE, Pres./CEO

410 ■ NPES: Association for Suppliers of Printing, Publishing and Converting Technologies (1589)
1899 Preston White Dr.
Reston, VA 20191
Ph: (703)264-7200
Fax: (703)620-0994
E-mail: npes@npes.org
URL: http://www.npes.org
Contact: Ralph J. Nappi, Pres.

Graphic Design

411 ■ Amalgamated Printers' Association (APA) (1745)
c/o Phillip Driscoll, Sec.
135 East Church St.
Clinton, MI 49236
E-mail: phil@phillipdriscoll.com
URL: http://www.apa-letterpress.com
Contact: Jim Daggs, Pres.

412 ■ Society of Publication Designers (SPD) (1749)
27 Union Sq. W, Ste.207
New York, NY 10003
Ph: (212)223-3332
Fax: (212)223-5880
E-mail: mail@spd.org
URL: http://www.spd.org
Contact: Nathalie Kirsheh, Pres.

Hardware

413 ■ Builders Hardware Manufacturers Association (BHMA) (1758)
355 Lexington Ave., 15th Fl.
New York, NY 10017
Ph: (212)297-2122
Fax: (212)370-9047
E-mail: bhma@kellencompany.com
URL: http://www.buildershardware.com
Contact: Don Baker, Pres.

414 ■ Industrial Fasteners Institute (IFI) (1651)
6363 Oak Tree Blvd.
Independence, OH 44131
Ph: (216)241-1482
E-mail: rharris@indfast.org
URL: http://www.indfast.org
Contact: Robert J. Harris, Managing Dir.

415 ■ North American Retail Hardware Association (NRHA) (1767)
6325 Digital Way, No. 300
Indianapolis, IN 46278-1787
Ph: (317)290-0338
Free: (800)772-4424
Fax: (317)328-4354
E-mail: pfbowman@nrha.org
URL: http://www.nrha.org
Contact: Patty Bowman, Contact

416 ■ Valve Repair Council (VRC) (241)
1050 17th St. NW, Ste.280
Washington, DC 20036
Ph: (202)331-8105
Fax: (202)296-0378
URL: http://www.unitedvalve.com/vr_council.htm
Contact: Marc Pasternak, VP/Exec. Dir.

Health Care

417 ■ National Association of Health and Educational Facilities Finance Authorities (NAHEFFA)
701 Pennsylvania Ave. NW, No. 900
Washington, DC 20004
Ph: (202)434-7311
Fax: (202)434-7400
E-mail: info@whefa.com
URL: http://www.naheffa.com
Contact: Marianne Remedios, Sec./Dir.

418 ■ National Council on Interpreting in Health Care (NCIHC)
5505 Connecticut Ave. NW, No. 119
Washington, DC 20015-2601
Ph: (202)596-2436
Fax: (425)963-0171

E-mail: info@ncihc.org
URL: http://www.ncihc.org
Contact: Gem P. Daus, Exec. Dir.

419 ■ National Organization of Life and Health Insurance Guaranty Associations (NOLHGA) (1791)
13873 Park Center Rd., Ste.329
Herndon, VA 20171
Ph: (703)481-5206
Fax: (703)481-5209
E-mail: info@nolhga.com
URL: http://www.nolhga.com
Contact: John R. Mathews Esq., Chm.

420 ■ PHI
349 E 149th St., 10th Fl.
Bronx, NY 10451
Ph: (718)402-7766
Free: (866)402-4138
Fax: (718)585-6852
E-mail: info@phinational.org
URL: http://phinational.org
Contact: Steven L. Dawson, Pres.
Status Note: Formerly Paraprofessional Healthcare Institute.

Health Care Products

421 ■ American Orthotic and Prosthetic Association (AOPA) (1855)
PO Box 34711
Alexandria, VA 22334-0711
Ph: (571)431-0876
Fax: (571)431-0899
E-mail: info@aopanet.org
URL: http://www.aopanet.org
Contact: Tom DiBello, Pres.

422 ■ Contact Lens Manufacturers Association (CLMA) (1795)
PO Box 29398
Lincoln, NE 68529
Ph: (402)465-4122
Free: (800)344-9060
Fax: (402)465-4187
E-mail: c_pantle@sbcglobal.net
URL: http://www.clma.net
Contact: Mr. Al Vaske, Pres.

423 ■ Dental Trade Alliance (DTA) (1797)
2300 Clarendon Blvd., Ste.1003
Arlington, VA 22201
Ph: (703)379-7755
Fax: (703)931-9429
E-mail: info@dentaltradealliance.org
URL: http://www.dentaltradealliance.org
Contact: Bret Wise, Chm.

424 ■ International Aloe Science Council (IASC) (1801)
8630 Fenton St., Ste.918
Silver Spring, MD 20910
Ph: (301)588-2420
Fax: (301)588-1174
E-mail: info@iasc.org
URL: http://www.iasc.org
Contact: Chris Hardy, Chm.

425 ■ Orthopedic Surgical Manufacturers Association (OSMA) (1803)
PO Box 38805
Germantown, TN 38183-0805
Ph: (901)758-0806
E-mail: secretary@osma.net
URL: http://www.osma.net
Contact: Al Alonzo, Pres.

426 ■ Vision Council of America (VCA) (1804)
225 Reinekers Ln., Ste.700
Alexandria, VA 22314
Ph: (703)548-4560
Free: (866)826-0290
Fax: (703)548-4580

E-mail: info@thevisioncouncil.org
URL: http://www.thevisioncouncil.org
Contact: Edward E. Greene, CEO

Heating and Cooling

427 ■ Air-Conditioning Heating and Refrigeration Institute (AHRI) (1809)
2111 Wilson Blvd., Ste.500
Arlington, VA 22201
Ph: (703)524-8800
Fax: **(703)562-1942**
E-mail: ahri@ahrinet.org
URL: http://www.ahrinet.org
Contact: Ray Hoglund, Chm.

428 ■ Air Diffusion Council (ADC) (1703)
1901 N Roselle Rd., Ste.800
Schaumburg, IL 60195
Ph: (847)706-6750
Fax: (847)706-6751
E-mail: info@flexibleduct.org
URL: http://www.flexibleduct.org
Contact: **Jason Lamborn, Pres.**

429 ■ Air Movement and Control Association International (AMCA International) (1803)
30 W Univ. Dr.
Arlington Heights, IL 60004
Ph: (847)394-0150
Fax: (847)253-0088
E-mail: mstevens@amca.org
URL: http://www.amca.org
Contact: **Wade Smith, Exec. Dir.**

430 ■ Hearth, Patio and Barbecue Foundation (HPBEF) (1815)
1901 N Moore St., Ste.600
Arlington, VA 22209
Ph: (703)524-8030
Fax: (703)522-0548
E-mail: info@hpbef.org
URL: http://hpbef.org
Contact: **Rick Vlahos, Exec. Dir.**

431 ■ Heating Airconditioning and Refrigeration Distributors International (HARDI) (1817)
3455 Mill Run Dr., Ste.820
Hilliard, OH 43026
Ph: (614)345-4328
Free: (888)253-2128
Fax: (614)345-9161
E-mail: hardimail@hardinet.org
URL: http://associationdatabase.com/aws/HARDI/pt/
sp/Home_Page
Contact: **Richard Cook, Pres.**

432 ■ International Air Filtration Certifiers Association (IAFCA)
129 S Gallatin
Liberty, MO 64068
Free: (888)679-1904
Fax: (816)792-8105
URL: **http://iafca.bestlabs.com**
Contact: **Michael Alleman, Contact**

433 ■ International Compressor Remanufacturers Association (ICRA) (1715)
1505 Carthage Rd.
Lumberton, NC 28358
Ph: **(910)301-7060**
Fax: **(910)738-6994**
E-mail: info@icracomp.com
URL: http://icracomp.com
Contact: James Pollock, Pres.

434 ■ Masonry Heater Association of North America (MHA) (1819)
2180 S Flying Q Ln.
Tucson, AZ 85713
Ph: (520)883-0191
Fax: **(480)371-1139**

E-mail: execdir@mha-net.org
URL: http://www.mha-net.org
Contact: Richard Smith, Exec. Dir.

435 ■ National Air Filtration Association (NAFA) (1830)
PO Box 68639
Virginia Beach, VA 23471
Ph: (757)313-7400
Fax: (757)497-1895
E-mail: nafa@nafahq.org
URL: http://www.nafahq.org
Contact: **Marisa Jimenez de Segovia CAFS, Pres.**

436 ■ North American Technician Excellence (NATE) (1824)
2111 Wilson Blvd., No. 510
Arlington, VA 22201
Ph: (703)276-7247
Free: (877)420-NATE
Fax: (703)527-2316
E-mail: pschwartz@natex.org
URL: http://www.natex.org
Contact: **Peter W. Schwartz, Pres./CEO**

437 ■ Radiant Professionals Alliance (RPA) (1833)
8512 Oswego Rd., Ste.180
Baldwinsville, NY 13027
Ph: (315)303-4735
Free: (800)660-7187
Fax: (315)303-5559
E-mail: info@rpa-info.com
URL: http://www.radiantpanelassociation.org
Contact: Ted Lowe, Exec. Dir.
Status Note: Formerly Radiant Panel Association.

438 ■ Refrigeration Service Engineers Society (RSES) (1834)
1666 Rand Rd.
Des Plaines, IL 60016-3552
Ph: (847)297-6464
Free: (800)297-5660
E-mail: bruceirma@aol.com
URL: http://www.rses.org
Contact: **Robert J. Sherman CM, Intl. Pres.**

Hobby Supplies

439 ■ American Stamp Dealers Association (ASDA) (1910)
217-14 Northern Blvd., Ste.205
Bayside, NY 11361
Ph: **(718)224-2500**
Fax: **(718)224-2501**
E-mail: asda@asdaonline.com
URL: **http://www.asdaonline.com**
Contact: Mr. Joseph B. Savarese, Exec. Dir.

Hospitality Industries

440 ■ American Hotel and Lodging Association (AH&LA) (1793)
1201 New York Ave. NW, No. 600
Washington, DC 20005-3931
Ph: (202)289-3100
Fax: (202)289-3199
E-mail: informationcenter@ahla.com
URL: http://www.ahla.com
Contact: **Joseph A. David, Pres./CEO**

441 ■ Association for Convention Marketing Executives (ACME) (1865)
204 E St., NE
Washington, DC 20002
Ph: **(202)547-8030**
Fax: **(202)547-6348**
E-mail: **smc@giuffrida.org**
URL: http://acmenet.org
Contact: **Sheila Crowley CMP, Exec. Dir.**

442 ■ Hotel Electronic Distribution Network Association (HEDNA) (1878)
750 Natl. Press Bldg.
529 14th St. NW
Washington, DC 20045
Ph: (202)204-8400
Fax: (703)223-9741
E-mail: info@hedna.org
URL: http://www.hedna.org
Contact: **Reed Hitchcock, Exec. Dir.**

443 ■ IAHI, the Owners' Association (1757)
3 Ravinia Dr., Ste.100
Atlanta, GA 30346
Ph: (770)604-5555
Free: **(877)500-4244**
Fax: (770)604-5684
URL: http://www.iahi.org
Contact: Eva Ferguson, Pres.
Status Note: Formerly International Association of Holiday Inns.

444 ■ International Concierge and Lifestyle Management Association (ICLMA)
3650 Rogers Rd., No. 328
Wake Forest, NC 27587
Ph: (804)368-1667
Free: (800)376-7020
Fax: **(637)267-4300**
E-mail: admin@iclma.org
URL: http://www.iclma.org
Contact: Katharine Giovanni CCS, Chair/Founder

445 ■ National Black McDonald's Operators Association (NBMOA) (1766)
PO Box 820668
South Florida, FL 33082-0668
Ph: (954)389-4487
Fax: (954)349-5408
E-mail: nbmoa1@aol.com
URL: http://www.nbmoa.org
Contact: **Roland G. Parrish, Chm./CEO**

446 ■ National Council of Chain Restaurants (NCCR) (1892)
325 7th St. NW, Ste.1100
Washington, DC 20004
Ph: (202)783-7971
Free: (800)673-4692
Fax: (202)737-2849
E-mail: **info@nrf.com**
URL: http://www.nccr.net
Contact: **Rob Green, Exec. Dir.**

447 ■ National Restaurant Association (NRA) (1931)
1200 17th St. NW
Washington, DC 20036
Ph: (202)331-5900
Free: (800)424-5156
Fax: (202)331-2429
URL: http://www.restaurant.org
Contact: **Sally Smith, Chair**

448 ■ National Restaurant Association Educational Foundation (NRAEF) (1894)
175 W Jackson Blvd., Ste.1500
Chicago, IL 60604-2702
Ph: (312)715-1010
Free: (800)765-2122
E-mail: info@restaurant.org
URL: http://www.nraef.org
Contact: **Linda Bacin, Interim Exec. Dir.**

449 ■ Professional Association of Innkeepers International (PAII) (1896)
207 White Horse Pike
Haddon Heights, NJ 08035
Ph: (856)310-1102
Free: (800)468-7244
Fax: **(856)895-0432**
E-mail: **jay@paii.org**
URL: http://www.paii.org
Contact: Jay Karen, Pres./CEO

Housewares

450 ■ American Brush Manufacturers Association (ABMA) (1940)
2111 Plum St., Ste.274
Aurora, IL 60506
Ph: **(720)392-2262**
Fax: **(866)837-8450**
E-mail: info@abma.org
URL: http://www.abma.org
Contact: **Ian P. Moss, Pres.**

451 ■ Cookware Manufacturers Association (CMA) (1780)
PO Box 531335
Birmingham, AL 35253-1335
Ph: **(205)592-0389**
Fax: **(205)599-5598**
E-mail: hrushing@usit.net
URL: http://www.cookware.org
Contact: Hugh J. Rushing, Exec. VP

Housing

452 ■ HomeFree - U.S.A.
3401A E W Hwy.
Hyattsville, MD 20782
Ph: (301)891-8400 (301)891-8423
Free: (866)OEN-2DAY
Fax: (301)891-8434
E-mail: **homefreeusa@homefreeusa.org**
URL: http://www.homefreeusa.org
Contact: Marcia Griffin, Pres./Founder

453 ■ National Association of Housing Counselors and Agencies (NAHCA)
PO Box 91873
Lafayette, LA 70509-1873
Fax: (337)232-8834
E-mail: slmoore@n-a-h-c-a.org
URL: http://www.n-a-h-c-a.org
Contact: **Sandra L. Moore, Pres.**

Human Resources

454 ■ National Association of African Americans in Human Resources (NAAAHR) (1916)
PO Box 311395
Atlanta, GA 31131
E-mail: **carl.jefferson@naaahr.org**
URL: **http://www.naaahr.us**
Contact: Carl C. Jefferson, Natl. Pres./CEO

455 ■ National Association of Professional Background Screeners (NAPBS)
2501 Aerial Center Pkwy., Ste.103
Morrisville, NC 27560
Ph: (919)459-2082
Free: (888)686-2727
Fax: (919)459-2075
E-mail: info@napbs.com
URL: http://www.napbs.com
Contact: **Stevie Hughes Kernick, Interim Exec. Dir.**

Industrial Equipment

456 ■ American Bearing Manufacturers Association (ABMA) (1923)
2025 M St. NW, Ste.800
Washington, DC 20036-2422
Ph: (202)367-1155
Fax: (202)367-2155
E-mail: info@americanbearings.org
URL: **http://www.americanbearings.org**
Contact: Scott Lynch, Pres./Sec.

457 ■ American Gear Manufacturers Association (AGMA) (1792)
1001 N Fairfax St., 5th Fl.
Alexandria, VA 22314-1587
Ph: (703)684-0211
Fax: (703)684-0242
E-mail: webmaster@agma.org
URL: http://www.agma.org
Contact: Joe T. Franklin Jr., Pres.

458 ■ American Mold Builders Association (AMBA) (1918)
3601 Algonquin Rd., Ste.304
Rolling Meadows, IL 60008
Ph: (847)222-9402
Fax: (847)222-9437
E-mail: info@amba.org
URL: http://www.amba.org
Contact: **Troy Nix, Exec. Dir.**

459 ■ Associated Wire Rope Fabricators (AWRF) (1937)
PO Box 748
Walled Lake, MI 48390-0748
Ph: (248)994-7753
Free: **(800)666-2973**
Fax: (248)994-7754
E-mail: awrf@att.net
URL: http://www.awrf.org
Contact: **Bruce Yoder, Pres.**

460 ■ Association of Ingersoll-Rand Distributors (AIRD) (1939)
1300 Sumner Ave.
Cleveland, OH 44115-2851
Ph: (216)241-7333 (407)677-4200
Fax: (216)241-0105
E-mail: aird@aird.org
URL: http://www.aird.org
Contact: **Richard Gau, Pres.**

461 ■ Contractors Pump Bureau (CPB) (1980)
6737 W Washington St., Ste.2400
Milwaukee, WI 53214-5647
Ph: (414)272-0943
Free: (866)236-0442
Fax: (414)272-1170
E-mail: **kedwards@aem.org**
URL: http://www.aem.org/Groups/Groups/Group.
   asp?G=22
Contact: Ben Rieboldt, Chm.

462 ■ Conveyor Equipment Manufacturers Association (CEMA) (264)
6724 Lone Oak Blvd.
Naples, FL 34109
Ph: (239)514-3441
Fax: (239)514-3470
E-mail: **kim@cemanet.org**
URL: http://www.cemanet.org
Contact: Phil Hannigan, Contact

463 ■ International Association of Elevator Consultants (IAEC) (1984)
15600 NE 8th St., Ste.B1
PMB 153
Bellevue, WA 98008
Ph: **(425)732-3328**
Fax: (425)957-0834
E-mail: **gernst@iaec.org**
URL: http://www.iaec.org/IAEC.html
Contact: Gordon Ernst, Exec. Dir.

464 ■ MAPI (1975)
1600 Wilson Blvd., 11th Fl.
Arlington, VA 22209-2594
Ph: (703)841-9000
Fax: (703)841-9514
URL: http://www.mapi.net
Contact: **Stephen Gold, Pres./CEO**

465 ■ Mechanical Power Transmission Association (MPTA) (1855)
6724 Lone Oak Blvd.
Naples, FL 34109
Ph: (239)514-3441
Fax: (239)514-3470
E-mail: **bob@mpta.org**
URL: http://www.mpta.org

466 ■ National Association of Hose and Accessories Distribution (NAHAD)
105 Eastern Ave., Ste.104
Annapolis, MD 21403
Ph: **(410)940-6350**
Free: (800)624-2227
Fax: (410)263-1659
E-mail: info@nahad.org
URL: http://www.nahad.org
Contact: **Tim O'Shaughnessy, Pres.**

467 ■ Power-Motion Technology Representatives Association (PTRA) (1994)
16A Journey, Ste.200
Aliso Viejo, CA 92656
Ph: (949)859-2885
Free: (888)817-7872
Fax: (949)855-2973
E-mail: info@ptra.org
URL: http://www.ptra.org
Contact: **Doug Bower, Exec. Dir.**

468 ■ Society of Professional Rope Access Technicians (SPRAT)
994 Old Eagle School Rd., Ste.1019
Wayne, PA 19087-1866
Ph: (610)971-4850
Fax: (610)971-4859
E-mail: info@sprat.org
URL: http://www.sprat.org
Contact: **Matt Hudson, Pres.**

469 ■ Wood Machinery Manufacturers of America (WMMA) (1999)
500 Citadel Dr., Ste.200
Commerce, CA 90040
Ph: **(323)215-0330**
Fax: **(323)215-0331**
E-mail: info@wmma.org
URL: http://www.wmma.org
Contact: **Mark Chappell, Pres.**

Industrial Security

470 ■ Computer Security Institute (CSI) (2023)
350 Hudson St., Ste.300
New York, NY 10014
Ph: (212)600-3026
E-mail: csi@ubm.com
URL: http://gocsi.com
Contact: Robert Richardson, Dir.

Information Management

471 ■ AIIM - The Enterprise Content Management Association (2065)
1100 Wayne Ave., Ste.1100
Silver Spring, MD 20910
Ph: (301)587-8202
Free: (800)477-2446
Fax: (301)587-2711
E-mail: aiim@aiim.org
URL: http://www.aiim.org
Contact: **John F. Mancini, Pres.**

472 ■ National Public Records Research Association (NPRRA) (1971)
2501 Aerial Center Pkwy., Ste.103
Morrisville, NC 27560
Ph: (919)459-2078 (303)863-1800
Fax: (919)459-2075

E-mail: info@nprra.org
URL: http://www.nprra.org
Contact: **Kelly McKown, Pres.**

473 ■ The Open Group (1928)
44 Montgomery St., Ste.960
San Francisco, CA 94104-4704
Ph: (415)374-8280
Fax: (415)374-8293
E-mail: **memberservices@opengroup.org**
URL: http://www.opengroup.org
Contact: Allen Brown, Pres./CEO

474 ■ Supply-Chain Council (SCC) (2046)
12320 Barker Cypress Rd., Ste.600
PMB 321
Cypress, TX 77429-8329
Ph: (202)962-0440
Fax: (202)540-9027
E-mail: info@supply-chain.org
URL: http://www.supply-chain.org
Contact: **John Sells, Chm.**

475 ■ World Organization of Webmasters (WOW)
PO Box 1743
Folsom, CA 95630
Ph: (916)989-2933
Fax: (916)987-3022
E-mail: info@joinwow.org
URL: **http://webprofessionals.org**
Contact: Bill Cullifer, Exec. Dir.

Inspectors

476 ■ Association of Construction Inspectors (ACI)
PO Box 879
Palm Springs, CA 92263
Ph: (760)327-5284
Free: (877)815-4174
Fax: (760)327-5631
E-mail: support@assoc-hdqts.org
URL: http://www.aci-assoc.org
Contact: **Ginny Foat, Ed.**

477 ■ Examination Board of Professional Home Inspectors (EBPHI) (2053)
53 Regional Dr., Ste.1
Concord, NH 03301-8500
Ph: (847)298-7750
E-mail: info@homeinspectionexam.org
URL: http://www.homeinspectionexam.org
Contact: **Don Lovering, Pres.**

Insurance

478 ■ American Association for Long-Term Care Insurance (AALTCI)
3835 E Thousand Oaks Blvd., Ste.336
Westlake Village, CA 91362
Ph: (818)597-3227 **(818)597-3205**
Fax: (818)597-3206
E-mail: info@aaltci.org
URL: http://www.aaltci.org
Contact: Jesse Slome, Contact

479 ■ American Insurance Marketing and Sales Society (AIMS) (2140)
PO Box 35718
Richmond, VA 23235
Ph: (804)674-6466
Free: (877)674-CPIA
Fax: (703)579-8896
E-mail: **info@aimssociety.org**
URL: http://www.aimssociety.org
Contact: Kitty Ambers, Exec. Dir.

480 ■ Association of Average Adjusters of the United States (AAAUS) (2080)
c/o Eileen M. Fellin, Sec.
126 Midwood Ave.
Farmingdale, NY 11735
E-mail: **joe.hughes@american-club.com**
URL: http://www.usaverageadjusters.org
Contact: Joseph E.M. Hughes, Chm.

481 ■ Association of Home Office Underwriters (AHOU) (2083)
2300 Windy Ridge Pkwy., Ste.600
Atlanta, GA 30339
Ph: (770)984-3715
Fax: (770)984-3758
E-mail: memberservices@ahou.org
URL: http://www.ahou.org
Contact: **Maureen Leydon, Pres.**

482 ■ Bank Insurance and Securities Association (BISA) (2086)
2025 M St. NW, Ste.800
Washington, DC 20036
Ph: **(202)367-1111**
Fax: **(202)367-1111**
E-mail: **info@bisanet.org**
URL: http://www.bisanet.org
Contact: **Jim McNeil, Exec. Dir.**

483 ■ Crop Insurance and Reinsurance Bureau (CIRB) (2026)
201 Massachusetts Ave. NE, Ste.C5
Washington, DC 20002
Ph: (202)544-0067
Fax: (202)330-5255
E-mail: mtorrey@cropinsurance.org
URL: http://www.cropinsurance.org
Contact: **Sam Scheef, Chm.**
Status Note: Formerly Crop Insurance Research Bureau.

484 ■ Fraternal Field Managers' Association (FFMA) (2100)
Catholic United Financial
3499 Lexington Ave. N
St. Paul, MN 55126
Ph: **(651)765-4150**
Fax: **(651)766-1077**
E-mail: **tschisler@catholic.org**
URL: http://www.ffma.info
Contact: **Thomas J. Schisler, Pres.**

485 ■ GAMA International (2032)
2901 Telestar Ct., Ste.140
Falls Church, VA 22042-1205
Free: (800)345-2687
Fax: **(703)770-8182**
E-mail: gamamail@gamaweb.com
URL: http://www.gamaweb.com
Contact: Kenneth G. Gallacher, Pres.-Elect

486 ■ Group Underwriters Association of America (GUAA)
PO Box 118
Weatogue, CT 06089-0118
E-mail: **czepeda@rgare.com**
URL: http://www.guaa.org
Contact: **Curt Zepeda, Pres.**

487 ■ Inland Marine Underwriters Association (IMUA) (1967)
14 Wall St., 8th Fl.
New York, NY 10005
Ph: (212)233-0550
Fax: (212)227-5102
E-mail: **kobrien@imua.org**
URL: http://www.imua.org
Contact: **Kevin O'Brien, Pres./CEO**

488 ■ Insurance Brokers and Agents of the West (IBA West) (2091)
7041 Koll Center Pkwy., Ste.290
Pleasanton, CA 94566-3128
Ph: (925)426-3310
Free: (800)772-8998

Fax: (925)484-6014
E-mail: info@ibawest.com
URL: http://www.ibawest.com
Contact: Clark Payan AAI, CEO

489 ■ Insurance Loss Control Association (ILCA) (2113)
118 Treetops Dr.
Lancaster, PA 17601-1790
Ph: (717)898-9056
E-mail: administration@insurancelosscontrol.org
URL: http://www.insurancelosscontrol.org
Contact: **Scot Gudenrath, Pres.**

490 ■ Insurance Regulatory Examiners Society (IRES) (2117)
1821 Univ. Ave. W, Ste.S256
St. Paul, MN 55104
Ph: **(651)917-6250**
Fax: **(651)917-1835**
E-mail: **info@go-ires.org**
URL: http://www.go-ires.org
Contact: **Leslie Krier AIE, Pres.**

491 ■ Insurance Society of New York (ISNY) (2119)
St. John's Univ.
8000 Utopia Pkwy.
Jamaica, NY 11439
Ph: **(718)990-6653**
Free: (888)9STJOHNS
Fax: **(718)990-8300**
E-mail: **ciel@stjohns.edu**
URL: http://new.stjohns.edu/academics/graduate/
   tobin/srm/isny
Contact: **Paula Edwards, Contact**

492 ■ Life Insurance Settlement Association (LISA)
1011 E Colonial Dr., Ste.500
Orlando, FL 32803
Ph: (407)894-3797
Fax: (407)897-1325
E-mail: support@lisassociation.org
URL: http://www.thevoiceoftheindustry.com
Contact: **Darwin Bayston, Exec. Dir.**

493 ■ National African-American Insurance Association (NAAIA)
1718 M St. NW, Box No. 1110
Washington, DC 20036
Free: (866)566-2242
Fax: (202)478-5181
E-mail: info@naaia.org
URL: http://www.naaia.org
Contact: **Don Davis, Chm.**

494 ■ National Association of Catastrophe Adjusters (NACA) (2139)
PO Box 821864
North Richland Hills, TX 76182
Ph: (817)498-3466
Fax: (817)498-0480
E-mail: naca@nacatadj.org
URL: http://www.nacatadj.org
Contact: **Warren Aplin, Pres.**

495 ■ National Association for Fixed Annuities (NAFA)
2300 E Kensington Blvd.
Milwaukee, WI 53211
Ph: (414)332-9306
Fax: **(888)884-6232**
E-mail: kim@nafa.com
URL: http://www.nafa.com
Contact: **Kim O'Brien MBA, Exec. Dir.**

496 ■ National Association of Fraternal Insurance Counsellors (NAFIC) (2143)
211 Canal Rd.
Waterloo, WI 53594
Free: (866)478-3880
E-mail: office@nafic.org
URL: **http://www.nafic.org**
Contact: Paul Hill FIC, Pres.

497 ■ National Association of Surety Bond Producers (NASBP) (2078)
1140 19th St., Ste.800
Washington, DC 20036-5104
Ph: (202)686-3700
Fax: (202)686-3656
E-mail: info@nasbp.org
URL: http://www.nasbp.org
Contact: Mark McCallum, CEO

498 ■ National Council of Self-Insurers (NCSI) (2011)
1253 Springfield Ave.
PMB 345
New Providence, NJ 07974
Ph: (908)665-2152
Fax: (908)665-4020
E-mail: natcouncil@aol.com
URL: http://www.natcouncil.com
Contact: David Kaplan, Pres.

499 ■ National Risk Retention Association (NRRA) (2144)
2214 Rock Hill Rd., Ste.315
Herndon, VA 20170
Ph: (703)297-0059
Free: (800)999-4505
Fax: (703)904-8008
E-mail: jennifer@riskretention.org
URL: http://www.nrra-usa.org
Contact: Jennifer C. Williamson, Pres.

500 ■ National Society of Insurance Premium Auditors (NSIPA) (2193)
PO Box 936
Columbus, OH 43216-0936
Free: (888)846-7472
Fax: (877)835-5798
E-mail: nsipa@nsipa.org
URL: http://www.nsipa.org
Contact: Edward Galloway, Pres.

501 ■ National Society of Professional Insurance Investigators (NSPII) (2164)
PO Box 88
Delaware, OH 43015
Free: (888)677-4498
Fax: (740)369-7155
E-mail: nspii@columbus.rr.com
URL: http://www.nspii.com
Contact: Carmen C. Sarge, Pres.

502 ■ Professional Risk Managers' International Association (PRMIA)
400 Washington St.
Northfield, MN 55057
E-mail: support@prmia.org
URL: http://prmia.org
Contact: Carol Alexander, Chair

503 ■ Reinsurance Association of America (RAA) (2023)
1445 New York Ave., 7th Fl.
Washington, DC 20005
Ph: (202)638-3690
Free: (800)570-1806
Fax: (202)638-0936
E-mail: infobox@reinsurance.org
URL: http://www.reinsurance.org
Contact: Franklin W. Nutter, Pres.

504 ■ Women in Insurance and Financial Services (WIFS) (2167)
136 Everett Rd.
Albany, NY 12205
Ph: (518)694-5506
Free: (866)264-9437
Fax: (518)935-9232
E-mail: office@wifsnational.org
URL: http://www.wifsnational.org
Contact: Nicole Lemperle Correia, Exec. Dir.

Interior Design

505 ■ American Society of Interior Designers (ASID) (2190)
608 Massachusetts Ave. NE
Washington, DC 20002-6006
Ph: (202)546-3480
Fax: (202)546-3240
E-mail: asid@asid.org
URL: http://www.interiors.org
Contact: Michael A. Thomas, Pres.

506 ■ Carpet and Rug Institute (CRI) (2039)
PO Box 2048
Dalton, GA 30722-2048
Ph: (706)278-3176 (706)428-2114
Fax: (706)278-8835
E-mail: snewberry@carpet-rug.org
URL: http://www.carpet-rug.org
Contact: Werner Braun, Pres.

507 ■ Interior Redesign Industry Specialists (IRIS)
1100-H Brandywine Blvd.
Zanesville, OH 43701-7303
Ph: (740)450-1330
Fax: (740)452-2552
E-mail: iris@irisorganization.org
URL: http://www.irisorganization.org
Contact: Anna Jacoby, Exec. Dir.

508 ■ International Association of Home Staging Professionals (IAHSP) (2180)
2420 Sand Creek Rd. C-1, No. 263
Brentwood, CA 94513
Free: (800)392-7161
Fax: (925)665-0322
E-mail: barb@iahsp.com
URL: http://www.iahsp.com
Contact: Barb Schwarz, CEO/Founder

509 ■ International Furnishings and Design Association (IFDA) (2202)
150 S Warner Rd., Ste.156
King of Prussia, PA 19406
Ph: (610)535-6422
Fax: (610)535-6423
E-mail: info@ifda.com
URL: http://www.ifda.com
Contact: Janet Stevenson, Pres.

510 ■ International Interior Design Association (IIDA) (2232)
222 Merchandise Mart, Ste.567
Chicago, IL 60654
Ph: (312)467-1950
Free: (888)799-4432
Fax: (312)467-0779
E-mail: iidahq@iida.org
URL: http://www.iida.org
Contact: Peter Conant, Pres.-Elect

511 ■ National Candle Association (NCA) (2206)
529 14th St. NW, Ste.750
Washington, DC 20045
Ph: (202)393-2210
Fax: (202)331-2714
E-mail: info@candles.org
URL: http://www.candles.org
Contact: Bob Nelson, Pres.-Elect

512 ■ National Kitchen and Bath Association (NKBA) (2059)
687 Willow Grove St.
Hackettstown, NJ 07840
Ph: (908)852-0033
Free: (800)843-6522
Fax: (908)852-1695
E-mail: feedback@nkba.org
URL: http://www.nkba.org
Contact: Bill Darcy, Exec. VP

513 ■ Paint and Decorating Retailers Association (PDRA) (2212)
1401 Triad Center Dr.
St. Peters, MO 63376-7353
Ph: (636)326-2636
E-mail: info@pdra.org
URL: http://www.pdra.org
Contact: Jeff Baggaley, Pres.

514 ■ Wallcoverings Association (WA) (2216)
401 N Michigan Ave., Ste.2200
Chicago, IL 60611
Ph: (312)321-5166
Fax: (312)673-6928
E-mail: info@wallcoverings.org
URL: http://www.wallcoverings.org
Contact: Phil Tarullo, Pres.

515 ■ Window Coverings Association of America (WCAA) (2218)
11230 Gold Express Dr., Ste.310-149
Gold River, CA 95670
Ph: (916)943-0979
Free: (888)298-9222
Fax: (888)496-0272
E-mail: info@wcaa.org
URL: http://www.wcaa.org
Contact: Jenna Abbott, Exec. Dir.

International Standards

516 ■ Moroccan American Business Council (MABC) (2177)
1085 Commonwealth Ave., Ste.194
Boston, MA 02215
Ph: (508)230-9943 (508)230-5985
Fax: (508)230-9943
E-mail: moulay@usa-morocco.org
URL: http://www.usa-morocco.org
Contact: Moulay M. Alaoui, Chm.

International Trade

517 ■ Emergency Committee for American Trade (ECAT) (2130)
900 17th St. NW, Ste.1150
Washington, DC 20006
Ph: (202)659-5147
Fax: (202)659-1347
URL: http://www.ecattrade.com
Contact: Calman J. Cohen, Pres.

518 ■ Joint Industry Group (JIG) (2242)
111 Rockville Pike, Ste.410
Rockville, MD 20850
Ph: (202)466-5490
Fax: (202)559-0131
E-mail: jig@moinc.com
URL: http://www.jig.org
Contact: Megan Giblin, Chair

519 ■ North America-Mongolia Business Council (NAMBC)
1015 Duke St.
Alexandria, VA 22314
Ph: (703)549-8444
Fax: (703)549-6526
E-mail: hqinfo@nambc.org
URL: http://www.nambc.org
Contact: Steve Saunders, Pres.

520 ■ U.S.-Bahrain Business Council (USBBC)
1615 H St. NW
Washington, DC 20062
Ph: (202)463-5628 (202)463-5401
Fax: (202)463-3114
E-mail: info@usbahrainbusiness.org
URL: http://www.usbahrainbusiness.org
Contact: Olivia Troye, Exec. Dir.

**521 ■ U.S. New Zealand Council (USNZC)
(2256)**
DACOR Bacon House
1801 F St. NW
Washington, DC 20006
Ph: (202)842-0772
Fax: (202)842-0749
E-mail: **ben.schaare@usnzcouncil.org**
URL: http://www.usnzcouncil.org
Contact: John E. Mullen, Pres.

Investigation

**522 ■ Council of International Investigators
(CII) (2265)**
2150 N 107th St., Ste.205
Seattle, WA 98133-9009
Ph: (206)361-8869
Free: (888)759-8884
Fax: (206)367-8777
E-mail: office@cii2.org
URL: http://www.cii2.org
Contact: **Nancy Barber, Chair**

**523 ■ International Association of Security
and Investigative Regulators (IASIR) (2266)**
PO Box 93
Waterloo, IA 50704
Free: (888)354-2747
Fax: (319)232-1488
E-mail: contact@iasir.org
URL: http://www.iasir.org
Contact: **Karen Forsyth, Pres.**

Investments

524 ■ Angel Capital Association (ACA) (2249)
10977 Granada Ln., Ste.103
Overland Park, KS 66211
Ph: (913)894-4700
E-mail: mhudson@angelcapitalassociation.org
URL: http://www.angelcapitalassociation.org
Contact: **Marianne Hudson, Exec. Dir.**

**525 ■ Hedge Fund Business Operations
Association (2256)**
1350 41st Ave., Ste.200
Capitola, CA 95010
Ph: (831)465-2298
E-mail: krodriguez@hfboa.org
URL: http://www.hfboa.org
Contact: **Daniel Federmann CPA, Bd. of Dir.**

**526 ■ National Association of Government
Defined Contribution Administrators
(NAGDCA) (2143)**
201 E Main St., Ste.1405
Lexington, KY 40507
Ph: (859)514-9161
Fax: (859)514-9188
E-mail: infonagdca@amrms.com
URL: http://www.nagdca.org
Contact: **Gay Lynn Bath, Pres.**

**527 ■ National Association of Publicly
Traded Partnerships (NAPTP) (2248)**
1940 Duke St., Ste.200
Alexandria, VA 22314
Ph: **(703)518-4185**
Fax: **(703)842-8333**
E-mail: **mlyman@naptp.org**
URL: http://www.naptp.org
Contact: Ms. Mary Lyman, Exec. Dir.

**528 ■ National Council of Real Estate
Investment Fiduciaries (NCREIF) (2289)**
2 Prudential Plz.
180 N Stetson Ave., Ste.2515
Chicago, IL 60601
Ph: (312)819-5890
Fax: (312)819-5891

E-mail: info@ncreif.org
URL: **http://www.ncreif.org**
Contact: **Catherine Polleys, Chair**

**529 ■ Professional Association for
Investment Communications Resources
(PAICR) (2294)**
12100 Sunset Hills Rd., Ste.130
Reston, VA 20190
Free: (866)993-0999
Fax: **(703)435-4390**
E-mail: **geistler.deann@principal.com**
URL: http://www.paicr.com
Contact: **Deann Geistler, Pres.**

Jewelry

**530 ■ Accredited Gemologists Association
(AGA) (2297)**
3315 Juanita St.
San Diego, CA 92105
Ph: (619)501-5444
E-mail: **5444@accreditedgemologists.org**
URL: http://accreditedgemologists.org
Contact: Donna Hawrelko FGA, Pres.

Landscaping

**531 ■ Coalition of Organic Landscapers
(COOL)**
1125 NE 152nd St.
Shoreline, WA 98155-7053
Ph: (206)362-8947
E-mail: info@organiclandscapers.org
URL: http://www.organiclandscapers.org
Contact: **David Stoller, Pres.**

**532 ■ Professional Landcare Network
(PLANET) (2336)**
950 Herndon Pkwy., Ste.450
Herndon, VA 20170
Ph: (703)736-9666
Free: (800)395-2522
Fax: (703)736-9668
E-mail: info@landcarenetwork.org
URL: http://www.landcarenetwork.org
Contact: **Gerald J. Grossi, Pres.**

**533 ■ Sports Turf Managers Association
(STMA) (2337)**
805 New Hampshire St., Ste.E
Lawrence, KS 66044
Free: (800)323-3875
Fax: (785)843-2977
E-mail: stmainfo@stma.org
URL: http://www.stma.org
Contact: **Troy Smith CSFM, Pres.**

Latin America

**534 ■ National Latina Business Women
Association (NLBWA)**
1740 W Katella Ave., Ste.Q
Orange, CA 92867
Ph: **(714)724-7762**
Free: (888)696-5292
URL: **http://www.nlbwaoc.org**
Contact: Cecilia Mota, Pres.

Laundry

**535 ■ Association for Linen Management
(ALM) (2401)**
2161 Lexington Rd., Ste.2
Richmond, KY 40475
Ph: (859)624-0177
Free: (800)669-0863
Fax: (859)624-3580

E-mail: **rwendland@egh.org**
URL: http://www.almnet.org
Contact: **Randy Wendland CLLM, Pres.**

536 ■ Coin Laundry Association (CLA) (2341)
1 S 660 Midwest Rd., Ste.205
Oakbrook Terrace, IL 60181
Ph: (630)953-7920
Free: **(800)570-5629**
Fax: (630)953-7925
E-mail: info@coinlaundry.org
URL: http://coinlaundry.org
Contact: Brian Wallace, Pres./CEO

**537 ■ Healthcare Laundry Accreditation
Council (HLAC)**
PO Box 1805
Frankfort, IL 60423
Ph: **(815)464-1404**
Fax: **(815)464-1405**
E-mail: **rbaras@hlacnet.org**
URL: **http://www.hlacnet.org**
Contact: **Regina Baras, Exec. Dir.**

Leadership

**538 ■ National Institute for Leadership
Development (NILD) (2322)**
1202 W Thomas Rd.
Phoenix, AZ 85013
Ph: (602)285-7495
Fax: (602)285-7439
E-mail: **nild@pcmail.maricopa.edu**
URL: http://www.pc.maricopa.edu/nild
Contact: Edna Baehre, Pres.

Leather

**539 ■ International Federation of Leather
Guilds (IFoLG) (2353)**
2264 Logan Dr.
New Palestine, IN 46163
Ph: **(317)861-9711**
E-mail: eddjanlucas@sbcglobal.net
URL: http://www.ifolg.org
Contact: Edd Lucas, Exec. Dir.

**540 ■ Sponge and Chamois Institute (SCI)
(2344)**
10024 Off. Center Ave., Ste.203
St. Louis, MO 63128
Ph: **(314)842-2230**
Fax: **(314)842-3999**
E-mail: **scwaters@swbell.net**
URL: http://www.chamoisinstitute.org
Contact: **Susan Waters, Contact**

Lending

**541 ■ American Financial Services
Association (AFSA) (2382)**
919 18th St. NW, Ste.300
Washington, DC 20006-5526
Ph: (202)296-5544
Fax: (202)223-0321
E-mail: **susie@afsamail.org**
URL: http://www.afsaonline.org
Contact: **Susie Irvine, Pres./CEO**

**542 ■ Commercial Finance Association (CFA)
(2285)**
370 7th Ave., Ste.1801
New York, NY 10001-3979
Ph: (212)792-9390 **(312)674-4547**
Fax: (212)564-6053
E-mail: info@cfa.com
URL: http://www.cfa.com
Contact: Randolph T. Abrahams, Pres./CEO

543 ■ National Foundation for Credit Counseling (NFCC) (2240)
2000 M St. NW, Ste.505
Washington, DC 20036
Free: (800)388-2227
URL: http://www.nfcc.org
Contact: Susan C. Keating, Pres./CEO

Lifesaving

544 ■ International Association of Dive Rescue Specialists (IADRS) (21100)
PO Box 877
Vero Beach, FL 32961
Ph: (970)482-1562
Free: (800)423-7791
Fax: **(234)564-2377**
E-mail: **brobinson@iadrs.org**
URL: http://www.iadrs.org
Contact: Blades Robinson, Exec. Dir.

Lighting

545 ■ Association of Outdoor Lighting Professionals (AOLP)
4305 N 6th St., Ste.A
Harrisburg, PA 17110
Ph: (717)238-2504
Fax: (717)238-9985
E-mail: info@aolponline.org
URL: http://www.aolponline.org
Contact: **Lisa Herron, Exec. Dir.**

546 ■ Professional Lighting and Sign Management Companies of America (PLASMA)
1100-H Brandywine Blvd.
Zanesville, OH 43701-7303
Ph: (740)452-4541
Fax: (740)452-2552
E-mail: **director@plasmalighting.org**
URL: http://plasmalighting.org
Contact: Amber Walls, Exec. Dir.

Luggage

547 ■ Travel Goods Association (TGA) (2350)
301 N Harrison St., No. 412
Princeton, NJ 08540-3512
Free: (877)TGA-1938
Fax: **(877)842-1938**
E-mail: info@travel-goods.org
URL: http://travel-goods.org
Contact: Michele Marini Pittenger, Pres.

Mail

548 ■ Association of Mailing, Shipping and Office Automation Specialists (AIMED) (2448)
11310 Wornall Rd.
Kansas City, MO 64114
Free: (888)750-6245
Fax: **(888)836-9561**
E-mail: **rick@aimedweb.org**
URL: http://www.aimedweb.org
Contact: **Rick Chambers, Exec. Dir.**

549 ■ Mail Systems Management Association (MSMA) (2374)
PO Box 1145
North Riverside, IL 60546-0545
Ph: (708)442-8589
Free: (800)714-6762
Fax: (708)853-0471
E-mail: **karen.cornelius@pb.com**
URL: http://www.msmanational.org
Contact: **Karen Cornelius, Pres.**

550 ■ National Association of Presort Mailers (NAPM) (2361)
1195 Mace Rd.
Annapolis, MD 21403-4330
Free: (877)620-6276
Fax: (410)990-1182
E-mail: **joel@presortmailer.org**
URL: **http://www.presortmailer.org**
Contact: Joel T. Thomas, Exec. Dir.

Maintenance

551 ■ Building Service Contractors Association International (BSCAI) (2419)
401 N Michigan Ave., Ste.2200
Chicago, IL 60611-4267
Ph: (312)321-5167
Free: (800)368-3414
Fax: (312)673-6735
E-mail: info@bscai.org
URL: http://www.bscai.org
Contact: **Chris Mundschenk, Exec. VP/CEO**

552 ■ Cleaning Equipment Trade Association (CETA) (2400)
PO Box 1710
Indian Trail, NC 28079
Ph: (704)635-7362
Free: (800)441-0111
Fax: (704)635-7363
E-mail: **roy@chappellsupply.com**
URL: http://www.ceta.org
Contact: **Roy Chappell, Pres.**

553 ■ International Executive Housekeepers Association (IEHA) (2403)
1001 Eastwind Dr., Ste.301
Westerville, OH 43081-3361
Ph: (614)895-7166
Free: (800)200-6342
Fax: (614)895-1248
E-mail: excel@ieha.org
URL: http://www.ieha.org
Contact: **Eric Bates REH, Pres.**

554 ■ Master Window Cleaners of America (MWCoA)
1220G Airport Fwy., No. 561
Bedford, TX 76022
E-mail: **president@mwcoa.com**
URL: http://www.mwcoa.com
Contact: Kraig Dyer, Pres.

555 ■ Restoration Industry Association (RIA) (2413)
9810 Patuxent Woods Dr., Ste.K
Columbia, MD 21046-1595
Ph: (443)878-1000
Free: (800)272-7012
Fax: (443)878-1010
E-mail: executiveoffice@restorationindustry.org
URL: http://www.ascr.org
Contact: **Timothy Shaw, Exec. Dir.**

556 ■ United Association of Mobile Contract Cleaners (UAmCc)
314 Marlow Ct.
Chesapeake, VA 23322
Free: (800)816-3240
E-mail: info@uamcc.org
URL: http://www.uamcc.org
Contact: **Michael Tessaro, Pres.**

Management

557 ■ Association of Productivity Specialists (APS) (2444)
521 5th Ave., Ste.1700
New York, NY 10175
Ph: (212)286-0943
URL: http://www.a-p-s.org
Contact: **Allen Evans, Contact**

558 ■ Association of Proposal Management Professionals (APMP) (2414)
PO Box 668
Dana Point, CA 92629-0668
E-mail: memberservices@apmp.org
URL: http://www.apmp.org
Contact: **Rick Harris, Exec. Dir.**

559 ■ Community Managers International Association (CMIA)
PO Box 848
Dana Point, CA 92629
Free: (888)900-2642
Fax: **(888)900-2642**
E-mail: cmiamanager@gmail.com
URL: http://www.cmiamanager.org
Contact: Mike Sibio, Pres.

560 ■ Emergency Management Professional Organization for Women's Enrichment (EMPOWER)
PO Box 10803
McLean, VA 22102
E-mail: information@empower-women.com
URL: http://www.empower-women.com
Contact: **Suzanne Boccia, Pres.**

561 ■ Financial Managers Society (FMS) (1370)
100 W Monroe St., Ste.1700
Chicago, IL 60603-1907
Ph: (312)578-1300 (312)630-3425
Free: (800)275-4367
Fax: (312)578-1308
E-mail: info@fmsinc.org
URL: http://www.fmsinc.org
Contact: Dick Yingst, Pres./CEO

562 ■ Institute of Certified Professional Managers (ICPM) (2497)
James Madison Univ.
MSC 5504
Harrisonburg, VA 22807
Ph: (540)568-3247 (540)568-3042
Free: (800)568-4120
Fax: (540)801-8650
E-mail: icpmcm@jmu.edu
URL: http://icpm.biz
Contact: **Robert D. Reid EdD, Exec. Dir.**

563 ■ Institute for Health and Productivity Management (IHPM) (2498)
17470 N Pacesetter Way
Scottsdale, AZ 85255
Ph: (480)305-2100 (804)527-1905
Fax: (480)305-2189
E-mail: **sean@ihpm.org**
URL: http://www.ihpm.org
Contact: **Sean Sullivan JD, Pres./CEO**

564 ■ Institute for Operations Research and the Management Sciences (INFORMS) (2283)
7240 Parkway. Dr., Ste.300
Hanover, MD 21076-1310
Ph: (443)757-3500
Free: (800)446-3676
Fax: (443)757-3515
E-mail: informs@informs.org
URL: http://www.informs.org
Contact: **Rina R. Schneur, Pres.**

565 ■ National Association of Electrical Distributors I National Education and Research Foundation (NERF) (2450)
1181 Corporate Lake Dr.
St. Louis, MO 63132
Ph: (314)991-9000
Free: (888)791-2512
Fax: (314)991-3060
E-mail: customerservice@naed.org
URL: http://www.naed.org
Contact: **Sandra Rosecrans, Chair**

566 ■ National Association of Senior Move Managers (NASMM) (2435)
PO Box 209
Hinsdale, IL 60522
Free: (877)606-2766
Fax: (630)230-3594
E-mail: **marykay@nasmm.org**
URL: http://www.nasmm.com
Contact: **Laura Feauto, Pres.-Elect**

567 ■ National Conference of Executives of the Arc (NCE) (2454)
1660 L St. NW, Ste.301
Washington, DC 20036
Ph: (225)927-0855
Free: (800)433-5255
Fax: (225)924-3935
E-mail: ncearc@thearc.org
URL: http://www.thearc.org/netcommunity/ncearc
Contact: **Mohan Meyer, Pres.**

568 ■ Product Development and Management Association (PDMA) (2458)
401 N Michigan Ave.
Chicago, IL 60611
Ph: (856)439-9052
Free: (800)232-5241
Fax: (856)439-0525
E-mail: pdma@pdma.org
URL: http://www.pdma.org
Contact: Robert E. Johnston Jr., Pres./Chm.

569 ■ Project Management Institute (PMI) (2299)
14 Campus Blvd.
Newtown Square, PA 19073-3299
Ph: (610)356-4600
Fax: **(610)482-9971**
E-mail: customercare@pmi.org
URL: http://www.pmi.org
Contact: **Mark Langley, Pres./CEO**

570 ■ Turnaround Management Association (TMA) (2464)
150 S Wacker Dr., Ste.900
Chicago, IL 60606
Ph: (312)578-6900 **(312)578-2020**
Fax: (312)578-8336
E-mail: info@turnaround.org
URL: http://www.turnaround.org
Contact: Linda Delgadillo CAE, Exec. Dir.

571 ■ Women in Management (WIM) (2326)
PO Box 1032
Dundee, IL 60118-7032
Ph: (708)386-0496
Free: (877)946-6285
Fax: (847)683-3751
E-mail: nationalwim@wimonline.org
URL: http://www.wimonline.org
Contact: **Katrina Laflin, Pres.**

Manufactured Housing

572 ■ Manufactured Housing Institute (MHI) (2312)
2111 Wilson Blvd., Ste.100
Arlington, VA 22201
Ph: (703)558-0400
Fax: (703)558-0401
E-mail: info@mfghome.org
URL: http://www.manufacturedhousing.org
Contact: **Thayer Long, Pres./CEO**

573 ■ National Association of Home Builders I Log Homes Council (LHC) (2468)
1201 15th St. NW
Washington, DC 20005
Free: (800)368-5242
Fax: (202)266-8141
URL: http://www.loghomes.org
Contact: **Jan Koepsell, Pres.**

574 ■ National Association of Home Builders I Modular Building Systems Council (MBSC) (2313)
1201 15th St. NW
Washington, DC 20005
Ph: (202)266-8200
Free: (800)368-5242
Fax: (202)266-8400
URL: http://www.nahb.org/category.aspx?sectionID=809
Contact: **Donna Peak, Contact**

Manufacturers Representatives

575 ■ Association of Independent Manufacturers'/Representatives (AIM/R) (2477)
16 A Journey, Ste.200
Aliso Viejo, CA 92656
Ph: (949)859-2884
Free: (866)729-0975
Fax: (949)855-2973
E-mail: info@aimr.net
URL: http://www.aimr.net
Contact: **Mark Creyer, Pres.**

576 ■ Incentive Manufacturers and Representatives Alliance (IMRA) (2493)
1601 N Bond St., Ste.303
Naperville, IL 60563
Ph: (630)369-7786
Fax: **(630)369-3773**
E-mail: katemarie@incentivemarketing.org
URL: http://www.imraorg.net
Contact: Kate Marie, Coor.

577 ■ Manufacturers' Agents National Association (MANA) (2480)
16 A Journey, Ste.200
Aliso Viejo, CA 92656-3317
Ph: (949)859-4040
Free: (877)626-2776
Fax: (949)855-2973
E-mail: mana@manaonline.org
URL: http://www.manaonline.org
Contact: **Charles Cohon, Pres./CEO**

578 ■ Manufacturers Representatives Educational Research Foundation (MRERF) (2342)
8329 Cole St.
Arvada, CO 80005
Ph: (303)463-1801
Fax: **(303)379-6024**
E-mail: certify@mrerf.org
URL: http://www.mrerf.org
Contact: Ms. Susannah E. Hart, Exec. Dir.

Manufacturing

579 ■ Alliance for American Manufacturing (AAM)
727 15th St. NW, Ste.700
Washington, DC 20005
Ph: (202)393-3430
Fax: (202)628-1864
E-mail: info@aamfg.org
URL: http://www.americanmanufacturing.org
Contact: **Scott Paul, Exec. Dir.**

580 ■ Association for Manufacturing Excellence (AME) (2327)
3701 Algonquin Rd., Ste.225
Rolling Meadows, IL 60008-3127
Ph: (224)232-5980
Fax: (224)232-5981
E-mail: info@ame.org
URL: http://www.ame.org
Contact: Phil Roether, Pres.

581 ■ Consortium for Advanced Management International (CAM-I) (2411)
6836 Bee Cave, Ste.256
Austin, TX 78746
Ph: (512)617-6428 **(512)296-6872**
E-mail: ashok@cam-i.org
URL: http://www.cam-i.org
Contact: Ashok Vadgama, Pres.

582 ■ International Surface Fabricators Association (ISFA) (2359)
165 N 1330 W, No. A3
Orem, UT 84057
Ph: (801)341-7360
Free: (877)464-7732
Fax: (801)341-7361
E-mail: **russ@isfanow.org**
URL: **http://www.isfanow.org**
Contact: Russ Lee, Exec. Dir.

583 ■ National Association of Manufacturers (NAM) (2488)
1331 Pennsylvania Ave. NW, Ste.600
Washington, DC 20004-1790
Ph: (202)637-3000
Free: (800)814-8468
Fax: (202)637-3182
E-mail: manufacturing@nam.org
URL: http://www.nam.org
Contact: **Jay Timmons, Pres./CEO**

584 ■ National Association of Manufacturers Council of Manufacturing Associations (NAM/CMA) (2489)
1331 Pennsylvania Ave. NW, Ste.600
Washington, DC 20004-1790
Ph: (202)637-3000
Free: (800)814-8468
Fax: (202)637-3182
E-mail: manufacturing@nam.org
URL: http://www.nam.org/council
Contact: **Jay Timmons, Pres./CEO**

585 ■ Tooling and Manufacturing Association (TMA) (2489)
1177 S Dee Rd.
Park Ridge, IL 60068
Ph: (847)825-1120
Fax: (847)825-0041
E-mail: **ccalabrese@tmanet.com**
URL: http://www.tmanet.com
Contact: Brian P. McGuire, Pres.

Marine

586 ■ Marine Retailers Association of America (MRAA) (2343)
PO Box 725
Boca Grande, FL 33921
Ph: **(941)964-2534**
Fax: **(941)531-6777**
E-mail: mraa@mraa.com
URL: http://www.mraa.com
Contact: Phil Keeter, Pres.

587 ■ National Marine Representatives Association (NMRA) (2515)
PO Box 360
Gurnee, IL 60031
Ph: (847)662-3167
Fax: (847)336-7126
E-mail: info@nmraonline.org
URL: http://www.nmraonline.org
Contact: **Mr. Rick Silverlake, Pres.**

588 ■ Offshore Marine Service Association (OMSA) (356)
990 N Corporate Dr., Ste.210
Harahan, LA 70123
Ph: (504)734-7622
Fax: (504)734-7134
E-mail: kenwells@offshoremarine.org
URL: http://www.offshoremarine.org
Contact: **Jim Adams, Pres.**

589 ■ Passenger Vessel Association (PVA) (2536)
103 Oronoco St., Ste.200
Alexandria, VA 22314
Ph: (703)518-5005
Free: (800)807-8360
Fax: (703)518-5151
E-mail: pvainfo@passengervessel.com
URL: http://www.passengervessel.com
Contact: **Jay Spence, Pres.**

590 ■ West Gulf Maritime Association (WGMA) (2459)
1717 E Loop
Portway Plz., Ste.200
Houston, TX 77029
Ph: (713)678-7655 (713)715-6423
Free: (800)435-5038
Fax: (713)672-7452
E-mail: barbara@wgma.org
URL: http://www.wgma.org
Contact: **Nathan Wesely, Pres.**

591 ■ Yacht Brokers Association of America (YBAA) (2542)
105 Eastern Ave., Ste.104
Annapolis, MD 21403
Ph: (410)940-6345
Fax: (410)263-1659
E-mail: info@ybaa.com
URL: http://www.ybaa.com
Contact: **Vincent J. Petrella, Exec. Dir.**

Marine Industries

592 ■ American Bureau of Shipping (ABS) (2399)
16855 Northchase Dr.
Houston, TX 77060
Ph: (281)877-5800
Fax: (281)877-5803
E-mail: abs-worldhq@eagle.org
URL: http://www.eagle.org
Contact: **Thomas H. Gilmour, Pres./COO**

593 ■ Association of Marina Industries (AMI) (2382)
50 Water St.
Warren, RI 02885
Free: (866)367-6622
Fax: (401)247-0074
E-mail: **malves@marinaassociation.org**
URL: http://www.marinaassociation.org
Contact: Jim Frye, Pres./Chm.

594 ■ Inland Rivers Ports and Terminals (IRPT) (360)
316 Bd. of Trade Pl.
New Orleans, LA 70130
Ph: (504)585-0715
Fax: (504)525-8197
E-mail: admin@irpt.net
URL: http://www.irpt.net
Contact: **Jerry Sailors, Chm.**

Marketing

595 ■ Association of Equipment Manufacturers | AEM Marketing Council (MC) (80)
6737 W Washington St., Ste.2400
Milwaukee, WI 53214-5647
Ph: **(414)298-4146**
Fax: (414)272-1170
URL: http://www.aem.org/CBC/JobSpec/MC
Contact: Sharon Holling, Chm.

596 ■ CUES Financial Suppliers Forum (FSF) (2421)
PO Box 14167
Madison, WI 53708-0167
Ph: (608)271-2664
Free: (800)252-2664
Fax: (608)271-2303
E-mail: cues@cues.org
URL: http://www.cues.org
Contact: **Fred Johnson, Pres./CEO**

597 ■ Diagnostic Marketing Association (DxMA) (2566)
10293 N Meridian St., Ste.175
Indianapolis, IN 46290
Ph: (317)816-1640
Free: (800)278-7886
Fax: (317)816-1633
E-mail: info@dxma.org
URL: http://dxma.org
Contact: **Brian P. Durkin, Pres.**

598 ■ Direct Marketing Association (DMA) (2390)
1120 Ave. of the Americas
New York, NY 10036-6700
Ph: (212)768-7277
Fax: (212)302-6714
E-mail: presiden@the-dma.org
URL: http://www.the-dma.org
Contact: **Lawrence M. Kimmel Jr., Pres./CEO**

599 ■ Electronic Retailing Association (ERA) (2568)
2000 N 14th St., Ste.300
Arlington, VA 22201
Ph: (703)841-1751
Free: (800)987-6462
Fax: (703)841-8290
E-mail: **info@retailing.org**
URL: http://www.retailing.org
Contact: Julie Coons, Pres./CEO

600 ■ Health Industry Representatives Association (HIRA) (2551)
8 The Meadows
Newnan, GA 30265
Ph: (303)756-8115
Fax: (912)598-7844
E-mail: mikepeters1@optonline.net
URL: http://www.hira.org
Contact: **Robin Fipps CPMR, Pres.**

601 ■ International Experiential Marketing Association (IXMA)
550 15th St., Ste.31
San Francisco, CA 94103
Ph: (415)355-1586
E-mail: director@ixma.org
URL: http://www.ixma.org
Contact: Erik Hauser, Dir.

602 ■ Legal Marketing Association (LMA) (2576)
401 N Michigan Ave., 22th Fl.
Chicago, IL 60611-6610
Ph: **(312)321-6898**
Free: (888)562-9494
Fax: **(312)673-6894**
E-mail: **membersupport@legalmarketing.org**
URL: http://www.legalmarketing.org
Contact: **Jeanne Hammerstrom, Pres.**

603 ■ Marketing Research Association (MRA) (2397)
110 Natl. Dr., 2nd Fl.
Glastonbury, CT 06033-1212
Ph: (860)682-1000
Fax: (860)682-1050
E-mail: **email@mra-net.org**
URL: http://www.mra-net.org
Contact: **Elisa Galloway, Pres.**

604 ■ Marketing Science Institute (MSI) (2591)
1000 Massachusetts Ave.
Cambridge, MA 02138-5396
Ph: (617)491-2060 **(617)491-6002**
Fax: (617)491-2065
E-mail: msi@msi.org
URL: http://www.msi.org
Contact: Ruth Bolton, Exec. Dir.

605 ■ Mystery Shopping Providers Association (MSPA) (2540)
4230 LBJ Freeway, Ste.414
Dallas, TX 75244
Fax: (972)755-2561
E-mail: info@mysteryshop.org
URL: http://www.mysteryshop.org
Contact: **Lynn Saladini, Pres.**

606 ■ Strategic Account Management Association (SAMA) (2401)
33 N LaSalle St., Ste.3700
Chicago, IL 60602
Ph: (312)251-3131
Fax: (312)251-3132
E-mail: **quancard@strategicaccounts.org**
URL: http://www.strategicaccounts.org
Contact: Bernard Quancard, Pres./CEO

607 ■ Word of Mouth Marketing Association (WOMMA) (2577)
65 E Wacker Pl., Ste.500
Chicago, IL 60601
Ph: (312)853-4400
Fax: (312)275-7687
E-mail: **kristen@womma.org**
URL: http://womma.org/main
Contact: **Rod Brooks, Pres.**

Meat

608 ■ National Meat Association (NMA) (369)
1970 Broadway, Ste.825
Oakland, CA 94612
Ph: (510)763-1533
Fax: (510)763-6186
E-mail: staff@nmaonline.org
URL: http://www.nmaonline.org
Contact: **Barry Carpenter, CEO**

Media

609 ■ National Association of Media and Technology Centers (NAMTC) (2614)
PO Box 9844
Cedar Rapids, IA 52409-9844
Ph: (319)654-0608
Fax: (319)654-0609
URL: http://www.namtc.org
Contact: **Beverly Knox-Pipes, Pres.-Elect**

Meeting Planners

610 ■ Association for Convention Operations Management (ACOM) (2620)
191 Clarksville Rd.
Princeton Junction, NJ 08550
Ph: (609)799-3712
Fax: (609)799-7032
E-mail: info@acomonline.org
URL: http://www.acomonline.org
Contact: **Eric Blanc, Pres.**

611 ■ Exposition Service Contractors Association (ESCA) (2624)
5068 W Plano Pkwy., Ste.300
Plano, TX 75093
Ph: **(972)447-8212 (972)447-8211**
Free: (877)792-3722
Fax: **(972)447-8209**

E-mail: info@esca.org
URL: http://www.esca.org
Contact: Larry Arnaudet, Exec. Dir.

612 ■ International Association of Hispanic Meeting Professionals (IAHMP) (2609)
2600 S Shore Blvd., Ste.300
League City, TX 77573
Ph: (281)245-3330
Fax: **(281)668-9199**
E-mail: membership@iahmp.org
URL: http://www.hispanicmeetingprofessionals.com
Contact: Margaret Gonzalez, Founder/Pres.

613 ■ National Coalition of Black Meeting Planners (NCBMP) (2643)
4401 Huntchase Dr.
Bowie, MD 20720
Ph: **(301)860-0200**
Fax: **(301)860-0500**
E-mail: ncbmp.hq@verizon.net
URL: http://www.ncbmp.com
Contact: Stella Beene-Venson, Pres.

Metal

614 ■ International Hard Anodizing Association (IHAA) (2499)
PO Box 579
Moorestown, NJ 08057-0579
Ph: (856)234-0330
Fax: (856)727-9504
E-mail: **denise@neffdowning.com**
URL: http://www.ihanodizing.com
Contact: Denise Downing, Sec./Exec. Dir.

Military

615 ■ International Military Community Executives Association (IMCEA) (291)
PO Box 91356
Austin, TX 78709-1356
Ph: **(512)814-6232**
Fax: **(866)369-2435**
E-mail: imcea@imcea.com
URL: http://www.imcea.com
Contact: Fred McKenney CMCE, Pres.

Minerals

616 ■ World Gold Council (WGC) (2669)
424 Madison Ave., 3rd Fl.
New York, NY 10017
Ph: (212)317-3800
Fax: (212)688-0410
E-mail: info@gold.org
URL: http://www.gold.org
Contact: **Ian Telfer, Chm.**

Mining

617 ■ Mining Electrical Maintenance and Safety Association (MEMSA) (2517)
c/o Bill Collins, Sec.-Treas.
PO Box 7163
Lakeland, FL 33807
Fax: (863)644-5531
E-mail: memsa@tampabay.rr.com
URL: http://www.miningelectrical.org
Contact: **John Toler, Pres.**

618 ■ Perlite Institute (PI) (2697)
4305 N 6th St., Ste.A
Harrisburg, PA 17110
Ph: (717)238-9723
Fax: (717)238-9985
E-mail: info@perlite.org
URL: http://www.perlite.org
Contact: **Kathryn Louis, Pres.**

Minority Business

619 ■ National Association of Investment Companies (NAIC) (2530)
1300 Pennsylvania Ave. NW, Ste.700
Washington, DC 20004
Ph: (202)204-3001
Fax: (202)204-3022
E-mail: **admin@naicvc.com**
URL: http://www.naicvc.com
Contact: Samuel J. Boyd Jr., Pres./CEO

Mortuary Science

620 ■ American Board of Funeral Service Education (ABFSE) (9040)
3414 Ashland Ave., Ste.G
St. Joseph, MO 64506
Ph: (816)233-3747
Fax: (816)233-3793
E-mail: exdir@abfse.org
URL: http://www.abfse.org
Contact: **Dr. Gretchen L. Warner, Exec. Dir.**

Mortuary Services

621 ■ Jewish Funeral Directors of America (JFDA) (2553)
385 Craig Ct.
Deerfield, IL 60015
Ph: **(847)607-9156**
Free: (888)477-5567
Fax: (847)607-9159
E-mail: jfdamer@aol.com
URL: http://www.jfda.org
Contact: **Danielle Hornick, Exec. Dir.**

622 ■ National Funeral Directors and Morticians Association (NFDMA) (2559)
6290 Shannon Pkwy.
Union City, GA 30291
Ph: (404)286-6740
Free: (800)434-0958
Fax: (404)286-6573
E-mail: info@nfdma.com
URL: http://www.nfdma.com
Contact: **Dr. Carol T. Williams, Interim Exec. Dir.**

Music

623 ■ International Computer Music Association (ICMA) (2750)
1819 Polk St., Ste.330
San Francisco, CA 94109
Fax: (734)878-3031
E-mail: **icma@umich.edu**
URL: http://www.computermusic.org
Contact: Tae Hong Park, Pres.

624 ■ National Association of School Music Dealers (NASMD) (2759)
14070 Proton Rd., Ste.100
Dallas, TX 75244-3601
Ph: (972)233-9107
Fax: (972)490-4219
E-mail: office@nasmd.com
URL: http://www.nasmd.com
Contact: **Joel Menchey, Pres.**

625 ■ SoundExchange (SX) (9045)
1121 Fourteenth St. NW, Ste.700
Washington, DC 20005
Ph: (202)640-5858 (202)507-4659
Fax: (202)640-5859
E-mail: info@soundexchange.com
URL: http://www.soundexchange.com
Contact: **Michael J. Huppe, Pres.**

Newspapers

626 ■ Newspaper Target Marketing Coalition (NTMC)
2969 Blackwood Rd.
Decatur, GA 30033
Ph: (202)386-6357
E-mail: philip.brown@newspapertmc.org
URL: http://www.newspapertmc.org
Contact: **Jane Comfort, Pres.**

Oils and Fats

627 ■ Institute of Shortening and Edible Oils (ISEO) (2851)
1319 F St. NW, Ste.600
Washington, DC 20004
Ph: (202)783-7960
Fax: (202)393-1367
E-mail: **contactus@iseo.org**
URL: http://www.iseo.org
Contact: Robert L. Collette, Pres.

Optical Equipment

628 ■ Optoelectronics Industry Development Association (OIDA) (2780)
2010 Massachusetts Ave. NW
Washington, DC 20036
Ph: **(202)416-1449**
Fax: **(202)558-7349**
E-mail: **oidainfo@osa.org**
URL: http://www.oida.org
Contact: Frederic Quan, Pres.

Organization Development

629 ■ Organization Development Network (ODN) (2619)
401 N Michigan Ave., Ste.2200
Chicago, IL 60611
Ph: **(312)321-5136**
Fax: (973)763-7488
URL: http://www.odnetwork.org
Contact: Peter F. Norlin, Exec. Dir.

Outdoor Recreation

630 ■ Outdoor Industry Association (OIA) (2705)
4909 Pearl East Cir., Ste.200
Boulder, CO 80301
Ph: (303)444-3353 **(303)327-3501**
Fax: (303)444-3284
E-mail: info@outdoorindustry.org
URL: http://www.outdoorindustry.org
Contact: Frank Hugelmeyer, Pres./CEO

Outsourcing

631 ■ Global Sourcing Council (GSC)
750 Third Ave., 11th Fl.
New York, NY 10017
Ph: **(631)398-3366**
E-mail: christine.bullen@gscouncil.org
URL: http://www.gscouncil.org
Contact: Wanda Lopuch, Pres.

Packaging

632 ■ Petroleum Packaging Council (PPC) (2807)
1519 via Tulipan
San Clemente, CA 92673
Ph: (949)369-7102
Fax: **(949)366-1057**

E-mail: ppc@atdmanagement.com
URL: http://www.ppcouncil.org
Contact: **Mr. Mike Profetto, Pres.**

633 ■ Women in Packaging (WMPKG) (2634)
4290 Bells Ferry Rd., Ste.106-17
Kennesaw, GA 30144-1300
Ph: (678)594-6872
E-mail: **joann@womeninpackaging.org**
URL: http://womeninpackaging.org
Contact: JoAnn R. Hines, Founder

Personnel

634 ■ National Association for Government Training and Development (NAGTAD) (2830)
156 Whispering Winds Dr.
Lexington, SC 29072
Ph: **(803)397-8468**
E-mail: **gotonagtad@gmail.com**
URL: http://www.nagtad.org
Contact: **Cheryl Tinsley, Pres.**

635 ■ National Human Resources Association (NHRA) (2821)
PO Box 7326
Nashua, NH 03060-7326
Free: (866)523-4417
Fax: (603)891-5760
E-mail: info@humanresources.org
URL: http://www.humanresources.org
Contact: **Jamie Rajotte-Tremblay, Pres.**

636 ■ Society for Human Resource Management (SHRM) (2833)
1800 Duke St.
Alexandria, VA 22314-3499
Ph: (703)548-3440 (703)548-6999
Free: (800)283-7476
Fax: (703)535-6490
E-mail: board@shrm.org
URL: http://www.shrm.org
Contact: **Jose A. Berrios SPHR, Chm.**

Pest Control

637 ■ Responsible Industry for a Sound Environment (RISE) (404)
1156 15th St. NW, Ste.400
Washington, DC 20005
Ph: (202)872-3860
Fax: (202)355-1467
E-mail: **kreardon@pestfacts.org**
URL: http://www.pestfacts.org
Contact: Angela B. Jamison, Pres.

Petroleum

638 ■ American Oil and Gas Historical Society (AOGHS)
3204 18th St. NW
Washington, DC 20010
Ph: (202)857-4785
Fax: (202)857-4799
E-mail: bawells@aoghs.org
URL: http://www.aoghs.org
Contact: Bruce Wells, Founder/Exec. Dir.

639 ■ America's Natural Gas Alliance (ANGA)
701 Eighth St. NW, Ste.800
Washington, DC 20001
Ph: (202)789-2642
E-mail: info@anga.us
URL: http://www.anga.us
Contact: James T. Hackett, Chm.
Description: Represents independent natural gas exploration and production companies. Aims to increase awareness of the economic, environmental and national security benefits of natural gas. Promotes the benefits of natural gas to a wide range of audiences, including electric power utilities, non-governmental organizations, federal and state policy-makers and regulators.

640 ■ Crude Oil Quality Association (COQA)
2324 N Dickerson St.
Arlington, VA 22207
E-mail: dir.coqa@verizon.net
URL: http://www.coqa-inc.org
Contact: Harry N. Giles, Dir.
Description: Strives to maintain the integrity and consistency of the refining characteristics of crude oil streams. Provides a forum for communication and sharing of information and ideas to better educate the crude oil industry.

641 ■ Energy Traffic Association (ETA) (2698)
935 Eldridge Rd., No. 604
Sugar Land, TX 77478-2809
Ph: **(832)474-3564**
E-mail: russell@energytraffic.org
URL: http://www.energytraffic.org
Contact: Ernest M. Powell, Exec. Dir.

642 ■ Gas Processors Association (GPA) (2849)
6526 E 60th St.
Tulsa, OK 74145-9202
Ph: (918)493-3872
Fax: (918)493-3875
E-mail: gpa@gpaglobal.org
URL: http://gpaglobal.org
Contact: **Mike Heim, Pres.**

643 ■ Gas Processors Suppliers Association (GPSA) (2850)
6526 E 60th St.
Tulsa, OK 74145
Ph: (918)493-3872
Fax: (918)493-3875
E-mail: msutton@gpaglobal.org
URL: **http://gpsa.gpaglobal.org**
Contact: Mark Sutton, Exec. Dir.

644 ■ Independent Lubricant Manufacturers Association (ILMA) (2851)
400 N Columbus St., Ste.201
Alexandria, VA 22314-2264
Ph: (703)684-5574
Fax: (703)836-8503
E-mail: ilma@ilma.org
URL: http://www.ilma.org
Contact: **Paul Aylor, Pres.**

645 ■ International Association of Geophysical Contractors (IAGC) (2855)
1225 N Loop West, Ste.220
Houston, TX 77008-1761
Ph: (713)957-8080
Free: **(866)558-1756**
Fax: (713)957-0008
E-mail: iagc@iagc.org
URL: http://www.iagc.org
Contact: Chip Gill, Pres.

646 ■ International Oil Scouts Association (IOSA) (2856)
PO Box 940310
Houston, TX 77094-7310
Ph: **(713)420-6257**
E-mail: **james.yorek@elpaso.com**
URL: http://www.oilscouts.com
Contact: **James Yorek, Pres.**

647 ■ National Association of Division Order Analysts (NADOA) (2858)
PO Box 6845
Edmond, OK 73083
Ph: **(432)685-4374**
E-mail: administrator@nadoa.org
URL: http://www.nadoa.org
Contact: **Noemi Taylor, Pres.**

648 ■ Petroleum Equipment Institute (PEI) (2784)
PO Box 2380
Tulsa, OK 74101-2380
Ph: (918)494-9696
Fax: (918)491-9895
E-mail: info@pei.org
URL: http://www.pei.org
Contact: **Dennis Rethmeier, Pres.**

649 ■ Service Station Dealers of America/National Coalition of Petroleum Retailers and Allied Trades (SSDA-AT) (2903)
1532 Pointer Ridge Pl., Ste.E
Bowie, MD 20716
Ph: (301)390-4405
Fax: (301)390-3161
E-mail: **pfiore@wmda.net**
URL: http://www.ssda-at.org
Contact: Mr. Paul Fiore, Exec. VP

650 ■ Society of Professional Women in Petroleum (SPWP) (2872)
PO Box 420957
Houston, TX 77242
E-mail: jbabin@spwp.org
URL: http://www.spwp.org
Contact: Jerri Babin, Pres.

651 ■ Western States Petroleum Association (WSPA) (2701)
1415 L St., Ste.600
Sacramento, CA 95814
Ph: (916)498-7750
Fax: (916)444-5745
E-mail: **elaine@wspa.org**
URL: http://www.wspa.org
Contact: Catherine Reheis-Boyd, Pres.

Pets

652 ■ American Pet Products Association (APPA) (2869)
255 Glenville Rd.
Greenwich, CT 06831
Ph: (203)532-0000 (203)532-3603
Free: **(800)452-1225**
Fax: (203)532-0551
E-mail: bob@americanpetproducts.org
URL: http://www.appma.org
Contact: Robert L. Vetere, Pres.

653 ■ Independent Pet and Animal Transportation Association International (IPATA) (2915)
745 Winding Trail
Holly Lake Ranch, TX 75765
Ph: (903)769-2267
Fax: (903)769-2867
E-mail: inquiries@ipata.com
URL: http://www.ipata.com
Contact: **Kim Cunningham, Contact**

654 ■ International Professional Groomers (IPG) (2883)
123 Manley Ave.
Greensboro, NC 27401
Ph: **(336)852-9867**
Fax: (336)299-7164
E-mail: **hayley@ipgicmg.com**
URL: **http://www.ipgicmg.com**
Contact: Hayley Keyes, Pres.

655 ■ Pet Industry Joint Advisory Council (PIJAC) (2808)
1140 19th St. NW, Ste.300
Washington, DC 20036
Ph: (202)452-1525
Free: (800)553-7387
Fax: **(202)452-1516**
E-mail: info@pijac.org
URL: http://www.pijac.org
Contact: James P. Heim, Chm.

656 ■ World Pet Association (WPA) (411)
135 W Lemon Ave.
Monrovia, CA 91016-2809
Ph: (626)447-2222
Free: (800)999-7295
Fax: (626)447-8350
E-mail: **info@wpamail.org**
URL: http://www.wwpia.org
Contact: Doug Poindexter CAE, Pres.

Pharmaceuticals

657 ■ Chain Drug Marketing Association (CDMA) (2731)
PO Box 995
43157 W Nine Mile Rd.
Novi, MI 48376-0995
Ph: (248)449-9300
Free: **(800)935-2362**
Fax: (248)449-9396
E-mail: customerservice@qualitychoice.com
URL: http://www.chaindrug.com
Contact: James R. Devine, Pres.

658 ■ Consumer Healthcare Products Association (CHPA) (2930)
900 19th St. NW, Ste.700
Washington, DC 20006
Ph: (202)429-9260
Fax: (202)223-6835
E-mail: **melville@chpa-info.org**
URL: http://www.chpa-info.org
Contact: **Scott M. Melville DPA, Pres./CEO**

659 ■ International Pharmaceutical Excipients Council of the Americas (IPEC-AMERICAS) (2820)
1655 N Ft. Myer Dr., Ste.700
Arlington, VA 22209
Ph: (703)875-2127
Fax: (703)525-5157
E-mail: info@ipecamericas.org
URL: http://www.ipecamericas.org
Contact: **Priscilla Zawislak, Chair**

660 ■ National Pharmaceutical Council (NPC) (2726)
1894 Preston White Dr.
Reston, VA 20191-5433
Ph: (703)620-6390 (703)715-2758
Fax: (703)476-0904
E-mail: **info@npcnow.org**
URL: http://www.npcnow.org
Contact: Dan Leonard, Pres.

661 ■ Pharmaceutical Research and Manufacturers of America (PhRMA) (2937)
950 F St. NW, Ste.300
Washington, DC 20004
Ph: (202)835-3400
Fax: (202)835-3414
URL: http://www.phrma.org
Contact: **John J. Castellani, Pres./CEO**

Pharmacy

662 ■ Nigerian Association of Pharmacists and Pharmaceutical Scientists in the Americas (NAPPSA)
1761 Tennessee Ave.
Cincinnati, OH 45229
Ph: (513)641-3300
Free: **(800)538-2171**
Fax: (513)861-3629
E-mail: contact@nappsa.org
URL: http://www.nappsa.org
Contact: Nnodum Iheme RPh, Pres.

Photography

663 ■ American Photographic Artists Guild (APAG) (2911)
2269 N 400 Rd.
Eudora, KS 66025
Ph: (785)883-4166
E-mail: **hancock69@peoplepc.com**
URL: http://apag.net
Contact: Quinn Hancock, Contact

664 ■ American Society of Picture Professionals (ASPP) (2763)
217 Palos Verdes Blvd., No. 700
Redondo Beach, CA 90277
Ph: **(424)247-9944**
Fax: **(424)247-9844**
E-mail: **michaeldmasterson@gmail.com**
URL: http://www.aspp.com
Contact: **Jain Lemos, Exec. Dir.**

665 ■ Antique and Amusement Photographers International (AAPI)
PO Box 15117
Arlington, VA 22215
Ph: (479)253-8554
Fax: (479)253-1052
E-mail: **info@oldtimephotos.org**
URL: http://www.oldtimephotos.org
Contact: **Mike Glasser, Pres.**

666 ■ Independent Photo Imagers (IPI) (2920)
2518 Anthem Village Dr., Ste.100
Henderson, NV 89052
Ph: (702)617-1141
Fax: (702)617-1181
E-mail: **brenda@ipiphoto.com**
URL: http://www.ipiphoto.com
Contact: Brent D. Bowyer, Pres./Exec. Dir.

667 ■ Professional Photographers of America (PPA) (2933)
229 Peachtree St. NE, Ste.2200
Atlanta, GA 30303-1608
Ph: (404)522-8600
Free: (800)786-6277
E-mail: csc@ppa.com
URL: http://www.ppa.com
Contact: **Louis Tonsmeire, Chm.**

668 ■ Professional Women Photographers (PWP) (2920)
119 W 72nd St., No. 223
New York, NY 10023
E-mail: **info@pwponline.org**
URL: http://www.pwponline.org
Contact: Maddi Ring, Pres.

669 ■ White House News Photographers Association (WHNPA) (2759)
7119 Ben Franklin Sta.
Washington, DC 20044-7119
Ph: (202)785-5230
E-mail: **john.harrington@whnpa.org**
URL: http://www.whnpa.org
Contact: John Harrington, Pres.

Pipes

670 ■ American Concrete Pressure Pipe Association (ACPPA) (2945)
3900 Univ. Dr., Ste.110
Fairfax, VA 22030-2513
Ph: (703)273-7227
Fax: (703)273-7230
URL: http://www.acppa.org
Contact: **Richard Mueller, Chm.**

671 ■ National Association of Steel Pipe Distributors (NASPD) (2951)
1501 E Mockingbird Ln., Ste.307
Victoria, TX 77904
Ph: (361)574-7878

Fax: (832)201-9479
E-mail: info@naspd.com
URL: http://www.naspd.com
Contact: **Balor Moore, Pres.**

672 ■ National Corrugated Steel Pipe Association (NCSPA) (2954)
14070 Proton Rd., Ste.100, LB 9
Dallas, TX 75244
Ph: (972)850-1907
Fax: (972)490-4219
E-mail: **mmcgough@ncspa.org**
URL: http://www.ncspa.org
Contact: Sean Waters, Pres.

673 ■ Pipe Fabrication Institute (PFI) (2955)
511 Avenue of the Americas, No. 601
New York, NY 10011
Ph: (514)634-3434
Fax: (514)634-9736
E-mail: pfi@pfi-institute.org
URL: http://www.pfi-institute.org
Contact: **Mark Habermann, Chm.**

674 ■ Plastics Pipe Institute (PPI) (2943)
105 Decker Ct., Ste.825
Irving, TX 75062
Ph: (469)499-1044 **(469)499-1046**
Fax: (469)499-1063
E-mail: info@plasticpipe.org
URL: http://www.plasticpipe.org
Contact: Tony Radoszewski, Exec. Dir.

Plastics

675 ■ Association of Rotational Molders International (ARM International) (2964)
800 Roosevelt Rd., Ste.C-312
Glen Ellyn, IL 60137
Ph: (630)942-6589
Fax: (630)790-3095
E-mail: info@rotomolding.org
URL: http://www.rotomolding.org
Contact: **David Smith, Pres.**

676 ■ Center for the Polyurethanes Industry (CPI) (2998)
1300 Wilson Blvd.
Arlington, VA 22209
Ph: **(703)741-5103**
Fax: (703)741-5655
E-mail: neeva_candelori@americanchemistry.com
URL: http://www.polyurethane.org
Contact: Ms. Neeva-Gayle Candelori, Dir.

677 ■ Society of the Plastics Industry (SPI) (2964)
1667 K St. NW, Ste.1000
Washington, DC 20006
Ph: (202)974-5200
Fax: (202)296-7005
E-mail: **spimembership@plasticsindustry.org**
URL: http://www.plasticsindustry.org
Contact: Mr. William R. Carteaux, Pres./CEO

Plumbing

678 ■ Decorative Plumbing and Hardware Association (DPHA)
401 N Michigan Ave., Ste.2200
Chicago, IL 60611
Ph: (312)321-5110
Free: (800)218-8047
Fax: (312)673-6666
E-mail: membersupport@dpha.net
URL: http://www.dpha.net
Contact: **Steven Weinberg, Pres.**

679 ■ Plumbing and Drainage Institute (PDI)
(2793)
800 Turnpike St., Ste.300
North Andover, MA 01845
Ph: (978)557-0720
Free: (800)589-8956
Fax: (978)557-0721
E-mail: pdi@pdionline.org
URL: http://www.pdionline.org
Contact: **Rand Ackroyd, Exec. Dir.**

680 ■ Plumbing Manufacturers Institute (PMI)
(2984)
1921 Rohlwing Rd., Unit G
Rolling Meadows, IL 60008
Ph: (847)481-5500
Fax: (847)481-5501
E-mail: **bhiggens@pmihome.org**
URL: http://www.pmihome.org
Contact: **Jack Krecek, Pres.**

Pollution Control

681 ■ Manufacturers of Emission Controls
Association (MECA) (2975)
2020 N 14th St., Ste.220
Arlington, VA 22201
Ph: (202)296-4797
Fax: **(202)331-1388**
E-mail: info@meca.org
URL: http://www.meca.org
Contact: Antonio Santos, Contact

682 ■ Spill Control Association of America
(SCAA) (2989)
2105 Laurel Bush Rd., Ste.200
Bel Air, MD 21015
Ph: (443)640-1085
Fax: (443)640-1086
E-mail: info@scaa-spill.org
URL: http://www.scaa-spill.org
Contact: **Andrew B. Altendorf, Pres.**

683 ■ Worldwide Pollution Control
Association (WPCA)
12190 Hubbard St.
Livonia, MI 48150
Ph: (734)525-0300
Fax: (734)525-0303
E-mail: rstaehle@marsulex.com
URL: http://wpca.info
Contact: **Susan D. Reinhold, Chm./CEO**

Postal Service

684 ■ National Association of College and
University Mail Services (NACUMS) (2977)
PO Box 270367
Fort Collins, CO 80527-0367
Free: (877)NAC-UMS1
E-mail: sburn@lamar.colostate.edu
URL: http://www.nacums.org
Contact: **Mark Goodrich, Pres.**

Press

685 ■ American Jewish Press Association
(AJPA) (2998)
107 S Southgate Dr.
Chandler, AZ 85226
Ph: (480)403-4602
E-mail: info@ajpa.org
URL: http://www.ajpa.org
Contact: **Amy Doty, Pres.**

686 ■ American News Women's Club (ANWC)
(3000)
1607 22nd St. NW
Washington, DC 20008
Ph: (202)332-6770
Fax: (202)265-6092

E-mail: anwclub@comcast.net
URL: http://www.anwc.org
Contact: **Lynn Gorton, Pres.**

687 ■ American Society of News Editors
(ASNE) (420)
11690B Sunrise Valley Dr.
Reston, VA 20191-1436
Ph: (703)453-1122 **(703)453-1120**
Fax: (703)453-1133
E-mail: asne@asne.org
URL: http://asne.org
Contact: Richard Karpel, Exec. Dir.

688 ■ Asian American Journalists
Association (AAJA) (3005)
5 Third St., Ste.1108
San Francisco, CA 94103
Ph: (415)346-2051
Fax: (415)346-6343
E-mail: national@aaja.org
URL: http://www.aaja.org
Contact: Sharon Pian Chan, Pres.

689 ■ Associated Press Managing Editors
(APME) (2817)
c/o Sally Jacobsen
450 W 33rd St.
New York, NY 10001
Ph: (212)621-1838
Fax: (212)506-6102
E-mail: apme@ap.org
URL: http://www.apme.com
Contact: **Hollis Towns, Pres.**

690 ■ Association of Alternative
Newsweeklies (AAN) (2856)
1156 15th St. NW, Ste.905
Washington, DC 20005
Ph: (202)289-8484
Fax: (202)289-2004
E-mail: web@aan.org
URL: http://www.altweeklies.com
Contact: Mr. Mark Zusman, Pres.

691 ■ Association of American Editorial
Cartoonists (AAEC) (2982)
3899 N Front St.
Harrisburg, PA 17110
Ph: **(717)703-3003**
Fax: **(717)703-3008**
URL: http://www.editorialcartoonists.com
Contact: Rex Babin, Pres.

692 ■ Association of Health Care Journalists
(AHCJ) (2985)
10 Neff Hall
Columbia, MO 65211
Ph: (573)884-5606
Fax: (573)884-5609
E-mail: info@healthjournalism.org
URL: http://www.healthjournalism.org
Contact: **Charles Ornstein, Pres.**

693 ■ Association for Women in Sports
Media (AWSM) (3014)
3899 N Front St.
Harrisburg, PA 17110
E-mail: **info@awsmonline.org**
URL: http://awsmonline.org
Contact: Amy Moritz, Pres.

694 ■ Automotive Aftermarket Industry
Association | National Catalog Managers
Association (NCMA) (3052)
7101 Wisconsin Ave., Ste.1300
Bethesda, MD 20814-3415
Ph: (301)654-6664
Fax: (301)654-3299
E-mail: ncma@aftermarket.org
URL: http://www.aftermarket.org/Segments/NCMA(-
2).aspx
Contact: **Milt Grimes, Pres.**

695 ■ International Center for Journalists
(ICFJ) (2940)
1616 H St. NW, 3rd Fl.
Washington, DC 20006
Ph: (202)737-3700
Fax: (202)737-0530
E-mail: editor@icfj.org
URL: http://www.icfj.org
Contact: **Michael Golden, Chm.**

696 ■ International Motor Press Association
(IMPA) (2850)
PO Box 146
Harrington Park, NJ 07640
Ph: (201)750-3533
Fax: (201)750-2010
E-mail: **mike@jalopnik.com**
URL: http://www.impa.org
Contact: **Mike Spinelli, Pres.**

697 ■ National Association of Black
Journalists (NABJ) (2976)
Univ. of Maryland
1100 Knight Hall, Ste.3100
College Park, MD 20742
Ph: (301)445-7100 (301)405-0248
Free: (866)479-NABJ
Fax: (301)314-1714
E-mail: nabj@nabj.org
URL: http://www.nabj.org
Contact: **Maurice Foster, Exec. Dir.**

698 ■ National Conference of Editorial
Writers (NCEW) (3054)
3899 N Front St.
Harrisburg, PA 17110
Ph: (717)703-3015
Fax: (717)703-3014
E-mail: ncew@pa-news.org
URL: http://www.ncew.org
Contact: **Froma Harrop, Pres.**

699 ■ National Newspaper Association (NNA)
(3093)
PO Box 7540
Columbia, MO 65205-7540
Ph: **(573)777-4980 (573)882-4021**
Free: (800)829-4662
Fax: **(573)777-4985**
E-mail: briansteffens@nna.org
URL: http://www.nnaweb.org
Contact: Brian L. Steffens, Exec. Dir.

700 ■ National Press Club (NPC) (3046)
Natl. Press Bldg.
529 14th St. NW, 13th Fl.
Washington, DC 20045
Ph: (202)662-7500 (202)662-7505
Fax: (202)662-7512
URL: http://www.press.org
Contact: **Mark Hamrick, Pres.**

701 ■ New York Financial Writers'
Association (NYFWA) (3066)
PO Box 338
Ridgewood, NJ 07451-0338
Ph: (201)612-0100
Fax: (201)612-9915
E-mail: **nyfwa@aol.com**
URL: http://www.nyfwa.org
Contact: **Imogen Rose Smith, Pres.**

702 ■ Organization of News Ombudsmen
(ONO) (3070)
c/o Debbie Kornmiller, Treas.
The Arizona Daily Star
4850 S Park Ave.
Tucson, AZ 85714
E-mail: jdvorkin46@gmail.com
URL: http://www.newsombudsmen.org
Contact: Jacob Mollerup, Pres.

703 ■ Outdoor Writers Association of America (OWAA) (3107)
615 Oak St., Ste.201
Missoula, MT 59801
Ph: (406)728-7434
Fax: (406)728-7445
E-mail: **info@owaa.org**
URL: http://www.owaa.org
Contact: Robin Giner, Exec. Dir.

704 ■ Overseas Press Club of America (OPC) (3059)
40 W 45 St.
New York, NY 10036
Ph: (212)626-9220
Fax: (212)626-9210
URL: http://www.opcofamerica.org
Contact: **David A. Andelman, Pres.**

705 ■ Regional Reporters Association (RRA) (3074)
Cincinnati Enquirer
1100 New York Ave. NW, Ste.2005
Washington, DC 20005
E-mail: president@rra.org
URL: http://www.rra.org
Contact: Joseph Morton, Pres.

706 ■ Society for Features Journalism (SFJ)
(2910)
200 E Las Olas Blvd., 9th Fl.
Fort Lauderdale, FL 33301
Ph: **(954)356-4718**
E-mail: **gday@sun-sentinel.com**
URL: http://featuresjournalism.org
Contact: **Gretchen Day-Bryant, Pres.**
Status Note: Formerly American Association of Sunday and Feature Editors.

707 ■ Society of Professional Journalists (SPJ) (3081)
Eugene S. Pulliam Natl. Journalism Center
3909 N Meridian St.
Indianapolis, IN 46208
Ph: (317)927-8000
Fax: (317)920-4789
E-mail: **hlimor@wcpo.com**
URL: http://www.spj.org
Contact: **Hagit Limor, Pres.**

708 ■ Society of the Silurians (3119)
PO Box 1195
Madison Square Sta.
New York, NY 10159
Ph: (212)532-0887
E-mail: silurians@aol.com
URL: http://www.silurians.com
Contact: **Tony Guida, Pres.**

709 ■ Travel Journalists Guild (TJG) (3072)
PO Box 10643
Chicago, IL 60610-4952
Ph: (312)664-9279 **(602)276-3111**
Fax: (312)664-9701
E-mail: pdhoffman32@msn.com
URL: http://www.tjgonline.com
Contact: **Kerrick James, Pres.**

710 ■ United Nations Correspondents Association (UNCA) (3085)
United Nations
405 E 42nd St., Rm. L-213
New York, NY 10017
Ph: (212)963-7137 **(212)355-6053**
E-mail: contactus@unca.com
URL: http://www.unca.com
Contact: Giampaolo Pioli, Pres.

Professionals

711 ■ American Association of Electronic Reporters and Transcribers (AAERT) (3086)
PO Box 9826
Wilmington, DE 19809-9826
Free: (800)233-5306
Fax: (302)241-2177
E-mail: **janet.harris@aaert.org**
URL: http://www.aaert.org
Contact: Janet B. Harris CERT, Pres.

712 ■ Upwardly Global
San Francisco Off.
582 Market St., Ste.1207
San Francisco, CA 94104
Ph: (415)834-9901
Fax: (415)840-0334
E-mail: **nikki@upwardlyglobal.org**
URL: http://www.upwardlyglobal.org
Contact: Nikki Cicerani, Exec. Dir.

Property Management

713 ■ Association of Green Property Owners and Managers (AGPOM)
3400 Capitol Blvd. SE, Ste.101
Tumwater, WA 98501
Ph: (425)646-6425
Fax: (425)454-8233
URL: http://agpom.org
Contact: Art Smith, Contact
Founded: 2009. **Membership Dues:** primary, $250 (annual) ● associate, $300 (annual). **Description:** Promotes environmental sustainability awareness and involvement among property owners and managers. Encourages the protection of the natural environment by promoting the benefits of going green. Offers financial incentives for property owners and managers to get involved in green practices. **Libraries: Type:** reference. **Subjects:** energy efficiency, water conservation, waste minimization, improved indoor air quality.

714 ■ International Facility Management Association (IFMA) (2909)
1 E Greenway Plz., Ste.1100
Houston, TX 77046-0104
Ph: (713)623-4362
Fax: (713)623-6124
E-mail: ifma@ifma.org
URL: http://www.ifma.org
Contact: **Tony Keane, Pres./CEO**

715 ■ National Association of Residential Property Managers (NARPM) (3107)
638 Independence Pkwy., Ste.100
Chesapeake, VA 23320
Free: (800)782-3452
Fax: (866)466-2776
E-mail: info@narpm.org
URL: http://www.narpm.org
Contact: **Tony A. Drost MPM, Pres.**

Public Lands

716 ■ National Brownfield Association (NBA)
1250 S Grove Ave., Ste.200
Barrington, IL 60010
Ph: (224)567-6790
Fax: (224)567-6795
E-mail: info@brownfieldassociation.org
URL: http://www.brownfieldassociation.org
Contact: Kenneth Cornell, Pres.

Public Relations

717 ■ National Black Public Relations Society (NBPRS) (3113)
14636 Runnymede St.
Van Nuys, CA 91405
Free: (888)976-0005

Fax: (888)976-0005
E-mail: **wynona.redmond@nbprs.org**
URL: http://www.nbprs.org
Contact: Wynona Redmond, Pres.

Publishing

718 ■ American Book Producers Association (ABPA) (3154)
151 W 19th St., 3rd Fl.
New York, NY 10011
Ph: (212)645-2368
Fax: **(212)675-1364**
E-mail: office@abpaonline.org
URL: http://www.abpaonline.org
Contact: Richard Rothschild, Pres.

719 ■ Associated Church Press (ACP) (3124)
PO Box 621001
Oviedo, FL 32762-1001
Ph: (407)341-6615
Fax: (407)386-3236
E-mail: contactacp@aol.com
URL: http://www.theacp.org
Contact: **Meinrad Scherer Emunds, Pres.**

720 ■ Custom Content Council (CCC)
30 W 26th St., 3rd Fl.
New York, NY 10010
Ph: (212)989-4631
Fax: **(212)255-8456**
E-mail: **info@customcontentcouncil.com**
URL: http://www.custompublishingcouncil.com
Contact: Lori Rosen, Exec. Dir.

721 ■ Great Lakes Independent Booksellers Association (GLiBA) (2950)
PO Box 901
Grand Haven, MI 49417
Ph: (616)847-2460
Free: (800)745-2460
Fax: (616)842-0051
E-mail: info@gliba.org
URL: http://www.gliba.org
Contact: **Deb Leonard, Exec. Dir.**

722 ■ The International Publication Planning Association (TIPPA)
1350 41st Ave., Ste.200
Capitola, CA 95010
Ph: **(831)465-2298**
E-mail: krodriguez@publicationplanningassociation.
org
URL: http://www.publicationplanningassociation.org
Contact: Kristin Rodriguez, Contact

723 ■ Livestock Publications Council (LPC) (3156)
910 Currie St.
Fort Worth, TX 76107
Ph: (817)336-1130
Fax: (817)232-4820
E-mail: **mobeef@sbcglobal.net**
URL: http://www.livestockpublications.com
Contact: **Andy Atzenweiler, Pres.**

724 ■ National Association of Independent Publishers Representatives (NAIPR) (2994)
111 E 14th St.
PMB 157
New York, NY 10003-4103
Ph: (646)414-2993
Free: (888)624-7779
Fax: (800)416-2586
E-mail: paulthebookman@verizon.net
URL: http://www.naipr.org
Contact: **Sean Concannon, Exec. Dir.**

725 ■ Protestant Church-Owned Publishers Association (PCPA) (3158)
6631 Westbury Oaks Ct.
Springfield, VA 22152
Ph: (703)220-5989

E-mail: mulder@pcpaonline.org
URL: http://www.pcpaonline.org
Contact: Gary Mulder, Assoc. Dir.

**726 ■ Small Publishers Association of North
America (SPAN) (3254)**
PO Box 9725
Colorado Springs, CO 80932-0725
Ph: (719)924-5534
Fax: (719)213-2602
E-mail: info@spannet.org
URL: http://www.spannet.org
Contact: Scott Flora, Exec. Dir.

Purchasing

**727 ■ Alliance of Supplier Diversity
Professionals (ASDP)**
c/o Lisa Barr, Treas.
PO Box 560211
Rockledge, FL 32955
Free: (877)405-6565
E-mail: info@asdp.us
URL: http://www.asdp.us
Contact: Greg Satoro, Pres.

**728 ■ Institute for Supply Management (ISM)
(3187)**
PO Box 22160
Tempe, AZ 85285-2160
Ph: (480)752-6276
Free: (800)888-6276
Fax: (480)752-7890
E-mail: sidney.johnson@delphi.com
URL: http://www.ism.ws
Contact: Sidney Johnson, Chm.

Quality Assurance

**729 ■ Society of Quality Assurance (SQA)
(3195)**
154 Hansen Rd., Ste.201
Charlottesville, VA 22911
Ph: (434)297-4772
Fax: (434)977-1856
E-mail: sqa@sqa.org
URL: http://www.sqa.org
Contact: James A. Ault RAC, Pres.

Radio

**730 ■ Public Radio Program Directors
Association** (PRPD) (3181)
38 Milford St.
Hamilton, NY 13346
Ph: (315)824-8226
Fax: (315)824-8227
E-mail: info@prpd.org
URL: http://www.prpd.org
Contact: Arthur Cohen, Pres./CEO

Railroads

**731 ■ American Association of Private
Railroad Car Owners (AAPRCO) (2992)**
622 N Reed St.
Joliet, IL 60435
Ph: (815)722-8877
E-mail: execdirector@aaprco.com
URL: http://www.aaprco.com
Contact: Diane Elliott, Exec. Dir.

**732 ■ National Association of Railway
Business Women (NARBW) (3237)**
621 Lippincott Ave.
Riverton, NJ 08077
E-mail: narbwinfo@narbw.org
URL: http://www.narbw.org
Contact: Ms. Krista L. Pohl, Natl. Chair

733 ■ Railway Supply Institute (RSI) (3242)
425 3rd St. SW, Ste.920
Washington, DC 20024-3229
Ph: (202)347-4664
Fax: (202)347-0047
E-mail: rsi@railwaysupply.org
URL: http://www.rsiweb.org
Contact: Thomas D. Simpson, Pres.

**734 ■ Tourist Railway Association (TRAIN)
(3016)**
1016 Rosser St.
Conyers, GA 30012
Ph: (770)278-0088
E-mail: train@valornet.com
URL: http://traininc.org
Contact: Suzanne Grace, Exec. Dir.

Real Estate

**735 ■ Association of Real Estate Women
(AREW) (3224)**
1201 Wakarusa Dr., Ste.C3
Lawrence, KS 66049
Ph: (212)599-6181
Free: (888)329-2739
Fax: (785)832-1551
E-mail: info@arew.org
URL: http://www.arew.org
Contact: Debra Cole, Pres.

736 ■ CCIM Institute (3226)
430 N Michigan Ave., Ste.800
Chicago, IL 60611-4092
Ph: (312)321-4460
Free: (800)621-7027
Fax: (312)321-4530
E-mail: webmaster@cciminstitute.com
URL: http://www.ccim.com
Contact: Frank N. Simpson, Pres.

737 ■ CoreNet Global (3229)
260 Peachtree St. NW, Ste.1500
Atlanta, GA 30303
Ph: (404)589-3200
Free: (800)726-8111
Fax: (404)589-3201
E-mail: acain@corenetglobal.org
URL: http://www.corenetglobal.org
Contact: Angela Cain, CEO

**738 ■ Council of Real Estate Brokerage
Managers (CRB) (3215)**
430 N Michigan Ave.
Chicago, IL 60611-4011
Ph: (312)321-4414
Free: (800)621-8738
Fax: (312)329-8882
E-mail: info@crb.com
URL: http://www.crb.com
Contact: Matthew Ferrara, CEO

**739 ■ Council of Residential Specialists
(CRS) (3231)**
430 N Michigan Ave.
Chicago, IL 60611
Ph: (312)321-4444
Free: (800)462-8841
Fax: (312)329-8851
E-mail: crshelp@crs.com
URL: http://www.crs.com
Contact: Franklin T. Serio CRS, Chm.

740 ■ CRE Finance Council (CMSA) (3228)
30 Broad St., 28th Fl.
New York, NY 10004
Ph: (212)509-1844
Fax: (212)509-1895
E-mail: info@crefc.org
URL: http://www.crefc.org
Contact: Stephen M. Renna, CEO

741 ■ CREW Network (3060)
1201 Wakarusa Dr., Ste.C3
Lawrence, KS 66049
Ph: (785)832-1808
Fax: (785)832-1551
E-mail: crewnetwork@crewnetwork.org
URL: http://www.crewnetwork.org
Contact: Gail Ayers PhD, CEO/Pres.

742 ■ FIABCI-U.S.A. (3234)
1961 Wilson Blvd., Ste.306
Arlington, VA 22201
Ph: (703)524-4279
Fax: (703)991-6256
E-mail: info@fiabci-usa.com
URL: http://www.fiabci-usa.com
Contact: Danielle Grossenbacher, Pres.

743 ■ Hotel Brokers International (HBI) (3237)
1420 NW Vivion Rd., Ste.111
Kansas City, MO 64118
Ph: (816)505-4315
Fax: (816)505-4319
E-mail: info@hbihotels.com
URL: http://www.hbihotels.com
Contact: Joseph R. McCann, Pres.

**744 ■ Industrial Asset Management Council
(IAMC)**
6625 The Corners Pkwy., Ste.200
Norcross, GA 30092
Ph: (770)325-3461
Fax: (770)263-8825
E-mail: info@iamc.org
URL: http://www.iamc.org
Contact: Doyle Shea, Chm.

**745 ■ Institute of Real Estate Management
(IREM) (3238)**
430 N Michigan Ave.
Chicago, IL 60611
Ph: (312)329-6000
Free: (800)837-0706
Fax: (312)338-4736
E-mail: custserv@irem.org
URL: http://www.irem.org
Contact: Ronald L. Goss, Pres.

**746 ■ International Business Brokers
Association (IBBA) (3240)**
401 N Michigan Ave., Ste.2200
Chicago, IL 60611-4267
Free: (888)686-4222
Fax: (312)673-6599
E-mail: admin@ibba.org
URL: http://www.ibba.org
Contact: Rob Firestone, Chm.

**747 ■ International Real Estate Institute
(IREI) (3034)**
PO Box 879
Palm Springs, CA 92263
Ph: (760)327-5284
Free: (877)743-6799
Fax: (760)327-5631
E-mail: support@assoc-hdqts.org
URL: http://irei-assoc.org
Contact: Snehal Jardosh, Consultant

**748 ■ National Association of Hispanic Real
Estate Professionals (NAHREP) (3244)**
5414 Oberlin Dr., Ste.230
San Diego, CA 92121
Ph: (858)622-9046
URL: http://www.nahrep.org
Contact: Carmen Mercado, Chair

**749 ■ National Association of Media Brokers
(NAMB) (462)**
2910 Electra Dr.
Colorado Springs, CO 80906-1073
Ph: (719)630-3111
Fax: (719)630-1871

E-mail: **jbmccoy@mediaservicesgroup.com**
URL: http://www.nambonline.com
Contact: **Jody McCoy, Pres.**

750 ■ National Association of Real Estate Brokers (NAREB) (3249)
5504 Brentwood Stair Rd.
Fort Worth, TX 76112
Ph: (817)446-7715
Fax: (817)446-7744
E-mail: **wvincent.wimbish@nareb.com**
URL: http://www.nareb.com
Contact: **Vincent Wimbish, Pres.**

751 ■ National Association of Real Estate Investment Managers (NAREIM) (3252)
900 7th St. NW, Ste.960
Washington, DC 20001
Ph: (202)789-4373
Fax: (202)789-4376
E-mail: info@nareim.org
URL: http://www.nareim.org
Contact: **Patrick G. Halter, Chm.**

752 ■ National Association of Real Estate Investment Trusts (NAREIT) (3045)
1875 I St. NW, Ste.600
Washington, DC 20006-5413
Ph: (202)739-9400
Free: (800)3NA-REIT
Fax: (202)739-9401
E-mail: baiken@nareit.com
URL: **http://www.reit.com**
Contact: Steven A. Wechsler, Pres./CEO

753 ■ National Association of Realtors (NAR) (3254)
430 N Michigan Ave.
Chicago, IL 60611-4087
Free: (800)874-6500
URL: http://www.realtor.org
Contact: **Ron Phipps, Pres.**

754 ■ Pension Real Estate Association (PREA) (3261)
100 Pearl St., 13th Fl.
Hartford, CT 06103
Ph: (860)692-6341
Fax: (860)692-6351
E-mail: prea@prea.org
URL: http://www.prea.org
Contact: **Raymond Torto, Chm.**

755 ■ Property Management Association (PMA) (3247)
7508 Wisconsin Ave., 4th Fl.
Bethesda, MD 20814
Ph: (301)657-9200
Fax: (301)907-9326
E-mail: info@pma-dc.org
URL: http://www.pma-dc.org
Contact: **Scott Skokan, Pres.**

756 ■ Real Estate Educators Association (REEA) (3264)
2000 Interstate Park Dr., Ste.306
Montgomery, AL 36109-5420
Ph: **(334)625-8650**
Fax: **(334)260-2903**
E-mail: **membercare@reea.org**
URL: http://www.reea.org
Contact: **Joe McClary, Exec. Dir.**

757 ■ Realtors Land Institute (RLI) (3268)
430 N Michigan Ave.
Chicago, IL 60611
Ph: (312)329-8446
Free: (800)441-5263
Fax: (312)329-8633
E-mail: rli@realtors.org
URL: http://www.rliland.com
Contact: **Ray Brownfield, Pres.-Elect**

758 ■ Vacation Rental Managers Association (VRMA) (3270)
9100 Purdue Rd., Ste.200
Indianapolis, IN 46268
Ph: (317)454-8315
Fax: (317)454-8316
E-mail: vrma@vrma.com
URL: http://www.vrma.com
Contact: **Steve Ingram, Exec. Dir.**

Recordings

759 ■ Audio Publishers Association (APA) (20976)
191 Clarksville Rd.
Princeton Junction, NJ 08550
Ph: (609)799-6327
Fax: (609)799-7032
E-mail: info@audiopub.org
URL: http://www.audiopub.org
Contact: **Jennifer Thayer, Exec. Dir.**

760 ■ Music Video Production Association (MVPA)
c/o Beth Sadler
Sony Pictures Studios
10202 W Washington Blvd., Cohn Bldg.
Culver City, CA 90232
Ph: **(310)244-6964** (310)202-3302
Fax: **(310)244-4080**
E-mail: **infomvpa@gmail.com**
URL: http://www.mvpa.com
Contact: Coleen Haynes, Pres.

Recreation

761 ■ International Amusement and Leisure Defense Association (IALDA)
PO Box 4563
Louisville, KY 40204
Ph: (502)473-0956
Fax: (502)473-7352
E-mail: info@ialda.org
URL: http://www.ialda.org
Contact: **Lambert J. Hassinger Jr., Pres.**

762 ■ National Association of RV Parks and Campgrounds (National ARVC) (3285)
9085 E Mineral Cir., Ste.200
Centennial, CO 80112
Ph: (303)681-0401
Free: **(800)395-2267**
Fax: (303)681-0426
E-mail: lprofaizer@arvc.org
URL: http://www.arvc.org
Contact: **Paul Bambei, Pres./CEO**

763 ■ National Swimming Pool Foundation (NSPF) (3360)
4775 Granby Cir.
Colorado Springs, CO 80919-3131
Ph: (719)540-9119
Fax: (719)540-2787
E-mail: **info@nspf.org**
URL: http://www.nspf.org
Contact: **Mr. Tom Lachocki, CEO**

Recycling

764 ■ Reusable Packaging Association (RPA)
1100 N Glebe Rd., Ste.1010
Arlington, VA 22201
Ph: (703)224-8284
Fax: (703)243-5612
E-mail: info@reusables.org
URL: http://reusables.org
Contact: Jon Kalin, Chm.
Founded: 1999. **Membership Dues:** regular (based on revenue from reusables), $3,000-$12,000 (annual) ● end user, $1,500 (annual) ● sole proprietor consultant, $2,000 (annual) ● institution, $1,000 (an-

nual). **Description:** Represents the collaborative effort between manufacturers, poolers, distributors, retailers and educators to promote the environmental, safety, and economic benefits of reusable packaging. Advances the adoption of reusable packaging and systems throughout the supply chain. Promotes the expansion of reusables as the preferred packaging solution across supply chains in all industries.

Renting and Leasing

765 ■ American Car Rental Association (ACRA) (3299)
PO Box 225
Clifton Park, NY 12065
Free: (888)200-2795
E-mail: sfaulkner@acraorg.com
URL: http://acraorg.com
Contact: Sharon Faulkner, Exec. Dir.

Retailing

766 ■ Association for Retail Technology Standards (ARTS)
325 7th St. NW, Ste.1100
Washington, DC 20004-2818
Ph: (202)626-8140 **(202)783-7971**
Free: (800)673-4692
Fax: (202)783-6520
E-mail: arts@nrf.com
URL: http://www.nrf-arts.org
Contact: Richard Mader, Exec. Dir.

767 ■ Consumer Electronics Retailers Coalition (CERC)
317 Massachusetts Ave. NE, Ste.200
Washington, DC 20006
Ph: (202)292-4600
Fax: **(202)292-4650**
E-mail: christopher.mclean@cercteam.com
URL: http://www.ceretailers.org
Contact: Christopher A. McLean, Exec. Dir.

768 ■ Consumer Goods Forum (3328)
8455 Colesville Rd., Ste.705
Silver Spring, MD 20910
Ph: (301)563-3383
Fax: (301)563-3386
E-mail: usa@ciesnet.com
URL: http://www.ciesnet.com
Contact: **Sabine Ritter, Exec. VP**

769 ■ Direct Gardening Association (DGA) (3413)
5836 Rockburn Woods Way
Elkridge, MD 21075
Ph: (410)540-9830
Fax: (410)540-9827
E-mail: **grow@directgardeningassociation.com**
URL: http://www.directgardeningassociation.com
Contact: **Val Gosset, Pres.**
Status Note: Formerly Mailorder Gardening Association.

770 ■ International League of Antiquarian Booksellers (ILAB) (3294)
c/o Tom Congalton, VP
35 W Maple Ave.
Merchantville, NJ 08109-5141
Ph: (856)665-2284 (856)456-8008
Fax: (856)665-3639
E-mail: mail@betweenthecovers.com
URL: **http://www.ilab.org**
Contact: **Arnoud Gerits, Pres.**

771 ■ International Mystery Shopping Alliance (IMSA)
210 Crossways Park Dr.
Woodbury, NY 11797
Ph: (516)576-1188
Fax: (516)576-1195

E-mail: veronica@betterbusiness.se
URL: http://www.theimsa.com
Contact: **Marcelo Tarica, Chm., Quality and Operations**

772 ■ National Association for Retail Marketing Services (NARMS)
2417 Post Rd.
Stevens Point, WI 54481
Ph: (715)342-0948
Fax: (715)342-1943
E-mail: admin@narms.com
URL: http://www.narms.com
Contact: **Mary Jo Bastuba, Chair**

773 ■ National Grocers Association (NGA) (3332)
1005 N Glebe Rd., Ste.250
Arlington, VA 22201-5758
Ph: (703)516-0700
Fax: (703)812-1821
E-mail: **feedback@nationalgrocers.org**
URL: http://www.nationalgrocers.org
Contact: **Peter J. Larkin, Pres./CEO**

774 ■ NATSO Foundation (8133)
1737 King St., Ste.200
Alexandria, VA 22314
Ph: (703)549-2100
Free: (888)275-6287
Fax: (703)684-9667
E-mail: foundation@natsofoundation.org
URL: http://www.natsofoundation.org
Contact: **Jeff Irwin, Chm.**

775 ■ Natural Products Association (NPA) (3376)
1773 T St. NW
Washington, DC 20009
Ph: (202)223-0101
Free: (800)966-6632
Fax: (202)223-0250
E-mail: natural@npainfo.org
URL: http://www.npainfo.org
Contact: **Ms. Sandra Jackson, Communications Mgr.**

776 ■ Retail Design Institute (ISP) (3241)
25 N Broadway
Tarrytown, NY 10591-3221
Free: (800)379-9912
Fax: (914)332-1541
E-mail: info@ispo.org
URL: http://www.retaildesigninstitute.org
Contact: **Brian Dyches FRDI, Pres.**

777 ■ Shop America Alliance (SAA)
1308 Westhampton Woods Ct.
Chesterfield, MO 63005
Ph: (707)224-3795
Fax: (636)821-3012
E-mail: shopamericatours@aol.com
URL: **http://www.shopamericatours.com**
Contact: Rosemary McCormick, Pres./Co-Founder

778 ■ Women Grocers of America (WGA) (3312)
1005 N Glebe Rd., Ste.250
Arlington, VA 22201-5758
Ph: (703)516-0700 **(703)516-8802**
Fax: (703)516-0115
E-mail: kcomley@nationalgrocers.org
URL: http://www.nationalgrocers.org/WGA/WGA.html
Contact: Kristen Comley, Liaison

Rubber

779 ■ American Chemical Society, Rubber Division (3345)
PO Box 499
Akron, OH 44309-0499
Ph: (330)972-6527 **(330)972-7814**
E-mail: emiller@rubber.org
URL: http://www.rubber.org
Contact: Edward L. Miller, Exec. Dir.

Safety

780 ■ American Biological Safety Association (ABSA) (3364)
1200 Allanson Rd.
Mundelein, IL 60060-3808
Ph: (847)949-1517
Free: (866)425-1385
Fax: (847)566-4580
E-mail: info@absa.org
URL: http://www.absa.org
Contact: **Karen Byers RBP, Pres.**

781 ■ International System Safety Society (3185)
PO Box 70
Unionville, VA 22567-0070
Ph: (540)854-8630
Fax: (540)854-4561
E-mail: systemsafety@system-safety.org
URL: http://www.system-safety.org
Contact: **Warren Naylor, Pres.**
Status Note: Formerly System Safety Society.

782 ■ Transportation Safety Equipment Institute (TSEI)
PO Box 13966
Research Triangle Park, NC 27709
Ph: **(919)406-8823**
Fax: (919)549-4824
E-mail: tsei@mema.org
URL: http://www.tsei.org
Contact: **Mark Iasiello, Admin.**

783 ■ United Lightning Protection Association (ULPA) (3189)
426 North Ave.
Libertyville, IL 60048
Free: (800)668-8572
Fax: (847)362-6443
E-mail: info@ulpa.org
URL: http://www.ulpa.org
Contact: **Mark Hicks, Pres.**

Sales

784 ■ Gift and Home Trade Association (GHTA)
2025 E Beltline Ave. SE, Ste.200
Grand Rapids, MI 49546
Ph: (616)949-9104
Free: (877)600-4872
Fax: **(509)479-5254**
E-mail: info@giftandhome.org
URL: http://www.giftandhome.org
Contact: Doug Cofiell, Chm.

785 ■ National Association of Sales Professionals (NASP) (3398)
555 Friendly St.
Livonia, MI 48152
Free: **(866)365-1520**
Fax: (248)256-0173
URL: http://www.nasp.com
Contact: Rod Hairston, CEO

786 ■ Professional Society for Sales and Marketing Training (SMT) (3423)
113 McHenry Rd., No. 141
Buffalo Grove, IL 60089
Ph: **(973)882-3931**
Free: (800)219-0096
E-mail: **smtpowerofe@gmail.com**
URL: http://www.smt.org
Contact: Teresa Hiatt, Pres.

787 ■ Sales and Marketing Executives International (SMEI) (3220)
PO Box 1390
Sumas, WA 98295-1390
Ph: (312)893-0751
Free: (800)999-1414
Fax: **(312)893-0751**

E-mail: admin@smei.org
URL: http://www.smei.org
Contact: Willis Turner CSE, Pres./CEO

School Services

788 ■ National School Supply and Equipment Association (NSSEA) (3390)
8380 Colesville Rd., Ste.250
Silver Spring, MD 20910
Ph: (301)495-0240
Free: (800)395-5550
Fax: (301)495-3330
E-mail: memberservices@nssea.org
URL: http://www.nssea.org
Contact: **Jim McGarry, Pres./CEO**

Scientific Products

789 ■ American Scientific Glassblowers Society (ASGS) (3409)
PO Box 453
Machias, NY 14101
Ph: **(716)353-8062**
Fax: **(716)353-4259**
E-mail: natl-office@asgs-glass.org
URL: http://www.asgs-glass.org
Contact: Curt Sexton, Pres.

790 ■ Association of Medical Diagnostics Manufacturers (AMDM) (3393)
c/o Rebecca Shames, Admin. Asst.
555 13th St. NW, Ste.7W-401
Washington, DC 20004
Ph: **(202)637-6837**
Fax: (202)637-5910
E-mail: **amdm_secretary@att.net**
URL: http://www.amdm.org
Contact: Judi Smith, Pres.

791 ■ Independent Laboratory Distributors Association (ILDA) (3394)
PO Box 1464
Fairplay, CO 80440
Ph: (719)836-9091
Free: (888)878-4532
Fax: (719)836-9112
E-mail: kbretcko@ilda.org
URL: http://www.ilda.org
Contact: **Jonathan DeMeis, Chm.**

792 ■ SAMA Group of Associations (SAMA) (3439)
PO Box 428
Fairfax, VA 22038
Ph: (703)836-1360
Fax: (703)836-6644
E-mail: info@lpanet.org
URL: http://www.lpanet.org
Contact: Steve Gound, Chm.

Seafood

793 ■ Northwest Fisheries Association (NWFA) (3409)
2208 NW Market St., Ste.318
Seattle, WA 98107
Ph: (206)789-6197
Fax: (206)789-8147
E-mail: info@northwestfisheries.org
URL: http://www.northwestfisheries.org
Contact: **Chris Adams, Pres.**

794 ■ Pacific Coast Shellfish Growers Association (PCSGA) (3239)
120 State Ave. NE
PMB No. 142
Olympia, WA 98501
Ph: (360)754-2744
Fax: (360)754-2743

E-mail: pcsga@pcsga.org
URL: http://www.pcsga.org
Contact: **Margaret Pilaro Barrette, Exec. Dir.**

795 ■ Pacific Seafood Processors Association (PSPA) (490)
1900 W Emerson Pl., No. 205
Seattle, WA 98119
Ph: (206)281-1667
Fax: **(206)283-2387**
E-mail: info@pspafish.net
URL: http://www.pspafish.net
Contact: Nancy Diaz, Contact

Securities

796 ■ Financial Industry Regulatory Authority (FINRA) (3469)
1735 K St.
Washington, DC 20006-1500
Ph: (301)590-6500
URL: **http://www.finra.org**
Contact: Richard G. Ketchum, Chm./CEO

797 ■ Mutual Fund Education Alliance (MFEA) (3259)
100 NW Englewood Rd., Ste.130
Kansas City, MO 64118
Ph: (816)454-9422
Fax: (816)454-9322
E-mail: mfea@mfea.com
URL: http://www.mfea.info
Contact: **Brian M. Smith, Dir.**

798 ■ National Association of Securities Professionals (NASP) (3518)
727 15th St., NW, Ste.750
Washington, DC 20005
Ph: (202)371-5535
Fax: (202)371-5536
E-mail: cmarrow@koried.com
URL: http://www.nasphq.org
Contact: **Gwendolyn Hatten Butler, Chm.**

799 ■ New York Society of Security Analysts (NYSSA) (3443)
1540 Broadway, Ste.1010
New York, NY 10036-2714
Ph: (212)541-4530
Fax: (212)541-4677
E-mail: webaccess@nyssa.org
URL: http://www.nyssa.org
Contact: **Amy Geffen PhD, Pres./CEO**

800 ■ Security Traders Association (STA) (3270)
80 Broad St., 5th Fl.
New York, NY 10004
Ph: (203)202-7680
Fax: (203)202-7681
E-mail: **sta@securitytraders.org**
URL: **http://securitytraders.info**
Contact: **Jim Toes, Pres./CEO**

Security

801 ■ Building Security Council (BSC)
1801 Alexander Bell Dr.
Reston, VA 20191
Ph: **(703)295-6314**
Fax: **(703)295-6415**
E-mail: **jschmid@burnsmcd.com**
URL: http://www.buildingsecuritycouncil.org
Contact: **Jon A. Schmidt, Chm.**

802 ■ Electronic Security Association (ESA) (3284)
2300 Valley View Ln., Ste.230
Irving, TX 75062
Ph: (214)260-5970
Free: (888)447-1689
Fax: (214)260-5979

E-mail: webmaster@alarm.org
URL: http://www.alarm.org
Contact: Merlin Guilbeau, Exec. Dir.
Status Note: Formerly National Burglar and Fire Alarm Association.

803 ■ International Association of Certified Surveillance Professionals (IACSP)
4333 Bell Rd., Apt. No. 1210
Newburgh, IN 47630
Ph: **(812)472-1744**
URL: http://www.iacsp.org
Contact: Derk Boss CSP, Pres.

804 ■ International Association of Professional Security Consultants (IAPSC) (3455)
575 Market St., Ste.2125
San Francisco, CA 94105
Ph: **(415)536-0288**
Fax: **(415)764-4915**
E-mail: iapsc@iapsc.org
URL: http://www.iapsc.org
Contact: **Richard Grassie CPP, Pres.**

805 ■ International Organization of Black Security Executives (IOBSE) (3414)
PO Box 1471
San Mateo, CA 94401
Free: (888)884-6273
Fax: **(630)236-3629**
E-mail: iobse@yahoo.com
URL: http://www.iobse.com
Contact: **Suni Shamapande, Pres.**

806 ■ National Association of Security Companies (NASCO) (3463)
444 N Capitol St. NW, Ste.345
Washington, DC 20001
Ph: (202)347-3257
Fax: (202)393-7006
E-mail: information@nasco.org
URL: http://www.nasco.org
Contact: **Jim McNulty, Chm.**

807 ■ North American Security Products Organization (NASPO)
1425 K St. NW, Ste.350
Washington, DC 20005
Ph: (202)587-5743
Fax: (604)921-9171
E-mail: **ustaginfo@naspo.info**
URL: http://www.naspo.info
Contact: Mike O'Neil, Exec. Dir.

808 ■ Safe and Vault Technicians Association (SAVTA) (3452)
3500 Easy St.
Dallas, TX 75247
Ph: (214)819-9771 (214)819-9733
Free: (800)532-2562
Fax: (214)819-9736
E-mail: **info@savta.org**
URL: http://www.savta.org
Contact: **Mr. Joseph Cortie, Pres.**

809 ■ Security Industry Association (SIA) (3288)
635 Slaters Ln., Ste.110
Alexandria, VA 22314
Ph: (703)683-2075
Free: (866)817-8888
Fax: (703)683-2469
E-mail: info@siaonline.org
URL: http://www.siaonline.org
Contact: **Gordon Hope, Chm.**

Service

810 ■ Coalition of Service Industries (CSI) (498)
1090 Vermont Ave. NW, Ste.420
Washington, DC 20005
Ph: (202)289-7460

Fax: **(202)379-9864**
E-mail: gololobov@uscsi.org
URL: http://www.uscsi.org
Contact: J. Robert Vastine, Pres.

811 ■ Custom Electronic Design Installation Association (CEDIA) (3548)
7150 Winton Dr., Ste.300
Indianapolis, IN 46268
Ph: (317)328-4336
Free: (800)669-5329
Fax: (317)735-4012
E-mail: member@cedia.org
URL: http://www.cedia.net
Contact: **Randy Stearns, Chm.**

812 ■ Equipment Service Association (ESA) (3500)
c/o Heather Phillips, Exec. Dir.
PO Box 1420
Cherry Hill, NJ 08034
Ph: (856)489-0753
Free: (866)372-3155
Fax: (856)424-9248
E-mail: esa@2esa.org
URL: http://www.2esa.org
Contact: Randy Valleroy, Pres.

813 ■ International Customer Service Association (ICSA) (3293)
1110 South Ave., Ste.No. 50
Staten Island, NY 10314
Ph: (374)273-1303
E-mail: info@icsatoday.org
URL: http://www.icsa.com
Contact: Bill Gessert, Pres.

814 ■ National Association of Service Managers (NASM) (3433)
PO Box 250796
Milwaukee, WI 53225
Ph: (414)466-6060 **(414)847-1200**
Fax: (414)466-0840
E-mail: **kenc@kencook.com**
URL: http://www.nasm.com
Contact: David Jones, Pres.

Shipping

815 ■ Independent Armored Car Operators Association (IACOA) (3494)
8000 Res. Forest Dr., Ste.115-155
The Woodlands, TX 77382-1504
Ph: (281)292-8208
Fax: **(281)292-9308**
E-mail: jmiacoa@yahoo.com
URL: http://www.iacoa.com
Contact: John Margaritis, Admin.

816 ■ International Furniture Transportation and Logistics Council (IFTLC) (3496)
282 N Ridge Rd.
Brooklyn, MI 49230
Ph: **(517)467-9355**
E-mail: russ111@comcast.net
URL: http://www.iftlc.org
Contact: Russ Matthews, Contact

817 ■ National Tank Truck Carriers (NTTC) (3506)
950 N Glebe Rd., Ste.520
Arlington, VA 22203
Ph: (703)838-1960
Fax: (703)838-8860
E-mail: **jconley@tanktruck.org**
URL: http://www.tanktruck.org
Contact: John Conley, Pres.

818 ■ Pacific Maritime Association (PMA) (3536)
555 Market St.
San Francisco, CA 94105-2800
Ph: (415)576-3200 (206)298-3434
Fax: (415)348-8392

E-mail: **cheryl.heinonen@bm.com**
URL: http://www.pmanet.org
Contact: James C. McKenna, Pres./CEO

819 ■ Propeller Club of the U.S. (PCUS) (3512)
3927 Old Lee Hwy., Ste.101A
Fairfax, VA 22030
Ph: (703)691-2777 (703)841-9300
Fax: **(703)691-4173**
E-mail: **info@propellerclubhq.com**
URL: http://www.propellerclubhq.com
Contact: Thomas A. Allegretti, Pres./CEO

820 ■ Transportation and Logistics Council (TLC) (3521)
120 Main St.
Huntington, NY 11743
Ph: (631)549-8988 (631)549-8984
Fax: (631)549-8962
E-mail: tlc@transportlaw.com
URL: http://www.tlcouncil.org
Contact: **Carol Wynstra, Chair**

Small Business

821 ■ Association for Enterprise Opportunity (AEO) (3531)
1111 16th St. NW, Ste.410
Washington, DC 20036
Ph: **(202)650-5580**
E-mail: cevans@aeoworks.org
URL: **http://www.aeoworks.org**
Contact: Connie Evans, Pres./CEO

822 ■ BEST Employers Association (BEA)
2505 McCabe Way
Irvine, CA 92614
Free: **(866)706-2225**
URL: **http://www.beassoc.org**

823 ■ International Council for Small Business (ICSB) (3537)
GWU School of Bus.
2201 G St. NW
Funger Hall, Ste.315
Washington, DC 20052
E-mail: aymanelt@icsb.org
URL: http://www.icsb.org
Contact: **David Smallbone, Pres.**

824 ■ SCORE (3535)
1175 Herndon Pkwy., Ste.900
Herndon, VA 20170
Ph: (703)487-3612
Free: (800)634-0245
Fax: (703)487-3066
E-mail: **kenneth.yancey@score.org**
URL: http://www.score.org
Contact: Kenneth W. Yancey Jr., CEO

825 ■ Small Business Service Bureau (SBSB)
554 Main St.
PO Box 15014
Worcester, MA 01615-0014
Free: (800)343-0939
Fax: (508)770-0528
E-mail: **info@sbsb.com**
URL: http://www.sbsb.com
Contact: Francis R. Carroll, Founder/CEO

Social Change

826 ■ Social Enterprise Alliance (SEA) (3543)
11525 Springridge Rd.
Potomac, MD 20854
Ph: (202)758-0194
Fax: (202)449-9611
E-mail: **info@se-alliance.org**
URL: http://www.se-alliance.org
Contact: **Lisa Nitze, Pres./CEO**

Sporting Goods

827 ■ American Fly-Fishing Trade Association (AFFTA) (3635)
901 Front St., Ste.B-125
Louisville, CO 80027
Ph: (303)604-6132
Fax: (303)604-6162
URL: http://www.affta.com
Contact: **Jim Klug, Chm.**

828 ■ Association of Golf Merchandisers (AGM) (3476)
PO Box 7247
Phoenix, AZ 85011-7247
Ph: (602)604-8250 **(602)687-5448**
Fax: (602)604-8251
E-mail: info@agmgolf.org
URL: http://www.agmgolf.org
Contact: Desane Blaney, Exec. Dir.

829 ■ Billiard and Bowling Institute of America (BBIA) (3551)
PO Box 6573
Arlington, TX 76005
Ph: (817)385-8120
Free: (800)343-1329
Fax: (817)633-2940
E-mail: answer@billiardandbowling.org
URL: http://www.billiardandbowling.org
Contact: **Phil Cardinale, Pres.**

830 ■ International Clubmakers' Guild (591)
95 Washington St., Ste.104-335
Canton, MA 02021
URL: http://www.clubmakersguild.com
Contact: **Ken Alterwitz, Pres.**

831 ■ National Association of Sporting Goods Wholesalers (NASGW) (3554)
1833 Centre Point Cir., Stem 123
Naperville, IL 60563
Ph: **(630)596-9006**
Fax: **(630)544-5055**
E-mail: nasgw@nasgw.org
URL: http://www.nasgw.org
Contact: Mr. Maurice A. Desmarais, Pres./Sec.

Sports

832 ■ Fantasy Sports Trade Association (FSTA)
c/o Charlie Wiegert, Treas.
11756 Borman Dr.
St. Louis, MO 63146
Ph: **(763)269-3609**
URL: http://www.fsta.org
Contact: Paul Charchian, Pres.

833 ■ Golf Course Builders Association of America (GCBAA) (3541)
727 O St.
Lincoln, NE 68508
Ph: (402)476-4444
Fax: (402)476-4489
E-mail: information@gcbaa.org
URL: **http://www.gcbaa.org**
Contact: **Justin Apel, Exec. Dir.**

834 ■ Golf Course Superintendents Association of America (GCSAA) (3573)
1421 Res. Park Dr.
Lawrence, KS 66049-3859
Ph: (785)841-2240
Free: (800)472-7878
Fax: (785)832-3643
E-mail: mbrhelp@gcsaa.org
URL: http://www.gcsaa.org
Contact: **Rhett Evans, CEO**

835 ■ Sport Marketing Association (SMA)
Univ. of Memphis
204B Fieldhouse
Memphis, TN 38152
Fax: (901)678-5014
E-mail: webmaster@sportmarketingassociation.com
URL: http://www.sportmarketingassociation.com
Contact: **Eric Schwarz, Pres.**

Stationery

836 ■ Business Solutions Association (BSA)
5024 Campbell Blvd., Ste.R
Baltimore, MD 21236-5943
Ph: (410)931-8100
Fax: (410)931-8111
E-mail: **calc@clemonsmgmt.com**
URL: http://businesssolutionsassociation.com
Contact: Calvin K. Clemons CAE, Exec. VP

837 ■ Greeting Card Association (GCA) (3607)
1133 Westchester Ave., Ste.N136
White Plains, NY 10604-3546
Ph: **(914)421-3331 (914)421-3225**
Fax: **(914)948-1484**
E-mail: **gca@gcamail.org**
URL: http://www.greetingcard.org
Contact: **Jack Withiam, Exec. VP**

838 ■ Print Services and Distribution Association (PSDA) (3592)
401 N Michigan Ave., Ste.2200
Chicago, IL 60611
Free: (800)230-0175
Fax: (312)673-6880
E-mail: psda@psda.org
URL: http://www.psda.org
Contact: **Mr. Matt Sanderson, Exec. VP**

Stone

839 ■ Allied Stone Industries (ASI) (3396)
c/o Butch Coleman, Dir.
PO Box 273
Susquehanna, PA 18847
Ph: (570)465-7200
Fax: **(800)672-3524**
E-mail: butchbluestone@gmail.com
URL: http://www.alliedstone.com
Contact: Mark Sawyer, Pres.

840 ■ Indiana Limestone Institute of America (ILIA) (3458)
400 Stone City Bank Bldg.
Bedford, IN 47421
Ph: (812)275-4426
Fax: (812)279-8682
E-mail: **todd@iliai.com**
URL: http://www.iliai.com
Contact: **Todd Schnatzmeyer, Exec. Dir.**

841 ■ National Stone, Sand and Gravel Association (NSSGA) (3624)
1605 King St.
Alexandria, VA 22314-2726
Ph: (703)525-8788 **(703)526-1098**
Free: (800)342-1415
Fax: (703)525-7782
E-mail: info@nssga.org
URL: http://www.nssga.org
Contact: Jennifer Joy Wilson, Pres./CEO

Surplus

842 ■ Investment Recovery Association (IRA) (3466)
638 W 39th St.
Kansas City, MO 64111-2910
Ph: (816)561-5323
Free: (800)728-2272

Fax: (816)561-1991
E-mail: **ira@invrecovery.org**
URL: http://www.invrecovery.org
Contact: Jane Male CAE, Exec. Dir.

Surveying

**843 ■ American Council of Engineering
Companies | Council of Professional
Surveyors** (COPS) (3615)
1015 15th St. NW, 8th Fl.
Washington, DC 20005-2605
Ph: (202)347-7474 **(202)682-4377**
Fax: (202)898-0068
E-mail: **htalbert@acec.org**
URL: http://www.acec.org/coalitions/COPS/index.cfm
Contact: **Tim Cawood, Chm.**

Tableware

844 ■ Society of American Silversmiths
(SAS) (3475)
PO Box 786
West Warwick, RI 02893
Ph: (401)461-6840
Free: **(800)461-6840**
Fax: (401)461-6841
E-mail: sas@silversmithing.com
URL: http://www.silversmithing.com
Contact: Jeffrey Herman, Founder/Exec. Dir.

Taxidermy

845 ■ National Taxidermists Association
(NTA) (3642)
108 Br. Dr.
Slidell, LA 70461-1912
Ph: (985)641-4682
Free: (866)662-9054
Fax: (985)641-9463
E-mail: ntahq@aol.com
URL: http://www.nationaltaxidermists.com
Contact: **Steve Wolk, Pres.**

Technology

**846 ■ 1394 High Performance Serial Bus
Trade Association (1394 TA)**
315 Lincoln, Ste.E
Mukilteo, WA 98275
Ph: **(425)870-6574**
Fax: **(425)320-3897**
E-mail: jsnider@1394ta.org
URL: http://www.1394ta.org
Contact: James Snider, Exec. Dir.

**847 ■ American Association of Professional
Technical Analysts (AAPTA)**
209 W Jackson Blvd., 6th Fl.
Chicago, IL 60606
Ph: **(972)213-5816**
E-mail: membership@aapta.com
URL: http://www.aapta.com
Contact: Jeanette Young, Pres.

848 ■ Global Technology Distribution Council
(GTDC)
141 Bay Point Dr. NE
St. Petersburg, FL 33704
Ph: (813)412-1148
Fax: (301)218-9406
E-mail: info@gtdc.org
URL: http://www.gtdc.org
Contact: Tim Curran, CEO
Founded: 1998. **Multinational. Description:** Represents the interests of computer industry distributors. Promotes the role of wholesale distribution in a healthy information technology channel. Offers as-
sistance to IT vendors in strengthening their partnerships and addresses industry-wide issues and opportunities.

Telecommunications

849 ■ Land Mobile Communications Council
(LMCC) (3665)
8484 Westpark Dr., Ste.630
McLean, VA 22102-5117
Ph: (703)528-5115
Fax: (703)524-1074
E-mail: mark.crosby@enterprisewireless.org
URL: http://www.lmcc.org
Contact: **Douglas M. Aiken, Pres.**

**850 ■ PCIA - The Wireless Infrastructure
Association (PCIA)** (3667)
901 N Washington St., Ste.600
Alexandria, VA 22314-1535
Ph: **(703)836-1608**
Free: (800)759-0300
Fax: (703)836-1608
E-mail: **nancy.touhill@pcia.com**
URL: http://www.pcia.com
Contact: Michael T.N. Fitch, Pres./CEO

851 ■ Telework Coalition (TelCoa)
204 E St. NE
Washington, DC 20002
Ph: **(202)266-0046**
E-mail: info@telcoa.org
URL: http://www.telcoa.org
Contact: Chuck Wilsker, Pres./CEO

**852 ■ Wireless Communications Association
International (WCA)** (3680)
1333 H St. NW, Ste.700 W
Washington, DC 20005-4754
Ph: (202)452-7823
Fax: (202)452-0041
E-mail: **susan@wcai.com**
URL: http://www.wcai.com
Contact: Fred Campbell, Pres./CEO

853 ■ ZigBee Alliance (3683)
2400 Camino Ramon, Ste.375
San Ramon, CA 94583
Ph: **(925)275-6607**
Fax: (925)886-3850
E-mail: help@zigbee.org
URL: http://www.zigbee.org
Contact: Bob Heile, Chm.

Textiles

854 ■ American Flock Association (AFA)
(3686)
6 Beacon St., Ste.1125
Boston, MA 02108
Ph: (617)303-6288
Fax: (617)542-2199
E-mail: **info@flocking.org**
URL: http://www.flocking.org
Contact: Todd Der Manouellian, Chm.

**855 ■ International Textile Market
Association (ITMA)**
PO Box 1208
High Point, NC 27261
Ph: (336)885-6842
Fax: (336)885-8926
E-mail: **info@itmashowtime.com**
URL: http://www.itma-showtime.com
Contact: **Bob Patton, Pres.**

**856 ■ National Association of Decorative
Fabric Distributors (NADFD)** (3553)
1 Windsor Cove, Ste.305
Columbia, SC 29223-1833
Ph: (803)252-5646
Free: (800)445-8629
Fax: (803)765-0860
E-mail: info@nadfd.com
URL: http://www.nadfd.com
Contact: **Anna Stinson, Pres.**

857 ■ The National Needle Arts Association
(TNNA) (3749)
1100-H Brandywine Blvd.
Zanesville, OH 43701-7303
Ph: **(740)455-6773**
Free: (800)889-8662
Fax: (740)452-2552
E-mail: tnna.info@offinger.com
URL: http://www.tnna.org
Contact: **Matt Bryant, Pres.**

858 ■ Spinning and Weaving Association
(SWA)
PO Box 7506
Loveland, CO 80537
Ph: (970)613-4629
E-mail: swa@spinweave.org
URL: http://www.spinweave.org
Contact: **Dave Van Stralen, Pres.**

859 ■ Surface Design Association (SDA)
(3722)
PO Box 360
Sebastopol, CA 95473-0360
Ph: (707)829-3110
Fax: (707)829-3285
E-mail: info@surfacedesign.org
URL: http://www.surfacedesign.org
Contact: **Candace Edgerley, Pres.**

**860 ■ United States Association of Importers
of Textiles and Apparel (USA-ITA)** (3648)
1140 Connecticut Ave., Ste.950
Washington, DC 20036
Ph: **(202)419-0444**
Fax: (202)783-0727
E-mail: info@usaita.com
URL: http://www.usaita.com
Contact: Laura E. Jones, Exec. Dir.

Timepieces

**861 ■ Independent Time and Labor
Management Association (ITLMA)** (3733)
c/o Michael Hoover, Sec.-Treas.
2049 Stout Dr., Ste.A-1
Warminster, PA 18974
Ph: **(215)443-8720**
Fax: **(215)443-8709**
E-mail: info@itlma.org
URL: http://www.itlma.org/1.5
Contact: **Sherry Evens, Pres.**

Tires

862 ■ Tire Industry Association (TIA) (3522)
1532 Pointer Ridge Pl., Ste.G
Bowie, MD 20716-1883
Ph: (301)430-7280
Free: (800)876-8372
Fax: (301)430-7283
E-mail: info@tireindustry.org
URL: http://www.tireindustry.org
Contact: **Gary Albright, Pres./CEO**

**863 ■ Tire Retread and Repair Information
Bureau (TRIB)** (3578)
1013 Birch St.
Falls Church, VA 22046
Ph: (703)533-7677
Free: **(877)394-6811**
Fax: (703)533-7678
E-mail: info@retread.org
URL: http://www.retread.org
Contact: **Mr. David Stevens, Managing Dir.**

Tourism

864 ■ Convention Industry Council (CIC) (3745)
700 N Fairfax St., Ste.510
Alexandria, VA 22314
Ph: (571)527-3116
Fax: (571)527-3105
E-mail: cichq@conventionindustry.org
URL: http://www.conventionindustry.org
Contact: **Stacey Tetschner CAE, Chm.**

Trade

865 ■ Fair Trade USA
1500 Broadway, Ste.400
Oakland, CA 94612
Ph: (510)663-5260
Fax: (510)663-5264
E-mail: info@transfairusa.org
URL: http://transfairusa.org
Contact: Paul Rice, Pres./CEO
Status Note: Formerly TransFair USA.

Transportation

866 ■ American Bus Association (ABA) (3776)
111 K St. NE, 9th Fl.
Washington, DC 20002
Ph: (202)842-1645
Fax: (202)842-0850
E-mail: abainfo@buses.org
URL: http://www.buses.org
Contact: Peter J. Pantuso, Pres./CEO

867 ■ American Public Transportation Association (APTA) (3777)
1666 K St. NW, Ste.1100
Washington, DC 20006
Ph: (202)496-4800
Fax: (202)496-4324
E-mail: info@apta.com
URL: http://www.apta.com
Contact: **Michael J. Scanlon, Chm.**

868 ■ Chinese Overseas Transportation Association (COTA)
Univ. of Washington
Dept. of Civil and Environmental Engg.
Seattle, WA 98195-2700
Ph: (206)616-2696
Fax: **(206)543-1543**
E-mail: yinhai@u.washington.edu
URL: **http://www.cota-home.org**
Contact: Dr. Yinhai Wang, Pres.

869 ■ Conference of Minority Transportation Officials (COMTO) (3752)
2025 M St. NW, Ste.800
Washington, DC 20036-3309
Ph: **(202)367-1181**
Fax: **(202)367-2181**
E-mail: jcunningham@comto.org
URL: http://www.comto.org
Contact: Ms. Julie A. Cunningham, Pres./CEO

870 ■ Driver Employment Council of America (DECA) (3615)
1150 17th St. NW, Ste.900
Washington, DC 20036
Ph: (202)842-3400
Fax: (202)842-0011
E-mail: **jcreager@vanguardservices.net**
URL: http://www.decausa.org
Contact: **Mr. John Creager, Pres.**

871 ■ Electrification Coalition
1111 19th St. NW, Ste.406
Washington, DC 20036
Ph: (202)461-2360
Fax: (202)461-2379
E-mail: info@electrificationcoalition.org
URL: http://www.electrificationcoalition.org
Contact: Robbie Diamond, Pres./CEO
Description: Represents business leaders in the electrified transportation industry. Promotes policies and actions that facilitate the deployment of electric vehicles on a mass scale. Strives to combat the economic, environmental and national security dangers caused by the nation's dependence on petroleum.

872 ■ Intelligent Transportation Society of America (ITSA) (3789)
1100 17th St. NW, Ste.1200
Washington, DC 20036
Ph: (202)484-4847 (202)721-4210
Free: (800)374-8472
Fax: (202)484-3483
E-mail: info@itsa.org
URL: http://www.itsa.org
Contact: **Ann Flemer, Chair**

873 ■ Light Electric Vehicle Association (LEVA)
PO Box 286
Orono, ME 04473
E-mail: sidneyk@levassociation.com
URL: http://www.levassociation.com
Contact: Sidney Kuropchak, Exec. Dir.

874 ■ National Association of Publicly Funded Truck Driving Schools (NAPFTDS) (3763)
c/o Tina Frindt, Treas.
Northampton Community Coll.
1900 Corporate Center Dr. E
Tobyhanna, PA 18466
Ph: (217)641-4914
Fax: (217)224-0741
E-mail: **tfrindt@northampton.edu**
URL: http://www.napftds.org
Contact: **Martin Garsee, Pres.**

875 ■ National Association of Show Trucks (NAST)
23227 Freedom Ave., Ste.7
Port Charlotte, FL 33980
Ph: **(734)604-3242**
E-mail: bogiesexpress@comcast.net
URL: http://www.nastshowtrucks.org
Contact: Bo Trout, Pres.

876 ■ Transportation Clubs International (TCI) (3649)
PO Box 2223
Ocean Shores, WA 98569
Free: (877)858-8627
Fax: (360)289-3188
E-mail: **dtam@transportationclubsinternational. com**
URL: http://www.transportationclubsinternational.com
Contact: Katie DeJonge, Exec. Dir.

877 ■ Trucking Industry Defense Association (TIDA) (3897)
6311 W Gross Point Rd.
Niles, IL 60714
Ph: (847)647-7226
Free: (866)856-7960
Fax: (847)647-8940
E-mail: **colleenp@tida.org**
URL: http://www.tida.org/tida
Contact: **Colleen Pedersen, Contact**

878 ■ Trucking Management, Inc. (TMI) (3719)
PO Box 860725
Shawnee, KS 66286
Ph: **(913)568-5873**
E-mail: info@tmiweb.org
URL: http://www.tmiweb.org
Contact: David Smith, Pres./CEO

879 ■ Truckload Carriers Association (TCA) (3819)
555 E Braddock Rd.
Alexandria, VA 22314-2182
Ph: (703)838-1950
Fax: (703)836-6610
E-mail: tca@truckload.org
URL: http://www.truckload.org
Contact: **Gary Salisbury, Chm.**

Travel

880 ■ American Small Business Travelers Alliance (ASBTA)
PO Box 270543
Flower Mound, TX 75027-0543
Ph: **(972)836-8064**
E-mail: info@asbta.com
URL: http://www.asbta.com
Contact: Chuck Sharp, Pres.

881 ■ Association of Corporate Travel Executives (ACTE) (3829)
515 King St., Ste.440
Alexandria, VA 22314
Ph: (703)683-5322
Fax: (703)683-2720
E-mail: **info1@acte.org**
URL: http://www.acte.org
Contact: Ron DiLeo, Exec. Dir.

882 ■ Association of Retail Travel Agents (ARTA) (3831)
4320 N Miller Rd.
Scottsdale, AZ 85251
Free: **(866)369-8969**
E-mail: pat@artonline.com
URL: http://www.artaonline.com
Contact: Pat Funk, Exec. Dir.

883 ■ Cruise Lines International Association (CLIA) (3666)
910 SE 17th St., Ste.400
Fort Lauderdale, FL 33316
Ph: (754)224-2200
Fax: (754)224-2250
E-mail: info@cruising.org
URL: http://www.cruising.org
Contact: **Christine Duffy, Pres./CEO**

884 ■ National Business Travel Association (NBTA) (3850)
110 N Royal St., 4th Fl.
Alexandria, VA 22314
Ph: (703)684-0836
Fax: (703)684-0263
E-mail: **info@gbta.org**
URL: http://www2.nbta.org/usa/Pages/default.aspx
Contact: Craig Banikowski CCTE, Pres./CEO

885 ■ Pacific Asia Travel Association (PATA) (3855)
164 Loop Pl.
Trinidad, CA 95570
Ph: (707)232-2102
Fax: (707)540-6259
E-mail: americas@pata.org
URL: http://www.pata.org
Contact: **Bill Calderwood, CEO**

886 ■ Society of Government Travel Professionals (SGTP) (6288)
PO Box 158
Glyndon, MD 21071-0158
Ph: (202)363-7487
Fax: (202)379-1775
E-mail: info@sgtp.org
URL: http://www.sgtp.org
Contact: Marc Stec, Pres.

887 ■ Student and Youth Travel Association (SYTA) (3822)
8400 Westpark Dr., 2nd Fl.
McLean, VA 22102
Ph: (703)610-1263
Fax: (703)610-0270
E-mail: cassante@syta.org
URL: http://www.syta.com
Contact: Carylann Assante, Exec. Dir.

888 ■ The Travel Institute (3649)
148 Linden St., Ste.305
Wellesley, MA 02482
Ph: (781)237-0280
Free: (800)542-4282
Fax: (781)237-3860
E-mail: info@thetravelinstitute.com
URL: http://www.thetravelinstitute.com
Contact: Jack E. Mannix, Chm.

889 ■ Travel and Tourism Research Association (TTRA) (3864)
3048 W Clarkston Rd.
Lake Orion, MI 48362
Ph: (248)708-8872
Fax: (248)814-7150
E-mail: admin@ttra.com
URL: http://www.ttra.com
Contact: Mr. Michael Palmer, Exec. Dir./CEO

890 ■ U.S. Travel Insurance Association (UStiA)
1333 H St. NW, Ste.820
Washington, DC 20005
Free: (800)224-6164
E-mail: information@ustia.org
URL: http://www.ustia.org
Contact: Mike Kelly, Pres.

Utilities

891 ■ 1-800 American Free Trade Association
PO Box 1049
Burlington, VT 05402-1049
Ph: (802)383-0816 (802)383-0724
Fax: (802)860-4821
E-mail: info@1800afta.org
URL: http://1800afta.org
Contact: Jay Carpenter, Pres.

892 ■ Association of Edison Illuminating Companies (AEIC) (3835)
c/o Earl B. Parsons, Jr., Exec. Dir./Sec.-Treas.
PO Box 2641
Birmingham, AL 35291
Ph: (205)257-2530
Fax: (205)257-2540
E-mail: aeicdir@bellsouth.net
URL: http://www.aeic.org
Contact: Donald J. Shippar, Pres.

893 ■ Edison Electric Institute (EEI) (3700)
701 Pennsylvania Ave. NW
Washington, DC 20004-2696
Ph: (202)508-5000
Fax: (202)508-5360
E-mail: bfarrell@eei.org
URL: http://www.eei.org
Contact: Thomas R. Kuhn, Pres.

894 ■ Electric Utility Industry Sustainable Supply Chain Alliance (EUISSCA)
PO Box 419164
Kansas City, MO 64141
Ph: (816)561-5323
Fax: (816)561-1991
E-mail: alliance@swassn.com
URL: http://www.euissca.org
Contact: Ms. Jane Male, Exec. Dir.
Founded: 2008. Description: Represents the interests of investor-owned electric utilities. Works to establish environmental criteria for supply chain practices. Collaborates with industry suppliers to

improve their environmental performance and advance sustainable business practices.

895 ■ NASSCO (3880)
11521 Cronridge Dr., Ste.J
Owings Mills, MD 21117
Ph: (410)486-3500
Fax: (410)486-6838
E-mail: kathy.romans@trelleborg.com
URL: http://www.nassco.org
Contact: Kathy Romans, Pres.

896 ■ National Telecommunications Cooperative Association (NTCA) (3845)
4121 Wilson Blvd., Ste.1000
Arlington, VA 22203
Ph: (703)351-2000 (703)351-2094
Fax: (703)351-2001
E-mail: mbrunner@ntca.org
URL: http://www.ntca.org
Contact: Shirley A. Bloomfield, CEO

897 ■ National Utility Training and Safety Education Association (NUTSEA) (3884)
c/o Melissa Wolf
1024 Steamboat Run
Newburgh, IN 47630
Ph: (812)508-1305
E-mail: info@nutsea.org
URL: http://www.nutsea.org
Contact: Mike Bergeaux, Chm.

898 ■ Underground Utility and Leak Locators Association (UULLA)
US Sewer and Drain
210 Field End St.
Sarasota, FL 34240
Free: (800)977-5325
Fax: (941)308-5326
E-mail: david@ussewer.com
URL: http://www.uulla.org
Contact: David Baker, Pres./Sec.
Founded: 1996. Description: Provides underground utilities and leak detection services to municipalities, private property owners, industries, engineers and architects. Fosters a high degree of professionalism among its members.

899 ■ Utilimetrics - The Utility Technology Association (3697)
1400 E Touhy Ave., Ste.258
Des Plaines, IL 60018-3345
Ph: (847)480-9628
Fax: (847)227-0411
E-mail: info@utilimetrics.org
URL: http://www.utilimetrics.org
Contact: Joel Hoiland, CEO
Status Note: Formerly Automatic Meter Reading Association.

Vending

900 ■ International Association of Ice Cream Distributors and Vendors (IAICDV) (3970)
5024-R Campbell Blvd.
Baltimore, MD 21236
Ph: (410)931-8100
Fax: (410)931-8111
E-mail: crista@iaicdv.org
URL: http://iaicdv.org
Contact: Crista LeGrand CAE, Exec. Dir.
Status Note: Formerly International Association of Ice Cream Vendors.

901 ■ Randolph-Sheppard Vendors of America (RSVA) (3713)
940 Parc Helene Dr.
Marrero, LA 70072-2421
Ph: (504)328-6373
Free: (800)467-5299
Fax: (504)328-6372
E-mail: kim.venable@att.net
URL: http://www.randolph-sheppard.org
Contact: Kim M. Venable, Treas.

Warehousing

902 ■ International Liquid Terminals Association (ILTA) (3718)
1005 N Glebe Rd., Ste.600
Arlington, VA 22201
Ph: (703)875-2011
Fax: (703)875-2018
E-mail: info@ilta.org
URL: http://www.ilta.org
Contact: Ms. Melinda Whitney, VP

903 ■ Order Fulfillment Council I Material Handling Industry of America (3815)
8720 Red Oak Blvd., Ste.201
Charlotte, NC 28217-3992
Ph: (704)676-1190
Free: (800)345-1815
Fax: (704)676-1199
E-mail: jnofsinger@mhia.org
URL: http://www.mhia.org/industrygroups/ofc
Contact: John Nofsinger, CEO

904 ■ Self Storage Association (SSA) (558)
1901 N Beauregard St., Ste.450
Alexandria, VA 22311
Ph: (703)575-8000
Free: (888)735-3784
Fax: (703)575-8901
E-mail: info@selfstorage.org
URL: http://www.selfstorage.org
Contact: Michael T. Scanlon Jr., Pres./CEO

Waste

905 ■ Association of Professional Animal Waste Specialists (aPaws)
PO Box 2325
Santa Clarita, CA 91386
Free: (800)787-7667
E-mail: president@apaws.org
URL: http://www.apaws.org
Contact: Paul Chesler, Pres.

906 ■ CHWMEG
470 William Pitt Way
Pittsburgh, PA 15238
Ph: (412)826-3055
Fax: (586)461-1856
E-mail: administrator@chwmeg.org
URL: http://www.chwmeg.org
Contact: Becky Hill, Deputy Admin.
Multinational. Description: Represents manufacturing and industrial companies interested in managing waste management aspects of their environmental stewardship programs. Conducts comprehensive, independent reviews of commercial facilities that treat, store, dispose, recycle or transport waste.

907 ■ Environmental Industry Associations (EIA)
4301 Connecticut Ave. NW, Ste.300
Washington, DC 20008-2304
Ph: (202)244-4700 (202)364-3730
Free: (800)424-2869
Fax: (202)966-4824
E-mail: membership@envasns.org
URL: http://www.environmentalistseveryday.org
Contact: Bruce Parker, Pres./CEO

908 ■ Paper Stock Industries Chapter of ISRI (PSI) (3925)
PO Box 64999
Fayetteville, NC 28306
Ph: (910)426-7400
E-mail: nktraders@tradersintl.net
URL: http://iguana191.securesites.net/paperstock
Contact: Mr. Kevin Duncombe, Pres.

909 ■ Steel Recycling Institute (SRI) (3701)
680 Andersen Dr.
Pittsburgh, PA 15220-2700
Ph: (412)922-2772
Free: (800)876-7274
E-mail: gcrawford@steel.org
URL: http://www.recycle-steel.org
Contact: **Mr. Gregory L. Crawford, Exec. Dir.**

Water

910 ■ Water Systems Council (WSC) (3937)
1101 30th St. NW, Ste.500
Washington, DC 20007
Ph: (202)625-4387
Free: (888)395-1033
Fax: (202)625-4363
E-mail: **memberservices@watersystemscouncil. org**
URL: http://www.watersystemscouncil.org
Contact: **Robert Stone, Pres.**

Weather

911 ■ Weather Risk Management Association (WRMA) (3940)
529 14th St. NW, Ste.750
Washington, DC 20045
Ph: (202)289-3800
Fax: **(202)591-2445**
E-mail: llemunyan@kellencompany.com
URL: http://www.wrma.org
Contact: Lauren LeMunyan, Exec. Dir.

Weighing

912 ■ International Society of Weighing and Measurement (ISWM) (3941)
9707 Key West Ave., Ste.100
Rockville, MD 20850
Ph: (301)258-1115
Fax: (301)990-9771
E-mail: **hughes819@midco.net**
URL: http://www.iswm.org
Contact: **John Hughes, Pres.**

Wind Energy

913 ■ Wind Energy Manufacturers Association (WEMA)
345 S High St.
Muncie, IN 47305
Ph: (317)733-9797
Fax: (317)733-9993

E-mail: info@wemawind.org
URL: http://www.wemawind.org
Contact: Frank Hoffman, Pres.
Description: Promotes the manufacturing base for the wind energy industry throughout the United States. Works to unite manufacturing operations engaged in or interested in wind energy manufacturing to enhance their opportunities and operations.

Women

914 ■ African-American Female Entrepreneurs Alliance (AAFEA)
45 Scottdale Ave.
Lansdowne, PA 19050
Ph: (215)747-9282 (610)986-8026
Fax: (610)394-0264
E-mail: aafea@prodigy.net
URL: http://www.aafea.net
Contact: Ms. Margo L. Davidson, Pres./Founder/ CEO

915 ■ Association for Women in Aviation Maintenance (AWAM) (3958)
PO Box 1030
Edgewater, FL 32132-1030
Ph: (386)416-0248 (386)424-5780
Fax: (386)236-0517
E-mail: whq@awam.org
URL: http://www.awam.org
Contact: **Denise Waters, Pres.**

916 ■ Center for Women's Business Research (3962)
1760 Old Meadow Rd., Ste.500
McLean, VA 22102
Ph: (703)556-7162
Fax: (703)506-3266
URL: http://www.cfwbr.org
Contact: **Dr. Patricia G. Greene, Chair**

917 ■ National Women's Business Council (NWBC) (3926)
409 3rd St. SW, Ste.210
Washington, DC 20024
Ph: (202)205-3850 (202)205-6828
Fax: (202)205-6825
E-mail: info@nwbc.gov
URL: http://www.nwbc.gov
Contact: **Dana M. Lewis, Exec. Dir.**

918 ■ Women Contractors Association (WCA) (3977)
10807 Jones Rd.
PMB 164
Houston, TX 77065
Ph: (713)807-9977
Fax: (713)807-9917
E-mail: director@womencontractors.org
URL: http://www.womencontractors.org
Contact: **Kellie Vazquez, Pres.**

919 ■ Women Entrepreneurs in Science and Technology (WEST) (3967)
485 Mass Ave., Ste.300
Cambridge, MA 02139
Ph: **(857)998-4040**
E-mail: info@westorg.org
URL: http://www.westorg.org
Contact: Gwen Acton PhD, Pres.

Workmen's Compensation

920 ■ Professionals in Workers' Compensation (PWC)
PO Box 4435
Federal Way, WA 98063
Ph: **(206)824-2899**
E-mail: **ruffs118@msn.com**
URL: http://www.pwc.org
Contact: **Christina Casady, Pres.**

Writers

921 ■ North American Case Research Association (NACRA) (3943)
c/o Robert C. Crowner, Sec.-Treas.
3719 Meadow Ln.
Saline, MI 48176
Ph: (734)429-5032
E-mail: rpcnacra@verizon.net
URL: http://www.nacra.net
Contact: **Armand Gilinsky, Pres.**

922 ■ Sisters in Crime (SinC) (3947)
PO Box 442124
Lawrence, KS 66044
Ph: (785)842-1325
E-mail: sinc@sistersincrime.org
URL: http://www.sistersincrime.org
Contact: **Cathy Pickens, Pres.**

923 ■ Women Writing the West (WWW)
8547 E Arapahoe Rd., No. J-541
Greenwood Village, CO 80112-1436
E-mail: **info@womenwritingthewest.org**
URL: http://www.womenwritingthewest.org
Contact: **Pam Tartaglio, Pres.-Elect**

Youth

924 ■ Youth Venture (YV) (3755)
1700 N Moore Ave., Ste.2000
Arlington, VA 22209
Ph: (703)527-4126
Fax: (703)527-8383
E-mail: **yvfellowship@youthventure.org**
URL: **http://www.genv.net**

Afghanistan

925 ■ Global Partnership for Afghanistan
PO Box 1237
New York, NY 10276
Ph: (212)735-2080
E-mail: info@gpfa.org
URL: http://www.gpfa.org
Contact: **Roger Hardister, Exec. Dir.**

Agribusiness

926 ■ Agribusiness Council (ABC) (3768)
3312 Porter St. NW
Washington, DC 20008
Ph: (202)296-4563
Fax: (202)887-9178
E-mail: **agenergy@aol.com**
URL: http://agribusinesscouncil.org
Contact: Nicholas E. Hollis, Pres./CEO

927 ■ National Council of Agricultural Employers (NCAE) (3998)
8233 Old Courthouse Rd., Ste.200
Vienna, VA 22182
Ph: (703)790-9039
E-mail: **matt@ncaeonline.org**
URL: http://www.ncaeonline.org
Contact: Frank Gasperini CAE, Exec. VP

928 ■ United Agribusiness League (UAL) (4003)
54 Corporate Park
Irvine, CA 92606-5105
Ph: (949)975-1424
Free: (800)223-4590
Fax: (949)975-1573
E-mail: info@aul.org
URL: http://www.ual.org
Contact: **Richard Schmidt, Pres./CEO**

Agricultural Development

929 ■ Farmers Market Coalition (FMC)
PO Box 331
Cockeysville, MD 21030
E-mail: info@farmersmarketcoalition.org
URL: http://www.farmersmarketcoalition.org
Contact: **Sharon Yeago, Pres.**

Agricultural Equipment

930 ■ Midwest Equipment Dealers Association (MEDA)
5330 Wall St., Ste.100
Madison, WI 53718
Ph: (608)240-4700
Fax: (608)240-2069

E-mail: gmanke@medaassn.com
URL: http://www.medaassn.com
Contact: **Sherry Wuebben, Pres.**

Agricultural Science

931 ■ Agriculture, Food and Human Values Society (AFHVS) (4011)
6802 SW 13th
Gainesville, FL 32608
Ph: (352)392-0958
Fax: (352)392-5577
E-mail: rhaynes@ufl.edu
URL: http://www.afhvs.org
Contact: Richard P. Haynes, Exec. Sec.

932 ■ Crop Science Society of America (CSSA) (4099)
5585 Guilford Rd.
Madison, WI 53711-5801
Ph: (608)273-8080
Fax: (608)273-2021
E-mail: **headquarters@sciencesocieties.org**
URL: http://www.crops.org
Contact: Ellen G.M. Bergfeld, CEO

933 ■ Ecological Farming Association (EFA) (4017)
2901 Park Ave., Ste.D-2
Soquel, CA 95073
Ph: (831)763-2111
E-mail: info@eco-farm.org
URL: http://www.eco-farm.org
Contact: **Ken Dickerson, Exec. Dir.**

934 ■ North American Weed Management Association (NAWMA) (4023)
PO Box 687
Meade, KS 67864
Ph: (620)873-8730
Fax: (620)873-8733
E-mail: nawma@sbcglobal.net
URL: http://www.nawma.org
Contact: **Fred Raish, Pres.**

Agriculture

935 ■ Agricultural Commodities Certification Association (ACCA)
PO Box 23175
Washington, DC 20026-3175
Ph: (571)377-0722
E-mail: info@agcca.org
URL: http://www.agcca.org
Contact: Dana Stahl, Pres.
Founded: 2000. **Membership Dues:** regular, $25 (annual). **Description:** Represents the interests of government certification professionals. Fosters professional development and working relationship of individuals who manages agricultural commodity

certification on behalf of government and state agencies. Provides technical advice and services that are responsive to the needs of the agricultural community.

936 ■ Farm Financial Standards Council (FFSC)
c/o Carroll Merry, Exec. Sec.
N78W14573 Appleton Ave., No. 287
Menomonee Falls, WI 53051
Ph: (262)253-6902
Fax: (262)253-6903
E-mail: cmerry@countryside-marketing.com
URL: http://www.ffsc.org
Contact: **Owen Thompson, Pres.**

937 ■ National Women in Agriculture Association (NWIAA)
1701 N Martin Luther King Ave.
Oklahoma City, OK 73119
Ph: (405)424-4623
E-mail: info@okwomeninag.org
URL: http://www.nationalwomeninag.org
Contact: Tammy Steele, Exec. Dir.

938 ■ Women Organizing for Change in Agriculture and NRM (WOCAN)
1775 K St. NW, Ste.410
Washington, DC 20006
Ph: (202)331-9099
E-mail: **jeannettegurung@wocan.org**
URL: http://www.wocan.org
Contact: Jeannette Gurung PhD, Dir.

Animal Breeding

939 ■ Alpaca Breeders of the Rockies (ABR) (4583)
PO Box 1965
Estes Park, CO 80517
Ph: (970)586-5589
Free: (888)993-9898
E-mail: president@alpacabreeders.org
URL: http://www.alpacabreeders.org
Contact: **Denise Haines, Pres.**

940 ■ American Legend (AL) (4008)
Motorcycle Trailers Inc.
903 S Prairieview Rd.
Mahomet, IL 61853
Ph: (217)586-2201
Free: (888)463-1917
Fax: (217)586-4830
E-mail: **officeadmin@legendaryinnovations.com**
URL: http://www.american-legend.com

941 ■ American Miniature Llama Association (AMLA) (20589)
PO Box 8
Kalispell, MT 59903
Ph: (406)755-3438

E-mail: info@carolinaminis.com
URL: http://www.miniaturellamas.com
Contact: **Pam Fink, Pres.**

**942 ■ American Mule Association (AMA)
(4049)**
260 Neilson Rd.
Reno, NV 89521
Ph: (775)849-9437 (775)867-3590
E-mail: **masmules@aol.com**
URL: http://www.americanmuleassociation.com
Contact: **Marsha Arthur, Pres.**

**943 ■ American Ostrich Association (AOA)
(4050)**
PO Box 166
Ranger, TX 76470
Ph: (254)647-1645
Fax: **(254)647-1645**
E-mail: aoa@ostriches.org
URL: http://www.ostriches.org
Contact: Pat McFadden, Pres.

**944 ■ Empress Chinchilla Breeders
Cooperative (ECBC) (4052)**
43188 Cottonwood Creek Rd.
Crawford, CO 81415
Ph: (970)921-7231
E-mail: empresschinchilla@gmail.com
URL: **http://www.empresschinchilla.org**
Contact: Mr. Gene Adcock, Pres.

**945 ■ Llama Association of North America
(LANA) (3813)**
1800 S Obenchain Rd.
Eagle Point, OR 97524
Ph: (541)830-5262
Fax: (541)830-5262
E-mail: llamainfo@gmail.com
URL: http://www.llamainfo.org
Contact: **Kathy Nichols, Pres.**

**946 ■ North American Potbellied Pig
Association (NAPPA) (4062)**
15525 E Via Del Palo
Gilbert, AZ 85298
Ph: **(480)899-8941**
E-mail: elliemaymun007@yahoo.com
URL: http://www.petpigs.com
Contact: Pam Munici, Pres.

Animal Science

**947 ■ American Embryo Transfer Association
(AETA) (4149)**
2441 Village Green Pl.
Champaign, IL 61822
Ph: (217)398-2217
Fax: (217)398-4119
E-mail: aeta@assochq.org
URL: http://www.aeta.org
Contact: **Dr. Richard Whitaker, Pres.**

**948 ■ International Marine Animal Trainers
Association (IMATA)**
1200 S Lake Shore Dr.
Chicago, IL 60605
Ph: (312)692-3193
Fax: (312)939-2216
E-mail: info@imata.org
URL: http://www.imata.org
Contact: **Michael Osborn, Pres.**

Animal Welfare

949 ■ Animal World USA (AWUSA)
5255 Brantford Dr.
Memphis, TN 38120
Ph: **(901)791-2455**
Free: (877)454-0807

E-mail: info@animalworldusa.org
URL: http://www.animalworldusa.org
Contact: Michelle Buckalew, Founder/Pres.

950 ■ Darwin Animal Doctors
222 E 89th St., No. 8
New York, NY 10128
E-mail: tod@darwinanimaldoctors.org
URL: http://darwinanimaldoctors.org
Contact: Tod Emko, Pres.
Multinational. Description: Provides professional
and comprehensive veterinary care for the animals of
the Galapagos Island. Aims to preserve the archipela-
go's biodiversity by humanely limiting the populations
of domestic animals.

951 ■ Global Animal Partnership
PO Box 21484
Washington, DC 20009
Ph: (202)540-9880
E-mail: info@globalanimalpartnership.org
URL: http://www.globalanimalpartnership.org
Contact: Joyce D'Silva, Chair
Founded: 2008. **Multinational. Description:** Facili-
tates and encourages improvement in animal agricul-
ture. Works to continually improve the lives of farm
animals through outreach, training and the develop-
ment and implementation of the 5-Step Animal
Welfare Rating system.

952 ■ Kids Making a Difference (KMAD)
1527 W State Hwy. 114, Ste.500, No. 106
Grapevine, TX 76051
E-mail: president_kmad@verizon.net
URL: http://www.kmad.org
Contact: Stephanie Cohen, Founder/Pres.
Founded: 2000. **Description:** Promotes the advancement of animal welfare. Encourages kids to
participate in environment-related activities. Helps to
preserve the environment with recycling efforts, public
education and coming to the aid of animals in need.

Apiculture

**953 ■ American Association of Professional
Apiculturists (AAPA) (4077)**
USDA ARS Honey Bee Lab
1157 Ben Hur Rd.
Baton Rouge, LA 70808
Ph: (225)767-9284
Fax: (225)766-9212
E-mail: jeffrey.harris@ars.usda.gov
URL: **http://www.masterbeekeeper.org/aapa**
Contact: Jeff Harris, Pres.

**954 ■ American Honey Producers
Association (AHPA)**
PO Box 162
Power, MT 59468
Ph: **(406)463-2227**
Fax: **(403)463-2583**
E-mail: **beeguy4jensen@yahoo.com**
URL: http://www.americanhoneyproducers.org
Contact: **Mark Jensen, Pres.**

Aquaculture

**955 ■ Aquaculture International (3877)
405 Union St.
Murfreesboro, NC 27855**
E-mail: aqua@dnet.net
URL: http://www.aquacultureinternational.org
Contact: Charles W. Johnson, Founder/Pres.

**956 ■ The Catfish Institute (TCI) (4086)
6311 Ridgewood Rd., Ste.W404**
Jackson, MS 39211
Ph: (601)977-9559
E-mail: info@catfishinstitute.com
URL: http://www.catfishinstitute.com
Contact: Roger Barlow, Pres.

957 ■ Global Aquaculture Alliance (GAA)
5661 Telegraph Rd., Ste.3A
St. Louis, MO 63129
Ph: (314)293-5500
Fax: (314)293-5525
E-mail: **wally.stevens@gaalliance.org**
URL: http://www.gaalliance.org
Contact: **Wally Stevens, Exec. Dir.**

958 ■ Marine Aquarium Council (MAC) (4090)
PO Box 90370
Los Angeles, CA 90009
Ph: (808)550-8217 (808)550-8517
Fax: (310)846-4040
E-mail: **certifiedfish@aquariumcouncil.org**
URL: http://www.aquariumcouncil.org
Contact: Steven Broad, Chm.

**959 ■ Sustainable Fisheries Partnership
(SFP)**
4348 Waialae Ave., No. 692
Honolulu, HI 96816
Ph: (202)580-8187
URL: http://www.sustainablefish.org
Contact: Jim Cannon, CEO/Founder
Founded: 2006. **Multinational. Description:** Strives
to catalyze global seafood supply chains in rebuilding
depleted fish stocks. Provides strategic and technical
guidance to seafood suppliers and producers. Educates seafood buyers and suppliers so they can help
improve fisheries and fish-farming regions, choose
their sources wisely and meet their own sustainability
commitments.

Arts

**960 ■ River of Words (ROW)
PO Box 4000-J
Berkeley, CA 94704**
Ph: (510)548-7636
Fax: (510)548-2095
E-mail: info@riverofwords.org
URL: http://www.riverofwords.org
Contact: Pamela Michael, Co-Founder/Exec. Dir.

Beekeeping

961 ■ Bee Native
Mantis Farm
68 Fingar Rd.
Hudson, NY 12534
Ph: (917)679-0567
E-mail: contact@beenative.org
URL: http://www.beenative.org
Contact: Helen Faraday Young, Co-Founder
Description: Provides education about bees and its
environment. Strengthens the honeybee population
and the health of the bees. Provides hive equipment,
bees and training in organic, chemical free beekeep-
ing methods.

Bird

962 ■ Environment for the Americas
2129 13th St., Ste.1
Boulder, CO 80302
Ph: (303)499-1950
Free: (866)334-3330
Fax: (303)499-9567
E-mail: bday@birdday.org
URL: http://birdday.org
Contact: Susan Bonfield, Exec. Dir.
Founded: 2006. **Multinational. Description:** Strives
to make bird conservation education available
throughout the Western Hemisphere. Develops
education materials about birds and their conserva-
tion. Serves as a network for the exchange of
information about successful bird conservation
education programs.

963 ■ Hummingbird Monitoring Network (HMN)
PO Box 115
Patagonia, AZ 85624
E-mail: swething@dakotacom.net
URL: http://www.hummonnet.org
Contact: Susan Wethington, Founder/Exec. Dir.
Founded: 2002. **Multinational. Description:** Promotes the conservation of hummingbird diversity and abundance throughout the Americas. Supports projects to improves hummingbird's ability to survive and reproduce. Maintains monitoring sites to detect hummingbird population.

Building Industries

964 ■ Clean Technology and Sustainable Industries Organization (CTSI)
3925 W Braker Ln.
Austin, TX 78759
Ph: (512)692-7267
E-mail: mlaudon@ct-si.org
URL: http://www.ct-si.org
Contact: Matthew Laudon, Pres./Chm.

Cat

965 ■ The International Bengal Cat Society (TIBCS) (4079)
PO Box 1894
Lake Dallas, TX 75065-1894
E-mail: info@tibcs.com
URL: http://www.bengalcat.com
Contact: Anthony Hutcherson, Pres.

966 ■ National Alliance of Burmese Breeders (NABB) (4083)
PO Box 100038
Cudahy, WI 53110
E-mail: dukecherry700@yahoo.com
URL: http://www.burmesecat.org
Contact: Renee Weinberger, Sec.

Cattle

967 ■ American Belgian Blue Breeders (ABBB) (3856)
245 W Main St.
Stanley, IA 50671
Ph: (319)230-0671
Fax: (319)634-3542
E-mail: info@belgianblue.org
URL: http://www.belgianblue.org
Contact: Connie Brooks, Pres.

968 ■ American Black Hereford Association (ABHA) (4086)
719 Walnut St.
Kansas City, MO 64106
Ph: (816)472-1111
Fax: (816)842-8998
E-mail: mail@blackhereford.com
URL: http://www.blackhereford.com
Contact: Joe Hoagland, Pres.

969 ■ American Brahman Breeders Association (ABBA) (4088)
3003 S Loop W, Ste.520
Houston, TX 77054
Ph: (713)349-0854
Fax: (713)349-9795
E-mail: abba@brahman.org
URL: http://www.brahman.org
Contact: Bob Hudgins, Pres.

970 ■ American British White Park Association (ABWPA) (4218)
PO Box 409
Myerstown, PA 17067
Ph: (270)563-9733
Free: (877)900-BEEF

Fax: (208)979-2008
E-mail: office@whitecattle.org
URL: http://www.whitecattle.org
Contact: Greg Powell, Pres.

971 ■ American Chianina Association (ACA) (4168)
1708 N Prairie View Rd.
PO Box 890
Platte City, MO 64079
Ph: (816)431-2808
Fax: (816)431-5381
E-mail: acaregistrations@earthlink.net
URL: http://www.chicattle.org
Contact: Stan Comer, CEO

972 ■ American Dexter Cattle Association (ADCA) (4221)
4150 Merino Ave.
Watertown, MN 55388
Ph: (952)215-2206 (281)692-0325
E-mail: adca@dextercattle.org
URL: http://dextercattle.org
Contact: Roberta Wieringa, Pres.

973 ■ American Guernsey Association (AGA) (4144)
1224 Alton Darby Creek Rd., Ste.G
Columbus, OH 43228
Ph: (614)864-2409 (614)339-5391
Fax: (614)864-5614
E-mail: info@usguernsey.com
URL: http://www.usguernsey.com
Contact: Seth Johnson, Exec. Sec.-Treas.

974 ■ American National CattleWomen (ANCW) (4159)
9110 E Nichols Ave., Ste.302
Centennial, CO 80112
Ph: (303)694-0313
Fax: (303)694-2390
E-mail: ancw@beef.org
URL: http://www.ancw.org
Contact: Lana Slaten, Pres.

975 ■ American Pinzgauer Association (APA) (4241)
PO Box 1097
Lake Ozark, MO 65049
Ph: (573)964-2389
Free: (800)914-9883
Fax: (509)471-4854
E-mail: info@pinzgauers.org
URL: http://www.pinzgauers.org
Contact: Donna Laney, Pres.

976 ■ American Red Brangus Association (ARBA) (4161)
3995 E Hwy. 290
Dripping Springs, TX 78620
Ph: (512)858-7285
Fax: (512)858-7084
E-mail: arba@texas.net
URL: http://www.americanredbrangus.org
Contact: Jimmy Brister, Pres.

977 ■ American Red Poll Association (ARPA) (4243)
PO Box 847
Frankton, IN 46044
Ph: (765)425-4515
E-mail: arpa@americanredpolls.com
URL: http://www.redpollusa.org
Contact: Mike Parks, Pres.

978 ■ American Wagyu Association (AWA) (4121)
PO Box 547
Pullman, WA 99163
Ph: (509)335-0519
Fax: (509)335-0519
E-mail: office@wagyu.org
URL: http://www.wagyu.org
Contact: Michael Beattie, Exec. Dir.

979 ■ Barzona Breeders Association of America (BBAA) (4173)
11477 E Warren Pl.
Aurora, CO 80014
Ph: (303)696-5799
Fax: (303)696-5799
E-mail: info@barzona.com
URL: http://www.barzona.com
Contact: Herb Young, Exec. Sec.

980 ■ Belted Galloway Society (4127)
Hav-A-Belt Galloways
New Glarus, WI 53574
Ph: (608)527-4811
Fax: (608)527-4811
E-mail: executivedirector@beltie.org
URL: http://www.beltie.org
Contact: Victor Eggleston, Exec. Dir.

981 ■ Braunvieh Association of America (BAA) (4176)
5750 Epsilon, Ste.200
San Antonio, TX 78249
Ph: (210)561-2892
Fax: (210)696-5031
E-mail: baaoffice@braunvieh.org
URL: http://www.braunvieh.org
Contact: Ron McBee, Pres.

982 ■ Buelingo Beef Cattle Society (BBCS) (4178)
15904 W Warren Rd.
Warren, IL 61087-9601
Ph: (815)745-2147
E-mail: office@buelingo.com
URL: http://www.buelingo.com
Contact: Joseph A. Steve, Pres.

983 ■ Cattlemen's Beef Promotion and Research Board (CBB) (4180)
9000 E Nichols Ave., Ste.215
Centennial, CO 80112-3450
Ph: (303)220-9890
Fax: (303)220-9280
E-mail: beefboard@beefboard.org
URL: http://www.mybeefcheckoff.com
Contact: Tom Jones, Chair

984 ■ International Brangus Breeders Association (IBBA) (4265)
5750 Epsilon
San Antonio, TX 78249
Ph: (210)696-4343
Fax: (210)696-8718
E-mail: info@int-brangus.org
URL: http://www.int-brangus.org
Contact: Dr. Joseph M. Massey, Exec. VP

985 ■ International Miniature Zebu Association (IMZA) (4187)
3571 Hwy. 20
Crawford, NE 69339
Ph: (308)665-1431
Fax: (308)665-1931
E-mail: thedemoors@aol.com
URL: http://www.imza.name
Contact: Steve DeMoor, Pres.

986 ■ International Texas Longhorn Association (ITLA)
PO Box 2610
Glen Rose, TX 76043
Ph: (254)898-0157
Fax: (254)898-0165
E-mail: staff@itla.com
URL: http://www.itla.com
Contact: Roger Hutton, Pres.

987 ■ Miniature Hereford Breeders Association (MHBA)
60885 Salt Creek Rd.
Collbran, CO 81624
E-mail: info@mhbaonline.org
URL: http://www.mhbaonline.org
Contact: Justin Grady, Pres.

988 ■ North American Limousin Foundation (NALF) (4198)
7383 S Alton Way, Ste.100
Centennial, CO 80112-2339
Ph: (303)220-1693
Fax: (303)220-1884
E-mail: limousin@nalf.org
URL: http://www.nalf.org
Contact: **Mike Smith, Pres.**

989 ■ North American South Devon Association (NASDA)
19590 E Main St., Ste.202
Parker, CO 80138
Ph: (303)770-3130
Fax: (303)770-9302
E-mail: nasouthdevon@aol.com
URL: http://www.southdevon.com
Contact: **Tony Matthis, Contact**

990 ■ Santa Gertrudis Breeders International (SGBI) (4163)
PO Box 1257
Kingsville, TX 78364
Ph: (361)592-9357
Fax: (361)592-8572
E-mail: info@santagertrudis.com
URL: http://santagertrudis.com
Contact: **John E. Ford, Exec. Dir.**

991 ■ Texas Longhorn Breeders Association of America (TLBAA) (4294)
2315 N Main St., Ste.402
PO Box 4430
Fort Worth, TX 76164
Ph: (817)625-6241
Fax: (817)625-1388
E-mail: tlbaa@tlbaa.org
URL: http://www.tlbaa.org
Contact: **Brent Bolen, Chm.**

992 ■ United Braford Breeders (UBB) (591)
422 E Main, No. 218
Nacogdoches, TX 75961
Ph: (936)569-8200
E-mail: **info@brafords.org**
URL: http://www.brafords.org
Contact: Rodney L. Roberson PhD, Exec. Dir.

993 ■ World Watusi Association (WWA) (4245)
PO Box 2610
Glen Rose, TX 76043
Ph: **(254)898-0157**
E-mail: mail@watusicattle.com
URL: http://watusicattle.com
Contact: Vernon Base, Pres.

Commodities

994 ■ Hop Growers of America (HGA) (4225)
PO Box 1207
Moxee, WA 98936
Ph: **(509)453-4749**
Fax: (509)457-8561
E-mail: info@usahops.org
URL: http://www.usahops.org

995 ■ International Cotton Advisory Committee (ICAC) (4241)
1629 K St. NW, Ste.702
Washington, DC 20006-1636
Ph: (202)463-6660
Fax: (202)463-6950
E-mail: secretariat@icac.org
URL: http://www.icac.org
Contact: **Mr. Patrick Packnett, Chm.**

996 ■ Kamut Association of North America (KANA) (4228)
PO Box 4903
Missoula, MT 59806
Ph: (406)251-9418

Fax: (406)251-9420
URL: http://www.kamut.com
Contact: **Trevor Blyth, CEO**

997 ■ National Sweet Sorghum Producers and Processors Association (NSSPPA) (844)
PO Box 1356
Cookeville, TN 38503-1356
Ph: **(931)644-7764**
E-mail: **nssppa@charter.net**
URL: http://www.ca.uky.edu/nssppa
Contact: **James Baier, Exec. Sec.**

998 ■ Soyfoods Association of North America (SANA) (4264)
1050 17th St. NW, Ste.600
Washington, DC 20036
Ph: (202)659-3520
Fax: (202)659-3522
E-mail: info@soyfoods.org
URL: http://www.soyfoods.org
Contact: **Kent Holt, Pres.**

999 ■ U.S. Wheat Associates (USW) (4239)
3103 10th St. N, Ste.300
Arlington, VA 22201
Ph: (202)463-0999
Fax: (703)524-4399
E-mail: info@uswheat.org
URL: http://www.uswheat.org
Contact: **Don Schieber, Chm.**

1000 ■ U.S.A. Rice Council (USARC) (4321)
4301 N Fairfax Dr., Ste.425
Arlington, VA 22203
Ph: (703)236-2300
Fax: (703)236-2301
E-mail: riceinfo@usarice.com
URL: http://www.usarice.com/industry/council/overview.html
Contact: **Charley Mathews, Chm.**

Conservation

1001 ■ Africa Environmental Watch (AEW)
4207 Plummers Promise Dr., Ste.100
Bowie, MD 20720
Ph: (240)417-2545 (215)828-2010
Fax: (301)464-1664
URL: http://www.africaenvironmentalwatch.org
Contact: Mr. Morris T. Koffa, Pres./Exec. Dir.
Founded: 2004. **Multinational. Description:** Promotes sustainability in Africa by advocating for a clean environment and sound natural resources management. Ensures the protection of the environment and the preservation as well as conservation of natural resources. Provides educational and public awareness for a healthy environment in Africa.

1002 ■ Alliance for International Reforestation (AIR) (4344)
1721 N Woodland Blvd.
DeLand, FL 32720
Ph: **(386)748-2454**
E-mail: **anne.hallum@airguatemala.org**
URL: **http://www.air-guatemala.org**
Contact: Anne Hallum, Founder/Pres.

1003 ■ Alliance for Tompotika Conservation (AlTo)
21416 86th Ave. SW
Vashon, WA 98070
Ph: (206)463-7720
Fax: (206)463-7720
E-mail: info@tompotika.org
URL: http://www.tompotika.org
Contact: Marcy Summers, Dir.
Founded: 2005. **Languages:** English, Indonesian. **Multinational. Description:** Aims to conserve the natural heritage of the lands and waters surrounding Mt. Tompotika, Sulawesi, Indonesia. Promotes innovative conservation strategies and a direct, people-to-people approach to prevent extinction and build a strong and enduring conservation ethic.

1004 ■ American Forests (4216)
PO Box 2000
Washington, DC 20013
Ph: (202)737-1944
Fax: (202)737-2457
E-mail: info@amfor.org
URL: http://www.americanforests.org
Contact: **Scott Steen, CEO**

1005 ■ Anglers for Conservation (AFC)
PO Box 373257
Satellite Beach, FL 32937
Ph: (321)446-8240
E-mail: **info@anglersforconservation.org**
URL: http://www.anglersforconservation.org
Contact: James R. Smith, Admin.

1006 ■ Association of Conservation Engineers (ACE)
c/o Kathy Dillmon, Sec.
Wyoming Game & Fish U.S. Department of
5400 Bishop Blvd.
Cheyenne, WY 82006
E-mail: kathy.dillmon@wgf.state.wy.us
URL: http://conservationengineers.org
Contact: **David Bumann, Pres.**

1007 ■ Association of Environmental and Resource Economists (AERE) (4359)
Iowa State Univ.
Dept. of Economics
568 Heady Hall
Ames, IA 50011-1070
Ph: **(515)294-5767**
E-mail: **ckling@iastate.edu**
URL: http://www.aere.org
Contact: **Dr. Catherine L. Kling, Pres.**

1008 ■ Association of Fish and Wildlife Agencies (4285)
444 N Capitol St. NW, Ste.725
Washington, DC 20001
Ph: (202)624-7890
Fax: (202)624-7891
E-mail: info@fishwildlife.org
URL: http://www.fishwildlife.org
Contact: **Curtis Taylor, Pres.**

1009 ■ Big Thicket Association (BTA) (4367)
PO Box 198
Saratoga, TX 77585
Ph: (936)274-1181
E-mail: **director@bigthicket.org**
URL: http://www.btatx.org
Contact: **Mary Catherine Johnston, Pres.**

1010 ■ BlueVoice.org
10 Sunfish Dr.
St. Augustine, FL 32080
E-mail: contact@bluevoice.org
URL: http://www.bluevoice.org
Contact: Hardy Jones, Exec. Dir.
Multinational. Description: Promotes ocean conservation and protection of dolphins, whales and other marine mammals. Addresses issues related to the plight of oceans and marine inhabitants.

1011 ■ CEDAM International (4006)
2 Fox Rd.
Croton-on-Hudson, NY 10520
Ph: (914)271-5365
E-mail: cedam@bestweb.net
URL: http://www.cedam.org
Contact: Susan Sammon, Contact

1012 ■ Climate, Community and Biodiversity Alliance (CCBA)
2011 Crystal Dr., Ste.500
Arlington, VA 22202
Ph: (703)341-2748
E-mail: info@climate-standards.org
URL: http://www.climate-standards.org
Contact: Gareth Wishart, Standards Coor.
Founded: 2003. **Multinational. Description:** Represents international non-governmental organizations

(NGOs) and research institutes that promote integrated solutions to land management. Promotes responsible land management activities that will benefit local communities, minimize climate change and conserve biodiversity.

1013 ■ Connecticut River Watershed Council (CRWC) (4049)
15 Bank Row
Greenfield, MA 01301
Ph: (413)772-2020
Fax: (413)772-2090
E-mail: **info@ctriver.org**
URL: http://www.ctriver.org
Contact: **Andrew Fisk, Exec. Dir.**

1014 ■ Conservation and Research Foundation (CRF) (4330)
PO Box 909
Shelburne, VT 05482-0909
E-mail: is_webmaster@conncoll.edu
URL: **http://www.conservationandresearchfoundation.org**
Contact: **Mary G. Wetzel, Pres.**

1015 ■ Cork Forest Conservation Alliance (CFCA)
565 Oxford St.
Salem, OR 97302
Ph: (503)931-9690
E-mail: info@corkforest.org
URL: http://www.corkforest.org
Contact: Patrick Spencer, Dir.
Founded: 2008. **Multinational. Description:** Works to protect and preserve the Mediterranean cork forests, its inhabitants and biodiversity. Promotes conservation through education, direct action, and partnerships with communities, businesses and governments.

1016 ■ ecoAmerica
1900 L St. NW, Ste.607
Washington, DC 20036
Ph: (202)457-1900
Fax: (509)351-1900
E-mail: info@ecoamerica.org
URL: http://www.ecoamerica.org
Contact: Amy Golden, Exec. Dir.
Description: Strives to build awareness, understanding and action for climate and environmental solutions among mainstream Americans. Aims to support the environmental movement and grow the base of public support for environment and climate solutions. Focuses on building public and leadership support for environmental and climate initiatives.

1017 ■ Ecological Research and Development Group (ERDG)
190 Main St.
Dover, DE 19901
Ph: (302)236-5383
E-mail: erdg@horseshoecrab.org
URL: http://www.horseshoecrab.org
Contact: Glenn Gauvry, Pres.
Founded: 1995. **Membership Dues:** individual, family, $25 (annual) ● non-profit organization, $35 (annual) ● corporation, business, $50 (annual) ● life, $1,000. **Multinational. Description:** Promotes the conservation of horseshoe crab species. Provides educational programs to create an atmosphere of learning to inspire and nurture curiosity about the horseshoe crabs species and their habitat. Seeks solutions that prevent the extinction of the horseshoe crab species through scientific research and development.

1018 ■ Efficiency First
70 Zoe St., Ste.201
San Francisco, CA 94107
Ph: **(415)449-0551**
Fax: **(415)449-0559**
E-mail: info@efficiencyfirst.org
URL: http://www.efficiencyfirst.org
Contact: Greg Thomas, Chm.

1019 ■ Environmental Commons
35501 S Hwy. 1, Unit No. 12
Gualala, CA 95445
E-mail: info@environmentalcommons.org
URL: http://www.environmentalcommons.org
Contact: Britt Bailey, Founder/Dir.
Founded: 2004. **Description:** Promotes the protection and conservation of rich biodiversity and genetic variability to better support ecological and human health. Educates the public about important environmental issues and policies.

1020 ■ Ethnobotanical Conservation Organization for South East Asia (ECO-SEA)
PO Box 77
Mendocino, CA 95460
Fax: (815)331-0850
E-mail: director@ecosea.org
URL: http://www.ecosea.org
Contact: Jeanine Pfeiffer, Exec. Dir.
Founded: 1995. **Description:** Promotes collaborative study and active preservation of native Southeast Asian plants and customs. Facilitates the conservation of biological and cultural diversity through partnerships with local, national and international organizations.

1021 ■ Experience International
PO Box 680
Everson, WA 98247
Ph: (360)966-3876
Fax: (360)966-4131
E-mail: info@expint.org
URL: **http://www.expint.org**
Contact: Charlie Walkinshaw, Dir.

1022 ■ Forest Bird Society
10969 SW 47th Terr.
Miami, FL 33165
Ph: (305)223-2680
Fax: (305)223-2680
E-mail: forestbirdsoc@aol.com
URL: http://www.forestbirdsociety.org
Contact: Francisco T. Sevilla, Pres./Exec. Dir.
Founded: 2001. **Membership Dues:** regular, $25 (annual) ● life, $1,000. **Multinational. Description:** Aims to protect native plants, animals and wild places, on land and in oceans. Promotes environmental education and the preservtion of natural ecosystems. Supports projects to study and protect the habitats of forest birds.

1023 ■ Forestry Conservation Communications Association (FCCA) (4019)
122 Baltimore St.
Gettysburg, PA 17325
Ph: (717)388-1505
Fax: (717)334-5656
E-mail: ed@fcca-usa.org
URL: http://www.fcca-usa.org
Contact: Ralph Haller, Exec. Dir.

1024 ■ Friends of the Everglades (FE) (4327)
11767 S Dixie Hwy., No. 232
Miami, FL 33156
Ph: (305)669-0858
Fax: **(305)479-2893**
E-mail: friends@everglades.org
URL: http://www.everglades.org
Contact: **Alan Farago, Pres.**

1025 ■ Friends of the Osa (FOO)
1822 R St. NW, 4th Fl.
Washington, DC 20009
Ph: (202)234-2356
E-mail: info@osaconservation.org
URL: http://www.osaconservation.org
Contact: **Adrian Forsyth, Founder/Pres.**

1026 ■ Global Parks
3803 Sulgrave Dr.
Alexandria, VA 22309
Ph: (703)317-1669

E-mail: todd@globalparks.org
URL: http://globalparks.org
Contact: Todd Koenings, Exec. Dir.
Founded: 2008. **Multinational. Description:** Aims to support retired senior conservation professionals to help strengthen protected areas and national park systems around the world. Collaborates with partners to plan activities for parks and protected areas. Provides analysis, advice and assistance in developing, reviewing, and implementing various protected areas plans, strategies and issues.

1027 ■ Grassland Heritage Foundation (GHF) (4026)
PO Box 394
Shawnee Mission, KS 66201
Ph: (785)887-6775 (785)748-0955
E-mail: **webadmin@grasslandheritage.org**
URL: http://www.grasslandheritage.org
Contact: **Joyce Wolf, Pres.**

1028 ■ Green Team America (GTA)
6300 Westpark Dr., Ste.210
Houston, TX 77057
Ph: (713)334-3000
E-mail: info@americasgreenteam.org
URL: http://americasgreenteam.org
Contact: Katherine Sharp, Assoc. Dir.
Founded: 2007. **Description:** Strives to unite American students in a green crusade that can achieve dramatic and measurable results. Works to help students and families become aware of the environmental issues that ensue the future generations of mankind. Raises public awareness of global warming and other environmental problems. Encourages people to lower the use of energy and become more active in their respective communities by planting trees or recycling materials.

1029 ■ International Union for the Conservation of Nature and Natural Resources U.S. (IUCN USA) (4161)
1630 Connecticut Ave. NW, 3rd Fl.
Washington, DC 20009
Ph: (202)387-4826
Fax: (202)387-4823
URL: http://www.iucn.org
Contact: **Mary Beth West, Dir.**

1030 ■ National Mitigation Banking Association (NMBA)
1155 15th St. NW, Ste.500
Washington, DC 20005
Ph: **(202)457-8409**
E-mail: info@mitigationbanking.org
URL: http://www.mitigationbanking.org
Contact: David Urban, Pres.

1031 ■ National Oceanic Society (NOS)
17300 Red Hill Ave., Ste.280
Irvine, CA 92614
Ph: (949)500-5451
Fax: (949)675-1366
URL: http://nationaloceanic.org
Contact: Gloria Sullivan, Contact
Founded: 1995. **Description:** Promotes the fundamental concepts of marine conservation and preservation. Supports the education, research and scientific study of marine environment. Assists governmental agencies in the monitoring and detection of activities that are hazardous and harmful to marine environment.

1032 ■ Network of Conservation Educators and Practitioners (NCEP)
Amer. Museum of Natural History
Center for Biodiversity and Conservation
Central Park West, 79th St.
New York, NY 10024
Ph: (212)769-5742
Fax: (212)769-5292

E-mail: ncep@amnh.org
URL: http://ncep.amnh.org
Contact: Dr. Ana Luz Porzecanski, Dir.
Multinational. Description: Aims to improve the practice of biodiversity conservation. Promotes educational resources on managing and sustaining biological and cultural diversity. Provides opportunities for communication and interaction among conservation educators and practitioners.

1033 ■ Ocean Research and Conservation Association (ORCA) (4384)
Duerr Lab. for Marine Conservation
1420 Seaway Dr., 2nd Fl.
Fort Pierce, FL 34949
Ph: (772)467-1600
Fax: (772)467-1602
E-mail: inquiries@teamorca.org
URL: http://www.teamorca.org
Contact: **Edie Widder PhD, Pres./CEO**

1034 ■ Oceanic Preservation Society (OPS)
3063 Sterling Cir. E, No. 7
Boulder, CO 80301
E-mail: thomas@sunshinesachs.com
URL: http://www.opsociety.org
Contact: Louie Psihoyos, Exec. Dir.

1035 ■ Pacific Islands Conservation Research Association (PICRA)
PO Box 302
South Beach, OR 97366
E-mail: grants@picra.net
URL: http://picra.net
Contact: Dr. Kevin Rhodes, Contact
Founded: 2004. **Description:** Advances the knowledge about insular Pacific species, populations, and ecosystems through scientific investigations. Facilitates and conducts research that focuses on understanding of the islands and the conservation issues they face.

1036 ■ Paso Pacifico
PO Box 1244
Ventura, CA 93002-1244
Ph: (805)643-7044
E-mail: info@pasopacifico.org
URL: http://www.pasopacifico.org
Contact: Sarah Otterstrom PhD, Exec. Dir.
Founded: 2005. **Multinational. Description:** Seeks to restore and conserve the natural ecosystems of Central America's Pacific slope. Addresses crucial issues pertaining to ecosystem conservation.

1037 ■ Renewable Natural Resources Foundation (RNRF) (4073)
5430 Grosvenor Ln.
Bethesda, MD 20814-2142
Ph: (301)493-9101
E-mail: info@rnrf.org
URL: http://www.rnrf.org
Contact: **Howard N. Rosen, Chm.**

1038 ■ Rising Tide North America (RTNA)
PO Box 3928
Oakland, CA 94609
Ph: (503)438-4697
E-mail: contact@risingtidenorthamerica.org
URL: http://www.risingtidenorthamerica.org
Contact: Mike Hudema, Contact

1039 ■ River Management Society (RMS) (4190)
PO Box 5750
Takoma Park, MD 20913-5750
Ph: **(301)585-4677**
Fax: **(301)585-4677**
E-mail: rms@river-management.org
URL: http://www.river-management.org
Contact: **Risa Shimoda, Exec. Dir.**

1040 ■ River Network (RN) (4191)
520 SW 6th Ave., Ste.1130
Portland, OR 97204
Ph: (503)241-3506

Fax: (503)241-9256
E-mail: info@rivernetwork.org
URL: http://www.rivernetwork.org
Contact: **Todd Ambs, Pres.**

1041 ■ Sailors for the Sea (4379)
18 Market Sq.
Newport, RI 02840
Ph: (401)846-8900
Fax: (401)846-7200
E-mail: **info@sailorsforthesea.org**
URL: http://www.sailorsforthesea.org
Contact: David Rockefeller Jr., Pres./Co-Founder

1042 ■ Sustainable World Coalition
Earth Island Inst.
2150 Allston Way. No. 460
Berkeley, CA 94704
Ph: **(415)737-0235**
E-mail: info@swcoalition.org
URL: http://www.swcoalition.org
Contact: Vinit Allen, Exec. Dir.

1043 ■ Tropical Forest Group
1125 Ft. Stockton Dr.
San Diego, CA 92103
E-mail: info@tropicalforestgroup.org
URL: http://tropicalforestgroup.org
Contact: John-O Niles, Dir.
Multinational. Description: Promotes the conservation and restoration of the planet's remaining tropical forests. Supports research and development of policies that help maintain the planet's most vital biome. Provides assistance to projects that restore and conserve tropical forests.

1044 ■ Turtle Island Restoration Network (TIRN)
PO Box 370
Forest Knolls, CA 94933
Ph: (415)663-8590
Free: (800)859-7283
Fax: (415)663-9534
E-mail: tsteiner@tirn.net
URL: http://www.tirn.net
Contact: Todd Steiner, Exec. Dir.
Founded: 1997. **Multinational. Description:** Aims to protect and restore marine species and their habitats. Encourages people in communities to advocate for conservation of sea turtles, salmon and other marine species. Raises an awareness about the protection of biodiversity and nature.

1045 ■ Wilderness International
PO Box 491
Canby, OR 97013
Ph: (503)593-0199
E-mail: info@wildernessintl.com
URL: http://www.wildernessintl.com
Contact: Russ Hall, Pres./Exec. Dir.
Membership Dues: individual, $25 (annual) ● family, $45 (annual) ● church, $250 (annual) ● life, $1,000.
Description: Aim to educate and encourage the public to enjoy the wonder of nature, observe God's majesty through His creation and enhance their lives through this knowledge and experience. Promotes conservation through habitat projects, adventure activities, multimedia presentations and public education.

1046 ■ The Wilderness Society (TWS) (4330)
1615 M St. NW
Washington, DC 20036
Ph: (202)833-2300
Free: (800)843-9453
E-mail: info@wilderness.org.au
URL: http://www.wilderness.org
Contact: **Douglas W. Walker, Chm.**

1047 ■ Wildlife Management Institute (WMI) (4085)
c/o Richard E. McCabe, VP
1424 NW Carlson Rd.
Topeka, KS 66614
Ph: **(410)562-5341**

E-mail: rmccabe@wildlifemgt.org
URL: http://www.wildlifemanagementinstitute.org
Contact: Steven A. Williams, Pres.

1048 ■ Wolf Haven International (4132)
3111 Offut Lake Rd.
Tenino, WA 98589
Ph: (360)264-4695
Free: (800)448-9653
Fax: (360)264-4639
E-mail: director@wolfhaven.org
URL: http://www.wolfhaven.org
Contact: **John Sleeter, Pres.**

1049 ■ World Federation for Coral Reef Conservation
PO Box 942
Safety Harbor, FL 34695
E-mail: vic.ferguson@wfcrc.org
URL: **http://wfcrc.org/default.aspx**
Contact: Vic Ferguson, Founder/CEO

Dairy Products

1050 ■ National Dairy Shrine (NDS) (4421)
PO Box 725
Denmark, WI 54208
Ph: (920)863-6333
Fax: (920)863-8328
E-mail: info@dairyshrine.org
URL: http://www.dairyshrine.org
Contact: Dr. David Selner, Exec. Dir.

Dog

1051 ■ Association of Pet Dog Trainers (APDT) (1160)
101 N Main St., Ste.610
Greenville, SC 29601
Free: (800)PET-DOGS
Fax: (864)331-0767
E-mail: information@apdt.com
URL: http://www.apdt.com
Contact: **Gail Fisher, Pres.**

Ecology

1052 ■ Association of Ecosystem Research Centers (AERC) (4155)
c/o Robin Graham, Sec.
Environmental Sciences Div.
Oak Ridge Natl. Lab.
PO Box 2008
Oak Ridge, TN 37831
Ph: (865)576-7756
E-mail: grahamrl@ornl.gov
URL: http://www.ecosystemresearch.org
Contact: **David E. Smith, Pres.**

1053 ■ Association for Fire Ecology (AFE)
PO Box 1054
Redlands, CA 92373
Ph: (541)852-7903 (510)642-7304
E-mail: office@fireecology.net
URL: http://fireecology.net
Contact: **Dr. Brian Oswald, Pres.**

1054 ■ International Association for Landscape Ecology I United States Regional Association (US-IALE)
Portland State Univ.
PO Box 751
Portland, OR 97207
Ph: (503)725-2494
E-mail: deanu@duke.edu
URL: http://www.usiale.org
Contact: **Robert M. Scheller, Treas.**

1055 ■ Planetwork
1230 Market St., No. 517
San Francisco, CA 94102
Ph: **(415)721-1591**
URL: http://www.planetwork.net
Contact: Jim Fournier, Pres./CFO

**1056 ■ Society for Ecological Restoration
International (SER) (4522)**
1017 O St. NW
Washington, DC 20001
Ph: **(202)299-9518**
Fax: (270)626-5485
E-mail: info@ser.org
URL: http://www.ser.org
Contact: Amanda Jorgenson, Exec. Dir.

Energy

1057 ■ GreenMotion
5795 S Sandhill Rd., Ste.F
Las Vegas, NV 89120
Ph: (310)663-9826
Fax: (310)388-8475
E-mail: info@greenmotion.org
URL: http://greenmotion.org
Contact: Leah Thompson, Pres./Exec. Dir.

Founded: 2006. **Description:** Aims to promote
sustainable environmental and economic development. Focuses on the research, development and
use of efficient and renewable energy solutions.

**1058 ■ Northwest Energy Efficiency Alliance
(NEEA)**
421 SW 6th Ave., Ste.600
Portland, OR 97204
Ph: **(503)688-5400**
Free: (800)411-0834
Fax: **(503)688-5447**
E-mail: **info@neea.org**
URL: http://www.nwalliance.org
Contact: Claire Fulenwider, Exec. Dir.

Environment

1059 ■ 41pounds.org
41 W Saratoga St.
Ferndale, MI 48220
Fax: (248)738-2761
E-mail: general@41pounds.org
URL: http://www.41pounds.org
Contact: Sander DeVries, Contact

Founded: 2006. **Description:** Seeks to protect the
environment by promoting the reduction of deforestation and consumption of other resources used to
produce junk mail. Works to mitigate the environmental hazard caused by unwanted and wasteful junk
mail.

1060 ■ Earth Island Institute (EII) (4506)
2150 Allston Way, Ste.460
Berkeley, CA 94704-1375
Ph: (510)859-9108 (510)859-9143
Fax: (510)859-9091
E-mail: **johnknox@earthisland.org**
URL: http://www.earthisland.org
Contact: John A. Knox, Exec. Dir.

**1061 ■ Earth Society Foundation (ESF)
(4488)**
238 E 58th St., Ste.2400
New York, NY 10022
Ph: (212)832-3659
Fax: (212)826-6213
E-mail: **earthsociety1@hotmail.com**
URL: http://www.earthsocietyfoundation.org
Contact: Thomas C. Dowd, Pres.

**1062 ■ Environmental Outreach and
Stewardship Alliance (EOS)**
230 NE Juniper St., Ste.201
Issaquah, WA 98027
Ph: (425)270-3274
Fax: **(425)526-2071**
E-mail: jworkman@eosalliance.org
URL: http://www.eosalliance.org
Contact: James Workman, Exec. Dir.

**1063 ■ International Center for the Solution
of Environmental Problems (ICSEP) (4522)**
5120 Woodway Dr., Ste.8009
Houston, TX 77056-1788
Ph: **(713)527-8711**
Fax: **(713)961-5157**
E-mail: icsep@airmail.net
URL: http://www.icsep.com
Contact: Joseph L. Goldman PhD, Technical Dir.

**1064 ■ International Society for
Environmental Ethics (ISEE) (4312)**
Colorado Coll.
Dept. of Philosophy
14 E Cache La Poudre St.
Colorado Springs, CO 80903
Ph: (719)227-8331
E-mail: marion.hourdequin@coloradocollege.edu
URL: **http://iseethics.org**
Contact: Marion Hourdequin, Treas.

**1065 ■ International Society for Reef Studies
(ISRS) (4540)**
Univ. of Hawaii at Manoa
Kewalo Marine Lab.
41 Ahui St.
Honolulu, HI 96813
E-mail: **richmond@hawaii.edu**
URL: **http://www.coralreefs.org/index.htm**
Contact: **Bob Richmond, Pres.**

**1066 ■ International Sonoran Desert Alliance
(ISDA)**
401 W Esperanza
Ajo, AZ 85321
Ph: (520)387-6823
Fax: (520)387-5626
E-mail: tracy@isdanet.org
URL: http://www.isdanet.org
Contact: Cathy Hutton, Pres.

1067 ■ Merck Family Fund (4524)
95 Eliot St., Ste.2
Milton, MA 02186
Ph: (617)696-3580
Fax: (617)696-7262
E-mail: merck@merckff.org
URL: http://www.merckff.org
Contact: **Nat Chamberlin, Pres.**

**1068 ■ Native American Fish and Wildlife
Society (NAFWS) (4455)**
8333 Greenwood Blvd., Ste.260
Denver, CO 80221
Ph: (303)466-1725 (303)800-4776
Free: (866)890-7258
Fax: (303)466-5414
URL: http://www.nafws.org
Contact: **D. Fred Matt, Exec. Dir.**

1069 ■ Nature Abounds
PO Box 241
Clearfield, PA 16830
E-mail: info@natureabounds.org
URL: http://www.natureabounds.org
Contact: Melinda Hughes-Wert, Pres.

Founded: 2008. **Membership Dues:** regular, $25
(annual). **Description:** Raises public awareness of
the natural world through education, action and
inspiration. Encourages volunteerism and environmental stewardship. Provides a forum for people who
are interested in protecting the environment.

1070 ■ Open Space Institute (OSI) (4536)
1350 Broadway, Ste.201
New York, NY 10018-7799
Ph: (212)290-8200
Fax: (212)244-3441
URL: http://www.osiny.org
Contact: **John H. Adams, Chm.**

1071 ■ People 4 Earth
1612 K St. NW, Ste.600
Washington, DC 20006
Ph: (484)919-1488
URL: http://www.people4earth.org
Contact: Nico Broersen, CEO

Multinational. Description: Aims to improve the
well-being of people and health of the planet by
transforming sustainable production and consumption from niche to mainstream markets. Encourages
companies to develop safe and healthier products
while protecting the environment and social labor
standards throughout the product chain.

1072 ■ Rock the Earth (4464)
1536 Wynkoop St., Ste.B200
Denver, CO 80202
Ph: (303)454-3304
Fax: (303)454-3306
E-mail: info@rocktheearth.org
URL: http://www.rocktheearth.net
Contact: **Marc Ross, Exec. Dir.**

1073 ■ Seventh Generation Advisors (SGA)
2601 Ocean Park Blvd., Ste.311
Santa Monica, CA 90405
Ph: (310)664-0300
E-mail: seventhgenerationadvisors@gmail.com
URL: http://www.seventhgenerationadvisors.org
Contact: Terry Tamminen, Pres.

Founded: 2007. **Multinational. Description:** Advocates environmental and clean energy policies for a
sustainable world seven generations into the future.
Promotes ways of transitioning to a sustainable, low
carbon economy. Guides climate change policy initiatives for non-profit organizations.

**1074 ■ Women's Voices for the Earth (WVE)
(4476)**
PO Box 8743
Missoula, MT 59807
Ph: (406)543-3747 (406)585-9009
Fax: (406)543-2557
E-mail: womensvoices@womensvoices.org
URL: **http://www.womensvoices.org**
Contact: Lisa Woll, Pres.

Environmental Education

1075 ■ EcoVentures International (EVI)
2122 P St. NW, Ste.302
Washington, DC 20037
Ph: (202)667-0802
Fax: (202)667-0803
E-mail: info@eco-ventures.org
URL: http://www.eco-ventures.org
Contact: Margie Brand, Founder

1076 ■ Kids Ecology Corps (KEC)
1350 E Sunrise Blvd.
Fort Lauderdale, FL 33304-2815
Ph: (954)524-0366
Free: (877)556-5437
Fax: **(954)524-0368**
E-mail: kec@kidsecologycorps.org
URL: http://www.kidsecologycorps.org
Contact: Emily Nell Lagerquist, Exec. Dir.

Environmental Quality

**1077 ■ Environmental Council of the States
(ECOS) (4569)**
50 F St. NW, Ste.350
Washington, DC 20001
Ph: **(202)266-4920**

Fax: **(202)266-4937**
E-mail: ecos@ecos.org
URL: http://www.ecos.org
Contact: R. Steven Brown, Exec. Dir.

**1078 ■ Environmental Research and
Education Foundation (EREF) (4218)**
3301 Benson Dr., Ste.301
Raleigh, NC 27609
Ph: (919)861-6876
Fax: (919)861-6878
E-mail: **bstaley@erefdn.org**
URL: http://www.erefdn.org
Contact: **Bryan F. Staley PhD, Pres./CEO**

**1079 ■ Filipino American Coalition for
Environmental Solidarity (FACES) (4571)**
PO Box 566
Berkeley, CA 94701-0566
Ph: **(415)496-6561**
E-mail: info@facessolidarity.org
URL: http://www.facessolidarity.org
Contact: Aileen Suzara, Co-Chair

**1080 ■ International Society of Sustainability
Professionals (ISSP)**
2515 NE 17th Ave., Ste.300
Portland, OR 97212
Ph: **(503)284-9132**
E-mail: mwillard@sustainabilityprofessionals.org
URL: http://sustainabilityprofessionals.org
Contact: Marsha Willard, Exec. Dir.

1081 ■ SkyTruth
PO Box 3283
Shepherdstown, WV 25443-3283
Ph: **(304)885-4581**
E-mail: info@skytruth.org
URL: http://www.skytruth.org
Contact: John F. Amos, Pres.

1082 ■ Transition United States
PO Box 917
Sebastopol, CA 95473
Ph: **(707)763-1100**
E-mail: info@transitionus.org
URL: http://www.transitionus.org
Contact: Carolyne Stayton, Exec. Dir.

Farming

**1083 ■ International Flying Farmers (IFF)
(4584)**
PO Box 309
Mansfield, IL 61854
Ph: **(217)489-9300**
Fax: **(217)489-9280**
E-mail: **iff1944@hotmail.com**
URL: http://www.flyingfarmers.org
Contact: **Eugene Shore, Pres.**

**1084 ■ National Farm-City Council (NFCC)
(4501)**
PO Box 6825
Reading, PA 19610
Free: **(877)611-8161**
E-mail: **contact@farmcity.org**
URL: http://www.farmcity.org
Contact: **Hugh Whaley, Chm.**

**1085 ■ National Farm and Ranch Business
Management Education Association
(NFRBMEA) (4577)**
1123 S Main St.
Rugby, ND 58368
Ph: **(701)776-5095**
E-mail: **allen.graner@dakotacollege.edu**
URL: http://www.nfrbmea.org
Contact: **Al Graner, Pres.**

1086 ■ National Farmers Union (NFU) (4225)
200 F St. NW, Ste.300
Washington, DC 20001
Ph: (202)554-1600

Fax: (202)554-1654
E-mail: sue.arends@nfu.org
URL: http://www.nfu.org
Contact: Roger Johnson, Pres.

**1087 ■ Organic Crop Improvement
Association (OCIA) (4507)**
1340 N Cotner Blvd.
Lincoln, NE 68505
Ph: (402)477-2323
Fax: (402)477-4325
E-mail: info@ocia.org
URL: http://www.ocia.org
Contact: **Peggy Linzmeier, Pres.**

Fishing Industries

**1088 ■ Gulf and Caribbean Fisheries Institute
(GCFI) (4668)**
Univ. of Florida
Picos Rd.
Fort Pierce, FL 34946
Ph: (561)462-1660
Fax: **(561)462-1510**
E-mail: leroy.creswell@gcfi.org
URL: http://www.gcfi.org
Contact: Leroy Creswell, Exec. Sec.

Forestry

**1089 ■ Alliance for Community Trees (ACT)
(4527)**
4603 Calvert Rd.
College Park, MD 20740-3421
Ph: (301)277-0040 (301)220-2251
Fax: (301)277-0042
E-mail: info@actrees.org
URL: http://www.actrees.org
Contact: **Carrie Gallagher, Exec. Dir.**

**1090 ■ American Forest and Paper
Association (AF&PA) (4620)**
1111 19th St. NW, Ste.800
Washington, DC 20036
Ph: (202)463-2700
Free: (800)878-8878
E-mail: info@afandpa.org
URL: http://www.afandpa.org
Contact: **James B. Hannan, Chm.**

**1091 ■ Association of Consulting Foresters
of America (ACF) (4310)**
312 Montgomery St., Ste.208
Alexandria, VA 22314
Ph: (703)548-0990
Fax: (703)548-6395
E-mail: director@acf-foresters.org
URL: http://www.acf-foresters.org
Contact: **Richard G. Carbonetti, Pres.**

**1092 ■ International Association of Wildland
Fire (IAWF) (4257)**
1418 Washburn St.
Missoula, MT 59801
Ph: **(406)531-8264**
Free: (888)440-IAWF
E-mail: iawf@iawfonline.org
URL: http://www.iawfonline.org
Contact: **Mikel Robinson, Exec. Dir.**

**1093 ■ International Society of Tropical
Foresters (ISTF) (4659)**
5400 Grosvenor Ln.
Bethesda, MD 20814
Ph: (301)530-4514
Fax: **(301)897-3690**
E-mail: webmaster@istf-bethesda.org
URL: http://www.istf-bethesda.org
Contact: **Gary S. Harshorn, Pres./Dir.-at-Large**

1094 ■ Planting Empowerment (PE)
1348 Euclid St. NW, No. 305
Washington, DC 20009
Ph: (202)470-2432
E-mail: dcroston@plantingempowerment.com
URL: http://www.plantingempowerment.com
Contact: Damion Croston, Dir. of Operations

1095 ■ Rights and Resources Initiative (RRI)
1238 Wisconsin Ave. NW, Ste.204
Washington, DC 20007
Ph: (202)470-3900 **(202)470-3890**
Fax: (202)944-3315
E-mail: info@rightsandresources.org
URL: http://www.rightsandresources.org
Contact: Andy White, Coor.

Fruits and Vegetables

**1096 ■ California Date Administrative
Committee (CDAC) (4711)**
PO Box 1736
Indio, CA 92202-1736
Ph: (760)347-4510
Free: (800)223-8748
Fax: (760)347-6374
E-mail: **info@datesaregreat.com**
URL: http://www.datesaregreat.com
Contact: Albert Keck, Chm.

1097 ■ Cranberry Institute (CI) (4725)
PO Box 497
Carver, MA 02330
Ph: **(508)866-1118**
Fax: **(508)866-1199**
E-mail: **cinews@cranberryinstitute.org**
URL: http://www.cranberryinstitute.org
Contact: **Terry Humfeld, Exec. Dir.**

**1098 ■ National Cherry Growers and
Industries Foundation (NCGIF) (4741)**
2667 Reed Rd.
Hood River, OR 97031
Ph: (541)386-5761
Fax: (541)386-3191
E-mail: **osweetcherry@gmail.com**
URL: http://www.nationalcherries.com

1099 ■ National Potato Council (NPC) (4683)
1300 L St. NW, No. 910
Washington, DC 20005
Ph: (202)682-9456
Fax: (202)682-0333
E-mail: johnk@nationalpotatocouncil.org
URL: http://www.nationalpotatocouncil.org
Contact: **Justin Dagen, Pres.**

**1100 ■ National Watermelon Association
(NWA)**
5129 S Lakeland Dr. Ste.1
Lakeland, FL 33813
Ph: **(813)619-7575**
Fax: (813)619-7577
E-mail: nwa@tampabay.rr.com
URL: http://www.nationalwatermelonassociation.com
Contact: Bob Morrissey, Dir.

**1101 ■ Potato Association of America (PAA)
(4704)**
Univ. of Maine
5719 Crossland Hall, Rm. 220
Orono, ME 04469-5719
Ph: (207)581-3042
Fax: (207)581-3015
E-mail: umpotato@maine.edu
URL: http://potatoassociation.org
Contact: **Don Halseth, Pres.**

1102 ■ United Soybean Board (USB) (4714)
16305 Swingley Ridge Rd., Ste.150
Chesterfield, MO 63017
Ph: (636)530-1777
Free: (800)989-8721
Fax: (636)530-1560

E-mail: **info@unitedsoybean.com**
URL: http://www.unitedsoybean.org
Contact: Lisa O'Brien, Exec. Dir.

1103 ■ U.S. Apple Association (4768)
8233 Old Courthouse Rd., Ste.200
Vienna, VA 22182
Ph: (703)442-8850
Free: (800)781-4443
Fax: (703)790-0845
E-mail: **info@usapple.org**
URL: http://www.usapple.org
Contact: Todd Hultquist, Contact

Fuel

1104 ■ American Gas Association (AGA) (1511)
400 N Capitol St. NW, Ste.450
Washington, DC 20001
Ph: (202)824-7000 (202)824-7024
Fax: (202)824-7081
URL: http://www.aga.org
Contact: **Dave McCurdy, Pres./CEO**

1105 ■ Interstate Natural Gas Association of America (INGAA) (4727)
20 F St. NW, Ste.450
Washington, DC 20001
Ph: (202)216-5900 (202)216-5901
Fax: (202)216-0870
E-mail: **webinfo@ingaa.org**
URL: http://www.ingaa.org
Contact: Donald F. Santa Jr., Pres.

Goats

1106 ■ American Kiko Goat Association (AKGA)
14551 County Rd. 7130
Moody, MO 65777
Ph: (254)423-5914
E-mail: **secretary@kikogoats.com**
URL: http://www.kikogoats.com
Contact: **Jean Gullion, Treas.**

1107 ■ International Boer Goat Association (4740)
PO Box 1045
Whitewright, TX 75491
Ph: (903)364-5735
Fax: (903)364-5741
E-mail: **officemgr@intlboergoat.org**
URL: http://www.intlboergoat.org
Contact: Jennifer Roberts, Pres./CEO

1108 ■ International Fainting Goat Association (IFGA) (4633)
1039 State Rte. 168
Darlington, PA 16115
Ph: **(724)843-2084**
Fax: **(724)891-1440**
E-mail: **ifga@accuregister.com**
URL: http://www.faintinggoat.com
Contact: **Yvonne Barker, Sec.**

1109 ■ North American Packgoat Association (NAPgA) (4746)
PO Box 170166
Boise, ID 83717
Ph: (435)764-1111
E-mail: **napga@napga.org**
URL: http://www.napga.org
Contact: Larry Robinson, Pres./Treas.

Hazardous Material

1110 ■ Institute of Hazardous Materials Management (IHMM) (4494)
11900 Parklawn Dr., Ste.450
Rockville, MD 20852-2624
Ph: (301)984-8969

Fax: (301)984-1516
E-mail: **info@ihmm.org**
URL: http://www.ihmm.org
Contact: **Jeffrey H. Greenwald CAE, Exec. Dir.**

Horses

1111 ■ American Azteca Horse International Association (AAHIA)
PO Box 1577
Rapid City, SD 57709
Ph: (605)342-2322 (605)347-4211
E-mail: **office@americanazteca.com**
URL: http://americanazteca.com
Contact: Rita Greslin, Pres.

1112 ■ American Bashkir Curly Registry (ABCR) (4812)
71 Cavalier Blvd., No. 124
Florence, KY 41042
Ph: (859)485-9700
Free: (877)324-0956
Fax: (859)485-9777
E-mail: cabincreekfarms@fuse.net
URL: http://www.abcregistry.org
Contact: **Sue Davis, Sec.**

1113 ■ American Drum Horse Association (ADHA)
3822 Bluff Cir.
Coarsegold, CA 93614
Ph: (559)676-7990
E-mail: americandrumhorse@yahoo.com
URL: http://www.drumhorseassociation.com
Contact: **Sarah Hollis, Pres.**

1114 ■ American Equestrian Trade Association (AETA) (4777)
107 W St. Rd.
Kennett Square, PA 19348-1613
Ph: (610)444-2025
Fax: (610)444-2027
E-mail: info@aeta.us
URL: http://www.aeta.us
Contact: **Tony Coppola, Pres.**

1115 ■ American Half Quarter Horse Registry (AHQHR) (4495)
PO Box 211
Carlsbad, NM 88221-0211
Ph: (480)982-1551
E-mail: lzmqhorses@earthlink.net
URL: http://www.halfquarterhorseregistry.com
Contact: James H. Averill, Pres.

1116 ■ American Morgan Horse Association (AMHA) (4766)
4066 Shelburne Rd., Ste.5
Shelburne, VT 05482-6908
Ph: (802)985-4944
Fax: (802)985-8897
E-mail: info@morganhorse.com
URL: http://www.morganhorse.com
Contact: **Harry Sebring, Pres.**

1117 ■ American Paint Horse Association (APHA) (4834)
PO Box 961023
Fort Worth, TX 76161-0023
Ph: (817)834-2742
Fax: (817)834-3152
E-mail: askapha@apha.com
URL: http://www.apha.com
Contact: **Dr. Travis Titlow, Pres.**

1118 ■ American Part-Blooded Horse Registry (APB) (4456)
PO Box 986
Oregon City, OR 97045
Ph: **(503)895-1680**
E-mail: **information@americanpartblooded-horseregistry.com**
URL: http://www.americanpartbloodedhorseregistry.com

1119 ■ American Quarter Horse Association (AQHA) (4459)
1600 Quarter Horse Dr.
Amarillo, TX 79168
Ph: (806)376-4811
URL: http://www.aqha.com
Contact: **Peter J. Cofrancesco III, Pres.**

1120 ■ American Ranch Horse Association (ARHA) (4687)
PO Box 186
Nancy, KY 42544
Ph: **(606)636-4112** (606)271-2963
Fax: (606)636-6197
E-mail: arhacontact@aol.com
URL: http://www.americanranchhorse.net
Contact: Randy Cope, Pres.

1121 ■ American Trakehner Association (ATA) (4695)
1536 W Church St.
Newark, OH 43055
Ph: (740)344-1111
Fax: (740)344-3225
E-mail: ata@americantrakehner.com
URL: http://www.americantrakehner.com
Contact: **Tim Holekamp MD, Pres.**

1122 ■ American Warmblood Registry (AWR) (4697)
PO Box 197
Carter, MT 59420
Ph: (406)734-5499
Fax: (775)667-0516
E-mail: **info@amerwarmblood.com**
URL: http://www.americanwarmblood.com

1123 ■ American Youth Horse Council (AYHC) (4474)
577 N Boyero Ave.
Pueblo West, CO 81007
Ph: (719)594-9778
Free: (800)TRY-AYHC
Fax: (775)256-0382
E-mail: info@ayhc.com
URL: http://www.ayhc.com
Contact: **Jill Montgomery, Exec. Dir.**

1124 ■ Belgian Draft Horse Corporation of America (BDHCA) (4710)
PO Box 335
Wabash, IN 46992
Ph: (260)563-3205
Fax: (260)563-3205
E-mail: belgian@belgiancorp.com
URL: http://www.belgiancorp.com
Contact: **Dr. Michael R. Stone, Pres.**

1125 ■ Caspian Horse Society of the Americas (CHSA) (4824)
c/o Vicki Hudgins, Registrar
PO Box 1589
Brenham, TX 77834-1589
Ph: (979)830-9046
URL: http://www.caspian.org
Contact: **Mary Harrison, Pres.**

1126 ■ Cleveland Bay Horse Society of North America (CBHSNA) (4826)
PO Box 483
Goshen, NH 03752
Ph: **(865)300-7133**
E-mail: info@clevelandbay.com
URL: http://www.clevelandbay.org
Contact: Tracie Traver, Pres.

1127 ■ Gypsy Vanner Horse Society (GVHS) (4842)
PO Box 65
Waynesfield, OH 45896
Free: (888)520-9777
E-mail: info@gypsyvannerhorsesociety.org
URL: http://www.gypsyvannerhorsesociety.org
Contact: **Wayne Hipsley, Interim Exec. Dir.**

1128 ■ Horse Protection League (HPL) (4497)
PO Box 741089
Arvada, CO 80006
Ph: (303)216-0141 (303)667-1007
E-mail: info@cohpl.org
URL: http://www.cohpl.org
Contact: **Lloyd Mower, Pres.**

1129 ■ Hungarian Horse Association of America (HHAA) (4498)
c/o George Cooksley, Treas.
HC 71, Box 108
Anselmo, NE 68813
Ph: (308)749-2411
E-mail: info@hungarianhorses.org
URL: http://hungarianhorses.org
Contact: **Rick Brandt, Pres.**

1130 ■ International Colored Appaloosa Association (ICAA) (4851)
PO Box 99
Shipshewana, IN 46565
Ph: **(574)238-4280**
E-mail: icaamail@aol.com
URL: http://www.icaainc.com
Contact: Penny Kowalski, Pres.

1131 ■ International Curly Horse Organization (ICHO) (4741)
HC 31 Box 102A
Williamsburg, NM 87942
Ph: (575)740-4159
E-mail: office@curlyhorses.org
URL: **http://ichocurlyhorses.weebly.com**
Contact: **Jackie Richardson, Registar**

1132 ■ International Friesian Show Horse Association (IFSHA)
PO Box 535
Santa Ynez, CA 93460
Ph: (805)448-3027 (951)677-9477
Fax: (951)696-9586
E-mail: ifsha@friesianshowhorse.com
URL: http://www.friesianshowhorse.com
Contact: Nancy Nathanson, Exec. Dir.

1133 ■ International Warlander Society and Registry (IWSR) (21068)
12218 26th Ave. NE
Tulalip, WA 98271
E-mail: **registry@warlander.org**
URL: http://www.warlander.org

1134 ■ Irish Draught Horse Society of North America (IDHS (NA))
c/o Rachel Cox, Information Off.
HC65 Box 45
Pleasant Mount, PA 18453-9605
Free: (866)434-7621
E-mail: rachael@nep.net
URL: http://www.irishdraught.com
Contact: **Bill Appel, Pres.**

1135 ■ Lipizzan Association of North America (LANA) (4911)
PO Box 1133
Anderson, IN 46015-1133
Ph: (765)215-6798
Fax: (765)641-1208
E-mail: **info@lipizzan.org**
URL: http://www.lipizzan.org
Contact: Sandy Heaberlin, Dir./Trustee

1136 ■ Lippitt Morgan Breeders Association (LMBA) (4867)
620 Millers Falls Rd.
Northfield, MA 01360
Ph: **(413)498-5553**
Fax: **(413)498-5553**
E-mail: **crescent@randallane.com**
URL: http://www.lippittmorganbreedersassociation.com
Contact: **Crescent Peirce, Pres.**

1137 ■ Mountain Pleasure Horse Association (MPHA) (4518)
PO Box 33
Wellington, KY 40387
Ph: (606)768-3847
E-mail: mphareg@ymail.com
URL: **http://www.mountainpleasurehorse.org**
Contact: **Ottis Jean Lane, Pres.**

1138 ■ National Cutting Horse Association (NCHA) (4873)
260 Bailey Ave.
Fort Worth, TX 76107-1862
Ph: (817)244-6188 (817)594-2068
Fax: (817)244-2015
E-mail: **dlrranch@airmail.net**
URL: http://www.nchacutting.com
Contact: **Chris Benedict, Pres.**

1139 ■ National Quarter Horse Registry (NQHR) (4854)
1497 S Staghorn
Toquerville, UT 84774
Ph: **(435)559-2069**
E-mail: questions@nqhr.org
URL: **http://www.nqhr.org/registry**
Contact: Tamara Holdaway, Exec. Dir.

1140 ■ National Reining Horse Association (NRHA) (4912)
3000 NW 10th St.
Oklahoma City, OK 73107-5302
Ph: (405)946-7400
Fax: (405)946-8425
E-mail: **allenmitchels@yahoo.com**
URL: http://www.nrha.com
Contact: **Allen Mitchels, Pres.**

1141 ■ National Show Horse Registry (NSHR) (4925)
PO Box 862
Lewisburg, OH 45338
Ph: **(937)962-4336**
Fax: **(937)962-4332**
E-mail: nshowhorse@aol.com
URL: http://www.nshregistry.org
Contact: Cindy Clinton, Contact

1142 ■ North American Danish Warmblood Association (NADWA)
32781 Chadlyn Ct.
Wildomar, CA 92595-9310
Ph: **(951)609-3787**
E-mail: **salsa@oakhillranch.com**
URL: http://www.danishwarmblood.org
Contact: **Sharon Londono, Pres.**

1143 ■ North American Peruvian Horse Association (NAPHA) (4866)
PO Box 2187
Santa Rosa, CA 95405
Ph: **(707)544-5807**
Fax: **(707)544-5857**
E-mail: **tsource@gte.net**
URL: http://www.napha.net
Contact: Edith Gandy, Pres.

1144 ■ Norwegian Fjord Horse Registry (NFHR) (4894)
1801 W County Rd. 4
Berthoud, CO 80513
Ph: (303)684-6466
Free: (888)646-5618
Fax: (888)646-5613
E-mail: info@nfhr.com
URL: http://www.nfhr.com
Contact: **Nancy Newport, Exec. Dir.**

1145 ■ Pony of the Americas Club (POAC) (4481)
3828 S Emerson Ave.
Indianapolis, IN 46203
Ph: (317)788-0107
Fax: (317)788-8974

E-mail: poac@poac.org
URL: http://www.poac.org
Contact: **Jackie Guthrie, Chair**

1146 ■ Rocky Mountain Horse Association (RMHA) (4549)
4037 Iron Works Pkwy., Ste.160
Lexington, KY 40511
Ph: (859)243-0260
Fax: **(859)243-0266**
E-mail: information@rmhorse.com
URL: http://www.rmhorse.com
Contact: Ms. Peggy Entrekin, Exec. Dir.

1147 ■ Spanish-Barb Breeders Association (SBBA) (4885)
PO Box 1628
Silver City, NM 88062
E-mail: info@spanishbarb.com
URL: http://www.spanishbarb.com
Contact: **Steve Dobrott, Pres.**

1148 ■ Spanish Mustang Registry (SMR) (4953)
323 County Rd. 419
Chilton, TX 76632
Ph: (254)546-2177 (512)461-8626
E-mail: **carol.dildine@yahoo.com**
URL: http://www.spanishmustang.org
Contact: Carol Dildine, Sec.

1149 ■ Spotted Saddle Horse Breeders' and Exhibitors' Association (SSHBEA)
PO Box 1046
Shelbyville, TN 37162
Ph: (931)684-7496
Fax: (931)684-7215
E-mail: **info@sshbea.org**
URL: http://www.sshbea.org
Contact: Janice Prince, Operations Mgr.

1150 ■ Tennessee Walking Horse Breeders' and Exhibitors' Association (TWHBEA) (4959)
PO Box 286
Lewisburg, TN 37091
Ph: (931)359-1574
Fax: (931)359-7530
E-mail: **rthomas@twhbea.com**
URL: http://www.twhbea.com
Contact: **Ron Thomas, Exec. Dir.**

1151 ■ Walking Horse Trainers Association (WHTA)
1101 N Main St.
PO Box 61
Shelbyville, TN 37162
Ph: (931)684-5866
Fax: (931)684-5895
E-mail: whtrainers@gmail.com
URL: http://www.walkinghorsetrainers.com
Contact: **Bill Cantrell, Pres.**

1152 ■ Western Saddle Clubs Association (WSCA) (4926)
c/o Teri Spence, Sec.
47009 Company Rd. 13
St. Peter, MN 56082
Ph: (507)345-5856
E-mail: secretary@wsca.org
URL: http://www.wsca.org
Contact: **Mark Spence, Pres.**

Horticulture

1153 ■ International Phalaenopsis Alliance (IPA)
c/o Lynn Fuller, Membership Sec.
1401 Pennsylvania Ave., No. 1604
Wilmington, DE 19806
Ph: (302)594-0765
E-mail: harper_svo@bellsouth.net
URL: http://www.phal.org
Contact: Tom Harper, Pres.

Landscaping

1154 ■ Northeastern Weed Science Society (NEWSS) (4582)
PO Box 307
Fredericksburg, PA 17026
Ph: (717)787-7204
E-mail: mbravo@state.pa.us
URL: http://www.newss.org
Contact: **Mark VanGessel, Pres.**

1155 ■ Project EverGreen
PO Box 156
New Prague, MN 56071
Ph: (952)758-9135
Free: (877)758-4835
E-mail: **cindycode@projectevergreen.com**
URL: http://www.projectevergreen.com
Contact: **Cindy Code, Exec. Dir.**

Livestock

1156 ■ American Emu Association (AEA) (4951)
1201 W Main St., Ste.2
Ottawa, IL 61350
Ph: (541)332-0675
E-mail: **info@aea-emu.org**
URL: http://www.aea-emu.org
Contact: I. Michael Eppley, Pres.

1157 ■ American Royal Association (ARA) (4586)
1701 Amer. Royal Ct.
Kansas City, MO 64102
Ph: (816)221-9800 (816)569-4003
Fax: (816)221-8189
E-mail: **bobp@americanroyal.com**
URL: http://www.americanroyal.com
Contact: **David Fowler, Chm.**

1158 ■ Food Animal Concerns Trust (FACT) (4997)
3525 W Peterson Ave., Ste.213
Chicago, IL 60659-3314
Ph: (773)525-4952
Fax: (773)525-5226
E-mail: info@foodanimalconcerns.org
URL: http://www.foodanimalconcerns.org
Contact: Richard Wood, Exec. Dir.

Marine

1159 ■ Global Underwater Explorers
15 S Main St.
High Springs, FL 32643
Ph: (386)454-0820
Free: (800)762-3483
Fax: (386)454-0654
E-mail: info@gue.com
URL: http://www.gue.com
Contact: Jarrod Jablonski, Pres.
Founded: 1998. **Membership Dues:** electronic, $39 (annual) ● silver, $125 (annual) ● gold, $275 (annual) ● scholar, $500 (annual) ● platinum, $1,000 (annual). **Description:** Aims to explore and protect the underwater world and to improve the quality of education and research in all things aquatic. Supports diver training, exploration and sustainable conservation initiatives.

1160 ■ PACON International (4853)
2525 Correa Rd., HIG 407A
Honolulu, HI 96822
Ph: (808)956-6163
Fax: (808)956-2580
E-mail: pacon@hawaii.edu
URL: http://www.hawaii.edu/pacon
Contact: **Dr. Lorenz Magaard, Pres.**

1161 ■ Reef Relief
PO Box 430
Key West, FL 33041
Ph: (305)294-3100
Fax: (305)294-9515
E-mail: reefrelief@gmail.com
URL: http://www.reefrelief.org
Contact: **Peter Anderson, Pres.**

Marine Biology

1162 ■ MarineBio Conservation Society
PO Box 235273
Encinitas, CA 92023
Ph: (713)248-2576
E-mail: info@marinebio.org
URL: http://marinebio.org
Contact: David Campbell, Founder/Dir.
Founded: 1998. **Multinational. Description:** Works to protect marine life and the ocean for future generations. Creates an awareness of marine conservation issues and their solutions. Supports marine conservation scientists and students involved in the marine life sciences.

Marketing

1163 ■ North American Farmers' Direct Marketing Association (NAFDMA) (4983)
62 White Loaf Rd.
Southampton, MA 01073
Ph: (413)529-0386
Free: (888)884-9270
Fax: (413)233-4285
E-mail: nafdma@map.com
URL: http://www.nafdma.com
Contact: Charlie Touchette, Exec. Dir.

1164 ■ Organic Trade Association (OTA) (4984)
28 Vernon St., Ste.413
Brattleboro, VT 05301
Ph: (802)275-3800
Fax: (802)275-3801
E-mail: info@ota.com
URL: http://www.ota.com
Contact: Julia Sabin, Pres.

Media

1165 ■ Science Communication Network (SCN)
2000 P St. NW, No. 740
Washington, DC 20036
Ph: (202)463-6670
E-mail: **gabriela@sciencecom.org**
URL: http://www.ems.org
Contact: Amy Kostant, Exec. Dir.

Microscopy

1166 ■ Optical Imaging Association (OPIA)
PO Box 428
Fairfax, VA 22038
Ph: (703)836-1360
Fax: (703)836-6644
E-mail: **cmulligan@lpanet.org**
URL: http://www.opia.org

Natural Resources

1167 ■ International Association for Society and Natural Resources (IASNR) (5028)
Penn State
Dept. of Agricultural Economics and Rural Sociology
114 Armsby Bldg.
University Park, PA 16802
Ph: (814)863-8643

E-mail: **ael3@psu.edu**
URL: http://www.iasnr.org
Contact: A.E. Luloff, Exec. Dir.

1168 ■ International Joint Commission (IJC) (4997)
2000 L St. NW, Ste.615
Washington, DC 20440
Ph: (202)736-9024
Fax: (202)632-2007
E-mail: bevacquaf@washington.ijc.org
URL: http://www.ijc.org
Contact: Frank Bevacqua, Public Information Off.

1169 ■ Rocky Mountain Institute (RMI) (18101)
2317 Snowmass Creek Rd.
Snowmass, CO 81654-9199
Ph: (970)927-3851
Fax: (970)927-3420
E-mail: ablovins@rmi.org
URL: http://www.rmi.org
Contact: Amory B. Lovins, Chm.

Nurseries

1170 ■ Horticultural Research Institute (HRI) (4528)
1000 Vermont Ave. NW, Ste.300
Washington, DC 20005-4914
Ph: (202)789-2900 (202)741-4852
Fax: (202)478-7288
E-mail: **tjodon@hriresearch.org**
URL: http://www.hriresearch.org
Contact: Teresa Jodon, Exec. Dir.

1171 ■ Nursery and Landscape Association Executives of North America (NLAE) (5004)
2130 Stella Ct.
Columbus, OH 43215
Ph: (614)487-1117
Fax: (614)487-1216
E-mail: nlae@nlae.org
URL: http://www.nlae.org
Contact: **Amy Graham, Pres.**

Nuts

1172 ■ National Peanut Festival Association (NPFA) (4633)
5622 Hwy. 231 S
Dothan, AL 36301
Ph: (334)793-4323
Free: (866)277-3962
Fax: (334)793-3247
E-mail: nationalpeanut@aol.com
URL: http://www.nationalpeanutfestival.com
Contact: **Ealey Brackin, Pres.**

1173 ■ Northern Nut Growers Association (NNGA) (2742)
c/o William Sachs, Treas.
PO Box 6216
Hamden, CT 06517-0216
E-mail: tuckerh@epix.net
URL: http://www.northernnutgrowers.org
Contact: Greg Miller, Pres.

Organic Farming

1174 ■ Independent Organic Inspectors Association (IOIA) (4907)
PO Box 6
Broadus, MT 59317-0006
Ph: (406)436-2031
E-mail: ioia@ioia.net
URL: http://www.ioia.net
Contact: **Michelle Durst, Chair**

1175 ■ Textile Exchange
822 Baldridge St.
O'Donnell, TX 79351
Ph: (806)428-3411
Fax: (806)428-3475
E-mail: **info@textileexchange.org**
URL: http://organicexchange.org/oecms
Contact: **Eraina Duffy, Chair**
Status Note: Formerly Organic Textile.

Parks and Recreation

1176 ■ Coalition of National Park Service Retirees (CNPSR)
5625 N Wilmot Rd.
Tucson, AZ 85750
Ph: (520)615-9417
Fax: (520)615-9474
E-mail: **rick_smith@npsretirees.org**
URL: http://www.npsretirees.org
Contact: **Richard B. Smith, Chair**

Pest Control

1177 ■ American Mosquito Control Association (AMCA) (5063)
15000 Commerce Pkwy., Ste.C
Mount Laurel, NJ 08054
Ph: (856)439-9222 (904)215-3008
Fax: (856)439-0525
E-mail: amca@mosquito.org
URL: http://www.mosquito.org
Contact: **William Meredith, Pres.**

1178 ■ Association of Natural Biocontrol Producers (ANBP) (5032)
c/o Lynn LeBeck, Exec. Dir.
PO Box 1609
Clovis, CA 93613-1609
Ph: (559)360-7111
Fax: (800)553-4817
E-mail: **exdir@anbp.org**
URL: http://www.anbp.org
Contact: **Eda Reinot, Pres.**

1179 ■ National Association of Exotic Pest Plant Councils (NAEPPC)
Univ. of Georgia
Center for Invasive Species and Ecosystem Hea.
PO Box 748
Tifton, GA 31793
Ph: **(229)386-3298**
Fax: **(229)386-3352**
E-mail: **cbargero@uga.edu**
URL: http://www.naeppc.org
Contact: **Chuck Bargeron, Chm.**

Plastics

1180 ■ Plastic Loose Fill Council (PLFC)
1298 Cronson Blvd., Ste.201
Crofton, MD 21114
Ph: (510)654-0756
Free: (800)828-2214
E-mail: join@loosefillpackaging.com
URL: http://www.loosefillpackaging.com
Contact: **John D. Mellott, Pres.**

Pollution Control

1181 ■ Climate Registry (5083)
523 W 6th St., Ste.445
Los Angeles, CA 90014
Ph: (213)891-6922
Free: (866)523-0764
Fax: (213)623-6716
E-mail: info@theclimateregistry.org
URL: http://www.theclimateregistry.org
Contact: **Denise Sheehan, Exec. Dir.**

1182 ■ National Pollution Prevention Roundtable (NPPR) (4599)
50 F St. NW, Ste.350
Washington, DC 20001
Ph: (202)299-9701
E-mail: **nppr@p2.org**
URL: http://www.p2.org
Contact: Jeffrey Burke, Exec. Dir.

1183 ■ Solar Cookers International (SCI) (5096)
1919 21st St., Ste.101
Sacramento, CA 95811
Ph: (916)455-4499
Fax: (916)455-4498
E-mail: info@solarcookers.org
URL: http://www.solarcookers.org
Contact: **Bev Blum, Pres.**

1184 ■ Water Environment Federation (WEF) (5101)
601 Wythe St.
Alexandria, VA 22314-1994
Ph: (703)684-2400
Free: (800)666-0206
Fax: (703)684-2492
E-mail: **jeger@wef.org**
URL: http://www.wef.org
Contact: **Jeff Eger, Exec. Dir./Sec.**

Poultry

1185 ■ National Chicken Council (NCC) (5070)
1015 15th St. NW, Ste.930
Washington, DC 20005-2622
Ph: (202)296-2622
Fax: (202)293-4005
E-mail: ncc@chickenusa.org
URL: http://www.nationalchickencouncil.com
Contact: **Michael J. Brown, Pres.**

Rabbits

1186 ■ American Belgian Hare Club (ABHC) (4613)
15330 Sharp Rd.
Rockton, IL 61072
Ph: **(815)629-2465**
E-mail: **rareharerabbits@aol.com**
URL: http://www.belgianhareclub.com
Contact: **Jeanne Walton, Pres.**

1187 ■ American Federation of New Zealand Rabbit Breeders (AFNZRB) (5135)
626 Alabama St.
Sulphur, LA 70663
Ph: **(337)533-9005**
E-mail: **suebord45@yahoo.com**
URL: http://www.newzealandrabbitclub.net
Contact: **Sue Borden, Pres.**

1188 ■ American Satin Rabbit Breeders' Association (ASRBA) (5100)
3500 S Wagner Rd.
Ann Arbor, MI 48103
Ph: **(734)668-6709**
E-mail: **paragonfarm@aol.com**
URL: http://www.asrba.org
Contact: **Sue Moessner, Pres.**

1189 ■ Havana Rabbit Breeders Association (HRBA) (5105)
N-9487 Walnut Rd.
Clintonville, WI 54929
Ph: **(715)823-5020**
E-mail: havanasecretary@yahoo.com
URL: http://www.havanarb.com
Contact: **Tanya Zimmerman, Sec.-Treas.**

1190 ■ National Jersey Wooly Rabbit Club (NJWRC)
309 S St. Paul
Sioux Falls, SD 57103
Ph: **(810)637-1537**
E-mail: **denise_geick@sio.midco.net**
URL: http://www.njwrc.net
Contact: Denise Geick, Pres.

1191 ■ North American Lionhead Rabbit Club (NALRC) (5117)
c/o Jennifer Hack, Sec.
4098 N Hwy. 67
Sedalia, CO 80135
Ph: **(765)346-7604**
E-mail: **jennifer@priderockrabbitry.net**
URL: http://www.lionhead.us
Contact: Arden Wetzel, Sec.

1192 ■ Rhinelander Rabbit Club of America (RRCA) (5088)
11237 Summit School Rd.
Huntingdon, PA 16652
Ph: **(814)667-2406**
E-mail: **wplanthaber@verizon.net**
URL: http://www.rhinelanderrabbits.com
Contact: **Wes Planthaber, Pres.**

Rain Forests

1193 ■ Rainforest Partnership
PO Box 49268
Austin, TX 78765
Ph: (512)420-0101
E-mail: info@rainforestpartnership.org
URL: http://www.rainforestpartnership.org
Contact: Niyanta Spelman, Exec. Dir.
Multinational. Description: Aims to protect tropical rainforests. Collaborates with communities in Latin America to develop sustainable economic alternatives to deforestation. Raises an awareness about the issues relevant to protecting the forest.

1194 ■ Tropical Forest and Climate Coalition (TFCC)
1616 P St. NW, Ste.403
Washington, DC 20036
Ph: **(202)552-1828**
E-mail: glenn@adpartners.org
URL: http://climateforest.org
Contact: Glenn Hurowitz, Dir.

Rangeland

1195 ■ Society for Range Management (SRM) (5166)
10030 W 27th Ave.
Wheat Ridge, CO 80215-6601
Ph: (303)986-3309
Fax: (303)986-3892
E-mail: **info@rangelands.org**
URL: http://www.rangelands.org
Contact: Jess Peterson, Exec. VP

Recycling

1196 ■ Cement Kiln Recycling Coalition (CKRC) (3967)
PO Box 7553
Arlington, VA 22207
Ph: **(703)869-4718**
URL: http://www.ckrc.org
Contact: Mike Benoit, Exec. Dir.

1197 ■ Clean the World
400A Pittman St.
Orlando, FL 32801
Ph: (407)574-8353
Fax: (732)847-5446

E-mail: info@cleantheworld.org
URL: http://www.cleantheworld.org
Contact: Shawn Seipler, Exec. Dir.
Founded: 2009. **Multinational. Description:** Aims to reduce waste by collecting and recycling soap and shampoo products. Distributes recycled soap products to impoverished countries and domestic homeless shelters suffering from high death rates due to acute respiratory infection and diarrheal disease.

1198 ■ Freecycle Network
PO Box 294
Tucson, AZ 85702
E-mail: info@freecycle.org
URL: http://www.freecycle.org
Contact: Deron Beal, Founder/Exec. Dir.
Founded: 2003. **Multinational. Description:** Promotes recycling and environmental sustainability. Advocates for the prevention of waste and saving of valuable resources.

Sheep

1199 ■ American Border Leicester Association (ABLA) (4762)
PO Box 500
Cuba, IL 61427
Ph: **(309)785-5058**
E-mail: **ads.banner@sybertech.net**
URL: http://www.ablasheep.org
Contact: **Greg Deakin, Pres.**

1200 ■ American Cheviot Sheep Society (ACSS) (4667)
10015 Flush Rd.
St. George, KS 66535
Ph: (785)494-2436
E-mail: ebertj@wamego.net
URL: http://www.cheviots.org
Contact: Jeff Ebert, Exec. Sec.

1201 ■ American Delaine and Merino Record Association (ADMRA) (4744)
7744 State Rte. 613
McComb, OH 45858
Ph: **(419)293-2871**
URL: http://www.admra.org
Contact: **Amy Schroeder, Sec.**

1202 ■ American Dorper Sheep Breeders' Society (ADSBS)
PO Box 259
Hallsville, MO 65255-0259
Ph: (573)696-2550
Fax: **(573)696-2030**
E-mail: adsbsoffice@centurytel.net
URL: http://www.dorperamerica.org
Contact: Ronda Sparks, Registrar

1203 ■ American Karakul Sheep Registry (AKSR) (4656)
11500 Hwy. 5
Boonville, MO 65233
Ph: (660)838-6340
Fax: (660)838-6322
E-mail: aksregistry@gmail.com
URL: http://www.karakulsheep.com
Contact: Rey Perera, Contact

1204 ■ American North Country Cheviot Sheep Association (ANCCSA) (5115)
1201 N 500 E
Rolling Prairie, IN 46371
Ph: **(574)323-3506**
URL: http://northcountrycheviot.com
Contact: **Brett Kessler, Pres.**

1205 ■ American Oxford Sheep Association (AOSA) (5154)
1960 E 2100 North Rd.
Stonington, IL 62567
Ph: (217)325-3515
Fax: **(217)325-3525**

E-mail: **oxfordassociation@ctitech.com**
URL: http://www.americanoxfords.org
Contact: Mary Blome, Sec.

1206 ■ American Rambouillet Sheep Breeders' Association (ARSBA) (4774)
15603 173rd Ave.
Milo, IA 50166
Ph: **(641)942-6402**
Fax: **(641)942-6502**
E-mail: **asregistry@yahoo.com**
URL: http://www.rambouilletsheep.org
Contact: Jane Gainer, Pres.

1207 ■ American Southdown Breeders' Association (ASBA) (5196)
100 Cornerstone Rd.
Fredonia, TX 76842
Ph: (325)429-6226
Fax: (325)429-6225
E-mail: gary@southdownsheep.org
URL: http://www.southdownsheep.org
Contact: **L.C. Scramlin, Pres.**

1208 ■ Barbados Blackbelly Sheep Association International (BBSAI)
1156 NE 50th Rd.
Lamar, MO 64759
Ph: **(417)398-2875**
E-mail: **president@blackbellysheep.org**
URL: http://www.blackbellysheep.org
Contact: **Mark Fleming, Pres.**

1209 ■ Natural Colored Wool Growers Association (NCWGA) (5172)
PO Box 406
New Palestine, IN 46163
Ph: **(317)681-4765**
E-mail: **john@merlau.com**
URL: http://www.ncwga.org
Contact: **John Merlau, Pres.**

1210 ■ North American Babydoll Southdown Sheep Association and Registry (NABSSAR)
PO Box 146
Wellsville, KS 66092
Ph: **(785)883-4811**
Fax: (785)883-4778
E-mail: spisak@embarqmail.com
URL: http://nabssar.org
Contact: Diane Spisak, Pres.

1211 ■ North American Shetland Sheepbreeders Association (NASSA)
NASSA Registry
15603 173rd Ave.
Milo, IA 50166
Ph: (641)942-6402
E-mail: membership@shetland-sheep.org
URL: http://www.shetland-sheep.org
Contact: **Mike Ludlum, Pres.**

1212 ■ North American Wensleydale Sheep Association (NAWSA)
4589 Fruitland Rd.
Loma Rica, CA 95901
Ph: **(530)745-5262**
E-mail: info@wensleydalesheep.org
URL: http://www.wensleydalesheep.org
Contact: Barbara Burrows, Pres.

1213 ■ United Suffolk Sheep Association (USSA) (5219)
PO Box 995
Ottumwa, IA 52501-0995
Ph: **(641)684-5291**
Fax: **(641)682-9449**
E-mail: **info@u-s-s-a.org**
URL: http://www.u-s-s-a.org
Contact: **Amanda Everts, Exec. Sec.**

Solar Energy

1214 ■ Global Possibilities
1955 Mandeville Canyon Rd.
Los Angeles, CA 90049
Ph: (310)656-1970
Fax: (310)656-1959
E-mail: casey@globalpossibilities.org
URL: http://www.globalpossibilities.org
Contact: Casey Coates Danson, Founder/Pres.
Founded: 1996. **Multinational. Description:** Promotes the use of solar and renewable energy to reduce dependency on fossil fuels and mitigate climate change through documentary films, consumer education and sustainable design curriculum development. Raises public awareness and understanding of the benefits of solar energy and sustainable design as it relates to humanly built environment and overall quality of life.

Sugar

1215 ■ American Society of Sugar Cane Technologists (ASSCT)
AgCenter
Sturgis Hall No. 128
Baton Rouge, LA 70803
Ph: (225)578-6930
Fax: (225)578-1403
E-mail: assct@assct.org
URL: http://www.assct.org
Contact: Freddie Martin PhD, Gen. Sec.-Treas.

Sustainable Agriculture

1216 ■ Community Agroecology Network (CAN)
PO Box 7653
Santa Cruz, CA 95061
Ph: (831)459-3619
E-mail: info@canunite.org
URL: http://www.canunite.org
Contact: Stephen Gliessman, Chm.
Founded: 2001. **Multinational. Description:** Aims to sustain rural livelihoods and environments by integrating research, education and trade innovations. Helps rural communities in Mexico and Central America to develop self-sufficiency and sustainable farming practices.

1217 ■ International Agro Alliance (IAA)
173 NW 89th St.
Miami, FL 33150
Free: (877)292-3921
Fax: (877)292-3921
E-mail: kone@interagroalliance.org
URL: http://www.interagroalliance.org
Contact: Kone Abdoulaye, Founder

1218 ■ Multinational Exchange for Sustainable Agriculture (MESA)
2362 Bancroft Way, No. 202
Berkeley, CA 94704
Ph: **(510)654-8858**
Free: **(888)834-7461**
Fax: (603)699-2459
E-mail: info@mesaprogram.org
URL: http://www.mesaprogram.org
Contact: Lauren Augusta, Exec. Dir.

Swine

1219 ■ American Guinea Hog Association (AGHA) (5196)
1820 P Ave.
Jefferson, IA 50129
Ph: **(515)370-1021**
E-mail: **kevinfall.agha@yahoo.com**
URL: http://www.americanguineahogassociation.org
Contact: **Kevin Fall, Pres.**

1220 ■ National Swine Registry (NSR) (4706)
2639 Yeager Rd.
West Lafayette, IN 47906
Ph: (765)463-3594
Fax: (765)497-2959
E-mail: **darrell@nationalswine.com**
URL: http://www.nationalswine.com
Contact: Darrell D. Anderson, CEO

Tobacco

1221 ■ Burley Stabilization Corporation (BSC) (4707)
1427 W Main St.
Greeneville, TN 37743
Ph: (865)525-9381
Fax: (865)525-8383
E-mail: connie@burleystabilization.com
URL: http://www.burleystabilization.com
Contact: Mr. George Marks, Pres.

Trees and Shrubs

1222 ■ American Society of Consulting Arborists (ASCA) (5221)
9707 Key W Ave., Ste.100
Rockville, MD 20850
Ph: (301)947-0483
Fax: (301)990-9771
E-mail: asca@mgmtsol.com
URL: http://www.asca-consultants.org
Contact: **Alan Jones, Pres.**

Waste

1223 ■ National Onsite Wastewater Recycling Association (NOWRA) (4821)
601 Wythe St.
Alexandria, VA 22314
Free: (800)966-2942
Fax: (703)535-5363
E-mail: info@nowra.org
URL: http://www.nowra.org
Contact: **Dick Otis, Pres.**

Water

1224 ■ Alliance for Water Efficiency (AWE)
300 W Adams St., Ste.601
Chicago, IL 60606
Ph: (773)360-5100
Free: (866)730-A4WE
Fax: (773)345-3636
E-mail: jeffrey@a4we.org
URL: http://www.a4we.org
Contact: Mary Ann Dickinson, Pres./CEO

1225 ■ National Utility Contractors Association [C]lean Water Council (CWC) (5251)
3925 Chain Bridge Rd., Ste.301
Fairfax, VA 22030
Ph: (703)358-9300
Fax: (703)358-9307
E-mail: bill@nuca.com
URL: http://www.nuca.com
Contact: Bill Hillman, CEO

Water Resources

1226 ■ Irrigation Water Management Society (IWMS)
2008 Sycamore Dr.
Eagle Mountain, UT 84005
Ph: **(509)981-6441**
E-mail: info@iwms.org
URL: http://www.iwms.org
Contact: Kurt Thompson, Contact

1227 ■ Puerto Rico Water and Environment Association (PRW&EA)
PO Box 13702
San Juan, PR 00908-3702
Ph: **(787)478-3716**
E-mail: membresias@prwea.org
URL: http://www.prwea.org
Contact: **Jaime Lopez, Pres.**

1228 ■ Save the Waves Coalition
PO Box 183
Davenport, CA 95017
Ph: (831)426-6169
Fax: (831)460-1256
E-mail: info@savethewaves.org
URL: http://www.savethewaves.org
Contact: **Greg Benoit, Pres.**

Wildlife Conservation

1229 ■ African Wild Dog Conservancy
208 N California Ave.
Silver City, NM 88061
E-mail: **lycaonpictus@awdconservancy.org**
URL: http://awdconservancy.org
Contact: Dr. Robert Robbins, Co-Founder

1230 ■ Amara Conservation
1531 Packard St., No. 12
Ann Arbor, MI 48104
Ph: (734)761-5357
URL: http://amaraconservation.org
Contact: Lori Bergemann, Exec. Dir.
Founded: 2001. **Multinational. Description:** Promotes the preservation of African wildlife. Provides education and community assistance to rural communities. Organizes and facilitates conservation-related projects.

1231 ■ Ape Action Africa
205 S Dixie Dr., No. 1014
Haines City, FL 33844
E-mail: info@apeactionafrica.org
URL: http://www.apeactionafrica.org
Contact: Rachel Hogan, Dir.
Multinational. Description: Works on the front-line of great ape protection. Addresses issues related to immediate threats faced by gorillas and chimps in Africa. Seeks to develop long-term solutions in ensuring the survival of apes in the wild.

1232 ■ Ape Conservation Effort (ACE)
800 Cherokee Ave. SE
Atlanta, GA 30315
Ph: (404)624-5963
E-mail: info@apeconservationeffort.org
URL: http://www.apeconservationeffort.org
Contact: Lynn Yakubinis, Pres.
Description: Aims to promote and support the conservation of apes. Conducts fundraising activities to save apes from extinction and conserve their native habitats.

1233 ■ Big Wildlife
PO Box 344
Williams, OR 97544
Ph: (541)846-1352
E-mail: **info@bigwildlife.org**
URL: http://www.bigwildlife.org
Contact: Brian Vincent, Communications Dir.

1234 ■ The Billfish Foundation (TBF) (4840)
5100 N Fed. Hwy., Ste.200
Fort Lauderdale, FL 33308
Ph: (954)938-0150
Free: (800)438-8247
Fax: (954)938-5311
E-mail: info@billfish.org
URL: http://www.billfish.org
Contact: **Mark O'Brien, Chm.**

1235 ■ Desert Tortoise Council (DTC) (5127)
PO Box 1568
Ridgecrest, CA 93556
E-mail: mojotort@yahoo.com
URL: http://www.deserttortoise.org
Contact: **Tracy Bailey, Corresponding Sec.**

1236 ■ EcoHealth Alliance (4937)
460 W 34th St., 17th Fl.
New York, NY 10001
Ph: (212)380-4460
Fax: (212)380-4465
E-mail: **homeoffice@ecohealthalliance.org**
URL: http://www.wildlifetrust.org
Contact: Peter Daszak PhD, Pres.
Status Note: Formerly Wildlife Trust.

1237 ■ Endangered Wolf Center (5368)
PO Box 760
Eureka, MO 63025
Ph: (636)938-5900
Fax: (636)938-6490
E-mail: **info@endangeredwolfcenter.org**
URL: http://www.endangeredwolfcenter.org
Contact: **Mac Sebaid, Exec. Dir.**
Status Note: Formerly Wild Canid Survival and Research Center.

1238 ■ Global Wildlife Conservation (GWC)
PO Box 129
Austin, TX 78767-0129
Ph: **(512)827-9418**
E-mail: info@globalwildlife.org
URL: http://globalwildlife.org
Contact: Wes Sechrest PhD, Contact

1239 ■ Human-Wildlife Conflict Collaboration (HWCC)
5410 Grosvenor Ln., Ste.200
Bethesda, MD 20814-2144
Ph: (202)986-0067
Fax: (301)530-2471
E-mail: francine@humanwildlifeconflict.org
URL: http://www.humanwildlifeconflict.org
Contact: Francine Madden, Exec. Dir.
Founded: 2006. **Multinational. Description:** Aims to improve the prevention and mitigation of human-wildlife conflict. Facilitates collaborative learning, innovation, scientific analysis and development of best practices. Addresses the practical and urgent needs in human-wildlife conflict, on both the local and global scale, through a global partnership.

1240 ■ Iemanya Oceanica
23293 Ventura Blvd.
Woodland Hills, CA 91364
Ph: **(818)224-4250**
Fax: **(818)224-4250**
E-mail: info@iemanya.org
URL: http://www.iemanya.org
Contact: Laleh Mohajerani, Pres./Exec. Dir.

1241 ■ International Association for Bear Research and Management (IBA) (5325)
Univ. of Tennessee
USGS-SAFL
274 Ellington Hall
Knoxville, TN 37996
Ph: **(865)974-0200**
Fax: (865)974-3555
URL: http://www.bearbiology.com
Contact: **Frank van Manen, Pres.**

1242 ■ International Bird Rescue Research Center (IBRRC) (5326)
San Francisco Oiled Wildlife Care and Educ. Center
4369 Cordelia Rd.
Fairfield, CA 94534
Ph: (707)207-0380
Fax: (707)207-0395
E-mail: info@ibrrc.org
URL: http://www.ibrrc.org
Contact: **Paul Kelway, Exec. Dir.**

1243 ■ International Snow Leopard Trust (ISLT) (4785)
4649 Sunnyside Ave. N, Ste.325
Seattle, WA 98103
Ph: (206)632-2421
Fax: (206)632-3967
E-mail: info@snowleopard.org
URL: http://www.snowleopard.org
Contact: **Carol Hosford, Pres.**

1244 ■ Jane Goodall Institute for Wildlife Research, Education, and Conservation (JGI) (4875)
4245 N Fairfax Dr., Ste.600
Arlington, VA 22203
Ph: (703)682-9220
Free: (800)592-5263
Fax: (703)682-9312
E-mail: info@janegoodall.org
URL: http://www.janegoodall.org
Contact: **Maureen P. Smith, Pres./CEO**

1245 ■ Keystone Conservation (5305)
PO Box 6733
Bozeman, MT 59771
Ph: (406)587-3389
Fax: (406)587-3178
E-mail: **info@keystoneconservation.us**
URL: http://www.keystoneconservation.us
Contact: **Lisa Upson, Exec. Dir.**

1246 ■ National Wild Turkey Federation (NWTF) (5343)
PO Box 530
Edgefield, SC 29824-0530
Ph: (803)637-3106
Free: (800)843-6983
E-mail: **info@nwtf.net**
URL: http://www.nwtf.org
Contact: George Thornton, CEO

1247 ■ National Wildlife Rehabilitators Association (NWRA) (5317)
2625 Clearwater Rd., Ste.110
St. Cloud, MN 56301
Ph: (320)230-9920
Fax: (320)230-3077
E-mail: nwra@nwrawildlife.org
URL: http://www.nwrawildlife.org
Contact: **Sandra Woltman, Pres.**

1248 ■ Orangutan Conservancy (5331)
PO Box 513
Los Angeles, CA 90036
E-mail: **info@orangutan.com**
URL: http://www.orangutan.com
Contact: **Norm Rosen, Pres.**

1249 ■ Organization for Bat Conservation (OBC)
PO Box 801
Bloomfield Hills, MI 48303
Ph: **(248)645-3232**
Free: (800)276-7074
Fax: **(248)645-2142**
E-mail: obcbats@aol.com
URL: http://www.batconservation.org
Contact: Kim Williams, Exec. Dir.

1250 ■ Pacific Seabird Group (PSG) (5335)
c/o Ron LeValley, Treas.
PO Box 324
Little River, CA 95456
Ph: (707)442-4302
Fax: (707)442-4303
E-mail: info@pacificseabirdgroup.org
URL: http://www.pacificseabirdgroup.org
Contact: **Pat Jodice, Chm.**

1251 ■ Panthera
8 W 40th St., 18th Fl.
New York, NY 10018
Ph: (646)786-0400
Fax: (646)786-0401
E-mail: info@panthera.org
URL: http://www.panthera.org/mission
Contact: Thomas S. Kaplan PhD, Founder/Chm.
Founded: 2006. **Description:** Ensures the future of wild cats through scientific leadership and global conservation action. Implements effective conservation strategies for the world's largest and most endangered cats such as tigers, lions, jaguars and snow leopards.

1252 ■ Quail Unlimited (QU) (4823)
PO Box 70518
Albany, GA 31708
Ph: (803)637-5731
Fax: (803)637-0037
E-mail: **bbowles@qu.org**
URL: http://www.qu.org
Contact: Bill Bowles, Pres.

1253 ■ Sea Turtle Conservancy (CCC) (5221)
4424 NW 13th St., Ste.B-11
Gainesville, FL 32609
Ph: (352)373-6441
Free: (800)678-7853
Fax: (352)375-2449
E-mail: **stc@conserveturtles.org**
URL: http://www.cccturtle.org
Contact: Mr. David Godfrey, Exec. Dir.

1254 ■ Shark Alliance
901 E St. NW, 10th Fl.
Washington, DC 20004
Ph: **(202)552-2000**
E-mail: info@sharkalliance.org
URL: http://www.sharkalliance.org
Contact: Dan Klotz, Communications Off.

1255 ■ Species Alliance
5200 San Pablo Ave.
Emeryville, CA 94608
Ph: **(510)594-8355**
E-mail: info@speciesalliance.org
URL: http://www.speciesalliance.org
Contact: **Monte Thompson, Exec. Dir.**

1256 ■ Turkey Vulture Society (5205)
2327 Polksville Rd.
Oakland, KY 42159
E-mail: vulturesociety@gmail.com
URL: http://vulturesociety.homestead.com
Contact: Bill Lynch, Pres.

1257 ■ Wild Animals Worldwide (WAW)
1100 Larkspur Landing Cir., Ste.340
Larkspur, CA 94939
Free: (866)439-0989
E-mail: info@savewildanimals.org
URL: http://www.savewildanimals.org
Contact: Carri Harte, Contact
Multinational. Description: Strives to address the protection of endangered animals and their habitats. Provides a sanctuary for rescued and threatened species.

1258 ■ Wild Felid Research and Management Association (WFA)
PO Box 3335
Montrose, CO 81402
Ph: (970)252-1928
E-mail: lsweanor@gmail.com
URL: http://www.wildfelid.com
Contact: Linda Sweanor, Interim Pres.
Membership Dues: standard, $35 (annual) ● student, $20 (annual) ● institution, $75 (annual). **Multinational. Description:** Represents researchers, wildlife managers, educators and others dedicated to effective conservation of wild cats. Promotes the sound management, conservation, and restoration of wild felids in the Western Hemisphere through science-based management and education. **Awards:** Wild Felid Legacy Scholarship. **Frequency:** annual. **Type:** scholarship. **Recipient:** to a graduate-level university student conducting research on wild felids.

1259 ■ Wild Gift
PO Box 3064
Sun Valley, ID 83353
Ph: (208)726-7475
Free: **(855)687-9453**
E-mail: info@wildgift.org
URL: http://www.wildgift.org
Contact: Bob Jonas, Founder

1260 ■ Wonderful World of Wildlife (WWOW)
88 E Main St., No. 134
Mendham, NJ 07945
Ph: (908)380-8810
Free: (800)863-5941
E-mail: **info@wonderfulworldofwildlife.org**
URL: http://www.wonderfulworldofwildlife.org
Contact: Charles Collins, Dir.

1261 ■ World Bird Sanctuary (WBS) (4938)
125 Bald Eagle Ridge Rd.
Valley Park, MO 63088
Ph: (636)861-3225
Fax: (636)861-3240
E-mail: info@worldbirdsanctuary.org
URL: http://www.worldbirdsanctuary.org
Contact: **Walter Crawford, Exec. Dir.**

1262 ■ World Nature Coalition (WNC)
601 Pennsylvania Ave. NW, South Bldg., Ste.900
Washington, DC 20004
Ph: **(202)379-2974**
Fax: **(202)618-6260**
E-mail: **info@naturecoalition.org**
URL: http://www.naturecoalition.org
Contact: Dan Stockdale, Pres.
Status Note: Formerly Conservation Alliance for Tigers.

Agriculture

1263 ■ National Association of Agriculture Employees (NAAE)
9080 Torrey Rd.
Willis, MI 48191
Ph: (734)942-9005
Fax: **(734)942-7691**
E-mail: mikeran@aloha.net
URL: http://www.aginspectors.org
Contact: Sarah Rehberg, Natl. Pres.

1264 ■ National Association of County Agricultural Agents (NACAA) (5414)
6584 W Duroc Rd.
Maroa, IL 61756
Ph: (217)794-3700 **(231)533-8818**
Fax: (217)794-5901
E-mail: exec-dir@nacaa.com
URL: http://www.nacaa.com
Contact: Stan Moore, Pres.

1265 ■ National Association of State Departments of Agriculture (NASDA) (5455)
1156 15th St. NW, Ste.1020
Washington, DC 20005
Ph: (202)296-9680
Fax: (202)296-9686
E-mail: nasda@nasda.org
URL: http://www.nasda.org
Contact: **Leonard Blackham, Pres.**

1266 ■ National Plant Board (NPB) (5353)
c/o Aurelio Posadas, Exec. Sec.
PO Box 847
Elk Grove, CA 95759
Ph: (916)709-3484 **(609)292-5441**
Fax: (916)689-2385
E-mail: aureliop@elkgrove.net
URL: http://www.nationalplantboard.org
Contact: Carl Schulze, Pres.

Arbitration and Mediation

1267 ■ Association for Conflict Resolution (ACR) (5426)
12100 Sunset Hills Rd., Ste.130
Reston, VA 20190
Ph: **(703)234-4141**
Fax: **(703)435-4390**
E-mail: membership@acrnet.org
URL: http://www.acrnet.org
Contact: **Lou Gieszl, Pres.**

Architecture

1268 ■ National Council of Architectural Registration Boards (NCARB) (5378)
1801 K St. NW, Ste.700-K
Washington, DC 20006-1310
Ph: (202)783-6500

Fax: (202)783-0290
E-mail: customerservice@ncarb.org
URL: http://www.ncarb.org
Contact: **Kenneth J. Naylor AIA, Pres./Chm.**

Armed Forces

1269 ■ Military Intelligence Corps Association (MICA)
PO Box 13020
Fort Huachuca, AZ 85670-3020
Ph: **(520)227-3894**
E-mail: **execdir@micorps.org**
URL: http://www.micorps.org
Contact: Lisa Camberos, Exec. Dir.

Attorneys

1270 ■ Croatian American Bar Association (CABA) (5466)
6 Papette Cir.
Ladera Ranch, CA 92694
Ph: (949)274-5360
E-mail: marko@croatianamericanbar.com
URL: http://www.croatianamericanbar.com
Contact: Marko Zoretic, Pres.

1271 ■ Fair Elections Legal Network (FELN)
1825 K St. NW, Ste.450
Washington, DC 20006
Ph: (202)331-0114
Fax: (202)331-1663
E-mail: **info@fairelectionsnetwork.com**
URL: http://www.fairelectionsnetwork.com
Contact: Robert M. Brandon, Pres./Co-Founder

1272 ■ Hispanic National Bar Association (HNBA) (5473)
1900 L St. NW, Ste.700
Washington, DC 20036
Ph: (202)223-4777
Fax: (202)223-2324
E-mail: **dsen29@gmail.com**
URL: http://www.hnba.com
Contact: **Diana Sen, Pres.**

1273 ■ International Academy of Trial Lawyers (IATL) (5523)
5841 Cedar Lake Rd., Ste.204
Minneapolis, MN 55416-5657
Ph: (952)546-2364
Free: (866)823-2443
Fax: (952)545-6073
E-mail: iatl@llmsi.com
URL: http://www.iatl.net
Contact: **Roberta D. Pichini, Pres.**

1274 ■ National Bar Association (NBA) (5492)
1225 11th St. NW
Washington, DC 20001
Ph: (202)842-3900
Fax: (202)289-6170
E-mail: **dsheltonjd@aol.com**
URL: http://www.nationalbar.org
Contact: **Demetrius D. Shelton, Pres.**

1275 ■ National Lawyers Guild (NLG) (731)
132 Nassau St., Rm. 922
New York, NY 10038
Ph: (212)679-5100
Fax: (212)679-2811
E-mail: **director@nlg.org**
URL: http://www.nlg.org
Contact: Heidi Boghosian, Exec. Dir.

1276 ■ Nigerian Lawyers Association (NLA)
321 Broadway, 3rd Fl.
New York, NY 10007
Ph: (212)566-9926
Fax: (212)571-4309
URL: http://www.nigerianlawyers.org
Contact: **Abayomi O. Ajaiyeoba, Pres.**

1277 ■ Serbian Bar Association of America (SBAA)
20 S Clark, Ste.700
Chicago, IL 60603
Ph: **(312)782-8500**
E-mail: apavich@monicopavich.com
URL: http://www.serbbar.org
Contact: Anastasia Pavich, Pres.

Civil Service

1278 ■ National Organization of Blacks in Government (BIG) (4987)
3005 Georgia Ave. NW
Washington, DC 20001-3807
Ph: (202)667-3280
Fax: (202)667-3705
E-mail: bignationa@aol.com
URL: http://www.bignet.org
Contact: **David A. Groves, Chm.**

1279 ■ Scientists and Engineers for America (SEA)
1850 M St. NW, Ste.1100
Washington, DC 20036
Ph: (202)223-6444
E-mail: contact@sefora.org
URL: http://www.sefora.org
Contact: **Tom Price, Exec. Dir.**

Commercial Law

1280 ■ Commercial Law League of America (CLLA) (5603)
205 N Michigan, Ste.2212
Chicago, IL 60601

Ph: **(312)240-1400**
Free: **(800)978-2552**
Fax: **(312)240-1408**
E-mail: info@clla.org
URL: http://www.clla.org
Contact: **James Hays, Pres.**

Communications

1281 ■ Scribes - The American Society of Legal Writers (736)
PO Box 13038
Lansing, MI 48901
Ph: (517)371-5140
Fax: (517)334-5781
E-mail: **executive-director@scribes.org**
URL: http://www.scribes.org
Contact: Prof. Norman E. Plate, Exec. Dir.

Consumers

1282 ■ National Association of Consumer Credit Administrators (NACCA) (5633)
PO Box 20871
Columbus, OH 43220-0871
Ph: (614)326-1165
Fax: (614)326-1162
E-mail: nacca2007@sbcglobal.net
URL: http://www.naccaonline.org
Contact: **Mark Tarpey, Pres.**

Corporate Law

1283 ■ Association of Corporate Counsel (ACC) (5637)
1025 Connecticut Ave. NW, Ste.200
Washington, DC 20036-5425
Ph: (202)293-4103
Fax: (202)293-4701
E-mail: acc.chair@acc.com
URL: http://www.acc.com
Contact: **J. Alberto Gonzalez Pita, Chm.**

County Government

1284 ■ National Association of Black County Officials (NABCO) (5640)
1090 Vermont Ave. NW, Ste.1290
Washington, DC 20005
Ph: (202)350-6696
Fax: (202)350-6699
E-mail: **nobco@nobcoinc.org**
URL: http://www.blackcountyofficials.com
Contact: **Arlanda J. Williams, Pres.**

Court Employees

1285 ■ United States Court Reporters Association (USCRA) (5654)
8430 Gross Point Rd., Ste.115
Skokie, IL 60077
Ph: **(847)470-9500**
Free: (800)628-2730
Fax: **(847)470-9505**
E-mail: info.uscra@gmail.com
URL: http://www.uscra.org
Contact: **Janet Davis, Pres.**

Crime

1286 ■ National Alliance of Gang Investigators Associations (NAGIA)
PO Box 782
Elkhorn, NE 68022
Ph: (402)510-8581

E-mail: **deathdet@cox.net**
URL: http://www.nagia.org
Contact: Bruce Ferrell, Pres.

Criminal Justice

1287 ■ International Association of Law Enforcement Planners (IALEP) (5613)
PO Box 11437
Torrance, CA 90510-1437
Ph: (310)225-5148 **(703)280-0737**
E-mail: **office@ialep.org**
URL: http://www.ialep.org
Contact: **Joseph Bui, Pres.**

Drug Policy

1288 ■ National Alliance for Model State Drug Laws (NAMSDL)
215 Lincoln Ave., Ste.201
Santa Fe, NM 87501
Ph: (703)836-6100
Fax: **(505)820-1750**
E-mail: info@natlalliance.org
URL: http://www.namsdl.org
Contact: Sherry Green, CEO

Economics

1289 ■ Society of Government Economists (SGE) (5565)
PO Box 77082
Washington, DC 20013
Ph: **(202)643-1743**
E-mail: **farhad.niami@sge-econ.org**
URL: http://www.sge-econ.org
Contact: **Farhad Niami, Pres.**

Emergency Aid

1290 ■ National Emergency Management Association (NEMA) (5595)
PO Box 11910
Lexington, KY 40578
Ph: (859)244-8000
Fax: (859)244-8239
E-mail: nemaadmin@csg.org
URL: http://www.nemaweb.org
Contact: **Jim Mullen, Pres.**

Employment

1291 ■ International Association of Workforce Professionals (IAWP) (5074)
1801 Louisville Rd.
Frankfort, KY 40601
Ph: (502)223-4459
Free: (888)898-9960
Fax: (502)223-4127
E-mail: iawp@iawponline.org
URL: http://www.iawponline.org
Contact: **Rich Vincent, Pres.**

Energy

1292 ■ Large Public Power Council (LPPC)
300 N Washington St., Ste.405
Alexandria, VA 22314
Ph: (703)740-1750
E-mail: lppc@lppc.org
URL: http://www.lppc.org
Contact: **Jorge Carrasco, Chm.**

Environmental Law

1293 ■ American College of Environmental Lawyers (ACOEL)
1300 SW 5th Ave., Ste.2300
Portland, OR 97201-5630
Ph: (207)774-1200
Fax: (207)774-1127
E-mail: jthaler@bernsteinshur.com
URL: http://www.acoel.org
Contact: Jeffrey A. Thaler, Pres.
Membership Dues: lawyer, $500 (annual). **Description:** Represents the interests of lawyers who practice in the field of environmental law. Maintains and improves the ethical practice of environmental law, the administration of justice, and the development of environmental law at both the state and federal level.

Family Law

1294 ■ American Academy of Matrimonial Lawyers (AAML) (5712)
150 N Michigan Ave., Ste.1420
Chicago, IL 60601
Ph: (312)263-6477
Fax: (312)263-7682
E-mail: office@aaml.org
URL: http://www.aaml.org
Contact: **Linda Lea M. Viken, Pres.**

1295 ■ Association of Family and Conciliation Courts (AFCC) (5713)
6525 Grand Teton Plz.
Madison, WI 53719
Ph: (608)664-3750
Fax: (608)664-3751
E-mail: afcc@afccnet.org
URL: http://www.afccnet.org
Contact: **Robert M. Smith, Pres.**

Federal Government

1296 ■ National Active and Retired Federal Employees Association (NARFE) (5724)
606 N Washington St.
Alexandria, VA 22314
Ph: (703)838-7760
Free: (800)627-3394
Fax: (703)838-7785
E-mail: hq@narfe.org
URL: http://www.narfe.org
Contact: **Joseph A. Beaudoin, Pres.**

Fire Fighting

1297 ■ International Association of Arson Investigators (IAAI) (5731)
2111 Baldwin Ave., Ste.203
Crofton, MD 21114
Ph: (410)451-3473
Free: **(800)468-4224**
Fax: (410)451-9049
E-mail: iaai@firearson.com
URL: http://www.firearson.com
Contact: **Gloria Guernsey Ryan, Dir.**

1298 ■ National Association of Hispanic Firefighters (NAHF) (5736)
1220 L St. NW, Ste.100-199
Washington, DC 20005
Free: **(877)342-6243**
Fax: **(855)759-6243**
E-mail: **d.valenzuela@nahf.org**
URL: http://www.nahf.org
Contact: **Daniel Valenzuela, Pres.**

Fishing

1299 ■ Atlantic States Marine Fisheries Commission (ASMFC) (5231)
1050 N Highlnd St., Ste.200 A-N
Arlington, VA 22201
Ph: (703)842-0740
Fax: (703)842-0741
E-mail: comments@asmfc.org
URL: http://www.asmfc.org
Contact: John V. O'Shea, Exec. Dir.

1300 ■ Western Association of Fish and Wildlife Agencies (WAFWA) (5751)
522 Notre Dame Ct.
Cheyenne, WY 82009
Ph: (307)638-1470
Fax: (307)638-1470
E-mail: larry.kruckenberg@wgf.state.wy.us
URL: http://www.wafwa.org
Contact: Larry L. Kruckenberg, Sec.

Forensic Sciences

1301 ■ American Society of Questioned Document Examiners (ASQDE) (5770)
PO Box 18298
Long Beach, CA 90807
Ph: (562)901-3376
Fax: (562)901-3378
E-mail: webeditor@asqde.org
URL: http://www.asqde.org
Contact: Linton A. Mohammed, Pres.

1302 ■ Society of Forensic Toxicologists (SOFT) (5782)
One MacDonald Center
1 N MacDonald St., Ste.15
Mesa, AZ 85201
Ph: (480)839-9106
Free: (888)866-7638
Fax: (480)839-9106
E-mail: office@soft-tox.org
URL: http://www.soft-tox.org
Contact: Sarah Kerrigan PhD, Pres.

Fundraising

1303 ■ National Association of State Charity Officials (NASCO) (5557)
815 Olive St.
St. Louis, MO 63101
E-mail: bob.carlson@ago.mo.gov
URL: http://www.nasconet.org
Contact: Bob Carlson, Pres.

Government

1304 ■ Worldwide Assurance for Employees of Public Agencies (WAEPA) (5792)
433 Park Ave.
Falls Church, VA 22046
Ph: (703)790-8010 (703)790-8011
Free: (800)368-3484
Fax: (703)790-4606
E-mail: info@waepa.org
URL: http://www.waepa.org
Contact: Debra Filippi, Pres.

Information Management

1305 ■ Association for Federal Information Resources Management (AFFIRM) (5825)
400 N Washington St., Ste.300
Alexandria, VA 22314
Ph: (703)778-4646
Fax: (703)683-5480

E-mail: info@affirm.org
URL: http://www.affirm.org
Contact: Peter Tseronis, Pres.

Insurance

1306 ■ Association of Defense Trial Attorneys (ADTA) (5836)
4135 Topsail Trail
New Port Richey, FL 34652
Ph: (727)859-0350
E-mail: gwalker@handarendall.com
URL: http://www.adtalaw.com
Contact: Mr. George M. Walker, Pres.

1307 ■ Association of Governmental Risk Pools (AGRiP)
PO Box J
Prague, OK 74864-1045
Ph: (405)567-2611
Fax: (405)567-3307
E-mail: info@agrip.org
URL: http://www.agrip.org
Contact: Johhnie Miller, CEO

1308 ■ Association of Life Insurance Counsel (ALIC) (5837)
3815 River Crossing Pkwy., Ste.100
Indianapolis, IN 46240
Ph: (317)566-2154
Fax: (317)566-2155
E-mail: pcarey@alic.cc
URL: http://alic.cc
Contact: Dennis Schoff, Pres.

1309 ■ Federation of Defense and Corporate Counsel (FDCC) (5838)
11812 N 56th St.
Tampa, FL 33617
Ph: (813)983-0022
Fax: (813)988-5837
E-mail: mstreeper@thefederation.org
URL: http://www.thefederation.org
Contact: F. Thomas Cordell, Pres.

1310 ■ National Association of Insurance Commissioners (NAIC) (5841)
2301 McGee St., Ste.800
Kansas City, MO 64108-2662
Ph: (816)842-3600
Fax: (816)783-8175
E-mail: news@naic.org
URL: http://www.naic.org
Contact: Susan E. Voss, Pres.

1311 ■ Public Agency Risk Managers Association (PARMA) (5844)
PO Box 6810
San Jose, CA 95150
Ph: (530)823-4957
Free: (888)412-5913
Fax: (530)823-4989
E-mail: brenda.reisinger@parma.com
URL: http://www.parma.com
Contact: David Pinnecker, Pres.

Intellectual Property

1312 ■ American Intellectual Property Law Association (AIPLA) (5846)
241 18th St. S, Ste.700
Arlington, VA 22202
Ph: (703)415-0780
Fax: (703)415-0786
E-mail: aipla@aipla.org
URL: http://www.aipla.org
Contact: David W. Hill, Pres.

1313 ■ Copyright Alliance
1224 M St. NW, Ste.301
Washington, DC 20005
Ph: (202)540-2243

E-mail: info@copyrightalliance.org
URL: http://www.copyrightalliance.org
Contact: Sandra Aistars, Exec. Dir.

1314 ■ Los Angeles Copyright Society (LACS) (5866)
c/o Michael Perlstein, Sec.
1875 Century Park E, Ste.1450
Los Angeles, CA 90067
E-mail: mperlstein@fpllaw.com
URL: http://www.copr.org
Contact: Larry Steinberg, Pres.

Investigation

1315 ■ Association of Certified Background Investigators (ACBI)
PO Box 80413
Staten Island, NY 10308
E-mail: president@acbi.net
URL: http://www.acbi.net
Contact: Robert A. Kuropkat, Pres.

1316 ■ National Association of Legal Investigators (NALI) (5897)
235 N Pine St.
Lansing, MI 48933
Ph: (517)702-9835
Free: (866)520-6254
Fax: (517)372-1501
E-mail: pjaeb@heartlandinfo.com
URL: http://www.nalionline.org
Contact: Paul Jaeb, Natl. Dir.

Judiciary

1317 ■ American Judges Association (AJA) (5905)
300 Newport Ave.
Williamsburg, VA 23185-4147
Ph: (757)259-1841
Fax: (757)259-1520
E-mail: aja@ncsc.dni.us
URL: http://aja.ncsc.dni.us
Contact: Mary A. Celeste, Pres.

1318 ■ American Judicature Society (AJS) (5906)
Drake Univ.
The Opperman Ctr.
2700 Univ. Ave.
Des Moines, IA 50311
Ph: (515)271-2281
Free: (800)626-4089
Fax: (515)279-3090
E-mail: sandersen@ajs.org
URL: http://www.ajs.org
Contact: William D. Johnston, Pres.

1319 ■ National Council of Juvenile and Family Court Judges (NCJFCJ) (5926)
PO Box 8970
Reno, NV 89507
Ph: (775)784-6012 (775)784-1548
Fax: (775)784-6628
E-mail: staff@ncjfcj.org
URL: http://www.ncjfcj.org
Contact: Mari Kay Bickett JD, Exec. Dir.

Labor

1320 ■ National Association of Governmental Labor Officials (NAGLO) (5929)
PO Box 29609
Atlanta, GA 30359
Ph: (404)679-1795
Fax: (678)222-7733
E-mail: jeannine.konieczny@dol.state.ga.us
URL: http://www.naglo.org
Contact: Lori Torres, Pres.

Law

1321 ■ Advocates International
9691 Main St., Ste.D
Fairfax, VA 22031-3754
Ph: (703)894-1084
Fax: (703)894-1074
E-mail: info@advocatesinternational.org
URL: http://www.advocatesinternational.org
Contact: **Brent McBurney, Pres./CEO**

1322 ■ American Veterinary Medical Law Association (AVMLA)
1666 K St. NW, Ste.260
Washington, DC 20006
Ph: **(202)449-3818**
Fax: **(202)449-8560**
E-mail: **admin@avmla.org**
URL: http://www.avmla.org
Contact: **Thomas Chandler, Pres.**

1323 ■ Foundation of the Federal Bar Association (FFBA) (5900)
1220 N Fillmore St., Ste.444
Arlington, VA 22201
Ph: (571)481-9100
Fax: (571)481-9090
E-mail: **fba@fedbar.org**
URL: http://www.fedbar.org/foundation.html
Contact: Jack D. Lockridge, Exec. Dir.

1324 ■ Inter-American Bar Association (IABA) (5827)
1211 Connecticut Ave. NW, Ste.202
Washington, DC 20036
Ph: (202)466-5944
Fax: (202)466-5946
E-mail: iaba@iaba.org
URL: http://www.iaba.org
Contact: **Beatriz Roxana Martorello, Pres.**

1325 ■ National Association of Bar Executives (NABE) (788)
321 N Clark St.
Chicago, IL 60654
Ph: **(312)988-6008**
Fax: (312)988-5492
E-mail: **haley.swilling@americanbar.org**
URL: **http://nabenet.org**
Contact: **Carolyn Witt, Pres.**

1326 ■ National Latino Officers Association (NLOA)
PO Box 02-0120
Brooklyn, NY 11201
Free: (866)579-5809
Fax: (646)772-3728
E-mail: **chairnloa@aol.com**
URL: http://nloaus.org/nl
Contact: Anthony Miranda, Exec. Chm.

1327 ■ National Organization of Bar Counsel (NOBC) (5917)
110 E Main St.
Madison, WI 53703
Ph: **(608)267-8915**
Fax: **(608)267-1959**
E-mail: **bill.weigel@wicourts.gov**
URL: http://www.nobc.org
Contact: **Bill Weigel, Pres.**

Law Enforcement

1328 ■ Association for Explosive Detection K-9s, International (AEDK9)
PO Box 176
Aquilla, TX 76622
Ph: (386)788-4083 (254)722-9310
E-mail: info@explk9.org
URL: http://www.explk9.org
Contact: **Hank Nolin, Pres.**

1329 ■ Commission on Accreditation for Law Enforcement Agencies (CALEA) (5326)
13575 Heathcote Blvd., Ste.320
Gainesville, VA 20155
Ph: (703)352-4225
Free: (800)368-3757
Fax: **(703)890-3126**
E-mail: calea@calea.org
URL: http://www.calea.org
Contact: Sylvester Daughtry Jr., Exec. Dir.

1330 ■ Law Enforcement Alliance of America (LEAA) (6005)
7700 Leesburg Pike, Ste.421
Falls Church, VA 22043
Ph: (703)847-2677
Free: (800)766-8578
Fax: (703)556-6485
E-mail: membership@leaa.org
URL: http://www.leaa.org
Contact: James J. Fotis, Dir./Exec. Dir.

1331 ■ Law Enforcement Thermographers' Association (LETA) (5759)
PO Box 6485
Edmond, OK 73083-6485
Ph: (405)330-6988 **(608)266-7702**
E-mail: wallef@doj.state.wi.us
URL: http://www.leta.org
Contact: Edward F. Wall, Pres.

1332 ■ National Association of Asian American Law Enforcement Commanders (NAAALEC)
PO Box 420496
San Francisco, CA 94142-0496
E-mail: **naaalecpresident@yahoo.com**
URL: http://www.naaalec.org
Contact: John Lee, Pres.

1333 ■ National Liquor Law Enforcement Association (NLLEA) (5960)
11720 Beltsville Dr., Ste.900
Calverton, MD 20705-3111
Ph: (301)755-2795
Fax: (301)755-2799
E-mail: support@nllea.org
URL: http://www.nllea.org
Contact: **Steve Ernst, Pres.**

1334 ■ National Narcotic Detector Dog Association (NNDDA) (5961)
379 CR 105
Carthage, TX 75633
Free: (888)289-0070
Fax: (409)284-7934
E-mail: thenndda@yahoo.com
URL: http://www.nndda.org
Contact: **Robin Fields, Pres.**

1335 ■ National Native American Law Enforcement Association (NNLEA) (5773)
PO Box 171
Washington, DC 20044
Ph: (202)204-3065
Free: (866)506-7631
E-mail: info@nnalea.org
URL: http://www.nnalea.org
Contact: **Michael Dillinger, Pres.**

1336 ■ National Police Canine Association (NPCA)
PO Box 538
Waddell, AZ 85355
Ph: **(713)562-7371**
Free: (877)362-1219
E-mail: info@npca.net
URL: http://www.npca.net
Contact: Terry Anderson, Pres.

1337 ■ National Tactical Officers Association (NTOA) (5946)
PO Box 797
Doylestown, PA 18901
Ph: **(215)230-7616**
Free: (800)279-9127
Fax: (215)230-7552
E-mail: membership@ntoa.org
URL: http://ntoa.org/site
Contact: John Gnagey, Exec. Dir.

1338 ■ United States Police Canine Association (USPCA) (5974)
PO Box 80
Springboro, OH 45066-0080
Ph: (937)751-6469
Free: (800)531-1614
E-mail: k9nord@aol.com
URL: http://www.uspcak9.com
Contact: **Kevin Johnson, Pres.**

Legal

1339 ■ National Legal Sanctuary for Community Advancement (NLSCA)
444 DeHaro St., Ste.205
San Francisco, CA 94107
Ph: (415)553-7100
Fax: **(415)553-7101**
E-mail: akhlaghilaw@sbcglobal.net
URL: http://www.legalsanctuary.org
Contact: Banafsheh Akhlaghi Esq., Pres./CEO

Legal Services

1340 ■ Alliance of Legal Document Assistant Professionals (ALDAP)
7290 Navajo Rd., Ste.113
San Diego, CA 92119
Free: (888)201-8622
E-mail: info@aldap.org
URL: **http://aldap.org**
Contact: **Suzanne Bowlby, Pres.**

1341 ■ Lawyers for Children America (LFCA) (5991)
151 Farmington Ave. RW61
Hartford, CT 06156
Ph: (860)273-0441
Free: (860)273-8340
E-mail: info@lawyersforchildrenamerica.org
URL: http://www.lawyersforchildrenamerica.org
Contact: **Richard Harris, Pres.**

1342 ■ National Center on Poverty Law (NCPL) (5913)
50 E Washington St., Ste.500
Chicago, IL 60602
Ph: (312)263-3830 **(312)368-2671**
Fax: (312)263-3846
E-mail: johnbouman@povertylaw.org
URL: http://www.povertylaw.org
Contact: John M. Bouman, Pres.

Liability

1343 ■ American Board of Professional Liability Attorneys (ABPLA) (6076)
4355 Cobb Pkwy., Ste.J-208
Atlanta, GA 30339
Ph: **(404)989-7663**
URL: http://www.abpla.org
Contact: **William F. McMurry, Pres.**

1344 ■ Defense Research Institute (DRI) (6077)
55 W Monroe, Ste.2000
Chicago, IL 60603
Ph: (312)795-1101
Fax: (312)795-0748

E-mail: dri@dri.org
URL: http://www.dri.org
Contact: **R. Matthew Cairns, Pres.**

Lotteries

1345 ■ North American Association of State and Provincial Lotteries (NASPL) (6081)
1 S Broadway
Geneva, OH 44041
Ph: (440)466-5630
Fax: (440)466-5649
E-mail: info@nasplhq.org
URL: http://www.naspl.org
Contact: **Jeff Anderson, Pres.**

Military

1346 ■ Air Force Association (AFA) (5387)
1501 Lee Hwy.
Arlington, VA 22209-1198
Ph: (703)247-5800
Free: (800)727-3337
Fax: (703)247-5853
E-mail: membership@afa.org
URL: http://www.afa.org
Contact: **S. Sanford Schlitt, Chm.**

1347 ■ Air Force Sergeants Association (AFSA) (6063)
5211 Auth Rd.
Suitland, MD 20746
Ph: (301)899-3500
Free: (800)638-0594
Fax: (301)899-8136
E-mail: **mccauslin@hqafsa.org**
URL: http://www.hqafsa.org
Contact: John McCauslin, CEO

1348 ■ American Logistics Association (ALA) (5390)
1133 15th St. NW, Ste.640
Washington, DC 20005
Ph: (202)466-2520
Fax: (202)296-4419
E-mail: membership@ala-national.org
URL: http://www.ala-national.org
Contact: **Frank Pecoraro, Pres.**

1349 ■ Civil Affairs Association (CAA) (5957)
10130 Hyla Brook Rd.
Columbia, MD 21044-1705
Ph: (410)992-7724
Fax: **(410)740-5046**
E-mail: civilaffairs@civilaffairsassoc.org
URL: http://www.civilaffairsassoc.org
Contact: **Michael E. Hess, Pres.**

1350 ■ Professional Loadmaster Association (PLA)
PO Box 4351
Tacoma, WA 98438
Ph: (253)215-0118 (253)620-6768
Free: **(800)239-4524**
E-mail: rpierce@bohenvironmental.com
URL: http://www.loadmasters.com
Contact: Ron Pierce, Pres.

Municipal Government

1351 ■ National Association of Towns and Townships (NATAT) (6158)
1130 Connecticut Ave. NW, Ste.300
Washington, DC 20036
Ph: (202)454-3954 (317)813-3240
Free: (866)830-0008
Fax: (202)331-1598
E-mail: jimo@tfgnet.com
URL: http://www.natat.org
Contact: **Mr. Jim Fisher, Pres.**

1352 ■ Women in Government (WIG) (6165)
1319 F St. NW, Ste.710
Washington, DC 20004
Ph: (202)333-0825
Free: (888)333-0164
Fax: (202)333-0875
E-mail: **mmaginn@womeningovernment.org**
URL: http://www.womeningovernment.org
Contact: **Marjorie Maginn, Pres./Exec. Dir.**

Natural Resources

1353 ■ Interstate Council on Water Policy (ICWP) (6021)
51 Monroe St., Ste.PE-08A
Rockville, MD 20850
Ph: (301)984-1908 **(703)243-7383**
Fax: (301)984-5841
E-mail: icwp2005@yahoo.com
URL: http://www.icwp.org
Contact: Peter Evans, Exec. Dir.

Paralegals

1354 ■ National Federation of Paralegal Associations (NFPA) (6182)
PO Box 2016
Edmonds, WA 98020
Ph: (425)967-0045
Fax: (425)771-9588
E-mail: info@paralegals.org
URL: http://www.paralegals.org
Contact: **Tracey L. Young RP, Pres.**

Parks and Recreation

1355 ■ Association of National Park Rangers (ANPR)
25958 Genesse Trail Rd.
PMB 222
Golden, CO 80401
E-mail: **anprbiz@aol.com**
URL: http://www.anpr.org
Contact: **Stacy Allen, Pres.**

1356 ■ National Association of State Park Directors (NASPD) (5597)
8829 Woodyhill Rd.
Raleigh, NC 27613
Ph: (919)676-8365 **(919)971-9300**
Fax: (919)676-8365
E-mail: naspd@me.com
URL: http://www.naspd.org
Contact: Philip K. McKnelly, Exec. Dir.

1357 ■ National Park Foundation (NPF) (5487)
1201 Eye St. NW, Ste.550B
Washington, DC 20005
Ph: (202)354-6460
Fax: (202)371-2066
E-mail: ask-npf@nationalparks.org
URL: http://www.nationalparks.org/npf-at-work/contact
Contact: **Chris Sullivan, Vice Chm.**

1358 ■ National Parks Conservation Association (NPCA) (5488)
1300 19th St. NW, Ste.300
Washington, DC 20036
Ph: (202)223-6722
Free: (800)628-7275
Fax: **(202)454-3333**
E-mail: npca@npca.org
URL: http://www.npca.org
Contact: **Thomas F. Secunda, Chm.**

Property

1359 ■ Unclaimed Property Professionals Organization (UPPO)
110 Wall St., 11th Fl., No. 0080
New York, NY 10005-3111
Ph: (508)883-9065
E-mail: info@uppo.org
URL: http://www.uppo.org
Contact: **Christa DeOliveira, Pres.**

Public Administration

1360 ■ National Academy of Public Administration (NAPA) (6154)
900 7th St. NW, Ste.600
Washington, DC 20001
Ph: (202)347-3190
Fax: (202)393-0993
E-mail: **kmarcy@napawash.org**
URL: http://www.napawash.org
Contact: **Kristine M. Marcy, Pres./CEO**

1361 ■ Section for Women in Public Administration (SWPA) (5520)
1301 Pennsylvania Ave. NW, Ste.840
Washington, DC 20004-1735
Ph: (202)393-7878
URL: http://www.swpanet.org
Contact: **Barbara Lewkowitz, Vice Chair**

Public Affairs

1362 ■ Air Force Public Affairs Alumni Association (AFPAAA) (6228)
PO Box 447
Locust Grove, VA 22508-0447
E-mail: boardnow@afpaaa.org
URL: http://www.afpaaa.org
Contact: **Christine Queen, Chair**

Public Finance

1363 ■ Association of Public Treasurers of the United States and Canada (APT US & C) (6231)
962 Wayne Ave., Ste.910
Silver Spring, MD 20910
Ph: (301)495-5560 **(440)826-5889**
Fax: (301)495-5561
E-mail: info@aptusc.org
URL: http://www.aptusc.org
Contact: Dana Kavander, Pres.

1364 ■ National Association of State Treasurers (NAST) (6236)
PO Box 11910
Lexington, KY 40578-1910
Ph: (859)244-8175
Fax: (859)244-8053
E-mail: nast@csg.org
URL: http://www.nast.net
Contact: **Kelly Schmidt, Pres.**

Public Health

1365 ■ Association of State and Territorial Local Health Liaison Officials (ASTLHLO)
PO Box 260451
Denver, CO 80226
Ph: (303)692-3479
Fax: (303)691-7746
E-mail: **info@astlhlo.org**
URL: http://www.astlhlo.org
Contact: Louise Merchant-Hannan, Sec.

1366 ■ National Association for Public Health Statistics and Information Systems (NAPHSIS) (824)
962 Wayne Ave., Ste.701
Silver Spring, MD 20910
Ph: (301)563-6001
Fax: (301)563-6012
E-mail: hq@naphsis.org
URL: http://www.naphsis.org
Contact: **Patricia Potrzebowski PhD, Exec. Dir.**

Public Interest Law

1367 ■ Equal Rights Advocates (ERA) (6248)
180 Howard St., Ste.300
San Francisco, CA 94105
Ph: (415)621-0672 (415)575-2395
Free: (800)839-4ERA
Fax: (415)621-6744
E-mail: info@equalrights.org
URL: http://www.equalrights.org
Contact: **Arcelia Hurtado, Exec. Dir.**

1368 ■ Public Justice (6109)
1825 K St. NW, Ste.200
Washington, DC 20006-1220
Ph: (202)797-8600
Fax: (202)232-7203
E-mail: **hgdeitzler@hpcbd.com**
URL: http://www.publicjustice.net
Contact: Harry G. Deitzler, Pres.

Public Works

1369 ■ American Public Works Association (APWA) (6115)
2345 Grand Blvd., Ste.700
Kansas City, MO 64108-2625
Ph: (816)472-6100 **(202)218-6700**
Free: (800)848-APWA
Fax: (816)472-1610
E-mail: pking@apwa.net
URL: http://www.apwa.net
Contact: Peter King, Exec. Dir.

1370 ■ National Alliance of Highway Beautification Agencies (NAHBA)
PO Box 191
Columbia, SC 29202
E-mail: contactnahba@nahba.org
URL: http://www.nahba.org
Contact: **Joyce Musick, Chair**

Purchasing

1371 ■ National Association of State Procurement Officials (NASPO) (6120)
201 E Main St., Ste.1405
Lexington, KY 40507-2004
Ph: (859)514-9159
E-mail: naspo@amrms.com
URL: http://www.naspo.org
Contact: **Greg Smith, Pres.**

Safety

1372 ■ Association of Public-Safety Communications Officials International (APCO) (6273)
351 N Williamson Blvd.
Daytona Beach, FL 32114-1112
Ph: (386)322-2500
Free: (888)272-6911
Fax: (386)322-2501

E-mail: apco@apcointl.org
URL: http://www.apco911.org
Contact: **William D. Carrow, Pres.**

1373 ■ REACT International (RI) (6136)
12114 Boydton Plank Rd.
Dinwiddie, VA 23841
Ph: (301)316-2900
E-mail: **brenda.cutchin@reactintl.org**
URL: http://www.reactintl.org
Contact: Brenda Cutchin, Office Mgr.

Social Security

1374 ■ National Council of Social Security Management Associations (NCSSMA) (6222)
418 C St. NE
Washington, DC 20002
Ph: (202)547-8530
Fax: (202)547-8532
E-mail: **joseph.dirago@ssa.gov**
URL: http://www.ncssma.org
Contact: Joe Dirago, Pres.

State Government

1375 ■ National Black Caucus of State Legislators (NBCSL) (5598)
444 N Capitol St. NW, Ste.622
Washington, DC 20001
Ph: (202)624-5457
Fax: (202)508-3826
URL: http://www.nbcsl.org
Contact: **Rep. Barbara W. Ballard, Pres.**

1376 ■ Republican Governors Association (RGA) (6286)
1747 Pennsylvania Ave. NW, Ste.250
Washington, DC 20006
Ph: (202)662-4140
E-mail: info@rga.org
URL: http://www.rga.org
Contact: **Phil Cox, Exec. Dir.**

Taxation

1377 ■ American Taxation Association (ATA) (6253)
9201 Univ. City Blvd.
Charlotte, NC 28223
Ph: **(704)687-7696**
E-mail: americantaxationassociation@aaahq.org
URL: http://aaahq.org/ata/index.htm
Contact: **Hughlene Burton, Pres.**

1378 ■ National Association of Enrolled Agents (NAEA) (6327)
1120 Connecticut Ave. NW, Ste.460
Washington, DC 20036-3953
Ph: (202)822-6232
Fax: (202)822-6270
E-mail: info@naea.org
URL: http://www.naea.org
Contact: **Sherrill Trovato EA, Pres.**

1379 ■ National Association of Tax Consultants (NATC) (6328)
321 W 13th Ave.
Eugene, OR 97401
Ph: **(541)298-2829**
Free: (800)745-6282
Fax: **(541)343-5353**
E-mail: office@natctax.org
URL: http://www.natctax.org
Contact: Mary Linebarger, Pres.

Telecommunications

1380 ■ National Association of Telecommunications Officers and Advisors (NATOA) (6335)
2121 Eisenhower Ave., Ste.401
Alexandria, VA 22314
Ph: (703)519-8035
Fax: **(703)997-7080**
E-mail: info@natoa.org
URL: http://www.natoa.org
Contact: Joanne Hovis, Pres.-Elect

Transportation

1381 ■ American Road and Transportation Builders Association (ARTBA) (6341)
1219 28th St. NW
Washington, DC 20007-3389
Ph: (202)289-4434
Fax: (202)289-4435
E-mail: general@artba.org
URL: http://www.artba.org
Contact: **Bill Cox, Chm.**

1382 ■ International Transportation Management Association (ITMA) (6086)
PO Box 62654
Houston, TX 77205
Ph: **(713)343-0889**
E-mail: president@itmahouston.org
URL: http://www.itmahouston.org/blog
Contact: Eloy Vazquez, Pres.

1383 ■ Transportation Lawyers Association (TLA) (6353)
PO Box 15122
Lenexa, KS 66285-5122
Ph: (913)895-4615
Fax: (913)895-4652
E-mail: tla-info@goamp.com
URL: http://www.translaw.org
Contact: **Sam Hallman, Pres.**

Trial Advocacy

1384 ■ American College of Trial Lawyers (ACTL) (6356)
19900 MacArthur Blvd., Ste.530
Irvine, CA 92612
Ph: (949)752-1801
Fax: (949)752-1674
E-mail: nationaloffice@actl.com
URL: http://www.actl.com
Contact: **Gregory P. Joseph, Pres.**

1385 ■ National Institute for Trial Advocacy (NITA) (6295)
1685 38th St., Ste.200
Boulder, CO 80301
Free: **(800)225-6482**
Fax: **(720)890-7069**
E-mail: jbaker@nita.org
URL: http://www.nita.org
Contact: John Baker, Pres./CEO

Utilities

1386 ■ Regulatory Assistance Project (RAP)
PO Box 507
Hallowell, ME 04347
Ph: **(207)319-6000**
E-mail: dmoskovitz@raponline.org
URL: http://raponline.org
Contact: David Moskovitz, Principal

Aerospace

1387 ■ High Frontier (HF) (5684)
2800 Shirlington Rd., Ste.405
Arlington, VA 22206
Ph: (703)671-4111
Fax: (703)931-6432
E-mail: high.frontier@verizon.net
URL: **http://users.erols.com/hifront**
Contact: Ambassador Henry F. Cooper, Chm.

1388 ■ Planetary Society (5693)
85 S Grand Ave.
Pasadena, CA 91106-2301
Ph: (626)793-5100
Fax: (626)793-5528
E-mail: tps@planetary.org
URL: http://www.planetary.org
Contact: **Bill Nye, Exec. Dir.**

1389 ■ Space Studies Institute (SSI)
1434 Flightline St.
Mojave, CA 93501
Ph: (661)750-2774
E-mail: **admin@ssi.org**
URL: http://www.ssi.org
Contact: **Ms. Robin Snelson, Exec. Dir./Sec.-Treas.**

Alternative Technology

1390 ■ American Biogas Council (ABC)
1211 Connecticut Ave. NW, Ste.600
Washington, DC 20036
Ph: (202)640-6595 (202)904-0220
E-mail: info@americanbiogascouncil.org
URL: http://www.americanbiogascouncil.org
Contact: Patrick Serfass, Exec. Dir.
Membership Dues: industry, international and renewable energy organization (based on revenues), $250-$20,000 (annual) ● farmer, sole proprietor, $250 (annual) ● utility, $5,000 (annual) ● support industry organization (media), $1,000 (annual) ● support industry organization (other - anyone not included in any other named category), $500 (annual) ● not-for-profit organization (public entity), $500 (annual) ● not-for-profit organization (other individual in not-for-profit sector), $150 (annual) ● non-profit organization (student), $100 (annual). **Description:** Represents the interests of the biogas industry. Promotes the advancement of anaerobic digestion technology in the United States. Increases biogas awareness through education and outreach.

1391 ■ Clean Technology Trade Alliance (CTTA)
2817 Wheaton Way, Ste.202
Bremerton, WA 98310
Ph: (360)692-7286

E-mail: info@cleantechtradealliance.org
URL: http://www.cleantechtradealliance.org
Contact: Mark D. Frost, Exec. Dir.
Founded: 2009. **Description:** Promotes the expansion of global clean technology. Connects companies and investors interested in clean technology with small to mid-sized clean technology businesses. Enhances the ability of small enterprises to access the growing markets in Europe and Asia, create green collar jobs and foster a sustainable business segment.

1392 ■ ClimateTalk Alliance
2400 Camino Ramon, Ste.375
San Ramon, CA 94583
Ph: (925)275-6641 (925)275-6681
Fax: (925)275-6691
E-mail: help@climatetalkalliance.org
URL: http://www.climatetalk.com
Contact: Susan Lowe, Exec. Dir.
Founded: 2009. **Membership Dues:** promoter, $35,000 (annual) ● contributor, $9,500 (annual) ● adopter, $2,500 (annual). **Description:** Represents companies committed to developing a common communication infrastructure for heating, ventilating and air conditioning (HVAC) and Smart Grid devices, enabling the interoperability of diverse systems. Aims to build a vendor neutral solution around a common information model for OEM differentiation. Enables interoperability of HVAC as a means of saving energy and improving user comfort in the residential market for all stakeholders.

1393 ■ FutureGen Alliance
73 E Central Park Plz.
Jacksonville, IL 62650
Ph: (217)243-8215
E-mail: info@futuregenalliance.org
URL: http://www.futuregenalliance.org
Contact: Steven Winberg, Chm.
Founded: 2005. **Multinational. Description:** Represents coal producers, coal users and coal equipment suppliers in the world. Works to benefit public interest and the interests of science through research, development and demonstration of near-zero emissions coal technology. Enables members to focus on developing innovative approaches to generating electricity from coal in a cleaner way. Strives to take more risks in experimenting with advanced technologies.

1394 ■ Innovation: Africa
520 8th Ave., 4th Fl.
New York, NY 10018
Ph: (212)710-6430
Fax: (212)481-4174
E-mail: info@innoafrica.org
URL: http://www.innoafrica.org
Contact: Sivan Ya'ari, Founder/Pres.
Founded: 2008. **Multinational. Description:** Works to bring sustainable technologies to African villages. Facilitates African development through the use of renewable technologies.

1395 ■ International Green Energy Council (IGEC)
1701 Pennsylvania Ave. NW, Ste.300
Washington, DC 20006
Ph: (202)349-7138
E-mail: info@greenenergycouncil.com
URL: http://www.greenenergycouncil.com
Contact: Ralph Avallone, Pres.
Membership Dues: petroleum company, $4,995 (annual) ● utility company, $2,995 (annual) ● green platinum corporate, $1,495 (annual) ● platinum corporate, $1,295 (annual) ● green gold corporate, $1,095 (annual) ● gold corporate, $995 (annual) ● non-green associate, $795 (annual) ● individual, $495 (annual) ● student, $50 (annual). **Multinational. Description:** Promotes green or sustainable forms of energy production, renewable energy sources and sustainable design practices. Educates legislators, corporate leaders and consumers about the green industry, alternative energy and green building.

1396 ■ Plug In America (PIA)
2370 Market St., No. 419
San Francisco, CA 94114
Ph: (415)323-3329
Fax: (415)796-0882
URL: http://www.pluginamerica.org
Contact: Dan Davids, Pres.
Founded: 2008. **Membership Dues:** regular, $25 (annual). **Description:** Promotes the use of plug-in vehicles powered by clean, affordable, domestic electricity. Encourages the development of battery electric vehicles, plug-in hybrid vehicles and other vehicles which utilize electricity. Advocates for the nation's dependence on petroleum and improvement of the global environment.

1397 ■ Sustainable Biomaterials Collaborative (SBC)
c/o Heeral Bhalala
Inst. for Local Self-Reliance
2001 S St. NW, Ste.570
Washington, DC 20009
Ph: (202)898-1610
E-mail: hbhalala@ilsr.org
URL: http://www.sustainablebiomaterials.org
Contact: Mark Rossi, Co-Coor.
Founded: 2006. **Description:** Promotes the introduction and use of biobased products that are sustainable throughout their lifecycle. Seeks to advance the development and diffusion of sustainable biomaterials by creating sustainability guidelines, engaging markets and promoting policy initiatives.

1398 ■ Sweet Sorghum Ethanol Association (SSEA)
8912 Brandon Sta. Rd.
Raleigh, NC 27613
Ph: (919)870-0782
URL: http://www.sseassociation.org
Contact: Scott W. Gibson, VP
Membership Dues: regular (voting), $100 (annual) ● sustaining (non-voting), $250-$500 (annual). **Multina-**

tional. **Description:** Promotes the development and use of sweet sorghum in processing ethanol and other bio-derivatives. Encourages the development of international standards for the measurement and reporting of sweet sorghum data. Facilitates the dissemination of educational and scientific information on ethanol and other bio-derivatives from sweet sorghum.

1399 ■ United States Water and Power
1179 Nelrose Ave.
Venice, CA 90291
E-mail: johncleddy@aol.com
URL: http://www.uswaterandpower.com
Contact: John C. Leddy, Co-Founder/Pres.
Description: Promotes sustainable water and energy technologies, policies and practices. Works to build a future based on sustainable resource management by focusing on energy efficiency, water use efficiency, water/energy conservation, water quality and clean energy production.

Anthropology

1400 ■ American Ethnological Society (AES) (856)
Univ. of Wisconsin
Dept. of Rural Sociology
Madison, WI 53701
Ph: (608)262-1217
E-mail: **jcollins@ssc.wisc.edu**
URL: http://www.aesonline.org
Contact: Jane Collins, Pres.

1401 ■ Council on Anthropology and Education (CAE) (6290)
Mills Coll.
5000 MacArthur Blvd.
Oakland, CA 94613
Ph: **(510)430-3384**
Fax: **(510)430-3379**
E-mail: **kschultz@mills.edu**
URL: http://www.aaanet.org/sections/cae/cae-home. html
Contact: **Kathy Schultz, Pres.**

1402 ■ Society for Visual Anthropology (SVA) (5736)
Reading Area Community Coll.
Soc. Sciences Div.
10 S 2nd St.
Reading, PA 19603
E-mail: **pblakely@racc.edu**
URL: http://www.societyforvisualanthropology.org
Contact: Kimberly Dukes, Treas.

Archaeology

1403 ■ Archaeological Institute of America (AIA) (6310)
656 Beacon St., 6th Fl.
Boston, MA 02215-2006
Ph: (617)353-9361 (617)353-8706
Free: (877)524-6300
Fax: (617)353-6550
E-mail: aia@aia.bu.edu
URL: http://www.archaeological.org
Contact: **Jarrett A. Lobell, Exec. Dir.**

1404 ■ Institute of Nautical Archaeology (INA) (6318)
PO Drawer HG
College Station, TX 77841-5137
Ph: (979)845-6694
Fax: (979)847-9260
E-mail: info@inadiscover.com
URL: **http://inadiscover.com**
Contact: **Deborah Carlson PhD, Pres.**

1405 ■ Society for Historical Archaeology (SHA) (6417)
9707 Key West Ave., Ste.100
Rockville, MD 20850
Ph: (301)990-2454
Fax: (301)990-9771
E-mail: hq@sha.org
URL: http://www.sha.org
Contact: **Bill Scott CAE, Exec. Dir.**

Architecture

1406 ■ American Institute of Building Design (AIBD) (6491)
7059 Blair Rd. NW, Ste.201
Washington, DC 20012
Free: (800)366-2423
Fax: (866)204-0293
E-mail: info@aibd.org
URL: http://www.aibd.org
Contact: **Steven Mickley CPBD, Pres.**

1407 ■ ArchVoices
1014 Curtis St.
Albany, CA 94706
Ph: (510)757-6213
E-mail: editors@archvoices.org
URL: http://www.archvoices.org
Contact: John Cary, Co-Founder/Operations Dir.
Founded: 1999. **Description:** Aims to advance the profession of architecture. Fosters a culture of communication through the collection and dissemination of architectural information and research. Compiles data and research on architecture and other licensed professions.

1408 ■ Council of Landscape Architectural Registration Boards (CLARB) (6500)
3949 Pender Dr., Ste.120
Fairfax, VA 22030
Ph: (571)432-0332
Fax: (571)432-0442
E-mail: info@clarb.org
URL: http://www.clarb.org
Contact: **Denise Husband, Pres.**

1409 ■ Ministry Architecture
1904 S Union Pl.
Lakewood, CO 80228
Ph: (720)937-9664 (303)989-4870
Fax: (303)989-0884
E-mail: ministryarchitecture@hotmail.com
URL: http://www.ministryarchitecture.com
Contact: Leonard C. Rosenberg AIA, Exec. Dir.
Founded: 1997. **Multinational. Description:** Represents design professionals and architecture students. Works primarily on giving architectural, engineering and planning services to evangelical ministries in developing countries.

1410 ■ National Organization of Minority Architects (NOMA) (6505)
Howard Univ.
Coll. of Engg., Architecture and Cmpt. Sciences
School of Architecture and Design
2366 Sixth St. NW, Rm. 100
Washington, DC 20059
Ph: (202)686-2780
E-mail: president@noma.net
URL: http://www.noma.net
Contact: **Sanford Garner, Pres.**

1411 ■ Society of American Registered Architects (SARA) (6440)
PO Box 280
Newport, TN 37822
Ph: (423)721-0129
Free: (888)385-7272
E-mail: cmoscato@sara-national.org
URL: **http://www.sara-national.org**
Contact: Cathie Moscato, Exec. Dir.

Astrology

1412 ■ International Society for Astrological Research (ISAR) (6521)
PO Box 38613
Los Angeles, CA 90038
Ph: (805)525-0461
Fax: (805)933-0301
E-mail: smootlips@gmail.com
URL: http://www.isarastrology.com
Contact: **Gisele Terry, Pres.**

Astronomy

1413 ■ Von Braun Astronomical Society (VBAS) (6538)
PO Box 1142
Huntsville, AL 35807
E-mail: **areisz@reiszeng.com**
URL: http://www.vbas.org
Contact: Al Reisz, Pres.

Automobile

1414 ■ SAE International (SAE) (6389)
400 Commonwealth Dr.
Warrendale, PA 15096-0001
Ph: (724)776-4841 (724)776-4970
Free: (877)606-7323
Fax: (724)776-0790
E-mail: customerservice@sae.org
URL: http://www.sae.org
Contact: **Richard E. Kleine EdD, Pres.**

Behavioral Sciences

1415 ■ International Society for Human Ethology (ISHE) (5932)
c/o Dori LeCroy, Treas.
175 King St.
Charleston, SC 29401
Fax: (843)577-9645
E-mail: **schiefen@orn.mpg.de**
URL: **http://media.anthro.univie.ac.at/ISHE**
Contact: Wulf Schiefenhovel, Pres.

1416 ■ International Society for Research on Aggression (ISRA) (6496)
The Univ. of Iowa
Dept. of Psychology
11 Seashore Hall E
Iowa City, IA 52240
Fax: (319)353-2919
E-mail: john-knutson@uiowa.edu
URL: http://www.israsociety.com
Contact: Prof. John F. Knutson PhD, Pres.-Elect

Biochemistry

1417 ■ American Society for Biochemistry and Molecular Biology (ASBMB) (5843)
11200 Rockville Pike, Ste.302
Rockville, MD 20852-3110
Ph: **(240)283-6600**
Fax: **(301)881-2080**
E-mail: asbmb@asbmb.org
URL: http://www.asbmb.org
Contact: Barbara A. Gordon, Exec. Dir.

1418 ■ International Society of Chemical Ecology (ISCE) (6580)
c/o Dr. Kenneth Haynes, Treas.
Univ. of Kentucky
Dept. of Entomology
Lexington, KY 40546
Ph: (859)257-1618
Fax: (859)323-1120

E-mail: khaynes@uky.edu
URL: http://www.chemecol.org
Contact: **Monika Hilker, Pres.**

Biology

1419 ■ American Academy of Microbiology (AAM) (6590)
1752 N St. NW
Washington, DC 20036-2804
Ph: **(202)737-3600**
Fax: (202)942-9353
E-mail: academy@asmusa.org
URL: http://academy.asm.org
Contact: R. John Collier, Chm.

1420 ■ Association of Genetic Technologists (AGT) (6438)
PO Box 19193
Lenexa, KS 66285
Ph: (913)895-4605
Fax: (913)895-4652
E-mail: agt-info@goamp.com
URL: http://www.agt-info.org
Contact: **Betty S. Dunn, Pres.**

1421 ■ International Organization for Mycoplasmology (IOM) (6582)
c/o Dr. Mitchell F. Balish, Treas.
80 Pearson Hall
Oxford, OH 45056
Ph: (513)528-0167
Fax: (513)529-2431
E-mail: balishmf@muohio.edu
URL: http://the-iom.org
Contact: **Joachim Frey, Chm.**

1422 ■ International Society of Differentiation (ISD) (6620)
c/o Jennifer Shultz, Admin. Off.
PO Box 55
Higganum, CT 06441
Ph: (860)554-5300
Fax: (860)838-4242
E-mail: office@isdifferentiation.org
URL: http://www.isdifferentiation.org
Contact: **Christine Mummery, Pres.**

1423 ■ Society for Developmental Biology (SDB) (6627)
9650 Rockville Pike
Bethesda, MD 20814-3998
Ph: (301)634-7815
Fax: (301)634-7825
E-mail: sdb@sdbonline.org
URL: http://www.sdbonline.org
Contact: **Alexandra Joyner, Pres.**

1424 ■ Society for In Vitro Biology (SIVB) (6466)
514 Daniels St., Ste.411
Raleigh, NC 27605-1317
Ph: (919)562-0600
Fax: (919)562-0608
E-mail: sivb@sivb.org
URL: http://www.sivb.org
Contact: **Ms. Marietta Ellis, Managing Dir.**

1425 ■ Teratology Society (TS) (6634)
1821 Michael Faraday Dr., Ste.300
Reston, VA 20190
Ph: (703)438-3104
Fax: (703)438-3113
E-mail: tshq@teratology.org
URL: http://www.teratology.org
Contact: **John M. Rogers PhD, Pres.**

Biomedical Engineering

1426 ■ Biomedical Engineering Society (BMES) (6640)
8201 Corporate Dr., Ste.1125
Landover, MD 20785-2224
Ph: (301)459-1999
Free: **(877)871-2637**
Fax: (301)459-2444
E-mail: info@bmes.org
URL: http://www.bmes.org
Contact: Edward L. Schilling III, Exec. Dir.

Botany

1427 ■ American Bamboo Society (ABS) (6002)
315 S Coast Hwy. 101, Ste.U
PMB 212
Encinitas, CA 92024-3555
E-mail: **help@bamboo.org**
URL: http://www.americanbamboo.org
Contact: David King, Sec.

1428 ■ American Bryological and Lichenological Society (ABLS) (6580)
c/o James Bennett, Sec.-Treas.
Univ. of Wisconsin
Dept. of Botany
430 Lincoln Dr.
Madison, WI 53706
Ph: **(608)262-5489**
E-mail: **jpbennet@wisc.edu**
URL: **http://www.abls.org**
Contact: Karen Renzaglia, Pres.

1429 ■ Aquatic Plant Management Society (APMS) (6663)
PO Box 821265
Vicksburg, MS 39182-1265
Ph: **(601)634-2656**
Fax: **(601)634-5502**
E-mail: **linda.s.nelson@erdc.usace.army.mil**
URL: http://www.apms.org
Contact: **Linda Nelson, Pres.**

1430 ■ International Bulb Society (IBS) (6596)
PO Box 336
Sanger, CA 93657-0336
E-mail: **info@bulbsociety.org**
URL: http://www.bulbsociety.org
Contact: Herbert Kelly Jr., Pres.

1431 ■ International Palm Society (IPS) (5922)
c/o Liz Stansfeld
9300 Sandstone St.
Austin, TX 78737
Ph: (512)301-2744
Fax: (512)607-6468
E-mail: info@palms.org
URL: http://www.palms.org
Contact: Bo-Goran Lundkvist, Pres.

1432 ■ Plant Growth Regulation Society of America (PGRSA) (6033)
1018 Duke St.
Alexandria, VA 22314
Ph: **(703)836-4606**
Fax: **(703)836-2024**
E-mail: **dmancini@ashs.org**
URL: http://www.pgrsa.org
Contact: **Ms. Dawn Mancini, Exec. Sec.**

1433 ■ Society for Economic Botany (SEB) (6514)
PO Box 299
St. Louis, MO 63166-0299
E-mail: **seb@econbot.org**
URL: http://www.econbot.org
Contact: **Mary Eubanks, Pres.**

Bridge

1434 ■ Short Span Steel Bridge Alliance (SSSBA)
1140 Connecticut Ave., Ste.705 NW
Washington, DC 20036
Ph: (301)367-6179
E-mail: sssba@steel.org
URL: http://www.shortspansteelbridges.org
Contact: Dan Snyder, Interim Dir.
Description: Aims to increase awareness of the benefits, cost-competitiveness and safety facts related to the use of short span steel bridges. Serves as an industry resource for short span steel bridge information.

Building Industries

1435 ■ Alliance for Building Regulatory Reform in the Digital Age
10702 Midsummer Dr.
Reston, VA 20191
Ph: (703)568-2323
Fax: (703)620-0015
E-mail: rcwible@comcast.net
URL: http://www.natlpartnerstreamline.org
Contact: Robert C. Wible, Contact
Founded: 2001. **Description:** Represents state and local governments as well as professionals in the building industry. Seeks to identify and share best practices that streamline the building regulatory processes. Enables communities to improve their effectiveness and efficiency by encouraging greater use of information technology.

Chemistry

1436 ■ American Institute of Chemists (AIC) (6703)
315 Chestnut St.
Philadelphia, PA 19106-2702
Ph: (215)873-8224
Fax: (215)629-5224
E-mail: info@theaic.org
URL: http://www.theaic.org
Contact: **Jerry Jasinski, Pres.**

1437 ■ Commercial Development and Marketing Association (CDMA) (6715)
15000 Commerce Pkwy., Ste.C
Mount Laurel, NJ 08054
Ph: (856)439-9052
Free: (800)232-5241
Fax: (856)439-0525
E-mail: cdma@pdma.org
URL: **http://pdma.org/chapter_home.cfm?pk_ chapter=61**
Contact: Theodore D. Goldman PhD, Pres./Treas.

1438 ■ Radiochemistry Society
PO Box 3091
Richland, WA 99354
Free: (800)371-0542
E-mail: rad-info@radiochemistry.org
URL: http://www.radiochemistry.org
Contact: Larry A. Burchfield PhD, Pres./CEO
Membership Dues: professional, $95 (annual) ● life, $1,500. **Description:** Aims to promote education and public outreach for the safe use, handling and benefits of radioisotopes in security, energy, agriculture, environment, food safety and medicine. Conducts seminars, trainings, scholarships, meetings and exchange of scientific information.

1439 ■ Societe de Chimie Industrielle, American Section (6733)
c/o Danielle Fraser, Admin.
80 Hathaway Dr.
Stratford, CT 06615
Ph: (212)725-9539
Fax: **(203)377-5408**

E-mail: societedechimie@yahoo.com
URL: http://www.societe.org
Contact: John E. Roberts, Pres.

Clinical Studies

**1440 ■ International Council on
Nanotechnology (ICON)**
PO Box 1892
Houston, TX 77251
Ph: (713)348-8210
Fax: (713)348-8218
E-mail: colvin@rice.edu
URL: http://icon.rice.edu
Contact: Vicki Colvin, Exec. Dir.
Founded: 2004. **Multinational. Description:** Aims
to communicate information regarding potential
environmental and health risks of nanotechnology.
Supports best practices in nanotechnology health
and environmental risk assessment and manage-
ment.

Computer Science

1441 ■ ACM SIGGRAPH (6780)
PO Box 30777
New York, NY 10087-0777
Ph: (212)626-0500
Fax: (212)944-1318
E-mail: acmhelp@acm.org
URL: http://www.siggraph.org
Contact: G. Scott Owen, Pres.

**1442 ■ Special Interest Group for Design
Automation (SIGDA) (6011)**
PO Box 6000
Binghamton, NY 13902
Ph: (607)777-2943
Fax: (607)777-4729
E-mail: pmadden@acm.org
URL: http://www.sigda.org
Contact: Prof. Patrick H. Madden, Chm.

Computer Users

**1443 ■ Special Interest Group on Accessible
Computing (SIGACCESS) (6100)**
2 Penn Plz., Ste.701
New York, NY 10121-0701
Ph: (212)626-0500
Free: (800)342-6626
Fax: (212)944-1318
E-mail: chair_sigaccess@acm.org
URL: http://www.sigaccess.org
Contact: Andrew Sears, Chm.

Computers

**1444 ■ Association of Service and Computer
Dealers International (ASCDI) (835)**
131 NW 1st Ave.
Delray Beach, FL 33444
Ph: (561)266-9016
Fax: (561)431-6302
E-mail: jmarion@ascdi.com
URL: http://www.ascdi.com
Contact: Joseph Marion, Pres.

**1445 ■ Computing Technology Industry
Association (CompTIA) (886)**
3500 Lacey Rd., Ste.100
Downers Grove, IL 60515
Ph: (630)678-8300
Fax: (630)678-8384
E-mail: membership@comptia.org
URL: http://www.comptia.org
Contact: Todd Thibodeaux, Pres./CEO

Construction

**1446 ■ American Institute of Constructors
(AIC) (6913)**
700 N Fairfax St., Ste.510
Alexandria, VA 22314
Ph: (703)683-4999
Fax: (571)527-3105
URL: http://www.professionalconstructor.org
Contact: Andi Wasiniak AIC, Pres.

**1447 ■ Construction Specifications Institute
(CSI) (6917)**
110 S Union St., Ste.100
Alexandria, VA 22314-3351
Free: (800)689-2900
Fax: (703)236-4600
E-mail: csi@csinet.org
URL: http://www.csinet.org
Contact: Dennis J. Hall FCSI, Pres.

Earth Sciences

**1448 ■ Drilling, Observation and Sampling of
the Earth's Continental Crust (DOSECC)**
PO Box 58857
Salt Lake City, UT 84158-0857
Ph: (801)583-2150
Fax: (801)583-2153
E-mail: dnielson@dosecc.org
URL: http://www.dosecc.org
Contact: Dennis Nielson, Pres.
Description: Provides leadership and technical sup-
port in subsurface sampling and monitoring technol-
ogy. Facilitates discussions of research drilling
programs that enhance the ability of the research
community to apply innovative drilling technology to
important earth science questions.

**1449 ■ Federation of Earth Science
Information Partners (ESIP Federation)**
6300 Creedmoor Rd., Ste.170-315
Raleigh, NC 27612
Ph: (919)870-7140
Free: (877)870-3747
Fax: (919)870-7141
E-mail: carolbmeyer@esipfed.org
URL: http://www.esipfed.org
Contact: Carol Beaton Meyer, Exec. Dir.
Founded: 1998. **Description:** Collects, interprets
and develops applications for earth observation
information. Works to make observation information
relating to a broad spectrum of earth science issues
more accessible to researchers, educators, policy
makers and the general public.

Economics

**1450 ■ National Economic Association (NEA)
(6613)**
Spelman Coll.
350 Spelman Ln.
Box 167
Atlanta, GA 30314
E-mail: jelu@spelman.edu
URL: http://www.neaecon.org/index.htm
Contact: Dr. Juliet Elu, Pres.-Elect

Energy

1451 ■ Alliance for Green Heat
6930 Carroll Ave., Ste.407
Takoma Park, MD 20912
Ph: (301)841-7755
Fax: (301)270-4000
E-mail: contact@forgreenheat.org
URL: http://www.forgreenheat.org
Contact: John Ackerly, Pres.
Founded: 2009. **Description:** Promotes clean and
efficient biomass heating systems, with a focus on

residential applications. Creates a public awareness
about the potential of wood and pellet heat and its
applications to low and middle-income populations.
Encourages tax credits and other incentives for the
cleanest wood and pellet stoves.

1452 ■ Alliance for Renewable Energy (ARE)
PO Box 63
Amherst, MA 01004
Ph: (413)549-8118
Fax: (413)256-8871
E-mail: contact@earthaction.org
URL: http://www.allianceforrenewableenergy.org
Contact: Lois Barber, Co-Chair
Founded: 2008. **Membership Dues:** individual, $50
(annual) ● business (based on revenue), $250-
$10,000 (annual) ● non-profit organization (based on
revenue), $100-$4,000 (annual). **Multinational. De-
scription:** Represents policymakers, renewable
energy experts, citizens, research institutions and
large and small businesses. Supports renewable
energy policies that will increase the shift from fossil
fuels to clean, renewable energy.

1453 ■ Citizens for Affordable Energy (CFAE)
1302 Waugh Dr., No. 940
Houston, TX 77019
Ph: (713)523-7333
Fax: (888)318-7818
E-mail: contact@cfaenergy.org
URL: http://www.citizensforaffordableenergy.org
Contact: Dr. Karen Hofmeister, Exec. Dir.
Membership Dues: advisory group, $500 (annual).
Description: Strives to educate citizens and govern-
ment officials about affordable energy solutions.
Promotes comprehensive energy and environmental
strategies at the local and national levels. Supports
energy from all sources and technology to increase
efficiency.

**1454 ■ Citizens' Alliance for Responsible
Energy (CARE)**
PO Box 52103
Albuquerque, NM 87181
Ph: (505)239-8998
E-mail: info@responsiblenergy.org
URL: http://www.responsiblenergy.org
Contact: Marita Noon, Exec. Dir.
Description: Aims to educate the public about the
need to guarantee access to affordable energy. Ad-
dresses energy issues focusing on oil, gas, coal and
nuclear/uranium.

1455 ■ Citizens for Energy Freedom (CEF)
2020 Pennsylvania Ave. NW, Ste.263
Washington, DC 20006
E-mail: info@citizensforenergyfreedom.org
URL: http://www.citizensforenergyfreedom.org
Contact: Dr. Robert Zubrin, Co-Founder
Description: Represents citizens, scientists, and
energy and transportation experts. Aims to free the
United States from the whims of the OPEC monopoly.
Addresses issues of energy security and oil depen-
dence.

1456 ■ Citizens Energy Plan (CEP)
MinnWest Tech. Campus
1700 Tech. Dr., Ste.212
Willmar, MN 56201
Ph: (320)222-3060
Fax: (320)222-3061
E-mail: contact@citizensenergyplan.com
URL: http://www.citizensenergyplan.com
Contact: V. Lee Byberg, Chm./Pres.
Membership Dues: individual, $10 (annual) ●
organization, $250 (annual) ● corporate, $500 (an-
nual). **Description:** Aims to develop a comprehensive
national energy plan. Promotes sufficient technology
and resources for a secure, affordable and
environmentally-balanced energy system. Supports
energy security through sound energy stewardship.

1457 ■ Eco Energy Finance (EEF)
2307 15th St. NW, Ste.1
Washington, DC 20009
Ph: (202)262-0412
E-mail: inquiries@ecoenergyfinance.org
URL: http://ecoenergyfinance.org
Contact: Ms. Shazia Khan Esq., Founder/Exec. Dir.
Multinational. Description: Provides clean and efficient energy solutions to the rural poor in Pakistan. Utilizes modern technology to install solar lighting systems in rural villages.

1458 ■ Energy Extraction Technologies (E2T)
7891 Wiggins Rd.
Howell, MI 48843
Ph: (517)548-3115
URL: http://www.energyextractiontechnologies.org
Contact: Mr. Thomas Wilmoth, Founder
Founded: 2005. **Description:** Aims to develop untapped sources of renewable energy in the United States. Promotes research of technologically-practical and commercially-viable solutions to address energy problems.

1459 ■ Energy Farm
PO Box 1834
Jackson, MS 39215
E-mail: projectdirector@energyfarm.org
URL: http://energyfarm.org
Contact: Richard Dortch, Project Dir.
Description: Aims to eliminate the energy dependence of the United States on foreign sources through the creation of domestic grid-distributed renewable energy infrastructure. Promotes application of renewable and sustainable energy technologies including solar, wind, hydro, tidal, geothermal, biomass, biofuels and ethanol.

1460 ■ New Energy Industry Association for Asia and the Pacific (NEIAAP)
2055 Junction Ave., Ste.225
San Jose, CA 95131
Ph: (408)434-1993
Fax: (408)434-1993
E-mail: shirley-snec@163.com
URL: http://www.neiaap.org
Contact: Shirley Chan, Contact
Multinational. Description: Aims to expand the market for new energy. Facilitates cooperation and exchange of information among members.

1461 ■ Research Partnership to Secure Energy for America (RPSEA)
1650 Hwy. 6, Ste.325
Sugar Land, TX 77478
Ph: (281)313-9555
URL: http://www.rpsea.org
Contact: Dr. Stephen A. Holditch, Chm.
Membership Dues: commercial company (based on annual revenue), $1,000-$10,000 (annual) ● academic institution, state/federal government entity, $2,500 (annual) ● non-profit organization/trade association, $1,000 (annual). **Description:** Facilitates the development of new methods and integrated systems for exploring, producing and transporting-to-market energy or other derivative products from ultra-deepwater and unconventional natural gas and other petroleum resources. Provides technical and knowledge resources about energy production in the United States.

1462 ■ Rural Renewable Energy Alliance (RREAL)
2330 Dancing Wind Rd. SW
Pine River, MN 56474
Ph: (218)587-4753
E-mail: info@rreal.org
URL: http://www.rreal.org
Contact: Jason Edens, Founding Dir.
Founded: 2000. **Description:** Addresses issues on availability of solar technologies to people of all income levels. Provides hands-on training and seminars in the field of solar energy.

1463 ■ Securing America's Future Energy (SAFE)
1111 19th St. NW, Ste.406
Washington, DC 20036
Ph: (202)461-2360
Fax: (202)461-2379
E-mail: info@secureenergy.org
URL: http://www.secureenergy.org
Contact: Robbie Diamond, Pres./CEO
Founded: 2005. **Description:** Aims to reduce America's dependence on oil and improve United States energy security. Educates policymakers and advocates for comprehensive energy reform. Raises public consciousness about the national security aspect of energy and practical solutions toward oil independence.

1464 ■ US-China Green Energy Council (UCGEC)
1964 Deodara Dr.
Los Altos, CA 94024-7054
E-mail: mike.zhang@ucgef.org
URL: http://www.ucgef.org
Contact: Robert S. Wu, Chm./CEO
Founded: 2008. **Membership Dues:** green, $20 (annual) ● senior, $500 (annual) ● VIP, $2,000 (annual).
Multinational. Description: Promotes and strengthens collaboration in green energy between United States and China. Provides a platform for government policy integration, business, investment, education and technology. Facilitates and sponsors high-impact cleantech collaborative initiatives and projects between the United States and China.

1465 ■ Young Professionals in Energy (YPE)
600 Travis St., Ste.2310
Houston, TX 77002
Ph: (832)429-6344
E-mail: contact@ypenergy.org
URL: http://www.ypenergy.org
Contact: Stephen Cravens, Founder
Founded: 2005. **Multinational. Description:** Facilitates the advancement of young professionals in the energy industry around the world. Provides a forum for networking and career development for professionals in the energy industry.

Engineering

1466 ■ American Society for Engineering Management (ASEM) (6331)
PO Box 820
Rolla, MO 65402-0820
Ph: (573)341-6228
Fax: (573)341-6567
E-mail: asem-hq@mst.edu
URL: http://www.asem.com
Contact: Kellie Davis, Mgr.

1467 ■ American Society of Plumbing Engineers (ASPE) (6334)
2980 S River Rd.
Des Plaines, IL 60018
Ph: (847)296-0002
E-mail: info@aspe.org
URL: http://aspe.org
Contact: **Jim Kendzel MPH, Exec. Dir.**

1468 ■ Association for Facilities Engineering (AFE) (6853)
12801 Worldgate Dr., Ste.500
Herndon, VA 20170
Ph: (571)203-7171
Fax: (571)766-2142
E-mail: info@afe.org
URL: http://www.afe.org
Contact: **Tom Baxter CPS, Chm.**

1469 ■ National Society of Black Engineers (NSBE) (6364)
205 Daingerfield Rd.
Alexandria, VA 22314
Ph: (703)549-2207
Fax: (703)683-5312

E-mail: info@nsbe.org
URL: **http://nsbe.org**
Contact: Calvin Phelps, Chm.

1470 ■ Society of Engineering Science (SES) (6890)
c/o S. White
Univ. of Illinois at Urbana-Champaign
Beckman Inst. for Advanced Sci. and Tech.
405 N Mathews Ave., Rm. 3361
Urbana, IL 61801
E-mail: swhite@uiuc.edu
URL: http://www.sesinc.org
Contact: Prof. Huajian Gao, Pres.

1471 ■ Society of Turkish American Architects, Engineers and Scientists (MIM) (6897)
821 United Nations Plz.
Turkish Ctr., 2nd Fl.
New York, NY 10017
Ph: (646)312-3366
E-mail: oalpoge@m-i-m.org
URL: http://www.m-i-m.org/mim2007-2.html
Contact: **Abdullah Uz Tansel, Pres.**

Entomology

1472 ■ The International Lepidoptera Survey (TILS)
PO Box 1124
Herndon, VA 20172
E-mail: tils-ttr-paypal@hotmail.com
URL: http://www.tils-ttr.org
Contact: Harry Pavulaan, Treas.
Founded: 1998. **Multinational. Description:** Aims to advance the study of Lepidoptera for the purpose of scientific discovery, determination and documentation. Maintains a vast collection of Lepidoptera.

Evolution

1473 ■ Society for the Study of Evolution (SSE) (6921)
c/o Judy Stone, Sec.
Colby Coll.
5720 Mayflower Hill Dr.
Waterville, ME 04901
Ph: (207)859-5736
Fax: (207)859-5705
E-mail: jstone@colby.edu
URL: http://www.evolutionsociety.org
Contact: **Scott V. Edwards, Pres.**

Explosives

1474 ■ International Association of Bomb Technicians and Investigators (IABTI) (6925)
1120 Intl. Pkwy., Ste.129
Goldvein, VA 22720-0160
Ph: (540)752-4533
Fax: (540)752-2796
E-mail: admin@iabti.org
URL: http://www.iabti.org
Contact: **David Glass, Intl. Dir.**

Fibers

1475 ■ Fiber Society (FS) (6926)
PO Box 8301
North Carolina State Univ.
Coll. of Textiles
2401 Res. Dr.
Raleigh, NC 27695-8301
Ph: (919)513-0143
Fax: **(919)515-3057**
E-mail: admin@thefibersociety.org
URL: http://www.thefibersociety.org
Contact: Dr. Michael Ellison, Sec.

Firearms

1476 ■ Association of Firearm and Tool Mark Examiners (AFTE) (7179)
c/o Andy G. Smith, Membership Sec.
San Francisco Police Dept.
PO Box 34426
San Francisco, CA 94134
Ph: (415)671-3264
Fax: (415)671-3290
E-mail: **aftemembership@gmail.com**
URL: http://www.afte.org
Contact: **John M. Finor, Pres.**

Fluid Power

1477 ■ International Fluid Power Society (IFPS) (7180)
PO Box 1420
Cherry Hill, NJ 08034-0054
Ph: (856)489-8983
Free: (800)308-6005
Fax: (856)424-9248
E-mail: **askus@ifps.org**
URL: http://www.ifps.org
Contact: **Jon Jensen, Pres./Chair**

Food

1478 ■ Sugar Industry Technologists (SIT) (6421)
201 Cypress Ave.
Clewiston, FL 33440
Ph: **(863)983-3637**
Fax: **(863)983-7855**
E-mail: **sitcontact@sucrose.com**
URL: http://www.sucrose.com/sit
Contact: **Mr. Leon A. Anhaiser, Exec. Dir.**

Gases

1479 ■ International Ozone Association (IOA) (7109)
PO Box 28873
Scottsdale, AZ 85255
Ph: (480)529-3787
Fax: (480)473-9068
E-mail: info3zone@io3a.org
URL: **http://www.io3a.org**
Contact: **Mr. Paul Overbeck, Exec. Dir.**

Genetics

1480 ■ American Genetic Association (AGA) (7209)
2030 SE Marine Sci. Dr.
Newport, OR 97365
Ph: (541)867-0334
E-mail: agajoh@oregonstate.edu
URL: http://www.theaga.org
Contact: **Dr. Scott Edwards, Pres.**

Geography

1481 ■ American Geographical Society (AGS) (6357)
32 Court St., Ste.201
Brooklyn, NY 11201-4404
Ph: **(718)624-2212**
Fax: **(718)624-2239**
E-mail: **ags@amergeog.org**
URL: http://www.amergeog.org
Contact: Mary Lynne Bird, Exec. Dir.

Geology

1482 ■ Association of American State Geologists (AASG) (6978)
Kentucky Geological Survey
228 Mining and Mineral Resources Bldg.
Lexington, KY 40506-0107
Ph: **(859)257-5500**
Fax: **(859)257-1147**
E-mail: **cobb@uky.edu**
URL: http://www.stategeologists.org
Contact: Mr. Jim Cobb, Pres.

Geoscience

1483 ■ ASFE (7234)
8811 Colesville Rd., Ste.G106
Silver Spring, MD 20910
Ph: (301)565-2733
Fax: (301)589-2017
E-mail: info@asfe.org
URL: http://www.asfe.org
Contact: **Mr. David R. Gaboury, Pres./CEO**

1484 ■ Society of Exploration Geophysicists (SEG) (7244)
PO Box 702740
Tulsa, OK 74170-2740
Ph: (918)497-5500 (918)497-5507
Fax: (918)497-5557
E-mail: **klaas.koster@apachecorp.com**
URL: http://www.seg.org
Contact: **Dr. Klaas Koster, Manuscript Tracking Specialist**

Graphics

1485 ■ American Design Drafting Association (ADDA) (7247)
105 E Main St.
Newbern, TN 38059
Ph: (731)627-0802
Fax: (731)627-9321
E-mail: **corporate@adda.org**
URL: http://www.adda.org
Contact: Floyd McWilliams, Pres.

1486 ■ Guild of Natural Science Illustrators (GNSI) (7003)
PO Box 652
Ben Franklin Sta.
Washington, DC 20044-0652
Ph: (301)309-1514
Fax: (301)309-1514
E-mail: **suewegener@comcast.net**
URL: http://www.gnsi.org
Contact: **Suzanne Wegener, Pres.**

1487 ■ Technical Association of the Graphic Arts (TAGA) (7005)
200 Deer Run Rd.
Sewickley, PA 15143
Ph: (412)259-1706
Fax: **(412)259-1765**
E-mail: jmeyers@printing.org
URL: http://www.printing.org/taga
Contact: Jessica Meyers, Admin.

Ichthyology

1488 ■ International Association of Astacology (IAA) (7269)
c/o Antonio Garza de Yta, Sec.
Auburn Univ.
Dept. of Fisheries and Allied Aquaculture
203 Swingle Hall
Auburn University, AL 36849-5419
Ph: **(334)844-4786**
Fax: (334)844-9208

E-mail: **garzaan@auburn.edu**
URL: http://iz.carnegiemnh.org/crayfish/iaa/index.htm
Contact: **James Fetzner, Pres.**

Industrial Engineering

1489 ■ SOLE - The International Society of Logistics (SOLE) (6422)
8100 Professional Pl., Ste.111
Hyattsville, MD 20785-2229
Ph: (301)459-8446
Fax: (301)459-1522
E-mail: solehq@erols.com
URL: http://www.sole.org
Contact: **Mr. Timothy H. Overstreet DML, Pres.**

Information Management

1490 ■ Association of Public Data Users (APDU) (7287)
PO Box 100155
Arlington, VA 22210
Ph: (703)522-4980
Fax: (703)522-4985
E-mail: info@apdu.org
URL: http://www.apdu.org
Contact: **Leonard M. Gaines, Pres.**

1491 ■ Special Interest Group on Information Retrieval (SIGIR) (7312)
140 Governors Dr.
Amherst, MA 01003-9264
Ph: **(413)545-3240**
Fax: **(413)545-1789**
E-mail: chair_sigir@acm.org
URL: http://www.sigir.org
Contact: **James Allan, Chm.**

Laboratory

1492 ■ Association of Laboratory Managers (ALMA) (6545)
8630 Guilford Rd., Ste.M
Columbia, MD 21046-2654
Free: **(800)985-7879**
Fax: **(800)985-7879**
E-mail: alma@labmanagers.org
URL: http://www.labmanagers.org
Contact: **Kelly John Mason, Pres.**

Manufacturing

1493 ■ Society of Manufacturing Engineers I North American Manufacturing Research Institution (NAMRI/SME) (6480)
1 SME Dr.
Dearborn, MI 48121
Ph: (313)425-3000
Free: (800)733-4763
Fax: (313)425-3400
E-mail: **membership@sme.org**
URL: http://www.sme.org/cgi-bin/communities.pl?/
  communities/namri/namrihome.htm
Contact: **Paul D. Bradley, Pres.**

Marine

1494 ■ American Littoral Society Northeast Region (ALS) (6483)
28 W 9th Rd.
Broad Channel, NY 11693
Ph: (718)318-9344
Fax: **(718)318-9345**
E-mail: driepe@nyc.rr.com
URL: http://www.alsnyc.org
Contact: **Don Riepe, Dir.**

1495 ■ Marine Technology Society (MTS) (7117)
5565 Sterrett Pl., Ste.108
Columbia, MD 21044
Ph: (410)884-5330
Fax: (410)884-9060
E-mail: membership@mtsociety.org
URL: http://www.mtsociety.org
Contact: **Jerry Boatman, Pres.**

Mathematics

1496 ■ Society for Natural Philosophy (SNP) (7398)
c/o Thomas J. Pence, Treas.
Michigan Sta. Univ.
Dept. of Mech. Engg.
2452 Engg. Bldg.
East Lansing, MI 48824-1226
E-mail: pence@egr.msu.edu
URL: http://www.ms.uky.edu/~snp
Contact: R.S. Rivlin, Chm.

Metallurgy

1497 ■ International Copper Association (ICA) (6524)
260 Madison Ave., 16th Fl.
New York, NY 10016-2401
Ph: **(212)251-7240**
Fax: **(212)251-7245**
E-mail: agkiretasr@cda.copper.org
URL: http://www.copperinfo.com
Contact: **Francis J. Kane, Pres./CEO**

1498 ■ Materials Properties Council (MPC) (6529)
PO Box 1942
New York, NY 10113-1941
Ph: (216)658-3847
Fax: (216)658-3854
E-mail: mprager@forengineers.org
URL: **http://foreng1.securesites.net/mpc**
Contact: Dr. Martin Prager, Contact

Mineralogy

1499 ■ Clay Minerals Society (CMS) (7446)
3635 Concorde Pkwy., Ste.500
Chantilly, VA 20151-1125
Ph: (703)652-9960
Fax: (703)652-9951
E-mail: cms@clays.org
URL: http://www.clays.org
Contact: **Paul A. Schroeder, Pres.**

Mining

1500 ■ Mining and Metallurgical Society of America (MMSA) (7452)
PO Box 810
Boulder, CO 80306-0810
Ph: (303)444-6032
E-mail: contactmmsa@mmsa.net
URL: http://www.mmsa.net
Contact: **Mark Jorgensen, Pres.**

1501 ■ Society for Mining, Metallurgy, and Exploration (SME) (7193)
12999 E Adam Aircraft Cir.
Englewood, CO 80112
Ph: (303)948-4200
Free: (800)763-3132
Fax: (303)973-3845
E-mail: cs@smenet.org
URL: http://www.smenet.org
Contact: **Drew A. Meyer, Pres.**

Natural Sciences

1502 ■ Academy of Natural Sciences (ANS) (7200)
1900 Benjamin Franklin Pkwy.
Philadelphia, PA 19103-1195
Ph: (215)299-1000
E-mail: presidentsoffice@ansp.org
URL: http://www.ansp.org
Contact: **George W. Gephart Jr., Pres./CEO**

1503 ■ American Quaternary Association (AMQUA) (7203)
c/o Brian Carter, Treas.
2209 W 104th St.
Perkins, OK 74059-4149
Ph: **(405)744-9585**
Fax: **(405)744-5269**
E-mail: treasurer@amqua.org
URL: http://www.amqua.org
Contact: **Stephen Jackson, Pres.**

1504 ■ Western Society of Naturalists (WSN) (7210)
San Diego State Univ.
Dept. of Biology
5500 Campanile Dr.
San Diego, CA 92182
E-mail: secretariat@wsn-online.org
URL: http://www.wsn-online.org
Contact: **Todd Anderson, Pres. -Elect**

Navigation

1505 ■ International Loran Association (ILA) (6582)
741 Cathedral Pointe Ln.
Santa Barbara, CA 93111
Ph: (805)967-8649
Fax: (805)967-8471
E-mail: ila@loran.org
URL: http://www.loran.org
Contact: **Sally Basker, Pres.**

Nuclear

1506 ■ Institute of Nuclear Materials Management (INMM) (7489)
111 Deer Lake Rd., Ste.100
Deerfield, IL 60015
Ph: (847)480-9573
Fax: (847)480-9282
E-mail: inmm@inmm.org
URL: http://www.inmm.org
Contact: **Mr. Scott Vance, Pres.**

1507 ■ Nuclear Information and Records Management Association (NIRMA) (7491)
10 Almas Rd.
Windham, NH 03087-1105
Ph: (603)432-6476
Fax: (603)432-3024
E-mail: **nirma@nirma.org**
URL: http://nirma.org/default.aspx
Contact: Jane Hannum, Exec. Dir.

1508 ■ Nuclear Information Technology Strategic Leadership (NITSL)
PO Box 262
Mohnton, PA 19540
Ph: (610)880-0055
E-mail: gregory.przyjemski@trmnet.com
URL: http://www.nitsl.org
Contact: Gregory Przyjemski, Contact
Founded: 1999. **Description:** Represents the interests of nuclear generation utilities that exchange information related to information technology management and quality issues. Provides strategic guidance on information technology solutions that support the business goals of nuclear generation.

Nuclear Energy

1509 ■ American Council on Global Nuclear Competitiveness
PO Box 4520
Washington, DC 20015
Ph: (301)656-1859
E-mail: scampbell@nuclearcompetitiveness.org
URL: http://www.nuclearcompetitiveness.org
Contact: Scott L. Campbell, Pres.
Founded: 2005. **Multinational. Description:** Aims to educate policymakers and the public on the need to restore United States leadership in nuclear energy. Promotes the return of American nuclear leadership to the world through the emergence of an U.S.-led global nuclear enterprise.

Ornithology

1510 ■ American Birding Association (ABA) (7515)
4945 N 30th St., Ste.200
Colorado Springs, CO 80919
Ph: (719)578-9703
Free: (800)850-2473
Fax: (719)578-1480
E-mail: member@aba.org
URL: http://www.aba.org
Contact: **Jeffrey A. Gordon, Pres./CEO**

1511 ■ American Ornithologists' Union (AOU) (6702)
c/o Scott Gillihan, Exec. Off.
5405 Villa View Dr.
Farmington, NM 87402
Ph: **(505)326-1579**
E-mail: aou@aou.org
URL: http://www.aou.org
Contact: John R. Faaborg, Pres.

1512 ■ Avicultural Society of America (ASA) (7518)
PO Box 5516
Riverside, CA 92517-5516
Ph: **(951)780-4102**
Fax: **(951)789-9366**
E-mail: info@asabirds.org
URL: http://www.asabirds.org
Contact: Helen Hanson, Membership Sec.

1513 ■ Inland Bird Banding Association (IBBA) (7265)
1833 S Winfield Dr.
Tiffin, OH 44883
E-mail: **hthomas.bartlett@gmail.com**
URL: http://ibbainfo.org
Contact: **H. Thomas Bartlett, Pres.**

Packaging

1514 ■ Institute of Packaging Professionals (IoPP) (6634)
1833 Centre Point Cir., Ste.123
Naperville, IL 60563
Ph: (630)544-5050
Fax: (630)544-5055
E-mail: info@iopp.org
URL: http://www.iopp.org
Contact: **Patrick Farrey, Exec. Dir.**

Parapsychology

1515 ■ Academy of Spirituality and Paranormal Studies, Inc. (ASPSI) (7440)
PO Box 614
Bloomfield, CT 06002-0614
Ph: (860)242-4593
E-mail: **execdir@aspsi.org**
URL: http://www.aspsi.org
Contact: Mr. Boyce Batey, Exec. Dir.

1516 ■ Parapsychological Association (PA) (7456)
PO Box 24173
Columbus, OH 43224
Ph: (202)318-2364
Fax: (202)318-2364
E-mail: business@parapsych.org
URL: http://www.parapsych.org
Contact: Ms. Annalisa Ventola, Exec. Sec.

Phenomena

1517 ■ American Society of Dowsers (ASD) (6685)
PO Box 24
Danville, VT 05828
Ph: (802)684-3417
Fax: (802)684-2565
E-mail: asd@dowsers.org
URL: http://www.dowsers.org
Contact: Nathan Platt, Operations Mgr.

1518 ■ National Investigations Committee on Unidentified Flying Objects (NICUFO) (6831)
9101 Topanga Canyon Blvd., No. 209
Chatsworth, CA 91311-5763
Ph: (818)882-0039
Fax: (818)998-6712
E-mail: info@nicufo.org
URL: http://www.nicufo.org
Contact: Julie Stranges, Founder

Polar Studies

1519 ■ American Polar Society (APS) (6735)
PO Box 300
Searsport, ME 04974
E-mail: aps@bluestreakme.com
URL: http://www.ampolarsociety.org
Contact: Charles Lagerbom, Membership Chm.

Power

1520 ■ GridWise Architecture Council (GWAC)
Pacific Northwest Natl. Lab.
PO Box 999
Richland, WA 99352
Ph: (509)372-6410
E-mail: gridwiseac.coordinator@pnl.gov
URL: http://www.gridwiseac.org
Contact: Ron Melton, Admin.
Description: Aims to promote and enable interoperability among the many entities that interact with the nation's electric power system. Provides resources for industry guidance and tools for the implementations of smart grid technology.

1521 ■ National Association of Power Engineers (NAPE) (7375)
1 Springfield St.
Chicopee, MA 01013
Ph: (413)592-6273
Fax: (413)592-1998
E-mail: nape@onecommail.com
URL: http://www.powerengineers.com
Contact: Barry Battista, Pres.

Radiation

1522 ■ Radiation Research Society (RRS) (7657)
PO Box 7050
Lawrence, KS 66044
Free: (800)627-0326

Fax: (785)843-1274
E-mail: info@radres.org
URL: http://www.radres.org
Contact: Jacqueline Williams PhD, Pres.

Research

1523 ■ Institute of Environmental Sciences and Technology (IEST) (7668)
2340 S Arlington Heights Rd., Ste.100
Arlington Heights, IL 60005-4516
Ph: (847)981-0100
Fax: (847)981-4130
E-mail: information@iest.org
URL: http://www.iest.org
Contact: Roberta Burrows, Exec. Dir.

1524 ■ Society of Research Administrators (SRA) (6783)
1901 N Moore St., Ste.1004
Arlington, VA 22209
Ph: (703)741-0140
Fax: (703)741-0142
E-mail: info@srainternational.org
URL: http://www.srainternational.org/sra03/index.cfm
Contact: Elliott Kulakowski, Interim Exec. Dir.

1525 ■ Universities Research Association (URA) (1014)
1111 19th St. NW, Ste.400
Washington, DC 20036
Ph: (202)293-1382
Fax: (202)293-5012
E-mail: info@ura-hq.org
URL: http://www.ura-hq.org
Contact: Eric Barron, Chm.

Robotics

1526 ■ Association for Unmanned Vehicle Systems International (AUVSI) (7678)
2700 S Quincy St., Ste.400
Arlington, VA 22206
Ph: (703)845-9671
Fax: (703)845-9679
E-mail: info@auvsi.org
URL: http://www.auvsi.org
Contact: Daryl Davidson, Exec. Dir.

1527 ■ Automated Imaging Association (AIA) (7418)
900 Victors Way, Ste.140
Ann Arbor, MI 48108
Ph: (734)994-6088
Free: (800)994-6099
Fax: (734)994-3338
E-mail: dwhalls@robotics.org
URL: http://www.machinevisiononline.org
Contact: Dana Whalls, Dir.

Sanitation

1528 ■ American Society of Sanitary Engineering (ASSE) (7688)
901 Canterbury Rd., Ste.A
Westlake, OH 44145
Ph: (440)835-3040
Fax: (440)835-3488
E-mail: info@asse-plumbing.org
URL: http://www.asse-plumbing.org
Contact: James Bickford, Pres.

Science

1529 ■ American Association for the Advancement of Science (AAAS) (7695)
1200 New York Ave. NW
Washington, DC 20005
Ph: (202)326-6400 (202)326-6640
Fax: (202)371-9526
E-mail: membership@aaas.org
URL: http://www.aaas.org
Contact: Alice Huang, Chair

1530 ■ American Philosophical Society (APS) (7697)
104 S 5th St.
Philadelphia, PA 19106-3387
Ph: (215)440-3400
Fax: (215)440-3423
E-mail: apsfund@amphilsoc.org
URL: http://www.amphilsoc.org
Contact: Mary Patterson McPherson, Exec. Off.

1531 ■ National Association of Academies of Science (NAAS) (6950)
c/o Mary E. Burke, Sec.
Acad. of Sci. of St. Louis
5050 Oakland Ave.
St. Louis, MO 63110
Ph: (314)533-8082
E-mail: mburke@academyofsciencestl.org
URL: http://www.academiesofscience.org
Contact: Dr. Peggy Connolly, Pres.

1532 ■ Society of Automotive Engineers (SAE) (7731)
400 Commonwealth Dr.
Warrendale, PA 15096-0001
Ph: (724)776-4970 (724)776-4841
Free: (877)606-7323
Fax: (724)776-0790
E-mail: customerservice@sae.org
URL: http://www.sae.org
Contact: Dr. Richard E. Kleine, Pres.

Seismology

1533 ■ International Tsunami Information Center (ITIC) (7742)
737 Bishop St., Ste.2200
Honolulu, HI 96813
Ph: (808)532-6423 (808)532-6422
Fax: (808)532-5576
E-mail: itic.tsunami@unesco.org
URL: http://itic.ioc-unesco.org
Contact: Dr. Laura S.L. Kong, Dir.

Soil

1534 ■ Soil Science Society of America (SSSA) (7776)
677 S Segoe Rd.
Madison, WI 53711
Ph: (608)273-8080 (608)268-4979
Fax: (608)273-2021
E-mail: headquarters@soils.org
URL: http://www.soils.org
Contact: Charles W. Rice, Pres.

Solar Energy

1535 ■ American Solar Energy Society (ASES) (7512)
4760 Walnut St., Ste.106
Boulder, CO 80301
Ph: (303)443-3130
Fax: (303)443-3212

E-mail: ases@ases.org
URL: http://www.ases.org
Contact: **Shaun McGrath, Exec. Dir.**

1536 ■ Solar Energy Industries Association (SEIA) (7781)
575 7th St. NW, Ste.400
Washington, DC 20004
Ph: (202)682-0556
Fax: **(202)682-0559**
E-mail: info@seia.org
URL: http://www.seia.org
Contact: Rhone Resch, Pres./CEO

1537 ■ Solar for Peace (SfP)
PO Box 764
Danville, CA 94526-0764
Ph: (925)208-4989
E-mail: info@solarforpeace.org
URL: http://www.solarforpeace.org
Contact: Vesna Heinze, Pres./Founder
Founded: 2009. **Multinational. Description:** Promotes development by harnessing solar energy that can provide electrical power and clean water to disadvantaged individuals and communities in the developing world. Fosters the use of solar technology for reduction in gaseous and solid emissions. Educates and provides technical assistance to promote alternative renewable energy.

Spectroscopy

1538 ■ Coblentz Society (CS) (7791)
Univ. of South Carolina
631 Sumter St.
Columbia, SC 29208
Ph: **(803)777-5264**
E-mail: **myrick@sc.edu**
URL: http://www.coblentz.org
Contact: **Prof. Michael L. Myrick, Pres.**

1539 ■ Society for Applied Spectroscopy (SAS) (7526)
5320 Spectrum Dr., Ste.C
Frederick, MD 21703
Ph: (301)694-8122 (513)627-2840
Fax: (301)694-6860
E-mail: **sasadmin@s-a-s.org**
URL: http://www.s-a-s.org
Contact: Bonnie A. Saylor, Exec. Dir.

Statistics

1540 ■ Caucus for Women in Statistics (CWS) (7806)
c/o Anna Nevius, Treas.
7732 Rydal Terr.
Rockville, MD 20855-2057
Ph: (301)827-0170 (301)258-0565
Fax: (301)827-6661
E-mail: anna.nevius@fda.hhs.gov
URL: http://caucusforwomeninstatistics.com
Contact: **Amanda L. Golbeck, Pres.**

1541 ■ Institute of Mathematical Statistics (IMS) (7809)
PO Box 22718
Beachwood, OH 44122
Ph: (216)295-2340 (301)634-7029
Free: (877)557-4674
Fax: (216)295-5661
E-mail: ims@imstat.org
URL: http://www.imstat.org
Contact: **Elyse Gustafson, Exec. Dir.**

1542 ■ International Biometric Society (IBS) (1027)
1444 I St. NW, Ste.700
Washington, DC 20005
Ph: (202)712-9049
Fax: (202)216-9646
E-mail: **ibs@tibs.org**
URL: http://www.tibs.org
Contact: Dee Ann Walker, Exec. Dir.

1543 ■ International Biometric Society, Western North American Region (7709)
1730 Minor Ave., Ste.1900
Cancer Res. and Biostatistics
Seattle, WA 98101-1468
E-mail: wnar@crab.org
URL: http://www.wnar.org
Contact: **Daniel Gillen, Pres.**

Surveying

1544 ■ American Association for Geodetic Surveying (AAGS) (7819)
6100 Ingleston Dr., No. 724
Sparks, NV 89436
Ph: **(775)626-6295**
E-mail: **blittell_aags@sbcglobal.net**
URL: http://www.aagsmo.org
Contact: **Barbara S. Littell, Pres.**

Telecommunications

1545 ■ Association of Federal Communications Consulting Engineers (AFCCE) (7873)
PO Box 19333
Washington, DC 20036
E-mail: afcce@cuenet.com
URL: http://www.afcce.org
Contact: **Stephen Lockwood, Pres.**

1546 ■ International Telecommunications Satellite Organization (ITSO) (7611)
3400 Intl. Dr. NW
Washington, DC 20008-3006
Ph: (202)243-5096 **(202)243-5050**
Fax: (202)243-5018
E-mail: **jtoscano@itso.int**
URL: http://www.itso.int
Contact: Jose Toscano, Dir. Gen./CEO

Telemetry

1547 ■ International Foundation for Telemetering (IFT) (7622)
5665 Oberlin Dr., Ste.200
San Diego, CA 92121
Ph: (858)225-4164
E-mail: **admin@telemetry.org**
URL: http://www.telemetry.org
Contact: Ms. Lena Moran, Exec. Coor.

Testing

1548 ■ ASTM International (6942)
PO Box C700
West Conshohocken, PA 19428-2959
Ph: (610)832-9500 **(610)832-9598**
Fax: (610)832-9555
E-mail: **jthomas@astm.org**
URL: http://www.astm.org
Contact: **James Thomas, Pres.**

Thermal Analysis

1549 ■ North American Thermal Analysis Society (NATAS) (7904)
c/o Lois Hall, Staff Management Dir.
Western Kentucky Univ.
Center for Res. and Development
Thermal Anal. Lab.
2413 Nashville Rd.
Bowling Green, KY 42101-4101
Ph: **(270)901-3490**
Fax: **(270)282-2096**
E-mail: natas@wku.edu
URL: http://www.natasinfo.org
Contact: **Tom Ramotowski, Exec. Councilor**

Toxicology

1550 ■ Society of Toxicology (SOT) (7640)
1821 Michael Faraday Dr., Ste.300
Reston, VA 20190-5348
Ph: (703)438-3115
Free: (800)826-6762
Fax: (703)438-3113
E-mail: sothq@toxicology.org
URL: http://www.toxicology.org
Contact: **Michael P. Holsapple, Pres.**

Transportation

1551 ■ Institute of Transportation Engineers (ITE) (7923)
1627 Eye St. NW, Ste.600
Washington, DC 20006
Ph: **(202)785-0060**
Fax: **(202)785-0609**
E-mail: ite_staff@ite.org
URL: http://www.ite.org
Contact: **Rock E. Miller, Intl. Pres.**

1552 ■ Transportation Research Forum (TRF) (7651)
NDSU Dept. 2880
PO Box 6050
Fargo, ND 58108-6050
Ph: (701)231-7766 **(701)231-8343**
Fax: (701)231-1945
E-mail: info@trforum.org
URL: http://www.trforum.org
Contact: Gene C. Griffin, Exec. Dir.

Tropical Studies

1553 ■ Organization for Tropical Studies, North American Office (OTS) (7652)
Duke Univ.
PO Box 90630
Durham, NC 27708-0630
Ph: (919)684-5774 **(919)684-3581**
Fax: (919)684-5661
E-mail: ots@duke.edu
URL: http://www.ots.ac.cr
Contact: Dr. Elizabeth Losos, Pres./CEO

Vacuum Technology

1554 ■ AVS Science and Technology Society (AVS) (7657)
c/o Angela Klink
125 Maiden Ln., 15th Fl.
New York, NY 10038
Ph: (212)248-0200
Fax: (212)248-0245

E-mail: yvonne@avs.org
URL: http://www.avs.org
Contact: **Angus Rockett, Pres.**

Water Resources

1555 ■ American Institute of Hydrology (AIH) (7933)
Southern Illinois Univ. Carbondale
1230 Lincoln Dr.
Carbondale, IL 62901
Ph: (618)453-7809
E-mail: aih@siu.edu
URL: http://www.aihydrology.org/whatisaih.htm
Contact: **Mr. Emitt C. Will III, Pres.**

Wind Energy

1556 ■ United States Offshore Wind Collaborative (USOWC)
1 Broadway, 14th Fl.
Cambridge, MA 02142

Ph: (617)401-3145
E-mail: info@usowc.org
URL: http://www.usowc.org
Contact: Fara Courtney, Exec. Dir.
Founded: 2009. **Description:** Facilitates the development and growth of a sustainable offshore wind industry in the United States. Addresses the technical, environmental, economic and regulatory issues to catalyze the sustainable development of offshore wind energy. Provides a forum for information-sharing, problem-solving, and capacity-building among government, industry, academia, energy and environment advocates.

1557 ■ The Wind Alliance (TWA)
1100 Louisiana St., Ste.5005
Houston, TX 77002
Ph: (713)600-9994
E-mail: info@thewindalliance.org
URL: http://www.thewindalliance.org
Contact: Dick Williams, Chm.
Description: Represents industrial, academic and public-sector entities working together to develop

infrastructure, technology and workforce within the wind industry. Provides sustainable and efficient clean power solutions through the use of wind energy as an alternative resource and technology.

Zoology

1558 ■ International Society of Protistologists (ISOP) (7979)
c/o Harriett Smith-Somerville
Univ. of Alabama
Dept. of Biological Sciences
Box 870344
Tuscaloosa, AL 35487
Ph: (205)348-1830
Fax: (205)348-1786
E-mail: hsmithso@ua.edu
URL: http://www.uga.edu/~protozoa
Contact: **Sina Adl, Pres.-Elect**

Administration

1559 ■ American Association of School Personnel Administrators (AASPA) (1201)
11863 W 112th St., Ste.100
Overland Park, KS 66210
Ph: (913)327-1222
Fax: (913)327-1223
E-mail: aaspa@aaspa.org
URL: http://www.aaspa.org
Contact: **Dr. Doug Gephart EdD, Interim Exec. Dir.**

1560 ■ American Conference of Academic Deans (ACAD) (7998)
c/o Laura A. Rzepka, Exec. Dir.
1818 R St. NW
Washington, DC 20009
Ph: (202)884-7419
Fax: (202)265-9532
E-mail: info@acad-edu.org
URL: http://www.acad-edu.org
Contact: **Carl Moses, Chm.**

1561 ■ Association of College and University Auditors (ACUA) (8001)
PO Box 14306
Lenexa, KS 66285-4306
Ph: (913)895-4620
Fax: (913)895-4652
E-mail: acua-info@goamp.com
URL: http://www.acua.org
Contact: **Mary M. Barnett, Pres.**

1562 ■ National Orientation Directors Association (NODA) (7736)
Univ. of Minnesota
1313 5th St. SE
Mail Unit 72
Minneapolis, MN 55414
Ph: (612)627-0150
Free: (866)521-NODA
Fax: (612)627-0153
E-mail: noda@umn.edu
URL: http://noda.orgsync.com
Contact: **Joyce Holl, Exec. Dir.**

Admissions

1563 ■ American Association of Collegiate Registrars and Admissions Officers (AACRAO) (8023)
1 Dupont Cir. NW, Ste.520
Washington, DC 20036
Ph: (202)293-9161
Fax: (202)872-8857
E-mail: **membership@aacrao.org**
URL: http://www.aacrao.org
Contact: **Jeffrey C. von Munkwitz-Smith, Pres.-Elect**

Agricultural Education

1564 ■ American Association for Agricultural Education (AAAE) (8050)
Ohio State Univ.
Human and Community Rsrc. Development
203A Ag. Admin. Bldg.
2120 Fyffe Rd.
Columbus, OH 43210
Ph: **(614)292-6321**
Fax: **(614)292-7007**
E-mail: **whittington.1@osu.edu**
URL: http://aaaeonline.org
Contact: **M. Susie Whittington, Pres.**

1565 ■ Association for International Agriculture and Rural Development (AIARD) (1053)
Univ. of California, Davis
Horticulture CRSP
190 EH Bldg.
1 Shields Ave.
Davis, CA 95616-5270
Ph: **(530)752-7975**
Fax: **(530)752-7182**
E-mail: **acrump@ucdavis.edu**
URL: http://www.aiard.org
Contact: **Amanda Crump, Sec.-Treas.**

1566 ■ National FFA Organization (NFFA) (7766)
PO Box 68960
Indianapolis, IN 46268-0960
Ph: (317)802-6060
Free: (800)772-0939
Fax: (317)802-6051
E-mail: **sbrown@ffa.org**
URL: http://www.ffa.org
Contact: **Steve A. Brown, Interim Advisor**

Alternative Medicine

1567 ■ American Commission for Accreditation of Reflexology Education and Training (ACARET)
1309 Hillcrest Dr.
Anchorage, AK 99503
Ph: (907)278-4646
Fax: (727)319-6911
E-mail: acaret@acaret.org
URL: http://www.acaret.org
Contact: Lilian Tibshraeny-Morten, Pres.

Founded: 1999. **Description:** Aims to uphold educational standards for the profession of reflexology. Provides voluntary accreditation for reflexology curricula and educators. Promotes standards of excellence in reflexology education.

Anti-Poverty

1568 ■ Out of Poverty thru Education (OPTE)
2128 William St., No. 107
Cape Girardeau, MO 63703
Ph: (573)334-0930
URL: http://www.outofpovertythrueducation.org
Contact: George Wrape, Founder
Multinational. Description: Aims to give children and orphans from Thomassique, Haiti access to basic education through the construction of a school. Provides a place where students can learn and eat at least one meal a day.

Arts

1569 ■ Association of Arts Administration Educators (AAAE) (7969)
4222 Oakland Dr.
Kalamazoo, MI 49008
Ph: **(608)561-2040**
E-mail: bharkins@artsadministration.org
URL: http://www.artsadministration.org
Contact: Barbara Harkins, Admin. Dir.

1570 ■ Council of Colleges of Arts and Sciences (CCAS) (8088)
Coll. of William and Mary
PO Box 8795
Williamsburg, VA 23187-8795
Ph: (757)221-1784
Fax: (757)221-1776
E-mail: ccas@wm.edu
URL: http://www.ccas.net
Contact: **Valerie Gray Hardcastle, Pres.-Elect**

1571 ■ National Art Education Association (NAEA) (8094)
1806 Robert Fulton Dr., Ste.300
Reston, VA 20191
Ph: (703)860-8000
Free: (800)299-8321
Fax: (703)860-2960
E-mail: info@arteducators.org
URL: **http://www.arteducators.org**
Contact: Ms. Melanie Dixon CAE, Chief Operating Off.

Bilingualism

1572 ■ National Association for Bilingual Education (NABE) (7824)
8701 Georgia Ave., Ste.611
Silver Spring, MD 20910
Ph: (240)450-3700
Fax: (240)450-3799
E-mail: nabe@nabe.org
URL: http://www.nabe.org
Contact: **Jose Agustin Ruiz-Escalante, Pres.**

Biology

1573 ■ National Association of Biology Teachers (NABT) (8119)
1313 Dolley Madison Blvd., Ste.402
McLean, VA 22101
Ph: (703)264-9696
Free: **(888)501-NABT**
Fax: **(703)790-2672**
E-mail: office@nabt.org
URL: http://www.nabt.org
Contact: **Daniel Ward, Pres.**

Broadcasting

1574 ■ Broadcast Education Association (BEA) (7140)
1771 N St. NW
Washington, DC 20036-2800
Ph: (202)429-3935
Fax: (202)775-2981
E-mail: **20hbirks@nab.org**
URL: http://www.beaweb.org
Contact: Heather Birks, Exec. Dir.

Business

1575 ■ Business-Higher Education Forum (BHEF) (7147)
2025 M St. NW, Ste.800
Washington, DC 20036-2422
Ph: (202)367-1189
Fax: (202)367-2269
E-mail: info@bhef.com
URL: http://www.bhef.com
Contact: **Brian K. Fitzgerald, CEO**

Business Education

1576 ■ Decision Sciences Institute (DSI) (7846)
75 Piedmont Ave., Ste.340
Atlanta, GA 30303
Ph: (404)413-7710 (404)413-7711
Fax: (404)413-7714
E-mail: clatta@gsu.edu
URL: http://www.decisionsciences.org
Contact: Carol J. Latta, Exec. Dir.

1577 ■ International Society for Business Education (ISBE) (8148)
2411 Lebanon Rd.
Pendleton, SC 29670
E-mail: **bosmanjanice@gmail.com**
URL: http://www.isbeusa.org
Contact: Janice Bosman, Pres.

1578 ■ National Association of Supervisor of Business Education (NASBE) (8156)
Colorado Community Coll. Sys.
9101 E Lowry Blvd.
Denver, CO 80230
Ph: **(720)858-2746**
Fax: **(303)904-2545**
E-mail: **laurie.urich@cccs.edu**
URL: http://www.nasbe.us
Contact: **Laurie Urich, Pres.-Elect**

Catholic

1579 ■ Association of Catholic Colleges and Universities (ACCU) (7180)
1 Dupont Cir., Ste.650
Washington, DC 20036
Ph: (202)457-0650
Fax: (202)728-0977
E-mail: accu@accunet.org
URL: http://www.accunet.org
Contact: **Michael Galligan-Stierle PhD, Pres./CEO**

Child Development

1580 ■ One Hen
PO Box 990781
Boston, MA 02199
E-mail: letters@onehen.org
URL: http://www.oneheninc.org
Contact: Amma Sefa-Dedeh, Exec. Dir.
Founded: 2009. **Multinational. Description:** Empowers kids to become social entrepreneurs who make a difference for themselves and the world. Equips educators with educational resources that will inspire kids to learn about financial responsibility, personal initiative, global awareness and giving back.

Childhood Education

1581 ■ Agami
PO Box 3178
Fremont, CA 94539
E-mail: education@agami.org
URL: http://www.agami.org
Contact: Dr. Babu S. Rahman, Pres.
Founded: 2003. **Membership Dues:** basic, $15 (annual) ● individual, $50 (annual) ● premium, $100 (annual) ● family, $80 (annual) ● student/senior, $35 (annual). **Multinational. Description:** Aims to promote basic education for the underprivileged children in Bangladesh. Provides educational materials to make projects in villages self-sufficient.

1582 ■ Battelle for Kids
1160 Dublin Rd., Ste.500
Columbus, OH 43215
Ph: (614)481-3141
Fax: (614)481-8997
E-mail: info@battelleforkids.org
URL: http://www.battelleforkids.org
Contact: Jim Mahoney PhD, Exec. Dir.
Founded: 2001. **Description:** Represents former superintendents, principals, teachers, curriculum staff and other professionals working collaboratively with school districts, state departments of education and other education-focused organizations. Provides strategic counsel for educational improvement. Supports training for teaching effectiveness and student progress.

1583 ■ Caring for Cambodia (CFC)
4815 W Braker Ln., Ste.502
Austin, TX 78759
E-mail: volunteers@caringforcambodia.org
URL: http://www.caringforcambodia.org
Contact: Bill Amelio, Chair
Membership Dues: family, $100 (annual) ● individual, $75 (annual) ● teacher, $50 (annual) ● student, $35 (annual). **Multinational. Description:** Aims to secure a better, brighter future for the children of Cambodia through education. Raises funds and builds schools to benefit Cambodian children.

1584 ■ NepalAama
PO Box 1565
Simi Valley, CA 93062
E-mail: info@nepalaama.org
URL: http://www.nepalaama.org
Contact: Suman Malla, Dir.
Founded: 2004. **Multinational. Description:** Aims to provide education to needy and underprivileged children in Nepal. Equips Nepalese children with higher quality of education, moral courage and academic excellence to impact society.

Chiropractic

1585 ■ Councils on Chiropractic Education International (CCEI)
PO Box 4943
Pocatello, ID 83205
Ph: (208)241-4855
E-mail: ccei@cceintl.org
URL: http://www.cceintl.org
Contact: Reed Phillips PhD, Exec. Dir.
Founded: 2001. **Multinational. Description:** Represents chiropractic accrediting bodies worldwide. Promotes excellence in chiropractic education through emphasis on quality in International Chiropractic Accreditation Standards. Advocates quality education through the dissemination and promotion of information to governments, professional organizations and others.

Christian

1586 ■ Association for Biblical Higher Education (ABHE) (8080)
5850 T.G. Lee Blvd., Ste.130
Orlando, FL 32822
Ph: (407)207-0808
Fax: (407)207-0840
E-mail: info@abhe.org
URL: http://www.abhe.org
Contact: Dr. Ralph E. Enlow Jr., Pres.

1587 ■ North American Professors of Christian Education (NAPCE) (8213)
Biola Univ.
13800 Biola Ave.
La Mirada, CA 90639
E-mail: mail@napce.org
URL: http://www.napce.org
Contact: **Dr. Freddy Cardoza, Exec. Admin.**

Communications

1588 ■ Religious Communication Association (RCA) (8149)
Univ. of Texas at Tyler
Dept. of Commun.
3900 Univ. Blvd.
Tyler, TX 75799
Ph: (903)566-7093
Fax: (903)566-7287
E-mail: **eiden@uttyler.edu**
URL: http://www.americanrhetoric.com/rca
Contact: Michael E. Eidenmuller, Coor. of Electronic Communication

Community Colleges

1589 ■ American Association of Community Colleges (AACC) (7271)
1 Dupont Cir. NW, Ste.410
Washington, DC 20036-1176
Ph: (202)728-0200
Fax: (202)833-2467
E-mail: **wbumphus@aacc.nche.edu**
URL: http://www.aacc.nche.edu
Contact: **Walter Bumphus, Pres./CEO**

1590 ■ National Council of State Directors of Community Colleges (8251)
1 Dupont Cir. NW, Ste.410
Washington, DC 20036
Ph: (202)728-0200
Fax: (202)833-2467
URL: http://www.statedirectors.org
Contact: **Edward Franklin, Chm.-Elect**

Community Development

1591 ■ International Organization for Haitian Development (IOHD)
1425 K St. NW, Ste.350
Washington, DC 20005
Ph: (305)735-3242
Free: (800)613-8262
URL: http://supporthaitieducation.org
Contact: Prof. Jefferson Miller JD, Pres.
Founded: 1999. **Membership Dues:** accredited Haiti higher educational institution (with enrollment under

5000), individual, $150 (annual) ● non-profit organization, accredited U.S. community college and higher educational institution, $250 (annual). **Multinational**. **Description:** Aims to develop a national community of educated professionals for the advancement of economic stability, sustainable governance and enrichment in Haiti. Offers educational, leadership and institutional development services to the Haitian people.

Community Education

1592 ■ National Community Education Association (NCEA) (7242)
3929 Old Lee Hwy., No. 91-A
Fairfax, VA 22030-2401
Ph: (703)359-8973
Fax: (703)359-0972
E-mail: ncea@ncea.com
URL: http://www.ncea.com
Contact: **Virginia Simmons, Pres.-Elect**

1593 ■ Under The Baobab Tree
1725 E Bayshore Rd., Ste.103
Redwood City, CA 94063
E-mail: info@underthebaobabtree.org
URL: http://www.underthebaobabtree.org
Contact: **Dr. Raj Patel, Co-Founder**
Founded: 2007. **Multinational**. **Description:** Aims to build sustainable communities and improve education in Malawi. Promotes education by building a bigger and better school for the children of Malawi. Supports projects on health, education, financial opportunity and raises awareness about issues in the local communities in Malawi.

Computer Science

1594 ■ Association of Information Technology Professionals (AITP) (7949)
401 N Michigan Ave., Ste.2400
Chicago, IL 60611-4267
Ph: (312)245-1070
Free: (800)224-9371
Fax: (312)673-6659
E-mail: aitp_hq@aitp.org
URL: http://www.aitp.org
Contact: **Jim Henry, Pres.**

1595 ■ Institute for Certification of Computing Professionals (ICCP) (8262)
2400 E Devon Ave., Ste.281
Des Plaines, IL 60018-4610
Ph: (847)299-4227
Free: (800)843-8227
Fax: (847)299-4280
E-mail: office2@iccp.org
URL: http://www.iccp.org
Contact: John Whitehouse, Dir. of Certification

1596 ■ International Association for Computer Information Systems (IACIS) (8263)
c/o Richard McCarthy, VP
Quinnipiac Univ.
School of Bus.
275 Mt. Carmel Ave.
Hamden, CT 06518
E-mail: richard.mccarthy@quinnipiac.edu
URL: http://www.iacis.org
Contact: **Lori Willoughby, Pres.**

Computers

1597 ■ Computers for Africa (CFA)
PO Box 34262
Omaha, NE 68134-0262
Ph: (402)933-6456

E-mail: info@computers4africa.org
URL: http://www.computers4africa.org
Contact: Timothy Leacock, Pres.
Founded: 2000. **Multinational**. **Description:** Promotes sustainable information and communications technology development (ICT) in rural African communities. Aims to bridge the digital divide by enhancing the technological education and training of African youth. Provides refurbished used computers to African high schools and non-profit organizations.

Cooperative Education

1598 ■ Cooperative Education and Internship Association (CEIA) (8289)
PO Box 42506
Cincinnati, OH 45242
Ph: (513)793-2342 (513)569-1624
Fax: (513)793-0463
E-mail: info@ceiainc.org
URL: http://www.ceiainc.org
Contact: **Robert S. Penkala, Pres.**

Curriculum

1599 ■ Association for Supervision and Curriculum Development (ASCD) (8307)
1703 N Beauregard St.
Alexandria, VA 22311-1714
Ph: (703)578-9600
Free: (800)933-2723
Fax: (703)575-5400
E-mail: member@ascd.org
URL: http://www.ascd.org
Contact: **Debra Hill, Pres.-Elect**

Driver Education

1600 ■ Driving School Association of the Americas (DSAA) (7851)
3090 E Gause Blvd., Ste.425
Slidell, LA 70461
Free: (800)270-DSAA
Fax: (985)649-9877
E-mail: info@thedsaa.org
URL: http://www.thedsaa.org
Contact: Ms. Sheila Varnado, Exec. VP

Earth Sciences

1601 ■ Rock Detective Geoscience Education
14655 Betz Ln.
Red Bluff, CA 96080
Ph: (530)529-4890
Fax: (530)529-6441
E-mail: kidsrx@rockdetective.org
URL: http://www.rockdetective.org
Contact: Ruth Deike, Exec. Dir.
Founded: 1996. **Description:** Fosters greater understanding and appreciation of earth science. Encourages students to develop curiosity that leads to further learning. Seeks to provide a carefully structured, hands-on program to enhance and complement K-12 Earth Science education.

Education

1602 ■ Academy for Educational Development (AED) (8039)
1825 Connecticut Ave. NW
Washington, DC 20009-5721
Ph: (202)884-8000 (202)884-8631
Fax: (202)884-8400
E-mail: web@aed.org
URL: http://www.aed.org
Contact: **Gregory R. Niblett, Pres./CEO**

1603 ■ American Educational Studies Association (AESA) (8228)
c/o Philip Kovacs, Communications Dir.
Univ. of Alabama in Huntsville
Dept. of Educ.
235 Morton Hall
Huntsville, AL 35899
E-mail: philip.kovacs@uah.edu
URL: http://www.educationalstudies.org
Contact: **Audrey Thompson, Pres.**

1604 ■ Creative Education Foundation (CEF) (7288)
48 N Pleasant St., Ste.301
Amherst, MA 01002
Ph: (508)960-0000
Fax: **(413)658-0046**
E-mail: contact@creativeeducationfoundation.org
URL: http://www.creativeeducationfoundation.org
Contact: Victoria Cliche, Pres./CEO

1605 ■ Education Development Center (EDC) (8382)
55 Chapel St.
Newton, MA 02458
Ph: (617)969-7100
Fax: (617)969-5979
E-mail: comment@edc.org
URL: http://www.edc.org
Contact: **Marvin J. Suomi, Pres./CEO**

1606 ■ International Listening Association (ILA) (7359)
PO Box 164
Belle Plaine, MN 56011-0164
Ph: (952)594-5697
Free: (877)8LI-STEN
E-mail: info@listen.org
URL: http://www.listen.org
Contact: **Christopher Bond, Pres.**

1607 ■ National Academy of Education (NAEd) (8100)
500 5th St. NW
Washington, DC 20001
Ph: (202)334-2341
Fax: (202)334-2350
E-mail: info@naeducation.org
URL: http://www.naeducation.org
Contact: Gregory White, Exec. Dir.

Educational Advocacy

1608 ■ International Association for Truancy and Dropout Prevention (IATDP) (8457)
c/o Henrietta Pryor, Sec.
10602 Holly Springs
Houston, TX 77042
Ph: **(713)802-4745**
Fax: **(713)802-4708**
E-mail: hpryor@houstonisd.org
URL: http://www.iatdp.org
Contact: **Alice Nichols, Pres.-Elect**

Educational Funding

1609 ■ Association for Education Finance and Policy (AEFP) (8471)
c/o Susanna Loeb, Pres.
524 Ceras, 520 Galvez Mall
Stanford, CA 94305
Ph: **(650)736-1258**
E-mail: **info@aefpweb.org**
URL: http://www.aefpweb.org
Contact: **Deborah Cunningham, Pres.-Elect**
Status Note: Formerly American Education Finance Association.

1610 ■ Council for Resource Development (CRD) (1103)
1 Dupont Cir. NW, Ste.365
Washington, DC 20036
Ph: (202)822-0750
Fax: (202)822-5014
E-mail: crd@crdnet.org
URL: http://www.crdnet.org
Contact: Polly Binns, Exec. Dir.

1611 ■ National Association of Student Financial Aid Administrators (NASFAA) (7419)
1101 Connecticut Ave. NW, Ste.1100
Washington, DC 20036-4312
Ph: (202)785-0453
Fax: (202)785-1487
E-mail: web@nasfaa.org
URL: http://www.nasfaa.org
Contact: Justin Draeger, Pres./CEO

Energy

1612 ■ Energy Conservation Organization (ECO)
965 Lanini Dr.
Hollister, CA 95023-6451
Ph: (408)804-2906
E-mail: info@energycharity.org
URL: http://www.energycharity.org
Contact: Darin Dingler, Contact
Founded: 2008. **Description:** Promotes energy conservation through increasing efficiencies and eliminating excessive waste. Aims to support expansion of renewable clean power sources, reduce dependence on foreign oil and decrease the effects of global warming.

1613 ■ Quantal Energy
97 Mt. Warner Rd.
Hadley, MA 01035
E-mail: info@quantalenergy.org
URL: http://quantalenergy.org
Contact: Matthew Breuer, Pres.
Multinational. Description: Addresses issues concerning environmental degradation, global conflicts and economic disparities. Investigates new and innovative alternative energy sources.

1614 ■ Strategic Energy, Environmental and Transportation Alternatives (SEETA)
18340 Yorba Linda Blvd., Ste.107-509
Yorba Linda, CA 92886-4058
Ph: (714)777-7729
Fax: (714)777-7728
E-mail: seetainfo@seeta.org
URL: http://www.seeta.org
Contact: Cynthia Verdugo-Peralta, Pres./CEO
Description: Promotes the education of clean energy and clean transportation technologies. Develops strategies to mitigate environmental problems through energy efficiency and cleaner, renewable technologies for energy generation and transportation. Educates public agencies, policy makers, legislators, stakeholders, industry, corporate executives and community organizations regarding environmental issues and how they affect the balance between public health and the economy.

Engineering

1615 ■ National Association of Peoplecultural Engineering Program Advocates (NAMEPA)
341 N Maitland Ave., Ste.130
Maitland, FL 32751-4761
Ph: (407)647-8839
Fax: (407)629-2502
E-mail: namepa@namepa.org
URL: http://www.namepa.org
Contact: Crystal S. Smith, Pres.

English

1616 ■ National Council of Teachers of English I Conference on English Education (CEE) (8509)
1111 W Kenyon Rd.
Urbana, IL 61801-1096
Ph: (217)328-3870
Free: (877)369-6283
Fax: (212)636-6452
URL: http://www.ncte.org/cee
Contact: Marshal George, Chair

1617 ■ Teachers of English to Speakers of Other Languages (TESOL) (8514)
1925 Ballenger Ave., Ste.550
Alexandria, VA 22314-6820
Ph: (703)836-0774
Free: (888)547-3369
Fax: (703)836-7864
E-mail: info@tesol.org
URL: http://www.tesol.org
Contact: Rosa Aronson, Exec. Dir.

Environment

1618 ■ American Society for Environmental History (ASEH) (8516)
Univ. of Washington
Interdisciplinary Arts and Sciences Prog.
1900 Commerce St.
Tacoma, WA 98402
E-mail: director@aseh.net
URL: http://www.aseh.net
Contact: Lisa Mighetto, Exec. Dir.

1619 ■ North American Association for Environmental Education (NAAEE)
2000 P St. NW, Ste.540
Washington, DC 20036
Ph: (202)419-0412
Fax: (202)419-0415
E-mail: info@naaee.org
URL: http://www.naaee.org
Contact: Linda Rhoads, Interim Exec. Dir.

Environmental Education

1620 ■ Alliance for Water Education (AWE)
120 Village Sq., Ste.137
Orinda, CA 94563
Ph: (925)386-0515
Fax: (925)386-0501
URL: http://allianceforwatereducation.org
Contact: Christie Batterman Jordan, Founder
Founded: 2009. **Description:** Aims to raise student awareness about fresh water and global sustainable water use. Improves environmental education for middle and high school students by providing programs about water literacy. Promotes sustainable fresh water use and empowers future generations to respond to global fresh water conditions.

1621 ■ Environmental Education and Conservation Global (EECG)
204 E Locust St.
Coudersport, PA 16915
Ph: (814)260-9138
E-mail: emccrea@eecg.org
URL: http://www.eecg.org
Contact: Edward J. McCrea, Pres./CEO
Founded: 2001. **Multinational. Description:** Promotes education as a tool to help conserve and enhance the earth's biological diversity. Provides training to educators and other professionals concerned about environmental quality to create more positive environmental attitudes and behaviors. **Awards:** John Judy Memorial Grants Project. **Frequency:** annual. **Type:** grant. **Recipient:** to an individual who dedicated his/her career to environmental education in the U.S. and abroad ● Linda Karbonit Memorial Grant Fund. **Frequency:** annual.

Type: grant. **Recipient:** for continuing education for women in environmental professions; for environmental medicine projects that include education as a focus; for small scale, particularly women-run, industries and economic activities; and for wildlife conservation education efforts.

1622 ■ Journey Toward Sustainability (JTS)
6585 Gatehouse Ct. NW
Concord, NC 28027
Ph: (704)641-7223 (704)960-9021
URL: http://www.journeytowardssustainability.org
Contact: Connie B. Harris, Exec. Dir.
Founded: 2009. **Multinational. Description:** Aims to educate elementary school children by utilizing an interactive mobile learning unit. Provides steps to reduce waste and to conserve water and energy, as well as explore other environmental initiatives.

Film

1623 ■ University Film and Video Association (UFVA) (7485)
3800 Barham Blvd., Ste.103
Los Angeles, CA 90068
Free: (866)647-8382
E-mail: ufvahome@aol.com
URL: http://www.ufva.org
Contact: Peter J. Bukalski, Treas.

Financial Aid

1624 ■ United Negro College Fund (UNCF) (8253)
8260 Willow Oaks Corporate Dr.
PO Box 10444
Fairfax, VA 22031-8044
Ph: (703)205-3400
Free: (800)331-2244
URL: http://www.uncf.org
Contact: Michael L. Lomax PhD, Pres./CEO

Gaming

1625 ■ International Simulation and Gaming Association (ISAGA) (7618)
George Washington Univ.
School of Bus. and Public Mgt.
Monroe Hall
Washington, DC 20052
Ph: (202)994-4930
E-mail: info@isaga.info
URL: http://www.isaga.info
Contact: Elizabeth Murf, Pres.

Gerontology

1626 ■ Association for Gerontology in Higher Education (AGHE) (8277)
1220 L St. NW, Ste.901
Washington, DC 20005-4018
Ph: (202)289-9806 (202)842-1275
Fax: (202)289-9824
E-mail: aghe@aghe.org
URL: http://www.aghe.org
Contact: Ms. M. Angela Baker, Dir.

Gifted

1627 ■ The Association for the Gifted (TAG)
Ball State Univ.
BU 109
Muncie, IN 47306
Ph: (765)285-5390
Free: (800)842-4251
Fax: (765)285-3783

E-mail: **cadams@bsu.edu**
URL: http://www.cectag.org
Contact: **Cheryll M. Adams PhD, Pres.**

Higher Education

1628 ■ Professional and Organizational Development Network in Higher Education (8117)
PO Box 3318
Nederland, CO 80466
Ph: (303)258-9521
Fax: (303)258-7377
E-mail: podoffice@podnetwork.org
URL: http://www.podnetwork.org
Contact: **Phyllis Worthy Dawkins PhD, Pres.**

History

1629 ■ Society for History Education (SHE) (8511)
California State Univ., Long Beach
1250 Bellflower Blvd.
Long Beach, CA 90840
Ph: (562)985-2573
Fax: (562)985-5431
E-mail: **trj@csulb.edu**
URL: http://www.thehistoryteacher.org
Contact: Troy Johnson, Pres.

Home Economics

1630 ■ National Association of Teacher Educators for Family and Consumer Sciences (NATEFACS) (8328)
Western Kentucky Univ.
1906 Coll. Heights Blvd., No. 11037
Bowling Green, KY 41201-1037
Ph: (270)745-3997
Fax: (270)745-3999
E-mail: dohner.1@osu.edu
URL: http://www.natefacs.org
Contact: **Kathy Croxall, Pres.-Elect/Program Chair**

Industrial Education

1631 ■ Association for sTEm Teacher Education (8355)
c/o Emily McKinley, Assoc. Mgr.
PO Box 2089
West Lafayette, IN 47996
E-mail: **astemte@gmail.com**
URL: http://www.astemte.org
Contact: **George E. Rogers EdD, Pres.**
Status Note: Formerly National Association of Industrial and Technical Teacher Educators.

1632 ■ Association of Technology, Management and Applied Engineering (ATMAE)
1390 Eisenhower Pl.
Ann Arbor, MI 48108
Ph: (734)677-0720
Fax: (734)677-0046
E-mail: atmae@atmae.org
URL: http://atmae.org
Contact: Mr. Rick Coscarelli, Exec. Dir.

1633 ■ International Technology Education Association | Council on Technology Teacher Education (CTTE) (7593)
1914 Assn. Dr.
Reston, VA 20191-1539
Ph: (703)860-2100
Fax: (703)860-0353
E-mail: ctte@list.appstate.edu
URL: **http://ctte.iweb.bsu.edu**
Contact: **Dr. Ed Reeve, Pres.**

Instructional Media

1634 ■ ACUTA: The Association for Communications Technology Professionals in Higher Education (ACUTA) (8689)
152 W Zandale Dr., Ste.200
Lexington, KY 40503
Ph: (859)278-3338
Fax: (859)278-3268
E-mail: **harrinjt@bc.edu**
URL: http://www.acuta.org
Contact: **Jennifer Van Horn, Pres.-Elect**

Insurance

1635 ■ Society of Insurance Trainers and Educators (SITE) (8389)
1821 Univ. Ave. W, Ste.S256
St. Paul, MN 55104
Ph: **(651)999-5354**
Fax: **(651)917-1835**
E-mail: ed@insurancetrainers.org
URL: http://www.insurancetrainers.org
Contact: **Brenda Davis AAI, Pres.**

International Exchange

1636 ■ Community Colleges for International Development (CCID) (8607)
PO Box 2068
Cedar Rapids, IA 52406-2068
Ph: (319)398-1257
Fax: (319)398-7113
E-mail: ccid@kirkwood.edu
URL: http://www.ccid.cc
Contact: **Dr. Carol Stax Brown, Exec. Dir.**

1637 ■ Council on International Educational Exchange USA (CIEE) (7669)
300 Fore St.
Portland, ME 04101
Ph: (207)553-4000
Free: (800)407-8839
Fax: (207)553-4299
E-mail: **contact@ciee.org**
URL: http://www.ciee.org
Contact: Robert E. Fallon, Chm.

1638 ■ Council for International Exchange of Scholars | Institute of International Education (CIES) (8750)
3007 Tilden St. NW, Ste.5L
Washington, DC 20008-3009
Ph: (202)686-4000
Fax: (202)362-3442
E-mail: cieswebmaster@iie.org
URL: http://www.cies.org
Contact: **James Ammons, Pres.**

1639 ■ Fulbright Association (FA) (8423)
1320 19th St. NW, Ste.350
Washington, DC 20036-1647
Ph: **(202)775-0725**
Fax: **(202)775-0727**
E-mail: jane.anderson@fulbright.org
URL: http://www.fulbright.org
Contact: Ms. Jane L. Anderson CAE, Exec. Dir.

1640 ■ National Registration Center for Study Abroad (NRCSA) (8638)
PO Box 1393
Milwaukee, WI 53201
Ph: (414)278-0631
Fax: (414)271-8884
E-mail: study@nrcsa.com
URL: **http://www.nrcsa.com**
Contact: **Mr. Mike Wittig, Dir.**

International Health

1641 ■ Universities Allied for Essential Medicines (UAEM)
2625 Alcatraz Ave., No. 180
Berkeley, CA 94705
Ph: (510)868-1159
Fax: (866)690-1178
E-mail: info@essentialmedicine.org
URL: http://essentialmedicine.org
Contact: Rachel Kiddell-Monroe, Pres.
Founded: 2001. **Multinational. Description:** Seeks to improve access to medicines in low-income and lower-middle income countries and to increase research and development of drugs for neglected tropical diseases. Promotes increased innovation and access to medicines and health-related technologies for public benefit.

International Relations

1642 ■ Building Bridges: Middle East-US
PO Box 1208
Norwich, VT 05055
Ph: (802)649-1601
E-mail: info@buildingbridgesmeus.org
URL: http://www.buildingbridgesmeus.org
Contact: Charles C. Buell, Pres./Treas.
Founded: 2002. **Multinational. Description:** Conducts a program of public education to improve mutual understanding between Middle East countries and the U.S. Creates opportunities for regular citizen dialogue via exchange visits.

1643 ■ Global China Connection (GCC)
PO Box 250860
New York, NY 10025
E-mail: info@gccglobal.org
URL: http://www.gccglobal.org
Contact: Daniel Tedesco, Pres.
Founded: 2008. **Multinational. Description:** Aims to promote cooperation between premier students in China and the international community. Works to create opportunities for students to develop life-changing relationships and leadership skills.

International Schools

1644 ■ Association for the Advancement of International Education (AAIE)
Nova Southeastern Univ.
Fischler School of Educ. and Human Services
3970 RCA Blvd., Ste.7000
Palm Beach Gardens, FL 33410
Ph: (954)262-5691 (954)262-5693
Fax: (954)262-2887
E-mail: aaie@nova.edu
URL: http://www.aaie.org
Contact: **Dr. Ronald Marino PhD, Treas.**

1645 ■ United Board for Christian Higher Education in Asia (7716)
475 Riverside Dr., Ste.1221
New York, NY 10115
Ph: (212)870-2600
Fax: (212)870-2322
E-mail: info@unitedboard.org
URL: http://www.unitedboard.org
Contact: **Nancy E. Chapman, Pres.**

Iranian

1646 ■ Association of Professors and Scholars of Iranian Heritage (APSIH)
PO Box 4175
Diamond Bar, CA 91765
Ph: (909)869-2569
Fax: (909)869-2564

E-mail: info@apsih.org
URL: http://www.apsih.org
Contact: Nasrin Rahimieh PhD, Pres.
Multinational. Description: Aims to create and promote scientific cooperation and enhancement within the social relationship of professors and scholars of Iranian heritage. Conducts scholarly and educational activities with professors of Iranian heritage and scholars. Offers scholarly and educational support to students of Iranian heritage.

Israeli

1647 ■ American Technion Society (ATS) (7743)
55 E 59th St.
New York, NY 10022-1112
Ph: (212)407-6300
Fax: (212)753-2925
E-mail: info@ats.org
URL: http://www.ats.org
Contact: **Stephen C. Crane, Exec. Dir.**

Jewish

1648 ■ Association for the Social Scientific Study of Jewry (ASSJ) (7925)
c/o Gail G. Glicksman, PhD, Pres.
429 Montgomery Ave., B-303
Haverford, PA 19041
E-mail: hartman@rowan.edu
URL: http://www.assj.org
Contact: Prof. Harriet Hartman PhD, Pres.

1649 ■ B'nai B'rith International's Center for Jewish Identity (8696)
801 2nd Ave., 14th Fl.
New York, NY 10017
Ph: (212)490-3290
Fax: (212)687-3429
E-mail: cji@bnaibrith.org
URL: http://www.bnaibrith.org/centers/jewish_identity.cfm
Contact: **Allan J. Jacobs, Pres.**

1650 ■ National Ramah Commission (NRC) (7937)
3080 Broadway
New York, NY 10027
Ph: (212)678-8881 (212)678-8883
Fax: (212)749-8251
E-mail: **info@campramah.org**
URL: http://www.campramah.org
Contact: **Rabbi Mitchell Cohen, Natl. Dir.**

Journalism

1651 ■ Journalism Education Association (JEA) (7807)
Kansas State Univ.
103 Kedzie Hall
Manhattan, KS 66506-1505
Ph: (785)532-5532 (785)532-7822
Free: (866)532-5532
Fax: (785)532-5563
E-mail: jea@spub.ksu.edu
URL: http://www.jea.org
Contact: **Kelly Furnas, Exec. Dir.**

Language

1652 ■ American Association of Teachers of Italian (AATI) (7782)
Indiana Univ.
Dept. of French and Italian
Ballentine Hall 642
1020 E Kirkwood Ave.
Bloomington, IN 47405-6601

E-mail: **ancvitti@indiana.edu**
URL: http://www.aati-online.org
Contact: Antonio C. Vitti, Pres.

1653 ■ American Council on the Teaching of Foreign Languages (ACTFL) (7793)
1001 N Fairfax St., Ste.200
Alexandria, VA 22314
Ph: (703)894-2900
Fax: (703)894-2905
E-mail: headquarters@actfl.org
URL: http://www.actfl.org
Contact: **David McAlpine, Pres.-Elect**

1654 ■ Association of Teachers of Japanese (ATJ) (8868)
240 Humanities Bldg.
279 UCB
Boulder, CO 80309-0279
Ph: (303)492-5487
Fax: (303)492-5856
E-mail: atj@colorado.edu
URL: http://www.aatj.org/atj
Contact: **Janet Ikeda, Pres.**

Legal Education

1655 ■ American Association for Paralegal Education (AAFPE) (7850)
19 Mantua Rd.
Mount Royal, NJ 08061
Ph: (856)423-2829
Fax: (856)423-3420
E-mail: info@aafpe.org
URL: http://www.aafpe.org
Contact: **Scott Hauert, Pres.-Elect**

1656 ■ Association of American Law Schools (AALS) (8901)
1201 Connecticut Ave. NW, Ste.800
Washington, DC 20036-2717
Ph: (202)296-8851
Fax: (202)296-8869
E-mail: aals@aals.org
URL: http://www.aals.org
Contact: **Lauren K. Robel, Pres.**

Liberal Arts

1657 ■ Association of Graduate Liberal Studies Programs (AGLSP) (7864)
Duke Univ.
Box 90095
Durham, NC 27708
Ph: (919)684-1987 (919)684-3222
Fax: (919)681-8905
E-mail: info@aglsp.org
URL: http://www.aglsp.org
Contact: **David L. Gitomer, Pres.**

Marine

1658 ■ National Marine Educators Association (NMEA) (8615)
PO Box 1470
Ocean Springs, MS 39566-1470
Ph: **(228)896-9182**
Fax: **(228)701-1771**
E-mail: nmea@usm.edu
URL: http://www.marine-ed.org
Contact: Adam Frederick, Pres.

Massage

1659 ■ Alliance for Massage Therapy Education
1760 Old Meadow Rd., Ste.500
McLean, VA 22102
Ph: (703)506-2888

Fax: (703)506-3266
E-mail: admin@afmte.org
URL: http://www.afmte.org
Contact: Pete Whitridge LMT, Pres.

Membership Dues: supporting, associate level - CE provider and teacher, $50 (annual) ● allied, $1,000 (annual) ● gold level - school, $500 (annual) ● gold level - CE provider, $150 (annual) ● gold level - teacher, associate level - school, $100 (annual). **Description:** Aims to advance massage therapy education by providing resources and educational opportunities to institutions, administrators, teachers and continuing education providers. Develops standards for effective teaching and training of massage therapy in schools.

Mathematics

1660 ■ Reasoning Mind (RM)
3050 Post Oak Blvd., Ste.1200
Houston, TX 77056
Ph: (281)579-1110
Fax: (281)200-0416
URL: http://www.reasoningmind.org
Contact: Alexander R. Khachatryan PhD, Pres./CEO

Founded: 2000. **Multinational. Description:** Provides quality math education for every child. Aims to develop students' math knowledge and thinking skills.

Medical Education

1661 ■ Association for Medical Education and Research in Substance Abuse (AMERSA) (7900)
PO Box 20160
Cranston, RI 02920
Ph: (401)243-8460
Fax: (877)418-8769
E-mail: admin@amersa.org
URL: http://www.amersa.org
Contact: Ms. Doreen MacLane-Baeder, Dir.

1662 ■ Association of Minority Health Professions Schools (AMHPS) (8850)
PO Box 13778
Atlanta, GA 30324
Ph: (678)904-4217
Free: (877)895-0902
Fax: (678)904-4518
E-mail: info@minorityhealth.org
URL: http://minorityhealth.org
Contact: **Wayne J. Riley MD, Pres./CEO**

1663 ■ Association of Professors of Medicine (APM) (8998)
330 John Carlyl St., Ste.610
Alexandria, VA 22314
Ph: (703)341-4540
Fax: (703)519-1893
E-mail: apm@im.org
URL: http://www.im.org/About/AllianceSites/APM/Pages/Default.aspx
Contact: Andrew I. Schafer MD, Pres.

Middle Schools

1664 ■ National Middle School Association (NMSA) (9024)
4151 Executive Pkwy., Ste.300
Westerville, OH 43081
Ph: (614)895-4730
Free: (800)528-6672
Fax: (614)895-4750
E-mail: info@nmsa.org
URL: http://www.nmsa.org
Contact: **Betty Greene-Bryant, Interim Dir.**

Music

**1665 ■ American School Band Directors'
Association (ASBDA) (9047)**
PO Box 696
Guttenberg, IA 52052
Ph: (563)252-2500
E-mail: asbda@alpinecom.net
URL: **http://www.asbda.com**
Contact: **Monte Dunnum, Natl. Pres.**

**1666 ■ College Band Directors National
Association (CBDNA) (7945)**
c/o Thomas Verrier, Sec.
Vanderbilt Univ.
Blair School of Music
2400 Blakemore Ave.
Nashville, TN 37212
Ph: (615)322-7651
Fax: (615)343-0324
E-mail: thomas.verrier@vanderbilt.edu
URL: http://www.cbdna.org
Contact: **Eric Rombach-Kendall, Pres.**

**1667 ■ National Association of College Wind
and Percussion Instructors (NACWPI) (8027)**
c/o Dr. Richard K. Weerts, Exec. Sec.-Treas.
308 Hillcrest Dr.
Kirksville, MO 63501
E-mail: dweerts@sbcglobal.net
URL: http://www.nacwpi.org
Contact: **Ken Broadway, Pres.**

**1668 ■ National Association of Schools of
Music (NASM) (9067)**
11250 Roger Bacon Dr., Ste.21
Reston, VA 20190-5248
Ph: (703)437-0700
Fax: (703)437-6312
E-mail: info@arts-accredit.org
URL: http://nasm.arts-accredit.org
Contact: **Don Gibson, Pres.**

Native American

**1669 ■ National Indian Education Association
(NIEA) (7977)**
110 Maryland Ave. NE, Ste.104
Washington, DC 20002
Ph: (202)544-7290
Fax: (202)544-7293
E-mail: niea@niea.org
URL: http://www.niea.org
Contact: **Quinton Roman Nose, Pres.-Elect**

Naturopathy

**1670 ■ Pediatric Association of Naturopathic
Physicians (PedANP)**
216 NE Fremont St.
Portland, OR 97212
E-mail: info@pedanp.org
URL: http://www.pedanp.org
Contact: Corey Harmon, Exec. Dir.
Membership Dues: associate, supporting, $85 (annual) ● student, $35 (annual). **Description:** Aims to disseminate knowledge and increase exposure of pediatric medicine to the naturopathic and conventional medical community. Elevates the standard of pediatric care and education in naturopathic medical programs. Encourages and facilitates dialogue on important pediatric issues within the medical community.

Nepalese

**1671 ■ Association of Nepal and Himalayan
Studies (ANHS) (9089)**
Macalester Coll.
Dept. of Anthropology
St. Paul, MN 55105-1801

Ph: **(651)696-6362**
Fax: **(651)696-6324**
E-mail: info@anhs-himalaya.org
URL: http://anhs-himalaya.org
Contact: **Geoff Childs, Pres.**

Peace

1672 ■ One Voice of Peace
522 S Sunrise Way, Ste.32
Palm Springs, CA 92264
Ph: (760)202-2330
E-mail: info@onevoiceofpeace.org
URL: http://www.onevoiceofpeace.org
Contact: Elena Chvany, Exec. Dir./Co-Founder
Description: Aims to promote peace throughout the world using educational programs and outreach. Works to provide practical tools that enhance communications and prevent conflict and misunderstanding before it can begin.

Physical Education

**1673 ■ American Alliance for Health,
Physical Education, Recreation and Dance
(AAHPERD) (8048)**
1900 Assn. Dr.
Reston, VA 20191-1598
Ph: (703)476-3400
Free: (800)213-7193
Fax: (703)476-9527
E-mail: membership@aahperd.org
URL: http://www.aahperd.org
Contact: **E. Paul Roetert, CEO**

Physics

**1674 ■ American Association of Physics
Teachers (AAPT) (8798)**
1 Physics Ellipse
College Park, MD 20740-3845
Ph: (301)209-3300 (301)209-3311
Fax: (301)209-0845
E-mail: eo@aapt.org
URL: http://www.aapt.org
Contact: **Beth A. Cunningham, Exec. Off.**

Preschool Education

1675 ■ Brick by Brick for Tanzania!
539 Braatz Dr.
Kewaskum, WI 53040
Ph: (262)573-9032
E-mail: johnk@brickbybrickfortanzania.org
URL: http://www.brickbybrickfortanzania.org/index.
html
Contact: John Kenworthy, Founder/Exec. Dir.
Founded: 2007. **Multinational. Description:** Aims to increase educational opportunities for the children of Tanzania, Africa by building preschools. Offers young students an academic headstart in a safe, nurturing and healthy environment.

Private Schools

**1676 ■ The Association of Boarding Schools
(TABS) (9018)**
1 N Pack Square., Ste.301
Asheville, NC 28801
Ph: (828)258-5354
Fax: (828)258-6428
E-mail: upham@tabs.org
URL: http://www.boardingschools.com
Contact: Peter Upham, Exec. Dir.

**1677 ■ Council for American Private
Education (CAPE) (8051)**
13017 Wisteria Dr., No. 457
Germantown, MD 20874-2607
Ph: (301)916-8460
Fax: (301)916-8485
E-mail: cape@capenet.org
URL: http://www.capenet.org
Contact: **Irene McHenry, Pres.**

Psychotherapy

1678 ■ Kate's Voice
PO Box 365
Sudbury, MA 01776
Ph: (978)440-9913
E-mail: katesvoice@comcast.net
URL: http://www.katesvoice.org
Contact: Laura Boyajian Rutherford, Dir./Pres.
Founded: 2007. **Description:** Provides music therapy services to students with special needs. Utilizes music therapy in interactive sessions as an effective way for students with special needs to develop their social, self-expression, communication and gross/fine motor skills.

Reading

**1679 ■ College Reading and Learning
Association (CRLA) (8848)**
2 Caracal St.
Belen, NM 87002
Ph: **(505)861-2142**
E-mail: **annwolf@crla.net**
URL: http://www.crla.net
Contact: **Ann Wolf, Pres.**

Real Estate

**1680 ■ American Real Estate and Urban
Economics Association (AREUEA) (8071)**
PO Box 9958
Richmond, VA 23228-9958
Free: (866)273-8321
Fax: (877)273-8323
E-mail: areuea@areuea.org
URL: http://www.areuea.org
Contact: **William C. Strange, Pres.**

Relief

1681 ■ Christ for the Poor
PO Box 60118
North Miami Beach, FL 33160
Ph: (305)891-2242
E-mail: atorres@christforthepoor.org
URL: http://christforthepoor.org
Contact: Mr. Alejandro Torres, Pres./CEO
Founded: 2007. **Multinational. Description:** Aims to assist communities devastated by war, poverty and hunger. Improves the quality of life of the poor by empowering young people, their families, and communities through education.

School Boards

**1682 ■ National School Boards Association
(NSBA) (9233)**
1680 Duke St.
Alexandria, VA 22314-3493
Ph: (703)838-6722
Fax: (703)683-7590
E-mail: info@nsba.org
URL: http://www.nsba.org
Contact: **Anne L. Bryant, Exec. Dir.**

Science

1683 ■ National Science Education Leadership Association (NSELA) (9268)
1219 N 54 St.
Omaha, NE 68132
Ph: (402)561-0176
E-mail: skoba@cox.net
URL: http://www.nsela.org
Contact: **Susan Koba, Pres.**

1684 ■ Triangle Coalition for Science and Technology Education (TCSTE) (8114)
1840 Wilson Blvd., Ste.201
Arlington, VA 22201
Ph: (703)516-5960
Free: (800)582-0115
Fax: (703)516-5969
E-mail: tricoal@triangle-coalition.org
URL: http://www.triangle-coalition.org
Contact: **Mary Burke, Pres.**

Social Welfare

1685 ■ National Organization for Human Services (NOHS) (9290)
5341 Old Hwy. 5, Ste.206, No. 214
Woodstock, GA 30188
Ph: (770)924-8899
Fax: (678)494-5076
E-mail: admin@nationalhumanservices.org
URL: http://www.nationalhumanservices.org
Contact: **Robert Olding, Pres.**

Special Education

1686 ■ Council for Children with Behavioral Disorders (CCBD)
1110 N Glebe Rd., Ste.300
Arlington, VA 22201-5704
Ph: (703)620-3660 (717)867-6389
Free: (800)224-6830
Fax: (703)264-9494
E-mail: peck@bc.edu
URL: http://www.ccbd.net
Contact: **Diana Rogers-Adkinson, Pres.-Elect**

1687 ■ Council for Exceptional Children (CEC) (9301)
2900 Crystal Dr., Ste.1000
Arlington, VA 22202-3557
Ph: (703)620-3660 (703)264-9415
Free: (866)509-0218
Fax: (703)264-9494
E-mail: service@cec.sped.org
URL: http://www.cec.sped.org
Contact: Bruce Ramirez, Exec. Dir.

Speech

1688 ■ American Forensic Association (AFA) (8142)
PO Box 256
River Falls, WI 54022
Free: (800)228-5424

Fax: (715)425-9533
E-mail: amforensicassoc@aol.com
URL: http://www.americanforensics.org
Contact: **Carol Winkler, Pres.**

Students

1689 ■ InterVarsity Link (8165)
PO Box 7895
Madison, WI 53707-7895
Ph: (608)274-9001
URL: http://www.intervarsity.org/link
Contact: **Renee Molitor, Staff Coor.**

Teachers

1690 ■ Association of Teacher Educators (ATE) (9005)
PO Box 793
Manassas, VA 20113
Ph: (703)331-0911
Fax: (703)331-3666
E-mail: info@ate1.org
URL: http://www.ate1.org
Contact: **James L. Alouf, Pres.**

Technical Education

1691 ■ General Society of Mechanics and Tradesmen of the City of New York (GSMT) (8204)
20 W 44th St.
New York, NY 10036
Ph: (212)840-1840
Fax: (212)840-2046
E-mail: info@generalsociety.org
URL: http://www.generalsociety.org
Contact: **Clinton W. Blume III, Exec. Dir.**

Testing

1692 ■ Educational Records Bureau (ERB) (1235)
220 E 42nd St.
New York, NY 10017
Free: (800)989-3721
E-mail: info@erbtest.org
URL: **http://erblearn.org**
Contact: **Dr. Lourdes Cowgill, Pres.**

Theology

1693 ■ National Association of Baptist Professors of Religion (NABPR) (8399)
Anderson Coll.
PO Box 1123
Anderson, SC 29621
E-mail: **mynatt@andersonuniversity.edu**
URL: http://www.nabpr.org
Contact: Danny S. Mynatt, Exec. Sec.-Treas.

Turkish

1694 ■ American Association of Teachers of Turkic Languages (AATT) (8295)
Princeton Univ.
Near Eastern Stud.
110 Jones Hall
Princeton, NJ 08544-1008
Ph: (609)258-1435
Fax: (609)258-1242
E-mail: ehgilson@princeton.edu
URL: http://www.princeton.edu/~turkish/aatt
Contact: **Dr. Uli Schamiloglu, Pres.**

Veterinary Medicine

1695 ■ Association of American Veterinary Medical Colleges (AAVMC) (1239)
1101 Vermont Ave. NW, Ste.301
Washington, DC 20005
Ph: (202)371-9195
Free: (877)862-2740
Fax: (202)842-0773
E-mail: tevanson@aavmc.org
URL: http://www.aavmc.org
Contact: **Dr. Willie Reed, Pres.**

Vocational Education

1696 ■ Association of Private Sector Colleges and Universities (APSCU) (9092)
1101 Connecticut Ave. NW, Ste.900
Washington, DC 20036
Ph: (202)336-6700
Free: (866)711-8574
Fax: (202)336-6828
E-mail: cca@career.org
URL: http://www.career.org
Contact: Haris N. Miller, Pres./CEO
Status Note: Formerly Career College Association.

1697 ■ National Association of State Directors of Career Technical Education Consortium (NASDCTEC) (9475)
8484 Georgia Ave., Ste.320
Silver Spring, MD 20910
Ph: (301)588-9630
Fax: (301)588-9631
E-mail: kgreen@nasdvtec.org
URL: http://www.careertech.org
Contact: **Dr. Phil Berkenbile, Pres.**

Women

1698 ■ American Association for Women in Community Colleges (AAWCC) (9480)
c/o Salt Lake Community College
PO Box 30808
Salt Lake City, UT 84130-0808
Ph: (801)975-4225
Fax: (801)957-4440
E-mail: aawccsupport@gmail.com
URL: http://www.aawccnatl.org
Contact: Dr. Cynthia A. Bioteau, Pres.

African

1699 ■ African Studies Association (ASA) (9134)
Rutgers Univ., Livingston Campus
54 Joyce Kilmer Ave.
Piscataway, NJ 08854-8045
Ph: (848)445-8173
Fax: (732)445-1366
E-mail: karen.jenkins@africanstudies.org
URL: http://www.africanstudies.org
Contact: Karen Jenkins, Exec. Dir.

1700 ■ Association of African Studies Programs (AASP) (7078)
c/o Judith A. Byfield
Cornell Univ.
Stud. and Res. Center
310 Triphammer Rd.
Ithaca, NY 14850
E-mail: jab632@cornell.edu
URL: http://aasp.asrc.cornell.edu
Contact: Dr. Ousseina Alidou, Chair

African-American

1701 ■ Association for the Study of African-American Life and History (ASALH) (8323)
Howard Center
2225 Georgia Ave. NW, Ste.331
Washington, DC 20059
Ph: (202)238-5910
Fax: (202)986-1506
E-mail: info@asalh.net
URL: http://www.asalh.org
Contact: Sylvia Cyrus-Albritton, Exec. Dir.

1702 ■ Charles H. Wright Museum of African American History (MAAH) (9530)
315 E Warren Ave.
Detroit, MI 48201
Ph: (313)494-5800 (313)494-5827
Fax: (313)494-5855
E-mail: membership@maah-detroit.org
URL: http://www.chwmuseum.org
Contact: Ms. Juanita Moore, Pres./CEO

American South

1703 ■ Institute for Southern Studies (ISS) (8355)
PO Box 531
Durham, NC 27702
Ph: (919)419-8311
Fax: (919)419-8315
E-mail: chris@southernstudies.org
URL: http://www.southernstudies.org
Contact: Chris Kromm, Exec. Dir./Publisher

1704 ■ Southern Historical Association (SHA) (9554)
Univ. of Georgia
Dept. of History, Rm. 111A
LeConte Hall
Athens, GA 30602-1602
Ph: (706)542-8848 (713)348-6039
E-mail: sdendy@uga.edu
URL: http://www.uga.edu/sha
Contact: Dr. John C. Inscoe, Sec.-Treas.

American West

1705 ■ Traditional Cowboy Arts Association (TCAA)
c/o Don Bellamy
PO Box 2002
Salmon, ID 83467
Ph: (208)865-2006
E-mail: tcowboyarts@gmail.com
URL: http://www.tcowboyarts.com
Contact: Scott Hardy, Pres.

Armenian

1706 ■ Armenian Film Foundation (AFF) (8382)
2219 Thousand Oaks Blvd., Ste.292
Thousand Oaks, CA 91362
Ph: (805)495-0717
Fax: (805)379-0667
E-mail: info@armenianfilm.org
URL: http://www.armenianfilm.org
Contact: Gerald S. Papazian Esq., Chm.

1707 ■ National Association for Armenian Studies and Research (NAASR) (8384)
395 Concord Ave.
Belmont, MA 02478
Ph: (617)489-1610
Fax: (617)484-1759
E-mail: hq@naasr.org
URL: http://www.naasr.org
Contact: Raffi P. Yeghiayan, Chm.

Art

1708 ■ American Guild of Judaic Art (AGJA) (9450)
135 Shaker Hallow
Alpharetta, GA 30022
Ph: (404)981-2308
E-mail: office@jewishart.org
URL: http://www.jewishart.org
Contact: Flora Rosefsky, Pres.

1709 ■ Independent Arts and Media
PO Box 420442
San Francisco, CA 94142
Ph: (415)738-4975
E-mail: clarisa@artsandmedia.net
URL: http://artsandmedia.net
Contact: Christine McClintock, Exec. Dir.

1710 ■ International Hajji Baba Society (IHBS) (9234)
c/o Kelvin Webb, Treas.
1105 D St. SE
Washington, DC 20003
E-mail: jeff@krauss.ws
URL: http://www.ihbs.org
Contact: Austin Doyle, Pres.

1711 ■ New Art Dealers Alliance (NADA)
55 Chrystie St. Ste.310
New York, NY 10002
Ph: (212)594-0883
E-mail: info@newartdealers.org
URL: http://www.newartdealers.org
Contact: Heather Hubbs, Dir.

1712 ■ Professional Picture Framers Association (PPFA) (8439)
3000 Picture Pl.
Jackson, MI 49201
Ph: (517)788-8100
Free: (800)762-9287
Fax: (517)788-8371
E-mail: nshaver@pmai.org
URL: http://www.pmai.org/ppfa
Contact: Kenneth Link, Pres.

1713 ■ Society for Asian Art (SAA) (1260)
Asian Art Museum
200 Larkin St.
San Francisco, CA 94102
Ph: (415)581-3701
Fax: (415)861-2358
E-mail: saa@asianart.org
URL: http://www.societyforasianart.org
Contact: Ehler Spliedt, Pres.

Artists

1714 ■ Allied Artists of America (AAA) (8477)
15 Gramercy Park S
New York, NY 10003
E-mail: thomasvalenti@alliedartistsofamerica.org
URL: http://www.alliedartistsofamerica.org
Contact: Thomas Valenti, Pres.

1715 ■ American Society of Artists (ASA) (9274)
PO Box 1326
Palatine, IL 60078
Ph: (312)751-2500 (847)991-4748
E-mail: asoa@webtv.net
URL: http://community-2.webtv.net/ASOA/ASA

1716 ■ Federation of Modern Painters and Sculptors (FMPS)
113 Greene St.
New York, NY 10012
Ph: (212)966-4864
Fax: (212)966-4864
E-mail: **info@fedart.org**
URL: http://www.fedart.org
Contact: Anneli Arms, Pres.

1717 ■ Graphic Artists Guild (The Guild) (8647)
32 Broadway, Ste.1114
New York, NY 10004-1612
Ph: (212)791-3400
Fax: (212)791-0333
E-mail: admin@gag.org
URL: **http://www.graphicartistsguild.org**
Contact: Ms. Patricia McKiernan, Exec. Dir.

1718 ■ National Cartoonists Society (NCS) (9550)
341 N Maitland Ave., Ste.130
Maitland, FL 32751
Ph: (407)647-8839
Fax: (407)629-2502
E-mail: info@reuben.org
URL: http://www.reuben.org
Contact: **Jeff Keane, Pres.**

1719 ■ Pollock-Krasner Foundation (PKF) (16651)
863 Park Ave.
New York, NY 10075
Ph: (212)517-5400
Fax: (212)288-2836
E-mail: **kbuitrago@pkf.org**
URL: http://www.pkf.org
Contact: Charles C. Bergman, Chm./CEO

1720 ■ Silk Painters International (SPIN)
PO Box 1074
East Point, FL 32328
Ph: **(850)670-8323**
E-mail: spin@silkpainters.org
URL: http://www.silkpainters.org
Contact: **Joyce Estes, Pres.**

1721 ■ Society of Illustrators (SI) (8489)
128 E 63rd St.
New York, NY 10021-7303
Ph: (212)838-2560
Fax: (212)838-2561
E-mail: info@societyillustrators.org
URL: http://www.societyillustrators.org
Contact: **Dennis Dittrich, Pres.**

1722 ■ Women's Caucus for Art (WCA) (9531)
Canal St. Sta.
PO Box 1498
New York, NY 10013
Ph: (212)634-0007
E-mail: **president@nationalwca.org**
URL: http://www.nationalwca.org
Contact: Mrs. Janice Nesser-Chu, Pres.

Arts

1723 ■ American Fired Arts Alliance (AFAA)
PO Box 14
Waupun, WI 53963
Ph: (920)296-5456
E-mail: **afaaonline@charter.com**
URL: **http://www.afaa.biz**
Contact: Mari Loomans, Pres.

1724 ■ Artfully AWARE (AfA)
201 E 17th St., 27D
New York, NY 10003
E-mail: create@artfullyaware.org
URL: http://www.artfullyaware.org
Contact: Hilary Wallis, Exec. Dir.

1725 ■ National Alliance for Media Arts and Culture (NAMAC) (1270)
145 9th St., Ste.102
San Francisco, CA 94103
Ph: (415)431-1391
Fax: (415)431-1392
E-mail: namac@namac.org
URL: http://www.namac.org
Contact: **David Dombrosky, Pres.**

1726 ■ National Assembly of State Arts Agencies (NASAA) (8530)
1029 Vermont Ave. NW, 2nd Fl.
Washington, DC 20005
Ph: (202)347-6352
Fax: (202)737-0526
E-mail: nasaa@nasaa-arts.org
URL: http://www.nasaa-arts.org
Contact: **Suzette M. Surkamer, Pres.**

1727 ■ Performing Arts Alliance (8675)
1211 Connecticut Ave. NW, Ste.200
Washington, DC 20036
Ph: (202)207-3850
Fax: (202)833-1543
E-mail: info@theperformingartsalliance.org
URL: http://theperformingartsalliance.org
Contact: Roche Schulfer, Chm.
Status Note: Formerly American Arts Alliance.

Arts and Sciences

1728 ■ Leonardo, The International Society for the Arts, Sciences and Technology (8575)
211 Sutter St., Ste.501
San Francisco, CA 94108
Ph: **(415)391-1110**
Fax: (415)391-2385
E-mail: isast@leonardo.info
URL: http://www.leonardo.info
Contact: Greg Harper, Chm./Treas.

Authors

1729 ■ American Christian Fiction Writers (ACFW)
PO Box 101066
Palm Bay, FL 32910-1066
E-mail: president@acfw.com
URL: http://www.acfw.com
Contact: **Margaret Daley, Pres.**

1730 ■ August Derleth Society (ADS) (8580)
PO Box 481
Sauk City, WI 53583
Ph: (608)643-3242
E-mail: augustderlethsociety@gmail.com
URL: http://www.derleth.org
Contact: **Ken Grant, Pres.**

1731 ■ D.H. Lawrence Society of North America (DHLSNA) (9427)
Loyola Univ. of Chicago
6525 N Sheridan
Chicago, IL 60626
E-mail: **jwexler@luc.edu**
URL: **http://dhlsna.com**
Contact: Joyce Wexler, Treas.

1732 ■ Ibsen Society of America (ISA) (8612)
c/o Prof. Arne Lunde, Treas.
Scandinavian Sect.
UCLA, 212 Royce Hall
Los Angeles, CA 90095
E-mail: **sandberg@berkeley.edu**
URL: http://www.ibsensociety.liu.edu
Contact: Mark Sandberg, Pres.

1733 ■ International Brecht Society (IBS) (8623)
Webster Univ.
470 E Lockwood
St. Louis, MO 63119
Ph: **(314)968-6900**
Fax: (314)963-6926
E-mail: hanssen@webster.edu
URL: **http://wiu.edu/users/brecht10**
Contact: Paula Hanssen, Sec.-Treas.

1734 ■ Kay Boyle Society
Columbia Coll.
Dept. of English
1301 Columbia Coll. Dr.
Columbia, SC 29203
E-mail: **anne.reynes@wannado.fr**
URL: http://homeweb1.unifr.ch/austenfe/pub/KBS/ KBS.htm
Contact: Prof. Christine Hait, Sec.-Treas.

1735 ■ Shakespeare Oxford Society (SOS) (9884)
PO Box 808
Yorktown Heights, NY 10598
Ph: (914)962-1717
Fax: (914)245-9713
E-mail: sosoffice@optonline.net
URL: http://www.shakespeare-oxford.com
Contact: **Richard Joyrich, Pres.**

1736 ■ Susan Glaspell Society
555 Jefferson St.
Northumberland, PA 17857
E-mail: powers@susqu.edu
URL: http://academic.shu.edu/glaspell
Contact: Dr. Doug Powers, Contact

Baltic

1737 ■ Association for the Advancement of Baltic Studies (AABS) (9905)
Univ. of Washington
Box 353420
Seattle, WA 98195-3420
E-mail: **aabs@uw.edu**
URL: **http://depts.washington.edu/aabs**
Contact: **Irena Blekys, Admin. Exec. Dir.**

Books

1738 ■ Antiquarian Booksellers Association of America (ABAA) (9521)
20 W 44th St., Ste.507
New York, NY 10036-6604
Ph: (212)944-8291
Fax: (212)944-8293
E-mail: **hq@abaa.org**
URL: http://www.abaa.org
Contact: Susan Benne, Exec. Dir.

1739 ■ Children's Book Council (CBC) (9919)
54 W 39th St., 14th Fl.
New York, NY 10018
Ph: (212)966-1990
Free: (800)807-9355
Fax: (212)966-2073
E-mail: cbc.info@cbcbooks.org
URL: http://www.cbcbooks.org
Contact: Robin Adelson, Exec. Dir.

1740 ■ Guild of Book Workers (GBW) (9923)
521 5th Ave.
New York, NY 10175-0038
E-mail: secretary@guildofbookworkers.org
URL: http://www.guildofbookworkers.org
Contact: **Andrew Huot, Pres.**

British

1741 ■ North American Conference on British Studies (NACBS) (8722)
Univ. of Texas at Austin
Harry Ransom Center
PO Box 7219
Austin, TX 78712-7219
Ph: (512)232-1236
Fax: (512)475-6978
E-mail: philippa@austin.utexas.edu
URL: http://www.nacbs.org
Contact: **Philippa Levine, Pres.**

Canals

1742 ■ Canal Society of New York State (CSNYS) (8743)
2527 Cherry Valley Tpke.
Marcellus, NY 13108
Ph: (315)730-4495
Fax: (315)673-1864
E-mail: **mbeilman@twcny.rr.com**
URL: http://www.newyorkcanals.org
Contact: Michele D. Beilman, Exec. Dir.

Catholic

1743 ■ Catholic Theological Society of America (CTSA) (9557)
c/o Dr. Dolores Christie, Exec. Dir.
John Carroll Univ.
20700 N Park Blvd.
University Heights, OH 44118
Ph: (216)397-1631
Fax: (216)397-1804
E-mail: dlchristie@aol.com
URL: http://www.ctsa-online.org
Contact: **Mary Ann Hinsdale IHM, Pres.**

Circus

1744 ■ American Youth Circus Organization (AYCO)
PO Box 96
Temple, NH 03084
Ph: (603)654-5523
E-mail: info@americanyouthcircus.org
URL: http://www.americanyouthcircus.org
Contact: **Chuck Johnson, Pres.**

Comics

1745 ■ Hero Initiative
11301 Olympic Blvd., No. 587
Los Angeles, CA 90064
Ph: **(818)776-1918**
E-mail: **james.mclauchlin.778@gmail.com**
URL: http://www.heroinitiative.org
Contact: Charlie Novinskie, Contact

Cultural Exchange

1746 ■ American Brazilian Cultural Exchange (ABCeX)
1075 E 33rd St.
Oakland, CA 94610
Ph: (510)280-4862
URL: http://www.abcex.org
Contact: Adam Stiles, CEO
Founded: 2009. **Multinational. Description:** Promotes cultural exchange between the United States and Brazil. Fosters cultural understanding and international cooperation by connecting individuals and organizations in Brazil and the United States.

1747 ■ American Telugu Association (ATA) (9869)
PO Box 4496
Naperville, IL 60567
Ph: (630)783-2250
Fax: (630)783-2251
E-mail: info@ataworld.org
URL: http://www.ataworld.org
Contact: **Dr. Rajender R. Jinna, Pres.**

1748 ■ Haiti Cultural Exchange
115 S Oxford St., No. 547
Brooklyn, NY 11217
Ph: (718)855-8514
E-mail: regine@haiticulturalx.org
URL: http://haiticulturalx.org
Contact: Regine M. Roumain, Exec. Dir.
Multinational. Description: Aims to develop, present and promote the cultural expressions of Haitian people. Raises an awareness of social issues and fosters cultural understanding and appreciation through programs in the arts, education and public affairs.

Dance

1749 ■ American Dance Guild (ADG) (9646)
240 W 14th St.
New York, NY 10011
Ph: **(212)627-9407**
E-mail: info@americandanceguild.org
URL: http://www.americandanceguild.org
Contact: **Gloria McLean, Pres.**

1750 ■ Congress on Research in Dance (CORD) (8975)
3416 Primm Ln.
Birmingham, AL 35216
Ph: (205)823-5517
Fax: (205)823-2760
E-mail: **ashanti@cordance.org**
URL: http://www.cordance.org
Contact: Marta Savigliano, Pres.

1751 ■ Dance Critics Association (DCA) (9655)
PO Box 1882
Old Chelsea Sta.
New York, NY 10011
E-mail: dancecritics@hotmail.com
URL: http://www.dancecritics.org
Contact: **Robert Abrams, Pres./Interim Exec. Dir.**

1752 ■ Dance Heritage Coalition (DHC) (9423)
1111 16th St. NW, Ste.300
Washington, DC 20036
Ph: **(202)223-8392**
Fax: (202)833-2686
E-mail: **lsmigel@danceheritage.org**
URL: http://www.danceheritage.org
Contact: Libby Smigel PhD, Exec. Dir.

English

1753 ■ ProEnglish
1601 N Kent St., Ste.1100
Arlington, VA 22209
Ph: (703)816-8821
Fax: **(571)527-2813**
E-mail: **dave@proenglish.org**
URL: http://www.proenglish.org
Contact: **Dave Louden, Exec. Dir.**

Ethnic Studies

1754 ■ American Society for Ethnohistory (ASE) (10080)
Duke Univ. Press
PO Box 906660
Durham, NC 27708-0660

Ph: **(919)687-3602**
Free: **(888)387-5687**
E-mail: membership@dukeupress.edu
URL: http://www.ethnohistory.org
Contact: **Dan Usner, Pres.**

1755 ■ National Association for Ethnic Studies (NAES) (1325)
Colorado State Univ.
Dept. of Ethnic Stud.
1790 Campus Delivery
Fort Collins, CO 80523-1790
E-mail: **naes@ethnicstudies.org**
URL: http://www.ethnicstudies.org
Contact: Maythee Rojas, Pres.

Film

1756 ■ Art Directors Guild (ADG) (8887)
11969 Ventura Blvd., 2nd Fl.
Studio City, CA 91604
Ph: (818)762-9995
Fax: (818)762-9997
E-mail: scott@artdirectors.org
URL: **http://www.adg.org**
Contact: Scott Roth, Exec. Dir.

Folk

1757 ■ American Folklore Society (AFS) (9049)
Ohio State Univ.
Mershon Center
1501 Neil Ave.
Columbus, OH 43201-2602
Ph: (614)292-3375 **(614)292-4715**
Fax: (614)292-2407
E-mail: lloyd.100@osu.edu
URL: http://www.afsnet.org
Contact: Timothy Lloyd, Exec. Dir.

1758 ■ Folk Alliance International (FAI) (10120)
510 S Main St., 1st Fl.
Memphis, TN 38103
Ph: (901)522-1170
Fax: (901)522-1172
E-mail: **anna@folk.org**
URL: http://www.folkalliance.org
Contact: **Renee Bodie, Pres.**

German

1759 ■ Goethe-Institut Inter Nationes (8907)
72 Spring St., 11th Fl.
New York, NY 10012
Ph: (212)439-8700
Fax: (212)439-8705
E-mail: info@newyork.goethe.org
URL: http://www.goethe.de/ins/us/ney/deindex.htm
Contact: **Ulrich Lindner, Acting Regional Dir.**

Historic Preservation

1760 ■ American Institute for Conservation of Historic and Artistic Works (AIC) (10174)
1156 15th St., Ste.320
Washington, DC 20005-1714
Ph: (202)452-9545 **(202)661-8060**
Fax: (202)452-9328
E-mail: info@conservation-us.org
URL: **http://www.conservation-us.org**
Contact: Ms. Eryl Wentworth, Exec. Dir.

1761 ■ American Overseas Schools Historical Society (AOSHS)
704 W Douglas Ave.
Wichita, KS 67203-6401
Ph: (316)265-6837

E-mail: overseasschools@aoshs.org
URL: **http://www.aoshs.org**
Contact: **Tina Calo, Pres.**

**1762 ■ APVA Preservation Virginia (APVA)
(9070)**
204 W Franklin St.
Richmond, VA 23220
Ph: (804)648-1889
Fax: **(804)775-0802**
E-mail: **info@preservationvirginia.org**
URL: **http://preservationvirginia.org**
Contact: Margaret Lam, Membership Coor.

1763 ■ Civil War Trust (CWT) (10182)
1156 15th St. NW, Ste.900
Washington, DC 20005
Ph: (202)367-1861
Free: (888)606-1400
Fax: (202)367-1865
E-mail: president@civilwar.org
URL: http://www.civilwar.org
Contact: James Lighthizer, Pres.
Status Note: Formerly Civil War Preservation Trust.

**1764 ■ Great Lakes Lighthouse Keepers
Association (GLLKA) (9575)**
PO Box 219
Mackinaw City, MI 49701-0219
Ph: (231)436-5580
Fax: (231)436-5466
E-mail: info@gllka.com
URL: http://www.gllka.com
Contact: **Mr. Dick Moehl, Pres.**

**1765 ■ International Coalition of Sites of
Conscience (ICSC)**
333 7th Ave., 14th Fl.
New York, NY 10001-5108
Ph: **(646)755-6180**
Fax: (646)755-6192
E-mail: coalition@tenement.org
URL: http://www.sitesofconscience.org
Contact: Maxim Novichenko, Admin. Mgr.

History

**1766 ■ Agricultural History Society (AHS)
(9860)**
c/o Alan I. Marcus, Treas.
**PO Box H
Mississippi State, MS 39762**
Ph: **(662)268-2247**
E-mail: **aimarcus@history.msstate.edu**
URL: http://www.aghistorysociety.org
Contact: James C. Giesen PhD, Exec. Sec.

**1767 ■ American Catholic Historical
Association (ACHA) (10258)**
Catholic Univ. of Am.
Mullen Lib., Rm. 320
Washington, DC 20064
Ph: (202)319-5079
Fax: (202)319-5079
E-mail: **acha@achahistory.org**
URL: http://research.cua.edu/acha
Contact: **Larissa Taylor, Pres.**

**1768 ■ American Society for Legal History
(ASLH) (10263)**
c/o Prof. Patricia Minter, Chair Membership Com-
mittee
**Western Kentucky Univ.
1906 Coll. Heights Blvd., No. 21086
Bowling Green, KY 42101-1086**
Fax: (270)793-0040
E-mail: **patricia.minter@wku.edu**
URL: http://www.aslh.net
Contact: Constance Backhouse, Pres.

1769 ■ Bostonian Society (TBS) (10132)
Old State House
206 Washington St.
Boston, MA 02109
Ph: (617)720-1713
E-mail: **ashley@bostonhistory.org**
URL: http://www.bostonhistory.org
Contact: Brian J. LeMay, Pres./Exec. Dir.

**1770 ■ Facing History and Ourselves
National Foundation (FHAO) (9888)**
16 Hurd Rd.
Brookline, MA 02445
Ph: (617)232-1595
Free: **(800)856-9039**
Fax: (617)232-0281
E-mail: info@facing.org
URL: http://www.facinghistory.org
Contact: **Margot Stern Strom, Exec. Dir.**

**1771 ■ Historical Society of Washington, DC
(HSW) (9894)**
Mt. Vernon Sq.
801 K St. NW
Washington, DC 20001
Ph: (202)383-1850 (202)383-1800
Fax: (202)383-1872
E-mail: info@historydc.org
URL: http://www.historydc.org
Contact: **Kenneth J. Brewer Sr., Chm.**

**1772 ■ History of Science Society (HSS)
(10154)
Univ. of Notre Dame
440 Geddes Hall
Notre Dame, IN 46556**
Ph: **(574)631-1194**
Fax: **(574)631-1533**
E-mail: info@hssonline.org
URL: http://www.hssonline.org
Contact: Robert Jay Malone, Exec. Dir.

**1773 ■ Organization of American Historians
(OAH) (9073)
112 N Bryan Ave.
Bloomington, IN 47408-4141**
Ph: (812)855-7311
Fax: (812)855-0696
E-mail: **questions@oah.org**
URL: http://www.oah.org
Contact: **Alice Kessler-Harris, Pres.**

**1774 ■ Society for French Historical Studies
(SFHS) (9087)**
551-101 Milton Ct.
Long Beach, CA 90803
Ph: (562)494-6764
E-mail: lclark2@csulb.edu
URL: **http://www.societyforfrenchhistorical-
studies.net**
Contact: Linda Clark, Exec. Dir.

**1775 ■ Society for Historians of American
Foreign Relations (SHAFR) (9088)**
Dept. of History
Ohio State Univ.
106 Dulles Hall
230 W 17th Ave.
Columbus, OH 43210
Ph: (614)292-1951 (614)292-7200
Fax: (614)292-2282
E-mail: shafr@osu.edu
URL: http://www.shafr.org
Contact: **Marilyn B. Young, Pres.**

**1776 ■ Society for Historians of the Early
American Republic (SHEAR) (9131)**
3355 Woodland Walk
Philadelphia, PA 19104-4531
Ph: (215)746-5393

Fax: (215)573-3391
E-mail: info@shear.org
URL: http://www.shear.org
Contact: **Harry Watson, Pres.**

**1777 ■ Society for History in the Federal
Government (SHFG) (9939)**
Box 14139
Benjamin Franklin Sta.
Washington, DC 20044
Ph: (301)279-9697
E-mail: **petedanielr@gmail.com**
URL: http://www.shfg.org
Contact: **Pete Daniel, Pres.**

Human Development

1778 ■ Cultural Survival (CS) (9951)
215 Prospect St.
Cambridge, MA 02139
Ph: (617)441-5400
Fax: (617)441-5417
E-mail: culturalsurvival@cs.org
URL: http://www.culturalsurvival.org
Contact: **Suzanne Benally, Exec. Dir.**

Humor

**1779 ■ International Society for Humor
Studies (ISHS) (9992)**
c/o Martin D. Lampert, PhD, Exec. Sec.
Holy Names Univ.
Psychology Dept.
3500 Mountain Blvd.
Oakland, CA 94619-1627
Ph: (510)436-1532
E-mail: ishs@hnu.edu
URL: **http://www.hnu.edu/ishs**
Contact: Elliott Oring, Pres.

Indian

**1780 ■ Leuva Patidar Samaj of USA (LPS of
USA)
716 Sweetwater Cir.
Old Hickory, TN 37138**
Ph: **(615)712-6999**
Fax: **(615)873-4650**
E-mail: **info@lpsofusa.com**
URL: http://www.leuvapatidarsamaj.com
Contact: Bharatbhai Patel, Pres.

**1781 ■ Uttaranchal Association of North
America (UANA)**
10560 Main St., Ste.LL-1
Fairfax, VA 22030
Ph: (703)273-7982
Fax: (703)385-3346
E-mail: **info@uttaranchal.org**
URL: http://www.uttaranchal.org
Contact: **Dr. Ajay Adhikari, Pres.**

Interdisciplinary Studies

**1782 ■ Society of Educators and Scholars
(SES) (10008)
Inter Amer. Univ. of Puerto Rico
Metropolitan Campus
PO Box 191293
San Juan, PR 00919-1293**
E-mail: **rakruse@charter.net**
URL: http://www.ses-online.org
Contact: **Tomas M. Jimenez, Exec. Dir.**

International Cooperation

1783 ■ Chinese American Cooperation Council (CACC)
PO Box 12028
Pleasanton, CA 94588
E-mail: bod@caccusa.org
URL: http://www.caccusa.org
Contact: Gary Li, Pres.
Founded: 2003. **Membership Dues:** executive, $25 (annual). **Multinational. Description:** Aims to promote cultural heritage and enhance friendship in the Chinese American community. Facilitates cultural and business exchanges and cooperation between the peoples of the United States and Greater China.

International Relations

1784 ■ Sino-American Bridge for Education and Health (SABEH)
c/o Anne S. Watt, EdD, Vice Chair
15R Sargent St.
Cambridge, MA 02140
E-mail: sthanas2001@yahoo.com
URL: http://sabeh.org
Contact: Susan C. Thanas, Chair
Founded: 2004. **Multinational. Description:** Develops and provides exchange programs for experienced American and Chinese teachers and healthcare workers. Creates a bridge between the cultures of the United States and China to achieve the common goals of mutual understanding, respect and friendship. **Additional Websites:** http://sino-americaneducation.org.

Irish

1785 ■ American Conference for Irish Studies (ACIS) (10408)
c/o Nicholas Wolf, Treas.
PO Box 842001
Richmond, VA 23284-2001
E-mail: sfarrel1@niu.edu
URL: http://www.acisweb.com/index.php
Contact: Mr. Sean Farrell, Pres.

Israeli

1786 ■ America-Israel Cultural Foundation (AICF) (10420)
1140 Broadway, Ste.No. 304
New York, NY 10001
Ph: (212)557-1600
Fax: (212)557-1611
E-mail: admin@aicf.org
URL: http://www.aicf.org
Contact: William A. Schwartz, Pres.

Italian

1787 ■ American Italian Historical Association (AIHA) (10032)
Queens College/City Univ. of New York
John D. Calandra Italiam Amer. Inst.
25 W 43rd St., 17th Fl.
New York, NY 10036
Ph: (708)756-7168
Fax: (708)756-7168
E-mail: gguida@citytech.cuny.edu
URL: http://www.aihaweb.org
Contact: George Guida, Pres.

Japan

1788 ■ Japan Studies Association (JSA)
c/o Dr. James Peoples, Sec.
Ohio Wesleyan Univ.
Dept. of Sociology/Anthropology
61 S Sandusky St.
Delaware, OH 43015
E-mail: overton@hawaii.edu
URL: http://www.japanstudies.org
Contact: Joe Overton, Pres.
Founded: 1995. **Membership Dues:** individual, $25 (annual) ● institution, $250 (annual). **Multinational. Description:** Aims to promote understanding of Japanese culture. Advocates and supports the infusion of Japan Studies at all levels of the educational system across the United States. Facilitates collaborative efforts in research and curricular development in Japan Studies.

Japanese

1789 ■ Japanese American Living Legacy
800 N State Coll. Blvd., RGC 8
Fullerton, CA 92831
Ph: (657)278-4483
E-mail: info@jalivinglegacy.org
URL: http://www.jalivinglegacy.org
Contact: Ms. Susan Uyemura, CEO/Pres.

Jewish

1790 ■ Leo Baeck Institute (LBI) (1382)
15 W 16th St.
New York, NY 10011-6301
Ph: (212)744-6400
Fax: (212)988-1305
E-mail: lbaeck@lbi.cjh.org
URL: http://www.lbi.org
Contact: Carol Kahn Strauss, Exec. Dir.

1791 ■ Yugntruf - Youth for Yiddish (YYY) (10463)
419 Lafayette St., 2nd Fl.
New York, NY 10003
Ph: (212)889-0381
E-mail: info@yugntruf.org
URL: http://www.yugntruf.org
Contact: Yankl-Perets Blum, Chm.

Latin America

1792 ■ Conference on Latin American History (CLAH) (10086)
Univ. of North Carolina at Charlotte
U.S. Department of of History and Prog. in Latin Amer. Studies
9201 Univ. City blvd.
Charlotte, NC 28223
Ph: (704)687-2027
Fax: (704)687-3218
E-mail: clah@uncc.edu
URL: http://clah.h-net.org
Contact: Jerry Davila, Exec. Sec.

1793 ■ Latin American Studies Association (LASA) (10481)
Univ. of Pittsburgh
416 Bellefield Hall
Pittsburgh, PA 15260
Ph: (412)648-7929
Fax: (412)624-7145
E-mail: lasa@pitt.edu
URL: http://lasa.international.pitt.edu
Contact: Maria Herminia Tavares de Almeida, Pres.

Libraries

1794 ■ American Association of Law Libraries (AALL) (10486)
105 W Adams St., Ste.3300
Chicago, IL 60603
Ph: (312)939-4764 (312)205-8016
Fax: (312)431-1097
E-mail: support@aall.org
URL: http://www.aallnet.org
Contact: Kate Hagan, Exec. Dir.

1795 ■ American Society for Indexing (ASI) (10492)
10200 W 44th Ave., Ste.304
Wheat Ridge, CO 80033
Ph: (303)463-2887
Fax: (303)422-8894
E-mail: info@asindexing.org
URL: http://www.asindexing.org/i4a/pages/index.cfm?pageid=1
Contact: Richard Shrout, Pres.

1796 ■ Asian Pacific American Librarians Association (APALA) (10327)
Loyola Law School
William M. Rains Lib.
919 Albany St.
Los Angeles, CA 90015
Ph: (213)736-1431
Fax: (213)487-2204
E-mail: florante.ibanez@lls.edu
URL: http://www.apalaweb.org
Contact: Florante Peter Ibanez, Pres.

1797 ■ Association of Research Libraries (ARL) (10115)
21 Dupont Cir. NW, Ste.800
Washington, DC 20036-1543
Ph: (202)296-2296
Fax: (202)872-0884
E-mail: clowry@arl.org
URL: http://www.arl.org
Contact: Charles B. Lowry, Exec. Dir.

1798 ■ Chief Officers of State Library Agencies (COSLA) (10516)
201 E Main St., Ste.1405
Lexington, KY 40507
Ph: (859)514-9151 (859)514-9210
Fax: (859)514-9166
E-mail: lveatch@georgialibraries.org
URL: http://www.cosla.org
Contact: Lamar Veatch, Pres.

1799 ■ Church and Synagogue Library Association (CSLA) (10125)
2920 SW Dolph Ct., Ste.3A
Portland, OR 97219-4055
Ph: (503)244-6919
Free: (800)LIB-CSLA
Fax: (503)977-3734
E-mail: csla@worldaccessnet.com
URL: http://cslainfo.org
Contact: Marjorie Smink, Pres.

1800 ■ Committee on Research Materials on Southeast Asia (CORMOSEA) (9304)
Ohio Univ.
Alden Lib.
Athens, OH 45701-2978
Ph: (740)593-2657
Fax: (740)597-1879
E-mail: comments@cormosea.org
URL: http://www.cormosea.org
Contact: Jeffrey R. Shane, Chm.

1801 ■ Library Leadership and Management Association (LLAMA) (9904)
50 E Huron St.
Chicago, IL 60611-2729
Ph: (312)280-5032 **(312)280-5036**
Free: (800)545-2433
Fax: (312)280-2169
E-mail: llama@ala.org
URL: http://ala.org/llama
Contact: **Kerry Ward, Exec. Dir.**

1802 ■ Middle East Librarians Association (MELA) (9291)
Harvard Univ.
Widener Lib., Rm. 5
1 Harvard Yard
Cambridge, MA 02138
Ph: **(617)496-3001**
Fax: **(617)496-2902**
E-mail: president@mela.us
URL: http://www.mela.us
Contact: **Michael Hopper, Pres.**

1803 ■ Music Library Association (MLA) (10544)
8551 Res. Way, Ste.180
Middleton, WI 53562-3567
Ph: (608)836-5825
Fax: (608)831-8200
E-mail: mla@areditions.com
URL: http://www.musiclibraryassoc.org
Contact: **Jerry L. McBride, Pres.**

Linguistics

1804 ■ American Association for Applied Linguistics (AAAL) (10570)
2900 Delk Rd., Ste.700
Marietta, GA 30067-5350
Ph: **(678)229-2892**
Free: (866)821-7700
Fax: **(678)560-9112**
E-mail: info@aaal.org
URL: http://www.aaal.org
Contact: **Suresh Canagarajah, Pres.**

1805 ■ Linguistic Society of America (LSA) (9377)
1325 18th St. NW, Ste.211
Washington, DC 20036-6501
Ph: (202)835-1714
Fax: (202)835-1717
E-mail: lsa@lsadc.org
URL: http://www.lsadc.org
Contact: **Sandra Chung, Pres.**

Literature

1806 ■ Children's Literature Association (ChLA) (1404)
PO Box 138
Battle Creek, MI 49016-0138
Ph: (269)965-8180
Fax: (269)965-3568
E-mail: **info@childlitassn.org**
URL: http://www.childlitassn.org
Contact: Kathryn Kiessling, Admin.

Marine

1807 ■ North American Society for Oceanic History (NASOH) (9500)
Dept. of History
Texas Christian Univ.
Box 297260
Fort Worth, TX 76129

E-mail: **amitchellcook@uwf.edu**
URL: http://www.nasoh.org
Contact: **Warren Riess, Pres.**

1808 ■ Titanic Historical Society (THS) (9418)
PO Box 51053
Indian Orchard, MA 01151-0053
Ph: (413)543-4770
Fax: (413)583-3633
E-mail: **titanicinfo@titanichistoricalsociety.org**
URL: http://titanichistoricalsociety.org
Contact: Edward S. Kamuda, Pres.

Medieval

1809 ■ International Center of Medieval Art (ICMA) (9427)
The Cloisters
Ft. Tryon Park
New York, NY 10040
Ph: (212)928-1146
Fax: (212)928-9946
E-mail: icma@medievalart.org
URL: http://www.medievalart.org
Contact: **Lawrence Nees, Pres.**

Mediterranean

1810 ■ Mediterranean Studies Association (MSA)
Box 79351
North Dartmouth, MA 02747
Ph: **(508)979-8687**
E-mail: btaggie@umassd.edu
URL: http://www.mediterraneanstudies.org
Contact: Benjamin F. Taggie, Exec. Dir./Treas.

Mexico

1811 ■ Mano A Mano: Mexican Culture Without Borders
126 St. Felix St.
Brooklyn, NY 11217
Ph: (212)587-3070
Fax: (212)587-3071
E-mail: info@manoamano.us
URL: http://www.manoamano.us
Contact: **Juan Carlos Aguirre, Exec. Dir.**

Museums

1812 ■ American Anthropological Association | Council for Museum Anthropology (CMA) (9577)
Univ. of Connecticut
Dept. of Anthropology
Academic Bldg. 114A
1084 Shennecossett Rd.
Groton, CT 06340
Ph: (860)405-9059
E-mail: margaret.bruchac@uconn.edu
URL: http://museumanthropology.org
Contact: Margaret Bruchac, Sec.

1813 ■ Association of Academic Museums and Galleries (AAMG) (10671)
Jordan Schnitzer Museum of Art
1223 Univ. of Oregon
Eugene, OR 97403-1223
Ph: (541)346-0972
Fax: **(541)346-0976**
E-mail: **hartz@uoregon.edu**
URL: http://www.aamg-us.org
Contact: **Jill Hartz, Pres.**

1814 ■ Association of Art Museum Directors (AAMD) (10669)
120 E 56th St., Ste.520
New York, NY 10022
Ph: (212)754-8084
Fax: (212)754-8087
URL: http://www.aamd.org
Contact: **Christine Anagnos, Exec. Dir.**

1815 ■ Council of American Jewish Museums (CAJM) (10675)
PO Box 12025
Jackson, MS 39236-2025
Ph: (303)871-3015
Fax: **(601)366-6293**
E-mail: **mhumphrey@cajm.net**
URL: http://www.cajm.net
Contact: **Judith Margles, Chair**

1816 ■ International Congress of Maritime Museums (ICMM) (10681)
329 High St.
Mystic, CT 06355
E-mail: **stuparnes@aol.com**
URL: http://www.icmmonline.org
Contact: Stuart Parnes, Sec. Gen.

1817 ■ Museum Education Roundtable (MER) (10684)
PO Box 15727
Washington, DC 20003
Ph: (202)547-8378
Fax: (202)547-8345
E-mail: **membership@museumeducation.info**
URL: http://museumeducation.info
Contact: Jill Overlie, Pres.

Music

1818 ■ American Composers Alliance (ACA) (10706)
802 W 190th St., 1st Fl.
New York, NY 10040
Ph: (212)925-0458
Fax: (212)925-6798
E-mail: info@composers.com
URL: http://www.composers.com
Contact: **Gina Genova, Exec. Dir./Gen. Mgr.**

1819 ■ Caledonian Foundation USA (CF) (9533)
PO Box 1242
Edgartown, MA 02539-1242
E-mail: **dm99mv@vineyard.net**
URL: http://www.caledonianfoundationusa.org
Contact: Ms. Duncan MacDonald, Exec. VP/Treas.

1820 ■ Chorus America (9554)
1156 15th St. NW, Ste.310
Washington, DC 20005
Ph: (202)331-7577
Fax: (202)331-7599
E-mail: service@chorusamerica.org
URL: http://www.chorusamerica.org
Contact: **Ann Meier Baker, Pres.**

1821 ■ International Clarinet Association (ICA) (10138)
PO Box 237
Longmont, CO 80502
Ph: **(405)651-6064**
Fax: (212)457-6124
E-mail: membership@clarinet.org
URL: http://www.clarinet.org
Contact: Ms. So Rhee, Exec. Dir.

1822 ■ International Tuba-Euphonium Association (ITEA) (10631)
PO Box 50867
Kalamazoo, MI 49005
Free: **(888)331-4832**
E-mail: adam@iteaonline.org
URL: http://www.iteaonline.org
Contact: Adam McFarlin, Exec. Dir.

1823 ■ Metropolitan Opera Guild (MOG) (10410)
70 Lincoln Center Plz.
New York, NY 10023
Ph: (212)769-7000 (212)362-0068
E-mail: info@metguild.org
URL: http://www.metoperafamily.org/guild
Contact: **Winthrop Rutherfurd Jr., Chm.**

1824 ■ Music Critics Association of North America (MCANA) (9614)
722 Dulaney Valley Rd., No. 259
Baltimore, MD 21204
Ph: (410)435-3881
Fax: (410)435-3881
E-mail: **info@mcana.org**
URL: http://mcana.org
Contact: Donald Rosenberg, Pres.

1825 ■ National Association for Civil War Brass Music (NACWBM)
124 Maiden Choice Ln.
Baltimore, MD 21228
Ph: (410)744-7708
E-mail: contact@nationalcivilwarbrassmusic.org
URL: http://www.nationalcivilwarbrassmusic.org
Contact: **Don Johnson, Pres.**

1826 ■ New Horizons International Music Association (NHIMA)
c/o Shirley Michaels, Ed.
1975 28th Ave., No. 18
Greeley, CO 80634
Ph: (970)301-4585
E-mail: smichaelsnhb@aol.com
URL: http://www.newhorizonsmusic.org
Contact: **Kathy Weber, Pres.**

1827 ■ New Violin Family Association (NVFA)
701 3rd St.
Encinitas, CA 92024
Ph: (760)632-0554
E-mail: info@hutchinsconsort.org
URL: **http://www.nvfa.org**
Contact: Dr. Carleen M. Hutchins, Exec. Dir./Founder

1828 ■ Society for Ethnomusicology (SEM)
The Musical Instrument Museum
8550 S Priest Dr.
Tempe, AZ 85284
Ph: **(480)309-4077**
E-mail: sem@indiana.edu
URL: http://webdb.iu.edu/sem/scripts/home.cfm
Contact: **Jennifer C. Post, Sec.**

1829 ■ Society for Music Perception and Cognition (SMPC)
c/o Scott Lipscomb, Treas.
Univ. of Minnesota School of Music
148 Ferguson Hall
2106 4th St. S
Minneapolis, MN 55455
Ph: (612)624-2843
Fax: (612)626-2200
E-mail: lipscomb@umn.edu
URL: http://www.musicperception.org
Contact: **Andrea Halpern, Pres.-Elect.**

Native American

1830 ■ Indian Arts and Crafts Association (IACA) (10507)
4010 Carlisle Blvd. NE, Ste.C
Albuquerque, NM 87107
Ph: (505)265-9149
Fax: (505)265-8251
E-mail: info@iaca.com
URL: http://www.iaca.com
Contact: **Joseph P. Zeller, Pres.**

Nudism

1831 ■ American Association for Nude Recreation (AANR) (9727)
1703 N Main St., Ste.E
Kissimmee, FL 34744
Ph: (407)933-2064
Free: (800)879-6833
Fax: (407)933-7577
E-mail: try-nude@aanr.com
URL: http://www.aanr.com
Contact: **Susan Weaver, Pres.**

Onomatology

1832 ■ American Name Society (ANS) (1459)
Binghamton Univ.
State Univ. of New York
Off. of the Provost
Binghamton, NY 13902-6000
Ph: (607)777-2143
Free: **(866)297-5154**
Fax: (607)777-4831
E-mail: mmcgoff@binghamton.edu
URL: http://www.wtsn.binghamton.edu/ans
Contact: Dr. Michael F. McGoff, Vice Provost/Treas.

Parliaments

1833 ■ American Institute of Parliamentarians (AIP) (10942)
550M Richie Hwy., No. 271
Severna Park, MD 21146
Free: (888)664-0428
Fax: (410)544-4640
E-mail: **aip@aippparl.org**
URL: http://www.aippparl.org
Contact: **Jeanette Williams, Dir.**

Performing Arts

1834 ■ International Performing Arts for Youth (IPAY)
1616 Walnut St., Ste.1800
Philadelphia, PA 19103
Ph: (267)690-1325
Fax: (215)413-7155
E-mail: **jane@ipayweb.org**
URL: http://www.ipayweb.org
Contact: **Jane Stojak, Gen. Mgr.**

1835 ■ Voices Breaking Boundaries (VBB)
PO Box 541247
Houston, TX 77254-1247
Ph: (713)524-7821
Fax: (713)630-5208
E-mail: info@vbbarts.org
URL: http://www.vbbarts.org
Contact: **Hosam Aboul-Ela, Pres.**

Philippines

1836 ■ Mamburao-U.S.A. Association (MUSA)
PO Box 17616
Beverly Hills, CA 90209-5616
Ph: **(310)286-2482**
Fax: **(310)286-9191**
E-mail: musatcom@aol.com
URL: http://www.musabulletin.com
Contact: Mrs. Thelma P. Calabio, Founder/Chair Emeritus

Philosophy

1837 ■ Association for Feminist Ethics and Social Theory (FEAST)
c/o Dr. Chris Frakes, Treas.
619 N Prospect St.
Colorado Springs, CO 80903
E-mail: **tessman@binghamton.edu**
URL: http://www.afeast.org
Contact: **Lisa Tessman, Chair**

1838 ■ International Society for Neoplatonic Studies (ISNS) (10804)
Univ. of Iowa
Dept. of Classics
210 Jefferson Bldg.
Iowa City, IA 52242
Ph: (319)335-0288
Free: **(800)444-2419**
Fax: (319)335-2326
E-mail: john-finamore@uiowa.edu
URL: http://www.isns.us
Contact: John F. Finamore, Pres.

1839 ■ North American Nietzsche Society (NANS) (9828)
Univ. of Illinois
Dept. of Philosophy
105 Gregory Hall
810 S Wright St.
Urbana, IL 61801
Ph: (217)333-1939 (217)333-2889
Fax: (217)244-8355
E-mail: northamericannietzschesociety@gmail.com
URL: http://nietzsche.philosophy.illinois.edu
Contact: Prof. Richard Schacht, Exec. Dir.

1840 ■ Society for Utopian Studies (SUS) (10839)
Univ. of Florida
PO Box 117310
Gainesville, FL 32611-7310
Ph: **(352)392-6650**
E-mail: pwegner@ufl.edu
URL: http://www.utoronto.ca/utopia
Contact: **Dr. Phillip E. Wegner, Pres.**

Photography

1841 ■ American Society of Photographers (ASP) (9805)
3120 N Argonne Dr.
Milwaukee, WI 53222
Ph: (414)871-6600
E-mail: jonallyn@aol.com
URL: **http://www.asofp.com**
Contact: Jon Allyn, Exec. Dir.

1842 ■ Blue Earth Alliance (BEA)
c/o Bart J. Cannon, Exec. Dir.
PO Box 4490
Seattle, WA 98194
Ph: **(206)569-8754**

E-mail: submissions10@blueearth.org
URL: http://www.blueearth.org
Contact: Malcolm L. Edwards, Co-Pres.

Play

1843 ■ The Association for the Study of Play (TASP) (11046)
St. Olaf Coll.
1520 St. Olaf Ave.
Northfield, MN 55057-1098
Ph: (507)786-3624
E-mail: **grossd@stolaf.edu**
URL: http://www.tasplay.org
Contact: **Dana Gross, Pres.**

Poetry

1844 ■ Academy of American Poets (10623)
75 Maiden Ln., Ste.901
New York, NY 10038
Ph: (212)274-0343
Fax: (212)274-9427
E-mail: **academy@poets.org**
URL: http://www.poets.org
Contact: Tree Swenson, Pres./Exec. Dir.

1845 ■ Tanka Society of America (TSA)
PO Box 521084
Tulsa, OK 74152
E-mail: **tankacat@gmail.com**
URL: http://www.tankasocietyofamerica.com
Contact: **Celia Stuart-Powles, Sec.**

Polish

1846 ■ Jozef Pilsudski Institute of America for Research in the Modern History of Poland (9900)
180 2nd Ave.
New York, NY 10003-5778
Ph: (212)505-9077
Fax: (212)505-9052
E-mail: **office@pilsudski.org**
URL: http://www.pilsudski.org
Contact: Dr. Iwona Korga, Exec. Dir.

1847 ■ Polish American Historical Association (PAHA) (10642)
Central Connecticut State Univ.
1615 Stanley St.
New Britain, CT 06050
Ph: (860)832-3010
E-mail: jacquesm@ccsu.edu
URL: http://www.polishamericanstudies.org
Contact: **Magda Jacques, Sec.**

Public Speaking

1848 ■ Toastmasters International (TI) (11090)
PO Box 9052
Mission Viejo, CA 92690-9052
Ph: (949)858-8255 (949)835-1300
Fax: (949)858-1207
E-mail: tminfo@toastmasters.org
URL: http://www.toastmasters.org
Contact: **Pat Johnson DTM, Pres.**

Railroads

1849 ■ Pacific Southwest Railway Museum (PSRM) (9959)
4695 Nebo Dr.
La Mesa, CA 91941-5259
Ph: (619)465-7776 (619)478-9937

E-mail: **support@sdrm.org**
URL: http://www.psrm.org
Contact: **Diana Hyatt, Pres.**

Reformation

1850 ■ Society for Reformation Research (SRR) (9914)
Luther Coll.
Dept. of History
700 Coll. Dr.
Decorah, IA 52101-1045
E-mail: **chrivi02@luther.edu**
URL: http://www.reformationresearch.org
Contact: **Mack P. Holt, Pres.**

Rhetoric

1851 ■ Rhetoric Society of America (RSA)
c/o Cara A. Finnegan, Committee Chair
Univ. of Illinois
103 Commun. Bldg. MC-456
1207 W Oregon Ave.
Urbana, IL 61801
E-mail: **info@rhetoricsociety.org**
URL: **http://associationdatabase.com/aws/RSA/pt/sp/Home_Page**
Contact: David Zarefsky, Pres.

Sculpture

1852 ■ Sculptors Guild (SG) (10720)
55 Washington St., Ste.256
Brooklyn, NY 11201
Ph: **(718)422-0555**
E-mail: sculptorsguild@gmail.com
URL: http://www.sculptorsguild.org
Contact: Mary Ellen Scherl, Pres.

Semantics

1853 ■ Institute of General Semantics (IGS) (10001)
3000 A Landers St.
Fort Worth, TX 76107
Ph: (817)922-9950
Fax: (817)922-9903
E-mail: **institute@general-semantics.org**
URL: **http://www.generalsemantics.org**
Contact: **Mr. Martin H. Levinson, Pres.**

Slavic

1854 ■ Association for Slavic, East European and Eurasian Studies (ASEEES) (10725)
203C Bellefield Hall
315 S Bellefield Ave.
Pittsburgh, PA 15260-6424
Ph: (412)648-9911 **(412)648-9788**
Fax: (412)648-9815
E-mail: aseees@pitt.edu
URL: http://www.aseees.org
Contact: **Lynda Park, Exec. Dir.**

Spanish

1855 ■ Queen Sofia Spanish Institute (9961)
684 Park Ave.
New York, NY 10065
Ph: (212)628-0420
Fax: (212)734-4177

E-mail: **press@queensofiasi.org**
URL: http://www.spanishinstitute.org
Contact: Oscar de la Renta, Chm.

Storytelling

1856 ■ Spellbinders (10489)
PO Box 1986
Basalt, CO 81621
Ph: (970)544-2389
Fax: (970)544-4761
E-mail: info@spellbinders.org
URL: http://www.spellbinders.org
Contact: Catherine Johnson, Exec. Dir.

Swedish

1857 ■ Swedish Colonial Society (SCS) (10749)
916 S Swanson St.
Philadelphia, PA 19147-4332
E-mail: **info@colonialswedes.org**
URL: http://www.colonialswedes.org
Contact: **Ms. Peg Berich, Registrar/Financial Sec.**

Theatre

1858 ■ Alliance of Resident Theatres/New York (ART/NY) (10754)
520 8th Ave., Ste.319
New York, NY 10018
Ph: (212)244-6667
Fax: (212)714-1918
E-mail: **tgramps@art-newyork.org**
URL: **http://www.art-newyork.org**
Contact: Robert LuPone, Pres.

1859 ■ New England Theatre Conference (NETC) (1499)
215 Knob Hill Dr.
Hamden, CT 06518
Ph: (617)851-8535
Fax: (203)288-5938
E-mail: **mail@netconline.org**
URL: http://netconline.org
Contact: **Jeffrey Watts, Pres.**

Time

1860 ■ International Society for the Study of Time (ISST) (9932)
c/o Jo Alyson Parker, Ed.
St. Joseph's Univ.
English Dept.
5600 City Ave.
Philadelphia, PA 19131-1395
E-mail: membership@studyoftime.org
URL: http://www.studyoftime.org
Contact: **Paul Harris, Pres.**

Translation

1861 ■ American Literary Translators Association (ALTA) (11058)
Univ. of Texas at Dallas
800 W Campbell Rd.
Mail Sta. J051
Richardson, TX 75080-3021
Ph: (972)883-2092
Fax: (972)883-6303
E-mail: **maria.suarez@utdallas.edu**
URL: http://www.utdallas.edu/alta
Contact: **Barbara Harshav, Pres.**

Turkish

1862 ■ Turkish Studies Association (TSA) (11062)
Princeton Univ.
110 Jones Hall
Princeton, NJ 08544
Ph: **(609)258-4280**
Fax: **(609)258-1242**
E-mail: **hanioglu@princeton.edu**
URL: http://www.h-net.org/~thetsa
Contact: **Sukru Hanioglu, Pres.**

Ukrainian

1863 ■ Ukrainian Academy of Arts and Sciences in the U.S. (UVAN) (10062)
206 W 100 St.
New York, NY 10021-1018
Ph: (212)222-1866
Fax: (212)864-3977
E-mail: **uvan@uvan.us**
URL: http://uvan.us
Contact: **Albert Kipa, Pres.**

1864 ■ Ukrainian Institute of America (UIA) (11248)
2 E 79th St.
New York, NY 10021
Ph: (212)288-8660
Fax: (212)288-2918
E-mail: **mail@ukrainianinstitute.org**
URL: http://www.ukrainianinstitute.org
Contact: Daniel Swistel, Pres.

Victorian

1865 ■ Research Society for Victorian Periodicals (RSVP) (10082)
939 Ridge Court, No. 2
Evanston, IL 60202
E-mail: **president@rs4vp.org**
URL: http://www.rs4vp.org
Contact: **Patrick Leary, Pres.**

World Notables

1866 ■ Harry S. Truman Library Institute for National and International Affairs (10880)
500 W U.S. Hwy. 24
Independence, MO 64050

Ph: **(816)268-8200 (816)268-8243**
Free: **(800)833-1225**
Fax: **(816)268-8295**
E-mail: truman.library@nara.gov
URL: http://www.trumanlibrary.org
Contact: **Mr. Alex Burden, Exec. Dir.**

1867 ■ William James Society (WJS) (11331)
c/o Todd Lekan, Sec.-Treas.
Muskingum Univ.
163 Stormont St.
New Concord, OH 43762
E-mail: **tmlekan@yahoo.com**
URL: http://www.wjsociety.org
Contact: **Ellen Suckiel, Pres.**

Writing

1868 ■ American Handwriting Analysis Foundation (AHAF) (10197)
PO Box 460385
Escondido, CA 92046-0385
Ph: **(760)489-0692**
Free: **(800)826-7774**
E-mail: **ahafpresident@gmail.com**
URL: **http://www.ahafhandwriting.org**
Contact: **Debra Peddy CG, Pres.**

Abortion

1869 ■ Elliot Institute
PO Box 7348
Springfield, IL 62791-7348
Ph: (217)525-8202
Free: (888)412-2676
Fax: **(217)525-8212**
URL: http://afterabortion.org
Contact: David C. Reardon PhD, Dir.

**1870 ■ National Network of Abortion Funds
(NNAF) (15989)**
PO Box 170280
Boston, MA 02117
Free: (800)772-9100
E-mail: **info@fundabortionnow.org**
URL: **http://www.fundabortionnow.org**
Contact: Stephanie Poggi, Exec. Dir.

Adoption

**1871 ■ Concerned Persons for Adoption
(CPFA) (11310)**
c/o Anna Marie O'Loughlin, Membership Chair
7 Elizabeth St.
Bloomingdale, NJ 07403
URL: http://www.cpfanj.org
Contact: **Pat Bennett, Contact**

**1872 ■ Joint Council on International
Children's Services (JCICS) (10732)**
117 S St. Asaph St.
Alexandria, VA 22314
Ph: (703)535-8045
Fax: (703)535-8049
E-mail: info@jointcouncil.org
URL: **http://www.jointcouncil.org**
Contact: Thomas DiFilipo, Pres./CEO

**1873 ■ National Council for Adoption (NCFA)
(10234)**
225 N Washington St.
Alexandria, VA 22314
Ph: (703)299-6633 **(301)751-3750**
Fax: (703)299-6004
E-mail: ncfa@adoptioncouncil.org
URL: http://www.adoptioncouncil.org
Contact: **Charles Johnson, Pres./CEO**

1874 ■ Operation Identity (OI) (11328)
1818 Somervell St. NE
Albuquerque, NM 87112-2836
Ph: (505)293-3144
E-mail: **president@nmoi.org**
URL: http://nmoi.org/index.html
Contact: **Connie Martin, Pres.**

**1875 ■ Stars of David International (SDI)
(10243)**
3175 Commercial Ave., Ste.100
Northbrook, IL 60062-1915
Free: (800)STAR-349
E-mail: **statsofdavid@aol.com**
URL: http://www.starsofdavid.org
Contact: Elyse Flack, Contact

Adventist

**1876 ■ Adventist World Aviation (AWA)
(10191)**
PO Box 251
Berrien Springs, MI 49103-0251
Ph: (269)473-0135
Fax: (269)471-4049
E-mail: info@flyawa.org
URL: http://www.flyawa.org
Contact: **Michael Porter, Interim Pres.**

Aging

**1877 ■ Alliance for Aging Research (AAR)
(10247)**
750 17th St. NW, Ste.1100
Washington, DC 20006
Ph: (202)293-2856
Fax: (202)785-8574
E-mail: info@agingresearch.org
URL: http://www.agingresearch.org
Contact: Daniel P. Perry, Pres./CEO

**1878 ■ Little Brothers - Friends of the Elderly
(LBFE) (11375)**
28 E Jackson Blvd., Ste.405
Chicago, IL 60604
Ph: **(312)829-3055**
Fax: **(312)829-3077**
E-mail: **national@littlebrothers.org**
URL: http://www.littlebrothers.org
Contact: **Elisa T. Drew, Natl. Exec. Dir.**

**1879 ■ National Adult Day Services
Association (11298)**
1421 E Broad St., Ste.425
Fuquay Varina, NC 27526
Free: (877)745-1440
Fax: **(919)552-0254**
E-mail: **nadsanews@gmail.com**
URL: http://www.nadsa.org
Contact: Linda Alexander-Lieblang, Chair

**1880 ■ National Association of Area
Agencies on Aging (N4A) (10144)**
1730 Rhode Island Ave. NW, Ste.1200
Washington, DC 20036
Ph: (202)872-0888
Free: (800)677-1116
Fax: (202)872-0057

E-mail: smarkwood@n4a.org
URL: http://www.n4a.org
Contact: **Dawn Simonson, Pres.**

**1881 ■ National Association of State United
for Aging and Disabilities (NASUAD) (11062)**
1201 15th St. NW, Ste.350
Washington, DC 20005
Ph: (202)898-2578
Fax: (202)898-2583
E-mail: **info@nasuad.org**
URL: http://www.nasuad.org
Contact: Irene Collins, Pres.
Status Note: Formerly National Association of State
Units on Aging.

**1882 ■ National Caucus and Center on Black
Aged (NCBA) (10284)**
1220 L St. NW, Ste.800
Washington, DC 20005
Ph: (202)637-8400
Fax: (202)347-0895
E-mail: **support@ncba-aged.org**
URL: http://www.ncba-aged.org
Contact: Karyne Jones, Pres./CEO

AIDS

**1883 ■ Design Industries Foundation
Fighting AIDS (DIFFA) (10252)**
200 Lexington Ave., Ste.910
New York, NY 10016
Ph: (212)727-3100
Fax: (212)727-2574
E-mail: info@diffa.org
URL: http://diffa.org
Contact: David Sheppard, Exec. Dir.

**1884 ■ Elton John AIDS Foundation
(EJAIDSF) (16963)**
584 Broadway, Ste.906
New York, NY 10012
E-mail: **info@ejaf.org**
URL: http://www.ejaf.org
Contact: Scott P. Campbell, Exec. Dir.

**1885 ■ National Alliance of State and
Territorial AIDS Directors (NASTAD) (14960)**
444 N Capitol St. NW, Ste.339
Washington, DC 20001
Ph: (202)434-8090
Fax: (202)434-8092
E-mail: nastad@nastad.org
URL: http://www.nastad.org
Contact: **Julie Scofield, Exec. Dir.**

**1886 ■ National Native American AIDS
Prevention Center (NNAAPC) (16968)**
720 S Colorado Blvd., Ste.650-S
Denver, CO 80246
Ph: (720)382-2244
Fax: (720)382-2248

E-mail: information@nnaapc.org
URL: http://www.nnaapc.org
Contact: **Stacy A. Bohlen, Pres.**

Animal Welfare

1887 ■ Animal Rights Coalition (ARC) (11447)
317 W 48th St.
Minneapolis, MN 55419
Ph: (612)822-6161
E-mail: animalrightscoalition@msn.com
URL: http://www.animalrightscoalition.com
Contact: **Charlotte Cozzetto, Pres.**

1888 ■ Animal Transportation Association (ATA) (10361)
12100 Sunset Hills Rd., Ste.130
Reston, VA 20190
Ph: (703)437-4377
Fax: (703)435-4390
E-mail: info@animaltransportationassociation.org
URL: **http://www.animaltransportationassociation.org**
Contact: **Erik Liebegott, Pres.**

1889 ■ Animal Welfare Advocacy (AWA)
PO Box 737
Mamaroneck, NY 10543
Ph: (914)381-6177
Fax: (914)381-6176
E-mail: brad@animalwelfareadvocacy.org
URL: http://www.animalwelfareadvocacy.org
Contact: Brad Goldberg, Pres./Dir.
Founded: 2003. **Description:** Works to alleviate animal suffering. Promotes the well being of animals through the legislative and political advocacy process. Provides education to the public regarding humane treatment of animals.

1890 ■ Animals Deserve Absolute Protection Today and Tomorrow (ADAPTT)
PO Box 725
Royal Oak, MI 48068
E-mail: garytofu@earthlink.net
URL: http://www.adaptt.org
Contact: Gary Yourofsky, Founder
Founded: 1996. **Description:** Advocates that all animals have an inherent right to be free and live completely unfettered by human dominance. Aims to assist in the abolition of vivisection, dissection, circuses, rodeos and other forms of enslavement, exploitation, abuse and murder. Encourages the public to take up the vegan lifestyle.

1891 ■ Animals and Society Institute (ASI) (11359)
2512 Carpenter Rd., Ste.202-A
Ann Arbor, MI 48108
Ph: (734)677-9240
Fax: **(734)677-9242**
E-mail: info@animalsandsociety.org
URL: http://www.animalsandsociety.org
Contact: Kenneth Shapiro, Exec. Dir.

1892 ■ Associated Humane Societies (AHS) (10363)
124 Evergreen Ave.
Newark, NJ 07114-2133
Ph: (973)824-7080
Fax: (973)824-2720
E-mail: contactus@ahscares.org
URL: **http://www.ahscares.org**
Contact: Roseann Trezza, Exec. Dir.

1893 ■ Bideawee (10335)
410 E 38th St.
New York, NY 10016
Ph: (212)532-6395 (212)532-4455
Free: (866)262-8133
E-mail: bideawee@bideawee.org
URL: http://www.bideawee.org
Contact: Nancy Taylor, Pres./CEO
Status Note: Formerly Bide-A-Wee Home Association.

1894 ■ Born Free USA (1545)
PO Box 22505
Sacramento, CA 95822
Ph: (916)447-3085
Fax: (916)447-3070
E-mail: **info@bornfreeusa.org**
URL: http://www.bornfreeusa.org
Contact: **Will Travers, Chm.**

1895 ■ DreamCatcher Wild Horse and Burro Sanctuary (11485)
PO Box 9
Ravendale, CA 96123
Ph: **(530)260-0148**
E-mail: mustangsb@hughes.net
URL: **http://www.dreamcatcherhorsesanctuary.org**
Contact: Barbara Clarke, Dir.

1896 ■ Humane Society of the United States (HSUS) (10242)
2100 L St. NW
Washington, DC 20037
Ph: (202)452-1100
E-mail: membership@humanesociety.org
URL: **http://www.humanesociety.org**
Contact: Wayne Pacelle, Pres./CEO

1897 ■ National Humane Education Society (NHES) (11195)
PO Box 340
Charles Town, WV 25414-0340
Ph: (304)725-0506
Fax: (304)725-1523
E-mail: **nhesinformation@nhes.org**
URL: http://www.nhes.org
Contact: James D. Taylor, Pres.

1898 ■ Prevent a Litter Coalition (PaLC) (10437)
PO Box 688
Great Falls, VA 22066
Ph: (703)818-8009
E-mail: contact@palc.org
URL: http://www.palc.org
Contact: Sara Khurody-Downs, Pres./CEO
Status Note: Defunct.

1899 ■ Primarily Primates, Inc. (PPI) (11685)
26099 Dull Knife Trail
San Antonio, TX 78255
Ph: (830)755-4616
Fax: **(830)755-4618**
E-mail: primarilyprimates@friendsofanimals.org
URL: http://primarilyprimates.org
Contact: Priscilla Feral, Pres.

1900 ■ SPCA International (SPCAI)
PO Box 8682
New York, NY 10001
E-mail: answers@spcai.org
URL: http://www.spcai.org
Contact: Donald Shultz, Operations Off.
Founded: 2006. **Multinational. Description:** Advocates for the humane treatment of animals. Promotes the safety and improvement of the well-being of animals. Seeks to develop and utilize a worldwide platform that supports independent animal shelters.

1901 ■ U.S.A. Defenders of Greyhounds (USADOG)
PO Box 1256
Carmel, IN 46082
Ph: (317)244-0113
E-mail: usadogpresident@aol.com
URL: **http://usadefendersofgreyhounds.org**
Contact: Ms. Sally Allen, Pres.

1902 ■ World Vets
802 1st Ave. N
Fargo, ND 58102
Free: (877)688-8387
Fax: (701)282-9324

E-mail: info@worldvets.org
URL: http://www.worldvets.org
Contact: Cathy King PhD, Exec. Dir.
Membership Dues: general, $40 (annual). **Multinational. Description:** Provides international veterinary assistance to impoverished nations outside of North America. Collaborates with animal advocacy groups, foreign governments and veterinary professionals in addressing veterinary and human health issues impacted by zoonotic diseases in developing countries.

Anti-Poverty

1903 ■ Children of Tanzania
3 Little Cove Ln.
Old Greenwich, CT 06870
Ph: (203)637-0191
E-mail: cotchildhelp@aol.com
URL: http://childrenoftanzania.com
Contact: Susan Rohrer, Chair
Founded: 2003. **Multinational. Description:** Provides support to children living in impoverished areas of Tanzania. Strives to help children access and stay within the educational system. Addresses crucial issues concerning the educational needs of the children.

1904 ■ Eliminate Poverty Now
PO Box 67
Mendham, NJ 07945
E-mail: judy.craig@eliminatepovertynow.org
URL: http://www.eliminatepovertynow.org
Contact: Judy Craig, Co-Founder
Founded: 2010. **Multinational. Description:** Advocates for the elimination of extreme poverty in Africa. Strives to create vast opportunities for Africans to find work and generate income. Encourages people to hone their skills and enhance their capabilities.

1905 ■ Haiti Outreach
15119 Minnetonka Blvd.
Minnetonka, MN 55345
Ph: (612)929-1122
Fax: (612)216-3777
E-mail: info@haitioutreach.org
URL: http://www.haitioutreach.org
Contact: Dale Snyder, Exec. Dir.
Founded: 1997. **Multinational. Description:** Provides essential public services that benefit the Haitian communities. Collaborates with the people of Haiti to build and maintain community-initiated projects that advance their development. Encourages active and responsible community participation among the Haitian population.

1906 ■ HavServe Volunteer Service Network
PO Box 4173
Silver Spring, MD 20914
E-mail: info@havserve.org
URL: http://www.havserve.org
Contact: Lianna Marmor, Exec. Dir.
Founded: 2010. **Multinational. Description:** Represents volunteers who strive to meet the goal of ending poverty in small towns and villages throughout Haiti. Supports community-led development through volunteerism in least developed countries. Empowers the villagers to put their knowledge and skills into practice.

1907 ■ Hearts for Kenya
1514 Norris Pl.
Louisville, KY 40205
Ph: (502)459-4582
E-mail: johnandalice@insightbb.com
URL: http://www.heartsforkenya.org
Contact: John Willingham, Pres.
Multinational. Description: Works to combat poverty, hunger and disease in small, agrarian communities in the Nyanza province of Kenya. Educates Kenyans to be self-sufficient in order to raise their standard of living.

1908 ■ Rising International
300 Potrero St.
Santa Cruz, CA 95060
Ph: (831)429-7473
Fax: (831)469-7473
URL: http://www.risinginternational.org
Contact: Carmel Jud, Pres./CEO

Multinational. Description: Focuses on women living in high-risk places worldwide. Aims to eradicate extreme poverty. Facilitates long-term projects designed to enhance the capabilities of disadvantaged people to sustain themselves or their families. Promotes ownership of craft-based businesses by women in impoverished areas of developed nations and developing nations.

Autism

1909 ■ Autism Community of Africa (ACA)
8775 Cloud Leap Ct., Ste.18
Columbia, MD 21045
Ph: (443)718-1824
Fax: (443)296-9185
E-mail: info@autismcommunityofafrica.org
URL: http://www.autismcommunityofafrica.org
Contact: Mrs. Brigitte Kobenan, Founder

Founded: 2007. **Multinational. Description:** Seeks to establish and maintain a comprehensive system of care and support to families affected by autism in Africa. Provides educational opportunities for children with autism based on applied behavior analysis (ABA) through the development of schools, inclusion and vocational programs, consumer advocacy and community outreach.

1910 ■ Global Communities of Support (GCOS)
475 Wall St.
Princeton, NJ 08540
Ph: (609)845-2340
Fax: (609)845-2329
E-mail: info@gcosinc.org
URL: http://www.gcosinc.org
Contact: Sue Repko, Pres.

Founded: 2001. **Description:** Supports the growth and development of individuals with autism and other developmental disabilities. Offers sservices and resources to individuals with autism and other developmental disabilities to ensure a meaningful and productive life.

1911 ■ Hands for Autistic Children of Ethiopia
621 Bushytail Dr.
Frederick, MD 21703
Ph: (240)429-8362
E-mail: zinashayele@autism-ethiopia.org
URL: http://autism-ethiopia.org
Contact: Zinash Ayele, Contact

Multinational. Description: Provides assistance to autistic children, their parents and siblings in Ethiopia. Offers basic needs such as education and living assistance.

Child Abuse

1912 ■ RedLight Children (RLC)
75 Rockefeller Plz., 17th Fl.
New York, NY 10019
E-mail: admin@redlightchildren.org
URL: http://redlightchildren.org
Contact: Guy Jacobson, Exec. Dir./Founder

Founded: 2004. **Description:** Aims to end the demand for child slavery and exploitation. Raises public awareness about child sexual slavery and exploitation. Collaborates with other organizations to create a joint effort to fight against child sexual slavery and exploitation.

Child Care

1913 ■ Council for Professional Recognition (11526)
2460 16th St. NW
Washington, DC 20009
Ph: (202)265-9090
Free: (800)424-4310
Fax: (202)265-9161
E-mail: webmaster@cdacouncil.org
URL: http://www.cdacouncil.org
Contact: Valora Washington, Pres./CEO/Chm.

1914 ■ National Coalition for Campus Children's Centers (NCCCC) (10378)
950 Glenn Dr., Ste.150
Folsom, CA 95630
Free: (877)736-6222
Fax: (916)932-2209
E-mail: info@campuschildren.org
URL: http://www.campuschildren.org
Contact: Betty Pearsall, Pres.

Child Welfare

1915 ■ Action for Children - Zambia (AFCZ)
20855 Kensington Blvd.
Lakeville, MN 55044
E-mail: c_mcbrady@hotmail.com
URL: http://www.afczambia.org
Contact: Carol McBrady, Dir.

Founded: 2005. **Multinational. Description:** Aims to reduce the difficulties that children face in Zambia. Addresses the immediate needs of vulnerable and displaced children in Zambia.

1916 ■ Africa Hope
PO Box 127
Dacula, GA 30019
Ph: (770)573-0676
Fax: (678)528-3025
E-mail: admin@africahopeinc.com
URL: http://www.africahopeinc.org
Contact: Felix Tshimanga MD, Pres.

Founded: 2007. **Multinational. Description:** Strives to improve the lives of orphans and disadvantaged children in the Democratic Republic of Congo. Provides shelter, basic health care and education.

1917 ■ AHOPE for Children
104 Hume Ave.
Alexandria, VA 22301
Ph: (703)683-7500
E-mail: rosemary@ahopeforchildren.org
URL: http://www.ahopeforchildren.org
Contact: Jennifer Olsen, Pres.

Founded: 2004. **Multinational. Description:** Aims to serve the children of Ethiopia by caring for orphans infected with HIV. Provides home, medical care, education, food, and other services.

1918 ■ Aiding Romania's Children (ARC)
212 W Lancaster Ave.
Paoli, PA 19301
E-mail: info@aidingromaniaschildren.org
URL: http://www.aidingromaniaschildren.org
Contact: Valerie H. Anewalt, Contact

Founded: 1999. **Multinational. Description:** Aims to provide financial and humanitarian support to Romanian children and families suffering from HIV/AIDS.

1919 ■ All the Children are Children (ATCAC)
PO Box 153012
Cape Coral, FL 33915
Ph: (239)214-4922
E-mail: kidsvoice@netzero.net
URL: http://www.atcac.net
Contact: Mr. Philocles Desir, Admin.

Founded: 2002. **Multinational. Description:** Aims to empower the lives of orphaned and underprivileged children living in rural communities in Haiti. Provides free basic education, training, food and shelter, and

medical assistance to those in need. Develops the working skills of young adults to become self-sufficient and productive in life.

1920 ■ All Our Children International Outreach
PO Box 1807
Claremont, CA 91711
Ph: (909)450-1177
URL: http://www.allourchildreninternational.com
Contact: Rachael Ranney, Founder/Pres.

Founded: 2007. **Multinational. Description:** Strives to create permanent change in the lives of children. Provides food, education and health care services to underprivileged children in Kenya and Ethiopia.

1921 ■ American Bar Association Center on Children and the Law
740 15th St. NW
Washington, DC 20005-1019
Ph: (202)662-1720
Free: (800)285-2221
Fax: (202)662-1755
E-mail: ctrchildlaw@americanbar.org
URL: http://www.americanbar.org/groups/child_law.html
Contact: Howard Davidson, Dir.

1922 ■ Ark Mission
830 S Buffalo Grove Rd., Ste.103
Buffalo Grove, IL 60089
Ph: (847)215-2755
Fax: (847)215-2757
E-mail: info@arkmission.org
URL: http://www.arkmission.org
Contact: Elina Filippova, Contact

Multinational. Description: Helps orphan children around the world. Supports programs to transform the lives of children.

1923 ■ Beanies for Baghdad
6401 Lincoln Ave.
Evansville, IN 47715
E-mail: info@beaniesforbaghdad.com
URL: http://www.beaniesforbaghdad.com
Contact: Donna Ward, Contact

Founded: 2003. **Multinational. Description:** Serves as a bridge between soldiers, sailors, airmen, marines, the children of Iraq, Kosovo, Afghanistan, Africa, Pakistan and other areas where children are in crisis. Supports young children who have suffered so much and have so little happiness in their lives.

1924 ■ Benefit4Kids
21660 23 Mile Rd.
Macomb, MI 48044
Free: (877)245-5430
E-mail: info@b4k.org
URL: http://www.b4k.org
Contact: Al Baggett, Pres.

Founded: 1998. **Description:** Aims to grant the outdoor wishes of children with life threatening and life limiting illnesses. Provides children's programs to help children experience the outdoors.

1925 ■ BLOOM Africa
4605 E Natl. Rd.
Springfield, OH 45505
E-mail: andrew.steele@bloomafrica.org
URL: http://www.bloomafrica.org
Contact: Andrew Steele, Founder/Exec. Dir.

Founded: 2010. **Multinational. Description:** Strives to improve the lives of orphans and vulnerable children in Africa. Provides resources to orphans in support of their basic needs through sustainable projects, educational programming and financial support.

1926 ■ Blue Nile Children's Organization (BNCO)
PO Box 28658
Seattle, WA 98118
Ph: (206)760-2873

E-mail: admin@bluenile.org
URL: http://www.bluenile.org
Contact: Selamawit Kifle, Exec. Dir.
Founded: 2001. **Multinational. Description:** Aims to address the health and educational needs of orphaned children in Bahir Dar and Addis Ababa, Ethiopia. Educates the local community on preventive methods for infectious diseases. Raises funds to support the sponsorship, medical and educational programs for the Ethiopian children.

1927 ■ A Bridge for Children (ABC)

PO Box 1054
New York, NY 10268
E-mail: info@abridgeforchildren.org
URL: http://abridgeforchildren.org
Contact: Steve Hwang, Exec. Dir.
Multinational. Description: Serves underprivileged children to reach their full potential. Works to place orphaned children with suitable families and to provide them with educational opportunities. Provides services for underprivileged children through strategic partnerships with other humanitarian organizations and social programs.

1928 ■ Bridge of Love

PO Box 1869
West Jordan, UT 84084
Ph: (801)867-9401
E-mail: romania.bridge@gmail.com
URL: http://www.bridgeoflove.net
Contact: Laurie Lundberg, Founder
Founded: 2001. **Multinational. Description:** Works to provide comfort and hope to the abandoned children of Romania. Provides support to sustain the children's physical, emotional and educational needs.

1929 ■ Bridges Cambodia International (BCI)

2970 Almond Dr.
San Jose, CA 95148
Ph: (408)223-2359 (408)472-3489
Fax: (408)531-9603
E-mail: info@bridgesinternational.org
URL: http://www.bridgesinternational.org
Contact: Hong Nayseap, Pres./Founder
Founded: 2007. **Multinational. Description:** Addresses the problems of access to vital resources experienced by the underprivileged people of Cambodia, especially the children. Seeks assistance from institutions and individuals sympathetic to the plight of the Cambodian population.

1930 ■ Camp To Belong (CTB)

PO Box 1146
Marana, AZ 85653
Ph: (520)413-1395
E-mail: info@camptobelong.org
URL: http://www.camptobelong.org
Contact: Karyn Schimmels, Chm.
Founded: 1995. **Multinational. Description:** Works to reunite brothers and sisters who are placed in separate foster homes and other out-of-home care for events of fun, emotional empowerment and sibling connection. Educates the public about the plight of foster siblings and the importance of keeping them together in foster care and/or adoption whenever possible. Seeks to develop a community awareness program for the purpose of recruiting foster homes suitable for sibling placements.

1931 ■ Catholic Guardian Society and Home Bureau (CGSHB)

1011 1st Ave., 10th Flr.
New York, NY 10022
Ph: (212)371-1000
Fax: **(212)758-5892**
E-mail: info@catholicguard.org
URL: http://www.cgshb.org
Contact: John J. Frein, Exec. Dir.

1932 ■ ChangeALife Uganda

58 Fairview Ave.
Brick, NJ 08724
Ph: (732)899-8483

E-mail: jsemler@changealifeuganda.org
URL: http://www.changealifeuganda.org
Contact: Jean Semler, Pres.
Founded: 2001. **Multinational. Description:** Aims to improve the lives of disadvantaged children and their families in Uganda. Provides assistance through a multi-sectoral approach including education, health and sanitation, and business development.

1933 ■ Child Aid Africa (CAA)

535 Rosaire Dr.
Hummelstown, PA 17036
Ph: (717)566-6118 (717)514-7597
E-mail: mnmbito@childaidafrica.org
URL: http://www.childaidafrica.org
Contact: Dr. Michael Njoroge Mbito, Pres./Founder
Multinational. Description: Aims to provide support to poor orphaned HIV/AIDS children in Africa. Assists children to pursue and earn secondary school education. Provides school fees, school books, uniforms, food and clothing and needed shelter to orphaned children.

1934 ■ Child Empowerment International (CEI)

PO Box 66274
Scotts Valley, CA 95067
Free: (800)725-8098
Fax: (206)284-7441
E-mail: info@childempowerment.org
URL: http://www.childempowerment.org
Contact: Adam Salmon, Founder/Pres.
Founded: 1998. **Multinational. Description:** Aims to reduce the cycle of poverty in areas of civil unrest through empowering and educating marginalized children. Provides schooling for underprivileged children and orphans.

1935 ■ Child Literacy

105 Greene St., No. 1202
Jersey City, NJ 07302
Ph: (212)531-1111
E-mail: info@childliteracy.org
URL: http://www.childliteracy.org
Contact: Naushard Cader, Exec. Dir.
Founded: 2005. **Multinational. Description:** Strives to provide the social, educational and psychological needs of disadvantaged or abused children. Undertakes, executes and supports projects and changes that make a substantial difference to the prospects of child welfare.

1936 ■ Child Protection International (CPI)

267 19th Ave. S, Ste.214
Minneapolis, MN 55455
E-mail: contact@childprotectioninternational.org
URL: http://www.childprotectioninternational.org
Contact: Robyn Skrebes, Founder
Multinational. Description: Aims to protect, promote, and advocate for the rights of all children. Creates an awareness about the rights of voiceless children around the world. Advocates for a healthy childhood free of violence and war in Southern Sudan.

1937 ■ Child Welfare League of America (CWLA) (11322)

1726 M St. NW, Ste.500
Washington, DC 20036-4522
Ph: (202)688-4200
Fax: **(202)833-1689**
E-mail: register@cwla.org
URL: http://www.cwla.org
Contact: Christine James-Brown, Pres./CEO

1938 ■ Children of Grace (COG)

PO Box 2394
Danville, CA 94526
Ph: (925)855-4697
E-mail: info@childrenofgrace.com
URL: http://www.children-of-grace.org
Contact: MaryAnn McCoy, Exec. Dir.
Founded: 2001. **Multinational. Description:** Aims to offer hope for orphaned children affected by HIV/AIDS in Uganda. Provides Ugandan orphans educa-

tion, nutrition, healthcare and empowerment programs to enable a better future. Raises awareness for the HIV/AIDS epidemic in Uganda.

1939 ■ Children of Nowhere

601 W 26th St., Ste.1105
New York, NY 10001
E-mail: info@childrenofnowhere.org
URL: http://www.childrenofnowhere.com
Contact: Richard Jonas, Contact
Founded: 2003. **Description:** Aims to help children with HIV and AIDS. Raises funds for healthcare, medications, food and other necessities.

1940 ■ Children's Future International (CFI)

22 Hartley Rd.
Great Neck, NY 11023
E-mail: info@childrensfutureinternational.org
URL: http://www.childrensfutureinternational.org
Contact: Andrew Wolf, Co-Founder/Exec. Dir.
Founded: 2007. **Multinational. Description:** Aims to serve marginalized and vulnerable children through access to quality education and well-being programs. Helps break the cycle of poverty by developing educated, self-reliant and compassionate individuals who will serve as positive role models and have the potential to become future community leaders.

1941 ■ Children's Medical Mission of Haiti

925 Hertzler Rd.
Mechanicsburg, PA 17055
Ph: (717)796-1852
E-mail: khquigley@comcast.net
URL: http://www.cmmh.org
Contact: Rev. Canon Bill Squire, Pres.
Multinational. Description: Provides support for the delivery of medical and educational services to the people of Haiti.

1942 ■ Children's Relief Mission

PO Box 597
Owensville, MO 65066
Ph: (818)502-1989
Fax: (818)502-9040
E-mail: info@childrensreliefmission.org
URL: http://www.childrensreliefmission.org
Contact: Michael Sholer, Asst. Sec.
Multinational. Description: Works to provide resources to create better lives for children. Offers relief and development assistance such as medical care, education, feeding programs and economic support for children and families.

1943 ■ Children's Welfare International (CWI)

223 Pacific Ave. S
Pacific, WA 98047
Ph: (206)859-3847
E-mail: info@thecwi.org
URL: http://www.thecwi.org
Contact: Joseph Fatinyan Jarbah, Founder/Exec. Dir.
Founded: 2008. **Multinational. Description:** Aims to improve the welfare of homeless and disadvantaged children in Liberia by providing support services. Focuses to protect and support the abandoned, abused, underprivileged and former child soldiers who are currently living in the streets of Liberia. Promotes full and fair access to basic needs and rights.

1944 ■ Chosen Children International (CCI)

PO Box 3046
Colorado Springs, CO 80934
Free: (866)599-5437
E-mail: chosenchildren@gmail.com
URL: http://www.ccikids.org
Contact: Marilyn Cohn, Dir.
Founded: 2007. **Multinational. Description:** Aims to break the cycle of poverty for orphans and destitute children in developing nations. Provides for the spiritual, physical and educational needs of homeless street children and orphans.

1945 ■ Committee for Children (CFC) (11691)
2815 2nd Ave., Ste.400
Seattle, WA 98121
Ph: (206)343-1223
Free: (800)634-4449
Fax: (206)438-6765
E-mail: info@cfchildren.org
URL: http://www.cfchildren.org
Contact: **Sarah Stanley, Pres.**

1946 ■ Crutches 4 Kids (C4K)
1350 Avenue of the Americas, 4th Fl.
New York, NY 10019
E-mail: info@crutches4kids.org
URL: http://www.crutches4kids.org
Contact: Ken Shubin Stein, Founder
Founded: 2009. **Multinational. Description:** Provides crutches for disabled children in low-income communities around the world. Works with a network of concerned citizens and humanitarian organizations to send crutches to children in need.

1947 ■ Empower Orphans
1415 Hidden Pond Dr.
Yardley, PA 19067
Ph: (610)909-1778
URL: http://www.empowerorphans.org
Contact: Neha Gupta, Contact
Multinational. Description: Aims to elevate the well being of orphaned children and empower them to succeed in life. Helps create self sufficiency by supplying children with the tools to gain a basic education and technical skills. Provides food, clothing, health care and medical supplies to establish an effective learning environment.

1948 ■ Ethiopian Orphan Relief (EOR)
3020 SW Christy Ave.
Beaverton, OR 97005
E-mail: info@ethiopianorphanrelief.org
URL: http://ethiopianorphanrelief.org
Contact: Kimberley Pasion, Pres.
Founded: 2008. **Multinational. Description:** Aims to improve the living conditions and lives of orphaned children in Ethiopia. Supports the emotional and physical needs of children. Works with local organizations to support the needs of the orphaned children.

1949 ■ Find the Children (11340)
2656 29th St., Ste.203
Santa Monica, CA 90405
Ph: **(310)314-3213**
Free: (888)477-6721
Fax: **(310)314-3169**
E-mail: findthechild@earthlink.net
URL: http://www.findthechildren.com
Contact: Alan Landsburg, Contact

1950 ■ Firefly
8317 Woodhaven Blvd.
Bethesda, MD 20817
Ph: (917)359-7207
Fax: (240)396-2107
E-mail: mrichards@fireflykids.org
URL: http://www.fireflykids.org
Contact: Nicole Levine, Pres.
Founded: 2000. **Multinational. Description:** Focuses on aiding orphans and children with disabilities. Strives to keep children under the care of birth families whenever possible instead of placing them in orphanages. Promotes the establishment of foster homes, small group homes and domestic adoption when living with birth families is not an option.

1951 ■ Forever Found
1464 Madera Rd., No. 158
Simi Valley, CA 93065
Ph: (805)304-6294
E-mail: info@foreverfound.org
URL: http://www.foreverfound.org
Contact: Shannon Sergey, Pres./Co-founder
Founded: 2010. **Multinational. Description:** Aids in the full rescue of children victimized by child prostitution and trafficking by supporting aftercare homes around the world that are effectively rescuing and restoring these victims. Raises support through the development and promotion of the works of musicians, artists and writers who are willing to donate all or some of their proceeds to help these children.

1952 ■ Friends of the Children of Angola (FOCOA)
6210 Homespun Ln.
Falls Church, VA 22044
Ph: (703)237-7468 (703)237-7466
Fax: (703)237-7467
URL: http://www.focoa-angola.org
Contact: Maria Luisa Abrantes, Chair
Founded: 1998. **Multinational. Description:** Aims to provide well-being of the children of the Republic of Angola in accordance with the United Nations Declaration of Human Rights and the Rights of the Children Convention.

1953 ■ Friends of Jamaica USA (FOJ)
6417 Commonwealth Dr.
Loves Park, IL 61111
E-mail: info@friendsofjamaicausa.org
URL: http://www.friendsofjamaicausa.org
Contact: Marcia Burke, Dir.
Founded: 2000. **Multinational. Description:** Aims to improve the lives of Jamaican children in need of medical care. Seeks to create educational opportunities for these children by supporting important community projects.

1954 ■ Friends of Kenyan Orphans
920 Berkshire Rd.
Grosse Pointe Park, MI 48230
Ph: (313)815-9900
Fax: (313)822-9380
E-mail: budozar@hotmail.com
URL: http://www.friendsofkenyanorphans.org
Contact: Sue Horrigan Ozar, Pres.
Multinational. Description: Works to rescue orphaned and abandoned street children by providing shelter, food and education. Raises funds in support of its mission to improve the lives of children in Kenya.

1955 ■ Ghana Relief Organization (GRO)
PO Box 1722
Baltimore, MD 21203
Ph: (410)486-6832
E-mail: grotamale@usdang.org
URL: http://www.usdang.org
Contact: Iddrisu Iliasu, Dir.
Multinational. Description: Aims to provide sufficient education and health needs of children in deprived communities of the world. Raises funds for the benefit of deprived and needy children in Northern Ghana. Creates an equitable living standard for all children.

1956 ■ Girls for a Change (GFC)
PO Box 1436
San Jose, CA 95109
Ph: (408)540-6432
Fax: **(831)425-1226**
E-mail: info@girlsforachange.org
URL: http://www.girlsforachange.org
Contact: Whitney Smith, Founder/Co-CEO

1957 ■ Global Centurion
2000 Clarendon Blvd.
Arlington, VA 22201
Ph: (703)276-3000
E-mail: info@globalcenturion.org
URL: http://www.globalcenturion.org
Contact: Laura J. Lederer, Pres.
Founded: 2008. **Multinational. Description:** Aims to abolish human trafficking, especially sex trafficking, forced labor and child slavery. Fights human trafficking by reducing the demand for sex trafficking. Assists communities, states and countries in eradicating child slavery.

1958 ■ Goods for Good
180 Varick St., Ste.1207
New York, NY 10014
Ph: (646)963-6076
Fax: (646)963-6076
E-mail: info@goods4good.org
URL: http://goods4good.org
Contact: Melissa Kushner, Exec. Dir./Founder
Founded: 2006. **Multinational. Description:** Promotes the development of orphans and vulnerable children. Advances the physical, emotional and educational growth of children. Provides school supplies, clothing, health and hygiene products and other necessities to orphans and vulnerable children.

1959 ■ Heart for Africa
PO Box 573
Alpharetta, GA 30009
Ph: (678)566-1589
Free: (800)901-7585
URL: http://www.heartforafrica.org
Contact: Ian Maxwell, Pres.
Founded: 2005. **Multinational. Description:** Aims to provide care and hope for children in Swaziland, Africa. Offers self sustainable homes for orphans and vulnerable children. Works to deliver quality care, shelter, food, water, clothing, health care and education.

1960 ■ Heart4Kids
13950 Mansarde Ave., Ste.186
Herndon, VA 20171
Ph: (404)957-9014
Fax: (800)704-8411
E-mail: info@heart4kids.org
URL: http://heart4kids.org
Contact: Sandra Danenga, Founder/Exec. Dir.
Founded: 2003. **Multinational. Description:** Strives to improve the quality of life of African children, particularly those in Zimbabwe. Provides educational and medical assistance to children in need. Seeks to bring a positive change to the future of abandoned or orphaned children whose lives have been devastated by the HIV/AIDS epidemic.

1961 ■ Hearts Across Romania
2544 Brookside Dr.
Irving, TX 75063
Ph: (214)213-9001
URL: http://www.heartsacrossromania.org
Contact: Mariana Achiriloaie, Co-Founder
Founded: 2003. **Multinational. Description:** Seeks to improve the lives of Romanian orphans through material, emotional and eductional support.

1962 ■ Helping Hands
2918 Churchill Way
Garland, TX 75044
Ph: (972)635-3903
Fax: (214)703-3283
URL: http://www.hhcharity.org
Contact: Mrs. Kaushalya Siriwardana, Founder
Founded: 2003. **Multinational. Description:** Aims to champion the causes of innocent children across the globe. Provides food, shelter, clothing, health care and education to the homeless and orphaned children of the world's most destitute areas.

1963 ■ Helping Honduras Kids
PO Box 111777
Campbell, CA 95011-1777
E-mail: info@helpinghonduraskids.org
URL: http://www.helpinghonduraskids.org
Contact: David Ashby, Pres./Chm.
Founded: 2006. **Multinational. Description:** Aims to improve the lives of orphaned, abandoned, abused and/or neglected children in Honduras. Supports programs to create educational opportunities to help children overcome poverty and become successful individuals.

1964 ■ Home of Hope
190 Tobin Clark Dr.
Hillsborough, CA 94010
Ph: (650)520-3204

E-mail: info@hohinc.org
URL: http://www.hohinc.org
Contact: Dr. Nilima Sabharwal, Chair
Founded: 1999. **Multinational. Description:** Provides care, education and support to orphaned and destitute children. Raises funds to improve the living conditions of these children.

1965 ■ Hope and Future for Children in Bolivia (HFCBolivia)
PO Box 4034
Mountain View, CA 94040
Ph: (650)962-0137
E-mail: hfcbolivia@yahoo.com
URL: http://www.hfcbolivia.org
Contact: Aydee Sickinger, Founder/Pres.
Founded: 2005. **Multinational. Description:** Seeks to provide basic necessities to impoverished children and families in Bolivia. Provides food, education, school supplies, clothes and shoes and hygienic supplies.

1966 ■ Hope for Haiti's Children (HFHC)
PO Box 936
Sugar Land, TX 77487
Free: (866)314-9330
Fax: (888)316-9646
E-mail: info@hopeforhaitischildren.org
URL: http://hopeforhaitischildren.org
Contact: Ken Bever, Chm.
Multinational. Description: Works to educate and care for the impoverished children in Haiti. Provides education sponsorship program, health care services, orphan care, and crisis relief efforts.

1967 ■ Horizon International
PO Box 180
Pendleton, IN 46064
Ph: (765)778-1016
Free: (866)778-7020
Fax: (765)778-9490
E-mail: info@horizoninternationalinc.com
URL: http://www.horizoninternationalinc.com
Contact: Robert W. Pearson, Founder/CEO
Founded: 2001. **Multinational. Description:** Works to create a world of hope for orphans affected by HIV/AIDS. Serves orphans and their communities by providing them opportunities to break the cycle of poverty and live free from the bonds of poverty and disease.

1968 ■ International Children Assistance Network (ICAN)
PO Box 5863
Santa Clara, CA 95056
Ph: (408)509-8788 (408)993-9445
Fax: (408)935-9657
E-mail: info@ican2.org
URL: http://www.ican2.org
Contact: Rev. Thich Phap Chon, Chm.
Founded: 2000. **Multinational. Description:** Aims to create strong family and community networks that support Vietnamese children. Helps children to realize their potential and become compassionate leaders by providing them with skills, confidence and opportunities to succeed in life.

1969 ■ Kids Home International (KHI)
2309 Plymouth Ave. N
Minneapolis, MN 55411
E-mail: kids@kidshomeinternational.org
URL: http://www.kidshomeinternational.org
Contact: Sharina McCants, Contact
Founded: 2002. **Multinational. Description:** Seeks to improve the quality of lives of the orphaned and vulnerable kids in Kenya through programs designed to develop their spirit, mind and body. Ensures access to essential services for orphans and vulnerable children. Raises an awareness to create a supportive environment for children affected by HIV/AIDS.

1970 ■ Kupenda for the Children
PO Box 473
Hampton, NH 03843
Ph: (410)456-2311

E-mail: kupenda@kupenda.org
URL: http://www.kupenda.org
Contact: Cynthia Bauer, Founder/Exec. Dir.
Founded: 2003. **Multinational. Description:** Works to meet the needs of children with disabilities. Promotes advocacy and creates an awareness to better assist children with disabilities. Provides the physical, spiritual and emotional needs of disabled children.

1971 ■ Loving Hands for the Needy (LHFN)
PO Box 243456
Boynton Beach, FL 33424
Ph: (561)283-3599
E-mail: info@lovefortheneedy.org
URL: http://lovefortheneedy.org
Contact: Rev. John Henry Miller, Pres./Exec. Dir.
Multinational. Description: Aims to protect and promote the welfare of the children and family in great needs. Works to provide shelter, build schools and other facilities to help needy children.

1972 ■ Malawi Children's Mission (MCM)
PO Box 313
Redwood City, CA 94064
E-mail: support@malawichildrensmission.org
URL: http://www.malawichildrensmission.org
Contact: Steven Koffman, Co-Founder/Dir.
Founded: 2007. **Multinational. Description:** Aims to serve orphaned and vulnerable children in Malawi, Africa. Provides assistance and humanity services in Malawi. Supports needy children with nutritious meals, educational assistance and basic health services.

1973 ■ Meds and Food for Kids (MFK)
4488 Forest Park Ave., Ste.230
St. Louis, MO 63108
Ph: (314)420-1634
E-mail: **info@mfkhaiti.org**
URL: **http://mfkhaiti.org**
Contact: Patricia B. Wolff MD, Founder/Exec. Dir.

1974 ■ Mike's Angels
2090 Dunwoody Club Dr., Ste.106-120
Atlanta, GA 30350-5424
Ph: (770)396-7858
E-mail: info@mikesangels.org
URL: http://www.mikesangels.org
Contact: Patricia Marcucci Sheeran, Pres.
Founded: 2010. **Multinational. Description:** Aims to improve the living conditions of orphans in Guatemala by providing them with life's basic necessities. Enhances the quality of care in orphanages.

1975 ■ Mothers Without Borders
125 E Main St., Ste.402
American Fork, UT 84003
Ph: **(801)607-5641**
E-mail: mail@motherswithoutborders.org
URL: http://www.motherswithoutborders.org
Contact: Kathy Headlee, Founder

1976 ■ National Center for Missing and Exploited Children (NCMEC) (11093)
Charles B. Wang Intl. Children's Bldg.
699 Prince St.
Alexandria, VA 22314-3175
Ph: (703)224-2150
Free: (800)843-5678
Fax: (703)224-2122
E-mail: careers@ncmec.org
URL: http://www.missingkids.com
Contact: **Ralph Parilla, Chm.**

1977 ■ National Center for Prosecution of Child Abuse (NCPCA) (11738)
44 Canal Center Plz., Ste.110
Alexandria, VA 22314
Ph: (703)549-9222 **(703)518-4385**
Fax: (703)836-3195
E-mail: ncpca@ndaa.org
URL: http://www.ndaa.org/ncpca_home.html
Contact: Scott Burns, Exec. Dir.

1978 ■ Options for Children in Zambia
8 Stonegate Ln.
Bedford, MA 01730
E-mail: optionsforchildren@gmail.com
URL: http://optionsforchildren.org
Contact: John Morgan, Contact
Founded: 2006. **Multinational. Description:** Seeks to improve the quality of life of children in Zambia. Raises money and develops partnerships to support the provision of health, education, cultural and microeconomic development of families in Zambia.

1979 ■ Orphan Support Africa (OSA)
2424 York St., Ste.248
Philadelphia, PA 19125
Ph: (215)454-2832
Fax: (917)677-8996
URL: http://orphansupportafrica.org
Contact: Tanya Prime, Dir.
Founded: 2006. **Multinational. Description:** Works to restore futures for children orphaned by HIV/AIDS throughout Sub-Saharan Africa. Works in partnership with community-based organizations to support orphaned and vulnerable children. Provides children with care and the tools they need to become self reliant adults.

1980 ■ Orphans Against AIDS (OAA)
1110 Knollwood Dr.
Buffalo Grove, IL 60089
E-mail: andrew.klaber@aya.yale.edu
URL: http://www.orphansagainstaids.org
Contact: Andrew Klaber, Founder/Pres.
Founded: 2002. **Multinational. Description:** Strives to help the orphaned and vulnerable children affected by HIV/AIDS. Works to break the cycle of HIV/AIDS by providing children with education, nutrition and healthcare.

1981 ■ Outreach Africa
PO Box 361
Union, IA 50258
Ph: (641)486-2550
Free: (800)513-0935
Fax: (641)486-2570
URL: http://www.outreachafrica.org
Contact: Floyd Hammer, Pres.
Founded: 2004. **Multinational. Description:** Provides safe water, food, medical care and education to children in need, with focus on developing countries. Facilitates community projects for the people of Singida Region in Tanzania.

1982 ■ Para Sa Bata
11331 Cedar Springs Dr.
Frisco, TX 75035
Ph: (469)579-4544
E-mail: parasabata@gmail.com
URL: http://parasabata.org
Contact: Dona Lontok Alvarez, Founder
Founded: 2005. **Multinational. Description:** Aims to bring joy to poor, sick, abused or neglected Filipino children by distributing clothes, shoes, toys, books, school supplies and other things that are no longer used. Organizes fundraising events.

1983 ■ Peace House Africa
6581 City W Pkwy.
Eden Prairie, MN 55344
Ph: (952)465-0050
Fax: (952)465-0051
E-mail: info@peacehouseafrica.org
URL: http://peacehouseafrica.org
Contact: Dan Grewe, Dir. of Operations
Founded: 2001. **Multinational. Description:** Promotes a brighter future for Africa's orphans, vulnerable children and their communities. Provides a quality and effective education for children who have lost parents to AIDS. Creates a sustainable economic growth in their communities through technology research and business development.

1984 ■ Pocketful of Joy
24 Goose Ln.
Tolland, CT 06084
E-mail: info@pocketfulofjoy.org
URL: http://pocketfulofjoy.org
Contact: Charlotte S. Hunter, Founder/Dir.
Founded: 2004. **Multinational. Description:** Provides healthcare and educational opportunities to children living in northern Tanzania. Empowers children in their pursuit of a happy, healthy and fulfilling life.

1985 ■ Seeds of HOPE International
PO Box 49458
Colorado Springs, CO 80949
Ph: (719)473-8494
E-mail: julietofwono@sohi.org
URL: http://www.sohi.org
Contact: Juliet Ofwono, Exec. Dir.
Founded: 2001. **Multinational. Description:** Works to bring hope to orphaned and street children in Uganda. Supports the education and physical well-being of Ugandan children by building Christian academies. Provides the children with the basic necessities of food, shelter and clothing.

1986 ■ Sky of Love
PO Box 170241
Brooklyn, NY 11217
E-mail: info@skyoflove.org
URL: http://skyoflove.org
Contact: Antonio D'Auria, Co-Founder/Pres.
Founded: 2008. **Multinational. Description:** Aims to nurture, mentor and educate orphaned, abused and neglected children in Ghana. Provides the needs of underprivileged and vulnerable children. Promotes and advocates for an environment of love and nonviolence, in accordance with the UN Convention of the Rights of the Child.

1987 ■ Sweet Sleep
PO Box 40486
Nashville, TN 37204-9998
Ph: (615)730-7671
Fax: (615)750-2789
E-mail: jon@sweetsleep.org
URL: http://www.sweetsleep.org
Contact: Jen Gash, Pres./Founder
Founded: 2003. **Multinational. Description:** Aims to provide beds to the world's orphaned and abandoned children. Improves their quality of life by providing them sufficient and healthy place to sleep.

1988 ■ To Love a Child
PO Box 165
Clifton Park, NY 12065
Ph: (518)859-4424
URL: http://www.toloveachild.net
Contact: Teresa Brobston, Pres.
Multinational. Description: Provides humanitarian assistance to impoverished children and their families. Helps create a better future and quality of life for all. Collaborates with academics, churches, and other organizations and experts to provide the most practical, sustainable and long term methods for project development.

1989 ■ Two Hearts for Hope
PO Box 1928
Lebanon, MO 65536
E-mail: info@twoheartsforhope.org
URL: http://www.twoheartsforhope.org
Contact: Kimberly Prud'homme, Founder/Exec. Dir.
Multinational. Description: Aims to support the needs of orphans in Kazakhstan. Raises funds to provide the basic necessities of orphaned children.

1990 ■ World Spark
1635 SE Malden St.
Portland, OR 97202
Ph: (503)245-7899
Fax: (503)245-7972

E-mail: info@worldspark.org
URL: http://www.worldspark.org
Contact: Michael Maslowsky, Pres.
Founded: 2002. **Multinational. Description:** Aims to provide the basic needs of homeless children. Collaborates with child advocates, social workers, community and religious leaders to develop a new approach to caring for orphaned children.

1991 ■ Zambia Hope International
Hope Mountain Found.
5235 Westview Dr., Ste.100
Frederick, MD 21703
Ph: (301)624-0061
E-mail: info@zambiahope.org
URL: http://zambiahope.org
Contact: Anne Musonda, Exec. Dir.
Founded: 2001. **Multinational. Description:** Assists the orphans and vulnerable children of Lusaka, Zambia. Provides children with the essentials of life, including food and medicine. Conducts program to combat the spread of HIV/AIDS through teaching responsible behavior to children.

Childhood Education

1992 ■ Caring Hand for Children
20315 Nordhoff St.
Chatsworth, CA 91311
Ph: (818)727-9740
Fax: (818)998-8239
E-mail: contact@caringhandforchildren.org
URL: http://www.caringhandforchildren.org
Contact: Vinay Chhabra, Contact
Founded: 2000. **Multinational. Description:** Strives to educate underprivileged children to help them become self-sufficient. Supports various programs to provide educational opportunities to Indian chidren.

1993 ■ Growing Liberia's Children (GLC)
PO Box 90676
San Diego, CA 92169
Ph: (858)539-0954
Free: (800)339-7005
E-mail: info@growingliberiaschildren.org
URL: http://www.growingliberiaschildren.org
Contact: Malia E. Harris, Founder
Founded: 2008. **Multinational. Description:** Aims to recruit people and mobilize resources in the United States and in Liberia to enhance the education and lives of Liberian children. Provides basic education and practical training for children and their teachers.

1994 ■ HELPSudan
5255 N Ashland Ave.
Chicago, IL 60640
E-mail: info@helpsudaninternational.org
URL: http://www.helpsudaninternational.org
Contact: Jok Kuol Wel, Founder/Pres.
Founded: 2005. **Multinational. Description:** Seeks to fulfill the educational needs of communities in Southern Sudan. Provides children in war-torn Southern Sudan with the educational opportunities.

Children

1995 ■ Better Boys Foundation (BBF) (11783)
1512 S Pulaski Rd.
Chicago, IL 60623
Ph: (773)542-7300 (773)542-7322
Fax: (773)521-4153
E-mail: **info@betterboys.org**
URL: **http://www.betterboys.org**
Contact: **John K. Holton PhD, Exec. Dir.**

1996 ■ Children, Inc. (CI)
4205 Dover Rd.
Richmond, VA 23221-3267
Ph: **(804)359-4565**
Free: (800)538-5381
E-mail: **sponsorship@childrenincorporated.org**
URL: **http://www.childrenincorporated.org**
Contact: **Richard E. Baltimore, Chm.**

1997 ■ Dream Factory (DF) (11797)
120 W Broadway, Ste.300
Louisville, KY 40202
Ph: (502)561-3001
Free: (800)456-7556
Fax: (502)561-3004
E-mail: dfinfo@dreamfactoryinc.org
URL: http://www.dreamfactoryinc.org
Contact: **Janice Harris, Pres.**

1998 ■ Jack and Jill of America (JJA) (11810)
1930 17th St. NW
Washington, DC 20009
Ph: (202)667-7010
E-mail: **edrenee@jack-and-jill.org**
URL: http://www.jack-and-jill.org
Contact: **Tara Joseph-Labrie, Pres.**

1999 ■ Orphan Foundation of America (OFA) (11462)
21351 Gentry Dr., Ste.130
Sterling, VA 20166
Ph: (571)203-0270
Fax: (571)203-0273
E-mail: **info@orphan.org**
URL: **http://fc2success.org**
Contact: Eileen McCaffrey, CEO

2000 ■ RAINBOWS (1590)
1360 Hamilton Pkwy.
Itasca, IL 60143
Ph: (847)952-1770
Free: (800)266-3206
Fax: (847)952-1774
E-mail: info@rainbows.org
URL: http://www.rainbows.org
Contact: Suzy Yehl Marta, Founder/Pres.

2001 ■ Save the Children (SCF) (11467)
54 Wilton Rd.
Westport, CT 06880
Ph: (203)221-4030
Free: (800)728-3843
E-mail: twebster@savethechildren.org
URL: http://www.savethechildren.org
Contact: **Charles F. MacCormack, CEO**

2002 ■ Southern Early Childhood Association (SECA) (11468)
PO Box 55930
Little Rock, AR 72215-5930
Ph: (501)221-1648
Free: (800)305-7322
Fax: (501)227-5297
E-mail: info@southernearlychildhood.org
URL: http://www.southernearlychildhood.org
Contact: **Janie Humphries, Pres.**

2003 ■ Starlight Children's Foundation (11470)
2049 Century Plz. E Ste.4320
Los Angeles, CA 90067
Ph: (310)479-1212
Fax: (310)479-1235
E-mail: info@starlight.org
URL: http://www.starlight.org
Contact: **Jacqueline Hart-Ibrahim, CEO**

Civil Rights and Liberties

2004 ■ A World of Difference Institute (10963)
605 3rd Ave.
New York, NY 10158
Ph: (212)885-7811
E-mail: webmaster@adl.org
URL: http://www.adl.org/education/edu_awod/default.asp
Contact: Erin Lee, Asst. Dir.

Community Action

2005 ■ Global Helps Network
PO Box 1238
Enumclaw, WA 98022
E-mail: info@globalhelpsnetwork.org
URL: http://www.globalhelpsnetwork.org
Contact: Mic McDaniel, Pres.

Multinational. Description: Aims to support non-profit and civic organizations, schools and churches in their global efforts to help disadvantaged people in developing countries, with particular focus on India. Fosters social, economic and spiritual development among communities. Offers opportunities for individuals and groups to participate in vision trips.

2006 ■ Midwest Academy (MA) (12045)
27 E Monroe, 11th Fl.
Chicago, IL 60603
Ph: (312)427-2304
Fax: (312)379-0313
E-mail: info@midwestacademy.com
URL: http://www.midwestacademy.com
Contact: **Judy Hertz, Exec. Dir.**

Community Development

2007 ■ Adopt-a-Village International (AaVI)
PO Box 26599
Colorado Springs, CO 80936
Ph: (719)492-8736
E-mail: info@adoptavillageinternational.org
URL: http://www.adoptavillageinternational.com
Contact: Dave Ruckman, Chm.

Founded: 2003. **Languages:** English, Spanish. **Multinational. Description:** Aims to break the cycle of poverty in impoverished villages. Provides sustainable improvements to meet basic human needs and improves quality of life, including medical care, educational and literacy programs, and water purification systems.

2008 ■ Alliance of Jamaican and American Humanitarians (AOJAH)
264 S La Cienega Blvd., Ste.1004
Beverly Hills, CA 90211
Ph: (424)249-8135
E-mail: info@aojah.org
URL: http://www.aojah.org
Contact: Joan Crawford, Pres.

Founded: 2010. **Multinational. Description:** Works to provide quality healthcare and education programs and services to the poor and the underprivileged. Facilitates the transfer of knowledge and innovations to local communities and the Carribean.

2009 ■ Breaking Ground
104 Neal St.
Portland, ME 04102
Ph: (206)351-7778
Fax: (207)772-7487
URL: http://breaking-ground.squarespace.com
Contact: Alexandra Moore, Exec. Dir.

Founded: 2006. **Multinational. Description:** Provides seed funding to projects of mobilized communities. Equips individuals and families with training and resources to increase their ability to earn money through primary income-generating activities.

2010 ■ Building Bridges Worldwide
5-09 48th Ave., Apt. 7B
Long Island City, NY 11101
E-mail: info@buildingbridgesworldwide.org
URL: http://www.buildingbridgesworldwide.org
Contact: Matthew Basile, Founder

Multinational. Description: Aims to help disadvantaged communities both domestically and abroad through a network of volunteers. Facilitates the planning, support and fund raising for a variety of service projects.

2011 ■ Building Community Bridges (BCB)
244 5th Ave., Ste.E283
New York, NY 10001
Free: (888)486-4218
Fax: (888)397-3717
E-mail: info@bcombridges.org
URL: http://www.bcombridges.org
Contact: Enyonam Nanevie, CEO/Founder

Founded: 2006. **Description:** Aims to improve the quality of life in underserved rural villages in West Africa by building clean-water pumps, new schools and medical clinics. Empowers rural populations to become self-reliant and self-sufficient by utilizing both indigenous knowledge and modern innovation and technology.

2012 ■ Burundi Friends International (BFI)
PO Box 927356
San Diego, CA 92192-7356
Ph: (619)800-2340
E-mail: info@bufri.org
URL: http://www.bufri.org
Contact: Jeanine Niyonzima-Aroian, Founder

Founded: 2007. **Multinational. Description:** Aims to help fight poverty in Burundi by providing education, health care and self sustaining enterprise opportunities on a village by village basis.

2013 ■ Chris Cares International (CCI)
119 Britton Ave.
Stoughton, MA 02072
E-mail: chris@chriscares.org
URL: http://www.chriscares.org
Contact: Christine Lott, Exec. Dir.

Founded: 2008. **Multinational. Description:** Aims to fight poverty through education in Tanzania by providing them with the tools they need to improve the lives of their families, villages and communities. Helps to sustain women in the rural villages of Tanzania in their small businesses.

2014 ■ Community Development International (CDI)
PO Box 3417
New York, NY 10163
E-mail: info@cd-international.org
URL: http://www.cd-international.org
Contact: Kevin Jamison, Pres.

Multinational. Description: Aims to build strong and sustainable urban and rural communities in both the worst off developing countries throughout the world and in disadvantaged local communities in the developed world. Implements innovative projects and programs to facilitate sustainable development in urban and rural locations.

2015 ■ Community Transportation Association of America (CTAA) (11513)
1341 G St. NW, 10th Fl.
Washington, DC 20005
Ph: (202)247-1922
Free: (800)891-0590
Fax: (202)737-9197
E-mail: marsico@ctaa.org
URL: **http://web1.ctaa.org/webmodules/webarticles/anmviewer.asp?a=23&z=2**
Contact: Dale J. Marsico CCTM, Exec. Dir.

2016 ■ Connecting Congo
1416 S 43rd St.
Tacoma, WA 98418
Ph: (206)351-9293 (208)860-7778
E-mail: contactus@connectingcongo.org
URL: http://www.connectingcongo.org
Contact: Dr. David Suze Manda, Chm.

Founded: 2009. **Multinational. Description:** Aims to improve the lives of the people of Democrative Republic of Congo. Focuses on improving the education system in the rural areas of Congo.

2017 ■ Education for Prosperity (EfP)
PO Box 302
East Lansing, MI 48826
Ph: (517)614-0501

E-mail: info@educationforprosperity.org
URL: http://www.educationforprosperity.org
Contact: David Smith, Pres.

Founded: 2004. **Multinational. Description:** Aims to improve the quality of life of disadvantaged communities. Provides education and service to increase prosperity in these communities. Fosters mutually beneficial and collaborative relationships between communities.

2018 ■ Funders' Network for Smart Growth and Livable Communities
1500 San Remo Ave., Ste.249
Coral Gables, FL 33146
Ph: (305)667-6350
Fax: (305)667-6355
E-mail: info@fundersnetwork.org
URL: http://www.fundersnetwork.org
Contact: Ben Starrett, Founder/Exec. Dir.

Founded: 1999. **Description:** Works to inspire, strengthen and expand funding and philanthropic leadership that yield environmentally sustainable, socially equitable and economically prosperous regions and communities. Strives to improve philanthropic understanding about connections between growth and development issues and environmental, economic and social outcomes. Seeks to encourage more funders to make investments to advance innovative solutions. Aims to strengthen relationships, connections and networks among funders.

2019 ■ Global Brigades
1099 E Champlain Dr., Ste.A176
Fresno, CA 93720
E-mail: admin@dglobalbrigades.org
URL: http://globalbrigades.org
Contact: Jeff Hay, Chm.

Founded: 2004. **Multinational. Description:** Aims to improve the quality of life in Honduran, Panamanian and Ghanaian communities by organizing a student-led social responsibility movement. Empowers volunteers to facilitate sustainable solutions in under resourced communities while fostering local cultures.

2020 ■ Global Partners Running Waters (GPRW)
13105 Watertown Plank Rd.
Elm Grove, WI 53122
Ph: (262)787-1010
E-mail: contact@globalpartnersrunningwaters.org
URL: http://www.globalpartnersrunningwaters.org
Contact: Sister Jan Gregorcich, Exec. Dir.

Founded: 2002. **Description:** Strives to build relationships through collaboration on water, food and health projects in Latin America. Fosters the education and empowerment of people in rural Latin America. Provides financial and other resources to assist with basic water distribution systems and solutions to shortages of healthful food and other basic needs.

2021 ■ HANDS for Cambodia
PO Box 940582
Plano, TX 75094-0582
E-mail: carolyn@handsforcambodia.com
URL: http://www.handsforcambodia.com
Contact: Carolyn Wyatt, Pres./Exec. Dir.

Founded: 2005. **Multinational. Description:** Provides health care, health education, clean water and community development services to those in need in Cambodia. Seeks to establish sustainable medical and health care education programs. Strives to create additional opportunities for health and neighborhood development services.

2022 ■ Help Aid Africa (HAA)
1132 Corrie Ln.
Walnut Creek, CA 94597
E-mail: info@helpaidafrica.org
URL: http://www.helpaidafrica.org
Contact: Abbas Moloo, Founder

Multinational. Description: Aims to build and empower communities in East Africa. Provides educational opportunities, infrastructure, affordable and available healthcare and humanitarian services.

2023 ■ Hope for Haiti
PO Box 496
Westminster, MD 21158-0496
Ph: (410)848-7343
E-mail: admin@hope-for-haiti.org
URL: http://hope-for-haiti.org
Contact: Brian House, Founder
Founded: 2005. **Multinational. Description:** Facilitates sustainable grassroots projects that provide long-term results to Haiti's current problems. Fosters self-sufficiency among communities through training and skill development.

2024 ■ Indigo Threads
PO Box 401
La Quinta, CA 92247
Ph: (760)564-2679
E-mail: mdmeyer@indigothreads.org
URL: http://www.indigothreads.org
Contact: Mary D. Meyer, Founder/Pres./Exec. Dir.
Founded: 2005. **Multinational. Description:** Aims to develop and support educational opportunities for desperately poor children in Southern Laos rural villages.

2025 ■ Jamaica Unite
3613 NW 194th Terr.
Miami Gardens, FL 33056
Ph: (954)353-7032
E-mail: contact@jamaicaunite.org
URL: http://jamaicaunite.org
Contact: Alecia Thompson, Pres./Founder
Founded: 2010. **Multinational. Description:** Helps Jamaica rebuild by working with youth, women and the poor. Provides educational resources for young people in Jamaica. Empowers women to stand up against abuse or discrimination.

2026 ■ Khadarlis for Sierra Leone (KFSL)
99 Acad. Ave.
Providence, RI 02908
Ph: (401)454-6916
URL: http://www.khadarlis.org
Contact: Dee Johnson, Founder
Founded: 2007. **Multinational. Description:** Works to rebuild villages in Sierra Leone destroyed by the civil war. Implements programs that will foster self esteem and self reliance among the community members. Provides villages with water supply housing, agriculture, education, basic health care and solar electricity.

2027 ■ Mama Hope
582 Market St., Ste.709
San Francisco, CA 94104
Ph: (415)686-6954
E-mail: info@mamahope.org
URL: http://www.mamahope.org
Contact: Nyla Rodgers, Founding Dir.
Multinational. Description: Works in partnership with African people to create self-sufficient communities. Fosters sustainable projects in communities that lead to healthy and productive lives. Provides access to the basic life resources of clean water, food security, health care and education.

2028 ■ Nepal SEEDS: Social Educational Environmental Development Services in Nepal
800 Kansas St.
San Francisco, CA 94107
Ph: (415)813-3331
E-mail: info@nepalseeds.org
URL: http://www.nepalseeds.org
Contact: KP Kafle, Founder/Exec. Dir.
Founded: 1997. **Multinational. Description:** Helps people improve their health and welfare by supporting grassroots projects that involve community partnerships in the areas of education, water, health services and the environment. Develops economically feasible and sustainable solutions that will benefit entire communities.

2029 ■ One Vision International (OVI)
PO Box 20608
Knoxville, TN 37940
Ph: (865)579-3353
E-mail: info@onevisionintl.org
URL: http://www.onevisionintl.org
Contact: John Miller, Founder/Exec. Dir.
Founded: 2005. **Multinational. Description:** Provides aid and support to forgotten areas of the world. Works with vulnerable people to meet their immediate physical needs and to bring hope to an entire community.

2030 ■ Operation HOPE, Inc. (OHI)
707 Wilshire Blvd., 30th Fl.
Los Angeles, CA 90017
Ph: (213)891-2900
Free: (877)592-4673
Fax: (213)489-7511
E-mail: leslie.alessandro@operationhope.org
URL: http://www.operationhope.org
Contact: John Hope Bryant, Founder/Chm./CEO

2031 ■ Orphans Africa (OA)
2610 N 8th St.
Tacoma, WA 98406-7207
Ph: (253)549-0089
E-mail: info@orphansafrica.org
URL: http://orphansafrica.org
Contact: Carl Gann, Co-Founder/Pres.
Founded: 2007. **Multinational. Description:** Helps to educate orphans by providing tuition fees and essential supplies. Enables widows to become self-sufficient through occupational training.

2032 ■ Reconstruction Efforts Aiding Children without Homes (REACH)
PO Box 4141
Winchester, VA 22604
E-mail: contact@reach4children.org
URL: http://reach4children.com
Contact: Donald Stevens, Founder
Founded: 2004. **Multinational. Description:** Aims to bring environmentally friendly and sustainable buildings to children affected by natural disaster, poverty, and war around the world.

2033 ■ Restoring Institutions Services and Empowering Liberia (RISE Liberia)
1250 4th St. SW
Washington, DC 20024
E-mail: info@riseliberia.org
URL: http://www.riseliberia.org
Contact: Ms. Fatu Kamara, Founder
Founded: 2009. **Multinational. Description:** Seeks to create opportunities for the disadvantaged people of Liberia. Provides assistance to Liberians in their literary, intellectual and socioeconomic wellbeing pursuits.

2034 ■ Service for the Love of God (SFLG)
291 Dutch Ln.
Pittsburgh, PA 15236
Ph: (412)650-6292
E-mail: sekearns1@msn.com
URL: http://sflgbenin.org
Contact: Sherri Kearns, Co-Founder/Chair
Founded: 2003. **Multinational. Description:** Aims to improve the lives of underprivileged people in Benin. Facilitates educational and health projects designed to address the needs of the people in Benin.

2035 ■ Shining Hope for Communities (SHOFCO)
14 Red Glen Rd.
Middletown, CT 06457
Ph: (860)218-9854
E-mail: info@hopetoshine.org
URL: http://www.hopetoshine.org
Contact: Kennedy Odede, Pres./CEO
Founded: 2009. **Multinational. Description:** Strives to combat intergenerational cycles of poverty and gender inequality. Links free schools for girls to holistic community centers that provide residents with essential services unavailable elsewhere.

2036 ■ Together for Tanzania
PO Box 395
Powhatan, VA 23139
E-mail: info@togetherfortanzania.org
URL: http://togetherfortanzania.org
Contact: Jeanette Brannan, Contact
Founded: 2008. **Multinational. Description:** Provides medical, educational and missional support to people in Tanzania through contributions, partnerships and sponsorships. Encourages Tanzanians to become self-sufficient in order for them to take care of their families and serve their communities.

2037 ■ Village Focus International (VFI)
14 Wall St., 20th Fl.
New York, NY 10005
Ph: (917)621-7167
E-mail: tms@villagefocus.org
URL: http://www.villagefocus.org
Contact: Todd Sigaty, Chm.
Founded: 2000. **Multinational. Description:** Works to serve the poorest, most vulnerable people of Laos and Cambodia. Fosters the development of local leadership in an effort to bring about positive fundamental social change. Addresses issues on anti-trafficking and child protection, integrated village development (education, health and food security) and land and natural resource rights.

2038 ■ The Waterfront Center (TWC) (11794)
PO Box 53351
Washington, DC 20009
Ph: (202)337-0356
Fax: (202)986-0448
E-mail: mail@waterfrontcenter.org
URL: http://www.waterfrontcenter.org
Contact: Ann E. Breen, Co-Dir./Co-Founder

2039 ■ Well Done Organization
10813 27th St. SE
Lake Stevens, WA 98258
Ph: (206)349-1574
URL: http://www.welldoneliberia.org
Contact: Daryl Finley, Founder
Founded: 2007. **Multinational. Description:** Aims to help people in Liberia, Africa gain access to basic human needs. Addresses poverty issues like clean water and sanitation. Provides food, clothing, shelter and mosquito nets for Liberians.

2040 ■ WorldHope Corps (WHC)
11 Ardsleigh Dr.
Madison, NJ 07940
Ph: (973)714-0023
E-mail: info@worldhopecorps.com
URL: http://www.worldhopecorps.com
Contact: Dr. Michael Christensen, Founder
Founded: 2007. **Multinational. Description:** Connects resources with needs to build capacity for sustainable community development. Facilitates community development and micro-enterprise projects. Offers peer training events in the areas of AIDS education and prevention, volunteer disaster response, community development and mental health promotion. Organizes volunteer missions.

Counseling

2041 ■ Association for Specialists in Group Work (ASGW) (11820)
c/o Amy Nitza, Sec.
Indiana University-Purdue Univ. Fort Wayne
2101 E Coliseum Blvd.
Fort Wayne, IN 46805-1499
Free: (800)347-6647
E-mail: nitzaa@ipfw.edu
URL: http://www.asgw.org
Contact: Bogusia Skudrzyk, Pres.

2042 ■ Commission on Rehabilitation Counselor Certification (CRCC) (12135)
1699 E Woodfield Rd., Ste.300
Schaumburg, IL 60173-4957
Ph: (847)944-1325
Fax: (847)944-1346
E-mail: info@crccertification.com
URL: http://www.crccertification.com
Contact: Cindy Chapman, Exec. Dir.

2043 ■ Employee Assistance Society of North America (EASNA) (11823)
2001 Jefferson Davis Hwy., Ste.1004
Arlington, VA 22202-3617
Ph: (703)416-0060
Fax: (703)416-0014
E-mail: bmclean@easna.org
URL: http://www.easna.org
Contact: Francois Legault, Pres.

2044 ■ International Association of Addictions and Offender Counselors (IAAOC) (10525)
Rider Univ.
Dept. of Graduate Educ., Leadership, and Counseling
Memorial 202
2083 Lawrenceville Rd.
Lawrenceville, NJ 08648
Free: (800)347-6647
Fax: (800)473-2329
E-mail: info@iaaoc.org
URL: http://www.iaaoc.org
Contact: Juleen K. Buser PhD, Pres.

2045 ■ National MultiCultural Institute (NMCI) (10599)
1666 K St. NW, Ste.440
Washington, DC 20006-1242
Ph: (202)483-0700
Fax: (202)483-5233
E-mail: nmci@nmci.org
URL: http://www.nmci.org
Contact: Elizabeth Pathy Salett MSW, Founder

Crime

2046 ■ Alliance of Guardian Angels
982 E 89th St.
Brooklyn, NY 11236
Ph: (212)860-5575
Free: (800)719-1917
Fax: (718)649-5705
E-mail: mary@guardianangels.org
URL: http://www.guardianangels.org
Contact: Mary Sliwa, Exec. Dir./COO

2047 ■ Black on Black Love Campaign (BOBL) (11966)
1000 E 87th St.
Chicago, IL 60619
Ph: (773)978-0868 (773)978-7265
Fax: (773)978-7345
E-mail: info@bobl.org
URL: http://www.bobl.org
Contact: Mrs. Frances Wright, Exec. Dir./Pres./CEO

2048 ■ National Crime Prevention Council (NCPC) (11844)
2001 Jefferson Davis Hwy., Ste.901
Arlington, VA 22202-4801
Ph: (202)466-6272
Fax: (202)296-1356
E-mail: webmaster@ncpc.org
URL: http://www.ncpc.org
Contact: Ann M. Harkins, Pres./CEO

Criminal Justice

2049 ■ Association of State Correctional Administrators (ASCA)
213 Court St., Ste.606
Middletown, CT 06457
Ph: (860)704-6410 (301)791-2722
Fax: (860)704-6420
E-mail: jfenton@asca.net
URL: http://www.asca.net
Contact: Camille Camp, Co-Exec. Dir.

2050 ■ International Association for Correctional and Forensic Psychology (IACFP)
c/o Mr. David Randall, Sec.-Treas.
PO Box 7642
Wilmington, NC 28406
E-mail: randall.david@mail.dc.state.fl.us
URL: http://www.aa4cfp.org
Contact: Dean Aufderhiede, Pres.

2051 ■ International Association of Correctional Training Personnel (IACTP) (11871)
PO Box 473254
Aurora, CO 80047
Ph: (719)738-9969
Free: (877)884-2287
Fax: (877)884-2287
E-mail: iactp@correctionsmail.com
URL: http://www.iactp.org
Contact: Linda Dunbar, Ed.

2052 ■ John Howard Association (JHA) (11324)
375 E Chicago Ave., Ste.529
Chicago, IL 60611
Ph: (312)503-6300
Fax: (312)503-6306
E-mail: dhoffman@thejha.org
URL: http://www.thejha.org
Contact: John Maki, Exec. Dir.

Disabled

2053 ■ Abilities! (12041)
201 I.U. Willets Rd.
Albertson, NY 11507-1599
Ph: (516)465-1400 (516)747-5400
Fax: (516)465-1591
E-mail: info@abilitiesonline.org
URL: http://www.ncds.org
Contact: John D. Kemp, Pres./CEO

2054 ■ Assistance Dogs International (ADI) (11923)
PO Box 5174
Santa Rosa, CA 95402
E-mail: info@assistancedogsinternational.org
URL: http://www.assistancedogsinternational.org
Contact: Peter Gorbing, Pres.

2055 ■ Association of Rehabilitation Programs in Computer Technology (ARPCT) (10813)
Western Michigan Univ.
Educational Leadership, Res. and Tech. Dept.
Kalamazoo, MI 49008
Ph: (269)387-2053
Fax: (269)387-3696
E-mail: dkret@dkajobs.com
URL: http://www.arpct.org
Contact: Dot Kret, Pres.

2056 ■ Council of Citizens With Low Vision International (CCLVI) (11934)
2200 Wilson Blvd., Ste.650
Arlington, VA 22201
Free: (800)733-2258
E-mail: webmaster@cclvi.org
URL: http://www.cclvi.org
Contact: Richard Rueda, Pres.

2057 ■ Disability Rights Education and Defense Fund (DREDF) (10708)
3075 Adeline St., Ste.210
Berkeley, CA 94703-2578
Ph: (510)644-2555
Free: (800)348-4232
Fax: (510)841-8645
E-mail: info@dredf.org
URL: http://www.dredf.org
Contact: Susan Henderson, Exec. Dir.

2058 ■ Foundation for Science and Disability (FSD) (12078)
503 NW 89 St.
Gainesville, FL 32607-1400
Ph: (352)374-5774
E-mail: rmankin1@aim.com
URL: http://www.sternd.org
Contact: Erica Penn, Pres.

2059 ■ Just One Break (JOB) (12090)
570 Seventh Ave.
New York, NY 10018
Ph: (212)785-7300
Fax: (212)785-4513
URL: http://www.justonebreak.com
Contact: John D. Kemp, Pres.

2060 ■ Lift Disability Network (11931)
PO Box 770607
Winter Garden, FL 34777
Ph: (407)228-8343
E-mail: info@liftdisability.net
URL: http://www.liftdisability.net
Contact: Jim Hukill, Exec. Dir.

2061 ■ National Amputation Foundation (NAF) (10729)
40 Church St.
Malverne, NY 11565
Ph: (516)887-3600
Fax: (516)887-3667
E-mail: amps76@aol.com
URL: http://www.nationalamputation.org
Contact: John Devine, Pres.

2062 ■ Society for Disability Studies (SDS) (12124)
Soc. for Disability Stud.
107 Commerce Center Dr., Ste.204
Huntersville, NC 28078
Ph: (704)274-9240
Fax: (704)948-7779
E-mail: info@disstudies.org
URL: http://disstudies.org
Contact: Stephan J. Hamlin-Smith, Exec. Off.

2063 ■ TASH (10875)
1001 Connecticut Ave. NW, Ste.235
Washington, DC 20036
Ph: (202)540-9020
Fax: (202)540-9019
E-mail: info@tash.org
URL: http://tash.org
Contact: Barbara Trader, Exec. Dir.

2064 ■ VSA - The International Organization on Arts and Disability (10836)
818 Connecticut Ave. NW, Ste.600
Washington, DC 20006
Ph: (202)628-2800
Free: (800)933-8721
Fax: (202)429-0868
E-mail: info@vsarts.org
URL: http://www.vsarts.org
Contact: Soula Antoniou, Pres.
Status Note: Formerly VSA arts.

2065 ■ Wheels for the World (11443)
Joni and Friends Intl. Disability Center
PO Box 3333
Agoura Hills, CA 91376-3333
Ph: (818)707-5664
Free: (800)523-5777

Fax: (818)707-2391
URL: **http://www.joniandfriends.org/wheels-for-the-world**
Contact: Joni Eareckson Tada, Founder/CEO

Disaster Aid

2066 ■ Aid Still Required (ASR)
PO Box 7353
Santa Monica, CA 90406
Ph: (310)454-4646
Free: (888)363-GIVE
E-mail: info@aidstillrequired.org
URL: http://aidstillrequired.org
Contact: Andrea Herz Payne, Founder/Chair
Multinational. Description: Focuses on bringing attention and providing humanitarian aid to areas suffering from natural disasters or human crises. Seeks to find innovative ways to build back regions affected with natural disasters through environmentally sustainable means.

2067 ■ Compassion into Action Network - Direct Outcome Organization (CAN-DO)
578 Washington Blvd., Ste.390
Marina Del Rey, CA 90292
Free: (877)226-3697
E-mail: press@can-do.org
URL: http://www.can-do.org
Contact: Eric Klein, Founder/CEO
Founded: 2004. **Multinational. Description:** Develops innovative methods to speed up the delivery of aid to communities in need by collaborating with local individuals and organizations. Works to provide lasting solutions to some of the world's most critical problems, including natural disasters, environmental degradation, humanitarian crises and educational inequity.

2068 ■ Great Commission Alliance (GCA)
4700 SW 188th Ave.
Southwest Ranches, FL 33332
Ph: (954)434-4500
E-mail: info@gcanet.org
URL: http://www.gcanet.org
Contact: Brian Kelso, Exec. Dir.
Founded: 2000. **Multinational. Description:** Works to bring temporary relief to many people in Haiti as they struggle with the aftermath of the earthquake. Collaborates with other charities to help establish orphanages, schools and economic enterprises for the people of Les Cayes. Supports humanitarian efforts in rebuilding and enhancing the lives of Haitians.

Divorce

2069 ■ Children's Rights Council (CRC) (12143)
9470 Annapolis Rd., Ste.310
Lanham, MD 20706-3022
Ph: (301)459-1220
Fax: (301)459-1227
E-mail: info@crckids.org
URL: http://www.crckids.org
Contact: Sal Frasca, CEO

2070 ■ North American Conference of Separated and Divorced Catholics (NACSDC) (11752)
PO Box 10
Hancock, MI 49930-0010
Ph: (906)482-0494
Fax: (906)482-7470
E-mail: office@nacsdc.org
URL: http://www.nacsdc.org
Contact: Mr. Greg Mills, Pres.

Domestic Violence

2071 ■ Emerge: Counseling and Education to Stop Domestic Violence (10746)
2464 Massachusetts Ave., Ste.101
Cambridge, MA 02140
Ph: (617)547-9879

E-mail: **info@emergedv.com**
URL: http://www.emergedv.com
Contact: David Adams, Co-Dir.

2072 ■ International Center for Assault Prevention (ICAP) (10787)
107 Gilbreth Pkwy., Ste.200
Mullica Hill, NJ 08062
Ph: **(856)582-7000**
Free: **(800)258-3189**
Fax: **(856)582-3588**
E-mail: **childassaultprevention@gmail.com**
URL: http://www.internationalcap.org
Contact: Jeannette Collins, Dir. of Curriculum and Programs

Economic Development

2073 ■ endPoverty.org (10872)
7910 Woodmont Ave., Ste.907
Bethesda, MD 20814
Ph: (240)396-1146
Fax: (240)235-3550
E-mail: info@endpoverty.org
URL: http://www.endpoverty.org
Contact: Larry Roadman, Chm.
Status Note: Formerly Enterprise Development International.

Employment

2074 ■ American Contract Compliance Association (ACCA) (17493)
17 E Monroe St., No. 150
Chicago, IL 60603
Free: (866)222-2298
Fax: (510)287-2158
E-mail: **jerry2@hapdx.org**
URL: http://www.acca298.org
Contact: **Jerry Walker, Pres.**

2075 ■ National Business and Disability Council (NBDC) (12233)
201 I.U. Willets Rd.
Albertson, NY 11507
Ph: (516)465-1516
E-mail: jtowles@abilitiesonline.org
URL: http://www.business-disability.com
Contact: **John Kemp, Pres./CEO**

2076 ■ National Career Development Association (NCDA) (12090)
305 N Beech Cir.
Broken Arrow, OK 74012
Ph: (918)663-7060
Free: (866)367-6232
Fax: (918)663-7058
E-mail: dpennington@ncda.org
URL: **http://associationdatabase.com/aws/NCDA/pt/sp/Home_Page**
Contact: Deneen Pennington, Exec. Dir.

2077 ■ National Employment Counseling Association (NECA) (12091)
6836 Bee Cave Rd., Ste.260
Austin, TX 78746
Free: (800)347-6647
E-mail: **kimberly@encompasswf.com**
URL: **http://www.employmentcounseling.org**
Contact: Kimberly Key, Pres.

2078 ■ POWER: People Organized to Win Employment Rights (15447)
335 S Van Ness Ave., 2nd Fl.
San Francisco, CA 94103
Ph: (415)864-8372
Fax: (415)864-8373
E-mail: power@peopleorganized.org
URL: **http://www.peopleorganized.org**
Contact: Steve Williams, Exec. Dir./Co-Founder

2079 ■ SER - Jobs for Progress National (12100)
100 E Royal Ln., Ste.130
Irving, TX 75039
Ph: **(469)549-3600**
Fax: **(469)549-3687**
E-mail: info@ser-national.org
URL: http://www.ser-national.org
Contact: Mr. Ignacio Salazar, Pres./CEO

2080 ■ W. E. Upjohn Institute for Employment Research (12249)
300 S Westnedge Ave.
Kalamazoo, MI 49007-4686
Ph: (269)343-5541 (269)343-4330
Free: (888)227-8569
Fax: (269)343-3308
E-mail: **communications@upjohn.org**
URL: http://www.upjohninstitute.org
Contact: Randall W. Eberts, Pres.

2081 ■ Wildcat Service Corporation (WSC) (10809)
2 Washington St., 3rd Fl.
New York, NY 10004
Ph: (212)209-6000
E-mail: **webresponses@wildcatnyc.org**
URL: http://www.wildcatnyc.org
Contact: Mary Ellen Boyd, Pres.

Euthanasia

2082 ■ Compassion and Choices (12281)
PO Box 101810
Denver, CO 80250-1810
Free: (800)247-7421
Fax: **(866)312-2690**
E-mail: info@compassionandchoices.org
URL: http://www.compassionandchoices.org
Contact: Barbara Coombs Lee, Pres.

Families

2083 ■ American College of Counselors (ACC) (12137)
273 Glossip Ave.
Highlandville, MO 65669-8133
Ph: **(417)885-4030**
Fax: **(417)443-3002**
URL: http://acconline.us
Contact: Raymond Bazemore Croskey, Pres.

2084 ■ American Mothers, Inc. (AMI) (12290)
1666 K St. NW, Ste.260
Washington, DC 20006
Free: (877)242-4264
E-mail: info@americanmothers.org
URL: http://www.americanmothers.org
Contact: **Connell Branan, Pres.**

2085 ■ Christian Family Movement (CFM) (10871)
PO Box 925
Evansville, IN 47706-0925
Ph: (812)962-5508
Fax: (812)962-5509
E-mail: office@cfm.org
URL: http://www.cfm.org
Contact: **Jane Leingang, Exec. Dir.**

2086 ■ Education and Enrichment Section of the National Council on Family Relations (EES) (10874)
1201 W River Pkwy., Ste.200
Minneapolis, MN 55454-1115
Ph: (763)781-9331
Free: (888)781-9331
Fax: (763)781-9348
E-mail: info@ncfr.org
URL: http://www.ncfr.org
Contact: **Susan K. Walker, Chair**

**2087 ■ National Council on Family Relations
(NCFR) (10824)**
1201 W River Pkwy., Ste.200
Minneapolis, MN 55454-1115
Ph: (763)781-9331
Free: (888)781-9331
Fax: (763)781-9348
E-mail: info@ncfr.org
URL: http://www.ncfr.org
Contact: Diane L. Cushman MPh, Exec. Dir.

Fundraising

**2088 ■ Association of Fundraising
Professionals (AFP) (11641)**
4300 Wilson Blvd., Ste.300
Arlington, VA 22203
Ph: (703)684-0410 (703)519-8445
Free: (800)666-FUND
Fax: (703)684-0540
E-mail: afp@afpnet.org
URL: http://www.afpnet.org
Contact: **Andrew Watt, Pres./CEO**

**2089 ■ Intimate Apparel Square Club (IASC)
(11062)**
326 Field Rd.
Clinton Corners, NY 12514
Ph: (845)758-5752
Fax: (845)758-2546
E-mail: amasry@yahoo.com
URL: http://thehugaward.org
Contact: **Adam Masry, Sec.**

2090 ■ Pioneers (12353)
930 15th St., 12th Fl.
Denver, CO 80202
Ph: (303)571-1200
Free: (800)872-5995
Fax: (303)572-0520
E-mail: info@pioneersvolunteer.org
URL: http://www.telecompioneers.org
Contact: **Carey Wirtzfeld, Interim Pres.**
Status Note: Formerly TelecomPioneers.

2091 ■ United Way of America (UWA) (12205)
701 N Fairfax St.
Alexandria, VA 22314
Ph: **(703)683-7800**
Fax: **(703)683-7846**
E-mail: **gallagher@uww.unitedway.org**
URL: **http://liveunited.org**
Contact: Mr. Brian A. Gallagher, Pres./CEO

Gay/Lesbian

**2092 ■ American Library Association | Gay,
Lesbian, Bisexual and Transgendered
Roundtable (ALA/GLBTRT)**
50 E Huron St.
Chicago, IL 60611
Free: (800)545-2433
Fax: (312)280-3255
E-mail: glbtrt@gmail.com
URL: http://www.ala.org/ala/mgrps/rts/glbtrt/index.cfm
Contact: **Anne Moore, Co-Chair**

**2093 ■ Association for Lesbian, Gay,
Bisexual and Transgender Issues in
Counseling (ALGBTIC) (12216)**
Oakland Univ.
440B Pawley Hall
Rochester, MI 48309
Ph: (508)531-2721 (248)370-3084
E-mail: **chaney@oakland.edu**
URL: http://www.algbtic.org
Contact: **Michael P. Chaney PhD, Pres.**

2094 ■ Couples National Network (15954)
PO Box 500699
Marathon, FL 33050-0699
Free: **(800)896-0717**

E-mail: couples@couples-national.org
URL: http://couples-national.org
Contact: **Jorg Gobel-Staib, Chm.**

2095 ■ Homosexual Information Center (HIC)
8721 Santa Monica Blvd., Ste.37
West Hollywood, CA 90069
Ph: **(818)527-5442**
E-mail: **chair@tangentgroup.org**
URL: http://www.tangentgroup.org
Contact: **C. Todd White, Chm.**

**2096 ■ Parents, Families, and Friends of
Lesbians and Gays (PFLAG) (1680)**
1828 L St. NW, Ste.660
Washington, DC 20036
Ph: (202)467-8180
Fax: **(202)349-0788**
E-mail: info@pflag.org
URL: http://community.pflag.org/Page.
aspx?pid=194&srcid=-2
Contact: Jody M. Huckaby, Exec. Dir.

Hispanic

**2097 ■ United States Conference of Catholic
Bishops | Secretariat for Hispanic Affairs
(SHA/USCCB) (12282)**
3211 4th St. NE
Washington, DC 20017
Ph: (202)541-3150 (202)541-3000
Fax: (202)722-8717
E-mail: **scha@usccb.org**
URL: http://www.usccb.org/hispanicaffairs
Contact: Father Allan F. Deck, Exec. Dir.

Home Economics

**2098 ■ American Association of Family and
Consumer Sciences (AAFCS) (12449)**
400 N Columbus St., Ste.202
Alexandria, VA 22314
Ph: (703)706-4600
Free: (800)424-8080
Fax: (703)706-4663
E-mail: staff@aafcs.org
URL: http://www.aafcs.org
Contact: **Sue Byrd CFCS, Pres.**

Homeless

**2099 ■ American Bar Association
Commission on Homelessness and Poverty**
740 15th St. NW
Washington, DC 20005-1022
Ph: **(202)662-1693** (202)662-1000
Fax: (202)638-3844
E-mail: **amy.hortonnewell@americanbar.org**
URL: **http://www.americanbar.org/groups/public_
services/homelessness_poverty.html**
Contact: Amy Horton-Newell, Dir.

Horses

2100 ■ American Horse League (AHL)
1612 Junction Ave., Ste.4
Sturgis, SD 57785
Ph: (605)347-1730
E-mail: ceo@americanhorseleague.com
URL: http://americanhorseleague.com
Contact: Chase R. Adams, CEO
Membership Dues: corporate, $500 (annual) ●
individual (non-voting), $100 (annual) ● industry
protector, $1,000 (annual). **Description:** Advocates
for the responsible management of horses in the
United States. Provides education and litigation to
ensure the humane treatment of horses.

Housing

**2101 ■ Cooperative Housing Foundation
(CHF) (12042)**
8601 Georgia Ave., Ste.800
Silver Spring, MD 20910
Ph: (301)587-4700
Fax: (301)587-7315
E-mail: mailbox@chfinternational.org
URL: http://www.chfinternational.org
Contact: **David A. Weiss, Pres./CEO**

**2102 ■ Enterprise Community Partners
(10977)**
10227 Wincopin Cir.
Columbia, MD 21044
Ph: (410)772-2404
Free: (800)624-4298
Fax: (410)964-1918
URL: http://www.enterprisecommunity.org
Contact: **Terri Ludwig, Pres./CEO**

**2103 ■ National Center for Housing
Management (NCHM) (11168)**
12021 Sunset Hills Rd., Ste.210
Reston, VA 20190
Ph: **(703)435-9393**
Free: (800)368-5625
Fax: **(703)435-9775**
E-mail: service@nchm.org
URL: http://www.nchm.org
Contact: Martha Abrams-Bell, Contact

**2104 ■ National Housing Conference (NHC)
(11116)**
1900 M St. NW, Ste.200
Washington, DC 20036
Ph: (202)466-2121
Fax: (202)466-2122
E-mail: mfriar@nhc.org
URL: http://www.nhc.org
Contact: Maureen Friar, Pres./CEO

**2105 ■ National Housing and Rehabilitation
Association (NH&RA)**
1400 16th St. NW, Ste.420
Washington, DC 20036-2244
Ph: (202)939-1750 (202)939-1741
Fax: (202)265-4435
E-mail: **info@housingonline.com**
URL: http://www.housingonline.com
Contact: Peter H. Bell, Pres./CEO

**2106 ■ National Rural Housing Coalition
(NRHC) (11029)**
1331 G St. NW, 10th Fl.
Washington, DC 20005
Ph: (202)393-5229
Fax: (202)393-3034
E-mail: **nrhc@ruralhousingcoalition.org**
URL: http://www.nrhcweb.org
Contact: **Selvin McGahee, Pres.**

2107 ■ Rebuilding Alliance
178 South Blvd.
San Mateo, CA 94402
Ph: **(650)325-4663**
Fax: **(650)325-4667**
E-mail: contact@rebuildingalliance.org
URL: **http://sandbox.rebuildingalliance.org**
Contact: Donna Baranski-Walker, Founder/Exec. Dir.

Human Development

**2108 ■ Institute of Cultural Affairs (ICA)
(11138)**
4750 N Sheridan Rd.
Chicago, IL 60640
Ph: (773)769-6363
Fax: **(773)944-1582**
E-mail: chicago@ica-usa.org
URL: http://www.ica-usa.org
Contact: Terry Bergdall PhD, CEO

2109 ■ Institute for the Development of the Harmonious Human Being (IDHHB) (12515)
PO Box 370
Nevada City, CA 95959
Ph: (530)271-2239
Free: (800)869-0658
Fax: **(530)272-0184**
E-mail: contact@idhhb.com
URL: http://www.idhhb.org
Contact: E.J. Gold, Founder

2110 ■ New Road Map Foundation (NRM) (12360)
PO Box 1363
Langley, WA 98260
E-mail: admin@financialintegrity.org
URL: **http://www.financialintegrity.org**

2111 ■ Sacred Passage and the Way of Nature Fellowship (10999)
PO Box 3388
Tucson, AZ 85722-3388
Ph: (520)623-3588 **(719)695-0153**
Free: (877)818-1881
E-mail: info@sacredpassage.com
URL: http://www.sacredpassage.com
Contact: John P. Milton, Founder

2112 ■ World Peace One (WPI) (11806)
5135 Dearborn St.
Pittsburgh, PA 15224
Ph: **(412)363-9792**
E-mail: info@proofthroughthenight.org
URL: http://www.missionball.org
Contact: Timothy L. Cimino, Contact

Humanities

2113 ■ Consortium of Humanities Centers and Institutes (CHCI) (11165)
Duke Univ.
John Hope Franklin Humanities Inst.
2204 Erwin Rd.
Durham, NC 27708-0403
Ph: (919)668-0107
Fax: **(919)664-1658**
E-mail: chci@duke.edu
URL: http://chcinetwork.org
Contact: Srinivas Aravamudan, Pres.

Hunger

2114 ■ American Outreach to Ethiopia
1121 S Diamond St.
Jacksonville, IL 62650
Ph: (217)245-8792
E-mail: aoe@ameroutreachethiopia.org
URL: http://www.ameroutreachethiopia.org
Contact: Amare Gizaw, Pres.

Multinational. Description: Establishes a direct link between American people and the people of Ethiopia. Solicits American support to help relieve suffering and restore human dignity in the country.

2115 ■ Feeding America (12560)
35 E Whacker Dr., No. 2000
Chicago, IL 60601
Ph: **(312)263-2303**
Free: (800)771-2303
Fax: (312)263-5626
E-mail: fundraise@secondharvest.org
URL: http://feedingamerica.org
Contact: Vicki B. Escarra, Pres./CEO

2116 ■ Global FoodBanking Network (GFN)
203 N LaSalle St., Ste.1900
Chicago, IL 60601
Ph: (312)782-4560
Fax: (312)782-4580

E-mail: info@foodbanking.org
URL: http://www.foodbanking.org
Contact: Jeffrey D. Klein, Pres./CEO
Founded: 2006. **Multinational. Description:** Aims to alleviate world hunger by creating, supplying and strengthening food banks and food bank networks. Addresses critical issues concerning the global food crisis.

2117 ■ National Student Campaign Against Hunger and Homelessness (NSCAHH)
328 S Jefferson St., Ste.620
Chicago, IL 60661
Ph: **(312)544-4436**
Free: (800)NO-HUNGR
Fax: (312)275-7150
E-mail: info@studentsagainsthunger.org
URL: http://www.studentsagainsthunger.org
Contact: **Megan Fitzgerald, Dir.**

International Development

2118 ■ Aid to Artisans (ATA) (12590)
1030 New Britain Ave., Ste.102
West Hartford, CT 06110
Ph: (860)756-5550
Fax: (860)756-7558
E-mail: info@aidtoartisans.org
URL: http://www.aidtoartisans.org
Contact: **Alfredo Espinosa, Pres.**

2119 ■ Glocal Ventures
1870 Rufe Snow Dr.
Keller, TX 76248
Ph: (817)656-5136
Fax: (817)656-4671
E-mail: info@glocalventures.org
URL: http://www.glocalventures.org
Contact: Bob Roberts Jr., Founder/Pres.
Founded: 1998. **Multinational. Description:** Aims to bring socio-economic development in Vietnam. Engages in the development process of promoting community-to-community relationships between the United States and Vietnam.

2120 ■ Haiti Works!
855 Main St., 5th Fl.
Bridgeport, CT 06604
Ph: (203)526-3542
Fax: (203)337-4588
E-mail: info@haiti-works.org
URL: http://www.haiti-works.org
Contact: Pierre F. d'Haiti MBS, Chm./Pres.
Founded: 2010. **Multinational. Description:** Seeks to assist Haiti in its long term recovery from an earthquake devastation. Develops long term strategies, planning, projects and partnerships that will aid in the redevelopment of Haiti.

2121 ■ Heifer International (HPI) (11114)
1 World Ave.
Little Rock, AR 72202
Free: (800)422-0474
Fax: (501)907-2902
E-mail: info@heifer.org
URL: http://www.heifer.org
Contact: **Jo Luck, Pres.**

2122 ■ New Forests Project (NFP) (12169)
737 8th St. SE, Ste.202
Washington, DC 20003
Ph: **(202)464-9386 (202)464-9384**
E-mail: piolster@ic-nfp.org
URL: http://www.newforestsproject.org
Contact: **Pia Iolster, Dir.**

Israel

2123 ■ Emunah of America (12633)
7 Penn Plz.
New York, NY 10001
Ph: (212)564-9045
Free: (800)368-6440

Fax: (212)643-9731
URL: http://www.emunah.org
Contact: **Pam Weiss, Contact**

Jewish

2124 ■ American Jewish Society for Service (AjSS) (12465)
10319 Westlake Blvd., Ste.193
Bethesda, MD 20817
Ph: **(240)205-5940**
Fax: (301)469-8115
E-mail: info@ajss.org
URL: http://www.ajss.org
Contact: Rena Convissor, Exec. Dir.

2125 ■ Association of Jewish Family and Children's Agencies (AJFCA) (11094)
5750 Park Heights Ave.
Baltimore, MD 21215
Ph: (410)843-7573
Free: (800)634-7346
Fax: (410)664-0551
E-mail: ajfca@ajfca.org
URL: http://ajfca.org
Contact: Lee Sherman, Pres./CEO

2126 ■ Jewish Council for Public Affairs (JCPA) (11907)
PO Box 1415
New York, NY 10156-1415
Ph: (212)684-6950
E-mail: contactus@thejcpa.org
URL: http://engage.jewishpublicaffairs.org
Contact: Rabbi Steve Gutow, Pres./CEO

2127 ■ Jewish Federations of North America (UJC) (11178)
PO Box 157
New York, NY 10268
Ph: (212)284-6500 (212)284-6903
Free: (866)844-0070
Fax: (212)284-6835
E-mail: info@jewishfederations.org
URL: **http://www.jewishfederations.org**
Contact: Jerry Silverman, Pres./CEO

2128 ■ Shomrim Society (12481)
c/o Murry Ellman, Financial Sec.
PO Box 598
Knickerbocker, NY 10002
Ph: (718)543-4825
E-mail: mail@nypdshomrim.org
URL: http://www.nypdshomrim.org
Contact: **Issac Franco, Pres.**

Lacrosse

2129 ■ Fields of Growth International
PO Box 751
Notre Dame, IN 46556
E-mail: info@fieldsofgrowth.org
URL: http://fieldsofgrowthintl.org
Contact: Kevin Dugan, Founder/Dir.
Founded: 2006. **Multinational. Description:** Promotes the game of lacrosse to bring community and human development in rural villages of Uganda, East Africa. Works to foster friendships and provides education, health care and various forms of human services.

Learning Disabled

2130 ■ Learning Disabilities Association of America (LDA) (11325)
4156 Lib. Rd.
Pittsburgh, PA 15234-1349
Ph: (412)341-1515
Fax: (412)344-0224

E-mail: info@ldaamerica.org
URL: http://www.ldaamerica.org
Contact: **Patricia Lillie, Pres.**

2131 ■ National Center for Learning Disabilities (NCLD) (11326)
381 Park Ave. S, Ste.1401
New York, NY 10016
Ph: (212)545-7510
Free: (888)575-7373
Fax: (212)545-9665
E-mail: **help@ncld.org**
URL: http://www.ncld.org
Contact: Mr. James H. Wendorf, Exec. Dir.

Medical Aid

2132 ■ CHOSEN (11347)
3638 W 26th St.
Erie, PA 16506-2037
Ph: (814)833-3023
Fax: (814)833-4091
E-mail: **rick@chosenmissionproject.org**
URL: **http://www.chosenmissionproject.com**
Contact: Mr. Richard King, Exec. Dir.

2133 ■ Gift of Life International (GOLI)
PO Box 650436
Fresh Meadows, NY 11365
Ph: **(845)546-2104**
Fax: (516)504-0828
E-mail: **rraylman@aol.com**
URL: http://www.giftoflifeinternational.org
Contact: William P. Currie, Pres.

2134 ■ Health For All Missions
9101 W Sahara Ave., Ste.105-F11
Las Vegas, NV 89117
Ph: (702)408-8269
E-mail: info@healthforallmissions.org
URL: http://www.healthforallmissions.org
Contact: Mary Joseph M. Angelina MA, Founder
Multinational. Description: Aims to help the rural and underprivileged areas of Africa through medical assistance and spiritual resources. Provides medical supplies to the local people who are often plagued with a variety of illnesses.

2135 ■ Kenya Medical Outreach (KMO)
4355 Suwanee Dam Rd., Ste.100
Suwanee, GA 30024
Ph: (678)858-3380
E-mail: info@kenyamo.com
URL: http://kenyamo.com
Contact: Brad Williams, Founder
Multinational. Description: Aims to improve the quality of life in Kenya through a combination of medicine and the love of Christ. Provides clean water, medical and dental care, emergency relief and discipleship for Kenyan communities to develop infrastructure for a sustainable, healthy future.

2136 ■ Liga International (LI) (1721)
19671 Lucaya Ct.
Apple Valley, CA 92308
Ph: (909)875-6300
Fax: (909)875-6900
E-mail: liga@ligainternational.org
URL: http://www.ligainternational.org
Contact: **Janet Lapp, Pres.**

2137 ■ MADRE (11206)
121 W 27th St., Ste.301
New York, NY 10001
Ph: (212)627-0444
Fax: (212)675-3704
E-mail: madre@madre.org
URL: http://www.madre.org
Contact: **Yifat Susskind, Exec. Dir.**

2138 ■ Mobile Medical Disaster Relief
5409 Maryland Way, Ste.119
Brentwood, TN 37027
Ph: (615)833-3002

E-mail: laurie@mmdr.org
URL: http://www.mmdr.org
Contact: David Vanderpool MD, Founder
Founded: 2005. **Multinational. Description:** Works to help fulfill the medical needs of vulnerable and underserved people in the United States and throughout the world. Provides medicines and other medical equipment to the clinics and hospitals.

2139 ■ NOVA Hope for Haiti
176 Palisade Ave.
Emerson, NJ 07630
Ph: (201)675-9413
E-mail: colette.mcdermott@novahopeforhaiti.org
URL: http://www.novahopeforhaiti.org
Contact: John Corcoran, Contact
Founded: 2004. **Multinational. Description:** Aims to bring needed humanitarian aid in the form of healthcare to the impoverished people of Haiti. Provides treatment of disease, prevention and health education to Haitian populace. Sponsors fundraising events for the maintenance of its various health and related educational programs.

2140 ■ Pan American Health and Education Foundation (PAHEF) (11169)
PO Box 27733
Washington, DC 20038-7733
Ph: (202)974-3416
Fax: (202)974-3636
E-mail: info@pahef.org
URL: http://www.pahef.org
Contact: **Rafael Perez-Escamilla PhD, Vice Chair**

Mentally Disabled

2141 ■ American Network of Community Options and Resources (ANCOR) (12560)
1101 King St., Ste.380
Alexandria, VA 22314
Ph: (703)535-7850 **(520)321-4477**
Fax: (703)535-7860
E-mail: ancor@ancor.org
URL: http://www.ancor.org
Contact: **Wendy Sokol, Pres.**

2142 ■ Little City Foundation (LCF) (11201)
1760 W Algonquin Rd.
Palatine, IL 60067-4799
Ph: (847)358-5510 (847)221-7810
Fax: **(847)358-3291**
E-mail: lreyes@littlecity.org
URL: http://www.littlecity.org
Contact: Mr. Fred G. Lebed, Pres.

2143 ■ National Association of Councils on Developmental Disabilities (NACCD) (11247)
1660 L St. NW, Ste.700
Washington, DC 20036
Ph: (202)506-5813
Fax: (202)506-5846
E-mail: info@nacdd.org
URL: http://www.nacdd.org
Contact: **Wanda Willis, Pres.**

Migrant Workers

2144 ■ Association of Farmworker Opportunity Programs (AFOP) (11412)
1726 M St. NW, Ste.602
Washington, DC 20036
Ph: (202)826-6006
URL: **http://afop.org**
Contact: Mr. David Strauss, Exec. Dir.

2145 ■ Global Workers Justice Alliance (17705)
789 Washington Ave.
Brooklyn, NY 11238
Ph: **(646)351-1160**

E-mail: info@globalworkers.org
URL: http://www.globalworkers.org
Contact: Cathleen Caron, Founder/Exec. Dir.

Native American

2146 ■ First Nations Development Institute (FNDI) (11439)
351 Coffman St., Ste.200
Longmont, CO 80501
Ph: (303)774-7836
Fax: (303)774-7841
E-mail: info@firstnations.org
URL: http://www.firstnations.org
Contact: Mike Roberts, Pres.

Natural Disasters

2147 ■ World Association of Natural Disaster Awareness and Assistance (WANDAA)
1865 SW 4th Ave., Ste.D5-A
Delray Beach, FL 33444
Ph: (561)450-5690
Fax: (561)330-8102
E-mail: info@wandaa.org
URL: http://www.wandaa.org
Contact: James Arnott, Pres./Dir.
Founded: 2010. **Multinational. Description:** Serves as a platform educating the public about various natural disasters. Provides a wide array of assistance to victims of natural disasters from food, water, clothing to education and the assistance to rebuild.

Obesity

2148 ■ National Association to Advance Fat Acceptance (NAAFA) (12647)
PO Box 22510
Oakland, CA 94609
Ph: (916)558-6880
URL: **http://www.naafaonline.com/dev2**
Contact: Jason Docherty, Co-Chm.

Organizations

2149 ■ BoardSource (12651)
750 9th St. NW, Ste.650
Washington, DC 20001-4793
Ph: **(202)349-2500**
Free: (877)892-6273
Fax: **(202)349-2599**
E-mail: mail@boardsource.org
URL: http://www.boardsource.org
Contact: Linda C. Crompton, Pres./CEO

2150 ■ Foundation Center (FC) (13049)
79 5th Ave., 16th St.
New York, NY 10003-3076
Ph: (212)620-4230 (212)807-2426
Free: (800)424-9836
Fax: (212)807-3677
E-mail: feedback@foundationcenter.org
URL: **http://foundationcenter.org**
Contact: Bradford K. Smith, Pres.

2151 ■ Management Assistance Group (MAG) (1739)
1629 K St. NW, Ste.300
Washington, DC 20006
Ph: (202)659-1963
Fax: **(866)403-6080**
E-mail: mag@magmail.org
URL: http://www.managementassistance.org
Contact: Inca A. Mohamed, Exec. Dir.

Parents

2152 ■ National Foster Parent Association (NFPA) (12677)
2021 E Hennepin Ave., Ste.320
Minneapolis, MN 55413-1865
Ph: (253)853-4000
Free: (800)557-5238
Fax: (253)238-4252
E-mail: info@nfpaonline.org
URL: http://www.nfpainc.org
Contact: Irene Clements, Pres.

2153 ■ Parents Without Partners (PWP) (12688)
1100-H Brandywine Blvd.
Zanesville, OH 43701-7303
Free: (800)637-7974
E-mail: intl.pres@parentswithoutpartners.org
URL: http://www.parentswithoutpartners.org
Contact: Garland Harris, Pres.

Peace

2154 ■ Sudan Sunrise
8643 Hauser Ct., Ste.240
Lenexa, KS 66215
Ph: (913)599-0800
E-mail: info@sudansunrise.org
URL: http://www.sudansunrise.org
Contact: John Zogby, Chm.
Founded: 2006. **Multinational. Description:** Aims to facilitate reconciliation and solidarity between Sudanese Christians, Darfurian Muslims and all Sudanese. Ensures lasting peace and the end of oppression in Sudan. Supports programs to provide education, health care and community development.

2155 ■ World Sound Healing Organization (WSHO)
PO Box 389
Ascutney, VT 05030
Ph: (802)674-9585
Fax: (802)674-9585
E-mail: info@worldsoundhealing.org
URL: http://www.worldsoundhealing.org
Contact: Zacciah Blackburn, Co-Dir.

Philanthropy

2156 ■ Bread for the Journey International (12131)
9 Santa Gabriella Ct.
Novato, CA 94945
Ph: (415)895-5357
E-mail: breadjourney@gmail.com
URL: http://www.breadforthejourney.org
Contact: Marianna Cacciatore, Exec. Dir.

2157 ■ Giving U.S.A. Foundation (12904)
303 W Madison St., Ste.2650
Chicago, IL 60606-3396
Ph: (312)981-6794
Free: (800)462-2372
Fax: (312)265-2908
E-mail: info@givinginstitute.org
URL: http://www.givinginstitute.org/gusa/mission.cfm
Contact: Edith H. Falk, Chair

2158 ■ Good360 (11520)
133 Braddock Pl., Ste.600
Alexandria, VA 22314
Ph: (703)836-2121
Fax: (877)798-3192
E-mail: serviceteam@giftsinkind.org
URL: http://www.giftsinkind.org
Contact: Gail E. Aldrich, Chair
Status Note: Formerly Gifts In Kind International.

2159 ■ Philanthropy Roundtable (11381)
1730 M St. NW, Ste.601
Washington, DC 20036
Ph: (202)822-8333
Fax: (202)822-8325
E-mail: main@philanthropyroundtable.org
URL: http://www.philanthropyroundtable.org
Contact: Adam Meyerson, Pres.

2160 ■ Twenty-First Century Foundation (21CF) (12467)
132 W 112th St., Lower Level, No. 1
New York, NY 10026
Ph: (212)662-3700
Fax: (212)662-6690
E-mail: info@21cf.org
URL: http://www.21cf.org
Contact: Chandra Y. Anderson, Interim Pres.

Phobias

2161 ■ Anxiety Disorders Association of America (ADAA) (12926)
8730 Georgia Ave., Ste.600
Silver Spring, MD 20910
Ph: (240)485-1001
Fax: (240)485-1035
E-mail: sgerfen@adaa.org
URL: http://www.adaa.org
Contact: Jerrold F. Rosenbaum MD, Pres.

Population

2162 ■ Population-Environment Balance (PEB) (11398)
PO Box 1059
Anaheim, CA 92815
Ph: (714)204-3466
Fax: (714)632-7221
E-mail: uspop@us.net
URL: http://www.balance.org

Poverty

2163 ■ Aid for the World
20 Murray St., Fl. 2
New York, NY 10007
Free: (877)424-3911
E-mail: ckeyes@aidfortheworld.org
URL: http://aidfortheworld.org
Contact: Carl Keyes, Founder
Multinational. Description: Works to establish effective local and international partnerships to address critical human needs. Seeks to develop sustainable local economies by providing assistance to individuals and families in impoverished communities.

2164 ■ Center for Community Change (CCC) (12769)
1536 U St. NW
Washington, DC 20009
Ph: (202)339-9300
Fax: (202)387-4892
E-mail: info@communitychange.org
URL: http://www.communitychange.org
Contact: Deepak Bhargava, Exec. Dir.

2165 ■ Community Action Partnership (12498)
1140 Connecticut Ave. NW, Ste.1210
Washington, DC 20036
Ph: (202)265-7546
Fax: (202)265-5048
E-mail: dmathis@communityactionpartnership.com
URL: http://www.communityactionpartnership.com
Contact: Donald W. Mathis, Pres./CEO

2166 ■ Helping Hearts Helping Hands
7060 Scenic Ridge
Clarkston, MI 48346
Ph: (248)660-4507
E-mail: helpingheartshelpinghands@hotmail.com
URL: http://www.helpingheartshelpinghands.org
Contact: Erica Cale, Founder
Founded: 2007. **Multinational. Description:** Aims to change the life of poverty stricken children and families in Honduras. Provides immediate assistance by delivering food, fresh water, clothing, shoes and vitamins to the village.

2167 ■ Inter-Faith Community Services (IFCS)
3370 S Irving St.
Englewood, CO 80110-1816
Ph: (303)789-0501
Fax: (303)789-3808
E-mail: ifcs@ifcs.org
URL: http://www.ifcs.org
Contact: Doug Applegate, Pres.

2168 ■ MDRC (11354)
16 E 34th St., 19th Fl.
New York, NY 10016-4326
Ph: (212)532-3200
Fax: (212)684-0832
E-mail: information@mdrc.org
URL: http://www.mdrc.org
Contact: Gordon Berlin, Pres.

2169 ■ Mercy Beyond Borders
1885 De La Cruz Blvd., Ste.101
Santa Clara, CA 95050
Ph: (650)815-1554
E-mail: info@mercybeyondborders.org
URL: http://www.mercybeyondborders.org
Contact: Marilyn Lacey, Exec. Dir./Chair
Founded: 2008. **Multinational. Description:** Aims to alleviate extreme poverty in Sudan by educating women and girls, providing funding for small entrepreneurial projects and promoting maternal and child health. Seeks to help rebuild communities devastated by years of war and famine.

2170 ■ Miracles in Action
241 Countryside Dr.
Naples, FL 34104
Ph: (239)348-0815
URL: http://www.miraclesinaction.org
Contact: Penny Rambacher, Chair/Pres.
Founded: 2004. **Multinational. Description:** Seeks to improve the lives of Guatemalans who are experiencing extreme poverty. Works in indigenous areas of rural Guatemala. Aids poor families to help themselves through education, vocation and sustainable development projects.

2171 ■ Partners in Sustainable Development International (PSDI)
9005 Greenridge Dr.
St. Louis, MO 63117
Ph: (314)993-5599
Fax: (314)993-5596
E-mail: v.klein@psdintl.org
URL: http://www.psdintl.org
Contact: Virginia Klein, Exec. Dir.
Multinational. Description: Addresses extreme poverty among rural populations in the developing world. Provides a model of poverty eradication through empowerment of the poor. Offers resources necessary for the poor to implement their own economic development to uplift them from poverty.

2172 ■ Reach Out to Romania
PO Box 18016
Anaheim, CA 92817-8016
E-mail: questions@reachouttoromania.org
URL: http://www.reachouttoromania.org
Contact: Rev. Paul Muresan, Contact
Founded: 2007. **Multinational. Description:** Aims to uproot the effects of poverty in Romania. Conducts and supports projects focusing on education, health and housing.

2173 ■ Tusubira - We Have Hope
PO Box 482
Mercer Island, WA 98040
E-mail: staff@wehavehope.org
URL: http://wehavehope.org
Contact: Kate Harris, Pres.
Founded: 2006. **Multinational. Description:** Works
to build relationships, remove barriers caused by
poverty and injustice and create opportunities for
vulnerable communities in Uganda. Conducts vision
trips.

2174 ■ Union Settlement Association (13195)
237 E 104th St.
New York, NY 10029
Ph: (212)828-6000 (212)828-6025
Fax: **(212)828-6022**
E-mail: dnocenti@unionsett.org
URL: http://www.unionsettlement.org
Contact: David Nocenti, Exec. Dir.

Recreation

**2175 ■ Employee Services Management
Foundation** (ESM) (12524)
PO Box 10517
Rockville, MD 20849
Ph: (630)559-0020
Fax: (630)559-0025
E-mail: esmahq@esmassn.org
URL: http://www.esmassn.org
Contact: Renee Mula, Exec. Dir.
Status Note: Formerly Employee Services Manage-
ment Association.

2176 ■ Prairie Club (13210)
12 E Willow St., Unit A
Lombard, IL 60148
Ph: **(630)620-9334**
Fax: **(630)620-9335**
E-mail: prairieclub@sbcglobal.net
URL: http://theprairieclub.org
Contact: Jane Walsh-Brown, Contact

Refugees

**2177 ■ American Refugee Committee (ARC)
(12805)**
430 Oak Grove St., Ste.204
Minneapolis, MN 55403
Ph: (612)872-7060
Free: (800)875-7060
Fax: (612)607-6499
E-mail: **info@archq.org**
URL: http://www.arcrelief.org
Contact: John Gappa, Chm.

**2178 ■ International Rescue Committee |
Spanish Refugee Aid** (SRA) (11612)
122 E 42nd St.
New York, NY 10168-1289
Ph: (212)551-3000
Fax: (212)551-3179
E-mail: **webmaster@rescue.org**
URL: **http://www.rescue.org**
Contact: George Rupp, Pres./CEO

**2179 ■ International Rescue Committee USA
(IRC) (12812)**
122 E 42nd St.
New York, NY 10168-1289
Ph: (212)551-3000 (202)822-0043
Free: (877)REF-UGEE
Fax: (212)551-3179
E-mail: fundraising@theirc.org
URL: **http://www.rescue.org**
Contact: George Rupp, Pres./CEO

**2180 ■ Lutheran Immigration and Refugee
Service (LIRS) (11448)**
700 Light St.
Baltimore, MD 21230
Ph: (410)230-2700
Fax: (410)230-2890
E-mail: lirs@lirs.org
URL: http://www.lirs.org
Contact: **Linda Hartke, Pres.**

Relief

**2181 ■ Alliance For Relief Mission in Haiti
(ARMH)**
PO Box 250028
Brooklyn, NY 11225
Ph: (516)499-7452
E-mail: armh@alliancehaiti.org
URL: http://www.alliancehaiti.org
Contact: Yvon Damour MD, Pres.
Founded: 2005. **Multinational. Description:** Aims
to assist the less fortunate living in Haiti. Provides for
the various needs of Haitians especially their health-
care needs.

2182 ■ Americans Care and Share
PO Box 600370
San Diego, CA 92160
Ph: (619)481-3085
Fax: (619)481-3089
E-mail: info@angelcare.org
URL: http://www.angelcare.org
Contact: Ana Espino, Founder
Founded: 2006. **Multinational. Description:** Fo-
cuses on relieving the suffering of poverty-stricken
children and their families. Promotes community self-
sufficiency and provides educational and training op-
portunities to children.

2183 ■ Baitulmaal
PO Box 166911
Irving, TX 75016
Ph: (972)257-2564
Free: (800)220-9554
Fax: (972)258-1396
E-mail: sec@baitulmaal.org
URL: http://www.baitulmaal.org
Contact: Ugas Jillaow, Pres.
Multinational. Description: Aims to restore dignity
and instill hope in communities affected by poverty
and disaster. Provides emergency disaster relief and
facilitates the distribution of basic necessities and
repair of social infrastructure.

2184 ■ Baptist Global Response (BGR)
402 BNA Dr., Ste.411
Nashville, TN 37217
Ph: (615)367-3678
Free: (866)974-5623
Fax: (615)290-5045
E-mail: info@gobgr.org
URL: http://www.baptistglobalresponse.com
Contact: Jeff Palmer, Exec. Dir.
Founded: 2006. **Multinational. Description:** Strives
to give the poor and suffering the opportunity to
experience a full and meaningful life. Responds to
people with critical needs that arise from disasters,
wars, epidemics, hunger, poverty and poor health.
Seeks to mobilize and involve the influence, prayer,
human and financial resources of Southern Baptists
for worldwide relief and development.

2185 ■ Covenant World Relief (CWR) (12261)
8303 W Higgins Rd.
Chicago, IL 60631
Ph: **(773)907-3301**
E-mail: **david.husby@covchurch.org**
URL: **http://www.covchurch.org/relief**
Contact: David Husby, Dir.

2186 ■ Global Action International (GAI)
PO Box 131269
Carlsbad, CA 92013
Ph: (760)438-3979

E-mail: dlee@globalactionintl.org
URL: http://www.global-action.com
Contact: Dwaine E. Lee, Pres.

**2187 ■ Hannah's Promise International Aid
(HPIA)**
PO Box 2102
Boone, NC 28607
Ph: (828)668-1434
E-mail: rad_kivette@hannahspromiseinternation-
alaid.org
URL: http://www.hannahspromiseinternationalaid.org
Contact: Rad Kivette, Founder/Chm.
Multinational. Description: Aims to improve the
health, education and human dignity of underserved
and disadvantaged individuals. Works to assist
orphanages and schools, provide scholarships to
poor children, supply medical equipment, implement
income generating projects and train doctors and
nurses.

2188 ■ Help Brings Hope for Haiti (HBHH)
3816 W Morrison Ave.
Tampa, FL 33629
Ph: (813)832-4244
E-mail: hbhh123@gmail.com
URL: http://www.hbhh.org
Contact: Patricia Eddy, Founder/Chair
Founded: 2003. **Multinational. Description:** Aims
to bring hope for a better life to Haitians by helping
them meet basic needs of food, water, sanitation,
education, medical care and clothing. Provides adult,
child and teen education, and creates jobs for the
people of Haiti.

2189 ■ Helping Hand for Nepal (HHN)
2930 Brittany Dr.
Anchorage, AK 99504
Ph: (907)338-8128
E-mail: info@hhnepal.org
URL: http://www.hhnepal.org
Contact: Linda Jackson MFA, Founder/Exec. Dir.
Founded: 2001. **Multinational. Description:** Aims
to alleviate poverty and suffering in Nepal. Provides
humanitarian projects in medicine, education and
water supply.

**2190 ■ Humanitarian African Relief
Organization (HARO)**
7364 El Cajon Blvd., Ste.208
San Diego, CA 92115
Ph: (619)741-9260 (619)564-2526
E-mail: haro@soomaalirelief.org
URL: http://www.soomaalirelief.org
Contact: Ali Haji Abdinur, Pres.
Founded: 2007. **Multinational. Description:** Aims
to empower the needy and the indigent in Somalia
and East Africa. Provides assistance in the form of
food, shelter and medicine.

2191 ■ International Aid (IA) (11575)
17011 Hickory St.
Spring Lake, MI 49456-9712
Ph: (616)846-7490
Free: (800)968-7490
Fax: (616)846-3842
E-mail: ia@internationalaid.org
URL: http://www.internationalaid.org
Contact: **Brian Anderson, CEO**

2192 ■ Islamic Relief U.S.A. (12278)
PO Box 22250
Alexandria, VA 22304
Ph: (703)370-7202
Free: (888)479-4968
Fax: (703)370-7201
E-mail: **info@islamicreliefusa.org**
URL: **http://www.islamicreliefusa.org**
Contact: Dr. Yaser Haddara, Chm.

**2193 ■ Korean American Sharing Movement
(KASM)**
7004 Little River Tpke., Ste.O
Annandale, VA 22003
Ph: (703)867-0846

Fax: (703)354-7093
E-mail: kasm.org@gmail.com
URL: http://www.kasm.org
Contact: Man Cho, Vice Chm.
Founded: 1997. **Multinational. Description:** Aims to help those in need, both in the United States and abroad. Provides relief and charity programs to help victims of natural and man-made disasters.

2194 ■ One Love Worldwide (OLW)
1223 El Caminito Dr.
Hobbs, NM 88240
E-mail: info@oneloveworldwide.org
URL: http://www.oneloveworldwide.org
Contact: Karli Sue McMurray, Pres./Founder
Multinational. Description: Provides aid and resources to underprivileged persons to rehabilitate their environment and create self sustainability. Implements projects and development programs to impoverished communities around the world.

2195 ■ People for Haiti
2132 Flameflower Ct.
Trinity, FL 34655
Ph: (727)457-7272
E-mail: peopleforhaiti@gmail.com
URL: http://www.peopleforhaiti.com
Contact: Guiga Vieira, Contact
Founded: 2010. **Multinational. Description:** Provides long-term support for the people devastated by the Haitian earthquake of 2010. Offers medical assistance to Haitian citizens. Raises funds to provide clean and safe drinking water for an entire community.

2196 ■ Reality Relief
834 Ave. F
Billings, MT 59102
Ph: (706)201-8520
E-mail: josephu@realityrelief.com
URL: http://www.realityrelief.com
Contact: Joseph Ulrich, Founder
Founded: 2010. **Description:** Aims to alleviate pain and suffering of people with life-threatening illnesses or those who are less fortunate. Inspires less fortunate people to get back on their feet and lead productive lives.

2197 ■ Rebuilding Haiti Now
2314 Alamance Dr.
West Chicago, IL 60185
E-mail: vdsaxe@comcast.net
URL: http://site.rebuildinghaitinow.org
Contact: Gladys Doebeli Rocourt, Founder
Founded: 2010. **Description:** Aims to help rebuild Haiti. Provides funding, equipment, supplies and leadership skills to rebuild and operate schools and other facilities that will help the Haitian people achieve human progress.

2198 ■ Relief Liberia International (RLI)
10186 Lancaster Ln. N
Maple Grove, MN 55369
Ph: (763)607-4233
URL: http://www.reliefliberiaintl.org
Contact: Mr. Jackson K. George, Exec. Dir.
Multinational. Description: Aims to serve impoverished and underserved communities throughout Liberia. Provides emergency relief, rehabilitation, development assistance and program services to vulnerable communities.

2199 ■ River International
2380 W Monte Vista Ave.
Turlock, CA 95382
E-mail: contactus@riverintl.org
URL: http://www.riverintl.org
Contact: Tom Hammond, Contact
Multinational. Description: Aims to improve the physical and spiritual quality of life for those in need of help worldwide. Provides humanitarian aid, education, vocational training and leadership development to communities around the globe.

2200 ■ Simple Hope
PO Box 4
Menomonee Falls, WI 53052
Ph: (262)569-9919
E-mail: simplehope1@gmail.com
URL: http://www.simple-hope.org
Contact: Pam Schwalbach, Contact
Founded: 2010. **Multinational. Description:** Aims to provide food and self-sustaining development for those in need in Tanzania, Africa. Raises funds to support projects to improve the quality of life of the people in Tanzania.

2201 ■ Vietnam Relief Effort (VRE)
845 United Nations Plz., 90A
New York, NY 10017
Ph: (917)668-2600
E-mail: inquiries@vietnamrelief.org
URL: http://www.vietnamrelief.org
Contact: Kathy Chu, Co-Founder
Founded: 1999. **Multinational. Description:** Seeks to bring aid to impoverished regions of Vietnam. Provides aid through medical, educational and disaster-relief projects.

2202 ■ World Emergency Relief (WER)
(11440)
PO Box 1760
Temecula, CA 92593
Ph: (951)225-6700
Free: (888)484-4543
E-mail: info@wer-us.org
URL: http://www.worldemergency.org
Contact: **Lawrence E. Cutting, Sec.**

Retirement

2203 ■ Institute for Retired Professionals (IRP) (11679)
New School Univ.
66 W 12th St., Rm. 502
New York, NY 10011
Ph: (212)229-5682
E-mail: irp@newschool.edu
URL: **http://www.newschool.edu/irp**
Contact: Michael I. Markowitz, Dir.

Right to Life

2204 ■ Baptists for Life (BFL) (13100)
PO Box 3158
Grand Rapids, MI 49501
Ph: (616)257-6800
Free: (800)968-6086
Fax: (616)257-6805
E-mail: **b4life@bfl.org**
URL: **http://www.bfl.org**
Contact: M. Thomas Lothamer, Exec. Dir.

2205 ■ Liberty Godparent Home (LGH) (1772)
PO Box 4199
Lynchburg, VA 24502
Ph: (434)845-3466
Free: **(800)54-CHILD**
Fax: (434)845-1751
URL: http://godparent.org
Contact: **Janelle Basham, Dir.**

2206 ■ National Right to Life Committee (NRLC) (11529)
512 10th St. NW
Washington, DC 20004
Ph: (202)626-8800
E-mail: nrlc@nrlc.org
URL: http://www.nrlc.org
Contact: **Carol Tobias, Pres.**

Runaways

2207 ■ National Network for Youth (NNY) (11717)
741 8th St. SE
Washington, DC 20003
Ph: (202)783-7949
Fax: (202)783-7955
E-mail: info@nn4youth.org
URL: http://www.nn4youth.org
Contact: **Jane Harper, Pres./CEO**

Rural Development

2208 ■ Abriendo Mentes
Opening Minds Latin America
3310 Crosspark Ln.
Houston, TX 77007
Ph: (713)893-8334
E-mail: opening.minds.project@gmail.com
URL: http://abriendomentes.org
Contact: Meradith Leebrick, Co-Founder
Founded: 2009. **Multinational. Description:** Aims to enhance education in rural Costa Rica. Strives to empower each community member with the knowledge and resources needed to achieve a better standard of living.

2209 ■ Act for Africa International
PO Box 2031
Manassas, VA 20108
Ph: (571)212-6167
Fax: (571)379-8600
E-mail: infos@actforafrica.org
URL: http://www.actforafrica.org
Contact: Papa Drame, Pres.
Founded: 2007. **Multinational. Description:** Aims to make a positive impact on the lives of people in rural communities in Sub-Saharan Africa through the improvement of their educational and health needs and the introduction of modern technologies. Provides a platform for rural communities to come together in order to identify their priority needs and find solution to their health and education issues.

2210 ■ Bridges to Prosperity (B2P)
5007 Victory Blvd., C-126
Yorktown, VA 23693
Fax: (757)234-0523
E-mail: avery@bridgestoprosperity.org
URL: http://www.bridgestoprosperity.org
Contact: Avery Louise Bang, Exec. Dir.
Founded: 2001. **Multinational. Description:** Seeks to empower poor African, Asian and South American rural communities through footbridge building. Encourages the poor to lift themselves from poverty on their own.

2211 ■ Community Empowerment Network (CEN)
1685 Grandview Pl.
Ferndale, WA 98248
Ph: (206)329-6244
Fax: (617)344-7868
E-mail: rbortner@endruralpoverty.org
URL: http://www.endruralpoverty.org
Contact: Robert Bortner, Founder/Dir.
Founded: 2004. **Multinational. Description:** Empowers rural communities in developing countries to break the cycle of poverty by becoming more self-reliant. Provides entrepreneurship skills development and encourages the creation of sustainable micro and small businesses.

2212 ■ Roots of Development
1325 18th St. NW, Ste.303
Washington, DC 20036
Ph: (202)466-0805

E-mail: info@rootsofdevelopment.org
URL: http://www.rootsofdevelopment.org
Contact: Chad W. Bissonnette, Co-Founder/Exec. Dir.
Founded: 2007. **Multinational. Description:** Helps impoverished communities in Haiti to manage their own development. Promotes an alternative approach to rural development by facilitating community-driven projects that lead to a more sustainable future.

2213 ■ Union MicroFinanza (UMF)
1485 Getty St.
Muskegon, MI 49442
E-mail: info@unionmicrofinanza.org
URL: http://www.unionmicrofinanza.org
Contact: Patrick Hughes, Dir. of Operations
Founded: 2009. **Multinational. Description:** Aims to improve the condition of impoverished rural communities in Honduras. Works with Honduran agricultural producers to overcome economic barriers and rise out of poverty. Conducts research on innovative strategies for a successful rural microfinance.

Rural Education

2214 ■ Haiti Convention Association (HCA)
272 Dunns Mill Rd., No. 254
Bordentown, NJ 08505
Ph: (201)532-2374
E-mail: projects@haiticonvention.org
URL: http://www.haiticonvention.org
Contact: Narha Nezius, Founder
Multinational. Description: Promotes literacy among various rural regions in Haiti to achieve social and economic development. Aims to support early childhood programs and built small schools and learning centers in rural areas. Provides teachers with training about teaching strategies and encourages them to acquire better and more skills.

2215 ■ Into Your Hands
PO Box 3981
Evergreen, CO 80437
Ph: (720)810-2837
E-mail: maria@intoyourhands.org
URL: http://www.intoyourhands.org
Contact: Maria Rosa Camp, Exec. Dir.
Founded: 1999. **Multinational. Description:** Seeks to improve rural communities of Uganda by developing financially sustainable solutions for affordable education. Empowers local school communities to implement self-funding education programs. Provides resources for school infrastructure and supports the development of school-based businesses.

Safety

2216 ■ Association for the Advancement of Automotive Medicine (AAAM) (11553)
PO Box 4176
Barrington, IL 60011-4176
Ph: (847)844-3880
Fax: (847)844-3884
E-mail: info@aaam.org
URL: http://www.carcrash.org
Contact: **Kristy B. Arbogast PhD, Sec.**

2217 ■ Recording Artists, Actors and Athletes Against Drunk Driving (RADD) (12395)
4370 Tujunga Ave., Ste.212
Studio City, CA 91604
Ph: (818)752-7799
Fax: (818)752-7792
E-mail: robert.pineda@radd.org
URL: http://www.radd.org
Contact: J.R. Sterling, Chm.

2218 ■ Veterans of Safety (VOS) (13186)
Univ. of Central Missouri
Humphreys 304
Warrensburg, MO 64093

Ph: (660)543-4971
E-mail: **bryant@ucmo.edu**
URL: http://www.vetsofsafety.org
Contact: Dianna Bryant, Exec. Dir.

Scouting

2219 ■ National Eagle Scout Association
(NESA) (12725)
c/o Boy Scouts of America
1325 W Walnut Hill Ln.
PO Box 152079
Irving, TX 75015-2079
Ph: (972)580-2183 **(972)580-2431**
Fax: (972)580-7870
E-mail: nesa@scouting.org
URL: http://www.nesa.org
Contact: Bill Steele, Natl. Dir.

Self Defense

2220 ■ Association for Women's Self Defense Advancement (AWSDA)
556 Rte. 17 N, Ste.7-209
Paramus, NJ 07652
Ph: (201)794-2153
Free: (888)STOP-RAPE
Fax: (201)791-6005
E-mail: info@awsda.org
URL: http://www.awsda.org
Contact: **Lisa M. Skvlara, Chair**

Selfhelp

2221 ■ Messies Anonymous (MA) (13218)
10525 NW 146th Pl.
Alachua, FL 32615-5723
E-mail: **nestbuilder@earthlink.net**
URL: http://www.messies.com
Contact: Sandra Felton, Founder

Service Clubs

2222 ■ Junior Optimist Octagon International (JOOI) (13045)
4494 Lindell Blvd.
St. Louis, MO 63108
Ph: (314)371-6000
Free: (800)500-8130
Fax: **(314)735-4118**
E-mail: **youthclubs@optimist.org**
URL: http://www.optimist.org
Contact: **Kayleigh White, Pres.**

2223 ■ Links Foundation (13049)
1200 Massachusetts Ave. NW
Washington, DC 20005-4501
Ph: (202)842-8686
Free: (800)574-3720
Fax: (202)842-4020
E-mail: techcom@linksinc.org
URL: http://www.linksinc.org
Contact: **Margot James Copeland, Pres.**

Sex Addiction

2224 ■ Sex Addicts Anonymous (SAA) (11624)
PO Box 70949
Houston, TX 77270
Ph: (713)869-4902
Free: (800)477-8191
E-mail: info@saa-recovery.org
URL: http://www.sexaa.org
Contact: **Joe H., Dir. of Operations**

Social Action

2225 ■ World Action for Humanity
PO Box 193584
San Francisco, CA 94119-3584
Ph: (415)321-0701
E-mail: info@worldactionforhumanity.org
URL: http://worldactionforhumanity.org
Contact: Nicole Carta, Chair
Founded: 2003. **Multinational. Description:** Aims to raise awareness and resources for small, grassroots projects in developing countries. Supports local leaders and their initiatives to improve lives in developing countries.

Social Issues

2226 ■ National Science and Technology Education Partnership (NSTEP) (13323)
2500 Wilson Blvd., Ste.210
Arlington, VA 22201-3834
Ph: (703)907-7400 (703)907-7431
Fax: (703)907-7991
E-mail: nstep@nstep-online.org
URL: **http://nstepstudybuddy.net**
Contact: Peter F. McCloskey, Pres.

2227 ■ Society for the Study of Social Problems (SSSP) (11721)
901 McClung Tower
Univ. of Tennessee
Knoxville, TN 37996-0490
Ph: **(865)689-1531**
Fax: (865)689-1534
E-mail: sssp@utk.edu
URL: http://www.sssp1.org
Contact: Kelley Flatford, Admin. Asst.

Social Service

2228 ■ Healing Hands International (HHI) (12556)
455 McNally Dr.
Nashville, TN 37211
Ph: (615)832-2000
Fax: (615)832-2002
E-mail: contact@hhi.org
URL: **http://www.hhi.org**
Contact: **Bill Merry Jr., Chm.**

Social Welfare

2229 ■ American Humane Association (AHA)
63 Inverness Dr. E
Englewood, CO 80112-5117
Ph: (303)792-9900
Free: (800)227-4645
Fax: (303)792-5333
E-mail: info@americanhumane.org
URL: http://www.americanhumane.org
Contact: **Robin R. Ganzert, Pres./CEO**

2230 ■ American Public Human Services Association (APHSA) (13151)
1133 19th St. NW, Ste.400
Washington, DC 20036
Ph: (202)682-0100
Fax: (202)289-6555
E-mail: **tracy.wareing@aphsa.org**
URL: http://www.aphsa.org
Contact: **Tracy Wareing, Exec. Dir.**

2231 ■ American Public Human Services Association I National Council of State Human Service Administrators (NCSHSA) (11954)
1133 19th St. NW, Ste.400
Washington, DC 20036
Ph: (202)682-0100

Fax: (202)289-6555
URL: http://www.aphsa.org
Contact: **Reggie Bicha, Chm.**

**2232 ■ American Rescue Workers (ARW)
(11728)**
25 Ross St.
Williamsport, PA 17701
Ph: (570)323-8693
Fax: (570)323-8694
E-mail: **arwus@arwus.org**
URL: http://www.arwus.com
Contact: Gen. Claude S. Astin Jr., Commander-in-
Chief

2233 ■ Council on Accreditation (COA)
45 Broadway 29th Fl.
New York, NY 10006
Ph: (212)797-3000
Free: (866)262-8088
Fax: (212)797-1428
E-mail: coainfo@coanet.org
URL: http://www.coanet.org
Contact: **Timothy F. Noelker, Chm.**

**2234 ■ Emergency Relief Response Fund
(19632)**
PO Box 2300
Redlands, CA 92373
Ph: (909)793-2009
Fax: (909)793-6880
E-mail: **email@emergencyreliefresponsefund.org**
URL: http://www.emergencyreliefresponsefund.org
Contact: Fred M. Johnson, Pres.

**2235 ■ National Staff Development and
Training Association (NSDTA) (11873)**
PO Box 112
Merced, CA 95341-0112
Ph: (209)385-3000
Fax: **(209)354-2501**
E-mail: apagan@hsa.co.merced.ca.us
URL: http://nsdta.aphsa.org
Contact: Ana Pagan, Pres.

Social Work

**2236 ■ Association of Oncology Social Work
(AOSW) (13199)**
100 N 20th St., 4th Fl.
Philadelphia, PA 19103
Ph: (215)599-6093
Fax: (215)564-2175
E-mail: info@aosw.org
URL: http://www.aosw.org
Contact: **Lisa Marquette Porat, Pres.**

**2237 ■ Clinical Social Work Association
(CSWA) (13201)**
PO Box 3740
Arlington, VA 22203
Ph: **(703)340-1456**
Fax: **(703)269-0707**
E-mail: administrator@clinicalsocialworkassociation.
org
URL: http://www.clinicalsocialworkassociation.org
Contact: Kevin Host, Pres.

**2238 ■ Employee Assistance Professionals
Association (EAPA) (13401)**
4350 N Fairfax Dr., Ste.410
Arlington, VA 22203
Ph: (703)387-1000
Fax: (703)522-4585
E-mail: **jeffrey.christie@halliburton.com**
URL: **http://www.eapassn.org**
Contact: **Jeffrey Christie CEAP, Pres.**

Substance Abuse

**2239 ■ Association of Halfway House
Alcoholism Programs of North America
(AHHAP) (13423)**
401 E Sangamon Ave.
Springfield, IL 62702
Ph: (217)523-0527
Fax: (217)698-8234
E-mail: jessica@iaodapca.org
URL: http://www.ahhap.org
Contact: **Susan O'Binns, Pres.**

**2240 ■ Center on Addiction and the Family
(COAF) (13228)**
50 Jay St.
Brooklyn, NY 11201
Ph: **(646)505-2061**
Fax: (718)222-6696
E-mail: coaf@phoenixhouse.org
URL: http://www.coaf.org
Contact: Naomi Weinstein MPH, Dir.

**2241 ■ Informed Families Education Center |
National Family Partnership** (NFP) (13471)
2490 Coral Way, Ste.501
Miami, FL 33145
Ph: (305)856-4886
Free: (800)705-8997
Fax: (305)856-4815
E-mail: **ireyes@nfp.org**
URL: http://www.nfp.org
Contact: Peggy B. Sapp, Pres./CEO

**2242 ■ International Lawyers in Alcoholics
Anonymous (ILAA) (13253)**
c/o Eli Gauna, Sec.
17216 Saticoy St., Ste.211
Van Nuys, CA 91406
Ph: **(818)343-2189**
Fax: **(888)269-6045**
E-mail: eligauna@yahoo.com
URL: http://www.ilaa.org
Contact: Eli Gauna, Sec.

**2243 ■ NALGAP: The Association of Lesbian,
Gay, Bisexual, and Transgender Addiction
Professionals and Their Allies** (11799)
1001 N Fairfax St., Ste.201
Alexandria, VA 22314
E-mail: joecd1@aol.com
URL: http://www.nalgap.org
Contact: Joseph M. Amico CAS, Pres.
Status Note: Formerly National Association of
Lesbian/Gay Addiction Professionals.

**2244 ■ National Association of Addiction
Treatment Providers (NAATP) (11834)**
313 W Liberty St., Ste.129
Lancaster, PA 17603-2748
Ph: (717)392-8480
Fax: (717)392-8481
E-mail: **kcarpenterpalumbo@naatp.org**
URL: http://www.naatp.org
Contact: **Karen Carpenter-Palumbo, Pres./CEO**

**2245 ■ National Association for Children of
Alcoholics (NACoA) (12987)**
10920 Connecticut Ave., Ste.100
Kensington, MD 20895
Ph: (301)468-0985
Free: (888)554-COAS
Fax: (301)468-0987
E-mail: nacoa@nacoa.org
URL: http://www.nacoa.org
Contact: Sis Wenger, Pres./CEO

2246 ■ Partnership at Drugfree.org (11961)
352 Park Ave. S 9th Fl.
New York, NY 10010
Ph: (212)922-1560 (212)973-3517
Free: (888)575-3115

Fax: (212)922-1570
URL: http://www.drugfree.org
Contact: Mr. Stephen J. Pasierb, Pres./CEO
Status Note: Formerly Partnership for a Drug-Free
America.

2247 ■ Project Renewal (13478)
200 Varick St.
New York, NY 10014
Ph: (212)620-0340
Fax: (212)243-4755
E-mail: **careers@projectrenewal.org**
URL: http://www.projectrenewal.org
Contact: Mitchell Netburn, Pres./CEO

**2248 ■ Recovered Alcoholic Clergy
Association (RACA) (11857)**
127 Inverness Rd.
Athens, GA 30606
Ph: **(706)546-5281**
E-mail: pc@petercourtney.net
URL: http://racapecusa.org
Contact: Fr. Peter Courtney, Dir.

2249 ■ Triangle Club (13484)
PO Box 65458
Washington, DC 20035
Ph: (202)659-8641
E-mail: club@triangleclub.org
URL: http://www.triangleclub.org
Contact: **Tom P., Pres.**

2250 ■ Women for Sobriety (WFS) (11870)
PO Box 618
Quakertown, PA 18951-0618
Ph: (215)536-8026
Fax: (215)538-9026
E-mail: **newlife@nni.com**
URL: http://www.womenforsobriety.org
Contact: Becky Fenner, Dir.

Suicide

**2251 ■ American Association of Suicidology
(AAS) (13486)**
5221 Wisconsin Ave. NW
Washington, DC 20015
Ph: (202)237-2280
Free: (800)273-TALK
Fax: (202)237-2282
E-mail: info@suicidology.org
URL: http://www.suicidology.org
Contact: **Michelle Linn-Gust, Pres.**

Toxic Exposure

2252 ■ Beyond Pesticides (11906)
701 E St. SE, Ste.200
Washington, DC 20003
Ph: (202)543-5450
Fax: (202)543-4791
E-mail: info@beyondpesticides.org
URL: http://www.beyondpesticides.org
Contact: Jay Feldman, Exec. Dir.

Veterans

**2253 ■ National Association of Atomic
Veterans (NAAV) (13555)**
11214 Sageland
Houston, TX 77089
Ph: (281)481-1357
E-mail: **naav.cmdr@naav.com**
URL: http://www.naav.com
Contact: R.J. Ritter CEM, Natl. Commander

**2254 ■ National Association of State
Veterans Homes (NASVH) (13556)**
3416 Columbus Ave.
Sandusky, OH 44870-5598
Ph: **(419)625-2454**

Fax: **(419)609-2583**
E-mail: info@nasvh.org
URL: http://www.nasvh.org
Contact: **Steve Matune, Pres.**

Victims

2255 ■ National Association of Crime Victim Compensation Boards (NACVCB) (13566)
PO Box 16003
Alexandria, VA 22302
Ph: (703)780-3200 (703)313-9500
Fax: (703)780-3261
E-mail: **dan.eddy@nacvcb.org**
URL: http://nacvcb.org
Contact: Dan Eddy, Exec. Dir.

2256 ■ Victims of Crime and Leniency (VOCAL) (12780)
PO Box 4449
Montgomery, AL 36103
Ph: **(334)262-7197**
Free: **(866)31-VOCAL**
Fax: **(334)834-5645**
E-mail: vocalonline@yahoo.com
URL: http://www.vocalonline.org
Contact: Joyce Miller, Contact

Voluntarism

2257 ■ AmeriCorps VISTA (13584)
1201 New York Ave. NW
Washington, DC 20005
Ph: (202)606-5000 (202)606-3472
Free: (800)942-2677
Fax: (202)606-3475
E-mail: **vista@americorps.gov**
URL: http://www.americorps.gov
Contact: **Paul Davis, Acting Dir.**

2258 ■ Association for Healthcare Volunteer Resource Professionals (AHVRP) (12137)
155 N Wacker Dr., Ste.400
Chicago, IL 60606-1725
Ph: **(312)422-3939**
Fax: **(312)278-0884**
E-mail: ahvrp@aha.org
URL: http://www.ahvrp.org
Contact: Audrey Harris, Exec. Dir.

2259 ■ Senior Corps (SCP) (13607)
1201 New York Ave. NW
Washington, DC 20525
Ph: (202)606-5000
Free: (800)424-8867
E-mail: **info@cns.gov**
URL: http://www.seniorcorps.gov/about/programs/sc.asp
Contact: **Patrick Corvington, CEO**

Water

2260 ■ Amman Imman: Water is Life
7700 Old Georgetown Rd., Ste.550
Bethesda, MD 20814
E-mail: info@ammanimman.org
URL: http://www.ammanimman.org
Contact: Ariane Alzhara Kirtley, Founder/Exec. Dir.

Founded: 2006. **Multinational. Description:** Aims to create permanent, sustainable and potable sources of water in Azawak of West Africa. Seeks to increase water security for the people living in the Azawak region in order to reduce incidence and prevalence of morbidity and mortality related to water insufficiency and poor water quality.

2261 ■ Clean Water for the World
3504 Madison St.
Kalamazoo, MI 49008
Ph: (269)342-1354
URL: http://www.cleanwaterfortheworld.org
Contact: Paul Flickinger, Exec. Dir.

Multinational. Description: Provides adaptable water purification systems to communities without access to clean drinking water.

2262 ■ Drinking Water for India (DWI)
PO Box 244
Plainsboro, NJ 08536-0244
Ph: (609)843-0176
E-mail: info@drinkingwaterforindia.org
URL: http://www.drinkingwaterforindia.org
Contact: Rujul Zaparde, Contact

Founded: 2007. **Multinational. Description:** Aims to bring clean water to rural Indian villages by providing tube-wells. Raises awareness about the water crisis in India.

2263 ■ Gift of Water (GoW)
1025 Pine Hill Way
Carmel, IN 46032-7701
Ph: (317)371-1656
E-mail: laura.moehling@giftofwater.org
URL: http://www.giftofwater.org
Contact: Laura Moehling, Contact

Founded: 1995. **Description:** Provides filtered and clean drinking water to third world countries. Focuses on the essential needs of children and families through community development.

2264 ■ Healing Waters International (HWI)
534 Commons Dr.
Golden, CO 80401
Ph: (303)526-7278
Free: (866)913-8522
Fax: (303)526-7288
E-mail: **info@healingwaters.org**
URL: **http://www.healingwaters.org**
Contact: Ed Anderson, CEO

2265 ■ In Our Own Quiet Way
110 S Main St.
Lindon, UT 84042
Ph: (801)669-7583
Fax: (801)830-0911
URL: http://www.quietway.org
Contact: Ron Hatfield, Chm.

Founded: 2002. **Multinational. Description:** Strives to ensure that Kenyans have sustainable access to clean water. Addresses critical issues concerning long-term solutions to Kenya's water scarcity.

2266 ■ International Action
819 L St. SE
Washington, DC 20003
Ph: (202)488-0735
Fax: (202)488-0736
E-mail: info@haitiwater.org
URL: http://www.iawater.org
Contact: Lindsay Mattison, Exec. Dir.

Founded: 2006. **Multinational. Description:** Aims to provide clean water in impoverished communities in Haiti. Implements sustainable water projects throughout Haiti.

2267 ■ Primero Agua
2675 Stonecrest Dr.
Washington, MO 63090
Ph: (636)239-1573
E-mail: primeroagua@gmail.com
URL: http://primeroagua.org
Contact: Jay L. Quattlebaum, Exec. Dir./Co-Founder

Founded: 2010. **Multinational. Description:** Strives to provide Honduran people with access to clean drinking water. Addresses important issues concerning access to safe drinking water and the implementation of sustainable solutions to the problem.

2268 ■ Water Alliance for Africa
3267 E 3300 S, No. 535
Salt Lake City, UT 84109
E-mail: kwaxis@hotmail.com
URL: http://wateralli.anceafrica.com
Contact: Brian Lloyd, Contact

Founded: 2006. **Multinational. Description:** Aims to provide pure and disease-free water to the world's most impoverished people.

2269 ■ Water for Sudan (WFS)
PO Box 25551
Rochester, NY 14625
Ph: (585)383-0410
E-mail: salva.dut@waterforsudan.org
URL: http://www.waterforsudan.org
Contact: Salva Dut, Founder/Pres.

Founded: 2003. **Multinational. Description:** Seeks to bring fresh, clean water to the people in Southern Sudan. Conducts well-drilling operations in remote villages.

Women

2270 ■ Finnish and American Women's Network (FAWN)
PO Box 3623
New York, NY 10163-3623
E-mail: information@fawnet.org
URL: http://www.fawnet.org
Contact: Kerstin Nordin, Chair

2271 ■ OWL - The Voice of Midlife and Older Women (13435)
1025 Connecticut Ave. NW Ste.701
Washington, DC 20036
Free: **(877)653-7966**
Fax: **(202)833-3472**
E-mail: **info@owl-national.org**
URL: http://www.owl-national.org
Contact: Bobbie A. Brinegar, Exec. Dir.

Status Note: Formerly Older Women's League.

2272 ■ Women's Funding Network (WFN) (11984)
505 Sansome St., 2nd Fl.
San Francisco, CA 94111
Ph: (415)441-0706
Fax: (415)441-0827
E-mail: info@womensfundingnetwork.org
URL: **http://www.womensfundingnetwork.org**
Contact: Chris Grumm, Pres./CEO

2273 ■ Women's International Center (WIC)
PO Box 669
Rancho Santa Fe, CA 92067-0669
Ph: (858)759-3567
Fax: (619)296-1633
E-mail: **team@wic.org**
URL: **http://www.wic.org**
Contact: Gloria J. Lane PhD, Pres./Founder

2274 ■ Women's Learning Partnership for Rights, Development, and Peace (WLP)
4343 Montgomery Ave., Ste.201
Bethesda, MD 20814
Ph: (301)654-2774
Fax: (301)654-2775
E-mail: wlp@learningpartnership.org
URL: **http://www.learningpartnership.org**
Contact: Mahnaz Afkhami, Pres./CEO

YMCA

2275 ■ Association of YMCA Professionals (AYP) (11958)
Springfield Coll.
263 Alden St.
Springfield, MA 01109
Ph: (413)748-3884
Fax: (413)748-3872

E-mail: **ddunn@ayponline.org**
URL: **http://www.ayponline.org**
Contact: Ms. Donna French Dunn CAE, Exec. Dir./
CEO

Youth

2276 ■ Boys' Towns of Italy (BTI)
250 E 63rd St., Ste.204
New York, NY 10021
Ph: (212)980-8770
Fax: (212)644-0766
E-mail: office@btiofny.org
URL: **http://www.boystownofitaly.org**
Contact: Lawrence Auriana, Pres.

2277 ■ I Have a Dream Foundation (13487)
330 7th Ave., 20th Fl.
New York, NY 10001
Ph: (212)293-5480
Fax: (212)293-5478
E-mail: info@ihaveadreamfoundation.org
URL: **http://www.ihaveadreamfoundation.org**
Contact: Iris Chen, Pres./CEO

2278 ■ National 4-H Council (N4-HC)
7100 Connecticut Ave.
Chevy Chase, MD 20815
Ph: (301)961-2801
Fax: (301)961-2894
E-mail: **info@4-h.org**
URL: http://www.4-h.org
Contact: Donald T. Floyd Jr., Pres./CEO

**2279 ■ National Association of Police
Athletic Leagues (12235)**
658 W Indiantown Rd., Ste.201
Jupiter, FL 33458
Ph: (561)745-5535
Fax: (561)745-3147
E-mail: **copnkid@nationalpal.org**
URL: http://www.nationalpal.org
Contact: Mr. Michael Dillhyon, Exec. Dir.

**2280 ■ Robert F. Kennedy Center for Justice
and Human Rights (RFKM) (12247)**
1367 Connecticut Ave. NW, Ste.200
Washington, DC 20036
Ph: (202)463-7575
Fax: (202)463-6606

E-mail: **jkarlen@rfkcenter.org**
URL: http://www.rfkcenter.org
Contact: Lynn Delaney, Exec. Dir.

**2281 ■ Youth to Youth International (Y2Y)
(12920)**
547 E 11th Ave.
Columbus, OH 43221
Ph: (614)224-4506
Fax: (614)224-8451
E-mail: **y2yinfo@compdrug.org**
URL: http://www.youthtoyouth.net
Contact: Robert E. Sweet, Pres./Founder

YWCA

**2282 ■ Young Women's Christian
Association of the United States of America
(12014)**
2025 M St. NW, Ste.550
Washington, DC 20036
Ph: (202)467-0801
Fax: (202)467-0802
E-mail: info@ywca.org
URL: http://www.ywca.org
Contact: **Gloria Lau, Interim CEO**

Acupuncture

2283 ■ American Abdominal Acupuncture Medical Association (AAAMA)
41790 Winchester Rd., Ste.B
Temecula, CA 92590
Ph: (951)296-1688
Fax: (951)296-6662
E-mail: info@aaama.us
URL: http://www.aaama.us
Contact: Prof. Zhiyun Bo, Honorary Pres.
Founded: 2007. **Description:** Aims to link together acupuncture professionals interested in or are currently practicing abdominal acupuncture in the United States. Promotes the science of abdominal acupuncture and its benefits across the United States. Seeks to exchange and share knowledge among all acupuncture professionals and academics around the globe.

2284 ■ Council for Acupuncture Research and Education (CARE)
3448 Horseshoe Bend Rd.
Charlottesville, VA 22901
E-mail: info@councilforacupuncture.org
URL: http://www.councilforacupuncture.com
Contact: John Dent MD, Contact
Multinational. Description: Promotes comprehensive integration of acupuncture treatment into the American healthcare system. Develops an evidence-based scientific model of the acupuncture system for a Western audience.

Aerospace Medicine

2285 ■ Airlines Medical Directors Association (AMDA) (12062)
c/o Ralph G. Fennell, MD, Sec.
46155 Black Spruce Ln.
Parker, CO 80138-4919
E-mail: **fennell@q.com**
URL: http://www.amda.aero
Contact: **Patrick C. Rodriguez MD, Pres.-Elect**

AIDS

2286 ■ The Foundation for AIDS Research
(12283)
120 Wall St., 13th Fl.
New York, NY 10005-3908
Ph: (212)806-1600
Fax: (212)806-1601
E-mail: **information@amfar.org**
URL: http://www.amfar.org
Contact: **Kenneth Cole, Chm.**

Allergy

2287 ■ American Academy of Allergy, Asthma and Immunology (AAAAI) (14053)
555 E Wells St., Ste.1100
Milwaukee, WI 53202-3823

Ph: (414)272-6071
Fax: (414)272-6070
E-mail: info@aaaai.org
URL: http://www.aaaai.org
Contact: **Dennis K. Ledford MD, Pres.**

2288 ■ American College of Allergy, Asthma and Immunology (ACAAI) (14056)
85 W Algonquin Rd., Ste.550
Arlington Heights, IL 60005-4425
Ph: (847)427-1200
Fax: (847)427-1294
E-mail: mail@acaai.org
URL: http://www.acaai.org
Contact: **Dana V. Wallace MD, Pres.**

Alternative Medicine

2289 ■ Alternative Medicine International (AMI)
7639 Houghton Rd.
Bakersfield, CA 93313
Ph: (661)330-2828
E-mail: dhealy3@gmail.com
URL: http://ami-wa.org
Contact: Dan Healy, Contact
Founded: 2008. **Multinational. Description:** Promotes alternative treatment to relieve the people living in Sub-Saharan Africa from diseases such as malaria, skin and dental problems.

2290 ■ American Association of Traditional Chinese Veterinary Medicine (AATCVM)
c/o Cheryl Chrisman, DVM
10145 SW 52nd Rd.
Gainesville, FL 32608
Ph: (352)672-6400
Fax: (352)672-6400
E-mail: chrismanc@ajtcvm.org
URL: http://www.aatcvm.org
Contact: Bruce Ferguson, Pres.
Founded: 2006. **Membership Dues:** veterinarian in U.S., $65 (annual) ● veterinarian outside U.S., $85 (annual). **Multinational. Description:** Represents traditional Chinese veterinary medicine practitioners worldwide. Aims to unite the global traditional Chinese veterinary medicine community. Supports research and development in all aspects of traditional Chinese veterinary medicine.

2291 ■ American Herbal Pharmacopoeia (AHP)
PO Box 66809
Scotts Valley, CA 95067
Ph: (831)461-6318
Fax: (831)438-2196
E-mail: ahpadmin@got.net
URL: http://www.herbal-ahp.org
Contact: Roy Upton RH, Exec. Dir.
Founded: 1995. **Description:** Represents experts in medicinal plants industry. Promotes the use of herbal

products and herbal medicines through producing monographs about Ayurvedic and Chinese botanicals.

2292 ■ Aromatherapy Registration Council (ARC)
530 1st St., Ste.A
Lake Oswego, OR 97034
Ph: (503)244-0726
E-mail: info@aromatherapycouncil.org
URL: http://aromatherapycouncil.org
Contact: Dorene Petersen, Chair
Founded: 1999. **Description:** Fosters the advancement of aromatherapy research and practice. Promotes safe and effective practices of aromatherapy.

2293 ■ Father Josef's Method of Reflexology (FJM)
1441 High Ridge Rd.
Stamford, CT 06903
Ph: (203)968-6824
E-mail: fjmreflexology@optonline.net
URL: http://www.fjmreflexology.com
Contact: Father Josef Eugster, Chm.
Founded: 2000. **Description:** Promotes the health benefits of reflexology through seminars and support of different reflexology organizations. Trains professional reflexologists as part of a continuing education program.

2294 ■ Global Natural Health Alliance (GNHA)
2442 NW Market St., No. 628
Seattle, WA 98107
Ph: (970)402-0575
E-mail: info@gnhalliance.org
URL: http://gnhalliance.org
Contact: Lindsay Herrera, Co-Founder
Founded: 2010. **Membership Dues:** community, $25 (annual) ● natural health care student, $30 (annual) ● natural health care provider, $50 (annual). **Multinational. Description:** Aims to provide free natural healthcare services to impoverished communities in developing nations by establishing natural healthcare centers and deploying circuit-based mobile natural health clinics. Promotes exchange of ideas between Western-trained natural health professionals and local traditional healers. Unites natural health professionals around the world.

2295 ■ International Society for Ayurveda and Health (ISAH)
PO Box 271737
West Hartford, CT 06127-1737
Ph: (860)561-4857
E-mail: aguha@att.net
URL: http://www.ayurvedahealth.org
Contact: Dr. Amala Guha, Contact
Membership Dues: individual, $50 (annual) ● library/institution, $90 (annual) ● student, $47 (annual) ● international, $100 (annual). **Multinational. Description:** Promotes understanding and knowledge of ayurvedic medicine. Combines the principle of the ancient science of ayurveda with advancement of

modern science. Provides lectures, workshops, research, publications, scientific meetings, related wellness programs and excursion tours.

2296 ■ OmSpring
550 Wisconsin St.
San Francisco, CA 94107
Ph: (415)206-9920
Fax: (415)826-0862
E-mail: suteja@omspring.org
URL: http://sites.google.com/site/omspringayurveda
Contact: Suteja Navarro, Contact
Description: Promotes natural healing through the use of different Ayurvedic therapies and other techniques. Conducts workshops and consultations on ayurveda and self-healing treatments.

2297 ■ Qigong Alliance International (QAI)
PO Box 750
Ely, MN 55731
Free: (800)341-8895
E-mail: kali@qicentral.org
URL: http://www.qigong-alliance.org
Contact: Rebecca Kali, Contact
Members: 700. **Multinational. Description:** Provides education and information about the benefits of Qigong. Supports networking, scientific research, sharing of information and cultural exchange.

2298 ■ Reiki Rays of Hope for Caregivers
9592 Dublin Ln.
Mentor, OH 44060
Ph: (440)357-6517
E-mail: reikiraysofhope@oh.rr.com
URL: http://www.reikiraysofhope.org
Contact: Judy McCracken, CEO
Founded: 2007. **Membership Dues:** basic, $75 (annual) ● full, $125 (annual). **Description:** Promotes Reiki as a method that enhances and complements traditional medicine. Fosters the professional development of caregivers by providing instructional classes in Reiki relaxation techniques.

2299 ■ Surfing Medicine International (SMI)
PO Box 548
Waialua, HI 96791
Ph: (518)635-0899
E-mail: surfingmedicine@gmail.com
URL: http://www.surfingmedicine.org
Contact: Dr. Summer Ragosta, Co-Founder
Multinational. Description: Aims to support, research and create botanical remedies for human disease and water pollution. Fosters international cooperation between traditional healers and surfers to develop medicinal plant systems for coastal communities.

2300 ■ Visionary Alternatives
7725 Kenway Pl. E
Boca Raton, FL 33433
Ph: (561)750-4551
Free: (866)750-4551
E-mail: jane@visionaryalternatives.com
URL: http://www.visionaryalternatives.org
Contact: Jane Tobal, Pres.
Founded: 1998. **Description:** Aims to provide the opportunity for individuals with life threatening illnesses to receive the treatment of their choice. Promotes an alternative health options for the critically ill and provides fund for proven unconventional treatment.

Anesthesiology

2301 ■ American Osteopathic College of Anesthesiologists (AOCA)
2260 E Saginaw St., Ste.B
East Lansing, MI 48823
Ph: (517)339-0919
Free: (800)842-2622
Fax: (517)339-0910
E-mail: **office@aocaonline.org**
URL: http://www.aocaonline.org
Contact: **James A. Skrabak DO, Pres.**

2302 ■ American Society for Advancement of Anesthesia and Sedation in Dentistry (ASAAD) (12329)
6 E Union Ave.
Bound Brook, NJ 08805
Ph: (732)469-9050
Fax: (732)271-1985
E-mail: dacryst1@aol.com
URL: http://www.sedation4dentists.net
Contact: David Crystal DDS, Exec. Sec.

2303 ■ American Society of Regional Anesthesia and Pain Medicine (ASRA) (14139)
520 N Northwest Hwy.
Park Ridge, IL 60068-2573
Ph: (847)825-7246
Fax: (847)825-5658
E-mail: **j.kahlfeldt@asahq.org**
URL: http://www.asra.com
Contact: **Julie Kahlfeldt CMP, Exec. Dir.**

2304 ■ Association of University Anesthesiologists (AUA) (12075)
520 N Northwest Hwy.
Park Ridge, IL 60068-2573
Ph: (847)825-5586 **(734)936-4235**
Fax: **(734)936-9091**
E-mail: aua@asahq.org
URL: http://www.auahq.org
Contact: Kevin K. Tremper MD, Pres.

2305 ■ Society of Cardiovascular Anesthesiologists (SCA) (14152)
2209 Dickens Rd.
Richmond, VA 23230-2005
Ph: (804)282-0084
Fax: (804)282-0090
E-mail: sca@societyhq.com
URL: http://www.scahq.org
Contact: **Solomon Aronson MD, Pres.**

Art

2306 ■ Association of Medical Illustrators (AMI) (12310)
201 E Main St., Ste.1405
Lexington, KY 40507
Free: (866)393-4264
Fax: **(859)514-9166**
E-mail: hq@ami.org
URL: http://www.ami.org
Contact: Ms. Tracy Tucker, Exec. Dir.

Autism

2307 ■ Aging with Autism
704 Marten Rd.
Princeton, NJ 08540
E-mail: cyndyhayes@gmail.com
URL: http://www.agingwithautism.org
Contact: Dr. Cyndy Hayes, Founder/Exec. Dir.
Founded: 2009. **Description:** Provides programs and services for individuals with classis autism as they transition to and through adulthood. Collaborates with other organizations to create a variety of residential, vocational and community options to ensure the wellbeing of individuals with autism and their families.

2308 ■ Autism Allies
2400 Prairie View Ln.
Buffalo, MN 55313-2450
Ph: (612)384-4265
E-mail: info@autismallies.org
URL: http://www.autismallies.org
Contact: Lisa Burke, Chair
Description: Aims to improve the lives of individuals with autism and their families by providing support, education and research. Conducts educational and informative activities to increase public awareness of autism.

2309 ■ Autism Care and Treatment Today! (ACT Today!)
19019 Ventura Blvd., Ste.200
Tarzana, CA 91356
Ph: (818)705-1625
Fax: (818)758-8015
E-mail: info@act-today.org
URL: http://www.act-today.org
Contact: Dr. Doreen Granpeesheh, Pres.
Founded: 2005. **Description:** Aims to raise awareness, provide treatment services and support families with children with autism. Helps facilitate early and on-going treatment by providing the necessary resources to individuals with autism and their families.

2310 ■ Autism Service Dogs of America (ASDA)
4248 Galewood St.
Lake Oswego, OR 97035
Ph: (503)314-6913
Fax: (503)675-4341
E-mail: info@autismservicedogsofamerica.org
URL: http://autismservicedogsofamerica.com
Contact: Priscilla Taylor, Founder/Dir.
Founded: 2002. **Description:** Seeks to make a positive impact on the lives of children living with autism by providing well trained service dogs. Serves as a physical and emotional anchor for children with autism.

2311 ■ Bailey's Team for Autism (BTA)
164 Westside Ave.
North Attleboro, MA 02760
Ph: (508)699-4483
E-mail: sammirobertson@comcast.net
URL: http://www.baileysteam.org
Contact: Sammi Robertson, Pres.
Founded: 2008. **Description:** Seeks to improve the lives of children with autism. Raises public awareness about autism and its effects. Supports organizations that fund and/or provide direct services to those living with autism.

2312 ■ Face Autism
5333 Rio Vista St.
Sarasota, FL 34232
E-mail: info@face-autism.org
URL: http://www.face-autism.org
Contact: Ms. Colleen Buccieri, Pres./Founder
Founded: 2009. **Description:** Provides Autism/ASD screenings and funding for the therapeutic services of autistic children. Works to give these children the opportunity to significantly improve and maintain a balanced quality of life.

2313 ■ Families with Autism Spectrum Disorders
5989 Meijer Dr., Ste.9
Milford, OH 45150
Ph: (513)444-4979
E-mail: helpingfamilieswithautism@yahoo.com
URL: http://www.familieswithasd.org
Contact: Mrs. Julia Ann Smith, Co-Founder
Founded: 2005. **Description:** Aims to raise awareness and promote understanding about families with Autism Spectrum Disorder (ASD). Offers support and resources to families effected by autism.

2314 ■ Fashion for Autism
274 Clinton Ave.
Brooklyn, NY 11205
Ph: (917)881-6259 (646)220-0611
E-mail: info@fashionforautism.com
URL: http://www.fashionforautism.org
Contact: Edwing D'Angelo, Founder
Founded: 2009. **Description:** Aims to increase public awareness of autism. Raises funds for other organizations committed to education, prevention, treatment and awareness of autism disorders. Supports resources and education of individuals and families living with and affected by autism spectrum disorders.

2315 ■ Generation Rescue
13636 Ventura Blvd., Ste.259
Sherman Oaks, CA 91423
Free: (877)98-AUTISM
E-mail: candace.mcdonald@generationrescue.org
URL: http://www.generationrescue.org
Contact: Candace McDonald, Exec. Dir.
Founded: 2005. **Description:** Aims to improve the quality of life of children with autism. Provides guidance and support for medical treatment of children with autism spectrum disorders.

2316 ■ Global Autism Collaboration (GAC)
Autism Res. Inst.
4182 Adams Ave.
San Diego, CA 92116
E-mail: researchpartners@globalautismcollaboration.
com
URL: http://www.autism.org
Contact: Stephen M. Edelson PhD, Pres.
Multinational. Description: Facilitates networking and communication among autism groups. Addresses issues pertaining to global autism health crisis.

2317 ■ Helping Autism through Learning and Outreach (HALO)
PO Box 303399
Austin, TX 78703
Ph: (512)465-9595
Free: (866)465-9595
Fax: (512)465-9598
E-mail: information@halo-soma.org
URL: http://www.halo-soma.org
Contact: Brian Jackson, Pres.
Founded: 2004. **Description:** Promotes the use of Soma Mukhopadhyay's Rapid Prompting Method for improving academic success and communication for persons with autism and similar disorders. Offers opportunities for professionals to train under Soma through donor-funded internship or apprentice programs.

2318 ■ International Coalition for Autism and All Abilities (ICAA)
200 Crestwood Plz.
St. Louis, MO 63126
E-mail: info@internationalautismcoalition.org
URL: http://www.internationalautismcoalition.org
Contact: Emily Malabey, Founder/Pres.
Multinational. Description: Advocates for and supports people on the autism spectrum and those with other disabilities. Encourages society to better understand, accommodate and include people with differences in ability.

2319 ■ Milestones Autism Organization
23880 Commerce Park, Ste.2
Beachwood, OH 44122
Ph: (216)464-7600
Fax: (216)464-7602
E-mail: info@milestones.org
URL: http://www.milestones.org
Contact: Ilana Hoffer Skoff MA, Exec. Dir.
Founded: 2003. **Description:** Promotes life long strategies of success for individuals with autism, from childhood through adulthood. Improves the level of educational and therapeutic programming available to individuals with autism. Provides training for parents and professionals in research-based educational interventions.

2320 ■ Stop Calling It Autism! (SCIA)
PO Box 155728
Fort Worth, TX 76155
Free: (888)SCIA-123
Fax: (888)724-2123
E-mail: scia@stopcallingitautism.org
URL: http://www.stopcallingitautism.org
Contact: Juan Rodriguez, Co-Founder
Founded: 2010. **Description:** Aims to build medical research to examine the evidence of immune system dysfunction in autism. Provides evidence to prove that autism is caused by medical disease.

2321 ■ Stories of Autism
13110 NE 177th Pl., No. 237
Woodinville, WA 98072
Ph: (425)485-9919
E-mail: info@storiesofautism.com
URL: http://www.storiesofautism.com
Contact: Charlie Cotugno, Pres.
Founded: 2009. **Description:** Aims to raise public awareness on autism through the exhibition of works, portraits and photographs created by people of the autism spectrum. Engages autism service providers and photographers to work with children and adults with autism spectrum disorders in sharing their unique stories.

2322 ■ S.U.C.C.E.S.S. for Autism (SFA)
28700 Euclid Ave.
Mailbox No. 120
Wickliffe, OH 44092
E-mail: lynettesw@yahoo.com
URL: http://successforautism.com
Contact: Lynette Scotese-Wojtila, Pres.
Founded: 2002. **Description:** Aims to raise public awareness on autism and related disorders. Raises funds to help provide financial support to qualified families and agencies. Provides access to professional training services for school personnel and families who care for children with autism and related disorders.

2323 ■ Talk About Curing Autism (TACA)
3070 Bristol St., Ste.340
Costa Mesa, CA 92626
Ph: (949)640-4401
Fax: (949)640-4424
URL: http://www.tacanow.org
Contact: Glen Ackerman, Pres.
Founded: 2000. **Members:** 20,000. **Description:** Provides information, resources and support to families affected by autism. Aims to speed up the cycle time from the autism diagnosis to effective treatments. Strengthens the autism community by connecting families and professionals to share stories and information to help people with autism.

Birth Defects

2324 ■ March of Dimes Foundation (13463)
1275 Mamaroneck Ave.
White Plains, NY 10605
Ph: (914)997-4488 (914)428-7100
E-mail: askus@marchofdimes.com
URL: http://www.marchofdimes.com
Contact: Dr. Jennifer L. Howse, Pres.

Blood

2325 ■ America's Blood Centers (ABC) (14230)
725 15th St. NW, Ste.700
Washington, DC 20005
Ph: (202)393-5725 (202)654-2915
Free: (888)US-BLOOD
Fax: (202)393-1282
E-mail: abc@americasblood.org
URL: http://www.americasblood.org
Contact: Dan A. Waxman, Pres.

Bronchoesophagology

2326 ■ American Broncho-Esophagological Association (ABEA) (14249)
Boston Medical Center, FGH Bldg.
Dept. of Otolaryngology-Head and Neck Surgery
820 Harrison Ave., 4th Fl.
Boston, MA 02118
Ph: (617)638-7934
Fax: (617)638-7965

E-mail: **gpostma@mail.mcg.edu**
URL: http://www.rothschilddesign.com/abea/website/
index.html
Contact: **Gregory Postma, Pres.**

Burns

2327 ■ American Burn Association (ABA) (13992)
311 S Wacker Dr., Ste.4150
Chicago, IL 60606
Ph: (312)642-9260
Fax: (312)642-9130
E-mail: info@ameriburn.org
URL: http://www.ameriburn.org
Contact: John A. Krichbaum JD, Exec. Dir.

Cancer

2328 ■ Association of Community Cancer Centers (ACCC) (14268)
11600 Nebel St., Ste.201
Rockville, MD 20852-2557
Ph: (301)984-9496
Fax: (301)770-1949
E-mail: membership@accc-cancer.org
URL: http://www.accc-cancer.org
Contact: **Thomas L. Whittaker MD, Pres.**

2329 ■ C-Change
1776 Eye St. NW, 9th Fl.
Washington, DC 20006
Ph: (202)756-1600 (202)756-1392
Free: (800)830-1827
Fax: (202)756-1512
E-mail: info@c-changetogether.org
URL: http://c-changetogether.org
Contact: Tom Kean MPH, Exec. Dir.
Founded: 1998. **Description:** Represents key cancer leaders from government, business and nonprofit sectors. Aims to eliminate cancer as a major public health problem by leveraging the expertise and resources of its multi-sector membership. Promotes primary cancer prevention and early detection. Provides access to high-quality care and enhances the quality of life of cancer patients.

2330 ■ International Society for Children with Cancer (ISCC)
16808 Armstrong Ave., Ste.170
Irvine, CA 92606
Ph: (949)679-9911 (818)775-9264
Fax: (949)679-3399
E-mail: info@iscc-charity.org
URL: http://iscc-charity.org
Contact: Mrs. Negin Tafazzoli, Pres.
Founded: 2004. **Multinational. Description:** Strives to make a difference in the lives of cancer-stricken children, adolescents and their families, by giving them access to quality care and service regardless of financial status. Aims to globally help reduce the mortality rate of impoverished children suffering from cancer through financial assistance.

2331 ■ Women Against Prostate Cancer (WAPC)
236 Massachusetts Ave. NE, Ste.301
Washington, DC 20002
Ph: (202)580-5730
Fax: (202)543-2727
E-mail: info@womenagainstprostatecancer.org
URL: http://www.womenagainstprostatecancer.org
Contact: Theresa Morrow, Pres.
Description: Aims to unite the voices and provide support for women affected by prostate cancer and their families. Advocates prostate cancer education, public awareness, screenings, legislation, and treatment options.

Cardiology

2332 ■ Heart Rhythm Society (HRS) (12261)
1400 K St. NW, Ste.500
Washington, DC 20005
Ph: (202)464-3400 **(202)464-3424**
Fax: (202)464-3401
E-mail: info@hrsonline.org
URL: http://www.hrsonline.org
Contact: James Youngblood, CEO

2333 ■ Michael E. DeBakey International Surgical Society (MEDISS) (12256)
c/o Kenneth L. Mattox, MD, Sec.-Treas.
1 Baylor Plz.
Houston, TX 77030
Ph: (713)798-4557
Free: (800)914-3709
Fax: (713)796-9605
E-mail: **redstart@aol.com**
URL: http://www.mediss.org
Contact: **Robert J. Salem MD, Pres.**

Child Health

2334 ■ Children's Health International
PO Box 3505
Silver Spring, MD 20918
Ph: (301)681-8307
Fax: (301)681-5056
E-mail: info@childrenshealthintl.org
URL: http://childrenshealthintl.org
Contact: Mrs. Grace Kumi Aaron, Founder
Founded: 1998. **Multinational. Description:** Aims to increase global awareness of the plight of children in underdeveloped countries. Provides adequate healthcare to children with infectious and communicable diseases. Raises funds and supplies to provide for the care and well-being of underserved children.

2335 ■ Children's International Health Relief
4218 S Steele St., Ste.220
Tacoma, WA 98409
Ph: (253)476-0556
E-mail: goddessrobin@aol.com
URL: http://www.childrenshealthrelief.org
Contact: Dr. Robin Jones, Pres.
Multinational. Description: Aims to improve the health care of needy children in the United States and developing countries. Provides dental and medical supplies, equipment, pharmaceuticals and educational materials to underserved populations. Conducts and organizes dental and medical mission to provide quality dental and medical care, preventive care, eye care, and maternal and child health care.

2336 ■ Childspring International
1328 Peachtree St. NE
Atlanta, GA 30309
Ph: (404)228-7744 (404)228-7733
E-mail: reb@childspringintl.org
URL: http://www.childspringintl.org
Contact: Rose Emily Bermudez, Exec. Dir.
Multinational. Description: Aims to provide medical care and opportunities for a better life to children around the world. Facilitates the medical treatment of children in need.

2337 ■ Medical Missions for Children (MMFC)
10-G Roessler Rd., Ste.500
Woburn, MA 01801
Ph: (508)697-5821
Fax: (781)501-5225
E-mail: info@mmfc.org
URL: http://www.mmfc.org
Contact: Elizabeth E. Desmarais Esq., Exec. Dir.
Multinational. Description: Provides surgical and dental services to poor and underprivileged children and young adults in countries throughout the world. Facilitates the transfer of medical education, knowledge and innovations to the local medical communities.

2338 ■ Society for Adolescent Health and Medicine (SAHM) (14465)
111 Deer lake Rd., Ste.100
Deerfield, IL 60015
Ph: (847)753-5226
Fax: **(847)480-9282**
E-mail: info@adolescenthealth.org
URL: http://www.adolescenthealth.org
Contact: **Leslie Walker, Pres.**
Status Note: Formerly Society for Adolescent Medicine.

Chiropractic

2339 ■ American College of Chiropractic Orthopedists (ACCO) (13694)
35 S Lake St.
North East, PA 16428
Ph: (781)665-1497 (814)725-2225
Fax: **(814)665-1032**
E-mail: **thomasmackdc@gmail.com**
URL: http://www.accoweb.org
Contact: **Thomas C. Mack DC, Pres.**

2340 ■ Chiropractic Diplomatic Corps
17602 17th St., Ste.102
Tustin, CA 92780
Free: (800)600-7032
E-mail: info@chiropracticdiplomatic.com
URL: http://www.chiropracticdiplomatic.com
Contact: Dr. Michel Tetrault, Exec. Dir.
Founded: 1997. **Multinational. Description:** Seeks to advance chiropractic training and services throughout the world. Aims to establish cooperative alliances with international organizations that are involved with the delivery of chiropractic care.

2341 ■ Chiropractic Orthopedists of North America (CONA)
c/o Dr. Philip Rake, Treas.
2048 Montrose Ave.
Montrose, CA 91020
Ph: (818)249-8326
E-mail: rakechiro@ca.rr.com
URL: http://www.conanet.org
Contact: Lewis Meltz DC, Pres.
Membership Dues: regular, $95 (annual). **Description:** Assists in the advancement of chiropractic using scientific and evidence-based research and information. Maintains highest standards of moral and ethical conduct among members. Promotes chiropractic orthopedics with other branches of the healing arts and professions.

2342 ■ Council of Chiropractic Acupuncture
510 Baxter Rd., Ste.8
Chesterfield, MO 63017
Ph: (636)207-6600
Fax: (636)207-6631
URL: http://councilofchiropracticacupuncture.org
Contact: Dr. Todd T. Frisch, Pres.
Founded: 2005. **Membership Dues:** student, $37 (annual) ● general, $150 (annual). **Description:** Aims to provide excellent educational opportunities to elevate the quality of care, life and practice of chiropractic acupuncture. Serves as a platform for professional communication regarding the practice of acupuncture in the chiropractic profession.

2343 ■ Council on Chiropractic Practice (CCP)
2950 N Dobson Rd., Ste.1
Chandler, AZ 85224
E-mail: ccp@ccp-guidelines.org
URL: http://www.ccp-guidelines.org
Contact: William M. Sloane PhD, Pres.
Founded: 1995. **Description:** Strives to develop evidence-based guidelines, conduct research and perform other functions to enhance chiropractic practice for the benefit of the consumer. Provides practice guidelines which serve the needs of the consumer and are consistent with chiropractic practice.

2344 ■ International Chiropractors Association (ICA) (12295)
6400 Arlington Blvd., Ste.800
Falls Church, VA 22042
Ph: (703)528-5000
Free: (800)423-4690
Fax: (703)528-5023
E-mail: chiro@chiropractic.org
URL: http://www.chiropractic.org
Contact: Dr. John Maltby, Pres.

2345 ■ Non-Profit Chiropractic Organization (NPCO)
601 Brady St., Ste.201
Davenport, IA 52803
Ph: (708)459-8080
E-mail: info@npco.org
URL: http://www.npco.org
Contact: Diane DaCruz, Exec. Dir.
Multinational. Description: Provides chiropractic healthcare services to people in underdeveloped countries. Seeks to educate the public about chiropractic through the implementation of various programs.

2346 ■ Sacro Occipital Research Society International (SORSI) (14236)
PO Box 24361
Overland Park, KS 66283
Ph: **(239)513-9800**
Free: (888)245-1011
E-mail: drkwaichang@msn.com
URL: http://www.sorsi.com
Contact: Suzanne Seekins DC, Past Pres.

Clinical Studies

2347 ■ American Society for Clinical Investigation (ASCI) (14515)
15 Res. Dr.
Ann Arbor, MI 48103
Ph: (734)222-6050
Fax: (734)222-6058
E-mail: staff@the-asci.org
URL: http://www.the-asci.org
Contact: **Elizabeth McNally, Pres.**

2348 ■ Association of Clinical Scientists (14247)
PO Box 1287
Middlebury, VT 05753
Ph: (802)458-3351
Fax: (802)458-3278
E-mail: clinsci@sover.net
URL: http://www.clinicalscience.org
Contact: **Dani S. Zander MD, Pres.**

2349 ■ Society for Clinical Trials (SCT) (14523)
100 N 20th St., 4th Fl.
Philadelphia, PA 19103
Ph: (215)564-3484
Fax: (215)564-2175
E-mail: sct@fernley.com
URL: http://www.sctweb.org
Contact: **Anne Lindblad PhD, Pres.-Elect**

Communications

2350 ■ Association of Biomedical Communications Directors (ABCD) (12309)
SUNY Downstate Medical Center
Box 18
Brooklyn, NY 11203
Ph: (423)439-2402 **(718)270-7551**
Fax: (423)439-7025
E-mail: ponnappa@etsu.org
URL: http://www.abcdirectors.org
Contact: Biddanda Ponnappa, Pres.

2351 ■ BioCommunications Association (BCA) (12681)
220 Southwind Ln.
Hillsborough, NC 27278
Ph: (919)245-0906 **(301)846-1546**
Fax: (919)245-0906
E-mail: office@bca.org
URL: http://www.bca.org
Contact: Nancy Hurtgen, Central Office Mgr.

2352 ■ Health Science Communications Association (HeSCA) (12313)
39 Wedgewood Dr., Ste.A
Jewett City, CT 06351-2420
Ph: (860)376-5915
Fax: (860)376-6621
E-mail: **hescaone@sbcglobal.net**
URL: http://www.hesca.org
Contact: **Jim Huff, Pres.-Elect**

Compensation Medicine

2353 ■ National Association of Disability Examiners (NADE) (14529)
1599 Green St., No. 303
San Francisco, CA 94123
Ph: **(510)622-3385**
Fax: **(510)622-3385**
E-mail: **andrew.martinez@dss.ca.gov**
URL: http://www.nade.org
Contact: **Andrew Martinez, Pres.**

Craniofacial Abnormalities

2354 ■ American Cleft Palate-Craniofacial Association (ACPA) (13410)
1504 E Franklin St., Ste.102
Chapel Hill, NC 27514-2820
Ph: (919)933-9044
Fax: **(919)933-9604**
E-mail: info@acpa-cpf.org
URL: http://www.acpa-cpf.org
Contact: **Jerald B. Moon PhD, Pres.**

2355 ■ Smile Network International
211 N First St., Ste.150
Minneapolis, MN 55401
Ph: (612)377-1800
Fax: (612)435-2677
E-mail: sara@smilenetwork.org
URL: http://www.smilenetwork.org
Contact: Greg Frankenfield, Chm.
Founded: 2003. **Description:** Provides free surgeries for impoverished children in developing countries who are born with cleft lips and palates. Conducts surgical missions to impart dignity and a better quality of life to individuals with birth defects and other conditions requiring surgical intervention.

Critical Care

2356 ■ Society of Critical Care Medicine (SCCM) (14071)
500 Midway Dr.
Mount Prospect, IL 60056
Ph: (847)827-6869 **(847)827-6888**
Fax: (847)827-6886
E-mail: info@sccm.org
URL: http://www.sccm.org
Contact: David Julian Martin CAE, CEO/Exec. VP

Cryonics

2357 ■ Alcor Life Extension Foundation (ALEF) (14573)
7895 E Acoma Dr., Ste.110
Scottsdale, AZ 85260-6916
Ph: (480)905-1906
Free: (877)462-5267

Fax: (480)922-9027
E-mail: **max@alcor.org**
URL: http://www.alcor.org
Contact: **Max More PhD, Pres./CEO**

Cytology

2358 ■ American Society for Cytotechnology (ASCT) (14579)
1500 Sunday Dr., Ste.102
Raleigh, NC 27607
Ph: (919)861-5571
Free: (800)948-3947
Fax: (919)787-4916
E-mail: info@asct.com
URL: http://www.asct.com
Contact: **Joan Rossi CT, Pres.**

Dentistry

2359 ■ Academy of Dental Materials (ADM) (14586)
c/o Thomas Hilton, Treas.
Oregon Hea. and Sci. Univ.
School of Dentistry
Dept. of Restorative Dentistry
611 SW Campus Dr.
Portland, OR 97239
Ph: (503)494-8672
Fax: (503)494-8260
E-mail: hiltont@ohsu.edu
URL: http://academydentalmaterials.org
Contact: **Alvaro Della Bona, Pres.**

2360 ■ Academy of Operative Dentistry (AOD) (14591)
c/o Dr. Richard G. Stevenson, III, Sec.
PO Box 34425
Los Angeles, CA 90034
Ph: (310)794-4387
Free: **(888)232-5011**
Fax: (310)825-2536
E-mail: **memberservices@academyofoperative-dentistry.com**
URL: **http://www.academyofoperativedentistry.com**
Contact: **Dr. J. William Robbins, Pres.**

2361 ■ American Academy of Dental Group Practice (AADGP) (14596)
2525 E Arizona Biltmore Cir., Ste.127
Phoenix, AZ 85016
Ph: (602)381-1185
Fax: (602)381-1093
E-mail: **aadgp@aadgp.org**
URL: http://www.aadgp.org
Contact: **Dr. Robert Bernstein, Pres.**

2362 ■ American Academy of Esthetic Dentistry (AAED) (13449)
303 W Madison St., Ste.2650
Chicago, IL 60606
Ph: (312)981-6770 (312)981-6772
Fax: **(312)265-2908**
E-mail: info@estheticacademy.org
URL: http://www.estheticacademy.org
Contact: Mr. Joseph M. Jackson CAE, Exec. Dir.

2363 ■ American Academy of Fixed Prosthodontics (AAFP) (12357)
c/o Dr. Richard D. Jordan, Treas.
36 N Mission Hills Ct.
Arden, NC 28704-5500
Free: (866)254-0280
Fax: (866)890-5657
E-mail: aafpjordan@bellsouth.net
URL: http://www.fixedprosthodontics.org
Contact: **Stephen F. Rosenstiel, Pres.**

2364 ■ American Academy of Gold Foil Operators (AAGFO) (14601)
c/o Dr. Robert C. Keene, Sec.
1 Woods End Rd.
Etna, NH 03750-4318
Ph: (603)643-2899
E-mail: dmdsmile@gmail.com
URL: http://www.aagfo.org
Contact: **Dr. Richard W. Nash, Pres.-Elect**

2365 ■ American Academy of the History of Dentistry (AAHD) (12359)
684 W Napa St.
Sonoma, CA 95476
Fax: (617)731-8724
E-mail: info@histden.org
URL: http://www.histden.org
Contact: **Peter Meyerhof PhD, Pres.**

2366 ■ American Academy of Maxillofacial Prosthetics (AAMP) (12749)
UT MD Anderson Cancer Center
1515 Holcomber Blvd., Unit 1445
Houston, TX 77030-4009
E-mail: mchamber@mdanderson.org
URL: http://www.maxillofacialprosth.org/Home.html
Contact: **Dr. Robert M. Taft, Pres.**

2367 ■ American Academy of Oral and Maxillofacial Radiology (AAOMR) (14606)
PO Box 231422
New York, NY 10023
Ph: **(304)293-3773**
Fax: **(304)293-2859**
E-mail: angelopoulosc@gmail.com
URL: http://www.aaomr.org
Contact: Dr. Christos Angelopoulos DDS, Exec. Dir.

2368 ■ American Academy of Oral Medicine (AAOM) (14607)
PO Box 2016
Edmonds, WA 98020-9516
Ph: (425)778-6162
Fax: (425)771-9588
E-mail: info@aaom.com
URL: http://www.aaom.com
Contact: **Carol Anne Murdoch-Kinch DDS, VP**

2369 ■ American Academy of Periodontology (AAP) (14611)
737 N Michigan Ave., Ste.800
Chicago, IL 60611-6660
Ph: (312)787-5518
Free: (800)282-4867
Fax: (312)787-3670
E-mail: member.services@perio.org
URL: http://www.perio.org
Contact: **Donald S. Clem, Pres.**

2370 ■ American Academy of Restorative Dentistry (AARD) (14110)
Southwestern Medical Found.
2305 Cedar Springs Rd., Ste.150
Dallas, TX 75201
E-mail: admin@restorativeacademy.com
URL: http://www.restorativeacademy.com
Contact: **Dr. Alan H. Brodine, Pres.**

2371 ■ American Association of Dental Boards (12344)
211 E Chicago Ave., Ste.760
Chicago, IL 60611
Ph: (312)440-7464
Fax: (312)440-3525
E-mail: info@dentalboards.org
URL: **http://dentalboards.org**
Contact: Ms. Molly Nadler, Exec. Dir.

2372 ■ American Association of Endodontists I American Board of Endodontics (ABE) (14351)
211 E Chicago Ave., Ste.1100
Chicago, IL 60611-2691
Ph: (312)266-7310
Free: (800)872-3636

Fax: (312)266-9867
E-mail: abe@aae.org
URL: http://www.aae.org/certboard
Contact: **Dr. Stephen J. Clark, Pres.**

2373 ■ American Association of Women Dentists (AAWD) (14622)
216 W Jackson Blvd., Ste.625
Chicago, IL 60606
Free: (800)920-2293
Fax: (312)750-1203
E-mail: info@aawd.org
URL: http://www.aawd.org
Contact: **Judith Belitz DDS, Pres.**

2374 ■ American Board of Orthodontics (ABO) (12383)
401 N Lindbergh Blvd., Ste.300
St. Louis, MO 63141-7839
Ph: (314)432-6130
Fax: (314)432-8170
E-mail: info@americanboardortho.com
URL: http://www.americanboardortho.com
Contact: **Dr. Barry S. Briss, Pres.**

2375 ■ American Endodontic Society (AES) (12366)
265 N Main St.
Glen Ellyn, IL 60137
Ph: (773)519-4879
Fax: (630)858-0525
E-mail: n2dontics@gmail.com
URL: http://www.aesoc.com
Contact: **Dr. Michael E. Bowman, Pres.**

2376 ■ American Equilibration Society (AES) (14638)
207 E Ohio St., Ste.399
Chicago, IL 60611
Ph: (847)965-2888
Fax: (609)573-5064
E-mail: exec@aes-tmj.org
URL: http://www.aes-tmj.org
Contact: **John T. Green, Pres.**

2377 ■ American Orthodontic Society (AOS) (12625)
11884 Greenville Ave., Ste.112
Dallas, TX 75243-3537
Free: (800)448-1601
Fax: **(972)234-4290**
E-mail: aos@orthodontics.com
URL: http://www.orthodontics.com
Contact: Tom Chapman, Exec. Dir.

2378 ■ American Prosthodontic Society (APS) (14642)
303 W Madison St., Ste.2650
Chicago, IL 60611
Ph: (312)981-6780
Fax: **(312)265-2908**
E-mail: **frank.lauciello@ivoclarvivadent.us.com**
URL: http://www.prostho.org
Contact: **Dr. Frank Lauciello, Exec. Dir.**

2379 ■ American Society of Master Dental Technologists (ASMDT) (14646)
146-21 13th Ave.
Whitestone, NY 11357-2420
Ph: (718)746-8355 **(631)539-8459**
Fax: (718)746-8355
E-mail: vinnie@asmdt.com
URL: http://www.asmdt.com
Contact: Sue Heppenheimer, Exec. Dir.

2380 ■ Association of State and Territorial Dental Directors (ASTDD) (14649)
1838 Fieldcrest Dr.
Sparks, NV 89434
Ph: (775)626-5008
Fax: (775)626-9268
E-mail: **mmsnow@dhhs.state.nh.us**
URL: http://www.astdd.org
Contact: **Margaret M. Snow DMD, Pres.**

2381 ■ Holistic Dental Association (HDA) (12416)
1825 Ponce de Leon Blvd., No. 148
Coral Gables, FL 33134
Ph: **(305)356-7338**
Fax: **(305)468-6359**
E-mail: **director@holisticdental.org**
URL: http://www.holisticdental.org
Contact: **Roberta Glasser, Exec. Dir.**

2382 ■ International College of Dentists (ICD) (14667)
1010 Rockville Pike, Ste.510
Rockville, MD 20852-1482
Ph: (240)403-7246
Fax: (240)403-7256
E-mail: centraloffice@icd.org
URL: http://www.icd.org
Contact: **Dr. John V. Hinterman, Sec. Gen.**

2383 ■ National Association of Dental Laboratories (NADL) (1921)
325 John Knox Rd., No. L103
Tallahassee, FL 32303
Ph: (850)205-5626 **(850)510-7948**
Free: (800)950-1150
Fax: (850)222-0053
E-mail: nadl@nadl.org
URL: http://www.nadl.org
Contact: Mr. Bennett Napier CAE, Exec. Dir.

2384 ■ National Board for Certification in Dental Laboratory Technology (NBC) (12656)
325 John Knox Rd., No. L103
Tallahassee, FL 32303
Ph: (850)205-5627
Free: (800)684-5310
Fax: (850)222-0053
E-mail: **bennett@nbccert.org**
URL: http://www.nbccert.org
Contact: Bennett Napier CAE, Exec. Dir.

2385 ■ National Dental Association (NDA) (12431)
3517 16th St. NW
Washington, DC 20010
Ph: (202)588-1697
Free: **(877)628-3368**
Fax: (202)588-1244
E-mail: **rsjohns@ndaonline.org**
URL: http://www.ndaonline.org
Contact: Robert S. Johns, Exec. Dir.

2386 ■ National Dental Hygienists' Association (NDHA) (12432)
PO Box 22463
Tampa, FL 33622
Free: (800)234-1096
E-mail: forndha@aol.com
URL: http://ndhaonline.org
Contact: **T. Carla Newbern RDH, Pres.-Elect**

2387 ■ National Denturist Association (NDA) (12433)
PO Box 308
Towanda, PA 18848
Free: (888)599-7958
Fax: (570)265-0239
E-mail: denture@sosbbs.com
URL: http://www.nationaldenturist.com
Contact: **Bruce Anderson, Pres.-Elect**

2388 ■ Pierre Fauchard Academy (PFA) (14687)
PO Box 3718
Mesquite, NV 89024-3718
Ph: (702)345-2950
Free: (800)232-0099
Fax: (702)345-5031
E-mail: centraloffice@fauchard.org
URL: http://www.fauchard.org
Contact: Judith D. Kozal, Exec. Dir.

2389 ■ Special Care Dentistry Association (SCDA) (12555)
401 N Michigan Ave., Ste.2200
Chicago, IL 60611
Ph: (312)527-6764
Fax: (312)673-6663
E-mail: scda@scdaonline.org
URL: http://www.scdonline.org
Contact: **Meghan Carey, Exec. Dir.**

Dermatology

2390 ■ American Academy of Dermatology (AAD) (14692)
PO Box 4014
Schaumburg, IL 60168
Ph: (847)240-1280
Free: (866)503-SKIN
Fax: (847)240-1859
E-mail: tsmith@aad.org
URL: http://www.aad.org
Contact: **Daniel M. Siegel MS, Pres.-Elect**

2391 ■ American Dermatological Association (ADA) (14422)
c/o Julie Odessky, Exec. Mgr.
PO Box 551301
Davie, FL 33355
Ph: (954)452-1113
Fax: (305)945-7063
E-mail: ameriderm1930@aol.com
URL: http://www.amer-derm-assn.org
Contact: **Marianne O'Donoghue, Pres.**

2392 ■ American Osteopathic College of Dermatology (AOCD) (14697)
PO Box 7525
Kirksville, MO 63501
Ph: (660)665-2184
Free: (800)449-2623
Fax: (660)627-2623
E-mail: execdirector@aocd.org
URL: http://www.aocd.org
Contact: **Marsha A. Wise, Exec. Dir.**

2393 ■ American Society for Dermatologic Surgery (ASDS) (12443)
5550 Meadowbrook Dr., Ste.120
Rolling Meadows, IL 60008
Ph: (847)956-0900 (847)956-9125
Fax: (847)956-0999
E-mail: **kduerdoth@asds.net**
URL: http://www.asds.net
Contact: Katherine J. Svedman Duerdoth CAE, Exec. Dir.

2394 ■ International Psoriasis Council (IPC)
2626 Cole Ave., Ste.400
Dallas, TX 75204
Ph: (214)369-0406
Fax: (214)242-3391
E-mail: info@psoriasiscouncil.org
URL: http://www.psoriasiscouncil.org
Contact: Dr. Peter Van de Kerkhof, Pres.
Founded: 2004. **Multinational. Description:** Aims to advance research and treatment of psoriasis. Provides a forum for collaboration, innovation and education among health professionals and researchers. Implements programs to promote a better understanding of psoriasis.

2395 ■ International Society of Dermatology (ISD) (14708)
2323 N State St., No. 30
Bunnell, FL 32110
Ph: (386)437-4405
Fax: (386)437-4427
E-mail: info@intsocderm.org
URL: http://www.intsocderm.org
Contact: **Francisco Kerdel MD, Pres.**

2396 ■ Pacific Dermatologic Association (PDA) (14716)
575 Market St., Ste.2125
San Francisco, CA 94105
Ph: (415)927-5729
Free: **(888)388-8815**
Fax: **(415)764-4915**
E-mail: pda@hp-assoc.com
URL: http://www.pacificderm.org
Contact: Kent Lindeman CMP, Exec. Dir.

Disease

2397 ■ Answer Africa
203 E Avenida San Juan
San Clemente, CA 92672
Ph: (949)498-5274
Fax: (949)498-5280
E-mail: answerafrica@gmail.com
URL: http://www.answerafrica.org
Contact: Makena Marangu, Co-Founder
Multinational. Description: Provides Africa with critical health interventions by focusing on fighting malaria through the distribution of insecticide treated mosquito nets. Offers cost-effective delivery of mosquito nets to the most remote, hard-to-reach rural areas.

2398 ■ Global Network for Neglected Tropical Diseases
2000 Pennsylvania Ave. NW, Ste.7100
Washington, DC 20006
Ph: (202)842-5025
E-mail: globalnetwork@sabin.org
URL: http://globalnetwork.org
Contact: Anjana Padmanabhan, Contact
Founded: 2006. **Multinational. Description:** Strives to raise awareness, political will and funding to control and eliminate the most common neglected tropical diseases (NTDs). Promotes the implementation, research, advocacy and policy efforts of the NTD community at the local, national, and international levels. Supports strategies to advocate for and implement NTD control and elimination programs.

2399 ■ Norrie Disease Association (NDA)
PO Box 3244
Munster, IN 46321
E-mail: joinnda@gmail.com
URL: http://www.norriedisease.org
Contact: Bruce Maguire, Pres.
Founded: 2006. **Membership Dues:** individual, $15 (annual). **Description:** Promotes public awareness about Norrie Disease. Provides support and information to people with Norrie Disease and their families. Encourages and helps fund research on Norrie Disease and its associated symptoms.

Electroencephalography

2400 ■ American Clinical Neurophysiology Society (ACNS) (12487)
PO Box 30
Bloomfield, CT 06002
Ph: (860)243-3977
Fax: (860)286-0787
E-mail: info@acns.org
URL: http://www.acns.org
Contact: **Douglas R. Nordli Jr., Pres.**

Electrolysis

2401 ■ American Electrology Association (AEA) (14308)
6 Market Pl., Ste.1
Essex Junction, VT 05452
Ph: **(802)879-1898**
E-mail: infoaea@electrology.com
URL: http://www.electrology.com
Contact: **Leslie Quinn Cody CPE, Contact**

2402 ■ Society for Clinical and Medical Hair Removal (SCMHR) (12494)
2424 Amer. Ln.
Madison, WI 53704-3102
Ph: (608)443-2470 **(361)991-6152**
Fax: (608)443-2474
E-mail: homeoffice@scmhr.org
URL: http://www.scmhr.org
Contact: Nedra D. Lockhart, Pres.

Emergency Aid

2403 ■ American Ambulance Association (AAA) (14823)
8400 Westpark Dr., 2nd Fl.
McLean, VA 22102
Ph: (703)610-9018
Free: (800)523-4447
Fax: (703)610-0210
E-mail: jjohnson@lifeemsinc.com
URL: http://www.the-aaa.org
Contact: **Jimmy Johnson, Pres.-Elect**

2404 ■ Association of Air Medical Services (AAMS) (14548)
909 N Washington St., Ste.410
Alexandria, VA 22314-3143
Ph: (703)836-8732
Fax: (703)836-8920
E-mail: dmancuso@aams.org
URL: http://www.aams.org
Contact: Dawn M. Mancuso CAE, Exec. Dir.

Emergency Medicine

2405 ■ American College of Emergency Physicians (ACEP) (12506)
PO Box 619911
Irving, TX 75038-2522
Ph: (972)550-0911
Free: (800)798-1822
Fax: (972)580-2816
E-mail: execdirector@acep.org
URL: http://www.acep.org
Contact: Dean Wilkerson MBA, Exec. Dir.

2406 ■ Emergency Nurses Association (ENA) (14568)
915 Lee St.
Des Plaines, IL 60016-6569
Ph: (847)460-4095
Free: (800)900-9659
Fax: (847)460-4002
E-mail: **execoffice@ena.org**
URL: http://www.ena.org
Contact: David A. Westman MBA, Exec. Dir.

2407 ■ Medics Without Borders (MWB)
PO Box 35
Woodbridge, VA 22194
Ph: (703)268-4774
E-mail: info@medicswithoutborders.org
URL: http://www.medicswithoutborders.org
Contact: Adomako Adjapong, Founder/Pres.
Multinational. Description: Aims to provide preventive medicine/primary healthcare, health education and emergency medical technology and services to care for the people in underserved communities in developing countries throughout the world. Promotes the creation of sustainable infrastructures which encourage local capacity building and professional development in health promotion and preventive medicine.

2408 ■ National Association of State EMS Officials (NASEMSO) (12515)
201 Park Washington Ct.
Falls Church, VA 22046-4527
Ph: (703)538-1799
Fax: (703)241-5603

E-mail: info@nasemso.org
URL: http://www.nasemso.org
Contact: **Dia Gainor, Exec. Dir.**

Endocrinology

2409 ■ Endocrine Society (14591)
8401 Connecticut Ave., Ste.900
Chevy Chase, MD 20815-5817
Ph: (301)941-0200 (301)941-0210
Free: (888)363-6274
Fax: (301)941-0259
E-mail: societyservices@endo-society.org
URL: http://www.endo-society.org
Contact: **Kelly E. Mayo PhD, Pres.**

Environmental Health

2410 ■ Environment and Human Health, Inc. (EHHI)
1191 Ridge Rd.
North Haven, CT 06473
Ph: (203)248-6582
Fax: (203)288-7571
E-mail: info@ehhi.org
URL: http://www.ehhi.org
Contact: Susan S. Addiss MPh, Contact
Founded: 1997. **Description:** Represents doctors, public health professionals and policy experts committed to the reduction of environmental health risks to individuals. Aims to protect human health from environmental harms through research, education and the promotion of sound public policy. Promotes effective communication of environmental health risks to those exposed and to responsible public and private officials.

Epidemiology

2411 ■ Society for Epidemiologic Research (SER) (14890)
PO Box 990
Clearfield, UT 84089
Ph: (801)525-0231
Fax: (801)525-6549
E-mail: membership@epiresearch.org
URL: http://www.epiresearch.org
Contact: **Mary Haan, Pres.**

Epilepsy

2412 ■ Epilepsy Foundation (13003)
8301 Professional Pl.
Landover, MD 20785-2223
Ph: (301)459-3700
Free: (800)332-1000
Fax: (301)577-2684
E-mail: info@efa.org
URL: http://www.epilepsyfoundation.org
Contact: **Richard P. Denness, Pres./CEO**

Family Planning

2413 ■ Society of Family Planning (SFP)
255 S 17th St., Ste.1102
Philadelphia, PA 19103
Free: (866)584-6758
E-mail: info@societyfp.org
URL: http://www.societyfp.org
Contact: Susan Higginbotham, Exec. Dir.
Founded: 2001. **Membership Dues:** fellowship, $400 (annual). ● junior fellowship, $200 (annual). **Description:** Promotes the advancement of family planning research and education. Provides evidence-based insight to improve clinical care in the areas of contraception and abortion. Fosters scholarly activity and leadership in reproductive health and family planning. **Awards:** Large and Small Research Grants.

Frequency: annual. **Type:** monetary. **Recipient:** for interdisciplinary research in the biological, medical, epidemiological, behavioral and social sciences related to family planning.

Gastroenterology

2414 ■ American Celiac Disease Alliance (ACDA)
2504 Duxbury Pl.
Alexandria, VA 22308
Ph: (703)622-3331
E-mail: info@americanceliac.org
URL: http://americanceliac.org
Contact: Andrea Levario, Exec. Dir.
Founded: 2003. **Members:** 27. **Description:** Represents the needs of patients, researchers, food manufacturers and others committed to serving the celiac community. Aims to improve the lives of individuals with celiac disease by raising awareness, education, advocacy and policy work.

2415 ■ American College of Gastroenterology (ACG) (14644)
PO Box 342260
Bethesda, MD 20827-2260
Ph: (301)263-9000
E-mail: mediaonly@acg.gi.org
URL: http://www.acg.gi.org
Contact: **Lawrence R. Schiller MD, Pres.-Elect**

2416 ■ American Neurogastroenterology and Motility Society (ANMS) (14922)
45685 Harmony Ln.
Belleville, MI 48111
Ph: (734)699-1130
Fax: (734)699-1136
E-mail: admin@motilitysociety.org
URL: http://www.motilitysociety.org
Contact: **Satish Rao MD, Pres.**

2417 ■ Society of American Gastrointestinal and Endoscopic Surgeons (SAGES) (1949)
11300 W Olympic Blvd., Ste.600
Los Angeles, CA 90064
Ph: (310)437-0544
Fax: (310)437-0585
E-mail: webmaster@sages.org
URL: http://www.sages.org
Contact: **Steven D. Schwaitzberg, Pres.-Elect**

2418 ■ Society of Gastroenterology Nurses and Associates (SGNA) (12582)
401 N Michigan Ave.
Chicago, IL 60611
Ph: (312)321-5165
Free: (800)245-7462
Fax: (312)673-6694
E-mail: sgna@smithbucklin.com
URL: http://www.sgna.org
Contact: **Dale West, Exec. Dir.**

Genetics

2419 ■ National Society of Genetic Counselors (NSGC) (14748)
401 N Michigan Ave.
Chicago, IL 60611
Ph: (312)321-6834 **(312)673-4710**
Fax: (312)673-6972
E-mail: nsgc@nsgc.org
URL: http://www.nsgc.org
Contact: Ms. Meghan Carey, Exec. Dir.

Gerontology

2420 ■ American Aging Association (AGE) (15029)
c/o Mark A. Smith, Exec. Dir.
Dept. of Pathology
2103 Cornell Rd., Rm. 5125
Cleveland, OH 44106
Ph: (216)368-3671
Free: (800)732-0999
Fax: (216)368-8964
E-mail: **ameraging@aol.com**
URL: http://www.americanaging.org
Contact: **Holly Brown-Borg PhD, Pres.**

2421 ■ American Geriatrics Society (AGS) (12618)
350 5th Ave., Ste.801
New York, NY 10118
Ph: (212)308-1414
Free: **(800)247-4779**
Fax: (212)832-8646
E-mail: info@americangeriatrics.org
URL: http://www.americangeriatrics.org
Contact: **Jennie Chin Hansen, CEO**

Hand

2422 ■ American Association for Hand Surgery (AAHS) (15048)
900 Cummings Ctr., Ste.221-U
Beverly, MA 01915
Ph: **(978)927-8330**
Free: (800)333-8835
Fax: **(978)524-8890**
E-mail: **steven.mccabe@louisville.edu**
URL: http://www.handsurgery.org
Contact: **Steven McCabe MD, Pres.**

2423 ■ American Society of Hand Therapists (ASHT) (14769)
15000 Commerce Pkwy., Ste.C
Mount Laurel, NJ 08054
Ph: (856)380-6856
Fax: (856)439-0525
E-mail: asht@asht.org
URL: http://www.asht.org
Contact: **Jerry Coverdale OTR, Pres.**

Health

2424 ■ AcademyHealth (12645)
1150 17th St. NW, Ste.600
Washington, DC 20036
Ph: (202)292-6700
Fax: (202)292-6800
URL: http://www.academyhealth.org
Contact: **Lisa Simpson MB, Pres./CEO**

2425 ■ American Health Planning Association (AHPA) (12956)
7245 Arlington Blvd., Ste.300
Falls Church, VA 22042
Ph: (703)573-3103 **(804)425-8867**
Fax: (703)573-3103
E-mail: info@ahpanet.org
URL: http://www.ahpanet.org
Contact: Karen Cameron MPH, Exec. Dir.

2426 ■ Federation of Associations of Regulatory Boards (FARB) (12653)
1466 Techny Rd.
Northbrook, IL 60062
Ph: (847)559-3272
Fax: (847)714-9796
E-mail: farb@farb.org
URL: http://www.farb.org
Contact: **Dale J. Atkinson, Exec. Dir.**

2427 ■ United Methodist Association of Health and Welfare Ministries (UMA) (12689)
407-B Corporate Center Dr., Ste.B
Vandalia, OH 45377
Ph: (937)415-3624
Free: (800)411-9901
Fax: (937)222-7364
E-mail: uma@umassociation.org
URL: http://www.umassociation.org
Contact: **Mr. Stephen L. Vinson, Pres./CEO**

Health Care

2428 ■ ACCESS Health International
3053 P St. NW
Washington, DC 20007
E-mail: info@accessh.org
URL: http://accessh.org
Contact: William A. Haseltine PhD, Founder/Pres.
Multinational. Description: Aims to improve the delivery of high quality, affordable health services in low, middle and high income countries. Supports initiatives and programs designed to create greater access to high quality affordable health care.

2429 ■ Amazonas Hope for Health
c/o Dr. Ruth A. Hayes, Treas.
15 Peterson Pl.
Wilmington, OH 45177
Ph: (937)383-3382
E-mail: kholten@cinci.rr.com
URL: http://amazonashopeforhealth.com
Contact: Dr. Sandra Riegler, Pres.
Founded: 2008. **Multinational. Description:** Aims to provide primary healthcare services in remote regions of the Brazil's Amazon State. Offers periodic primary health and dental care for adults and children.

2430 ■ Ambassadors for Sustained Health (ASH)
3 Petrel St.
West Roxbury, MA 02132
Ph: (646)481-0844
URL: http://weareash.org
Contact: Michelle Milee Chang, Founder/CEO
Multinational. Description: Aims to build community centers to holistically improve health in impoverished areas. Works to provide quality healthcare, prevent the perpetuation of disease and empower the community.

2431 ■ American Chinese Medical Exchange Society (ACMES)
15 New England Executive Park
Burlington, MA 01803
Ph: (781)791-5066
Fax: (781)402-0284
E-mail: info@acmes.net
URL: http://acmes2.info
Contact: Dr. June Kong, Pres.
Founded: 2008. **Multinational. Description:** Represents Chinese American physicians and researchers in diverse medical and healthcare fields. Contributes to the improvement of overall quality of healthcare and spread of evidence-based medicine in China through various exchange and professional education programs and medical publications. **Additional Websites:** http://www.acmes.net.

2432 ■ Cambodian Health Professionals Association of America (CHPAA)
1025 Atlantic Ave.
Long Beach, CA 90813
Ph: (562)491-9292
Fax: (562)495-1878
E-mail: membership@chpaa.org
URL: http://www.chpaa.org
Contact: Song Tan MD, Pres.
Multinational. Description: Aims to promote health through service and education. Provides a network of communication among all Cambodian health professionals living in America and abroad. Conducts health mission to provide primary medical care to underserved areas in Cambodia.

2433 ■ Forward in Health (FIH)
192 Lawrence St.
Gardner, MA 01440
Ph: (978)632-7166
E-mail: metzmn6@gmail.com
URL: http://www.forwardinhealth.org
Contact: John Mulqueen MD, Pres.
Founded: 2006. **Multinational. Description:** Aims to improve the health conditions and dignity of the people in and around Les Cayes, Haiti. Provides life-

sustaining healthcare by working hand-in-hand with local institutions in Les Cayes.

2434 ■ Friends for Health in Haiti (FHH)
PO Box 122
Pewaukee, WI 53072
Ph: (262)227-9581
Fax: (866)491-5406
E-mail: friendsforhealth@gmail.com
URL: http://www.friendsforhealthinhaiti.org
Contact: Dr. Catherine Wolf, Exec. Dir.
Founded: 2006. **Multinational. Description:** Aims to improve the health status of the people of Haiti by providing high quality health care. Develops community-based model of care by empowering local communities to achieve better access to primary and preventive medical services.

2435 ■ Global Flying Hospitals (GFH)
4440 PGA Blvd., Ste.600
Palm Beach Gardens, FL 33410
Ph: (855)434-4747
E-mail: contactus@globalflyinghospitals.org
URL: http://www.globalflyinghospitals.org
Contact: Neill F. Newton, Chm./Founder
Founded: 2001. **Multinational. Description:** Aims to bring hope, healing and healthcare in developing countries on board aircraft equipped with self-contained surgical suites and roll-off medical support. Works to provide medical treatment for the needy, train medical professionals and supply modular transportable field clinics and hospitals, as well as medical equipment and medicines.

2436 ■ Health Empowering Humanity (HEH)
PO Box 300551
Houston, TX 77230
Free: (888)210-3438
Fax: (888)210-3438
E-mail: info@heh.org
URL: http://www.heh.org
Contact: Geoff Preidis, Co-Founder/Pres.
Multinational. Description: Empowers the most underprivileged communities to improve their quality of life through access to quality basic medical care. Aims to develop a sustainable model of community-based healthcare by collaborating with local populations in resource-poor nations and benefactors and expert volunteers in resource-rich nations.

2437 ■ I Care Grace International (ICGI)
400 Riverside Ave.
Charlottesville, VA 22902
Ph: (434)973-6889
URL: http://icaregrace.org
Contact: Jenifer Kilel, Pres./Founder
Multinational. Description: Promotes long term healthcare in rural areas. Organizes a medical mission internationally to reach and assist disadvantaged people through community outreach.

2438 ■ Inter-American Health Alliance
2301 Vanderbilt Pl.
PMB 351804
Nashville, TN 37235
Ph: (703)725-9320
E-mail: interamericanhealth@gmail.com
URL: http://www.interamericanhealth.org
Contact: Brent Savoie, Pres.
Multinational. Description: Aims to support community health organizations working with marginalized populations in the western highlands of Guatemala. Improves access to health care and health education through the development of innovative collaborations between governmental, non-governmental and educational institutions.

2439 ■ International Healthcare Volunteers (IHCV)
PO Box 8231
Trenton, NJ 08650
Ph: (609)259-8807
Fax: (609)259-6108

E-mail: ihcvinfo@gmail.com
URL: http://www.ihcv.org
Contact: Charletta Ayers, Chair
Founded: 2001. **Multinational. Description:** Provides health care to women and their families in underserved areas of the world. Supports sustainable programs and offers continuing medical education for health professionals.

2440 ■ MED25 International
PO Box 1459
Mercer Island, WA 98040
Ph: (206)779-0655
Fax: (206)275-4616
E-mail: rebecca@med25.org
URL: http://med25.org
Contact: Rebecca Conte Okelo, Exec. Dir.
Founded: 2006. **Multinational. Description:** Strives to provide all individuals with access to affordable healthcare. Promotes access to competent, culturally appropriate and affordable health care in impoverished communities.

2441 ■ A Promise of Health
419 E Fraser Dr.
Pueblo West, CO 81007
Ph: (719)547-1995
E-mail: info@promiseofhealth.org
URL: http://www.promiseofhealth.org
Contact: Barbara Grannell, Co-Founder/Exec. Dir.
Founded: 2001. **Multinational. Description:** Aims to bring safe, effective and affordable healthcare to the poor and needy of rural Mexico. Provides healthcare solutions using homeopathic medicine and practitioners.

2442 ■ Women for World Health
16291 Fantasia Ln.
Huntington Beach, CA 92649
Ph: (714)846-4524
E-mail: information@womenforworldhealth.org
URL: http://www.womenforworldhealth.org
Contact: Denise Cucurny, Pres./Co-founder
Founded: 2006. **Multinational. Description:** Aims to evaluate and identify community health care needs in the United States and in developing nations. Provides support through volunteer medical missions.

2443 ■ World Health Ambassador (WHA)
7611 Little River Tpke., Ste.108W
Annandale, VA 22003
Ph: (703)658-7060
E-mail: info@whausa.org
URL: http://www.whausa.org
Contact: Thien Do, Dir.
Founded: 2007. **Multinational. Description:** Seeks to deliver health care and emergency relief to underserved and underprivileged populations in the United States and abroad, as well as to the victims of natural disasters. Provides humanitarian relief to communities that are in desperate need of medical and dental assistance.

Health Care Products

2444 ■ American Association for Homecare (AAHomecare) (12963)
2011 Crystal Dr., Ste.725
Arlington, VA 22202
Ph: (703)836-6263 **(703)535-1880**
Fax: (703)836-6730
E-mail: info@aahomecare.org
URL: http://www.aahomecare.org
Contact: Mr. Tyler Wilson, Pres./CEO

Health Professionals

2445 ■ International Healthcare Leadership
Columbia Univ. Medical Center
3959 Broadway, 8 N
New York, NY 10032
Ph: (212)305-5475

E-mail: info@ihleaders.org
URL: http://ihleaders.org
Contact: Dr. David P. Roye Jr., Pres./CEO
Founded: 2006. **Multinational. Description:** Aims to train Chinese healthcare professionals on incorporating healthcare public policy into healthcare reform and hospital management. Offers tools, training and forums to provide better health services for underserved communities.

Health Services

2446 ■ American Correctional Health Services Association (ACHSA) (15249)
3990 Bullard Rd.
Monticello, GA 31064
Free: **(855)825-5559**
Fax: **(866)365-3838**
E-mail: admin@achsa.org
URL: http://www.achsa.org
Contact: **Ron McCuan, Pres.**

2447 ■ American Medical Group Association (AMGA) (12707)
One Prince St.
Alexandria, VA 22314-3318
Ph: (703)838-0033
Fax: (703)548-1890
E-mail: dfisher@amga.org
URL: http://www.amga.org
Contact: Dr. Donald W. Fisher CAE, Pres./CEO

2448 ■ Community Health International (CHI)
59 Windsor Rd.
Brookline, MA 02445
Ph: (617)739-2638
E-mail: contact@communityhealthinternational.org
URL: http://www.communityhealthinternational.org
Contact: Pierre Cremieux PhD, Pres.
Founded: 2007. **Multinational. Description:** Aims to support the provision of health care to communities affected by conflict, natural disasters and epidemics. Improves the health and well being of communities emerging from crises by providing primary health care programs, access to safe, clean water, preventative health education and programs for traumatized individuals and communities.

Hearing Impaired

2449 ■ Academy of Rehabilitative Audiology (ARA)
PO Box 2323
Albany, NY 12220-0323
Fax: (866)547-3073
E-mail: ara@audrehab.org
URL: http://www.audrehab.org
Contact: **Joseph J. Montano EdD, Pres.**

2450 ■ ADARA: Professionals Networking for Excellence in Service Delivery with Individuals who are Deaf or Hard of Hearing (ADARA) (12717)
PO Box 480
Myersville, MD 21773
E-mail: abcritchfield@dhr.state.ga.us
URL: http://www.adara.org
Contact: **Barry Critchfield, Pres.-Elect**

2451 ■ Conference of Educational Administrators of Schools and Programs for the Deaf (CEASD) (12725)
PO Box 1778
St. Augustine, FL 32085-1778
Ph: (904)810-5200 (904)823-9013
Free: **(866)697-8805**
Fax: (904)810-5525
E-mail: nationaloffice@ceasd.org
URL: http://www.ceasd.org
Contact: Joseph P. Finnegan Jr., Exec. Dir.

2452 ■ Council of American Instructors of the Deaf (CAID) (12726)
PO Box 377
Bedford, TX 76095-0377
Ph: (817)354-8414 **(585)230-3369**
Fax: **(585)533-1552**
E-mail: caid@swbell.net
URL: http://www.caid.org
Contact: Helen Lovato, Office Mgr.

2453 ■ Council on Education of the Deaf (CED) (14069)
Eastern Kentucky Univ.
Wallace 245
Richmond, KY 40475
Ph: (859)622-1043
Fax: (859)622-4443
E-mail: karen.dilka@eku.edu
URL: **http://councilondeafed.org**
Contact: Dr. Karen Dilka, Exec. Dir.

2454 ■ International Hearing Dog (IHDI) (15304)
5901 E 89th Ave.
Henderson, CO 80640
Ph: (303)287-3277
Fax: (303)287-3425
E-mail: ihdi@aol.com
URL: http://www.ihdi.org
Contact: **Valerie Foss-Brugger, Exec. Dir.**

2455 ■ International Hearing Society (IHS) (12735)
16880 Middlebelt Rd., Ste.4
Livonia, MI 48154-3374
Ph: (734)522-7200
E-mail: **kmennillo@ihsinfo.org**
URL: http://ihsinfo.org
Contact: Kathleen Mennillo MBA, Exec. Dir.

2456 ■ Registry of Interpreters for the Deaf (RID) (13117)
333 Commerce St.
Alexandria, VA 22314
Ph: (703)838-0030 **(703)838-0459**
Fax: (703)838-0454
E-mail: admin@rid.org
URL: http://www.rid.org
Contact: Clay Nettles MA, Exec. Dir.

Heart Disease

2457 ■ Society for Heart Valve Disease (SHVD)
900 Cummings Ctr., Ste.221-U
Beverly, MA 01915
Ph: (978)927-8330
Fax: (978)524-8890
E-mail: secretrariat@shvd.org
URL: http://www.shvd.org
Contact: Robert O. Bonow, Pres.
Founded: 1999. **Multinational. Description:** Advances the practice, science and art of treating heart valve disease. Aims to undertake, promote, support and encourage research, in the causes, prevention, and the treatment of heart valve disease. Creates a public awareness about heart valve disease or any related cardiac disease, illness or condition.

Hematology

2458 ■ American Society of Pediatric Hematology/Oncology (ASPHO) (12754)
4700 W Lake Ave.
Glenview, IL 60025-1485
Ph: (847)375-4716
Fax: **(877)734-9557**
E-mail: info@aspho.org
URL: http://www.aspho.org
Contact: Cynthia Porter, Exec. Dir.

Hepatology

2459 ■ American Liver Foundation (ALF) (1977)
39 Broadway, Ste.2700
New York, NY 10006
Ph: (212)668-1000
Free: (800)223-0179
Fax: (212)483-8179
URL: http://www.liverfoundation.org
Contact: **Newton Guerin, Pres./CEO**

Holistic Medicine

2460 ■ Holistic Mentorship Network (HMN)
55 Newton Sparta Rd.
Newton, NJ 07860
Ph: (973)300-1184
Fax: (973)300-1189
E-mail: linda@holisticmentorshipnetwork.com
URL: http://www.holisticmentorshipnetwork.com
Contact: Linda Mitchell, Founder/Exec. Dir.
Founded: 2004. **Multinational. Description:** Represents and lobbies for the entire array of health professionals who practice holistically or with a holistic philosophy in their practice. Facilitates the growth of the holistic profession. Provides a forum for members to connect with other practitioners and create opportunities for business and personal development.

2461 ■ National Association for Holistic Aromatherapy (NAHA) (15083)
PO Box 1868
Banner Elk, NC 28604
Ph: (828)898-6161
Fax: (828)898-1965
E-mail: info@naha.org
URL: http://www.naha.org
Contact: **Kelly Holland Azzaro, Pres.**

Home Care

2462 ■ National Association for Home Care and Hospice (NAHC) (13107)
228 7th St. SE
Washington, DC 20003
Ph: (202)547-7424
Fax: (202)547-3540
E-mail: exec@nahc.org
URL: http://www.nahc.org
Contact: **Andrea Devoti, Chair**

Homeopathy

2463 ■ American Institute of Homeopathy (AIH) (15389)
101 S Whiting St., Ste.16
Alexandria, VA 22304
Ph: **(703)273-5250**
Free: (888)445-9988
Fax: (703)548-7792
E-mail: admin@homeopathyusa.org
URL: http://www.homeopathyusa.org
Contact: **Sandra Chase MD, Pres.**

Hospital

2464 ■ American Association of Healthcare Consultants (AAHC) (12858)
1205 Johnson Ferry Rd., Ste.136-420
Marietta, GA 30068
Ph: **(770)635-8758**
Fax: **(770)874-4401**
E-mail: info@aahcmail.org
URL: http://www.aahc.net

2465 ■ American Hospital Association I Association for Healthcare Resource and Materials Management (AHRMM) (15415)
155 N Wacker Dr.
Chicago, IL 60606
Ph: (312)422-3840 (312)422-3842
Fax: (312)422-4573
E-mail: ahrmm@aha.org
URL: http://www.ahrmm.org
Contact: Deborah Sprindzunas, Exec. Dir.

2466 ■ American Hospital Association I Society for Healthcare Strategy and Market Development (SHSMD) (15439)
155 N Wacker Dr., Ste.400
Chicago, IL 60606
Ph: (312)422-3888
Fax: **(312)278-0883**
E-mail: shsmd@aha.org
URL: http://www.shsmd.org
Contact: Lauren Barnett, Exec. Dir.

2467 ■ Association for Healthcare Foodservice (AHF) (12813)
455 S Fourth St., Ste.650
Louisville, KY 40202
Ph: (502)574-9930 **(502)574-9934**
Free: (888)528-9552
Fax: (502)589-3602
E-mail: info@healthcarefoodservice.org
URL: http://www.healthcarefoodservice.org
Contact: Keith Howard, Exec. VP

2468 ■ Association for Healthcare Philanthropy (AHP) (15414)
313 Park Ave., Ste.400
Falls Church, VA 22046-3303
Ph: (703)532-6243
Fax: (703)532-7170
E-mail: ahp@ahp.org
URL: http://www.ahp.org
Contact: **Ms. Susan J. Doliner FAHP, Chair-Elect**

2469 ■ International Association for Healthcare Security and Safety (IAHSS) (15430)
PO Box 5038
Glendale Heights, IL 60139
Ph: (630)529-3913
Free: (888)353-0990
Fax: (630)529-4139
E-mail: info@iahss.org
URL: http://www.iahss.org
Contact: **Jim Stankevich CHPA, Pres.**

2470 ■ National Association of Healthcare Access Management (NAHAM) (15433)
2025 M St. NW, Ste.800
Washington, DC 20036-2422
Ph: (202)367-1125
Fax: (202)367-2125
E-mail: info@naham.org
URL: http://www.naham.org
Contact: **Steven C. Kemp CAE, Exec. Dir.**

Infectious Diseases

2471 ■ Association for Professionals in Infection Control and Epidemiology (APIC) (15490)
1275 K St. NW, Ste.1000
Washington, DC 20005-4006
Ph: (202)789-1890
Fax: (202)789-1899
E-mail: apicinfo@apic.org
URL: http://www.apic.org
Contact: **Russell N. Olmsted MPH, Pres.**

2472 ■ Global Solutions for Infectious Diseases (GSID)
830 Dubuque Ave.
South San Francisco, CA 94080
Ph: (650)228-7900
Fax: (650)228-7901

E-mail: inquiry@gsid.org
URL: http://www.gsid.org
Contact: Donald P. Francis MD, Co-Founder/Exec.
Dir.
Founded: 2004. **Multinational. Description:** Promotes the development of vaccines and other products to help prevent the spread of infectious diseases in developing countries. Provides assistance and collaborates with organizations focused on public health issues and infectious diseases. Facilitates the access to affordable health solutions for the benefit of the people most in need.

2473 ■ Infectious Diseases Society of America (IDSA) (15491)
1300 Wilson Blvd., Ste.300
Arlington, VA 22209
Ph: (703)299-0200
Free: (866)889-7318
Fax: (703)299-0204
E-mail: info@idsociety.org
URL: http://www.idsociety.org
Contact: **James M. Hughes MD, Pres.**

2474 ■ National Foundation for Infectious Diseases (NFID) (12896)
4733 Bethesda Ave., Ste.750
Bethesda, MD 20814-5278
Ph: (301)656-0003
Fax: (301)907-0878
E-mail: info@nfid.org
URL: http://www.nfid.org
Contact: **Thomas M. File Jr., Pres.-Elect**

International Health

2475 ■ African Medical and Research Foundation (AMREF USA) (2006)
4 W 43rd St., 2nd Fl.
New York, NY 10036
Ph: (212)768-2440
Fax: (212)768-4230
E-mail: **info@amrefusa.org**
URL: **http://www.amrefusa.org**
Contact: Lisa K. Meadowcroft, Exec. Dir.

2476 ■ Ahoto Partnership for Ghana
366 Winthtrop Mail Ctr.
32 Mill St.
Cambridge, MA 02138
E-mail: contact@ahotopartnership.org
URL: http://ahotopartnership.org/ahoto
Contact: Michael Kapps, Pres./Founder
Founded: 2009. **Multinational. Description:** Promotes better health practices and improves health care access in the developing regions of Ghana. Provides information and resources through conferences and health programs.

2477 ■ American College of International Physicians (ACIP) (14270)
9323 Old Mt. Vernon Rd.
Alexandria, VA 22309-2714
Ph: (703)221-1500
Fax: **(703)221-1500**
E-mail: walkwithgod7@gmail.com
URL: http://acip.org
Contact: Alex Yadao MD, Chm./Pres.

2478 ■ American Friends of Guinea (AFG)
12012 Wickchester Ln., Ste.475
Houston, TX 77079
Ph: (713)353-9400
Fax: (713)353-9421
E-mail: info@afguinea.org
URL: http://www.afguinea.org
Contact: Michael P. Carson, Exec. Dir.
Founded: 2006. **Multinational. Description:** Seeks to improve the quality of life of Guinean people by providing medical care and infrastructure. Administers installation of water wells for the provision of safe drinking water. Promotes programs on disease prevention and sanitation.

2479 ■ Andean Health and Development (AHD)
2039 Winnebago St., No. 8
Madison, WI 53704
Ph: (619)788-6833
E-mail: info@andeanhealth.org
URL: http://www.andeanhealth.org
Contact: Dr. David Gaus, Founder/Exec. Dir.
Founded: 1995. **Multinational. Description:** Works to build self-sustaining primary health care systems in rural Ecuador. Provides high quality medical care and training for rural healthcare leaders.

2480 ■ Arise Medical Missions
1350 Grantham Dr.
Sarasota, FL 34234
Ph: (253)355-0179
E-mail: carl@arise.ms
URL: http://www.arise.ms
Contact: Carl Bottorf, Dir.
Multinational. Description: Provides healthcare in restricted access countries. Conducts medical outreaches and trains national and international workers.

2481 ■ Caribbean Health Outreach
4300 W 58th Pl.
Los Angeles, CA 90043
Ph: (626)274-3282
Fax: (323)291-7806
E-mail: healthoutreachinc@sbcglobal.net
URL: http://www.caribbeanhealthoutreachinc.org
Contact: Hope Miller RN, Pres.
Founded: 2001. **Multinational. Description:** Represents professionals and paraprofessionals in the fields of health and education. Promotes health and wellness in the Caribbean region, particularly the underserved, vulnerable and special-need population. Provides health care assistance through educational sessions and symposia, health screenings and distribution of medical equipment and supplies.

2482 ■ ChildAlive
14505 Gilpin Rd.
Silver Spring, MD 20906
Ph: (301)598-1163
E-mail: ian@childalive.net
URL: http://www.childalive.net
Contact: Donald Ian Macdonald MD, Founder/Chm.
Founded: 2004. **Multinational. Description:** Aims to fill the unmet health needs of children and families in the world's poorest countries. Promotes sustainable global health initiatives to make a difference in the health of poor people.

2483 ■ Clinic at a Time (CAAT)
PO Box 14457
Madison, WI 53708
Ph: (608)239-3091
E-mail: mulu@clinicatatime.org
URL: http://clinicatatime.org
Contact: Mulusew Yayehyirad, Founder/Exec. Dir.
Founded: 2007. **Multinational. Description:** Aims to improve the quality of health care for the poor and underprivileged communities in the Province of Gojjam, Ethiopia. Collects and provides medical supplies to those in need. Strives to enhance existing public health care facilities and build new ones. Provides educational materials on disease prevention and health promotion.

2484 ■ Clinicians of the World (COW)
PO Box 116
Rochester, MN 55903
Ph: (612)353-8632
E-mail: help@cliniciansoftheworld.org
URL: http://www.cliniciansoftheworld.org
Contact: Rowlens M. Melduni MD, Pres./CEO
Founded: 2010. **Multinational. Description:** Improves the health of underserved people around the world regardless of culture, religion or political affiliation. Provides specialized medical care, health education and humanitarian aid to underserved population. Offers training and health education to individuals and health care professionals to meet their healthcare needs.

2485 ■ Doctors for United Medical Missions (DrUMM)
313 Tidewater Dr.
Havre de Grace, MD 21078
Ph: (410)688-0691
Fax: (240)331-2417
E-mail: drumm@healingdrumm.org
URL: http://www.healingdrumm.org
Contact: John B. Sampson MD, Founder
Multinational. Description: Aims to improve medical care in developing countries through the performance of collaborative medical projects. Provides medical and surgical care to patients in developing countries. Offers instruction in state-of-the-art medical practices and continuing medical education for healthcare providers abroad.

2486 ■ Dorcas Medical Mission
907 Utica Ave.
Brooklyn, NY 11203
Ph: (718)342-2928
Fax: (718)342-2809
E-mail: info@dorcasmedicalmission.org
URL: http://www.dorcasmedicalmission.org
Contact: Lorna Mullings RN, Pres.
Founded: 2000. **Multinational. Description:** Seeks to alleviate suffering in the developing world through the provision of free medical care. Promotes health and well-being and disease prevention among the economically-disadvantaged, using a holistic approach to the delivery of healthcare in a community setting.

2487 ■ Emofra Africa
1815-B Chain Bridge Rd., Ste.34
McLean, VA 22102
URL: http://www.emofraafrica.org
Contact: Grace Kofi E. Marabe, Founder/Pres.
Multinational. Description: Focuses on improving public health in West Africa. Educates the youth population on HIV prevention. Works with health care professionals to lower the risk of HIV contamination from mother to child.

2488 ■ Engineering World Health (EWH)
The Prizery, Ste.230
302 E Pettigrew St.
Durham, NC 27701
Ph: (919)682-7788
E-mail: info@ewh.org
URL: http://www.ewh.org
Contact: Melissa Beard, Exec. Dir.
Founded: 2001. **Membership Dues:** student, $35 (annual) ● professional, faculty, $125 (annual). **Multinational. Description:** Mobilizes the biomedical engineering community to improve the quality of health care in vulnerable communities of the developing world. Seeks to provide and maintain appropriate medical expertise and technology to underserved nations.

2489 ■ Ghana Medical Mission
248 McNear Dr.
San Rafael, CA 94901
E-mail: info@ghanamedicalmission.org
URL: http://ghanamedicalmission.org
Contact: Dr. Antonia Nicosia, Co-Founder
Multinational. Description: Provides health care services to disadvantaged people in the Central Region of Ghana. Works with local governments and university institutions in fostering knowledge exchange and research collaborations pertaining to medical care.

2490 ■ Global Emergency Care Collaborative (GECC)
2033 W Iowa St., No. 3
Chicago, IL 60622
E-mail: contact@globalemergencycare.org
URL: http://globalemergencycare.org
Contact: Stacey Chamberlain, Contact
Multinational. Description: Aims to improve global health by creating or improving access to quality emergency care in the developing world. Improves access to emergency care for the local people by

training local providers and introducing appropriate medical technology.

2491 ■ Global Health Corps
5 Penn Plz., 2nd Fl.
New York, NY 10001
E-mail: applyinfo@ghcorps.org
URL: http://www.ghcorps.org
Contact: Barbara Bush, Co-Founder/Pres.
Multinational. Description: Aims to mobilize a global community of emerging leaders to build the movement for health equity. Addresses issues of global health, including disparities in access to health care. Fosters an equitable and just global distribution of health services.

2492 ■ Global Health through Education, Training and Service (GHETS)
8 N Main St., Ste.404
Attleboro, MA 02703
Ph: (508)226-5091
URL: http://www.ghets.org
Contact: Caroline Mailloux, Exec. Dir.
Founded: 2002. **Multinational. Description:** Aims to improve health in developing countries through innovations in education and service. Provides start-up grants to local training institutions in low-income countries. Offers technical help to launch and improve programs that prepare and support healthcare workers in rural and poor communities.

2493 ■ Global Health Informatics Partnership (GHIP)
4915 St. Elmo Ave., Ste.402
Bethesda, MD 20814
Ph: (301)657-1291
Fax: (301)657-1296
E-mail: info@ghip.net
URL: http://www.ghip.net
Contact: John H. Holmes PhD, Chm.
Founded: 2010. **Multinational. Description:** Aims to support healthcare systems worldwide through information that improves the quality, safety and effectiveness of services. Establishes and supports an international collaborative learning community focused on the use of healthcare information to improve healthcare delivery. Cultivates networks of health informatics advocates to foster understanding of the benefits, policy implications and resources available to health systems.

2494 ■ Global Health Linkages, Inc. (GHLI)
10810 Hickory Ridge Rd.
Columbia, MD 21044
Ph: (410)202-8868
Fax: (410)992-7553
E-mail: info@globalhealthlinkages.org
URL: http://www.globalhealthlinkages.org
Contact: Suni Jani, CEO
Multinational. Description: Provides people and patients with top quality health care services and information. Works to address health care disparities in a cost efficient technologically innovative and feasible manner.

2495 ■ Global Physicians Corps (GPC)
PO Box 25772
Los Angeles, CA 90025
E-mail: maria@globalphysicians.org
URL: http://www.globalphysicians.org
Contact: Dr. Maria Alikakos, Co-Founder/CEO
Founded: 2006. **Multinational. Description:** Aims to understand and address all factors attributing to global health issues. Provides sustainable solutions to the delivery of healthcare in underserved areas of the global community.

2496 ■ Haiti Healthcare Partners (HHP)
4607 Lakeview Canyon Ave., No. 640
Westlake Village, CA 91361
E-mail: cindigortner@mindspring.com
URL: http://www.haitihealthcare.org
Contact: Cindi Gortner, Contact
Founded: 2005. **Multinational. Description:** Focuses on healthcare and overall welfare of Grande

Colline in Haiti. Funds primary care services through a medical clinic in rural areas of Grande Colline and seeks partnership with other charitable organizations.

2497 ■ Healing Across the Divides
72 Laurel Dr.
Northampton, PA 18067
E-mail: norbert@healingdivides.org
URL: http://www.healingdivides.org
Contact: Norbert Goldfield MD, Exec. Dir.
Founded: 2004. **Multinational. Description:** Supports health care organizations in bridge-building programs to improve health for both Israelis and Palestinians. Seeks to increase clinical knowledge base for both Palestinian and Israeli health professionals. Strives to enhance awareness of health and human rights, in light of the current conflict.

2498 ■ Health and Education Relief for Guyana (HERG)
245-07 Francis Lewis Blvd.
Rosedale, NY 11422
Ph: (347)528-2794
E-mail: info@hergweb.org
URL: http://www.hergweb.org
Contact: Wayne Sampson MD, Founder/Pres.
Founded: 2000. **Multinational. Description:** Seeks to improve the health and well being of communities in need through medical and educational outreach programs in Guyana.

2499 ■ Health Horizons International
Tufts Univ.
Community Health Prog.
112 Packard Ave.
Medford, MA 02155
Ph: (617)627-4299
Fax: (617)627-3072
E-mail: info@hhidr.org
URL: http://hhidr.org
Contact: Laura McNulty, Co-Founder/Exec. Dir.
Founded: 2009. **Multinational. Description:** Aims to improve community health and expand access to quality health care in impoverished communities of the Dominican Republic. Promotes well-being and access to health care through medical service trips with community-based health initiatives.

2500 ■ Health Horizons International
1112 Brown Dr.
Pflugerville, TX 78660
Ph: (512)989-1297
Fax: (512)989-1297
URL: http://healthhi.org
Contact: Dr. Roger Tappa, Contact
Founded: 2002. **Multinational. Description:** Empowers local communities in developing countries to achieve, live and sustain a comfortable life. Promotes primary health care and increases coverage of medical and health care services. Assists in the implementation of local health projects.

2501 ■ Health through Walls (HtW)
12555 Biscayne Blvd., No. 955
North Miami, FL 33181
E-mail: info@healththroughwalls.org
URL: http://www.healththroughwalls.org
Contact: John P. May MD, Pres.
Founded: 2001. **Multinational. Description:** Represents volunteer doctors, nurses and correctional professionals. Provides medical assistance and health care to prisoners of economically disadvantaged countries through public service. Focuses on prevention, identification and management of infectious diseases such as AIDS and tuberculosis.

2502 ■ Honduras Outreach Medical Brigada Relief Effort (HOMBRE)
West Hosp., 14th Fl.
1200 E Broad St.
Richmond, VA 23298-0251

E-mail: hombremcv@gmail.com
URL: http://www.hombremedicine.org
Contact: Dr. Steve Crossman, Contact
Founded: 2000. **Multinational. Description:** Represents an organized team of students, doctors and health professionals working to provide direct medical care and healthcare education to the impoverished population of Honduras. Conducts healthcare programs that the communities can adopt and sustain.

2503 ■ Hope Beyond Hope (HBH)
4230 Harding Rd., Ste.307
Nashville, TN 37205
Ph: (615)292-8299
Fax: (615)835-7993
E-mail: info@hopebeyondhope.com
URL: http://hopebeyondhope.org
Contact: Bruce Wolf, Founder
Founded: 2009. **Multinational. Description:** Works to find innovative solutions to maximize healthcare delivery to the less fortunate in the United States and the world. Aims to minimize and redirect waste of usable medication.

2504 ■ Hope Through Healing Hands (HTHH)
2033 Richard Jones Rd.
Nashville, TN 37215
Ph: (615)386-0045
Fax: (615)386-3041
E-mail: jenny@hopethroughhealinghands.org
URL: http://www.hopethroughhealinghands.org
Contact: Jenny Eaton Dyer PhD, Exec. Dir.
Founded: 2004. **Multinational. Description:** Promotes improved quality of life for citizens and communities around the world using health as a currency for peace. Supports efforts to address issues of child survival and maternal health, clean water, extreme poverty and global diseases such as HIV/AIDS, tuberculosis and Malaria. Sponsors young health professionals, including students, residents and fellows, to participate in its various campaigns and programs.

2505 ■ Horizon International Medical Mission (HIMM)
111 Lions Gate Rd.
Savannah, GA 31419
Ph: (912)308-8799
E-mail: kennedy@himm.org
URL: http://www.himm.org/index.htm
Contact: Dr. Kennedy Kelechi Okere, Founder
Founded: 2000. **Multinational. Description:** Provides free medical care to rural areas in African and Caribbean countries. Sets up local clinics that will involve local healthcare workers in continuous care of patients and maintenance of medical facilities. Works with healthcare institutions in organizing international medical missions for students.

2506 ■ Intermed International (14672)
125-28 Queens Blvd., Ste.538
Kew Gardens, NY 11415
Ph: (212)327-4940 **(646)820-7360**
Fax: (212)327-4940
E-mail: info@dooleyintermed.org
URL: http://www.dooleyintermed.org
Contact: Dr. Verne E. Chaney Jr., Pres./Founder

2507 ■ International Health and Development Network (IHDN)
PO Box 7488
Springfield, IL 62791
E-mail: ihdn@aol.com
URL: http://www.ihdn.org
Contact: Dr. Edem Agamah, Pres.
Founded: 1996. **Multinational. Description:** Aims to help poor villages in developing countries. Supports effective and sustainable primary healthcare programs. Conducts medical missions in small towns and villages in developing countries.

2508 ■ International Medical Alliance (IMA)
PO Box 2727
Rancho Mirage, CA 92270
Ph: (760)485-8963
E-mail: inesallen@internationalmedicalalliance.org
URL: http://www.internationalmedicalalliance.org
Contact: Ines Allen, Founder/Pres.
Founded: 2000. **Multinational. Description:** Provides free medical and dental assistance, training and care for impoverished communities in the developing world. Renders services to hospitals and clinics with the help of medical professionals. Solicits donations of medical equipment and supplies from local hospitals, corporations, foundations and charitable organizations.

2509 ■ Medical Mission Group (MMG)
134 Grove St.
Pearl River, NY 10965
Ph: (845)920-9001
E-mail: dupton@medicalmissiongroup.org
URL: http://www.medicalmissiongroup.org
Contact: Devin Upton, Pres.
Multinational. Description: Provides specialized healthcare services to individuals worldwide who lack sufficient access or financial resources to obtain medical care. Educates and trains local physicians on medical and surgical skills.

2510 ■ mHealth Alliance (mHA)
1800 Massachusetts Ave. NW, Ste.400
Washington, DC 20036
Ph: (202)887-9040
E-mail: info@mhealthalliance.org
URL: http://www.mhealthalliance.org
Contact: Clive Smith, Dir., Global Operations
Founded: 2009. **Multinational. Description:** Seeks to mobilize innovation to deliver quality health services to the furthest reaches of the wireless networks. Advances mHealth through research, advocacy and support for the development of interoperable solutions and sustainable deployment models. Hosts a global online community for resource sharing and collaborative solution generation.

2511 ■ Network Ethiopia
2401 Virginia Ave. NW
Washington, DC 20037
Ph: (202)835-8383
E-mail: info@networke.org
URL: http://www.networke.org
Contact: Rev. John W. Wimberly Jr., Pres.
Founded: 2009. **Multinational. Description:** Seeks to improve the well-being of Ethiopian people by addressing their healthcare needs. Works by identifying small clinics in Ethiopia that need additional funding to expand their services to poor women and children.

2512 ■ Partners for World Health
7 Glasgow Rd.
Scarborough, ME 04074
Ph: (207)885-1011
E-mail: mclellan.elizabeth@gmail.com
URL: http://www.partnersforworldhealth.org
Contact: Elizabeth McLellan, Founder/Pres.
Multinational. Description: Provides primary care services to third world countries and educates people about global health. Collects and distributes discarded medical supplies to reduce environmental waste.

2513 ■ Progressive Health Partnership (PHP)
PO Box 98025
Durham, NC 27708
Ph: (708)365-9564
E-mail: info@proghealth.org
URL: http://www.proghealth.org
Contact: Josh Greenberg, CEO
Founded: 2007. **Multinational. Description:** Aims to decrease the burden of disease on the global poor. Works to provide comprehensive healthcare for communities in need.

2514 ■ Project Concern International (PCI)
(12920)
5151 Murphy Canyon Rd., Ste.320
San Diego, CA 92123-4339
Ph: (858)279-9690
Free: (877)PCI-HOPE
Fax: (858)694-0294
E-mail: **postmaster@pciglobal.org**
URL: **http://www.pciglobal.org**
Contact: George Guimaraes, Pres./CEO

2515 ■ Reach International Healthcare and Training
PO Box 152
Caulfield, MO 65626
E-mail: sherbox3@gmail.com
URL: http://reachinternationalhealthcareandtraining. com
Contact: Samuel C. Evans MD, Dir.
Multinational. Description: Responds to the needs of impoverished Filipinos and others who have limited or no access to medical care. Provides free medical outreach clinics and surgeries to remote areas.

2516 ■ Sharing Resources Worldwide (SRW)
4417 Robertson Rd.
Madison, WI 53714
Fax: (608)437-7662
E-mail: info@sharingresourcesworldwide.org
URL: http://www.sharingresourcesworldwide.org
Contact: Richard Thompson, Pres.
Founded: 2002. **Multinational. Description:** Seeks to improve the quality of life of disadvantaged populations around the world by delivering quality health care. Organizes medical teams that provide surgical, dental and eye care for people in need.

2517 ■ Shout Global Health
103 Azalea Ct., No. 18-2
Largo, MD 20774
Ph: (240)293-3652
E-mail: info@shouthealth.com
URL: http://www.shouthealth.com
Contact: Olufunke Akiyode, Exec. Dir.
Multinational. Description: Aims to improve global health through education, advocacy and research. Conducts research on global health issues and educates the public about prevention, causes and treatments of diseases.

2518 ■ Soft Power Health
2887 Purchase St.
Purchase, NY 10577
Ph: (914)694-2442
E-mail: jessie@softpowerhealth.org
URL: http://www.softpowerhealth.org
Contact: Dr. Jessie Stone, Founder/Dir.
Founded: 2002. **Multinational. Description:** Provides primary and preventive healthcare services to Ugandans. Conducts education programs pertaining to malaria prevention and family planning.

2519 ■ UHAI for Health
37 Sophia Dr.
Worcester, MA 01607
E-mail: uhaiforhealth@gmail.com
URL: http://www.uhai.org
Contact: Jane Kimani-Chomba, Pres.
Founded: 2010. **Multinational. Description:** Aims to improve the lives of the marginalized African population through health education and promotion, research, screening and referral. Promotes health in the African born community in Worcester and in Kenya.

2520 ■ Unified for Global Healing
487 Myrtle Ave., Unit B-7
Brooklyn, NY 11205
E-mail: zbruce@unifiedforglobalhealing.org
URL: http://www.unifiedforglobalhealing.org
Contact: Zola Z. Bruce, Exec. Dir.
Founded: 2007. **Multinational. Description:** Provides culturally-competent health services and promotes the advancement of health education. Aims

to improve the lives of underserved communities internationally.

2521 ■ Upenyu
1 Mary Ct.
Cranbury, NJ 08512
Ph: (317)460-6792
E-mail: info@upenyu.org
URL: http://www.upenyu.org
Contact: Lisa Bevilacqua, Contact
Founded: 2009. **Multinational. Description:** Aims to address health problems in developing countries. Seeks to create effective health programs to support disadvantaged people living in the communities.

2522 ■ Uplift International
PO Box 27696
Seattle, WA 98165
Ph: (206)455-0916
E-mail: info@upliftinternational.org
URL: http://upliftinternational.org
Contact: Mark Schlansky, Founder/CEO
Founded: 1997. **Multinational. Description:** Aims to improve the well being of the world's most vulnerable populations by promoting the universal human right to health through education, advocacy and humanitarian efforts. Promotes corporate social responsibility and develops sustainable health programs that contribute to economic development in developing countries. Strives to develop stronger and more collaborations with universities, governments, professional organizations, NGOs and the business community that will bring much needed technical expertise in healthcare.

2523 ■ Waves of Health
206 Bergen Ave., Ste.203
Kearny, NJ 07032
Ph: (201)436-8888
URL: http://www.thewavesofhealth.org
Contact: Chris Boni, Pres.
Founded: 2007. **Multinational. Description:** Works to provide modern medical care to communities in developing countries. Educates healthcare professionals about health problems of underserved communities in the developing world.

2524 ■ World Health Imaging, Telemedicine and Informatics Alliance (WHITIA)
47 W Polk St., Ste.100-289
Chicago, IL 60605
Ph: (312)994-9940
E-mail: ivy@whitia.org
URL: http://www.worldhealthimaging.org
Contact: Ivy Walker, CEO
Multinational. Description: Seeks to improve the health status and quality of healthcare received by people in resource-limited areas worldwide. Provides communities access to digital medical technologies and the necessary coordination to sustain the systems. Helps find a solution to the lack of availability of low-cost digital X-ray equipment in the developing world.

2525 ■ World Health Partners (WHP)
2140 Shattuck Ave., Ste.1110
Berkeley, CA 94704
E-mail: info@worldhealthpartners.org
URL: http://www.worldhealthpartners.org
Contact: Gopi Gopalakrishnan, Pres./Founder
Founded: 2008. **Multinational. Description:** Aims to provide access to health care and family planning in developing countries. Provides health and reproductive health services to rural and vulnerable communities. Utilizes the latest advances in communication, diagnostic and medical technology to estabish large scale, cost effective health service networks.

2526 ■ World Health Services
21122 Cabin Point Rd.
Disputanta, VA 23842
Ph: (817)933-2088

E-mail: rbendall@worldhealthservices.org
URL: http://www.worldhealthservices.org
Contact: Richard W. Bendall, Pres.
Founded: 2002. **Multinational. Description:** Seeks to enhance the quality of life of disadvantaged people. Assists local medical personnel in the creation and presentation of effective preventive health education programs. Conducts health screenings of local populations, live public lecturing and mass media presentations.

2527 ■ Wuqu' Kawoq
PO Box 91
Bethel, VT 05032
E-mail: contact@wuqukawoq.org
URL: http://www.wuqukawoq.org
Contact: Emily Tummons, Chair
Founded: 2007. **Multinational. Description:** Aims to improve the health and vitality of Mayan communities. Works to fund projects in order to provide medical care. Supports indigenous medical workers, develops first language health services and disseminates knowledge about traditional health practices, including herbal medicine and midwifery.

2528 ■ Wyman Worldwide Health Partners (WWHPS)
227 Mechanic St., Ste.3
Lebanon, NH 03766
E-mail: rwyman@wwhps.org
URL: http://www.wwhps.org
Contact: Rosalie S. Wyman, Founder/CEO
Founded: 2004. **Multinational. Description:** Creates a self-sustaining improvement in the healthcare delivery system for rural health centers in Rwanda. Ensures that Rwandans have access to quality health services.

Laboratory

2529 ■ Clinical Laboratory Management Association (CLMA) (15540)
401 N Michigan Ave., Ste.2200
Chicago, IL 60611
Ph: (312)321-5111 (312)673-4962
Fax: (312)673-6927
E-mail: info@clma.org
URL: http://www.clma.org
Contact: C. Anne Pontius, Pres.

2530 ■ Clinical and Laboratory Standards Institute (CLSI) (14288)
940 W Valley Rd., Ste.1400
Wayne, PA 19087-1898
Ph: (610)688-0100 **(484)588-5905**
Free: (877)447-1888
Fax: (610)688-0700
E-mail: customerservice@clsi.org
URL: http://www.clsi.org
Contact: Glen Fine MS, Exec. VP

Legal

2531 ■ American Association of Nurse Attorneys (TAANA) (15547)
PO Box 14218
Lenexa, KS 66285-4218
Free: (877)538-2262
Fax: (913)895-4652
E-mail: taana_executive_office@goamp.com
URL: http://www.taana.org
Contact: **Edie Brous BSN, Pres.**

2532 ■ American College of Legal Medicine (ACLM) (15548)
2 Woodfield Lake
1100 E Woodfield Rd., Ste.520
Schaumburg, IL 60173-5125
Ph: (847)969-0283
Fax: (847)517-7229

E-mail: info@aclm.org
URL: http://www.aclm.org
Contact: **Gary I. Birnbaum MD, Pres.**

2533 ■ American Hospital Association | Society for Healthcare Consumer Advocacy (SHCA) (15552)
155 N Wacker Dr., Ste.155
Chicago, IL 60606
Ph: (312)422-3700
Fax: (312)278-0881
E-mail: shca@aha.org
URL: http://www.shca-aha.org
Contact: **Amy Wellington, Pres.**

2534 ■ American Society of Law, Medicine and Ethics (ASLME) (15549)
765 Commonwealth Ave., Ste.1634
Boston, MA 02215-1401
Ph: (617)262-4990
Fax: (617)437-7596
E-mail: **thutchinson@aslme.org**
URL: http://www.aslme.org
Contact: **Ted Hutchinson, Exec. Dir.**

Leprosy

2535 ■ American Leprosy Missions (ALM) (12940)
1 ALM Way
Greenville, SC 29601
Ph: (864)271-7040
Free: (800)543-3135
Fax: (864)271-7062
E-mail: amlep@leprosy.org
URL: http://www.leprosy.org
Contact: **Bill Simmons, Pres.**

Massage

2536 ■ American Massage Therapy Association (AMTA) (15569)
500 Davis St., Ste.900
Evanston, IL 60201-4695
Ph: (847)864-0123
Free: **(877)905-0577**
Fax: (847)864-5196
E-mail: info@amtamassage.org
URL: http://www.amtamassage.org
Contact: **Shelly Johnson, Exec. Dir.**

2537 ■ Emergency Response Massage International (ERMI)
227 S Peak St.
Columbus, NC 28722
Ph: (704)763-6099
E-mail: info@ermassage.org
URL: http://www.ermassage.org
Contact: Abbie G. Yandle, Pres.
Founded: 2005. **Multinational. Description:** Seeks to provide stress relief to emergency responders and caregivers following a disaster or critical incident. Aims to set standards for emergency response stress management in the massage therapy profession.

Medical Administration

2538 ■ American Academy of Medical Administrators (AAMA) (15584)
701 Lee St., Ste.600
Des Plaines, IL 60016-4516
Ph: (847)759-8601
Fax: (847)759-8602
E-mail: info@aameda.org
URL: http://www.aameda.org
Contact: **Mr. Alan J. Burgess, Chm.**

2539 ■ American Association of Healthcare Administrative Management (AAHAM) (15586)
11240 Waples Mill Rd., Ste.200
Fairfax, VA 22030
Ph: (703)281-4043 **(336)617-6354**
Fax: (703)359-7562
E-mail: moayad@aaham.org
URL: http://www.aaham.org
Contact: Laurie A. Shoaf CPAM, Pres.

2540 ■ Association of Otolaryngology Administrators (AOA) (15602)
2400 Ardmore Blvd., Ste.302
Pittsburgh, PA 15221
Ph: (412)243-5156 (419)289-8919
Fax: (412)243-5160
E-mail: aoa@oto-online.org
URL: http://www.oto-online.org
Contact: **Todd Blum MHA, Pres.**

2541 ■ Medical Group Management Association (MGMA) (15607)
104 Inverness Terr. E
Englewood, CO 80112-5306
Ph: (303)799-1111
Free: (877)275-6462
E-mail: support@mgma.com
URL: http://www.mgma.com
Contact: **Shena J. Scott MBA, Chair**

2542 ■ National Renal Administrators Association (NRAA) (15613)
100 N 20th St., 4th Fl.
Philadelphia, PA 19103
Ph: (215)320-4655 **(216)295-7003**
Fax: (215)564-2175
E-mail: nraa@nraa.org
URL: http://www.nraa.org
Contact: **Diane Wish, Pres.**

2543 ■ Radiology Business Management Association (RBMA) (12975)
10300 Eaton Pl., Ste.460
Fairfax, VA 22030
Ph: (703)621-3355
Free: (888)224-7262
Fax: (703)621-3356
E-mail: info@rbma.org
URL: http://www.rbma.org
Contact: **Alicia Vasquez CRA, Pres.**

Medical Aid

2544 ■ Doctors in Christ
14359 Miramar Pkwy., Ste.140
Miramar, FL 33027
Ph: (954)483-1215
E-mail: jorgegomezmd@doctorsinchrist.org
URL: http://www.doctorsinchrist.org
Contact: Jorge W. Gomez MD, Pres.
Founded: 2008. **Multinational. Description:** Aims to improve health care and bring needed medications to the poor throughout the world. Conducts medical missions to poor communities and provides medicines and supplies.

Medical Assistants

2545 ■ Association for Healthcare Documentation Integrity (AHDI) (12981)
4230 Kiernan Ave., Ste.130
Modesto, CA 95356
Ph: (209)527-9620
Free: (800)982-2182
Fax: (209)527-9633
E-mail: ahdi@ahdionline.org
URL: http://www.ahdionline.org
Contact: **Wendy Carriegan, Dir. of Admin.**

Medicine

2546 ■ American Association of Medical Society Executives (AAMSE) (15416)
555 E Wells St., Ste.1100
Milwaukee, WI 53202-3823
Ph: (414)221-9275
Fax: (414)276-3449
E-mail: aamse@aamse.org
URL: http://www.aamse.org
Contact: **Jay W. Millson, Pres.-Elect**

2547 ■ Chinese American Medical Society (CAMS) (13031)
41 Elizabeth St., Ste.403
New York, NY 10013
Ph: (212)334-4760
Fax: (212)965-1876
E-mail: **jseto@camsociety.org**
URL: http://www.camsociety.org
Contact: Warren W. Chin MD, Pres.

2548 ■ Harvey Society (HS) (13443)
c/o Marie Filbin, PhD, Sec.
City Univ. of New York
Hunter Coll.
695 Park Ave.
New York, NY 10065
Ph: **(212)772-5472**
E-mail: filbin@genectr.hunter.cuny.edu
URL: http://www.harveysociety.org
Contact: **John H. Morrison PhD, Pres.**

2549 ■ National Medical Association (NMA) (15738)
8403 Colesville Rd., Ste.920
Silver Spring, MD 20910
Ph: (202)347-1895
Fax: (202)347-0722
E-mail: **publicaffairs@nmanet.org**
URL: http://www.nmanet.org
Contact: **Leonard Weather MD, Pres.**

Mental Health

2550 ■ All Healers Mental Health Alliance (AHMHA)
2 W 64th St., Rm. 505
New York, NY 10023
Ph: (917)677-8550
Fax: (917)677-8550
E-mail: ssbec@nysec.org
URL: http://www.ahmha.net
Contact: Dr. Phyllis Harrison-Ross, Pres.
Description: Represents psychiatrists, faith-based leaders, social workers, psychologists, allied associates and other mental health professionals committed to developing timely and sustainable responses to the mental health needs of survivors of catastrophic events and the caregivers who come to their aid. Establishes a local and national network of culturally-competent mental health professionals and allied associates.

2551 ■ International Association for Women's Mental Health (IAWMH)
8213 Lakenheath Way
Potomac, MD 20854
Ph: (301)983-6282
Fax: (301)983-6288
E-mail: info@iawmh.org
URL: http://www.iawmh.org
Contact: Debra Tucker CMP, Exec. Dir.
Founded: 2001. **Multinational. Description:** Aims to improve the mental health of women throughout the world. Seeks to create a network of national and international societies and sections devoted to mental health of women. Promotes research through international collaboration and networks.

Military

2552 ■ Association of Military Surgeons of the U.S. (AMSUS) (15829)
9320 Old Georgetown Rd.
Bethesda, MD 20814-1653
Ph: (301)897-8800
Free: **(800)761-9320**
Fax: (301)530-5446
E-mail: **amsus@amsus.org**
URL: http://www.amsus.org
Contact: **Robert A. Petzel MD, Pres.**

Naturopathy

2553 ■ American Association of Naturopathic Midwives (AANM)
PO Box 672
Meredith, NH 03253
E-mail: sao@imagina.com
URL: http://www.naturopathicmidwives.com
Contact: Sara Ohgushi ND, Pres.
Membership Dues: ND new/renewal, $50 (annual) ● ND retired/supporting, $40 (annual) ● student, $15 (annual). **Description:** Represents the interests of naturopathic midwives. Aims to unify, support, safeguard, build and educate the current and future community of naturopathic midwives. Provides clinical support, continuing education, licensing standards and mentoring programs for its members.

2554 ■ Naturopathic Medical Student Association (NMSA)
2828 Naito Pkwy., Ste.401
Portland, OR 97201
Ph: (503)334-4153
E-mail: president@naturopathicstudent.org
URL: http://www.naturopathicstudent.org
Contact: Malea MacOdrum, Pres.
Founded: 2004. **Description:** Supports students' enthusiasm and passion for the naturopathic medical profession. Helps students through their academic journey by providing useful resources regarding study tools, residencies, preceptorships, career development and philosophy.

2555 ■ Naturopathic Medicine for Global Health (NMGH)
37 Mulberry Row
Princeton, NJ 08540
Ph: (609)310-1340
E-mail: info@natmedglobalhealth.org
URL: http://www.natmedglobalhealth.org
Contact: Carlos Cunningham ND, CEO/Founder
Founded: 2008. **Multinational. Description:** Works to provide sustainable healthcare and humanitarian assistance in developing countries. Promotes naturopathic medicine as a feasible and cost-effective means of healthcare in developing nations.

2556 ■ Oncology Association of Naturopathic Physicians (OncANP)
216 NE Fremont St.
Portland, OR 97212
Free: (800)490-8509
E-mail: oncanp@gmail.com
URL: http://www.oncanp.org
Contact: Corey Harmon, Exec. Dir.
Founded: 2004. **Membership Dues:** associate, supporting (non-student), $135 (annual) ● student, $40 (annual). **Description:** Aims to advance the philosophy, science and practice of naturopathic oncology. Supports naturopathic oncology residency education and enhances the survival and quality of life for people living with cancer through the integration of naturopathic oncology into cancer care.

Nephrology

2557 ■ American Association of Kidney Patients (AAKP) (13184)
3505 E Frontage Rd., Ste.315
Tampa, FL 33607-1796
Free: (800)749-2257

Fax: (813)636-8122
E-mail: info@aakp.org
URL: http://www.aakp.org
Contact: **Sam M. Pederson, Pres.-Elect**

2558 ■ American Nephrology Nurses' Association (ANNA) (15559)
E Holly Ave.
Box 56
Pitman, NJ 08071
Ph: (856)256-2320 **(856)256-2312**
Free: (888)600-2662
Fax: (856)589-7463
E-mail: anna.webeditor@inurse.com
URL: http://www.annanurse.org
Contact: **Mike Cunningham, Exec. Dir.**

2559 ■ Children's Dialysis International (CDI)
25604 NW 2nd Ave.
Newberry, FL 32669
Ph: (352)472-2651
E-mail: info@childrensdialysis.org
URL: http://www.childrensdialysis.org
Contact: Robert Roberge, Founder/Program Dir.
Multinational. Description: Assists dialysis centers in countries with developing economies expand their services to help children receive treatment.

2560 ■ National Kidney Foundation (NKF) (15868)
30 E 33rd St.
New York, NY 10016-5337
Ph: (212)889-2210
Free: (800)622-9010
Fax: (212)689-9261
URL: http://www.kidney.org
Contact: **John Davis, CEO**

Neurological Disorders

2561 ■ American Academy for Cerebral Palsy and Developmental Medicine (AACPDM) (15876)
555 E Wells St., Ste.1100
Milwaukee, WI 53202
Ph: (414)918-3014
Fax: (414)276-2146
E-mail: info@aacpdm.org
URL: http://www.aacpdm.org/index?service=page/ Home
Contact: **Scott Hoffinger MD, Pres.**

2562 ■ American Asperger's Association (AAA)
1301 Seminole Blvd., Ste.B-112
Largo, FL 33770
Ph: (727)518-7294
E-mail: ron.knaus@gmail.com
URL: http://www.americanaspergers.org
Contact: Dr. Ron Knaus, Founder
Founded: 2009. **Description:** Aims to initiate, sponsor, support and promote activities and projects for the care, treatment and education of children and adults afflicted with autism and asperger's syndrome. Raises funds to provide free hyperbaric oxygen therapy to those with autism and aspergers syndrome.

Neurosurgery

2563 ■ Society for Neuroscience in Anesthesiology and Critical Care (SNACC) (13223)
520 N Northwest Hwy.
Park Ridge, IL 60068-2573
Ph: (847)825-5586
Fax: (847)825-5658
E-mail: snacc@snacc.org
URL: http://www.snacc.org
Contact: **Monica S. Vavilala MD, Pres.**
Status Note: Formerly Society of Neurosurgical Anesthesia and Critical Care.

Nuclear Medicine

2564 ■ American College of Nuclear Medicine (ACNM) (13227)
1850 Samuel Morse Dr.
Reston, VA 20190
Ph: (703)326-1190
Fax: **(703)708-9015**
E-mail: vpappas@snm.org
URL: http://www.acnmonline.org
Contact: **Virginia Pappas CAE, CEO**

Nursing

2565 ■ American Association of Critical-Care Nurses (AACN) (16021)
101 Columbia
Aliso Viejo, CA 92656-4109
Ph: (949)362-2000 (949)362-2050
Free: (800)899-2226
Fax: (949)362-2020
E-mail: info@aacn.org
URL: http://www.aacn.org
Contact: **Mary Stahl, Pres.-Elect**

2566 ■ Vietnamese-American Nurses Association
PO Box 691994
Houston, TX 77269-1994
E-mail: vho03@yahoo.com
URL: http://www.thevana.org
Contact: **Vi Ho PhD, Pres./Founder**
Founded: 2007. **Membership Dues:** nurse, healthcare professional, $25 (annual) ● nursing student, $10 (annual). **Description:** Aims to unite Vietnamese-American nurses in the United States. Promotes the health of Vietnamese communities through research, education and prevention. Serves as a forum for Vietnamese-American nurses to exchange ideas and voice their concerns.

Obstetrics and Gynecology

2567 ■ Endometriosis Association (EA) (13436)
8585 N 76th Pl.
Milwaukee, WI 53223
Ph: (414)355-2200
Free: (800)992-3636
Fax: (414)355-6065
URL: http://www.endometriosisassn.org
Contact: Mary Lou Ballweg, Pres./Exec. Dir.

2568 ■ Society for Gynecologic Investigation (SGI) (16219)
888 Bestgate Rd., Ste.420
Annapolis, MD 21401
Ph: (404)727-8600 (410)571-1152
Fax: **(404)727-8609**
E-mail: sgiava@aol.com
URL: http://www.sgionline.org
Contact: **Sarah L. Berga MD, Pres.-Elect**

2569 ■ Society for Menstrual Cycle Research (SMCR) (15619)
Eastern Washington Univ.
229 Communications Bldg.
Cheney, WA 99004
E-mail: **ekissling@ewu.edu**
URL: http://menstruationresearch.org
Contact: **Elizabeth A. Kissling PhD, Pres.**

Oncology

2570 ■ American College of Mohs Surgery (ACMS) (16236)
555 E Wells St., Ste.1100
Milwaukee, WI 53202-3823
Ph: (414)347-1103
Free: (800)500-7224

Fax: (414)276-2146
E-mail: info@mohscollege.org
URL: http://www.mohscollege.org
Contact: **Kim Schardin CAE, Exec. Dir.**

2571 ■ National Foundation for Cancer Research (NFCR) (2098)
4600 E West Hwy., Ste.525
Bethesda, MD 20814
Ph: (301)654-1250
Free: (800)321-2873
Fax: (301)654-5824
E-mail: info@nfcr.org
URL: http://www.nfcr.org
Contact: **Franklin C. Salisbury Jr., Pres.**

Oral and Maxillofacial Surgery

2572 ■ American Society of Maxillofacial Surgeons (ASMS) (16336)
900 Cummings Ctr., Ste.221-U
Beverly, MA 01915
Ph: **(978)927-8330**
Fax: **(978)524-8890**
URL: http://www.maxface.org
Contact: **Steven R. Buchman MD, Pres.**

Otorhinolaryngology

2573 ■ American Head and Neck Society (AHNS) (16105)
11300 W Olympic Blvd., Ste.600
Los Angeles, CA 90064
Ph: (310)437-0559
Fax: (310)437-0585
E-mail: admin@ahns.info
URL: http://www.ahns.info
Contact: **Carol R. Bradford MD, Pres.**

2574 ■ American Laryngological, Rhinological and Otological Society (ALROS) (16420)
13930 Gold Cir., Ste.103
Omaha, NE 68144
Ph: (402)346-5500
Fax: (402)346-5300
E-mail: info@triological.org
URL: http://www.triological.org
Contact: **Robert H. Ossoff DMD, Pres.**

Pathology

2575 ■ Renal Pathology Society (RPS) (16473)
UNC Division of Nephropathology
409 Brinkhous-Bullitt Bldg., CB No. 7525
Chapel Hill, NC 27599
Ph: **(919)966-2421**
Fax: **(919)966-4542**
E-mail: **hsingh@med.unc.edu**
URL: http://www.renalpathsoc.org
Contact: **Dr. Harsharan K. Singh, Sec.**

Pharmacy

2576 ■ Healthcare Distribution Management Association (HDMA) (16226)
901 N Glebe Rd., Ste.1000
Arlington, VA 22203
Ph: (703)787-0000
Fax: (703)812-5282
E-mail: **lkanfer@hdmanet.org**
URL: http://www.healthcaredistribution.org
Contact: **David Moody, Chm.**

2577 ■ National Association of Chain Drug Stores (NACDS) (16550)
413 N Lee St.
Alexandria, VA 22314
Ph: (703)549-3001 (703)837-4111
Fax: **(703)683-1451**
URL: http://www.nacds.org
Contact: Steven C. Anderson, Pres./CEO

2578 ■ National Community Pharmacists Association (NCPA) (2880)
100 Daingerfield Rd.
Alexandria, VA 22314
Ph: (703)683-8200
Free: (800)544-7447
Fax: (703)683-3619
E-mail: info@ncpanet.org
URL: http://www.ncpanet.org
Contact: **Robert Greenwood, Pres.**

2579 ■ Pharmaceutical Care Management Association (PCMA) (2730)
601 Pennsylvania Ave. NW, Ste.740 S
Washington, DC 20004
Ph: (202)207-3610
E-mail: kpumphrey@pcmanet.org
URL: http://www.pcmanet.org
Contact: Mark Merritt, Pres./CEO

Physicians

2580 ■ Catholic Medical Association (CMA) (16610)
29 Bala Ave., Ste.205
Bala Cynwyd, PA 19004-3206
Ph: (484)270-8002
Fax: (866)666-2319
E-mail: info@cathmed.org
URL: http://www.cathmed.org
Contact: **Jan R. Hemstad MD, Pres.**

Physics

2581 ■ American Association of Physicists in Medicine (AAPM) (13700)
1 Physics Ellipse
College Park, MD 20740
Ph: (301)209-3350
Fax: (301)209-0862
E-mail: **2011.aapm@aapm.org**
URL: http://www.aapm.org
Contact: Angela R. Keyser, Exec. Dir.

Psychology

2582 ■ American Psychological Association I Division of Family Psychology (16738)
750 1st St. NE
Washington, DC 20002-4242
Ph: (202)216-7602
Fax: (202)218-3599
E-mail: kcooke@apa.org
URL: **http://www.apa.org/about/division/div43.**
aspx
Contact: **George K. Hong PhD, Pres.**

2583 ■ Association of Black Psychologists (ABPsi) (14541)
PO Box 55999
Washington, DC 20040-5999
Ph: (202)722-0808
Fax: (202)722-5941
E-mail: **info@abpsi.org**
URL: http://www.abpsi.org
Contact: **Benson G. Cooke EdD, Pres.**

2584 ■ Association for Humanistic Psychology (AHP) (16753)
PO Box 1190
Tiburon, CA 94920
Ph: (415)435-1604 **(617)287-7232**

Fax: (415)435-1654
E-mail: ahpoffice@aol.com
URL: http://www.ahpweb.org
Contact: Mr. Carroy U. Ferguson, Co-Pres.

**2585 ■ Association for Psychological Type
International (APTi) (13810)**
9650 Rockville Pike
Bethesda, MD 20814-3998
Ph: (301)634-7450
Free: (800)847-9943
Fax: (301)634-7099
E-mail: info@aptinternational.org
URL: http://www.aptinternational.org
Contact: John Lord, Exec. Dir.

2586 ■ Psychonomic Society (PS) (16781)
2424 Amer. Ln.
Madison, WI 53704-3102
Ph: (608)441-1070
Fax: (608)443-2474
E-mail: info@psychonomic.org
URL: http://www.psychonomic.org
Contact: Kathy Kuehn, Exec. Dir.

**2587 ■ Society for Personality Assessment
(SPA) (13839)**
6109H Arlington Blvd.
Falls Church, VA 22044
Ph: (703)534-4772
Free: (866)849-3725
Fax: (703)534-6905
E-mail: manager@spaonline.org
URL: http://www.personality.org
Contact: Dr. Paula J. Garber, Admin. Dir.

Psychotherapy

2588 ■ Angel Harps
PO Box 704
Wildomar, CA 92595
Ph: (951)246-0320
E-mail: info@angelharps.org
URL: http://www.angelharps.org
Contact: Dianna Woodley, Contact
Founded: 2003. **Description:** Promotes harp music
therapy. Provides therapeutic harps to disabled
children to assist them in the healing process.
Conducts annual non-profit benefit concerts and other
fundraising efforts.

2589 ■ Music Therapy for Healing
6688 Nolensville Rd., Ste.111, No. 165
Brentwood, TN 37027
Ph: (615)216-0589
Fax: (866)618-6112
E-mail: info@musictherapyforhealing.org
URL: http://musictherapyforhealing.org
Contact: Don Reed, Contact
Description: Promotes and endorses the power of
healing through music. Engages and trains musicians
to perform therapeutic music for patients nationwide.

Public Health

**2590 ■ Caribbean Public Health Coalition
(CPHC)**
15515 Symondsbury Way
Upper Marlboro, MD 20774
Ph: (240)602-0103
E-mail: cphcinc@gmail.com
URL: http://cphca.netfirms.com
Contact: Dr. Ludmilla F. Wikkeling-Scott, CEO/
    Founder/Chair
Founded: 2002. **Multinational. Description:** Aims
to provide better and more accessible health care
solutions to Caribbean and Latin American communi-
ties. Supports comprehensive approach to improve
healthcare and healthcare delivery services through
technology, infrastructure and education.

**2591 ■ South Asian Public Health
Association (SAPHA)**
c/o Mayur A. Patel, MS, Treas.
1105 Grant St.
Evanston, IL 60201
E-mail: mpatel@next-source.com
URL: http://www.sapha.org
Contact: Umair Shah MD, Chm.
Founded: 1999. **Multinational. Description:** Promotes the health and well-being of South Asian communities by advancing the field of South Asian public
health. Addresses public health issues that affect
South Asians and their communities in the United
States. Provides a forum for mentorship, dialogue
and resource-sharing among public health professionals working with South Asians and their communities.

Reproductive Health

2592 ■ Family Health Alliance (FHA)
6520 Platt Ave., Ste.433
West Hills, CA 91307
Ph: (818)610-7278
E-mail: info@familyhealthalliance.org
URL: http://familyhealthalliance.org
Contact: Taraneh R. Salke, Exec. Dir.
Founded: 2005. **Multinational. Description:** Seeks
to improve and enhance the health of women and
families in resource-poor environments through
education, training and research. Promotes the
advancement of reproductive health and rights and
recognizes the role of women in the promotion and
improvement of family health.

**2593 ■ International Partnership for
Reproductive Health (IPRH)**
PO Box 510
Chesterton, IN 46304
E-mail: sharon.ransom@gmail.com
URL: http://www.iprh.org
Contact: Sharon A. Ransom MD, Pres./Exec. Dir.
Multinational. Description: Represents medical
professionals and service providers, community
outreach organizations and personnel dedicated to
supporting the development of cervical cancer and
HIV/AIDS screening for women in Ethiopia. Strives to
improve the reproductive health and wellness of
women in Ethiopia. Seeks to enhance the knowledge
and skills of medical professionals who are actively
engaged in supporting community-based healthcare
services.

Spinal Injury

2594 ■ Spinal Health International (SHI)
2221 NW 3rd Pl.
Gainesville, FL 32603
E-mail: info@spinalhealthinternational.org
URL: http://www.spinalhealthinternational.org
Contact: Mindy Gregory, Contact
Founded: 2009. **Multinational. Description:** Focuses on improving the availability and quality of
healthcare related to disorders and diseases of the
spine in underprivileged countries. Facilitates education and training that focus on relevant and realistic
goals. Strives to maximize use of locally available
equipment and supplies.

2595 ■ World Spine Care (WSC)
801 N Tustin Ave., Ste.202
Santa Ana, CA 92705
Ph: (714)547-9822
E-mail: scott.haldeman@worldspinecare.org
URL: http://worldspinecare.org
Contact: Dr. Scott Haldeman, Pres./CEO
Founded: 2008. **Multinational. Description:** Aims
to bring together healthcare professionals involved in
spinal health. Provides evidence-based, culturally
integrated prevention, assessment and treatment of
spinal disorders in the developing world.

Substance Abuse

**2596 ■ American Society of Addiction
Medicine (ASAM) (14573)**
4601 N Park Ave., Upper Arcade No. 101
Chevy Chase, MD 20815
Ph: (301)656-3920
Fax: (301)656-3815
E-mail: email@asam.org
URL: http://www.asam.org
Contact: Donald J. Kurth MD, Pres.

**2597 ■ Society for Prevention Research
(SPR) (17144)**
11240 Waples Mill Rd., Ste.200
Fairfax, VA 22030
Ph: (703)934-4850
Fax: (703)359-7562
E-mail: jenniferlewis@preventionresearch.org
URL: http://www.preventionresearch.org
Contact: Jennifer Lewis, Exec. Dir.

Surgery

**2598 ■ American Society of Abdominal
Surgeons (ASAS) (16568)**
824 Main St., 2nd Fl., Ste.1
Melrose, MA 02176
Ph: (781)665-6102
Fax: (781)665-4127
E-mail: office@abdominalsurg.org
URL: http://www.abdominalsurg.org
Contact: Diane Pothier, Newsletter Ed.

Veterinary Medicine

**2599 ■ United States Animal Health
Association (USAHA) (16458)**
4221 Mitchell Ave.
St. Joseph, MO 64507
Ph: (816)671-1144
Fax: (816)671-1201
E-mail: usaha@usaha.org
URL: http://www.usaha.org
Contact: Benjamin Richey, Exec. Dir.

Visually Impaired

**2600 ■ Association for Education and
Rehabilitation of the Blind and Visually
Impaired (AERBVI) (16480)**
1703 N Beauregard St., Ste.440
Alexandria, VA 22311
Ph: (703)671-4500
Free: (877)492-2708
Fax: (703)671-6391
E-mail: lou@aerbvi.org
URL: http://www.aerbvi.org
Contact: Lou Tutt, Exec. Dir.

2601 ■ Global Vision 2020
PO Box 3332
Easton, MD 21601
Ph: (410)822-6170
E-mail: info@gv2020.org
URL: http://www.gv2020.org
Contact: Kevin White, Exec. Dir.
Multinational. Description: Works to address the
unfulfilled worldwide need for corrective eyeglasses.
Addresses the issues of vision correction globally.

**2602 ■ Guiding Eyes for the Blind (GEB)
(17155)**
611 Granite Springs Rd.
Yorktown Heights, NY 10598
Ph: (914)245-4024 (845)878-3330
Free: (800)942-0149
Fax: (914)245-1609

E-mail: **mbrier@guidingeyes.org**
URL: http://www.guidingeyes.org
Contact: William D. Badger, Pres./CEO

**2603 ■ Lutheran Braille Evangelism
Association (LBEA) (17494)**
1740 Eugene St.
White Bear Lake, MN 55110-3312
Ph: (651)426-0469
E-mail: lbea@qwest.net
URL: http://www.users.qwest.net/~lbea
Contact: **Rev. Scott McLaughlin, Pres.**

**2604 ■ Lutheran Braille Workers (LBW)
(2249)**
PO Box 5000
Yucaipa, CA 92399

Ph: (909)795-8977
Free: (800)925-6092
Fax: **(909)795-8970**
E-mail: lbw@lbwinc.org
URL: http://www.lbwinc.org
Contact: Rev. Dr. Phil Pledger, Pres.

**2605 ■ National Industries for the Blind (NIB)
(16525)**
1310 Braddock Pl.
Alexandria, VA 22314-1691
Ph: (703)310-0500
E-mail: 508team@nib.org
URL: http://www.nib.org
Contact: **Kevin A. Lynch, Pres./CEO**

Yoga

2606 ■ Silver Age Yoga
7968 Arjons Dr., Ste.213
San Diego, CA 92126
Ph: (858)693-3110
Free: (877)313-3110
E-mail: info@silverageyoga.org
URL: http://www.silverageyoga.org
Contact: Frank Iszak, Dir./Founder

Founded: 2003. **Description:** Provides free yoga classes to underserved seniors throughout the country. Offers certification to yoga teachers.

Africa

2607 ■ Africa Faith and Justice Network (AFJN) (16567)
125 Michigan Ave. NE, Ste.480
Washington, DC 20017
Ph: (202)884-9780
Fax: (202)884-9774
E-mail: **allisonburket@afjn.org**
URL: http://www.afjn.org
Contact: Rev. Rocco Puopolo, Exec. Dir.

2608 ■ Operation Crossroads Africa (OCA) (14410)
PO Box 5570
New York, NY 10027
Ph: (212)289-1949
Fax: (212)289-2526
E-mail: oca@igc.org
URL: http://operationcrossroadsafrica.org
Contact: **Dr. James Robinson, Founder**

Agriculture

2609 ■ Women Involved in Farm Economics (WIFE) (16607)
8463 20th St. SW
Richardton, ND 58652
Ph: **(702)938-4246** (406)557-2400
Fax: (605)985-5205
E-mail: **debdressler1@gmail.com**
URL: http://www.wifeline.com
Contact: **Deb Dressler, Pres.**

Americas

2610 ■ Americas Society (AS) (16621)
680 Park Ave.
New York, NY 10021
Ph: (212)249-8950 **(212)277-8342**
Fax: (212)249-1880
E-mail: inforequest@as-coa.org
URL: http://www.americas-society.org
Contact: Susan L. Segal, Pres./CEO

2611 ■ Partners of the Americas (16980)
1424 K St. NW, Ste.700
Washington, DC 20005
Ph: (202)628-3300 **(202)637-6202**
Free: **(800)322-7844**
Fax: (202)628-3306
E-mail: info@partners.net
URL: http://www.partners.net
Contact: Stephen G. Vetter, Pres./CEO

Anti-Poverty

2612 ■ Green for All
1611 Telegraph Ave., Ste.600
Oakland, CA 94612
Ph: (510)663-6500

E-mail: officeofthepresident@greenforall.org
URL: http://www.greenforall.org
Contact: Phaedra Ellis-Lamkins, CEO
Description: Works to build a strong green economy to lift people out of poverty. Seeks to improve the lives of all Americans through a clean energy economy. Builds new coalitions that leverage public and private investment to create quality green jobs.

2613 ■ Innovations for Poverty Action (IPA)
101 Whitney Ave.
New Haven, CT 06510
Ph: (203)772-2216
E-mail: contact@poverty-action.org
URL: http://www.poverty-action.org
Contact: Prof. Dean Karlan, Pres.
Founded: 2002. **Multinational. Description:** Utilizes randomized evaluations to develop and test innovative solutions to real problems faced by the poor in developing countries. Works to effectively promote poverty reduction.

2614 ■ Millennium Campus Network (MCN)
1330 Beacon St., Ste.249
Brookline, MA 02446
E-mail: contact@mcnpartners.org
URL: http://www.millenniumcampusnetwork.org
Contact: Will Herberich, Exec. Dir./Pres.
Founded: 2007. **Description:** Represents student organizations dedicated to the eradication of extreme poverty. Encourages students to work together in raising awareness, sharing ideas and best practices, pressuring policy makers and taking collective action in efforts to end extreme poverty.

Appropriate Technology

2615 ■ Aprovecho Research Center (15321)
80574 Hazelton Rd.
Cottage Grove, OR 97424
Ph: (541)942-8198
E-mail: **aprovecho.mail@gmail.com**
URL: http://www.aprovecho.net
Contact: **Jeremy Roth, Contact**

Asian

2616 ■ U.S.-Vietnam Trade Council (USVTC) (16657)
1025 Vermont Ave. NW, Ste.300
Washington, DC 20005
Ph: (202)580-6950
Fax: (202)580-6958
E-mail: **vbfoote@usvtc.org**
URL: http://www.usvtc.org
Contact: Virginia B. Foote, Pres./Co-Founder

Baltic

2617 ■ Joint Baltic American National Committee (JBANC) (14505)
400 Hurley Ave.
Rockville, MD 20850-3121
Ph: (301)340-1954
Fax: (301)309-1405
E-mail: jbanc@jbanc.org
URL: http://www.jbanc.org
Contact: **Marju Rink-Abel, Pres.**

Censorship

2618 ■ National Coalition Against Censorship (NCAC) (16179)
19 Fulton St., Ste.407
New York, NY 10038
Ph: (212)807-6222
Fax: (212)807-6245
E-mail: ncac@ncac.org
URL: http://www.ncac.org
Contact: Joan E. Bertin, Exec. Dir.

Central America

2619 ■ Neighbor to Neighbor (N2N) (16694)
1550 Blue Spruce Dr.
Fort Collins, CO 80524
Ph: (970)484-7498
Fax: (970)488-2355
E-mail: wrobinson@n2n.org
URL: http://www.n2n.org
Contact: **Dave Armstrong, Pres.**

Chinese

2620 ■ U.S.-China Peoples Friendship Association (USCPFA) (2280)
402 E 43rd St.
Indianapolis, IN 46205
Ph: (317)283-7735 (561)747-9487
Fax: (561)747-9487
E-mail: **robert@uscpfa.org**
URL: http://www.uscpfa.org
Contact: Robert Sanborn, Pres.

Citizenship

2621 ■ American Legion Auxiliary Girls Nation
8945 N Meridian St., 2nd Fl.
Indianapolis, IN 46260
Ph: (317)569-4500
Fax: **(317)569-4502**

E-mail: **alahq@alaforveterans.org**
URL: **http://www.alaforveterans.org**
Contact: Mary Davis, Chair

2622 ■ Close Up Foundation
1220 Braddock Pl., Ste.400
Alexandria, VA 22314
Ph: **(703)706-3300**
Free: (800)256-7387
E-mail: info@closeup.org
URL: http://www.closeup.org
Contact: Timothy S. Davis, Pres./CEO

Civil Rights and Liberties

2623 ■ American Civil Rights Union (ACRU)
3213 Duke St., No. 625
Alexandria, VA 22314
Ph: (703)807-0242
Free: (877)730-2278
E-mail: info@theacru.org
URL: http://www.theacru.org
Contact: Robert A. Knight, Exec. Dir.
Description: Aims to protect the civil rights of all
Americans by publicly advancing a Constitutional
understanding of the essential rights and freedoms.
Monitors and counters organizations that threaten
the constitutional rights. Fights against harmful anti-
Constitutional ideologies that have taken hold in
nation's courts, law schools and bureaucracies.

**2624 ■ National Organization for the Reform
of Marijuana Laws (NORML) (2294)**
1600 K St. NW, Ste.501
Washington, DC 20006-2832
Ph: (202)483-5500
Free: (888)676-6765
Fax: (202)483-0057
E-mail: norml@norml.org
URL: http://www.norml.org
Contact: **Stephen W. Dillon ESQ, Chm.**

Communications

**2625 ■ Inter American Press Association
(IAPA) (14685)**
Jules Dubois Bldg.
1801 SW 3rd Ave.
Miami, FL 33129
Ph: (305)634-2465
Fax: (305)635-2272
E-mail: **pdirube@sipiapa.org**
URL: http://www.sipiapa.com
Contact: Julio E. Munoz, Exec. Dir.

2626 ■ Media Watch (MW) (15147)
PO Box 618
Santa Cruz, CA 95061-0618
Ph: (831)423-6355
Free: (800)631-6355
E-mail: info@mediawatch.com
URL: http://www.mediawatch.com
Contact: **Ann Simonton, Dir./Founder**

Community Development

**2627 ■ Community Associations Institute
(CAI)**
6402 Arlington Blvd., Ste.500
Falls Church, VA 22042
Ph: **(703)970-9220**
Free: (888)CAI-4321
Fax: (703)684-1581
E-mail: **cai-info@caionline.org**
URL: http://www.caionline.org
Contact: Thomas M. Skiba, CEO

2628 ■ Opportunity Finance Network (15543)
Public Ledger Bldg.
620 Chestnut St., Ste.572
Philadelphia, PA 19106

Ph: (215)923-4754
Fax: (215)923-4755
E-mail: info@opportunityfinance.net
URL: http://www.opportunityfinance.net
Contact: **Ignacio Esteban, Chair**

Conflict Resolution

**2629 ■ Alliance for Peacebuilding (AfP)
(17248)**
1320 19th St. NW, Ste.410
Washington, DC 20036
Ph: (202)822-2047
Fax: (202)822-2049
E-mail: **afp-info@allianceforpeacebuilding.org**
URL: http://www.allianceforpeacebuilding.org
Contact: **Rob Ricigliano, Chm.**

Conservation

2630 ■ Ocean Champions
PO Box 381596
Cambridge, MA 02238
Ph: (617)661-6647
E-mail: rob@oceanchampions.org
URL: http://www.oceanchampions.org
Contact: Rob Moir PhD, Chm.
Founded: 2003. **Description:** Aims to create a politi-
cal environment wherein the protection and restora-
tion of oceans is a priority of federal and state govern-
ments. Works with the U.S. Congress to ensure
ocean health through electoral and legislative action.

Conservative

2631 ■ Freedom House (14802)
1301 Connecticut Ave. NW, 6th Fl.
Washington, DC 20036
Ph: (202)296-5101
Fax: (202)293-2840
E-mail: info@freedomhouse.org
URL: http://www.freedomhouse.org
Contact: **David J. Kramer, Exec. Dir.**

Consumers

**2632 ■ Consumer Federation of America
(CFA) (17606)**
1620 I St. NW, Ste.200
Washington, DC 20006
Ph: (202)387-6121 (202)737-0766
E-mail: cfa@consumerfed.org
URL: http://www.consumerfed.org
Contact: **Irene Leech, Pres.**

**2633 ■ Funeral Service Consumer Assistance
Program (FSCAP) (17617)**
c/o Celine Clark Haga, Exec. Dir.
13625 Bishop Dr.
Brookfield, WI 53005-6607
Free: (877)402-5900
Fax: (262)789-6977
E-mail: info@funeralservicefoundation.org
URL: http://www.FuneralServiceFoundation.org
Contact: **Shaun Myers, Chm.-Elect**

Cuba

**2634 ■ Directorio Democratico Cubano
(16502)**
PO Box 110235
Hialeah, FL 33011
Ph: (305)220-2713
Fax: **(305)220-2716**
E-mail: info@directorio.org
URL: http://www.directorio.org
Contact: Javier de Cespedes, Pres./Co-Founder

Defense

**2635 ■ Inter-American Defense Board (IADB)
(14960)**
2600 NW 16th St.
Washington, DC 20441
Ph: (202)939-6041
Fax: **(202)319-2791**
E-mail: personnel@jid.org
URL: http://www.jid.org
Contact: Lt. Gen. Jose Roberto Machado E. Silva,
Chm.

Democracy

2636 ■ American Libyan Freedom Alliance
PO Box 22262
Lehigh Valley, PA 18002
Ph: (610)703-1382
E-mail: info@alfa-online.net
URL: http://alfa-online.net
Contact: Mohammed M. Bugaighis PhD, Chm.
Founded: 2003. **Membership Dues:** regular, $100
(annual). **Description:** Promotes human rights and
democracy in Libya through advocacy and education.
Informs the American public and international com-
munity about Libyan history, culture, concerns and
aspirations.

**2637 ■ International People's Democratic
Uhuru Movement (InPDUM) (17395)**
1245 18th Ave. S
St. Petersburg, FL 33705
E-mail: info@inpdum.org
URL: http://www.inpdum.org
Contact: Chimurenga Waller, Intl. Pres.

Democratic Party

2638 ■ Democrats Abroad (DA) (15362)
430 S Capitol St. SE
Washington, DC 20003
Ph: (202)488-5073
Fax: (202)572-7836
E-mail: info@democratsabroad.org
URL: http://www.democratsabroad.org
Contact: **Ken Sherman, Chm.**

Disarmament

2639 ■ Clear Path International (CPI) (16560)
321 High School Rd. NE, No. 574
Bainbridge Island, WA 98110
Ph: (206)780-5964
E-mail: **info@cpi.org**
URL: http://www.cpi.org
Contact: Sherry Larsen Holmes, Dir. of Admin.

**2640 ■ NGO Committee on Disarmament,
Peace and Security (16568)**
777 UN Plz., Ste.3-B
New York, NY 10017
Ph: (212)687-5340
Fax: (212)687-1643
E-mail: **disarmtimes@gmail.com**
URL: http://disarm.igc.org
Contact: Hiroyuki Sakurai, Pres.

Draft

2641 ■ Center on Conscience and War (CCW)
1830 Connecticut Ave. NW
Washington, DC 20009-5732
Ph: (202)483-2220
Free: (800)379-2679
Fax: (202)483-1246
E-mail: ccw@centeronconscience.org
URL: http://www.centeronconscience.org
Contact: **Maria Santelli, Exec. Dir.**

Energy

2642 ■ Focus the Nation
240 N Broadway, Ste.212
Portland, OR 97227
Ph: (503)224-9440
Fax: (503)980-7905
E-mail: info@focusthenation.org
URL: http://www.focusthenation.org
Contact: Garett Brennan, Exec. Dir.
Founded: 1999. **Description:** Advocates for a just and prosperous clean energy future. Educates the public on matters of clean energy development. Empowers young people through education, civic engagement and action.

2643 ■ Set America Free
7811 Montrose Rd., Ste.505
Potomac, MD 20854-3368
E-mail: info@setamericafree.org
URL: http://www.setamericafree.org
Contact: Anne Korin, Chair
Description: Aims to educate the public about the danger of the United States dependence on foreign oil and the need for fuel choice. Increases public demand for and use of flexible fuel vehicles and plug-in hybrids. Supports policy solutions to increase fuel choice.

European

2644 ■ European Union Delegation to the United States (15047)
2175 K St. SW
Washington, DC 20037
Ph: (202)862-9500
Fax: (202)429-1766
E-mail: delegation-usa-info@eeas.europa.eu
URL: http://www.eurunion.org
Contact: Joao Vale de Almeida, Ambassador

Feminism

2645 ■ Federally Employed Women (FEW) (16666)
700 N Fairfax St., No. 510
Alexandria, VA 22314
Ph: (202)898-0994
Fax: (202)898-1535
E-mail: few@few.org
URL: http://www.few.org
Contact: Sue Webster, Pres.

2646 ■ Global Fund for Women (GFW) (15841)
222 Sutter St., Ste.500
San Francisco, CA 94109
Ph: (415)248-4800
Fax: (415)248-4801
E-mail: americas@globalfundforwomen.org
URL: http://www.globalfundforwomen.org
Contact: Ms. Musimbi Kanyoro, CEO

2647 ■ International Center for Research on Women (ICRW) (17543)
1120 20th St. NW, Ste.500 N
Washington, DC 20036
Ph: (202)797-0007 (202)742-1227
Fax: (202)797-0020
E-mail: info@icrw.org
URL: http://www.icrw.org
Contact: Dr. Sarah Degnan Kambou, Pres.

2648 ■ Ms. Foundation for Women (MFW) (15131)
12 MetroTech Center, 26th Fl.
Brooklyn, NY 11201
Ph: (212)742-2300
Fax: (212)742-1653
E-mail: info@ms.foundation.org
URL: http://www.ms.foundation.org
Contact: Anika Rahman, Pres./CEO

2649 ■ National Association of Commissions for Women (NACW) (17189)
401 N Washington St., Ste.100
Rockville, MD 20850-1737
Ph: (240)777-8308
Free: (800)338-9267
Fax: (301)279-1318
E-mail: info@nacw.org
URL: http://www.nacw.org
Contact: Mary Molina Mescall, Pres.

2650 ■ Women's Environment and Development Organization (WEDO) (2368)
355 Lexington Ave., 3rd Fl.
New York, NY 10017
Ph: (212)973-0325
Fax: (212)973-0335
E-mail: cate@wedo.org
URL: http://www.wedo.org
Contact: Monique Essed Fernandes, Chair

Foreign Policy

2651 ■ Council on Foreign Relations (CFR) (17608)
The Harold Pratt House
58 E 68th St.
New York, NY 10065
Ph: (212)434-9400 (212)434-9797
Fax: (212)434-9800
E-mail: corporate@cfr.org
URL: http://www.cfr.org
Contact: Richard N. Haas, Pres.

Free Enterprise

2652 ■ Americanism Educational League (AEL) (17262)
PO Box 1287
Monrovia, CA 91017
Ph: (626)357-7733
E-mail: aelmain@americanism.org
URL: http://www.americanism.org
Contact: Gideon Lowe III, Sec.

2653 ■ Fisher Institute for Medical Research (FI)
580 Decker Dr., Ste.100
Irving, TX 75062
Ph: (972)660-3219 (972)887-9456
Fax: (972)660-1245
URL: http://www.fisherinstitute.org
Contact: Candace F. McDaniel, Medical Dir.

2654 ■ Private Enterprise Research Center (PERC) (15173)
Texas A&M Univ.
4231 TAMU
College Station, TX 77843-4231
Ph: (979)845-7722
Fax: (979)845-6636
E-mail: perc@tamu.edu
URL: http://www.tamu.edu/perc
Contact: Dr. Thomas R. Saving, Dir.

2655 ■ Professional Services Council (PSC) (18201)
4401 Wilson Blvd., Ste.1110
Arlington, VA 22203
Ph: (703)875-8059 (703)875-3123
Fax: (703)875-8922
E-mail: chvotkin@pscouncil.org
URL: http://www.pscouncil.org
Contact: Alan Chvotkin, Exec. VP/Counsel

Government Relations

2656 ■ Women in Government Relations (WGR) (16814)
801 N Fairfax St., Ste.211
Alexandria, VA 22314-1757
Ph: (703)299-8546 (703)770-8156
Fax: (703)299-9233
E-mail: info@wgr.org
URL: http://wgr.org
Contact: Ms. Emily Bardach, Exec. Dir.

Honduras

2657 ■ Honduras Outreach, Inc. (HOI) (17728)
4105 Briarcliff Rd. NE
Atlanta, GA 30345
Ph: (404)327-5770 (404)327-5769
E-mail: info@hoi.org
URL: http://www.hoi.org
Contact: Laurie Willing, Exec. Dir.

Human Rights

2658 ■ Advancing Human Rights (AHR)
277 Park Ave., 49th Fl.
New York, NY 10172
Ph: (212)207-5042 (212)207-5062
Fax: (212)207-5047
E-mail: david.keyes@advancinghumanrights.org
URL: http://advancinghumanrights.org
Contact: David Keyes, Exec. Dir.
Founded: 2011. **Description:** Promotes individual liberty and good governance. Conducts research and advocacy on human rights. Encourages accountability, fairness and transparency in human rights organizations' work.

2659 ■ Center for International Policy (CIP) (15351)
1717 Massachusetts Ave. NW, Ste.801
Washington, DC 20036
Ph: (202)232-3317
Fax: (202)232-3440
E-mail: cip@ciponline.org
URL: http://www.ciponline.org
Contact: William Goodfellow, Exec. Dir.

2660 ■ CorpWatch (CW) (17756)
PO Box 29198
San Francisco, CA 94129
Ph: (415)800-4004
E-mail: pratap@corpwatch.org
URL: http://www.corpwatch.org
Contact: Pratap Chatterjee, Senior Ed.

2661 ■ Dalit Freedom Network (DFN)
631 Pennsylvania Ave. SE, Ste.2
Washington, DC 20003
Ph: (202)375-5000
Fax: (202)280-1340
E-mail: info@dalitnetwork.org
URL: http://www.dalitnetwork.org
Contact: Dr. Joseph D'Souza, Pres.
Founded: 2002. **Multinational. Description:** Aims to bring an end to the injustices perpetrated against the Dalit people of India. Promotes social freedom and human dignity by networking human, financial and informational resources.

2662 ■ Dalit Solidarity
PO Box 112
Hines, IL 60141
Ph: (708)612-4248
E-mail: dalitsolidarity@gmail.com
URL: http://www.dalitsolidarity.org
Contact: Benjamin Chinnappan, Pres.
Founded: 2000. **Multinational. Description:** Promotes equality and justice for Dalits who have been marginalized and segregated under the shadow of Caste oppression in the sub-continent of India. Empower the Dalits through social awareness, educational program, economical opportunities and developmental projects. Supports activism in the Dalit movement and provides resources.

2663 ■ Dwa Fanm
PO Box 23505
Brooklyn, NY 11202
Ph: (718)222-6320 (347)677-3135
Free: (866)345-3266
Fax: (718)222-1014
E-mail: dwafanm@dwafanm.org
URL: http://www.dwafanm.org
Contact: Farah Tanis, Co-Founder/Exec. Dir.
Founded: 1999. **Multinational. Description:** Empowers all Haitian women and girls with the freedom to control and define their lives. Works to end discrimination, violence and other forms of injustice in the U.S. and in Haiti through service, education, advocacy and grassroots programs.

2664 ■ Global Rights (15370)
1200 18th St. NW, Ste.602
Washington, DC 20036
Ph: (202)822-4600
Fax: (202)822-4606
E-mail: info@globalrights.org
URL: http://gr.convio.net/site/
    PageServer?pagename=gr_index
Contact: **Susan M. Farnsworth, Exec. Dir.**

2665 ■ Human Rights Watch (HRW) (15364)
350 5th Ave., 34th Fl.
New York, NY 10118-3299
Ph: (212)290-4700 **(212)216-1877**
Fax: (212)736-1300
E-mail: hrwnyc@hrw.org
URL: http://www.hrw.org
Contact: Kenneth Roth, Exec. Dir.

2666 ■ International Center for Transitional Justice (ICTJ) (17767)
5 Hanover Sq., 24th Fl.
New York, NY 10004
Ph: (917)637-3800 (917)637-3845
Fax: (917)637-3900
E-mail: info@ictj.org
URL: http://www.ictj.org
Contact: **Refik Hodzic, Dir. of Communications**

2667 ■ Iran Democratic Union (IDU)
PO Box 61551
Potomac, MD 20859-1551
Ph: (202)618-1438
Fax: (404)393-5279
E-mail: info@irandemocraticunion.org
URL: http://www.irandemocraticunion.org
Contact: Reza Pahlavi, Honorary Chm.
Description: Works for a free and secular Iran that honors the individual rights of all its citizens. Educates the public about the human rights crisis in Iran to gain international support.

2668 ■ Physicians for Human Rights (PHR) (17419)
2 Arrow St., Ste.301
Cambridge, MA 02138
Ph: (617)301-4200
Fax: (617)301-4250
E-mail: **web@phrusa.org**
URL: http://physiciansforhumanrights.org
Contact: A. Frank Donahue, CEO

Hunger

2669 ■ Bread for the World (BFW) (15390)
425 3rd St. SW, Ste.1200
Washington, DC 20024
Ph: (202)639-9400
Free: (800)822-7323
Fax: (202)639-9401
E-mail: bread@bread.org
URL: http://www.bread.org
Contact: David Beckmann, Pres.

International Affairs

2670 ■ EastWest Institute (EWI) (16961)
700 Broadway, 2nd Fl.
New York, NY 10003-9536
Ph: (212)824-4100 **(212)824-4112**
Fax: (212)824-4149
E-mail: communications@ewi.info
URL: http://www.ewi.info
Contact: John Edwin Mroz, Pres./Founder/CEO

International Development

2671 ■ Consultative Group to Assist the Poor (CGAP) (16972)
900 19th St. NW, Ste.300
Washington, DC 20006
Ph: (202)473-9594
Fax: (202)522-3744
E-mail: pibarra@worldbank.org
URL: http://www.cgap.org
Contact: **Mr. Tilman Ehrbeck, CEO**

2672 ■ Counterpart - United States Office (16973)
2345 Crystal Dr., Ste.301
Arlington, VA 22202
Ph: (703)236-1200
Fax: (703)412-5035
E-mail: communications@counterpart.org
URL: http://www.counterpart.org
Contact: **Joan C. Parker, Pres./CEO**

2673 ■ Development Group for Alternative Policies (15436)
3179 18th St. NW
Washington, DC 20010
Ph: **(202)898-1566**
E-mail: dgap@developmentgap.org
URL: http://www.developmentgap.org
Contact: Stephen Hellinger, Exec. Dir./Co-Founder

2674 ■ Financial Services Volunteer Corps (FSVC) (17837)
10 E 53rd St., 36th Fl.
New York, NY 10022
Ph: (212)771-1400 (212)771-1443
Fax: **(212)421-2162**
E-mail: jpompay@fsvc.org
URL: http://www.fsvc.org
Contact: J. Andrew Spindler, Pres./CEO

2675 ■ International Professional Partnerships for Sierra Leone (IPPSL)
2042 Swans Neck Way
Reston, VA 20191-4030
Ph: (202)390-5375
Fax: (888)IPPSL-99
E-mail: info@ippsl.org
URL: http://ippsl.org
Contact: Mr. Jamie O'Connell JD, Pres.
Founded: 2009. **Multinational. Description:** Aims to establish a program of professional exchange and assistance to provide capacity-building and public policy development in Sierra Leone. Supports the progress of Sierra Leone's public sector development through technical assistance, fellowships with government agencies, and other international professional partnerships.

2676 ■ TechnoServe (TNS) (16145)
1120 19th St. NW, 8th Fl.
South Tower
Washington, DC 20036
Ph: (202)785-4515
Free: (800)99-WORKS
Fax: (202)785-4544
E-mail: technoserve@tns.org
URL: http://www.technoserve.org
Contact: Bruce McNamer, Pres./CEO

International Relations

2677 ■ American MidEast Leadership Network (AMLN)
PO Box 2156
Long Island City, NY 11102
Ph: (347)924-9674
Fax: (917)591-2177
E-mail: info@amln.org
URL: http://www.amln.org
Contact: Rami Nuseir, Founder/Dir.
Multinational. Description: Aims to empower the Arab-American community in the United States. Enhances cultural, economic and political understanding between the United States and the Arab world. Provides cultural exchange programs to bring together American and Middle Eastern students and young professionals.

2678 ■ American Turkish Friendship Council (ATFC)
1266 W Paces Ferry Rd., No. 257
Atlanta, GA 30327-2306
Ph: (404)848-9600
Fax: (404)364-0777
E-mail: info@theatfc.org
URL: http://www.theatfc.org
Contact: Mona Diamond, Contact
Founded: 2005. **Multinational. Description:** Aims to build relationships and mutual understanding between the citizens of the United States and the Republic of Turkey. Promotes and expands educational, economic and humanitarian relationships.

2679 ■ Friends of Taiwan International (FOTI)
12 S 1st St., Ste.205
San Jose, CA 95113
E-mail: info@fotinternational.org
URL: http://www.fotinternational.org
Contact: Dr. Frank Fiscalini, Chm.
Multinational. Description: Fosters effective relationships between the people of Taiwan and of the United States. Supports the freedom and security of Taiwan.

2680 ■ United Burundian-American Community Association (UBACA)
14339 Rosetree Ct.
Silver Spring, MD 20906
Ph: (240)669-6305
Fax: (240)669-6305
E-mail: president@ubaca.org
URL: http://ubaca.org
Contact: Oscar Niyiragira, Pres.
Membership Dues: general, $30 (annual). **Description:** Seeks to assist in achieving excellence for the betterment of lives of the Burundian community living in the United States. Strengthens the ties of friendship and cooperation between the people of the United States and Burundi. Provides a forum for people of Burundian descent living in the United States.

2681 ■ U.S.-Japan Council (USJC)
1225 Nineteenth St. NW, Ste.700
Washington, DC 20036
Ph: (202)223-6840
Fax: (202)429-0027
E-mail: stakasu@usjapancouncil.org
URL: http://www.usjapancouncil.org
Contact: Irene Hirano, Pres.
Founded: 2009. **Multinational. Description:** Seeks to build a dynamic international network of Japanese Americans committed to strong U.S.-Japan relations. Develops educational and policy programs focused on key bilateral issues and initiatives. Creates a dialogue and exchange on leading U.S.-Japan issues.

International Understanding

2682 ■ Friendship Force International (FFI) (17523)
127 Peachtree St., Ste.501
Atlanta, GA 30303
Ph: (404)522-9490 (404)965-4335

Fax: (404)688-6148
E-mail: **payments@thefriendshipforce.org**
URL: http://www.thefriendshipforce.org
Contact: Dr. George T. Brown Jr., Pres./CEO

2683 ■ National Council for International Visitors (NCIV)
1420 K St. NW, Ste.800
Washington, DC 20005
Ph: (202)842-1414
Free: **(800)523-8101**
Fax: (202)289-4625
E-mail: info@nciv.org
URL: http://www.nciv.org
Contact: Sherry L. Mueller PhD, Pres.

2684 ■ Perhaps Kids Meeting Kids Can Make a Difference (15425)
380 Riverside Dr.
Box 8H
New York, NY 10025
E-mail: info@kidsmeetingkids.org
URL: http://kidsmeetingkids.org
Contact: **Mary Sochet, Chair**

2685 ■ Sister Cities International (SCI) (17547)
915 15th St. NW, 4th Fl.
Washington, DC 20005
Ph: (202)347-8630
Fax: (202)393-6524
E-mail: info@sister-cities.org
URL: http://www.sister-cities.org
Contact: **Brad Cole, Chm.**

2686 ■ Volunteers for Peace (VFP) (15553)
7 Kilburn St., Ste.316
Burlington, VT 05401
Ph: **(802)540-3060**
Fax: (802)259-2922
E-mail: info@vfp.org
URL: http://www.vfp.org
Contact: **Ms. Megan Brook, CEO**

Iran

2687 ■ Iran Policy Committee (IPC)
3700 Massachusetts Ave. NW, Ste.507
Washington, DC 20016
Ph: (202)333-7346
E-mail: info@iranpolicy.org
URL: http://www.iranpolicy.org
Contact: Prof. Raymond Tanter, Pres./Co-Founder
Founded: 2005. **Description:** Represents former officials from the White House, State Department, Pentagon, intelligence agencies and experts from think tanks and universities. Advocates for the facilitation of democratic change in Iran.

Irish

2688 ■ Irish American Unity Conference (IAUC)
PO Box 55573
Washington, DC 20040
Free: (800)947-4282
E-mail: **tjburkejr@gmail.com**
URL: http://www.iauc.org
Contact: **Tom Burke, Pres.**

Israel

2689 ■ Americans for Peace Now (APN)
1101 14th St. NW, 6th Fl.
Washington, DC 20005
Ph: (202)408-9898 (323)934-3480
Fax: **(202)408-9899**
E-mail: apndc@peacenow.org
URL: http://www.peacenow.org
Contact: Debra DeLee, Pres./CEO

Jewish

2690 ■ Jewish Telegraphic Agency (JTA) (17584)
330 7th Ave., 17th Fl.
New York, NY 10001
Ph: (212)643-1890
Fax: (212)643-8498
E-mail: **support@jta.org**
URL: http://www.jta.org
Contact: **David J. Rudis, Pres.**

2691 ■ North American Conference on Ethiopian Jewry (NACOEJ) (15888)
255 W 36th St., Ste.701
New York, NY 10018
Ph: (212)233-5200
Fax: **(212)233-5243**
E-mail: nacoej@nacoej.org
URL: http://www.nacoej.org
Contact: Barbara Ribakove Gordon, Exec. Dir.

Judicial Reform

2692 ■ HALT
1612 K St. NW, Ste.510
Washington, DC 20006-2849
Ph: (202)887-8255
Free: (888)FOR-HALT
Fax: (202)887-9699
E-mail: halt@halt.org
URL: http://www.halt.org
Contact: **Rodd M. Santomauro, Exec. Dir.**

Labor

2693 ■ California Public Employee Relations Program (CPER)
2521 Channing Way, No. 5555
Berkeley, CA 94720-5555
Ph: (510)643-7096 (510)643-7093
Fax: **(510)643-8754**
E-mail: cvendril@berkeley.edu
URL: http://cper.berkeley.edu
Contact: Carol Vendrillo JD, Dir./Ed.

2694 ■ International Labor Rights Forum (ILRF) (17973)
1634 I St. NW, No. 1001
Washington, DC 20006
Ph: (202)347-4100 (207)262-7277
Fax: (202)347-4885
E-mail: laborrights@ilrf.org
URL: http://www.laborrights.org
Contact: **Judy Gearhart, Exec. Dir.**

Latin America

2695 ■ Fellowship of Reconciliation Task Force on Latin America and Caribbean (FOR TFLAC) (15954)
PO Box 271
Nyack, NY 10960
Ph: (845)358-4601
Fax: (845)358-4924
E-mail: **mjohnson@forusa.org**
URL: http://www.forusa.org
Contact: Mark C. Johnson, Exec. Dir.

2696 ■ Washington Office on Latin America (WOLA)
1666 Connecticut Ave. NW, Ste.400
Washington, DC 20009
Ph: (202)797-2171
Fax: (202)797-2172
E-mail: **employment@wola.org**
URL: http://www.wola.org
Contact: Joy Olson, Exec. Dir.

Leadership

2697 ■ American Council of Young Political Leaders (ACYPL) (18000)
2131 K St. NW, Ste.400
Washington, DC 20037
Ph: (202)857-0999
Fax: (202)857-0027
E-mail: **qlide@acypl.org**
URL: http://www.acypl.org
Contact: Linda Rotunno, CEO

Marriage

2698 ■ Alternatives to Marriage Project (AtMP) (17656)
358 7th Ave.
PMB 131
Brooklyn, NY 11215
Ph: **(347)987-1068**
URL: http://www.unmarried.org
Contact: **Nicky Grist, Exec. Dir.**

Middle East

2699 ■ America-MidEast Educational and Training Services (AMIDEAST) (15699)
1730 M St. NW, Ste.1100
Washington, DC 20036
Ph: (202)776-9600
Free: **(800)368-5720**
Fax: (202)776-7000
E-mail: inquiries@amideast.org
URL: http://www.amideast.org
Contact: Ambassador Theodore H. Kattouf, Pres./ CEO

2700 ■ Americans for a Safe Israel (AFSI) (17683)
1751 2nd Ave.
New York, NY 10128-5363
Free: (800)235-3658
Fax: **(212)828-1717**
E-mail: afsi@rcn.com
URL: http://afsi.org
Contact: Barry Freedman, Exec. Dir.

2701 ■ International Council for Middle East Studies (ICMES)
1055 Thomas Jefferson St. NW, Ste.M100
Washington, DC 20009
Ph: (202)315-8680
E-mail: robert.keating@icmes.net
URL: http://www.icmes.net
Contact: Don Wallace, Chm.
Founded: 2010. **Multinational. Description:** Aims to inform and enlighten American citizens about the current states of mind in the Middle East. Promotes peaceful solutions and outcomes of Middle East social, political, economic, cultural and educational problems and concerns. Provides a better understanding of major religious and non-religious beliefs that are relevant to the Middle East.

2702 ■ Ishmael and Isaac
One Bratenahl Pl., Ste.1302
Bratenahl, OH 44108
Ph: (216)233-7333
E-mail: info@ishmaelandisaac.org
URL: http://www.ishmaelandisaac.org
Contact: Anita Gray, Pres.
Founded: 2003. **Multinational. Description:** Aims to promote the reconciliation of Israelis and Palestinians. Encourages collaboration between the American Arab and Jewish communities in the United States to build the foundation for sustainable economic development and peace.

2703 ■ Middle East Studies Association of North America (MESA) (17696)
Univ. of Arizona
1219 N Santa Rita Ave.
Tucson, AZ 85721
Ph: (520)621-5850 (520)626-6290
Fax: (520)626-9095
E-mail: **mesana@email.arizona.edu**
URL: http://mesa.wns.ccit.arizona.edu
Contact: Amy W. Newhall, Exec. Dir./Treas.

Military

2704 ■ Center for Strategic and Budgetary Assessments (CSBA) (17706)
1667 K St. NW, Ste.900
Washington, DC 20006
Ph: (202)331-7990 **(202)719-1341**
Fax: (202)331-8019
E-mail: info@csbaonline.org
URL: http://www.csbaonline.org
Contact: Dr. Andrew F. Krepinevich, Pres.

Missing-in-Action

2705 ■ National League of Families of American Prisoners and Missing in Southeast Asia (17211)
5673 Columbia Pike, Ste.100
Falls Church, VA 22041
Ph: (703)465-7432
Fax: (703)465-7433
E-mail: **powmiafam@aol.com**
URL: http://www.pow-miafamilies.org
Contact: Ann Mills Griffiths, Exec. Dir.

Muslim

2706 ■ Free Muslims Coalition (FMC) (18084)
1050 17th St. NW, Ste.1000
Washington, DC 20036
Ph: (202)776-7190 **(202)907-5724**
E-mail: info@freemuslims.org
URL: http://www.freemuslims.org
Contact: Kamal Nawash, Pres.

Native American

2707 ■ United Indians of All Tribes Foundation (UIATF) (17731)
Discovery Park
PO Box 99100
Seattle, WA 98199
Ph: (206)285-4425
Fax: **(206)282-3640**
E-mail: info@unitedindians.org
URL: http://www.unitedindians.org
Contact: **Henry Cagey, Chm.**

Nicaragua

2708 ■ Bikes Not Bombs (BNB) (15762)
284 Amory St.
Jamaica Plain, MA 02130
Ph: (617)522-0222
Fax: (617)522-0922
E-mail: **sam@bikesnotbombs.org**
URL: http://www.bikesnotbombs.org
Contact: Samantha Wechsler, Exec. Dir.

Nuclear War and Weapons

2709 ■ Global Security Institute (GSI) (17282)
GSB Bldg., Ste.400
One Belmont Ave.
Bala Cynwyd, PA 19004

Ph: (610)668-5488 **(610)668-5470**
Fax: (610)668-5489
E-mail: general@gsinstitute.org
URL: http://www.gsinstitute.org
Contact: Jonathan Granoff, Pres.

2710 ■ Psychologists for Social Responsibility (PsySR) (17300)
258 Harvard St.
PMB 282
Brookline, MA 02446
Ph: (202)543-5347
Fax: **(617)274-8048**
E-mail: info@psysr.org
URL: http://www.psysr.org
Contact: Colleen Cordes, Exec. Dir.

2711 ■ United Against Nuclear Iran (UANI)
PO Box 1028
New York, NY 10008-1021
Ph: (212)554-3296
Fax: (212)554-3299
E-mail: info@unitedagainstnucleariran.com
URL: http://www.unitedagainstnucleariran.com
Contact: Mark Wallace, Pres.
Founded: 2008. **Description:** Aims to prevent Iran into becoming regional super-power possessing nuclear weapons. Creates awareness about the danger a nuclear-armed Iran poses to the region and the world.

Parents

2712 ■ National Center for Fathering (NCF)
PO Box 413888
Kansas City, MO 64141
Free: (800)593-DADS
Fax: (913)384-4665
E-mail: dads@fathers.com
URL: http://www.fathers.com
Contact: **Carey Casey, CEO**

Peace

2713 ■ The Children of War (TCOW) (18197)
PO Box 223602
Chantilly, VA 20153-3602
Ph: (703)625-9147
E-mail: info@thechildrenofwar.org
URL: http://thechildrenofwar.org/web1
Contact: **Najib Aziz, Pres./Founder**

2714 ■ Fellowship of Reconciliation - USA (FOR) (17832)
PO Box 271
Nyack, NY 10960
Ph: (845)358-4601
Fax: (845)358-4924
E-mail: mjohnson@forusa.org
URL: http://www.forusa.org
Contact: Mark C. Johnson PhD, Exec. Dir.

2715 ■ Global Ambassadors for Children (GAFC)
7399 N Shadeland Ave., No. 116
Indianapolis, IN 46250
Ph: (317)814-5318
Free: (866)338-3468
Fax: (317)814-2116
E-mail: contact@ambassadorsforchildren.org
URL: http://ambassadorsforchildren.org
Contact: David Gorsage, CEO
Founded: 1998. **Multinational. Description:** Promotes peace and understanding through face to face cultural exchange opportunities. Provides hands-on interaction with disadvantaged children, balanced by opportunities for sightseeing and immersion in the native culture of the community served. Serves children around the world through short-term humanitarian service trips and sustainable programs.

2716 ■ Jane Addams Peace Association (JAPA) (2455)
777 United Nations Plz., 6th Fl.
New York, NY 10017
Ph: (212)682-8830
Fax: (212)286-8211
E-mail: japa@igc.org
URL: http://www.janeaddamspeace.org
Contact: **Jane Addams, Exec. Dir.**

2717 ■ Kids for Peace
3303 James Dr.
Carlsbad, CA 92008
Ph: (760)730-3320
E-mail: info@kidsforpeaceglobal.org
URL: http://www.kidsforpeaceglobal.org
Contact: Jill McManigal, Exec. Dir.
Multinational. Description: Aims to cultivate every child's innate ability to promote peace and make the world a better place. Fosters peace through cross-cultural experiences and hands-on arts, service and environmental projects. **Awards:** Peace Hero. **Frequency:** annual. **Type:** recognition. **Recipient:** for promoting peace.

2718 ■ Peace and Justice Studies Association (PJSA) (18507)
Prescott Coll.
220 Grove Ave.
Prescott, AZ 86301
Ph: (928)350-2008
E-mail: **info@peacejusticestudies.org**
URL: http://www.peacejusticestudies.org
Contact: Randall Amster, Exec. Dir.

2719 ■ Peaceworkers Nonviolent Peaceforce (NP) (16185)
425 Oak Grove St.
Minneapolis, MN 55403
Ph: (612)871-0005
Fax: (612)871-0006
E-mail: information@nonviolentpeaceforce.org
URL: http://www.nonviolentpeaceforce.org
Contact: **Dr. Tim Wallis, Exec. Dir.**

2720 ■ Student Peace Alliance (SPA)
PO Box 27601
Washington, DC 20038
Ph: (202)684-2553
E-mail: aaron@thepeacealliance.org
URL: http://www.studentpeacealliance.org
Contact: Aaron Voldman, Exec. Dir.
Founded: 2006. **Description:** Seeks to engage communities and policy makers in building sustainable peace. Advocates for evidence-based legislation and policy pertaining to effective peacebuilding.

2721 ■ Veterans for Peace (VFP) (17385)
216 S Meramec Ave.
St. Louis, MO 63105
Ph: (314)725-6005
Fax: (314)725-7103
E-mail: vfped@veteransforpeace.org
URL: http://www.veteransforpeace.org
Contact: **Elliott Adams, Pres.**

2722 ■ Voters for Peace
2842 N Calvert St.
Baltimore, MD 21218
Ph: (443)708-8360
Fax: (877)637-3335
E-mail: action@votersforpeace.org
URL: http://votersforpeace.us
Contact: Kevin Martin, Exec. Dir.
Founded: 2006. **Description:** Educates and encourages voters to end the occupation of Iraq and prevent future wars of aggression. Aims to mobilize anti-war voters to become effective peace advocates.

Political Parties

2723 ■ Working Families Party (WFP) (18608)
2 Nevins St., 3rd Fl.
Brooklyn, NY 11217
Ph: (718)222-3796
Fax: (718)246-3718
E-mail: wfp@workingfamiliesparty.org
URL: http://www.workingfamiliesparty.org
Contact: **T.J. Helmstetter, Contact**

Politics

2724 ■ American Association of Political Consultants (AAPC) (17976)
8400 Westpark Dr., 2nd Fl.
Washington, DC 20003
Ph: **(703)245-8020**
Fax: **(703)610-9005**
E-mail: **info@aapc.org**
URL: http://www.theaapc.org
Contact: Anthony Fazio, Chm.

2725 ■ American League of Lobbyists (ALL) (16044)
c/o Patti Jo Baber, Exec. Dir.
PO Box 30005
Alexandria, VA 22310
Ph: (703)960-3011
E-mail: alldc.org@erols.com
URL: http://www.alldc.org
Contact: **Gina Bancroft, Acting Exec. Dir.**

2726 ■ Arab American Institute (AAI) (18344)
1600 K St. NW, Ste.601
Washington, DC 20006
Ph: (202)429-9210
Fax: (202)429-9214
E-mail: **webmaster@aaiusa.org**
URL: http://www.aaiusa.org
Contact: Dr. James Zogby, Pres.

Polls

2727 ■ American Association for Public Opinion Research (AAPOR) (18638)
111 Deer Lake Rd., Ste.100
Deerfield, IL 60015
Ph: (847)205-2651
Fax: (847)480-9282
E-mail: info@aapor.org
URL: http://www.aapor.org
Contact: **Scott Keeter, Pres.**

Public Affairs

2728 ■ The Asia Foundation (TAF) (14996)
PO Box 193223
San Francisco, CA 94119-3223
Ph: (415)982-4640
Free: (866)581-GIVE
Fax: (415)392-8863
E-mail: info@asiafound.org
URL: http://www.asiafoundation.org
Contact: **David D. Arbold, Pres.**

2729 ■ Ford Foundation (18028)
320 E 43rd St.
New York, NY 10017
Ph: (212)573-5000
Fax: (212)351-3677
E-mail: office-of-communications@fordfound.org
URL: http://www.fordfound.org
Contact: **Mr. Nancy P. Feller, VP/Sec./Gen. Counsel**

Public Finance

2730 ■ Business Roundtable (BR) (18673)
1717 Rhode Island Ave. NW, Ste.800
Washington, DC 20036
Ph: (202)872-1260
Fax: (202)466-3509
E-mail: info@businessroundtable.org
URL: http://businessroundtable.org
Contact: **John Engler, Pres.**

Public Information

2731 ■ National Freedom of Information Coalition (18413)
Univ. of Missouri-Columbia
Journalism Inst.
101 Reynolds
Columbia, MO 65211
Ph: **(573)882-4856 (573)882-3075**
Fax: (573)884-6204
E-mail: buntingk@missouri.edu
URL: http://www.nfoic.org
Contact: Ken Bunting, Exec.Dir.

Public Policy

2732 ■ Economic Policy Institute (EPI) (16703)
1333 H St. NW, Ste.300
East Tower
Washington, DC 20005-4707
Ph: (202)775-8810
Free: **(800)374-4844**
Fax: (202)775-0819
E-mail: epi@epi.org
URL: http://www.epi.org
Contact: Lawrence Mishel, Pres.

2733 ■ Institute for Policy Studies (IPS) (18089)
1112 16th St. NW, Ste.600
Washington, DC 20036
Ph: (202)234-9382
E-mail: info@ips-dc.org
URL: http://www.ips-dc.org
Contact: **Sarah Anderson, Dir.**

2734 ■ Northeast-Midwest Institute (NMI) (17606)
50 F St. NW, Ste.950
Washington, DC 20001
Ph: (202)464-4014 **(202)464-4005**
Fax: (202)544-0043
E-mail: info@nemw.org
URL: http://www.nemw.org
Contact: **Allegra Cangelosi, Pres.**

Radio

2735 ■ Mainstream Media Project (MMP)
854 9th St., Ste.B
Arcata, CA 95521
Ph: (707)826-9111 **(707)923-1177**
Fax: (707)826-9112
E-mail: info@mainstream-media.net
URL: http://www.mainstream-media.net
Contact: Jimmy Durchslag, Exec. Dir.

Refugees

2736 ■ Church World Service, Immigration and Refugee Program (CWS/IRP) (18497)
475 Riverside Dr., Ste.700
New York, NY 10115
Ph: (212)870-2061 **(212)870-2676**
Free: (800)297-1516
Fax: (212)870-3523

E-mail: info@churchworldservice.org
URL: http://www.churchworldservice.org/Immigration
Contact: Erol Kekic, Dir.

2737 ■ Refugee Council U.S.A. (18134)
1628 16th St. NW
Washington, DC 20009
Ph: (202)319-2102
Fax: (202)319-2104
E-mail: info@rcusa.org
URL: http://www.rcusa.org
Contact: **Dan Kosten, Chm.**

Reproductive Rights

2738 ■ Center for Reproductive Rights (16248)
120 Wall St.
New York, NY 10005
Ph: (917)637-3600 **(917)637-3791**
Fax: (917)637-3666
E-mail: info@reprorights.org
URL: http://reproductiverights.org
Contact: Ms. Nancy Northup, Pres.

Right to Life

2739 ■ Pro-Life Action League (PLAL) (16306)
6160 N Cicero Ave., Ste.600
Chicago, IL 60646
Ph: (773)777-2900 **(773)777-2525**
Fax: (773)777-3061
E-mail: info@prolifeaction.org
URL: http://www.prolifeaction.org
Contact: Joseph M. Scheidler, Natl. Dir./Publisher

Rural Development

2740 ■ Inter-American Foundation (IAF) (18203)
901 N Stuart St., 10th Fl.
Balston
Arlington, VA 22203-1821
Ph: (703)306-4301
Fax: (703)306-4365
E-mail: info@iaf.gov
URL: http://www.iaf.gov
Contact: **Robert N. Kaplan, Pres.**

Security

2741 ■ Business Executives for National Security (BENS) (18217)
1030 15th St., NW, Ste.200 E
Washington, DC 20005
Ph: (202)296-2125
Fax: **(202)296-2490**
E-mail: bens@bens.org
URL: http://www.bens.org/home.html
Contact: **Montgomery C. Meigs, Pres./CEO**

2742 ■ Defense Orientation Conference Association (DOCA) (16845)
9271 Old Keene Mill Rd., Ste.200
Burke, VA 22015-4202
Ph: (703)451-1200
URL: http://www.doca.org
Contact: **Frank M. Weinberg, Pres.**

2743 ■ OPSEC Professionals Society (OPS) (18594)
PO Box 150515
Alexandria, VA 22315-0515
Fax: **(503)907-7511**
E-mail: president@opsecsociety.org
URL: http://www.opsecsociety.org
Contact: Daryl Haegley, Pres.

2744 ■ **Women in International Security (WIIS) (16336)**
3600 North St. NW, Lower Level
Washington, DC 20007
Ph: (202)687-3366 (202)687-2817
Fax: **(202)687-4303**
E-mail: wiisinfo@georgetown.edu
URL: http://wiis.georgetown.edu
Contact: Jolynn Shoemaker, Exec. Dir.

Social Action

2745 ■ **Fuel for Truth (FFT)**
165 E 56th St., 2nd Fl.
New York, NY 10022
Ph: (212)594-4435
E-mail: info@fuelfortruth.org
URL: http://www.fuelfortruth.org
Contact: Meredith Weiss, Exec. Dir.

Founded: 2001. **Description:** Aims to furnish young Americans with basic facts and necessary skills to advocate on behalf of Israel and the United States. Supports Israel's fight against radical Islamic terror.

2746 ■ **Vote Hemp (VH)**
PO Box 1571
Brattleboro, VT 05302
Ph: (202)318-8999
Fax: (202)318-8999
E-mail: hempinfo@votehemp.com
URL: http://www.votehemp.com
Contact: Eric Steenstra, Pres.

Founded: 2000. **Description:** Advocates for the acceptance of and free market for industrial hemp, low-THC oilseed and fiber varieties of Cannabis. Works to defend against any new laws, regulations or policies that would prohibit or restrict hemp commerce or imports.

Social Change

2747 ■ **Graduation Pledge Alliance (GPA) (19144)**
c/o Heidi Gross, Coor.
Bentley Univ.
175 Forest St.
Waltham, MA 02452
Ph: (781)891-2529
Fax: **(781)891-2896**
E-mail: gpa@bentley.edu
URL: http://www.graduationpledge.org
Contact: **Tim Rairdon, Exec. Dir.**

Social Justice

2748 ■ **Ensaaf**
811 1st Ave., Ste.401
Seattle, WA 98104
Ph: (206)866-5642
Fax: (270)916-7074
E-mail: info@ensaaf.org
URL: http://www.ensaaf.org
Contact: Jaskaran Kaur, Co-Dir./Co-Founder

Founded: 2004. **Multinational. Description:** Seeks to end impunity and achieve justice for mass state crimes in India, with a focus on Punjab. Documents abuses to counter official denials and build evidence for accountability. Engages in strategic litigation to remove perpetrators from power and set national precedents on human rights norms.

Sociology

2749 ■ **Sociologists Without Borders (SSF) (18293)**
c/o David Brunsma, Treas.
Univ. of Missouri
312 Middlebush Hall
Columbia, MO 65211
Ph: **(537)882-1067**
Fax: **(537)355-0599**
E-mail: **jrblau@email.unc.edu**
URL: http://www.sociologistswithoutborders.org
Contact: Judith Blau, Pres.

Terrorism

2750 ■ **International Counter-Terrorism Officers Association (ICTOA) (17856)**
PO Box 580009
Flushing, NY 11358
Ph: (212)564-5048
Fax: (718)661-4044
E-mail: info@ictoa.org
URL: http://www.ictoa.org
Contact: Brian J. Corrigan, Exec. Dir.

Tibet

2751 ■ **Tibet Justice Center (TJC) (2528)**
440 Grand Ave., Ste.425
Oakland, CA 94610
Ph: (510)486-0588
Fax: **(510)548-3785**

E-mail: tjc@tibetjustice.org
URL: http://www.tibetjustice.org
Contact: Robert D. Sloane, Pres.

Ukrainian

2752 ■ **Saint Andrew's Ukrainian Orthodox Society (SAUOS) (16184)**
c/o Vitali Vizir
1023 Yorkshire Dr.
Los Altos, CA 94024
Ph: **(440)582-1051**
E-mail: **imahlay@yahoo.com**
URL: http://www.uocofusa.org/st_andrew_uos.html
Contact: Rev. Deacon Ihor Mahlay, Pres.

2753 ■ **U.S. Ukraine Foundation (USUF)**
1 Thomas Cir. NW, Ste.900-B
Washington, DC 20005
Ph: (202)223-2228
Fax: (202)223-1224
E-mail: info@usukraine.org
URL: http://usukraine.org
Contact: Nadia K. McConnell, Pres.

Waste

2754 ■ **Basel Action Network (BAN) (17918)**
206 First Ave. S., Ste.410
Seattle, WA 98104
Ph: (206)652-5555
Fax: (206)652-5750
E-mail: inform@ban.org
URL: http://www.ban.org
Contact: Mr. Jim Puckett, Contact

Widowhood

2755 ■ **Global Action on Widowhood (GLoW)**
3 Newport Rd., Ste.1
Cambridge, MA 02140
Ph: (617)441-8892
E-mail: ladarelkg@verizon.net
URL: http://www.globalactiononwidowhood.org
Contact: Margaret Owen, Founder/Dir.
Founded: 2010. **Multinational. Description:** Aims to advocate for the human rights of widows around the world and to enforce widows' rights. Raises the issues of widowhood in the UN system and in various forums.

Youth

2756 ■ **Global Youth Action Network (GYAN)**
540 Pres. St., 3rd Fl.
Brooklyn, NY 11215
Ph: (212)661-6111
URL: http://gyan.tigweb.org
Contact: **Dr. Poonam Ahluwalia, Exec. Dir.**

Afghan

2757 ■ Afghan American Muslim Outreach (AAMO)
1339 E Katella Ave., No. 333
Orange, CA 92867
Free: **(877)663-2266**
E-mail: info@aamo-net.org
URL: http://www.aamo-net.org
Contact: Jawid Habib, Sec.

2758 ■ Afghan Friends Network (AFN)
PO Box 170368
San Francisco, CA 94117
Ph: (650)931-4527
Fax: (866)330-2342
E-mail: info@afghanfriends.net
URL: http://afghanfriends.net
Contact: **John Bortner, Pres.**

Alumni

2759 ■ Defense Intel Alumni Association (DIAA) (18892)
256 Morris Creek Rd.
Cullen, VA 23934
Ph: (571)426-0098
Fax: (703)738-7487
E-mail: admin@diaalumni.org
URL: http://www.dialumni.org
Contact: **Judi Demulling, Pres.**

2760 ■ Marquette University Alumni Association (MUAA) (18527)
Marquette Univ.
PO Box 1881
Milwaukee, WI 53201-1881
Ph: (414)288-7441 (414)351-1998
Free: (800)344-7544
Fax: (414)288-3956
E-mail: muconnect@marquette.edu
URL: http://www.marquette.edu/alumni
Contact: **Valerie Wilson Reed, Pres.**

2761 ■ North Dakota State University Alumni Association (NDSUAA) (16304)
1241 N Univ. Dr.
Fargo, ND 58102-2524
Ph: (701)231-6800 (701)231-6834
Free: (800)279-8971
Fax: (701)231-6801
E-mail: office@ndsualumni.com
URL: http://www.ndsualumni.com
Contact: **Barry Batcheller, Chm.**

2762 ■ Ouachita Baptist University Alumni Association (OBUAA) (18539)
410 Ouachita St.
Arkadelphia, AR 71998
Ph: (870)245-5506 (870)245-5000
Free: (800)342-5628

Fax: (870)245-5500
E-mail: alumni@obu.edu
URL: http://www.obualumni.org/netcommunity
Contact: **Dr. Wesley Kluck, Pres.**

2763 ■ University of Texas at Brownsville and Texas Southmost College Alumni Association
80 Ft. Brown
Brownsville, TX 78520-4956
Ph: (956)882-4327 **(956)982-0106**
Fax: (956)983-7990
E-mail: veronica.m.garcia@utb.edu
URL: http://blue.utb.edu/alumni
Contact: Veronica M. Garcia, Program Dir.

2764 ■ University of Texas I Pan-American Alumni Association (18558)
1201 W Univ. Dr., UC108
Edinburg, TX 78541
Ph: (956)381-2500
Fax: (956)381-2385
E-mail: alumni@utpa.edu
URL: http://www.utpaalumni.com
Contact: **Jose Gonzalez, Pres.**

2765 ■ University of Wisconsin I Eau Claire Alumni Association (UWECAA) (18559)
PO Box 4004
Eau Claire, WI 54702-4004
Ph: (715)836-3266
Fax: (715)836-4375
E-mail: alumni@uwec.edu
URL: http://www.uwec.edu/alumni
Contact: **Larry Allen, Pres.**

Appalachian

2766 ■ Melungeon Heritage Association (MHA)
PO Box 1253
Danville, VA 24543
E-mail: mhainc2000@yahoo.com
URL: http://www.melungeon.org
Contact: S.J. Arthur, Pres.

Arabic

2767 ■ Arab American Women's Council (18951)
c/o American Arab Chamber of Commerce
12740 W Warren Ave., Ste.101
Dearborn, MI 48126
Ph: (313)945-1700
Fax: (313)945-6697
E-mail: chamber@americanarab.com
URL: http://www.americanarab.com
Contact: **Ahmad Chebbani, Chm./Co-Founder**

Armed Forces

2768 ■ Army and Air Force Mutual Aid Association (AAFMAA) (19235)
102 Sheridan Ave., Bldg. 468
Fort Myer, VA 22211-1110
Ph: **(703)707-4600**
Free: (800)336-4538
Fax: (703)522-1336
E-mail: info@aafmaa.com
URL: http://www.aafmaa.com
Contact: Ret. Major Walt Lincoln CFP, Pres./Treas.

2769 ■ USO World Headquarters (19240)
PO Box 96322
Washington, DC 20090
Ph: (703)908-6400
Free: **(888)484-3876**
Fax: **(703)908-6433**
E-mail: info@uso.org
URL: http://www.uso.org
Contact: Sloan D. Gibson, Pres./CEO

Asian

2770 ■ Asian/Pacific American Heritage Association (APAHA) (19250)
6220 Westpark, Ste.245B
Houston, TX 77057
Ph: (713)784-1112
Fax: **(832)201-8228**
E-mail: info@apaha.org
URL: http://www.apaha.org
Contact: Shehla Zakaullah, Exec. Dir.

Austrian

2771 ■ American-Austrian Cultural Society (A-ACS) (17208)
c/o Mr. Michael Korenchuk, Treas.
116 E Melrose St.
Chevy Chase, MD 20815
E-mail: american_austrian_society@yahoo.com
URL: http://american-austrian-cultural-society.com
Contact: Ms. Ulrike Wiesner, Pres.

Awards

2772 ■ International Foodservice Manufacturers Association I International Gold and Silver Plate Society (IGSPS) (19499)
2 Prudential Plz.
180 N Stetson Ave., Ste.4400
Chicago, IL 60601-6766
Ph: (312)540-4400
Fax: (312)540-4401

E-mail: ifma@ifmaworld.com
URL: http://www.ifmaworld.com/index.
 php?idrub=55&idmeta=65&idlang=2&idsite=1
Contact: **Sally Luck, Chair**

Catholic

2773 ■ Daughters of Isabella, International Circle (D of I) (18118)
PO Box 9585
New Haven, CT 06535
Ph: (203)865-2570
Fax: (203)865-5586
E-mail: membership@daughtersofisabella.org
URL: http://www.daughtersofisabella.org
Contact: **Christiane Chagnon, Intl. Regent**

2774 ■ Junior Knights of Peter Claver (JKPC) (18121)
c/o Knights of Peter Claver, Inc.
1825 Orleans Ave.
New Orleans, LA 70116-2825
Ph: (504)821-4425
Fax: (504)821-4253
E-mail: info@kofpc.org
URL: http://www.kofpc.org
Contact: **Fredron Dekarlos Blackmon, Supreme Knight/CEO**

2775 ■ Knights of Peter Claver (KPC) (19522)
1825 Orleans Ave.
New Orleans, LA 70116
Ph: (504)821-4225
Fax: (504)821-4253
E-mail: info@kofpc.org
URL: http://www.kofpc.org
Contact: **Mr. Michael J. Taylor, Exec. Dir.**

Chinese

2776 ■ Association of Chinese-American Professionals (ACAP) (17244)
10303 Westoffice Dr.
Houston, TX 77042-5306
E-mail: dchen@njclaw.com
URL: http://www.acap-usa.org
Contact: **Janet Chung, Pres.**

2777 ■ Council of Overseas Chinese Services (COCS)
PO Box 6940
New York, NY 10150
Ph: (347)617-2687
E-mail: contact@cocservices.org
URL: http://www.cocservices.org
Contact: **Ge Li, Pres.**

Czech

2778 ■ American Friends of the Czech Republic (AFoCR)
4410 Massachusetts Ave. NW, No. 391
Washington, DC 20016-5572
Ph: (202)413-5528
Fax: **(703)549-0224**
E-mail: afocr@afocr.org
URL: http://www.afocr.org
Contact: **Fred Malek, Chm.**

Dominican Republic

2779 ■ Dominican American National Roundtable (DANR)
1050 17th St. NW, Ste.600
Washington, DC 20036
Ph: (202)238-0097
Fax: (202)536-5253

E-mail: info@danr.org
URL: http://www.danr.org
Contact: **Dr. Maria Teresa Feliciano, Pres.**

Finnish

2780 ■ Finlandia Foundation National (FF) (16926)
PO Box 92298
Pasadena, CA 91109-2298
Ph: (626)795-2081
Fax: (626)795-6533
E-mail: **smileys.place@juno.com**
URL: http://www.finlandiafoundation.org
Contact: Anita Smiley, Pres.

French

2781 ■ Committee of French Speaking Societies (CFSS) (19062)
30 E 40th St., Ste.906
New York, NY 10016
E-mail: contact@cafusa.org
URL: http://www.cafusa.org
Contact: **Dr. Gerard Epelbaum, Pres.**

2782 ■ French-American Aid for Children (FAAFC) (19064)
150 E 58th St., 23rd Fl.
New York, NY 10155
Ph: (212)486-9593
Fax: (212)486-9594
E-mail: info@faafc.org
URL: http://www.aidforchildren.org
Contact: **Mrs. Joerg Klebe, Pres.**

Georgian

2783 ■ Georgian Association in the United States of America (GAUSA) (19070)
2300 M St. NW, Ste.800
Washington, DC 20037
Ph: (202)234-2441
E-mail: **mamukagt@aol.com**
URL: http://www.georgianassociation.org
Contact: Mamuka Tsereteli, Pres.

German

2784 ■ American Council on Germany (ACG) (16958)
14 E 60th St., Ste.1000
New York, NY 10022
Ph: (212)826-3636
Fax: (212)758-3445
E-mail: info@acgusa.org
URL: http://www.acgusa.org
Contact: **Robert M. Kimmitt, Chm.**

2785 ■ American Historical Society of Germans From Russia (AHSGR) (18686)
631 D St.
Lincoln, NE 68502-1199
Ph: (402)474-3363
Fax: (402)474-7229
E-mail: ahsgr@ahsgr.org
URL: http://www.ahsgr.org
Contact: **Donald C. Schenk, Pres.**

2786 ■ Germans From Russia Heritage Society (GRHS) (19579)
1125 W Turnpike Ave.
Bismarck, ND 58501-8115
Ph: (701)223-6167
Fax: **(701)223-4421**
E-mail: grhs@grhs.org
URL: **http://www.grhs.org**
Contact: **Don Ehreth, Pres.**

Greek

2787 ■ Daughters of Penelope (DP) (19087)
1909 Q St. NW, Ste.500
Washington, DC 20009
Ph: (202)234-9741
Fax: (202)483-6983
E-mail: **christinekc2011@gmail.com**
URL: http://daughtersofpenelope.org
Contact: Christine K. Constantine, Pres.

Hispanic

2788 ■ League of United Latin American Citizens (LULAC) (17323)
2000 L St. NW, Ste.610
Washington, DC 20036
Ph: (202)833-6130
Free: (877)LUL-AC01
Fax: (202)833-6135
E-mail: **mmoran@lulac.org**
URL: http://lulac.org
Contact: **Margaret Moran, Natl. Pres.**

2789 ■ National Image (19602)
PO Box 1368
Bonita, CA 91908
Ph: (858)495-7407
Fax: (858)495-7664
E-mail: chair_natlimage@live.com
URL: http://www.nationalimageinc.org
Contact: Sylvia Chavez-Metoyer, Chair/CEO

Hungarian

2790 ■ American Hungarian Foundation (AHF) (9166)
PO Box 1084
New Brunswick, NJ 08903
Ph: (732)846-5777
Fax: (732)249-7033
E-mail: info@ahfoundation.org
URL: http://www.ahfoundation.org
Contact: **Gergely Hajdu-Nemeth, Exec. Dir.**

Indian

2791 ■ Association of Indian Muslims of America (AIM) (2562)
PO Box 10654
Silver Spring, MD 20914
E-mail: info@aimamerica.org
URL: http://www.aimamerica.org
Contact: **Dr. Mohammad Thahir, Sec.**

2792 ■ Network of Indian Professionals (NetIP)
PO Box 06362
Chicago, IL 60606
Ph: (312)952-0254
E-mail: **ashwin.janakiram@netip.org**
URL: http://na.netip.org
Contact: **Ashwin Janakiram, Pres.**

Insurance

2793 ■ Degree of Honor Protective Association (DHPA) (16992)
400 Robert St. N, Ste.1600
St. Paul, MN 55101-2029
Ph: (651)228-7600 **(651)228-7620**
Free: (800)947-5812
Fax: (651)224-7446
E-mail: jfelling@degreeofhonor.com
URL: http://www.degreeofhonor.com
Contact: Jacqueline A. Felling, CEO/Natl. Pres.

2794 ■ Equitable Reserve Association (16494)
116 S Commercial St.
PO Box 448
Neenah, WI 54957-0448
Free: (800)722-1574
Fax: (920)725-2869
E-mail: generalinfo@equitablereserve.com
URL: http://www.equitablereserve.com
Contact: Melvin L. Rambo, Pres./CEO

2795 ■ Independent Order of Vikings (IOV) (17349)
5250 S Sixth St.
PO Box 5147
Springfield, IL 62705-5147
Free: (877)241-6006
Fax: (217)241-6574
E-mail: member_services@iovikings.org
URL: http://www.iovikings.org
Contact: Dewey Bringedahl, Grand Chief

Iranian

2796 ■ Iranian Alliances Across Borders (IAAB)
PO Box 20429
New York, NY 10009
E-mail: join@iranianalliances.org
URL: http://www.iranianalliances.org
Contact: Mana Kharrazi, Exec. Dir.

Italian

2797 ■ Unico National (UN) (19436)
271 U.S. Hwy. 46 W, Ste.A-108
Fairfield, NJ 07004
Ph: (973)808-0035 (570)348-4921
Free: (800)877-1492
Fax: (973)808-0043
E-mail: uniconational@unico.org
URL: http://www.unico.org
Contact: Christopher DiMattio, Pres.

Jewelry

2798 ■ Gemological Institute of America Alumni Association (GIA) (18283)
The Robert Mouawad Campus
5345 Armada Dr.
Carlsbad, CA 92008
Ph: (760)603-4135 (760)603-4000
Free: (800)421-7250
Fax: (760)603-4199
E-mail: alumni@gia.edu
URL: http://www.gia.edu
Contact: **Susan M. Jacques, Chair**

Law Enforcement

2799 ■ Society of Former Special Agents of the Federal Bureau of Investigation (SFSAFBI) (19697)
3717 Fettler Park Dr.
Dumfries, VA 22025
Ph: (703)445-0026
Free: (800)527-7372
Fax: (703)445-0039
E-mail: socxfbi@socxfbi.org
URL: http://www.socxfbi.org
Contact: **Lester A. Davis, Pres.**

Leadership

2800 ■ National Community for Latino Leadership (NCLL)
1701 K St. NW, Ste.301
Washington, DC 20006
Ph: **(202)257-4419**

Fax: (202)721-8296
E-mail: ncll@latinoleadership.org
URL: http://www.latinoleadership.org
Contact: Alfred Ramirez, Pres.

Macedonian

2801 ■ Macedonian Patriotic Organization of United States and Canada (MPO) (16858)
124 W Wayne St.
Fort Wayne, IN 46802
Ph: (260)422-5900
Fax: (260)422-1348
E-mail: info@macedonian.org
URL: http://www.macedonian.org
Contact: **Mr. Nick Nicoloff, Pres.**

Marine Corps

2802 ■ Marine Corps CounterIntelligence Association (MCCIA) (18334)
PO Box 19125
Washington, DC 20036-9125
URL: http://www.mccia.org
Contact: Neal Duckworth, Chm.

2803 ■ Marine Corps Interrogator Translator Teams Association (MCITTA)
1900 S Ocean Blvd., Apt. 14L
Pompano Beach, FL 33062-8030
E-mail: **vburdelski@gmail.com**
URL: http://www.mcitta.org
Contact: **Vince Burdelski, Chm.**

Masons

2804 ■ Ancient and Accepted Scottish Rite of Free Masonry, Southern Jurisdiction I Supreme Council 33rd Degree (AASR-SJ) (17465)
1733 16th St. NW
Washington, DC 20009-3103
Ph: (202)232-3579
Fax: (202)464-0487
E-mail: **council@scottishrite.org**
URL: http://www.scottishrite.org
Contact: Ronald A. Seale, Sovereign Grand Commander

2805 ■ High Twelve International (HI-12) (18845)
Bettendorf Masonic Center
2412 Grand St.
Bettendorf, IA 52722
Ph: **(563)514-3270**
Fax: **(563)514-3270**
E-mail: secretary@high12.org
URL: http://high12.org
Contact: **Mervyn J. Harris, Pres.**

2806 ■ Philalethes Society (PS) (17107)
c/o John C. Householder, Jr., Business Mgr.
800 S 15th St., No. 1803
Sebring, OH 44672
Ph: (330)938-7582
E-mail: **terrytilton@q.com**
URL: http://www.freemasonry.org
Contact: Terry L. Tilton, Pres.

2807 ■ Tall Cedars of Lebanon of North America (TCLNA) (18863)
2609 N Front St.
Harrisburg, PA 17110
Ph: (717)232-5991
Fax: (717)232-5997
E-mail: tclsf@tallcedars.org
URL: http://www.tallcedars.org
Contact: **Norman L. Clark, Chm.**

Native American

2808 ■ Institute for Tribal Environmental Professionals (ITEP) (19274)
PO Box 15004
Flagstaff, AZ 86011
Ph: (928)523-9555 (928)523-0946
Free: (866)248-4576
Fax: (928)523-1266
E-mail: itep@nau.edu
URL: http://www4.nau.edu/itep
Contact: **Ann Marie Chischilly, Exec. Dir.**

2809 ■ Red Earth (17142)
6 Santa Fe Plz.
Oklahoma City, OK 73102
Ph: (405)427-5228
Fax: (405)427-8079
E-mail: info@redearth.org
URL: http://www.redearth.org
Contact: **Janet Dyke, Pres. Elect**

Nigerian

2810 ■ Egbe Omo Yoruba: National Association of Yoruba Descendants in North America (18398)
PO Box 204
White Marsh, MD 21162-0204
Ph: (314)974-3604 (925)858-2565
E-mail: info@yorubanation.org
URL: http://www.yorubanation.org
Contact: Ola Oduwole, Pres.

2811 ■ Friends of Nigeria (FON) (18896)
c/o Peter J. Hansen, Treas.
1 Oaknoll Ct., Apt. 439
Iowa City, IA 52246
Ph: (319)351-3375
E-mail: pjhansen@ia.net
URL: http://friendsofnigeria.org
Contact: Mike Goodkind, Pres.

2812 ■ Idoma Association USA
PO Box 7211342
Houston, TX 77272-1342
E-mail: scholarship@idomausa.org
URL: http://www.idomausa.org
Contact: **Grace Dama Ogwuche, Pres.**

Polish

2813 ■ Polish American Congress (PAC) (19788)
5711 N Milwaukee Ave.
Chicago, IL 60646-6215
Ph: (773)763-9944
Free: **(800)621-3723**
Fax: (773)763-7114
E-mail: pacchgo@pac1944.org
URL: http://www.pac1944.org
Contact: Frank J. Spula, Pres.

2814 ■ Polish Arts and Culture Foundation (PACF)
4077 Waterhouse Rd.
Oakland, CA 94602
Ph: (510)599-2244
Fax: (510)531-2721
E-mail: **polishartssf@yahoo.com**
URL: http://www.polishculturesf.org
Contact: Caria Tomczykowska, Pres.

2815 ■ Polish Assistance, Inc. (PAI) (19308)
15 E 65th St.
New York, NY 10065-6501
Ph: (212)570-5560
Fax: (212)570-5561
E-mail: **office@polishassistance.org**
URL: http://www.polishassistance.org
Contact: Jadwiga Palade, Pres.

2816 ■ Polish Beneficial Association (PBA) (17519)
2595 Orthodox St.
Philadelphia, PA 19137
Ph: (215)535-2626
Free: (800)599-2917
Fax: (215)535-0169
E-mail: **mail@polishbeneficialassoc.com**
URL: **http://polishbeneficialassoc.com**
Contact: Loretta Zekanis, Pres.

2817 ■ Polish Falcons of America (PFA) (19792)
381 Mansfield Ave.
Pittsburgh, PA 15220-2751
Ph: (412)922-2244
Free: (800)535-2071
Fax: (412)922-5029
E-mail: **info@polishfalcons.org**
URL: http://www.polishfalcons.org
Contact: Timothy L. Kuzma, CEO/Pres.

2818 ■ Union of Poles in America (UPA) (16649)
9999 Granger Rd.
Garfield Heights, OH 44125
Ph: (216)478-0120
Fax: (216)478-0122
E-mail: **upahomeoffice@yahoo.com**
URL: http://www.unionofpoles.com
Contact: David Milcinovic, VP

Professions

2819 ■ Black Career Women (BCW) (17191)
PO Box 19332
Cincinnati, OH 45219-0332
Ph: (513)531-1932
Fax: (513)531-2166
E-mail: **keelinae@ucmail.uc.edu**
URL: http://www.bcw.org
Contact: Linda Bates Parker, Pres.

Puerto Rico

2820 ■ Puerto Rican Studies Association (PRSA) (18931)
Cornell Univ.
Latino Studies Program
434 Rockefeller Hall
Ithaca, NY 14853-2502
Ph: **(607)255-3197**
Fax: **(607)255-2433**
E-mail: prsa@cornell.edu
URL: http://www.puertoricanstudies.org
Contact: **Roberto Marquez, Pres.**

Refugees

2821 ■ Shelter for Life International (SFL) (19329)
10201 Wayzata Blvd., Ste.230
Hopkins, MN 55305
Ph: **(763)253-4082**
Fax: **(763)253-4085**
E-mail: info@shelter.org
URL: http://www.shelter.org
Contact: **Brint Patrick, Chm.**

Scandinavian

2822 ■ Independent Order of Svithiod (IOS) (19605)
5518 W Lawrence Ave.
Chicago, IL 60630
Ph: (773)736-1191

E-mail: **iosvithiod@sbcglobal.net**
URL: http://www.svithiod.org
Contact: **Janet Nelson, Grand Master**

Scottish

2823 ■ Saint Andrew's Society of the State of New York (17561)
150 E 55th St., Ste.3
New York, NY 10022
Ph: (212)223-4248
Fax: (212)223-0748
E-mail: office@standrewsny.org
URL: http://www.standrewsny.org
Contact: **William T. Maitland, Pres.**

Slovak

2824 ■ Slovak Catholic Sokol (SCS) (17212)
205 Madison St.
PO Box 899
Passaic, NJ 07055
Free: (800)886-7656
Fax: (973)779-8245
E-mail: **life@slovakcatholicsokol.org**
URL: http://www.slovakcatholicsokol.org
Contact: **Larry M. Glugosh, Pres.**

Social Clubs

2825 ■ Chemists' Club (19634)
30 W 44th St.
New York, NY 10036
Ph: (212)582-5454
E-mail: **membership@chemistsclub.org**
URL: http://www.thechemistsclub.com
Contact: **Edward Werner Cook, Chm.**

2826 ■ Jim Smith Society (JSS) (17225)
256 Lake Meade Dr.
East Berlin, PA 17316
E-mail: **smithjj@embargmail.com**
URL: http://jimsmithsociety.com
Contact: **Jim Eden, Pres.**

2827 ■ The Moles (18487)
577 Chestnut Ridge Rd.
Woodcliff Lake, NJ 07677
Ph: (201)930-1923
Fax: (201)930-8501
E-mail: carty.moles@verizon.net
URL: http://themoles.info
Contact: **Stephen J. Barlow, Pres.**

2828 ■ Stunts Unlimited (SU) (17054)
15233 Ventura Blvd., Ste.425
Sherman Oaks, CA 91403
Ph: **(818)501-1970**
Fax: **(818)501-1009**
E-mail: info@stuntsunlimited.com
URL: http://www.stuntsunlimited.com
Contact: Scott Waugh, Pres.

Ukrainian

2829 ■ Ukrainian National Association (UNA) (19020)
2200 Rte. 10 W
Parsippany, NJ 07054
Ph: (973)292-9800
Free: (800)253-9862
Fax: **(973)292-0900**
E-mail: **una@unamember.com**
URL: http://www.unamember.com
Contact: Roma Lisovich, Treas.

2830 ■ The Washington Group (TWG)
PO Box 11248
Washington, DC 20008
Ph: (202)586-7227
Fax: (202)586-3617
E-mail: **president@thewashingtongroup.org**
URL: http://www.thewashingtongroup.org
Contact: Andrew Bihun, Pres.

Vietnamese

2831 ■ National Congress of Vietnamese Americans (NCVA) (19027)
6433 Northanna Dr.
Springfield, VA 22150
Ph: (703)971-9178
Free: (877)592-4140
Fax: (703)719-5764
E-mail: **nguyennbich37726@aol.com**
URL: http://www.ncvaonline.org
Contact: Hung Quoc Nguyen, Pres./CEO

2832 ■ Union of North American Vietnamese Students Association (UNAVSA)
PO Box 433
Westminster, CA 92684
Fax: (563)405-1621
E-mail: info@unavsa.org
URL: http://www.unavsa.org
Contact: **Dan Huynh, Pres.**

Welsh

2833 ■ Welsh National Gymanfa Ganu Association (WNGGA) (19897)
PO Box 410
Granville, OH 43023
Ph: (740)587-3936
E-mail: **exec_dir@wngga.org**
URL: http://www.wngga.org
Contact: Rev. Stacy Evans, Exec. Dir.

West Indian

2834 ■ Montserrat Progressive Society of New York (MPSNY) (17636)
The Montserrat Bldg.
207 W 137th St.
New York, NY 10030-2425
Ph: (212)283-3346
Fax: (212)368-3165
E-mail: society@mpsofny.org
URL: http://www.mpsofny.org
Contact: **Llewellyn White, Pres.**

Women

2835 ■ United Order True Sisters (UOTS) (19437)
Linton Intl. Plaza
660 Linton Blvd., Ste.6
Delray Beach, FL 33444
Ph: (561)265-1557 **(561)276-7017**
E-mail: info@uots.org
URL: http://www.uots.org
Contact: Betty Peyser, Natl. Pres.

Alternative Medicine

2836 ■ Commission on Religious Counseling and Healing (19702)
4202 Newark Ave.
Cleveland, OH 44109
Ph: (216)543-6377
E-mail: rbsocc@juno.com
URL: http://crch.rbsocc.org
Contact: **Rev. Dr. Stephen Lawrence, Commission Moderator**

Anglican Catholic

2837 ■ American Friends of the Anglican Centre in Rome (19707)
PO Box 300
St. Francisville, LA 70775
Ph: **(225)252-3231**
E-mail: **cjenkins1468@gmail.com**
URL: http://www.americanfriendsacr.org
Contact: **Rev. Charles Jenkins III, Chm.**

2838 ■ Fellowship of Concerned Churchmen (FCC) (19054)
192 Wellesley Dr.
Spartanburg, SC 29307
Ph: (864)582-2657
E-mail: info@anglicanchurches.net
URL: http://www.anglicanchurches.net/index.html
Contact: **Wallace H. Spaulding, Pres.**

Baptist

2839 ■ American Baptist Homes and Caring Ministries (ABHCM) (2598)
Judson Park
23600 Marine View Dr. S
Des Moines, WA 98198
Free: **(800)ABC-3USA**
E-mail: **bpainter@abhow.com**
URL: http://www.abhcm.org
Contact: **Bill Painter, Pres.**

2840 ■ Association of Baptists for World Evangelism (ABWE) (19072)
PO Box 8585
Harrisburg, PA 17105-8585
Ph: (717)774-7000 (717)909-2326
Free: **(800)921-2293**
Fax: (717)774-1919
E-mail: info@abwe.org
URL: http://www.abwe.org
Contact: Dr. Michael Loftis, Pres.

2841 ■ Baptist Bible Fellowship International (BBFI) (19732)
PO Box 191
Springfield, MO 65801-0191
Ph: (417)862-5001

Fax: (417)865-0794
E-mail: info@bbfimissions.com
URL: http://www.bbfi.org
Contact: **Linzy Slayden, Pres.**

2842 ■ Baptist Communicators Association (BCA) (19077)
c/o Margaret M. Dempsey
1519 Menlo Dr.
Kennesaw, GA 30152
Ph: (770)425-3728
E-mail: office@baptistcommunicators.org
URL: http://www.baptistcommunicators.org
Contact: **Julie McGowan, Pres.**

2843 ■ Conservative Baptist Association of America (17325)
3686 Stagecoach Rd., Ste.F
Longmont, CO 80504-5660
Ph: (303)772-1205 (303)827-3583
Free: **(888)366-3010**
Fax: (303)772-5690
E-mail: info@cbamerica.org
URL: http://www.cbamerica.org
Contact: **Rev. Stan Rieb, Contact**

2844 ■ National Association of Free Will Baptists (NAFWB) (17143)
5233 Mt. View Rd.
Antioch, TN 37013-2306
Ph: (615)731-6812
Free: (877)767-7659
Fax: (615)731-0771
E-mail: keith@nafwb.org
URL: **http://www.nafwb.org**
Contact: Keith Burden, Exec. Sec.

2845 ■ Seventh Day Baptist General Conference (SDBGC) (17334)
PO Box 1678
Janesville, WI 53547-1678
Ph: (608)752-5055
Fax: (608)752-7711
E-mail: **robappel@seventhdaybaptist.org**
URL: http://www.seventhdaybaptist.org
Contact: Robert F. Appel, Exec. Dir.

2846 ■ Seventh Day Baptist General Conference of the United States and Canada (20801)
PO Box 1678
Janesville, WI 53547-1678
Ph: (608)752-5055
Fax: (608)752-7711
E-mail: **robappel@seventhdaybaptist.org**
URL: http://www.seventhdaybaptist.org
Contact: **Robert Appel, Exec. Dir.**

2847 ■ Seventh Day Baptist World Federation (SDBWF)
88 Terrace Ave.
Salem, WV 26426
Ph: **(304)782-1727**

E-mail: president@sdbwf.org
URL: **http://www.sdbwf.org**
Contact: Rev. Dr. Dale Thorngate, Pres.

2848 ■ Women Nationally Active for Christ (WNAC) (19757)
PO Box 5002
Antioch, TN 37011-5002
Ph: **(615)731-6812**
Free: (877)767-7662
E-mail: info@wnac.org
URL: http://www.wnac.org
Contact: **Elizabeth Hodges, Exec. Dir.**

Bible

2849 ■ BCM International
201 Granite Run Dr., Ste.260
Lancaster, PA 17601
Ph: **(717)560-9601**
Free: (888)226-4685
Fax: **(717)560-9607**
E-mail: **donations@bcmintl.org**
URL: http://bcmintl.org
Contact: Rev. Martin Windle, Pres.

2850 ■ Bible League International (BLI) (19765)
PO Box 28000
Chicago, IL 60628
Free: (866)825-4636
Fax: (708)367-8600
E-mail: info@bibleleague.org
URL: http://www.bibleleague.org
Contact: **Rob Frank, CEO**

Brethren

2851 ■ Association of Grace Brethren Ministers (AGBM) (17730)
PO Box 694
Winona Lake, IN 46590
E-mail: **jerichards@sbcglobal.net**
URL: http://www.agbm.org
Contact: **Pastor Joel Richards, Pres.**

Buddhist

2852 ■ Cambodian Buddhist Society (CBS) (8741)
13800 New Hampshire Ave.
Silver Spring, MD 20904
Ph: (301)622-6544 (301)384-3319
Fax: (301)622-6544
E-mail: sovantun@cambodian-buddhist.org
URL: http://www.cambodian-buddhist.org
Contact: **Mr. Sovan Tun, VP**

Catholic

2853 ■ All Roads Ministry (ARM) (19564)
55 Pallen Rd., No. 3
Hopewell Junction, NY 12533
Ph: (845)226-4172
E-mail: **vin@vinlewis.com**
URL: http://www.allroadsministry.com
Contact: Vincent P. Lewis, Co-Founder/Pres.

2854 ■ Apostolate for Family Consecration (AFC) (19571)
3375 County Rd. 36
Bloomingdale, OH 43910
Ph: (740)765-5500
Free: (800)773-2645
Fax: **(740)765-5561**
E-mail: info@familyland.org
URL: http://www.familyland.org
Contact: Jerry Coniker, Founder/Pres.

2855 ■ Association for the Rights of Catholics in the Church (ARCC) (17774)
3150 Newgate Dr.
Florissant, MO 63033
Ph: **(413)527-9929**
Free: (877)700-2722
Fax: (413)527-5877
E-mail: arcc@arccsites.org
URL: http://arcc-catholic-rights.org
Contact: Patrick B. Edgar, Pres.

2856 ■ Canon Law Society of America (CLSA) (19847)
The Hecker Center, Ste.111
3025 Fourth St. NE
Washington, DC 20017-1102
Ph: (202)832-2350
Fax: (202)832-2331
E-mail: info@clsa.org
URL: http://www.clsa.org
Contact: **Rev. Michael Joyce JCD, Pres.**

2857 ■ Capuchin-Franciscans (CFPSJ) (17258)
3407 S Archer Ave.
Chicago, IL 60608
Ph: (773)475-6206
Fax: **(773)847-7409**
E-mail: vocation@capuchinfranciscans.org
URL: http://www.capuchinfranciscans.org
Contact: **Fr. William Hugo, Contact**

2858 ■ Catholic Church Extension Society of the U.S.A. (19851)
150 S Wacker Dr., 20th Fl.
Chicago, IL 60606
Ph: **(312)795-5112**
Free: (800)842-7804
Fax: (312)236-5276
E-mail: info@catholicextension.org
URL: http://www.catholicextension.org
Contact: Fr. John J. Wall, Pres./CEO

2859 ■ Catholic Golden Age (CGA) (16931)
PO Box 249
Olyphant, PA 18447
Free: (800)836-5699
Fax: (570)586-7721
E-mail: **info@catholicgoldenage.org**
URL: http://www.catholicgoldenage.org
Contact: Rev. Gerald N. Dino, Pres.

2860 ■ Catholic Kolping Society of America (CKSA) (19198)
1223 Van Houten Ave.
Clifton, NJ 07013
Ph: (201)666-1169
Free: (877)659-7237
Fax: (201)666-5262
E-mail: patfarkas@optonline.net
URL: http://kolping.org/main.htm
Contact: Patricia Farkas, Natl. Admin.

2861 ■ Catholic Traditionalist Movement (CTM) (17271)
210 Maple Ave.
Westbury, NY 11590-3117
Ph: (516)333-6470
Fax: (516)333-7535
URL: http://www.latinmass-ctm.org
Contact: **Richard A. Cuneo, Pres.**

2862 ■ Catholics in Alliance for the Common Good
1612 K St. NW, Ste.400
Washington, DC 20006
Ph: (202)466-1665
E-mail: **information@catholicsinalliance.org**
URL: http://www.catholicsinalliance.org
Contact: **Alfred M. Rotondaro, Chm.**

2863 ■ Catholics United for the Faith (CUF) (2616)
827 N 4th St.
Steubenville, OH 43952
Ph: (740)283-2484
Free: (800)693-2484
Fax: (740)283-4011
E-mail: info@cuf.org
URL: http://www.cuf.org
Contact: **Michael Mohr, Chm.**

2864 ■ Central Association of the Miraculous Medal (CAMM) (16943)
475 E Chelten Ave.
Philadelphia, PA 19144-5758
Ph: (215)848-1010
Free: (800)523-3674
Fax: (215)848-1014
E-mail: stewart@cammonline.org
URL: http://www.cammonline.org
Contact: **Rev. Carl L. Pieber PhD, Exec. Dir.**

2865 ■ Conference of Major Superiors of Men (CMSM) (17215)
8808 Cameron St.
Silver Spring, MD 20910
Ph: (301)588-4030
Fax: (301)587-4575
E-mail: postmaster@cmsm.org
URL: http://www.cmsm.org
Contact: **Thomas P. Cassidy SCJ, Pres.**

2866 ■ Congregation of Sisters of Saint Agnes (CSA) (17456)
320 County Rd. K
Fond du Lac, WI 54937-8158
Ph: (920)907-2300 (920)907-2302
Fax: **(920)923-4551**
E-mail: jquinn@csasisters.org
URL: http://www.csasisters.org
Contact: Sister Jeremy Quinn CSA, Gen. Sec.

2867 ■ Glenmary Research Center (GRC) (19884)
Glenmary Home Missioners
PO Box 465618
Cincinnati, OH 45246
Ph: **(513)874-8900**
Fax: (513)874-1690
E-mail: grc@glenmary.org
URL: http://www.glenmary.org/site/epage/95967_919.htm

2868 ■ International Catholic Deaf Association United States Section (ICDA-US)
7202 Buchanan St.
Landover Hills, MD 20784-2236
Ph: (301)429-0697
Fax: (301)429-0698
E-mail: homeoffice@icda-us.org
URL: http://www.icda-us.org
Contact: **Peter Un, Pres.**

2869 ■ Laity for Life
PO Box 111478
Naples, FL 34108
Ph: (239)352-6333

E-mail: info@laityforlife.org
URL: http://www.laityforlife.org
Contact: Patricia Bucalo, Co-Founder/Pres.

2870 ■ Lay Mission-Helpers Association (LMH) (19903)
3435 Wilshire Blvd., Ste.1940
Los Angeles, CA 90010
Ph: (213)368-1870 **(213)368-1873**
Fax: (213)368-1871
E-mail: info@laymissionhelpers.org
URL: http://www.laymissionhelpers.org
Contact: Janice England, Program Dir.

2871 ■ Mariological Society of America (MSA) (20102)
Univ. of Dayton
The Marian Lib.
Dayton, OH 45469-1390
Ph: (937)229-4294
Fax: (937)229-4258
E-mail: cecilia.mushenheim@notes.udayton.edu
URL: http://www.mariologicalsociety.com
Contact: **Fr. Thomas Buffer, Pres.**

2872 ■ National Association of the Holy Name Society (NAHNS) (19919)
c/o Cleveland Cosom, Dir.
PO Box 12012
Baltimore, MD 21281-2012
Ph: (410)325-1523
Fax: (410)325-1524
E-mail: **info@nahns.com**
URL: http://www.nahns.com
Contact: **Joseph W. Lapointe, Pres.**

2873 ■ National Black Catholic Clergy Caucus (NBCCC) (17508)
2815 Forbes Dr.
Montgomery, AL 36110
Ph: **(404)226-8170**
E-mail: franthonyb@aol.com
URL: http://www.nbccc-us.com
Contact: Rev. Anthony Bozeman, Pres.

2874 ■ National Catholic Office for the Deaf (NCOD) (19274)
7202 Buchanan St.
Landover Hills, MD 20784
Ph: (301)577-1684
Free: **(866)395-6353**
Fax: (301)577-1684
E-mail: info@ncod.org
URL: http://www.ncod.org
Contact: Rev. Kevin C. Rhoades, Rep.

2875 ■ National Christ Child Society (NCCS) (20124)
4340 E West Hwy., Ste.202
Bethesda, MD 20814
Ph: (301)718-0220
Free: (800)814-2149
Fax: (301)718-8822
E-mail: office@nationalchristchildsoc.org
URL: http://www.nationalchristchildsoc.org
Contact: **Patricia Myler, Pres.**

2876 ■ North American Association for the Catechumenate (NAAC) (19296)
2915 NE Flanders
Portland, OR 97232
Ph: (503)502-6251 **(503)284-7141**
E-mail: webcurator@catechumenate.org
URL: http://www.catechumenate.org
Contact: Rev. Mary E. Peterson, Membership Chair

2877 ■ Pontifical Mission Societies in the United States (PMS) (20145)
70 W 36th St., 8th Fl.
New York, NY 10018
Ph: (212)563-8700
Fax: (212)563-8725
E-mail: pmsusa@propfaith.org
URL: http://www.onefamilyinmission.org
Contact: **Rev. Andrew Small, Natl. Dir.**

2878 ■ Raskob Foundation for Catholic Activities (17544)
PO Box 4019
Wilmington, DE 19807-0019
Ph: (302)655-4440
Fax: (302)655-3223
E-mail: info@rfca.org
URL: http://www.rfca.org
Contact: **Paul A. Zambernardi, Exec. VP**

2879 ■ Sacred Heart League (SHL) (19711)
PO Box 300
Walls, MS 38680-0300
Free: (800)232-9079
E-mail: comments@shl.org
URL: **http://www.shsm.org/site/PageServer**
Contact: Rev. Jack Kurps, Spiritual Dir.

2880 ■ Society of African Missions (SMA) (19719)
23 Bliss Ave.
Tenafly, NJ 07670-3001
Ph: (201)567-0450 **(201)567-9085**
Free: (800)318-1209
Fax: (201)541-1280
E-mail: tenaflyhouse@smafathers.org
URL: http://www.smafathers.org
Contact: Ms. Martha Paladino, Mgr.

2881 ■ Society of Missionaries of Africa (19972)
1624 21st St. NW
Washington, DC 20009-1003
Ph: (202)232-5154
Free: (877)523-4MOA
Fax: **(202)232-0120**
E-mail: info@missionariesofafrica.org
URL: http://www.missionariesofafrica.org
Contact: Fr. John P. Lynch, Exec. Dir.

2882 ■ Society of Our Lady of the Most Holy Trinity (SOLT) (17560)
PO Box 152
3816 County Rd. 61
Robstown, TX 78380
Ph: (361)387-2754 (361)387-8090
Fax: **(361)387-8800**
E-mail: soltlaity@societyofourlady.net
URL: http://societyofourlady.net
Contact: **Fr. Tito Ayo, Contact**

2883 ■ United States Conference of Catholic Bishops (USCCB) (17929)
3211 4th St. NE
Washington, DC 20017-1104
Ph: (202)541-3000
Fax: (202)541-3322
E-mail: webcoordinator@usccb.org
URL: http://www.usccb.org
Contact: **Archbishop Timothy Dolan, Pres.**

2884 ■ Volunteer Missionary Movement - U.S. Office (VMM-USA) (17931)
5980 W Loomis Rd.
Greendale, WI 53129-1824
Ph: (414)423-8660
Fax: (414)423-8964
E-mail: vmm@vmmusa.org
URL: http://www.vmmusa.org
Contact: **Vic Doucette, Exec. Dir.**

Chaplains

2885 ■ American Catholic Correctional Chaplains Association (ACCCA) (19989)
738 Guernsey Ct.
Slinger, WI 53086
Ph: **(262)627-0636**
E-mail: paul.rogers@wisconsin.gov
URL: http://www.catholiccorrectionalchaplains.org
Contact: Paul E. Rogers, Pres.

2886 ■ American Correctional Chaplains Association (ACCA) (18843)
PO Box 85840
Seattle, WA 98145-1840
Ph: **(206)985-0577** (920)689-2280
Fax: **(206)526-7113**
E-mail: **dale_hale@usc.salvationarmy.org**
URL: http://www.correctionalchaplains.org
Contact: **Dale L. Hale, Pres.**

2887 ■ Federation of Fire Chaplains (FFC) (19747)
PO Box 437
Meridian, TX 76665
Ph: **(254)435-2256**
Fax: **(254)435-2256**
E-mail: chapdir1@aol.com
URL: http://firechaplains.org
Contact: Steve Kay, Pres.

2888 ■ International Conference of Police Chaplains (ICPC) (17446)
PO Box 5590
Destin, FL 32540-5590
Ph: (850)654-9736
Fax: (850)654-9742
E-mail: icpc@icpc.gccoxmail.com
URL: http://www.icpc4cops.org
Contact: **Chaplain Cyndee Thomas, Pres.**

2889 ■ National Association of Catholic Chaplains (NACC) (20001)
4915 S Howell Ave., Ste.501
Milwaukee, WI 53207
Ph: (414)483-4898
Fax: (414)483-6712
E-mail: info@nacc.org
URL: http://www.nacc.org
Contact: **Alan Bowman, Chm.**

2890 ■ Race Track Chaplaincy of America (RTCA) (19354)
2365 Harrodsburg Rd., Ste.A120
Lexington, KY 40504
Ph: **(859)410-7822**
E-mail: info@rtcanational.org
URL: http://www.rtcanational.org
Contact: **Mr. Gary Cartwright, Pres.**

Christian

2891 ■ A Christian Ministry in the National Parks (ACMNP) (17473)
9185 E Kenyon Ave., Ste.230
Denver, CO 80237
Ph: **(303)220-2808**
Free: (800)786-3450
Fax: **(303)220-0128**
E-mail: info@acmnp.com
URL: http://www.acmnp.com
Contact: Rev. Spencer L. Lundgaard, Exec. Dir.

2892 ■ CLOUT - Christian Lesbians Out (20043)
3653-F Flakes Mill Rd., No. 306
Decatur, GA 30034-5255
E-mail: **office@cloutsisters.org**
URL: http://www.cloutsisters.org
Contact: **Shawn MacDonald, Co-Moderator**

2893 ■ Fellowship of Christian Peace Officers U.S.A. (FCPO-USA) (17483)
PO Box 3686
Chattanooga, TN 37404-0686
Ph: (423)622-1234 **(423)553-8806**
Fax: (423)622-9725
E-mail: **fcpo@fcpo.org**
URL: http://www.fcpo.org
Contact: Lamar Moore, Exec. Dir.

2894 ■ Fellowship of Saint James (FSJ) (17992)
PO Box 410788
Chicago, IL 60641
Ph: (773)481-1090
Fax: (773)481-1095
E-mail: **patricia@fsj.org**
URL: http://www.fsj.org

2895 ■ International Network of Children's Ministry (INCM) (19758)
PO Box 190
Castle Rock, CO 80104
Free: (800)324-4543
Fax: (303)660-6444
E-mail: **webmaster@incm.org**
URL: http://www.incm.org
Contact: **Michael Chanley, Exec. Dir.**

2896 ■ International Orthodox Christian Charities (IOCC) (19409)
PO Box 630225
Baltimore, MD 21263-0225
Ph: (410)243-9820
Free: (877)803-4622
Fax: (410)243-9824
E-mail: relief@iocc.org
URL: **http://www.iocc.org**
Contact: **Michael S. Homsey, Chm.**

2897 ■ National Alliance Against Christian Discrimination (NAACD)
PO Box 62685
Colorado Springs, CO 80962
E-mail: heathenhooey@yahoo.com
URL: http://www.naacd.com
Contact: Rev. Thomas L. Pedigo, Exec. Dir.

2898 ■ Nazarene Compassionate Ministries International (NCM) (17651)
17001 Prairie Star Pkwy.
Lenexa, KS 66220
Ph: **(913)768-4808**
Free: (800)310-6362
E-mail: info@ncm.org
URL: http://www.ncm.org
Contact: Dr. Richard Schubert, Chm.

Church and State

2899 ■ Americans United for Separation of Church and State (AUSCS) (2650)
1301 K St. NW, Ste.850, E Tower
Washington, DC 20005
Ph: (202)466-3234
Fax: (202)466-2587
E-mail: americansunited@au.org
URL: http://www.au.org
Contact: Barry W. Lynn, Exec. Dir.

Churches

2900 ■ IFCA International (17520)
PO Box 810
Grandville, MI 49468-0810
Ph: (616)531-1840
Free: (800)347-1840
Fax: **(616)531-1814**
E-mail: office@ifca.org
URL: http://www.ifca.org
Contact: Dr. Les Lofquist, Exec. Dir.

Counseling

2901 ■ Association of Biblical Counselors (ABC)
209 N Indus. Blvd., Ste.237
Bedford, TX 76021
Free: (877)222-4551

E-mail: **info@christiancounseling.com**
URL: http://www.christiancounseling.com
Contact: Jeremy Lelek, Pres.

2902 ■ Damien Ministries (DM)
PO Box 10202
Washington, DC 20018-0202
Ph: (202)526-3020
Fax: (202)526-9770
E-mail: **info@damienministries.org**
URL: http://www.damienministries.org
Contact: Otis Sutson, Exec. Dir.

Divine Science

2903 ■ Divine Science Federation International (DSFI) (17554)
110 Merchants Row, Ste.4
Rutland, VT 05701
Ph: (802)779-9019
Free: (800)644-9680
E-mail: dsfi@me.com
URL: http://www.divinesciencefederation.org
Contact: **Mary Emma Dryden, Pres.**

Eastern Orthodox

2904 ■ Fellowship of St. John the Divine (19882)
Antiochian Orthodox Christian Archdiocese
PO Box 5238
Englewood, NJ 07631-5238
Ph: (201)871-1355
Fax: (201)871-7954
E-mail: editor@antiochian.org
URL: http://www.antiochian.org/fellowship-of-st-john
Contact: **Jane Tadros, Pres.**

2905 ■ Standing Conference of the Canonical Orthodox Bishops in the Americas (SCOBA) (19478)
10 E 79th St.
New York, NY 10075
Ph: (212)774-0526 (212)570-3593
Fax: (212)774-0202
E-mail: scoba@scoba.us
URL: http://www.scoba.us
Contact: **Fr. Mark Arey, Gen. Sec.**

Ecumenical

2906 ■ Churches Uniting in Christ (CUIC) (20148)
c/o Elder James N. Tse, Treas.
8717 85th St.
Woodhaven, NY 11421-1913
Ph: (718)849-1608
Fax: (718)849-1608
E-mail: tomsamed@msn.com
URL: http://www.cuicinfo.org
Contact: **Rev. Dr. Suzanne Webb, Pres.**

2907 ■ Graymoor Ecumenical and Interreligious Institute (GEII) (17571)
475 Riverside Dr., Rm. 1960
New York, NY 10115
Ph: (212)870-2330
Free: (800)338-2620
Fax: (212)870-2001
E-mail: **lmnygeii@aol.com**
URL: http://www.geii.org
Contact: Ms. Veronica Sullivan, Business Mgr.

2908 ■ International Association of Ministers Wives and Ministers Widows (IAMWMW) (19489)
105 River Knoll
Macon, GA 31211
Ph: **(478)743-5126**
Fax: **(478)745-5504**

E-mail: **bevglove@bellsouth.net**
URL: http://www.iamwmw.com
Contact: **Dr. Beverly W. Glover, Pres.**

2909 ■ Lumunos (18071)
PO Box 307
Marlborough, NH 03455-0307
Ph: **(603)876-4121**
Free: (800)245-7378
Fax: **(603)876-4300**
E-mail: info@lumunos.org
URL: http://www.lumunos.org
Contact: Doug Wysockey-Johnson, Exec. Dir.

2910 ■ National Council of Churches of Christ in the U.S.A. (NCC) (20162)
475 Riverside Dr., Ste.880
New York, NY 10115
Ph: **(212)870-2228**
Fax: (212)870-2030
E-mail: info@ncccusa.org
URL: http://www.ncccusa.org
Contact: Rev. Michael Kinnamon, Gen. Sec.

2911 ■ Societas Liturgica (SL) (19003)
c/o Alan Barthel, Sec.
100 Witherspoon St.
Louisville, KY 40202
Ph: (502)569-5759
E-mail: alnbarthel@aol.com
URL: http://societas-liturgica.org
Contact: **Dr. Karen Westerfield, Pres.**

Education

2912 ■ Ecumenical Theological Seminary (ETS) (20181)
2930 Woodward Ave.
Detroit, MI 48201
Ph: (313)831-5200
Fax: (313)831-1353
E-mail: **lofficer@etseminary.edu**
URL: http://www.etseminary.edu
Contact: **Ms. Katherine A.M. Nyberg, Chair**

2913 ■ National Council of Churches, Education and Leadership Ministries Commission (NCC ELMC) (17627)
475 Riverside Dr., 8th Fl.
New York, NY 10115-0500
Ph: (212)870-2267 **(212)870-2297**
Fax: (212)870-3112
E-mail: gpierce@ncccusa.org
URL: http://www.ncccusa.org/elmc
Contact: Garland F. Pierce, Contact

2914 ■ Religious Education Association: An Association of Professors, Practitioners, and Researchers in Religious Education (REA: APRRE) (18116)
PO Box 200392
Evans, CO 80620-0392
Ph: (765)225-8836
Fax: (970)351-1269
E-mail: **secretary@religiouseducation.net**
URL: http://www.religiouseducation.net
Contact: Dr. Lucinda Huffaker, Exec. Sec.

Episcopal

2915 ■ Associated Parishes for Liturgy and Mission (APLM) (19537)
PO Box 543
Hughsonville, NY 12537
E-mail: info@associatedparishes.org
URL: http://www.associatedparishes.org
Contact: **Jay Koyle, Pres.**

2916 ■ Church Army (CA) (20204)
115 W Atlantic St., Ste.104
Branson, MO 65616
Ph: **(417)544-9019**
Free: (888)412-5442
URL: http://www.churcharmyusa.org
Contact: **Tami Mckinney, Admin.**

2917 ■ Episcopalians for Global Reconciliation (EGR)
2202 Willwood Hollow Dr.
Valrico, FL 33596
Ph: **(813)333-1832**
E-mail: **admin@e4gr.org**
URL: http://www.e4gr.org
Contact: **Dr. John Hammock, Chm.**

2918 ■ Faith Alive (FA) (19957)
431 Richmond Pl. NE
Albuquerque, NM 87106
Ph: (505)255-3233
Fax: (505)255-2282
E-mail: faofficenm@aol.com
URL: http://www.faithalive.org
Contact: **Tom Riley, Pres.**

2919 ■ Historical Society of the Episcopal Church (HSEC) (20219)
c/o Susan Johnson, Dir. of Operations
PO Box 1749
Harlingen, TX 78551
Free: (866)989-5851
Fax: (956)412-8780
E-mail: administrator@hsec.us
URL: http://www.hsec.us
Contact: Rev. Dr. Robert W. Prichard, Pres.

2920 ■ National Network of Episcopal Clergy Associations (NNECA) (18143)
c/o Rev. Michael R. Link
11844 Orense Dr.
Las Vegas, NV 89138
E-mail: **pstrohl@diocesecpa.org**
URL: http://www.nneca.org
Contact: **Patrick Strohl, Pres.**

Evangelical

2921 ■ Evangelical and Ecumenical Women's Caucus (EEWC) (17673)
PO Box 78171
Indianapolis, IN 46278-0171
E-mail: office@eewc.com
URL: http://www.eewc.com
Contact: **Linda Bieze, Coord.**

2922 ■ Evangelical Philosophical Society (EPS) (19979)
PO Box 1298
La Mirada, CA 90637
Ph: (562)906-4570
Fax: (562)777-4063
E-mail: philchristi@biola.edu
URL: http://www.epsociety.org
Contact: **Dr. Paul Copan, Pres.**

2923 ■ World Relief (18162)
7 E Baltimore St.
Baltimore, MD 21202
Ph: (443)451-1900
Free: (800)535-5433
Fax: (443)451-1975
E-mail: worldrelief@wr.org
URL: http://worldrelief.org
Contact: **Stephan Bauman, Pres./CEO**

Evangelism

2924 ■ Action International Ministries (ACTION) (19578)
PO Box 398
Mountlake Terrace, WA 98043-0398
Ph: (425)775-4800
Free: **(800)775-6918**

Fax: (425)775-0634
E-mail: info@actionusa.org
URL: http://www.actionintl.org
Contact: Rex Lee, Dir.

2925 ■ Artists in Christian Testimony (ACT) (19989)
PO Box 1649
Brentwood, TN 37024-1649
Ph: (615)376-7861
Fax: (615)376-7863
E-mail: larry@actinternational.org
URL: http://www.actinternational.org
Contact: **Rev. Byron Spradlin, Pres./CEO**

2926 ■ Christian Boaters Association (CBA) (20000)
193 Plantation Dr.
Tavernier, FL 33070
Ph: **(305)852-4799**
URL: http://christianboater.com
Contact: Marlin Simon, Pres.

2927 ■ COME International Baptist Ministries (17823)
PO Box 88085
Grand Rapids, MI 49518
Ph: **(616)868-9906** (616)455-8228
E-mail: stevens1943@gmail.com
URL: http://comemissions.org
Contact: Dr. Eldon W. Stevens, Pres.

2928 ■ Evangelical Press Association (EPA) (17590)
PO Box 28129
Crystal, MN 55428
Ph: (763)535-4793
Fax: (763)535-4794
E-mail: **director@epassoc.org**
URL: http://www.epassoc.org
Contact: Doug Trouten, Exec. Dir.

2929 ■ The Gideons International (TGI) (17833)
PO Box 140800
Nashville, TN 37214-0800
Ph: (615)564-5000
E-mail: tgi@gideons.org
URL: http://www.gideons.org
Contact: **Ivan Gow, Natl. Pres.**

2930 ■ International Messianic Jewish Alliance (IMJA) (17838)
5480 Baltimore Dr., Ste.203
La Mesa, CA 91942-2015
Ph: (619)464-9793
Fax: (619)464-9725
E-mail: **ravjoel@pacbell.net**
URL: http://www.imja.com
Contact: **Joel Liberman, Exec. Dir.**

2931 ■ International Students, Inc. (ISI) (2678)
PO Box C
Colorado Springs, CO 80901
Ph: (719)576-2700
Free: (800)474-4147
Fax: **(719)576-5363**
E-mail: team@isionline.org
URL: http://www.isionline.org
Contact: Dr. Douglas Shaw, Pres./CEO

2932 ■ Maranatha Volunteers International (MVI)
990 Reserve Dr., Ste.100
Roseville, CA 95678
Ph: (916)774-7700
Fax: (916)774-7701
E-mail: leaders@maranatha.org
URL: http://www.maranatha.org
Contact: John Freeman, Founder

2933 ■ Morris Cerullo World Evangelism (MCWE) (20025)
PO Box 85277
San Diego, CA 92186-5277
Ph: (858)277-2200
E-mail: partnerservices@mcwe.com
URL: http://www.mcwe.com
Contact: **Dr. Morris Cerullo, Pres.**

2934 ■ Pro Athletes Outreach (PAO) (19621)
PO Box 801
Palo Alto, CA 94302
Ph: **(650)206-2962**
Free: (800)733-7306
Fax: **(650)206-2959**
E-mail: office@pao.org
URL: http://www.pao.org
Contact: Steve Stenstrom, Pres.

2935 ■ WEC International (17741)
PO Box 1707
Fort Washington, PA 19034
Ph: (215)646-2322
Free: **(888)646-6202**
URL: http://www.wec-usa.org
Contact: David Hall, Link Dir.

Gay/Lesbian

2936 ■ Integrity USA (20058)
620 Park Ave., No. 311
Rochester, NY 14607-2943
Ph: (585)360-4512
Free: (800)462-9498
Fax: (585)486-6529
E-mail: info@integrityusa.org
URL: http://www.integrityusa.org
Contact: **Mr. Max Niedzwiecki, Exec. Dir.**

2937 ■ LIFE Ministries
250 Meadow Ln.
Conestoga, PA 17516
Ph: (717)871-0540
Fax: (717)871-0547
E-mail: info@life-ministries.com
URL: http://www.life-ministries.com
Contact: **Vera Mae Zimmerman, Sec.**

2938 ■ Lutherans Concerned/North America (LC/NA) (17882)
PO Box 4707
St. Paul, MN 55104-0707
Ph: (651)665-0861
Fax: (651)665-0863
E-mail: **admin@lcna.org**
URL: http://www.lcna.org
Contact: **Emily Eastwood, Exec. Dir.**

2939 ■ Metropolitan Community Churches (MCC) (20062)
PO Box 1374
Abilene, TX 79604
Ph: (310)360-8640 **(325)261-1531**
Fax: (325)690-6328
E-mail: info@mccchurch.net
URL: http://mccchurch.org
Contact: Barbara Crabtree, Dir. of Operations

2940 ■ United Church of Christ Coalition for Lesbian, Gay, Bisexual and Transgender Concerns (18243)
2592 W 14th St.
Cleveland, OH 44113
Ph: (216)861-0799
Free: (800)653-0799
Fax: (216)861-0782
E-mail: office@ucccoalition.org
URL: http://www.ucccoalition.org
Contact: **Andy Lang, Interim Exec. Dir.**

History

2941 ■ American Society of Church History (ASCH) (17784)
PO Box 2216
Hewitt, TX 76643-2216
Ph: (254)666-2457
Fax: (254)666-8010
E-mail: asch@churchhistory.org
URL: http://www.churchhistory.org
Contact: **Barbara Newman, Pres.**

2942 ■ Conference on Faith and History (CFH) (17785)
c/o Paul E. Michelson, Sec.
Huntington Univ.
Dept. of History
2303 Coll. Ave.
Huntington, IN 46750
Ph: (260)359-4242
E-mail: pmichelson@huntington.edu
URL: http://www.huntington.edu/cfh/conference.htm
Contact: **Barry Hankins, Pres.**

Humanism

2943 ■ American Ethical Union (AEU) (19672)
2 W 64th St.
New York, NY 10023-7104
Ph: (212)873-6500
Fax: (212)362-0850
E-mail: **lmiller.aeu@gmail.com**
URL: http://www.aeu.org
Contact: Jennifer Scates, Pres.

2944 ■ International Federation for Secular Humanistic Judaism (IFSHJ) (20521)
1777 T St. NW
Washington, DC 20009
Ph: (202)248-4880
E-mail: info@ifshj.org
URL: **http://www.ifshj.net**
Contact: Marvin Rosenblum, Pres.

Interfaith

2945 ■ Abrahamic Alliance International (AAi)
1900 Camden Ave., Ste.201-E
San Jose, CA 95124
Ph: (408)728-8943
Fax: (206)600-4978
E-mail: info@abrahamicalliance.org
URL: http://www.abrahamicalliance.org
Contact: Rod Cardoza, Founder/Exec. Dir.

2946 ■ Monks Without Borders
1750 Grant St.
Eugene, OR 97402
Ph: **(562)448-2012**
E-mail: info@monkswithoutborders.org
URL: http://monkswithoutborders.org
Contact: Zachary Perlman, Chm.

Jewish

2947 ■ AMIT (19708)
817 Broadway
New York, NY 10003
Ph: (212)477-4720 **(212)792-5698**
Free: (800)989-AMIT
Fax: (212)353-2312
E-mail: info@amitchildren.org
URL: http://www.amitchildren.org
Contact: Dr. Francine S. Stein, Pres.

2948 ■ B'nai B'rith International (BBI) (20125)
2020 K St. NW, 7th Fl.
Washington, DC 20006
Ph: (202)857-6600
Free: (888)388-4224

Fax: (202)857-6609
E-mail: **president@bnaibrith.org**
URL: http://bnaibrith.org/index.cfm
Contact: **Allan J. Jacobs, Interim Pres.**

2949 ■ Central Conference of American Rabbis (CCAR) (17837)
355 Lexington Ave.
New York, NY 10017
Ph: (212)972-3636
Fax: (212)692-0819
E-mail: info@ccarnet.org
URL: http://ccarnet.org
Contact: **Jonathan Stein, Pres.**

2950 ■ CLAL - The National Jewish Center for Learning and Leadership (17949)
440 Park Ave. S, 4th Fl.
New York, NY 10016-8012
Ph: (212)779-3300
Fax: (212)779-1009
E-mail: **info@clal.org**
URL: http://www.clal.org
Contact: **Irwin Kula, Pres.**

2951 ■ Coalition on the Environment and Jewish Life (COEJL)
116 E 27th St., 10th Fl.
New York, NY 10016
Ph: (212)532-7436 (212)684-2513
Fax: **(212)686-1353**
E-mail: info@coejl.org
URL: http://www.coejl.org
Contact: Rabbi Steve Gutow, Exec. Dir.

2952 ■ Habonim Dror North America (HDNA) (17851)
114 W 26th St., Ste.1004
New York, NY 10001
Ph: (212)255-1796
Fax: (212)929-3459
E-mail: mazkir@habonimdror.org
URL: http://www.habonimdror.org
Contact: **Talia Spear, Natl. Dir.**

2953 ■ Hadassah, The Women's Zionist Organization of America (HWZOA) (20139)
50 W 58th St.
New York, NY 10019
Ph: (212)355-7900
Free: **(800)303-3640**
Fax: (212)303-8282
E-mail: **webmaster@hadassah.org**
URL: http://www.hadassah.org
Contact: Ms. Nancy Falchuk, Pres.

2954 ■ International Federation of Rabbis (IFR) (19733)
5600 Wisconsin Ave., No. 1107
Chevy Chase, MD 20815
Fax: **(561)499-6316**
E-mail: rabbis@bellsouth.net
URL: http://www.intfedrabbis.org
Contact: Rabbi Suzanne H. Carter, Pres.

2955 ■ Jewish National Fund (JNF) (20150)
42 E 69th St.
New York, NY 10021
Ph: (212)879-9305 (212)879-9300
Free: (888)JNF-0099
Fax: (212)570-1673
E-mail: **customerservice@jnf.org**
URL: http://www.jnf.org
Contact: Russell F. Robinson, CEO

2956 ■ Jewish Reconstructionist Federation (JRF) (20151)
101 Greenwood Ave., Ste.430
Jenkintown, PA 19046
Ph: (215)885-5601
Fax: (215)885-5603
E-mail: csheingold@jrf.org
URL: http://jrf.org
Contact: **Mr. Robert A. Barkin, Exec. VP**

2957 ■ League for Yiddish (20414)
64 Fulton St., Ste.1101
New York, NY 10038
Ph: (212)889-0380
Fax: **(212)889-0380**
E-mail: info@leagueforyiddish.org
URL: http://leagueforyiddish.org
Contact: Dr. Sheva Zucker, Exec. Dir.

2958 ■ MERCAZ USA (19749)
820 Second Ave., 10th Fl.
New York, NY 10017-4504
Ph: (212)533-2061
Fax: (212)533-2601
E-mail: info@mercazusa.org
URL: http://www.mercazusa.org
Contact: **Janet Tobin, Pres.**

2959 ■ Na'amat U.S.A. (17874)
505 8th Ave., Ste.2302
New York, NY 10118
Ph: (212)563-5222
Fax: (212)563-5710
E-mail: naamat@naamat.org
URL: http://www.naamat.org
Contact: Liz Raider, Natl. Pres.

2960 ■ National Association of Temple Administrators (NATA) (20163)
PO Box 936
Ridgefield, WA 98642
Ph: (360)887-0464
Free: (800)966-NATA
Fax: (866)767-3791
E-mail: nataoffice@natanet.org
URL: http://natanet.org
Contact: **Livia Thompson FTA, Pres.**

2961 ■ National Council of Jewish Women (NCJW) (20423)
475 Riverside Dr., Ste.250
New York, NY 10115
Ph: (212)645-4048
Fax: (212)645-7466
E-mail: action@ncjw.org
URL: http://www.ncjw.org
Contact: **Linda Slucker, Pres.**

2962 ■ Rabbinical Assembly (RA) (19762)
3080 Broadway
New York, NY 10027
Ph: (212)280-6000 **(212)280-6058**
Fax: (212)749-9166
E-mail: info@rabbinicalassembly.org
URL: http://www.rabbinicalassembly.org
Contact: Rabbi Julie Schonfeld, Exec. VP

2963 ■ Rabbinical Council of America (RCA) (17895)
305 7th Ave., 12th Fl.
New York, NY 10001
Ph: (212)807-9000
Fax: (212)727-8452
E-mail: office@rabbis.org
URL: http://www.rabbis.org
Contact: **Rabbi Shmuel Goldin, Pres.**

2964 ■ Society of Jewish Ethics (SJE)
1531 Dickey Dr.
Atlanta, GA 30322
Ph: **(404)712-8550**
Fax: (404)727-7399
E-mail: kjohn9@emory.edu
URL: http://societyofjewishethics.org
Contact: Kristina Johnson, Program Coor.

2965 ■ Union for Traditional Judaism (UTJ) (17910)
668 Amer. Legion Dr., Ste.B
Teaneck, NJ 07666
Ph: (201)801-0707
Fax: (201)801-0449
E-mail: office@utj.org
URL: http://www.utj.org
Contact: Rabbi Ronald D. Price, Exec. VP

2966 ■ Women of Reform Judaism (WRJ) (19781)
633 3rd Ave.
New York, NY 10017
Ph: (212)650-4050
Free: (866)975-5924
Fax: (212)650-4059
E-mail: wrj@urj.org
URL: http://www.womenofreformjudaism.org
Contact: **Robin E. Cohen, Interim Exec. Dir.**

2967 ■ Women's League for Conservative Judaism (WLCJ) (20451)
475 Riverside Dr., Ste.820
New York, NY 10115
Ph: (212)870-1260
Fax: (212)870-1261
E-mail: **scrane@wlcj.org**
URL: http://www.wlcj.org
Contact: **Sarrae G. Crane, Exec. Dir.**

2968 ■ World Council of Conservative/Masorti Synagogues (WCS) (19785)
3080 Broadway
New York, NY 10027
Ph: (212)280-6039
Fax: (212)678-5321
E-mail: **worldcouncil@masortiworld.org**
URL: http://www.masortiworld.org
Contact: Alan H. Silberman, Pres.

Laity

2969 ■ National Association for Lay Ministry (NALM) (18123)
6896 Laurel St. NW
Washington, DC 20012
Ph: (202)291-4100 **(202)541-5300**
Fax: (202)291-8550
E-mail: nalm@nalm.org
URL: http://www.nalm.org
Contact: Christopher C. Anderson, Exec. Dir.

Lutheran

2970 ■ Concordia Historical Institute (CHI) (17937)
804 Seminary Pl.
St. Louis, MO 63105-3014
Ph: (314)505-7900 **(314)505-7911**
Fax: (314)505-7901
E-mail: chi@lutheranhistory.org
URL: **http://www.lutheranhistory.org**
Contact: Larry Lumpe, Exec. Dir.

2971 ■ Lutheran Deaconess Association (LDA) (2701)
1304 LaPorte Ave.
Valparaiso, IN 46383
Ph: (219)464-6925
Fax: (219)464-6928
E-mail: deacserv@valpo.edu
URL: http://www.thelda.org
Contact: **Deaconess Roberta Hillhouse, Pres.**

2972 ■ Lutheran Deaconess Conference (LDC) (2702)
1304 LaPorte Ave.
Valparaiso, IN 46383
Ph: (219)464-6925
Fax: (219)464-6928
E-mail: deacserv@valpo.edu
URL: **http://www.thelda.org/about/ldc.php**

2973 ■ Lutheran Historical Conference (LHC) (19811)
c/o Marvin A. Huggins, Membership Sec.
5732 White Pine Dr.
St. Louis, MO 63129-2936
Ph: (314)505-7921 (314)487-9884
Fax: (314)505-7901

E-mail: marvinh@pobox.com
URL: http://www.luthhist.org
Contact: **Susan Wilds McArver, Pres.**

2974 ■ Lutheran Human Relations Association (LHRA) (18038)
1821 N 16th St.
Milwaukee, WI 53205
Ph: (414)536-0585 **(414)536-0636**
Fax: (414)536-0690
E-mail: lhra@lhra.org
URL: http://www.lhra.org
Contact: Marilyn Miller, Exec. Dir.

2975 ■ Lutheran Men in Mission (LMM) (20480)
Evangelical Lutheran Church in Am.
8765 W Higgins Rd.
Chicago, IL 60631
Free: (800)638-3522
Fax: (773)380-2632
E-mail: **doug.haugen@elca.org**
URL: **http://www.lutheranmeninmission.org**
Contact: Doug Haugen, Dir.

Macedonian

2976 ■ Macedonian Outreach (18087)
PO Box 398
Danville, CA 94526-0398
Ph: (925)820-4107
Fax: (925)820-4107
E-mail: macout@acts.org
URL: http://www.macedonianoutreach.org
Contact: **Terry L. Thompson, Chm.**

Medicine

2977 ■ MAP International (MAP) (20499)
4700 Glynco Pkwy.
Brunswick, GA 31525-6800
Ph: (912)265-6010
Free: (800)225-8550
E-mail: **map@map.org**
URL: http://www.map.org
Contact: Immanuel Thangaraj MD, Chm.

Mennonite

2978 ■ Mennonite Central Committee (MCC) (20503)
21 S 12th St.
PO Box 500
Akron, PA 17501-0500
Ph: (717)859-1151
Free: (888)563-4676
Fax: (717)859-2171
E-mail: ebn@mcc.org
URL: http://mcc.org
Contact: **Arli Klassen, Exec. Dir.**

2979 ■ Mennonite Church USA Historical Committee (17967)
1700 S Main St.
Goshen, IN 46526
Ph: (574)523-3080
Free: **(866)866-2872**
Fax: (574)535-7756
E-mail: history@mennoniteusa.org
URL: http://www.mcusa-archives.org
Contact: Rich Preheim, Dir.

Messianic Judaism

2980 ■ Messianic Jewish Alliance of America (MJAA) (18426)
PO Box 274
Springfield, PA 19064
Ph: **(610)338-0451**
Free: (800)225-6522

Fax: (610)338-0471
E-mail: office@mjaa.org
URL: http://www.mjaa.org
Contact: Rabbi Frank Lowinger, Pres.

Methodist

2981 ■ Methodist Federation for Social Action (MFSA) (17985)
212 E Capitol St. NE
Washington, DC 20003
Ph: (202)546-8806
Fax: (202)546-6811
E-mail: mfsa@mfsaweb.org
URL: http://mfsaweb.org
Contact: **Rev. Vicki Woods, Co-Pres.**

Ministry

2982 ■ Academy of Parish Clergy (APC) (17995)
2249 Florinda St.
Sarasota, FL 34231-4414
Ph: **(941)922-8633**
E-mail: **pjbinder2@juno.com**
URL: http://www.apclergy.org
Contact: **Rev. David Imhoff, Pres.**

2983 ■ Christ for the City International (CFCI) (19362)
PO Box 390395
Omaha, NE 68139
Ph: (402)592-8332
Free: (888)526-7551
Fax: **(402)592-8312**
E-mail: info@cfci.org
URL: http://www.cfci.org
Contact: Dr. Duane Anderson, Pres./CEO

2984 ■ International Network of Prison Ministries (INPM)
Box 227475
Dallas, TX 75222
URL: http://prisonministry.net
Contact: **Beth Mitchel, Contact**

2985 ■ LifeWind International (20709)
PO Box 1302
Salida, CA 95368
Ph: (209)543-7500
Fax: (209)543-7550
E-mail: info@lifewind.org
URL: http://www.lifewind.org
Contact: Dr. John C. Payne MD, Pres.

2986 ■ World Hope International (20718)
PO Box 17151
Baltimore, MD 21297-1151
Ph: (703)923-9414
Free: (888)466-4673
Fax: (703)923-9418
E-mail: whi@worldhope.net
URL: **http://www.worldhope.org**
Contact: Karl D. Eastlack, Pres./CEO

Mission

2987 ■ Africa Inland Mission International (AIM) (18004)
PO Box 178
Pearl River, NY 10965
Ph: (845)735-4014
Free: (800)254-0010
Fax: (845)735-1814
URL: http://www.aimint.org/usa
Contact: **Katie Spiguzza, Rep.**

2988 ■ Agricultural Missions, Inc. (AMI) (18107)
475 Riverside Dr., Rm. 725
New York, NY 10115
Ph: (212)870-2553
Fax: (212)870-2959
E-mail: info@ag-missions.org
URL: http://www.agriculturalmissions.org
Contact: **Winston Carroo, Exec. Dir.**

2989 ■ American Society of Missiology (ASM) (18466)
2100 S Summit Ave.
Sioux Falls, SD 57105
Ph: **(605)336-6588**
Fax: **(605)335-9090**
E-mail: **sec_treas@asmweb.org**
URL: http://www.asmweb.org
Contact: **W. Jay Moon, Sec.-Treas.**

2990 ■ Avant Ministries (18062)
10000 N Oak Trafficway
Kansas City, MO 64155
Ph: (816)734-8500
Free: (800)468-1892
Fax: (816)734-4601
E-mail: **info@avmi.org**
URL: http://www.avantministries.org
Contact: Jack Elwood, Pres./CEO

2991 ■ Bibles For The World (BFTW) (20561)
PO Box 49759
Colorado Springs, CO 80949-9759
Ph: **(719)630-7733**
Free: (888)382-4253
Fax: (719)630-1449
E-mail: info@bftw.org
URL: http://www.bftw.org
Contact: **Dr. Lalrimawii Pudaite, Pres./Co-Founder**

2992 ■ Catholic Committee of Appalachia (CCA) (20567)
885 Orchard Run Rd.
Spencer, WV 25276
Ph: (304)927-5798
E-mail: ccappal@citynet.net
URL: http://www.ccappal.org
Contact: **Arnie Simonse, Chm.**

2993 ■ Christian Aid Mission (18033)
PO Box 9037
Charlottesville, VA 22906
Ph: (434)977-5650
Free: (800)977-5650
E-mail: **friends@christianaid.org**
URL: **http://www.christianaid.org**
Contact: Bob Finley, Founder/Chm.

2994 ■ Christian Missions in Many Lands (CMML) (18037)
PO Box 13
Spring Lake, NJ 07762-0013
Ph: (732)449-8880
Fax: (732)974-0888
E-mail: **cmml@cmml.us**
URL: http://www.cmmlusa.org
Contact: Robert F. Dadd, Pres.

2995 ■ Christian Pilots Association (CPA) (18490)
PO Box 90452
Los Angeles, CA 90009
Ph: (562)208-2912
Free: **(800)637-2945**
E-mail: info@christianpilots.org
URL: http://www.christianpilots.org

2996 ■ Evangelical Free Church of America (EFCA) (19921)
901 E 78th St.
Minneapolis, MN 55420-1334
Ph: (952)854-1300 **(952)853-8491**
Free: (800)745-2202
Fax: (952)853-8474

E-mail: **webmaster@efca.org**
URL: http://www.efca.org
Contact: Dr. William J. Hamel, Pres.

**2997 ▪ Evangelical Missiological Society
(EMS) (19922)**
PO Box 794
Wheaton, IL 60187
Ph: **(630)752-5949**
Fax: **(630)752-7125**
E-mail: info@emsweb.org
URL: http://www.emsweb.org
Contact: Enoch Wan, Pres.

2998 ▪ Fellowship International Mission (FIM)
555 S 24th St.
Allentown, PA 18104-6666
Ph: (610)435-9099
Free: (888)346-9099
Fax: (610)435-2641
E-mail: **swilt@fim.org**
URL: http://fim.org
Contact: Mr. Steve Wilt, Gen. Dir.

**2999 ▪ Global Economic Outreach (GEO)
(18188)**
PO Box 12778
Wilmington, NC 28405
E-mail: **geomail@geo360.org**
URL: **http://www.geo360.org**

**3000 ▪ Gospel Literature International
(GLINT) (18061)**
PO Box 4060
Ontario, CA 91761-1003
Ph: (909)481-5222
Free: (800)434-5468
Fax: (909)481-5216
E-mail: **info@glint.org**
URL: http://www.glint.org
Contact: Dr. Georgalyn Wilkinson, Pres.

**3001 ▪ Inter Varsity Christian Fellowship
(18067)**
PO Box 7895
Madison, WI 53707-7895
Ph: (608)274-9001
Fax: (608)274-7882
E-mail: **info@intervarsity.org**
URL: http://www.intervarsity.org
Contact: Alec D. Hill, Pres./CEO

**3002 ▪ International Mission Board (IMB)
(20350)**
PO Box 6767
Richmond, VA 23230-0767
Free: (800)999-3113
E-mail: **imb@imb.org**
URL: http://www.imb.org
Contact: **Tom Elliff, Pres.**

3003 ▪ Latin America Mission (LAM) (18075)
PO Box 527900
Miami, FL 33152-7900
Ph: (305)884-8400
Free: (800)275-8410
Fax: (305)885-8649
E-mail: **short-term@lam.org**
URL: http://www.lam.org
Contact: Steve Johnson, Pres.

3004 ▪ Moody Bible Institute (MBI) (18094)
820 N LaSalle Blvd.
Chicago, IL 60610
Ph: (312)329-4000 **(312)329-4223**
Free: (800)356-6639
Fax: **(312)329-4419**
E-mail: pr@moody.edu
URL: http://www.moody.edu
Contact: Dr. Paul Nyquist, Pres.

3005 ▪ Mustard Seed Foundation (18095)
7115 Leesburg Pike, Ste.304
Falls Church, VA 22043
Ph: (703)524-5620

Fax: (703)533-7340
URL: http://www.msfdn.org
Contact: **Dennis Bakke, Co-Chm./Treas.**

3006 ▪ New Tribes Mission (NTM) (20374)
1000 E 1st St.
Sanford, FL 32771-1441
Ph: (407)323-3430
Free: (866)547-2460
Fax: (407)330-0376
E-mail: ntm@ntm.org
URL: **http://usa.ntm.org**
Contact: Mr. Larry Brown, Chm.

**3007 ▪ North America Indigenous Ministries
(NAIM) (18096)**
PO Box 499
Sumas, WA 98295
Ph: **(604)850-3052**
Free: **(888)942-5468**
Fax: **(604)504-0178**
E-mail: office@naim.ca
URL: http://www.naim.ca
Contact: Clyde Cowan, Exec. Dir.

3008 ▪ O.C. International (OCI) (17686)
PO Box 36900
Colorado Springs, CO 80936
Ph: (719)592-9292
Free: (800)676-7837
Fax: (719)592-0693
E-mail: **info@oci.org**
URL: http://www.onechallenge.org
Contact: Mr. Bob Malouf, Pres.

3009 ▪ OMF International U.S.A. (18106)
10 W Dry Creek Cir.
Littleton, CO 80120-4413
Ph: (303)730-4160
Free: (800)422-5330
Fax: (303)730-4165
E-mail: info@omf.org
URL: http://www.omf.org/us
Contact: **David Barlow, Pres./CEO**

3010 ▪ OMS International (19464)
PO Box A
Greenwood, IN 46142
Ph: **(317)888-3333**
Fax: (317)888-5275
E-mail: **info@onemissionsociety.org**
URL: **http://www.onemissionsociety.org**
Contact: David Long, Pres.

3011 ▪ Reach Across
PO Box 2047
Lexington, SC 29071-2047
Ph: **(803)358-2330**
E-mail: accountsmanager.us@reachacross.net
URL: http://us.reachacross.net

3012 ▪ Samaritans International (18119)
370 E Cedar St.
Mooresville, NC 28115-2806
Ph: (704)663-7951 **(704)663-5485**
E-mail: info@samaritaninternational.org
URL: http://www.samaritansinternational.org
Contact: Stephen Ferguson, Pres.

**3013 ▪ Spanish World Ministries (SWM)
(18127)**
PO Box 542
Winona Lake, IN 46590-0542
Ph: (574)267-8821
E-mail: info@spanishworld.org
URL: http://spanishworld.org
Contact: **Daniel Sandoval, Exec. Dir.**

**3014 ▪ United Indian Missions International
(UIMI) (20660)**
PO Box 336010
Greeley, CO 80633-0601
Ph: **(970)785-1176**

E-mail: uim@uim.org
URL: http://www.uim.org
Contact: **Mr. Daniel P. Fredericks, Exec. Dir.**

**3015 ▪ World for Christ Crusade (WCC)
(20835)**
1005 Union Valley Rd.
West Milford, NJ 07480
Ph: (973)728-3267
URL: http://www.worldforchristcrusade.org
Contact: **Rev. William Stelpstra, Contact**

3016 ▪ World Team (WT) (20839)
1431 Stuckert Rd.
Warrington, PA 18976
Ph: (215)491-4900
Free: (800)967-7109
Fax: (215)491-4910
E-mail: wt-usa@worldteam.org
URL: http://www.worldteam.org
Contact: **David Riddell, International Dir.**

3017 ▪ Youth With a Mission (YWAM) (18234)
PO Box 26479
Colorado Springs, CO 80936-6479
Ph: (719)380-0505
Fax: (719)380-0936
E-mail: **info@ywamicn.org**
URL: http://www.ywam.org
Contact: Mr. Rob Abraham, Dir.

Music

**3018 ▪ Association of Anglican Musicians
(AAM) (17737)**
PO Box 7530
Little Rock, AR 72217
Ph: **(501)661-9925**
Fax: **(501)661-9925**
E-mail: **anglicanm@aol.com**
URL: http://anglicanmusicians.org
Contact: Bryan K. Mock DMA, Pres.

3019 ▪ Choristers Guild (CG) (20014)
12404 Park Central Dr., Ste.100
Dallas, TX 75251-1802
Ph: (469)398-3606
Free: (800)246-7478
Fax: (469)398-3611
E-mail: **jrindelaub@mailcg.org**
URL: http://www.choristersguild.org
Contact: Jim Rindelaub, Exec. Dir.

**3020 ▪ Church Music Association of America
(CMAA) (20683)**
12421 New Point Dr.
Richmond, VA 23233
Ph: **(334)703-0884 (334)444-5584**
Fax: (334)460-9924
E-mail: contact@musicasacra.com
URL: http://musicasacra.com
Contact: William P. Mahrt, Pres.

**3021 ▪ Hymn Society in the United States
and Canada (HSUSC) (18163)**
Baptist Theological Seminary at Richmond
3400 Brook Rd.
Richmond, VA 23227-4536
Ph: **(804)204-1226**
Free: (800)843-4966
Fax: (804)355-9208
E-mail: **office@thehymnsociety.org**
URL: http://www.thehymnsociety.org
Contact: **Deborah Carlton Loftis, Exec. Dir.**

Muslim

**3022 ▪ Imam Mahdi Association of Marjaeya
(IMAM)**
835 Mason St.
Dearborn, MI 48124
Ph: (313)303-9280 (313)914-7042
Free: (888)747-8264

Fax: (313)447-2037
E-mail: info@imam-us.org
URL: http://www.imam-us.org
Contact: Sayyid Mohammad Baqir Kashmiri, Chm.

Mysticism

3023 ▪ Astara (18609)
10700 Jersey Blvd., Ste.450
Rancho Cucamonga, CA 91730
Ph: (909)948-7412
Free: (800)964-4941
Fax: (909)948-2016
E-mail: mail@astara.org
URL: http://www.astara.org
Contact: **Dean Zakich, Gen. Mgr.**

Pentecostal

3024 ▪ Society for Pentecostal Studies (SPS) (18312)
1435 N Glenstone Ave.
Springfield, MO 65802
Ph: **(417)268-1084**
E-mail: **lolena@agts.edu**
URL: http://www.sps-usa.org
Contact: **Lois E. Olena, Exec. Dir.**

Presbyterian

3025 ▪ Independent Board for Presbyterian Foreign Missions (IBPFM) (20053)
PO Box 1346
Blue Bell, PA 19422-0435
Ph: (610)279-0952
Fax: (610)279-0954
E-mail: info@ibpfm.org
URL: http://www.ibpfm.org
Contact: **Brad Gsell, Pres.**

Relief

3026 ▪ World Vision International (20488)
800 W Chestnut Ave.
Monrovia, CA 91016-3198
Ph: (626)303-8811
Fax: (626)301-7786
E-mail: worvis@wvi.org
URL: http://www.wvi.org
Contact: **Kevin Jenkins, Pres./CEO**

Religion

3027 ▪ Church Universal and Triumphant (CUT) (17121)
63 Summit Way
Gardiner, MT 59030
Ph: (406)848-9500
Free: (800)245-5445
Fax: **(406)848-9555**
E-mail: tslinfo@tsl.org
URL: http://tsl.org
Contact: Mr. Thomas Schumacher, Marketing/Communications Dir.

3028 ▪ Health Ministries Association (HMA)
PO Box 60042
Dayton, OH 45406
Free: **(800)723-4291**
Fax: **(937)558-0453**
E-mail: **info@hmassoc.org**
URL: http://www.hmassoc.org
Contact: Marlene Feagan, Pres.

3029 ▪ International Order of Saint Luke the Physician (OSL)
PO Box 780909
San Antonio, TX 78278-0909
Ph: (210)492-5222
Free: (877)992-5222
E-mail: osl2@satx.rr.com
URL: http://www.orderofstluke.org
Contact: **Hazel Kundinger, Pres.**

3030 ▪ Maclellan Foundation (18343)
820 Broad St., Ste.300
Chattanooga, TN 37402
Ph: (423)755-1366
Fax: (423)755-1640
E-mail: **support@maclellan.net**
URL: http://www.maclellan.net
Contact: Mr. Hugh O. Maclellan Jr., Chm.

Research

3031 ▪ Religious Research Association (RRA) (18333)
618 SW 2nd Ave.
Galva, IL 61434-1912
Ph: (309)932-2727
Fax: (309)932-2282
E-mail: **williamswatos@augustana.edu**
URL: http://rra.hartsem.edu
Contact: Dr. William H. Swatos Jr., Exec. Off.

Rosicrucian

3032 ▪ Rosicrucian Fellowship (20962)
2222 Mission Ave.
Oceanside, CA 92058-2329
Ph: (760)757-6600
Fax: (760)721-3806
E-mail: **rf@rosicrucian.com**
URL: http://www.rosicrucian.com

Sabbath

3033 ▪ Lord's Day Alliance of the United States (LDA) (20965)
PO Box 941745
Atlanta, GA 31145-0745
Ph: (404)693-5530
E-mail: tnorton@ldausa.org
URL: http://www.ldausa.org
Contact: **Brian W. Hanse, Pres.**

Science

3034 ▪ Institute on Religion in an Age of Science (IRAS) (17820)
744 DuBois Dr.
Baton Rouge, LA 70808
E-mail: **michaelcav@aol.com**
URL: http://www.iras.org
Contact: **Michael Cavanaugh, Contact**

Spiritual Understanding

3035 ▪ Thanks-Giving Square (TGS) (18257)
PO Box 131770
Dallas, TX 75313-1770
Ph: (214)969-1977
Free: (888)305-1205
Fax: (214)754-0152
E-mail: tgs@thanksgiving.org
URL: http://www.thanksgiving.org
Contact: **Chris Slaughter, Pres.**

Unitarian Universalist

3036 ▪ Unitarian Universalist Historical Society (UUHS) (18747)
27 Grove St.
Scituate, MA 02066
E-mail: gjgibson@juno.com
URL: **http://www.uuhs.org**
Contact: Rev. Gordon Gibson, Pres.

3037 ▪ Unitarian Universalist Ministers Association (UUMA) (20179)
25 Beacon St.
Boston, MA 02108
Ph: (617)848-0498 **(617)848-0416**
Fax: (617)848-0973
E-mail: administrator@uuma.org
URL: http://www.uuma.org
Contact: **Janette M. Lallier, Admin.**

Waldensian

3038 ▪ American Waldensian Society (AWS) (18299)
PO Box 398
Valdese, NC 28690
Ph: (828)874-3500
Free: (866)825-3373
Fax: (828)874-0880
E-mail: info@waldensian.org
URL: http://www.waldensian.org
Contact: **Dr. Brad Lewis, Pres.**

Water

3039 ▪ A Cup of Water International (ACOWI)
PO Box 9809
Kansas City, MO 64134
Ph: (267)242-1798
E-mail: biblicalhot@hotmail.com
URL: http://www.givetodrink.org
Contact: Jong S. Kweon, Contact

Women

3040 ▪ Women Church Convergence (WCC) (18413)
PO Box 806
Mill Valley, CA 94942
Ph: (908)753-4636
Fax: (718)368-4887
E-mail: **info@women-churchconvergence.org**
URL: http://www.women-churchconvergence.org
Contact: **Susan Paweski, Co-Coor.**

3041 ▪ Women's Missionary Society, AME Church (WMS) (18317)
1134 11th St. NW
Washington, DC 20001
Ph: (202)371-8886
Fax: (202)371-8820
E-mail: **wmsamec@aol.com**
URL: http://www.wms-amec.org
Contact: **Dr. Shirley Hopkins Davis, Pres.**

3042 ▪ World Day of Prayer International Committee (WDPIC) (18309)
475 Riverside Dr., Rm. 729
New York, NY 10115
Ph: (212)870-3049
Fax: (212)864-8648
E-mail: wdpic@worlddayofprayer.net
URL: http://www.worlddayofprayer.net
Contact: **Eileen King, Exec. Dir.**

Yoga

3043 ■ Self-Realization Fellowship (SRF) (18322)
3880 San Rafael Ave., Dept. 9W
Los Angeles, CA 90065-3298
Ph: (818)549-5151 **(323)225-2471**
Free: (800)801-1952
Fax: (818)549-5100
E-mail: **publicaffairs@yogananda-srf.org**
URL: http://www.yogananda-srf.org
Contact: **Sri Mrinalini Mata, Pres.**

3044 ■ Yoga Research Foundation (YRF) (20637)
6111 SW 74th Ave.
Miami, FL 33143
Ph: (305)666-2006
Fax: (305)666-4443
E-mail: **info@yrf.org**
URL: http://www.yrf.org
Contact: Swami Jyotirmayananda, Founder

Youth

3045 ■ American Youth Foundation (AYF) (20892)
6357 Clayton Rd.
St. Louis, MO 63117
Ph: (314)963-1321 **(314)719-4343**
Fax: (314)963-9243
E-mail: **annakay.vorsteg@ayf.com**
URL: http://www.ayf.com
Contact: Anna Kay Vorsteg, Pres./CEO

3046 ■ Youth for Christ/U.S.A. (YFC/USA) (20222)
PO Box 4478
Englewood, CO 80155
Ph: (303)843-9000
Fax: (303)843-9002
E-mail: **info@yfc.net**
URL: http://www.yfc.net
Contact: Daniel S. Wolgemuth, Pres.

Aerospace

3047 ■ Tuskegee Airmen, Inc. (TAI) (18796)
PO Box 830060
Tuskegee, AL 36083
Ph: **(334)421-0198**
Fax: **(334)725-8205**
E-mail: **mthomas@tuskegeeairmen.org**
URL: http://tuskegeeairmen.org
Contact: **Leon A. Johnson, Pres.**

American Revolution

3048 ■ Descendants of the Signers of the Declaration of Independence (DSDI) (18460)
103 Elmsford Ct.
Brentwood, TN 37027-4753
E-mail: president@dsdi1776.com
URL: http://dsdi1776.com
Contact: **John C. Glynn Jr., Pres. Gen.**

3049 ■ National Society, Daughters of the American Revolution (DAR) (18365)
1776 D St. NW
Washington, DC 20006-5303
Ph: (202)628-1776 (202)628-4780
Free: **(888)673-2732**
E-mail: **membership@dar.org**
URL: http://www.dar.org
Contact: Merry Ann T. Wright, Pres. Gen.

3050 ■ National Society, Sons of the American Revolution (NSSAR) (21082)
1000 S 4th St.
Louisville, KY 40203
Ph: (502)589-1776
Fax: (502)589-1671
E-mail: **jharris@sar.org**
URL: http://www.sar.org
Contact: **Joe E. Harris Jr., Exec. Dir.**

Army

3051 ■ 25th Infantry Division Association (18388)
PO Box 7
Flourtown, PA 19031-0007
E-mail: tropicltn@aol.com
URL: http://www.25thida.com
Contact: **Tom Jones, Pres.**

3052 ■ National 4th Infantry Ivy Division Association (20957)
c/o Don Kelby, Exec. Dir.
PO Box 1914
St. Peters, MO 63376-0035
Ph: (314)606-1969
E-mail: 4thidaed@swbell.net
URL: http://www.4thinfantry.org
Contact: **Phil Menendez, Pres.**

Awards

3053 ■ Ladies Auxiliary of the Military Order of the Purple Heart United States of America (LAMOPH) (20287)
19138 Bedford Dr.
Oregon City, OR 97045
Ph: **(503)657-7085**
E-mail: **karenh417@hotmail.com**
URL: http://www.purpleheart.org/LAMOPH/default.
aspx
Contact: **Karen Haltiner, Pres.**

Civil War

3054 ■ Auxiliary to Sons of Union Veterans of the Civil War (ASUVCW) (18868)
2966 Hayts Corners East Rd.
Ovid, NY 14521
Ph: **(607)869-3720**
E-mail: president@asuvcw.org
URL: http://www.asuvcw.org
Contact: **Virginia L. Twist, Pres.**

3055 ■ Daughters of Union Veterans of the Civil War, 1861-1865 (DUVCW) (18513)
c/o Sharon R. Patton, Membership Chair
1932 Clifton Ave.
Lansing, MI 48910-3531
Ph: (517)484-7795
E-mail: duvcw2009@live.com
URL: http://www.duvcw.org
Contact: **Patricia Kotteman, Pres.**

3056 ■ Military Order of the Stars and Bars (MOSB)
PO Box 1700
White House, TN 37188-1700
Free: (877)790-6672
E-mail: headquarters@mosbihq.org
URL: http://www.mosbihq.org
Contact: **Max L. Waldrop Jr., Commander Gen.**

Colonial

3057 ■ Holland Society of New York (HSNY) (21141)
20 W 44th St., 5th Fl.
New York, NY 10036
Ph: (212)758-1675
Fax: (212)758-2232
E-mail: **info@hollandsociety.org**
URL: http://www.hollandsociety.org
Contact: **Charles Zabriskie Jr., Pres.**

Family Name Societies

3058 ■ Boone Society (19879)
1303 Hunter Ace Way
Cedar Park, TX 78613
E-mail: **samcomptons@cs.com**
URL: http://www.boonesociety.org
Contact: **Sam Compton, Pres.**

3059 ■ Clan Currie Society (18484)
PO Box 541
Summit, NJ 07902-0541
Ph: (908)273-3509
Fax: (908)273-4342
E-mail: clancurrie@mail.com
URL: **http://www.clancurrie.com**
Contact: Robert Currie, Pres.

3060 ■ Clan Fergusson Society of North America (CFSNA) (21111)
c/o B. J. Ferguson, Sec.
192 Hawthorne Hill Rd.
Jasper, GA 30143
E-mail: **rfurgerson2@juno.com**
URL: http://www.cfsna.net
Contact: **Rupert H. Furgerson II, Pres.**

3061 ■ Clan Moncreiffe Society (CMS) (20853)
c/o Charlotte Moncrief, Treas.
1405 Plaza St. SE
Decatur, AL 35603
E-mail: sgiandhu@aol.com
URL: http://www.moncreiffe.org
Contact: **Robert V. Dawes, Pres.**

3062 ■ Clan Montgomery Society International (CMSI) (20429)
2803 Kinnett Rd.
Bethel, OH 45106
E-mail: president@clanmontgomery.org
URL: http://www.clanmontgomery.org
Contact: Hugh Montgomery Jr., Pres.

Genealogy

3063 ■ American Society of Genealogists (ASG) (19277)
PO Box 26836
San Diego, CA 92196
E-mail: asg.sec@gmail.com
URL: http://www.fasg.org
Contact: **Melinde Lutz Sanborn, Pres.**

3064 ■ International Association of Jewish Genealogical Societies (IAJGS) (21339)
c/o Paul Silverstone, Treas.
PO Box 3624
Cherry Hill, NJ 08034-0556
E-mail: president@iajgs.org
URL: http://www.iajgs.org
Contact: Michael Goldstein, Pres.

3065 ■ International Society for British Genealogy and Family History (ISBGFH) (19297)
PO Box 350459
Westminster, CO 80035-0459
Ph: (303)422-9371
E-mail: admin@isbgfh.org
URL: http://www.isbgfh.org
Contact: **Ann Wells, Pres.**

3066 ■ Lancaster Mennonite Historical Society (LMHS) (18649)
2215 Millstream Rd.
Lancaster, PA 17602-1499
Ph: (717)393-9745
Fax: (717)393-8751
E-mail: lmhs@lmhs.org
URL: http://www.lmhs.org
Contact: **Charles G. Bauman, Chm.**

3067 ■ New York Genealogical and Biographical Society (NYG&B) (21434)
36 W 44th St., 7th Fl.
New York, NY 10036-8105
Ph: (212)755-8532
Fax: (212)754-4218
E-mail: **msmith@nygbs.org**
URL: http://www.newyorkfamilyhistory.org
Contact: McKelden Smith, Pres.

3068 ■ Ohio Genealogical Society (OGS) (2899)
611 State Rte. 97 W
Bellville, OH 44813-8813
Ph: (419)886-1903
Fax: **(419)886-0092**
E-mail: ogs@ogs.org
URL: http://www.ogs.org
Contact: Sunda Anderson Peters, Pres.

3069 ■ Palatines to America: Researching German-Speaking Ancestry (Pal-Am) (18659)
PO Box 141260
Columbus, OH 43214
Ph: (614)267-4700
E-mail: **membership@palam.org**
URL: http://www.palam.org

3070 ■ Saint Nicholas Society of the City of New York (SNSCNY) (21148)
c/o Jill Spiller, Exec. Dir.
20 W 44th St., Rm. 508
New York, NY 10036-6603
Ph: (212)991-9944
Fax: (646)237-2767
E-mail: info@saintnicholassociety.org
URL: http://www.saintnicholassociety.org
Contact: **Rev. Thomas F. Pike, Pres.**

Huguenot

3071 ■ Huguenot Historical Society (HHS) (21376)
18 Broadhead Ave.
New Paltz, NY 12561-1403
Ph: (845)255-1660 (845)255-1889

Fax: (845)255-0376
E-mail: info@huguenotstreet.org
URL: http://www.huguenotstreet.org
Contact: **Mary Etta Schneider, Pres.**

Korean War

3072 ■ 2nd Infantry Division, Korean War Veterans Alliance (20254)
c/o Ralph Hockley, Sec.
10027 Pine Forest Rd.
Houston, TX 77042-1531
Ph: (713)334-0271
Fax: (713)334-0272
E-mail: rmh-2id-kwva@earthlink.net
URL: http://www.2id.org
Contact: Charles E. Hankins, Pres.
Status Note: Defunct.

Martial Arts

3073 ■ Special Military Active Retired Travel Club (SMART) (20839)
600 Univ. Off. Blvd., Ste.1A
Pensacola, FL 32504
Ph: (850)478-1986
Free: (800)354-7681
E-mail: **smart@smartrving.org**
URL: http://www.smartrving.net
Contact: **Melissa Wade, Exec. Mgr.**

Military Families

3074 ■ American Legion Auxiliary (ALA) (21406)
8945 N Meridian St., 2nd Fl.
Indianapolis, IN 46260
Ph: (317)569-4500
Fax: (317)569-4502
E-mail: **alahq@alaforveterans.org**
URL: http://www.legion-aux.org
Contact: Carlene Ashworth, Natl. Pres.

3075 ■ Sons of the American Legion (SAL) (2911)
PO Box 1055
Indianapolis, IN 46206
Ph: **(317)630-1200**
Fax: (317)630-1413
E-mail: sal@legion.org
URL: http://www.sal.legion.org
Contact: Brian O'Hearne, Adjutant

3076 ■ World War II War Brides Association (WWIIWBA) (18547)
1125 Pinon Oak Dr.
Prescott, AZ 86305
Ph: **(928)237-1581**
E-mail: **theladydiane@gmail.com**
URL: http://uswarbrides.com
Contact: **Ms. Diane Reddy, Membership Dir.**

Pilgrims

3077 ■ General Society of Mayflower Descendants (GSMD) (21464)
PO Box 3297
Plymouth, MA 02361-3297
Ph: (508)746-3188
Fax: (508)746-2488
E-mail: **gsmd.libr@verizon.net**
URL: http://www.themayflowersociety.com
Contact: Judith Haddock Swan, Governor Gen.

Pioneers

3078 ■ National Society of the Sons of Utah Pioneers (NSSUP) (21469)
3301 E 2920 S
Salt Lake City, UT 84109
Ph: (801)484-4441
Free: (888)724-1847
Fax: (801)484-2067
E-mail: sup1847@comcast.net
URL: http://www.sonsofutahpioneers.org
Contact: **La Mar Adams, Pres.**

Veterans

3079 ■ American GI Forum of United States (AGIF) (21494)
c/o Dottie Bruton, Mgr.
2870 Speed Blvd., No. 103
Denver, CO 80211
Free: (866)244-3628
Fax: (303)458-1634
E-mail: agifnat@gmail.com
URL: http://www.agifusa.org
Contact: **Albert Gonzales, Natl. Commander**

3080 ■ Catholic War Veterans of the U.S.A. (CWV)
441 N Lee St.
Alexandria, VA 22314
Ph: (703)549-3622
Fax: (703)684-5196
E-mail: cwvlmt@aol.com
URL: http://www.cwv.org
Contact: **Mrs. Lupita Martinez, Pres.**

3081 ■ National Association of Veterans Program Administrators (NAVPA) (9292)
2020 Pennsylvania Ave. NW, Ste.1975
Washington, DC 20006-1846
Ph: (517)483-1932
E-mail: info@navpa.org
URL: http://www.navpa.org
Contact: **Dorothy Gillman, Pres.**

World War II

3082 ■ 509th Parachute Infantry Association (19181)
PO Box 860
Huntsville, AL 35804-0860
E-mail: webmaster@509thgeronimo.org
URL: http://www.509thgeronimo.org
Contact: **Mike Monroe, Pres.**

Aerospace

3083 ■ **American Aviation Historical Society (AAHS) (20992)**
PO Box 3023
Huntington Beach, CA 92605-3023
E-mail: websmaster@aahs-online.org
URL: http://www.aahs-online.org
Contact: Robert Brockmeier, Pres.

3084 ■ **F-4 Phantom II Society (21445)**
3053 Rancho Vista Blvd., Ste.H-102
Palmdale, CA 93551
E-mail: president@f4phantom.com
URL: http://www.f4phantom.com
Contact: **Helen Thompson, VP, Admin.**

3085 ■ **International Wheelchair Aviators (IWA) (21023)**
923 W Sherwood Blvd.
Big Bear City, CA 92314
Ph: (951)529-2644 (530)258-6709
E-mail: **dwight_leiss@yahoo.com**
URL: http://wheelchairaviators.org
Contact: **Dwight Leiss, Pres.**

3086 ■ **League of World War I Aviation Historians (21459)**
16820 25th Ave. N
Plymouth, MN 55447
E-mail: otf-membership@overthefront.com
URL: http://www.overthefront.com
Contact: **J.R. Williams, Pres./Chm.**

3087 ■ **National InterCollegiate Flying Association (NIFA) (21670)**
PO Box 15081
Monroe, LA 71207
Ph: (318)325-6156
Fax: (318)325-6156
E-mail: nifahq@hotmail.com
URL: http://www.nifa.us
Contact: **Brad Hock, Pres.**

3088 ■ **Society of Antique Modelers (SAM) (21681)**
3379 Crystal Ct.
Napa, CA 94558
Ph: **(707)255-3547**
E-mail: **ehamler@comcast.net**
URL: http://www.antiquemodeler.org
Contact: **Ed Hamler, Pres.**

3089 ■ **World Airline Historical Society (WAHS)**
PO Box 489
Ocoee, FL 34761
Fax: (407)522-9352
E-mail: **information@wahsonline.com**
URL: http://www.wahsonline.com
Contact: Duane Young, Pres.

Amateur Radio

3090 ■ **ARRL Foundation (ARRLF)**
225 Main St.
Newington, CT 06111
Ph: (860)594-0397 (860)594-0228
Fax: (860)594-0259
E-mail: **hq@arrl.org**
URL: http://www.arrl.org/the-arrl-foundation
Contact: **Kay C. Craigie, Pres.**

Antiques

3091 ■ **The Questers (TQ) (20608)**
210 S Quince St.
Philadelphia, PA 19107-5534
Ph: (215)923-5183
E-mail: **contactus@questers1944.org**
URL: http://www.questers1944.org
Contact: Joan LoCasale, Pres.

Arms

3092 ■ **Japanese Sword Society of the United States (JSSUS) (19036)**
PO Box 5216
Albuquerque, NM 87181
E-mail: barry@hennick.ca
URL: http://www.jssus.org
Contact: Barry Hennick, Ombudsman

Astronomy

3093 ■ **Association of Lunar and Planetary Observers (ALPO) (21550)**
c/o Matthew L. Will, Sec.-Treas.
PO Box 13456
Springfield, IL 62791-3456
E-mail: will008@attglobal.net
URL: http://alpo-astronomy.org
Contact: **Richard W. Schmude Jr., Exec. Dir.**

Automobile

3094 ■ **American Bugatti Club (ABC) (21770)**
600 Lakeview Terr.
Glen Ellyn, IL 60137
Ph: (630)469-4920 (773)380-5480
E-mail: **abcpcsimms@gmail.com**
URL: http://www.americanbugatticlub.org
Contact: Paul Simms, Sec.

3095 ■ **Antique Automobile Club of America (AACA) (19375)**
PO Box 417
Hershey, PA 17033
Ph: (717)534-1910

Fax: (717)534-9101
E-mail: general@aaca.org
URL: http://www.aaca.org
Contact: **Joseph Gagliano, Pres.**

3096 ■ **Auburn-Cord-Duesenberg Club (ACD) (21145)**
24218 E Arapahoe Pl.
Aurora, CO 80016
Ph: **(303)748-3579**
E-mail: auburncars@verizon.net
URL: http://www.acdclub.org
Contact: **Bill Hummel, Pres.**

3097 ■ **Cadillac-LaSalle Club (CLC) (2967)**
PO Box 360835
Columbus, OH 43236-0835
Ph: (614)478-4622
Fax: (614)472-3222
E-mail: clcoffice@cadillaclasalleclub.org
URL: http://www.cadillaclasalleclub.org
Contact: **Lars Kneller, Pres.**

3098 ■ **Classic Car Club of America (CCCA) (21614)**
1645 Des Plaines River Rd., Ste.7A
Des Plaines, IL 60018-2206
Ph: (847)390-0443
Fax: (847)390-7118
E-mail: **info@classiccarclub.org**
URL: http://www.classiccarclub.org
Contact: Al Kroemer, Pres.

3099 ■ **Classic Thunderbird Club International (CTCI) (21617)**
1308 E 29th St.
Signal Hill, CA 90755-1842
Ph: (562)426-2709
Free: (800)488-2709
Fax: (562)426-7023
E-mail: ctcioffice@ctci.org
URL: http://www.ctci.org
Contact: **Chuck Korenko, Pres.**

3100 ■ **Corvair Society of America (CORSA)**
PO Box 607
Lemont, IL 60439-0607
Ph: (630)403-5010
Fax: (630)257-5540
E-mail: corvair@corvair.org
URL: http://www.corvair.org
Contact: **Jamie Reinhart, Pres.**

3101 ■ **Early Ford V-8 Club of America (21633)**
PO Box 1715
Maple Grove, MN 55311
Ph: (763)420-7829
Free: (866)427-7583
Fax: (763)420-7849
E-mail: registration@cornerstonereg.com
URL: http://www.earlyfordv8.org
Contact: **Bob York, Pres.**

3102 ■ Edsel Club (19430)
19296 Tuckaway Ct.
Fort Myers, FL 33903-1244
Ph: (239)731-8027
E-mail: **edselworld@comcast.net**
URL: http://www.edselworld.com
Contact: Robert Allen Mayer, Contact

3103 ■ Elgin Motorcar Owners Registry (21201)
2226 E Apache Ln.
Vincennes, IN 47591
Ph: **(812)888-4172**
Fax: **(812)888-5471**
E-mail: jwolf@indian.vinu.edu
URL: http://beaver.vinu.edu/Eowners.HTM
Contact: Mr. Jay Wolf, Contact

3104 ■ Ferrari Club of America (FCA) (21845)
PO Box 720597
Atlanta, GA 30358
Free: (800)328-0444
Fax: (800)328-0444
E-mail: **membership@ferrariclubofamerica.org**
URL: http://www.ferrariclubofamerica.org
Contact: Don Ambrose, Chm.

3105 ■ Ferrari Owners Club (FOC) (19778)
19051 Goldenwest St., Ste.106-328
Huntington Beach, CA 92648
Ph: (714)213-4775
Fax: (714)960-4262
E-mail: **info@ferrariownersclub.org**
URL: http://www.ferrariownersclub.org
Contact: **Richard Adams, Chm.**

3106 ■ Ford Owners' Association (FOA)
3875 Thornhill Dr.
Lilburn, GA 30047
E-mail: foa005@yahoo.com
URL: http://www.fordowners.org
Contact: **Randy Church, Contact**

3107 ■ Graham Owners Club International (GOCI) (19464)
c/o Gloria Reid, Treas.
4028 Empire Creek Cir.
Georgetown, CA 95634
Ph: **(530)333-4105**
Fax: (510)733-5081
E-mail: **rjsill@graham-paige.com**
URL: http://www.graham-paige.com
Contact: David Spence, Pres.

3108 ■ H.H. Franklin Club (HHFC) (21858)
Cazenovia Coll.
Cazenovia, NY 13035
E-mail: **webmaster@franklincar.org**
URL: http://www.franklincar.org
Contact: **Marvin Gage, Pres.**

3109 ■ Horseless Carriage Club of America (HCCA) (21220)
5709 Oak Ave.
Temple City, CA 91780-2431
Ph: (626)287-4222
E-mail: office@hcca.org
URL: http://www.hcca.org
Contact: **Richard Cutler, Pres.**

3110 ■ International Amphicar Owners Club (IAOC) (21664)
c/o Ina Cabanas, Treas.
11 Pemberton St.
Pemberton, NJ 08068-1111
E-mail: **prez@amphicar.com**
URL: http://www.amphicar.com
Contact: **Mike Clark, Pres.**

3111 ■ International King Midget Car Club (IKMCC)
c/o Teresa Harris, Sec.
5198 Happy Hollow Rd.
Nelsonville, OH 45764
Ph: **(740)591-0084**

E-mail: secretary@kingmidgetcarclub.org
URL: http://www.kingmidgetcarclub.org
Contact: Lee Seats, Pres.

3112 ■ Iso and Bizzarrini Owners Club (IBOC) (19164)
2025 Drake Dr.
Oakland, CA 94611
E-mail: ibocmembership@cox.net
URL: http://home.tiscali.nl/isorivolta/isoclubs.htm

3113 ■ Jaguar Clubs of North America (JCNA) (2977)
c/o Nancy Rath
234 Buckland Trace
Louisville, KY 40245
Ph: (502)244-1672
Free: (888)258-2524
E-mail: nrath@jcna.com
URL: http://www.jcna.com
Contact: **Steve Kennedy, Sec.**

3114 ■ Lincoln Zephyr Owner's Club (LZOC) (21889)
25609 N Forrest Rd., Ste.10
Rio Verde, AZ 85263
E-mail: **mead@vallnet.com**
URL: http://www.lzoc.org
Contact: **Mr. Thomas Brunner, Contact**

3115 ■ Lotus, Ltd. (18973)
PO Box L
College Park, MD 20741
Ph: (301)982-4054
Fax: (301)982-4054
E-mail: hq@lotuscarclub.org
URL: http://www.lotuscarclub.org
Contact: **Dominick Munofo, Pres.**

3116 ■ Mercedes-Benz Club of America (MBCA) (19190)
1907 Lelaray St.
Colorado Springs, CO 80909-2872
Ph: (719)633-6427
Free: (800)637-2360
Fax: **(719)633-9283**
E-mail: rvann40398@aol.com
URL: http://www.mbca.org
Contact: Douglas Truitt, Exec. Dir.

3117 ■ Midstates Jeepster Association (MJA)
7721 Howick Rd.
Celina, OH 45822
E-mail: **gconrad@bright.net**
URL: http://midstatesjeepster.com
Contact: Barb Conrad, Sec.-Treas.

3118 ■ Model A Ford Club of America (MAFCA) (19524)
250 S Cypress St.
La Habra, CA 90631-5515
Ph: (562)697-2712 (562)697-2737
Fax: (562)690-7452
E-mail: info@mafca.com
URL: http://www.mafca.com
Contact: **Alex Janke, Pres.**

3119 ■ Morgan 3/4 Group (21972)
PO Box 1208
Ridgefield, CT 06877
Ph: (917)880-2962 **(203)727-8566**
URL: http://www.morgan34.org
Contact: Laurence E. Sheehan, Pres.

3120 ■ Morgan Car Club (MCC)
c/o Lisa Shriver
45070 Brae Terr.
Ashburn, VA 20147
E-mail: **bccdocs@gmail.com**
URL: http://www.morgandc.com
Contact: Paul Warren, Pres.

3121 ■ Motor Bus Society (MBS) (19401)
PO Box 261
Paramus, NJ 07653-0261
E-mail: **mca-editor@pixlyn.com**
URL: http://www.motorbussociety.org
Contact: Richard Phillippi, Treas.

3122 ■ Mustang Club of America (MCA) (21722)
4051 Barrancas Ave.
PMB 102
Pensacola, FL 32507
Ph: (850)438-0626
URL: http://www.mustang.org
Contact: **Steve Prewitt, Pres.**

3123 ■ National Council of Corvette Clubs (NCCC) (21730)
c/o Larry Morrison, VP of Membership
492 Meadowlark Way
Clifton, CO 81520-8811
E-mail: **membership@corvettesnccc.org**
URL: http://www.corvettesnccc.org
Contact: Richard Yanko, Pres.

3124 ■ Packard Automobile Classics (PAC) (21755)
PO Box 360806
Columbus, OH 43236-0806
Ph: (614)478-4946
Free: (800)478-0012
Fax: (614)472-3222
E-mail: pacnatoffice@aol.com
URL: http://www.packardclub.org
Contact: **Bonnie Franko, Pres.**

3125 ■ Plymouth Barracuda/Cuda Owners Club (PB/COC) (21324)
c/o Ann M. Curman, Sec.
36 Woodland Rd.
East Greenwich, RI 02818-3430
Ph: **(401)884-4449**
E-mail: amc7268@verizon.net
URL: http://www.pbcoc.com
Contact: Jay M. Fisher, Founder/Dir.

3126 ■ Porsche Club of America (PCA) (22017)
PO Box 6400
Columbia, MD 21045
Ph: **(410)381-0911**
Fax: **(410)381-0924**
E-mail: admin@pca.org
URL: http://www.pca.org
Contact: **Manny Alban, Pres.**

3127 ■ Rolls-Royce Owners' Club (RROC) (19289)
191 Hempt Rd.
Mechanicsburg, PA 17050
Ph: (717)697-4671
Free: (800)879-7762
Fax: (717)697-7820
E-mail: rrochq@rroc.org
URL: http://www.rroc.org
Contact: **Gil Fuqua, Exec. Chair**

3128 ■ Saleen Club of America (SCOA)
6181 Linden Dr. E
West Bend, WI 53095
Ph: (414)234-7472
E-mail: **president@saleenclubofamerica.com**
URL: http://www.saleenclubofamerica.com
Contact: Charlie Smith, Pres.

3129 ■ Shelby American Automobile Club (SAAC) (21977)
PO Box 788
Sharon, CT 06069
Fax: (860)364-0769
E-mail: **pitcrew@saac.com**
URL: http://www.saac.com
Contact: Rick Kopec, Dir.

3130 ■ Society of Automotive Historians (SAH) (21785)
c/o Patrick D. Bisson, Treas.
8537 Tim Tam Trail
Flushing, MI 48433
URL: http://www.autohistory.org
Contact: Susan Davis, Pres.

3131 ■ Subaru 360 Drivers' Club (19581)
23251 Hansen Rd.
Tracy, CA 95304
E-mail: subaru360club@gmail.com
URL: http://www.subaru360club.org
Contact: Brian Kliment, Contact

3132 ■ Thunderbird and Cougar Club of America (TCCoA)
422 Cooper St.
Mountain Home, AR 72653
E-mail: sirwilliam@tccoa.com
URL: http://www.tccoa.com
Contact: Bill William, Pres./Founder

3133 ■ Triumph Register of America (TRA) (21358)
934 Coachway
Annapolis, MD 21401
Ph: (410)974-6707
E-mail: jdwtrxk@verizon.net
URL: http://www.triumphregister.com
Contact: John Warfield, Pres.

3134 ■ Tucker Automobile Club of America (TACA) (19588)
9509 Hinton Dr.
Santee, CA 92071-2760
E-mail: shop@tuckerclub.org
URL: http://www.tuckerclub.org/index.php
Contact: Larry Clark, Contact

3135 ■ United Four-Wheel Drive Associations (UFWDA)
PO Box 316
Swartz Creek, MI 48473
Free: (800)448-3932
E-mail: info@ufwda.org
URL: http://www.ufwda.org
Contact: Jim Mazzola III, Pres.

3136 ■ Veteran Motor Car Club of America (VMCCA) (19595)
c/o Mike Welsh, Sec.
7501 Manchester Ave.
Kansas City, MO 64138
Ph: (816)298-6412
Fax: (816)298-6412
E-mail: vsecretary@vmcca.org
URL: http://www.vmcca.org
Contact: B.D. Berryhill, Pres.

3137 ■ Vintage Chevrolet Club of America (VCCA) (21367)
c/o Mike McGowan, Membership Sec.
PO Box 609
Lemont, IL 60439-0609
Ph: (708)455-8222
E-mail: membershipsecretary@vcca.org
URL: http://www.vcca.org
Contact: Don Williams, Pres.

Bird

3138 ■ American Cockatiel Society (ACS)
PO Box 980055
Houston, TX 77098-0055
Free: (888)221-1161
E-mail: membership@acstiels.com
URL: http://www.acstiels.com
Contact: Bert McAulay, Pres.

3139 ■ American Waterslager Society (AWS) (21842)
556 S Cactus Wren St.
Gilbert, AZ 85296
Ph: (480)892-5464
E-mail: thomas.trujillo@elpaso.com
URL: http://www.waterslagers.com
Contact: Tom Trujillo, Pres.

3140 ■ International Parrotlet Society (IPS) (21406)
PO Box 2446
Aptos, CA 95003-2446
Ph: (831)688-5560 (919)552-6312
E-mail: sandee@parrotletranch.com
URL: http://www.internationalparrotletsociety.org
Contact: Leslie Huegerich, Pres.

Bottles

3141 ■ Federation of Historical Bottle Collectors (FOHBC) (19153)
c/o June Lowry, Business Mgr.
401 Johnston Ct.
Raymore, MO 64083
Ph: (816)318-0160
E-mail: osubuckeyes71@aol.com
URL: http://www.fohbc.com
Contact: Gene Bradberry, Pres.

Bridge

3142 ■ American Bridge Teachers' Association (ABTA) (20001)
490 N Winnebago Dr.
Lake Winnebago, MO 64034-9321
Ph: (816)537-5165
E-mail: krolfe5@comcast.net
URL: http://www.abtahome.com
Contact: Joyce Penn, Pres.

3143 ■ United States Bridge Federation (USBF)
2990 Airways Blvd.
Memphis, TN 38116-3828
E-mail: joanandron@att.net
URL: http://usbf.org
Contact: Joan Gerard, Pres.

Cat

3144 ■ Cat Fanciers' Association (CFA) (19408)
1805 Atlantic Ave.
Manasquan, NJ 08736
Ph: (732)528-9797 (732)528-6443
Fax: (732)528-7391
E-mail: cfa@cfa.org
URL: http://www.cfainc.org
Contact: Jerold Hamza, Pres.

3145 ■ Cat Fanciers' Federation (CFF) (20013)
PO Box 661
Gratis, OH 45330
Ph: (937)787-9009
Fax: (937)787-9009
E-mail: lcestee@aol.com
URL: http://www.cffinc.org
Contact: Linda Neilsen, Pres.

Ceramics

3146 ■ International Association of Duncan Certified Ceramic Teachers (IADCCT) (21477)
510 Salem St.
Risingsun, OH 43457
Ph: (419)457-7281

E-mail: cdog1281@aol.com
URL: http://www.iadcct.com
Contact: Clair Morse, Pres.

Clowns

3147 ■ International Shrine Clown Association (ISCA)
PO Box 102
Marine, IL 62061-0102
Ph: (618)887-4544
E-mail: cy-lo@comcast.net
URL: http://www.shrineclowns.com
Contact: Rupert Solis, Sec.

3148 ■ World Clown Association (WCA) (22130)
PO Box 12215
Merrillville, IN 46410
Ph: (219)487-5317
Free: (800)336-7922
Fax: (866)686-7716
E-mail: wca_manager@att.net
URL: http://worldclown.com
Contact: Joyce Payne, Pres.

Collectors

3149 ■ American Bell Association International (ABAII) (22175)
7210 Bellbrook Dr.
San Antonio, TX 78227-1002
E-mail: coordinator@americanbell.org
URL: http://www.americanbell.org
Contact: Ms. Betty Goodson, Pres.

3150 ■ American Collectors of Infant Feeders (ACIF) (19598)
c/o Sara Jean Binder, Treas.
13851 Belle Chasse Blvd., Ste.412
Laurel, MD 20707
E-mail: eiboquckim@mac.com
URL: http://www.acif.org
Contact: Victoria Moore, Sec.

3151 ■ Czech Collector's Association (CCA) (19253)
810 - 11th St., Ste.201
Miami Beach, FL 33139-4834
URL: http://www.czechcollectors.org
Contact: David Fein, Contact

3152 ■ German Gun Collectors' Association (GGCA)
PO Box 429
Mayfield, UT 84643
Ph: (435)979-9723
Fax: (435)528-7966
E-mail: sales@germanguns.com
URL: http://www.germanguns.com
Contact: Dietrich Apel, Founder

3153 ■ International Association of R.S. Prussia Collectors (22043)
PO Box 624
Mayfield, KY 42066
E-mail: mlkbougher@hotmail.com
URL: http://www.rsprussia.com

3154 ■ International Association of Silver Art Collectors (IASAC) (19505)
PO Box 3987
Clarksville, TN 37043
E-mail: iasacnancy@comcast.net
URL: http://thesilverbugle.com
Contact: Ed Lantz, Sec.-Treas.

3155 ■ International Match Safe Association (IMSA) (21105)
PO Box 4212
Bartonville, IL 61607-4212
E-mail: imsaoc@aol.com
URL: http://www.matchsafe.org
Contact: Mr. George Sparacio, Treas.

3156 ■ International Scouting Collectors Association (ISCA) (22231)
c/o Tod Johnson
PO Box 10008
South Lake Tahoe, CA 96158
E-mail: craig.leighty@gmail.com
URL: http://www.scouttrader.org
Contact: Craig Leighty, Pres.

3157 ■ International Swizzle Stick Collectors Association (ISSCA) (21606)
PO Box 5205
Bellingham, WA 98227-5205
Ph: (604)936-7636
E-mail: veray.issca@shaw.ca
URL: http://members.shaw.ca/veray.issca
Contact: Ray P. Hoare, Co-Chm.

3158 ■ M&M's Collectors Club (22067)
612 Head of River Rd.
Chesapeake, VA 23322
E-mail: mnms.club@gmail.com
URL: http://www.mnmclub.com
Contact: Elizabeth Dixon, Treas.

3159 ■ Midwest Decoy Collectors Association (MDCA) (19530)
6 E Scott St., No. 3
Chicago, IL 60610
Ph: (312)337-7957 (847)842-8847
Fax: (847)842-1915
E-mail: mdc@midwestdecoy.org
URL: http://www.midwestdecoy.org
Contact: Rick Sandstrom, Pres.

3160 ■ On the Lighter Side, International Lighter Collectors (OTLS) (19851)
PO Box 1733
Quitman, TX 75783-2733
Ph: (903)763-2795
URL: http://www.otls.com
Contact: Rob Giaretta, Pres.

3161 ■ Society of Inkwell Collectors (SOIC) (21659)
2203 39th St. SE
Puyallup, WA 98372
Ph: (301)919-6322
E-mail: soic@soic.com
URL: http://soic.com
Contact: Jeffrey Pisetzner, Exec. Dir.

Crafts

3162 ■ American Bladesmith Society (ABS) (9606)
PO Box 905
Salida, CO 81201
Ph: (419)832-0400 (719)539-1033
E-mail: membership@americanbladesmith.com
URL: http://www.americanbladesmith.com
Contact: Greg Neely, Chm.

3163 ■ American Made Alliance
3000 Chestnut Ave., Ste.300
Baltimore, MD 21211
Ph: (410)889-2933 (410)262-2872
Free: (800)432-7238
E-mail: wendy@rosengrp.com
URL: http://www.americanmadealliance.org
Contact: Jean Thompson, Media Relations Off.

3164 ■ Caricature Carvers of America (CCA)
c/o Donald K. Mertz, Sec.
729 Prairie Rd.
Wilmington, OH 45177-9683

Ph: (316)788-0175
E-mail: splaters@hotmail.com
URL: http://www.cca-carvers.org
Contact: Floyd Rhadigan, Pres.

3165 ■ Craft Organization Development Association (CODA)
PO Box 51
Onia, AR 72663
Ph: (870)746-5159
E-mail: coda@codacraft.org
URL: http://www.codacraft.org
Contact: Linda Van Trump, Managing Dir.

3166 ■ International Guild of Miniature Artisans (IGMA) (19624)
PO Box 629
Freedom, CA 95019-0629
Ph: (831)724-7974
Free: (800)711-IGMA
Fax: (831)724-8605
E-mail: info@igma.org
URL: http://www.igma.org
Contact: Carol Hardy, Guild Admin.

3167 ■ International Wildfowl Carvers Association (21217)
194 Summerside Dr.
Centralia, WA 98531
Ph: (360)736-1082
E-mail: jobyrn@comcast.net
URL: http://iwfca.com
Contact: Bob L. Sutton, Chm.

3168 ■ Knifemakers' Guild (KG) (8795)
2914 Winters Ln.
La Grange, KY 40031
Ph: (502)222-1397
Fax: (502)222-2676
E-mail: gil@hibbenknives.com
URL: http://www.knifemakersguild.com
Contact: Gil Hibben, Pres.

3169 ■ National Academy of Needlearts (NAN) (19917)
c/o Debbie Stiehler
1 Riverbanks Ct.
Greer, SC 29651
URL: http://www.needleart.org
Contact: Debbie Stiehler, Contact

3170 ■ National Association of Wheat Weavers (NAWW) (19388)
46 Ophir Ave.
Lincoln, IL 62656
Ph: (217)732-1957
E-mail: webmaster@nawwstraw.org
URL: http://www.nawwstraw.org
Contact: Dianne Ruff, Pres.

3171 ■ Northwest Regional Spinners' Association (NwRSA) (21717)
c/o Diane Du Bray, Membership Chair
22440 SE, 419th St.
Enumclaw, WA 98022
Ph: (360)825-1634
E-mail: nwrsamail@hotmail.com
URL: http://www.nwregionalspinners.org
Contact: Diane Bentley-Baker, Pres.

3172 ■ World Organization of China Painters (WOCP) (22177)
2641 NW 10th St.
Oklahoma City, OK 73107-5407
Ph: (405)521-1234
Fax: (405)521-1265
E-mail: wocporg@theshop.net
URL: http://www.theshop.net/wocporg
Contact: Pat Dickerson, Exec. Dir.

Dog

3173 ■ All American Premier Breeds Administration (AAPBA)
141 3rd Ave. SW
Castle Rock, WA 98611
Ph: (360)274-4209
Fax: (360)274-7694
E-mail: aapba@aapba.com
URL: http://www.aapba.com
Contact: John C. Booker, Pres.

3174 ■ Boykin Spaniel Club and Breeders Association of America (BSCBAA)
PO Box 42
Gilbert, SC 29054
Ph: (803)532-0990
E-mail: bscbaa@aol.com
URL: http://theboykinspanielclub.com
Contact: Butch Norckauer, Pres.

3175 ■ Danish/Swedish Farmdog Club of America (DSFCA)
PO Box 1184
Ramona, CA 92065
E-mail: cs@dsfca.org
URL: http://www.farmdogs.org
Contact: Brita Lemmon, Pres.

3176 ■ Havana Silk Dog Association of America (HSDAA)
c/o Cathy Dillahunty, Treas.
4435 14th St. NE
St. Petersburg, FL 33703
E-mail: havanasilkdog@aol.com
URL: http://www.havanasilkdog.org
Contact: Bill Klumb, Pres.

3177 ■ Hovawart Club of North America (HCNA)
c/o Utah Felhaber-Smith, Membership Dir.
4718 NE 14th Pl.
Portland, OR 97211
E-mail: info@mulburninn.com
URL: http://www.hovawartclub.org
Contact: Christina Ferraro, Corresponding Sec.

3178 ■ International Kennel Club of Chicago (IKC) (21822)
6222 W North Ave.
Chicago, IL 60639
Ph: (773)237-5100
Fax: (773)237-5126
E-mail: office@ikcdogshow.com
URL: http://www.ikcdogshow.com
Contact: Mr. Louis Auslander, Pres.

3179 ■ Miniature Australian Shepherd Club of America (MASCA)
PO Box 248
Roanoke, IN 46783
E-mail: masca@mascaonline.net
URL: http://www.mascaonline.net
Contact: A. Katherine Szafran, Contact

3180 ■ National Association of Dog Obedience Instructors (NADOI) (19742)
PO Box 1439
Socorro, NM 87801
Ph: (505)850-5957
URL: http://www.nadoi.org
Contact: Helen Cariotis, Pres.

3181 ■ North American Gun Dog Association (NAGDA)
17850 County Rd. 54
Burlington, CO 80807
Ph: (719)342-0776
Fax: (719)348-5999
E-mail: nagda@plains.net
URL: http://www.nagdog.com
Contact: Mike Hatfield, Pres.

3182 ■ North American Ring Association (NARA) (21355)
PO Box 146
Gig Harbor, WA 98335
Ph: (206)219-9072
E-mail: **cory@dhart.com**
URL: http://www.ringsport.org
Contact: **Cory Hart, Treas.**

3183 ■ Polish Tatra Sheepdog Club of America (PTSCA)
c/o Anita Liebl, Sec.
7119 W Lakefield Dr.
Milwaukee, WI 53219
Ph: (414)329-1373
E-mail: hurricane@chinookdogs.com
URL: http://www.ptsca.org
Contact: **David Wishowsky, Pres.**

3184 ■ Portuguese Podengo Club of America (PPCA)
c/o Becky Berkley, Membership Chair
11655 Vaca Pl.
San Diego, CA 92124
E-mail: podengosusa@aol.com
URL: http://www.podengos.com
Contact: **Bob Brawders, Pres.**

3185 ■ Toy Australian Shepherd Association of America (TASAA)
557 Forest Way Dr.
Fort Mill, SC 29715
Ph: (803)548-7048
E-mail: **tasaa_bod@comporium.net**
URL: http://whoward.homestead.com/index.html
Contact: Shirley Shannon, Pres.

3186 ■ United States of America Coton de Tulear Club (USACTC)
c/o J.J. Walker, Sec.
PO Box 3792
Pikeville, KY 41502
Ph: (606)639-0364 (606)478-8295
E-mail: pamosborne@bellsouth.net
URL: http://www.usactc.org
Contact: **Ruth Weidrick, Pres.**

3187 ■ United States Complete Shooting Dog Association (USCSDA)
3329 Redlawn Rd.
Boydton, VA 23917
Ph: (434)738-9757 **(434)738-5646**
E-mail: uscsda@hotmail.com
URL: http://www.uscomplete.org
Contact: Yvonne McKeag, Sec.-Treas./Futurity Sec.

3188 ■ Working Riesenschnauzer Federation (WRSF) (22386)
c/o Martha Galuszka, Membership Dir.
324 Oakwood Ave.
West Hartford, CT 06110
Ph: (860)233-2286
E-mail: mjgaluszka@aol.com
URL: http://www.workingriesenschnauzer.com
Contact: **Tim Nyx, Pres.**

Dolls

3189 ■ Doll Artisan Guild (DAG) (21916)
PO Box 1113
Oneonta, NY 13820-5113
Ph: (607)432-4977 **(315)691-9922**
Fax: (607)432-2042
E-mail: info@dollartisanguild.org
URL: http://www.dollsbeautiful.com
Contact: Karlyn Grzmkowski, Pres.

3190 ■ National Institute of American Doll Artists (NIADA) (22403)
109 Ladder Hill North
Weston, CT 06883
Ph: **(203)557-3169**

E-mail: **donnamaydolls@optonline.net**
URL: http://www.niada.org
Contact: Donna May Robinson, Pres.

Electrical

3191 ■ National Insulator Association (NIA) (20441)
PO Box 188
Providence, UT 84332
E-mail: **don.briel@comcast.net**
URL: http://www.nia.org
Contact: Donald Briel, Membership Dir.

Fire Fighting

3192 ■ International Fire Buff Associates (IFBA) (20451)
11017 N Redwood Tree Ct.
Mequon, WI 53092
Fax: (262)236-0095
E-mail: **wmokros@wi.rr.com**
URL: http://www.ifba.org
Contact: Mr. William M. Mokros, Exec. VP

Firearms

3193 ■ Parker Gun Collectors Association (PGCA)
PO Box 115
Mayodan, NC 27027
E-mail: pgcamembership@gmail.com
URL: http://www.parkerguns.org
Contact: **Bill Mullins, Pres.**

3194 ■ Thompson Collectors Association (TCA) (22431)
PO Box 1675
Ellicott City, MD 21041-1675
E-mail: **billtroy@thetca.net**
URL: http://thetca.net/default.aspx
Contact: Bill Troy, Pres.

3195 ■ Weatherby Collectors Association (WCA) (22432)
PO Box 1217
Washington, MO 63090
Ph: (636)239-0348
E-mail: wcasecretary@aol.com
URL: http://www.weatherbycollectors.com
Contact: **J.D. Morgan, Pres.**

Fish

3196 ■ Associated Koi Clubs of America (AKCA) (19833)
40211 Redbud Dr.
Oakhurst, CA 93644
Ph: (559)658-5295
Fax: (559)658-5295
E-mail: judgedahl@hotmail.com
URL: http://www.akca.org
Contact: Doug Dahl, Contact

3197 ■ International Betta Congress (IBC) (20131)
c/o Steve Van Camp, Membership Chm./Sec.
923 Wadsworth St.
Syracuse, NY 13208
Ph: (315)454-4792
E-mail: bettacongress@yahoo.com
URL: http://www.ibcbettas.org
Contact: **Jennifer Lapello, Pres.**

Games

3198 ■ National 42 Players Association (N42PA)
c/o David Roberts, Treas.
215 Sunday Cir.
Fredericksburg, TX 78624
Ph: (830)990-0123
E-mail: treasurer@n42pa.com
URL: http://www.n42pa.com
Contact: **Jody Badum, Pres.**

3199 ■ Valley International Foosball Association (VIFA)
PO Box 656
Bay City, MI 48707
Free: (800)544-1346
Fax: (989)893-0103
E-mail: info@vifa.com
URL: http://www.vifa.com

Gaming

3200 ■ Pro vs. GI Joe
4 Montage
Irvine, CA 92614-8112
Ph: (818)371-1283
E-mail: **prosvsgijoes@gmail.com**
URL: http://www.provsgijoe.com
Contact: Greg Zinone, Pres./Co-Founder

Gardening

3201 ■ American Hibiscus Society (AHS) (19877)
PO Box 1580
Venice, FL 34284-1580
E-mail: **erndtcg@aol.com**
URL: http://www.americanhibiscus.org
Contact: **Don Mixon, Pres.**

3202 ■ Bonsai Clubs International (BCI) (22017)
PO Box 8445
Metairie, LA 70011-8445
Ph: (504)832-8071
Fax: (504)832-8071
E-mail: **bci.manager@yahoo.com**
URL: http://www.bonsai-bci.com
Contact: Donna Banting, Managing Ed.

3203 ■ Bromeliad Society International (BSI) (19891)
713 Breckenridge Dr.
Port Orange, FL 32127-7528
E-mail: president@bsi.org
URL: http://www.bsi.org
Contact: **Jay Thurrott, Pres.**

3204 ■ Cymbidium Society of America (CSA) (22021)
6639 Ibex Woods Ct.
Citrus Heights, CA 95621
Ph: (510)537-8923
E-mail: melclaramoura@aol.com
URL: http://cymbidium.org
Contact: **Anthony Barcellos, Membership Sec.**

3205 ■ Gesneriad Society (22028)
1122 E Pike St.
PMB 637
Seattle, WA 98122-3916
E-mail: **president@gesneriadsociety.org**
URL: http://www.gesneriadsociety.org
Contact: Peter Shalit, Pres.

**3206 ■ International Lilac Society (ILS)
(22035)**
c/o Karen McCauley, Treas./Interim Membership
Sec.
325 W 82nd St.
Chaska, MN 55318
Ph: **(952)443-3703**
E-mail: **mccauleytk@aol.com**
URL: http://www.internationallilacsociety.org
Contact: **Brad Bittorf, Exec. VP**

**3207 ■ Society for Pacific Coast Native Iris
(SPCNI) (19934)**
7417 92nd Pl. SE
Mercer Island, WA 98040
Ph: (206)232-7745
E-mail: **ksayce@willapabay.org**
URL: http://www.pacificcoastiris.org
Contact: Debby Cole, Pres.

3208 ■ Tall Bearded Iris Society (TBIS)
PO Box 6991
Lubbock, TX 79493
Ph: (806)792-1878
E-mail: **stoutgarden@cox.net**
URL: http://www.tbisonline.com
Contact: **Hugh Stout, Pres.**

Glass

**3209 ■ International Carnival Glass
Association (ICGA) (3096)**
c/o Lee Markley, Sec.
Box 306
Mentone, IN 46539
Ph: **(574)353-7678**
E-mail: **bpitman@woodsland.com**
URL: http://www.internationalcarnivalglass.com
Contact: Brian Pitman, Pres.

Gourmets

**3210 ■ American Institute of Wine and Food
(AIWF) (22082)**
26384 Carmel Rancho Ln., Ste.200E
Carmel, CA 93923
Ph: **(831)250-7595**
Free: (800)274-2493
Fax: **(831)250-7641**
E-mail: info@aiwf.org
URL: http://www.aiwf.com
Contact: Ms. Lisa Lipton, Chair

Machinery

**3211 ■ Antique Caterpillar Machinery Owners
Club (ACMOC)**
7501 N Univ., Ste.119
Peoria, IL 61614
Ph: (309)691-5002 **(309)453-1364**
Fax: (309)296-4518
E-mail: cat@acmoc.org
URL: http://www.acmoc.org
Contact: Tricia Potts, Exec. Dir.

Magic

**3212 ■ Society of American Magicians (SAM)
(22623)**
PO Box 505
Parker, CO 80134
Ph: **(303)362-0575**
E-mail: samadministrator@magicsam.com
URL: http://www.magicsam.com
Contact: Manon Rodriguez, Natl. Admin.

Military

**3213 ■ Orders and Medals Society of
America (OMSA) (20032)**
PO Box 198
San Ramon, CA 94583
E-mail: dpeck9696@aol.com
URL: http://www.omsa.org
Contact: Douglas M. Peck, Sec.

Model Trains

3214 ■ Toy Train Collectors Society (TTCS)
c/o Louis A. Bohn, Membership Chm.
109 Howedale Dr.
Rochester, NY 14616-1534
Ph: (585)663-4188
E-mail: ttcs_ltd@yahoo.com
URL: http://www.ttcsltd.org
Contact: **Robert D. Richter, Pres.**

3215 ■ Youth in Model Railroading (YMR)
12990 Prince Ct.
Broomfield, CO 80020-5419
Ph: **(303)466-2857**
E-mail: **info@ymr-online.org**
URL: http://www.ymr-online.org
Contact: Larry Price, Pres./Founder

Models

**3216 ■ International Scale Soaring
Association (ISSA)**
c/o Rick Briggs, Treas./Webmaster
3015 Volk Ave.
Long Beach, CA 90808
Ph: (562)421-4864
E-mail: scalebldr1@verizon.net
URL: http://www.soaringissa.org
Contact: **Larry Jolly, Pres.**

Motorcycle

**3217 ■ Antique Motorcycle Club of America
(AMCA)**
c/o Trudi Johnson-Richards, National Sec.
3295 Victoria St.
Shoreview, MN 55126
Ph: **(651)482-0096**
E-mail: **trudijr@visi.com**
URL: http://www.antiquemotorcycle.org
Contact: **Peter Gagan, Pres.**

**3218 ■ British Biker Cooperative (BBC)
(22881)**
PO Box 371021
Milwaukee, WI 53237-2121
Ph: **(262)514-2073**
E-mail: **kasper.peggy@gmail.com**
URL: http://www.britishbiker.net
Contact: **Peggy Kasper, Contact**

**3219 ■ International CBX Owners
Association (ICOA) (22196)**
PO Box 546
Knox, PA 16232
Ph: (717)697-5559
E-mail: icoamembership@hargray.com
URL: http://www.cbxclub.com
Contact: Bill Hertling, Membership Dir.

**3220 ■ Vintage BMW Motorcycle Owners
(VBMWMO) (22904)**
c/o Roland Slabon
PO Box 599
Troy, OH 45373-0599
Ph: **(770)235-5281**
E-mail: vintagebmw@comcast.net
URL: http://www.vintagebmw.org
Contact: **Jeffery L. Yost, Pres.**

Numismatic

3221 ■ Challenge Coin Association (CCA)
1375 Mistletoe Ridge Pl. NW
Concord, NC 28027
Ph: (704)723-1170
Fax: (704)723-9202
E-mail: coincheck@challengecoinassociation.org
URL: http://challengecoinassociation.org
Contact: Jesse L. Medford, Pres.

3222 ■ Colonial Coin Collectors Club (C4)
c/o Charlie Rohrer, Treas.
PO Box 25
Mountville, PA 17554
E-mail: rohrerc@cadmus.com
URL: http://www.colonialcoins.org
Contact: **Jim Rosen, Pres.**

**3223 ■ Professional Currency Dealers
Association (PCDA) (22753)**
c/o James A. Simek, Sec.
PO Box 7157
Westchester, IL 60154
E-mail: nge3@comcast.net
URL: http://www.pcdaonline.com
Contact: **Sergio Sanches Jr., Pres.**

**3224 ■ Professional Numismatists Guild
(PNG) (20150)**
28441 Rancho California Rd., Ste.106
Temecula, CA 92590
Ph: **(951)587-8300**
Free: (800)375-4653
Fax: **(951)587-8301**
E-mail: info@pngdealers.com
URL: http://www.pngdealers.com
Contact: Robert Brueggeman, Exec. Dir.

Philatelic

**3225 ■ American Revenue Association (ARA)
(20174)**
PO Box 74
Grosse Ile, MI 48138
Ph: (734)676-2649
Fax: (734)676-2959
E-mail: ara@northfieldmail.com
URL: http://www.revenuer.org
Contact: Robert Hohertz, Pres.

3226 ■ First Issues Collectors Club (FICC)
PO Box 453
Brentwood, TN 37024-0453
E-mail: president@firstissues.org
URL: http://www.firstissues.org
Contact: **E. Clark Buchi, Pres.**

**3227 ■ International Society of Worldwide
Stamp Collectors (ISWSC)**
PO Box 580
Whittier, CA 90608
E-mail: **desoto1947@yahoo.com**
URL: http://www.iswsc.org
Contact: **Mike Crump, Pres.**

3228 ■ Korea Stamp Society (KSS)
c/o John E. Talmage, Jr., Sec.-Treas.
PO Box 6889
Oak Ridge, TN 37831
E-mail: **jtalmage@usit.net**
URL: http://www.pennfamily.org/KSS-USA
Contact: Peter M. Beck, Pres.

**3229 ■ National Duck Stamp Collectors
Society (NDSCS)**
PO Box 43
Harleysville, PA 19438-0043
E-mail: ndscs@hwcn.org
URL: http://www.hwcn.org/link/ndscs
Contact: Anthony J. Monico, Sec.

3230 ■ Rotary on Stamps Fellowship (ROS) (22863)
1327 Prince Albert Dr.
St. Louis, MO 63146
E-mail: contact@rotaryonstamps.org
URL: http://www.rotaryonstamps.org
Contact: Robert Kriegshauser, Chm.

3231 ■ Scandinavian Collectors Club (SCC) (20315)
c/o Donald Brent, Exec. Sec.
PO Box 13196
El Cajon, CA 92020
E-mail: dbrent47@sprynet.com
URL: http://www.scc-online.org
Contact: **Roger Quinby, Pres.**

3232 ■ Society of Australasian Specialists/Oceania (SASO)
PO Box 24764
San Jose, CA 95154-4764
Ph: **(408)978-0193**
E-mail: stulev@ix.netcom.com
URL: http://www.sasoceania.org
Contact: Stuart Leven, Sec.-Treas.

3233 ■ Society for Hungarian Philately (SHP) (19943)
c/o Jim Gaul, Auction Chm.
1920 Fawn Ln.
Hellertown, PA 18055-2117
Ph: (610)838-8162
E-mail: **terrynjim@verizon.net**
URL: http://www.hungarianphilately.org
Contact: Bill Wilson, Pres.

3234 ■ Space Topic Study Unit
c/o Carmine Torrisi, Sec.
PO Box 780241
Maspeth, NY 11378
E-mail: ctorrisi@nyc.rr.com
URL: http://www.space-unit.com
Contact: **Reuben A. Ramkisson, Pres. Emeritus**

3235 ■ Sports Philatelists International (SPI) (20329)
c/o Norman Jacobs, Advertising
2712 N Decatur Rd.
Decatur, GA 30033
E-mail: member@sportstamps.org
URL: http://www.sportstamps.org
Contact: Mark C. Maestrone, Pres.

Photography

3236 ■ Photographic Society of America (PSA) (20348)
3000 United Founders Blvd., Ste.103
Oklahoma City, OK 73112-3940
Ph: (405)843-1437
Free: **(866)772-4636**
Fax: (405)843-1438
E-mail: hq@psa-photo.org
URL: http://www.psa-photo.org
Contact: Fred Greene FPSA, Pres.

Plastics

3237 ■ Plasticville Collectors Association (PCA)
c/o John Niehaus, Sec.-Treas.
601 SE Second St.
Ankeny, IA 50021-3207
E-mail: secretary@plasticvilleusa.org
URL: http://www.plasticvilleusa.org
Contact: **Jim Dawes, Pres.**

Postal Service

3238 ■ Carriers and Locals Society
PO Box 74
Grosse Ile, MI 48138
Ph: **(734)676-2649**
Fax: **(734)676-2959**
E-mail: martinr362@aol.com
URL: http://www.pennypost.org
Contact: Martin D. Richardson, Sec.-Treas.

Postcards

3239 ■ International Federation of Postcard Dealers (IFPD) (22906)
PO Box 399
Neosho, MO 64850
E-mail: **postcards@courthousesquare.net**
URL: http://www.playle.com/IFPD
Contact: **Dr. Jim Taylor, Pres.**

Recreational Vehicles

3240 ■ SunnyTravelers
58800 Executive Dr.
Mishawaka, IN 46544
Ph: (574)258-0571
Free: (800)262-5178
Fax: (574)259-7105
URL: http://www.sunnybrookrvclub.com

Shooting

3241 ■ Fifty Caliber Shooters Association (FCSA) (22470)
PO Box 111
Monroe, UT 84754-0111
Ph: (435)527-9245
Fax: (435)527-0948
E-mail: **fcsa@qwestoffice.net**
URL: http://www.fcsa.org

Steam Engines

3242 ■ Northwest Steam Society (NSS) (22475)
PO Box 73
Hansville, WA 98340-0073
Ph: (206)310-4565
E-mail: **jerrynjudyross@comcast.net**
URL: http://www.northweststeamsociety.org
Contact: Jerry Ross, Pres.

Telephones

3243 ■ Telephone Collectors International (TCI) (22986)
3805 Spurr Cir.
Brea, CA 92823
Ph: (714)528-3561
E-mail: info@telephonecollectors.org
URL: http://www.telephonecollectors.org
Contact: **Paul Wills MD, Pres.**

Timepieces

3244 ■ International Watch Fob Association (IWFA) (20423)
601 Patriot Pl.
Holmen, WI 54636
Ph: (608)385-7237
E-mail: **freemansspec@hotmail.com**
URL: http://www.watchfob.com
Contact: Louise Harting, Sec.-Treas.

Tractors

3245 ■ Gravely Tractor Club of America (GTCOA)
PO Box 119
McLean, VA 22101
Ph: (610)518-1028
E-mail: jhowlandgravely@gmail.com
URL: http://www.gravelytractorclub.org
Contact: Jim Cherry, Registrar

3246 ■ Vintage Garden Tractor Club of America (VGTCOA)
412 W Chestnut
Pardeeville, WI 53954
Ph: (608)429-4520
E-mail: **shewfeltfamily@sympatico.ca**
URL: http://www.vgtcoa.com
Contact: Jim Cunzenheim Sr., Pres.

Trucks

3247 ■ Dodge Pilothouse Era Truck Club of America (DPETCA)
3778 Hoen Ave.
Santa Rosa, CA 95405
E-mail: info@dodgepilothouseclub.org
URL: http://www.dodgepilothouseclub.org
Contact: Robert Koch, Treas.

3248 ■ North American Truck Camper Owners Association (NATCOA) (23200)
PO Box 30408
Bellingham, WA 98228
E-mail: paul@natcoa.com
URL: http://www.natcoa.com
Contact: **Bonnie Passcucc, Membership Sec.**

Wood

3249 ■ International Wood Collectors Society (IWCS)
2300 W Rangeline Rd.
Greencastle, IN 46135-7875
Ph: (765)653-6483
E-mail: **treasurer@woodcollectors.org**
URL: http://woodcollectors.org
Contact: William Cockrell, Sec.-Treas.

Aerospace

3250 ■ United States Hang Gliding and Paragliding Association (USHPA) (20476)
PO Box 1330
Colorado Springs, CO 80901-1330
Ph: (719)632-8300
Free: (800)616-6888
Fax: (719)632-6417
E-mail: info@ushpa.aero
URL: http://www.ushga.org
Contact: **Nick Greece, Contact**

Aikido

3251 ■ United States Aikido Federation (USAF) (20478)
New York Aikikai
142 W 18th St.
New York, NY 10011
Ph: (212)242-6246
Fax: **(212)242-9749**
E-mail: **yamadasensei@usaikifed.com**
URL: http://www.usaikifed.com
Contact: Mr. Yoshimitsu Yamada, Contact

Athletes

3252 ■ National Coalition Against Violent Athletes (NCAVA)
PO Box 620453
Littleton, CO 80162
Ph: **(303)524-9853**
E-mail: info@ncava.org
URL: http://www.ncava.org
Contact: Katherine Redmond, Contact

Ball Games

3253 ■ National Amateur Dodgeball Association (NADA) (22583)
1223 W Sharon Ln.
Schaumburg, IL 60193
Ph: **(847)985-2120**
Fax: (847)985-2466
E-mail: dodgeball@parkfun.com
URL: http://www.dodgeballusa.com

3254 ■ U.S.A Team Handball (USATH) (23282)
2330 W California Ave.
Salt Lake City, UT 84104
Ph: (801)463-2000
E-mail: info@usateamhandball.org
URL: http://www.usateamhandball.org
Contact: Steve Pastorino, Gen. Mgr.

Ballooning

3255 ■ Balloon Federation of America (BFA) (20524)
PO Box 400
Indianola, IA 50125
Ph: (515)961-8809
Fax: (515)961-3537
E-mail: bfaoffice@bfa.net
URL: http://www.bfa.net
Contact: **Troy Bradley, Pres.**

Baseball

3256 ■ American Baseball Coaches Association (ABCA) (3160)
108 S Univ. Ave., Ste.3
Mount Pleasant, MI 48858-2327
Ph: (989)775-3300
Fax: (989)775-3600
E-mail: abca@abca.org
URL: http://www.abca.org
Contact: **Tim Mead, Pres.**

3257 ■ American Legion Baseball (ALB)
700 N Pennsylvania St.
Indianapolis, IN 46204
Ph: (317)630-1200
Fax: (317)630-1369
E-mail: baseball@legion.org
URL: http://www.legion.org/baseball
Contact: **Jimmie Foster, Natl. Commander**

3258 ■ Little League Foundation (LLF) (23112)
539 U.S. Rte. 15 Hwy.
PO Box 3485
Williamsport, PA 17701-0485
Ph: (570)326-1921
Fax: (570)326-1074
E-mail: **bbassett@littleleague.org**
URL: http://www.littleleague.org
Contact: Stephen D. Keener, Pres./CEO

3259 ■ National Amateur Baseball Federation (NABF) (23115)
c/o Charles M. Blackburn, Jr., Exec. Dir.
PO Box 705
Bowie, MD 20715
Ph: (410)721-4727
Fax: (410)721-4940
E-mail: nabf1914@aol.com
URL: http://www.nabf.com
Contact: **Gregory Reddington, Pres.**

3260 ■ National Association of Professional Baseball Leagues (NAPBL) (20546)
PO Box A
St. Petersburg, FL 33731
Ph: (727)822-6937
Fax: (727)821-5819

E-mail: admin@minorleaguebaseball.com
URL: http://web.minorleaguebaseball.com/index.jsp
Contact: **Pat O'Conner, Pres./CEO**

3261 ■ Professional Baseball Athletic Trainers Society (PBATS) (23125)
PO Box 386
Atlanta, GA 30361
E-mail: bball@chisox.com
URL: http://www.pbats.com
Contact: **Richie Bancells, Pres.**

3262 ■ Society for American Baseball Research (SABR) (23126)
4455 E Camelback Rd., Ste.D-140
Phoenix, AZ 85018
Ph: **(602)343-6455**
Free: (800)969-7227
Fax: **(602)702-5192**
E-mail: info@sabr.org
URL: http://www.sabr.org
Contact: **Marc Appleman, Exec. Dir.**

3263 ■ U.S.A. Baseball (USBF) (22615)
403 Blackwell St.
Durham, NC 27701
Ph: (919)474-8721
Fax: (919)474-8822
E-mail: info@usabaseball.com
URL: http://web.usabaseball.com/index.jsp
Contact: Paul V. Seiler, Exec. Dir./CEO

Basketball

3264 ■ National Basketball Association (NBA) (20562)
645 5th Ave., 10th Fl.
New York, NY 10022
Ph: **(212)407-8000**
Free: (800)NBA-0548
Fax: **(212)832-3861**
E-mail: fanrelations@nba.com
URL: http://www.nba.com
Contact: David J. Stern, Commissioner

3265 ■ National Basketball Athletic Trainers Association (NBATA) (20563)
400 Colony Sq., Ste.1750
Atlanta, GA 30361
Ph: (404)892-8919 (404)875-4000
Fax: (404)892-8560
E-mail: **rmallernee@mallernee-branch.com**
URL: http://nbata.com
Contact: Rollin Mallernee, Gen. Counsel

3266 ■ Women's Basketball Coaches Association (WBCA) (22627)
4646 Lawrenceville Hwy.
Lilburn, GA 30047
Ph: (770)279-8027
Fax: (770)279-8473

E-mail: **membership@wbca.org**
URL: http://www.wbca.org
Contact: Geno Auriemma, Pres.

Baton Twirling

**3267 ■ United States Twirling Association
(USTA)**
1608 Wortell Dr.
Lincoln, CA 95648
Ph: **(916)343-0062**
E-mail: **president@ustwirling.com**
URL: http://www.ustwirling.com
Contact: **Ms. Mark Nash, Pres.**

Billiards

**3268 ■ United States Billiard Association
(USBA) (23146)**
c/o Jim Shovak, Sec.-Treas.
58 Hawthorne Ave.
East Islip, NY 11730
Ph: (516)238-6193
E-mail: **president@usba.net**
URL: http://www.usba.net
Contact: **Henry Ugartechea, Pres.**

Boating

**3269 ■ American Y-Flyer Yacht Racing
Association (AYFYRA) (20372)**
7349 Scarborough Blvd., East Dr.
Indianapolis, IN 46256-2052
Ph: (317)849-7588
E-mail: **president@yflyer.org**
URL: http://www.yflyer.org
Contact: Anthony Passafiume, Pres.

**3270 ■ Antique and Classic Boat Society
(ACBS) (19377)**
422 James St.
Clayton, NY 13624
Ph: (315)686-2628
Fax: (315)686-2680
E-mail: hqs@acbs.org
URL: http://www.acbs.org
Contact: **John Bergstrom, Pres.**

**3271 ■ Classic Yacht Association (CYA)
(21426)**
5267 Shilshole Ave. NW, Ste.107
Seattle, WA 98107
Ph: (206)937-6211
E-mail: pnwcommodore@classicyacht.org
URL: http://www.classicyacht.org
Contact: **Larry Benson, Commodore**

**3272 ■ El Toro International Yacht Racing
Association (ETIYRA) (20184)**
1014 Hopper Ave., No. 419
Santa Rosa, CA 95403-1613
Ph: (707)526-6621
Fax: (707)526-3838
E-mail: **steve@swiftsail.net**
URL: http://www.eltoroyra.org
Contact: Steve Lowry, Sec.

**3273 ■ Highlander Class International
Association (HCIA)**
410 Holiday Rd.
Lexington, KY 40502
Ph: **(859)806-5908**
E-mail: **pilot@sailhighlander.org**
URL: http://www.sailhighlander.org
Contact: Bryan Hollingsworth, Exec. Sec.-Treas.

**3274 ■ International Flying Dutchman Class
Association of the U.S. (IFDCAUS) (23185)**
c/o Jonathan Clapp, Sec.-Treas.
PO Box 223
Amherst, MA 01004-0223

Ph: (978)660-4497 **(215)815-4179**
E-mail: **tfsayles@advanceddma.com**
URL: http://www.sailfd.org/USA
Contact: Tim Sayles, Pres.

**3275 ■ International Lightning Class
Association (ILCA) (23188)**
7625 S Yampa St.
Centennial, CO 80016
Ph: (303)325-5886
Fax: (303)699-2178
E-mail: office@lightningclass.org
URL: http://www.lightningclass.org
Contact: **Robert Ruhlman, Pres.**

**3276 ■ International Mobjack Association
(IMA) (23189)**
3720 Blue Heron Ln.
West Point, VA 23181
Ph: (804)843-2682 **(757)312-0768**
E-mail: **mobjack20@aol.com**
URL: http://mobjack.tripod.com
Contact: **Al Williamson, Pres.**

**3277 ■ International Penguin Class Dinghy
Association (IPCDA) (23191)**
c/o Charles Krafft, Treas.
8300 Waverly Rd.
Owings, MD 20736
E-mail: **michael.hecky@verizonwireless.com**
URL: http://www.penguinclass.com
Contact: **Mike Hecky, Sec.**

**3278 ■ International Sunfish Class
Association (ISCA) (23194)**
PO Box 300128
Waterford, MI 48330-0128
Ph: (248)673-2750
Fax: (248)673-2750
E-mail: sunfishoff@aol.com
URL: http://www.sunfishclass.org
Contact: **Paul-Jon Patin, Pres.**

**3279 ■ Joshua Slocum Society International
(JSSI) (21037)**
15 Codfish Hill Rd. Extension
Bethel, CT 06801
Ph: (203)790-6616
Fax: (203)778-9917
E-mail: **jone402@att.net**
URL: http://www.joshuaslocumsocietyintl.org
Contact: Ted Jones, Commodore

3280 ■ Lido 14 Class Association (20810)
PO Box 1252
Newport Beach, CA 92663
Ph: (714)437-1370
Fax: **(714)437-1374**
E-mail: shaddowwoman@sbcglobal.net
URL: http://www.lido14.org
Contact: Sharon Young, Exec. Sec.

**3281 ■ National Boating Federation (NBF)
(23387)**
PO Box 4111
Annapolis, MD 21403-4111
Fax: (866)239-2070
URL: http://www.n-b-f.org
Contact: **Fred W. Poppe, Pres.**

3282 ■ Santana 20 Class Association (21157)
1266 Napa Creek Dr.
Eugene, OR 97404
Ph: **(541)517-8690**
E-mail: dsmartin737@sbcglobal.net
URL: http://www.s20.org
Contact: Derek Martin, Pres.

**3283 ■ Shields National Class Association
(20814)**
3225 W St. Joseph
Lansing, MI 48917
Ph: (517)372-9207
Fax: **(517)321-0495**

E-mail: mschwartz10@sbcglobal.net
URL: http://www.shieldsclass.com
Contact: Michael Schwartz, Pres.

**3284 ■ Thistle Class Association (TCA)
(21164)**
c/o Patty Lawrence, Sec.-Treas.
6758 Little River Ln.
Loveland, OH 45140
Ph: (513)583-5080
E-mail: secretary@thistleclass.com
URL: http://www.thistleclass.com
Contact: **Lloyd Litchin, Pres.**

**3285 ■ Traditional Small Craft Association
(TSCA) (21437)**
PO Box 350
Mystic, CT 06355
Ph: **(425)361-7758**
E-mail: **jrweiss98155@comcast.net**
URL: http://www.tsca.net
Contact: John Weiss, Pres./Coor.

**3286 ■ U.S. Albacore Association (USAA)
(20725)**
1031 Graham St.
Bethlehem, PA 18015-2520
E-mail: **secretary@usaa.albacore.org**
URL: **http://usaa.albacore.org**
Contact: Kay Marsh, Membership Sec./Ed.

**3287 ■ United States J/24 Class Association
(USJCA) (23227)**
900 Old Koenig Ln., Ste.114
Austin, TX 78756
Ph: (512)266-0033
E-mail: director@j24class.org
URL: http://www.j24class.org/usa
Contact: Paul Scalisi, Pres.

**3288 ■ U.S. Mariner Class Association
(20834)**
PO Box 273
Ship Bottom, NJ 08008
E-mail: president@usmariner.org
URL: http://www.usmariner.org
Contact: **Nathan Bayreuther, Pres.**

**3289 ■ United States Optimist Dinghy
Association (USODA) (21170)**
PO Box 311
North Kingstown, RI 02852
Ph: **(609)510-0798**
E-mail: usoda@usoda.org
URL: http://www.usoda.org
Contact: Robin Kuebel, Pres.

**3290 ■ United States Power Squadrons
(USPS)**
1504 Blue Ridge Rd.
Raleigh, NC 27607
Free: (888)367-8777
URL: http://www.usps.org
Contact: **Lt/C James Hoffee, Exec. Off.**

**3291 ■ United States Sailing Association I
Council of Sailing Associations (CSA) (20590)**
15 Maritime Dr.
PO Box 1260
Portsmouth, RI 02871-0907
Ph: (401)683-0800
Free: **(800)877-2451**
Fax: (401)683-0840
E-mail: info@ussailing.org
URL: **http://about.ussailing.org/Directory/
Councils/Council_of_Sailing_Associations.htm**
Contact: **Bob Counihan, Contact**

3292 ■ Windmill Class Association (WCA) (23239)
1571 Quarrier St.
Charleston, WV 25311
E-mail: achauvenet@gmail.com
URL: http://www.windmillclass.org
Contact: **Lon Ethington, Pres.**

Bodybuilding

3293 ■ International Natural Bodybuilding and Fitness Federation (INBF)
PO Box 4
Pocono Lake, PA 18347
E-mail: **fitter@exercisegroup.com**
URL: http://www.inbf.net
Contact: Steve Downs CSCS, VP

Bowling

3294 ■ National Duckpin Bowling Congress (NDBC) (20255)
c/o Sue Burucker, Exec. Dir./Sec.
4991 Fairview Ave.
Linthicum, MD 21090
Ph: (410)636-2695 (410)444-4058
Fax: (410)636-3256
E-mail: **executivedirector@ndbc.org**
URL: http://ndbc.org
Contact: **Stan Kellum, Pres.**

3295 ■ United States Lawn Bowls Association (USLBA)
10639 Lindamere Dr.
Los Angeles, CA 90077
Ph: (310)440-9400
E-mail: **martyssr@aol.com**
URL: http://www.uslba.org
Contact: **Marty Schans, Pres.**

Boxing

3296 ■ International Boxing Federation (IBF) (20714)
899 Mountain Ave., Ste.2C
Springfield, NJ 07081
Ph: **(973)564-8046**
Fax: **(973)564-8751**
E-mail: **jsalazar@ibfboxing.com**
URL: http://www.ibf-usba-boxing.com
Contact: Daryl J. Peoples, Pres.

3297 ■ International Chinese Boxing Association (ICBA) (23262)
3308 Preston Rd., Ste.350-356
Plano, TX 75093
E-mail: **grandmaster@wingpai.com**
URL: http://www.wingpai.com/ICBA_World_Wide_
WSHT.php
Contact: GM David M. Grago Sr., Chm.

3298 ■ International Female Boxers Association (IFBA)
701 N Green Valley Pkwy., Ste.200
Henderson, NV 89074
Ph: (310)428-1403
Fax: (310)541-9708
E-mail: **info@ifba.com**
URL: http://www.ifba.com

3299 ■ U.S.A. Boxing (23267)
30 Cimino Dr.
Colorado Springs, CO 80903
Ph: (719)866-2300
Fax: (719)866-2132
E-mail: **abartkowski@me.com**
URL: http://www.usaboxing.org
Contact: **Dr. Anthony Bartkowski, Exec. Dir.**

Camping

3300 ■ American Camp Association (ACA) (20874)
5000 State Rd., 67 N
Martinsville, IN 46151-7902
Ph: (765)342-8456
Free: (800)428-CAMP
Fax: (765)342-2065
E-mail: **2020@acacamps.org**
URL: http://www.acacamps.org
Contact: Peter Surgenor CCD, Pres.

3301 ■ Camping Women (CW)
PO Box 1402
Twain Harte, CA 95383
E-mail: karen.mcvey@twinriversusd.org
URL: http://www.campingwomen.org
Contact: Karen McVey, Pres.

3302 ■ Christian Camp and Conference Association (CCCA) (23477)
PO Box 62189
Colorado Springs, CO 80962-2189
Ph: (719)260-9400
Fax: (719)260-6398
E-mail: info@ccca.org
URL: http://www.ccca.org
Contact: **Greg Anderson, Chm.**

3303 ■ North American Family Campers Association (NAFCA)
PO Box 318
Lunenburg, MA 01462
Ph: (401)828-0579 **(401)580-1428**
E-mail: ka1rcy1@msn.com
URL: http://www.nafca.org
Contact: Ron Barratt, Pres.

Cheerleading

3304 ■ Christian Cheerleaders of America (CCA)
PO Box 49
Bethania, NC 27010
Free: (877)243-3722
Fax: **(866)222-1093**
E-mail: info@cheercca.com
URL: http://www.cheercca.com
Contact: Rose Clevenger, Pres.

Coaching

3305 ■ Creativity Coaching Association (CCA)
PO Box 328
Lake George, NY 12845
Ph: **(518)798-6933**
E-mail: publisher@creativitycoachingassociation.com
URL: http://www.creativitycoachingassociation.com
Contact: Beverly Down, Pres./CEO

3306 ■ National High School Athletic Coaches Association (NHSACA) (21221)
c/o Jerome Garry
PO Box 5921
Rochester, MN 55903
E-mail: **jg.nhsaca@charter.net**
URL: http://www.hscoaches.org
Contact: Virg Polak, Pres.

3307 ■ Professional Coaches, Mentors and Advisors (PCMA)
PO Box 265
Palos Verdes Estates, CA 90274-0265
Free: (800)768-6017
E-mail: admin@pcmacoaches.com
URL: **http://www.pcmacoaches.com**
Contact: Reri MacLean MEd, Pres.

Croquet

3308 ■ Croquet Foundation of America (CFA) (20881)
700 Florida Mango Rd.
West Palm Beach, FL 33406-4461
Ph: (561)478-0760
Fax: **(561)686-5507**
E-mail: usca@msn.com
URL: http://www.croquetamerica.com
Contact: Gene Young, Pres.

3309 ■ United States Croquet Association (USCA) (20741)
700 Florida Mango Rd.
West Palm Beach, FL 33406-4461
Ph: (561)478-0760
Fax: **(561)686-5507**
E-mail: usca@msn.com
URL: http://www.croquetamerica.com
Contact: Gene Young, Pres.

Curling

3310 ■ United States Women's Curling Association (USWCA) (20743)
Cleveland Skating Club
Shaker Heights, OH 44120
E-mail: president@uswca.org
URL: http://www.uswca.org
Contact: **Nancy Seitz, Pres.**

Cycling

3311 ■ International Unicycling Federation (IUF) (23311)
PO Box 2082
Spring Valley, CA 91979
E-mail: contact@iufinc.org
URL: **http://iufinc.org**
Contact: Ryan Woessner, Pres.

3312 ■ Ultra Marathon Cycling Association (UMCA) (21239)
PO Box 18028
Boulder, CO 80308-1028
Ph: **(303)545-9566**
Fax: **(303)545-9619**
E-mail: director@ultracycling.com
URL: http://www.ultracycling.com
Contact: Merry Vander Linden, Pres.

3313 ■ Unicycling Society of America (USA) (23525)
PO Box 21487
Minneapolis, MN 55421-0487
E-mail: wgrzych@comcast.net
URL: http://www.unicyclingusa.org
Contact: Wendy Grzych, Pres.

3314 ■ The Wheelmen (23322)
1552 Autumn Ridge Cir.
Reston, VA 20194-1563
E-mail: **keturner@thewheelmen.org**
URL: http://www.thewheelmen.org
Contact: Kenneth Gray, Commander/Membership Chm.

Darts

3315 ■ AMOA National Dart Association (AMOA-NDA) (20767)
9100 Purdue Rd., Ste.200
Indianapolis, IN 46268
Ph: (317)387-1299
Free: (800)808-9884
Fax: (317)387-0999
E-mail: **info@ndadarts.com**
URL: http://www.ndadarts.com
Contact: Leslie Murphy CAE, Exec. Dir.

Disabled

3316 ■ BlazeSports America
535 N McDonough St.
Decatur, GA 30030
Ph: (404)270-2000
Fax: **(404)270-2039**
E-mail: info@blazesports.org
URL: http://www.blazesports.org
Contact: Carol Mushett Johnson, CEO

**3317 ■ National Wheelchair Basketball
Association (NWBA) (20925)**
1130 Elkton St., Ste.C
Colorado Springs, CO 80907
Ph: (719)266-4082
Fax: (719)266-4876
E-mail: **nwbapresident@gmail.com**
URL: http://www.nwba.org
Contact: **Dickie Bryant, Pres.**

**3318 ■ United States Deaf Ski and
Snowboard Association (USDSSA) (22848)**
PO Box 4
Cambridge, VT 05444
E-mail: **shira@usdssa.org**
URL: http://www.usdssa.org
Contact: Rachel Boll, Pres.

**3319 ■ Wheelchair and Ambulatory Sports,
USA (WASUSA) (21281)**
c/o Ralph Armento, Operations Mgr.
PO Box 5266
Kendall Park, NJ 08824-5266
Ph: **(732)266-2634**
Fax: **(732)355-6500**
E-mail: office@wsusa.org
URL: http://www.wsusa.org
Contact: Barbara Chambers, Chair
Status Note: Formerly Wheelchair Sports U.S.A.

Disc Sports

**3320 ■ Freestyle Players Association (FPA)
(22854)**
864 Grand Ave.
Box 475
San Diego, CA 92109
Free: (800)321-8833
E-mail: info@freestyledisc.org
URL: http://www.freestyledisc.org
Contact: **Lori Daniels, Exec. Dir.**

Diving

3321 ■ USA Diving
132 E Washington St., Ste.850
Indianapolis, IN 46204
Ph: (317)237-5252
Fax: (317)237-5257
E-mail: linda.paul@usadiving.org
URL: http://www.usadiving.org
Contact: **Linda Paul, Pres./CEO**

Dog Racing

**3322 ■ American Greyhound Track Operators
Association (AGTOA) (21292)**
Palm Beach Kennel Club
1111 N Cong. Ave.
West Palm Beach, FL 33409
Ph: (561)688-5799
Fax: (801)751-2404
URL: http://www.agtoa.com
Contact: **Tim Leuschner, Pres.**

**3323 ■ International Federation of Sleddog
Sports (IFSS) (23591)**
c/o Sally O'Sullivan Bair, Sec. Gen.
8554 Gateway Cir.
Monticello, MN 55362
Ph: (763)295-5465
Fax: (763)295-3290
E-mail: sbair@tds.net
URL: **http://sleddogsport.net**
Contact: Bengt Ponten, Pres.

**3324 ■ Lakes Region Sled Dog Club (LRSDC)
(21295)**
c/o Peter Colbath, Treas.
PO Box 341
Laconia, NH 03247-0382
Ph: (603)524-4314 **(603)524-8560**
E-mail: **lyman@lrsdc.org**
URL: http://www.lrsdc.org
Contact: James Lyman, Pres.

Fencing

**3325 ■ United States Fencing Association
(USFA) (20819)**
1 Olympic Plz.
Colorado Springs, CO 80909-5780
Ph: (719)866-4511
Fax: **(719)325-8998**
E-mail: info@usfencing.org
URL: http://www.usfencing.org
Contact: **Greg Dilworth, Exec. Dir.**

Fishing

**3326 ■ Bass Anglers Sportsman Society
(20826)**
1170 Celebration Blvd., Ste.200
Celebration, FL 34747
Free: (877)BAS-SUSA
E-mail: **bassmaster@emailcustomerservice.com**
URL: http://sports.espn.go.com/outdoors/bassmaster/
  index
Contact: Mr. Don Rucks, VP/Gen. Mgr.

**3327 ■ International Underwater Spearfishing
Association (IUSA)**
2515 NW 29th Dr.
Boca Raton, FL 33434
E-mail: **sheri.daye@yahoo.com**
URL: http://www.iusarecords.com
Contact: **Sheri Daye, Pres.**

**3328 ■ International Women's Fishing
Association (IWFA) (20369)**
PO Box 21066
Fort Lauderdale, FL 33335-1066
E-mail: **iwfapresident@iwfa.org**
URL: http://www.iwfa.org
Contact: **Kate Burke, Pres.**

Football

**3329 ■ National Football Foundation and
College Hall of Fame (NFF) (21324)**
433 E Las Colinas Blvd., Ste.1130
Irving, TX 75039
Ph: **(972)556-1000**
Fax: (972)556-9032
E-mail: membership@footballfoundation.com
URL: http://www.footballfoundation.com
Contact: Mr. Steven Hatchell, Pres./CEO

**3330 ■ National Football League Alumni (NFL
Alumni) (20851)**
1 Washington Park
1 Washington St., 14th Fl.
Newark, NJ 07102
Ph: **(973)718-7350**
Free: **(877)258-6635**
Fax: **(862)772-0277**

E-mail: **katie.hilder@nflalumni.org**
URL: http://www.nflalumni.org
Contact: **George Martin, Pres./CEO**

**3331 ■ North American Football League
(NAFL)**
5775 Glenridge Dr. NE, Ste.100B
Atlanta, GA 30328
Ph: (404)475-1803
Fax: (866)505-9208
E-mail: info@nafl.org
URL: http://www.nafl.org
Contact: **Robin Williams, Conference Commis-
sioner**

**3332 ■ Professional Football Writers of
America (PFWA) (20992)**
12030 Cedar Lake Ct.
Maryland Heights, MO 63043
E-mail: **alexmarvez@pfwa.org**
URL: http://www.pfwa.org
Contact: **Alex Marvez, Pres.**

**3333 ■ United States Flag Football League
(USFFL)**
763 Ridge Rd.
Angier, NC 27501
Ph: (919)894-7976 **(919)412-2155**
Fax: **(919)894-4517**
E-mail: info@flagfootball.org
URL: http://www.flagfootball.org/usffl.htm
Contact: Tim Langdon, Contact

Golf

**3334 ■ American Junior Golf Association
(AJGA) (20865)**
1980 Sports Club Dr.
Braselton, GA 30517
Ph: (770)868-4200
Free: **(877)373-2542**
Fax: (770)868-4211
E-mail: ajga@ajga.org
URL: http://www.ajga.org
Contact: Stephen A. Hamblin, Exec. Dir.

**3335 ■ Golf Coaches Association of America
(GCAA)**
1225 W Main St., Ste.110
Norman, OK 73069
Ph: (405)329-4222
Free: (866)422-2669
Fax: (405)573-7888
E-mail: **info@collegiategolf.com**
URL: http://www.collegiategolf.com
Contact: **Bruce Brockbank, Pres.**

**3336 ■ International Association of Golf
Administrators (IAGA) (320)**
1974 Sproul Rd., Ste.400
Broomall, PA 19008
Ph: **(610)687-2340**
E-mail: **jgarber@gapgolf.org**
URL: http://www.iaga.org
Contact: Robert Markionni, Pres.

**3337 ■ Professional Golfers' Association of
America (PGA) (20877)**
100 Ave. of the Champions
Palm Beach Gardens, FL 33418
Ph: (561)624-8400
E-mail: **webmaster.pga@turner.com**
URL: http://www.pga.com
Contact: **Allen Wronowski, Pres.**

**3338 ■ Professional Putters Association
(PPA)**
28 Sioux Trail
Ransom Canyon, TX 79366
Ph: (434)237-7888
E-mail: **joe@proputters.com**
URL: http://www.proputters.com
Contact: Joe Aboid, Commissioner

3339 ■ Salute Military Golf Association (SMGA)
PO Box 83893
Gaithersburg, MD 20883
Ph: (301)500-7449
E-mail: jcmay245@verizon.net
URL: http://www.golfsalute.org
Contact: Jim Estes, Founder/Pres.

Gymnastics

3340 ■ Eastern Intercollegiate Gymnastic League (EIGL) (20884)
Eastern Coll. Athletic Conf.
1311 Craigville Beach Rd.
Centerville, MA 02632
Ph: (508)771-5060
Fax: (508)771-9486
E-mail: mletzeisen@ecac.org
URL: http://www.ecac.org/affiliates/EIGL/index
Contact: Michael Letzeisen, Dir. of Sports Administration

Handball

3341 ■ United States Handball Association (USHA) (21365)
2333 N Tucson Blvd.
Tucson, AZ 85716
Ph: (520)795-0434
Free: (800)289-8742
Fax: (520)795-0465
E-mail: handball@ushandball.org
URL: http://ushandball.org
Contact: Vern Roberts, Exec. Dir.

Hockey

3342 ■ Eastern College Athletic Conference (ECAC)
PO Box 3
Centerville, MA 02632
Ph: (508)771-5060
Fax: (508)771-9486
E-mail: sbamford@ecac.org
URL: http://www.ecac.org
Contact: Fredina Ingold, Pres.

3343 ■ Western Collegiate Hockey Association (WCHA) (21373)
2211 S Josephine St.
Denver, CO 80208
Ph: (303)871-4223
Fax: (303)871-4770
E-mail: info@wcha.com
URL: http://www.wcha.com
Contact: Carol LaBelle-Ehrhardt, Asst. Commissioner of Operations

Horse Racing

3344 ■ Harness Tracks of America (HTA) (20906)
12025 E Dry Gulch Pl.
Tucson, AZ 85749
Ph: (520)529-2525
Fax: (520)529-3235
E-mail: info@harnesstracks.com
URL: http://www.harnesstracks.com
Contact: Paul J. Estok, Exec. VP/Gen. Counsel

3345 ■ International Trotting and Pacing Association (ITPA)
5140 County Rd. 56
Auburn, IN 46706
Ph: (260)337-5808
Fax: (260)337-5808
E-mail: janinezehr.itpa@yahoo.com
URL: http://trottingbreds.homestead.com

3346 ■ Jockeys' Guild (JG) (23503)
103 Wind Haven Dr., Ste.200
Nicholasville, KY 40356
Ph: (859)523-5625
Free: (866)435-6257
Fax: (859)219-9892
E-mail: info@jockeysguild.com
URL: http://www.jockeysguild.com
Contact: John R. Velazquez, Chm.

3347 ■ National Museum of Racing and Hall of Fame (NMR) (22981)
191 Union Ave.
Saratoga Springs, NY 12866-3566
Ph: (518)584-0400
Free: (800)562-5394
Fax: (518)584-4574
E-mail: nmrmedia@racingmuseum.net
URL: http://www.racingmuseum.org
Contact: Christopher Dragone, Dir.

3348 ■ Thoroughbred Club of America (TCA)
PO Box 8098
Lexington, KY 40533-8098
Ph: (859)254-4282
Fax: (859)231-6131
E-mail: memberservices@thethoroughbredclub.com
URL: http://www.thethoroughbredclub.com
Contact: Edwin S. Saunier, Pres.

3349 ■ United States Team Penning Association (USTPA) (23719)
3609 Acton Hwy., Ste.21
Granbury, TX 76049
Ph: (817)326-4444
Fax: (817)326-4469
E-mail: jana.sain@ustpa.com
URL: http://www.ustpa.com
Contact: Jake Wells, Pres.

Horseback Riding

3350 ■ CHA - Certified Horsemanship Association (23738)
4037 Iron Works Pkwy., Ste.180
Lexington, KY 40511
Ph: (859)259-3399 (720)857-9550
Free: (800)399-0138
Fax: (859)255-0726
E-mail: office@cha-ahse.org
URL: http://www.cha-ahse.org
Contact: Mr. Christy Landwehr, CEO

3351 ■ International Side Saddle Organization (ISSO) (23002)
PO Box 161
Stevensville, MD 21666-0161
Ph: (918)685-0072
Fax: (410)643-1497
E-mail: info@sidesaddle.com
URL: http://www.sidesaddle.com
Contact: Janet Brown, Pres.

3352 ■ National Versatility Ranch Horse Association (NVRHA)
590 Hwy. 105, Box 150
Monument, CO 80132
Ph: (719)487-9014
Free: (866)430-8114
Fax: (719)487-9014
E-mail: timwrose@aol.com
URL: http://nvrha.org
Contact: Dave Currin, Pres.

3353 ■ Trail Riders of Today (TROT) (23532)
c/o Margaret Scarff, Membership Committee
4406 Carico Ln.
White Hall, MD 21161
Ph: (301)622-4157
E-mail: rmacnab@comcast.net
URL: http://www.trot-md.org
Contact: Ron MacNab, Pres.

Horses

3354 ■ American Driving Society (ADS) (21375)
PO Box 278
Cross Plains, WI 53528
Ph: (608)237-7382
Fax: (608)237-6468
E-mail: info@americandrivingsociety.org
URL: http://www.americandrivingsociety.org
Contact: John Freiburger, Pres.

Hunting

3355 ■ American Coon Hunters Association (ACHA)
PO Box 453
Grayson, KY 41143
Ph: (606)474-9740
E-mail: mheath@worldhunt.org
URL: http://www.worldhunt.org
Contact: Mike Heath, Pres.

3356 ■ Masters of Foxhounds Association of America (MFHA) (3209)
PO Box 363
Millwood, VA 22646
Ph: (540)955-5680
Fax: (540)955-5682
E-mail: office@mfha.com
URL: http://www.mfha.com
Contact: Edward W. Kelly MFH, Pres.

Lacrosse

3357 ■ Federation of International Lacrosse (FIL) (20965)
911 Overbrook Rd.
Wilmington, DE 19807
Ph: (302)652-4530
Fax: (302)652-4530
E-mail: info@filacrosse.com
URL: http://www.filacrosse.com
Contact: Stan Cockerton, Pres.

Luge

3358 ■ United States Luge Association (USLA) (23047)
57 Church St.
Lake Placid, NY 12946
Ph: (518)523-2071
Free: (800)USA-LUGE
Fax: (518)523-4106
E-mail: info@usaluge.org
URL: http://www.usaluge.org
Contact: John Fee, Pres.

Martial Arts

3359 ■ All Japan Ju-Jitsu International Federation (AJJIF)
5460 White Oak Ave., Unit F207
Encino, CA 91316
Ph: (818)578-6671
E-mail: secretary.ajjif@gmail.com
URL: http://www.ajjif.org
Contact: Grand Master Alexey Kunin, Pres.

3360 ■ International Association of Gay and Lesbian Martial Artists (IAGLMA) (3267)
PO Box 590601
San Francisco, CA 94159-0601
Ph: (610)940-1434
Fax: (610)940-1434
E-mail: peobumjong@aol.com
URL: http://www.iaglma.org
Contact: Teresa Galetti, Co-Pres.

3361 ■ Martial Arts International Federation (MAIF)
1850 Columbia Pike, Ste.No. 612
Arlington, VA 22204
Ph: (703)920-1590
Fax: (703)920-1590
E-mail: info@maintlfed.org
URL: **http://www.itkj.org**
Contact: Bruce R. Bethers, Sec. Gen.

3362 ■ Universal Martial Arts Brotherhood (UMAB)
2427 Buckingham Rd.
Ann Arbor, MI 48104
Ph: (734)971-7040
E-mail: **assyakh@gmail.com**
URL: http://utbtaekwondo.org/page3.htm
Contact: Grandmaster Eugene A. Humesky PhD, Founder/CEO/Chm.

3363 ■ The World Kuoshu Federation (TWKSF)
PO Box 20269
Baltimore, MD 21284-0269
Ph: **(443)394-9222**
Fax: (443)394-9202
E-mail: **twksf@verizon.net**
URL: http://www.twksf.org
Contact: Chien Liang Huang, Chm./Pres.

3364 ■ World Martial Arts Association (WMAA) (20978)
Redeemer St. John's Church
939 - 83rd St.
Brooklyn, NY 11228
Ph: (718)833-9039
URL: http://www.wmaa.com
Contact: **Michael T. Dealy, Contact**

3365 ■ World Traditional Karate Organization (WTKO)
138 Bradley Ave.
Staten Island, NY 10314
E-mail: **johnmullin@wtko.org**
URL: http://www.wtko.org
Contact: Mr. John J. Mullin, Exec. Chm.

Motorcycle

3366 ■ American Motorcyclist Association (AMA) (23622)
13515 Yarmouth Dr.
Pickerington, OH 43147-8214
Ph: **(614)856-1900**
Free: (800)262-5646
Fax: (614)856-1920
E-mail: ama@ama-cycle.org
URL: http://www.ama-cycle.org
Contact: Stan Simpson, Chm.

3367 ■ International Brotherhood of Motorcycle Campers (IBMC) (22550)
PO Box 375
Helper, UT 84526
Ph: (805)278-9244 **(719)873-5466**
E-mail: camp@ibmc.org
URL: http://www.ibmc.org

Olympic Games

3368 ■ United States Olympic Committee (USOC) (21124)
27 S Tejon
Colorado Springs, CO 80903
Ph: **(719)866-4529**
Free: **(888)222-2313**

E-mail: media@usoc.org
URL: http://www.olympic-usa.org
Contact: **Lawrence F. Probst, Chm.**

3369 ■ Virgin Islands Olympic Committee (VIOC)
PO Box 366
Frederiksted, VI 00841
Ph: **(340)719-8462**
Fax: (340)778-0270
E-mail: virginislandsolympic@attglobal.net
URL: http://www.virginislandsolympics.com
Contact: Hans Lawaetz, Pres.

Orienteering

3370 ■ National Association of Competitive Mounted Orienteering (NACMO) (20996)
4309 Laura St. NW
Comstock Park, MI 49321
Ph: (616)784-1645
E-mail: **alisonannebennett@gmail.com**
URL: http://www.nacmo.org
Contact: Alison Bennett, Pres.

3371 ■ United States Orienteering Federation (USOF) (23103)
PO Box 505
Riderwood, MD 21139
Ph: (410)802-1125
E-mail: **gjs@orienteeringusa.org**
URL: http://www.us.orienteering.org
Contact: Glen Schorr, Exec. Dir.

Psychology

3372 ■ North American Society for the Psychology of Sport and Physical Activity (NASPSPA) (23885)
1607 N Market St.
Champaign, IL 61820
Fax: **(217)351-1549**
E-mail: **dstmarie@uottawa.ca**
URL: http://www.naspspa.org
Contact: **Prof. Diane Ste-Marie, Pres.**

Recreation

3373 ■ International Association of Skateboard Companies (IASC) (22600)
22431 Antonio Pkwy., Ste.B160-412
Rancho Santa Margarita, CA 92688
Ph: (949)455-1112
Fax: (949)455-1712
URL: http://www.skateboardiasc.org
Contact: **Josh Friedberg, Exec. Dir.**

Rodeo

3374 ■ Professional Armed Forces Rodeo Association (PAFRA) (23693)
c/o Val Baker, Sec.
1985 1st St. W, No. 2523
Randolph, TX 78150-4312
E-mail: **pafra_pres@hotmail.com**
URL: http://www.pafra2000.com
Contact: **R.J. Eppers, Pres.**

3375 ■ Professional Rodeo Cowboys Association (PRCA) (23694)
101 Pro Rodeo Dr.
Colorado Springs, CO 80919-2301
Ph: (719)593-8840
Free: **(800)234-7722**
Fax: (719)548-4876

E-mail: prorodeo@prorodeo.com
URL: http://www.prorodeo.com

Rowing

3376 ■ Eastern Association of Rowing Colleges (EARC) (23157)
Easter Coll. Athletic Conf.
1311 Craigville Beach Rd.
Centerville, MA 02632
Ph: (508)771-5060 (857)257-3728
Fax: (508)771-9468
E-mail: gary.caldwell@tufts.edu
URL: http://www.ecac.org/affiliates/EARC/index
Contact: Gary Caldwell, Dir. of Rowing

3377 ■ Intercollegiate Rowing Association (IRA) (23158)
Eastern Coll. Athletic Conf.
1311 Craigville Beach Rd.
Centerville, MA 02632-4129
Ph: (508)771-5060 (857)257-3728
Fax: (508)771-9486
E-mail: gcaldwell@ecac.org
URL: http://www.ecac.org/affiliates/IRA
Contact: Clayton Chapman, Dir.

Rugby

3378 ■ United States Rugby Football Union (USARFU) (23706)
2500 Arapahoe Ave., Ste.200
Boulder, CO 80302
Ph: (303)539-0300
Free: (800)280-6302
Fax: (303)539-0311
E-mail: **nmelville@usarugby.org**
URL: http://www.usarugby.org
Contact: **Nigel Melville, CEO/Pres.**

Running

3379 ■ Girls on the Run International (GOTR)
120 Cottage Pl.
Charlotte, NC 28207
Ph: (704)376-9817
Free: (800)901-9965
Fax: (704)376-1039
E-mail: **sponsorships@girlsontherun.org**
URL: http://girlsontherun.org
Contact: Elizabeth Kunz, Pres.

Shooting

3380 ■ Cast Bullet Association (CBA) (22631)
c/o Paul Gans, Membership Dir.
7600 SE Maple Ave.
Vancouver, WA 98664-1737
Ph: (360)882-0502
E-mail: **1pres@castbulletassoc.org**
URL: http://www.castbulletassoc.org
Contact: John Alexander, Pres.

3381 ■ International Handgun Metallic Silhouette Association (IHMSA) (23719)
c/o Lorene Thompson
PO Box 95690
South Jordan, UT 84095-5690
Ph: (801)733-8423
Fax: (801)733-8424
E-mail: **headquarters@ihmsa.org**
URL: http://www.ihmsa.org
Contact: Nancy LaCroix, Pres.

3382 ■ National Bench Rest Shooters Association (NBRSA) (23721)
2835 Guilford Ln.
Oklahoma City, OK 73120-4404
Ph: (405)842-9585
E-mail: **nbrsa.manager@gmail.com**
URL: http://nbrsa.org
Contact: Mrs. Pat Ferrell, Business Mgr.

3383 ■ National Rifle Association of America (NRA) (21187)
11250 Waples Mill Rd.
Fairfax, VA 22030
Ph: (703)267-1600
Free: (800)672-3888
E-mail: membership@nrahq.org
URL: **http://home.nra.org**

3384 ■ North-South Skirmish Association (N-SSA)
PO Box 218
Crozet, VA 22932-0218
E-mail: **pspaugy@aol.com**
URL: http://www.n-ssa.org
Contact: Charlie Smithgall, Commander

3385 ■ United States Revolver Association (USRA) (22645)
RR 1 Box 548
Scotrun, PA 18355
E-mail: **dave@usra1.net**
URL: http://www.usra1.org

Skating

3386 ■ Professional Figure Skaters Cooperative (PFSC)
PO Box 893
Park Forest, IL 60466
Ph: (312)296-7864
Fax: **(312)896-9119**
E-mail: info@proskaters.org
URL: http://www.proskaters.org
Contact: Ashley Clark, Pres.

3387 ■ U.S. Speedskating (USS) (23196)
PO Box 18370
Kearns, UT 84118
Ph: (801)417-5360
Fax: (801)417-5361
E-mail: **bbissell@usspeedskating.org**
URL: http://www.usspeedskating.org
Contact: Brad Goskowicz, Pres.

Skiing

3388 ■ National Brotherhood of Skiers (NBS) (21078)
1525 E 53rd St., Ste.418
Chicago, IL 60615
Ph: (773)955-4100
URL: http://www.nbs.org
Contact: **Haymon T. Jahi, Pres.**

3389 ■ Professional Ski Instructors of America (PSIA) (21082)
133 S Van Gordon St., Ste.200
Lakewood, CO 80228
Ph: (303)987-9390
Fax: (303)988-9489
E-mail: **mist@thesnowpros.org**
URL: http://www.psia.org
Contact: **Eric Sheckleton, Chm.**

Snow Sports

3390 ■ U.S. Bobsled and Skeleton Federation (USBSF) (21577)
196 Old Military Rd.
Lake Placid, NY 12946
Ph: (518)523-1842
Fax: (518)523-9491
E-mail: **asmith@usbsf.com**
URL: http://www.usbsf.com
Contact: Adelle Smith, Operation Mgr.

3391 ■ United States Snowshoe Association (USSSA) (21223)
678 County Rte. 25
Corinth, NY 12822
Ph: (518)654-7648 **(518)420-6961**
E-mail: **usssa2@roadrunner.com**
URL: http://www.snowshoeracing.com
Contact: Mark Elmore, Sports Dir.

Soap Box Derby

3392 ■ National Derby Rallies (NDR) (23216)
6644 Switzer Ln.
Shawnee, KS 66203
Ph: (913)962-6360
E-mail: **derek@zero-error.com**
URL: http://www.ndr.org
Contact: **Derek Fitzgerald, Exec. Dir.**

Soccer

3393 ■ American Youth Soccer Organization (AYSO) (23774)
19750 S Vermont Ave., Ste.200
Torrance, CA 90502
Free: (800)872-2976
Fax: (310)643-5310
E-mail: suitup@ayso.org
URL: http://www.ayso.org/home.aspx
Contact: Mike Wade, Pres.

3394 ■ National Intercollegiate Soccer Officials Association (NISOA) (23778)
1030 Ohio Ave.
Cape May, NJ 08204
E-mail: **calcioref@aol.com**
URL: http://www.nisoa.com
Contact: **Manny Ortiz Jr., Pres.**

Softball

3395 ■ Amateur Softball Association of America (ASA) (21235)
2801 NE 50th St.
Oklahoma City, OK 73111
Ph: (405)424-5266
E-mail: **piedmontasa@verizon.net**
URL: http://www.softball.org
Contact: Andy Dooley, Pres.

3396 ■ International Senior Softball Association (ISSA)
9401 East St.
Manassas, VA 20110
Ph: **(571)436-9704**
Fax: (703)361-0344
URL: http://www.seniorsoftball.org
Contact: R.B. Thomas Jr., Exec. Dir.

Sports

3397 ■ Athletic Equipment Managers Association (AEMA) (21122)
460 Hunt Hill Rd.
Freeville, NY 13068
Ph: **(607)539-6300**
Fax: **(607)539-6340**
E-mail: aema@frontiernet.net
URL: http://www.equipmentmanagers.org
Contact: Dorothy Cutting, Office Mgr.

3398 ■ Atlantic Coast Conference (ACC) (24024)
4512 Weybridge Ln.
Greensboro, NC 27407
Ph: (336)854-8787
URL: http://www.theacc.com/sports/m-footbl/2009-
    this-week-in-ACC-football.html
Contact: John D. Swofford, Commissioner

3399 ■ Big East Conference (BEC) (24025)
222 Richmond St., Ste.110
Providence, RI 02903
Ph: **(401)453-0660**
Fax: **(401)751-8540**
E-mail: **webmaster@bigeast.org**
URL: http://www.bigeast.org
Contact: Michael A. Tranghese, Commissioner

3400 ■ College Athletic Business Management Association (CABMA) (23255)
c/o Pat Manak, Asst. Sec.
24651 Detroit Rd.
Westlake, OH 44145
Ph: (440)892-4000
Fax: (440)892-4007
E-mail: pmanak@nacda.com
URL: http://nacda.ocsn.com/cabma/nacda-cabma.
    html
Contact: **Ross Cobb, Pres.**

3401 ■ Intercollegiate Association of Amateur Athletes of America (IC4A) (23262)
Eastern Coll. Athletic Conf.
PO Box 3
Centerville, MA 02632
Ph: (508)771-5060
Fax: (508)771-9486
E-mail: stevebartold@sbcglobal.net
URL: http://www.ecac.org/affiliates/IC4A/index
Contact: Steve Bartold, Contact

3402 ■ Maccabi USA/Sports for Israel
1926 Arch St., No. 4R
Philadelphia, PA 19103
Ph: (215)561-6900
Fax: (215)561-5470
E-mail: **jchurylo@maccabiusa.com**
URL: http://www.maccabiusa.com
Contact: Jed Margolis, Exec. Dir.

3403 ■ National Association of Collegiate Directors of Athletics (NACDA) (21142)
24651 Detroit Rd.
Westlake, OH 44145
Ph: **(440)892-4000**
Fax: **(440)892-4007**
E-mail: rspetman@fsu.edu
URL: **http://www.nacda.com**
Contact: **Mike Cleary, Exec. Dir.**

3404 ■ National Collegiate Athletic Association (NCAA) (21631)
PO Box 6222
Indianapolis, IN 46206-6222
Ph: (317)917-6222
Fax: (317)917-6888

E-mail: pmr@ncaa.org
URL: **http://www.ncaa.org**
Contact: **Dr. Mark A. Emmert, Pres.**

3405 ■ National Intramural-Recreational Sports Association (NIRSA) (23842)
4185 SW Res. Way
Corvallis, OR 97333-1067
Ph: (541)766-8211
Fax: (541)766-8284
E-mail: nirsa@nirsa.org
URL: http://www.nirsa.org
Contact: **R. Kevin Marbury, Pres.**

3406 ■ National Junior College Athletic Association (NJCAA) (21278)
1631 Mesa Ave., Ste.B
Colorado Springs, CO 80906
Ph: (719)590-9788
Fax: (719)590-7324
E-mail: meleicht@njcaa.org
URL: http://www.njcaa.org
Contact: **Mary Ellen Leicht, Exec. Dir.**

3407 ■ Pacific 10 Conference (PAC-10) (23289)
1350 Treat Blvd., Ste.500
Walnut Creek, CA 94597-8853
Ph: (925)932-4411
Fax: (925)932-4601
E-mail: **pac-10@pac-10.org**
URL: http://www.pac-10.org
Contact: Larry Scott, Commissioner

3408 ■ RollerSoccer International Federation (RSIF) (23292)
PO Box 423318
San Francisco, CA 94142-3318
Ph: (415)864-6879
Fax: (415)437-0859
E-mail: **rsif2@rollersoccer.com**
URL: http://www.rollersoccer.com
Contact: Zack Phillips, Founder

3409 ■ United States Collegiate Athletic Association (USCAA) (22761)
4101 Washington Ave., Bldg. 601
Newport News, VA 23607
Ph: **(757)706-3756 (757)706-3757**
Fax: **(757)706-3758**
E-mail: **info@theuscaa.com**
URL: http://www.theuscaa.com
Contact: Mr. Bill Casto, Exec. Dir./Commissioner

3410 ■ United States Sports Academy (USSA) (21166)
One Acad. Dr.
Daphne, AL 36526-7055
Ph: (251)626-3303
Free: (800)223-2668
Fax: (251)625-1035
E-mail: **president@ussa.edu**
URL: http://www.ussa.edu
Contact: Dr. Thomas P. Rosandich, Pres./CEO

3411 ■ Western Athletic Conference (WAC) (20674)
9250 E Costilla Ave., Ste.300
Englewood, CO 80112
Ph: (303)799-9221 (303)792-3199
Fax: (303)799-3888
E-mail: **kbenson@wac.org**
URL: http://www.wacsports.com
Contact: Karl Benson, Commissioner

3412 ■ World Sport Stacking Association (WSSA) (23868)
11 Inverness Way S
Englewood, CO 80112
Ph: (303)962-5672

E-mail: **info@thewssa.com**
URL: http://www.worldsportstackingassociation.org
Contact: Roger Washburn, Contact

Sports Officials

3413 ■ National Association of Sports Officials (NASO) (23312)
2017 Lathrop Ave.
Racine, WI 53405
Ph: (262)632-5448
Free: (800)733-6100
Fax: (262)632-5460
E-mail: **cservice@naso.org**
URL: http://www.naso.org
Contact: Barry Mano, Pres.

Surfing

3414 ■ Eastern Surfing Association (ESA) (21180)
PO Box 625
Virginia Beach, VA 23451
Ph: (757)233-1790
Fax: (757)233-1396
E-mail: **centralhq@surfesa.org**
URL: http://www.surfesa.org
Contact: Debbie Hodges, Exec. Dir.

Swimming

3415 ■ College Swimming Coaches Association of America (CSCAA) (23324)
1640 Maple Ave., No. 803
Evanston, IL 60201
Ph: (847)833-3478
E-mail: r-groseth@northwestern.edu
URL: **http://www.cscaa.org**
Contact: Bob Groseth, Exec. Dir.

3416 ■ National InterScholastic Swimming Coaches Association of America (NISCA) (23328)
29 Fairview Ave.
Great Neck, NY 11023-1206
E-mail: **president@niscaonline.org**
URL: http://www.niscaonline.org
Contact: **Arvel McElroy, Pres.**

3417 ■ U.S. Aquatic Sports (USAS) (21323)
c/o Debra Turner, Coor.
325 Rolling Trails Rd.
Greenwood, IN 46142
Ph: (317)223-0702
Fax: (317)968-5105
E-mail: **jim-wood-bac@juno.com**
URL: http://www.usaquaticsports.org
Contact: **Jim Wood, Pres.**

3418 ■ United States Swim School Association (21674)
PO Box 17208
Fountain Hills, AZ 85269
Ph: (480)837-5525
Fax: (480)836-8277
E-mail: office@usswimschools.org
URL: **http://www.usswimschools.org**
Contact: Sue Mackie, Exec. Dir.

3419 ■ United States Synchronized Swimming (USSS) (21202)
132 E Washington St., Ste.820
Indianapolis, IN 46204
Ph: (317)237-5700
Fax: (317)237-5705

E-mail: **president@usasynchro.org**
URL: http://www.usasynchro.org
Contact: Duke Zielinski, Pres.

Tennis

3420 ■ American Medical Tennis Association (AMTA) (21206)
1803 Cobblestone Dr.
Provo, UT 84604
Free: (800)326-2682
Fax: (801)374-0135
E-mail: amta@mdtennis.org
URL: http://www.mdtennis.org
Contact: **Bonnie Sidoff MD, Pres.**

3421 ■ American Tennis Association (ATA) (21325)
9701 Apollo Dr., Ste.301
Largo, MD 20774
Ph: **(240)487-5953**
E-mail: **fscott@americantennisassociation.org**
URL: **http://www.americantennisassociation.org**
Contact: **Dr. Franklyn Scott Jr., Pres.**

3422 ■ United States National Tennis Academy (USNTA) (21336)
3523 McKinney Ave., No. 208
Dallas, TX 75204
Free: (800)452-8519
Fax: **(214)231-2986**
E-mail: usnta@usnta.com
URL: http://www.usnta.com

Track and Field

3423 ■ Lifelong Fitness Alliance (LFA) (23920)
2682 Middlefield Rd., Ste.Z
Redwood City, CA 94063
Ph: (650)361-8282
Free: **(855)361-8282**
Fax: (650)529-9592
E-mail: **step@lifelongfitnessalliance.org**
URL: http://www.50plus.org
Contact: Christopher P. Berka, Pres.

Trails

3424 ■ Adirondack Trail Improvement Society (ATIS) (21249)
PO Box 565
Keene Valley, NY 12943
Ph: (518)576-9949
E-mail: tgoodwin@kvvi.net
URL: http://www.atis-web.com
Contact: **Bobbie Burchenal Landers, Pres.**

3425 ■ American Hiking Society (AHS) (23372)
1422 Fenwick Ln.
Silver Spring, MD 20910
Ph: (301)565-6704
Free: (800)972-8608
Fax: (301)565-6714
E-mail: **info@americanhiking.org**
URL: http://www.americanhiking.org
Contact: Mr. Peter Olsen, Dir. of Operations/ Membership

3426 ■ InterCollegiate Outing Club Association (IOCA) (23941)
c/o Don Wade, Direct Mail Chair
35-41 72 St.
Jackson Heights, NY 11372

E-mail: info@ioca.org
URL: http://www.ioca.org
Contact: **Kelly Barrat, Exec. Sec.**

3427 ■ IOCALUM (24160)
597 State Hwy. 162
Sprakers, NY 12166-4008
Ph: (518)673-3212
Fax: (518)673-3219
E-mail: **rvinyard@frontiernet.net**
URL: http://www.ioca.org/iocalum
Contact: Roland Vinyard, Exec. Sec.

3428 ■ New England Trails Conference (NETC) (23386)
PO Box 550
Charlestown, NH 03603
Ph: (603)543-1700
E-mail: **marsha@sca-inc.org**
URL: http://www.wapack.org/netrails
Contact: Bob Spoerl, Pres.

Triathlon

3429 ■ U.S.A. Triathlon (USAT) (21706)
5825 Delmonico Dr.
Colorado Springs, CO 80919
Ph: (719)597-9090 **(719)955-2807**

Fax: (719)597-2121
E-mail: info@usatriathlon.org
URL: http://www.usatriathlon.org
Contact: **Mr. Rob Urbach, Exec. Dir.**

Tug of War

3430 ■ United States Amateur Tug of War Association (USATOWA) (23959)
c/o Amy Breuscher, Sec.
PO Box 68
Hollandale, WI 53544
Free: (800)TUGOWAR
E-mail: shelbytow@msn.com
URL: **http://www.usatowa.com**
Contact: Mrs. Shelby Richardson, Pres.

Underwater Sports

3431 ■ Professional Association of Diving Instructors (PADI) (21286)
30151 Tomas St.
Rancho Santa Margarita, CA 92688-2125
Ph: (949)858-7234
Free: (800)729-7234
Fax: (949)267-1267

E-mail: webmaster@padi.com
URL: http://www.padi.com
Contact: **Brian Cronin, CEO**

Water Polo

3432 ■ United States Water Polo (USWP) (23411)
2124 Maine St., Ste.240
Huntington Beach, CA 92648
Ph: (714)500-5445 (714)500-5449
Fax: (714)960-2431
E-mail: **media@usawaterpolo.org**
URL: http://www.usawaterpolo.com
Contact: Christopher Ramsey, CEO

Water Sports

3433 ■ United States Canoe Association (USCA) (23279)
c/o Paula Thiel, Membership Chair
487 Wylie School Rd.
Voluntown, CT 06384
Ph: **(860)564-2443**
E-mail: **ladyjustice@erols.com**
URL: http://www.uscanoe.com
Contact: **Susan Williams, Pres.**

Administrative Services

3434 ■ AFL-CIO | SEIU | District 925 (23429)
1914 N 34th St., Ste.100
Seattle, WA 98103
Ph: (206)322-3010
Free: (866)734-8925
Fax: (206)547-5581
E-mail: **khart@seiu925.org**
URL: http://www.seiu925.org
Contact: **Karen Hart, Pres.**

3435 ■ Office and Professional Employees International Union (OPEIU) (21307)
c/o Mary Mahoney, Sec.-Treas.
80 Eighth Ave., Ste.610
New York, NY 10011
Ph: **(212)367-0902**
Fax: **(212)727-2087**
URL: http://www.opeiu.org
Contact: Michael Goodwin, Pres.

Aviation

3436 ■ Air Line Pilots Association International (ALPA) (23439)
1625 Massachusetts Ave. NW
Washington, DC 20036
Ph: (703)689-2270
Free: **(888)359-2572**
URL: http://www.alpa.org
Contact: **Capt. Lee Moak, Pres.**

3437 ■ Aircraft Mechanics Fraternal Association (AMFA) (24225)
14001 E Iliff Ave., Ste.217
Aurora, CO 80014
Ph: (303)752-2632
Free: (800)520-2632
Fax: (303)362-7736
E-mail: **louie.key@amfanatl.org**
URL: http://www.amfanatl.org
Contact: Louie Key, Natl. Dir.

3438 ■ Association of Flight Attendants - CWA (AFA-CWA) (24241)
501 3rd St. NW
Washington, DC 20001
Ph: (202)434-1300
Free: (800)424-2401
Fax: (202)434-1319
E-mail: info@afacwa.org
URL: http://www.afanet.org
Contact: **Veda Shook, Pres.**

3439 ■ National Air Traffic Controllers Association (NATCA) (24013)
1325 Massachusetts Ave. NW
Washington, DC 20005
Ph: (202)628-5451
Free: (800)266-0895
Fax: (202)628-5767

E-mail: dchurch@natcadc.org
URL: http://www.natca.org
Contact: **Paul Rinaldi, Pres.**

Broadcasting

3440 ■ American Federation of Television and Radio Artists (AFTRA) (23456)
260 Madison Ave., 9th Fl.
New York, NY 10016-2401
Ph: (212)532-0800
Free: (866)855-5191
Fax: (212)532-2242
E-mail: membership@aftra.com
URL: http://www.aftra.com
Contact: **Roberta Reardon, Natl. Pres.**

Building Trades

3441 ■ AFL-CIO | Building and Construction Trades Department (BCTD) (24257)
815 16th St., Ste.600
Washington, DC 20006
Ph: (202)347-1461
URL: http://www.bctd.org
Contact: **Mark H. Ayers, Pres.**

Christian

3442 ■ Christian Labor Association of the U.S.A. (CLA) (23469)
PO Box 65
Zeeland, MI 49464
Ph: (616)772-9164
Free: (877)CLA-1018
Fax: (616)772-9830
E-mail: michigan@cla-usa.com
URL: http://www.cla-usa.com
Contact: **Clarence Merrill, Natl. Pres.**

Construction

3443 ■ CPWR - The Center for Construction Research and Training (21445)
8484 Georgia Ave., Ste.1000
Silver Spring, MD 20910
Ph: (301)578-8500
Fax: (301)578-8572
E-mail: cpwrwebsite@cpwr.com
URL: http://www.cpwr.com
Contact: **Mark H. Ayers, Pres./Chm.**

Education

3444 ■ National Council on Teacher Retirement (NCTR) (24277)
7600 Greenhaven Dr., Ste.302
Sacramento, CA 95831
Ph: (916)394-2075

Fax: (916)392-0295
URL: http://www.nctr.org
Contact: **Ronnie Jung, Pres.**

Emergency Medicine

3445 ■ International Association of EMTs and Paramedics (IAEP)
159 Burgin Pkwy.
Quincy, MA 02169
Ph: (617)376-0220
Free: (866)412-7762
Fax: **(617)472-7566**
E-mail: **ppetit@nage.org**
URL: http://www.iaep.org
Contact: **David J. Holway, Natl. Pres.**

Government Employees

3446 ■ National Council of Field Labor Locals (NCFLL) (24292)
8 N 3rd St., Rm. 207
Lafayette, IN 47901
Ph: (765)423-2152 (606)432-0943
Fax: (765)423-2194
E-mail: demay.dennis2@dol.gov
URL: http://www.ncfll.org
Contact: Denny DeMay, Pres.

Health Care

3447 ■ Committee of Interns and Residents (CIR) (24089)
520 8th Ave., Ste.1200
New York, NY 10018-4183
Ph: (212)356-8100 (212)356-8180
Free: (800)247-8877
Fax: (212)356-8111
E-mail: info@cirseiu.org
URL: http://www.cirseiu.org
Contact: **Hillary Tompkins MD, Pres.**

Labor

3448 ■ Asian Pacific American Labor Alliance (APALA) (24235)
815 16th St. NW
Washington, DC 20006
Ph: (202)508-3733
Fax: (202)508-3716
E-mail: apala@apalanet.org
URL: http://www.apalanet.org
Contact: **Gregory A. Cendana, Exec. Dir.**

3449 ■ Just Transition Alliance (JTA)
2810 Camino Del Rio S, Ste.116
San Diego, CA 92108
Ph: (619)573-4934
Fax: (619)546-9910

E-mail: **jtawest@yahoo.com**
URL: http://www.jtalliance.org
Contact: Jose T. Bravo, Exec. Dir.

Labor Studies

3450 ■ Association of Labor Relations Agencies (ALRA)
Natl. Labor Relations Bd.
1099 14th St. NW, Ste.11600
Washington, DC 20570
Ph: **(202)273-1067**
Fax: (202)273-4270
E-mail: lester.heltzer@nlrb.gov
URL: http://www.alra.org
Contact: **Lester A. Heltzer, Pres.**

3451 ■ Labor Notes (LN) (24116)
7435 Michigan Ave.
Detroit, MI 48210
Ph: (313)842-6262
Fax: (313)842-0227
E-mail: **mark@labornotes.org**
URL: http://www.labornotes.org
Contact: Mark Brenner, Dir.

Law Enforcement

3452 ■ National Union of Law Enforcement Associations (NULEA)
7700 Authur Dr.
McCalla, AL 35111
Ph: **(757)630-0202**
Free: **(800)888-4099**
Fax: **(205)277-8122**
E-mail: contact@nulea.com
URL: http://www.nulea.com
Contact: Don McDonald, Pres.

Marine

3453 ■ International Longshoremen's Association (ILA) (23556)
5000 W Side Ave.
North Bergen, NJ 07047
Ph: (212)425-1200
Fax: (212)425-2928
E-mail: **sknott@acdila.org**
URL: http://www.ilaunion.org
Contact: **Stephen Knott, Pres.**

Paints and Finishes

3454 ■ International Union of Painters and Allied Trades (IUPAT) (21898)
7234 Parkway Dr.
Hanover, MD 21076
Ph: (410)564-5900
Free: (800)554-2479
E-mail: mail@iupat.org
URL: http://www.iupat.org/nonflash.htm
Contact: James A. Williams, Gen. Pres.

Pensions

3455 ■ Association of Public Pension Fund Auditors (APPFA)
PO Box 16064
Columbus, OH 43216
E-mail: rbendall@lacera.com
URL: http://www.appfa.org
Contact: Richard Bendall, Pres.

Performing Arts

3456 ■ American Federation of Musicians of the United States and Canada (AFM) (21545)
1501 Broadway, Ste.600
New York, NY 10036
Ph: (212)869-1330

Fax: **(212)764-6134**
E-mail: presoffice@afm.org
URL: http://www.afm.org
Contact: Ray Hair, Pres.

3457 ■ Screen Actors Guild (SAG) (24158)
5757 Wilshire Blvd., 7th Fl.
Los Angeles, CA 90036-3600
Ph: (323)954-1600 **(323)549-6409**
Free: (800)SAG-0767
Fax: (323)549-6603
E-mail: saginfo@sag.org
URL: http://www.sag.org
Contact: **Ken Howard, Pres.**

3458 ■ Stage Directors and Choreographers Society (SDC) (24159)
1501 Broadway, Ste.1701
New York, NY 10036
Ph: (212)391-1070
Free: (800)541-5204
Fax: (212)302-6195
E-mail: info@ssdcweb.org
URL: http://www.sdcweb.org
Contact: **Karen Azenberg, Pres.**

Petroleum

3459 ■ Distribution Contractors Association (DCA) (21914)
101 W Renner Rd., Ste.460
Richardson, TX 75082-2024
Ph: (972)680-0261
Fax: (972)680-0461
E-mail: dca@dca-online.org
URL: http://www.dca-online.org
Contact: **Kevin G. Miller, Pres.**

Postal Service

3460 ■ American Postal Workers Union (APWU) (21562)
1300 L St. NW
Washington, DC 20005
Ph: (202)842-4200 **(202)842-4250**
Fax: (202)842-4297
URL: http://www.apwu.org
Contact: **Cliff Guffey, Pres.**

3461 ■ National Association of Postal Supervisors (NAPS) (21921)
1727 King St., Ste.400
Alexandria, VA 22314-2700
Ph: (703)836-9660
Fax: (703)836-9665
E-mail: napshq@naps.org
URL: http://www.naps.org
Contact: **Louis M. Atkins, Pres.**

Railroads

3462 ■ Brotherhood of Locomotive Engineers and Trainmen (BLET) (24406)
1370 Ontario St., Mezzanine
Cleveland, OH 44113-1701
Ph: (216)241-2630
Fax: (216)241-6516
E-mail: **pierce@ble-t.org**
URL: http://www.ble.org
Contact: **Dennis R. Pierce, Natl. Pres.**

3463 ■ Transportation Communications Union I Brotherhood Railway Carmen Division (BRC/TCU)
3 Res. Pl.
Rockville, MD 20850
Ph: (301)948-4910
Fax: (301)948-1369
URL: http://tcu6760.homestead.com/6760index.htm
Contact: **Robert A. Scardelletti, Pres.**

Retailing

3464 ■ Retail, Wholesale and Department Store Union (RWDSU) (24412)
30 E 29th St.
New York, NY 10016
Ph: **(212)684-5300**
Fax: (212)779-2809
E-mail: **info@rwdsu.org**
URL: http://www.rwdsu.info
Contact: Stuart Applebaum, Pres.

Service

3465 ■ Service Employees International Union (SEIU) (24419)
1800 Massachusetts Ave. NW
Washington, DC 20036
Ph: (202)730-7000 (202)730-7481
Free: (800)424-8592
E-mail: **media@seiu.org**
URL: http://www.seiu.org
Contact: Mary Kay Henry, Pres.

Transportation

3466 ■ Amalgamated Transit Union (ATU) (21594)
5025 Wisconsin Ave. NW
Washington, DC 20016
Ph: (202)537-1645
Free: (888)240-1196
Fax: (202)244-7824
E-mail: dispatch@atu.org
URL: http://www.atu.org
Contact: **Lawrence J. Hanley, Pres.**

3467 ■ Transport Workers Union of America (TWU) (21951)
501 3rd St. NW, 9th Fl.
Washington, DC 20001
Ph: **(202)719-3900**
Fax: **(202)347-0454**
URL: http://www.twu.org
Contact: James C. Little, Pres.

Unions

3468 ■ Coalition of Labor Union Women (CLUW) (23631)
815 16th St. NW, 2nd Fl. S
Washington, DC 20006
Ph: (202)508-6969 **(202)508-6958**
Fax: (202)508-6968
E-mail: **ksee@cluw.org**
URL: http://www.cluw.org
Contact: **Karen See, Pres.**

3469 ■ Coalition of Labor Union Women Center for Education and Research (23632)
815 16th St. NW, 2nd Fl. S
Washington, DC 20006
Ph: (202)508-6969 (202)508-6951
Fax: (202)508-6968
E-mail: getinfo@cluw.org
URL: http://www.cluw.org
Contact: **Karen J. See, Pres.**

Writers

3470 ■ Writers Guild of America West (WGA) (24454)
7000 W Third St.
Los Angeles, CA 90048
Ph: (323)951-4000 **(323)782-4532**
Free: (800)548-4532
Fax: (323)782-4800
URL: http://www.wga.org
Contact: John Wells, Pres.

Chambers of Commerce

3471 ■ American-Uzbekistan Chamber of Commerce (AUCC) (21051)
1300 Connecticut Ave. NW, Ste.501
Washington, DC 20036
Ph: (202)223-1770
E-mail: info@aucconline.com
URL: http://www.aucconline.com
Contact: **Carolyn B. Lamm, Chair**

3472 ■ Argentine-American Chamber of Commerce (AACC)
630 5th Ave., 25th Fl.
Rockefeller Ctr.
New York, NY 10111
Ph: (212)698-2238
Fax: (212)698-2239
E-mail: **info@argentinechamber.org**
URL: http://www.argentinechamber.org
Contact: Claudia Schaefer-Farre, Exec. Dir.

3473 ■ Armenian American Chamber of Commerce (AACC)
225 E Broadway, Ste.313C
Glendale, CA 91205
Ph: (818)247-0196
Fax: (818)247-7668
E-mail: **aacc@armenianchamber.com**
URL: http://www.armenianchamber.org
Contact: **Alissa Asmarian, Pres.**

3474 ■ Belgian American Chamber of Commerce (BACC) (24441)
1177 Ave. of the Americas, 8th Fl.
New York, NY 10018
Ph: (212)541-0779
E-mail: info@belcham.org
URL: http://www.belcham.org
Contact: **Mr. Vincent Herbert, Chm.**

3475 ■ Brazil-U.S. Business Council (BUSBC)
1615 H St. NW
Washington, DC 20062
Ph: **(202)463-5729**
Fax: (202)463-3126
E-mail: brazilcouncil@uschamber.com
URL: http://www.brazilcouncil.org
Contact: Steven Bipes, Exec. Dir.

3476 ■ Brazilian-American Chamber of Commerce (BACC) (21578)
509 Madison Ave., Ste.304
New York, NY 10022
Ph: (212)751-4691
Fax: (212)751-7692
E-mail: info@brazilcham.com
URL: http://www.brazilcham.com
Contact: **John D. Landers, Pres./Chm.**

3477 ■ Chile-U.S. Chamber of Commerce
PO Box 560181
Miami, FL 33256-0181
Ph: (305)890-3547
Fax: (786)472-8799
E-mail: camara@chileus.org
URL: http://www.chileus.org
Contact: **Sebastian Estades, Exec. Sec.**

3478 ■ Council for Community and Economic Research (C2ER) (23696)
PO Box 100127
Arlington, VA 22210
Ph: (703)522-4980
Fax: **(480)393-5098**
E-mail: **info@c2er.org**
URL: http://www.c2er.org
Contact: **Tom Tveidt, Chm.**

3479 ■ European-American Business Council (EABC) (24478)
919 18th St. NW, No. 220
Washington, DC 20006
Ph: (202)828-9104 **(202)828-9101**
Fax: (202)828-9106
URL: http://www.eabc.org
Contact: Michael C. Maibach, Pres./CEO

3480 ■ Federation of Philippine American Chambers of Commerce (FPACC)
Philippine Consulate Bldg., Stes. 700-701
447 Sutter St.
San Francisco, CA 94108-4601
Ph: (415)398-3043
Fax: (415)398-3043
E-mail: president@fpacc.com
URL: http://fpacc.com
Contact: **Jaime Lim, Pres.**

3481 ■ Greek American Chamber of Commerce
PO Box 1147
Kearny, NJ 07032
E-mail: info@greekamericanchamber.com
URL: http://www.greekamericanchamber.com
Contact: **Stavros Antonakakis, Chm.**

3482 ■ Innovation Norway - United States (24515)
655 3rd Ave., Rm. 1810
New York, NY 10017-9111
Ph: (212)885-9700
Fax: (212)885-9710
E-mail: **newyork@innovationnorway.no**
URL: http://www.innovasjonnorge.no/system/Global-
   toppmeny/English
Contact: Kristin Dahle, Dir. for Tourism Americas

3483 ■ Iraqi American Chamber of Commerce and Industry (IACCI) (24517)
15265 Maturin Dr., No. 184
San Diego, CA 92127
Ph: (858)613-9215
Free: (877)684-5162
Fax: (858)408-2624
E-mail: **info@iacci.org**
URL: http://www.i-acci.org
Contact: Yousif Al-Hardan, Exec. VP

3484 ■ Jamaica USA Chamber of Commerce (JAUSACC)
4770 Biscayne Blvd., Ste.1050
Miami, FL 33137
Ph: **(305)576-7888**
Free: **(866)577-3236**
Fax: (305)576-0089
E-mail: **marie@mgillonline.com**
URL: http://www.jamaicausachamber.org
Contact: Ms. Marie Gill, Pres.

3485 ■ Norwegian-American Chamber of Commerce (NACC) (24524)
655 3rd Ave., Ste.1810
New York, NY 10017
Ph: **(212)885-9737**
E-mail: shipping@ntcny.org
URL: http://www.naccusa.org
Contact: Blaine Collins, Pres.

3486 ■ Spain-United States Chamber of Commerce (24527)
Empire State Bldg.
350 5th Ave., Ste.2600
New York, NY 10118
Ph: (212)967-2170
Fax: (212)564-1415
E-mail: info@spainuscc.org
URL: http://www.spainuscc.org
Contact: **Xavier Ruiz, Chm.**

3487 ■ Swedish-American Chambers of Commerce, U.S.A. (SACC-USA) (24499)
2900 K St. NW, Ste.403
Washington, DC 20007
Ph: (202)536-1520
E-mail: info@sacc-usa.org
URL: http://www.sacc-usa.org
Contact: **Therese Linde, Pres.**

3488 ■ U.S.-Angola Chamber of Commerce (USACC) (24501)
1100 17th St. NW, Ste.1000
Washington, DC 20036
Ph: (202)857-0789
Fax: **(202)223-0551**
E-mail: mdacruz@us-angola.org
URL: http://www.us-angola.org
Contact: Maria da Cruz, Exec. Dir.

3489 ■ United States Qatar Business Council (USQBC) (21676)
1341 Connecticut Ave. NW, Ste.4A
Washington, DC 20036
Ph: (202)457-8555
Fax: (202)457-1919

E-mail: **members@usqbc.org**
URL: http://www.usqbc.org
Contact: Ambassador Patrick N. Theros, Pres./Exec.
Dir.

**3490 ■ Venezuelan-American Chamber of
Commerce (24305)**
1600 Ponce de Leon, Ste.1004
Coral Gables, FL 33134
Ph: (786)350-1190
Fax: (786)350-1191
URL: http://www.venamcham.org
Contact: **Lesly Simon, Pres.**

Christian

3491 ■ Kingdom Chamber of Commerce
383 N Kings Highway, Ste.201
Cherry Hill, NJ 08034
Ph: (856)414-0818
Fax: (856)414-6140
E-mail: angela@christianchambercommerce.com
URL: http://www.kingdomchamberofcommerce.org
Status Note: Formerly Christian Chamber of Commerce.

France

**3492 ■ French-American Chamber of
Commerce (FACC) (24521)**
1350 Broadway, Ste.2101
New York, NY 10018
Ph: (212)867-0123
Fax: (212)867-9050
E-mail: info@faccnyc.org
URL: http://www.faccnyc.org
Contact: **Christopher Gallagher, Exec. Dir.**

Gay/Lesbian

**3493 ■ National Gay and Lesbian Chamber of
Commerce (NGLCC) (23114)**
729 15th St. NW, 9th Fl.
Washington, DC 20005
Ph: (202)234-9181
Fax: (202)234-9185
E-mail: info@nglcc.org
URL: http://www.nglcc.org
Contact: Justin G. Nelson, Co-Founder

Greek

**3494 ■ Hellenic-American Chamber of
Commerce (24557)**
780 3rd Ave., 16 Fl.
New York, NY 10017
Ph: (212)629-6380
Fax: (212)564-9281
E-mail: hellenicchamber-nyc@att.net
URL: http://www.hellenicamerican.cc
Contact: **John C. Stratakis, Chm.**

Hispanic

**3495 ■ United States Hispanic Chamber of
Commerce (USHCC) (24528)**
1424 K St. NW, Ste.401
Washington, DC 20005
Ph: (202)842-1212 **(202)715-0481**
Free: (800)874-2286

Fax: (202)842-3221
E-mail: **palomarez@ushcc.com**
URL: http://www.ushcc.com
Contact: Javier Palomarez, Pres./CEO

Indian

**3496 ■ United States Indian American
Chamber of Commerce (USIACC)**
6030 Daybreak Cir., Ste.A150/164
Clarksville, MD 21029
Ph: (240)393-2945
Fax: (410)772-8018
E-mail: **suresh@mayurtech.com**
URL: http://www.usiacc.com
Contact: Suresh Ramachandra, Natl. Pres./CEO

International Standards

**3497 ■ Albanian-American Trade and
Development Association (AATDA) (21119)**
159 E 4th St.
Dunkirk, NY 14048
Ph: (954)802-3166
Fax: (716)366-1516
E-mail: aatda1991@yahoo.com
URL: http://www.albaniabiz.org
Contact: **James V. Elias, Chm./CEO**

Investments

**3498 ■ Managed Funds Association (MFA)
(24334)**
600 14th St. NW, Ste.900
Washington, DC 20005
Ph: **(202)730-2600**
E-mail: **rbaker@managedfunds.org**
URL: http://www.managedfunds.org
Contact: Richard H. Baker, Pres./CEO

Japan

**3499 ■ U.S.-Japan Business Council (USJBC)
(22067)**
2101 L St. NW, Ste.1000
Washington, DC 20037
Ph: (202)728-0068
E-mail: **jwfatheree@usjbc.org**
URL: http://www.usjbc.org
Contact: Jean-Luc Butel, Chm.

Japanese

**3500 ■ Japanese Chamber of Commerce and
Industry of New York (JCCINY) (24544)**
145 W 57th St.
New York, NY 10019
Ph: (212)246-8001
Fax: (212)246-8002
E-mail: info@jcciny.org
URL: http://www.jcciny.org
Contact: **Seiei Ono, Pres.**

Latin America

**3501 ■ Council of the Americas (CoA)
(24582)**
680 Park Ave.
New York, NY 10065
Ph: (212)628-3200
Fax: **(212)517-6247**
E-mail: inforequest@as-coa.org
URL: http://coa.counciloftheamericas.org
Contact: Susan L. Segal, Pres./CEO

Pakistan

**3502 ■ Pakistan Chamber of Commerce USA
(PCC-USA)**
11110 Bellaire Blvd., Ste.202
Houston, TX 77072-2600
Ph: **(832)877-1234 (832)877-0520**
E-mail: **info@pakistanchamberusa.com**
URL: http://www.pcc-usa.org
Contact: **Waseem Rahim, Pres.-Elect**

Tourism

**3503 ■ National Council of State Tourism
Directors (NCSTD) (24579)**
1100 New York Ave. NW, Ste.450
Washington, DC 20005-3934
Ph: (202)408-8422
Fax: (202)408-1255
E-mail: **ncstd@ustravel.org**
URL: http://www.ustravel.org
Contact: George Zimmermann, Chm.

Trade

**3504 ■ American Chamber of Commerce
Executives (ACCE) (21650)**
4875 Eisenhower Ave., Ste.250
Alexandria, VA 22304
Ph: (703)998-0072 **(703)998-3553**
Fax: (703)212-9512
E-mail: mfleming@acce.org
URL: http://www.acce.org
Contact: Mike Fleming, Pres.

Travel

**3505 ■ International Galapagos Tour
Operators Association (IGTOA) (24613)**
PO Box 1713
Lolo, MT 59847
E-mail: **exd@igtoa.org**
URL: http://www.igtoa.org
Contact: **Matt Kareus, Exec. Dir.**

Youth

**3506 ■ U.S. Junior Chamber of Commerce
(USJCC) (24590)**
7447 S Lewis Ave.
Tulsa, OK 74136-6808
Ph: (918)584-2481
Free: (800)JAY-CEES
Fax: (918)584-4422
E-mail: **execdirector@usjaycees.org**
URL: http://www.usjaycees.org
Contact: **Joel Harper, Exec. Dir.**

Agriculture

3507 ■ Alpha Gamma Rho (AGR) (24624)
10101 NW Ambassador Dr.
Kansas City, MO 64153-1395
Ph: (816)891-9200
Fax: (816)891-9401
E-mail: agr@alphagammarho.org
URL: http://www.alphagammarho.org
Contact: **Sandy Belden, Grand Pres.**

Anthropology

3508 ■ Lambda Alpha (21173)
Ball State Univ.
Dept. of Anthropology
Muncie, IN 47306
Ph: (765)285-1575
E-mail: 01bkswartz@bsu.edu
URL: http://www.lambdaalpha.com
Contact: Dr. B.K. Swartz Jr., Exec. Sec.

Athletics

3509 ■ Sigma Delta Pi (21735)
Coll. of Charleston
66 George St.
Charleston, SC 29424-0001
Ph: (843)953-5253 (843)953-6748
Fax: (866)920-7011
E-mail: delmastrom@citadel.edu
URL: http://www.citadel.edu
Contact: Mark P. Del Mastro, Exec. Dir.

Biology

3510 ■ Phi Sigma (22121)
Quinnipiac Univ.
Dept. of Biological Sciences
275 Mt. Carmel Ave.
Hamden, CT 06518-1905
E-mail: **phisigmasociety@gmail.com**
URL: http://www.phisigmasociety.org
Contact: **Catherine Wong, Exec. Co-Dir.**

Chemistry

3511 ■ Iota Sigma Pi (23839)
Angelo State Univ.
Dept. of Chemistry & Biochemistry
Cavness Sci. Bldg., Rm. 204B
San Angelo, TX 76909-0892
Ph: **(325)486-6662**
Fax: (325)942-2184
E-mail: **kathryn.louie@angelo.edu**
URL: http://www.iotasigmapi.info
Contact: Kathryn Louie, Pres.

Communications

3512 ■ Zeta Phi Eta (21793)
95 Park Ave.
Washington, NJ 07882
E-mail: coed@zetaphieta.org
URL: http://zetaphieta.org
Contact: Ms. Tara Sapienza, Exec. Dir.

Computer Science

3513 ■ Upsilon Pi Epsilon Association
(23845)
158 Wetlands Edge Rd.
American Canyon, CA 94503
Ph: **(530)518-8488**
Fax: **(707)647-3560**
E-mail: upe@acm.org
URL: http://upe.acm.org
Contact: Orlando S. Madrigal PhD, Exec. Dir.

Dentistry

3514 ■ Alpha Omega International Dental
Fraternity (24634)
50 W Edmonston Dr., No. 303
Rockville, MD 20852
Ph: **(301)738-6400**
Free: (877)677-8468
Fax: **(301)738-6403**
E-mail: **drmds@spektor.com**
URL: http://www.ao.org
Contact: **Michael D. Spektor, Intl. Pres.-Elect**

3515 ■ Sigma Phi Alpha (SPA) (24669)
Northern Arizona Univ.
PO Box 15065
Flagstaff, AZ 86011-5065
Ph: **(928)523-0520**
Fax: **(928)523-6195**
E-mail: marjorie.reveal@nau.edu
URL: http://www.sigmaphialpha.org
Contact: **Marjorie R. Reveal RDH, Pres.**

Editors

3516 ■ National Panhellenic Conference I
National Panhellenic Editors Conference
(NPEC) (21808)
3901 W 86th St., Ste.398
Indianapolis, IN 46268
Ph: (317)872-3185
Fax: (317)872-3192
E-mail: jsiler@chartertn.net
URL: http://www.npcwomen.org/about/npc.aspx
Contact: Mrs. Jennifer M. Siler, Pres.

Education

3517 ■ Alpha Delta Kappa (24646)
1615 W 92nd St.
Kansas City, MO 64114
Ph: (816)363-5525
Free: (800)247-2311
Fax: (816)363-4010
E-mail: headquarters@alphadeltakappa.org
URL: http://www.alphadeltakappa.org
Contact: **Arnold Bjorkman, Pres.**

3518 ■ Delphi Foundation (24647)
2020 Pennsylvania Ave. NW, No. 355
Washington, DC 20006-1811
Ph: (202)558-2801
Free: (800)587-3728
Fax: (202)318-2277
E-mail: **helpdesk@dlp.org**
URL: http://sites.dlp.org/sites/national
Contact: **Chris Newman, Exec. Dir.**

3519 ■ National Kappa Kappa Iota (21787)
1875 E 15th St.
Tulsa, OK 74104-4610
Ph: (918)744-0389
Free: (800)678-0389
Fax: (918)744-0578
E-mail: kappa@galstar.com
URL: http://nationalkappakappaiota.org
Contact: **Marcelle Bridgeman, Pres.**

3520 ■ Pi Lambda Theta (23867)
408 N Union St.
PO Box 7888
Bloomington, IN 47407-7888
Ph: **(812)339-1156**
Free: **(800)766-1156**
Fax: **(812)339-0018**
E-mail: **plt@pdkintl.org**
URL: http://www.pilambda.org
Contact: Elizabeth Douglass, Pres.

Engineering

3521 ■ Alpha Epsilon (AE)
Univ. of Illinois in Urbana-Champaign
Dept. of Agricultural and Biological Engg.
1304 W Pennsylvania Ave.
Urbana, IL 61801
Ph: **(217)333-3570**
Fax: **(217)244-0323**
E-mail: **oldani1@illinois.edu**
URL: http://www.alpha-epsilon.org
Contact: **Anna Oldani, Pres.**

3522 ■ Eta Kappa Nu (HKN) (23869)
445 Hoes Ln.
Piscataway, NJ 08854
Free: **(800)406-2590**
Fax: **(800)864-2051**

E-mail: info@hkn.org
URL: http://www.hkn.org
Contact: **Stephen M. Goodnick, Pres.**

Fraternities and Sororities

3523 ■ **Association of Fraternity Advisors (AFA) (24475)**
9640 N Augusta Dr., Ste.433
Carmel, IN 46032
Ph: (317)876-1632 (317)876-1870
Fax: (317)876-3981
E-mail: info@fraternityadvisors.org
URL: http://www.fraternityadvisors.org
Contact: **Monica Miranda Smalls, Pres.**

3524 ■ **Fraternity Executives Association (FEA) (23889)**
c/o Sydney N. Dunn, Admin.
1750 Royalton Dr.
Carmel, IN 46032
Ph: **(317)496-2411**
E-mail: fea.inc@gmail.com
URL: http://www.fea-inc.org
Contact: Mark A. Williams CAE, Pres.

3525 ■ **National Panhellenic Conference (NPC) (21817)**
3901 W 86th St., Ste.398
Indianapolis, IN 46268
Ph: (317)872-3185
Fax: (317)872-3192
E-mail: npccentral@npcwomen.org
URL: http://www.npcwomen.org
Contact: Nicki Meneley, Exec. Dir.

3526 ■ **Professional Fraternity Association (PFA) (24684)**
1011 San Jacinto, Ste.205
Austin, TX 78701
Ph: (512)789-9530
E-mail: info@profraternity.org
URL: **http://www.professionalfraternity.org**
Contact: Michael Abraham, Exec. Dir.

Geology

3527 ■ **Sigma Gamma Epsilon (SGE) (21850)**
Univ. of Norther Iowa
Dept. of Earth Sci.
Cedar Falls, IA 50614-0335
Ph: **(319)273-2707**
Fax: **(319)273-7124**
E-mail: **walters@uni.edu**
URL: **http://www.sigmagammaepsilon.com**
Contact: **Dr. James C. Walters, Pres.**

Honor Societies

3528 ■ **Omicron Delta Kappa Society (ODK) (24515)**
224 McLaughlin St.
Lexington, VA 24450-2002
Ph: **(540)458-5336**
Free: **(877)ODK-NHDQ**
Fax: **(540)458-5342**
E-mail: odknhdq@odk.org
URL: http://www.odk.org
Contact: Thomas G. Goodale, Exec. Dir.

3529 ■ **Phi Beta Delta (23926)**
1630 Connecticut Ave. NW, 3rd Fl.
Washington, DC 20009
Ph: (202)518-2052 (202)544-3501
Fax: (202)387-4823
E-mail: **staff@phibetadelta.org**
URL: http://www.phibetadelta.org
Contact: Yvonne Captain-Hidalgo PhD, Exec. Dir.

3530 ■ **Phi Kappa Phi (23927)**
7576 Goodwood Blvd.
Baton Rouge, LA 70806
Ph: (225)388-4917
Free: (800)804-9880
Fax: (225)388-4900
E-mail: info@phikappaphi.org
URL: http://www.phikappaphi.org
Contact: **William A. Bloodworth Jr., Pres.**

3531 ■ **Sigma Alpha Lambda (SAL) (24519)**
501 Village Green Pkwy., Ste.1
Bradenton, FL 34209
Ph: (941)866-5614
Fax: (941)827-2924
E-mail: info@sigmaalphalambda.org
URL: http://www.salhonors.org
Contact: **D. Mark Pickhardt, Exec. Dir.**

Insurance

3532 ■ **Gamma Iota Sigma (23928)**
PO Box 227
Norristown, PA 19404
Ph: (484)991-4471
URL: http://www.gammaiotasigma.org
Contact: **Noelle Codispoti, Exec. Dir.**

Japanese

3533 ■ **Japanese National Honor Society (JNHS) (24521)**
PO Box 3719
Boulder, CO 80307-3719
E-mail: jfujimoto@ou.edu
URL: http://www.ncjlt.net
Contact: Junko Fujimoto, Dir.

Law

3534 ■ **Delta Theta Phi (21883)**
PO Box 117
Elyria, OH 44036-0117
Ph: (919)866-4667
Free: (800)783-2600
E-mail: dtpdirector@gmail.com
URL: http://www.deltathetaphi.org
Contact: **Vito M. Evola, Exec. Dir.**

Management

3535 ■ **Sigma Iota Epsilon (SIE) (21890)**
Colorado State Univ.
312 Rockwell Hall
Fort Collins, CO 80521
Ph: (970)491-6265 (970)491-7200
Fax: (970)491-3522
E-mail: **jimf@lamar.colostate.edu**
URL: http://www.sienational.com
Contact: Dr. G. James Francis, Pres.

Marketing

3536 ■ **Mu Kappa Tau (MKT) (24535)**
Univ. of Wisconsin-Madison
Grainger Hall
975 Univ. Ave.
Madison, WI 53706
E-mail: mktpresident@gmail.com
URL: **http://www.wix.com/mukappatau/mkt**
Contact: Seonah Iverson, Pres.

Mathematics

3537 ■ **Pi Mu Epsilon (PME) (24539)**
Hendrix Coll.
Dept. of Mathematics and Cmpt. Sci.
Conway, AR 72032
Ph: **(501)450-1253**
E-mail: **sutherlandd@hendrix.edu**
URL: http://www.pme-math.org
Contact: **David C. Sutherland, Pres.**

Medicine

3538 ■ **Alpha Epsilon Delta (AED) (24768)**
Texas Christian Univ.
Box 298810
Fort Worth, TX 76129
Ph: **(817)257-4550**
Fax: **(817)257-0201**
E-mail: **aed@nationalaed.org**
URL: http://nationalaed.org
Contact: Rev. Joseph L. Walter CSC, Pres.

3539 ■ **Phi Chi Medical Fraternity (PCMF)**
2039 Ridgeview Dr.
Floyds Knobs, IN 47119
Ph: **(812)923-7270**
E-mail: **phichi@phi-chi.org**
URL: **http://www.phichimed.org/public/history/**
  history.htm
Contact: **Dana Murphy, Sec.**

Military

3540 ■ **National Society of Pershing Rifles (NSPR) (24740)**
PO Box 25057
Baton Rouge, LA 70894
E-mail: nhq@pershingriflessociety.org
URL: http://www.pershingriflessociety.org
Contact: **Major Gen. Rebecca Scholand, Natl. Commander**

Music

3541 ■ **Society of Pi Kappa Lambda (24556)**
Capital Univ.
Conservatory of Music
1 Coll. and Main
Columbus, OH 43209
Ph: (614)236-7211
Fax: (614)236-6935
E-mail: **execdir@pikappalambda.org**
URL: http://www.pikappalambda.org
Contact: Dr. Mark Lochstampfor, Exec. Dir.

Pharmacy

3542 ■ **Alpha Zeta Omega (AZO) (24567)**
140 Hepburn Rd., Apt. 15B
Clifton, NJ 07012
E-mail: **salsarx@optonline.net**
URL: http://www.alphazetaomega.net
Contact: **Leonardo Ortega, Supreme Dir.**

3543 ■ **Phi Delta Chi (24570)**
116 N Lafayette, Ste.B
South Lyon, MI 48178
Free: (800)PDC-1883
Fax: (248)486-1906
E-mail: execdir@phideltachi.org
URL: http://www.phideltachi.org
Contact: Kenny Walkup, Exec. Dir.

Physical Education

3544 ■ Phi Epsilon Kappa (23982)
901 W New York St.
Indianapolis, IN 46202
Ph: (317)627-8745
Fax: (317)278-2041
E-mail: jvessel@iupui.edu
URL: http://www.phiepsilonkappa.org
Contact: Jeff Vessely, Exec. Dir.

Science

3545 ■ Sigma Delta Epsilon, Graduate Women in Science (SDE/GWIS) (23995)
PO Box 240607
St. Paul, MN 55124
Ph: (952)236-9112 (319)384-1816
E-mail: gwised@mac.com
URL: http://www.gwis.org
Contact: **Ms. Dee McManus, Exec. Dir.**

Service Fraternities

3546 ■ Alpha Phi Omega National Service Fraternity (21938)
14901 E 42nd St.
Independence, MO 64055-7347
Ph: (816)373-8667
Fax: (816)373-5975
E-mail: executive.director@apo.org
URL: http://www.apo.org
Contact: **Mark Stratton, Pres.**

Service Sororities

3547 ■ Beta Sigma Phi (24003)
1800 W 91st Pl.
Kansas City, MO 64114
Ph: (816)444-6800
Free: (800)821-3989
E-mail: **laura@betasigmaphi.org**
URL: http://www.betasigmaphi.org
Contact: Laura Ross Wingfield, Contact

3548 ■ Gamma Alpha Omega Sorority
PO Box 427
Tempe, AZ 85280
E-mail: national_president@gammaalphaomega.com
URL: http://www.gammaalphaomega.com
Contact: **Ms. Thasanee McGuffey, Natl. Pres.**

3549 ■ Gamma Sigma Sigma (21923)
PO Box 248
Rindge, NH 03461-0248
Free: (800)585-7508
Fax: (216)803-3065
E-mail: **info@gammasigmasigma.org**
URL: http://www.gammasigmasigma.org
Contact: Keli Connor, Pres.

Social Fraternities

3550 ■ Alpha Psi Lambda National (21968)
PO Box 804835
Chicago, IL 60680

E-mail: **nationaloffice@alphapsilambda.net**
URL: http://www.alphapsilambda.net
Contact: Michelle L. Maday, Natl. Pres.

3551 ■ Delta Lambda Phi National Social Fraternity (21976)
2020 Pennsylvania Ave. NW, No. 355
Washington, DC 20006-1811
Ph: (202)527-9453 (202)558-2801
Free: (800)587-FRAT
Fax: (202)318-2277
E-mail: helpdesk@dlp.org
URL: http://sites.dlp.org/sites/national
Contact: **Alexandre Chepeaux, Natl. Sec.**

3552 ■ Kappa Delta Rho (21986)
331 S Main St.
Greensburg, PA 15601-3111
Ph: (724)838-7100
Free: (800)536-5371
Fax: (724)838-7101
E-mail: president@kdr.com
URL: http://www.kdr.com
Contact: **Brian J. Stumm, Pres.**

3553 ■ Pi Beta Phi (24053)
1154 Town and Country Commons Dr.
Town and Country, MO 63017-8200
Ph: (636)256-0680
Fax: (636)256-8095
E-mail: **juli@pibetaphi.org**
URL: http://www.pibetaphi.org
Contact: Juli Willeman, Exec. Dir.

3554 ■ Pi Delta Psi Fraternity (PDPsi)
PO Box 520269
Flushing, NY 11352-0269
Fax: (917)421-3900
E-mail: president@pideltapsi.com
URL: http://www.pideltapsi.com
Contact: **Kenji Yanagisawa, Pres.**

3555 ■ Pi Kappa Alpha (21993)
8347 W Range Cove
Memphis, TN 38125
Ph: (901)748-1868
Fax: (901)748-3100
E-mail: **pikeinfo@pikes.org**
URL: http://www.pka.com
Contact: Justin A. Buck, Exec. VP/CEO

3556 ■ Pi Lambda Phi Fraternity (PiLam) (24652)
60 Newtown Rd., No. 118
Danbury, CT 06810
Ph: (203)740-1044
Free: (800)394-7573
Fax: (203)740-1644
E-mail: headquarters@pilambdaphi.org
URL: http://www.pilambdaphi.org
Contact: **Jeff Buhler, Pres.**

3557 ■ Sigma Beta Rho Fraternity (24060)
PO Box 4668
New York, NY 10163
Free: (888)333-1449
Fax: (484)233-7117
E-mail: kunal.patel@sigmabetarho.com
URL: http://www.sigmabetarho.com
Contact: **Ari Stillman, Pres.**

3558 ■ Sigma Phi Epsilon (SIGEP) (24660)
310 S Blvd.
PO Box 1901
Richmond, VA 23218
Ph: (804)353-1901 **(804)612-1417**
Free: (800)767-1901
Fax: (804)359-8160
E-mail: journal@sigep.net
URL: http://www.sigep.org
Contact: Brian Warren, Exec. Dir.

3559 ■ Tau Kappa Epsilon (TKE) (24666)
7439 Woodland Dr.
Indianapolis, IN 46268
Ph: (317)872-6533
Fax: (317)875-8353
E-mail: tkeogc@tke.org
URL: http://www.tke.org
Contact: Joyce-Ann Anderson, Exec. Sec.

Social Sororities

3560 ■ Alpha Sigma Tau (AST) (22022)
3334 Founders Rd.
Indianapolis, IN 46268
Ph: (205)978-2179 (317)613-7575
Free: (877)505-1899
Fax: **(317)613-7111**
E-mail: ccovington@alphasigmatau.org
URL: http://www.alphasigmatau.org
Contact: Christina Duggan Covington, Pres.

3561 ■ Gamma Phi Beta (22033)
12737 E Euclid Dr.
Centennial, CO 80111-6437
Ph: (303)799-1874
Fax: (303)799-1876
E-mail: **lveldhuizen@gammaphibeta.org**
URL: http://www.gammaphibeta.org
Contact: **Laurie Velhuizen, Exec. Dir.**

3562 ■ Kappa Kappa Gamma (22386)
PO Box 38
Columbus, OH 43216-0038
Ph: (614)228-6515
Free: (866)KKG-1870
Fax: (614)228-7809
E-mail: kkghq@kappa.org
URL: http://kappakappagamma.org
Contact: **Ann Truesdell, Exec. Dir.**

Sororities

3563 ■ Sigma Lambda Gamma National Sorority
125 E Zeller St., Suites D & E
North Liberty, IA 52317
Ph: (319)626-7679
Free: (888)486-2382
Fax: (319)626-7688
E-mail: director@sigmalambdagamma.com
URL: http://www.sigmalambdagamma.com
Contact: Mary Peterson, Exec. Dir.

3564 ■ Theta Nu Xi Multicultural Sorority
c/o Rashida Rawls, Dir. of Communications
PO Box 32987
Phoenix, AZ 85064
E-mail: **national.administrator@thetanuxi.org**
URL: http://thetanuxi.org
Contact: Monica Copeland, Admin.

Actors

3565 ■ Beyond the Rainbow (22415)
PO Box 31672
St. Louis, MO 63131-0672
Ph: (314)799-1724
Fax: **(314)596-4549**
E-mail: elaine@beyondtherainbow2oz.com
URL: http://www.beyondtherainbow2oz.com
Contact: Elaine Willingham, Founder

Animals

3566 ■ Princess Kitty Fan Club (PKFC) (24959)
PO Box 430784
Miami, FL 33243-0784
Ph: **(305)661-0528**
E-mail: **info@princesskittyinc.com**
URL: **http://www.princesskitty.com**
Contact: Karen Payne, Pres.

Cartoons

3567 ■ Disneyana Fan Club (DFC) (23590)
PO Box 19212
Irvine, CA 92623-9212
Ph: (714)731-4705
E-mail: **info@disneyanafanclub.org**
URL: http://www.disneyanafanclub.org
Contact: Mr. Gary Schaengold, Pres.
Status Note: Formerly National Fantasy Fan Club for Disneyana Enthusiasts.

Comedy

3568 ■ Three Stooges Fan Club (TSFC) (25019)
PO Box 747
Gwynedd Valley, PA 19437
Ph: (267)468-0810
E-mail: **garystooge@aol.com**
URL: http://www.stoogeum.com
Contact: Gary Lassin, Pres.

Humor

3569 ■ Marx Brotherhood (22509)
335 Fieldstone Dr.
New Hope, PA 18938-1012
E-mail: **webcontact@marx-brothers.org**
URL: http://www.marx-brothers.org
Contact: Paul G. Wesolowski, Dir.

Music

3570 ■ Alabama Fan Club (AFC) (22202)
PO Box 680529
Fort Payne, AL 35968-1606
Ph: (256)845-1646
Free: (800)557-8223
Fax: (256)845-5650
E-mail: **contact@thealabamaband.com**
URL: http://www.thealabamaband.com

3571 ■ Always Patsy Cline World Wide Fan Organization (APC) (23636)
PO Box 462
Joelton, TN 37080
URL: http://www.patsycline.info/apc.html
Contact: Mel Dick, Contact

3572 ■ Amy Beth Fan Club (ABFC) (23637)
Peridot Records
PO Box 8846
Cranston, RI 02920
Ph: (401)785-2677
E-mail: **peridot@peridotrecords.com**
URL: http://www.peridotrecords.com/home.html
Contact: T. Parravano, Dir.

3573 ■ Beach Boys Fan Club (BBFC) (23640)
631 N Stephanie St., No. 546
Henderson, NV 89014
E-mail: webworksz95@beachboysfanclub.com
URL: http://www.beachboysfanclub.com
Contact: Brian Wilson, Contact

3574 ■ Billy "Crash" Craddock Fan Club (BCCFC) (23644)
4101 Pickfair Rd.
Springfield, IL 62703
Ph: (336)339-9928
E-mail: **info@billycrashcraddock.com**
URL: http://www.billycrashcraddock.net
Contact: Judy Plummer, Pres.

3575 ■ Charley Pride Fan Club (CPFC) (22197)
3198 Royal Ln., No. 200
Dallas, TX 75229
Ph: (214)350-8477
Fax: (214)350-0534
E-mail: **john@charleypride.com**
URL: http://www.charleypride.com
Contact: John Daines, Contact

3576 ■ Chicago True Advocates (CTA)
PO Box 195
Landing, NJ 07850
E-mail: **roatz1@gmail.com**
URL: http://www.ctaofficialfanclub.net
Contact: Bob Dillon, Pres.

3577 ■ Chris LeDoux International Fan Club (CLIFC) (25019)
PO Box 41052
San Jose, CA 95160
E-mail: **robfairjr@gmail.com**
URL: http://www.chrisledoux.com/home.cfm
Contact: Rob Fair, Pres.

3578 ■ Gene Pitney International Fan Club (GPIFC) (22289)
6201 - 39th Ave.
Kenosha, WI 53142
URL: http://www.genepitney.com
Contact: **Dave Guida, Contact**

3579 ■ George Strait Fan Club (GSFC)
PO Box 2119
Hendersonville, TN 37077
Ph: (615)824-7176
Fax: (615)826-7052
E-mail: **customerservice@georgestraitfans.com**
URL: http://www.georgestrait.com
Contact: Anita O'Brian, Pres.

3580 ■ Glenn Miller Birthplace Society (GMBS) (22577)
122 W Clark St.
PO Box 61
Clarinda, IA 51632
Ph: (712)542-2461
Fax: **(712)542-2868**
E-mail: **gmbs@glennmiller.org**
URL: http://www.glennmiller.org
Contact: Marvin Negley, Pres.

3581 ■ Hank Williams International Fan Club (25060)
103 Summit Cir.
Daphne, AL 36526
Ph: **(251)626-1645**
E-mail: **johnr749@bellsouth.net**
URL: http://www.hankwilliamsinternationalfanclub.com
Contact: **Ed Kirby, Pres.**

3582 ■ International Crosby Circle (ICC)
5608 N 34th St.
Arlington, VA 22207
Ph: (703)241-5608
E-mail: **wigbing@hotmail.com**
URL: http://www.mdcrampton.f2s.com/index.html
Contact: Wig Wiggins, Contact

3583 ■ Kate Smith Commemorative Society (25079)
PO Box 242
Syracuse, NY 13214-0242
E-mail: **suesann413@aol.com**
URL: http://www.katesmith.org
Contact: Rev. Raymond B. Wood, Pres.

3584 ■ KISS Rocks Fan Club (KRFC)
15 Maple Rd.
Briarcliff Manor, NY 10510
E-mail: **jon@kissrocks.net**
URL: http://www.kissrocks.net
Contact: Jon Rubin, Pres./Founder

3585 ■ Lesley Gore International Fan Club (22269)
PO Box 1548
Ocean Pines, MD 21811
Ph: (410)208-6369
Fax: (410)208-6967
E-mail: **lesley@lesleygorefanclub.com**
URL: http://lesleygorefanclub.com/index.html
Contact: Jack Natoli, Pres.

3586 ■ Official Fan Club of the Grand Ole Opry (22299)
2804 Opryland Dr.
Nashville, TN 37214
Ph: (615)871-OPRY (615)871-5043
Free: (800)SEE-OPRY
Fax: (615)458-8540
E-mail: **oprymail@opry.com**
URL: http://www.opry.com

3587 ■ Roy Rogers - Dale Evans Collectors Association (RRDECA)
PO Box 1166
Portsmouth, OH 45662
Ph: (740)353-0900 (740)354-7711
E-mail: **gardondavis@yahoo.com**
URL: http://www.royrogersfestival.org
Contact: Nancy Horsley, Exec. Sec.

Sports

3588 ■ Cleveland Hockey Booster Club (CHBC) (25137)
c/o Marsha Hess
13118 Tyler Ave.
Cleveland, OH 44111
Ph: (216)251-0606
E-mail: **bsjhockey@yahoo.com**
URL: http://www.clevelandhockeybc.org
Contact: **Bonnie Johnson, Pres.**

3589 ■ Dale Jarrett Fan Club (DJFC) (22381)
PO Box 279
Conover, NC 28613
Ph: (828)464-8818
Free: (888)325-3527
Fax: (828)465-5088
E-mail: **patb@dalejarrett.com**
URL: **http://www.dalejarrettfans.com**

3590 ■ Hartford Whalers Booster Club (HWBC) (22449)
PO Box 273
Hartford, CT 06141
Ph: **(860)956-3839** (860)890-1301
E-mail: **forever11@snet.net**
URL: http://www.whalerwatch.com
Contact: **Marty Evtushek, Pres.**

3591 ■ Los Angeles Kings Booster Club (LAKBC) (25141)
555 N Nash St.
El Segundo, CA 90245
E-mail: **prez@lakbc.com**
URL: http://www.lakbc.com
Contact: Kim Southard, Pres.

3592 ■ National Hockey League Booster Clubs (NHLBC) (22455)
PO Box 805
St. Louis, MO 63188
E-mail: **heythars@cox.net**
URL: **http://www.nhlboosterclub.org**
Contact: **Melinda Harty, Pres.**

3593 ■ Philadelphia Flyers Fan Club (PFFC) (22458)
PO Box 610
Plymouth Meeting, PA 19462
E-mail: flyers212@verizon.net
URL: http://www.flyersfanclub.org
Contact: Joe Fisher III, Pres.

3594 ■ Pittsburgh Penguins Booster Club (PPBC) (22459)
PO Box 903
Pittsburgh, PA 15230
E-mail: **pens_bc@lycos.com**
URL: http://www.members.tripod.com/~pens_bc/main.html
Contact: Melinda Harty, Pres.

3595 ■ Washington Capitals Fan Club (WCFC) (25148)
PO Box 2802
Springfield, VA 22152-0802
E-mail: nancy@capsfanclub.org
URL: **http://67.199.38.190**
Contact: Nancy Rogers, Pres.

Star Trek

3596 ■ STARFLEET (25217)
PO Box 8213
Bangor, ME 04402
Free: (888)734-8735
E-mail: **cs@sfi.org**
URL: http://www.sfi.org
Contact: **Dave Blaser, Commander**

3597 ■ Starfleet Command (SFC) (24392)
PO Box 33565
Indianapolis, IN 46203-0565
Ph: (317)508-9351
Fax: (317)845-5095
E-mail: **cadv@starfleet-command.com**
URL: **http://www.sfcq1.com**
Contact: Roseann Packer, Chief Advisor

Television

3598 ■ Rin Tin Tin Fan Club (25169)
PO Box 27
Crockett, TX 75835
Ph: (936)545-0471
E-mail: **rintintin@rintintin.com**
URL: http://www.rintintin.com
Contact: Ms. Daphne Hereford, Pres./CEO

3599 ■ Six of One Club: The Prisoner Appreciation Society (25043)
871 Clover Dr.
North Wales, PA 19454-2749
Ph: (215)699-2527
E-mail: **sixofone@netreach.net**
URL: http://www.netreach.net/~sixofone
Contact: Bruce A. Clark, Coor.

Association names are listed alphabetically by name and by keyword subheading (in bold). Index numbers refer to entry numbers, not to page numbers. A star ★ before an entry number signifies that the name is not listed separately, but is mentioned or described within the entry indicated by the entry number.

NUMERIC

1-800 Amer. Free Trade Assn. **[891]**, PO Box 1049, Burlington, VT 05402-1049, (802)383-0816

2nd Infantry Div., Korean War Veterans Alliance **[3072]**, c/o Ralph Hockley, Sec., 10027 Pine Forest Rd., Houston, TX 77042-1531, (713)334-0271

25th Infantry Div. Assn. **[3051]**, PO Box 7, Flourtown, PA 19031-0007

41pounds.org **[1059]**, 41 W Saratoga St., Ferndale, MI 48220

509th Parachute Infantry Assn. **[3082]**, PO Box 860, Huntsville, AL 35804-0860

911 Indus. Alliance **[195]**, c/o Reid French, Vice Chm., 1611 N Kent St., Ste. 802, Arlington, VA 22209, (202)737-6001

1394 High Performance Serial Bus Trade Assn. **[846]**, 315 Lincoln, Ste. E, Mukilteo, WA 98275, (425)870-6574

A

Abdominal Surgeons; Amer. Soc. of **[2598]**

Abilities! **[2053]**, 201 I.U. Willets Rd., Albertson, NY 11507-1599, (516)465-1400

Abortion
Elliot Inst. **[1869]**
Natl. Network of Abortion Funds **[1870]**

Abrahamic Alliance Intl. **[2945]**, 1900 Camden Ave., Ste. 201-E, San Jose, CA 95124, (408)728-8943

Abriendo Mentes **[2208]**, Opening Minds Latin America, 3310 Crosspark Ln., Houston, TX 77007, (713)893-8334

Acad. of Amer. Poets **[1844]**, 75 Maiden Ln., Ste. 901, New York, NY 10038, (212)274-0343

Acad. of Certified Archivists **[57]**, 1450 Western Ave., Ste. 101, Albany, NY 12203, (518)694-8471

Acad. of Dental Materials **[2359]**, c/o Thomas Hilton, Treas., Oregon Hea. and Sci. Univ., School of Dentistry, Dept. of Restorative Dentistry, 611 SW Campus Dr., Portland, OR 97239, (503)494-8672

Acad. for Educational Development **[1602]**, 1825 Connecticut Ave. NW, Washington, DC 20009-5721, (202)884-8000

Acad. of Motion Picture Arts and Sciences **[319]**, 8949 Wilshire Blvd., Beverly Hills, CA 90211, (310)247-3000

Acad. of Natural Sciences **[1502]**, 1900 Benjamin Franklin Pkwy., Philadelphia, PA 19103-1195, (215)299-1000

Acad. of Operative Dentistry **[2360]**, c/o Dr. Richard G. Stevenson, III, Sec., PO Box 34425, Los Angeles, CA 90034, (310)794-4387

Acad. of Parish Clergy **[2982]**, 2249 Florinda St., Sarasota, FL 34231-4414, (941)922-8633

Acad. of Rehabilitative Audiology **[2449]**, PO Box 2323, Albany, NY 12220-0323

Acad. of Spirituality and Paranormal Stud., Inc. **[1515]**, PO Box 614, Bloomfield, CT 06002-0614, (860)242-4593

AcademyHealth **[2424]**, 1150 17th St. NW, Ste. 600, Washington, DC 20036, (202)292-6700

ACCESS Hea. Intl. **[2428]**, 3053 P St. NW, Washington, DC 20007

Accounting
Amer. Soc. of Women Accountants **[1]**

Amer. Woman's Soc. of Certified Public Accountants **[2]**
Assn. of Chartered Accountants in the U.S. **[3]**
Assn. of Insolvency and Restructuring Advisors **[4]**
DFK International/USA **[5]**
Inst. of Internal Auditors **[6]**
Intl. Fed. of Accountants **[7]**
Intl. Soc. of Filipinos in Finance and Accounting **[8]**
Natl. Soc. of Accountants for Cooperatives **[9]**
Professional Assn. of Small Bus. Accountants **[10]**
Soc. of Depreciation Professionals **[11]**

Accreditation
Amer. Commn. for Accreditation of Reflexology Educ. and Training **[1567]**
Healthcare Laundry Accreditation Coun. **[537]**

Accredited Gemologists Assn. **[530]**, 3315 Juanita St., San Diego, CA 92105, (619)501-5444

ACM SIGGRAPH **[1441]**, PO Box 30777, New York, NY 10087-0777, (212)626-0500

Act for Africa Intl. **[2209]**, PO Box 2031, Manassas, VA 20108, (571)212-6167

Action for Children - Zambia **[1915]**, 20855 Kensington Blvd., Lakeville, MN 55044

Action Intl. Ministries **[2924]**, PO Box 398, Mountlake Terrace, WA 98043-0398, (425)775-4800

Actors
Beyond the Rainbow **[3565]**
Intl. Crosby Circle **[3582]**

Acupuncture
Amer. Abdominal Acupuncture Medical Assn. **[2283]**
Coun. for Acupuncture Res. and Educ. **[2284]**
Amer. Assn. of Traditional Chinese Veterinary Medicine **[2290]**
Coun. of Chiropractic Acupuncture **[2342]**

ACUTA: The Assn. for Communications Tech. Professionals in Higher Educ. **[1634]**, 152 W Zandale Dr., Ste. 200, Lexington, KY 40503, (859)278-3338

ADARA: Professionals Networking for Excellence in Ser. Delivery with Individuals who are Deaf or Hard of Hearing **[2450]**, PO Box 480, Myersville, MD 21773

Addiction Medicine; Amer. Soc. of **[2596]**

Adirondack Trail Improvement Soc. **[3424]**, PO Box 565, Keene Valley, NY 12943, (518)576-9949

Administration
Amer. Assn. of School Personnel Administrators **[1559]**
Amer. Conf. of Academic Deans **[1560]**
Assn. of Coll. and Univ. Auditors **[1561]**
Natl. Orientation Directors Assn. **[1562]**
Assn. for the Advancement of Intl. Educ. **[1644]**
Natl. Assn. of Peoplecultural Engg. Prog. Advocates **[1615]**

Administrative Services
AFL-CIO I SEIU I District 925 **[3434]**
Assn. for Financial Tech. **[12]**
Assn. of Healthcare Administrative Professionals **[13]**
Black Data Processing Associates **[14]**
Intl. Virtual Assistants Assn. **[15]**

Off. Bus. Center Assn. Intl. **[16]**
Off. and Professional Employees Intl. Union **[3435]**
Soc. of Corporate Secretaries and Governance Professionals **[17]**

Admissions
Amer. Assn. of Collegiate Registrars and Admissions Officers **[1563]**

Adopt-a-Village Intl. **[2007]**, PO Box 26599, Colorado Springs, CO 80936, (719)492-8736

Adopt a Building Prog. **[★2047]**

Adoption
Concerned Persons for Adoption **[1871]**
Joint Coun. on Intl. Children's Services **[1872]**
Natl. Coun. for Adoption **[1873]**
Oper. Identity **[1874]**
Stars of David Intl. **[1875]**
Catholic Guardian Soc. and Home Bur. **[1931]**

ADSC: The Intl. Assn. of Found. Drilling **[214]**, 8445 Freeport Pkwy., Ste. 325, Irving, TX 75063, (469)359-6000

Advanced Biofuels Assn. **[391]**, 2099 Pennsylvania Ave. NW Ste. 100, Washington, DC 20006, (202)469-5140

Advancing Human Rights **[2658]**, 277 Park Ave., 49th Fl., New York, NY 10172, (212)207-5042

Adventist
Adventist World Aviation **[1876]**

Adventist World Aviation **[1876]**, PO Box 251, Berrien Springs, MI 49103-0251, (269)473-0135

Advertising
Advt. Club of New York **[18]**
Antique Advt. Assn. of Am. **[19]**
Mobile Marketing Assn. **[20]**
Natl. Agri-Marketing Assn. **[21]**
Point-of-Purchase Advt. Intl. **[22]**
Retail Advt. and Marketing Assn. **[23]**
Newspaper Target Marketing Coalition **[626]**

Advertising Auditors
Publishers Info. Bur. **[24]**

Advt. Club of New York **[18]**, 235 Park Ave. S, 6th Fl., New York, NY 10003-1450, (212)533-8080

Advocates Intl. **[1321]**, 9691 Main St., Ste. D, Fairfax, VA 22031-3754, (703)894-1084

Aerospace
Air Transport Assn. of Am. **[25]**
Amer. Aviation Historical Soc. **[3083]**
Aviation Distributors and Mfrs. Assn. **[26]**
Aviation Indus. CBT Comm. **[27]**
F-4 Phantom II Soc. **[3084]**
Flight Safety Found. **[28]**
Helicopter Found. Intl. **[29]**
High Frontier **[1387]**
Intl. Assn. of Space Entrepreneurs **[30]**
Intl. Soc. of Transport Aircraft Trading **[31]**
Intl. Wheelchair Aviators **[3085]**
League of World War I Aviation Historians **[3086]**
Natl. Aeronautic Assn. **[32]**
Natl. Aircraft Resale Assn. **[33]**
Natl. InterCollegiate Flying Assn. **[3087]**
Org. of Black Airline Pilots **[34]**
Pilatus Owners and Pilots Assn. **[35]**
Planetary Soc. **[1388]**
Professional Aviation Maintenance Assn. **[36]**

Regional Airline Assn. [37]
Soc. of Antique Modelers [3088]
Space Stud. Inst. [1389]
Tuskegee Airmen, Inc. [3047]
U.S. Hang Gliding and Paragliding Assn. [3250]
U.S. Pilots Assn. [38]
World Airline Historical Soc. [3089]
Intl. Scale Soaring Assn. [3216]
Space Topic Stud. Unit [3234]

Aerospace Medicine
Airlines Medical Directors Assn. [2285]
Affordable Housing Investors Coun. [131], c/o Toni
Sylvester, Exec. Admin., PO Box 986, Irmo, SC
29063, (803)781-1638
Affordable Housing Tax Credit Coalition [132], 401
9th St. NW, Ste. 900, Washington, DC 20004,
(202)585-8162

Afghan
Afghan Amer. Muslim Outreach [2757]
Afghan Friends Network [2758]
Global Partnership for Afghanistan [925]
Afghan Amer. Muslim Outreach [2757], 1339 E Ka-
tella Ave., No. 333, Orange, CA 92867, (877)663-
2266
Afghan Friends Network [2758], PO Box 170368,
San Francisco, CA 94117, (650)931-4527

Afghanistan
Global Partnership for Afghanistan [925]
AFL-CIO I Building and Constr. Trades Dept. [3441],
815 16th St., Ste. 600, Washington, DC 20006,
(202)347-1461
AFL-CIO I SEIU I District 925 [3434], 1914 N 34th
St., Ste. 100, Seattle, WA 98103, (206)322-3010

Africa
Africa Faith and Justice Network [2607]
Oper. Crossroads Africa [2608]
Act for Africa Intl. [2209]
Africa Environmental Watch [1001]
Alternative Medicine Intl. [2289]
Amara Conservation [1230]
Amman Imman: Water is Life [2260]
Answer Africa [2397]
BLOOM Africa [1925]
Child Aid Africa [1933]
Computers for Africa [1597]
Eliminate Poverty Now [1904]
Emofra Africa [2487]
Heart for Africa [1959]
Help Aid Africa [2022]
Idoma Assn. USA [2812]
Innovation: Africa [1394]
Intl. Agro Alliance [1217]
Intl. Partnership for Reproductive Hea. [2593]
Orphans Africa [2031]
Water Alliance for Africa [2268]
Africa Environmental Watch [1001], 4207 Plummers
Promise Dr., Ste. 100, Bowie, MD 20720,
(240)417-2545
Africa Faith and Justice Network [2607], 125
Michigan Ave. NE, Ste. 480, Washington, DC
20017, (202)884-9780
Africa Hope [1916], PO Box 127, Dacula, GA 30019,
(770)573-0676
Africa Inland Mission Intl. [2987], PO Box 178, Pearl
River, NY 10965, (845)735-4014

African
African Stud. Assn. [1699]
Assn. of African Stud. Programs [1700]
Idoma Assn. USA [2812]
UHAI for Hea. [2519]

African-American
Assn. for the Stud. of African-American Life and
History [1701]
Charles H. Wright Museum of African Amer. His-
tory [1702]
Natl. Assn. of Black Women in Constr. [206]
African-American Female Entrepreneurs Alliance
[914], 45 Scottdale Ave., Lansdowne, PA 19050,
(215)747-9282
African Medical and Res. Found. [2475], 4 W 43rd
St., 2nd Fl., New York, NY 10036, (212)768-2440
African Stud. Assn. [1699], Rutgers Univ., Livingston
Campus, 54 Joyce Kilmer Ave., Piscataway, NJ
08854-8045, (848)445-8173
African Wild Dog Conservancy [1229], 208 N
California Ave., Silver City, NM 88061
Agami [1581], PO Box 3178, Fremont, CA 94539

Agents
North Amer. Performing Arts Managers and
Agents [39]

Aging
Alliance for Aging Res. [1877]
Little Bros. - Friends of the Elderly [1878]
Natl. Adult Day Services Assn. [1879]
Natl. Assn. of Area Agencies on Aging [1880]
Natl. Assn. of State United for Aging and Dis-
abilities [1881]
Natl. Caucus and Center on Black Aged [1882]
Silver Age Yoga [2606]
Aging with Autism [2307], 704 Marten Rd., Princ-
eton, NJ 08540

Agribusiness
Agribusiness Coun. [926]
Natl. Coun. of Agricultural Employers [927]
United Agribusiness League [928]
Food Trade Sustainability Leadership Assn. [362]
Agribusiness Coun. [926], 3312 Porter St. NW,
Washington, DC 20008, (202)296-4563
Agricultural Commodities Certification Assn. [935],
PO Box 23175, Washington, DC 20026-3175,
(571)377-0722

Agricultural Development
Farmers Market Coalition [929]
Agricultural Commodities Certification Assn. [935]
Community Agroecology Network [1216]
Intl. Agro Alliance [1217]
Multinational Exchange for Sustainable Agriculture
[1218]
Natl. Women in Agriculture Assn. [937]
Reach Across [3011]
Women Organizing for Change in Agriculture and
NRM [938]

Agricultural Education
Amer. Assn. for Agricultural Educ. [1564]
Assn. for Intl. Agriculture and Rural Development
[1565]
Natl. FFA Org. [1566]
Multinational Exchange for Sustainable Agriculture
[1218]
North Amer. South Devon Assn. [989]

Agricultural Engineering
Alpha Epsilon [3521]

Agricultural Equipment
Farm Equip. Mfrs. Assn. [40]
Midwest Equip. Dealers Assn. [930]
North Amer. Equip. Dealers Assn. [41]
Agricultural History Soc. [1766], c/o Alan I. Marcus,
Treas., PO Box H, Mississippi State, MS 39762,
(662)268-2247
Agricultural Missions, Inc. [2988], 475 Riverside Dr.,
Rm. 725, New York, NY 10115, (212)870-2553

Agricultural Science
Agriculture, Food and Human Values Soc. [931]
Crop Sci. Soc. of Am. [932]
Ecological Farming Assn. [933]
North Amer. Weed Mgt. Assn. [934]

Agriculture
Agricultural Commodities Certification Assn. [935]
Alpha Gamma Rho [3507]
Farm Financial Standards Coun. [936]
Natl. Assn. of Agriculture Employees [1263]
Natl. Assn. of County Agricultural Agents [1264]
Natl. Assn. of State Departments of Agriculture
[1265]
Natl. Plant Bd. [1266]
Natl. Women in Agriculture Assn. [937]
Women Involved in Farm Economics [2609]
Women Organizing for Change in Agriculture and
NRM [938]
Alpha Epsilon [3521]
Community Agroecology Network [1216]
Experience Intl. [1021]
Food Trade Sustainability Leadership Assn. [362]
Intl. Agro Alliance [1217]
Multinational Exchange for Sustainable Agriculture
[1218]
Planting Empowerment [1094]
Agriculture, Food and Human Values Soc. [931],
6802 SW 13th, Gainesville, FL 32608, (352)392-
0958
AHOPE for Children [1917], 104 Hume Ave.,
Alexandria, VA 22301, (703)683-7500
Ahoto Partnership for Ghana [2476], 366 Winthrop
Mail Ctr., 32 Mill St., Cambridge, MA 02138

AIC Foundation [★1436]
Aid to Artisans [2118], 1030 New Britain Ave., Ste.
102, West Hartford, CT 06110, (860)756-5550
Aid Still Required [2066], PO Box 7353, Santa
Monica, CA 90406, (310)454-4646
Aid for the World [2163], 20 Murray St., Fl. 2, New
York, NY 10007, (877)424-3911
Aiding Romania's Children [1918], 212 W Lancaster
Ave., Paoli, PA 19301

AIDS
Design Indus. Found. Fighting AIDS [1883]
Elton John AIDS Found. [1884]
The Found. for AIDS Res. [2286]
Natl. Alliance of State and Territorial AIDS Direc-
tors [1885]
Natl. Native Amer. AIDS Prevention Center [1886]
AHOPE for Children [1917]
Aiding Romania's Children [1918]
Children of Grace [1938]
Children of Nowhere [1939]
Damien Ministries [2902]
Emofra Africa [2487]
Horizon Intl. [1967]
Orphan Support Africa [1979]
Orphans Against AIDS [1980]
Peace House Africa [1983]
AIIM - The Enterprise Content Mgt. Assn. [471],
1100 Wayne Ave., Ste. 1100, Silver Spring, MD
20910, (301)587-8202

Aikido
U.S. Aikido Fed. [3251]
World Martial Arts Assn. [3364]
Aikikai Found. [★3251]
Air-Conditioning Heating and Refrigeration Inst.
[427], 2111 Wilson Blvd., Ste. 500, Arlington, VA
22201, (703)524-8800
Air Diffusion Coun. [428], 1901 N Roselle Rd., Ste.
800, Schaumburg, IL 60195, (847)706-6750
Air Force Assn. [1346], 1501 Lee Hwy., Arlington,
VA 22209-1198, (703)247-5800
Air Force Public Affairs Alumni Assn. [1362], PO Box
447, Locust Grove, VA 22508-0447
Air Force Sergeants Assn. [1347], 5211 Auth Rd.,
Suitland, MD 20746, (301)899-3500
Air Line Pilots Assn. Intl. [3436], 1625 Mas-
sachusetts Ave. NW, Washington, DC 20036,
(703)689-2270
Air Movement and Control Assn. Intl. [429], 30 W
Univ. Dr., Arlington Heights, IL 60004, (847)394-
0150
Air Transport Assn. of Am. [25], 1301 Pennsylvania
Ave. NW, Ste. 1100, Washington, DC 20004-7017,
(202)626-4000

Aircraft
Intl. Scale Soaring Assn. [3216]
World Airline Historical Soc. [3089]
Aircraft Mechanics Fraternal Assn. [3437], 14001 E
Iliff Ave., Ste. 217, Aurora, CO 80014, (303)752-
2632
Airline Passenger Experience Assn. [101], 355
Lexington Ave., 15th Fl., New York, NY 10017,
(212)297-2177
Airlines Medical Directors Assn. [2285], c/o Ralph G.
Fennell, MD, Sec., 46155 Black Spruce Ln.,
Parker, CO 80138-4919
Alabama Fan Club [3570], PO Box 680529, Fort
Payne, AL 35968-1606, (256)845-1646
Albanian-American Trade and Development Assn.
[3497], 159 E 4th St., Dunkirk, NY 14048,
(954)802-3166

Alcohol Abuse
Intl. Assn. of Addictions and Offender Counselors
[2044]

Alcoholic Beverages
Fermenters Intl. Trade Assn. [42]
U.S. Sommelier Assn. [43]
Wine and Spirits Shippers Assn. [44]
Alcoholic Clergy Assn; Recovered [2248]
Alcoholics; Natl. Assn. for Children of [2245]
Alcor Life Extension Found. [2357], 7895 E Acoma
Dr., Ste. 110, Scottsdale, AZ 85260-6916,
(480)905-1906
All Amer. Premier Breeds Admin. [3173], 141 3rd
Ave. SW, Castle Rock, WA 98611, (360)274-4209
All the Children are Children [1919], PO Box
153012, Cape Coral, FL 33915, (239)214-4922
All Healers Mental Hea. Alliance [2550], 2 W 64th
St., Rm. 505, New York, NY 10023, (917)677-8550

All Japan Ju-Jitsu Intl. Fed. **[3359]**, 5460 White Oak Ave., Unit F207, Encino, CA 91316, (818)578-6671

All Our Children Intl. Outreach **[1920]**, PO Box 1807, Claremont, CA 91711, (909)450-1177

All Roads Ministry **[2853]**, 55 Pallen Rd., No. 3, Hopewell Junction, NY 12533, (845)226-4172

Allergy
Amer. Acad. of Allergy, Asthma and Immunology **[2287]**
Amer. Coll. of Allergy, Asthma and Immunology **[2288]**

Alliance for Aging Res. **[1877]**, 750 17th St. NW, Ste. 1100, Washington, DC 20006, (202)293-2856

Alliance for Amer. Mfg. **[579]**, 727 15th St. NW, Ste. 700, Washington, DC 20005, (202)393-3430

Alliance for Building Regulatory Reform in the Digital Age **[1435]**, 10702 Midsummer Dr., Reston, VA 20191, (703)568-2323

Alliance for Community Trees **[1089]**, 4603 Calvert Rd., College Park, MD 20740-3421, (301)277-0040

Alliance for Fire and Smoke Containment and Control **[351]**, 4 Brookhollow Rd. SW, Rome, GA 30165-6509, (706)291-9355

Alliance For Relief Mission in Haiti **[2181]**, PO Box 250028, Brooklyn, NY 11225, (516)499-7452

Alliance for Green Heat **[1451]**, 6930 Carroll Ave., Ste. 407, Takoma Park, MD 20912, (301)841-7755

Alliance of Guardian Angels **[2046]**, 982 E 89th St., Brooklyn, NY 11236, (212)860-5575

Alliance for Intl. Reforestation **[1002]**, 1721 N Woodland Blvd., DeLand, FL 32720, (386)748-2454

Alliance of Jamaican and Amer. Humanitarians **[2008]**, 264 S La Cienega Blvd., Ste. 1004, Beverly Hills, CA 90211, (424)249-8135

Alliance of Legal Document Asst. Professionals **[1340]**, 7290 Navajo Rd., Ste. 113, San Diego, CA 92119, (888)201-8622

Alliance for Massage Therapy Educ. **[1659]**, 1760 Old Meadow Rd., Ste. 500, McLean, VA 22102, (703)506-2888

Alliance of Motion Picture and TV Producers **[320]**, 15301 Ventura Blvd., Bldg. E, Sherman Oaks, CA 91403, (818)995-3600

Alliance for Nonprofit Mgt. **[61]**, 731 Market St., Ste. 200, San Francisco, CA 94103, (415)704-5058

Alliance for Peacebuilding **[2629]**, 1320 19th St. NW, Ste. 410, Washington, DC 20036, (202)822-2047

Alliance for Renewable Energy **[1452]**, PO Box 63, Amherst, MA 01004, (413)549-8118

Alliance of Resident Theatres/New York **[1858]**, 520 8th Ave., Ste. 319, New York, NY 10018, (212)244-6667

Alliance of Supplier Diversity Professionals **[727]**, c/o Lisa Barr, Treas., PO Box 560211, Rockledge, FL 32955, (877)405-6565

Alliance for Sustainable Built Environments **[133]**, 5150 N Port Washington Rd., Ste. 260, Milwaukee, WI 53217, (866)913-9473

Alliance for Tompotika Conservation **[1003]**, 21416 86th Ave. SW, Vashon, WA 98070, (206)463-7720

Alliance for Water Educ. **[1620]**, 120 Village Sq., Ste. 137, Orinda, CA 94563, (925)386-0515

Alliance for Water Efficiency **[1224]**, 300 W Adams St., Ste. 601, Chicago, IL 60606, (773)360-5100

Alliance for Women in Media **[125]**, 1760 Old Meadow Rd., Ste. 500, McLean, VA 22102, (703)506-3290

Allied Artists of Am. **[1714]**, 15 Gramercy Park S, New York, NY 10003

Allied Hea. Assn. **[239]**, 5420 S Quebec St., Ste. 102, Englewood, CO 80111, (800)444-7546

Allied Stone Indus. **[839]**, c/o Butch Coleman, Dir., PO Box 273, Susquehanna, PA 18847, (570)465-7200

ALMA - The Intl. Loudspeaker Assn. **[276]**, 55 Littleton Rd., 13B, Ayer, MA 01432, (617)314-6977

Alpaca Breeders of the Rockies **[939]**, PO Box 1965, Estes Park, CO 80517, (970)586-5589

Alpha Delta Kappa **[3517]**, 1615 W 92nd St., Kansas City, MO 64114, (816)363-5525

Alpha Epsilon **[3521]**, Univ. of Illinois in Urbana-Champaign, Dept. of Agricultural and Biological Engg., 1304 W Pennsylvania Ave., Urbana, IL 61801, (217)333-3570

Alpha Epsilon Delta **[3538]**, Texas Christian Univ., Box 298810, Fort Worth, TX 76129, (817)257-4550

Alpha Gamma Rho **[3507]**, 10101 NW Ambassador Dr., Kansas City, MO 64153-1395, (816)891-9200

Alpha Omega Intl. Dental Fraternity **[3514]**, 50 W Edmonston Dr., No. 303, Rockville, MD 20852, (301)738-6400

Alpha Phi Omega Natl. Ser. Fraternity **[3546]**, 14901 E 42nd St., Independence, MO 64055-7347, (816)373-8667

Alpha Psi Lambda Natl. **[3550]**, PO Box 804835, Chicago, IL 60680

Alpha Sigma Tau **[3560]**, 3334 Founders Rd., Indianapolis, IN 46268, (205)978-2179

Alpha Zeta Omega **[3542]**, 140 Hepburn Rd., Apt. 15B, Clifton, NJ 07012

Alternative Medicine
Alternative Medicine Intl. **[2289]**
Amer. Assn. of Traditional Chinese Veterinary Medicine **[2290]**
Amer. Commn. for Accreditation of Reflexology Educ. and Training **[1567]**
Amer. Herbal Pharmacopoeia **[2291]**
Aromatherapy Registration Coun. **[2292]**
Commn. on Religious Counseling and Healing **[2836]**
Father Josef's Method of Reflexology **[2293]**
Global Natural Hea. Alliance **[2294]**
Intl. Soc. for Ayurveda and Hea. **[2295]**
OmSpring **[2296]**
Qigong Alliance Intl. **[2297]**
Reiki Rays of Hope for Caregivers **[2298]**
Surfing Medicine Intl. **[2299]**
Visionary Alternatives **[2300]**
Alliance for Massage Therapy Educ. **[1659]**
Amer. Abdominal Acupuncture Medical Assn. **[2283]**
Amer. Assn. of Naturopathic Midwives **[2553]**
Angel Harps **[2588]**
Chiropractic Diplomatic Corps **[2340]**
Chiropractic Orthopedists of North Am. **[2341]**
Coun. for Acupuncture Res. and Educ. **[2284]**
Coun. of Chiropractic Acupuncture **[2342]**
Coun. on Chiropractic Practice **[2343]**
Councils on Chiropractic Educ. Intl. **[1585]**
Emergency Response Massage Intl. **[2537]**
Holistic Mentorship Network **[2460]**
Kate's Voice **[1678]**
Music Therapy for Healing **[2589]**
Naturopathic Medical Student Assn. **[2554]**
Naturopathic Medicine for Global Hea. **[2555]**
Non-Profit Chiropractic Org. **[2345]**
Oncology Assn. of Naturopathic Physicians **[2556]**
Pediatric Assn. of Naturopathic Physicians **[1670]**
A Promise of Hea. **[2441]**
Silver Age Yoga **[2606]**
World Sound Healing Org. **[2155]**

Alternative Medicine Intl. **[2289]**, 7639 Houghton Rd., Bakersfield, CA 93313, (661)330-2828

Alternative Technology
Amer. Biogas Coun. **[1390]**
Clean Tech. Trade Alliance **[1391]**
ClimateTalk Alliance **[1392]**
FutureGen Alliance **[1393]**
Innovation: Africa **[1394]**
Intl. Green Energy Coun. **[1395]**
Plug In Am. **[1396]**
Sustainable Biomaterials Collaborative **[1397]**
Sweet Sorghum Ethanol Assn. **[1398]**
U.S. Water and Power **[1399]**
Advanced Biofuels Assn. **[391]**
Alliance for Green Heat **[1451]**
Alliance for Renewable Energy **[1452]**
Citizens for Affordable Energy **[1453]**
Electrification Coalition **[871]**
Energy Extraction Technologies **[1458]**
Energy Farm **[1459]**
Focus the Nation **[2642]**
Global Biofuels Alliance **[392]**
GreenMotion **[1057]**
Light Elec. Vehicle Assn. **[873]**
Quantal Energy **[1613]**
Rural Renewable Energy Alliance **[1462]**
Seventh Generation Advisors **[1073]**
Strategic Energy, Environmental and Trans. Alternatives **[1614]**

The Wind Alliance **[1557]**

Alternatives to Marriage Proj. **[2698]**, 358 7th Ave., PMB 131, Brooklyn, NY 11215, (347)987-1068

Aluminum Anodizers Coun. **[192]**, 1000 N Rand Rd., No. 214, Wauconda, IL 60084, (847)526-2010

Alumni
Defense Intel Alumni Assn. **[2759]**
Marquette Univ. Alumni Assn. **[2760]**
North Dakota State Univ. Alumni Assn. **[2761]**
Ouachita Baptist Univ. Alumni Assn. **[2762]**
Univ. of Texas at Brownsville and Texas Southmost Coll. Alumni Assn. **[2763]**
Univ. of Texas I Pan-American Alumni Assn. **[2764]**
Univ. of Wisconsin I Eau Claire Alumni Assn. **[2765]**

Always Patsy Cline World Wide Fan Org. **[3571]**, PO Box 462, Joelton, TN 37080

Amalgamated Printers' Assn. **[411]**, c/o Phillip Driscoll, Sec., 135 East Church St., Clinton, MI 49236

Amalgamated Transit Union **[3466]**, 5025 Wisconsin Ave. NW, Washington, DC 20016, (202)537-1645

Amara Conservation **[1230]**, 1531 Packard St., No. 12, Ann Arbor, MI 48104, (734)761-5357

Amateur Radio
ARRL Found. **[3090]**

Amateur Softball Assn. of Am. **[3395]**, 2801 NE 50th St., Oklahoma City, OK 73111, (405)424-5266

Amazonas Hope for Hea. **[2429]**, c/o Dr. Ruth A. Hayes, Treas., 15 Peterson Pl., Wilmington, OH 45177, (937)383-3382

Ambassadors for Sustained Hea. **[2430]**, 3 Petrel St., West Roxbury, MA 02132, (646)481-0844

America-Israel Cultural Found. **[1786]**, 1140 Broadway, Ste. No. 304, New York, NY 10001, (212)557-1600

America-MidEast Educational and Training Services **[2699]**, 1730 M St. NW, Ste. 1100, Washington, DC 20036, (202)776-9600

American
Alliance for Amer. Mfg. **[579]**
Americans for Peace Now **[2689]**
Armenian Amer. Chamber of Commerce **[3473]**
Irish Amer. Unity Conf. **[2688]**
Pakistan Chamber of Commerce USA **[3502]**

Amer. Abdominal Acupuncture Medical Assn. **[2283]**, 41790 Winchester Rd., Ste. B, Temecula, CA 92590, (951)296-1688

Amer. Acad. of Allergy, Asthma and Immunology **[2287]**, 555 E Wells St., Ste. 1100, Milwaukee, WI 53202-3823, (414)272-6071

Amer. Acad. for Cerebral Palsy and Developmental Medicine **[2561]**, 555 E Wells St., Ste. 1100, Milwaukee, WI 53202, (414)918-3014

Amer. Acad. of Dental Gp. Practice **[2361]**, 2525 E Arizona Biltmore Cir., Ste. 127, Phoenix, AZ 85016, (602)381-1185

Amer. Acad. of Dermatology **[2390]**, PO Box 4014, Schaumburg, IL 60168, (847)240-1280

Amer. Acad. of Esthetic Dentistry **[2362]**, 303 W Madison St., Ste. 2650, Chicago, IL 60606, (312)981-6770

Amer. Acad. of Fixed Prosthodontics **[2363]**, c/o Dr. Richard D. Jordan, Treas., 36 N Mission Hills Ct., Arden, NC 28704-5500, (866)254-0280

Amer. Acad. of Gold Foil Operators **[2364]**, c/o Dr. Robert C. Keene, Sec., 1 Woods End Rd., Etna, NH 03750-4318, (603)643-2899

Amer. Acad. of the History of Dentistry **[2365]**, 684 W Napa St., Sonoma, CA 95476

Amer. Acad. of Matrimonial Lawyers **[1294]**, 150 N Michigan Ave., Ste. 1420, Chicago, IL 60601, (312)263-6477

Amer. Acad. of Maxillofacial Prosthetics **[2366]**, UT MD Anderson Cancer Center, 1515 Holcomber Blvd., Unit 1445, Houston, TX 77030-4009

Amer. Acad. of Medical Administrators **[2538]**, 701 Lee St., Ste. 600, Des Plaines, IL 60016-4516, (847)759-8601

Amer. Acad. of Microbiology **[1419]**, 1752 N St. NW, Washington, DC 20036-2804, (202)737-3600

Amer. Acad. of Oral and Maxillofacial Radiology **[2367]**, PO Box 231422, New York, NY 10023, (304)293-3773

A star before a book entry number signifies that the name is not listed separately, but is mentioned within the entry.

Amer. Acad. of Oral Medicine **[2368]**, PO Box 2016, Edmonds, WA 98020-9516, (425)778-6162

Amer. Acad. of Periodontology **[2369]**, 737 N Michigan Ave., Ste. 800, Chicago, IL 60611-6660, (312)787-5518

Amer. Acad. of Restorative Dentistry **[2370]**, Southwestern Medical Found., 2305 Cedar Springs Rd., Ste. 150, Dallas, TX 75201

Amer. Aging Assn. **[2420]**, c/o Mark A. Smith, Exec. Dir., Dept. of Pathology, 2103 Cornell Rd., Rm. 5125, Cleveland, OH 44106, (216)368-3671

Amer. Albacore Fishing Assn. **[353]**, 4364 Bonita Rd., Box 311, Bonita, CA 91902, (619)941-2307

Amer. Alliance for Hea., Physical Educ., Recreation and Dance **[1673]**, 1900 Assn. Dr., Reston, VA 20191-1598, (703)476-3400

Amer. Ambulance Assn. **[2403]**, 8400 Westpark Dr., 2nd Fl., McLean, VA 22102, (703)610-9018

Amer. Anthropological Assn. I Coun. for Museum Anthropology **[1812]**, Univ. of Connecticut, Dept. of Anthropology, Academic Bldg. 114A, 1084 Shennecossett Rds., Groton, CT 06340, (860)405-9059

American Arts Alliance **[★1727]**

Amer. Asperger's Assn. **[2562]**, 1301 Seminole Blvd., Ste. B-112, Largo, FL 33770, (727)518-7294

Amer. Assn. for the Advancement of Sci. **[1529]**, 1200 New York Ave. NW, Washington, DC 20005, (202)326-6400

Amer. Assn. for Agricultural Educ. **[1564]**, Ohio State Univ., Human and Community Rsrc. Development, 203A Ag. Admin. Bldg., 2120 Fyffe Rd., Columbus, OH 43210, (614)292-6321

Amer. Assn. for Applied Linguistics **[1804]**, 2900 Delk Rd., Ste. 700, Marietta, GA 30067-5350, (678)229-2892

Amer. Assn. of Automatic Door Mfrs. **[259]**, 1300 Sumner Ave., Cleveland, OH 44115-2851, (216)241-7333

American Assn. of Colleges **[★2157]**

Amer. Assn. of Collegiate Registrars and Admissions Officers **[1563]**, 1 Dupont Cir. NW, Ste. 520, Washington, DC 20036, (202)293-9161

Amer. Assn. of Community Colleges **[1589]**, 1 Dupont Cir. NW, Ste. 410, Washington, DC 20036-1176, (202)728-0200

Amer. Assn. of Critical-Care Nurses **[2565]**, 101 Columbia, Aliso Viejo, CA 92656-4109, (949)362-2000

Amer. Assn. of Daily Money Managers **[346]**, 174 Crestview Dr., Bellefonte, PA 16823, (877)326-5991

Amer. Assn. of Dental Boards **[2371]**, 211 E Chicago Ave., Ste. 760, Chicago, IL 60611, (312)440-7464

Amer. Assn. of Electronic Reporters and Transcribers **[711]**, PO Box 9826, Wilmington, DE 19809-9826, (800)233-5306

Amer. Assn. of Endodontists I Amer. Bd. of Endodontics **[2372]**, 211 E Chicago Ave., Ste. 1100, Chicago, IL 60611-2691, (312)266-7310

Amer. Assn. of Family and Consumer Sciences **[2098]**, 400 N Columbus St., Ste. 202, Alexandria, VA 22314, (703)706-4600

Amer. Assn. for Geodetic Surveying **[1544]**, 6100 Ingleston Dr., No. 724, Sparks, NV 89436, (775)626-6295

Amer. Assn. of Grain Inspection and Weighing Agencies **[402]**, PO Box 26426, Kansas City, MO 64196, (816)569-4020

Amer. Assn. for Hand Surgery **[2422]**, 900 Cummings Ctr., Ste. 221-U, Beverly, MA 01915, (978)927-8330

Amer. Assn. of Healthcare Administrative Mgt. **[2539]**, 11240 Waples Mill Rd., Ste. 200, Fairfax, VA 22030, (703)281-4043

Amer. Assn. of Healthcare Consultants **[2464]**, 1205 Johnson Ferry Rd., Ste. 136-420, Marietta, GA 30068, (770)635-8758

Amer. Assn. for Homecare **[2444]**, 2011 Crystal Dr., Ste. 725, Arlington, VA 22202, (703)836-6263

Amer. Assn. of Human Design Practitioners **[253]**, PO Box 195, Ranchos de Taos, NM 87557-0195

Amer. Assn. of Insurance Mgt. Consultants **[208]**, Texas Insurance Consulting, 8980 Lakes at 610 Dr., Ste. 100, Houston, TX 77054, (713)664-6424

Amer. Assn. of Kidney Patients **[2557]**, 3505 E Frontage Rd., Ste. 315, Tampa, FL 33607-1796, (800)749-2257

Amer. Assn. of Law Libraries **[1794]**, 105 W Adams St., Ste. 3300, Chicago, IL 60603, (312)939-4764

Amer. Assn. for Long-Term Care Insurance **[478]**, 3835 E Thousand Oaks Blvd., Ste. 336, Westlake Village, CA 91362, (818)597-3227

Amer. Assn. of Medical Soc. Executives **[2546]**, 555 E Wells St., Ste. 1100, Milwaukee, WI 53202-3823, (414)221-9275

Amer. Assn. of Naturopathic Midwives **[2553]**, PO Box 672, Meredith, NH 03253

Amer. Assn. for Nude Recreation **[1831]**, 1703 N Main St., Ste. E, Kissimmee, FL 34744, (407)933-2064

Amer. Assn. of Nurse Attorneys **[2531]**, PO Box 14218, Lenexa, KS 66285-4218, (877)538-2262

Amer. Assn. for Paralegal Educ. **[1655]**, 19 Mantua Rd., Mount Royal, NJ 08061, (856)423-2829

Amer. Assn. of Physicists in Medicine **[2581]**, 1 Physics Ellipse, College Park, MD 20740, (301)209-3350

Amer. Assn. of Physics Teachers **[1674]**, 1 Physics Ellipse, College Park, MD 20740-3845, (301)209-3300

Amer. Assn. of Political Consultants **[2724]**, 8400 Westpark Dr., 2nd Fl., Washington, DC 20003, (703)245-8020

Amer. Assn. of Private Railroad Car Owners **[731]**, 622 N Reed St., Joliet, IL 60435, (815)722-8877

Amer. Assn. of Professional Apiculturists **[953]**, USDA ARS Honey Bee Lab, 1157 Ben Hur Rd., Baton Rouge, LA 70808, (225)767-9284

Amer. Assn. of Professional Tech. Analysts **[847]**, 209 W Jackson Blvd., 6th Fl., Chicago, IL 60606, (972)213-5816

Amer. Assn. for Public Opinion Res. **[2727]**, 111 Deer Lake Rd., Ste. 100, Deerfield, IL 60015, (847)205-2651

Amer. Assn. of School Personnel Administrators **[1559]**, 11863 W 112th St., Ste. 100, Overland Park, KS 66210, (913)327-1222

Amer. Assn. of Suicidology **[2251]**, 5221 Wisconsin Ave. NW, Washington, DC 20015, (202)237-2280

American Assn. of Sunday and Feature Editors **[★706]**

Amer. Assn. of Teachers of Italian **[1652]**, Indiana Univ., Dept. of French and Italian, Ballentine Hall 642, 1020 E Kirkwood Ave., Bloomington, IN 47405-6601

Amer. Assn. of Teachers of Turkic Languages **[1694]**, Princeton Univ., Near Eastern Stud., 110 Jones Hall, Princeton, NJ 08544-1008, (609)258-1435

Amer. Assn. of Traditional Chinese Veterinary Medicine **[2290]**, c/o Cheryl Chrisman, DVM, 10145 SW 52nd Rd., Gainesville, FL 32608, (352)672-6400

Amer. Assn. for Women in Community Colleges **[1698]**, c/o Salt Lake Community Coll., PO Box 30808, Salt Lake City, UT 84130-0808, (801)975-4225

Amer. Assn. of Women Dentists **[2373]**, 216 W Jackson Blvd., Ste. 625, Chicago, IL 60606, (800)920-2293

American-Austrian Cultural Soc. **[2771]**, c/o Mr. Michael Korenchuk, Treas., 116 E Melrose St., Chevy Chase, MD 20815

Amer. Aviation Historical Soc. **[3083]**, PO Box 3023, Huntington Beach, CA 92605-3023

Amer. Azteca Horse Intl. Assn. **[1111]**, PO Box 1577, Rapid City, SD 57709, (605)342-2322

Amer. Bamboo Soc. **[1427]**, 315 S Coast Hwy. 101, Ste. U, PMB 212, Encinitas, CA 92024-3555

Amer. Baptist Homes and Caring Ministries **[2839]**, Judson Park, 23600 Marine View Dr. S, Des Moines, WA 98198, (800)ABC-3USA

Amer. Bar Assn. Center on Children and the Law **[1921]**, 740 15th St. NW, Washington, DC 20005-1019, (202)662-1720

Amer. Bar Assn. Commn. on Homelessness and Poverty **[2099]**, 740 15th St. NW, Washington, DC 20005-1022, (202)662-1693

Amer. Baseball Coaches Assn. **[3256]**, 108 S Univ. Ave., Ste. 3, Mount Pleasant, MI 48858-2327, (989)775-3300

Amer. Bashkir Curly Registry **[1112]**, 71 Cavalier Blvd., No. 124, Florence, KY 41042, (859)485-9700

Amer. Bearing Mfrs. Assn. **[456]**, 2025 M St. NW, Ste. 800, Washington, DC 20036-2422, (202)367-1155

Amer. Belgian Blue Breeders **[967]**, 245 W Main St., Stanley, IA 50671, (319)230-0671

Amer. Belgian Hare Club **[1186]**, 15330 Sharp Rd., Rockton, IL 61072, (815)629-2465

Amer. Bell Assn. Intl. **[3149]**, 7210 Bellbrook Dr., San Antonio, TX 78227-1002

Amer. Biogas Coun. **[1390]**, 1211 Connecticut Ave. NW, Ste. 600, Washington, DC 20036, (202)640-6595

Amer. Biological Safety Assn. **[780]**, 1200 Allanson Rds., Mundelein, IL 60060-3808, (847)949-1517

Amer. Birding Assn. **[1510]**, 4945 N 30th St., Ste. 200, Colorado Springs, CO 80919, (719)578-9703

Amer. Black Hereford Assn. **[968]**, 719 Walnut St., Kansas City, MO 64106, (816)472-1111

Amer. Bladesmith Soc. **[3162]**, PO Box 905, Salida, CO 81201, (419)832-0400

Amer. Bd. of Funeral Ser. Educ. **[620]**, 3414 Ashland Ave., Ste. G, St. Joseph, MO 64506, (816)233-3747

American Bd. of Medical Lab. Immunology **[★1419]**

American Bd. of Medical Microbiology **[★1419]**

Amer. Bd. of Orthodontics **[2374]**, 401 N Lindbergh Blvd., Ste. 300, St. Louis, MO 63141-7839, (314)432-6130

Amer. Bd. of Professional Liability Attorneys **[1343]**, 4355 Cobb Pkwy., Ste. J-208, Atlanta, GA 30339, (404)989-7663

Amer. Book Producers Assn. **[718]**, 151 W 19th St., 3rd Fl., New York, NY 10011, (212)645-2368

Amer. Border Leicester Assn. **[1199]**, PO Box 500, Cuba, IL 61427, (309)785-5058

Amer. Brahman Breeders Assn. **[969]**, 3003 S Loop W, Ste. 520, Houston, TX 77054, (713)349-0854

Amer. Brazilian Cultural Exchange **[1746]**, 1075 E 33rd St., Oakland, CA 94610, (510)280-4862

Amer. Bridge Teachers' Assn. **[3142]**, 490 N Winnebago Dr., Lake Winnebago, MO 64034-9321, (816)537-5165

Amer. British White Park Assn. **[970]**, PO Box 409, Myerstown, PA 17067, (270)563-9733

Amer. Broncho-Esophagological Assn. **[2326]**, Boston Medical Center, FGH Bldg., Dept. of Otolaryngology-Head and Neck Surgery, 820 Harrison Ave., 4th Fl., Boston, MA 02118, (617)638-7934

Amer. Brush Mfrs. Assn. **[450]**, 2111 Plum St., Ste. 274, Aurora, IL 60506, (720)392-2262

Amer. Bryological and Lichenological Soc. **[1428]**, c/o James Bennett, Sec.-Treas., Univ. of Wisconsin, Dept. of Botany, 430 Lincoln Dr., Madison, WI 53706, (608)262-5489

Amer. Bugatti Club **[3094]**, 600 Lakeview Terr., Glen Ellyn, IL 60137, (630)469-4920

Amer. Bur. of Shipping **[592]**, 16855 Northchase Dr., Houston, TX 77060, (281)877-5800

Amer. Burn Assn. **[2327]**, 311 S Wacker Dr., Ste. 4150, Chicago, IL 60606, (312)642-9260

Amer. Bus Assn. **[866]**, 111 K St. NE, 9th Fl., Washington, DC 20002, (202)842-1645

Amer. Bus. Women's Assn. **[162]**, PO Box 8728, Kansas City, MO 64114-0728, (800)228-0007

Amer. Camp Assn. **[3300]**, 5000 State Rd., 67 N, Martinsville, IN 46151-7902, (765)342-8456

Amer. Car Rental Assn. **[765]**, PO Box 225, Clifton Park, NY 12065, (888)200-2795

Amer. Catholic Correctional Chaplains Assn. **[2885]**, 738 Guernsey Ct., Slinger, WI 53086, (262)627-0636

Amer. Catholic Historical Assn. **[1767]**, Catholic Univ. of Am., Mullen Lib., Rm. 320, Washington, DC 20064, (202)319-5079

Amer. Celiac Disease Alliance **[2414]**, 2504 Duxbury Pl., Alexandria, VA 22308, (703)622-3331

Amer. Chamber of Commerce Executives **[3504]**, 4875 Eisenhower Ave., Ste. 250, Alexandria, VA 22304, (703)998-0072

Amer. Cheese Soc. **[251]**, 2696 S Colorado Blvd., Ste. 570, Denver, CO 80222-5954, (720)328-2788

Amer. Chem. Soc., Rubber Div. **[779]**, PO Box 499, Akron, OH 44309-0499, (330)972-6527

Amer. Chemistry Coun. **[182]**, 700 2nd St. NE, Washington, DC 20002, (202)249-7000

Amer. Cheviot Sheep Soc. **[1200]**, 10015 Flush Rd., St. George, KS 66535, (785)494-2436

Amer. Chianina Assn. **[971]**, 1708 N Prairie View Rd., PO Box 890, Platte City, MO 64079, (816)431-2808

Amer. Chinese Medical Exchange Soc. **[2431]**, 15 New England Executive Park, Burlington, MA 01803, (781)791-5066

Amer. Christian Fiction Writers **[1729]**, PO Box 101066, Palm Bay, FL 32910-1066

Amer. Civil Rights Union **[2623]**, 3213 Duke St., No. 625, Alexandria, VA 22314, (703)807-0242

Amer. Cleaning Inst. **[183]**, 1331 L St. NW, Ste. 650, Washington, DC 20005, (202)347-2900

Amer. Cleft Palate-Craniofacial Assn. **[2354]**, 1504 E Franklin St., Ste. 102, Chapel Hill, NC 27514-2820, (919)933-9044

Amer. Clinical Neurophysiology Soc. **[2400]**, PO Box 30, Bloomfield, CT 06002, (860)243-3977

Amer. Cockatiel Soc. **[3138]**, PO Box 980055, Houston, TX 77098-0055, (888)221-1161

Amer. Coke and Coal Chemicals Inst. **[191]**, 1140 Connecticut Ave. NW, Ste. 705, Washington, DC 20036, (202)452-7198

Amer. Collectors of Infant Feeders **[3150]**, c/o Sara Jean Binder, Treas., 13851 Belle Chasse Blvd., Ste. 412, Laurel, MD 20707

Amer. Coll. of Allergy, Asthma and Immunology **[2288]**, 85 W Algonquin Rd., Ste. 550, Arlington Heights, IL 60005-4425, (847)427-1200

Amer. Coll. of Chiropractic Orthopedists **[2339]**, 35 S Lake St., North East, PA 16428, (781)665-1497

Amer. Coll. of Counselors **[2083]**, 273 Glossip Ave., Highlandville, MO 65669-8133, (417)885-4030

Amer. Coll. of Emergency Physicians **[2405]**, PO Box 619911, Irving, TX 75038-2522, (972)550-0911

Amer. Coll. of Environmental Lawyers **[1293]**, 1300 SW 5th Ave., Ste. 2300, Portland, OR 97201-5630, (207)774-1200

Amer. Coll. of Gastroenterology **[2415]**, PO Box 342260, Bethesda, MD 20827-2260, (301)263-9000

Amer. Coll. of Intl. Physicians **[2477]**, 9323 Old Mt. Vernon Rd., Alexandria, VA 22309-2714, (703)221-1500

Amer. Coll. of Legal Medicine **[2532]**, 2 Woodfield Lake, 1100 E Woodfield Rd., Ste. 520, Schaumburg, IL 60173-5125, (847)969-0283

Amer. Coll. of Mohs Surgery **[2570]**, 555 E Wells St., Ste. 1100, Milwaukee, WI 53202-3823, (414)347-1103

Amer. Coll. of Nuclear Medicine **[2564]**, 1850 Samuel Morse Dr., Reston, VA 20190, (703)326-1190

Amer. Coll. of Trial Lawyers **[1384]**, 19900 MacArthur Blvd., Ste. 530, Irvine, CA 92612, (949)752-1801

Amer. Commn. for Accreditation of Reflexology Educ. and Training **[1567]**, 1309 Hillcrest Dr., Anchorage, AK 99503, (907)278-4646

Amer. Composers Alliance **[1818]**, 802 W 190th St., 1st Fl., New York, NY 10040, (212)925-0458

Amer. Concrete Pressure Pipe Assn. **[670]**, 3900 Univ. Dr., Ste. 110, Fairfax, VA 22030-2513, (703)273-7227

Amer. Conf. of Academic Deans **[1560]**, c/o Laura A. Rzepka, Exec. Dir., 1818 R St. NW, Washington, DC 20009, (202)884-7419

Amer. Conf. for Irish Stud. **[1785]**, c/o Nicholas Wolf, Treas., PO Box 842001, Richmond, VA 23284-2001

Amer. Constr. Inspectors Assn. **[202]**, 530 S Lake Ave., No. 431, Pasadena, CA 91101, (626)797-2242

Amer. Contract Compliance Assn. **[2074]**, 17 E Monroe St., No. 150, Chicago, IL 60603, (866)222-2298

Amer. Coon Hunters Assn. **[3355]**, PO Box 453, Grayson, KY 41143, (606)474-9740

Amer. Correctional Chaplains Assn. **[2886]**, PO Box 85840, Seattle, WA 98145-1840, (206)985-0577

Amer. Correctional Hea. Services Assn. **[2446]**, 3990 Bullard Rd., Monticello, GA 31064, (855)825-5559

Amer. Coun. of Engg. Companies I Coun. of Professional Surveyors **[843]**, 1015 15th St. NW, 8th Fl., Washington, DC 20005-2605, (202)347-7474

Amer. Coun. on Germany **[2784]**, 14 E 60th St., Ste. 1000, New York, NY 10022, (212)826-3636

Amer. Coun. on Global Nuclear Competitiveness **[1509]**, PO Box 4520, Washington, DC 20015, (301)656-1859

Amer. Coun. of State Savings Supervisors **[108]**, 1129 20th St. NW, 9th Fl., Washington, DC 20036-3403, (202)728-5757

Amer. Coun. on the Teaching of Foreign Languages **[1653]**, 1001 N Fairfax St., Ste. 200, Alexandria, VA 22314, (703)894-2900

Amer. Coun. of Young Political Leaders **[2697]**, 2131 K St. NW, Ste. 400, Washington, DC 20037, (202)857-0999

Amer. Dance Guild **[1749]**, 240 W 14th St., New York, NY 10011, (212)627-9407

Amer. Delaine and Merino Record Assn. **[1201]**, 7744 State Rte. 613, McComb, OH 45858, (419)293-2871

Amer. Dermatological Assn. **[2391]**, c/o Julie Odessky, Exec. Mgr., PO Box 551301, Davie, FL 33355, (954)452-1113

Amer. Design Drafting Assn. **[1485]**, 105 E Main St., Newbern, TN 38059, (731)627-0802

Amer. Dexter Cattle Assn. **[972]**, 4150 Merino Ave., Watertown, MN 55388, (952)215-2206

Amer. Dorper Sheep Breeders' Soc. **[1202]**, PO Box 259, Hallsville, MO 65255-0259, (573)696-2550

Amer. Driving Soc. **[3354]**, PO Box 278, Cross Plains, WI 53528, (608)237-7382

Amer. Drum Horse Assn. **[1113]**, 3822 Bluff Cir., Coarsegold, CA 93614, (559)676-7990

American Educ. Finance Assn. **[★1609]**

Amer. Educational Stud. Assn. **[1603]**, c/o Philip Kovacs, Communications Dir., Univ. of Alabama in Huntsville, Dept. of Educ., 235 Morton Hall, Huntsville, AL 35899

Amer. Electrology Assn. **[2401]**, 6 Market Pl., Ste. 1, Essex Junction, VT 05452, (802)879-1898

Amer. Embryo Transfer Assn. **[947]**, 2441 Village Green Pl., Champaign, IL 61822, (217)398-2217

Amer. Enameling Assn. **[1156]**, 1201 W Main St., Ste. 2, Ottawa, IL 61350, (541)332-0675

Amer. Endodontic Soc. **[2375]**, 265 N Main St., Glen Ellyn, IL 60137, (773)519-4879

Amer. Equestrian Trade Assn. **[1114]**, 107 W St. Rd., Kennett Square, PA 19348-1613, (610)444-2025

Amer. Equilibration Soc. **[2376]**, 207 E Ohio St., Ste. 399, Chicago, IL 60611, (847)965-2888

Amer. Ethical Union **[2943]**, 2 W 64th St., New York, NY 10023-7104, (212)873-6500

Amer. Ethnological Soc. **[1400]**, Univ. of Wisconsin, Dept. of Rural Sociology, Madison, WI 53701, (608)262-1217

Amer. Farrier's Assn. **[118]**, 4059 Iron Works Pkwy., Ste. 1, Lexington, KY 40511, (859)233-7411

Amer. Fed. of Musicians of the U.S. and Canada **[3456]**, 1501 Broadway, Ste. 600, New York, NY 10036, (212)869-1330

Amer. Fed. of New Zealand Rabbit Breeders **[1187]**, 626 Alabama St., Sulphur, LA 70663, (337)533-9005

Amer. Fed. of TV and Radio Artists **[3440]**, 260 Madison Ave., 9th Fl., New York, NY 10016-2401, (212)532-0800

Amer. Fence Assn. **[203]**, 800 Roosevelt Rd., Bldg. C-312, Glen Ellyn, IL 60137, (630)942-6598

Amer. Fiberboard Assn. **[134]**, 1935 S Plum Grove Rd., No. 283, Palatine, IL 60067, (847)934-8394

Amer. Finance Assn. **[325]**, Univ. of California, Haas School of Bus., Berkeley, CA 94720-1900, (800)835-6770

Amer. Financial Services Assn. **[541]**, 919 18th St. NW, Ste. 300, Washington, DC 20006-5526, (202)296-5544

Amer. Fired Arts Alliance **[1723]**, PO Box 14, Waupun, WI 53963, (920)296-5456

Amer. Flock Assn. **[854]**, 6 Beacon St., Ste. 1125, Boston, MA 02108, (617)303-6288

American Floral Indus. Assn. **[★358]**

Amer. Fly-Fishing Trade Assn. **[827]**, 901 Front St., Ste. B-125, Louisville, CO 80027, (303)604-6132

Amer. Folklore Soc. **[1757]**, Ohio State Univ., Mershon Center, 1501 Neil Ave., Columbus, OH 43201-2602, (614)292-3375

Amer. Forensic Assn. **[1688]**, PO Box 256, River Falls, WI 54022, (800)228-5424

Amer. Forest and Paper Assn. **[1090]**, 1111 19th St. NW, Ste. 800, Washington, DC 20036, (202)463-2700

Amer. Forests **[1004]**, PO Box 2000, Washington, DC 20013, (202)737-1944

Amer. Friends of the Anglican Centre in Rome **[2837]**, PO Box 300, St. Francisville, LA 70775, (225)252-3231

Amer. Friends of the Czech Republic **[2778]**, 4410 Massachusetts Ave. NW, No. 391, Washington, DC 20016-5572, (202)413-5528

Amer. Friends of Guinea **[2478]**, 12012 Wickchester Ln., Ste. 475, Houston, TX 77079, (713)353-9400

Amer. Gas Assn. **[1104]**, 400 N Capitol St. NW, Ste. 450, Washington, DC 20001, (202)824-7000

Amer. Gear Mfrs. Assn. **[457]**, 1001 N Fairfax St., 5th Fl., Alexandria, VA 22314-1587, (703)684-0211

Amer. Genetic Assn. **[1480]**, 2030 SE Marine Sci. Dr., Newport, OR 97365, (541)867-0334

Amer. Geographical Soc. **[1481]**, 32 Court St., Ste. 201, Brooklyn, NY 11201-4404, (718)624-2212

Amer. Geriatrics Soc. **[2421]**, 350 5th Ave., Ste. 801, New York, NY 10118, (212)308-1414

Amer. GI Forum of U.S. **[3079]**, c/o Dottie Bruton, Mgr., 2870 Speed Blvd., No. 103, Denver, CO 80211, (866)244-3628

Amer. Greyhound Track Operators Assn. **[3322]**, Palm Beach Kennel Club, 1111 N Cong. Ave., West Palm Beach, FL 33409, (561)688-5799

Amer. Guernsey Assn. **[973]**, 1224 Alton Darby Creek Rd., Ste. G, Columbus, OH 43228, (614)864-2409

Amer. Guild of Judaic Art **[1708]**, 135 Shaker Hallow, Alpharetta, GA 30022, (404)981-2308

Amer. Guinea Hog Assn. **[1219]**, 1820 P Ave., Jefferson, IA 50129, (515)370-1021

Amer. Half Quarter Horse Registry **[1115]**, PO Box 211, Carlsbad, NM 88221-0211, (480)982-1551

Amer. Handwriting Anal. Found. **[1868]**, PO Box 460385, Escondido, CA 92046-0385, (760)489-0692

Amer. Head and Neck Soc. **[2573]**, 11300 W Olympic Blvd., Ste. 600, Los Angeles, CA 90064, (310)437-0559

Amer. Hea. Planning Assn. **[2425]**, 7245 Arlington Blvd., Ste. 300, Falls Church, VA 22042, (703)573-3103

Amer. Herbal Pharmacopoeia **[2291]**, PO Box 66809, Scotts Valley, CA 95067, (831)461-6318

Amer. Hibiscus Soc. **[3201]**, PO Box 1580, Venice, FL 34284-1580

Amer. Hiking Soc. **[3425]**, 1422 Fenwick Ln., Silver Spring, MD 20910, (301)565-6704

Amer. Historical Soc. of Germans From Russia **[2785]**, 631 D St., Lincoln, NE 68502-1199, (402)474-3363

Amer. Honey Producers Assn. **[954]**, PO Box 162, Power, MT 59468, (406)463-2227

Amer. Horse League **[2100]**, 1612 Junction Ave., Ste. 4, Sturgis, SD 57785, (605)347-1730

Amer. Hosp. Assn. I Assn. for Healthcare Rsrc. and Materials Mgt. **[2465]**, 155 N Wacker Dr., Chicago, IL 60606, (312)422-3840

Amer. Hosp. Assn. I Soc. for Healthcare Consumer Advocacy **[2533]**, 155 N Wacker Dr., Ste. 155, Chicago, IL 60606, (312)422-3700

Amer. Hosp. Assn. I Soc. for Healthcare Strategy and Market Development **[2466]**, 155 N Wacker Dr., Ste. 400, Chicago, IL 60606, (312)422-3888

Amer. Hotel and Lodging Assn. **[440]**, 1201 New York Ave. NW, No. 600, Washington, DC 20005-3931, (202)289-3100

Amer. Humane Assn. **[2229]**, 63 Inverness Dr. E, Englewood, CO 80112-5117, (303)792-9900

Amer. Hungarian Found. **[2790]**, PO Box 1084, New Brunswick, NJ 08903, (732)846-5777

American Indian
United Indian Missions Intl. **[3014]**

Amer. Inst. of Building Design **[1406]**, 7059 Blair Rd. NW, Ste. 201, Washington, DC 20012, (800)366-2423

Amer. Inst. of Chemists **[1436]**, 315 Chestnut St., Philadelphia, PA 19106-2702, (215)873-8224

Amer. Inst. for Conservation of Historic and Artistic Works **[1760]**, 1156 15th St., Ste. 320, Washington, DC 20005-1714, (202)452-9545

A star before a book entry number signifies that the name is not listed separately, but is mentioned within the entry.

Amer. Inst. of Constructors **[1446]**, 700 N Fairfax St., Ste. 510, Alexandria, VA 22314, (703)683-4999

Amer. Inst. of Floral Designers **[357]**, 720 Light St., Baltimore, MD 21230, (410)752-3318

Amer. Inst. of Homeopathy **[2463]**, 101 S Whiting St., Ste. 16, Alexandria, VA 22304, (703)273-5250

Amer. Inst. of Hydrology **[1555]**, Southern Illinois Univ. Carbondale, 1230 Lincoln Dr., Carbondale, IL 62901, (618)453-7809

Amer. Inst. of Parliamentarians **[1833]**, 550M Richie Hwy., No. 271, Severna Park, MD 21146, (888)664-0428

Amer. Inst. of Wine and Food **[3210]**, 26384 Carmel Rancho Ln., Ste. 200E, Carmel, CA 93923, (831)250-7595

Amer. Insurance Marketing and Sales Soc. **[479]**, PO Box 35718, Richmond, VA 23235, (804)674-6466

Amer. Intellectual Property Law Assn. **[1312]**, 241 18th St. S, Ste. 700, Arlington, VA 22202, (703)415-0780

Amer. Italian Historical Assn. **[1787]**, Queens College/City Univ. of New York, John D. Calandra Italiam Amer. Inst., 25 W 43rd St., 17th Fl., New York, NY 10036, (708)756-7168

Amer. Jewish Press Assn. **[685]**, 107 S Southgate Dr., Chandler, AZ 85226, (480)403-4602

Amer. Jewish Soc. for Ser. **[2124]**, 10319 Westlake Blvd., Ste. 193, Bethesda, MD 20817, (240)205-5940

Amer. Judges Assn. **[1317]**, 300 Newport Ave., Williamsburg, VA 23185-4147, (757)259-1841

Amer. Judicature Soc. **[1318]**, Drake Univ., The Opperman Ctr., 2700 Univ. Ave., Des Moines, IA 50311, (515)271-2281

American Junior Acad. of Sci. **[★1531]**

Amer. Junior Golf Assn. **[3334]**, 1980 Sports Club Dr., Braselton, GA 30517, (770)868-4200

Amer. Karakul Sheep Registry **[1203]**, 11500 Hwy. 5, Boonville, MO 65233, (660)838-6340

Amer. Kiko Goat Assn. **[1106]**, 14551 County Rd. 7130, Moody, MO 65777, (254)423-5914

Amer. Laryngological, Rhinological and Otological Soc. **[2574]**, 13930 Gold Cir., Ste. 103, Omaha, NE 68144, (402)346-5500

Amer. League of Lobbyists **[2725]**, c/o Patti Jo Baber, Exec. Dir., PO Box 30005, Alexandria, VA 22310, (703)960-3011

Amer. Legend **[940]**, Motorcycle Trailers Inc., 903 S Prairieview Rd., Mahomet, IL 61853, (217)586-2201

Amer. Legion Auxiliary **[3074]**, 8945 N Meridian St., 2nd Fl., Indianapolis, IN 46260, (317)569-4500

Amer. Legion Auxiliary Girls Nation **[2621]**, 8945 N Meridian St., 2nd Fl., Indianapolis, IN 46260, (317)569-4500

Amer. Legion Baseball **[3257]**, 700 N Pennsylvania St., Indianapolis, IN 46204, (317)630-1200

Amer. Leprosy Missions **[2535]**, 1 ALM Way, Greenville, SC 29601, (864)271-7040

Amer. Lib. Assn. I Gay, Lesbian, Bisexual and Transgendered Roundtable **[2092]**, 50 E Huron St., Chicago, IL 60611, (800)545-2433

Amer. Libyan Freedom Alliance **[2636]**, PO Box 22262, Lehigh Valley, PA 18002, (610)703-1382

Amer. Literary Translators Assn. **[1861]**, Univ. of Texas at Dallas, 800 W Campbell Rd., Mail Sta. J051, Richardson, TX 75080-3021, (972)883-2092

Amer. Littoral Soc. Northeast Region **[1494]**, 28 W 9th Rd., Broad Channel, NY 11693, (718)318-9344

Amer. Liver Found. **[2459]**, 28 Broadway, Ste. 2700, New York, NY 10006, (212)668-1000

Amer. Loggers Coun. **[384]**, PO Box 966, Hemphill, TX 75948, (409)625-0206

Amer. Logistics Assn. **[1348]**, 1133 15th St. NW, Ste. 640, Washington, DC 20005, (202)466-2520

Amer. Made Alliance **[3163]**, 3000 Chestnut Ave., Ste. 300, Baltimore, MD 21211, (410)889-2933

Amer. Massage Therapy Assn. **[2536]**, 500 Davis St., Ste. 900, Evanston, IL 60201-4695, (847)864-0123

Amer. Medical Gp. Assn. **[2447]**, One Prince St., Alexandria, VA 22314-3318, (703)838-0033

Amer. Medical Tennis Assn. **[3420]**, 1803 Cobblestone Dr., Provo, UT 84604, (800)326-2682

Amer. MidEast Leadership Network **[2677]**, PO Box 2156, Long Island City, NY 11102, (347)924-9674

Amer. Miniature Llama Assn. **[941]**, PO Box 8, Kalispell, MT 59903, (406)755-3438

Amer. Mold Builders Assn. **[458]**, 3601 Algonquin Rd., Ste. 304, Rolling Meadows, IL 60008, (847)222-9402

Amer. Morgan Horse Assn. **[1116]**, 4066 Shelburne Rd., Ste. 5, Shelburne, VT 05482-6908, (802)985-4944

Amer. Mosquito Control Assn. **[1177]**, 15000 Commerce Pkwy., Ste. C, Mount Laurel, NJ 08054, (856)439-9222

Amer. Mothers, Inc. **[2084]**, 1666 K St. NW, Ste. 260, Washington, DC 20006, (877)242-4264

Amer. Motorcyclist Assn. **[3366]**, 13515 Yarmouth Dr., Pickerington, OH 43147-8214, (614)856-1900

Amer. Mule Assn. **[942]**, 260 Neilson Rd., Reno, NV 89521, (775)849-9437

Amer. Name Soc. **[1832]**, Binghamton Univ., State Univ. of New York, Off. of the Provost, Binghamton, NY 13902-6000, (607)777-2143

Amer. Natl. CattleWomen **[974]**, 9110 E Nichols Ave., Ste. 302, Centennial, CO 80112, (303)694-0313

Amer. Nephrology Nurses' Assn. **[2558]**, E Holly Ave., Box 56, Pitman, NJ 08071, (856)256-2320

Amer. Network of Community Options and Resources **[2141]**, 1101 King St., Ste. 380, Alexandria, VA 22314, (703)535-7850

Amer. Neurogastroenterology and Motility Soc. **[2416]**, 45685 Harmony Ln., Belleville, MI 48111, (734)699-1130

Amer. News Women's Club **[686]**, 1607 22nd St. NW, Washington, DC 20008, (202)332-6770

Amer. North Country Cheviot Sheep Assn. **[1204]**, 1201 N 500 E, Rolling Prairie, IN 46371, (574)323-3506

Amer. Oil and Gas Historical Soc. **[638]**, 3204 18th St. NW, Washington, DC 20010, (202)857-4785

Amer. Ornithologists' Union **[1511]**, c/o Scott Gillihan, Exec. Off., 5405 Villa View Dr., Farmington, NM 87402, (505)326-1579

Amer. Orthodontic Soc. **[2377]**, 11884 Greenville Ave., Ste. 112, Dallas, TX 75243-3537, (800)448-1601

Amer. Orthotic and Prosthetic Assn. **[421]**, PO Box 34711, Alexandria, VA 22334-0711, (571)431-0876

Amer. Osteopathic Coll. of Anesthesiologists **[2301]**, 2260 E Saginaw St., Ste. B, East Lansing, MI 48823, (517)339-0919

Amer. Osteopathic Coll. of Dermatology **[2392]**, PO Box 7525, Kirksville, MO 63501, (660)665-2184

Amer. Ostrich Assn. **[943]**, PO Box 166, Ranger, TX 76470, (254)647-1645

Amer. Outreach to Ethiopia **[2114]**, 1121 S Diamond St., Jacksonville, IL 62650, (217)245-8792

Amer. Overseas Schools Historical Soc. **[1761]**, 704 W Douglas Ave., Wichita, KS 67203-6401, (316)265-6837

Amer. Oxford Sheep Assn. **[1205]**, 1960 E 2100 North Rd., Stonington, IL 62567, (217)325-3515

Amer. Paint Horse Assn. **[1117]**, PO Box 961023, Fort Worth, TX 76161-0023, (817)834-2742

Amer. Part-Blooded Horse Registry **[1118]**, PO Box 986, Oregon City, OR 97045, (503)895-1680

Amer. Pet Products Assn. **[652]**, 255 Glenville Rd., Greenwich, CT 06831, (203)532-0000

Amer. Philosophical Soc. **[1530]**, 104 S 5th St., Philadelphia, PA 19106-3387, (215)440-3400

Amer. Photographic Artists Guild **[663]**, 2269 N 400 Rd., Eudora, KS 66025, (785)883-4166

Amer. Pinzgauer Assn. **[975]**, PO Box 1097, Lake Ozark, MO 65049, (573)964-2389

Amer. Polar Soc. **[1519]**, PO Box 300, Searsport, ME 04974

Amer. Postal Workers Union **[3460]**, 1300 L St. NW, Washington, DC 20005, (202)842-4200

Amer. Prosthodontic Soc. **[2378]**, 303 W Madison St., Ste. 2650, Chicago, IL 60611, (312)981-6780

Amer. Psychological Assn. I Division of Family Psychology **[2582]**, 750 1st St. NE, Washington, DC 20002-4242, (202)216-7602

Amer. Public Human Services Assn. **[2230]**, 1133 19th St. NW, Ste. 400, Washington, DC 20036, (202)682-0100

Amer. Public Human Services Assn. I Natl. Coun. of State Human Ser. Administrators **[2231]**, 1133 19th St. NW, Ste. 400, Washington, DC 20036, (202)682-0100

Amer. Public Trans. Assn. **[867]**, 1666 K St. NW, Ste. 1100, Washington, DC 20006, (202)496-4800

Amer. Public Works Assn. **[1369]**, 2345 Grand Blvd., Ste. 700, Kansas City, MO 64108-2625, (816)472-6100

Amer. Quarter Horse Assn. **[1119]**, 1600 Quarter Horse Dr., Amarillo, TX 79168, (806)376-4811

Amer. Quaternary Assn. **[1503]**, c/o Brian Carter, Treas., 2209 W 104th St., Perkins, OK 74059-4149, (405)744-9585

Amer. Rambouillet Sheep Breeders' Assn. **[1206]**, 15603 173rd Ave., Milo, IA 50166, (641)942-6402

Amer. Ranch Horse Assn. **[1120]**, PO Box 186, Nancy, KY 42544, (606)636-4112

Amer. Real Estate and Urban Economics Assn. **[1680]**, PO Box 9958, Richmond, VA 23228-9958, (866)273-8321

Amer. Red Brangus Assn. **[976]**, 3995 E Hwy. 290, Dripping Springs, TX 78620, (512)858-7285

Amer. Red Poll Assn. **[977]**, PO Box 847, Frankton, IN 46044, (765)425-4515

Amer. Refugee Comm. **[2177]**, 430 Oak Grove St., Ste. 204, Minneapolis, MN 55403, (612)872-7060

Amer. Rescue Workers **[2232]**, 25 Ross St., Williamsport, PA 17701, (570)323-8693

Amer. Revenue Assn. **[3225]**, PO Box 74, Grosse Ile, MI 48138, (734)676-2649

American Revolution

Descendants of the Signers of the Declaration of Independence **[3048]**

Natl. Soc., Daughters of the Amer. Revolution **[3049]**

Natl. Soc., Sons of the Amer. Revolution **[3050]**

Gen. Soc. of Mayflower Descendants **[3077]**

Amer. Road and Trans. Builders Assn. **[1381]**, 1219 28th St. NW, Washington, DC 20007-3389, (202)289-4434

Amer. Royal Assn. **[1157]**, 1701 Amer. Royal Ct., Kansas City, MO 64102, (816)221-9800

Amer. Salvage Pool Assn. **[69]**, PMB 709, 2900 Delk Rd., Ste. 700, Marietta, GA 30067, (678)560-6678

Amer. Satin Rabbit Breeders' Assn. **[1188]**, 3500 S Wagner Rd., Ann Arbor, MI 48103, (734)668-6709

Amer. School Band Directors' Assn. **[1665]**, PO Box 696, Guttenberg, IA 52052, (563)252-2500

Amer. Sci. Glassblowers Soc. **[789]**, PO Box 453, Machias, NY 14101, (716)353-8062

Amer. Small Bus. Travelers Alliance **[880]**, PO Box 270543, Flower Mound, TX 75027-0543, (972)836-8064

Amer. Soc. of Abdominal Surgeons **[2598]**, 824 Main St., 2nd Fl., Ste. 1, Melrose, MA 02176, (781)665-6102

Amer. Soc. of Addiction Medicine **[2596]**, 4601 N Park Ave., Upper Arcade No. 101, Chevy Chase, MD 20815, (301)656-3920

Amer. Soc. for Advancement of Anesthesia and Sedation in Dentistry **[2302]**, 6 E Union Ave., Bound Brook, NJ 08805, (732)469-9050

Amer. Soc. of Agricultural Appraisers **[49]**, PO Box 186, Twin Falls, ID 83303-0186, (208)733-1122

Amer. Soc. of Artists **[1715]**, PO Box 1326, Palatine, IL 60078, (312)751-2500

Amer. Soc. for Biochemistry and Molecular Biology **[1417]**, 11200 Rockville Pike, Ste. 302, Rockville, MD 20852-3110, (240)283-6600

Amer. Soc. of Church History **[2941]**, PO Box 2216, Hewitt, TX 76643-2216, (254)666-2457

Amer. Soc. for Clinical Investigation **[2347]**, 15 Res. Dr., Ann Arbor, MI 48103, (734)222-6050

Amer. Soc. of Concrete Contractors **[215]**, 2025 S Brentwood Blvd., Ste. 105, St. Louis, MO 63144, (314)962-0210

Amer. Soc. of Consulting Arborists **[1222]**, 9707 Key W Ave., Ste. 100, Rockville, MD 20850, (301)947-0483

Amer. Soc. for Cytotechnology **[2358]**, 1500 Sunday Dr., Ste. 102, Raleigh, NC 27607, (919)861-5571

Amer. Soc. for Dermatologic Surgery **[2393]**, 5550 Meadowbrook Dr., Ste. 120, Rolling Meadows, IL 60008, (847)956-0900

Amer. Soc. of Dowsers **[1517]**, PO Box 24, Danville, VT 05828, (802)684-3417

Amer. Soc. for Engg. Mgt. **[1466]**, PO Box 820, Rolla, MO 65402-0820, (573)341-6228

Amer. Soc. for Environmental History **[1618]**, Univ. of Washington, Interdisciplinary Arts and Sciences Prog., 1900 Commerce St., Tacoma, WA 98402

Amer. Soc. for Ethnohistory [1754], Duke Univ. Press, PO Box 906660, Durham, NC 27708-0660, (919)687-3602

Amer. Soc. of Genealogists [3063], PO Box 26836, San Diego, CA 92196

Amer. Soc. of Hand Therapists [2423], 15000 Commerce Pkwy., Ste. C, Mount Laurel, NJ 08054, (856)380-6856

Amer. Soc. for Indexing [1795], 10200 W 44th Ave., Ste. 304, Wheat Ridge, CO 80033, (303)463-2887

Amer. Soc. of Interior Designers [505], 608 Massachusetts Ave. NE, Washington, DC 20002-6006, (202)546-3480

Amer. Soc. of Law, Medicine and Ethics [2534], 765 Commonwealth Ave., Ste. 1634, Boston, MA 02215-1401, (617)262-4990

Amer. Soc. for Legal History [1768], c/o Prof. Patricia Minter, Chair Membership Comm., Western Kentucky Univ., 1906 Coll. Heights Blvd., No. 21086, Bowling Green, KY 42101-1086

Amer. Soc. of Master Dental Technologists [2379], 146-21 13th Ave., Whitestone, NY 11357-2420, (718)746-8355

Amer. Soc. of Maxillofacial Surgeons [2572], 900 Cummings Ctr., Ste. 221-U, Beverly, MA 01915, (978)927-8330

Amer. Soc. of Missiology [2989], 2100 S Summit Ave., Sioux Falls, SD 57105, (605)336-6588

Amer. Soc. of News Editors [687], 11690B Sunrise Valley Dr., Reston, VA 20191-1436, (703)453-1122

Amer. Soc. of Pediatric Hematology/Oncology [2458], 4700 W Lake Ave., Glenview, IL 60025-1485, (847)375-4716

Amer. Soc. of Photographers [1841], 3120 N Argonne Dr., Milwaukee, WI 53222, (414)871-6600

Amer. Soc. of Picture Professionals [664], 217 Palos Verdes Blvd., No. 700, Redondo Beach, CA 90277, (424)247-9944

Amer. Soc. of Plumbing Engineers [1467], 2980 S River Rd., Des Plaines, IL 60018, (847)296-0002

American Soc. of Plumbing Engineers Res. Foundation [★1467]

Amer. Soc. of Questioned Document Examiners [1301], PO Box 18298, Long Beach, CA 90807, (562)901-3376

Amer. Soc. of Regional Anesthesia and Pain Medicine [2303], 520 N Northwest Hwy., Park Ridge, IL 60068-2573, (847)825-7246

Amer. Soc. of Sanitary Engg. [1528], 901 Canterbury Rd., Ste. A, Westlake, OH 44145, (440)835-3040

Amer. Soc. of Sugar Cane Technologists [1215], AgCenter, Sturgis Hall No. 128, Baton Rouge, LA 70803, (225)578-6930

Amer. Soc. of Theatre Consultants [209], c/o Edgar L. Lustig, Sec./CFO, 12226 Mentz Hill Rd., St. Louis, MO 63128, (314)843-9218

Amer. Soc. of Women Accountants [1], 1760 Old Meadow Rd., Ste. 500, McLean, VA 22102, (703)506-3265

Amer. Solar Energy Soc. [1535], 4760 Walnut St., Ste. 106, Boulder, CO 80301, (303)443-3130

American South

Inst. for Southern Stud. [1703]

Southern Historical Assn. [1704]

Amer. Southdown Breeders' Assn. [1207], 100 Cornerstone Rd., Fredonia, TX 76842, (325)429-6226

Amer. Spice Trade Assn. [359], 2025 M St. NW, Ste. 800, Washington, DC 20036, (202)367-1127

Amer. Stamp Dealers Assn. [439], 217-14 Northern Blvd., Ste. 205, Bayside, NY 11361, (718)224-2500

Amer. Subcontractors Assn. [216], 1004 Duke St., Alexandria, VA 22314-3588, (703)684-3450

Amer. Taxation Assn. [1377], 9201 Univ. City Blvd., Charlotte, NC 28223, (704)687-7696

Amer. Technion Soc. [1647], 55 E 59th St., New York, NY 10022-1112, (212)407-6300

Amer. Telugu Assn. [1747], PO Box 4496, Naperville, IL 60567, (630)783-2250

Amer. Tennis Assn. [3421], 9701 Apollo Dr., Ste. 301, Largo, MD 20774, (240)487-5953

Amer. Trakehner Assn. [1121], 1536 W Church St., Newark, OH 43055, (740)344-1111

Amer. Turkish Friendship Coun. [2678], 1266 W Paces Ferry Rd., No. 257, Atlanta, GA 30327-2306, (404)848-9600

American-Uzbekistan Chamber of Commerce [3471], 1300 Connecticut Ave. NW, Ste. 501, Washington, DC 20036, (202)223-1770

Amer. Veterinary Medical Law Assn. [1322], 1666 K St. NW, Ste. 260, Washington, DC 20006, (202)449-3818

Amer. Wagyu Assn. [978], PO Box 547, Pullman, WA 99163, (509)335-0519

Amer. Waldensian Soc. [3038], PO Box 398, Valdese, NC 28690, (828)874-3500

Amer. Walnut Mfrs. Assn. [386], 1007 N 725 W, West Lafayette, IN 47906-9431

Amer. Warmblood Registry [1122], PO Box 197, Carter, MT 59420, (406)734-5499

Amer. Waterslager Soc. [3139], 556 S Cactus Wren St., Gilbert, AZ 85296, (480)892-5464

American West

Traditional Cowboy Arts Assn. [1705]

Amer. Wholesale Marketers Assn. [360], 2750 Prosperity Ave., Ste. 530, Fairfax, VA 22031, (703)208-3358

Amer. Woman's Soc. of Certified Public Accountants [2], 136 S Keowee St., Dayton, OH 45402, (937)222-1872

American Women in Radio and TV [★125]

Amer. Y-Flyer Yacht Racing Assn. [3269], 7349 Scarborough Blvd., East Dr., Indianapolis, IN 46256-2052, (317)849-7588

Amer. Youth Circus Org. [1744], PO Box 96, Temple, NH 03084, (603)654-5523

Amer. Youth Found. [3045], 6357 Clayton Rd., St. Louis, MO 63117, (314)963-1321

Amer. Youth Horse Coun. [1123], 577 N Boyero Ave., Pueblo West, CO 81007, (719)594-9778

Amer. Youth Soccer Org. [3393], 19750 S Vermont Ave., Ste. 200, Torrance, CA 90502, (800)872-2976

Americanism Educational League [2652], PO Box 1287, Monrovia, CA 91017, (626)357-7733

Americans Care and Share [300], PO Box 600370, San Diego, CA 92160, (619)481-3085

Americans for Peace Now [2689], 1101 14th St. NW, 6th Fl., Washington, DC 20005, (202)408-9898

Americans for a Safe Israel [2700], 1751 2nd Ave., New York, NY 10128-5363, (800)235-3658

Americans United for Separation of Church and State [2899], 1301 K St. NW, Ste. 850, E Tower, Washington, DC 20005, (202)466-3234

Americas

Americas Soc. [2610]

Partners of the Americas [2611]

America's Blood Centers [2325], 725 15th St. NW, Ste. 700, Washington, DC 20005, (202)393-5725

America's Natural Gas Alliance [639], 701 Eighth St. NW, Ste. 800, Washington, DC 20001, (202)789-2642

Americas Soc. [2610], 680 Park Ave., New York, NY 10021, (212)249-8950

AmeriCorps VISTA [2257], 1201 New York Ave. NW, Washington, DC 20005, (202)606-5000

AMIT [2947], 817 Broadway, New York, NY 10003, (212)477-4720

Amman Imman: Water is Life [2260], 7700 Old Georgetown Rd., Ste. 550, Bethesda, MD 20814

AMOA Natl. Dart Assn. [3315], 9100 Purdue Rd., Ste. 200, Indianapolis, IN 46268, (317)387-1299

Amputation Found; Natl. [2061]

Amusement and Music Operators Assn. [308], 600 Spring Hill Ring Rd., Ste. 111, West Dundee, IL 60118, (847)428-7699

Amy Beth Fan Club [3572], Peridot Records, PO Box 8846, Cranston, RI 02920, (401)785-2677

Ancient and Accepted Scottish Rite of Free Masonry, Southern Jurisdiction l Supreme Coun. 33rd Degree [2804], 1733 16th St. NW, Washington, DC 20009-3103, (202)232-3579

Andean Hea. and Development [2479], 2039 Winnebago St., No. 8, Madison, WI 53704, (619)788-6833

Anesthesiology

Amer. Osteopathic Coll. of Anesthesiologists [2301]

Amer. Soc. for Advancement of Anesthesia and Sedation in Dentistry [2302]

Amer. Soc. of Regional Anesthesia and Pain Medicine [2303]

Assn. of Univ. Anesthesiologists [2304]

Soc. of Cardiovascular Anesthesiologists [2305]

Angel Capital Assn. [524], 10977 Granada Ln., Ste. 103, Overland Park, KS 66211, (913)894-4700

Angel Harps [2588], PO Box 704, Wildomar, CA 92595, (951)246-0320

Anglers for Conservation [1005], PO Box 373257, Satellite Beach, FL 32937, (321)446-8240

Anglican Catholic

Amer. Friends of the Anglican Centre in Rome [2837]

Fellowship of Concerned Churchmen [2838]

Animal Breeding

Alpaca Breeders of the Rockies [939]

Amer. Legend [940]

Amer. Miniature Llama Assn. [941]

Amer. Mule Assn. [942]

Amer. Ostrich Assn. [943]

Empress Chinchilla Breeders Cooperative [944]

Llama Assn. of North Am. [945]

North Amer. Potbellied Pig Assn. [946]

Amer. Azteca Horse Intl. Assn. [1111]

Amer. Cockatiel Soc. [3138]

Boykin Spaniel Club and Breeders Assn. of Am. [3174]

Havana Silk Dog Assn. of Am. [3176]

Intl. Trotting and Pacing Assn. [3345]

North Amer. South Devon Assn. [989]

Thoroughbred Club of Am. [3348]

U.S.A. Coton de Tular Club [3186]

Animal Research

Boykin Spaniel Club and Breeders Assn. of Am. [3174]

Walking Horse Trainers Assn. [1151]

Animal Rights

Amer. Horse League [2100]

Animal Welfare Advocacy [1889]

Animals Deserve Absolute Protection Today and Tomorrow [1890]

Born Free USA [1894]

DreamCatcher Wild Horse and Burro Sanctuary [1895]

Global Animal Partnership [951]

SPCA Intl. [1900]

U.S.A. Defenders of Greyhounds [1901]

Animal Rights Coalition [1887], 317 W 48th St., Minneapolis, MN 55419, (612)822-6161

Animal Science

Amer. Embryo Transfer Assn. [947]

Intl. Marine Animal Trainers Assn. [948]

Animal Trans. Assn. [1888], 12100 Sunset Hills Rd., Ste. 130, Reston, VA 20190, (703)437-4377

Animal Welfare

Animal Rights Coalition [1887]

Animal Trans. Assn. [1888]

Animal Welfare Advocacy [1889]

Animal World USA [949]

Animals Deserve Absolute Protection Today and Tomorrow [1890]

Animals and Soc. Inst. [1891]

Assoc. Humane Societies [1892]

Bideawee [1893]

Born Free USA [1894]

Darwin Animal Doctors [950]

DreamCatcher Wild Horse and Burro Sanctuary [1895]

Global Animal Partnership [951]

Humane Soc. of the U.S. [1896]

Kids Making a Difference [952]

Natl. Humane Educ. Soc. [1897]

Prevent a Litter Coalition [1898]

Primarily Primates, Inc. [1899]

SPCA Intl. [1900]

U.S.A. Defenders of Greyhounds [1901]

World Vets [1902]

Amer. Azteca Horse Intl. Assn. [1111]

Amer. Cockatiel Soc. [3138]

Amer. Horse League [2100]

Amer. Humane Assn. [2229]

Ape Action Africa [1231]

Ape Conservation Effort [1232]

Intl. Trotting and Pacing Assn. [3345]

Panthera [1251]

Thoroughbred Club of Am. [3348]

Turtle Island Restoration Network [1044]

A star before a book entry number signifies that the name is not listed separately, but is mentioned within the entry.

Wild Animals Worldwide **[1257]**
World Nature Coalition **[1262]**
Animal Welfare Advocacy **[1889]**, PO Box 737,
Mamaroneck, NY 10543, (914)381-6177
Animal World USA **[949]**, 5255 Brantford Dr.,
Memphis, TN 38120, (901)791-2455

Animals
Princess Kitty Fan Club **[3566]**
Amer. Azteca Horse Intl. Assn. **[1111]**
Amer. Cockatiel Soc. **[3138]**
Amer. Horse League **[2100]**
Amer. Kiko Goat Assn. **[1106]**
Animal Welfare Advocacy **[1889]**
Animal World USA **[949]**
Animals Deserve Absolute Protection Today and
Tomorrow **[1890]**
Ape Action Africa **[1231]**
Ape Conservation Effort **[1232]**
Big Wildlife **[1233]**
Born Free USA **[1894]**
Boykin Spaniel Club and Breeders Assn. of Am.
[3174]
Darwin Animal Doctors **[950]**
Global Animal Partnership **[951]**
Havana Silk Dog Assn. of Am. **[3176]**
Intl. Trotting and Pacing Assn. **[3345]**
Kids Making a Difference **[952]**
Natl. Versatility Ranch Horse Assn. **[3352]**
Panthera **[1251]**
Shark Alliance **[1254]**
SPCA Intl. **[1900]**
Thoroughbred Club of Am. **[3348]**
U.S.A. Coton de Tulear Club **[3186]**
U.S. Complete Shooting Dog Assn. **[3187]**
U.S.A. Defenders of Greyhounds **[1901]**
Walking Horse Trainers Assn. **[1151]**
Wild Animals Worldwide **[1257]**
Wild Felid Res. and Mgt. Assn. **[1258]**
Wonderful World of Wildlife **[1260]**
World Nature Coalition **[1262]**
World Vets **[1902]**
Animals Deserve Absolute Protection Today and
Tomorrow **[1890]**, PO Box 725, Royal Oak, MI
48068
Animals and Soc. Inst. **[1891]**, 2512 Carpenter Rd.,
Ste. 202-A, Ann Arbor, MI 48108, (734)677-9240
Answer Africa **[2397]**, 203 E Avenida San Juan, San
Clemente, CA 92672, (949)498-5274

Anthropology
Amer. Ethnological Soc. **[1400]**
Coun. on Anthropology and Educ. **[1401]**
Lambda Alpha **[3508]**
Soc. for Visual Anthropology **[1402]**
Soc. for Ethnomusicology **[1828]**

Anti-Poverty
Children of Tanzania **[1903]**
Eliminate Poverty Now **[1904]**
Green for All **[2612]**
Haiti Outreach **[1905]**
HavServe Volunteer Ser. Network **[1906]**
Hearts for Kenya **[1907]**
Innovations for Poverty Action **[2613]**
Millennium Campus Network **[2614]**
Out of Poverty thru Educ. **[1568]**
Rising Intl. **[1908]**
Americans Care and Share **[2182]**
Community Empowerment Network **[2211]**
Jamaica Unite **[2025]**
Partners in Sustainable Development Intl. **[2171]**
Shining Hope for Communities **[2035]**
Tusubira - We Have Hope **[2173]**
Union MicroFinanza **[2213]**
Village Focus Intl. **[2037]**
Antiquarian Booksellers Assn. of Am. **[1738]**, 20 W
44th St., Ste. 507, New York, NY 10036-6604,
(212)944-8291
Antique Advt. Assn. of Am. **[19]**, 13915 David Rd.,
Woodstock, IL 60098
Antique and Amusement Photographers Intl. **[665]**,
PO Box 15117, Arlington, VA 22215, (479)253-
8554
Antique Auto. Club of Am. **[3095]**, PO Box 417, Her-
shey, PA 17033, (717)534-1910
Antique Caterpillar Machinery Owners Club **[3211]**,
7501 N Univ., Ste. 119, Peoria, IL 61614,
(309)691-5002
Antique and Classic Boat Soc. **[3270]**, 422 James
St., Clayton, NY 13624, (315)686-2628

Antique Motorcycle Club of Am. **[3217]**, c/o Trudi
Johnson-Richards, Natl. Sec., 3295 Victoria St.,
Shoreview, MN 55126, (651)482-0096

Antiques
The Questers **[3091]**
Antique Advt. Assn. of Am. **[19]**
Antique Caterpillar Machinery Owners Club **[3211]**
Antique Motorcycle Club of Am. **[3217]**
Colonial Coin Collectors Club **[3222]**
Corvair Soc. of Am. **[3100]**
First Issues Collectors Club **[3226]**
Intl. Fire Buff Associates **[3192]**
Korea Stamp Soc. **[3228]**
Midstates Jeepster Assn. **[3117]**
Morgan Car Club **[3120]**
Plasticville Collectors Assn. **[3237]**
United Four-Wheel Drive Associations **[3135]**
Vintage Garden Tractor Club of Am. **[3246]**
World Airline Historical Soc. **[3089]**

Antiquities
Antique Caterpillar Machinery Owners Club **[3211]**
Colonial Coin Collectors Club **[3222]**

Anti-Racism
A World of Difference Inst. **[2004]**

Anti-Semitism
A World of Difference Inst. **[2004]**
Anxiety Disorders Assn. of Am. **[2161]**, 8730
Georgia Ave., Ste. 600, Silver Spring, MD 20910,
(240)485-1001
Ape Action Africa **[1231]**, 205 S Dixie Dr., No. 1014,
Haines City, FL 33844
Ape Conservation Effort **[1232]**, 800 Cherokee Ave.
SE, Atlanta, GA 30315, (404)624-5963

Apiculture
Amer. Assn. of Professional Apiculturists **[953]**
Amer. Honey Producers Assn. **[954]**
Apostolate for Family Consecration **[2854]**, 3375
County Rd. 36, Bloomingdale, OH 43910,
(740)765-5500

Appalachian
Melungeon Heritage Assn. **[2766]**

Apparel
Custom Tailors and Designers Assn. of Am. **[45]**
World Shoe Assn. **[46]**
Appliance Parts Distributors Assn. **[47]**, 3621 N Oak-
ley Ave., Chicago, IL 60618, (773)230-9851

Appliances
Appliance Parts Distributors Assn. **[47]**
Natl. Appliance Parts Suppliers Assn. **[48]**
TopTen USA **[305]**

Appraisers
Amer. Soc. of Agricultural Appraisers **[49]**
Assn. of Appraiser Regulatory Officials **[50]**
Independent Automotive Damage Appraisers
Assn. **[51]**
Intl. Soc. of Appraisers **[52]**
Natl. Assn. of Real Estate Appraisers **[53]**

Appropriate Technology
Aprovecho Res. Center **[2615]**
Aprovecho Res. Center **[2615]**, 80574 Hazelton Rd.,
Cottage Grove, OR 97424, (541)942-8198
APVA Preservation Virginia **[1762]**, 204 W Franklin
St., Richmond, VA 23220, (804)648-1889

Aquaculture
Aquaculture Intl. **[955]**
The Catfish Inst. **[956]**
Global Aquaculture Alliance **[957]**
Intl. Professional Pond Contractors Assn. **[54]**
Marine Aquarium Coun. **[958]**
Sustainable Fisheries Partnership **[959]**
Intl. Seafood Sustainability Assn. **[355]**
Aquaculture Intl. **[955]**, 405 Union St., Murfreesboro,
NC 27855
Aquatic Plant Mgt. Soc. **[1429]**, PO Box 821265,
Vicksburg, MS 39182-1265, (601)634-2656

Arab
Amer. MidEast Leadership Network **[2677]**
Arab Amer. Inst. **[2726]**, 1600 K St. NW, Ste. 601,
Washington, DC 20006, (202)429-9210
Arab Amer. Women's Coun. **[2767]**, c/o Amer. Arab
Chamber of Commerce, 12740 W Warren Ave.,
Ste. 101, Dearborn, MI 48126, (313)945-1700
Arab Bankers Assn. of North Am. **[109]**, 150 W 28th
St., Ste. 801, New York, NY 10001, (212)599-3030

Arab-Israeli Relations
Ishmael and Isaac **[2702]**

Arabic
Arab Amer. Women's Coun. **[2767]**

Arbitration and Mediation
Assn. for Conflict Resolution **[1267]**
Archaeological Inst. of Am. **[1403]**, 656 Beacon St.,
6th Fl., Boston, MA 02215-2006, (617)353-9361

Archaeology
Archaeological Inst. of Am. **[1403]**
Inst. of Nautical Archaeology **[1404]**
Soc. for Historical Archaeology **[1405]**

Architectural Education
ArchVoices **[1407]**

Architecture
Amer. Inst. of Building Design **[1406]**
ArchVoices **[1407]**
Assn. of Licensed Architects **[55]**
Coun. of Landscape Architectural Registration
Boards **[1408]**
Graham Found. **[56]**
Ministry Architecture **[1409]**
Natl. Coun. of Architectural Registration Boards
[1268]
Natl. Org. of Minority Architects **[1410]**
Soc. of Amer. Registered Architects **[1411]**
Building Commissioning Assn. **[141]**
Coalition of Organic Landscapers **[531]**
Community Associations Inst. **[2627]**
Short Span Steel Bridge Alliance **[1434]**

Archives
Acad. of Certified Archivists **[57]**
ArchVoices **[1407]**, 1014 Curtis St., Albany, CA
94706, (510)757-6213

Argentina
Argentine-American Chamber of Commerce
[3472]
Argentine-American Chamber of Commerce **[3472]**,
630 5th Ave., 25th Fl., Rockefeller Ctr., New York,
NY 10111, (212)698-2238
Arise Medical Missions **[2480]**, 1350 Grantham Dr.,
Sarasota, FL 34234, (253)355-0179
Ark Mission **[1922]**, 830 S Buffalo Grove Rd., Ste.
103, Buffalo Grove, IL 60089, (847)215-2755

Armed Forces
Army and Air Force Mutual Aid Assn. **[2768]**
Military Intelligence Corps Assn. **[1269]**
USO World HQ **[2769]**
Salute Military Golf Assn. **[3339]**

Armenia
Armenian Amer. Chamber of Commerce **[3473]**

Armenian
Armenian Film Found. **[1706]**
Natl. Assn. for Armenian Stud. and Res. **[1707]**
Armenian Amer. Chamber of Commerce **[3473]**
Armenian Amer. Chamber of Commerce **[3473]**, 225
E Broadway, Ste. 313C, Glendale, CA 91205,
(818)247-0196
Armenian Film Found. **[1706]**, 2219 Thousand Oaks
Blvd., Ste. 292, Thousand Oaks, CA 91362,
(805)495-0717

Arms
Japanese Sword Soc. of the U.S. **[3092]**

Army
25th Infantry Div. Assn. **[3051]**
Natl. 4th Infantry Ivy Div. Assn. **[3052]**
Army and Air Force Mutual Aid Assn. **[2768]**, 102
Sheridan Ave., Bldg. 468, Fort Myer, VA 22211-
1110, (703)707-4600
Aromatherapy; Natl. Assn. for Holistic **[2461]**
Aromatherapy Registration Coun. **[2292]**, 530 1st
St., Ste. A, Lake Oswego, OR 97034, (503)244-
0726
ARRL Found. **[3090]**, 225 Main St., Newington, CT
06111, (860)594-0397

Art
Amer. Guild of Judaic Art **[1708]**
Assn. of Medical Illustrators **[2306]**
Assn. of Sci. Fiction and Fantasy Artists **[58]**
Fine Art Dealers Assn. **[59]**
Independent Arts and Media **[1709]**
Intl. Hajji Baba Soc. **[1710]**
New Art Dealers Alliance **[1711]**
Private Art Dealers Assn. **[60]**
Professional Picture Framers Assn. **[1712]**
Soc. for Asian Art **[1713]**
Artfully AWARE **[1724]**
Fed. of Modern Painters and Sculptors **[1716]**
Hero Initiative **[1745]**
Intl. Performing Arts for Youth **[1834]**
Polish Arts and Culture Found. **[2814]**

Spinning and Weaving Assn. **[858]**

Art Directors Guild **[1756]**, 11969 Ventura Blvd., 2nd Fl., Studio City, CA 91604, (818)762-9995

Art Therapy

Artfully AWARE **[1724]**

Artfully AWARE **[1724]**, 201 E 17th St., 27D, New York, NY 10003

Artist-Blacksmith's Assn. of North Am. **[119]**, 259 Muddy Fork Rd., Jonesborough, TN 37659, (423)913-1022

Artists

Allied Artists of Am. **[1714]**

Amer. Soc. of Artists **[1715]**

Fed. of Modern Painters and Sculptors **[1716]**

Graphic Artists Guild **[1717]**

Natl. Cartoonists Soc. **[1718]**

Pollock-Krasner Found. **[1719]**

Silk Painters Intl. **[1720]**

Soc. of Illustrators **[1721]**

Women's Caucus for Art **[1722]**

Creativity Coaching Assn. **[3305]**

Hero Initiative **[1745]**

Independent Arts and Media **[1709]**

Intl. Performing Arts for Youth **[1834]**

Artists in Christian Testimony **[2925]**, PO Box 1649, Brentwood, TN 37024-1649, (615)376-7861

Arts

Amer. Fired Arts Alliance **[1723]**

Artfully AWARE **[1724]**

Assn. of Arts Admin. Educators **[1569]**

Coun. of Colleges of Arts and Sciences **[1570]**

Natl. Alliance for Media Arts and Culture **[1725]**

Natl. Art Educ. Assn. **[1571]**

Natl. Assembly of State Arts Agencies **[1726]**

Performing Arts Alliance **[1727]**

River of Words **[960]**

Creativity Coaching Assn. **[3305]**

Independent Arts and Media **[1709]**

Intl. Performing Arts for Youth **[1834]**

Arts and Sciences

Leonardo, The Intl. Soc. for the Arts, Sciences and Tech. **[1728]**

ASFE **[1483]**, 8811 Colesville Rd., Ste. G106, Silver Spring, MD 20910, (301)565-2733

The Asia Found. **[2728]**, PO Box 193223, San Francisco, CA 94119-3223, (415)982-4640

Asian

Asian/Pacific Amer. Heritage Assn. **[2770]**

U.S.-Vietnam Trade Coun. **[2616]**

Intl. Soc. of Filipinos in Finance and Accounting **[8]**

Asian Am. MultiTechnology Assn. **[277]**, 3 W 37th Ave., Ste. 19, San Mateo, CA 94403-4470, (650)350-1124

Asian-American

Union of North Am. Vietnamese Students Assn. **[2832]**

Asian Amer. Journalists Assn. **[688]**, 5 Third St., Ste. 1108, San Francisco, CA 94103, (415)346-2051

Asian Financial Soc. **[326]**, 32 Broadway, Ste. 1701, New York, NY 10004, (646)580-5066

Asian/Pacific Amer. Heritage Assn. **[2770]**, 6220 Westpark, Ste. 245B, Houston, TX 77057, (713)784-1112

Asian Pacific Amer. Labor Alliance **[3448]**, 815 16th St. NW, Washington, DC 20006, (202)508-3733

Asian Pacific Amer. Librarians Assn. **[1796]**, Loyola Law School, William M. Rains Lib., 919 Albany St., Los Angeles, CA 90015, (213)736-1431

Asphalt Emulsion Mfrs. Assn. **[135]**, 3 Church Cir., PMB 250, Annapolis, MD 21401, (410)267-0023

Assault

Intl. Center for Assault Prevention **[2072]**

Assistance Dogs Intl. **[2054]**, PO Box 5174, Santa Rosa, CA 95402

Assoc. Air Balance Coun. **[136]**, 1518 K St. NW, Washington, DC 20005, (202)737-0202

Assoc. Builders and Contractors **[217]**, 4250 N Fairfax Dr., 9th Fl., Arlington, VA 22203-1607, (703)812-2000

Assoc. Builders and Contractors I Natl. Elecl. Contractors Coun. **[218]**, 4250 N Fairfax Dr., 9th Fl., Arlington, VA 22203-1607, (703)812-2000

Assoc. Church Press **[719]**, PO Box 621001, Oviedo, FL 32762-1001, (407)341-6615

Assoc. Constr. Distributors Intl. **[137]**, 1605 SE Delaware Ave., Ste. B, Ankeny, IA 50021, (515)964-1335

Assoc. Humane Societies **[1892]**, 124 Evergreen Ave., Newark, NJ 07114-2133, (973)824-7080

Assoc. Koi Clubs of Am. **[3196]**, 40211 Redbud Dr., Oakhurst, CA 93644, (559)658-5295

Assoc. Parishes for Liturgy and Mission **[2915]**, PO Box 543, Hughsonville, NY 12537

Assoc. Press Managing Editors **[689]**, c/o Sally Jacobsen, 450 W 33rd St., New York, NY 10001, (212)621-1838

Assoc. Wire Rope Fabricators **[459]**, PO Box 748, Walled Lake, MI 48390-0748, (248)994-7753

Assn. of Academic Museums and Galleries **[1813]**, Jordan Schnitzer Museum of Art, 1223 Univ. of Oregon, Eugene, OR 97403-1223, (541)346-0972

Assn. for the Advancement of Automotive Medicine **[2216]**, PO Box 4176, Barrington, IL 60011-4176, (847)844-3880

Assn. for the Advancement of Baltic Stud. **[1737]**, Univ. of Washington, Box 353420, Seattle, WA 98195-3420

Assn. for the Advancement of Intl. Educ. **[1644]**, Nova Southeastern Univ., Fischler School of Educ. and Human Services, 3970 RCA Blvd., Ste. 7000, Palm Beach Gardens, FL 33410, (954)262-5691

Assn. of African Stud. Programs **[1700]**, c/o Judith A. Byfield, Cornell Univ., Stud. and Res. Center, 310 Triphammer Rd., Ithaca, NY 14850

Assn. of Air Medical Services **[2404]**, 909 N Washington St., Ste. 410, Alexandria, VA 22314-3143, (703)836-8732

Assn. of Alternative Newsweeklies **[690]**, 1156 15th St. NW, Ste. 905, Washington, DC 20005, (202)289-8484

Assn. of Amer. Editorial Cartoonists **[691]**, 3899 N Front St., Harrisburg, PA 17110, (717)703-3003

Assn. of Amer. Law Schools **[1656]**, 1201 Connecticut Ave. NW, Ste. 800, Washington, DC 20036-2717, (202)296-8851

Assn. of Amer. State Geologists **[1482]**, Kentucky Geological Survey, 228 Mining and Mineral Resources Bldg., Lexington, KY 40506-0107, (859)257-5500

Assn. of Amer. Veterinary Medical Colleges **[1695]**, 1101 Vermont Ave. NW, Ste. 301, Washington, DC 20005, (202)371-9195

Assn. of Anglican Musicians **[3018]**, PO Box 7530, Little Rock, AR 72217, (501)661-9925

Assn. of Appraiser Regulatory Officials **[50]**, 13200 Strickland Rd., Ste. 114-264, Raleigh, NC 27613, (919)235-4544

Assn. of Art Museum Directors **[1814]**, 120 E 56th St., Ste. 520, New York, NY 10022, (212)754-8084

Assn. of Arts Admin. Educators **[1569]**, 4222 Oakland Dr., Kalamazoo, MI 49008, (608)561-2040

Assn. for Automatic Identification and Mobility North Am. **[66]**, 1 Landmark N, 20399 Rte., Ste. 203, Cranberry Township, PA 16066, (724)742-4473

Assn. of Average Adjusters of the U.S. **[480]**, c/o Eileen M. Fellin, Sec., 126 Midwood Ave., Farmingdale, NY 11735

Assn. of Baptists for World Evangelism **[2840]**, PO Box 8585, Harrisburg, PA 17105-8585, (717)774-7000

Assn. for Better Insulation **[138]**, 3906 Auburn Hills Dr., Greensboro, NC 27407, (603)768-3984

Assn. of Biblical Counselors **[2901]**, 209 N Indus. Blvd., Ste. 237, Bedford, TX 76021, (877)222-4551

Assn. for Biblical Higher Educ. **[1586]**, 5850 T.G. Lee Blvd., Ste. 130, Orlando, FL 32822, (407)207-0808

Assn. of Biomedical Communications Directors **[2350]**, SUNY Downstate Medical Center, Box 18, Brooklyn, NY 11203, (423)439-2402

Assn. of Black Psychologists **[2583]**, PO Box 55999, Washington, DC 20040-5999, (202)722-0808

The Assn. of Boarding Schools **[1676]**, 1 N Pack Square., Ste. 301, Asheville, NC 28801, (828)258-5354

Assn. of Bridal Consultants **[122]**, 56 Danbury Rd., Ste. 11, New Milford, CT 06776, (860)355-7000

Assn. of Catholic Colleges and Universities **[1579]**, 1 Dupont Cir., Ste. 650, Washington, DC 20036, (202)457-0650

Assn. of Certified Background Investigators **[1315]**, PO Box 80413, Staten Island, NY 10308

Assn. of Chartered Accountants in the U.S. **[3]**, 1050 Winter St., Ste. 1000, Waltham, MA 02451, (508)395-0224

Assn. of Chinese-American Professionals **[2776]**, 10303 Westoffice Dr., Houston, TX 77042-5306

Assn. of Cinema and Video Labs. **[321]**, c/o Peter Bulcke, Treas., 1833 Centinela Ave., Santa Monica, CA 90404, (310)828-1098

Assn. of Clinical Scientists **[2348]**, PO Box 1287, Middlebury, VT 05753, (802)458-3351

Assn. of Coll. and Univ. Auditors **[1561]**, PO Box 14306, Lenexa, KS 66285-4306, (913)895-4620

Assn. for Communications Tech. Professionals in Higher Educ; ACUTA: The **[1634]**

Assn. of Community Cancer Centers **[2328]**, 11600 Nebel St., Ste. 201, Rockville, MD 20852-2557, (301)984-9496

Assn. for Conflict Resolution **[1267]**, 12100 Sunset Hills Rd., Ste. 130, Reston, VA 20190, (703)234-4141

Assn. for Conservation Engineers **[1006]**, c/o Kathy Dillmon, Sec., Wyoming Game & Fish U.S. Department of, 5400 Bishop Blvd., Cheyenne, WY 82006

Assn. of Constr. Inspectors **[476]**, PO Box 879, Palm Springs, CA 92263, (760)327-5284

Assn. of Consulting Foresters of Am. **[1091]**, 312 Montgomery St., Ste. 208, Alexandria, VA 22314, (703)548-0990

Assn. for Convention Marketing Executives **[441]**, 204 E St., NE, Washington, DC 20002, (202)547-8030

Assn. for Convention Operations Mgt. **[610]**, 191 Clarksville Rd., Princeton Junction, NJ 08550, (609)799-3712

Assn. of Corporate Counsel **[1283]**, 1025 Connecticut Ave. NW, Ste. 200, Washington, DC 20036-5425, (202)293-4103

Assn. of Corporate Travel Executives **[881]**, 515 King St., Ste. 440, Alexandria, VA 22314, (703)683-5322

Assn. of Credit Union Internal Auditors **[247]**, 815 King St., Ste. 308, Alexandria, VA 22314, (703)535-5757

Assn. of Defense Trial Attorneys **[1306]**, 4135 Topsail Trail, New Port Richey, FL 34652, (727)859-0350

Assn. of Divorce Financial Planners **[347]**, 514 Fourth St., East Northport, NY 11731, (631)754-6125

Assn. of Ecosystem Res. Centers **[1052]**, c/o Robin Graham, Sec., Environmental Sciences Div., Oak Ridge Natl. Lab., PO Box 2008, Oak Ridge, TN 37831, (865)576-7756

Assn. of Edison Illuminating Companies **[892]**, c/o Earl B. Parsons, Jr., Exec. Dir./Sec.-Treas., PO Box 2641, Birmingham, AL 35291, (205)257-2530

Assn. for Educ. Finance and Policy **[1609]**, c/o Susanna Loeb, Pres., 524 Ceras, 520 Galvez Mall, Stanford, CA 94305, (650)736-1258

Assn. for Educ. and Rehabilitation of the Blind and Visually Impaired **[2600]**, 1703 N Beauregard St., Ste. 440, Alexandria, VA 22311, (703)671-4500

Assn. for Enterprise Info. **[163]**, 2111 Wilson Blvd., Ste. 400, Arlington, VA 22201, (703)247-9474

Assn. for Enterprise Opportunity **[821]**, 1111 16th St. NW, Ste. 410, Washington, DC 20036, (202)650-5580

Assn. of Environmental and Rsrc. Economists **[1007]**, Iowa State Univ., Dept. of Economics, 568 Heady Hall, Ames, IA 50011-1070, (515)294-5767

Assn. of Equip. Mfrs. I AEM Marketing Coun. **[595]**, 6737 W Washington St., Ste. 2400, Milwaukee, WI 53214-5647, (414)298-4146

Assn. for Explosive Detection K-9s, Intl. **[1328]**, PO Box 176, Aquilla, TX 76622, (386)788-4083

Assn. for Facilities Engg. **[1468]**, 12801 Worldgate Dr., Ste. 500, Herndon, VA 20170, (571)203-7111

Assn. of Family and Conciliation Courts **[1295]**, 6525 Grand Teton Plz., Madison, WI 53719, (608)664-3750

Assn. of Farmworker Opportunity Programs **[2144]**, 1726 M St. NW, Ste. 602, Washington, DC 20036, (202)826-6006

A star before a book entry number signifies that the name is not listed separately, but is mentioned within the entry.

Assn. of Fed. Communications Consulting Engineers **[1545]**, PO Box 19333, Washington, DC 20036

Assn. for Fed. Info. Resources Mgt. **[1305]**, 400 N Washington St., Ste. 300, Alexandria, VA 22314, (703)778-4646

Assn. for Feminist Ethics and Social Theory **[1837]**, c/o Dr. Chris Frakes, Treas., 619 N Prospect St., Colorado Springs, CO 80903

Assn. for Financial Professionals **[327]**, 4520 E West Hwy., Ste. 750, Bethesda, MD 20814, (301)907-2862

Assn. for Financial Tech. **[12]**, 34 N High St., New Albany, OH 43054, (614)895-1208

Assn. for Fire Ecology **[1053]**, PO Box 1054, Redlands, CA 92373, (541)852-7903

Assn. of Firearm and Tool Mark Examiners **[1476]**, c/o Andy G. Smith, Membership Sec., San Francisco Police Dept., PO Box 34426, San Francisco, CA 94134, (415)671-3264

Assn. of Fish and Wildlife Agencies **[1008]**, 444 N Capitol St. NW, Ste. 725, Washington, DC 20001, (202)624-7890

Assn. of Flight Attendants - CWA **[3438]**, 501 3rd St. NW, Washington, DC 20001, (202)434-1300

Assn. of Fraternity Advisors **[3523]**, 9640 N Augusta Dr., Ste. 433, Carmel, IN 46032, (317)876-1632

Assn. of Fundraising Professionals **[2088]**, 4300 Wilson Blvd., Ste. 300, Arlington, VA 22203, (703)684-0410

Assn. of Genetic Technologists **[1420]**, PO Box 19193, Lenexa, KS 66285, (913)895-4605

Assn. for Gerontology in Higher Educ. **[1626]**, 1220 L St. NW, Ste. 901, Washington, DC 20005-4018, (202)289-9806

The Assn. for the Gifted **[1627]**, Ball State Univ., BU 109, Muncie, IN 47306, (765)285-5390

Assn. of Golf Merchandisers **[828]**, PO Box 7247, Phoenix, AZ 85011-7247, (602)604-8250

Assn. of Governmental Risk Pools **[1307]**, PO Box J, Prague, OK 74864-1045, (405)567-2611

Assn. of Grace Brethren Ministers **[2851]**, PO Box 694, Winona Lake, IN 46590

Assn. of Graduate Liberal Stud. Programs **[1657]**, Duke Univ., Box 90095, Durham, NC 27708, (919)684-1987

Assn. of Green Property Owners and Managers **[713]**, 3400 Capitol Blvd. SE, Ste. 101, Tumwater, WA 98501, (425)646-6425

Assn. of Halfway House Alcoholism Programs of North Am. **[2239]**, 401 E Sangamon Ave., Springfield, IL 62702, (217)523-0527

Assn. of Hea. Care Journalists **[692]**, 10 Neff Hall, Columbia, MO 65211, (573)884-5606

Assn. of Healthcare Administrative Professionals **[13]**, 455 S 4th St., Ste. 650, Louisville, KY 40202, (502)574-9040

Assn. for Healthcare Documentation Integrity **[2545]**, 4230 Kiernan Ave., Ste. 130, Modesto, CA 95356, (209)527-9620

Assn. for Healthcare Foodservice **[2467]**, 455 S Fourth St., Ste. 650, Louisville, KY 40202, (502)574-9930

Assn. for Healthcare Philanthropy **[2468]**, 313 Park Ave., Ste. 400, Falls Church, VA 22046-3303, (703)532-6243

Assn. for Healthcare Volunteer Rsrc. Professionals **[2258]**, 155 N Wacker Dr., Ste. 400, Chicago, IL 60606-1725, (312)422-3939

Assn. for High Tech. Distribution **[278]**, N19 W24400 Riverwood Dr., Waukesha, WI 53188, (262)696-3645

Assn. of Home Off. Underwriters **[481]**, 2300 Windy Ridge Pkwy., Ste. 600, Atlanta, GA 30339, (770)984-3715

Assn. for Humanistic Psychology **[2584]**, PO Box 1190, Tiburon, CA 94920, (415)435-1604

Assn. of Independent Manufacturers'/Representatives **[575]**, 16 A Journey, Ste. 200, Aliso Viejo, CA 92656, (949)859-2884

Assn. of Indian Muslims of Am. **[2791]**, PO Box 10654, Silver Spring, MD 20914

Assn. for Info. Media and Equip. **[65]**, PO Box 9844, Cedar Rapids, IA 52409-9844, (319)654-0608

Assn. of Info. Tech. Professionals **[1594]**, 401 N Michigan Ave., Ste. 2400, Chicago, IL 60611-4267, (312)245-1070

Assn. of Ingersoll-Rand Distributors **[460]**, 1300 Sumner Ave., Cleveland, OH 44115-2851, (216)241-7333

Assn. of Insolvency and Restructuring Advisors **[4]**, 221 Stewart Ave., Ste. 207, Medford, OR 97501, (541)858-1665

Assn. for Intl. Agriculture and Rural Development **[1565]**, Univ. of California, Davis, Horticulture CRSP, 190 EH Bldg., 1 Shields Ave., Davis, CA 95616-5270, (530)752-7975

Association of Intl. Auto. Mfrs. **[★76]**

Assn. of Jewish Family and Children's Agencies **[2125]**, 5750 Park Heights Ave., Baltimore, MD 21215, (410)843-7573

Assn. of Labor Relations Agencies **[3450]**, Natl. Labor Relations Bd., 1099 14th St. NW, Ste. 11600, Washington, DC 20570, (202)273-1067

Assn. of Lab. Managers **[1492]**, 8630 Guilford Rd., Ste. M, Columbia, MD 21046-2654, (800)985-7879

Assn. for Lesbian, Gay, Bisexual and Transgender Issues in Counseling **[2093]**, Oakland Univ., 440B Pawley Hall, Rochester, MI 48309, (508)531-2721

Assn. of Licensed Architects **[55]**, 22159 N Pepper Rd., Ste. 2N, Barrington, IL 60010, (847)382-0630

Assn. of Life Insurance Counsel **[1308]**, 3815 River Crossing Pkwy., Ste. 100, Indianapolis, IN 46240, (317)566-2154

Assn. for Linen Mgt. **[535]**, 2161 Lexington Rd., Ste. 2, Richmond, KY 40475, (859)624-0177

Assn. of Lunar and Planetary Observers **[3093]**, c/o Matthew L. Will, Sec.-Treas., PO Box 13456, Springfield, IL 62791-3456

Assn. of Mailing, Shipping and Off. Automation Specialists **[548]**, 11310 Wornall Rd., Kansas City, MO 64114, (888)750-6245

Assn. for Mfg. Excellence **[580]**, 3701 Algonquin Rd., Ste. 225, Rolling Meadows, IL 60008-3127, (224)232-5980

Assn. of Marina Indus. **[593]**, 50 Water St., Warren, RI 02885, (866)367-6622

Assn. Media and Publishing **[62]**, 1760 Old Meadow Rd., Ste. 500, McLean, VA 22102, (703)506-3285

Assn. of Medical Diagnostics Mfrs. **[790]**, c/o Rebecca Shames, Admin. Asst., 555 13th St. NW, Ste. 7W-401, Washington, DC 20004, (202)637-6837

Assn. for Medical Educ. and Res. in Substance Abuse **[1661]**, PO Box 20160, Cranston, RI 02920, (401)243-8460

Assn. of Medical Illustrators **[2306]**, 201 E Main St., Ste. 1405, Lexington, KY 40507, (866)393-4264

Assn. of Military Surgeons of the U.S. **[2552]**, 9320 Old Georgetown Rd., Bethesda, MD 20814-1653, (301)897-8800

Assn. of Millwork Distributors **[139]**, 10047 Robert Trent Jones Pkwy., New Port Richey, FL 34655-4649, (727)372-3665

Assn. of Minority Hea. Professions Schools **[1662]**, PO Box 13778, Atlanta, GA 30324, (678)904-4217

Assn. of Moroccan Professionals in Am. **[164]**, 5301 Pooks Hill Rd., Bethesda, MD 20814

Assn. of Natl. Park Rangers **[1355]**, 25958 Genesse Trail Rd., PMB 222, Golden, CO 80401

Assn. of Natural Biocontrol Producers **[1178]**, c/o Lynn LeBeck, Exec. Dir., PO Box 1609, Clovis, CA 93613-1609, (559)360-7111

Assn. of Nepal and Himalayan Stud. **[1671]**, Macalester Coll., Dept. of Anthropology, St. Paul, MN 55105-1801, (651)696-6362

Assn. of Oncology Social Work **[2236]**, 100 N 20th St., 4th Fl., Philadelphia, PA 19103, (215)599-6093

Assn. of Otolaryngology Administrators **[2540]**, 2400 Ardmore Blvd., Ste. 302, Pittsburgh, PA 15221, (412)243-5156

Assn. of Outdoor Lighting Professionals **[545]**, 4305 N 6th St., Ste. A, Harrisburg, PA 17110, (717)238-2504

Assn. of Pet Dog Trainers **[1051]**, 101 N Main St., Ste. 610, Greenville, SC 29601, (800)PET-DOGS

Assn. of Premier Nanny Agencies **[190]**, c/o Ginger Swift, 400 S Colorado Blvd., Ste. 300, Denver, CO 80246

Assn. of Private Sector Colleges and Universities **[1696]**, 1101 Connecticut Ave. NW, Ste. 900, Washington, DC 20036, (202)336-6700

Assn. of Productivity Specialists **[557]**, 521 5th Ave., Ste. 1700, New York, NY 10175, (212)286-0943

Assn. of Professional Animal Waste Specialists **[905]**, PO Box 2325, Santa Clarita, CA 91386, (800)787-7667

Assn. of Professional Consultants **[210]**, PO Box 51193, Irvine, CA 92619-1193, (800)745-5050

Assn. of Professional Material Handling Consultants **[211]**, 8720 Red Oak Blvd., Ste. 201, Charlotte, NC 28217-3992, (704)676-1184

Assn. for Professionals in Infection Control and Epidemiology **[2471]**, 1275 K St. NW, Ste. 1000, Washington, DC 20005-4006, (202)789-1890

Assn. of Professors of Medicine **[1663]**, 330 John Carlylr St., Ste. 610, Alexandria, VA 22314, (703)341-4540

Assn. of Professors, Practitioners, and Researchers in Religious Educ; Religious Educ. Assn.: An **[2914]**

Assn. of Professors and Scholars of Iranian Heritage **[1646]**, PO Box 4175, Diamond Bar, CA 91765, (909)869-2569

Assn. of Proposal Mgt. Professionals **[558]**, PO Box 668, Dana Point, CA 92629-0668

Assn. for Psychological Type Intl. **[2585]**, 9650 Rockville Pike, Bethesda, MD 20814-3998, (301)634-7450

Assn. of Public Data Users **[1490]**, PO Box 100155, Arlington, VA 22210, (703)522-4980

Assn. of Public Pension Fund Auditors **[3455]**, PO Box 16064, Columbus, OH 43216

Assn. of Public-Safety Communications Officials Intl. **[1372]**, 351 N Williamson Blvd., Daytona Beach, FL 32114-1112, (386)322-2500

Assn. of Public TV Stations **[126]**, 2100 Crystal Dr., Ste. 700, Arlington, VA 22202, (202)654-4200

Assn. of Public Treasurers of the U.S. and Canada **[1363]**, 962 Wayne Ave., Ste. 910, Silver Spring, MD 20910, (301)495-5560

Assn. of Real Estate Women **[735]**, 1201 Wakarusa Dr., Ste. C3, Lawrence, KS 66049, (212)599-6181

Assn. of Rehabilitation Programs in Cmpt. Tech. **[2055]**, Western Michigan Univ., Educational Leadership, Res. and Tech. Dept., Kalamazoo, MI 49008, (269)387-2053

Assn. of Res. Libraries **[1797]**, 21 Dupont Cir. NW, Ste. 800, Washington, DC 20036-1543, (202)296-2296

Assn. for Retail Tech. Standards **[766]**, 325 7th St. NW, Ste. 1100, Washington, DC 20004-2818, (202)626-8140

Assn. for Retail Travel Agents **[882]**, 4320 N Miller Rd., Scottsdale, AZ 85251, (866)369-8969

Assn. for the Rights of Catholics in the Church **[2855]**, 3150 Newgate Dr., Florissant, MO 63033, (413)527-9929

Assn. of Rotational Molders Intl. **[675]**, 800 Roosevelt Rd., Ste. C-312, Glen Ellyn, IL 60137, (630)942-6589

Assn. of Sci. Fiction and Fantasy Artists **[58]**, PO Box 65011, Phoenix, AZ 85082-5011

Assn. of Ser. and Cmpt. Dealers Intl. **[1444]**, 131 NW 1st Ave., Delray Beach, FL 33444, (561)266-9016

Assn. for Slavic, East European and Eurasian Stud. **[1854]**, 203C Bellefield Hall, 315 S Bellefield Ave., Pittsburgh, PA 15260-6424, (412)648-9911

Assn. for the Social Sci. Stud. of Jewry **[1648]**, c/o Gail G. Glicksman, PhD, Pres., 429 Montgomery Ave., B-303, Haverford, PA 19041

Assn. for Specialists in Gp. Work **[2041]**, c/o Amy Nitza, Sec., Indiana University-Purdue Univ. Fort Wayne, 2101 E Coliseum Blvd., Fort Wayne, IN 46805-1499, (800)347-6647

Assn. of Specialized and Professional Accreditors **[266]**, 3304 N Broadway St., No. 214, Chicago, IL 60657, (773)857-7900

Assn. of State Correctional Administrators **[2049]**, 213 Court St., Ste. 606, Middletown, CT 06457, (860)704-6410

Assn. of State and Territorial Dental Directors **[2380]**, 1838 Fieldcrest Dr., Sparks, NV 89434, (775)626-5008

Assn. of State and Territorial Local Hea. Liaison Officials **[1365]**, PO Box 260451, Denver, CO 80226, (303)692-3479

Assn. for sTEm Teacher Educ. **[1631]**, c/o Emily McKinley, Assoc. Mgr., PO Box 2089, West Lafayette, IN 47996

Assn. for the Stud. of African-American Life and History **[1701]**, Howard Center, 2225 Georgia Ave. NW, Ste. 331, Washington, DC 20059, (202)238-5910

The Assn. for the Stud. of Play **[1843]**, St. Olaf Coll., 1520 St. Olaf Ave., Northfield, MN 55057-1098, (507)786-3624

Assn. for Supervision and Curriculum Development **[1599]**, 1703 N Beauregard St., Alexandria, VA 22311-1714, (703)578-9600

Assn. of Synthetic Grass Installers **[140]**, 17487 Penn Valley Dr., Ste. B103, Penn Valley, CA 95946, (530)432-5851

Assn. of Teacher Educators **[1690]**, PO Box 793, Manassas, VA 20113, (703)331-0911

Assn. of Teachers of Japanese **[1654]**, 240 Humanities Bldg., 279 UCB, Boulder, CO 80309-0279, (303)492-5487

Assn. of Tech., Mgt. and Applied Engg. **[1632]**, 1390 Eisenhower Pl., Ann Arbor, MI 48108, (734)677-0720

Assn. of Univ. Anesthesiologists **[2304]**, 520 N Northwest Hwy., Park Ridge, IL 60068-2573, (847)825-5586

Assn. for Unmanned Vehicle Systems Intl. **[1526]**, 2700 S Quincy St., Ste. 400, Arlington, VA 22206, (703)845-9671

Assn. for Women in Aviation Maintenance **[915]**, PO Box 1030, Edgewater, FL 32132-1030, (386)416-0248

Assn. for Women in Sports Media **[693]**, 3899 N Front St., Harrisburg, PA 17110

Assn. for Women's Self Defense Advancement **[2220]**, 556 Rte. 17 N, Ste. 7-209, Paramus, NJ 07652, (201)794-2153

Assn. of YMCA Professionals **[2275]**, Springfield Coll., 263 Alden St., Springfield, MA 01109, (413)748-3884

Associations
Alliance for Nonprofit Mgt. **[61]**
Assn. Media and Publishing **[62]**
Natl. Coun. of Nonprofits **[63]**

Astara **[3023]**, 10700 Jersey Blvd., Ste. 450, Rancho Cucamonga, CA 91730, (909)948-7412

Asthma and Immunology; Amer. Acad. of Allergy, **[2287]**

Asthma and Immunology; Amer. Coll. of Allergy, **[2288]**

ASTM Intl. **[1548]**, PO Box C700, West Conshohocken, PA 19428-2959, (610)832-9500

Astrology
Intl. Soc. for Astrological Res. **[1412]**

Astronomy
Assn. of Lunar and Planetary Observers **[3093]**
Von Braun Astronomical Soc. **[1413]**

At-sea Processors Assn. **[354]**, PO Box 32817, Juneau, AK 99803, (907)523-0970

Athletes
Natl. Coalition Against Violent Athletes **[3252]**
All Japan Ju-Jitsu Intl. Fed. **[3359]**
Amer. Legion Baseball **[3257]**
BlazeSports Am. **[3316]**
Christian Cheerleaders of Am. **[3304]**
Eastern Coll. Athletic Conf. **[3342]**
Fed. of Intl. Lacrosse **[3357]**
Golf Coaches Assn. of Am. **[3335]**
Intl. Assn. of Gay and Lesbian Martial Artists **[3360]**
Intl. Female Boxers Assn. **[3298]**
Intl. Natural Bodybuilding and Fitness Fed. **[3293]**
Maccabi USA/Sports for Israel **[3402]**
Martial Arts Intl. Fed. **[3361]**
Natl. Assn. of Professional Baseball Leagues **[3260]**
New England Trails Conf. **[3428]**
North Amer. Football League **[3331]**
Professional Baseball Athletic Trainers Soc. **[3261]**
Professional Figure Skaters Cooperative **[3386]**
Professional Putters Assn. **[3338]**
U.S. Bobsled and Skeleton Fed. **[3390]**
U.S. Flag Football League **[3333]**
U.S. Olympic Comm. **[3368]**
U.S. Women's Curling Assn. **[3310]**
USA Diving **[3321]**
The World Kuoshu Fed. **[3363]**
World Martial Arts Assn. **[3364]**

Athletic Equip. Managers Assn. **[3397]**, 460 Hunt Hill Rd., Freeville, NY 13068, (607)539-6300

Athletics
Sigma Delta Pi **[3509]**
All Japan Ju-Jitsu Intl. Fed. **[3359]**
Amer. Legion Baseball **[3257]**
BlazeSports Am. **[3316]**
Christian Cheerleaders of Am. **[3304]**
Eastern Coll. Athletic Conf. **[3342]**
Fed. of Intl. Lacrosse **[3357]**
Golf Coaches Assn. of Am. **[3335]**
Intl. Assn. of Gay and Lesbian Martial Artists **[3360]**
Intl. Female Boxers Assn. **[3298]**
Intl. Natural Bodybuilding and Fitness Fed. **[3293]**
Maccabi USA/Sports for Israel **[3402]**
Martial Arts Intl. Fed. **[3361]**
Natl. Assn. of Professional Baseball Leagues **[3260]**
Natl. Coalition Against Violent Athletes **[3252]**
New England Trails Conf. **[3428]**
North Amer. Football League **[3331]**
Professional Baseball Athletic Trainers Soc. **[3261]**
Professional Figure Skaters Cooperative **[3386]**
Professional Putters Assn. **[3338]**
U.S. Bobsled and Skeleton Fed. **[3390]**
U.S. Flag Football League **[3333]**
U.S. Olympic Comm. **[3368]**
U.S. Women's Curling Assn. **[3310]**
USA Diving **[3321]**
The World Kuoshu Fed. **[3363]**
World Martial Arts Assn. **[3364]**

Atlantic Coast Conf. **[3398]**, 4512 Weybridge Ln., Greensboro, NC 27407, (336)854-8787

Atlantic States Marine Fisheries Commn. **[1299]**, 1050 N Highlnd St., Ste. 200 A-N, Arlington, VA 22201, (703)842-0740

Attorneys
Croatian Amer. Bar Assn. **[1270]**
Fair Elections Legal Network **[1271]**
Hispanic Natl. Bar Assn. **[1272]**
Intl. Acad. of Trial Lawyers **[1273]**
Natl. Bar Assn. **[1274]**
Natl. Lawyers Guild **[1275]**
Nigerian Lawyers Assn. **[1276]**
Serbian Bar Assn. of Am. **[1277]**
Intl. Amusement and Leisure Defense Assn. **[761]**

Auburn-Cord-Duesenberg Club **[3096]**, 24218 E Arapahoe Pl., Aurora, CO 80016, (303)748-3579

Auctions
Indus. Auctioneers Assn. **[64]**

Audio Publishers Assn. **[759]**, 191 Clarksville Rd., Princeton Junction, NJ 08550, (609)799-6327

Audiology
Acad. of Rehabilitative Audiology **[2449]**

Audiovisual
Assn. for Info. Media and Equip. **[65]**

August Derleth Soc. **[1730]**, PO Box 481, Sauk City, WI 53583, (608)643-3242

Australia
Soc. of Australasian Specialists/Oceania **[3232]**

Australian
Soc. of Australasian Specialists/Oceania **[3232]**

Austrian
American-Austrian Cultural Soc. **[2771]**

Authors
Amer. Christian Fiction Writers **[1729]**
August Derleth Soc. **[1730]**
D.H. Lawrence Soc. of North Am. **[1731]**
Ibsen Soc. of Am. **[1732]**
Intl. Brecht Soc. **[1733]**
Kay Boyle Soc. **[1734]**
Shakespeare Oxford Soc. **[1735]**
Susan Glaspell Soc. **[1736]**

Autism
Aging with Autism **[2307]**
Autism Allies **[2308]**
Autism Care and Treatment Today! **[2309]**
Autism Community of Africa **[1909]**
Autism Ser. Dogs of Am. **[2310]**
Bailey's Team for Autism **[2311]**
Face Autism **[2312]**
Families with Autism Spectrum Disorders **[2313]**
Fashion for Autism **[2314]**
Generation Rescue **[2315]**
Global Autism Collaboration **[2316]**

Global Communities of Support **[1910]**
Hands for Autistic Children of Ethiopia **[1911]**
Helping Autism through Learning and Outreach **[2317]**
Intl. Coalition for Autism and All Abilities **[2318]**
Milestones Autism Org. **[2319]**
Stop Calling It Autism! **[2320]**
Stories of Autism **[2321]**
S.U.C.C.E.S.S. for Autism **[2322]**
Talk About Curing Autism **[2323]**
Amer. Asperger's Assn. **[2562]**

Autism Allies **[2308]**, 2400 Prairie View Ln., Buffalo, MN 55313-2450, (612)384-4265

Autism Care and Treatment Today! **[2309]**, 19019 Ventura Blvd., Ste. 200, Tarzana, CA 91356, (818)705-1625

Autism Community of Africa **[1909]**, 8775 Cloud Leap Ct., Ste. 18, Columbia, MD 21045, (443)718-1824

Autism Ser. Dogs of Am. **[2310]**, 4248 Galewood St., Lake Oswego, OR 97035, (503)314-6913

Auto Intl. Assn. **[80]**, 7101 Wisconsin Ave., Ste. 1300, Bethesda, MD 20814, (301)654-6664

Automated Imaging Assn. **[1527]**, 900 Victors Way, Ste. 140, Ann Arbor, MI 48108, (734)994-6088

Automatic Identification
Assn. for Automatic Identification and Mobility North Am. **[66]**
GS1 US **[67]**
Intl. RFID Bus. Assn. **[68]**

Automatic Meter Reading Assn. **[★899]**

Automobile
Amer. Bugatti Club **[3094]**
Antique Auto. Club of Am. **[3095]**
Auburn-Cord-Duesenberg Club **[3096]**
Cadillac-LaSalle Club **[3097]**
Classic Car Club of Am. **[3098]**
Classic Thunderbird Club Intl. **[3099]**
Corvair Soc. of Am. **[3100]**
Early Ford V-8 Club of Am. **[3101]**
Edsel Club **[3102]**
Elgin Motorcar Owners Registry **[3103]**
Ferrari Club of Am. **[3104]**
Ferrari Owners Club **[3105]**
Ford Owners' Assn. **[3106]**
Graham Owners Club Intl. **[3107]**
H.H. Franklin Club **[3108]**
Horseless Carriage Club of Am. **[3109]**
Intl. Amphicar Owners Club **[3110]**
Intl. King Midget Car Club **[3111]**
Iso and Bizzarrini Owners Club **[3112]**
Jaguar Clubs of North Am. **[3113]**
Lincoln Zephyr Owner's Club **[3114]**
Lotus, Ltd. **[3115]**
Mercedes-Benz Club of Am. **[3116]**
Midstates Jeepster Assn. **[3117]**
Model A Ford Club of Am. **[3118]**
Morgan 3/4 Gp. **[3119]**
Morgan Car Club **[3120]**
Motor Bus Soc. **[3121]**
Mustang Club of Am. **[3122]**
Natl. Coun. of Corvette Clubs **[3123]**
Packard Auto. Classics **[3124]**
Plymouth Barracuda/Cuda Owners Club **[3125]**
Porsche Club of Am. **[3126]**
Rolls-Royce Owners' Club **[3127]**
SAE Intl. **[1414]**
Saleen Club of Am. **[3128]**
Shelby Amer. Auto. Club **[3129]**
Soc. of Automotive Historians **[3130]**
Subaru 360 Drivers' Club **[3131]**
Thunderbird and Cougar Club of Am. **[3132]**
Triumph Register of Am. **[3133]**
Tucker Auto. Club of Am. **[3134]**
United Four-Wheel Drive Associations **[3135]**
Veteran Motor Car Club of Am. **[3136]**
Vintage Chevrolet Club of Am. **[3137]**
PGI **[90]**

Automotive
Corvair Soc. of Am. **[3100]**
Electrification Coalition **[871]**
Light Elec. Vehicle Assn. **[873]**
Midstates Jeepster Assn. **[3117]**
Morgan Car Club **[3120]**
PGI **[90]**

A star before a book entry number signifies that the name is not listed separately, but is mentioned within the entry.

United Four-Wheel Drive Associations **[3135]**
Automotive Aftermarket Indus. Assn. I Heavy Duty Distribution Assn. **[70]**, 7101 Wisconsin Ave., Ste. 1300, Bethesda, MD 20814, (301)654-6664
Automotive Aftermarket Indus. Assn. I Natl. Catalog Managers Assn. **[694]**, 7101 Wisconsin Ave., Ste. 1300, Bethesda, MD 20814-3415, (301)654-6664
Automotive Aftermarket Suppliers Assn. I Brake Mfrs. Coun. **[81]**, PO Box 13966, Research Triangle Park, NC 27709-3966, (919)549-4800
Automotive Communications Coun. **[71]**, 7101 Wisconsin Ave., Ste. 1300, Bethesda, MD 20814, (240)333-1089
Automotive Engine Rebuilders Assn. **[82]**, 500 Coventry Ln., Ste. 180, Crystal Lake, IL 60014-7592, (815)526-7600
Automotive Hall of Fame **[72]**, 21400 Oakwood Blvd., Dearborn, MI 48124, (313)240-4000
Automotive Industries
Amer. Salvage Pool Assn. **[69]**
Automotive Aftermarket Indus. Assn. I Heavy Duty Distribution Assn. **[70]**
Automotive Communications Coun. **[71]**
Automotive Hall of Fame **[72]**
Automotive Indus. Action Gp. **[73]**
Automotive Trade Assn. Executives **[74]**
Automotive Training Managers Coun. **[75]**
Global Automakers **[76]**
Heavy Duty Mfrs. Assn. I Heavy-Duty Bus. Forum **[77]**
Natl. Auto Body Coun. **[78]**
Overseas Automotive Coun. **[79]**
Corvair Soc. of Am. **[3100]**
Electrification Coalition **[871]**
Light Elec. Vehicle Assn. **[873]**
Midstates Jeepster Assn. **[3117]**
Morgan Car Club **[3120]**
Plug In Am. **[1396]**
United Four-Wheel Drive Associations **[3135]**
Automotive Indus. Action Gp. **[73]**, 26200 Lahser Rd., Ste. 200, Southfield, MI 48033-7100, (248)358-3003
Automotive Maintenance and Repair Assn. **[94]**, 201 Park Washington Ct., Falls Church, VA 22046, (703)532-2027
Automotive Manufacturers
Auto Intl. Assn. **[80]**
Automotive Aftermarket Suppliers Assn. I Brake Mfrs. Coun. **[81]**
Automotive Engine Rebuilders Assn. **[82]**
Automotive Occupant Restraints Coun. **[83]**
Battery Coun. Intl. **[84]**
Elecl. Rebuilder's Assn. **[85]**
Equip. and Tool Inst. **[86]**
Filter Mfrs. Coun. **[87]**
Heavy Duty Representatives Assn. **[88]**
Natl. Truck Equip. Assn. **[89]**
PGI **[90]**
Specialty Equip. Market Assn. **[91]**
Spring Res. Inst. **[92]**
Truck Trailer Mfrs. Assn. **[93]**
Corvair Soc. of Am. **[3100]**
Midstates Jeepster Assn. **[3117]**
Morgan Car Club **[3120]**
United Four-Wheel Drive Associations **[3135]**
Automotive Occupant Restraints Coun. **[83]**, 1081 Dove Run Rd., Ste. 403, Lexington, KY 40502, (859)269-4240
Automotive Parts Remanufacturers Assn. **[95]**, 4215 Lafayette Center Dr., Ste. 3, Chantilly, VA 20151-1243, (703)968-2772
Automotive Services
Automotive Maintenance and Repair Assn. **[94]**
Automotive Parts Remanufacturers Assn. **[95]**
Gasoline and Automotive Ser. Dealers Assn. **[96]**
Inter-Industry Conf. on Auto Collision Repair **[97]**
Ser. Specialists Assn. **[98]**
Truck-Frame and Axle Repair Assn. **[99]**
Used Truck Assn. **[100]**
Automotive Trade Assn. Executives **[74]**, 8400 Westpark Dr., McLean, VA 22102, (703)821-7072
Automotive Training Managers Coun. **[75]**, 101 Blue Seal Dr. SE, Ste. 101, Leesburg, VA 20175, (703)669-6670
Auxiliary to Sons of Union Veterans of the Civil War **[3054]**, 2966 Hayts Corners East Rd., Ovid, NY 14521, (607)869-3720

Avant Ministries **[2990]**, 10000 N Oak Trafficway, Kansas City, MO 64155, (816)734-8500
Aviation
Air Line Pilots Assn. Intl. **[3436]**
Aircraft Mechanics Fraternal Assn. **[3437]**
Airline Passenger Experience Assn. **[101]**
Assn. of Flight Attendants - CWA **[3438]**
Black Pilots of Am. **[102]**
Intl. Aviation Womens Assn. **[103]**
Natl. Air Traffic Controllers Assn. **[3439]**
Intl. Scale Soaring Assn. **[3216]**
World Airline Historical Soc. **[3089]**
Aviation Distributors and Mfrs. Assn. **[26]**, 100 N 20th St., 4th Fl., Philadelphia, PA 19103-1443, (215)564-3484
Aviation Historical Soc; Amer. **[3083]**
Aviation Indus. CBT Comm. **[27]**, PO Box 4067, Federal Way, WA 98063, (253)218-1408
Avicultural Soc. of Am. **[1512]**, PO Box 5516, Riverside, CA 92517-5516, (951)780-4102
AVS Sci. and Tech. Soc. **[1554]**, c/o Angela Klink, 125 Maiden Ln., 15th Fl., New York, NY 10038, (212)248-0200
Awards
Awards and Recognition Assn. **[104]**
Intl. Foodservice Mfrs. Assn. I Intl. Gold and Silver Plate Soc. **[2772]**
Ladies Auxiliary of the Military Order of the Purple Heart U.S.A. **[3053]**
Phi Chi Medical Fraternity **[3539]**
Awards and Recognition Assn. **[104]**, 4700 W Lake Ave., Glenview, IL 60025, (847)375-4800

B

Bailey's Team for Autism **[2311]**, 164 Westside Ave., North Attleboro, MA 02760, (508)699-4483
Baitulmaal **[2183]**, PO Box 166911, Irving, TX 75016, (972)257-2564
Baking
Bread Bakers Guild of Am. **[105]**
Independent Bakers Assn. **[106]**
Retail Bakers of Am. **[107]**
Ball Games
Natl. Amateur Dodgeball Assn. **[3253]**
U.S.A Team Handball **[3254]**
Balloon Fed. of Am. **[3255]**, PO Box 400, Indianola, IA 50125, (515)961-8809
Ballooning
Balloon Fed. of Am. **[3255]**
Baltic
Assn. for the Advancement of Baltic Stud. **[1737]**
Joint Baltic Amer. Natl. Comm. **[2617]**
Bank Insurance and Securities Assn. **[482]**, 2025 M St. NW, Ste. 800, Washington, DC 20036, (202)367-1111
Banking
Amer. Coun. of State Savings Supervisors **[108]**
Arab Bankers Assn. of North Am. **[109]**
Electronic Transactions Assn. **[110]**
Hellenic Amer. Bankers Assn. **[111]**
Natl. Assn. of Affordable Housing Lenders **[112]**
Natl. Assn. of Mortgage Processors **[113]**
Natl. Investment Banking Assn. **[114]**
Retirement Indus. Trust Assn. **[115]**
Colonial Coin Collectors Club **[3222]**
Banks
Colonial Coin Collectors Club **[3222]**
Baptist
Amer. Baptist Homes and Caring Ministries **[2839]**
Assn. of Baptists for World Evangelism **[2840]**
Baptist Bible Fellowship Intl. **[2841]**
Baptist Communicators Assn. **[2842]**
Conservative Baptist Assn. of Am. **[2843]**
Natl. Assn. of Free Will Baptists **[2844]**
Seventh Day Baptist Gen. Conf. **[2845]**
Seventh Day Baptist Gen. Conf. of the U.S. and Canada **[2846]**
Seventh Day Baptist World Fed. **[2847]**
Women Nationally Active for Christ **[2848]**
Baptist Global Response **[2184]**
Baptist Bible Fellowship Intl. **[2841]**, PO Box 191, Springfield, MO 65801-0191, (417)862-5001
Baptist Communicators Assn. **[2842]**, c/o Margaret M. Dempsey, 1519 Menlo Dr., Kennesaw, GA 30152, (770)425-3728
Baptist Global Response **[2184]**, 402 BNA Dr., Ste. 411, Nashville, TN 37217, (615)367-3678

Baptists for Life **[2204]**, PO Box 3158, Grand Rapids, MI 49501, (616)257-6800
Bar Assn. Commn. on Homelessness and Poverty; Amer. **[2099]**
Barbados Blackbelly Sheep Assn. Intl. **[1208]**, 1156 NE 50th Rd., Lamar, MO 64759, (417)398-2875
Barzona Breeders Assn. of Am. **[979]**, 11477 E Warren Pl., Aurora, CO 80014, (303)696-5799
Baseball
Amer. Baseball Coaches Assn. **[3256]**
Amer. Legion Baseball **[3257]**
Little League Found. **[3258]**
Natl. Amateur Baseball Fed. **[3259]**
Natl. Assn. of Professional Baseball Leagues **[3260]**
Professional Baseball Athletic Trainers Soc. **[3261]**
Soc. for Amer. Baseball Res. **[3262]**
U.S.A. Baseball **[3263]**
Basel Action Network **[2754]**, 206 First Ave. S., Ste. 410, Seattle, WA 98104, (206)652-5555
Basketball
Natl. Basketball Assn. **[3264]**
Natl. Basketball Athletic Trainers Assn. **[3265]**
Women's Basketball Coaches Assn. **[3266]**
Basketball Assn; Natl. Wheelchair **[3317]**
Bass Anglers Sportsman Soc. **[3326]**, 1170 Celebration Blvd., Ste. 200, Celebration, FL 34747, (877)BAS-SUSA
Baton Twirling
U.S. Twirling Assn. **[3267]**
Battelle for Kids **[1582]**, 1160 Dublin Rd., Ste. 500, Columbus, OH 43215, (614)481-3141
Batteries
Natl. Alliance for Advanced Tech. Batteries **[116]**
Battery Coun. Intl. **[84]**, 401 N Michigan Ave., 24th Fl., Chicago, IL 60611-4267, (312)644-6610
BCM Intl. **[2849]**, 201 Granite Run Dr., Ste. 260, Lancaster, PA 17601, (717)560-9601
Beach Boys Fan Club **[3573]**, 631 N Stephanie St., No. 546, Henderson, NV 89014
Beanies for Baghdad **[1923]**, 6401 Lincoln Ave., Evansville, IN 47715
Bee Native **[961]**, Mantis Farm, 68 Fingar Rd., Hudson, NY 12534, (917)679-0567
Beekeeping
Bee Native **[961]**
Amer. Honey Producers Assn. **[954]**
Behavioral Sciences
Intl. Soc. for Human Ethology **[1415]**
Intl. Soc. for Res. on Aggression **[1416]**
Belgian
Belgian Amer. Chamber of Commerce **[3474]**
Belgian Amer. Chamber of Commerce **[3474]**, 1177 Ave. of the Americas, 8th Fl., New York, NY 10018, (212)541-0779
Belgian Draft Horse Corp. of Am. **[1124]**, PO Box 335, Wabash, IN 46992, (260)563-3205
Belted Galloway Soc. **[980]**, Hav-A-Belt Galloways, New Glarus, WI 53574, (608)527-4811
Benefit4Kids **[1924]**, 21660 23 Mile Rd., Macomb, MI 48044, (877)245-5430
BEST Employers Assn. **[822]**, 2505 McCabe Way, Irvine, CA 92614, (866)706-2225
Beta Sigma Phi **[3547]**, 1800 W 91st Pl., Kansas City, MO 64114, (816)444-6800
Better Boys Found. **[1995]**, 1512 S Pulaski Rd., Chicago, IL 60623, (773)542-7300
Beyond Pesticides **[2252]**, 701 E St. SE, Ste. 200, Washington, DC 20003, (202)543-5450
Beyond the Rainbow **[3565]**, PO Box 31672, St. Louis, MO 63131-0672, (314)799-1724
Bible
BCM Intl. **[2849]**
Bible League Intl. **[2850]**
Assn. of Biblical Counselors **[2901]**
Fellowship Intl. Mission **[2998]**
Seventh Day Baptist World Fed. **[2847]**
Bible Inst; Moody **[3004]**
Bible League Intl. **[2850]**, PO Box 28000, Chicago, IL 60628, (866)825-4636
Bibles For The World **[2991]**, PO Box 49759, Colorado Springs, CO 80949-9759, (719)630-7733
Bicycle
Light Elec. Vehicle Assn. **[873]**
Bide-A-Wee Home Assn. **[★1893]**
Bideawee **[1893]**, 410 E 38th St., New York, NY 10016, (212)532-6395

Big East Conf. **[3399]**, 222 Richmond St., Ste. 110, Providence, RI 02903, (401)453-0660

Big Thicket Assn. **[1009]**, PO Box 198, Saratoga, TX 77585, (936)274-1181

Big Wildlife **[1233]**, PO Box 344, Williams, OR 97544, (541)846-1352

Bikes Not Bombs **[2708]**, 284 Amory St., Jamaica Plain, MA 02130, (617)522-0222

Bilingualism
Natl. Assn. for Bilingual Educ. **[1572]**

The Billfish Found. **[1234]**, 5100 N Fed. Hwy., Ste. 200, Fort Lauderdale, FL 33308, (954)938-0150

Billiard and Bowling Inst. of Am. **[829]**, PO Box 6573, Arlington, TX 76005, (817)385-8120

Billiards
U.S. Billiard Assn. **[3268]**

Billy "Crash" Craddock Fan Club **[3574]**, 4101 Pick-fair Rd., Springfield, IL 62703, (336)339-9928

Biochemistry
Amer. Soc. for Biochemistry and Molecular Biology **[1417]**
Intl. Soc. of Chem. Ecology **[1418]**

BioCommunications Assn. **[2351]**, 220 Southwind Ln., Hillsborough, NC 27278, (919)245-0906

Biology
Amer. Acad. of Microbiology **[1419]**
Assn. of Genetic Technologists **[1420]**
Intl. Org. for Mycoplasmology **[1421]**
Intl. Soc. of Differentiation **[1422]**
Natl. Assn. of Biology Teachers **[1573]**
Phi Sigma **[3510]**
Soc. for Developmental Biology **[1423]**
Soc. for In Vitro Biology **[1424]**
Teratology Soc. **[1425]**

Biomedical Engineering
Biomedical Engg. Soc. **[1426]**
Engg. World Hea. **[2488]**

Biomedical Engg. Soc. **[1426]**, 8201 Corporate Dr., Ste. 1125, Landover, MD 20785-2224, (301)459-1999

Biotechnology
Org. of Regulatory and Clinical Associates **[117]**

Bird
Amer. Cockatiel Soc. **[3138]**
Amer. Waterslager Soc. **[3139]**
Env. for the Americas **[962]**
Hummingbird Monitoring Network **[963]**
Intl. Parrotlet Soc. **[3140]**
Forest Bird Soc. **[1022]**

Birth Defects
March of Dimes Found. **[2324]**
Smile Network Intl. **[2355]**

Black on Black Love Campaign **[2047]**, 1000 E 87th St., Chicago, IL 60619, (773)978-0868

Black Career Women **[2819]**, PO Box 19332, Cincinnati, OH 45219-0332, (513)531-1932

Black Data Processing Associates **[14]**, 9500 Arena Dr., Ste. 350, Largo, MD 20774, (301)584-3135

Black Pilots of Am. **[102]**, PO Box 7463, Pine Bluff, AR 71611, (504)214-7346

Blacksmiths
Amer. Farrier's Assn. **[118]**
Artist-Blacksmith's Assn. of North Am. **[119]**

BlazeSports Am. **[3316]**, 535 N McDonough St., Decatur, GA 30030, (404)270-2000

Blind
Norrie Disease Assn. **[2399]**

Blind; Guiding Eyes for the **[2602]**

Blind; Natl. Indus. for the **[2605]**

Blind and Visually Impaired; Assn. for Educ. and Rehabilitation of the **[2600]**

Blood
America's Blood Centers **[2325]**

BLOOM Africa **[1925]**, 4605 E Natl. Rd., Springfield, OH 45505

Blue Earth Alliance **[1842]**, c/o Bart J. Cannon, Exec. Dir., PO Box 4490, Seattle, WA 98194, (206)569-8754

Blue Nile Children's Org. **[1926]**, PO Box 28658, Seattle, WA 98118, (206)760-2873

BlueVoice.org **[1010]**, 10 Sunfish Dr., St. Augustine, FL 32080

B'nai B'rith Intl. **[2948]**, 2020 K St. NW, 7th Fl., Washington, DC 20006, (202)857-6600

B'nai B'rith International's Center for Jewish Identity **[1649]**, 801 2nd Ave., 14th Fl., New York, NY 10017, (212)490-3290

BoardSource **[2149]**, 750 9th St. NW, Ste. 650, Washington, DC 20001-4793, (202)349-2500

Boating
Amer. Y-Flyer Yacht Racing Assn. **[3269]**
Antique and Classic Boat Soc. **[3270]**
Classic Yacht Assn. **[3271]**
El Toro Intl. Yacht Racing Assn. **[3272]**
Highlander Class Intl. Assn. **[3273]**
Intl. Flying Dutchman Class Assn. of the U.S. **[3274]**
Intl. Lightning Class Assn. **[3275]**
Intl. Mobjack Assn. **[3276]**
Intl. Penguin Class Dinghy Assn. **[3277]**
Intl. Sunfish Class Assn. **[3278]**
Joshua Slocum Soc. Intl. **[3279]**
Lido 14 Class Assn. **[3280]**
Natl. Boating Fed. **[3281]**
Santana 20 Class Assn. **[3282]**
Shields Natl. Class Assn. **[3283]**
States Org. for Boating Access **[120]**
Thistle Class Assn. **[3284]**
Traditional Small Craft Assn. **[3285]**
U.S. Albacore Assn. **[3286]**
U.S. J/24 Class Assn. **[3287]**
U.S. Mariner Class Assn. **[3288]**
U.S. Optimist Dinghy Assn. **[3289]**
U.S. Power Squadrons **[3290]**
U.S. Sailing Assn. I Coun. of Sailing Associations **[3291]**
Windmill Class Assn. **[3292]**

Bobsled and Skeleton Fed; U.S. **[3390]**

Bobsleigh
U.S. Bobsled and Skeleton Fed. **[3390]**

Bodybuilding
Intl. Natural Bodybuilding and Fitness Fed. **[3293]**

Bonsai Clubs Intl. **[3202]**, PO Box 8445, Metairie, LA 70011-8445, (504)832-8071

Books
Antiquarian Booksellers Assn. of Am. **[1738]**
Children's Book Coun. **[1739]**
Guild of Book Workers **[1740]**

Boone Soc. **[3058]**, 1303 Hunter Ace Way, Cedar Park, TX 78613

Born Free USA **[1894]**, PO Box 22505, Sacramento, CA 95822, (916)447-3085

Bostonian Soc. **[1769]**, Old State House, 206 Washington St., Boston, MA 02109, (617)720-1713

Botany
Amer. Bamboo Soc. **[1427]**
Amer. Bryological and Lichenological Soc. **[1428]**
Aquatic Plant Mgt. Soc. **[1429]**
Intl. Bulb Soc. **[1430]**
Intl. Palm Soc. **[1431]**
Plant Growth Regulation Soc. of Am. **[1432]**
Soc. for Economic Botany **[1433]**
Ethnobotanical Conservation Org. for South East Asia **[1020]**
Intl. Phalaenopsis Alliance **[1153]**

Bottles
Fed. of Historical Bottle Collectors **[3141]**

Bowling
Intl. Bowling Pro Shop and Instructors Assn. **[121]**
Natl. Duckpin Bowling Cong. **[3294]**
U.S. Lawn Bowls Assn. **[3295]**

Boxing
Intl. Boxing Fed. **[3296]**
Intl. Chinese Boxing Assn. **[3297]**
Intl. Female Boxers Assn. **[3298]**
U.S.A. Boxing **[3299]**

Boykin Spaniel Club and Breeders Assn. of Am. **[3174]**, PO Box 42, Gilbert, SC 29054, (803)532-0990

Boys' Town of Rome **[★2276]**

Boys' Towns of Italy **[2276]**, 250 E 63rd St., Ste. 204, New York, NY 10021, (212)980-8770

Braille Evangelism Assn; Lutheran **[2603]**

Braunvieh Assn. of Am. **[981]**, 5750 Epsilon, Ste. 200, San Antonio, TX 78249, (210)561-2892

Brazil
Amazonas Hope for Hea. **[2429]**
Amer. Brazilian Cultural Exchange **[1746]**
Brazil-U.S. Bus. Coun. **[3475]**
Brazilian-American Chamber of Commerce **[3476]**

Brazil-U.S. Bus. Coun. **[3475]**, 1615 H St. NW, Washington, DC 20062, (202)463-5729

Brazilian
Brazil-U.S. Bus. Coun. **[3475]**

Brazilian-American Chamber of Commerce **[3476]**, 509 Madison Ave., Ste. 304, New York, NY 10022, (212)751-4691

Bread Bakers Guild of Am. **[105]**, 670 W Napa St., Ste. B, Sonoma, CA 95476, (707)935-1468

Bread for the Journey Intl. **[2156]**, 9 Santa Gabriella Ct., Novato, CA 94945, (415)895-5357

Bread for the World **[2669]**, 425 3rd St. SW, Ste. 1200, Washington, DC 20024, (202)639-9400

Breaking Ground **[2009]**, 104 Neal St., Portland, ME 04102, (206)351-7778

Brethren
Assn. of Grace Brethren Ministers **[2851]**

Brick by Brick for Tanzania! **[1675]**, 539 Braatz Dr., Kewaskum, WI 53040, (262)573-9032

Bridal Services
Assn. of Bridal Consultants **[122]**
Bridal Show Producers Intl. **[123]**
Wedding Indus. Professionals Assn. **[124]**

Bridal Show Producers Intl. **[123]**, 17730 W Center Rd., Ste. 110-311, Omaha, NE 68130, (402)330-8900

Bridge
Amer. Bridge Teachers' Assn. **[3142]**
Short Span Steel Bridge Alliance **[1434]**
U.S. Bridge Fed. **[3143]**

A Bridge for Children **[1927]**, PO Box 1054, New York, NY 10268

Bridge of Love **[1928]**, PO Box 1869, West Jordan, UT 84084, (801)867-9401

Bridges Cambodia Intl. **[1929]**, 2970 Almond Dr., San Jose, CA 95148, (408)223-2359

Bridges to Prosperity **[2210]**, 5007 Victory Blvd., C-126, Yorktown, VA 23693

British
North Amer. Conf. on British Stud. **[1741]**

British Biker Cooperative **[3218]**, PO Box 371021, Milwaukee, WI 53237-2121, (262)514-2073

Broadcast Educ. Assn. **[1574]**, 1771 N St. NW, Washington, DC 20036-2800, (202)429-3935

Broadcasters
ARRL Found. **[3090]**

Broadcasting
Alliance for Women in Media **[125]**
Amer. Fed. of TV and Radio Artists **[3440]**
Assn. of Public TV Stations **[126]**
Broadcast Educ. Assn. **[1574]**
CTAM - Cable and Telecommunications Assn. for Marketing **[127]**
MRFAC **[128]**
Natl. Assn. of Black Owned Broadcasters **[129]**
Natl. Translator Assn. **[130]**
ARRL Found. **[3090]**

Bromeliad Identification Center **[★3203]**

Bromeliad Soc. Intl. **[3203]**, 713 Breckenridge Dr., Port Orange, FL 32127-7528

Bronchoesophagology
Amer. Broncho-Esophagological Assn. **[2326]**

Brotherhood of Locomotive Engineers and Trainmen **[3462]**, 1370 Ontario St., Mezzanine, Cleveland, OH 44113-1701, (216)241-2630

Buddhist
Cambodian Buddhist Soc. **[2852]**

Buelingo Beef Cattle Soc. **[982]**, 15904 W Warren Rd., Warren, IL 61087-9601, (815)745-2147

Builders Hardware Mfrs. Assn. **[413]**, 355 Lexington Ave., 15th Fl., New York, NY 10017, (212)297-2122

Building Bridges: Middle East-US **[1642]**, PO Box 1208, Norwich, VT 05055, (802)649-1601

Building Bridges Worldwide **[2010]**, 5-09 48th Ave., Apt. 7B, Long Island City, NY 11101

Building Codes
Alliance for Building Regulatory Reform in the Digital Age **[1435]**
Building Security Coun. **[801]**

Building Commissioning Assn. **[141]**, 100 SW Main St., Ste. 1600, Portland, OR 97204, (877)666-2292

Building Community Bridges **[2011]**, 244 5th Ave., Ste. E283, New York, NY 10001, (888)486-4218

Building Industries
Affordable Housing Investors Coun. **[131]**
Affordable Housing Tax Credit Coalition **[132]**

A star before a book entry number signifies that the name is not listed separately, but is mentioned within the entry.

Alliance for Building Regulatory Reform in the
    Digital Age **[1435]**
Alliance for Sustainable Built Environments **[133]**
Amer. Fiberboard Assn. **[134]**
Asphalt Emulsion Mfrs. Assn. **[135]**
Assoc. Air Balance Coun. **[136]**
Assoc. Constr. Distributors Intl. **[137]**
Assn. for Better Insulation **[138]**
Assn. of Millwork Distributors **[139]**
Assn. of Synthetic Grass Installers **[140]**
Building Commissioning Assn. **[141]**
Ceramic Tile Distributors Assn. **[142]**
Clean Tech. and Sustainable Indus. Org. **[964]**
Constr. Employers Assn. **[143]**
Cool Metal Roofing Coalition **[144]**
Elevator U **[145]**
Green Builder Coalition **[146]**
Intl. Cast Polymer Assn. **[147]**
Intl. Soc. for Concrete Pavements **[148]**
Leading Builders of Am. **[149]**
Materials and Methods Standards Assn. **[150]**
Moulding and Millwork Producers Assn. **[151]**
Natl. Assn. of Constr. Contractors Cooperation
    [152]
Natl. Assn. of the Remodeling Indus. **[153]**
Natl. Coun. of Acoustical Consultants **[154]**
Natl. Roof Certification and Inspection Assn. **[155]**
Natl. Sunroom Assn. **[156]**
Natl. Wood Flooring Assn. **[157]**
North Amer. Building Material Distribution Assn.
    [158]
Preservation Trades Network **[159]**
Scaffold Indus. Assn. **[160]**
Structural Insulated Panel Assn. **[161]**
Building Security Coun. **[801]**
Natl. Assn. of Black Women in Constr. **[206]**
Short Span Steel Bridge Alliance **[1434]**
Building Security Coun. **[801]**, 1801 Alexander Bell
    Dr., Reston, VA 20191, (703)295-6314
Building Ser. Contractors Assn. Intl. **[551]**, 401 N
    Michigan Ave., Ste. 2200, Chicago, IL 60611-4267,
    (312)321-5167
Building Trades
    AFL-CIO | Building and Constr. Trades Dept.
        [3441]
    Assn. of Synthetic Grass Installers **[140]**
    Cool Metal Roofing Coalition **[144]**
    Intl. Soc. for Concrete Pavements **[148]**
    Leading Builders of Am. **[149]**
    Ministry Architecture **[1409]**
    Natl. Roof Certification and Inspection Assn. **[155]**
Burley Stabilization Corp. **[1221]**, 1427 W Main St.,
    Greeneville, TN 37743, (865)525-9381
Burns
    Amer. Burn Assn. **[2327]**
Burundi Friends Intl. **[2012]**, PO Box 927356, San
    Diego, CA 92192-7356, (619)800-2340
Business
    Amer. Bus. Women's Assn. **[162]**
    Assn. for Enterprise Info. **[163]**
    Assn. of Moroccan Professionals in Am. **[164]**
    Business-Higher Educ. Forum **[1575]**
    Canadian-American Bus. Coun. **[165]**
    Inst. of Certified Bus. Counselors **[166]**
    Intl. Downtown Assn. **[167]**
    Intl. Executive Ser. Corps **[168]**
    Intl. Ombudsman Assn. **[169]**
    Italian Amer. Alliance for Bus. and Tech. **[170]**
    Mountains and Plains Independent Booksellers
        Assn. **[171]**
    Natl. Assn. for Female Executives **[172]**
    Natl. Soc. of Hispanic MBAs **[173]**
    Representative of German Indus. and Trade **[174]**
    Singapore Am. Bus. Assn. **[175]**
    U.S. Coun. for Intl. Bus. **[176]**
    United States-Indonesia Soc. **[177]**
    U.S.-Ukraine Bus. Coun. **[178]**
    US-Ireland Alliance **[179]**
    911 Indus. Alliance **[195]**
    Alliance for Amer. Mfg. **[579]**
    Alliance of Supplier Diversity Professionals **[727]**
    Alliance for Sustainable Built Environments **[133]**
    Armenian Amer. Chamber of Commerce **[3473]**
    Assn. of Appraiser Regulatory Officials **[50]**
    Assn. for Better Insulation **[138]**
    Assn. of Synthetic Grass Installers **[140]**
    BEST Employers Assn. **[822]**

Brazil-U.S. Bus. Coun. **[3475]**
Bridal Show Producers Intl. **[123]**
Building Security Coun. **[801]**
CEO Netweavers **[236]**
Chinese Amer. Cooperation Coun. **[1783]**
CHWMEG **[906]**
Clean Tech. and Sustainable Indus. Org. **[964]**
Cool Metal Roofing Coalition **[144]**
Corporate Responsibility Officers Assn. **[237]**
Corporate Social Responsibility Assn. **[238]**
Crude Oil Quality Assn. **[640]**
Decorative Plumbing and Hardware Assn. **[678]**
Electronic Indus. Citizenship Coalition **[280]**
Energy Efficiency Bus. Coalition **[301]**
Energy Info. Standards Alliance **[302]**
Enterprise for a Sustainable World **[263]**
Fisher Inst. for Medical Res. **[2653]**
Food Trade Sustainability Leadership Assn. **[362]**
Gift and Home Trade Assn. **[784]**
Global Sourcing Coun. **[631]**
Global Tech. Distribution Coun. **[848]**
Gp. Underwriters Assn. of Am. **[486]**
Holistic Mentorship Network **[2460]**
Indus. Auctioneers Assn. **[64]**
Innovation Norway - U.S. **[3482]**
Intl. Air Filtration Certifiers Assn. **[432]**
Intl. Amusement and Leisure Defense Assn. **[761]**
Intl. Assn. of Space Entrepreneurs **[30]**
Iraqi Amer. Chamber of Commerce and Indus.
    [3483]
Kingdom Chamber of Commerce **[3491]**
Middle East Investment Initiative **[336]**
Natl. Assn. of Small Bus. Contractors **[222]**
Natl. Latina Bus. Women Assn. **[534]**
North Am. Chinese Clean-tech and Semiconduc-
    tor Assn. **[287]**
North Amer. Security Products Org. **[807]**
Pakistan Chamber of Commerce USA **[3502]**
Planting Empowerment **[1094]**
Professional Lighting and Sign Mgt. Companies of
    Am. **[546]**
Retail Energy Supply Assn. **[304]**
Reusable Packaging Assn. **[764]**
Rising Tide Capital **[265]**
Small Bus. Ser. Bur. **[825]**
TopTen USA **[305]**
Underground Utility and Leak Locators Assn.
    [898]
U.S. Indian Amer. Chamber of Commerce **[3496]**
U.S.-Ukraine Bus. Coun. **[178]**
Women in Mgt. **[571]**
Youth Venture **[924]**
Business and Commerce
    911 Indus. Alliance **[195]**
    Alliance for Amer. Mfg. **[579]**
    Alliance of Supplier Diversity Professionals **[727]**
    Argentine-American Chamber of Commerce
        [3472]
    Armenian Amer. Chamber of Commerce **[3473]**
    Assn. for Better Insulation **[138]**
    Assn. of Synthetic Grass Installers **[140]**
    Brazil-U.S. Bus. Coun. **[3475]**
    Bridal Show Producers Intl. **[123]**
    CEO Netweavers **[236]**
    Corporate Responsibility Officers Assn. **[237]**
    Crude Oil Quality Assn. **[640]**
    Decorative Plumbing and Hardware Assn. **[678]**
    Electronic Indus. Citizenship Coalition **[280]**
    Global Sourcing Coun. **[631]**
    Indus. Auctioneers Assn. **[64]**
    Innovation Norway - U.S. **[3482]**
    Intl. Amusement and Leisure Defense Assn. **[761]**
    Intl. Assn. of Space Entrepreneurs **[30]**
    Iraqi Amer. Chamber of Commerce and Indus.
        [3483]
    Leadership for Energy Automated Processing
        [303]
    Middle East Investment Initiative **[336]**
    Natl. Assn. of Small Bus. Contractors **[222]**
    Natl. Latina Bus. Women Assn. **[534]**
    North Amer. Security Products Org. **[807]**
    Pakistan Chamber of Commerce USA **[3502]**
    Professional Lighting and Sign Mgt. Companies of
        Am. **[546]**
    Retail Energy Supply Assn. **[304]**
    Rising Tide Capital **[265]**
    Underground Utility and Leak Locators Assn.
        [898]

U.S. Indian Amer. Chamber of Commerce **[3496]**
Business Education
    Decision Sciences Inst. **[1576]**
    Intl. Soc. for Bus. Educ. **[1577]**
    Natl. Assn. of Supervisor of Bus. Educ. **[1578]**
    Natl. Assn. of Small Bus. Contractors **[222]**
Bus. Executives for Natl. Security **[2741]**, 1030 15th
    St., NW, Ste. 200 E, Washington, DC 20005,
    (202)296-2125
Business-Higher Educ. Forum **[1575]**, 2025 M St.
    NW, Ste. 800, Washington, DC 20036-2422,
    (202)367-1189
Business Products
    North Amer. Security Products Org. **[807]**
    TopTen USA **[305]**
Bus. Products Credit Assn. **[328]**, 607 Westridge Dr.,
    O'Fallon, MO 63366, (636)294-5775
Bus. Roundtable **[2730]**, 1717 Rhode Island Ave.
    NW, Ste. 800, Washington, DC 20036, (202)872-
    1260
Bus. Solutions Assn. **[836]**, 5024 Campbell Blvd.,
    Ste. R, Baltimore, MD 21236-5943, (410)931-8100

C

C-Change **[2329]**, 1776 Eye St. NW, 9th Fl.,
    Washington, DC 20006, (202)756-1600
Cadillac-LaSalle Club **[3097]**, PO Box 360835,
    Columbus, OH 43236-0835, (614)478-4622
Caledonian Found. USA **[1819]**, PO Box 1242,
    Edgartown, MA 02539-1242
California Date Administrative Comm. **[1096]**, PO
    Box 1736, Indio, CA 92202-1736, (760)347-4510
California Public Employee Relations Prog. **[2693]**,
    2521 Channing Way, No. 5555, Berkeley, CA
    94720-5555, (510)643-7096
California Soc. of Printmakers **[404]**, PO Box
    194202, San Francisco, CA 94119
Cambodian Buddhist Soc. **[2852]**, 13800 New
    Hampshire Ave., Silver Spring, MD 20904,
    (301)622-6544
Cambodian Hea. Professionals Assn. of Am. **[2432]**,
    1025 Atlantic Ave., Long Beach, CA 90813,
    (562)491-9292
Camp To Belong **[1930]**, PO Box 1146, Marana, AZ
    85653, (520)413-1395
Camping
    Amer. Camp Assn. **[3300]**
    Camping Women **[3301]**
    Christian Camp and Conf. Assn. **[3302]**
    North Amer. Family Campers Assn. **[3303]**
Camping Women **[3301]**, PO Box 1402, Twain
    Harte, CA 95383
Camps
    Camping Women **[3301]**
    Christian Camp and Conf. Assn. **[3302]**
    North Amer. Family Campers Assn. **[3303]**
Canadian-American Bus. Coun. **[165]**, 1900 K St.
    NW, Ste. 100, Washington, DC 20006, (202)496-
    7906
Canal Soc. of New York State **[1742]**, 2527 Cherry
    Valley Tpke., Marcellus, NY 13108, (315)730-4495
Canals
    Canal Soc. of New York State **[1742]**
Cancer
    Assn. of Community Cancer Centers **[2328]**
    C-Change **[2329]**
    Intl. Soc. for Children with Cancer **[2330]**
    Women Against Prostate Cancer **[2331]**
    Intl. Partnership for Reproductive Hea. **[2593]**
    Oncology Assn. of Naturopathic Physicians **[2556]**
Canoeing
    Camping Women **[3301]**
Canon Law Soc. of Am. **[2856]**, The Hecker Center,
    Ste. 111, 3025 Fourth St. NE, Washington, DC
    20017-1102, (202)832-2350
Capuchin-Franciscans **[2857]**, 3407 S Archer Ave.,
    Chicago, IL 60608, (773)475-6206
Cardiology
    Heart Rhythm Soc. **[2332]**
    Michael E. DeBakey Intl. Surgical Soc. **[2333]**
Cardiovascular Disease
    Heart Rhythm Soc. **[2332]**
Career Coll. Assn. **[★1696]**
Caribbean
    Caribbean Hea. Outreach **[2481]**
Caribbean Hea. Outreach **[2481]**, 4300 W 58th Pl.,
    Los Angeles, CA 90043, (626)274-3282

Caribbean Public Hea. Coalition **[2590]**, 15515 Symondsbury Way, Upper Marlboro, MD 20774, (240)602-0103

Caricature Carvers of Am. **[3164]**, c/o Donald K. Mertz, Sec., 729 Prairie Rd., Wilmington, OH 45177-9683, (316)788-0175

Caring for Cambodia **[1583]**, 4815 W Braker Ln., Ste. 502, Austin, TX 78759

Caring Hand for Children **[1992]**, 20315 Nordhoff St., Chatsworth, CA 91311, (818)727-9740

Carpet and Rug Inst. **[506]**, PO Box 2048, Dalton, GA 30722-2048, (706)278-3176

Carriers and Locals Soc. **[3238]**, PO Box 74, Grosse Ile, MI 48138, (734)676-2649

Cartoonists Soc; Natl. **[1718]**

Cartoons

   Disneyana Fan Club **[3567]**

Caspian Horse Soc. of the Americas **[1125]**, c/o Vicki Hudgins, Registrar, PO Box 1589, Brenham, TX 77834-1589, (979)830-9046

Cast Bullet Assn. **[3380]**, c/o Paul Gans, Membership Dir., 7600 SE Maple Ave., Vancouver, WA 98664-1737, (360)882-0502

Cat

   Cat Fanciers' Assn. **[3144]**

   Cat Fanciers' Fed. **[3145]**

   The Intl. Bengal Cat Soc. **[965]**

   Natl. Alliance of Burmese Breeders **[966]**

   Wild Felid Res. and Mgt. Assn. **[1258]**

Cat Fanciers' Assn. **[3144]**, 1805 Atlantic Ave., Manasquan, NJ 08736, (732)528-9797

Cat Fanciers' Fed. **[3145]**, PO Box 661, Gratis, OH 45330, (937)787-9009

The Catfish Inst. **[956]**, 6311 Ridgewood Rd., Ste. W404, Jackson, MS 39211, (601)977-9559

Catholic

   All Roads Ministry **[2853]**

   Apostolate for Family Consecration **[2854]**

   Assn. of Catholic Colleges and Universities **[1579]**

   Assn. for the Rights of Catholics in the Church **[2855]**

   Canon Law Soc. of Am. **[2856]**

   Capuchin-Franciscans **[2857]**

   Catholic Church Extension Soc. of the U.S.A. **[2858]**

   Catholic Golden Age **[2859]**

   Catholic Kolping Soc. of Am. **[2860]**

   Catholic Theological Soc. of Am. **[1743]**

   Catholic Traditionalist Movement **[2861]**

   Catholics in Alliance for the Common Good **[2862]**

   Catholics United for the Faith **[2863]**

   Central Assn. of the Miraculous Medal **[2864]**

   Conf. of Major Superiors of Men **[2865]**

   Congregation of Sisters of Saint Agnes **[2866]**

   Daughters of Isabella, Intl. Circle **[2773]**

   Glenmary Res. Center **[2867]**

   Intl. Catholic Deaf Assn. U.S. Sect. **[2868]**

   Junior Knights of Peter Claver **[2774]**

   Knights of Peter Claver **[2775]**

   Laity for Life **[2869]**

   Lay Mission-Helpers Assn. **[2870]**

   Mariological Soc. of Am. **[2871]**

   Natl. Assn. of the Holy Name Soc. **[2872]**

   Natl. Black Catholic Clergy Caucus **[2873]**

   Natl. Catholic Off. for the Deaf **[2874]**

   Natl. Christ Child Soc. **[2875]**

   North Amer. Assn. for the Catechumenate **[2876]**

   Pontifical Mission Societies in the U.S. **[2877]**

   Raskob Found. for Catholic Activities **[2878]**

   Sacred Heart League **[2879]**

   Soc. of African Missions **[2880]**

   Soc. of Missionaries of Africa **[2881]**

   Soc. of Our Lady of the Most Holy Trinity **[2882]**

   U.S. Conf. of Catholic Bishops **[2883]**

   Volunteer Missionary Movement - U.S. Off. **[2884]**

   Catholic Guardian Soc. and Home Bur. **[1931]**

   Catholic War Veterans of the U.S.A. **[3080]**

Catholic Chaplains; Natl. Assn. of **[2889]**

Catholic Church Extension Soc. of the U.S.A. **[2858]**, 150 S Wacker Dr., 20th Fl., Chicago, IL 60606, (312)795-5112

Catholic Comm. of Appalachia **[2992]**, 885 Orchard Run Rd., Spencer, WV 25276, (304)927-5798

Catholic Golden Age **[2859]**, PO Box 249, Olyphant, PA 18447, (800)836-5699

Catholic Guardian Soc. and Home Bur. **[1931]**, 1011 1st Ave., 10th Flr., New York, NY 10022, (212)371-1000

Catholic Historical Assn; Amer. **[1767]**

Catholic Kolping Soc. of Am. **[2860]**, 1223 Van Houten Ave., Clifton, NJ 07013, (201)666-1169

Catholic Medical Assn. **[2580]**, 29 Bala Ave., Ste. 205, Bala Cynwyd, PA 19004-3206, (484)270-8002

Catholic Theological Soc. of Am. **[1743]**, c/o Dr. Dolores Christie, Exec. Dir., John Carroll Univ., 20700 N Park Blvd., University Heights, OH 44118, (216)397-1631

Catholic Traditionalist Movement **[2861]**, 210 Maple Ave., Westbury, NY 11590-3117, (516)333-6470

Catholic War Veterans of the U.S.A. **[3080]**, 441 N Lee St., Alexandria, VA 22314, (703)549-3622

Catholics in Alliance for the Common Good **[2862]**, 1612 K St. NW, Ste. 400, Washington, DC 20006, (202)466-1665

Catholics United for the Faith **[2863]**, 827 N 4th St., Steubenville, OH 43952, (740)283-2484

Cattle

   Amer. Belgian Blue Breeders **[967]**

   Amer. Black Hereford Assn. **[968]**

   Amer. Brahman Breeders Assn. **[969]**

   Amer. British White Park Assn. **[970]**

   Amer. Chianina Assn. **[971]**

   Amer. Dexter Cattle Assn. **[972]**

   Amer. Guernsey Assn. **[973]**

   Amer. Natl. CattleWomen **[974]**

   Amer. Pinzgauer Assn. **[975]**

   Amer. Red Brangus Assn. **[976]**

   Amer. Red Poll Assn. **[977]**

   Amer. Wagyu Assn. **[978]**

   Barzona Breeders Assn. of Am. **[979]**

   Belted Galloway Soc. **[980]**

   Braunvieh Assn. of Am. **[981]**

   Buelingo Beef Cattle Soc. **[982]**

   Cattlemen's Beef Promotion and Res. Bd. **[983]**

   Intl. Brangus Breeders Assn. **[984]**

   Intl. Miniature Zebu Assn. **[985]**

   Intl. Texas Longhorn Assn. **[986]**

   Miniature Hereford Breeders Assn. **[987]**

   North Amer. Limousin Found. **[988]**

   North Amer. South Devon Assn. **[989]**

   Santa Gertrudis Breeders Intl. **[990]**

   Texas Longhorn Breeders Assn. of Am. **[991]**

   United Braford Breeders **[992]**

   World Watusi Assn. **[993]**

Cattlemen's Beef Promotion and Res. Bd. **[983]**, 9000 E Nichols Ave., Ste. 215, Centennial, CO 80112-3450, (303)220-9890

Caucus for Women in Statistics **[1540]**, c/o Anna Nevius, Treas., 7732 Rydal Terr., Rockville, MD 20855-2057, (301)827-0170

CCIM Inst. **[736]**, 430 N Michigan Ave., Ste. 800, Chicago, IL 60611-4092, (312)321-4460

CEDAM Intl. **[1011]**, 2 Fox Rd., Croton-on-Hudson, NY 10520, (914)271-5365

Ceilings and Interior Systems Constr. Assn. **[219]**, 405 Illinois Ave., Unit 2B, St. Charles, IL 60174, (630)584-1919

Celtic

   North Amer. Celtic Buyers Assn. **[180]**

Cement Kiln Recycling Coalition **[1196]**, PO Box 7553, Arlington, VA 22207, (703)869-4718

Censorship

   Natl. Coalition Against Censorship **[2618]**

Center on Addiction and the Family **[2240]**, 50 Jay St., Brooklyn, NY 11201, (646)505-2061

Center for Community Change **[2164]**, 1536 U St. NW, Washington, DC 20009, (202)339-9300

Center on Conscience and War **[2641]**, 1830 Connecticut Ave. NW, Washington, DC 20009-5732, (202)483-2220

Center for Intl. Policy **[2659]**, 1717 Massachusetts Ave. NW, Ste. 801, Washington, DC 20036, (202)232-3317

Center for the Polyurethanes Indus. **[676]**, 1300 Wilson Blvd., Arlington, VA 22209, (703)741-5103

Center to Protect Workers Rights **[★3441]**

Center for Reproductive Rights **[2738]**, 120 Wall St., New York, NY 10005, (917)637-3600

Center for Strategic and Budgetary Assessments **[2704]**, 1667 K St. NW, Ste. 900, Washington, DC 20006, (202)331-7990

Center for Women's Bus. Res. **[916]**, 1760 Old Meadow Rd., Ste. 500, McLean, VA 22102, (703)556-7162

Central America

   Neighbor to Neighbor **[2619]**

   Paso Pacifico **[1036]**

Central Assn. of the Miraculous Medal **[2864]**, 475 E Chelten Ave., Philadelphia, PA 19144-5758, (215)848-1010

Central Conf. of Amer. Rabbis **[2949]**, 355 Lexington Ave., New York, NY 10017, (212)972-3636

CEO Netweavers **[236]**, PO Box 700393, Dallas, TX 75370

Ceramic Tile Distributors Assn. **[142]**, 800 Roosevelt Rd., Bldg. C, Ste. 312, Glen Ellyn, IL 60137, (630)545-9415

Ceramics

   Intl. Assn. of Duncan Certified Ceramic Teachers **[3146]**

CHA - Certified Horsemanship Assn. **[3350]**, 4037 Iron Works Pkwy., Ste. 180, Lexington, KY 40511, (859)259-3399

Chain Drug Marketing Assn. **[657]**, PO Box 995, 43157 W Nine Mile Rd., Novi, MI 48376-0995, (248)449-9300

Challenge Coin Assn. **[3221]**, 1375 Mistletoe Ridge Pl. NW, Concord, NC 28027, (704)723-1170

Chamber of Commerce; Brazilian-American **[3476]**

Chamber of Commerce Executives; Amer. **[3504]**

Chamber of Commerce; French-American **[3492]**

Chamber of Commerce and Indus. of New York; Japanese **[3500]**

Chamber of Commerce; U.S. Hispanic **[3495]**

Chambers of Commerce

   American-Uzbekistan Chamber of Commerce **[3471]**

   Argentine-American Chamber of Commerce **[3472]**

   Armenian Amer. Chamber of Commerce **[3473]**

   Belgian Amer. Chamber of Commerce **[3474]**

   Brazil-U.S. Bus. Coun. **[3475]**

   Brazilian-American Chamber of Commerce **[3476]**

   Chile-U.S. Chamber of Commerce **[3477]**

   Coun. for Community and Economic Res. **[3478]**

   European-American Bus. Coun. **[3479]**

   Fed. of Philippine Amer. Chambers of Commerce **[3480]**

   Greek Amer. Chamber of Commerce **[3481]**

   Innovation Norway - U.S. **[3482]**

   Iraqi Amer. Chamber of Commerce and Indus. **[3483]**

   Jamaica USA Chamber of Commerce **[3484]**

   Norwegian-American Chamber of Commerce **[3485]**

   Spain-United States Chamber of Commerce **[3486]**

   Swedish-American Chambers of Commerce, U.S.A. **[3487]**

   U.S.-Angola Chamber of Commerce **[3488]**

   U.S. Qatar Bus. Coun. **[3489]**

   Venezuelan-American Chamber of Commerce **[3490]**

   Pakistan Chamber of Commerce USA **[3502]**

   U.S. Indian Amer. Chamber of Commerce **[3496]**

ChangeALife Uganda **[1932]**, 58 Fairview Ave., Brick, NJ 08724, (732)899-8483

Chaplains

   Amer. Catholic Correctional Chaplains Assn. **[2885]**

   Amer. Correctional Chaplains Assn. **[2886]**

   Fed. of Fire Chaplains **[2887]**

   Intl. Conf. of Police Chaplains **[2888]**

   Natl. Assn. of Catholic Chaplains **[2889]**

   Race Track Chaplaincy of Am. **[2890]**

Charles H. Wright Museum of African Amer. History **[1702]**, 315 E Warren Ave., Detroit, MI 48201, (313)494-5800

Charley Pride Fan Club **[3575]**, 3198 Royal Ln., No. 200, Dallas, TX 75229, (214)350-8477

Cheerleading

   Christian Cheerleaders of Am. **[3304]**

Chefs

   U.S. Personal Chef Assn. **[181]**

Chemicals

   Amer. Chemistry Coun. **[182]**

A star before a book entry number signifies that the name is not listed separately, but is mentioned within the entry.

Amer. Cleaning Inst. [183]
Halogenated Solvents Indus. Alliance [184]
Inst. for Polyacrylate Absorbents [185]
Methacrylate Producers Assn. [186]
Pine Chemicals Assn. [187]
SB Latex Coun. [188]
Soc. for Chem. Hazard Commun. [189]

Chemistry
Amer. Inst. of Chemists [1436]
Commercial Development and Marketing Assn. [1437]
Iota Sigma Pi [3511]
Radiochemistry Soc. [1438]
Societe de Chimie Industrielle, Amer. Sect. [1439]
Chemists' Club [2825], 30 W 44th St., New York, NY 10036, (212)582-5454
Chicago True Advocates [3576], PO Box 195, Landing, NJ 07850
Chief Officers of State Lib. Agencies [1798], 201 E Main St., Ste. 1405, Lexington, KY 40507, (859)514-9151

Child Abuse
RedLight Children [1912]
Catholic Guardian Soc. and Home Bur. [1931]
Child Aid Africa [1933], 535 Rosaire Dr., Hummelstown, PA 17036, (717)566-6118

Child Care
Assn. of Premier Nanny Agencies [190]
Coun. for Professional Recognition [1913]
Natl. Coalition for Campus Children's Centers [1914]
Action for Children - Zambia [1915]
Africa Hope [1916]
AHOPE for Children [1917]
Aiding Romania's Children [1918]
All the Children are Children [1919]
Amer. Bar Assn. Center on Children and the Law [1921]
Ark Mission [1922]
Beanies for Baghdad [1923]
Benefit4Kids [1924]
BLOOM Africa [1925]
Blue Nile Children's Org. [1926]
Boys' Towns of Italy [2276]
A Bridge for Children [1927]
Camp To Belong [1930]
Catholic Guardian Soc. and Home Bur. [1931]
ChangeALife Uganda [1932]
Child Aid Africa [1933]
Child Literacy [1935]
Child Protection Intl. [1936]
Children of Grace [1938]
Children, Inc. [1996]
Children of Nowhere [1939]
Children's Hea. Intl. [2334]
Children's Intl. Hea. Relief [2335]
Children's Medical Mission of Haiti [1941]
Children's Relief Mission [1942]
Children's Welfare Intl. [1943]
Chosen Children Intl. [1944]
Empower Orphans [1947]
Ethiopian Orphan Relief [1948]
Firefly [1950]
Forever Found [1951]
Friends of the Children of Angola [1952]
Friends of Jamaica USA [1953]
Friends of Kenyan Orphans [1954]
Ghana Relief Org. [1955]
Goods for Good [1958]
Hands for Autistic Children of Ethiopia [1911]
Heart for Africa [1959]
Heart4Kids [1960]
Hearts Across Romania [1961]
Helping Hands [1962]
Helping Honduras Kids [1963]
Home of Hope [1964]
Hope and Future for Children in Bolivia [1965]
Horizon Intl. [1967]
Intl. Children Assistance Network [1968]
Intl. Soc. for Children with Cancer [2330]
Kids Home Intl. [1969]
Kupenda for the Children [1970]
Loving Hands for the Needy [1971]
Malawi Children's Mission [1972]
Medical Missions for Children [2337]
Meds and Food for Kids [1973]
Mike's Angels [1974]

Orphan Support Africa [1979]
Orphans Against AIDS [1980]
Outreach Africa [1981]
Para Sa Bata [1982]
Peace House Africa [1983]
Pocketful of Joy [1984]
RedLight Children [1912]
Sky of Love [1986]
Sweet Sleep [1987]
Two Hearts for Hope [1989]
World Spark [1990]
Zambia Hope Intl. [1991]

Child Custody
Catholic Guardian Soc. and Home Bur. [1931]

Child Development
One Hen [1580]
Action for Children - Zambia [1915]
Africa Hope [1916]
Agami [1581]
Aging with Autism [2307]
All Our Children Intl. Outreach [1920]
Americans Care and Share [2182]
Autism Community of Africa [1909]
Bailey's Team for Autism [2311]
Battelle for Kids [1582]
BLOOM Africa [1925]
Blue Nile Children's Org. [1926]
Brick by Brick for Tanzania! [1675]
Camp To Belong [1930]
Caring for Cambodia [1583]
ChangeALife Uganda [1932]
Child Aid Africa [1933]
Child Empowerment Intl. [1934]
Child Literacy [1935]
Children of Grace [1938]
Children, Inc. [1996]
Children's Future Intl. [1940]
Children's Medical Mission of Haiti [1941]
Children's Welfare Intl. [1943]
Empower Orphans [1947]
Firefly [1950]
Friends of Jamaica USA [1953]
Friends of Kenyan Orphans [1954]
Ghana Relief Org. [1955]
Goods for Good [1958]
Growing Liberia's Children [1993]
Hands for Autistic Children of Ethiopia [1911]
Heart4Kids [1960]
Hearts Across Romania [1961]
Helping Hands [1962]
HELPSudan [1994]
Home of Hope [1964]
Hope and Future for Children in Bolivia [1965]
Intl. Children Assistance Network [1968]
Kids Home Intl. [1969]
Kupenda for the Children [1970]
Loving Hands for the Needy [1971]
Milestones Autism Org. [2319]
NepalAama [1584]
Orphan Support Africa [1979]
Orphans Against AIDS [1980]
Pocketful of Joy [1984]
Talk About Curing Autism [2323]
Two Hearts for Hope [1989]
Child Empowerment Intl. [1934], PO Box 66274, Scotts Valley, CA 95067, (800)725-8098

Child Health
Children's Hea. Intl. [2334]
Children's Intl. Hea. Relief [2335]
Childspring Intl. [2336]
Medical Missions for Children [2337]
Soc. for Adolescent Hea. and Medicine [2338]
Action for Children - Zambia [1915]
Aging with Autism [2307]
Autism Allies [2308]
Autism Community of Africa [1909]
Autism Ser. Dogs of Am. [2310]
Bailey's Team for Autism [2311]
Benefit4Kids [1924]
Blue Nile Children's Org. [1926]
Catholic Guardian Soc. and Home Bur. [1931]
ChildAlive [2482]
Children, Inc. [1996]
Children's Dialysis Intl. [2559]
Children's Medical Mission of Haiti [1941]
Face Autism [2312]
Fashion for Autism [2314]

Friends of Jamaica USA [1953]
Generation Rescue [2315]
Heart4Kids [1960]
Hearts Across Romania [1961]
Home of Hope [1964]
Intl. Soc. for Children with Cancer [2330]
Meds and Food for Kids [1973]
Milestones Autism Org. [2319]
Network Ethiopia [2511]
Options for Children in Zambia [1978]
Outreach Africa [1981]
Smile Network Intl. [2355]
Talk About Curing Autism [2323]
Child Literacy [1935], 105 Greene St., No. 1202, Jersey City, NJ 07302, (212)531-1111
Child Protection Intl. [1936], 267 19th Ave. S, Ste. 214, Minneapolis, MN 55455

Child Welfare
Action for Children - Zambia [1915]
Africa Hope [1916]
AHOPE for Children [1917]
Aiding Romania's Children [1918]
All the Children are Children [1919]
All Our Children Intl. Outreach [1920]
Amer. Bar Assn. Center on Children and the Law [1921]
Ark Mission [1922]
Beanies for Baghdad [1923]
Benefit4Kids [1924]
BLOOM Africa [1925]
Blue Nile Children's Org. [1926]
A Bridge for Children [1927]
Bridge of Love [1928]
Bridges Cambodia Intl. [1929]
Camp To Belong [1930]
Catholic Guardian Soc. and Home Bur. [1931]
ChangeALife Uganda [1932]
Child Aid Africa [1933]
Child Empowerment Intl. [1934]
Child Literacy [1935]
Child Protection Intl. [1936]
Child Welfare League of Am. [1937]
Children of Grace [1938]
Children of Nowhere [1939]
Children's Future Intl. [1940]
Children's Medical Mission of Haiti [1941]
Children's Relief Mission [1942]
Children's Welfare Intl. [1943]
Chosen Children Intl. [1944]
Comm. for Children [1945]
Crutches 4 Kids [1946]
Empower Orphans [1947]
Ethiopian Orphan Relief [1948]
Find the Children [1949]
Firefly [1950]
Forever Found [1951]
Friends of the Children of Angola [1952]
Friends of Jamaica USA [1953]
Friends of Kenyan Orphans [1954]
Ghana Relief Org. [1955]
Girls for a Change [1956]
Global Centurion [1957]
Goods for Good [1958]
Heart for Africa [1959]
Heart4Kids [1960]
Hearts Across Romania [1961]
Helping Hands [1962]
Helping Honduras Kids [1963]
Home of Hope [1964]
Hope and Future for Children in Bolivia [1965]
Hope for Haiti's Children [1966]
Horizon Intl. [1967]
Intl. Children Assistance Network [1968]
Kids Home Intl. [1969]
Kupenda for the Children [1970]
Loving Hands for the Needy [1971]
Malawi Children's Mission [1972]
Meds and Food for Kids [1973]
Mike's Angels [1974]
Mothers Without Borders [1975]
Natl. Center for Missing and Exploited Children [1976]
Natl. Center for Prosecution of Child Abuse [1977]
Options for Children in Zambia [1978]
Orphan Support Africa [1979]
Orphans Against AIDS [1980]
Outreach Africa [1981]

Para Sa Bata [1982]
Peace House Africa [1983]
Pocketful of Joy [1984]
Seeds of HOPE Intl. [1985]
Sky of Love [1986]
Sweet Sleep [1987]
To Love a Child [1988]
Two Hearts for Hope [1989]
World Spark [1990]
Zambia Hope Intl. [1991]
Amer. Humane Assn. [2229]
Americans Care and Share [2182]
Bailey's Team for Autism [2311]
Boys' Towns of Italy [2276]
Brick by Brick for Tanzania! [1675]
Caring for Cambodia [1583]
Caring Hand for Children [1992]
Children, Inc. [1996]
Children of Tanzania [1903]
Children's Hea. Intl. [2334]
Growing Liberia's Children [1993]
HELPSudan [1994]
Medical Missions for Children [2337]
NepalAama [1584]
Orphans Africa [2031]
Out of Poverty thru Educ. [1568]
Reconstruction Efforts Aiding Children without
  Homes [2032]
RedLight Children [1912]
Robert F. Kennedy Center for Justice and Human
  Rights [2280]
Smile Network Intl. [2355]
Child Welfare League of Am. [1937], 1726 M St.
  NW, Ste. 500, Washington, DC 20036-4522,
  (202)688-4200
ChildAlive [2482], 14505 Gilpin Rd., Silver Spring,
  MD 20906, (301)598-1163
Childhood Education
Agami [1581]
Battelle for Kids [1582]
Caring for Cambodia [1583]
Caring Hand for Children [1992]
Growing Liberia's Children [1993]
HELPSudan [1994]
NepalAama [1584]
Blue Nile Children's Org. [1926]
Brick by Brick for Tanzania! [1675]
Child Empowerment Intl. [1934]
Children, Inc. [1996]
Children of Tanzania [1903]
Children's Future Intl. [1940]
Children's Medical Mission of Haiti [1941]
Friends of Jamaica USA [1953]
Friends of Kenyan Orphans [1954]
One Hen [1580]
Orphans Against AIDS [1980]
Out of Poverty thru Educ. [1568]
Children
Better Boys Found. [1995]
Children, Inc. [1996]
Dream Factory [1997]
Jack and Jill of Am. [1998]
Orphan Found. of Am. [1999]
RAINBOWS [2000]
Save the Children [2001]
Southern Early Childhood Assn. [2002]
Starlight Children's Found. [2003]
Action for Children - Zambia [1915]
Africa Hope [1916]
AHOPE for Children [1917]
Aiding Romania's Children [1918]
All the Children are Children [1919]
All Our Children Intl. Outreach [1920]
Amer. Bar Assn. Center on Children and the Law
  [1921]
Ark Mission [1922]
Beanies for Baghdad [1923]
Benefit4Kids [1924]
BLOOM Africa [1925]
Blue Nile Children's Org. [1926]
Boys' Towns of Italy [2276]
A Bridge for Children [1927]
Bridge of Love [1928]
Bridges Cambodia Intl. [1929]
Caring for Cambodia [1583]

Caring Hand for Children [1992]
Catholic Guardian Soc. and Home Bur. [1931]
ChangeALife Uganda [1932]
Child Aid Africa [1933]
Child Empowerment Intl. [1934]
Child Literacy [1935]
Child Protection Intl. [1936]
Children of Grace [1938]
Children of Nowhere [1939]
Children's Future Intl. [1940]
Children's Hea. Intl. [2334]
Children's Medical Mission of Haiti [1941]
Children's Relief Mission [1942]
Children's Welfare Intl. [1943]
Childspring Intl. [2336]
Chosen Children Intl. [1944]
Coun. on Accreditation [2233]
Coun. for Children with Behavioral Disorders
  [1686]
Crutches 4 Kids [1946]
Empower Orphans [1947]
Ethiopian Orphan Relief [1948]
Face Autism [2312]
Firefly [1950]
Forever Found [1951]
Friends of the Children of Angola [1952]
Friends of Jamaica USA [1953]
Friends of Kenyan Orphans [1954]
Ghana Relief Org. [1955]
Global Ambassadors for Children [2715]
Global Centurion [1957]
Goods for Good [1958]
Growing Liberia's Children [1993]
Heart for Africa [1959]
Heart4Kids [1960]
Hearts Across Romania [1961]
Helping Hands [1962]
Helping Honduras Kids [1963]
Home of Hope [1964]
Hope and Future for Children in Bolivia [1965]
Hope for Haiti's Children [1966]
Horizon Intl. [1967]
Intl. Children Assistance Network [1968]
Kids Ecology Corps [1076]
Kids Home Intl. [1969]
Kids Making a Difference [952]
Kids for Peace [2717]
Kupenda for the Children [1970]
Loving Hands for the Needy [1971]
Malawi Children's Mission [1972]
Medical Missions for Children [2337]
Meds and Food for Kids [1973]
Mike's Angels [1974]
NepalAama [1584]
One Hen [1580]
Orphan Support Africa [1979]
Orphans Africa [2031]
Orphans Against AIDS [1980]
Out of Poverty thru Educ. [1568]
Outreach Africa [1981]
Para Sa Bata [1982]
Peace House Africa [1983]
Pocketful of Joy [1984]
Reconstruction Efforts Aiding Children without
  Homes [2032]
RedLight Children [1912]
Robert F. Kennedy Center for Justice and Human
  Rights [2280]
Seeds of HOPE Intl. [1985]
Sky of Love [1986]
Smile Network Intl. [2355]
Sweet Sleep [1987]
To Love a Child [1988]
Two Hearts for Hope [1989]
World Spark [1990]
Zambia Hope Intl. [1991]
Children of Grace [1938], PO Box 2394, Danville,
  CA 94526, (925)855-4697
Children, Inc. [1996], 4205 Dover Rd., Richmond,
  VA 23221-3267, (804)359-4565
Children of Nowhere [1939], 601 W 26th St., Ste.
  1105, New York, NY 10001
Children of Tanzania [1903], 3 Little Cove Ln., Old
  Greenwich, CT 06870, (203)637-0191
The Children of War [2713], PO Box 223602, Chan-
  tilly, VA 20153-3602, (703)625-9147

Children's Book Coun. [1739], 54 W 39th St., 14th
  Fl., New York, NY 10018, (212)966-1990
Children's Dialysis Intl. [2559], 25604 NW 2nd Ave.,
  Newberry, FL 32669, (352)472-2651
Children's Future Intl. [1940], 22 Hartley Rd., Great
  Neck, NY 11023
Children's Hea. Intl. [2334], PO Box 3505, Silver
  Spring, MD 20918, (301)681-8307
Children's Intl. Hea. Relief [2335], 4218 S Steele St.,
  Ste. 220, Tacoma, WA 98409, (253)476-0556
Children's Literature Assn. [1806], PO Box 138,
  Battle Creek, MI 49016-0138, (269)965-8180
Children's Medical Mission of Haiti [1941], 925 Hertz-
  zler Rd., Mechanicsburg, PA 17055, (717)796-1852
Children's Relief Mission [1942], PO Box 597,
  Owensville, MO 65066, (818)502-1989
Children's Rights Coun. [2069], 9470 Annapolis Rd.,
  Ste. 310, Lanham, MD 20706-3022, (301)459-1220
Children's Welfare Intl. [1943], 223 Pacific Ave. S,
  Pacific, WA 98047, (206)859-3847
Childspring Intl. [2336], 1328 Peachtree St. NE,
  Atlanta, GA 30309, (404)228-7744
Chile-U.S. Chamber of Commerce [3477], PO Box
  560181, Miami, FL 33256-0181, (305)890-3547
China
Chinese Amer. Cooperation Coun. [1783]
Global China Connection [1643]
Sino-American Bridge for Educ. and Hea. [1784]
US-China Green Energy Coun. [1464]
Chinese
Assn. of Chinese-American Professionals [2776]
Coun. of Overseas Chinese Services [2777]
U.S.-China Peoples Friendship Assn. [2620]
Amer. Chinese Medical Exchange Soc. [2431]
Intl. Chinese Boxing Assn. [3297]
North Am. Chinese Clean-tech and Semiconduc-
  tor Assn. [287]
Chinese Amer. Cooperation Coun. [1783], PO Box
  12028, Pleasanton, CA 94588
Chinese Amer. Medical Soc. [2547], 41 Elizabeth
  St., Ste. 403, New York, NY 10013, (212)334-4760
Chinese Overseas Trans. Assn. [868], Univ. of
  Washington, Dept. of Civil and Environmental
  Engg., Seattle, WA 98195-2700, (206)616-2696
Chiropractic
Amer. Coll. of Chiropractic Orthopedists [2339]
Chiropractic Diplomatic Corps [2340]
Chiropractic Orthopedists of North Am. [2341]
Coun. of Chiropractic Acupuncture [2342]
Coun. on Chiropractic Practice [2343]
Councils on Chiropractic Educ. Intl. [1585]
Intl. Chiropractors Assn. [2344]
Non-Profit Chiropractic Org. [2345]
Sacro Occipital Res. Soc. Intl. [2346]
Chiropractic Diplomatic Corps [2340], 17602 17th
  St., Ste. 102, Tustin, CA 92780, (800)600-7032
Chiropractic Orthopedists of North Am. [2341], c/o
  Dr. Philip Rake, Treas., 2048 Montrose Ave., Mon-
  trose, CA 91020, (818)249-8326
Choristers Guild [3019], 12404 Park Central Dr., Ste.
  100, Dallas, TX 75251-1802, (469)398-3606
Chorus Am. [1820], 1156 15th St. NW, Ste. 310,
  Washington, DC 20005, (202)331-7577
CHOSEN [2132], 3638 W 26th St., Erie, PA 16506-
  2037, (814)833-3023
Chosen Children Intl. [1944], PO Box 3046,
  Colorado Springs, CO 80934, (866)599-5437
Chris Cares Intl. [2013], 119 Britton Ave., Stoughton,
  MA 02072
Chris LeDoux Intl. Fan Club [3577], PO Box 41052,
  San Jose, CA 95160
Christ for the City Intl. [2983], PO Box 390395,
  Omaha, NE 68139, (402)592-8332
Christ for the Poor [1681], PO Box 60118, North
  Miami Beach, FL 33160, (305)891-2242
Christian
Assn. for Biblical Higher Educ. [1586]
Christian Labor Assn. of the U.S.A. [3442]
A Christian Ministry in the Natl. Parks [2891]
CLOUT - Christian Lesbians Out [2892]
Fellowship of Christian Peace Officers U.S.A.
  [2893]
Fellowship of Saint James [2894]
Intl. Network of Children's Ministry [2895]
Intl. Orthodox Christian Charities [2896]

A star before a book entry number signifies that the name is not listed separately, but is mentioned within the entry.

Kingdom Chamber of Commerce [3491]
Natl. Alliance Against Christian Discrimination [2897]
Nazarene Compassionate Ministries Intl. [2898]
North Amer. Professors of Christian Educ. [1587]
Abrahamic Alliance Intl. [2945]
Assn. of Biblical Counselors [2901]
BCM Intl. [2849]
Catholic War Veterans of the U.S.A. [3080]
Christian Camp and Conf. Assn. [3302]
Christian Cheerleaders of Am. [3304]
A Cup of Water Intl. [3039]
Episcopalians for Global Reconciliation [2917]
Intl. Catholic Deaf Assn. U.S. Sect. [2868]
Reach Across [3011]
Seventh Day Baptist World Fed. [2847]
Christian Aid Mission [2993], PO Box 9037, Charlottesville, VA 22906, (434)977-5650
Christian Boaters Assn. [2926], 193 Plantation Dr., Tavernier, FL 33070, (305)852-4799
Christian Camp and Conf. Assn. [3302], PO Box 62189, Colorado Springs, CO 80962-2189, (719)260-9400
Christian Chamber of Commerce [★3491]
Christian Cheerleaders of Am. [3304], PO Box 49, Bethania, NC 27010, (877)243-3722
Christian Family Movement [2085], PO Box 925, Evansville, IN 47706-0925, (812)962-5508
Christian Labor Assn. of the U.S.A. [3442], PO Box 65, Zeeland, MI 49464, (616)772-9164
A Christian Ministry in the Natl. Parks [2891], 9185 E Kenyon Ave., Ste. 230, Denver, CO 80237, (303)220-2808
Christian Missions in Many Lands [2994], PO Box 13, Spring Lake, NJ 07762-0013, (732)449-8880
Christian Pilots Assn. [2995], PO Box 90452, Los Angeles, CA 90009, (562)208-2912
Christianity
BCM Intl. [2849]
Catholic War Veterans of the U.S.A. [3080]
Episcopalians for Global Reconciliation [2917]
Intl. Catholic Deaf Assn. U.S. Sect. [2868]
Natl. Alliance Against Christian Discrimination [2897]
Seventh Day Baptist World Fed. [2847]
Church Army [2916], 115 W Atlantic St., Ste. 104, Branson, MO 65616, (417)544-9019
Church Music Assn. of Am. [3020], 12421 New Point Dr., Richmond, VA 23233, (334)703-0884
Church and State
Americans United for Separation of Church and State [2899]
Church and Synagogue Lib. Assn. [1799], 2920 SW Dolph Ct., Ste. 3A, Portland, OR 97219-4055, (503)244-6919
Church Universal and Triumphant [3027], 63 Summit Way, Gardiner, MT 59030, (406)848-9500
Church World Ser., Immigration and Refugee Prog. [2736], 475 Riverside Dr., Ste. 700, New York, NY 10115, (212)870-2061
Churches
IFCA Intl. [2900]
BCM Intl. [2849]
Episcopalians for Global Reconciliation [2917]
Fellowship Intl. Mission [2998]
Seventh Day Baptist World Fed. [2847]
United Indian Missions Intl. [3014]
Churches Uniting in Christ [2906], c/o Elder James N. Tse, Treas., 8717 85th St., Woodhaven, NY 11421-1913, (718)849-1608
CHWMEG [906], 470 William Pitt Way, Pittsburgh, PA 15238, (412)826-3055
Circus
Amer. Youth Circus Org. [1744]
Citizens for Affordable Energy [1453], 1302 Waugh Dr., No. 940, Houston, TX 77019, (713)523-7333
Citizens' Alliance for Responsible Energy [1454], PO Box 52103, Albuquerque, NM 87181, (505)239-8998
Citizens for Energy Freedom [1455], 2020 Pennsylvania Ave. NW, Ste. 263, Washington, DC 20006
Citizens Energy Plan [1456], MinnWest Tech. Campus, 1700 Tech. Dr., Ste. 212, Willmar, MN 56201, (320)222-3060
Citizenship
Amer. Legion Auxiliary Girls Nation [2621]

Close Up Found. [2622]
Civil Affairs Assn. [1349], 10130 Hyla Brook Rd., Columbia, MD 21044-1705, (410)992-7724
Civil Rights and Liberties
Amer. Civil Rights Union [2623]
Natl. Org. for the Reform of Marijuana Laws [2624]
A World of Difference Inst. [2004]
Advancing Human Rights [2658]
Amer. Libyan Freedom Alliance [2636]
Dalit Freedom Network [2661]
Dalit Solidarity [2662]
Iran Democratic Union [2667]
Natl. Alliance Against Christian Discrimination [2897]
Civil Rights Trail [★2622]
Civil Service
Natl. Org. of Blacks in Govt. [1278]
Scientists and Engineers for Am. [1279]
Civil War
Auxiliary to Sons of Union Veterans of the Civil War [3054]
Daughters of Union Veterans of the Civil War, 1861-1865 [3055]
Military Order of the Stars and Bars [3056]
Natl. Assn. for Civil War Brass Music [1825]
North-South Skirmish Assn. [3384]
Civil War Preservation Trust [★1763]
Civil War Trust [1763], 1156 15th St. NW, Ste. 900, Washington, DC 20005, (202)367-1861
CLAL - The Natl. Jewish Center for Learning and Leadership [2950], 440 Park Ave. S, 4th Fl., New York, NY 10016-8012, (212)779-3300
Clan Currie Soc. [3059], PO Box 541, Summit, NJ 07902-0541, (908)273-3509
Clan Fergusson Soc. of North Am. [3060], c/o B. J. Ferguson, Sec., 192 Hawthorne Hill Rd., Jasper, GA 30143
Clan Moncreiffe Soc. [3061], c/o Charlotte Moncrief, Treas., 1405 Plaza St. SE, Decatur, AL 35603
Clan Montgomery Soc. Intl. [3062], 2803 Kinnett Rd., Bethel, OH 45106
Classic Car Club of Am. [3098], 1645 Des Plaines River Rd., Ste. 7A, Des Plaines, IL 60018-2206, (847)390-0443
Classic Thunderbird Club Intl. [3099], 1308 E 29th St., Signal Hill, CA 90755-1842, (562)426-2709
Classic Yacht Assn. [3271], 5267 Shilshole Ave. NW, Ste. 107, Seattle, WA 98107, (206)937-6211
Clay Minerals Soc. [1499], 3635 Concorde Pkwy., Ste. 500, Chantilly, VA 20151-1125, (703)652-9960
Clean Tech. and Sustainable Indus. Org. [964], 3925 W Braker Ln., Austin, TX 78759, (512)692-7267
Clean Tech. Trade Alliance [1391], 2817 Wheaton Way, Ste. 202, Bremerton, WA 98310, (360)692-7286
Clean Water for the World [2261], 3504 Madison St., Kalamazoo, MI 49008, (269)342-1354
Clean the World [1197], 400A Pittman St., Orlando, FL 32801, (407)574-8353
Cleaning Equip. Trade Assn. [552], PO Box 1710, Indian Trail, NC 28079, (704)635-7362
Clear Path Intl. [2639], 321 High School Rd. NE, No. 574, Bainbridge Island, WA 98110, (206)780-5964
Clearpoint Financial Solutions [329], 8000 Franklin Farms Dr., Richmond, VA 23229-5004, (877)422-9040
Cleft Palate-Craniofacial Assn; Amer. [2354]
Cleveland Bay Horse Soc. of North Am. [1126], PO Box 483, Goshen, NH 03752, (865)300-7133
Cleveland Hockey Booster Club [3588], c/o Marsha Hess, 13118 Tyler Ave., Cleveland, OH 44111, (216)251-0606
Climate, Community and Biodiversity Alliance [1012], 2011 Crystal Dr., Ste. 500, Arlington, VA 22202, (703)341-2748
Climate Registry [1181], 523 W 6th St., Ste. 445, Los Angeles, CA 90014, (213)891-6922
ClimateTalk Alliance [1392], 2400 Camino Ramon, Ste. 375, San Ramon, CA 94583, (925)275-6641
Climbing
New England Trails Conf. [3428]
Clinic at a Time [2483], PO Box 14457, Madison, WI 53708, (608)239-3091
Clinical Lab. Mgt. Assn. [2529], 401 N Michigan Ave., Ste. 2200, Chicago, IL 60611, (312)321-5111
Clinical and Lab. Standards Inst. [2530], 940 W Valley Rd., Ste. 1400, Wayne, PA 19087-1898, (610)688-0100

Clinical Neurophysiology Soc; Amer. [2400]
Clinical Social Work Assn. [2237], PO Box 3740, Arlington, VA 22203, (703)340-1456
Clinical Studies
Amer. Soc. for Clinical Investigation [2347]
Assn. of Clinical Scientists [2348]
Intl. Coun. on Nanotechnology [1440]
Soc. for Clinical Trials [2349]
Clinicians of the World [2484], PO Box 116, Rochester, MN 55903, (612)353-8632
Close Up Found. [2622], 1220 Braddock Pl., Ste. 400, Alexandria, VA 22314, (703)706-3300
CLOUT - Christian Lesbians Out [2892], 3653-F Flakes Mill Rd., No. 306, Decatur, GA 30034-5255
Clowns
Intl. Shrine Clown Assn. [3147]
World Clown Assn. [3148]
Clubs
Fed. of Intl. Lacrosse [3357]
Intl. Assn. of Gay and Lesbian Martial Artists [3360]
Maccabi USA/Sports for Israel [3402]
New England Trails Conf. [3428]
Professional Baseball Athletic Trainers Soc. [3261]
U.S. Bobsled and Skeleton Fed. [3390]
USA Diving [3321]
Coaching
Creativity Coaching Assn. [3305]
Natl. High School Athletic Coaches Assn. [3306]
Professional Coaches, Mentors and Advisors [3307]
Golf Coaches Assn. of Am. [3335]
U.S. Twirling Assn. [3267]
Coal
Amer. Coke and Coal Chemicals Inst. [191]
FutureGen Alliance [1393]
Coalition on the Env. and Jewish Life [2951], 116 E 27th St., 10th Fl., New York, NY 10016, (212)532-7436
Coalition for Govt. Procurement [401], 1990 M St. NW, Ste. 450, Washington, DC 20036, (202)331-0975
Coalition of Labor Union Women [3468], 815 16th St. NW, 2nd Fl. S, Washington, DC 20006, (202)508-6969
Coalition of Labor Union Women Center for Educ. and Res. [3469], 815 16th St. NW, 2nd Fl. S, Washington, DC 20006, (202)508-6969
Coalition of Natl. Park Ser. Retirees [1176], 5625 N Wilmot Rd., Tucson, AZ 85750, (520)615-9417
Coalition of Organic Landscapers [531], 1125 NE 152nd St., Shoreline, WA 98155-7053, (206)362-8947
Coalition of Ser. Indus. [810], 1090 Vermont Ave. NW, Ste. 420, Washington, DC 20005, (202)289-7460
Coatings
Aluminum Anodizers Coun. [192]
Coblentz Soc. [1538], Univ. of South Carolina, 631 Sumter St., Columbia, SC 29208, (803)777-5264
Coin Laundry Assn. [536], 1 S 660 Midwest Rd., Ste. 205, Oakbrook Terrace, IL 60181, (630)953-7920
Coins
Colonial Coin Collectors Club [3222]
Collectibles
Antique Advt. Assn. of Am. [19]
Antique Caterpillar Machinery Owners Club [3211]
Antique Motorcycle Club of Am. [3217]
Colonial Coin Collectors Club [3222]
Corvair Soc. of Am. [3100]
First Issues Collectors Club [3226]
Intl. Fire Buff Associates [3192]
Intl. Soc. of Worldwide Stamp Collectors [3227]
Korea Stamp Soc. [3228]
Midstates Jeepster Assn. [3117]
Morgan Car Club [3120]
Plasticville Collectors Assn. [3237]
Soc. of Australasian Specialists/Oceania [3232]
Space Topic Stud. Unit [3234]
Toy Train Collectors Soc. [3214]
United Four-Wheel Drive Associations [3135]
Vintage Garden Tractor Club of Am. [3246]
World Airline Historical Soc. [3089]
Youth in Model Railroading [3215]
Collectors
Amer. Bell Assn. Intl. [3149]

Amer. Collectors of Infant Feeders [3150]
Czech Collector's Assn. [3151]
German Gun Collectors' Assn. [3152]
Intl. Assn. of R.S. Prussia Collectors [3153]
Intl. Assn. of Silver Art Collectors [3154]
Intl. Match Safe Assn. [3155]
Intl. Scouting Collectors Assn. [3156]
Intl. Swizzle Stick Collectors Assn. [3157]
M&M's Collectors Club [3158]
Midwest Decoy Collectors Assn. [3159]
On the Lighter Side, Intl. Lighter Collectors [3160]
Soc. of Inkwell Collectors [3161]
Antique Advt. Assn. of Am. [19]
Antique Caterpillar Machinery Owners Club [3211]
Antique Motorcycle Club of Am. [3217]
Colonial Coin Collectors Club [3222]
Corvair Soc. of Am. [3100]
First Issues Collectors Club [3226]
Intl. Fire Buff Associates [3192]
Intl. Soc. of Worldwide Stamp Collectors [3227]
Korea Stamp Soc. [3228]
Midstates Jeepster Assn. [3117]
Morgan Car Club [3120]
Plasticville Collectors Assn. [3237]
Soc. of Australasian Specialists/Oceania [3232]
Space Topic Stud. Unit [3234]
Toy Train Collectors Soc. [3214]
United Four-Wheel Drive Associations [3135]
Vintage Garden Tractor Club of Am. [3246]
World Airline Historical Soc. [3089]
Youth in Model Railroading [3215]
Coll. Athletic Bus. Mgt. Assn. [3400], c/o Pat Manak,
  Asst. Sec., 24651 Detroit Rd., Westlake, OH
  44145, (440)892-4000
Coll. Band Directors Natl. Assn. [1666], c/o Thomas
  Verrier, Sec., Vanderbilt Univ., Blair School of
  Music, 2400 Blakemore Ave., Nashville, TN 37212,
  (615)322-7651
Coll. Reading and Learning Assn. [1679], 2 Caracal
  St., Belen, NM 87002, (505)861-2142
Coll. Swimming Coaches Assn. of Am. [3415], 1640
  Maple Ave., No. 803, Evanston, IL 60201,
  (847)833-3478
Colleges and Universities
  Eastern Coll. Athletic Conf. [3342]
  Golf Coaches Assn. of Am. [3335]
  Natl. Assn. of Peoplecultural Engg. Prog.
    Advocates [1615]
  Union of North Amer. Vietnamese Students Assn.
    [2832]
  Universities Allied for Essential Medicines [1641]
Colonial
  Holland Soc. of New York [3057]
  Colonial Coin Collectors Club [3222]
  Gen. Soc. of Mayflower Descendants [3077]
Colonial Coin Collectors Club [3222], c/o Charlie
  Rohrer, Treas., PO Box 25, Mountville, PA 17554
Color
  Color Marketing Gp. [193]
Color Marketing Gp. [193], 1908 Mt. Vernon Ave.,
  Alexandria, VA 22301, (703)329-8500
COME Intl. Baptist Ministries [2927], PO Box 88085,
  Grand Rapids, MI 49518, (616)868-9906
Comedy
  Three Stooges Fan Club [3568]
Comics
  Comics Professional Retailers Org. [194]
  Hero Initiative [1745]
Comics Professional Retailers Org. [194], PO Box
  75446, Colorado Springs, CO 80970, (877)574-
  8618
Commercial Development and Marketing Assn.
  [1437], 15000 Commerce Pkwy., Ste. C, Mount
  Laurel, NJ 08054, (856)439-9052
Commercial Finance Assn. [542], 370 7th Ave., Ste.
  1801, New York, NY 10001-3979, (212)792-9390
Commercial Law
  Commercial Law League of Am. [1280]
Commercial Law League of Am. [1280], 205 N
  Michigan, Ste. 2212, Chicago, IL 60601, (312)240-
  1400
Commn. on Accreditation for Law Enforcement
  Agencies [1329], 13575 Heathcote Blvd., Ste. 320,
  Gainesville, VA 20155, (703)352-4225
Commission on Dental Accreditation [★2372]

Commn. on Rehabilitation Counselor Certification
  [2042], 1699 E Woodfield Rd., Ste. 300, Schaum-
  burg, IL 60173-4957, (847)944-1325
Commn. on Religious Counseling and Healing
  [2836], 4202 Newark Ave., Cleveland, OH 44109,
  (216)543-6377
Comm. for Children [1945], 2815 2nd Ave., Ste. 400,
  Seattle, WA 98121, (206)343-1223
Comm. of French Speaking Societies [2781], 30 E
  40th St., Ste. 906, New York, NY 10016
Comm. of Interns and Residents [3447], 520 8th
  Ave., Ste. 1200, New York, NY 10018-4183,
  (212)356-8100
Committee on Postgraduate Educational Programs
  [★1419]
Committee for Purchase From People Who Are Blind
  or Severely Disabled [★2605]
Comm. on Res. Materials on Southeast Asia [1800],
  Ohio Univ., Alden Lib., Athens, OH 45701-2978,
  (740)593-2657
Commodities
  Hop Growers of Am. [994]
  Intl. Cotton Advisory Comm. [995]
  Kamut Assn. of North Am. [996]
  Natl. Sweet Sorghum Producers and Processors
    Assn. [997]
  Soyfoods Assn. of North Am. [998]
  U.S. Wheat Associates [999]
  U.S.A. Rice Coun. [1000]
Communications
  911 Indus. Alliance [195]
  Assn. of Biomedical Communications Directors
    [2350]
  BioCommunications Assn. [2351]
  Hea. Sci. Communications Assn. [2352]
  Inter Amer. Press Assn. [2625]
  Media Watch [2626]
  MultiService Forum [196]
  Religious Commun. Assn. [1588]
  Scribes - The Amer. Soc. of Legal Writers [1281]
  Soc. for Tech. Commun. [197]
  Zeta Phi Eta [3512]
  ARRL Found. [3090]
  Electronic Indus. Citizenship Coalition [280]
  Mainstream Media Proj. [2735]
  Rhetoric Soc. of Am. [1851]
Community
  Climate, Community and Biodiversity Alliance
    [1012]
  Community Associations Inst. [2627]
  Natl. Community for Latino Leadership [2800]
Community Action
  Global Helps Network [2005]
  Midwest Acad. [2006]
  Breaking Ground [2009]
  Building Bridges Worldwide [2010]
  Burundi Friends Intl. [2012]
  Children of Tanzania [1903]
  ecoAmerica [1016]
  Girls for a Change [1956]
  Green Team Am. [1028]
  Help Brings Hope for Haiti [2188]
  Khadarlis for Sierra Leone [2026]
  Mama Hope [2027]
  Miracles in Action [2170]
  Mobile Medical Disaster Relief [2138]
  One Love Worldwide [2194]
  People for Haiti [2195]
  Transition U.S. [1082]
Community Action Partnership [2165], 1140 Con-
  necticut Ave. NW, Ste. 1210, Washington, DC
  20036, (202)265-7546
Community Agroecology Network [1216], PO Box
  7653, Santa Cruz, CA 95061, (831)459-3619
Community Associations Inst. [2627], 6402 Arlington
  Blvd., Ste. 500, Falls Church, VA 22042, (703)970-
  9220
Community Colleges
  Amer. Assn. of Community Colleges [1589]
  Natl. Coun. of State Directors of Community Col-
    leges [1590]
Community Colleges for Intl. Development [1636],
  PO Box 2068, Cedar Rapids, IA 52406-2068,
  (319)398-1257
Community Development
  Adopt-a-Village Intl. [2007]

Alliance of Jamaican and Amer. Humanitarians
  [2008]
Breaking Ground [2009]
Building Bridges Worldwide [2010]
Building Community Bridges [2011]
Burundi Friends Intl. [2012]
Chris Cares Intl. [2013]
Community Associations Inst. [2627]
Community Development Intl. [2014]
Community Trans. Assn. of Am. [2015]
Connecting Congo [2016]
Educ. for Prosperity [2017]
Funders' Network for Smart Growth and Livable
  Communities [2018]
Global Brigades [2019]
Global Partners Running Waters [2020]
HANDS for Cambodia [2021]
Help Aid Africa [2022]
Hope for Haiti [2023]
Indigo Threads [2024]
Intl. Org. for Haitian Development [1591]
Jamaica Unite [2025]
Khadarlis for Sierra Leone [2026]
Mama Hope [2027]
Nepal SEEDS: Social Educational Environmental
  Development Services in Nepal [2028]
One Vision Intl. [2029]
Oper. HOPE, Inc. [2030]
Opportunity Finance Network [2628]
Orphans Africa [2031]
Reconstruction Efforts Aiding Children without
  Homes [2032]
Restoring Institutions Services and Empowering
  Liberia [2033]
Ser. for the Love of God [2034]
Shining Hope for Communities [2035]
Together for Tanzania [2036]
Village Focus Intl. [2037]
The Waterfront Center [2038]
Well Done Org. [2039]
WorldHope Corps [2040]
Abriendo Mentes [2208]
Act for Africa Intl. [2209]
Agami [1581]
Alliance For Relief Mission in Haiti [2181]
Amer. Bar Assn. Commn. on Homelessness and
  Poverty [2099]
Amer. Friends of Guinea [2478]
Americans Care and Share [2182]
Artfully AWARE [1724]
Bridges Cambodia Intl. [1929]
Bridges to Prosperity [2210]
Christ for the Poor [1681]
Clean Tech. and Sustainable Indus. Org. [964]
Clean Water for the World [2261]
Community Empowerment Network [2211]
Community Hea. Intl. [2448]
Community Managers Intl. Assn. [559]
Computers for Africa [1597]
Drinking Water for India [2262]
Fields of Growth Intl. [2129]
Gift of Water [2263]
Global Helps Network [2005]
Haiti Convention Assn. [2214]
Haiti Outreach [1905]
Hearts for Kenya [1907]
Help Brings Hope for Haiti [2188]
Helping Hand for Nepal [2189]
Helping Hearts Helping Hands [2166]
HELPSudan [1994]
Idoma Assn. USA [2812]
In Our Own Quiet Way [2265]
Innovation: Africa [1394]
Intl. Action [2266]
Into Your Hands [2215]
Junior Optimist Octagon Intl. [2222]
Kids Home Intl. [1969]
Malawi Children's Mission [1972]
Mercy Beyond Borders [2169]
Miracles in Action [2170]
Natl. Community for Latino Leadership [2800]
Natl. Housing and Rehabilitation Assn. [2105]
Natl. Student Campaign Against Hunger and
  Homelessness [2117]
One Love Worldwide [2194]

A star before a book entry number signifies that the name is not listed separately, but is mentioned within the entry.

Outreach Africa **[1981]**
Partners in Sustainable Development Intl. **[2171]**
Peace House Africa **[1983]**
Reach Intl. Healthcare and Training **[2515]**
Reach Out to Romania **[2172]**
Rebuilding Haiti Now **[2197]**
Rights and Resources Initiative **[1095]**
Rising Intl. **[1908]**
River Intl. **[2199]**
Roots of Development **[2212]**
Simple Hope **[2200]**
Solar for Peace **[1537]**
Sudan Sunrise **[2154]**
To Love a Child **[1988]**
Tusubira - We Have Hope **[2173]**
Under The Baobab Tree **[1593]**
Union MicroFinanza **[2213]**
Vietnam Relief Effort **[2201]**
Water Alliance for Africa **[2268]**
Wild Gift **[1259]**
Community Development Intl. **[2014]**, PO Box 3417,
New York, NY 10163
Community Education
Natl. Community Educ. Assn. **[1592]**
Under The Baobab Tree **[1593]**
Abriendo Mentes **[2208]**
Alliance of Jamaican and Amer. Humanitarians
[2008]
Christ for the Poor **[1681]**
Educ. for Prosperity **[2017]**
HELPSudan **[1994]**
Intl. Org. for Haitian Development **[1591]**
Into Your Hands **[2215]**
Ser. for the Love of God **[2034]**
Community Empowerment Network **[2211]**, 1685
Grandview Pl., Ferndale, WA 98248, (206)329-
6244
Community Financial Services Assn. **[330]**, 515 King
St., Ste. 300, Alexandria, VA 22314, (888)572-9329
Community Hea. Intl. **[2448]**, 59 Windsor Rd.,
Brookline, MA 02445, (617)739-2638
Community Improvement
Act for Africa Intl. **[2209]**
Adopt-a-Village Intl. **[2007]**
Amer. Bar Assn. Commn. on Homelessness and
Poverty **[2099]**
Breaking Ground **[2009]**
Bridges to Prosperity **[2210]**
Burundi Friends Intl. **[2012]**
Chris Cares Intl. **[2013]**
Clean Water for the World **[2261]**
Community Development Intl. **[2014]**
Community Managers Intl. Assn. **[559]**
Educ. for Prosperity **[2017]**
Funders' Network for Smart Growth and Livable
Communities **[2018]**
Global Brigades **[2019]**
Global Helps Network **[2005]**
Global Partners Running Waters **[2020]**
Haiti Convention Assn. **[2214]**
HANDS for Cambodia **[2021]**
Help Aid Africa **[2022]**
Help Brings Hope for Haiti **[2188]**
Hope for Haiti **[2023]**
Into Your Hands **[2215]**
Junior Optimist Octagon Intl. **[2222]**
Khadarlis for Sierra Leone **[2026]**
Mama Hope **[2027]**
Mercy Beyond Borders **[2169]**
Natl. Alliance of Highway Beautification Agencies
[1370]
Nepal SEEDS: Social Educational Environmental
Development Services in Nepal **[2028]**
One Vision Intl. **[2029]**
Planetwork **[1055]**
Ser. for the Love of God **[2034]**
Shining Hope for Communities **[2035]**
Together for Tanzania **[2036]**
Tusubira - We Have Hope **[2173]**
Under The Baobab Tree **[1593]**
Vietnam Relief Effort **[2201]**
Village Focus Intl. **[2037]**
WorldHope Corps **[2040]**
Community Managers Intl. Assn. **[559]**, PO Box 848,
Dana Point, CA 92629, (888)900-2642
Community Service
Abrahamic Alliance Intl. **[2945]**

Act for Africa Intl. **[2209]**
Adopt-a-Village Intl. **[2007]**
Amer. Bar Assn. Commn. on Homelessness and
Poverty **[2099]**
Americans Care and Share **[2182]**
Artfully AWARE **[1724]**
Breaking Ground **[2009]**
Bridges to Prosperity **[2210]**
Building Bridges Worldwide **[2010]**
Building Community Bridges **[2011]**
Burundi Friends Intl. **[2012]**
Community Managers Intl. Assn. **[559]**
Educ. for Prosperity **[2017]**
Gift of Water **[2263]**
Global Helps Network **[2005]**
Haiti Healthcare Partners **[2496]**
Haiti Outreach **[1905]**
HANDS for Cambodia **[2021]**
HavServe Volunteer Ser. Network **[1906]**
Helping Hand for Nepal **[2189]**
Helping Hearts Helping Hands **[2166]**
Indigo Threads **[2024]**
Junior Optimist Octagon Intl. **[2222]**
Mama Hope **[2027]**
Miracles in Action **[2170]**
Nepal SEEDS: Social Educational Environmental
Development Services in Nepal **[2028]**
One Vision Intl. **[2029]**
Outreach Africa **[1981]**
Restoring Institutions Services and Empowering
Liberia **[2033]**
Rights and Resources Initiative **[1095]**
Roots of Development **[2212]**
Tusubira - We Have Hope **[2173]**
Community Trans. Assn. of Am. **[2015]**, 1341 G St.
NW, 10th Fl., Washington, DC 20005, (202)247-
1922
Compassion into Action Network - Direct Outcome
Org. **[2067]**, 578 Washington Blvd., Ste. 390,
Marina Del Rey, CA 90292, (877)226-3697
Compassion and Choices **[2082]**, PO Box 101810,
Denver, CO 80250-1810, (800)247-7421
Compensation Medicine
Natl. Assn. of Disability Examiners **[2353]**
Computer Science
ACM SIGGRAPH **[1441]**
Assn. of Info. Tech. Professionals **[1594]**
Inst. for Certification of Computing Professionals
[1595]
Intl. Assn. for Cmpt. Info. Systems **[1596]**
Special Interest Gp. for Design Automation **[1442]**
Upsilon Pi Epsilon Assn. **[3513]**
Cmpt. Security Inst. **[470]**, 350 Hudson St., Ste.
300, New York, NY 10014, (212)600-3026
Computer Users
Special Interest Gp. on Accessible Computing
[1443]
Global Tech. Distribution Coun. **[848]**
Computers
Assn. of Ser. and Cmpt. Dealers Intl. **[1444]**
Computers for Africa **[1597]**
Computing Tech. Indus. Assn. **[1445]**
Pro vs. GI Joe **[3200]**
Computers for Africa **[1597]**, PO Box 34262,
Omaha, NE 68134-0262, (402)933-6456
Computing Tech. Indus. Assn. **[1445]**, 3500 Lacey
Rd., Ste. 100, Downers Grove, IL 60515,
(630)678-8300
Concerned Persons for Adoption **[1871]**, c/o Anna
Marie O'Loughlin, Membership Chair, 7 Elizabeth
St., Bloomingdale, NJ 07403
Concordia Historical Inst. **[2970]**, 804 Seminary Pl.,
St. Louis, MO 63105-3014, (314)505-7900
Concrete
Intl. Concrete Repair Inst. **[198]**
Natl. Concrete Masonry Assn. **[199]**
Natl. Precast Concrete Assn. **[200]**
Precast/Prestressed Concrete Inst. **[201]**
Intl. Soc. for Concrete Pavements **[148]**
Conf. of Educational Administrators of Schools and
Programs for the Deaf **[2451]**, PO Box 1778, St.
Augustine, FL 32085-1778, (904)810-5200
Conf. on Faith and History **[2942]**, c/o Paul E. Mich-
elson, Sec., Huntington Univ., Dept. of History,
2303 Coll. Ave., Huntington, IN 46750, (260)359-
4242
Conf. on Latin Amer. History **[1792]**, Univ. of North
Carolina at Charlotte, U.S. Department of of His-
tory and Prog. in Latin Amer. Studies, 9201 Univ.
City blvd., Charlotte, NC 28223, (704)687-2027

Conf. of Major Superiors of Men **[2865]**, 8808 Cam-
eron St., Silver Spring, MD 20910, (301)588-4030
Conf. of Minority Trans. Officials **[869]**, 2025 M St.
NW, Ste. 800, Washington, DC 20036-3309,
(202)367-1181
Conflict Resolution
Alliance for Peacebuilding **[2629]**
Congregation of Sisters of Saint Agnes **[2866]**, 320
County Rd. K, Fond du Lac, WI 54937-8158,
(920)907-2300
Cong. on Res. in Dance **[1750]**, 3416 Primm Ln.,
Birmingham, AL 35216, (205)823-5517
Connecticut River Watershed Coun. **[1013]**, 15 Bank
Row, Greenfield, MA 01301, (413)772-2020
Connecting Congo **[2016]**, 1416 S 43rd St., Tacoma,
WA 98418, (206)351-9293
Conscientious Objectors
Center on Conscience and War **[2641]**
Conservation
Africa Environmental Watch **[1001]**
Alliance for Intl. Reforestation **[1002]**
Alliance for Tompotika Conservation **[1003]**
Amer. Forests **[1004]**
Anglers for Conservation **[1005]**
Assn. of Conservation Engineers **[1006]**
Assn. of Environmental and Rsrc. Economists
[1007]
Assn. of Fish and Wildlife Agencies **[1008]**
Big Thicket Assn. **[1009]**
BlueVoice.org **[1010]**
CEDAM Intl. **[1011]**
Climate, Community and Biodiversity Alliance
[1012]
Connecticut River Watershed Coun. **[1013]**
Conservation and Res. Found. **[1014]**
Cork Forest Conservation Alliance **[1015]**
ecoAmerica **[1016]**
Ecological Res. and Development Gp. **[1017]**
Efficiency First **[1018]**
Environmental Commons **[1019]**
Ethnobotanical Conservation Org. for South East
Asia **[1020]**
Experience Intl. **[1021]**
Forest Bird Soc. **[1022]**
Forestry Conservation Communications Assn.
[1023]
Friends of the Everglades **[1024]**
Friends of the Osa **[1025]**
Global Parks **[1026]**
Grassland Heritage Found. **[1027]**
Green Team Am. **[1028]**
Intl. Union for the Conservation of Nature and
Natural Resources U.S. **[1029]**
Natl. Mitigation Banking Assn. **[1030]**
Natl. Oceanic Soc. **[1031]**
Network of Conservation Educators and
Practitioners **[1032]**
Ocean Champions **[2630]**
Ocean Res. and Conservation Assn. **[1033]**
Oceanic Preservation Soc. **[1034]**
Pacific Islands Conservation Res. Assn. **[1035]**
Paso Pacifico **[1036]**
Renewable Natural Resources Found. **[1037]**
Rising Tide North Am. **[1038]**
River Mgt. Soc. **[1039]**
River Network **[1040]**
Sailors for the Sea **[1041]**
Sustainable World Coalition **[1042]**
Tropical Forest Gp. **[1043]**
Turtle Island Restoration Network **[1044]**
Wilderness Intl. **[1045]**
The Wilderness Soc. **[1046]**
Wildlife Mgt. Inst. **[1047]**
Wolf Haven Intl. **[1048]**
World Fed. for Coral Reef Conservation **[1049]**
Alliance for Water Educ. **[1620]**
Alliance for Water Efficiency **[1224]**
Amara Conservation **[1230]**
Animal World USA **[949]**
Ape Action Africa **[1231]**
Ape Conservation Effort **[1232]**
Bee Native **[961]**
Big Wildlife **[1233]**
Coalition of Natl. Park Ser. Retirees **[1176]**
Community Agroecology Network **[1216]**
Darwin Animal Doctors **[950]**
Energy Conservation Org. **[1612]**

Env. for the Americas **[962]**
Environmental Educ. and Conservation Global **[1621]**
Global Underwater Explorers **[1159]**
Global Wildlife Conservation **[1238]**
Human-Wildlife Conflict Collaboration **[1239]**
Hummingbird Monitoring Network **[963]**
Iemanya Oceanica **[1240]**
Intl. Soc. of Sustainability Professionals **[1080]**
Irrigation Water Mgt. Soc. **[1226]**
Journey Toward Sustainability **[1622]**
Kids Ecology Corps **[1076]**
MarineBio Conservation Soc. **[1162]**
Nature Abounds **[1069]**
Panthera **[1251]**
Planetwork **[1055]**
Rainforest Partnership **[1193]**
Responsible Purchasing Network **[316]**
Rights and Resources Initiative **[1095]**
Shark Alliance **[1254]**
TopTen USA **[305]**
Wild Animals Worldwide **[1257]**
Wild Gift **[1259]**
Women Organizing for Change in Agriculture and NRM **[938]**
Wonderful World of Wildlife **[1260]**
World Nature Coalition **[1262]**
Conservation Alliance for Tigers **[★1262]**
Conservation and Res. Found. **[1014]**, PO Box 909, Shelburne, VT 05482-0909
Conservationists
Assn. of Conservation Engineers **[1006]**
Conservative
Freedom House **[2631]**
Conservative Baptist Assn. of Am. **[2843]**, 3686 Stagecoach Rd., Ste. F, Longmont, CO 80504-5660, (303)772-1205
Consortium for Advanced Mgt. Intl. **[581]**, 6836 Bee Cave, Ste. 256, Austin, TX 78746, (512)617-6428
Consortium of Humanities Centers and Institutes **[2113]**, Duke Univ., John Hope Franklin Humanities Inst., 2204 Erwin Rd., Durham, NC 27708-0403, (919)668-0107
Constitution
Amer. Civil Rights Union **[2623]**
Construction
Amer. Constr. Inspectors Assn. **[202]**
Amer. Fence Assn. **[203]**
Amer. Inst. of Constructors **[1446]**
Constr. Specifications Inst. **[1447]**
CPWR - The Center for Constr. Res. and Training **[3443]**
Equip. Managers Coun. of Am. **[204]**
Firestop Contractors Intl. Assn. **[205]**
Natl. Assn. of Black Women in Constr. **[206]**
Quartzite Rock Assn. **[207]**
Assn. for Better Insulation **[138]**
Assn. of Constr. Inspectors **[476]**
Building Commissioning Assn. **[141]**
Building Security Coun. **[801]**
Green Builder Coalition **[146]**
Intl. Soc. for Concrete Pavements **[148]**
Natl. Alliance of Highway Beautification Agencies **[1370]**
Natl. Assn. of Constr. Contractors Cooperation **[152]**
Natl. Roof Certification and Inspection Assn. **[155]**
Short Span Steel Bridge Alliance **[1434]**
Wood I-Joist Mfrs. Assn. **[389]**
Constr. Employers Assn. **[143]**, c/o Michael Walton, Sec., 1646 N California Blvd., Ste. 500, Walnut Creek, CA 94596-4148, (925)930-8184
Constr. Financial Mgt. Assn. **[220]**, 100 Village Blvd., Ste. 200, Princeton, NJ 08542, (609)452-8000
Constr. Specifications Inst. **[1447]**, 110 S Union St., Ste. 100, Alexandria, VA 22314-3351, (800)689-2900
Consultative Gp. to Assist the Poor **[2671]**, 900 19th St. NW, Ste. 300, Washington, DC 20006, (202)473-9594
Consulting
Amer. Assn. of Insurance Mgt. Consultants **[208]**
Amer. Soc. of Theatre Consultants **[209]**
Assn. of Professional Consultants **[210]**
Assn. of Professional Material Handling Consultants **[211]**

Professional and Tech. Consultants Assn. **[212]**
Consumer Electronics Retailers Coalition **[767]**, 317 Massachusetts Ave. NE, Ste. 200, Washington, DC 20006, (202)292-4600
Consumer Fed. of Am. **[2632]**, 1620 I St. NW, Ste. 200, Washington, DC 20006, (202)387-6121
Consumer Goods Forum **[768]**, 8455 Colesville Rd., Ste. 705, Silver Spring, MD 20910, (301)563-3383
Consumer Healthcare Products Assn. **[658]**, 900 19th St. NW, Ste. 700, Washington, DC 20006, (202)429-9260
Consumers
Consumer Fed. of Am. **[2632]**
Funeral Ser. Consumer Assistance Prog. **[2633]**
Natl. Assn. of Consumer Credit Administrators **[1282]**
Farmers Market Coalition **[929]**
Natl. Found. for Credit Counseling **[543]**
TopTen USA **[305]**
Contact Lens Mfrs. Assn. **[422]**, PO Box 29398, Lincoln, NE 68529, (402)465-4122
Containers
Recycled Paperboard Tech. Assn. **[213]**
Contractors
ADSC: The Intl. Assn. of Found. Drilling **[214]**
Amer. Soc. of Concrete Contractors **[215]**
Amer. Subcontractors Assn. **[216]**
Assoc. Builders and Contractors **[217]**
Assoc. Builders and Contractors I Natl. Elecl. Contractors Coun. **[218]**
Ceilings and Interior Systems Constr. Assn. **[219]**
Constr. Financial Mgt. Assn. **[220]**
Joint Indus. Bd. of the Elecl. Indus. **[221]**
Natl. Assn. of Small Bus. Contractors **[222]**
Natl. Assn. of State Contractors Licensing Agencies **[223]**
Natl. Assn. of Women in Constr. **[224]**
Natl. Demolition Assn. **[225]**
Natl. Frame Builders Assn. **[226]**
Natl. Utility Contractors Assn. **[227]**
Natl. Utility Locating Contractors Assn. **[228]**
Power and Commun. Contractors Assn. **[229]**
Professional Constr. Estimators Assn. of Am. **[230]**
Professional Women in Constr. **[231]**
Tilt-Up Concrete Assn. **[232]**
Women Constr. Owners and Executives U.S.A. **[233]**
Alliance for Building Regulatory Reform in the Digital Age **[1435]**
Assn. for Better Insulation **[138]**
Intl. Soc. for Concrete Pavements **[148]**
Natl. Assn. of Constr. Contractors Cooperation **[152]**
Contractors Pump Bur. **[461]**, 6737 W Washington St., Ste. 2400, Milwaukee, WI 53214-5647, (414)272-0943
Convention Indus. Coun. **[864]**, 700 N Fairfax St., Ste. 510, Alexandria, VA 22314, (571)527-3116
Conveyor Equip. Mfrs. Assn. **[462]**, 6724 Lone Oak Blvd., Naples, FL 34109, (239)514-3441
Cookware Mfrs. Assn. **[451]**, PO Box 531335, Birmingham, AL 35253-1335, (205)592-0389
Cool Metal Roofing Coalition **[144]**, 680 Andersen Dr., Pittsburgh, PA 15220, (412)922-2772
Cooperative Education
Cooperative Educ. and Internship Assn. **[1598]**
Cooperative Educ. and Internship Assn. **[1598]**, PO Box 42506, Cincinnati, OH 45242, (513)793-2342
Cooperative Housing Found. **[2101]**, 8601 Georgia Ave., Ste. 800, Silver Spring, MD 20910, (301)587-4700
Cooperatives
Natl. Cooperative Bus. Assn. **[234]**
Natl. Cooperative Grocers Assn. **[235]**
Copyright Alliance **[1313]**, 1224 M St. NW, Ste. 301, Washington, DC 20005, (202)540-2243
CoreNet Global **[737]**, 260 Peachtree St. NW, Ste. 1500, Atlanta, GA 30303, (404)589-3200
Cork Forest Conservation Alliance **[1015]**, 565 Oxford St., Salem, OR 97302, (503)931-9690
Cork Inst. of Am. **[387]**, 715 Fountain Ave., Lancaster, PA 17601, (717)295-3400
Corporate Law
Assn. of Corporate Counsel **[1283]**

Corporate Responsibility
CEO Netweavers **[236]**
Corporate Responsibility Officers Assn. **[237]**
Corporate Social Responsibility Assn. **[238]**
Uplift Intl. **[2522]**
Corporate Responsibility Officers Assn. **[237]**, 343 Thornall St., Ste. 515, Edison, NJ 08837-2209, (732)476-6160
Corporate Social Responsibility Assn. **[238]**, 155 E Boardwalk Dr., No. 544, Fort Collins, CO 80525, (303)944-4225
CorpWatch **[2660]**, PO Box 29198, San Francisco, CA 94129, (415)800-4004
Correctional
Assn. of State Correctional Administrators **[2049]**
Intl. Assn. for Correctional and Forensic Psychology **[2050]**
Corvair Soc. of Am. **[3100]**, PO Box 607, Lemont, IL 60439-0607, (630)403-5010
Corvette Clubs; Natl. Coun. of **[3123]**
Cosmetology
Allied Hea. Assn. **[239]**
Natl. - Interstate Coun. of State Boards of Cosmetology **[240]**
Professional Beauty Assn. I Nail Mfrs. Coun. **[241]**
Soc. of Permanent Cosmetic Professionals **[242]**
Cotton
Cotton Coun. Intl. **[243]**
Natl. Cotton Coun. of Am. **[244]**
Cotton Coun. Intl. **[243]**, 1521 New Hampshire Ave. NW, Washington, DC 20036, (202)745-7805
Coun. on Accreditation **[2233]**, 45 Broadway 29th Fl., New York, NY 10006, (212)797-3000
Coun. for Acupuncture Res. and Educ. **[2284]**, 3448 Horseshoe Bend Rd., Charlottesville, VA 22901
Coun. of Amer. Instructors of the Deaf **[2452]**, PO Box 377, Bedford, TX 76095-0377, (817)354-8414
Coun. of Amer. Jewish Museums **[1815]**, PO Box 12025, Jackson, MS 39236-2025, (303)871-3015
Coun. for Amer. Private Educ. **[1677]**, 13017 Wisteria Dr., No. 457, Germantown, MD 20874-2607, (301)916-8460
Coun. of the Americas **[3501]**, 680 Park Ave., New York, NY 10065, (212)628-3200
Coun. on Anthropology and Educ. **[1401]**, Mills Coll., 5000 MacArthur Blvd., Oakland, CA 94613, (510)430-3384
Coun. for Children with Behavioral Disorders **[1686]**, 1110 N Glebe Rd., Ste. 300, Arlington, VA 22201-5704, (703)620-3660
Coun. of Chiropractic Acupuncture **[2342]**, 510 Baxter Rd., Ste. 8, Chesterfield, MO 63017, (636)207-6600
Coun. on Chiropractic Practice **[2343]**, 2950 N Dobson Rd., Ste. 1, Chandler, AZ 85224
Coun. of Citizens With Low Vision Intl. **[2056]**, 2200 Wilson Blvd., Ste. 650, Arlington, VA 22201, (800)733-2258
Coun. of Colleges of Arts and Sciences **[1570]**, Coll. of William and Mary, PO Box 8795, Williamsburg, VA 23187-8795, (757)221-1784
Coun. for Community and Economic Res. **[3478]**, PO Box 100127, Arlington, VA 22210, (703)522-4980
Coun. on Educ. of the Deaf **[2453]**, Eastern Kentucky Univ., Wallace 245, Richmond, KY 40475, (859)622-1043
Coun. for Exceptional Children **[1687]**, 2900 Crystal Dr., Ste. 1000, Arlington, VA 22202-3557, (703)620-3660
Coun. on Foreign Relations **[2651]**, The Harold Pratt House, 58 E 68th St., New York, NY 10065, (212)434-9400
Coun. on Intl. Educational Exchange USA **[1637]**, 300 Fore St., Portland, ME 04101, (207)553-4000
Coun. for Intl. Exchange of Scholars I Inst. of Intl. Educ. **[1638]**, 3007 Tilden St. NW, Ste. 5L, Washington, DC 20008-3009, (202)686-4000
Coun. of Intl. Investigators **[522]**, 2150 N 107th St., Ste. 205, Seattle, WA 98133-9009, (206)361-8869
Coun. of Landscape Architectural Registration Boards **[1408]**, 3949 Pender Dr., Ste. 120, Fairfax, VA 22030, (571)432-0332
Coun. of Overseas Chinese Services **[2777]**, PO Box 6940, New York, NY 10150, (347)617-2687

A star before a book entry number signifies that the name is not listed separately, but is mentioned within the entry.

Coun. for Professional Recognition [1913], 2460 16th St. NW, Washington, DC 20009, (202)265-9090

Coun. of Real Estate Brokerage Managers [738], 430 N Michigan Ave., Chicago, IL 60611-4011, (312)321-4414

Coun. of Residential Specialists [739], 430 N Michigan Ave., Chicago, IL 60611, (312)321-4444

Coun. for Rsrc. Development [1610], 1 Dupont Cir. NW, Ste. 365, Washington, DC 20036, (202)822-0750

Councils on Chiropractic Educ. Intl. [1585], PO Box 4943, Pocatello, ID 83205, (208)241-4855

Counseling
Assn. of Biblical Counselors [2901]
Assn. for Specialists in Gp. Work [2041]
Commn. on Rehabilitation Counselor Certification [2042]
Damien Ministries [2902]
Employee Assistance Soc. of North Am. [2043]
Intl. Assn. of Addictions and Offender Counselors [2044]
Natl. MultiCultural Inst. [2045]
Creativity Coaching Assn. [3305]
LIFE Ministries [2937]

CounterIntelligence Assn; Marine Corps [2802]

Counterpart - U.S. Off. [2672], 2345 Crystal Dr., Ste. 301, Arlington, VA 22202, (703)236-1200

Country-Western Music
George Strait Fan Club [3579]
Roy Rogers - Dale Evans Collectors Assn. [3587]

County Government
Natl. Assn. of Black County Officials [1284]

Couples Natl. Network [2094], PO Box 500699, Marathon, FL 33050-0699, (800)896-0717

Court Employees
U.S. Court Reporters Assn. [1285]

Covenant World Relief [2185], 8303 W Higgins Rd., Chicago, IL 60631, (773)907-3301

CPWR - The Center for Constr. Res. and Training [3443], 8484 Georgia Ave., Ste. 1000, Silver Spring, MD 20910, (301)578-8500

Craft Org. Development Assn. [3165], PO Box 51, Onia, AR 72663, (870)746-5159

Crafts
Amer. Bladesmith Soc. [3162]
Amer. Made Alliance [3163]
Caricature Carvers of Am. [3164]
Craft Org. Development Assn. [3165]
Intl. Guild of Miniature Artisans [3166]
Intl. Wildfowl Carvers Assn. [3167]
Knifemakers' Guild [3168]
Natl. Acad. of Needlearts [3169]
Natl. Assn. of Wheat Weavers [3170]
Northwest Regional Spinners' Assn. [3171]
World Org. of China Painters [3172]
Intl. Wood Collectors Soc. [3249]
Spinning and Weaving Assn. [858]

Cranberry Inst. [1097], PO Box 497, Carver, MA 02330, (508)866-1118

Craniofacial Abnormalities
Amer. Cleft Palate-Craniofacial Assn. [2354]
Smile Network Intl. [2355]

CRE Finance Coun. [740], 30 Broad St., 28th Fl., New York, NY 10004, (212)509-1844

Creative Educ. Found. [1604], 48 N Pleasant St., Ste. 301, Amherst, MA 01002, (508)960-0000

Creativity
Creativity Coaching Assn. [3305]

Creativity Coaching Assn. [3305], PO Box 328, Lake George, NY 12845, (518)798-6933

Credit
Intl. Assn. of Credit Portfolio Managers [245]
Printing Indus. Credit Executives [246]
Natl. Assn. of Mortgage Processors [113]
Natl. Found. for Credit Counseling [543]

Credit Professionals Intl. [331], 10726 Manchester Rd., Ste. 210, St. Louis, MO 63122, (314)821-9393

Credit Unions
Assn. of Credit Union Internal Auditors [247]
Natl. Assn. of Credit Union Services Organizations [248]
Natl. Assn. of Fed. Credit Unions [249]
World Coun. of Credit Unions [250]

CREW Network [741], 1201 Wakarusa Dr., Ste. C3, Lawrence, KS 66049, (785)832-1808

Crime
Alliance of Guardian Angels [2046]

Black on Black Love Campaign [2047]
Natl. Alliance of Gang Investigators Associations [1286]
Natl. Crime Prevention Coun. [2048]
Assn. of State Correctional Administrators [2049]
Intl. Assn. for Correctional and Forensic Psychology [2050]
Robert F. Kennedy Center for Justice and Human Rights [2280]

Crime Prevention Coalition [★2048]

Criminal Justice
Assn. of State Correctional Administrators [2049]
Intl. Assn. for Correctional and Forensic Psychology [2050]
Intl. Assn. of Correctional Training Personnel [2051]
Intl. Assn. of Law Enforcement Planners [1287]
John Howard Assn. [2052]
Robert F. Kennedy Center for Justice and Human Rights [2280]

Criminal Law
Assn. of State Correctional Administrators [2049]
Intl. Assn. for Correctional and Forensic Psychology [2050]

Crisis Intervention
Transition U.S. [1082]

Critical Care
Soc. of Critical Care Medicine [2356]

Croatian Amer. Bar Assn. [1270], 6 Papette Cir., Ladera Ranch, CA 92694, (949)274-5360

Crop Insurance and Reinsurance Bur. [483], 201 Massachusetts Ave. NE, Ste. C5, Washington, DC 20002, (202)544-0067

Crop Insurance Res. Bur. [★483]

Crop Sci. Soc. of Am. [932], 5585 Guilford Rd., Madison, WI 53711-5801, (608)273-8080

Croquet
Croquet Found. of Am. [3308]
U.S. Croquet Assn. [3309]

Croquet Found. of Am. [3308], 700 Florida Mango Rd., West Palm Beach, FL 33406-4461, (561)478-0760

Crude Oil Quality Assn. [640], 2324 N Dickerson St., Arlington, VA 22207

Cruise Lines Intl. Assn. [883], 910 SE 17th St., Ste. 400, Fort Lauderdale, FL 33316, (754)224-2200

Crutches 4 Kids [1946], 1350 Avenue of the Americas, 4th Fl., New York, NY 10019

Cryonics
Alcor Life Extension Found. [2357]

CTAM - Cable and Telecommunications Assn. for Marketing [127], 201 N Union St., Ste. 440, Alexandria, VA 22314, (703)549-4200

Cuba
Directorio Democratico Cubano [2634]

Cuban
Havana Silk Dog Assn. of Am. [3176]

CUES Financial Suppliers Forum [596], PO Box 14167, Madison, WI 53708-0167, (608)271-2664

Cultural Exchange
Amer. Brazilian Cultural Exchange [1746]
Amer. Telugu Assn. [1747]
Haiti Cultural Exchange [1748]
Amer. MidEast Leadership Network [2677]
Chinese Amer. Cooperation Coun. [1783]
Multinational Exchange for Sustainable Agriculture [1218]
Qigong Alliance Intl. [2297]
Sino-American Bridge for Educ. and Hea. [1784]
United Burundian-American Community Assn. [2680]

Cultural Survival [1778], 215 Prospect St., Cambridge, MA 02139, (617)441-5400

A Cup of Water Intl. [3039], PO Box 9809, Kansas City, MO 64134, (267)242-1798

Curling
U.S. Women's Curling Assn. [3310]

Curriculum
Assn. for Supervision and Curriculum Development [1599]

Custom Content Coun. [720], 30 W 26th St., 3rd Fl., New York, NY 10010, (212)989-4631

Custom Electronic Design Installation Assn. [811], 7150 Winton Dr., Ste. 300, Indianapolis, IN 46268, (317)328-4336

Custom Tailors and Designers Assn. of Am. [45], 42732 Ridgeway Dr., Broadlands, VA 20148, (888)248-2832

Cycling
Intl. Unicycling Fed. [3311]
Ultra Marathon Cycling Assn. [3312]
Unicycling Soc. of Am. [3313]
The Wheelmen [3314]
Camping Women [3301]

Cymbidium Soc. of Am. [3204], 6639 Ibex Woods Ct., Citrus Heights, CA 95621, (510)537-8923

Cytology
Amer. Soc. for Cytotechnology [2358]

Czech
Amer. Friends of the Czech Republic [2778]

Czech Collector's Assn. [3151], 810 - 11th St., Ste. 201, Miami Beach, FL 33139-4834

D

Dairy Products
Amer. Cheese Soc. [251]
Natl. Dairy Shrine [1050]
Natl. Yogurt Assn. [252]

Dale Jarrett Fan Club [3589], PO Box 279, Conover, NC 28613, (828)464-8818

Dalit Freedom Network [2661], 631 Pennsylvania Ave. SE, Ste. 2, Washington, DC 20003, (202)375-5000

Dalit Solidarity [2662], PO Box 112, Hines, IL 60141, (708)612-4248

Damien Ministries [2902], PO Box 10202, Washington, DC 20018-0202, (202)526-3020

Dance
Amer. Dance Guild [1749]
Cong. on Res. in Dance [1750]
Dance Critics Assn. [1751]
Dance Heritage Coalition [1752]

Dance Critics Assn. [1751], PO Box 1882, Old Chelsea Sta., New York, NY 10011

Dance Heritage Coalition [1752], 1111 16th St. NW, Ste. 300, Washington, DC 20036, (202)223-8392

Danish/Swedish Farmdog Club of Am. [3175], PO Box 1184, Ramona, CA 92065

Darts
AMOA Natl. Dart Assn. [3315]

Darwin Animal Doctors [950], 222 E 89th St., No. 8, New York, NY 10128

Daughters of Isabella, Intl. Circle [2773], PO Box 9585, New Haven, CT 06535, (203)865-2570

Daughters of Penelope [2787], 1909 Q St. NW, Ste. 500, Washington, DC 20009, (202)234-9741

Daughters of Penelope Foundation [★2787]

Daughters of Union Veterans of the Civil War, 1861-1865 [3055], c/o Sharon R. Patton, Membership Chair, 1932 Clifton Ave., Lansing, MI 48910-3531, (517)484-7795

Deaf
Acad. of Rehabilitative Audiology [2449]
Intl. Catholic Deaf Assn. U.S. Sect. [2868]

Decision Sciences Inst. [1576], 75 Piedmont Ave., Ste. 340, Atlanta, GA 30303, (404)413-7710

Decorative Plumbing and Hardware Assn. [678], 401 N Michigan Ave., Ste. 2200, Chicago, IL 60611, (312)321-5110

Defense
Inter-American Defense Bd. [2635]

Defense Intel Alumni Assn. [2759], 256 Morris Creek Rd., Cullen, VA 23934, (571)426-0098

Defense Orientation Conf. Assn. [2742], 9271 Old Keene Mill Rd., Ste. 200, Burke, VA 22015-4202, (703)451-1200

Defense Res. Inst. [1344], 55 W Monroe, Ste. 2000, Chicago, IL 60603, (312)795-1101

Degree of Honor Protective Assn. [2793], 400 Robert St. N, Ste. 1600, St. Paul, MN 55101-2029, (651)228-7600

Delphi Found. [3518], 2020 Pennsylvania Ave. NW, No. 355, Washington, DC 20006-1811, (202)558-2801

Delta Lambda Phi Natl. Social Fraternity [3551], 2020 Pennsylvania Ave. NW, No. 355, Washington, DC 20006-1811, (202)527-9453

Delta Theta Phi [3534], PO Box 117, Elyria, OH 44036-0117, (919)866-4667

Democracy
Amer. Libyan Freedom Alliance [2636]
Intl. People's Democratic Uhuru Movement [2637]

Democratic Party
Democrats Abroad [2638]

Democrats Abroad **[2638]**, 430 S Capitol St. SE, Washington, DC 20003, (202)488-5073

Dental Hygiene
Amer. Acad. of Restorative Dentistry **[2370]**
Amer. Assn. of Endodontists I Amer. Bd. of Endodontics **[2372]**

Dental Trade Alliance **[423]**, 2300 Clarendon Blvd., Ste. 1003, Arlington, VA 22201, (703)379-7755

Dentistry
Acad. of Dental Materials **[2359]**
Acad. of Operative Dentistry **[2360]**
Alpha Omega Intl. Dental Fraternity **[3514]**
Amer. Acad. of Dental Gp. Practice **[2361]**
Amer. Acad. of Esthetic Dentistry **[2362]**
Amer. Acad. of Fixed Prosthodontics **[2363]**
Amer. Acad. of Gold Foil Operators **[2364]**
Amer. Acad. of the History of Dentistry **[2365]**
Amer. Acad. of Maxillofacial Prosthetics **[2366]**
Amer. Acad. of Oral and Maxillofacial Radiology **[2367]**
Amer. Acad. of Oral Medicine **[2368]**
Amer. Acad. of Periodontology **[2369]**
Amer. Acad. of Restorative Dentistry **[2370]**
Amer. Assn. of Dental Boards **[2371]**
Amer. Assn. of Endodontists I Amer. Bd. of Endodontics **[2372]**
Amer. Assn. of Women Dentists **[2373]**
Amer. Bd. of Orthodontics **[2374]**
Amer. Endodontic Soc. **[2375]**
Amer. Equilibration Soc. **[2376]**
Amer. Orthodontic Soc. **[2377]**
Amer. Prosthodontic Soc. **[2378]**
Amer. Soc. of Master Dental Technologists **[2379]**
Assn. of State and Territorial Dental Directors **[2380]**
Holistic Dental Assn. **[2381]**
Intl. Coll. of Dentists **[2382]**
Natl. Assn. of Dental Labs. **[2383]**
Natl. Bd. for Certification in Dental Lab. Tech. **[2384]**
Natl. Dental Assn. **[2385]**
Natl. Dental Hygienists' Assn. **[2386]**
Natl. Denturist Assn. **[2387]**
Pierre Fauchard Acad. **[2388]**
Sigma Phi Alpha **[3515]**
Special Care Dentistry Assn. **[2389]**

Dermatology
Amer. Acad. of Dermatology **[2390]**
Amer. Dermatological Assn. **[2391]**
Amer. Osteopathic Coll. of Dermatology **[2392]**
Amer. Soc. for Dermatologic Surgery **[2393]**
Intl. Psoriasis Coun. **[2394]**
Intl. Soc. of Dermatology **[2395]**
Pacific Dermatologic Assn. **[2396]**

Descendants of the Signers of the Declaration of Independence **[3048]**, 103 Elmsford Ct., Brentwood, TN 37027-4753

Desert Tortoise Coun. **[1235]**, PO Box 1568, Ridgecrest, CA 93556

Design
Amer. Assn. of Human Design Practitioners **[253]**
Universal Design Alliance **[254]**
Building Commissioning Assn. **[141]**
Decorative Plumbing and Hardware Assn. **[678]**
Interior Redesign Indus. Specialists **[507]**

Design Automation; Special Interest Gp. for **[1442]**

Design Indus. Found. Fighting AIDS **[1883]**, 200 Lexington Ave., Ste. 910, New York, NY 10016, (212)727-3100

Development Gp. for Alternative Policies **[2673]**, 3179 18th St. NW, Washington, DC 20010, (202)898-1566

Developmental Education
Amer. Assn. of Human Design Practitioners **[253]**

DFK International/USA **[5]**, 1025 Thomas Jefferson St. NW, Ste. 500 E, Washington, DC 20007, (202)452-8100

D.H. Lawrence Soc. of North Am. **[1731]**, Loyola Univ. of Chicago, 6525 N Sheridan, Chicago, IL 60626

Diagnostic Marketing Assn. **[597]**, 10293 N Meridian St., Ste. 175, Indianapolis, IN 46290, (317)816-1640

Digital Living Network Alliance **[279]**, 400 Kruse Way Pl., Bldg. 2, Ste. 250, Lake Oswego, OR 97035, (503)908-1115

Direct Gardening Assn. **[769]**, 5836 Rockburn Woods Way, Elkridge, MD 21075, (410)540-9830

Direct Marketing Assn. **[598]**, 1120 Ave. of the Americas, New York, NY 10036-6700, (212)768-7277

Direct Marketing Fundraisers Assn. **[393]**, PO Box 1038, New York, NY 10028, (646)675-7314

Directorio Democratico Cubano **[2634]**, PO Box 110235, Hialeah, FL 33011, (305)220-2713

Disabilities
Acad. of Rehabilitative Audiology **[2449]**
Amer. Asperger's Assn. **[2562]**
BlazeSports Am. **[3316]**
Families with Autism Spectrum Disorders **[2313]**
Global Communities of Support **[1910]**
Kupenda for the Children **[1970]**

Disability Rights Educ. and Defense Fund **[2057]**, 3075 Adeline St., Ste. 210, Berkeley, CA 94703-2578, (510)644-2555

Disabled
Abilities! **[2053]**
Assistance Dogs Intl. **[2054]**
Assn. of Rehabilitation Programs in Cmpt. Tech. **[2055]**
BlazeSports Am. **[3316]**
Coun. of Citizens With Low Vision Intl. **[2056]**
Disability Rights Educ. and Defense Fund **[2057]**
Found. for Sci. and Disability **[2058]**
Just One Break **[2059]**
Lift Disability Network **[2060]**
Natl. Amputation Found. **[2061]**
Natl. Wheelchair Basketball Assn. **[3317]**
Soc. for Disability Stud. **[2062]**
TASH **[2063]**
U.S. Deaf Ski and Snowboard Assn. **[3318]**
VSA - The Intl. Org. on Arts and Disability **[2064]**
Wheelchair and Ambulatory Sports, USA **[3319]**
Wheels for the World **[2065]**
Acad. of Rehabilitative Audiology **[2449]**
Angel Harps **[2588]**
Catholic Guardian Soc. and Home Bur. **[1931]**
Crutches 4 Kids **[1946]**
Global Communities of Support **[1910]**
Kupenda for the Children **[1970]**

Disabled Veterans
Salute Military Golf Assn. **[3339]**

Disarmament
Clear Path Intl. **[2639]**
NGO Comm. on Disarmament, Peace and Security **[2640]**

Disaster Aid
Aid Still Required **[2066]**
Compassion into Action Network - Direct Outcome Org. **[2067]**
Great Commn. Alliance **[2068]**
Baitulmaal **[2183]**
Baptist Global Response **[2184]**
Haiti Works! **[2120]**
Korean Amer. Sharing Movement **[2193]**
Mobile Medical Disaster Relief **[2138]**
Reconstruction Efforts Aiding Children without Homes **[2032]**
World Assn. of Natural Disaster Awareness and Assistance **[2147]**

Disc Sports
Freestyle Players Assn. **[3320]**

Discipline
Natl. Coalition Against Violent Athletes **[3252]**

Disease
Answer Africa **[2397]**
Global Network for Neglected Tropical Diseases **[2398]**
Norrie Disease Assn. **[2399]**
Amer. Celiac Disease Alliance **[2414]**
C-Change **[2329]**
Global Solutions for Infectious Diseases **[2472]**
Heart Rhythm Soc. **[2332]**
Intl. Psoriasis Coun. **[2394]**
Intl. Soc. for Children with Cancer **[2330]**
Soc. for Heart Valve Disease **[2457]**

Disneyana Fan Club **[3567]**, PO Box 19212, Irvine, CA 92623-9212, (714)731-4705

Disposable Products
Foodservice and Packaging Inst. **[255]**
Mfrs. Representatives of Am. **[256]**

Distribution Contractors Assn. **[3459]**, 101 W Renner Rd., Ste. 460, Richardson, TX 75082-2024, (972)680-0261

Divine Science
Divine Sci. Fed. Intl. **[2903]**

Divine Sci. Fed. Intl. **[2903]**, 110 Merchants Row, Ste. 4, Rutland, VT 05701, (802)779-9019

Diving
USA Diving **[3321]**

Divorce
Children's Rights Coun. **[2069]**
North Amer. Conf. of Separated and Divorced Catholics **[2070]**
Assn. of Divorce Financial Planners **[347]**

Do It Yourself Aids
Home Improvement Res. Inst. **[257]**

Doctors in Christ **[2544]**, 14359 Miramar Pkwy., Ste. 140, Miramar, FL 33027, (954)483-1215

Doctors for United Medical Missions **[2485]**, 313 Tidewater Dr., Havre de Grace, MD 21078, (410)688-0691

Dodge Pilothouse Era Truck Club of Am. **[3247]**, 3778 Hoen Ave., Santa Rosa, CA 95405

Dog
All Amer. Premier Breeds Admin. **[3173]**
Assn. of Pet Dog Trainers **[1051]**
Boykin Spaniel Club and Breeders Assn. of Am. **[3174]**
Danish/Swedish Farmdog Club of Am. **[3175]**
Havana Silk Dog Assn. of Am. **[3176]**
Hovawart Club of North Am. **[3177]**
Intl. Kennel Club of Chicago **[3178]**
Miniature Australian Shepherd Club of Am. **[3179]**
Natl. Assn. of Dog Obedience Instructors **[3180]**
North Amer. Gun Dog Assn. **[3181]**
North Amer. Ring Assn. **[3182]**
Polish Tatra Sheepdog Club of Am. **[3183]**
Portuguese Podengo Club of Am. **[3184]**
Toy Australian Shepherd Assn. of Am. **[3185]**
U.S.A. Coton de Tulear Club **[3186]**
U.S. Complete Shooting Dog Assn. **[3187]**
Working Riesenschnauzer Fed. **[3188]**
Autism Ser. Dogs of Am. **[2310]**
U.S.A. Defenders of Greyhounds **[1901]**

Dog Racing
Amer. Greyhound Track Operators Assn. **[3322]**
Intl. Fed. of Sleddog Sports **[3323]**
Lakes Region Sled Dog Club **[3324]**
U.S.A. Defenders of Greyhounds **[1901]**

Doll Artisan Guild **[3189]**, PO Box 1113, Oneonta, NY 13820-5113, (607)432-4977

The Doll Center **[★3189]**

Dolls
Doll Artisan Guild **[3189]**
Natl. Inst. of Amer. Doll Artists **[3190]**

Domestic Energy Producers Alliance **[300]**, PO Box 18359, Oklahoma City, OK 73154, (405)424-1699

Domestic Services
Vacation Rental Housekeeping Professionals **[258]**

Domestic Violence
Emerge: Counseling and Educ. to Stop Domestic Violence **[2071]**
Intl. Center for Assault Prevention **[2072]**

Dominican Amer. Natl. Roundtable **[2779]**, 1050 17th St. NW, Ste. 600, Washington, DC 20036, (202)238-0097

Dominican Republic
Dominican Amer. Natl. Roundtable **[2779]**

Door
Amer. Assn. of Automatic Door Mfrs. **[259]**
Institutional Locksmiths' Assn. **[260]**

Dorcas Medical Mission **[2486]**, 907 Utica Ave., Brooklyn, NY 11203, (718)342-2928

Draft
Center on Conscience and War **[2641]**

Dream Factory **[1997]**, 120 W Broadway, Ste. 300, Louisville, KY 40202, (502)561-3001

DreamCatcher Wild Horse and Burro Sanctuary **[1895]**, PO Box 9, Ravendale, CA 96123, (530)260-0148

Drilling, Observation and Sampling of the Earth's Continental Crust **[1448]**, PO Box 58857, Salt Lake City, UT 84158-0857, (801)583-2150

Drinking Water for India **[2262]**, PO Box 244, Plainsboro, NJ 08536-0244, (609)843-0176

A star before a book entry number signifies that the name is not listed separately, but is mentioned within the entry.

Driver Education
Driving School Assn. of the Americas **[1600]**
Driver Employment Coun. of Am. **[870]**, 1150 17th St. NW, Ste. 900, Washington, DC 20036, (202)842-3400
Driving School Assn. of the Americas **[1600]**, 3090 E Gause Blvd., Ste. 425, Slidell, LA 70461, (800)270-DSAA

Drug Abuse
Intl. Assn. of Addictions and Offender Counselors **[2044]**

Drug Policy
Natl. Alliance for Model State Drug Laws **[1288]**

Drug Rehabilitation
Intl. Assn. of Addictions and Offender Counselors **[2044]**
Dwa Fanm **[2663]**, PO Box 23505, Brooklyn, NY 11202, (718)222-6320

E

E-Commerce
Merchant Risk Coun. **[261]**
WECAI Network **[262]**
Early Ford V-8 Club of Am. **[3101]**, PO Box 1715, Maple Grove, MN 55311, (763)420-7829
Earth Island Inst. **[1060]**, 2150 Allston Way, Ste. 460, Berkeley, CA 94704-1375, (510)859-9108

Earth Sciences
Drilling, Observation and Sampling of the Earth's Continental Crust **[1448]**
Fed. of Earth Sci. Info. Partners **[1449]**
Rock Detective Geoscience Educ. **[1601]**
Earth Soc. Found. **[1061]**, 238 E 58th St., Ste. 2400, New York, NY 10022, (212)832-3659
Eastern Assn. of Rowing Colleges **[3376]**, Easter Coll. Athletic Conf., 1311 Craigville Beach Rd., Centerville, MA 02632, (508)771-5060
Eastern Coll. Athletic Conf. **[3342]**, PO Box 3, Centerville, MA 02632, (508)771-5060
Eastern Intercollegiate Gymnastic League **[3340]**, Eastern Coll. Athletic Conf., 1311 Craigville Beach Rd., Centerville, MA 02632, (508)771-5060

Eastern Orthodox
Fellowship of St. John the Divine **[2904]**
Standing Conf. of the Canonical Orthodox Bishops in the Americas **[2905]**
Eastern Surfing Assn. **[3414]**, PO Box 625, Virginia Beach, VA 23451, (757)233-1790
EastWest Inst. **[2670]**, 700 Broadway, 2nd Fl., New York, NY 10003-9536, (212)824-4100
Eco Energy Finance **[1457]**, 2307 15th St. NW, Ste. 1, Washington, DC 20009, (202)262-0412
ecoAmerica **[1016]**, 1900 L St. NW, Ste. 607, Washington, DC 20036, (202)457-1900
EcoHealth Alliance **[1236]**, 460 W 34th St., 17th Fl., New York, NY 10001, (212)380-4460
Ecological Farming Assn. **[933]**, 2901 Park Ave., Ste. D-2, Soquel, CA 95073, (831)763-2111
Ecological Res. and Development Gp. **[1017]**, 190 Main St., Dover, DE 19901, (302)236-5383

Ecology
Assn. of Ecosystem Res. Centers **[1052]**
Assn. for Fire Ecology **[1053]**
Intl. Assn. for Landscape Ecology I U.S. Regional Assn. **[1054]**
Planetwork **[1055]**
Soc. for Ecological Restoration Intl. **[1056]**
Climate, Community and Biodiversity Alliance **[1012]**
Coalition on the Env. and Jewish Life **[2951]**
Community Agroecology Network **[1216]**
Ecological Res. and Development Gp. **[1017]**
Ethnobotanical Conservation Org. for South East Asia **[1020]**
Freecycle Network **[1198]**
Friends of the Osa **[1025]**
Global Underwater Explorers **[1159]**
Kids Ecology Corps **[1076]**
Network of Conservation Educators and Practitioners **[1032]**
Pacific Islands Conservation Res. Assn. **[1035]**
Wonderful World of Wildlife **[1260]**

Economic Development
endPoverty.org **[2073]**
Enterprise for a Sustainable World **[263]**
New Am. Alliance **[264]**

Rising Tide Capital **[265]**
Armenian Amer. Chamber of Commerce **[3473]**
Clean Tech. Trade Alliance **[1391]**
Community Development Intl. **[2014]**
Community Empowerment Network **[2211]**
Glocal Ventures **[2119]**
Green Collar Assn. **[296]**
Iraqi Amer. Chamber of Commerce and Indus. **[3483]**
Middle East Investment Initiative **[336]**
Pakistan Chamber of Commerce USA **[3502]**
Roots of Development **[2212]**
U.S. Indian Amer. Chamber of Commerce **[3496]**
Economic Policy Inst. **[2732]**, 1333 H St. NW, Ste. 300, East Tower, Washington, DC 20005-4707, (202)775-8810

Economics
Assn. of Specialized and Professional Accreditors **[266]**
Intl. Soc. for Ecological Economics **[267]**
Natl. Economic Assn. **[1450]**
Soc. of Govt. Economists **[1289]**
Armenian Amer. Chamber of Commerce **[3473]**
Brazil-U.S. Bus. Coun. **[3475]**
Fisher Inst. for Medical Res. **[2653]**
Innovation Norway - U.S. **[3482]**
Iraqi Amer. Chamber of Commerce and Indus. **[3483]**
Pakistan Chamber of Commerce USA **[3502]**
U.S. Indian Amer. Chamber of Commerce **[3496]**
EcoVentures Intl. **[1075]**, 2122 P St. NW, Ste. 302, Washington, DC 20037, (202)667-0802

Ecumenical
Churches Uniting in Christ **[2906]**
Graymoor Ecumenical and Interreligious Inst. **[2907]**
Intl. Assn. of Ministers Wives and Ministers Widows **[2908]**
Lumunos **[2909]**
Natl. Coun. of Churches of Christ in the U.S.A. **[2910]**
Societas Liturgica **[2911]**
Seventh Day Baptist World Fed. **[2847]**
Ecumenical Theological Seminary **[2912]**, 2930 Woodward Ave., Detroit, MI 48201, (313)831-5200
Ecumenical Women's Caucus; Evangelical and **[2921]**
Edison Elec. Inst. **[893]**, 701 Pennsylvania Ave. NW, Washington, DC 20004-2696, (202)508-5000

Editors
Natl. Panhellenic Conf. I Natl. Panhellenic Editors Conf. **[3516]**
Edsel Club **[3102]**, 19296 Tuckaway Ct., Fort Myers, FL 33903-1244, (239)731-8027

Education
Acad. for Educational Development **[1602]**
Alpha Delta Kappa **[3517]**
Amer. Educational Stud. Assn. **[1603]**
Creative Educ. Found. **[1604]**
Delphi Found. **[3518]**
Ecumenical Theological Seminary **[2912]**
Educ. Development Center **[1605]**
Intl. Listening Assn. **[1606]**
Natl. Acad. of Educ. **[1607]**
Natl. Coun. of Churches, Educ. and Leadership Ministries Commn. **[2913]**
Natl. Coun. on Teacher Retirement **[3444]**
Natl. Kappa Kappa Iota **[3519]**
Pi Lambda Theta **[3520]**
Religious Educ. Assn.: An Assn. of Professors, Practitioners, and Researchers in Religious Educ. **[2914]**
Agami **[1581]**
Alpha Epsilon **[3521]**
Amer. Assn. of Human Design Practitioners **[253]**
Americans Care and Share **[2182]**
Assn. for the Advancement of Intl. Educ. **[1644]**
The Assn. for the Gifted **[1627]**
Assn. of Professors and Scholars of Iranian Heritage **[1646]**
Assn. of State Correctional Administrators **[2049]**
Assn. of Tech., Mgt. and Applied Engg. **[1632]**
Battelle for Kids **[1582]**
Building Bridges: Middle East-US **[1642]**
Caring for Cambodia **[1583]**
Caring Hand for Children **[1992]**
Child Aid Africa **[1933]**

Close Up Found. **[2622]**
Coun. for Children with Behavioral Disorders **[1686]**
Environmental Educ. and Conservation Global **[1621]**
Indigo Threads **[2024]**
Intl. Assn. for Correctional and Forensic Psychology **[2050]**
Intl. Org. for Haitian Development **[1591]**
Kate's Voice **[1678]**
Mercy Beyond Borders **[2169]**
Natl. 4-H Coun. **[2278]**
Natl. Assn. of Peoplecultural Engg. Prog. Advocates **[1615]**
NepalAama **[1584]**
North Amer. Assn. for Environmental Educ. **[1619]**
One Hen **[1580]**
One Voice of Peace **[1672]**
Out of Poverty thru Educ. **[1568]**
Phi Chi Medical Fraternity **[3539]**
Reasoning Mind **[1660]**
Restoring Institutions Services and Empowering Liberia **[2033]**
Rock Detective Geoscience Educ. **[1601]**
Under The Baobab Tree **[1593]**

Education, Alternative
Reasoning Mind **[1660]**
Educ. Development Center **[1605]**, 55 Chapel St., Newton, MA 02458, (617)969-7100
Educ. and Enrichment Sect. of the Natl. Coun. on Family Relations **[2086]**, 1201 W River Pkwy., Ste. 200, Minneapolis, MN 55454-1115, (763)781-9331
Educ. for Prosperity **[2017]**, PO Box 302, East Lansing, MI 48826, (517)614-0501

Education Youth
Caring Hand for Children **[1992]**
Child Literacy **[1935]**
Coun. for Children with Behavioral Disorders **[1686]**
Global China Connection **[1643]**
Natl. 4-H Coun. **[2278]**

Educational Advocacy
Intl. Assn. for Truancy and Dropout Prevention **[1608]**

Educational Funding
Assn. for Educ. Finance and Policy **[1609]**
Coun. for Rsrc. Development **[1610]**
Natl. Assn. of Student Financial Aid Administrators **[1611]**
Educational Records Bur. **[1692]**, 220 E 42nd St., New York, NY 10017, (800)989-3721

Educators
Assn. for the Advancement of Intl. Educ. **[1644]**
Efficiency First **[1018]**, 70 Zoe St., Ste. 201, San Francisco, CA 94107, (415)449-0551
Egbe Omo Yoruba: Natl. Assn. of Yoruba Descendants in North America **[2810]**, PO Box 204, White Marsh, MD 21162-0204, (314)974-3604
El Toro Intl. Yacht Racing Assn. **[3272]**, 1014 Hopper Ave., No. 419, Santa Rosa, CA 95403-1613, (707)526-6621
Elder Support Network **[★2125]**

Elections
Natl. Assn. of State Election Directors **[268]**
Elec. Utility Indus. Sustainable Supply Chain Alliance **[894]**, PO Box 419164, Kansas City, MO 64141, (816)561-5323

Electrical
Elecl. Equip. Representatives Assn. **[269]**
Energy Telecommunications and Elecl. Assn. **[270]**
Intl. Assn. of Elecl. Inspectors **[271]**
Natl. Insulator Assn. **[3191]**
Natl. Rural Elec. Cooperative Assn. **[272]**
North Amer. Elec. Reliability Corp. **[273]**
Professional Elecl. Apparatus Recyclers League **[274]**
Women's Intl. Network of Utility Professionals **[275]**
Electronic Indus. Citizenship Coalition **[280]**
Large Public Power Coun. **[1292]**
Professional Lighting and Sign Mgt. Companies of Am. **[546]**
Elecl. Equip. Representatives Assn. **[269]**, 638 W 39th St., Kansas City, MO 64111, (816)561-5323
Elecl. Rebuilder's Assn. **[85]**, PO Box 906, Union, MO 63084, (636)584-7400

Electricity
Elec. Utility Indus. Sustainable Supply Chain Alliance [894]
Electrification Coalition [871]
GridWise Architecture Coun. [1520]
Natl. Alliance for Advanced Tech. Batteries [116]
Solar for Peace [1537]
Electrification Coalition [871], 1111 19th St. NW, Ste. 406, Washington, DC 20036, (202)461-2360

Electroencephalography
Amer. Clinical Neurophysiology Soc. [2400]

Electrolysis
Amer. Electrology Assn. [2401]
Soc. for Clinical and Medical Hair Removal [2402]
Electronic Indus. Citizenship Coalition [280], c/o Carrie Hoffman, Dir. of Communications, 1155 15th St. NW, Ste. 500, Washington, DC 20005, (202)962-0167
Electronic Retailing Assn. [599], 2000 N 14th St., Ste. 300, Arlington, VA 22201, (703)841-1751
Electronic Security Assn. [802], 2300 Valley View Ln., Ste. 230, Irving, TX 75062, (214)260-5970
Electronic Transactions Assn. [110], 1101 16th St. NW, Washington, DC 20036, (202)828-2635

Electronics
ALMA - The Intl. Loudspeaker Assn. [276]
Asian Am. MultiTechnology Assn. [277]
Assn. for High Tech. Distribution [278]
Digital Living Network Alliance [279]
Electronic Indus. Citizenship Coalition [280]
Electronics Representatives Assn. [281]
Intl. Soc. of Certified Electronics Technicians [282]
IPC - Assn. Connecting Electronics Indus. [283]
JEDEC [284]
Natl. Electronics Ser. Dealers Assn. [285]
Natl. Systems Contractors Assn. [286]
North Am. Chinese Clean-tech and Semiconductor Assn. [287]
North Amer. Retail Dealers Assn. [288]
Professional Audio Mfrs. Alliance [289]
Variable Electronic Components Inst. [290]
Electronics Representatives Assn. [281], 111 N Canal St., Ste. 885, Chicago, IL 60606, (312)559-3050
Elevator U [145], 751 N Olcott Ave., Harwood Heights, IL 60706

Elevators
Elevator U [145]
Elgin Motorcar Owners Registry [3103], 2226 E Apache Ln., Vincennes, IN 47591, (812)888-4172
Eliminate Poverty Now [1904], PO Box 67, Mendham, NJ 07945
Elliot Inst. [1869], PO Box 7348, Springfield, IL 62791-7348, (217)525-8202
Elton John AIDS Found. [1884], 584 Broadway, Ste. 906, New York, NY 10012
Emerge: Counseling and Educ. to Stop Domestic Violence [2071], 2464 Massachusetts Ave., Ste. 101, Cambridge, MA 02140, (617)547-9879

Emergency Aid
Amer. Ambulance Assn. [2403]
Assn. of Air Medical Services [2404]
Natl. Emergency Mgt. Assn. [1290]
Baptist Global Response [2184]
Compassion into Action Network - Direct Outcome Org. [2067]
Intl. Fire Buff Associates [3192]
Kenya Medical Outreach [2135]
Medics Without Borders [2407]
Relief Liberia Intl. [2198]
World Assn. of Natural Disaster Awareness and Assistance [2147]
Emergency Comm. for Amer. Trade [517], 900 17th St. NW, Ste. 1150, Washington, DC 20006, (202)659-5147
Emergency Mgt. Professional Org. for Women's Enrichment [560], PO Box 10803, McLean, VA 22102

Emergency Medicine
Amer. Coll. of Emergency Physicians [2405]
Emergency Nurses Assn. [2406]
Intl. Assn. of EMTs and Paramedics [3445]
Medics Without Borders [2407]
Natl. Assn. of State EMS Officials [2408]
Emergency Response Massage Intl. [2537]

Global Emergency Care Collaborative [2490]
Intl. Fire Buff Associates [3192]
Emergency Nurses Assn. [2406], 915 Lee St., Des Plaines, IL 60016-6569, (847)460-4095
Emergency Relief Response Fund [2234], PO Box 2300, Redlands, CA 92373, (909)793-2009
Emergency Response Massage Intl. [2537], 227 S Peak St., Columbus, NC 28722, (704)763-6099

Emergency Services
Intl. Fire Buff Associates [3192]
Emerging Markets Private Equity Assn. [332], 1077 30th St. NW, Ste. 100, Washington, DC 20007, (202)333-8171
Emofra Africa [2487], 1815-B Chain Bridge Rd., Ste. 34, McLean, VA 22102
Employee Assistance Professionals Assn. [2238], 4350 N Fairfax Dr., Ste. 410, Arlington, VA 22203, (703)387-1000
Employee Assistance Soc. of North Am. [2043], 2001 Jefferson Davis Hwy., Ste. 1004, Arlington, VA 22202-3617, (703)416-0060

Employee Benefits
Employers Coun. on Flexible Compensation [291]
Intl. Found. of Employee Benefit Plans [292]
Intl. Soc. of Certified Employee Benefit Specialists [293]
Natl. Assn. of Benefits and Work Incentive Specialists [294]
Professionals in Workers' Compensation [920]

Employee Ownership
Natl. Center for Employee Ownership [295]
Employee Services Mgt. Assn. [★2175]
Employee Services Mgt. Found. [2175], PO Box 10517, Rockville, MD 20849, (630)559-0020
Employers Coun. on Flexible Compensation [291], 927 15th St. NW, Ste. 1000, Washington, DC 20005, (202)659-4300

Employment
Amer. Contract Compliance Assn. [2074]
Green Collar Assn. [296]
Indus. Found. of Am. [297]
Intl. Assn. of Workforce Professionals [1291]
Natl. Assn. of Professional Employer Organizations [298]
Natl. Bus. and Disability Coun. [2075]
Natl. Career Development Assn. [2076]
Natl. Employment Counseling Assn. [2077]
POWER: People Organized to Win Employment Rights [2078]
SER - Jobs for Progress Natl. [2079]
W. E. Upjohn Inst. for Employment Res. [2080]
Wildcat Ser. Corp. [2081]
WorldatWork [299]
Professionals in Workers' Compensation [920]
Empower Orphans [1947], 1415 Hidden Pond Dr., Yardley, PA 19067, (610)909-1778
Empress Chinchilla Breeders Cooperative [944], 43188 Cottonwood Creek Rd., Crawford, CO 81415, (970)921-7231
Emunah of Am. [2123], 7 Penn Plz., New York, NY 10001, (212)564-9045
Endangered Wolf Center [1237], PO Box 760, Eureka, MO 63025, (636)938-5900
Endocrine Soc. [2409], 8401 Connecticut Ave., Ste. 900, Chevy Chase, MD 20815-5817, (301)941-0200

Endocrinology
Endocrine Soc. [2409]
Endodontic Soc; Amer. [2375]
Endometriosis Assn. [2567], 8585 N 76th Pl., Milwaukee, WI 53223, (414)355-2200
endPoverty.org [2073], 7910 Woodmont Ave., Ste. 907, Bethesda, MD 20814, (240)396-1146

Energy
Alliance for Green Heat [1451]
Alliance for Renewable Energy [1452]
Citizens for Affordable Energy [1453]
Citizens' Alliance for Responsible Energy [1454]
Citizens for Energy Freedom [1455]
Citizens Energy Plan [1456]
Domestic Energy Producers Alliance [300]
Eco Energy Finance [1457]
Energy Conservation Org. [1612]
Energy Efficiency Bus. Coalition [301]
Energy Extraction Technologies [1458]

Energy Farm [1459]
Energy Info. Standards Alliance [302]
Focus the Nation [2642]
GreenMotion [1057]
Large Public Power Coun. [1292]
Leadership for Energy Automated Processing [303]
New Energy Indus. Assn. for Asia and the Pacific [1460]
Northwest Energy Efficiency Alliance [1058]
Quantal Energy [1613]
Res. Partnership to Secure Energy for Am. [1461]
Retail Energy Supply Assn. [304]
Rural Renewable Energy Alliance [1462]
Securing America's Future Energy [1463]
Set Am. Free [2643]
Strategic Energy, Environmental and Trans. Alternatives [1614]
TopTen USA [305]
US-China Green Energy Coun. [1464]
Young Professionals in Energy [1465]
Advanced Biofuels Assn. [391]
Amer. Biogas Coun. [1390]
Amer. Coun. on Global Nuclear Competitiveness [1509]
America's Natural Gas Alliance [639]
ClimateTalk Alliance [1392]
Efficiency First [1018]
Elec. Utility Indus. Sustainable Supply Chain Alliance [894]
Electrification Coalition [871]
FutureGen Alliance [1393]
Global Biofuels Alliance [392]
Global Possibilities [1214]
Green for All [2612]
GridWise Architecture Coun. [1520]
Innovation: Africa [1394]
Intl. Green Energy Coun. [1395]
Natl. Alliance for Advanced Tech. Batteries [116]
Solar for Peace [1537]
Sweet Sorghum Ethanol Assn. [1398]
U.S. Offshore Wind Collaborative [1556]
U.S. Water and Power [1399]
The Wind Alliance [1557]
Wind Energy Mfrs. Assn. [913]
Energy Conservation Org. [1612], 965 Lanini Dr., Hollister, CA 95023-6451, (408)804-2906
Energy Efficiency Bus. Coalition [301], 5500 E Yale St., Ste. 360, Denver, CO 80222, (720)445-3728
Energy Extraction Technologies [1458], 7891 Wiggins Rd., Howell, MI 48843, (517)548-3115
Energy Farm [1459], PO Box 1834, Jackson, MS 39215
Energy Info. Standards Alliance [302], 65 Washington St., Ste. 170, Santa Clara, CA 95050, (650)938-6945
Energy Telecommunications and Elecl. Assn. [270], 5005 Royal Ln., Ste. 116, Irving, TX 75063, (888)503-8700
Energy Traffic Assn. [641], 935 Eldridge Rd., No. 604, Sugar Land, TX 77478-2809, (832)474-3564
Engine Mfrs. Assn. [306], 333 W Wacker Dr., Ste. 810, Chicago, IL 60606, (312)929-1970

Engineering
Alpha Epsilon [3521]
Amer. Soc. for Engg. Mgt. [1466]
Amer. Soc. of Plumbing Engineers [1467]
Assn. for Facilities Engg. [1468]
Eta Kappa Nu [3522]
Natl. Assn. of Peoplecultural Engg. Prog. Advocates [1615]
Natl. Soc. of Black Engineers [1469]
Soc. of Engg. Sci. [1470]
Soc. of Turkish Amer. Architects, Engineers and Scientists [1471]
Assn. of Conservation Engineers [1006]
Building Commissioning Assn. [141]
Drilling, Observation and Sampling of the Earth's Continental Crust [1448]
Quantal Energy [1613]
Scientists and Engineers for Am. [1279]
Short Span Steel Bridge Alliance [1434]
Engg. World Hea. [2488], The Prizery, Ste. 230, 302 E Pettigrew St., Durham, NC 27701, (919)682-7788

A star before a book entry number signifies that the name is not listed separately, but is mentioned within the entry.

Equip. Ser. Assn. **[812]**, c/o Heather Phillips, Exec. Dir., PO Box 1420, Cherry Hill, NJ 08034, (856)489-0753

Equip. and Tool Inst. **[86]**, 134 W Univ. Dr., Ste. 205, Rochester, MI 48307, (248)656-5080

Equitable Reserve Assn. **[2794]**, 116 S Commercial St., PO Box 448, Neenah, WI 54957-0448, (800)722-1574

ERIC CH on Disabilities and Gifted Education **[★1687]**

Estate Management
Natl. Assn. of Financial and Estate Planning **[338]**

Eta Kappa Nu **[3522]**, 445 Hoes Ln., Piscataway, NJ 08854, (800)406-2590

Ethiopia
Amer. Outreach to Ethiopia **[2114]**
Clinic at a Time **[2483]**
Ethiopian Orphan Relief **[1948]**
Hands for Autistic Children of Ethiopia **[1911]**
Intl. Partnership for Reproductive Hea. **[2593]**
Network Ethiopia **[2511]**

Ethiopian
Ethiopian Orphan Relief **[1948]**

Ethiopian Orphan Relief **[1948]**, 3020 SW Christy Ave., Beaverton, OR 97005

Ethnic Studies
Amer. Soc. for Ethnohistory **[1754]**
Natl. Assn. for Ethnic Stud. **[1755]**

Ethnobotanical Conservation Org. for South East Asia **[1020]**, PO Box 77, Mendocino, CA 95460

European
European Union Delegation to the U.S. **[2644]**

European-American Bus. Coun. **[3479]**, 919 18th St. NW, No. 220, Washington, DC 20006, (202)828-9104

European Union Delegation to the U.S. **[2644]**, 2175 K St. SW, Washington, DC 20037, (202)862-9500

Euthanasia
Compassion and Choices **[2082]**

Evangelical
Evangelical and Ecumenical Women's Caucus **[2921]**
Evangelical Philosophical Soc. **[2922]**
World Relief **[2923]**
BCM Intl. **[2849]**
A Cup of Water Intl. **[3039]**
Fellowship Intl. Mission **[2998]**

Evangelical and Ecumenical Women's Caucus **[2921]**, PO Box 78171, Indianapolis, IN 46278-0171

Evangelical Free Church of Am. **[2996]**, 901 E 78th St., Minneapolis, MN 55420-1334, (952)854-1300

Evangelical Missiological Soc. **[2997]**, PO Box 794, Wheaton, IL 60187, (630)752-5949

Evangelical Philosophical Soc. **[2922]**, PO Box 1298, La Mirada, CA 90637, (562)906-4570

Evangelical Press Assn. **[2928]**, PO Box 28129, Crystal, MN 55428, (763)535-4793

Evangelism
Action Intl. Ministries **[2924]**
Artists in Christian Testimony **[2925]**
Christian Boaters Assn. **[2926]**
COME Intl. Baptist Ministries **[2927]**
Evangelical Press Assn. **[2928]**
The Gideons Intl. **[2929]**
Intl. Messianic Jewish Alliance **[2930]**
Intl. Students, Inc. **[2931]**
Maranatha Volunteers Intl. **[2932]**
Morris Cerullo World Evangelism **[2933]**
Pro Athletes Outreach **[2934]**
WEC Intl. **[2935]**
BCM Intl. **[2849]**
Fellowship Intl. Mission **[2998]**
Ministry Architecture **[1409]**

Evangelism Assn; Lutheran Braille **[2603]**

Evangelization
BCM Intl. **[2849]**
Fellowship Intl. Mission **[2998]**

Evolution
Soc. for the Stud. of Evolution **[1473]**

Examination Bd. of Professional Home Inspectors **[477]**, 53 Regional Dr., Ste. 1, Concord, NH 03301-8500, (847)298-7750

Exhibitors
Intl. Sport Show Producers Assn. **[317]**

Bridal Show Producers Intl. **[123]**

Experience Intl. **[1021]**, PO Box 680, Everson, WA 98247, (360)966-3876

Explosives
Intl. Assn. of Bomb Technicians and Investigators **[1474]**

Exposition Ser. Contractors Assn. **[611]**, 5068 W Plano Pkwy., Ste. 300, Plano, TX 75093, (972)447-8212

F

F-4 Phantom II Soc. **[3084]**, 3053 Rancho Vista Blvd., Ste. H-102, Palmdale, CA 93551

Face Autism **[2312]**, 5333 Rio Vista St., Sarasota, FL 34232

Facing History and Ourselves Natl. Found. **[1770]**, 16 Hurd Rd., Brookline, MA 02445, (617)232-1595

Fair Elections Legal Network **[1271]**, 1825 K St. NW, Ste. 450, Washington, DC 20006, (202)331-0114

Fair Trade USA **[865]**, 1500 Broadway, Ste. 400, Oakland, CA 94612, (510)663-5260

Faith Alive **[2918]**, 431 Richmond Pl. NE, Albuquerque, NM 87106, (505)255-3233

Families
Amer. Coll. of Counselors **[2083]**
Amer. Mothers, Inc. **[2084]**
Christian Family Movement **[2085]**
Educ. and Enrichment Sect. of the Natl. Coun. on Family Relations **[2086]**
Natl. Coun. on Family Relations **[2087]**
Coun. on Accreditation **[2233]**
Family Hea. Alliance **[2592]**
North Amer. Family Campers Assn. **[3303]**

Families with Autism Spectrum Disorders **[2313]**, 5989 Meijer Dr., Ste. 9, Milford, OH 45150, (513)444-4979

Family Hea. Alliance **[2592]**, 6520 Platt Ave., Ste. 433, West Hills, CA 91307, (818)610-7278

Family Law
Amer. Acad. of Matrimonial Lawyers **[1294]**
Assn. of Family and Conciliation Courts **[1295]**

Family Name Societies
Boone Soc. **[3058]**
Clan Currie Soc. **[3059]**
Clan Fergusson Soc. of North Am. **[3060]**
Clan Moncreiffe Soc. **[3061]**
Clan Montgomery Soc. Intl. **[3062]**

Family Planning
Soc. of Family Planning **[2413]**
Family Hea. Alliance **[2592]**
Soft Power Hea. **[2518]**
World Hea. Partners **[2525]**

Fantasy Sports Trade Assn. **[832]**, c/o Charlie Wiegert, Treas., 11756 Borman Dr., St. Louis, MO 63146, (763)269-3609

Farm Equip. Mfrs. Assn. **[40]**, 1000 Executive Pkwy., Ste. 100, St. Louis, MO 63141-6369, (314)878-2304

Farm Financial Standards Coun. **[936]**, c/o Carroll Merry, Exec. Sec., N78W14573 Appleton Ave., No. 287, Menomonee Falls, WI 53051, (262)253-6902

Farm Management
Farm Financial Standards Coun. **[936]**
Multinational Exchange for Sustainable Agriculture **[1218]**

Farmers Market Coalition **[929]**, PO Box 331, Cockeysville, MD 21030

Farming
Intl. Flying Farmers **[1083]**
Natl. Farm-City Coun. **[1084]**
Natl. Farm and Ranch Bus. Mgt. Educ. Assn. **[1085]**
Natl. Farmers Union **[1086]**
Organic Crop Improvement Assn. **[1087]**
Community Agroecology Network **[1216]**
Farm Financial Standards Coun. **[936]**
Farmers Market Coalition **[929]**
Food Trade Sustainability Leadership Assn. **[362]**
Global Partnership for Afghanistan **[925]**
Multinational Exchange for Sustainable Agriculture **[1218]**
Natl. Women in Agriculture Assn. **[937]**
Planting Empowerment **[1094]**
Vote Hemp **[2746]**

Farriers
Guild of Professional Farriers **[318]**

Fashion for Autism **[2314]**, 274 Clinton Ave., Brooklyn, NY 11205, (917)881-6259

Father Josef's Method of Reflexology **[2293]**, 1441 High Ridge Rd., Stamford, CT 06903, (203)968-6824

Federal Government
Natl. Active and Retired Fed. Employees Assn. **[1296]**

Federally Employed Women **[2645]**, 700 N Fairfax St., No. 510, Alexandria, VA 22314, (888)898-0994

Fed. of Associations of Regulatory Boards **[2426]**, 1466 Techny Rd., Northbrook, IL 60062, (847)559-3272

Fed. of Defense and Corporate Counsel **[1309]**, 11812 N 56th St., Tampa, FL 33617, (813)983-0022

Fed. of Earth Sci. Info. Partners **[1449]**, 6300 Creedmoor Rd., Ste. 170-315, Raleigh, NC 27612, (919)870-7140

Fed. of Fire Chaplains **[2887]**, PO Box 437, Meridian, TX 76665, (254)435-2256

Fed. of Historical Bottle Collectors **[3141]**, c/o June Lowry, Bus. Mgr., 401 Johnston Ct., Raymore, MO 64083, (816)318-0160

Fed. of Intl. Lacrosse **[3357]**, 911 Overbrook Rd., Wilmington, DE 19807, (302)652-4530

Fed. of Modern Painters and Sculptors **[1716]**, 113 Greene St., New York, NY 10012, (212)966-4864

Fed. of Philippine Amer. Chambers of Commerce **[3480]**, Philippine Consulate Bldg., Stes. 700-701, 447 Sutter St., San Francisco, CA 94108-4601, (415)398-3043

Feeding Am. **[2115]**, 35 E Whacker Dr., No. 2000, Chicago, IL 60601, (312)263-2303

Fellowship of Christian Peace Officers U.S.A. **[2893]**, PO Box 3686, Chattanooga, TN 37404-0686, (423)622-1234

Fellowship of Concerned Churchmen **[2838]**, 192 Wellesley Dr., Spartanburg, SC 29307, (864)582-2657

Fellowship Intl. Mission **[2998]**, 555 S 24th St., Allentown, PA 18104-6666, (610)435-9099

Fellowship of Reconciliation Task Force on Latin Am. and Caribbean **[2695]**, PO Box 271, Nyack, NY 10960, (845)358-4601

Fellowship of Reconciliation - USA **[2714]**, PO Box 271, Nyack, NY 10960, (845)358-4601

Fellowship of Saint James **[2894]**, PO Box 410788, Chicago, IL 60641, (773)481-1090

Fellowship of St. John the Divine **[2904]**, Antiochian Orthodox Christian Archdiocese, PO Box 5238, Englewood, NJ 07631-5238, (201)871-1355

Feminism
Federally Employed Women **[2645]**
Global Fund for Women **[2646]**
Intl. Center for Res. on Women **[2647]**
Ms. Found. for Women **[2648]**
Natl. Assn. of Commissions for Women **[2649]**
Women's Env. and Development Org. **[2650]**

Fencing
U.S. Fencing Assn. **[3325]**

Fermenters Intl. Trade Assn. **[42]**, c/o Dee Roberson, Sec.-Treas., PO Box 1373, Valrico, FL 33595, (813)685-4261

Ferrari Club of Am. **[3104]**, PO Box 720597, Atlanta, GA 30358, (800)328-0444

Ferrari Owners Club **[3105]**, 19051 Goldenwest St., Ste. 106-328, Huntington Beach, CA 92648, (714)213-4775

FIABCI-U.S.A. **[742]**, 1961 Wilson Blvd., Ste. 306, Arlington, VA 22201, (703)524-4279

Fiber Soc. **[1475]**, PO Box 8301, North Carolina State Univ., Coll. of Textiles, 2401 Res. Dr., Raleigh, NC 27695-8301, (919)513-0143

Fibers
Fiber Soc. **[1475]**
Vote Hemp **[2746]**

Fields of Growth Intl. **[2129]**, PO Box 751, Notre Dame, IN 46556

Fifty Caliber Shooters Assn. **[3241]**, PO Box 111, Monroe, UT 84754-0111, (435)527-9245

Filipino Amer. Coalition for Environmental Solidarity **[1079]**, PO Box 566, Berkeley, CA 94701-0566, (415)496-6561

A star before a book entry number signifies that the name is not listed separately, but is mentioned within the entry.

Found. for Sci. and Disability **[2058]**, 503 NW 89 St., Gainesville, FL 32607-1400, (352)374-5774

Fragrances
Aromatherapy Registration Coun. **[2292]**

France
French-American Chamber of Commerce **[3492]**

Franchising
Natl. Franchisee Assn. **[390]**
Fraternal Field Managers' Assn. **[484]**, Catholic United Financial, 3499 Lexington Ave. N, St. Paul, MN 55126, (651)765-4150

Fraternities, Service
Alpha Epsilon **[3521]**
Phi Chi Medical Fraternity **[3539]**

Fraternities, Social
Alpha Epsilon **[3521]**
Phi Chi Medical Fraternity **[3539]**

Fraternities and Sororities
Assn. of Fraternity Advisors **[3523]**
Fraternity Executives Assn. **[3524]**
Natl. Panhellenic Conf. **[3525]**
Professional Fraternity Assn. **[3526]**
Fraternity Executives Assn. **[3524]**, c/o Sydney N. Dunn, Admin., 1750 Royalton Dr., Carmel, IN 46032, (317)496-2411

Free Enterprise
Americanism Educational League **[2652]**
Fisher Inst. for Medical Res. **[2653]**
Private Enterprise Res. Center **[2654]**
Professional Services Coun. **[2655]**

Free Expression
Natl. Freedom of Info. Coalition **[2731]**
Free Muslims Coalition **[2706]**, 1050 17th St. NW, Ste. 1000, Washington, DC 20036, (202)776-7190
Freecycle Network **[1198]**, PO Box 294, Tucson, AZ 85702

Freedom
Advancing Human Rights **[2658]**
Amer. Civil Rights Union **[2623]**
Amer. Libyan Freedom Alliance **[2636]**
Dalit Freedom Network **[2661]**
Dalit Solidarity **[2662]**
Dwa Fanm **[2663]**
Ensaaf **[2748]**
Iran Democratic Union **[2667]**
Freedom House **[2631]**, 1301 Connecticut Ave. NW, 6th Fl., Washington, DC 20036, (202)296-5101
Freestyle Players Assn. **[3320]**, 864 Grand Ave., Box 475, San Diego, CA 92109, (800)321-8833

French
Comm. of French Speaking Societies **[2781]**
French-American Aid for Children **[2782]**
French-American Aid for Children **[2782]**, 150 E 58th St., 23rd Fl., New York, NY 10155, (212)486-9593
French-American Chamber of Commerce **[3492]**, 1350 Broadway, Ste. 2101, New York, NY 10018, (212)867-0123
Friends of ARCC **[★2855]**
Friends of the Children of Angola **[1952]**, 6210 Homespun Ln., Falls Church, VA 22044, (703)237-7468
Friends of the Everglades **[1024]**, 11767 S Dixie Hwy., No. 232, Miami, FL 33156, (305)669-0858
Friends for Hea. in Haiti **[2434]**, PO Box 122, Pewaukee, WI 53072, (262)227-9581
Friends of Jamaica USA **[1953]**, 6417 Commonwealth Dr., Loves Park, IL 61111
Friends of Kenyan Orphans **[1954]**, 920 Berkshire Rd., Grosse Pointe Park, MI 48230, (313)815-9900
Friends of Nigeria **[2811]**, c/o Peter J. Hansen, Treas., 1 Oaknoll Ct., Apt. 439, Iowa City, IA 52246, (319)351-3375
Friends of the Osa **[1025]**, 1822 R St. NW, 4th Fl., Washington, DC 20009, (202)234-2356
Friends of Taiwan Intl. **[2679]**, 12 S 1st St., Ste. 205, San Jose, CA 95113
Friendship Force Intl. **[2682]**, 127 Peachtree St., Ste. 501, Atlanta, GA 30303, (404)522-9490

Fruits and Vegetables
California Date Administrative Comm. **[1096]**
Cranberry Inst. **[1097]**
Natl. Cherry Growers and Indus. Found. **[1098]**
Natl. Potato Coun. **[1099]**
Natl. Watermelon Assn. **[1100]**
Potato Assn. of Am. **[1101]**

United Soybean Bd. **[1102]**
U.S. Apple Assn. **[1103]**

Fuel
Advanced Biofuels Assn. **[391]**
Amer. Gas Assn. **[1104]**
Global Biofuels Alliance **[392]**
Interstate Natural Gas Assn. of Am. **[1105]**
Alliance for Green Heat **[1451]**
Amer. Biogas Coun. **[1390]**
America's Natural Gas Alliance **[639]**
Citizens' Alliance for Responsible Energy **[1454]**
Citizens for Energy Freedom **[1455]**
Domestic Energy Producers Alliance **[300]**
Res. Partnership to Secure Energy for Am. **[1461]**
Set Am. Free **[2643]**
Sweet Sorghum Ethanol Assn. **[1398]**
Transition U.S. **[1082]**
Fuel for Truth **[2745]**, 165 E 56th St., 2nd Fl., New York, NY 10022, (212)594-4435
Fulbright Assn. **[1639]**, 1320 19th St. NW, Ste. 350, Washington, DC 20036-1647, (202)775-0725
Funders' Network for Smart Growth and Livable Communities **[2018]**, 1500 San Remo Ave., Ste. 249, Coral Gables, FL 33146, (305)667-6350

Fundraising
Assn. of Fundraising Professionals **[2088]**
Direct Marketing Fundraisers Assn. **[393]**
Giving Inst. **[394]**
Intimate Apparel Square Club **[2089]**
Natl. Assn. of State Charity Officials **[1303]**
Pioneers **[2090]**
United Way of Am. **[2091]**
Hero Initiative **[1745]**
Funeral Ser. Consumer Assistance Prog. **[2633]**, c/o Celine Clark Haga, Exec. Dir., 13625 Bishop Dr., Brookfield, WI 53005-6607, (877)402-5900

Furniture
Futon Assn. Intl. **[395]**
High Point Market Authority **[396]**
Sustainable Furnishings Coun. **[397]**
Futon Assn. Intl. **[395]**, 10705-7 Rocket Blvd., Orlando, FL 32824, (407)447-1706
FutureGen Alliance **[1393]**, 73 E Central Park Plz., Jacksonville, IL 62650, (217)243-8215

G

GAMA Intl. **[485]**, 2901 Telestar Ct., Ste. 140, Falls Church, VA 22042-1205, (800)345-2687

Games
Natl. 42 Players Assn. **[3198]**
Valley Intl. Foosball Assn. **[3199]**
Natl. Amateur Dodgeball Assn. **[3253]**
Pro vs. GI Joe **[3200]**
U.S. Bridge Fed. **[3143]**

Gaming
Intl. Simulation and Gaming Assn. **[1625]**
Pro vs. GI Joe **[3200]**
Natl. 42 Players Assn. **[3198]**
U.S. Bridge Fed. **[3143]**
Gamma Alpha Omega Sorority **[3548]**, PO Box 427, Tempe, AZ 85280
Gamma Iota Sigma **[3532]**, PO Box 227, Norristown, PA 19404, (484)991-4471
Gamma Phi Beta **[3561]**, 12737 E Euclid Dr., Centennial, CO 80111-6437, (303)799-1874
Gamma Sigma Sigma **[3549]**, PO Box 248, Rindge, NH 03461-0248, (800)585-7508

Gardening
Amer. Hibiscus Soc. **[3201]**
Bonsai Clubs Intl. **[3202]**
Bromeliad Soc. Intl. **[3203]**
Cymbidium Soc. of Am. **[3204]**
Gesneriad Soc. **[3205]**
Intl. Lilac Soc. **[3206]**
Soc. for Pacific Coast Native Iris **[3207]**
Tall Bearded Iris Soc. **[3208]**
Coalition of Organic Landscapers **[531]**
Gas Processors Assn. **[642]**, 6526 E 60th St., Tulsa, OK 74145-9202, (918)493-3872
Gas Processors Suppliers Assn. **[643]**, 6526 E 60th St., Tulsa, OK 74145, (918)493-3872

Gases
Intl. Ozone Assn. **[1479]**
Domestic Energy Producers Alliance **[300]**

Gasoline and Automotive Ser. Dealers Assn. **[96]**, 372 Doughty Blvd., Ste. 2C, Inwood, NY 11096, (516)371-6201

Gastroenterology
Amer. Celiac Disease Alliance **[2414]**
Amer. Coll. of Gastroenterology **[2415]**
Amer. Neurogastroenterology and Motility Soc. **[2416]**
Soc. of Amer. Gastrointestinal and Endoscopic Surgeons **[2417]**
Soc. of Gastroenterology Nurses and Associates **[2418]**

Gay/Lesbian
Amer. Lib. Assn. I Gay, Lesbian, Bisexual and Transgendered Roundtable **[2092]**
Assn. for Lesbian, Gay, Bisexual and Transgender Issues in Counseling **[2093]**
Couples Natl. Network **[2094]**
Homosexual Info. Center **[2095]**
Integrity USA **[2936]**
LIFE Ministries **[2937]**
Lutherans Concerned/North Am. **[2938]**
Metropolitan Community Churches **[2939]**
Natl. Gay and Lesbian Chamber of Commerce **[3493]**
Parents, Families, and Friends of Lesbians and Gays **[2096]**
United Church of Christ Coalition for Lesbian, Gay, Bisexual and Transgender Concerns **[2940]**
Intl. Assn. of Gay and Lesbian Martial Artists **[3360]**
Gemological Inst. of Am. Alumni Assn. **[2798]**, The Robert Mouawad Campus, 5345 Armada Dr., Carlsbad, CA 92008, (760)603-4135
Gene Pitney Intl. Fan Club **[3578]**, 6201 - 39th Ave., Kenosha, WI 53142

Genealogy
Amer. Soc. of Genealogists **[3063]**
Intl. Assn. of Jewish Genealogical Societies **[3064]**
Intl. Soc. for British Genealogy and Family History **[3065]**
Lancaster Mennonite Historical Soc. **[3066]**
New York Genealogical and Biographical Soc. **[3067]**
Ohio Genealogical Soc. **[3068]**
Palatines to Am.: Researching German-Speaking Ancestry **[3069]**
Saint Nicholas Soc. of the City of New York **[3070]**
Gen. Soc. of Mayflower Descendants **[3077]**
Gen. Soc. of Mayflower Descendants **[3077]**, PO Box 3297, Plymouth, MA 02361-3297, (508)746-3188
Gen. Soc. of Mechanics and Tradesmen of the City of New York **[1691]**, 20 W 44th St., New York, NY 10036, (212)840-1840
Generation Rescue **[2315]**, 13636 Ventura Blvd., Ste. 259, Sherman Oaks, CA 91423, (877)98-AUTISM
Genetic Technologists; Assn. of **[1420]**

Genetics
Amer. Genetic Assn. **[1480]**
Natl. Soc. of Genetic Counselors **[2419]**

Genocide
Facing History and Ourselves Natl. Found. **[1770]**
Geodetic Surveying; Amer. Assn. for **[1544]**

Geography
Amer. Geographical Soc. **[1481]**

Geology
Assn. of Amer. State Geologists **[1482]**
Sigma Gamma Epsilon **[3527]**
George Strait Fan Club **[3579]**, PO Box 2119, Hendersonville, TN 37077, (615)824-7176

Georgian
Georgian Assn. in the U.S.A. **[2783]**
Georgian Assn. in the U.S.A. **[2783]**, 2300 M St. NW, Ste. 800, Washington, DC 20037, (202)234-2441

Geoscience
ASFE **[1483]**
Soc. of Exploration Geophysicists **[1484]**
Fed. of Earth Sci. Info. Partners **[1449]**

German
Amer. Coun. on Germany **[2784]**

A star before a book entry number signifies that the name is not listed separately, but is mentioned within the entry.

Amer. Historical Soc. of Germans From Russia [2785]
Germans From Russia Heritage Soc. [2786]
Goethe-Institut Inter Nationes [1759]
German Gun Collectors' Assn. [3152], PO Box 429, Mayfield, UT 84643, (435)979-9723
Germans From Russia Heritage Soc. [2786], 1125 W Turnpike Ave., Bismarck, ND 58501-8115, (701)223-6167

Gerontology
Amer. Aging Assn. [2420]
Amer. Geriatrics Soc. [2421]
Assn. for Gerontology in Higher Educ. [1626]
Gesneriad Soc. [3205], 1122 E Pike St., PMB 637, Seattle, WA 98122-3916

Ghana
Ahoto Partnership for Ghana [2476]
Ghana Medical Mission [2489]
Ghana Relief Org. [1955]
Global Brigades [2019]
Ghana Medical Mission [2489], 248 McNear Dr., San Rafael, CA 94901
Ghana Relief Org. [1955], PO Box 1722, Baltimore, MD 21203, (410)486-6832
The Gideons Intl. [2929], PO Box 140800, Nashville, TN 37214-0800, (615)564-5000
Gift and Home Trade Assn. [784], 2025 E Beltline Ave. SE, Ste. 200, Grand Rapids, MI 49546, (616)949-9104
Gift of Life Intl. [2133], PO Box 650436, Fresh Meadows, NY 11365, (845)546-2104
Gift of Water [2263], 1025 Pine Hill Way, Carmel, IN 46032-7701, (317)371-1656

Gifted
The Assn. for the Gifted [1627]

Gifts
Natl. Specialty Gift Assn. [398]
Gifts In Kind Intl. [★2158]

Girls
Amer. Legion Auxiliary Girls Nation [2621]
Dwa Fanm [2663]
Girls for a Change [1956], PO Box 1436, San Jose, CA 95109, (408)540-6432
Girls on the Run Intl. [3379], 120 Cottage Pl., Charlotte, NC 28207, (704)376-9817
Girls State [★2621]
Girls' Town of Rome [★2276]
Giving Inst. [394], 303 W Madison St., Ste. 2650, Chicago, IL 60606, (312)981-6794
Giving U.S.A. Found. [2157], 303 W Madison St., Ste. 2650, Chicago, IL 60606-3396, (312)981-6794

Glass
Glass Assn. of North Am. [399]
Intl. Carnival Glass Assn. [3209]
Natl. Glass Assn. [400]
Glass Assn. of North Am. [399], 800 SW Jackson St., Ste. 1500, Topeka, KS 66612-1200, (785)271-0208
Glenmary Res. Center [2867], Glenmary Home Missioners, PO Box 465618, Cincinnati, OH 45246, (513)874-8900
Glenn Miller Birthplace Soc. [3580], 122 W Clark St., PO Box 61, Clarinda, IA 51632, (712)542-2461
Global Action Intl. [2186], PO Box 131269, Carlsbad, CA 92013, (760)438-3979
Global Action on Widowhood [2755], 3 Newport Rd., Ste. 1, Cambridge, MA 02140, (617)441-8892
Global Ambassadors for Children [2715], 7399 N Shadeland Ave., No. 116, Indianapolis, IN 46250, (317)814-5318
Global Animal Partnership [951], PO Box 21484, Washington, DC 20009, (202)540-9880
Global Aquaculture Alliance [957], 5661 Telegraph Rd., Ste. 3A, St. Louis, MO 63129, (314)293-5500
Global Autism Collaboration [2316], Autism Res. Inst., 4182 Adams Ave., San Diego, CA 92116
Global Automakers [76], 1050 K St. NW, Ste. 650, Washington, DC 20001, (202)650-5555
Global Biofuels Alliance [392], 1540 E Lake Rd., Erie, PA 16511, (814)528-9067
Global Brigades [2019], 1099 E Champlain Dr., Ste. A176, Fresno, CA 93720
Global Centurion [1957], 2000 Clarendon Blvd., Arlington, VA 22201, (703)276-3000
Global China Connection [1643], PO Box 250860, New York, NY 10025
Global Communities of Support [1910], 475 Wall St., Princeton, NJ 08540, (609)845-2340

Global Economic Outreach [2999], PO Box 12778, Wilmington, NC 28405
Global Emergency Care Collaborative [2490], 2033 W Iowa St., No. 3, Chicago, IL 60622
Global Flying Hospitals [2435], 4440 PGA Blvd., Ste. 600, Palm Beach Gardens, FL 33410, (855)434-4747
Global FoodBanking Network [2116], 203 N LaSalle St., Ste. 1900, Chicago, IL 60601, (312)782-4560
Global Fund for Women [2646], 222 Sutter St., Ste. 500, San Francisco, CA 94109, (415)248-4800
Global Hea. Corps [2491], 5 Penn Plz., 2nd Fl., New York, NY 10001
Global Hea. through Educ., Training and Ser. [2492], 8 N Main St., Ste. 404, Attleboro, MA 02703, (508)226-5091
Global Hea. Informatics Partnership [2493], 4915 St. Elmo Ave., Ste. 402, Bethesda, MD 20814, (301)657-1291
Global Hea. Linkages, Inc. [2494], 10810 Hickory Ridge Rd., Columbia, MD 21044, (410)202-8868
Global Helps Network [2005], PO Box 1238, Enumclaw, WA 98022
Global Natural Hea. Alliance [2294], 2442 NW Market St., No. 628, Seattle, WA 98107, (970)402-0575
Global Network for Neglected Tropical Diseases [2398], 2000 Pennsylvania Ave. NW, Ste. 7100, Washington, DC 20006, (202)842-5025
Global Parks [1026], 3803 Sulgrave Dr., Alexandria, VA 22309, (703)317-1669
Global Partners Running Waters [2020], 13105 Watertown Plank Rd., Elm Grove, WI 53122, (262)787-1010
Global Partnership for Afghanistan [925], PO Box 1237, New York, NY 10276, (212)735-2080
Global Physicians Corps [2495], PO Box 25772, Los Angeles, CA 90025
Global Possibilities [1214], 1955 Mandeville Canyon Rd., Los Angeles, CA 90049, (310)656-1970
Global Rights [2664], 1200 18th St. NW, Ste. 602, Washington, DC 20036, (202)822-4600
Global Security Inst. [2709], GSB Bldg., Ste. 400, One Belmont Ave., Bala Cynwyd, PA 19004, (610)668-5488
Global Solutions for Infectious Diseases [2472], 830 Dubuque Ave., South San Francisco, CA 94080, (650)228-7900
Global Sourcing Coun. [631], 750 Third Ave., 11th Fl., New York, NY 10017, (631)398-3366
Global Tech. Distribution Coun. [848], 141 Bay Point Dr. NE, St. Petersburg, FL 33704, (813)412-1148
Global Underwater Explorers [1159], 15 S Main St., High Springs, FL 32643, (386)454-0820
Global Vision 2020 [2601], PO Box 3332, Easton, MD 21601, (410)822-6170
Global Wildlife Conservation [1238], PO Box 129, Austin, TX 78767-0129, (512)827-9418
Global Workers Justice Alliance [2145], 789 Washington Ave., Brooklyn, NY 11238, (646)351-1160
Global Youth Action Network [2756], 540 Pres. St., 3rd Fl., Brooklyn, NY 11215, (212)661-6111
Glocal Ventures [2119], 1870 Rufe Snow Dr., Keller, TX 76248, (817)656-5136

Goats
Amer. Kiko Goat Assn. [1106]
Intl. Boer Goat Assn. [1107]
Intl. Fainting Goat Assn. [1108]
North Amer. Packgoat Assn. [1109]
Goethe-Institut Inter Nationes [1759], 72 Spring St., 11th Fl., New York, NY 10012, (212)439-8700

Golf
Amer. Junior Golf Assn. [3334]
Golf Coaches Assn. of Am. [3335]
Intl. Assn. of Golf Administrators [3336]
Professional Golfers' Assn. of Am. [3337]
Professional Putters Assn. [3338]
Salute Military Golf Assn. [3339]
Golf Coaches Assn. of Am. [3335], 1225 W Main St., Ste. 110, Norman, OK 73069, (405)329-4222
Golf Course Builders Assn. of Am. [833], 727 O St., Lincoln, NE 68508, (402)476-4444
Golf Course Superintendents Assn. of Am. [834], 1421 Res. Park Dr., Lawrence, KS 66049-3859, (785)841-2240
Good360 [2158], 133 Braddock Pl., Ste. 600, Alexandria, VA 22314, (703)836-2121

Goods for Good [1958], 180 Varick St., Ste. 1207, New York, NY 10014, (646)963-6076

Gospel
BCM Intl. [2849]
Gospel Literature Intl. [3000], PO Box 4060, Ontario, CA 91761-1003, (909)481-5222

Gourmets
Amer. Inst. of Wine and Food [3210]

Government
Worldwide Assurance for Employees of Public Agencies [1304]
Amer. Legion Auxiliary Girls Nation [2621]
Assn. of Governmental Risk Pools [1307]
Close Up Found. [2622]
Fisher Inst. for Medical Res. [2653]
Intl. Professional Partnerships for Sierra Leone [2675]
Natl. Coun. for Intl. Visitors [2683]
Scientists and Engineers for Am. [1279]

Government Contracts
Coalition for Govt. Procurement [401]

Government Employees
Natl. Coun. of Field Labor Locals [3446]

Government Relations
Women in Govt. Relations [2656]
Graduation Pledge Alliance [2747], c/o Heidi Gross, Coor., Bentley Univ., 175 Forest St., Waltham, MA 02452, (781)891-2529
Graham Found. [56], 4 W Burton Pl., Chicago, IL 60610-1416, (312)787-4071
Graham Owners Club Intl. [3107], c/o Gloria Reid, Treas., 4028 Empire Creek Cir., Georgetown, CA 95634, (530)333-4105

Grain
Amer. Assn. of Grain Inspection and Weighing Agencies [402]
Trans., Elevator and Grain Merchants Assn. [403]
Graphic Artists Guild [1717], 32 Broadway, Ste. 1114, New York, NY 10004-1612, (212)791-3400

Graphic Arts
California Soc. of Printmakers [404]
Graphic Arts Educ. and Res. Found. [405]
Gravure Assn. of Am. [406]
IDEAlliance - Intl. Digital Enterprise Alliance [407]
Natl. Assn. of Litho Clubs [408]
Natl. Assn. for Printing Leadership [409]
NPES: Assn. for Suppliers of Printing, Publishing and Converting Technologies [410]
Graphic Arts Educ. and Res. Found. [405], 1899 Preston White Dr., Reston, VA 20191, (703)264-7200

Graphic Design
Amalgamated Printers' Assn. [411]
Soc. of Publication Designers [412]

Graphics
Amer. Design Drafting Assn. [1485]
Guild of Natural Sci. Illustrators [1486]
Tech. Assn. of the Graphic Arts [1487]
Grassland Heritage Found. [1027], PO Box 394, Shawnee Mission, KS 66201, (785)887-6775
Gravely Tractor Club of Am. [3245], PO Box 119, McLean, VA 22101, (610)518-1028
Gravure Assn. of Am. [406], PO Box 25617, Rochester, NY 14625, (201)523-6042
Graymoor Ecumenical and Interreligious Inst. [2907], 475 Riverside Dr., Rm. 1960, New York, NY 10115, (212)870-2330
Great Commn. Alliance [2068], 4700 SW 188th Ave., Southwest Ranches, FL 33332, (954)434-4500
Great Lakes Independent Booksellers Assn. [721], PO Box 901, Grand Haven, MI 49417, (616)847-2460
Great Lakes Lighthouse Keepers Assn. [1764], PO Box 219, Mackinaw City, MI 49701-0219, (231)436-5580

Greek
Daughters of Penelope [2787]
Hellenic-American Chamber of Commerce [3494]
Alpha Epsilon [3521]
Phi Chi Medical Fraternity [3539]
Greek Amer. Chamber of Commerce [3481], PO Box 1147, Kearny, NJ 07032
Green for All [2612], 1611 Telegraph Ave., Ste. 600, Oakland, CA 94612, (510)663-6500
Green Builder Coalition [146], PO Box 7507, Gurnee, IL 60031
Green Collar Assn. [296], PO Box 2093, Washington, DC 20013, (866)262-5735

Green Team Am. **[1028]**, 6300 Westpark Dr., Ste. 210, Houston, TX 77057, (713)334-3000

GreenMotion **[1057]**, 5795 S Sandhill Rd., Ste. F, Las Vegas, NV 89120, (310)663-9826

Greeting Card Assn. **[837]**, 1133 Westchester Ave., Ste. N136, White Plains, NY 10604-3546, (914)421-3331

Greyhound
   U.S.A. Defenders of Greyhounds **[1901]**

GridWise Architecture Coun. **[1520]**, Pacific Northwest Natl. Lab., PO Box 999, Richland, WA 99352, (509)372-6410

Gritchenko Foundation **[★1864]**

Gp. Underwriters Assn. of Am. **[486]**, PO Box 118, Weatogue, CT 06089-0118

Growing Liberia's Children **[1993]**, PO Box 90676, San Diego, CA 92169, (858)539-0954

GS1 US **[67]**, Princeton Pike Corporate Center, 1009 Lenox Dr., Ste. 202, Lawrenceville, NJ 08648, (609)620-0200

Guatemala
   Mike's Angels **[1974]**
   Miracles in Action **[2170]**
   Wuqu' Kawoq **[2527]**

Guiding Eyes for the Blind **[2602]**, 611 Granite Springs Rd., Yorktown Heights, NY 10598, (914)245-4024

Guild of Book Workers **[1740]**, 521 5th Ave., New York, NY 10175-0038

Guild of Natural Sci. Illustrators **[1486]**, PO Box 652, Ben Franklin Sta., Washington, DC 20044-0652, (301)309-1514

Guild of Professional Farriers **[318]**, PO Box 4541, Midway, KY 40347

Gulf and Caribbean Fisheries Inst. **[1088]**, Univ. of Florida, Picos Rd., Fort Pierce, FL 34946, (561)462-1660

Gymnastics
   Eastern Intercollegiate Gymnastic League **[3340]**

Gynecologic Investigation; Soc. for **[2568]**

Gypsy Vanner Horse Soc. **[1127]**, PO Box 65, Waynesfield, OH 45896, (888)520-9777

H

Habonim Dror North Am. **[2952]**, 114 W 26th St., Ste. 1004, New York, NY 10001, (212)255-1796

Hadassah, The Women's Zionist Org. of Am. **[2953]**, 50 W 58th St., New York, NY 10019, (212)355-7900

Haiti
   All the Children are Children **[1919]**
   Alliance For Relief Mission in Haiti **[2181]**
   Forward in Hea. **[2433]**
   Friends for Hea. in Haiti **[2434]**
   Great Commn. Alliance **[2068]**
   Haiti Convention Assn. **[2214]**
   Haiti Cultural Exchange **[1748]**
   Haiti Healthcare Partners **[2496]**
   Haiti Outreach **[1905]**
   Haiti Works! **[2120]**
   HavServe Volunteer Ser. Network **[1906]**
   Help Brings Hope for Haiti **[2188]**
   Hope for Haiti **[2023]**
   Hope for Haiti's Children **[1966]**
   Intl. Org. for Haitian Development **[1591]**
   Meds and Food for Kids **[1973]**
   NOVA Hope for Haiti **[2139]**
   People for Haiti **[2195]**
   Rebuilding Haiti Now **[2197]**

Haiti Convention Assn. **[2214]**, 272 Dunns Mill Rd., No. 254, Bordentown, NJ 08505, (201)532-2374

Haiti Cultural Exchange **[1748]**, 115 S Oxford St., No. 547, Brooklyn, NY 11217, (718)855-8514

Haiti Healthcare Partners **[2496]**, 4607 Lakeview Canyon Ave., No. 640, Westlake Village, CA 91361

Haiti Outreach **[1905]**, 15119 Minnetonka Blvd., Minnetonka, MN 55345, (612)929-1122

Haiti Works! **[2120]**, 855 Main St., 5th Fl., Bridgeport, CT 06604, (203)526-3542

Halogenated Solvents Indus. Alliance **[184]**, 1530 Wilson Blvd., Ste. 690, Arlington, VA 22209, (703)875-0683

HALT **[2692]**, 1612 K St. NW, Ste. 510, Washington, DC 20006-2849, (202)887-8255

Hand
   Amer. Assn. for Hand Surgery **[2422]**
   Amer. Soc. of Hand Therapists **[2423]**

Handball
   U.S. Handball Assn. **[3341]**

Handicapped
   Acad. of Rehabilitative Audiology **[2449]**
   BlazeSports Am. **[3316]**

Hands for Autistic Children of Ethiopia **[1911]**, 621 Bushytail Dr., Frederick, MD 21703, (240)429-8362

HANDS for Cambodia **[2021]**, PO Box 940582, Plano, TX 75094-0582

Hank Williams Intl. Fan Club **[3581]**, 103 Summit Cir., Daphne, AL 36526, (251)626-1645

Hannah's Promise Intl. Aid **[2187]**, PO Box 2102, Boone, NC 28607, (828)668-1434

Hardware
   Builders Hardware Mfrs. Assn. **[413]**
   Indus. Fasteners Inst. **[414]**
   North Amer. Retail Hardware Assn. **[415]**
   Valve Repair Coun. **[416]**
   Decorative Plumbing and Hardware Assn. **[678]**

Harness Tracks of Am. **[3344]**, 12025 E Dry Gulch Pl., Tucson, AZ 85749, (520)529-2525

Harry S. Truman Lib. Inst. for Natl. and Intl. Affairs **[1866]**, 500 W U.S. Hwy. 24, Independence, MO 64050, (816)268-8200

Hartford Whalers Booster Club **[3590]**, PO Box 273, Hartford, CT 06141, (860)956-3839

Harvey Soc. **[2548]**, c/o Marie Filbin, PhD, Sec., City Univ. of New York, Hunter Coll., 695 Park Ave., New York, NY 10065, (212)772-5472

Havana Rabbit Breeders Assn. **[1189]**, N-9487 Walnut Rd., Clintonville, WI 54929, (715)823-5020

Havana Silk Dog Assn. of Am. **[3176]**, c/o Cathy Dillahunty, Treas., 4435 14th St. NE, St. Petersburg, FL 33703

HavServe Volunteer Ser. Network **[1906]**, PO Box 4173, Silver Spring, MD 20914

Hazardous Material
   Inst. of Hazardous Materials Mgt. **[1110]**

Head and Neck Soc; Amer. **[2573]**

Healing Across the Divides **[2497]**, 72 Laurel Dr., Northampton, PA 18067

Healing Hands Intl. **[2228]**, 455 McNally Dr., Nashville, TN 37211, (615)832-2000

Healing Waters Intl. **[2264]**, 534 Commons Dr., Golden, CO 80401, (303)526-7278

Health
   AcademyHealth **[2424]**
   Amer. Hea. Planning Assn. **[2425]**
   Fed. of Associations of Regulatory Boards **[2426]**
   United Methodist Assn. of Hea. and Welfare Ministries **[2427]**
   ACCESS Hea. Intl. **[2428]**
   Ahoto Partnership for Ghana **[2476]**
   All Healers Mental Hea. Alliance **[2550]**
   Alliance of Jamaican and Amer. Humanitarians **[2008]**
   Alliance for Massage Therapy Educ. **[1659]**
   Ambassadors for Sustained Hea. **[2430]**
   Amer. Abdominal Acupuncture Medical Assn. **[2283]**
   Amer. Acad. of Restorative Dentistry **[2370]**
   Amer. Assn. of Endodontists ∣ Amer. Bd. of Endodontics **[2372]**
   Amer. Celiac Disease Alliance **[2414]**
   Amer. Friends of Guinea **[2478]**
   Amer. Herbal Pharmacopoeia **[2291]**
   Amer. Osteopathic Coll. of Anesthesiologists **[2301]**
   Andean Hea. and Development **[2479]**
   Angel Harps **[2588]**
   Answer Africa **[2397]**
   Aromatherapy Registration Coun. **[2292]**
   Assn. of Biomedical Communications Directors **[2350]**
   Assn. for Healthcare Volunteer Rsrc. Professionals **[2258]**
   Autism Allies **[2308]**
   Autism Ser. Dogs of Am. **[2310]**
   Bailey's Team for Autism **[2311]**
   C-Change **[2329]**
   Caribbean Public Hea. Coalition **[2590]**
   Catholic Guardian Soc. and Home Bur. **[1931]**

Children's Dialysis Intl. **[2559]**
Chiropractic Diplomatic Corps **[2340]**
Coun. on Accreditation **[2233]**
Coun. for Acupuncture Res. and Educ. **[2284]**
Dorcas Medical Mission **[2486]**
Emofra Africa **[2487]**
Engg. World Hea. **[2488]**
Env. and Human Hea., Inc. **[2410]**
Face Autism **[2312]**
Fashion for Autism **[2314]**
Father Josef's Method of Reflexology **[2293]**
Generation Rescue **[2315]**
Ghana Medical Mission **[2489]**
Global Autism Collaboration **[2316]**
Global Hea. through Educ., Training and Ser. **[2492]**
Global Hea. Informatics Partnership **[2493]**
Global Hea. Linkages, Inc. **[2494]**
Global Natural Hea. Alliance **[2294]**
Global Network for Neglected Tropical Diseases **[2398]**
Global Physicians Corps **[2495]**
Global Solutions for Infectious Diseases **[2472]**
Haiti Healthcare Partners **[2496]**
Healing Across the Divides **[2497]**
Hea. and Educ. Relief for Guyana **[2498]**
Hea. Empowering Humanity **[2436]**
Hea. Horizons Intl. **[2499]**
Hea. through Walls **[2501]**
Healthcare Laundry Accreditation Coun. **[537]**
Heart Rhythm Soc. **[2332]**
Helping Autism through Learning and Outreach **[2317]**
Holistic Mentorship Network **[2460]**
Hope Beyond Hope **[2503]**
Hope Through Healing Hands **[2504]**
Horizon Intl. Medical Mission **[2505]**
Intl. Coalition for Autism and All Abilities **[2318]**
Intl. Coun. on Nanotechnology **[1440]**
Intl. Medical Alliance **[2508]**
Intl. Psoriasis Coun. **[2394]**
Intl. Soc. for Children with Cancer **[2330]**
MED25 Intl. **[2440]**
Medical Mission Gp. **[2509]**
Meds and Food for Kids **[1973]**
mHealth Alliance **[2510]**
Naturopathic Medicine for Global Hea. **[2555]**
Network Ethiopia **[2511]**
OmSpring **[2296]**
Phi Chi Medical Fraternity **[3539]**
Progressive Hea. Partnership **[2513]**
Qigong Alliance Intl. **[2297]**
Reach Intl. Healthcare and Training **[2515]**
Reiki Rays of Hope for Caregivers **[2298]**
Ser. for the Love of God **[2034]**
Sharing Resources Worldwide **[2516]**
Shout Global Hea. **[2517]**
Silver Age Yoga **[2606]**
Soc. of Family Planning **[2413]**
Soc. for Heart Valve Disease **[2457]**
Soft Power Hea. **[2518]**
South Asian Public Hea. Assn. **[2591]**
Spinal Hea. Intl. **[2594]**
Stories of Autism **[2321]**
S.U.C.C.E.S.S. for Autism **[2322]**
Surfing Medicine Intl. **[2299]**
UHAI for Hea. **[2519]**
Unified for Global Healing **[2520]**
Upenyu **[2521]**
Uplift Intl. **[2522]**
Vietnamese-American Nurses Assn. **[2566]**
Visionary Alternatives **[2300]**
Waves of Hea. **[2523]**
Women Against Prostate Cancer **[2331]**
Women for World Hea. **[2442]**
World Hea. Ambassador **[2443]**
World Hea. Imaging, Telemedicine and Informatics Alliance **[2524]**
World Hea. Services **[2526]**
World Spine Care **[2595]**
Wuqu' Kawoq **[2527]**
Wyman Worldwide Hea. Partners **[2528]**

Health Care
   ACCESS Hea. Intl. **[2428]**
   Amazonas Hope for Hea. **[2429]**

A star before a book entry number signifies that the name is not listed separately, but is mentioned within the entry.

Dorcas Medical Mission [2486]
Engg. World Hea. [2488]
Forward in Hea. [2433]
Friends for Hea. in Haiti [2434]
Ghana Medical Mission [2489]
Global Emergency Care Collaborative [2490]
Global Flying Hospitals [2435]
Global Hea. Corps [2491]
Global Hea. through Educ., Training and Ser. [2492]
Global Hea. Informatics Partnership [2493]
Global Hea. Linkages, Inc. [2494]
Global Natural Hea. Alliance [2294]
Hea. and Educ. Relief for Guyana [2498]
Hea. Empowering Humanity [2436]
Hea. For All Missions [2134]
Hea. Horizons Intl. [2500]
Hea. Horizons Intl. [2499]
Hea. through Walls [2501]
Honduras Outreach Medical Brigada Relief Effort [2502]
Hope Beyond Hope [2503]
Hope Through Healing Hands [2504]
Horizon Intl. Medical Mission [2505]
I Care Grace Intl. [2437]
Inter-American Hea. Alliance [2438]
Intl. Hea. and Development Network [2507]
Intl. Healthcare Volunteers [2439]
Intl. Medical Alliance [2508]
MED25 Intl. [2440]
Medical Mission Gp. [2509]
Medics Without Borders [2407]
mHealth Alliance [2510]
Mobile Medical Disaster Relief [2138]
Non-Profit Chiropractic Org. [2345]
Norrie Disease Assn. [2399]
NOVA Hope for Haiti [2139]
Partners for World Hea. [2512]
Progressive Hea. Partnership [2513]
A Promise of Hea. [2441]
Reach Intl. Healthcare and Training [2515]
Sharing Resources Worldwide [2516]
Soft Power Hea. [2518]
UHAI for Hea. [2519]
Unified for Global Healing [2520]
Upenyu [2521]
Visionary Alternatives [2300]
Waves of Hea. [2523]
Women Against Prostate Cancer [2331]
Women for World Hea. [2442]
World Hea. Ambassador [2443]
World Hea. Imaging, Telemedicine and Informatics Alliance [2524]
World Hea. Partners [2525]
World Hea. Services [2526]
World Spine Care [2595]
Wuqu' Kawoq [2527]
Wyman Worldwide Hea. Partners [2528]
Hea. through Walls [2501], 12555 Biscayne Blvd., No. 955, North Miami, FL 33181
Healthcare Distribution Mgt. Assn. [2576], 901 N Glebe Rd., Ste. 1000, Arlington, VA 22203, (703)787-0000
Healthcare Laundry Accreditation Coun. [537], PO Box 1805, Frankfort, IL 60423, (815)464-1404

Hearing Impaired
Acad. of Rehabilitative Audiology [2449]
ADARA: Professionals Networking for Excellence in Ser. Delivery with Individuals who are Deaf or Hard of Hearing [2450]
Conf. of Educational Administrators of Schools and Programs for the Deaf [2451]
Coun. of Amer. Instructors of the Deaf [2452]
Coun. on Educ. of the Deaf [2453]
Intl. Hearing Dog [2454]
Intl. Hearing Soc. [2455]
Registry of Interpreters for the Deaf [2456]
Intl. Catholic Deaf Assn. U.S. Sect. [2868]
Hearing, Speech and
Intl. Catholic Deaf Assn. U.S. Sect. [2868]
Heart for Africa [1959], PO Box 573, Alpharetta, GA 30009, (678)566-1589
Heart Disease
Soc. for Heart Valve Disease [2457]
Heart Rhythm Soc. [2332]

Heart Rhythm Soc. [2332], 1400 K St. NW, Ste. 500, Washington, DC 20005, (202)464-3400
Heart4Kids [1960], 13950 Mansarde Ave., Ste. 186, Herndon, VA 20171, (404)957-9014
Hearth, Patio and Barbecue Found. [430], 1901 N Moore St., Ste. 600, Arlington, VA 22209, (703)524-8030
Hearts Across Romania [1961], 2544 Brookside Dr., Irving, TX 75063, (214)213-9001
Hearts for Kenya [1907], 1514 Norris Pl., Louisville, KY 40205, (502)459-4582
Heating Airconditioning and Refrigeration Distributors Intl. [431], 3455 Mill Run Dr., Ste. 820, Hilliard, OH 43026, (614)345-4328
Heating and Cooling
Air-Conditioning Heating and Refrigeration Inst. [427]
Air Diffusion Coun. [428]
Air Movement and Control Assn. Intl. [429]
Hearth, Patio and Barbecue Found. [430]
Heating Airconditioning and Refrigeration Distributors Intl. [431]
Intl. Air Filtration Certifiers Assn. [432]
Intl. Compressor Remanufacturers Assn. [433]
Masonry Heater Assn. of North Am. [434]
Natl. Air Filtration Assn. [435]
North Amer. Technician Excellence [436]
Radiant Professionals Alliance [437]
Refrigeration Ser. Engineers Soc. [438]
ClimateTalk Alliance [1392]
Heavy Duty Mfrs. Assn. I Heavy-Duty Bus. Forum [77], 10 Lab. Dr., PO Box 13966, Research Triangle Park, NC 27709-3966, (919)549-4800
Heavy Duty Representatives Assn. [88], 160 Symphony Way, Elgin, IL 60120, (847)760-0067
Heavy Metal Music
KISS Rocks Fan Club [3584]
Hedge Fund Bus. Operations Assn. [525], 1350 41st Ave., Ste. 200, Capitola, CA 95010, (831)465-2298
Heifer Intl. [2121], 1 World Ave., Little Rock, AR 72202, (800)422-0474
Helicopter Found. Intl. [29], 1635 Prince St., Alexandria, VA 22314-2818, (703)683-4646
Hellenic Amer. Bankers Assn. [111], PO Box 7244, New York, NY 10150-7201, (212)421-1057
Hellenic-American Chamber of Commerce [3494], 780 3rd Ave., 16 Fl., New York, NY 10017, (212)629-6380
Help Aid Africa [2022], 1132 Corrie Ln., Walnut Creek, CA 94597
Help Brings Hope for Haiti [2188], 3816 W Morrison Ave., Tampa, FL 33629, (813)832-4244
Helping Autism through Learning and Outreach [2317], PO Box 303399, Austin, TX 78703, (512)465-9595
Helping Hand for Nepal [2189], 2930 Brittany Dr., Anchorage, AK 99504, (907)338-8128
Helping Hands [1962], 2918 Churchill Way, Garland, TX 75044, (972)635-3903
Helping Hearts Helping Hands [2166], 7060 Scenic Ridge, Clarkston, MI 48346, (248)660-4507
Helping Honduras Kids [1963], PO Box 111777, Campbell, CA 95011-1777
HELPSudan [1994], 5255 N Ashland Ave., Chicago, IL 60640
Hematology
Amer. Soc. of Pediatric Hematology/Oncology [2458]
Hepatology
Amer. Liver Found. [2459]
Herbs
Alternative Medicine Intl. [2289]
Amer. Herbal Pharmacopoeia [2291]
Hero Initiative [1745], 11301 Olympic Blvd., No. 587, Los Angeles, CA 90064, (818)776-1918
H.H. Franklin Club [3108], Cazenovia Coll., Cazenovia, NY 13035
High Frontier [1387], 2800 Shirlington Rd., Ste. 405, Arlington, VA 22206, (703)671-4111
High Point Market Authority [396], 164 S Main St., Ste. 700, High Point, NC 27260, (336)869-1000
High Twelve Intl. [2805], Bettendorf Masonic Center, 2412 Grand St., Bettendorf, IA 52722, (563)514-3270
Higher Education
Professional and Organizational Development Network in Higher Educ. [1628]

Intl. Org. for Haitian Development [1591]
Natl. Assn. of Peoplecultural Engg. Prog. Advocates [1615]
Highlander Class Intl. Assn. [3273], 410 Holiday Rd., Lexington, KY 40502, (859)806-5908
Hiking
Camping Women [3301]
New England Trails Conf. [3428]
Hiking Soc; Amer. [3425]
Hispanic
League of United Latin Amer. Citizens [2788]
Natl. Image [2789]
U.S. Conf. of Catholic Bishops I Secretariat for Hispanic Affairs [2097]
U.S. Hispanic Chamber of Commerce [3495]
Natl. Community for Latino Leadership [2800]
Hispanic Natl. Bar Assn. [1272], 1900 L St. NW, Ste. 700, Washington, DC 20036, (202)223-4777
Historic Preservation
Amer. Inst. for Conservation of Historic and Artistic Works [1760]
Amer. Overseas Schools Historical Soc. [1761]
APVA Preservation Virginia [1762]
Civil War Trust [1763]
Great Lakes Lighthouse Keepers Assn. [1764]
Intl. Coalition of Sites of Conscience [1765]
Corvair Soc. of Am. [3100]
Intl. Fire Buff Associates [3192]
Midstates Jeepster Assn. [3117]
Morgan Car Club [3120]
Natl. Alliance of Highway Beautification Agencies [1370]
Natl. Assn. for Civil War Brass Music [1825]
North-South Skirmish Assn. [3384]
United Four-Wheel Drive Associations [3135]
Vintage Garden Tractor Club of Am. [3246]
World Airline Historical Soc. [3089]
Historical Reenactment
North-South Skirmish Assn. [3384]
Historical Soc. of the Episcopal Church [2919], c/o Susan Johnson, Dir. of Operations, PO Box 1749, Harlingen, TX 78551, (866)989-5851
Historical Soc. of Washington, DC [1771], Mt. Vernon Sq., 801 K St. NW, Washington, DC 20001, (202)383-1850
History
Agricultural History Soc. [1766]
Amer. Catholic Historical Assn. [1767]
Amer. Soc. of Church History [2941]
Amer. Soc. for Legal History [1768]
Bostonian Soc. [1769]
Conf. on Faith and History [2942]
Facing History and Ourselves Natl. Found. [1770]
Historical Soc. of Washington, DC [1771]
History of Sci. Soc. [1772]
Org. of Amer. Historians [1773]
Soc. for French Historical Stud. [1774]
Soc. for Historians of Amer. Foreign Relations [1775]
Soc. for Historians of the Early Amer. Republic [1776]
Soc. for History Educ. [1629]
Soc. for History in the Fed. Govt. [1777]
Colonial Coin Collectors Club [3222]
Corvair Soc. of Am. [3100]
Gen. Soc. of Mayflower Descendants [3077]
Intl. Fire Buff Associates [3192]
Midstates Jeepster Assn. [3117]
Morgan Car Club [3120]
North-South Skirmish Assn. [3384]
Soc. of Australasian Specialists/Oceania [3232]
Space Topic Stud. Unit [3234]
United Four-Wheel Drive Associations [3135]
Vintage Garden Tractor Club of Am. [3246]
World Airline Historical Soc. [3089]
History of Sci. Soc. [1772], Univ. of Notre Dame, 440 Geddes Hall, Notre Dame, IN 46556, (574)631-1194
Hobbies
First Issues Collectors Club [3226]
Intl. Scale Soaring Assn. [3216]
Natl. 42 Players Assn. [3198]
Plasticville Collectors Assn. [3237]
Hobby Supplies
Amer. Stamp Dealers Assn. [439]

A star before a book entry number signifies that the name is not listed separately, but is mentioned within the entry.

Plasticville Collectors Assn. [3237]
Hockey
Eastern Coll. Athletic Conf. [3342]
Western Collegiate Hockey Assn. [3343]
Natl. Hockey League Booster Clubs [3592]
Holiday and Decorative Assn. [358], PO Box
420244, Dallas, TX 75342-0244, (214)742-2747
Holistic Dental Assn. [2381], 1825 Ponce de Leon
Blvd., No. 148, Coral Gables, FL 33134, (305)356-
7338
Holistic Medicine
Holistic Mentorship Network [2460]
Natl. Assn. for Holistic Aromatherapy [2461]
Holistic Mentorship Network [2460], 55 Newton
Sparta Rd., Newton, NJ 07860, (973)300-1184
Holland Soc. of New York [3057], 20 W 44th St., 5th
Fl., New York, NY 10036, (212)758-1675
Home
Community Associations Inst. [2627]
Leading Builders of Am. [149]
Home Care
Natl. Assn. for Home Care and Hospice [2462]
Home Economics
Amer. Assn. of Family and Consumer Sciences
[2098]
Natl. Assn. of Teacher Educators for Family and
Consumer Sciences [1630]
Home of Hope [1964], 190 Tobin Clark Dr., Hillsbor-
ough, CA 94010, (650)520-3204
Home Improvement Res. Inst. [257], 3922 Coconut
Palm Dr., 3rd Fl., Tampa, FL 33619, (813)627-6750
HomeFree - U.S.A. [452], 3401A E W Hwy., Hyatts-
ville, MD 20782, (301)891-8400
Homeless
Amer. Bar Assn. Commn. on Homelessness and
Poverty [2099]
Natl. Student Campaign Against Hunger and
Homelessness [2117]
Homeopathy
Amer. Inst. of Homeopathy [2463]
A Promise of Hea. [2441]
Homosexual Info. Center [2095], 8721 Santa Monica
Blvd., Ste. 37, West Hollywood, CA 90069,
(818)527-5442
Honda
Intl. CBX Owners Assn. [3219]
Honduras
Honduras Outreach, Inc. [2657]
Global Brigades [2019]
Honduras Outreach Medical Brigada Relief Effort
[2502]
Primero Agua [2267]
Union MicroFinanza [2213]
Honduras Outreach, Inc. [2657], 4105 Briarcliff Rd.
NE, Atlanta, GA 30345, (404)327-5770
Honduras Outreach Medical Brigada Relief Effort
[2502], West Hosp., 14th Fl., 1200 E Broad St.,
Richmond, VA 23298-0251
Honor Societies
Omicron Delta Kappa Soc. [3528]
Phi Beta Delta [3529]
Phi Kappa Phi [3530]
Sigma Alpha Lambda [3531]
Alpha Epsilon [3521]
Phi Chi Medical Fraternity [3539]
Hop Growers of Am. [994], PO Box 1207, Moxee,
WA 98936, (509)453-4749
Hope Beyond Hope [2503], 4230 Harding Rd., Ste.
307, Nashville, TN 37205, (615)292-8299
Hope and Future for Children in Bolivia [1965], PO
Box 4034, Mountain View, CA 94040, (650)962-
0137
Hope for Haiti [2023], PO Box 496, Westminster,
MD 21158-0496, (410)848-7343
Hope for Haiti's Children [1966], PO Box 936, Sugar
Land, TX 77487, (866)314-9330
Hope Through Healing Hands [2504], 2033 Richard
Jones Rd., Nashville, TN 37215, (615)386-0045
Horizon Intl. [1967], PO Box 180, Pendleton, IN
46064, (765)778-1016
Horizon Intl. Medical Mission [2505], 111 Lions Gate
Rd., Savannah, GA 31419, (912)308-8799
Horse Protection League [1128], PO Box 741089,
Arvada, CO 80006, (303)216-0141
Horse Racing
Harness Tracks of Am. [3344]
Intl. Trotting and Pacing Assn. [3345]

Jockeys' Guild [3346]
Natl. Museum of Racing and Hall of Fame [3347]
Thoroughbred Club of Am. [3348]
U.S. Team Penning Assn. [3349]
Horseback Riding
CHA - Certified Horsemanship Assn. [3350]
Intl. Side Saddle Org. [3351]
Natl. Versatility Ranch Horse Assn. [3352]
Trail Riders of Today [3353]
Horseless Carriage Club of Am. [3109], 5709 Oak
Ave., Temple City, CA 91780-2431, (626)287-4222
Horses
Amer. Azteca Horse Intl. Assn. [1111]
Amer. Bashkir Curly Registry [1112]
Amer. Driving Soc. [3354]
Amer. Drum Horse Assn. [1113]
Amer. Equestrian Trade Assn. [1114]
Amer. Half Quarter Horse Registry [1115]
Amer. Horse League [2100]
Amer. Morgan Horse Assn. [1116]
Amer. Paint Horse Assn. [1117]
Amer. Part-Blooded Horse Registry [1118]
Amer. Quarter Horse Assn. [1119]
Amer. Ranch Horse Assn. [1120]
Amer. Trakehner Assn. [1121]
Amer. Warmblood Registry [1122]
Amer. Youth Horse Coun. [1123]
Belgian Draft Horse Corp. of Am. [1124]
Caspian Horse Soc. of the Americas [1125]
Cleveland Bay Horse Soc. of North Am. [1126]
Gypsy Vanner Horse Soc. [1127]
Horse Protection League [1128]
Hungarian Horse Assn. of Am. [1129]
Intl. Colored Appaloosa Assn. [1130]
Intl. Curly Horse Org. [1131]
Intl. Friesian Show Horse Assn. [1132]
Intl. Warlander Soc. and Registry [1133]
Irish Draught Horse Soc. of North Am. [1134]
Lipizzan Assn. of North Am. [1135]
Lippitt Morgan Breeders Assn. [1136]
Mountain Pleasure Horse Assn. [1137]
Natl. Cutting Horse Assn. [1138]
Natl. Quarter Horse Registry [1139]
Natl. Reining Horse Assn. [1140]
Natl. Show Horse Registry [1141]
North Amer. Danish Warmblood Assn. [1142]
North Amer. Peruvian Horse Assn. [1143]
Norwegian Fjord Horse Registry [1144]
Pony of the Americas Club [1145]
Rocky Mountain Horse Assn. [1146]
Spanish-Barb Breeders Assn. [1147]
Spanish Mustang Registry [1148]
Spotted Saddle Horse Breeders' and Exhibitors'
Assn. [1149]
Tennessee Walking Horse Breeders' and Exhibi-
tors' Assn. [1150]
Walking Horse Trainers Assn. [1151]
Western Saddle Clubs Assn. [1152]
Intl. Trotting and Pacing Assn. [3345]
Natl. Versatility Ranch Horse Assn. [3352]
Thoroughbred Club of Am. [3348]
Horticultural Res. Inst. [1170], 1000 Vermont Ave.
NW, Ste. 300, Washington, DC 20005-4914,
(202)789-2900
Horticulture
Intl. Phalaenopsis Alliance [1153]
Coalition of Organic Landscapers [531]
Hospital
Amer. Assn. of Healthcare Consultants [2464]
Amer. Hosp. Assn. | Assn. for Healthcare Rsrc.
and Materials Mgt. [2465]
Amer. Hosp. Assn. | Soc. for Healthcare Strategy
and Market Development [2466]
Assn. for Healthcare Foodservice [2467]
Assn. for Healthcare Philanthropy [2468]
Intl. Assn. for Healthcare Security and Safety
[2469]
Natl. Assn. of Healthcare Access Mgt. [2470]
Assn. for Healthcare Volunteer Rsrc. Profession-
als [2258]
Healthcare Laundry Accreditation Coun. [537]
Hospitality Industries
Amer. Hotel and Lodging Assn. [440]
Assn. for Convention Marketing Executives [441]
Hotel Electronic Distribution Network Assn. [442]
IAHI, the Owners' Assn. [443]
Intl. Concierge and Lifestyle Mgt. Assn. [444]

Natl. Black McDonald's Operators Assn. [445]
Natl. Coun. of Chain Restaurants [446]
Natl. Restaurant Assn. [447]
Natl. Restaurant Assn. Educational Found. [448]
Professional Assn. of Innkeepers Intl. [449]
Intl. Galapagos Tour Operators Assn. [3505]
Hotel Brokers Intl. [743], 1420 NW Vivion Rd., Ste.
111, Kansas City, MO 64118, (816)505-4315
Hotel Electronic Distribution Network Assn. [442],
750 Natl. Press Bldg., 529 14th St. NW,
Washington, DC 20045, (202)204-8400
Housewares
Amer. Brush Mfrs. Assn. [450]
Cookware Mfrs. Assn. [451]
Housing
Cooperative Housing Found. [2101]
Enterprise Community Partners [2102]
HomeFree - U.S.A. [452]
Natl. Assn. of Housing Counselors and Agencies
[453]
Natl. Center for Housing Mgt. [2103]
Natl. Housing Conf. [2104]
Natl. Housing and Rehabilitation Assn. [2105]
Natl. Rural Housing Coalition [2106]
Rebuilding Alliance [2107]
Community Associations Inst. [2627]
Efficiency First [1018]
Leading Builders of Am. [149]
Natl. Assn. of Constr. Contractors Cooperation
[152]
Hovawart Club of North Am. [3177], c/o Utah
Felhaber-Smith, Membership Dir., 4718 NE 14th
Pl., Portland, OR 97211
HSUS Animal Control Acad. [★1896]
Huguenot
Huguenot Historical Soc. [3071]
Huguenot Historical Soc. [3071], 18 Broadhead
Ave., New Paltz, NY 12561-1403, (845)255-1660
Human Development
Cultural Survival [1778]
Inst. of Cultural Affairs [2108]
Inst. for the Development of the Harmonious Hu-
man Being [2109]
New Road Map Found. [2110]
Sacred Passage and the Way of Nature Fellow-
ship [2111]
World Peace One [2112]
Abriendo Mentes [2208]
All Our Children Intl. Outreach [1920]
Amer. Assn. of Human Design Practitioners [253]
Breaking Ground [2009]
Fields of Growth Intl. [2129]
Friends of the Children of Angola [1952]
Intl. Children Assistance Network [1968]
Kids Home Intl. [1969]
Orphans Africa [2031]
Seeds of HOPE Intl. [1985]
Sky of Love [1986]
Human Resources
Natl. Assn. of African Americans in Human
Resources [454]
Natl. Assn. of Professional Background Screeners
[455]
Human Rights
Advancing Human Rights [2658]
Center for Intl. Policy [2659]
CorpWatch [2660]
Dalit Freedom Network [2661]
Dalit Solidarity [2662]
Dwa Fanm [2663]
Global Rights [2664]
Human Rights Watch [2665]
Intl. Center for Transitional Justice [2666]
Iran Democratic Union [2667]
Physicians for Human Rights [2668]
Advocates Intl. [1321]
Amer. Civil Rights Union [2623]
Amer. Libyan Freedom Alliance [2636]
Child Protection Intl. [1936]
Ensaaf [2748]
Facing History and Ourselves Natl. Found. [1770]
Global Action on Widowhood [2755]
Uplift Intl. [2522]
Washington Off. on Latin Am. [2696]
Human Rights Watch [2665], 350 5th Ave., 34th Fl.,
New York, NY 10118-3299, (212)290-4700
Human Services
Amer. Public Human Services Assn. | Natl. Coun.
of State Human Ser. Administrators [2231]

Breaking Ground **[2009]**
Ethiopian Orphan Relief **[1948]**
Friends of the Children of Angola **[1952]**
Helping Hand for Nepal **[2189]**
Mercy Beyond Borders **[2169]**
Nepal SEEDS: Social Educational Environmental
Development Services in Nepal **[2028]**
Outreach Africa **[1981]**
Rebuilding Haiti Now **[2197]**
Seeds of HOPE Intl. **[1985]**
Tusubira - We Have Hope **[2173]**
Village Focus Intl. **[2037]**
World Action for Humanity **[2225]**
Human Services Assn; Amer. Public **[2230]**
Human-Wildlife Conflict Collaboration **[1239]**, 5410
Grosvenor Ln., Ste. 200, Bethesda, MD 20814-
2144, (202)986-0067
Humane Soc. of the U.S. **[1896]**, 2100 L St. NW,
Washington, DC 20037, (202)452-1100
Humanism
Amer. Ethical Union **[2943]**
Intl. Fed. for Secular Humanistic Judaism **[2944]**
Humanitarian African Relief Org. **[2190]**, 7364 El Ca-
jon Blvd., Ste. 208, San Diego, CA 92115,
(619)741-9260
Humanities
Consortium of Humanities Centers and Institutes
[2113]
Hummingbird Monitoring Network **[963]**, PO Box
115, Patagonia, AZ 85624
Humor
Intl. Soc. for Humor Stud. **[1779]**
Marx Brotherhood **[3569]**
Hungarian
Amer. Hungarian Found. **[2790]**
Hungarian Horse Assn. of Am. **[1129]**, c/o George
Cooksley, Treas., HC 71, Box 108, Anselmo, NE
68813, (308)749-2411
Hunger
Amer. Outreach to Ethiopia **[2114]**
Bread for the World **[2669]**
Feeding Am. **[2115]**
Global FoodBanking Network **[2116]**
Natl. Student Campaign Against Hunger and
Homelessness **[2117]**
Aid for the World **[2163]**
Hearts for Kenya **[1907]**
Simple Hope **[2200]**
Hunting
Amer. Coon Hunters Assn. **[3355]**
Masters of Foxhounds Assn. of Am. **[3356]**
North-South Skirmish Assn. **[3384]**
Hunting Dogs
U.S. Complete Shooting Dog Assn. **[3187]**
Hydrology; Amer. Inst. of **[1555]**
Hygienists' Assn; Natl. Dental **[2386]**
Hymn Soc. in the U.S. and Canada **[3021]**, Baptist
Theological Seminary at Richmond, 3400 Brook
Rd., Richmond, VA 23227-4536, (804)204-1226

I

I Care Grace Intl. **[2437]**, 400 Riverside Ave., Char-
lottesville, VA 22902, (434)973-6889
I Have a Dream Found. **[2277]**, 330 7th Ave., 20th
Fl., New York, NY 10001, (212)293-5480
IAHI, the Owners' Assn. **[443]**, 3 Ravinia Dr., Ste.
100, Atlanta, GA 30346, (770)604-5555
Ibsen Soc. of Am. **[1732]**, c/o Prof. Arne Lunde,
Treas., Scandinavian Sect., UCLA, 212 Royce
Hall, Los Angeles, CA 90095
Ichthyology
Intl. Assn. of Astacology **[1488]**
IDEAlliance - Intl. Digital Enterprise Alliance **[407]**,
1421 Prince St., Ste. 230, Alexandria, VA 22314-
2805, (703)837-1070
Idoma Assn. USA **[2812]**, PO Box 7211342,
Houston, TX 77272-1342
Iemanya Oceanica **[1240]**, 23293 Ventura Blvd.,
Woodland Hills, CA 91364, (818)224-4250
IFCA Intl. **[2900]**, PO Box 810, Grandville, MI 49468-
0810, (616)531-1840
Imam Mahdi Assn. of Marjaeya **[3022]**, 835 Mason
St., Dearborn, MI 48124, (313)303-9280
Immigration
Iranian Alliances Across Borders **[2796]**

In Our Own Quiet Way **[2265]**, 110 S Main St., Lindon, UT 84042, (801)669-7583
Incentive Mfrs. and Representatives Alliance **[576]**,
1601 N Bond St., Ste. 303, Naperville, IL 60563,
(630)369-7786
Independent Armored Car Operators Assn. **[815]**,
8000 Res. Forest Dr., Ste. 115-155, The
Woodlands, TX 77382-1504, (281)292-8208
Independent Arts and Media **[1709]**, PO Box
420442, San Francisco, CA 94142, (415)738-4975
Independent Automotive Damage Appraisers Assn.
[51], PO Box 12291, Columbus, GA 31917-2291,
(800)369-4232
Independent Bakers Assn. **[106]**, PO Box 3731,
Washington, DC 20007, (202)333-8190
Independent Bd. for Presbyterian Foreign Missions
[3025], PO Box 1346, Blue Bell, PA 19422-0435,
(610)279-0952
Independent Film and TV Alliance **[322]**, 10850
Wilshire Blvd., 9th Fl., Los Angeles, CA 90024-
4321, (310)446-1000
Independent Lab. Distributors Assn. **[791]**, PO Box
1464, Fairplay, CO 80440, (719)836-9091
Independent Lubricant Mfrs. Assn. **[644]**, 400 N
Columbus St., Ste. 201, Alexandria, VA 22314-
2264, (703)684-5574
Independent Order of Svithiod **[2822]**, 5518 W
Lawrence Ave., Chicago, IL 60630, (773)736-1191
Independent Order of Vikings **[2795]**, 5250 S Sixth
St., PO Box 5147, Springfield, IL 62705-5147,
(877)241-6006
Independent Organic Inspectors Assn. **[1174]**, PO
Box 6, Broadus, MT 59317-0006, (406)436-2031
Independent Pet and Animal Trans. Assn. Intl. **[653]**,
745 Winding Trail, Holly Lake Ranch, TX 75765,
(903)769-2267
Independent Photo Imagers **[666]**, 2518 Anthem Vil-
lage Dr., Ste. 100, Henderson, NV 89052,
(702)617-1141
Independent Time and Labor Mgt. Assn. **[861]**, c/o
Michael Hoover, Sec.-Treas., 2049 Stout Dr., Ste.
A-1, Warminster, PA 18974, (215)443-8720
India
Ensaaf **[2748]**
Global Helps Network **[2005]**
Indian
Assn. of Indian Muslims of Am. **[2791]**
Leuva Patidar Samaj of USA **[1780]**
Network of Indian Professionals **[2792]**
U.S. Indian Amer. Chamber of Commerce **[3496]**
Uttaranchal Assn. of North Am. **[1781]**
United Indian Missions Intl. **[3014]**
Indian Arts and Crafts Assn. **[1830]**, 4010 Carlisle
Blvd. NE, Ste. C, Albuquerque, NM 87107,
(505)265-9149
Indiana Limestone Inst. of Am. **[840]**, 400 Stone City
Bank Bldg., Bedford, IN 47421, (812)275-4426
Indigenous Peoples
World Sound Healing Org. **[2155]**
Indigo Threads **[2024]**, PO Box 401, La Quinta, CA
92247, (760)564-2679
Indonesia
Alliance for Tompotika Conservation **[1003]**
Indus. Asset Mgt. Coun. **[744]**, 6625 The Corners
Pkwy., Ste. 200, Norcross, GA 30092, (770)325-
3461
Indus. Auctioneers Assn. **[64]**, 3213 Ayr Ln.,
Dresher, PA 19025, (215)366-5450
Industrial Design
Alliance for Sustainable Built Environments **[133]**
Green Builder Coalition **[146]**
Industrial Development
ClimateTalk Alliance **[1392]**
Industrial Education
Assn. for sTem Teacher Educ. **[1631]**
Assn. of Tech., Mgt. and Applied Engg. **[1632]**
Intl. Tech. Educ. Assn. l Coun. on Tech. Teacher
Educ. **[1633]**
Industrial Engineering
SOLE - The Intl. Soc. of Logistics **[1489]**
Industrial Equipment
Amer. Bearing Mfrs. Assn. **[456]**
Amer. Gear Mfrs. Assn. **[457]**
Amer. Mold Builders Assn. **[458]**
Assoc. Wire Rope Fabricators **[459]**

Assn. of Ingersoll-Rand Distributors **[460]**
Contractors Pump Bur. **[461]**
Conveyor Equip. Mfrs. Assn. **[462]**
Intl. Assn. of Elevator Consultants **[463]**
MAPI **[464]**
Mech. Power Transmission Assn. **[465]**
Natl. Assn. of Hose and Accessories Distribution
[466]
Power-Motion Tech. Representatives Assn. **[467]**
Soc. of Professional Rope Access Technicians
[468]
Wood Machinery Mfrs. of Am. **[469]**
Antique Caterpillar Machinery Owners Club **[3211]**
Indus. Auctioneers Assn. **[64]**
Intl. Soc. for Concrete Pavements **[148]**
Indus. Fasteners Inst. **[414]**, 6363 Oak Tree Blvd.,
Independence, OH 44131, (216)241-1482
Indus. Found. of Am. **[297]**, 179 Enterprise Pkwy.,
Ste. 200, Boerne, TX 78006, (830)249-7899
Industrial Security
Cmpt. Security Inst. **[470]**
Infectious Diseases
Assn. for Professionals in Infection Control and
Epidemiology **[2471]**
Global Solutions for Infectious Diseases **[2472]**
Infectious Diseases Soc. of Am. **[2473]**
Natl. Found. for Infectious Diseases **[2474]**
Infectious Diseases Soc. of Am. **[2473]**, 1300 Wilson
Blvd., Ste. 300, Arlington, VA 22209, (703)299-
0200
Information Management
AIIM - The Enterprise Content Mgt. Assn. **[471]**
Assn. for Fed. Info. Resources Mgt. **[1305]**
Assn. of Public Data Users **[1490]**
Natl. Public Records Res. Assn. **[472]**
The Open Gp. **[473]**
Special Interest Gp. on Info. Retrieval **[1491]**
Supply-Chain Coun. **[474]**
World Org. of Webmasters **[475]**
Global Tech. Distribution Coun. **[848]**
Natl. Freedom of Info. Coalition **[2731]**
Nuclear Info. Tech. Strategic Leadership **[1508]**
Informed Families Educ. Center l Natl. Family
Partnership **[2241]**, 2490 Coral Way, Ste. 501,
Miami, FL 33145, (305)856-4886
Inland Bird Banding Assn. **[1513]**, 1833 S Winfield
Dr., Tiffin, OH 44883
Inland Marine Underwriters Assn. **[487]**, 14 Wall St.,
8th Fl., New York, NY 10005, (212)233-0550
Inland Rivers Ports and Terminals **[594]**, 316 Bd. of
Trade Pl., New Orleans, LA 70130, (504)585-0715
Innovation
ClimateTalk Alliance **[1392]**
Innovation: Africa **[1394]**
Innovations for Poverty Action **[2613]**
mHealth Alliance **[2510]**
Innovation: Africa **[1394]**, 520 8th Ave., 4th Fl., New
York, NY 10018, (212)710-6430
Innovation Norway - U.S. **[3482]**, 655 3rd Ave., Rm.
1810, New York, NY 10017-9111, (212)885-9700
Innovations for Poverty Action **[2613]**, 101 Whitney
Ave., New Haven, CT 06510, (203)772-2216
Insects
Bee Native **[961]**
The Intl. Lepidoptera Survey **[1472]**
Inspectors
Assn. of Constr. Inspectors **[476]**
Examination Bd. of Professional Home Inspectors
[477]
Healthcare Laundry Accreditation Coun. **[537]**
Inst. for Certification of Computing Professionals
[1595], 2400 E Devon Ave., Ste. 281, Des Plaines,
IL 60018-4610, (847)299-4227
Inst. of Certified Bus. Counselors **[166]**, 18831 Wil-
lamette Dr., West Linn, OR 97068, (877)422-2674
Inst. of Certified Professional Managers **[562]**,
James Madison Univ., MSC 5504, Harrisonburg,
VA 22807, (540)568-3247
Inst. of Cultural Affairs **[2108]**, 4750 N Sheridan Rd.,
Chicago, IL 60640, (773)769-6363
Inst. for the Development of the Harmonious Human
Being **[2109]**, PO Box 370, Nevada City, CA
95959, (530)271-2239
Inst. of Environmental Sciences and Tech. **[1523]**,
2340 S Arlington Heights Rd., Ste. 100, Arlington
Heights, IL 60005-4516, (847)981-0100

A star before a book entry number signifies that the name is not listed separately, but is mentioned within the entry.

Inst. for Food Safety and Hea. **[363]**, 6502 S Archer Rd., Summit, IL 60501-1957, (708)563-1576

Inst. of Gen. Semantics **[1853]**, 3000 A Landers St., Fort Worth, TX 76107, (817)922-9950

Inst. of Hazardous Materials Mgt. **[1110]**, 11900 Parklawn Dr., Ste. 450, Rockville, MD 20852-2624, (301)984-8969

Inst. for Hea. and Productivity Mgt. **[563]**, 17470 N Pacesetter Way, Scottsdale, AZ 85255, (480)305-2100

Inst. of Internal Auditors **[6]**, 247 Maitland Ave., Altamonte Springs, FL 32701-4907, (407)937-1100

Inst. of Mathematical Statistics **[1541]**, PO Box 22718, Beachwood, OH 44122, (216)295-2340

Inst. of Nautical Archaeology **[1404]**, PO Drawer HG, College Station, TX 77841-5137, (979)845-6694

Inst. of Nuclear Materials Mgt. **[1506]**, 111 Deer Lake Rd., Ste. 100, Deerfield, IL 60015, (847)480-9573

Inst. for Operations Res. and the Mgt. Sciences **[564]**, 7240 Parkway. Dr., Ste. 300, Hanover, MD 21076-1310, (443)757-3500

Inst. of Packaging Professionals **[1514]**, 1833 Centre Point Cir., Ste. 123, Naperville, IL 60563, (630)544-5050

Inst. for Policy Stud. **[2733]**, 1112 16th St. NW, Ste. 600, Washington, DC 20036, (202)234-9382

Inst. for Polyacrylate Absorbents **[185]**, 1850 M St. NW, Ste. 700, Washington, DC 20036-5810, (202)721-4154

Inst. of Real Estate Mgt. **[745]**, 430 N Michigan Ave., Chicago, IL 60611, (312)329-6000

Inst. on Religion in an Age of Sci. **[3034]**, 744 DuBois Dr., Baton Rouge, LA 70808

Institute for Res. in Modern History of Poland **[★1846]**

Inst. for Retired Professionals **[2203]**, New School Univ., 66 W 12th St., Rm. 502, New York, NY 10011, (212)229-5682

Inst. of Shortening and Edible Oils **[627]**, 1319 F St. NW, Ste. 600, Washington, DC 20004, (202)783-7960

Inst. for Southern Stud. **[1703]**, PO Box 531, Durham, NC 27702, (919)419-8311

Inst. for Supply Mgt. **[728]**, PO Box 22160, Tempe, AZ 85285-2160, (480)752-6276

Inst. of Trans. Engineers **[1551]**, 1627 Eye St. NW, Ste. 600, Washington, DC 20006, (202)785-0060

Inst. for Tribal Environmental Professionals **[2808]**, PO Box 15004, Flagstaff, AZ 86011, (928)523-9555

Institutional Locksmiths' Assn. **[260]**, PO Box 9560, Naperville, IL 60567-9560

Instructional Media

ACUTA: The Assn. for Communications Tech. Professionals in Higher Educ. **[1634]**

Instructional Technology

Reasoning Mind **[1660]**

Instrumentation

Natl. Assn. for Civil War Brass Music **[1825]**

Insurance

Amer. Assn. for Long-Term Care Insurance **[478]**

Amer. Insurance Marketing and Sales Soc. **[479]**

Assn. of Average Adjusters of the U.S. **[480]**

Assn. of Defense Trial Attorneys **[1306]**

Assn. of Governmental Risk Pools **[1307]**

Assn. of Home Off. Underwriters **[481]**

Assn. of Life Insurance Counsel **[1308]**

Bank Insurance and Securities Assn. **[482]**

Crop Insurance and Reinsurance Bur. **[483]**

Degree of Honor Protective Assn. **[2793]**

Equitable Reserve Assn. **[2794]**

Fed. of Defense and Corporate Counsel **[1309]**

Fraternal Field Managers' Assn. **[484]**

GAMA Intl. **[485]**

Gamma Iota Sigma **[3532]**

Gp. Underwriters Assn. of Am. **[486]**

Independent Order of Vikings **[2795]**

Inland Marine Underwriters Assn. **[487]**

Insurance Brokers and Agents of the West **[488]**

Insurance Loss Control Assn. **[489]**

Insurance Regulatory Examiners Soc. **[490]**

Insurance Soc. of New York **[491]**

Life Insurance Settlement Assn. **[492]**

Natl. African-American Insurance Assn. **[493]**

Natl. Assn. of Catastrophe Adjusters **[494]**

Natl. Assn. for Fixed Annuities **[495]**

Natl. Assn. of Fraternal Insurance Counsellors **[496]**

Natl. Assn. of Insurance Commissioners **[1310]**

Natl. Assn. of Surety Bond Producers **[497]**

Natl. Coun. of Self-Insurers **[498]**

Natl. Risk Retention Assn. **[499]**

Natl. Soc. of Insurance Premium Auditors **[500]**

Natl. Soc. of Professional Insurance Investigators **[501]**

Professional Risk Managers' Intl. Assn. **[502]**

Public Agency Risk Managers Assn. **[1311]**

Reinsurance Assn. of Am. **[503]**

Soc. of Insurance Trainers and Educators **[1635]**

Women in Insurance and Financial Services **[504]**

Insurance Brokers and Agents of the West **[488]**, 7041 Koll Center Pkwy., Ste. 290, Pleasanton, CA 94566-3128, (925)426-3310

Insurance Loss Control Assn. **[489]**, 118 Treetops Dr., Lancaster, PA 17601-1790, (717)898-9056

Insurance Regulatory Examiners Soc. **[490]**, 1821 Univ. Ave. W, Ste. S256, St. Paul, MN 55104, (651)917-6250

Insurance Soc. of New York **[491]**, St. John's Univ., 8000 Utopia Pkwy., Jamaica, NY 11439, (718)990-6653

Integrity USA **[2936]**, 620 Park Ave., No. 311, Rochester, NY 14607-2943, (585)360-4512

Intellectual Property

Amer. Intellectual Property Law Assn. **[1312]**

Copyright Alliance **[1313]**

Los Angeles Copyright Soc. **[1314]**

Intelligent Trans. Soc. of Am. **[872]**, 1100 17th St. NW, Ste. 1200, Washington, DC 20036, (202)484-4847

Inter-American Bar Assn. **[1324]**, 1211 Connecticut Ave. NW, Ste. 202, Washington, DC 20036, (202)466-5944

Inter-American Defense Bd. **[2635]**, 2600 NW 16th St., Washington, DC 20441, (202)939-6041

Inter-American Found. **[2740]**, 901 N Stuart St., 10th Fl., Balston, Arlington, VA 22203-1821, (703)306-4301

Inter-American Hea. Alliance **[2438]**, 2301 Vanderbilt Pl., PMB 351804, Nashville, TN 37235, (703)725-9320

Inter Amer. Press Assn. **[2625]**, Jules Dubois Bldg., 1801 SW 3rd Ave., Miami, FL 33129, (305)634-2465

Inter-Faith Community Services **[2167]**, 3370 S Irving St., Englewood, CO 80110-1816, (303)789-0501

Inter-Industry Conf. on Auto Collision Repair **[97]**, 5125 Trillium Blvd., Hoffman Estates, IL 60192-3600, (847)590-1198

Inter Varsity Christian Fellowship **[3001]**, PO Box 7895, Madison, WI 53707-7895, (608)274-9001

Intercollegiate Assn. of Amateur Athletes of Am. **[3401]**, Eastern Coll. Athletic Conf., PO Box 3, Centerville, MA 02632, (508)771-5060

InterCollegiate Outing Club Assn. **[3426]**, c/o Don Wade, Direct Mail Chair, 35-41 72 St., Jackson Heights, NY 11372

Intercollegiate Rowing Assn. **[3377]**, Eastern Coll. Athletic Conf., 1311 Craigville Beach Rd., Centerville, MA 02632-4129, (508)771-5060

Intercultural

Haiti Cultural Exchange **[1748]**

Interdisciplinary Studies

Soc. of Educators and Scholars **[1782]**

Interfaith

Abrahamic Alliance Intl. **[2945]**

Monks Without Borders **[2946]**

Interior Design

Amer. Soc. of Interior Designers **[505]**

Carpet and Rug Inst. **[506]**

Interior Redesign Indus. Specialists **[507]**

Intl. Assn. of Home Staging Professionals **[508]**

Intl. Furnishings and Design Assn. **[509]**

Intl. Interior Design Assn. **[510]**

Natl. Candle Assn. **[511]**

Natl. Kitchen and Bath Assn. **[512]**

Paint and Decorating Retailers Assn. **[513]**

Wallcoverings Assn. **[514]**

Window Coverings Assn. of Am. **[515]**

Decorative Plumbing and Hardware Assn. **[678]**

Interior Redesign Indus. Specialists **[507]**, 1100-H Brandywine Blvd., Zanesville, OH 43701-7303, (740)450-1330

Intermed Intl. **[2506]**, 125-28 Queens Blvd., Ste. 538, Kew Gardens, NY 11415, (212)327-4940

Intl. Acad. of Trial Lawyers **[1273]**, 5841 Cedar Lake Rd., Ste. 204, Minneapolis, MN 55416-5657, (952)546-2364

Intl. Action **[2266]**, 819 L St. SE, Washington, DC 20003, (202)488-0735

International Affairs

EastWest Inst. **[2670]**

Friends of Taiwan Intl. **[2679]**

Idoma Assn. USA **[2812]**

Intl. Assn. of Space Entrepreneurs **[30]**

Intl. Coun. for Middle East Stud. **[2701]**

Irish Amer. Unity Conf. **[2688]**

United Burundian-American Community Assn. **[2680]**

Intl. Agro Alliance **[1217]**, 173 NW 89th St., Miami, FL 33150, (877)292-3921

Intl. Aid **[2191]**, 17011 Hickory St., Spring Lake, MI 49456-9712, (616)846-7490

Intl. Air Filtration Certifiers Assn. **[432]**, 129 S Gallatin, Liberty, MO 64068, (888)679-1904

Intl. Aloe Sci. Coun. **[424]**, 8630 Fenton St., Ste. 918, Silver Spring, MD 20910, (301)588-2420

Intl. Amphicar Owners Club **[3110]**, c/o Ina Cabanas, Treas., 11 Pemberton St., Pemberton, NJ 08068-1111

Intl. Amusement and Leisure Defense Assn. **[761]**, PO Box 4563, Louisville, KY 40204, (502)473-0956

Intl. Assn. of Addictions and Offender Counselors **[2044]**, Rider Univ., Dept. of Graduate Educ., Leadership, and Counseling, Memorial 202, 2083 Lawrenceville Rd., Lawrenceville, NJ 08648, (800)347-6647

Intl. Assn. of Amusement Parks and Attractions **[309]**, 1448 Duke St., Alexandria, VA 22314, (703)836-4800

Intl. Assn. of Arson Investigators **[1297]**, 2111 Baldwin Ave., Ste. 203, Crofton, MD 21114, (410)451-3473

Intl. Assn. of Astacology **[1488]**, c/o Antonio Garza de Yta, Sec., Auburn Univ., Dept. of Fisheries and Allied Aquaculture, 203 Swingle Hall, Auburn University, AL 36849-5419, (334)844-4786

Intl. Assn. for Bear Res. and Mgt. **[1241]**, Univ. of Tennessee, USGS-SAFL, 274 Ellington Hall, Knoxville, TN 37996, (865)974-0200

Intl. Assn. of Bomb Technicians and Investigators **[1474]**, 1120 Intl. Pkwy., Ste. 129, Goldvein, VA 22720-0160, (540)752-4533

Intl. Assn. of Certified Surveillance Professionals **[803]**, 4333 Bell Rd., Apt. No. 1210, Newburgh, IN 47630, (812)472-1744

Intl. Assn. for Cmpt. Info. Systems **[1596]**, c/o Richard McCarthy, VP, Quinnipiac Univ., School of Bus., 275 Mt. Carmel Ave., Hamden, CT 06518

Intl. Assn. for Correctional and Forensic Psychology **[2050]**, c/o Mr. David Randall, Sec.-Treas., PO Box 7642, Wilmington, NC 28406

Intl. Assn. of Correctional Training Personnel **[2051]**, PO Box 473254, Aurora, CO 80047, (719)738-9969

Intl. Assn. of Credit Portfolio Managers **[245]**, 360 Madison Ave., 17th Fl., New York, NY 10017-7111, (646)289-5430

Intl. Assn. of Dive Rescue Specialists **[544]**, PO Box 877, Vero Beach, FL 32961, (970)482-1562

Intl. Assn. of Duncan Certified Ceramic Teachers **[3146]**, 510 Salem St., Risingsun, OH 43457, (419)457-7281

Intl. Assn. of Elecl. Inspectors **[271]**, PO Box 830848, Richardson, TX 75083-0848, (972)235-1455

Intl. Assn. of Elevator Consultants **[463]**, 15600 NE 8th St., Ste. B1, PMB 153, Bellevue, WA 98008, (425)732-3328

Intl. Assn. of EMTs and Paramedics **[3445]**, 159 Burgin Pkwy., Quincy, MA 02169, (617)376-0220

Intl. Assn. of Gay and Lesbian Martial Artists **[3360]**, PO Box 590601, San Francisco, CA 94159-0601, (610)940-1434

Intl. Assn. of Geophysical Contractors **[645]**, 1225 N Loop West, Ste. 220, Houston, TX 77008-1761, (713)957-8080

Intl. Assn. of Golf Administrators **[3336]**, 1974 Sproul Rd., Ste. 400, Broomall, PA 19008, (610)687-2340

Intl. Assn. for Healthcare Security and Safety **[2469]**, PO Box 5038, Glendale Heights, IL 60139, (630)529-3913

Intl. Assn. of Hispanic Meeting Professionals **[612]**, 2600 S Shore Blvd., Ste. 300, League City, TX 77573, (281)245-3330

International Assn. of Holiday Inns **[★443]**

Intl. Assn. of Home Staging Professionals **[508]**, 2420 Sand Creek Rd. C-1, No. 263, Brentwood, CA 94513, (800)392-7161

Intl. Assn. of Ice Cream Distributors and Vendors **[900]**, 5024-R Campbell Blvd., Baltimore, MD 21236, (410)931-8100

International Assn. of Ice Cream Vendors **[★900]**

Intl. Assn. of Jewish Genealogical Societies **[3064]**, c/o Paul Silverstone, Treas., PO Box 3624, Cherry Hill, NJ 08034-0556

Intl. Assn. for Landscape Ecology I U.S. Regional Assn. **[1054]**, Portland State Univ., PO Box 751, Portland, OR 97207, (503)725-2494

Intl. Assn. of Law Enforcement Planners **[1287]**, PO Box 11437, Torrance, CA 90510-1437, (310)225-5148

Intl. Assn. of Ministers Wives and Ministers Widows **[2908]**, 105 River Knoll, Macon, GA 31211, (478)743-5126

Intl. Assn. of Professional Security Consultants **[804]**, 575 Market St., Ste. 2125, San Francisco, CA 94105, (415)536-0288

Intl. Assn. of R.S. Prussia Collectors **[3153]**, PO Box 624, Mayfield, KY 42066

Intl. Assn. of Security and Investigative Regulators **[523]**, PO Box 93, Waterloo, IA 50704, (888)354-2747

Intl. Assn. of Silver Art Collectors **[3154]**, PO Box 3987, Clarksville, TN 37043

Intl. Assn. of Skateboard Companies **[3373]**, 22431 Antonio Pkwy., Ste. B160-412, Rancho Santa Margarita, CA 92688, (949)455-1112

Intl. Assn. for Soc. and Natural Resources **[1167]**, Penn State, Dept. of Agricultural Economics and Rural Sociology, 114 Armsby Bldg., University Park, PA 16802, (814)863-8643

Intl. Assn. of Space Entrepreneurs **[30]**, 16 First Ave., Nyack, NY 10960

Intl. Assn. for Truancy and Dropout Prevention **[1608]**, c/o Henrietta Pryor, Sec., 10602 Holly Springs, Houston, TX 77042, (713)802-4745

Intl. Assn. of Wildland Fire **[1092]**, 1418 Washburn St., Missoula, MT 59801, (406)531-8264

Intl. Assn. for Women's Mental Hea. **[2551]**, 8213 Lakenheath Way, Potomac, MD 20854, (301)983-6282

Intl. Assn. of Workforce Professionals **[1291]**, 1801 Louisville Rd., Frankfort, KY 40601, (502)223-4459

Intl. Aviation Womens Assn. **[103]**, PO Box 1088, Edgewater, MD 21037, (410)571-1990

The Intl. Bengal Cat Soc. **[965]**, PO Box 1894, Lake Dallas, TX 75065-1894

Intl. Betta Cong. **[3197]**, c/o Steve Van Camp, Membership Chm./Sec., 923 Wadsworth St., Syracuse, NY 13208, (315)454-4792

Intl. Biometric Soc. **[1542]**, 1444 I St. NW, Ste. 700, Washington, DC 20005, (202)712-9049

Intl. Biometric Soc., Western North Amer. Region **[1543]**, 1730 Minor Ave., Ste. 1900, Cancer Res. and Biostatistics, Seattle, WA 98101-1468

Intl. Bird Rescue Res. Center **[1242]**, San Francisco Oiled Wildlife Care and Educ. Center, 4369 Cordelia Rd., Fairfield, CA 94534, (707)207-0380

International Bd. of Electrologist Certification **[★2401]**

Intl. Boer Goat Assn. **[1107]**, PO Box 1045, Whitewright, TX 75491, (903)364-5735

Intl. Bowling Pro Shop and Instructors Assn. **[121]**, PO Box 6574, Arlington, TX 76005-6574, (817)649-0079

Intl. Boxing Fed. **[3296]**, 899 Mountain Ave., Ste. 2C, Springfield, NJ 07081, (973)564-8046

Intl. Brangus Breeders Assn. **[984]**, 5750 Epsilon, San Antonio, TX 78249, (210)696-4343

Intl. Brecht Soc. **[1733]**, Webster Univ., 470 E Lockwood, St. Louis, MO 63119, (314)968-6900

Intl. Brotherhood of Motorcycle Campers **[3367]**, PO Box 375, Helper, UT 84526, (805)278-9244

Intl. Bulb Soc. **[1430]**, PO Box 336, Sanger, CA 93657-0336

Intl. Bus. Brokers Assn. **[746]**, 401 N Michigan Ave., Ste. 2200, Chicago, IL 60611-4267, (888)686-4222

Intl. Carnival Glass Assn. **[3209]**, c/o Lee Markley, Sec., Box 306, Mentone, IN 46539, (574)353-7678

Intl. Cast Polymer Assn. **[147]**, 1010 N Glebe Rd., Ste. 450, Arlington, VA 22201, (703)525-0320

Intl. Catholic Deaf Assn. U.S. Sect. **[2868]**, 7202 Buchanan St., Landover Hills, MD 20784-2236, (301)429-0697

Intl. CBX Owners Assn. **[3219]**, PO Box 546, Knox, PA 16232, (717)697-5559

Intl. Center for Assault Prevention **[2072]**, 107 Gilbreth Pkwy., Ste. 200, Mullica Hill, NJ 08062, (856)582-7000

Intl. Center for Journalists **[695]**, 1616 H St. NW, 3rd Fl., Washington, DC 20006, (202)737-3700

Intl. Center of Medieval Art **[1809]**, The Cloisters, Ft. Tryon Park, New York, NY 10040, (212)928-1146

Intl. Center for Res. on Women **[2647]**, 1120 20th St. NW, Ste. 500 N, Washington, DC 20036, (202)797-0007

Intl. Center for the Solution of Environmental Problems **[1063]**, 5120 Woodway Dr., Ste. 8009, Houston, TX 77056-1788, (713)527-8711

Intl. Center for Transitional Justice **[2666]**, 5 Hanover Sq., 24th Fl., New York, NY 10004, (917)637-3800

International Center for Youth Studies **[★2276]**

Intl. Children Assistance Network **[1968]**, PO Box 5863, Santa Clara, CA 95056, (408)509-8788

Intl. Chinese Boxing Assn. **[3297]**, 3308 Preston Rd., Ste. 350-356, Plano, TX 75093

Intl. Chiropractors Assn. **[2344]**, 6400 Arlington Blvd., Ste. 800, Falls Church, VA 22042, (703)528-5000

Intl. Cinema Tech. Assn. **[323]**, 770 Broadway, 7th Fl., New York, NY 10003-9522, (212)493-4097

Intl. Clarinet Assn. **[1821]**, PO Box 237, Longmont, CO 80502, (405)651-6064

Intl. Clubmakers' Guild **[830]**, 95 Washington St., Ste. 104-335, Canton, MA 02021

Intl. Coalition for Autism and All Abilities **[2318]**, 200 Crestwood Plz., St. Louis, MO 63126

Intl. Coalition of Sites of Conscience **[1765]**, 333 7th Ave., 14th Fl., New York, NY 10001-5108, (646)755-6180

Intl. Coll. of Dentists **[2382]**, 1010 Rockville Pike, Ste. 510, Rockville, MD 20852-1482, (240)403-7246

Intl. Colored Appaloosa Assn. **[1130]**, PO Box 99, Shipshewana, IN 46565, (574)238-4280

Intl. Compressor Remanufacturers Assn. **[433]**, 1505 Carthage Rd., Lumberton, NC 28358, (910)301-7060

Intl. Cmpt. Music Assn. **[623]**, 1819 Polk St., Ste. 330, San Francisco, CA 94109

Intl. Concierge and Lifestyle Mgt. Assn. **[444]**, 3650 Rogers Rd., No. 328, Wake Forest, NC 27587, (804)368-1667

Intl. Concrete Repair Inst. **[198]**, 10600 W Higgins Rd., Ste. 607, Rosemont, IL 60018, (847)827-0830

Intl. Conf. of Police Chaplains **[2888]**, PO Box 5590, Destin, FL 32540-5590, (850)654-9736

Intl. Cong. of Maritime Museums **[1816]**, 329 High St., Mystic, CT 06355

Intl. Consortium on Governmental Financial Mgt. **[334]**, PO Box 1077, St. Michaels, MD 21663, (410)745-8570

International Cooperation

Chinese Amer. Cooperation Coun. **[1783]**

Amer. Brazilian Cultural Exchange **[1746]**

Amer. MidEast Leadership Network **[2677]**

Building Bridges: Middle East-US **[1642]**

Friends of Taiwan Intl. **[2679]**

Global China Connection **[1643]**

Intl. Assn. of Space Entrepreneurs **[30]**

Ishmael and Isaac **[2702]**

United Burundian-American Community Assn. **[2680]**

U.S.-Japan Coun. **[2681]**

Intl. Copper Assn. **[1497]**, 260 Madison Ave., 16th Fl., New York, NY 10016-2401, (212)251-7240

Intl. Cotton Advisory Comm. **[995]**, 1629 K St. NW, Ste. 702, Washington, DC 20006-1636, (202)463-6660

Intl. Coun. for Middle East Stud. **[2701]**, 1055 Thomas Jefferson St. NW, Ste. M100, Washington, DC 20009, (202)315-8680

Intl. Coun. on Nanotechnology **[1440]**, PO Box 1892, Houston, TX 77251, (713)348-8210

Intl. Coun. for Small Bus. **[823]**, GWU School of Bus., 2201 G St. NW, Funger Hall, Ste. 315, Washington, DC 20052

Intl. Counter-Terrorism Officers Assn. **[2750]**, PO Box 580009, Flushing, NY 11358, (212)564-5048

Intl. Crosby Circle **[3582]**, 5608 N 34th St., Arlington, VA 22207, (703)241-5608

Intl. Curly Horse Org. **[1131]**, HC 31 Box 102A, Williamsburg, NM 87942, (575)740-4159

Intl. Customer Ser. Assn. **[813]**, 1110 South Ave., Ste. No. 50, Staten Island, NY 10314, (374)273-1303

International Development

Aid to Artisans **[2118]**

Consultative Gp. to Assist the Poor **[2671]**

Counterpart - U.S. Off. **[2672]**

Development Gp. for Alternative Policies **[2673]**

Financial Services Volunteer Corps **[2674]**

Glocal Ventures **[2119]**

Haiti Works! **[2120]**

Heifer Intl. **[2121]**

Intl. Professional Partnerships for Sierra Leone **[2675]**

New Forests Proj. **[2122]**

TechnoServe **[2676]**

Fellowship Intl. Mission **[2998]**

Global China Connection **[1643]**

Hea. Horizons Intl. **[2500]**

Idoma Assn. USA **[2812]**

Intl. Agro Alliance **[1217]**

Natl. Student Campaign Against Hunger and Homelessness **[2117]**

Reach Across **[3011]**

Intl. Downtown Assn. **[167]**, 1025 Thomas Jefferson St. NW, Ste. 500W, Washington, DC 20007, (202)393-6801

Intl. Entertainment Buyers Assn. **[310]**, 9 Music Sq. W, Nashville, TN 37203, (615)251-9000

International Exchange

Community Colleges for Intl. Development **[1636]**

Coun. on Intl. Educational Exchange USA **[1637]**

Coun. for Intl. Exchange of Scholars I Inst. of Intl. Educ. **[1638]**

Fulbright Assn. **[1639]**

Natl. Registration Center for Stud. Abroad **[1640]**

Amer. Turkish Friendship Coun. **[2678]**

U.S.-Japan Coun. **[2681]**

Intl. Executive Housekeepers Assn. **[553]**, 1001 Eastwind Dr., Ste. 301, Westerville, OH 43081-3361, (614)895-7166

Intl. Executive Ser. Corps **[168]**, 1900 M St. NW, Ste. 500, Washington, DC 20036, (202)589-2600

Intl. Experiential Marketing Assn. **[601]**, 550 15th St., Ste. 31, San Francisco, CA 94103, (415)355-1586

Intl. Fac. Mgt. Assn. **[714]**, 1 E Greenway Plz., Ste. 1100, Houston, TX 77046-0104, (713)623-4362

Intl. Factoring Assn. **[335]**, 2665 Shell Beach Rd., Ste. 3, Pismo Beach, CA 93449-1778, (805)773-0011

Intl. Fainting Goat Assn. **[1108]**, 1039 State Rte. 168, Darlington, PA 16115, (724)843-2084

Intl. Fed. of Accountants **[7]**, 545 5th Ave., 14th Fl., New York, NY 10017, (212)286-9344

Intl. Fed. of Leather Guilds **[539]**, 2264 Logan Dr., New Palestine, IN 46163, (317)861-9711

Intl. Fed. of Postcard Dealers **[3239]**, PO Box 399, Neosho, MO 64850

Intl. Fed. of Rabbis **[2954]**, 5600 Wisconsin Ave., No. 1107, Chevy Chase, MD 20815

Intl. Fed. for Secular Humanistic Judaism **[2944]**, 1777 T St. NW, Washington, DC 20009, (202)248-4880

Intl. Fed. of Sleddog Sports **[3323]**, c/o Sally O'Sullivan Bair, Sec. Gen., 8554 Gateway Cir., Monticello, MN 55362, (763)295-5465

Intl. Female Boxers Assn. **[3298]**, 701 N Green Valley Pkwy., Ste. 200, Henderson, NV 89074, (310)428-1403

Intl. Fire Buff Associates **[3192]**, 11017 N Redwood Tree Ct., Mequon, WI 53092

Intl. Fluid Power Soc. **[1477]**, PO Box 1420, Cherry Hill, NJ 08034-0054, (856)489-8983

Intl. Flying Dutchman Class Assn. of the U.S. **[3274]**, c/o Jonathan Clapp, Sec.-Treas., PO Box 223, Amherst, MA 01004-0223, (978)660-4497

A star before a book entry number signifies that the name is not listed separately, but is mentioned within the entry.

Intl. Flying Farmers **[1083]**, PO Box 309, Mansfield, IL 61854, (217)489-9300

Intl. Food and Agribusiness Mgt. Assn. **[364]**, PO Box 14145, College Station, TX 77841-4145, (979)845-2118

Intl. Food Ser. Executive's Assn. **[374]**, 4955 Miller St., Ste. 107, Wheat Ridge, CO 80033, (800)893-5499

Intl. Foodservice Mfrs. Assn. | Intl. Gold and Silver Plate Soc. **[2772]**, 2 Prudential Plz., 180 N Stetson Ave., Ste. 4400, Chicago, IL 60601-6766, (312)540-4400

Intl. Found. of Employee Benefit Plans **[292]**, PO Box 69, Brookfield, WI 53008-0069, (262)786-6700

Intl. Found. for Telemetering **[1547]**, 5665 Oberlin Dr., Ste. 200, San Diego, CA 92121, (858)225-4164

Intl. Friesian Show Horse Assn. **[1132]**, PO Box 535, Santa Ynez, CA 93460, (805)448-3027

Intl. Furnishings and Design Assn. **[509]**, 150 S Warner Rd., Ste. 156, King of Prussia, PA 19406, (610)535-6422

Intl. Furniture Trans. and Logistics Coun. **[816]**, 282 N Ridge Rd., Brooklyn, MI 49230, (517)467-9355

Intl. Galapagos Tour Operators Assn. **[3505]**, PO Box 1713, Lolo, MT 59847

Intl. Green Energy Coun. **[1395]**, 1701 Pennsylvania Ave. NW, Ste. 300, Washington, DC 20006, (202)349-7138

Intl. Guild of Miniature Artisans **[3166]**, PO Box 629, Freedom, CA 95019-0629, (831)724-7974

Intl. Hajji Baba Soc. **[1710]**, c/o Kelvin Webb, Treas., 1105 D St. SE, Washington, DC 20003

Intl. Handgun Metallic Silhouette Assn. **[3381]**, c/o Lorene Thompson, PO Box 95690, South Jordan, UT 84095-5690, (801)733-8423

Intl. Hard Anodizing Assn. **[614]**, PO Box 579, Moorestown, NJ 08057-0579, (856)234-0330

International Health

African Medical and Res. Found. **[2475]**
Ahoto Partnership for Ghana **[2476]**
Amer. Coll. of Intl. Physicians **[2477]**
Amer. Friends of Guinea **[2478]**
Andean Hea. and Development **[2479]**
Arise Medical Missions **[2480]**
Caribbean Hea. Outreach **[2481]**
ChildAlive **[2482]**
Clinic at a Time **[2483]**
Clinicians of the World **[2484]**
Doctors for United Medical Missions **[2485]**
Dorcas Medical Mission **[2486]**
Emofra Africa **[2487]**
Engg. World Hea. **[2488]**
Ghana Medical Mission **[2489]**
Global Emergency Care Collaborative **[2490]**
Global Hea. Corps **[2491]**
Global Hea. through Educ., Training and Ser. **[2492]**
Global Hea. Informatics Partnership **[2493]**
Global Hea. Linkages, Inc. **[2494]**
Global Physicians Corps **[2495]**
Haiti Healthcare Partners **[2496]**
Healing Across the Divides **[2497]**
Hea. and Educ. Relief for Guyana **[2498]**
Hea. Horizons Intl. **[2500]**
Hea. Horizons Intl. **[2499]**
Hea. through Walls **[2501]**
Honduras Outreach Medical Brigada Relief Effort **[2502]**
Hope Beyond Hope **[2503]**
Hope Through Healing Hands **[2504]**
Horizon Intl. Medical Mission **[2505]**
Intermed Intl. **[2506]**
Intl. Hea. and Development Network **[2507]**
Intl. Medical Alliance **[2508]**
Medical Mission Gp. **[2509]**
mHealth Alliance **[2510]**
Network Ethiopia **[2511]**
Partners for World Hea. **[2512]**
Progressive Hea. Partnership **[2513]**
Proj. Concern Intl. **[2514]**
Reach Intl. Healthcare and Training **[2515]**
Sharing Resources Worldwide **[2516]**
Shout Global Hea. **[2517]**
Soft Power Hea. **[2518]**
UHAI for Hea. **[2519]**
Unified for Global Healing **[2520]**

Universities Allied for Essential Medicines **[1641]**
Upenyu **[2521]**
Uplift Intl. **[2522]**
Waves of Hea. **[2523]**
World Hea. Imaging, Telemedicine and Informatics Alliance **[2524]**
World Hea. Partners **[2525]**
World Hea. Services **[2526]**
Wuqu' Kawoq **[2527]**
Wyman Worldwide Hea. Partners **[2528]**
ACCESS Hea. Intl. **[2428]**
Amazonas Hope for Hea. **[2429]**
Ambassadors for Sustained Hea. **[2430]**
Amer. Chinese Medical Exchange Soc. **[2431]**
Answer Africa **[2397]**
Cambodian Hea. Professionals Assn. of Am. **[2432]**
Caribbean Public Hea. Coalition **[2590]**
Children's Intl. Hea. Relief **[2335]**
Childspring Intl. **[2336]**
Community Hea. Intl. **[2448]**
Forward in Hea. **[2433]**
Friends for Hea. in Haiti **[2434]**
Global Flying Hospitals **[2435]**
Global Natural Hea. Alliance **[2294]**
Global Network for Neglected Tropical Diseases **[2398]**
Global Solutions for Infectious Diseases **[2472]**
Global Vision 2020 **[2601]**
Hea. Empowering Humanity **[2436]**
I Care Grace Intl. **[2437]**
Inter-American Hea. Alliance **[2438]**
Intl. Assn. for Women's Mental Hea. **[2551]**
Intl. Healthcare Leadership **[2445]**
Intl. Healthcare Volunteers **[2439]**
Intl. Partnership for Reproductive Hea. **[2593]**
MED25 Intl. **[2440]**
Medics Without Borders **[2407]**
Natl. Student Campaign Against Hunger and Homelessness **[2117]**
Naturopathic Medicine for Global Hea. **[2555]**
South Asian Public Hea. Assn. **[2591]**
Spinal Hea. Intl. **[2594]**
Women for World Hea. **[2442]**
World Hea. Ambassador **[2443]**
World Spine Care **[2595]**

Intl. Hea. and Development Network **[2507]**, PO Box 7488, Springfield, IL 62791

Intl. Healthcare Leadership **[2445]**, Columbia Univ. Medical Center, 3959 Broadway, 8 N, New York, NY 10032, (212)305-5475

Intl. Healthcare Volunteers **[2439]**, PO Box 8231, Trenton, NJ 08650, (609)259-8807

Intl. Hearing Dog **[2454]**, 5901 E 89th Ave., Henderson, CO 80640, (303)287-3277

Intl. Hearing Soc. **[2455]**, 16880 Middlebelt Rd., Ste. 4, Livonia, MI 48154-3374, (734)522-7200

International Inst. for Hearing Instruments Stud. **[★2455]**

Intl. Interior Design Assn. **[510]**, 222 Merchandise Mart, Ste. 567, Chicago, IL 60654, (312)467-1950

Intl. Joint Commn. **[1168]**, 2000 L St. NW, Ste. 615, Washington, DC 20440, (202)736-9024

Intl. Kennel Club of Chicago **[3178]**, 6222 W North Ave., Chicago, IL 60639, (773)237-5100

Intl. King Midget Car Club **[3111]**, c/o Teresa Harris, Sec., 5198 Happy Hollow Rd., Nelsonville, OH 45764, (740)591-0084

Intl. Labor Rights Forum **[2694]**, 1634 I St. NW, No. 1001, Washington, DC 20006, (202)347-4100

Intl. Lawyers in Alcoholics Anonymous **[2242]**, c/o Eli Gauna, Sec., 17216 Saticoy St., Ste. 211, Van Nuys, CA 91406, (818)343-2189

Intl. League of Antiquarian Booksellers **[770]**, c/o Tom Congalton, VP, 35 W Maple Ave., Merchantville, NJ 08109-5141, (856)665-2284

The Intl. Lepidoptera Survey **[1472]**, PO Box 1124, Herndon, VA 20172

Intl. Lightning Class Assn. **[3275]**, 7625 S Yampa St., Centennial, CO 80016, (303)325-5886

Intl. Lilac Soc. **[3206]**, c/o Karen McCauley, Treas./ Interim Membership Sec., 325 W 82nd St., Chaska, MN 55318, (952)443-3703

Intl. Liquid Terminals Assn. **[902]**, 1005 N Glebe Rd., Ste. 600, Arlington, VA 22201, (703)875-2011

Intl. Listening Assn. **[1606]**, PO Box 164, Belle Plaine, MN 56011-0164, (952)594-5697

Intl. Longshoremen's Assn. **[3453]**, 5000 W Side Ave., North Bergen, NJ 07047, (212)425-1200

Intl. Loran Assn. **[1505]**, 741 Cathedral Pointe Ln., Santa Barbara, CA 93111, (805)967-8649

Intl. Maple Syrup Inst. **[365]**, 387 County Rd., Woodstock, CT 06281, (860)974-1235

Intl. Marine Animal Trainers Assn. **[948]**, 1200 S Lake Shore Dr., Chicago, IL 60605, (312)692-3193

Intl. Match Safe Assn. **[3155]**, PO Box 4212, Bartonville, IL 61607-4212

Intl. Medical Alliance **[2508]**, PO Box 2727, Rancho Mirage, CA 92270, (760)485-8963

Intl. Messianic Jewish Alliance **[2930]**, 5480 Baltimore Dr., Ste. 203, La Mesa, CA 91942-2015, (619)464-9793

Intl. Military Community Executives Assn. **[615]**, PO Box 91356, Austin, TX 78709-1356, (512)814-6232

Intl. Miniature Zebu Assn. **[985]**, 3571 Hwy. 20, Crawford, NE 69339, (308)665-1431

Intl. Mission Bd. **[3002]**, PO Box 6767, Richmond, VA 23230-0767, (800)999-3113

Intl. Mobjack Assn. **[3276]**, 3720 Blue Heron Ln., West Point, VA 23181, (804)843-2682

Intl. Motor Press Assn. **[696]**, PO Box 146, Harrington Park, NJ 07640, (201)750-3533

Intl. Mystery Shopping Alliance **[771]**, 210 Crossways Park Dr., Woodbury, NY 11797, (516)576-1188

Intl. Natural Bodybuilding and Fitness Fed. **[3293]**, PO Box 4, Pocono Lake, PA 18347

Intl. Network of Children's Ministry **[2895]**, PO Box 190, Castle Rock, CO 80104, (800)324-4543

Intl. Network of Prison Ministries **[2984]**, Box 227475, Dallas, TX 75222

Intl. Oil Scouts Assn. **[646]**, PO Box 940310, Houston, TX 77094-7310, (713)420-6257

Intl. Ombudsman Assn. **[169]**, 390 Amwell Rd., Ste. 403, Hillsborough, NJ 08844, (908)359-0246

Intl. Order of Saint Luke the Physician **[3029]**, PO Box 780909, San Antonio, TX 78278-0909, (210)492-5222

Intl. Org. of Black Security Executives **[805]**, PO Box 1471, San Mateo, CA 94401, (888)884-6273

Intl. Org. for Haitian Development **[1591]**, 1425 K St. NW, Ste. 350, Washington, DC 20005, (305)735-3242

Intl. Org. for Mycoplasmology **[1421]**, c/o Dr. Mitchell F. Balish, Treas., 80 Pearson Hall, Oxford, OH 45056, (513)528-0167

Intl. Orthodox Christian Charities **[2896]**, PO Box 630225, Baltimore, MD 21263-0225, (410)243-9820

Intl. Ozone Assn. **[1479]**, PO Box 28873, Scottsdale, AZ 85255, (480)529-3787

Intl. Palm Soc. **[1431]**, c/o Liz Stansfeld, 9300 Sandstone St., Austin, TX 78737, (512)301-2744

Intl. Parrotlet Soc. **[3140]**, PO Box 2446, Aptos, CA 95003-2446, (831)688-5560

Intl. Partnership for Reproductive Hea. **[2593]**, PO Box 510, Chesterton, IN 46304

Intl. Penguin Class Dinghy Assn. **[3277]**, c/o Charles Krafft, Treas., 8300 Waverly Rd., Owings, MD 20736

Intl. People's Democratic Uhuru Movement **[2637]**, 1245 18th Ave. S, St. Petersburg, FL 33705

Intl. Performing Arts for Youth **[1834]**, 1616 Walnut St., Ste. 1800, Philadelphia, PA 19103, (267)690-1325

Intl. Phalaenopsis Alliance **[1153]**, c/o Lynn Fuller, Membership Sec., 1401 Pennsylvania Ave., No. 1604, Wilmington, DE 19806, (302)594-0765

Intl. Pharmaceutical Excipients Coun. of the Americas **[659]**, 1655 N Ft. Myer Dr., Ste. 700, Arlington, VA 22209, (703)875-2127

Intl. Professional Groomers **[654]**, 123 Manley Ave., Greensboro, NC 27401, (336)852-9867

Intl. Professional Partnerships for Sierra Leone **[2675]**, 2042 Swans Neck Way, Reston, VA 20191-4030, (202)390-5375

Intl. Professional Pond Contractors Assn. **[54]**, 4045 N Arnold Mill Rd., Woodstock, GA 30188, (770)592-9790

Intl. Psoriasis Coun. **[2394]**, 2626 Cole Ave., Ste. 400, Dallas, TX 75204, (214)369-0406

The Intl. Publication Planning Assn. **[722]**, 1350 41st Ave., Ste. 200, Capitola, CA 95010, (831)465-2298

Intl. Real Estate Inst. **[747]**, PO Box 879, Palm Springs, CA 92263, (760)327-5284

A star before a book entry number signifies that the name is not listed separately, but is mentioned within the entry.

Intl. Assn. of Space Entrepreneurs **[30]**
Iraqi Amer. Chamber of Commerce and Indus.
[3483]
Middle East Investment Initiative **[336]**
Pakistan Chamber of Commerce USA **[3502]**
IOCALUM **[3427]**, 597 State Hwy. 162, Sprakers,
NY 12166-4008, (518)673-3212
Iota Sigma Pi **[3511]**, Angelo State Univ., Dept. of
Chemistry & Biochemistry, Cavness Sci. Bldg.,
Rm. 204B, San Angelo, TX 76909-0892, (325)486-
6662
IPC - Assn. Connecting Electronics Indus. **[283]**,
3000 Lakeside Dr., 309 S, Bannockburn, IL 60015,
(847)615-7100
Iran
Iran Policy Comm. **[2687]**
Assn. of Professors and Scholars of Iranian
Heritage **[1646]**
Iran Democratic Union **[2667]**
United Against Nuclear Iran **[2711]**
Iran Democratic Union **[2667]**, PO Box 61551, Poto-
mac, MD 20859-1551, (202)618-1438
Iran Policy Comm. **[2687]**, 3700 Massachusetts Ave.
NW, Ste. 507, Washington, DC 20016, (202)333-
7346
Iranian
Assn. of Professors and Scholars of Iranian
Heritage **[1646]**
Iranian Alliances Across Borders **[2796]**
Iran Policy Comm. **[2687]**
Iranian Alliances Across Borders **[2796]**, PO Box
20429, New York, NY 10009
Iraq
Iraqi Amer. Chamber of Commerce and Indus.
[3483]
Iraqi Amer. Chamber of Commerce and Indus.
[3483], 15265 Maturin Dr., No. 184, San Diego,
CA 92127, (858)613-9215
Irish
Amer. Conf. for Irish Stud. **[1785]**
Irish Amer. Unity Conf. **[2688]**
Irish Amer. Unity Conf. **[2688]**, PO Box 55573,
Washington, DC 20040, (800)947-4282
Irish Draught Horse Soc. of North Am. **[1134]**, c/o
Rachel Cox, Info. Off., HC65 Box 45, Pleasant
Mount, PA 18453-9605, (866)434-7621
Irrigation
Irrigation Water Mgt. Soc. **[1226]**
Irrigation Water Mgt. Soc. **[1226]**, 2008 Sycamore
Dr., Eagle Mountain, UT 84005, (509)981-6441
Ishmael and Isaac **[2702]**, One Bratenahl Pl., Ste.
1302, Bratenahl, OH 44108, (216)233-7333
Islamic Relief U.S.A. **[2192]**, PO Box 22250,
Alexandria, VA 22304, (703)370-7202
Iso and Bizzarrini Owners Club **[3112]**, 2025 Drake
Dr., Oakland, CA 94611
Israel
Americans for Peace Now **[2689]**
Emunah of Am. **[2123]**
Fuel for Truth **[2745]**
Maccabi USA/Sports for Israel **[3402]**
Israel; Americans for a Safe **[2700]**
Israeli
America-Israel Cultural Found. **[1786]**
Amer. Technion Soc. **[1647]**
Healing Across the Divides **[2497]**
Maccabi USA/Sports for Israel **[3402]**
Italian
Amer. Italian Historical Assn. **[1787]**
Unico Natl. **[2797]**
Italian Amer. Alliance for Bus. and Tech. **[170]**, 74 W
Long Lake Rd., Ste. 204, Bloomfield Hills, MI
48304, (248)227-6143
Italy
Boys' Towns of Italy **[2276]**

J

Jack and Jill of Am. **[1998]**, 1930 17th St. NW,
Washington, DC 20009, (202)667-7010
Jaguar Clubs of North Am. **[3113]**, c/o Nancy Rath,
234 Buckland Trace, Louisville, KY 40245,
(502)244-1672
Jamaica
Friends of Jamaica USA **[1953]**
Jamaica Unite **[2025]**
Jamaica Unite **[2025]**, 3613 NW 194th Terr., Miami
Gardens, FL 33056, (954)353-7032

Jamaica USA Chamber of Commerce **[3484]**, 4770
Biscayne Blvd., Ste. 1050, Miami, FL 33137,
(305)576-7888
Jane Addams Peace Assn. **[2716]**, 777 United Na-
tions Plz., 6th Fl., New York, NY 10017, (212)682-
8830
Jane Goodall Inst. for Wildlife Res., Educ., and
Conservation **[1244]**, 4245 N Fairfax Dr., Ste. 600,
Arlington, VA 22203, (703)682-9220
Japan
Japan Stud. Assn. **[1788]**
U.S.-Japan Bus. Coun. **[3499]**
All Japan Ju-Jitsu Intl. Fed. **[3359]**
U.S.-Japan Coun. **[2681]**
Japan Stud. Assn. **[1788]**, c/o Dr. James Peoples,
Sec., Ohio Wesleyan Univ., Dept. of Sociology/
Anthropology, 61 S Sandusky St., Delaware, OH
43015
Japanese
Japanese Amer. Living Legacy **[1789]**
Japanese Chamber of Commerce and Indus. of
New York **[3500]**
Japanese Natl. Honor Soc. **[3533]**
All Japan Ju-Jitsu Intl. Fed. **[3359]**
Japan Stud. Assn. **[1788]**
Japanese Amer. Living Legacy **[1789]**, 800 N State
Coll. Blvd., RGC 8, Fullerton, CA 92831, (657)278-
4483
Japanese Chamber of Commerce and Indus. of New
York **[3500]**, 145 W 57th St., New York, NY 10019,
(212)246-8001
Japanese Natl. Honor Soc. **[3533]**, PO Box 3719,
Boulder, CO 80307-3719
Japanese Sword Soc. of the U.S. **[3092]**, PO Box
5216, Albuquerque, NM 87181
JEDEC **[284]**, 3103 N 10th St., Ste. 240-S,
Arlington, VA 22201-2107, (703)907-7540
Jewelry
Accredited Gemologists Assn. **[530]**
Gemological Inst. of Am. Alumni Assn. **[2798]**
Jewish
Amer. Jewish Soc. for Ser. **[2124]**
AMIT **[2947]**
Assn. of Jewish Family and Children's Agencies
[2125]
Assn. for the Social Sci. Stud. of Jewry **[1648]**
B'nai B'rith Intl. **[2948]**
B'nai B'rith International's Center for Jewish
Identity **[1649]**
Central Conf. of Amer. Rabbis **[2949]**
CLAL - The Natl. Jewish Center for Learning and
Leadership **[2950]**
Coalition on the Env. and Jewish Life **[2951]**
Habonim Dror North Am. **[2952]**
Hadassah, The Women's Zionist Org. of Am.
[2953]
Intl. Fed. of Rabbis **[2954]**
Jewish Coun. for Public Affairs **[2126]**
Jewish Federations of North Am. **[2127]**
Jewish Natl. Fund **[2955]**
Jewish Reconstructionist Fed. **[2956]**
Jewish Telegraphic Agency **[2690]**
League for Yiddish **[2957]**
Leo Baeck Inst. **[1790]**
MERCAZ USA **[2958]**
Na'amat U.S.A. **[2959]**
Natl. Assn. of Temple Administrators **[2960]**
Natl. Coun. of Jewish Women **[2961]**
Natl. Ramah Commn. **[1650]**
North Amer. Conf. on Ethiopian Jewry **[2691]**
Rabbinical Assembly **[2962]**
Rabbinical Coun. of Am. **[2963]**
Shomrim Soc. **[2128]**
Soc. of Jewish Ethics **[2964]**
Union for Traditional Judaism **[2965]**
Women of Reform Judaism **[2966]**
Women's League for Conservative Judaism
[2967]
World Coun. of Conservative/Masorti Synagogues
[2968]
Yugntruf - Youth for Yiddish **[1791]**
Abrahamic Alliance Intl. **[2945]**
Americans for Peace Now **[2689]**
Maccabi USA/Sports for Israel **[3402]**
Jewish Coun. for Public Affairs **[2126]**, PO Box
1415, New York, NY 10156-1415, (212)684-6950
Jewish Federations of North Am. **[2127]**, PO Box
157, New York, NY 10268, (212)284-6500

Jewish Funeral Directors of Am. **[621]**, 385 Craig
Ct., Deerfield, IL 60015, (847)607-9156
Jewish Museums; Coun. of Amer. **[1815]**
Jewish Natl. Fund **[2955]**, 42 E 69th St., New York,
NY 10021, (212)879-9305
Jewish Reconstructionist Fed. **[2956]**, 101
Greenwood Ave., Ste. 430, Jenkintown, PA 19046,
(215)885-5601
Jewish Telegraphic Agency **[2690]**, 330 7th Ave.,
17th Fl., New York, NY 10001, (212)643-1890
Jim Smith Soc. **[2826]**, 256 Lake Meade Dr., East
Berlin, PA 17316
Jockeys' Guild **[3346]**, 103 Wind Haven Dr., Ste.
200, Nicholasville, KY 40356, (859)523-5625
John Howard Assn. **[2052]**, 375 E Chicago Ave.,
Ste. 529, Chicago, IL 60611, (312)503-6300
Joint Baltic Amer. Natl. Comm. **[2617]**, 400 Hurley
Ave., Rockville, MD 20850-3121, (301)340-1954
Joint Coun. on Intl. Children's Services **[1872]**, 117
S St. Asaph St., Alexandria, VA 22314, (703)535-
8045
Joint Indus. Bd. of the Elecl. Indus. **[221]**, 158-11
Harry Van Arsdale Jr. Ave., Flushing, NY 11365,
(718)591-2000
Joint Indus. Gp. **[518]**, 111 Rockville Pike, Ste. 410,
Rockville, MD 20850, (202)466-5490
Joshua Slocum Soc. Intl. **[3279]**, 15 Codfish Hill Rd.
Extension, Bethel, CT 06801, (203)790-6616
Journalism
Journalism Educ. Assn. **[1651]**
Journalism Educ. Assn. **[1651]**, Kansas State Univ.,
103 Kedzie Hall, Manhattan, KS 66506-1505,
(785)532-5532
Journey Toward Sustainability **[1622]**, 6585 Gate-
house Ct. NW, Concord, NC 28027, (704)641-7223
Jozef Pilsudski Inst. of Am. for Res. in the Modern
History of Poland **[1846]**, 180 2nd Ave., New York,
NY 10003-5778, (212)505-9077
Judicial Reform
HALT **[2692]**
Judiciary
Amer. Judges Assn. **[1317]**
Amer. Judicature Soc. **[1318]**
Natl. Coun. of Juvenile and Family Court Judges
[1319]
Judo
World Martial Arts Assn. **[3364]**
Junior Knights of Peter Claver **[2774]**, c/o Knights of
Peter Claver, Inc., 1825 Orleans Ave., New
Orleans, LA 70116-2825, (504)821-4425
Junior Optimist Octagon Intl. **[2222]**, 4494 Lindell
Blvd., St. Louis, MO 63108, (314)371-6000
Just One Break **[2059]**, 570 Seventh Ave., New
York, NY 10018, (212)785-7300
Just Transition Alliance **[3449]**, 2810 Camino Del Rio
S, Ste. 116, San Diego, CA 92108, (619)573-4934
Juvenile
Robert F. Kennedy Center for Justice and Human
Rights **[2280]**
Juvenile Delinquency
Robert F. Kennedy Center for Justice and Human
Rights **[2280]**

K

Kamut Assn. of North Am. **[996]**, PO Box 4903, Mis-
soula, MT 59806, (406)251-9418
Kappa Delta Rho **[3552]**, 331 S Main St., Greens-
burg, PA 15601-3111, (724)838-7100
Kappa Delta Rho Found. **[★3552]**
Kappa Kappa Gamma **[3562]**, PO Box 38,
Columbus, OH 43216-0038, (614)228-6515
Karate
World Martial Arts Assn. **[3364]**
Kate Smith Commemorative Soc. **[3583]**, PO Box
242, Syracuse, NY 13214-0242
Kate's Voice **[1678]**, PO Box 365, Sudbury, MA
01776, (978)440-9913
Kay Boyle Soc. **[1734]**, Columbia Coll., Dept. of
English, 1301 Columbia Coll. Dr., Columbia, SC
29203
Kenya Medical Outreach **[2135]**, 4355 Suwanee
Dam Rd., Ste. 100, Suwanee, GA 30024,
(678)858-3380
Keystone Conservation **[1245]**, PO Box 6733, Boze-
man, MT 59771, (406)587-3389
Khadarlis for Sierra Leone **[2026]**, 99 Acad. Ave.,
Providence, RI 02908, (401)454-6916

Kidney
Children's Dialysis Intl. **[2559]**
Kidney Found; Natl. **[2560]**
Kidney Patients; Amer. Assn. of **[2557]**
Kids Ecology Corps **[1076]**, 1350 E Sunrise Blvd., Fort Lauderdale, FL 33304-2815, (954)524-0366
Kids Home Intl. **[1969]**, 2309 Plymouth Ave. N, Minneapolis, MN 55411
Kids Making a Difference **[952]**, 1527 W State Hwy. 114, Ste. 500, No. 106, Grapevine, TX 76051
Kids for Peace **[2717]**, 3303 James Dr., Carlsbad, CA 92008, (760)730-3320
Kingdom Chamber of Commerce **[3491]**, 383 N Kings Highway, Ste. 201, Cherry Hill, NJ 08034, (856)414-0818
KISS Rocks Fan Club **[3584]**, 15 Maple Rd., Briarcliff Manor, NY 10510
Knifemakers' Guild **[3168]**, 2914 Winters Ln., La Grange, KY 40031, (502)222-1397
Knights of Peter Claver **[2775]**, 1825 Orleans Ave., New Orleans, LA 70116, (504)821-4225

Korea
Korea Stamp Soc. **[3228]**
Korea Stamp Soc. **[3228]**, c/o John E. Talmage, Jr., Sec.-Treas., PO Box 6889, Oak Ridge, TN 37831

Korean
Korea Stamp Soc. **[3228]**
Korean Amer. Sharing Movement **[2193]**, 7004 Little River Tpke., Ste. O, Annandale, VA 22003, (703)867-0846

Korean War
2nd Infantry Div., Korean War Veterans Alliance **[3072]**
Kupenda for the Children **[1970]**, PO Box 473, Hampton, NH 03843, (410)456-2311

L

Labor
Asian Pacific Amer. Labor Alliance **[3448]**
California Public Employee Relations Prog. **[2693]**
Intl. Labor Rights Forum **[2694]**
Just Transition Alliance **[3449]**
Natl. Assn. of Governmental Labor Officials **[1320]**
Trans. Communications Union I Brotherhood Railway Carmen Div. **[3463]**

Labor Management
Trans. Communications Union I Brotherhood Railway Carmen Div. **[3463]**
Labor Notes **[3451]**, 7435 Michigan Ave., Detroit, MI 48210, (313)842-6262

Labor Studies
Assn. of Labor Relations Agencies **[3450]**
Labor Notes **[3451]**
Trans. Communications Union I Brotherhood Railway Carmen Div. **[3463]**

Labor Unions
Trans. Communications Union I Brotherhood Railway Carmen Div. **[3463]**

Laboratory
Assn. of Lab. Managers **[1492]**
Clinical Lab. Mgt. Assn. **[2529]**
Clinical and Lab. Standards Inst. **[2530]**

Lacrosse
Fed. of Intl. Lacrosse **[3357]**
Fields of Growth Intl. **[2129]**
Ladies Auxiliary of the Military Order of the Purple Heart U.S.A. **[3053]**, 19138 Bedford Dr., Oregon City, OR 97045, (503)657-7085

Laity
Natl. Assn. for Lay Ministry **[2969]**
Laity for Life **[2869]**, PO Box 111478, Naples, FL 34108, (239)352-6333
Lakes Region Sled Dog Club **[3324]**, c/o Peter Colbath, Treas., PO Box 341, Laconia, NH 03247-0382, (603)524-4314
Lambda Alpha **[3508]**, Ball State Univ., Dept. of Anthropology, Muncie, IN 47306, (765)285-1575
Lancaster Mennonite Historical Soc. **[3066]**, 2215 Millstream Rd., Lancaster, PA 17602-1499, (717)393-9745
Land Mobile Communications Coun. **[849]**, 8484 Westpark Dr., Ste. 630, McLean, VA 22102-5117, (703)528-5115

Landscaping
Coalition of Organic Landscapers **[531]**

Northeastern Weed Sci. Soc. **[1154]**
Professional Landcare Network **[532]**
Proj. EverGreen **[1155]**
Sports Turf Managers Assn. **[533]**
Assn. of Synthetic Grass Installers **[140]**

Language
Amer. Assn. of Teachers of Italian **[1652]**
Amer. Coun. on the Teaching of Foreign Languages **[1653]**
Assn. of Teachers of Japanese **[1654]**
Acad. of Rehabilitative Audiology **[2449]**
Rhetoric Soc. of Am. **[1851]**
Large Public Power Coun. **[1292]**, 300 N Washington St., Ste. 405, Alexandria, VA 22314, (703)740-1750
Laryngological, Rhinological and Otological Soc; Amer. **[2574]**

Latin America
Conf. on Latin Amer. History **[1792]**
Coun. of the Americas **[3501]**
Fellowship of Reconciliation Task Force on Latin Am. and Caribbean **[2695]**
Latin Amer. Stud. Assn. **[1793]**
Natl. Latina Bus. Women Assn. **[534]**
Washington Off. on Latin Am. **[2696]**
Latin Am. Mission **[3003]**, PO Box 527900, Miami, FL 33152-7900, (305)884-8400

Latin American
Natl. Community for Latino Leadership **[2800]**
Latin Amer. Stud. Assn. **[1793]**, Univ. of Pittsburgh, 416 Bellefield Hall, Pittsburgh, PA 15260, (412)648-7929

Laundry
Assn. for Linen Mgt. **[535]**
Coin Laundry Assn. **[536]**
Healthcare Laundry Accreditation Coun. **[537]**

Law
Advocates Intl. **[1321]**
Amer. Veterinary Medical Law Assn. **[1322]**
Delta Theta Phi **[3534]**
Found. of the Fed. Bar Assn. **[1323]**
Inter-American Bar Assn. **[1324]**
Natl. Assn. of Bar Executives **[1325]**
Natl. Latino Officers Assn. **[1326]**
Natl. Org. of Bar Counsel **[1327]**
Alliance of Guardian Angels **[2046]**
Alliance of Legal Document Asst. Professionals **[1340]**
Amer. Bar Assn. Center on Children and the Law **[1921]**
Amer. Coll. of Environmental Lawyers **[1293]**
Assn. of State Correctional Administrators **[2049]**
Intl. Assn. for Correctional and Forensic Psychology **[2050]**

Law Enforcement
Assn. for Explosive Detection K-9s, Intl. **[1328]**
Commn. on Accreditation for Law Enforcement Agencies **[1329]**
Law Enforcement Alliance of Am. **[1330]**
Law Enforcement Thermographers' Assn. **[1331]**
Natl. Assn. of Asian Amer. Law Enforcement Commanders **[1332]**
Natl. Liquor Law Enforcement Assn. **[1333]**
Natl. Narcotic Detector Dog Assn. **[1334]**
Natl. Native Amer. Law Enforcement Assn. **[1335]**
Natl. Police Canine Assn. **[1336]**
Natl. Tactical Officers Assn. **[1337]**
Natl. Union of Law Enforcement Associations **[3452]**
Soc. of Former Special Agents of the Fed. Bur. of Investigation **[2799]**
U.S. Police Canine Assn. **[1338]**
Alliance of Guardian Angels **[2046]**
Law Enforcement Alliance of Am. **[1330]**, 7700 Leesburg Pike, Ste. 421, Falls Church, VA 22043, (703)847-2677
Law Enforcement Thermographers' Assn. **[1331]**, PO Box 6485, Edmond, OK 73083-6485, (405)330-6988
Law, Medicine and Ethics; Amer. Soc. of **[2534]**
Lawyers for Children Am. **[1341]**, 151 Farmington Ave. RW61, Hartford, CT 06156, (860)273-0441
Lay Mission-Helpers Assn. **[2870]**, 3435 Wilshire Blvd., Ste. 1940, Los Angeles, CA 90010, (213)368-1870

Leadership
Amer. Coun. of Young Political Leaders **[2697]**
Natl. Community for Latino Leadership **[2800]**
Natl. Inst. for Leadership Development **[538]**
CEO Netweavers **[236]**
Intl. Org. for Haitian Development **[1591]**
Leadership for Energy Automated Processing **[303]**, c/o Mary Dortenzio, Treas., Glencore, 301 Tresser Blvd., Stamford, CT 06901, (203)846-1300

Leadership Training
Natl. Community for Latino Leadership **[2800]**
Leading Builders of Am. **[149]**, 1455 Pennsylvania Ave. NW, Ste. 400, Washington, DC 20004, (202)621-1815
League of United Latin Amer. Citizens **[2788]**, 2000 L St. NW, Ste. 610, Washington, DC 20036, (202)833-6130
League of World War I Aviation Historians **[3086]**, 16820 25th Ave. N, Plymouth, MN 55447
League for Yiddish **[2957]**, 64 Fulton St., Ste. 1101, New York, NY 10038, (212)889-0380
Learning Disabilities Assn. of Am. **[2130]**, 4156 Lib. Rd., Pittsburgh, PA 15234-1349, (412)341-1515

Learning Disabled
Learning Disabilities Assn. of Am. **[2130]**
Natl. Center for Learning Disabilities **[2131]**

Leather
Intl. Fed. of Leather Guilds **[539]**
Sponge and Chamois Inst. **[540]**

Legal
Amer. Assn. of Nurse Attorneys **[2531]**
Amer. Coll. of Legal Medicine **[2532]**
Amer. Hosp. Assn. I Soc. for Healthcare Consumer Advocacy **[2533]**
Amer. Soc. of Law, Medicine and Ethics **[2534]**
Natl. Legal Sanctuary for Community Advancement **[1339]**
Alliance of Legal Document Asst. Professionals **[1340]**
Amer. Bar Assn. Center on Children and the Law **[1921]**
Amer. Coll. of Environmental Lawyers **[1293]**
Assn. of State Correctional Administrators **[2049]**
HALT **[2692]**
Intl. Amusement and Leisure Defense Assn. **[761]**
Intl. Assn. for Correctional and Forensic Psychology **[2050]**

Legal Education
Amer. Assn. for Paralegal Educ. **[1655]**
Assn. of Amer. Law Schools **[1656]**
Legal Marketing Assn. **[602]**, 401 N Michigan Ave., 22th Fl., Chicago, IL 60611-6610, (312)321-6898

Legal Services
Alliance of Legal Document Asst. Professionals **[1340]**
Lawyers for Children Am. **[1341]**
Natl. Center on Poverty Law **[1342]**
Assn. of State Correctional Administrators **[2049]**
Intl. Amusement and Leisure Defense Assn. **[761]**
Intl. Assn. for Correctional and Forensic Psychology **[2050]**

Legislative Reform
HALT **[2692]**

Lending
Amer. Financial Services Assn. **[541]**
Commercial Finance Assn. **[542]**
Natl. Found. for Credit Counseling **[543]**
Natl. Assn. of Mortgage Processors **[113]**
Leo Baeck Inst. **[1790]**, 15 W 16th St., New York, NY 10011-6301, (212)744-6400
Leonardo, The Intl. Soc. for the Arts, Sciences and Tech. **[1728]**, 211 Sutter St., Ste. 501, San Francisco, CA 94108, (415)391-1110

Leprosy
Amer. Leprosy Missions **[2535]**
Lesley Gore Intl. Fan Club **[3585]**, PO Box 1548, Ocean Pines, MD 21811, (410)208-6369
Leuva Patidar Samaj of USA **[1780]**, 716 Sweetwater Cir., Old Hickory, TN 37138, (615)712-6999

Liability
Amer. Bd. of Professional Liability Attorneys **[1343]**
Defense Res. Inst. **[1344]**

Liberal Arts
Assn. of Graduate Liberal Stud. Programs **[1657]**

A star before a book entry number signifies that the name is not listed separately, but is mentioned within the entry.

Liberia
    Children's Welfare Intl. **[1943]**
    Relief Liberia Intl. **[2198]**
Liberty Godparent Home **[2205]**, PO Box 4199, Lynchburg, VA 24502, (434)845-3466
Libraries
    Amer. Assn. of Law Libraries **[1794]**
    Amer. Soc. for Indexing **[1795]**
    Asian Pacific Amer. Librarians Assn. **[1796]**
    Assn. of Res. Libraries **[1797]**
    Chief Officers of State Lib. Agencies **[1798]**
    Church and Synagogue Lib. Assn. **[1799]**
    Comm. on Res. Materials on Southeast Asia **[1800]**
    Lib. Leadership and Mgt. Assn. **[1801]**
    Middle East Librarians Assn. **[1802]**
    Music Lib. Assn. **[1803]**
    Amer. Lib. Assn. | Gay, Lesbian, Bisexual and Transgendered Roundtable **[2092]**
Lib. Leadership and Mgt. Assn. **[1801]**, 50 E Huron St., Chicago, IL 60611-2729, (312)280-5032
Libyan
    Amer. Libyan Freedom Alliance **[2636]**
Lido 14 Class Assn. **[3280]**, PO Box 1252, Newport Beach, CA 92663, (714)437-1370
Life Insurance Settlement Assn. **[492]**, 1011 E Colonial Dr., Ste. 500, Orlando, FL 32803, (407)894-3797
LIFE Ministries **[2937]**, 250 Meadow Ln., Conestoga, PA 17516, (717)871-0540
Lifelong Fitness Alliance **[3423]**, 2682 Middlefield Rd., Ste. Z, Redwood City, CA 94063, (650)361-8282
Lifesaving
    Intl. Assn. of Dive Rescue Specialists **[544]**
LifeWind Intl. **[2985]**, PO Box 1302, Salida, CA 95368, (209)543-7500
Lift Disability Network **[2060]**, PO Box 770607, Winter Garden, FL 34777, (407)228-8343
Liga Intl. **[2136]**, 19671 Lucaya Ct., Apple Valley, CA 92308, (909)875-6300
Light Elec. Vehicle Assn. **[873]**, PO Box 286, Orono, ME 04473
Lighthouse Keepers Assn; Great Lakes **[1764]**
Lighting
    Assn. of Outdoor Lighting Professionals **[545]**
    Professional Lighting and Sign Mgt. Companies of Am. **[546]**
Lincoln Zephyr Owner's Club **[3114]**, 25609 N Forrest Rd., Ste. 10, Rio Verde, AZ 85263
Linguistic Institute **[★1805]**
Linguistic Soc. of Am. **[1805]**, 1325 18th St. NW, Ste. 211, Washington, DC 20036-6501, (202)835-1714
Linguistics
    Amer. Assn. for Applied Linguistics **[1804]**
    Linguistic Soc. of Am. **[1805]**
Links Found. **[2223]**, 1200 Massachusetts Ave. NW, Washington, DC 20005-4501, (202)842-8686
Lipizzan Assn. of North Am. **[1135]**, PO Box 1133, Anderson, IN 46015-1133, (765)215-6798
Lippitt Morgan Breeders Assn. **[1136]**, 620 Millers Falls Rd., Northfield, MA 01360, (413)498-5553
Literacy
    Abriendo Mentes **[2208]**
    Children of Tanzania **[1903]**
    Haiti Convention Assn. **[2214]**
Literature
    Children's Literature Assn. **[1806]**
Little Bros. - Friends of the Elderly **[1878]**, 28 E Jackson Blvd., Ste. 405, Chicago, IL 60604, (312)829-3055
Little City Found. **[2142]**, 1760 W Algonquin Rd., Palatine, IL 60067-4799, (847)358-5510
Little League Found. **[3258]**, 539 U.S. Rte. 15 Hwy., PO Box 3485, Williamsport, PA 17701-0485, (570)326-1921
Liver Found; Amer. **[2459]**
Livestock
    Amer. Emu Assn. **[1156]**
    Amer. Royal Assn. **[1157]**
    Food Animal Concerns Trust **[1158]**
    Amer. Kiko Goat Assn. **[1106]**
    Global Animal Partnership **[951]**
Livestock Publications Coun. **[723]**, 910 Currie St., Fort Worth, TX 76107, (817)336-1130
Llama Assn. of North Am. **[945]**, 1800 S Obenchain Rd., Eagle Point, OR 97524, (541)830-5262

Longshoremen's Assn; Intl. **[3453]**
Lord's Day Alliance of the U.S. **[3033]**, PO Box 941745, Atlanta, GA 31145-0745, (404)693-5530
Los Angeles Copyright Soc. **[1314]**, c/o Michael Perlstein, Sec., 1875 Century Park E, Ste. 1450, Los Angeles, CA 90067
Los Angeles Kings Booster Club **[3591]**, 555 N Nash St., El Segundo, CA 90245
Lotteries
    North Amer. Assn. of State and Provincial Lotteries **[1345]**
Lotus, Ltd. **[3115]**, PO Box L, College Park, MD 20741, (301)982-4054
Loving Hands for the Needy **[1971]**, PO Box 243456, Boynton Beach, FL 33424, (561)283-3599
Luge
    U.S. Luge Assn. **[3358]**
Luggage
    Travel Goods Assn. **[547]**
Lumunos **[2909]**, PO Box 307, Marlborough, NH 03455-0307, (603)876-4121
Lutheran
    Concordia Historical Inst. **[2970]**
    Lutheran Deaconess Assn. **[2971]**
    Lutheran Deaconess Conf. **[2972]**
    Lutheran Historical Conf. **[2973]**
    Lutheran Human Relations Assn. **[2974]**
    Lutheran Men in Mission **[2975]**
Lutheran Braille Evangelism Assn. **[2603]**, 1740 Eugene St., White Bear Lake, MN 55110-3312, (651)426-0469
Lutheran Braille Workers **[2604]**, PO Box 5000, Yucaipa, CA 92399, (909)795-8977
Lutheran Deaconess Assn. **[2971]**, 1304 LaPorte Ave., Valparaiso, IN 46383, (219)464-6925
Lutheran Deaconess Conf. **[2972]**, 1304 LaPorte Ave., Valparaiso, IN 46383, (219)464-6925
Lutheran Historical Conf. **[2973]**, c/o Marvin A. Huggins, Membership Sec., 5732 White Pine Dr., St. Louis, MO 63129-2936, (314)505-7921
Lutheran Human Relations Assn. **[2974]**, 1821 N 16th St., Milwaukee, WI 53205, (414)536-0585
Lutheran Immigration and Refugee Ser. **[2180]**, 700 Light St., Baltimore, MD 21230, (410)230-2700
Lutheran Men in Mission **[2975]**, Evangelical Lutheran Church in Am., 8765 W Higgins Rd., Chicago, IL 60631, (800)638-3522
Lutherans Concerned/North Am. **[2938]**, PO Box 4707, St. Paul, MN 55104-0707, (651)665-0861

M

Maccabi USA/Sports for Israel **[3402]**, 1926 Arch St., No. 4R, Philadelphia, PA 19103, (215)561-6900
Macedonian
    Macedonian Outreach **[2976]**
    Macedonian Patriotic Org. of U.S. and Canada **[2801]**
Macedonian Outreach **[2976]**, PO Box 398, Danville, CA 94526-0398, (925)820-4107
Macedonian Patriotic Org. of U.S. and Canada **[2801]**, 124 W Wayne St., Fort Wayne, IN 46802, (260)422-5900
Machinery
    Antique Caterpillar Machinery Owners Club **[3211]**
    Indus. Auctioneers Assn. **[64]**
Maclellan Found. **[3030]**, 820 Broad St., Ste. 300, Chattanooga, TN 37402, (423)755-1366
MADRE **[2137]**, 121 W 27th St., Ste. 301, New York, NY 10001, (212)627-0444
Magic
    Soc. of Amer. Magicians **[3212]**
Mail
    Assn. of Mailing, Shipping and Off. Automation Specialists **[548]**
    Mail Systems Mgt. Assn. **[549]**
    Natl. Assn. of Presort Mailers **[550]**
    41pounds.org **[1059]**
    First Issues Collectors Club **[3226]**
    Intl. Soc. of Worldwide Stamp Collectors **[3227]**
    Korea Stamp Soc. **[3228]**
    Soc. of Australasian Specialists/Oceania **[3232]**
    Space Topic Stud. Unit **[3234]**
Mail Systems Mgt. Assn. **[549]**, PO Box 1145, North Riverside, IL 60546-0545, (708)442-8589
Mailorder Gardening Assn. **[★769]**
Mainstream Media Proj. **[2735]**, 854 9th St., Ste. B, Arcata, CA 95521, (707)826-9111

Maintenance
    Building Ser. Contractors Assn. Intl. **[551]**
    Cleaning Equip. Trade Assn. **[552]**
    Intl. Executive Housekeepers Assn. **[553]**
    Master Window Cleaners of Am. **[554]**
    Restoration Indus. Assn. **[555]**
    United Assn. of Mobile Contract Cleaners **[556]**
    Healthcare Laundry Accreditation Coun. **[537]**
Malawi Children's Mission **[1972]**, PO Box 313, Redwood City, CA 94064
Mama Hope **[2027]**, 582 Market St., Ste. 709, San Francisco, CA 94104, (415)686-6954
Mamburao-U.S.A. Assn. **[1836]**, PO Box 17616, Beverly Hills, CA 90209-5616, (310)286-2482
Managed Funds Assn. **[3498]**, 600 14th St. NW, Ste. 900, Washington, DC 20005, (202)730-2600
Management
    Assn. of Productivity Specialists **[557]**
    Assn. of Proposal Mgt. Professionals **[558]**
    Community Managers Intl. Assn. **[559]**
    Emergency Mgt. Professional Org. for Women's Enrichment **[560]**
    Financial Managers Soc. **[561]**
    Inst. of Certified Professional Managers **[562]**
    Inst. for Hea. and Productivity Mgt. **[563]**
    Inst. for Operations Res. and the Mgt. Sciences **[564]**
    Natl. Assn. of Elecl. Distributors | Natl. Educ. and Res. Found. **[565]**
    Natl. Assn. of Senior Move Managers **[566]**
    Natl. Conf. of Executives of the Arc **[567]**
    Prdt. Development and Mgt. Assn. **[568]**
    Proj. Mgt. Inst. **[569]**
    Sigma Iota Epsilon **[3535]**
    Turnaround Mgt. Assn. **[570]**
    Women in Mgt. **[571]**
    Assn. of Governmental Risk Pools **[1307]**
    Corporate Responsibility Officers Assn. **[237]**
    Corporate Social Responsibility Assn. **[238]**
    Indus. Asset Mgt. Coun. **[744]**
    Professional Lighting and Sign Mgt. Companies of Am. **[546]**
    Women Organizing for Change in Agriculture and NRM **[938]**
Mgt. Assistance Gp. **[2151]**, 1629 K St. NW, Ste. 300, Washington, DC 20006, (202)659-1963
Managers
    CEO Netweavers **[236]**
M&M's Collectors Club **[3158]**, 612 Head of River Rd., Chesapeake, VA 23322
Mano A Mano: Mexican Culture Without Borders **[1811]**, 126 St. Felix St., Brooklyn, NY 11217, (212)587-3070
Manufactured Housing
    Manufactured Housing Inst. **[572]**
    Natl. Assn. of Home Builders | Log Homes Coun. **[573]**
    Natl. Assn. of Home Builders | Modular Building Systems Coun. **[574]**
Manufactured Housing Inst. **[572]**, 2111 Wilson Blvd., Ste. 100, Arlington, VA 22201, (703)558-0400
Mfrs'. Agents Natl. Assn. **[577]**, 16 A Journey, Ste. 200, Aliso Viejo, CA 92656-3317, (949)859-4040
Mfrs. of Emission Controls Assn. **[681]**, 2020 N 14th St., Ste. 220, Arlington, VA 22201, (202)296-4797
Manufacturers Representatives
    Assn. of Independent Manufacturers'/Representatives **[575]**
    Incentive Mfrs. and Representatives Alliance **[576]**
    Mfrs'. Agents Natl. Assn. **[577]**
    Mfrs. Representatives Educational Res. Found. **[578]**
Mfrs. Representatives of Am. **[256]**, 1111 Jupiter Rd., Ste. 204D, Plano, TX 75074, (972)422-0428
Mfrs. Representatives Educational Res. Found. **[578]**, 8329 Cole St., Arvada, CO 80005, (303)463-1801
Manufacturing
    Alliance for Amer. Mfg. **[579]**
    Assn. for Mfg. Excellence **[580]**
    Consortium for Advanced Mgt. Intl. **[581]**
    Intl. Surface Fabricators Assn. **[582]**
    Natl. Assn. of Mfrs. **[583]**
    Natl. Assn. of Mfrs. Coun. of Mfg. Associations **[584]**
    Soc. of Mfg. Engineers | North Amer. Mfg. Res. Institution **[1493]**

Tooling and Mfg. Assn. [585]
911 Indus. Alliance [195]
Alliance of Supplier Diversity Professionals [727]
Wind Energy Mfrs. Assn. [913]
MAP Intl. [2977], 4700 Glynco Pkwy., Brunswick, GA 31525-6800, (912)265-6010
MAPI [464], 1600 Wilson Blvd., 11th Fl., Arlington, VA 22209-2594, (703)841-9000
Maranatha Volunteers Intl. [2932], 990 Reserve Dr., Ste. 100, Roseville, CA 95678, (916)774-7700
March of Dimes Found. [2324], 1275 Mamaroneck Ave., White Plains, NY 10605, (914)997-4488
Marijuana Laws; Natl. Org. for the Reform of [2624]

Marine
Amer. Littoral Soc. Northeast Region [1494]
Global Underwater Explorers [1159]
Intl. Longshoremen's Assn. [3453]
Marine Retailers Assn. of Am. [586]
Marine Tech. Soc. [1495]
Natl. Marine Educators Assn. [1658]
Natl. Marine Representatives Assn. [587]
North Amer. Soc. for Oceanic History [1807]
Offshore Marine Ser. Assn. [588]
PACON Intl. [1160]
Passenger Vessel Assn. [589]
Reef Relief [1161]
Titanic Historical Soc. [1808]
West Gulf Maritime Assn. [590]
Yacht Brokers Assn. of Am. [591]
Iemanya Oceanica [1240]
MarineBio Conservation Soc. [1162]
Natl. Oceanic Soc. [1031]
Oceanic Preservation Soc. [1034]
Sustainable Fisheries Partnership [959]
Turtle Island Restoration Network [1044]
World Fed. for Coral Reef Conservation [1049]
Marine Aquarium Coun. [958], PO Box 90370, Los Angeles, CA 90009, (808)550-8217

Marine Biology
MarineBio Conservation Soc. [1162]
World Fed. for Coral Reef Conservation [1049]

Marine Corps
Marine Corps CounterIntelligence Assn. [2802]
Marine Corps Interrogator Translator Teams Assn. [2803]
Marine Corps CounterIntelligence Assn. [2802], PO Box 19125, Washington, DC 20036-9125
Marine Corps Interrogator Translator Teams Assn. [2803], 1900 S Ocean Blvd., Apt. 14L, Pompano Beach, FL 33062-8030

Marine Industries
Amer. Bur. of Shipping [592]
Assn. of Marina Indus. [593]
Inland Rivers Ports and Terminals [594]
Marine Retailers Assn. of Am. [586], PO Box 725, Boca Grande, FL 33921, (941)964-2534
Marine Tech. Soc. [1495], 5565 Sterrett Pl., Ste. 108, Columbia, MD 21044, (410)884-5330
MarineBio Conservation Soc. [1162], PO Box 235273, Encinitas, CA 92023, (713)248-2576
Mariological Soc. of Am. [2871], Univ. of Dayton, The Marian Lib., Dayton, OH 45469-1390, (937)229-4294

Maritime
Highlander Class Intl. Assn. [3273]
U.S. Albacore Assn. [3286]
U.S. Power Squadrons [3290]

Marketing
Assn. of Equip. Mfrs. l AEM Marketing Coun. [595]
CUES Financial Suppliers Forum [596]
Diagnostic Marketing Assn. [597]
Direct Marketing Assn. [598]
Electronic Retailing Assn. [599]
Hea. Indus. Representatives Assn. [600]
Intl. Experiential Marketing Assn. [601]
Legal Marketing Assn. [602]
Marketing Res. Assn. [603]
Marketing Sci. Inst. [604]
Mu Kappa Tau [3536]
Mystery Shopping Providers Assn. [605]
North Amer. Farmers' Direct Marketing Assn. [1163]
Organic Trade Assn. [1164]
Strategic Account Mgt. Assn. [606]

Word of Mouth Marketing Assn. [607]
Farmers Market Coalition [929]
Natl. Watermelon Assn. [1100]
Newspaper Target Marketing Coalition [626]
Retail Energy Supply Assn. [304]
Rising Tide Capital [265]
Marketing Res. Assn. [603], 110 Natl. Dr., 2nd Fl., Glastonbury, CT 06033-1212, (860)682-1000
Marketing Sci. Inst. [604], 1000 Massachusetts Ave., Cambridge, MA 02138-5396, (617)491-2060
Marquette Univ. Alumni Assn. [2760], Marquette Univ., PO Box 1881, Milwaukee, WI 53201-1881, (414)288-7441

Marriage
Alternatives to Marriage Proj. [2698]
Wedding Indus. Professionals Assn. [124]

Martial Arts
All Japan Ju-Jitsu Intl. Fed. [3359]
Intl. Assn. of Gay and Lesbian Martial Artists [3360]
Martial Arts Intl. Fed. [3361]
Special Military Active Retired Travel Club [3073]
Universal Martial Arts Brotherhood [3362]
The World Kuoshu Fed. [3363]
World Martial Arts Assn. [3364]
World Traditional Karate Org. [3365]
Intl. Chinese Boxing Assn. [3297]
Martial Arts Intl. Fed. [3361], 1850 Columbia Pike, Ste. No. 612, Arlington, VA 22204, (703)920-1590
Marx Brotherhood [3569], 335 Fieldstone Dr., New Hope, PA 18938-1012
Masonry Heater Assn. of North Am. [434], 2180 S Flying Q Ln., Tucson, AZ 85713, (520)883-0191

Masons
Ancient and Accepted Scottish Rite of Free Masonry, Southern Jurisdiction l Supreme Coun. 33rd Degree [2804]
High Twelve Intl. [2805]
Philalethes Soc. [2806]
Tall Cedars of Lebanon of North Am. [2807]

Massage
Alliance for Massage Therapy Educ. [1659]
Amer. Massage Therapy Assn. [2536]
Emergency Response Massage Intl. [2537]
Father Josef's Method of Reflexology [2293]
OmSpring [2296]
Master Window Cleaners of Am. [554], 1220G Airport Fwy., No. 561, Bedford, TX 76022
Masters of Foxhounds Assn. of Am. [3356], PO Box 363, Millwood, VA 22646, (540)955-5680
Materials and Methods Standards Assn. [150], 4125 LaPalma Ave., No. 250, Anaheim, CA 92807
Materials Properties Coun. [1498], PO Box 1942, New York, NY 10113-1941, (216)658-3847

Mathematics
Pi Mu Epsilon [3537]
Reasoning Mind [1660]
Soc. for Natural Philosophy [1496]
Maxillofacial Prosthetics; Amer. Acad. of [2366]
Mayflower Descendants; Gen. Soc. of [3077]
MDRC [2168], 16 E 34th St., 19th Fl., New York, NY 10016-4326, (212)532-3200

Meat
Natl. Meat Assn. [608]
Mech. Power Transmission Assn. [465], 6724 Lone Oak Blvd., Naples, FL 34109, (239)514-3441
Mechanics and Tradesmen of the City of New York; Gen. Soc. of [1691]
MED25 Intl. [2440], PO Box 1459, Mercer Island, WA 98040, (206)779-0655

Media
Natl. Assn. of Media and Tech. Centers [609]
Sci. Commun. Network [1165]
Independent Arts and Media [1709]
Mainstream Media Proj. [2735]
Natl. Assn. of Media Brokers [749]
Newspaper Target Marketing Coalition [626]
Media Communications Assn. Intl. [324], PO Box 5135, Madison, WI 53705-0135, (888)899-6224
Media Watch [2626], PO Box 618, Santa Cruz, CA 95061-0618, (831)423-6355

Medical
Amer. Acad. of Restorative Dentistry [2370]
Amer. Assn. of Endodontists l Amer. Bd. of Endodontics [2372]

Amer. Osteopathic Coll. of Anesthesiologists [2301]
Assn. of Biomedical Communications Directors [2350]
Heart Rhythm Soc. [2332]
Phi Chi Medical Fraternity [3539]

Medical Accreditation
Amer. Commn. for Accreditation of Reflexology Educ. and Training [1567]
Councils on Chiropractic Educ. Intl. [1585]

Medical Administration
Amer. Acad. of Medical Administrators [2538]
Amer. Assn. of Healthcare Administrative Mgt. [2539]
Assn. of Otolaryngology Administrators [2540]
Medical Gp. Mgt. Assn. [2541]
Natl. Renal Administrators Assn. [2542]
Radiology Bus. Mgt. Assn. [2543]
Assn. of Biomedical Communications Directors [2350]

Medical Aid
CHOSEN [2132]
Doctors in Christ [2544]
Gift of Life Intl. [2133]
Hea. For All Missions [2134]
Kenya Medical Outreach [2135]
Liga Intl. [2136]
MADRE [2137]
Mobile Medical Disaster Relief [2138]
NOVA Hope for Haiti [2139]
Pan Amer. Hea. and Educ. Found. [2140]
Alternative Medicine Intl. [2289]
Amazonas Hope for Hea. [2429]
Arise Medical Missions [2480]
Cambodian Hea. Professionals Assn. of Am. [2432]
Children's Intl. Hea. Relief [2335]
Children's Medical Mission of Haiti [1941]
Childspring Intl. [2336]
Clinicians of the World [2484]
Community Hea. Intl. [2448]
Doctors for United Medical Missions [2485]
Dorcas Medical Mission [2486]
Engg. World Hea. [2488]
Forward in Hea. [2433]
Friends for Hea. in Haiti [2434]
Global Flying Hospitals [2435]
Global Vision 2020 [2601]
Hannah's Promise Intl. Aid [2187]
Hea. Empowering Humanity [2436]
Hea. Horizons Intl. [2500]
Hea. through Walls [2501]
Honduras Outreach Medical Brigada Relief Effort [2502]
Hope Beyond Hope [2503]
Horizon Intl. Medical Mission [2505]
I Care Grace Intl. [2437]
Intl. Hea. and Development Network [2507]
Intl. Medical Alliance [2508]
Medical Missions for Children [2337]
Medics Without Borders [2407]
Meds and Food for Kids [1973]
Partners for World Hea. [2512]
Reach Across [3011]
Sharing Resources Worldwide [2516]
Women for World Hea. [2442]
World Hea. Ambassador [2443]

Medical Assistants
Assn. for Healthcare Documentation Integrity [2545]

Medical Education
Assn. for Medical Educ. and Res. in Substance Abuse [1661]
Assn. of Minority Hea. Professions Schools [1662]
Assn. of Professors of Medicine [1663]
Alliance for Massage Therapy Educ. [1659]
Amer. Chinese Medical Exchange Soc. [2431]
Chiropractic Diplomatic Corps [2340]
Coun. for Acupuncture Res. and Educ. [2284]
Councils on Chiropractic Educ. Intl. [1585]
Naturopathic Medical Student Assn. [2554]
Universities Allied for Essential Medicines [1641]
Medical Gp. Mgt. Assn. [2541], 104 Inverness Terr. E, Englewood, CO 80112-5306, (303)799-1111
Medical Mission Gp. [2509], 134 Grove St., Pearl River, NY 10965, (845)920-9001

A star before a book entry number signifies that the name is not listed separately, but is mentioned within the entry.

Medical Missions for Children **[2337]**, 10-G Roessler Rd., Ste. 500, Woburn, MA 01801, (508)697-5821

Medical Research
Heart Rhythm Soc. **[2332]**
Intl. Psoriasis Coun. **[2394]**
Surfing Medicine Intl. **[2299]**
Universities Allied for Essential Medicines **[1641]**

Medical Specialties
Amer. Osteopathic Coll. of Anesthesiologists **[2301]**

Medical Technology
Engg. World Hea. **[2488]**
Universities Allied for Essential Medicines **[1641]**
World Hea. Imaging, Telemedicine and Informatics Alliance **[2524]**

Medicine
Alpha Epsilon Delta **[3538]**
Amer. Assn. of Medical Soc. Executives **[2546]**
Chinese Amer. Medical Soc. **[2547]**
Harvey Soc. **[2548]**
MAP Intl. **[2977]**
Natl. Medical Assn. **[2549]**
Phi Chi Medical Fraternity **[3539]**
Amer. Abdominal Acupuncture Medical Assn. **[2283]**
Amer. Herbal Pharmacopoeia **[2291]**
Doctors in Christ **[2544]**
Global Solutions for Infectious Diseases **[2472]**
Heart Rhythm Soc. **[2332]**
Intl. Soc. for Ayurveda and Hea. **[2295]**
Surfing Medicine Intl. **[2299]**
Universities Allied for Essential Medicines **[1641]**
Medics Without Borders **[2407]**, PO Box 35, Woodbridge, VA 22194, (703)268-4774

Medieval
Intl. Center of Medieval Art **[1809]**

Mediterranean
Mediterranean Stud. Assn. **[1810]**
Mediterranean Stud. Assn. **[1810]**, Box 79351, North Dartmouth, MA 02747, (508)979-8687
Meds and Food for Kids **[1973]**, 4488 Forest Park Ave., Ste. 230, St. Louis, MO 63108, (314)420-1634

Meeting Planners
Assn. for Convention Operations Mgt. **[610]**
Exposition Ser. Contractors Assn. **[611]**
Intl. Assn. of Hispanic Meeting Professionals **[612]**
Natl. Coalition of Black Meeting Planners **[613]**
Melungeon Heritage Assn. **[2766]**, PO Box 1253, Danville, VA 24543

Mennonite
Mennonite Central Comm. **[2978]**
Mennonite Church USA Historical Comm. **[2979]**
Mennonite Central Comm. **[2978]**, 21 S 12th St., PO Box 500, Akron, PA 17501-0500, (717)859-1151
Mennonite Church USA Historical Comm. **[2979]**, 1700 S Main St., Goshen, IN 46526, (574)523-3080

Mental Health
All Healers Mental Hea. Alliance **[2550]**
Intl. Assn. for Women's Mental Hea. **[2551]**
Aging with Autism **[2307]**
Amer. Asperger's Assn. **[2562]**
Autism Care and Treatment Today! **[2309]**
Autism Community of Africa **[1909]**
Coun. on Accreditation **[2233]**
Global Autism Collaboration **[2316]**
Milestones Autism Org. **[2319]**
Stop Calling It Autism! **[2320]**
Talk About Curing Autism **[2323]**

Mentally Disabled
Amer. Network of Community Options and Resources **[2141]**
Little City Found. **[2142]**
Natl. Assn. of Councils on Developmental Disabilities **[2143]**
Aging with Autism **[2307]**
Amer. Asperger's Assn. **[2562]**
Autism Community of Africa **[1909]**
Families with Autism Spectrum Disorders **[2313]**
Global Communities of Support **[1910]**
Hands for Autistic Children of Ethiopia **[1911]**
Milestones Autism Org. **[2319]**
Stop Calling It Autism! **[2320]**
Talk About Curing Autism **[2323]**
MERCAZ USA **[2958]**, 820 Second Ave., 10th Fl., New York, NY 10017-4504, (212)533-2061

Mercedes-Benz Club of Am. **[3116]**, 1907 Lelaray St., Colorado Springs, CO 80909-2872, (719)633-6427
Merchant Risk Coun. **[261]**, 2400 N 45th St., Ste. 15, Seattle, WA 98103, (206)364-2789
Merck Family Fund **[1067]**, 95 Eliot St., Ste. 2, Milton, MA 02186, (617)696-3580
Mercy Beyond Borders **[2169]**, 1885 De La Cruz Blvd., Ste. 101, Santa Clara, CA 95050, (650)815-1554
Messianic Jewish Alliance of Am. **[2980]**, PO Box 274, Springfield, PA 19064, (610)338-0451

Messianic Judaism
Messianic Jewish Alliance of Am. **[2980]**
Messies Anonymous **[2221]**, 10525 NW 146th Pl., Alachua, FL 32615-5723

Metal
Intl. Hard Anodizing Assn. **[614]**
Cool Metal Roofing Coalition **[144]**
Natl. Assn. of Hose and Accessories Distribution **[466]**
Metallurgical Soc. of Am; Mining and **[1500]**

Metallurgy
Intl. Copper Assn. **[1497]**
Materials Properties Coun. **[1498]**
Methacrylate Producers Assn. **[186]**, 17260 Vannes Ct., Hamilton, VA 20158, (540)751-2093

Methodist
Methodist Fed. for Social Action **[2981]**
Methodist Assn. of Hea. and Welfare Ministries; United **[2427]**
Methodist Fed. for Social Action **[2981]**, 212 E Capitol St. NE, Washington, DC 20003, (202)546-8806
Metropolitan Community Churches **[2939]**, PO Box 1374, Abilene, TX 79604, (310)360-8640
Metropolitan Opera Guild **[1823]**, 70 Lincoln Center Plz., New York, NY 10023, (212)769-7000

Mexico
Mano A Mano: Mexican Culture Without Borders **[1811]**
mHealth Alliance **[2510]**, 1800 Massachusetts Ave. NW, Ste. 400, Washington, DC 20036, (202)887-9040
Michael E. DeBakey Intl. Surgical Soc. **[2333]**, c/o Kenneth L. Mattox, MD, Sec.-Treas., 1 Baylor Plz., Houston, TX 77030, (713)798-4557
Microbiology; Amer. Acad. of **[1419]**

Microscopy
Optical Imaging Assn. **[1166]**

Middle East
America-MidEast Educational and Training Services **[2699]**
Americans for a Safe Israel **[2700]**
Intl. Coun. for Middle East Stud. **[2701]**
Ishmael and Isaac **[2702]**
Middle East Stud. Assn. of North Am. **[2703]**
Amer. MidEast Leadership Network **[2677]**
Building Bridges: Middle East-US **[1642]**
Middle East Investment Initiative **[336]**
Middle East Investment Initiative **[336]**, 500 Eighth St. NW, Washington, DC 20004, (202)741-6283
Middle East Librarians Assn. **[1802]**, Harvard Univ., Widener Lib., Rm. 5, 1 Harvard Yard, Cambridge, MA 02138, (617)496-3001
Middle East Stud. Assn. of North Am. **[2703]**, Univ. of Arizona, 1219 N Santa Rita Ave., Tucson, AZ 85721, (520)621-5850

Middle Schools
Natl. Middle School Assn. **[1664]**
Midstates Jeepster Assn. **[3117]**, 7721 Howick Rd., Celina, OH 45822
Midwest Acad. **[2006]**, 27 E Monroe, 11th Fl., Chicago, IL 60603, (312)427-2304
Midwest Decoy Collectors Assn. **[3159]**, 6 E Scott St., No. 3, Chicago, IL 60610, (312)337-7957
Midwest Equip. Dealers Assn. **[930]**, 5330 Wall St., Ste. 100, Madison, WI 53718, (608)240-4700
Midwest Rugby Football Union **[★3378]**

Migrant Workers
Assn. of Farmworker Opportunity Programs **[2144]**
Global Workers Justice Alliance **[2145]**
Mike's Angels **[1974]**, 2090 Dunwoody Club Dr., Ste. 106-120, Atlanta, GA 30350-5424, (770)396-7858
Milestones Autism Org. **[2319]**, 23880 Commerce Park, Ste. 2, Beachwood, OH 44122, (216)464-7600

Military
Air Force Assn. **[1346]**
Air Force Sergeants Assn. **[1347]**
Amer. Logistics Assn. **[1348]**
Assn. of Military Surgeons of the U.S. **[2552]**
Center for Strategic and Budgetary Assessments **[2704]**
Civil Affairs Assn. **[1349]**
Intl. Military Community Executives Assn. **[615]**
Natl. Soc. of Pershing Rifles **[3540]**
Orders and Medals Soc. of Am. **[3213]**
Professional Loadmaster Assn. **[1350]**
Catholic War Veterans of the U.S.A. **[3080]**
Center on Conscience and War **[2641]**
Military Order of the Stars and Bars **[3056]**
Natl. Assn. for Civil War Brass Music **[1825]**
North-South Skirmish Assn. **[3384]**
Pro vs. GI Joe **[3200]**
Salute Military Golf Assn. **[3339]**

Military Families
Amer. Legion Auxiliary **[3074]**
Sons of the Amer. Legion **[3075]**
World War II War Brides Assn. **[3076]**
Catholic War Veterans of the U.S.A. **[3080]**

Military History
Catholic War Veterans of the U.S.A. **[3080]**
Military Order of the Stars and Bars **[3056]**
Natl. Assn. for Civil War Brass Music **[1825]**
North-South Skirmish Assn. **[3384]**
Military Intelligence Corps Assn. **[1269]**, PO Box 13020, Fort Huachuca, AZ 85670-3020, (520)227-3894
Military Order of the Stars and Bars **[3056]**, PO Box 1700, White House, TN 37188-1700, (877)790-6672
Millennium Campus Network **[2614]**, 1330 Beacon St., Ste. 249, Brookline, MA 02446

Mineralogy
Clay Minerals Soc. **[1499]**

Minerals
World Gold Coun. **[616]**
Miniature Australian Shepherd Club of Am. **[3179]**, PO Box 248, Roanoke, IN 46783
Miniature Hereford Breeders Assn. **[987]**, 60885 Salt Creek Rd., Collbran, CO 81624

Mining
Mining Elecl. Maintenance and Safety Assn. **[617]**
Mining and Metallurgical Soc. of Am. **[1500]**
Perlite Inst. **[618]**
Soc. for Mining, Metallurgy, and Exploration **[1501]**
Equip. Managers Coun. of Am. **[204]**
Mining Elecl. Maintenance and Safety Assn. **[617]**, c/o Bill Collins, Sec.-Treas., PO Box 7163, Lakeland, FL 33807
Mining and Metallurgical Soc. of Am. **[1500]**, PO Box 810, Boulder, CO 80306-0810, (303)444-6032

Ministry
Acad. of Parish Clergy **[2982]**
Christ for the City Intl. **[2983]**
Intl. Network of Prison Ministries **[2984]**
LifeWind Intl. **[2985]**
World Hope Intl. **[2986]**
Ministry Architecture **[1409]**
Ministry Architecture **[1409]**, 1904 S Union Pl., Lakewood, CO 80228, (720)937-9664

Minorities
Idoma Assn. USA **[2812]**
Intl. Soc. of Filipinos in Finance and Accounting **[8]**
Iranian Alliances Across Borders **[2796]**
Natl. Assn. of Peoplecultural Engg. Prog. Advocates **[1615]**
Natl. Community for Latino Leadership **[2800]**
Natl. Latina Bus. Women Assn. **[534]**
Union of North Am. Vietnamese Students Assn. **[2832]**

Minority Business
Natl. Assn. of Investment Companies **[619]**

Minority Students
Union of North Am. Vietnamese Students Assn. **[2832]**
Miracles in Action **[2170]**, 241 Countryside Dr., Naples, FL 34104, (239)348-0815
Missing and Exploited Children; Natl. Center for **[1976]**

Missing-in-Action
Natl. League of Families of Amer. Prisoners and Missing in Southeast Asia **[2705]**

Mission

Africa Inland Mission Intl. **[2987]**
Agricultural Missions, Inc. **[2988]**
Amer. Soc. of Missiology **[2989]**
Avant Ministries **[2990]**
Bibles For The World **[2991]**
Catholic Comm. of Appalachia **[2992]**
Christian Aid Mission **[2993]**
Christian Missions in Many Lands **[2994]**
Christian Pilots Assn. **[2995]**
Evangelical Free Church of Am. **[2996]**
Evangelical Missiological Soc. **[2997]**
Fellowship Intl. Mission **[2998]**
Global Economic Outreach **[2999]**
Gospel Literature Intl. **[3000]**
Inter Varsity Christian Fellowship **[3001]**
Intl. Mission Bd. **[3002]**
Latin Am. Mission **[3003]**
Moody Bible Inst. **[3004]**
Mustard Seed Found. **[3005]**
New Tribes Mission **[3006]**
North Am. Indigenous Ministries **[3007]**
O.C. Intl. **[3008]**
OMF Intl. U.S.A. **[3009]**
OMS Intl. **[3010]**
Reach Across **[3011]**
Samaritans Intl. **[3012]**
Spanish World Ministries **[3013]**
United Indian Missions Intl. **[3014]**
World for Christ Crusade **[3015]**
World Team **[3016]**
Youth With a Mission **[3017]**
BCM Intl. **[2849]**
CHOSEN **[2132]**
Coalition on the Env. and Jewish Life **[2951]**
A Cup of Water Intl. **[3039]**
Intl. Catholic Deaf Assn. U.S. Sect. **[2868]**
Mobile Marketing Assn. **[20]**, 8 W 38th St., Ste. 200, New York, NY 10018, (646)257-4515
Mobile Medical Disaster Relief **[2138]**, 5409 Maryland Way, Ste. 119, Brentwood, TN 37027, (615)833-3002
Model A Ford Club of Am. **[3118]**, 250 S Cypress St., La Habra, CA 90631-5515, (562)697-2712

Model Trains

Toy Train Collectors Soc. **[3214]**
Youth in Model Railroading **[3215]**

Models

Intl. Scale Soaring Assn. **[3216]**
Toy Train Collectors Soc. **[3214]**
World Airline Historical Soc. **[3089]**
Youth in Model Railroading **[3215]**
Molecular Biology; Amer. Soc. for Biochemistry and **[1417]**
The Moles **[2827]**, 577 Chestnut Ridge Rd., Woodcliff Lake, NJ 07677, (201)930-1923
Monks Without Borders **[2946]**, 1750 Grant St., Eugene, OR 97402, (562)448-2012
Montserrat Progressive Soc. of New York **[2834]**, The Montserrat Bldg., 207 W 137th St., New York, NY 10030-2425, (212)283-3346
Moody Bible Inst. **[3004]**, 820 N LaSalle Blvd., Chicago, IL 60610, (312)329-4000
Morgan 3/4 Gp. **[3119]**, PO Box 1208, Ridgefield, CT 06877, (917)880-2962
Morgan Car Club **[3120]**, c/o Lisa Shriver, 45070 Brae Terr., Ashburn, VA 20147
Moroccan Amer. Bus. Coun. **[516]**, 1085 Commonwealth Ave., Ste. 194, Boston, MA 02215, (508)230-9943
Morris Cerullo World Evangelism **[2933]**, PO Box 85277, San Diego, CA 92186-5277, (858)277-2200

Mortuary Science

Amer. Bd. of Funeral Ser. Educ. **[620]**

Mortuary Services

Jewish Funeral Directors of Am. **[621]**
Natl. Funeral Directors and Morticians Assn. **[622]**
Mothers Without Borders **[1975]**, 125 E Main St., Ste. 402, American Fork, UT 84003, (801)607-5641
Motor Bus Soc. **[3121]**, PO Box 261, Paramus, NJ 07653-0261

Motorcycle

Amer. Motorcyclist Assn. **[3366]**
Antique Motorcycle Club of Am. **[3217]**
British Biker Cooperative **[3218]**
Intl. Brotherhood of Motorcycle Campers **[3367]**
Intl. CBX Owners Assn. **[3219]**
Vintage BMW Motorcycle Owners **[3220]**
Light Elec. Vehicle Assn. **[873]**
Moulding and Millwork Producers Assn. **[151]**, 507 1st St., Woodland, CA 95695, (530)661-9591
Mountain Pleasure Horse Assn. **[1137]**, PO Box 33, Wellington, KY 40387, (606)768-3847
Mountains and Plains Independent Booksellers Assn. **[171]**, 8020 Springshire Dr., Park City, UT 84098, (435)649-6079
MRFAC **[128]**, 899-A Harrison St. SE, Leesburg, VA 20175, (703)669-0320
Ms. Found. for Women **[2648]**, 12 MetroTech Center, 26th Fl., Brooklyn, NY 11201, (212)742-2300
Mu Kappa Tau **[3536]**, Univ. of Wisconsin-Madison, Grainger Hall, 975 Univ. Ave., Madison, WI 53706
Multicultural Foodservice and Hospitality Alliance **[375]**, 1144 Narragansett Blvd., Providence, RI 02905, (401)461-6342
Multinational Exchange for Sustainable Agriculture **[1218]**, 2362 Bancroft Way, No. 202, Berkeley, CA 94704, (510)654-8858
MultiService Forum **[196]**, 48377 Fremont Blvd., Ste. 117, Fremont, CA 94538, (510)492-4050

Municipal Government

Natl. Assn. of Towns and Townships **[1351]**
Women in Govt. **[1352]**
Equip. Managers Coun. of Am. **[204]**
Museum Educ. Roundtable **[1817]**, PO Box 15727, Washington, DC 20003, (202)547-8378

Museums

Amer. Anthropological Assn. | Coun. for Museum Anthropology **[1812]**
Assn. of Academic Museums and Galleries **[1813]**
Assn. of Art Museum Directors **[1814]**
Coun. of Amer. Jewish Museums **[1815]**
Intl. Cong. of Maritime Museums **[1816]**
Museum Educ. Roundtable **[1817]**

Music

Alabama Fan Club **[3570]**
Always Patsy Cline World Wide Fan Org. **[3571]**
Amer. Composers Alliance **[1818]**
Amer. School Band Directors' Assn. **[1665]**
Amy Beth Fan Club **[3572]**
Assn. of Anglican Musicians **[3018]**
Beach Boys Fan Club **[3573]**
Billy "Crash" Craddock Fan Club **[3574]**
Caledonian Found. USA **[1819]**
Charley Pride Fan Club **[3575]**
Chicago True Advocates **[3576]**
Choristers Guild **[3019]**
Chorus Am. **[1820]**
Chris LeDoux Intl. Fan Club **[3577]**
Church Music Assn. of Am. **[3020]**
Coll. Band Directors Natl. Assn. **[1666]**
Gene Pitney Intl. Fan Club **[3578]**
George Strait Fan Club **[3579]**
Glenn Miller Birthplace Soc. **[3580]**
Hank Williams Intl. Fan Club **[3581]**
Hymn Soc. in the U.S. and Canada **[3021]**
Intl. Clarinet Assn. **[1821]**
Intl. Cmpt. Music Assn. **[623]**
Intl. Crosby Circle **[3582]**
Intl. Tuba-Euphonium Assn. **[1822]**
Kate Smith Commemorative Soc. **[3583]**
KISS Rocks Fan Club **[3584]**
Lesley Gore Intl. Fan Club **[3585]**
Metropolitan Opera Guild **[1823]**
Music Critics Assn. of North Am. **[1824]**
Natl. Assn. for Civil War Brass Music **[1825]**
Natl. Assn. of Coll. Wind and Percussion Instructors **[1667]**
Natl. Assn. of School Music Dealers **[624]**
Natl. Assn. of Schools of Music **[1668]**
New Horizons Intl. Music Assn. **[1826]**
New Violin Family Assn. **[1827]**
Official Fan Club of the Grand Ole Opry **[3586]**
Roy Rogers - Dale Evans Collectors Assn. **[3587]**
Soc. for Ethnomusicology **[1828]**
Soc. for Music Perception and Cognition **[1829]**
Soc. of Pi Kappa Lambda **[3541]**
SoundExchange **[625]**

Angel Harps **[2588]**
Kate's Voice **[1678]**
Music Therapy for Healing **[2589]**
Music Critics Assn. of North Am. **[1824]**, 722 Dulaney Valley Rd., No. 259, Baltimore, MD 21204, (410)435-3881
Music Lib. Assn. **[1803]**, 8551 Res. Way, Ste. 180, Middleton, WI 53562-3567, (608)836-5825
Music Therapy for Healing **[2589]**, 6688 Nolensville Rd., Ste. 111, No. 165, Brentwood, TN 37027, (615)216-0589
Music Video Production Assn. **[760]**, c/o Beth Sadler, Sony Pictures Studios, 10202 W Washington Blvd., Cohn Bldg., Culver City, CA 90232, (310)244-6964

Musicians

Intl. Crosby Circle **[3582]**
Music Therapy for Healing **[2589]**

Muslim

Free Muslims Coalition **[2706]**
Imam Mahdi Assn. of Marjaeya **[3022]**
Abrahamic Alliance Intl. **[2945]**
Reach Across **[3011]**
Mustang Club of Am. **[3122]**, 4051 Barrancas Ave., PMB 102, Pensacola, FL 32507, (850)438-0626
Mustard Seed Found. **[3005]**, 7115 Leesburg Pike, Ste. 304, Falls Church, VA 22043, (703)524-5620
Mutual Fund Educ. Alliance **[797]**, 100 NW Englewood Rd., Ste. 130, Kansas City, MO 64118, (816)454-9422
Mystery Shopping Providers Assn. **[605]**, 4230 LBJ Freeway, Ste. 414, Dallas, TX 75244

Mysticism

Astara **[3023]**

N

Na'amat U.S.A. **[2959]**, 505 8th Ave., Ste. 2302, New York, NY 10118, (212)563-5222
NALGAP: The Assn. of Lesbian, Gay, Bisexual, and Transgender Addiction Professionals and Their Allies **[2243]**, 1001 N Fairfax St., Ste. 201, Alexandria, VA 22314
NASSCO **[895]**, 11521 Cronridge Dr., Ste. J, Owings Mills, MD 21117, (410)486-3500
Natl. 4-H Coun. **[2278]**, 7100 Connecticut Ave., Chevy Chase, MD 20815, (301)961-2801
Natl. 4th Infantry Ivy Div. Assn. **[3052]**, c/o Don Kelby, Exec. Dir., PO Box 1914, St. Peters, MO 63376-0035, (314)606-1969
Natl. 42 Players Assn. **[3198]**, c/o David Roberts, Treas., 215 Sunday Cir., Fredericksburg, TX 78624, (830)990-0123
Natl. Acad. of Educ. **[1607]**, 500 5th St. NW, Washington, DC 20001, (202)334-2341
Natl. Acad. of Needlearts **[3169]**, c/o Debbie Stiehler, 1 Riverbanks Ct., Greer, SC 29651
Natl. Acad. of Public Admin. **[1360]**, 900 7th St. NW, Ste. 600, Washington, DC 20001, (202)347-3190
National Acad. for Voluntarism **[★2091]**
Natl. Active and Retired Fed. Employees Assn. **[1296]**, 606 N Washington St., Alexandria, VA 22314, (703)838-7760
Natl. Adult Day Services Assn. **[1879]**, 1421 E Broad St., Ste. 425, Fuquay Varina, NC 27526, (877)745-1440
Natl. Aeronautic Assn. **[32]**, 1 Reagan Natl. Airport, Hangar 7, Ste. 202, Washington, DC 20001-6015, (703)416-4888
Natl. African-American Insurance Assn. **[493]**, 1718 M St. NW, Box No. 1110, Washington, DC 20036, (866)566-2242
Natl. Agri-Marketing Assn. **[21]**, 11020 King St., Ste. 205, Overland Park, KS 66210, (913)491-6500
Natl. Air Filtration Assn. **[435]**, PO Box 68639, Virginia Beach, VA 23471, (757)313-7400
Natl. Air Traffic Controllers Assn. **[3439]**, 1325 Massachusetts Ave. NW, Washington, DC 20005, (202)628-5451
Natl. Aircraft Resale Assn. **[33]**, PO Box 3860, Grapevine, TX 76099, (402)475-7611
Natl. Alliance for Advanced Tech. Batteries **[116]**, 122 S Michigan Ave., Ste. 1700, Chicago, IL 60603, (312)588-0477
Natl. Alliance Against Christian Discrimination **[2897]**, PO Box 62685, Colorado Springs, CO 80962

A star before a book entry number signifies that the name is not listed separately, but is mentioned within the entry.

Natl. Alliance of Burmese Breeders **[966]**, PO Box 100038, Cudahy, WI 53110

Natl. Alliance of Gang Investigators Associations **[1286]**, PO Box 782, Elkhorn, NE 68022, (402)510-8581

Natl. Alliance of Highway Beautification Agencies **[1370]**, PO Box 191, Columbia, SC 29202

Natl. Alliance for Media Arts and Culture **[1725]**, 145 9th St., Ste. 102, San Francisco, CA 94103, (415)431-1391

Natl. Alliance for Model State Drug Laws **[1288]**, 215 Lincoln Ave., Ste. 201, Santa Fe, NM 87501, (703)836-6100

Natl. Alliance of State and Territorial AIDS Directors **[1885]**, 444 N Capitol St. NW, Ste. 339, Washington, DC 20001, (202)434-8090

Natl. Amateur Baseball Fed. **[3259]**, c/o Charles M. Blackburn, Jr., Exec. Dir., PO Box 705, Bowie, MD 20715, (410)721-4727

Natl. Amateur Dodgeball Assn. **[3253]**, 1223 W Sharon Ln., Schaumburg, IL 60193, (847)985-2120

Natl. Amputation Found. **[2061]**, 40 Church St., Malverne, NY 11565, (516)887-3600

Natl. Appliance Parts Suppliers Assn. **[48]**, 4015 W Marshall Ave., Longview, TX 75604

Natl. Art Educ. Assn. **[1571]**, 1806 Robert Fulton Dr., Ste. 300, Reston, VA 20191, (703)860-8000

Natl. Assembly of State Arts Agencies **[1726]**, 1029 Vermont Ave. NW, 2nd Fl., Washington, DC 20005, (202)347-6352

Natl. Assn. of Academies of Sci. **[1531]**, c/o Mary E. Burke, Sec., Acad. of Sci. of St. Louis, 5050 Oakland Ave., St. Louis, MO 63110, (314)533-8082

Natl. Assn. of Addiction Treatment Providers **[2244]**, 313 W Liberty St., Ste. 129, Lancaster, PA 17603-2748, (717)392-8480

Natl. Assn. to Advance Fat Acceptance **[2148]**, PO Box 22510, Oakland, CA 94609, (916)558-6880

Natl. Assn. of Affordable Housing Lenders **[112]**, 1667 K St., Ste. 210, Washington, DC 20006, (202)293-9850

Natl. Assn. of African Americans in Human Resources **[454]**, PO Box 311395, Atlanta, GA 31131

Natl. Assn. of Agriculture Employees **[1263]**, 9080 Torrey Rd., Willis, MI 48191, (734)942-9005

Natl. Assn. of Area Agencies on Aging **[1880]**, 1730 Rhode Island Ave. NW, Ste. 1200, Washington, DC 20036, (202)872-0888

Natl. Assn. for Armenian Stud. and Res. **[1707]**, 395 Concord Ave., Belmont, MA 02478, (617)489-1610

Natl. Assn. of Asian Amer. Law Enforcement Commanders **[1332]**, PO Box 420496, San Francisco, CA 94142-0496

Natl. Assn. of Atomic Veterans **[2253]**, 11214 Sageland, Houston, TX 77089, (281)481-1357

Natl. Assn. of Baptist Professors of Religion **[1693]**, Anderson Coll., PO Box 1123, Anderson, SC 29621

Natl. Assn. of Bar Executives **[1325]**, 321 N Clark St., Chicago, IL 60654, (312)988-6008

Natl. Assn. of Benefits and Work Incentive Specialists **[294]**, 12009 Shallot St., Orlando, FL 32837, (407)859-7767

Natl. Assn. for Bilingual Educ. **[1572]**, 8701 Georgia Ave., Ste. 611, Silver Spring, MD 20910, (240)450-3700

Natl. Assn. of Biology Teachers **[1573]**, 1313 Dolley Madison Blvd., Ste. 402, McLean, VA 22101, (703)264-9696

Natl. Assn. of Black County Officials **[1284]**, 1090 Vermont Ave. NW, Ste. 1290, Washington, DC 20005, (202)350-6696

Natl. Assn. of Black Female Executives in Music and Entertainment **[311]**, 59 Maiden Ln., 27th Fl., New York, NY 10038, (212)424-9568

Natl. Assn. of Black Journalists **[697]**, Univ. of Maryland, 1100 Knight Hall, Ste. 3100, College Park, MD 20742, (301)445-7100

Natl. Assn. of Black Owned Broadcasters **[129]**, 1201 Connecticut Ave. NW, Ste. 200, Washington, DC 20036, (202)463-8970

Natl. Assn. of Black Women in Constr. **[206]**, 1910 NW 105 Ave., Pembroke Pines, FL 33026

Natl. Assn. of Casino Party Operators **[312]**, PO Box 5626, South San Francisco, CA 94083, (888)922-0777

Natl. Assn. of Catastrophe Adjusters **[494]**, PO Box 821864, North Richland Hills, TX 76182, (817)498-3466

Natl. Assn. of Catholic Chaplains **[2889]**, 4915 S Howell Ave., Ste. 501, Milwaukee, WI 53207, (414)483-4898

Natl. Assn. of Chain Drug Stores **[2577]**, 413 N Lee St., Alexandria, VA 22314, (703)549-3001

Natl. Assn. for Children of Alcoholics **[2245]**, 10920 Connecticut Ave., Ste. 100, Kensington, MD 20895, (301)468-0985

Natl. Assn. of Christian Financial Consultants **[349]**, 1055 Maitland Center Commons Blvd., Maitland, FL 32751, (407)644-9793

Natl. Assn. for Civil War Brass Music **[1825]**, 124 Maiden Choice Ln., Baltimore, MD 21228, (410)744-7708

Natl. Assn. of Coll. and Univ. Mail Services **[684]**, PO Box 270367, Fort Collins, CO 80527-0367, (877)NAC-UMS1

Natl. Assn. of Coll. Wind and Percussion Instructors **[1667]**, c/o Dr. Richard K. Weerts, Exec. Sec.-Treas., 308 Hillcrest Dr., Kirksville, MO 63501

Natl. Assn. of Collegiate Directors of Athletics **[3403]**, 24651 Detroit Rd., Westlake, OH 44145, (440)892-4000

Natl. Assn. of Commissions for Women **[2649]**, 401 N Washington St., Ste. 100, Rockville, MD 20850-1737, (240)777-8308

Natl. Assn. of Competitive Mounted Orienteering **[3370]**, 4309 Laura St. NW, Comstock Park, MI 49321, (616)784-1645

Natl. Assn. of Constr. Contractors Cooperation **[152]**, 7447 Holmes Rd., Ste. 300, Kansas City, MO 64131, (816)442-8680

Natl. Assn. of Consumer Credit Administrators **[1282]**, PO Box 20871, Columbus, OH 43220-0871, (614)326-1165

Natl. Assn. of Corporate Treasurers **[337]**, 12100 Sunset Hills Rd., Ste. 130, Reston, VA 20190, (703)437-4377

Natl. Assn. of Councils on Developmental Disabilities **[2143]**, 1660 L St. NW, Ste. 700, Washington, DC 20036, (202)506-5813

Natl. Assn. of County Agricultural Agents **[1264]**, 6584 W Duroc Rd., Maroa, IL 61756, (217)794-3700

Natl. Assn. of Credit Union Services Organizations **[248]**, 3419 Via Lido, PMB 135, Newport Beach, CA 92663, (949)645-5296

Natl. Assn. of Crime Victim Compensation Boards **[2255]**, PO Box 16003, Alexandria, VA 22302, (703)780-3200

Natl. Assn. of Decorative Fabric Distributors **[856]**, 1 Windsor Cove, Ste. 305, Columbia, SC 29223-1833, (803)252-5646

Natl. Assn. of Dental Labs. **[2383]**, 325 John Knox Rd., No. L103, Tallahassee, FL 32303, (850)205-5626

Natl. Assn. of Disability Examiners **[2353]**, 1599 Green St., No. 303, San Francisco, CA 94123, (510)622-3385

Natl. Assn. of Div. Order Analysts **[647]**, PO Box 6845, Edmond, OK 73083, (432)685-4374

Natl. Assn. of Dog Obedience Instructors **[3180]**, PO Box 1439, Socorro, NM 87801, (505)850-5957

Natl. Assn. of Elecl. Distributors I Natl. Educ. and Res. Found. **[565]**, 1181 Corporate Lake Dr., St. Louis, MO 63132, (314)991-9000

Natl. Assn. of Enrolled Agents **[1378]**, 1120 Connecticut Ave. NW, Ste. 460, Washington, DC 20036-3953, (202)822-6232

Natl. Assn. of Estate Planners and Councils **[350]**, 1120 Chester Ave., Ste. 470, Cleveland, OH 44114, (866)226-2224

Natl. Assn. for Ethnic Stud. **[1755]**, Colorado State Univ., Dept. of Ethnic Stud., 1790 Campus Delivery, Fort Collins, CO 80523-1790

Natl. Assn. of Exotic Pest Plant Councils **[1179]**, Univ. of Georgia, Center for Invasive Species and Ecosystem Hea., PO Box 748, Tifton, GA 31793, (229)386-3298

Natl. Assn. of Fed. Credit Unions **[249]**, 3138 10th St. N, Arlington, VA 22201-2149, (703)522-4770

Natl. Assn. for Female Executives **[172]**, PO Box 3052, Langhorne, PA 19047, (800)927-6233

Natl. Assn. of Financial and Estate Planning **[338]**, 515 E 4500 S, No. G-200, Salt Lake City, UT 84107, (800)454-2649

Natl. Assn. for Fixed Annuities **[495]**, 2300 E Kensington Blvd., Milwaukee, WI 53211, (414)332-9306

Natl. Assn. of Fraternal Insurance Counsellors **[496]**, 211 Canal Rd., Waterloo, WI 53594, (866)478-3880

Natl. Assn. of Free Will Baptists **[2844]**, 5233 Mt. View Rd., Antioch, TN 37013-2306, (615)731-6812

Natl. Assn. of Govt. Defined Contribution Administrators **[526]**, 201 E Main St., Ste. 1405, Lexington, KY 40507, (859)514-9161

Natl. Assn. for Govt. Training and Development **[634]**, 156 Whispering Winds Dr., Lexington, SC 29072, (803)397-8468

Natl. Assn. of Governmental Labor Officials **[1320]**, PO Box 29609, Atlanta, GA 30359, (404)679-1795

Natl. Assn. of Hea. and Educational Facilities Finance Authorities **[417]**, 701 Pennsylvania Ave. NW, No. 900, Washington, DC 20004, (202)434-7311

Natl. Assn. of Healthcare Access Mgt. **[2470]**, 2025 M St. NW, Ste. 800, Washington, DC 20036-2422, (202)367-1125

Natl. Assn. of Hispanic Firefighters **[1298]**, 1220 L St. NW, Ste. 100-199, Washington, DC 20005, (877)342-6243

Natl. Assn. of Hispanic Real Estate Professionals **[748]**, 5414 Oberlin Dr., Ste. 230, San Diego, CA 92121, (858)622-9046

Natl. Assn. for Holistic Aromatherapy **[2461]**, PO Box 1868, Banner Elk, NC 28604, (828)898-6161

Natl. Assn. of the Holy Name Soc. **[2872]**, c/o Cleveland Cosom, Dir., PO Box 12012, Baltimore, MD 21281-2012, (410)325-1523

Natl. Assn. of Home Builders I Log Homes Coun. **[573]**, 1201 15th St. NW, Washington, DC 20005, (800)368-5242

Natl. Assn. of Home Builders I Modular Building Systems Coun. **[574]**, 1201 15th St. NW, Washington, DC 20005, (202)266-8200

Natl. Assn. for Home Care and Hospice **[2462]**, 228 7th St. SE, Washington, DC 20003, (202)547-7424

Natl. Assn. of Hose and Accessories Distribution **[466]**, 105 Eastern Ave., Ste. 104, Annapolis, MD 21403, (410)940-6350

Natl. Assn. of Housing Counselors and Agencies **[453]**, PO Box 91873, Lafayette, LA 70509-1873

Natl. Assn. of Independent Publishers Representatives **[724]**, 111 E 14th St., PMB 157, New York, NY 10003-4103, (646)414-2993

National Assn. of Indus. and Tech. Teacher Educators **[★1631]**

Natl. Assn. of Insurance Commissioners **[1310]**, 2301 McGee St., Ste. 800, Kansas City, MO 64108-2662, (816)842-3600

Natl. Assn. of Investment Companies **[619]**, 1300 Pennsylvania Ave. NW, Ste. 700, Washington, DC 20004, (202)204-3001

Natl. Assn. for Lay Ministry **[2969]**, 6896 Laurel St. NW, Washington, DC 20012, (202)291-4100

Natl. Assn. of Legal Investigators **[1316]**, 235 N Pine St., Lansing, MI 48933, (517)702-9835

National Assn. of Lesbian/Gay Addiction Professionals **[★2243]**

Natl. Assn. of Litho Clubs **[408]**, 3268 N 147th Ln., Goodyear, AZ 85395, (650)339-4007

Natl. Assn. of Mfrs. **[583]**, 1331 Pennsylvania Ave. NW, Ste. 600, Washington, DC 20004-1790, (202)637-3000

Natl. Assn. of Mfrs. Coun. of Mfg. Associations **[584]**, 1331 Pennsylvania Ave. NW, Ste. 600, Washington, DC 20004-1790, (202)637-3000

Natl. Assn. of Media Brokers **[749]**, 2910 Electra Dr., Colorado Springs, CO 80906-1073, (719)630-3111

Natl. Assn. of Media and Tech. Centers **[609]**, PO Box 9844, Cedar Rapids, IA 52409-9844, (319)654-0608

Natl. Assn. of Mortgage Processors **[113]**, 1250 Connecticut Ave. NW, Ste. 200, Washington, DC 20036, (202)261-6505

Natl. Assn. of Peoplecultural Engg. Prog. Advocates **[1615]**, 341 N Maitland Ave., Ste. 130, Maitland, FL 32751-4761, (407)647-8839

Natl. Assn. of Police Athletic Leagues **[2279]**, 658 W Indiantown Rd., Ste. 201, Jupiter, FL 33458, (561)745-5535

Natl. Assn. of Postal Supervisors **[3461]**, 1727 King St., Ste. 400, Alexandria, VA 22314-2700, (703)836-9660

Natl. Assn. of Power Engineers **[1521]**, 1 Springfield St., Chicopee, MA 01013, (413)592-6273

Natl. Assn. of Presort Mailers **[550]**, 1195 Mace Rd., Annapolis, MD 21403-4330, (877)620-6276

Natl. Assn. for Printing Leadership **[409]**, 75 W Century Rd., Ste. 100, Paramus, NJ 07652-1408, (201)634-9600

Natl. Assn. of Professional Background Screeners **[455]**, 2501 Aerial Center Pkwy., Ste. 103, Morrisville, NC 27560, (919)459-2082

Natl. Assn. of Professional Baseball Leagues **[3260]**, PO Box A, St. Petersburg, FL 33731, (727)822-6937

Natl. Assn. of Professional Employer Organizations **[298]**, 707 N St. Asaph St., Alexandria, VA 22314, (703)836-0466

Natl. Assn. for Public Hea. Statistics and Info. Systems **[1366]**, 962 Wayne Ave., Ste. 701, Silver Spring, MD 20910, (301)563-6001

Natl. Assn. of Publicly Funded Truck Driving Schools **[874]**, c/o Tina Frindt, Treas., Northampton Community Coll., 1900 Corporate Center Dr. E, Tobyhanna, PA 18466, (217)641-4914

Natl. Assn. of Publicly Traded Partnerships **[527]**, 1940 Duke St., Ste. 200, Alexandria, VA 22314, (703)518-4185

Natl. Assn. of Railway Bus. Women **[732]**, 621 Lippincott Ave., Riverton, NJ 08077

Natl. Assn. of Real Estate Appraisers **[53]**, PO Box 879, Palm Springs, CA 92263, (760)327-5284

Natl. Assn. of Real Estate Brokers **[750]**, 5504 Brentwood Stair Rd., Fort Worth, TX 76112, (817)446-7715

Natl. Assn. of Real Estate Investment Managers **[751]**, 900 7th St. NW, Ste. 960, Washington, DC 20001, (202)789-4373

Natl. Assn. of Real Estate Investment Trusts **[752]**, 1875 I St. NW, Ste. 600, Washington, DC 20006-5413, (202)739-9400

Natl. Assn. of Realtors **[753]**, 430 N Michigan Ave., Chicago, IL 60611-4087, (800)874-6500

Natl. Assn. of the Remodeling Indus. **[153]**, 780 Lee St., Ste. 200, Des Plaines, IL 60016, (847)298-9200

Natl. Assn. of Residential Property Managers **[715]**, 638 Independence Pkwy., Ste. 100, Chesapeake, VA 23320, (800)782-3452

Natl. Assn. for Retail Marketing Services **[772]**, 2417 Post Rd., Stevens Point, WI 54481, (715)342-0948

Natl. Assn. of RV Parks and Campgrounds **[762]**, 9085 E Mineral Cir., Ste. 200, Centennial, CO 80112, (303)681-0401

Natl. Assn. of Sales Professionals **[785]**, 555 Friendly St., Livonia, MI 48152, (866)365-1520

Natl. Assn. of School Music Dealers **[624]**, 14070 Proton Rd., Ste. 100, Dallas, TX 75244-3601, (972)233-9107

Natl. Assn. of Schools of Music **[1668]**, 11250 Roger Bacon Dr., Ste. 21, Reston, VA 20190-5248, (703)437-0700

Natl. Assn. of Securities Professionals **[798]**, 727 15th St., NW, Ste. 750, Washington, DC 20005, (202)371-5535

Natl. Assn. of Security Companies **[806]**, 444 N Capitol St. NW, Ste. 345, Washington, DC 20001, (202)347-3257

Natl. Assn. of Senior Move Managers **[566]**, PO Box 209, Hinsdale, IL 60522, (877)606-2766

Natl. Assn. of Ser. Managers **[814]**, PO Box 250796, Milwaukee, WI 53225, (414)466-6060

Natl. Assn. of Show Trucks **[875]**, 23227 Freedom Ave., Ste. 7, Port Charlotte, FL 33980, (734)604-3242

Natl. Assn. of Small Bus. Contractors **[222]**, 1200 G St. NW, Ste. 800, Washington, DC 20005, (888)861-9290

Natl. Assn. of Sporting Goods Wholesalers **[831]**, 1833 Centre Point Cir., Stem 123, Naperville, IL 60563, (630)596-9006

Natl. Assn. of Sports Officials **[3413]**, 2017 Lathrop Ave., Racine, WI 53405, (262)632-5448

Natl. Assn. of State Charity Officials **[1303]**, 815 Olive St., St. Louis, MO 63101

Natl. Assn. of State Contractors Licensing Agencies **[223]**, 23309 N 17th Dr., Bldg. 1, Unit 10, Phoenix, AZ 85027, (623)587-9354

Natl. Assn. of State Departments of Agriculture **[1265]**, 1156 15th St. NW, Ste. 1020, Washington, DC 20005, (202)296-9680

Natl. Assn. of State Directors of Career Tech. Educ. Consortium **[1697]**, 8484 Georgia Ave., Ste. 320, Silver Spring, MD 20910, (301)588-9630

Natl. Assn. of State Election Directors **[268]**, 12543 Westella Dr., Ste. 100, Houston, TX 77077-3929, (281)752-6200

Natl. Assn. of State EMS Officials **[2408]**, 201 Park Washington Ct., Falls Church, VA 22046-4527, (703)538-1799

Natl. Assn. of State and Local Equity Funds **[339]**, 1970 Broadway, Ste. 250, Oakland, CA 94612, (510)444-1101

Natl. Assn. of State Park Directors **[1356]**, 8829 Woodyhill Rd., Raleigh, NC 27613, (919)676-8365

Natl. Assn. of State Procurement Officials **[1371]**, 201 E Main St., Ste. 1405, Lexington, KY 40507-2004, (859)514-9159

Natl. Assn. of State Treasurers **[1364]**, PO Box 11910, Lexington, KY 40578-1910, (859)244-8175

Natl. Assn. of State United for Aging and Disabilities **[1881]**, 1201 15th St. NW, Ste. 350, Washington, DC 20005, (202)898-2578

National Assn. of State Units on Aging **[★1881]**

Natl. Assn. of State Veterans Homes **[2254]**, 3416 Columbus Ave., Sandusky, OH 44870-5598, (419)625-2454

Natl. Assn. of Steel Pipe Distributors **[671]**, 1501 E Mockingbird Ln., Ste. 307, Victoria, TX 77904, (361)574-7878

Natl. Assn. of Student Financial Aid Administrators **[1611]**, 1101 Connecticut Ave. NW, Ste. 1100, Washington, DC 20036-4312, (202)785-0453

Natl. Assn. of Supervisor of Bus. Educ. **[1578]**, Colorado Community Coll. Sys., 9101 E Lowry Blvd., Denver, CO 80230, (720)858-2746

Natl. Assn. of Surety Bond Producers **[497]**, 1140 19th St., Ste. 800, Washington, DC 20036-5104, (202)686-3700

Natl. Assn. of Tax Consultants **[1379]**, 321 W 13th Ave., Eugene, OR 97401, (541)298-2829

Natl. Assn. of Teacher Educators for Family and Consumer Sciences **[1630]**, Western Kentucky Univ., 1906 Coll. Heights Blvd., No. 11037, Bowling Green, KY 41201-1037, (270)745-3997

Natl. Assn. of Telecommunications Officers and Advisors **[1380]**, 2121 Eisenhower Ave., Ste. 401, Alexandria, VA 22314, (703)519-8035

Natl. Assn. of Temple Administrators **[2960]**, PO Box 936, Ridgefield, WA 98642, (360)887-0464

Natl. Assn. of Theatre Owners **[313]**, 750 1st St. NE, Ste. 1130, Washington, DC 20002, (202)962-0054

Natl. Assn. of Towns and Townships **[1351]**, 1130 Connecticut Ave. NW, Ste. 300, Washington, DC 20036, (202)454-3954

Natl. Assn. of Veterans Prog. Administrators **[3081]**, 2020 Pennsylvania Ave. NW, Ste. 1975, Washington, DC 20006-1846, (517)483-1932

Natl. Assn. of Wheat Weavers **[3170]**, 46 Ophir Ave., Lincoln, IL 62656, (217)732-1957

Natl. Assn. of Women in Constr. **[224]**, 327 S Adams St., Fort Worth, TX 76104, (817)877-5551

Natl. Auto Body Coun. **[78]**, 191 Clarksville Rd., Princeton Junction, NJ 08550, (888)667-7433

Natl. Bar Assn. **[1274]**, 1225 11th St. NW, Washington, DC 20001, (202)842-3900

Natl. Barbecue Assn. **[366]**, 455 S Fourth St., Ste. 650, Louisville, KY 40202, (888)909-2121

Natl. Basketball Assn. **[3264]**, 645 5th Ave., 10th Fl., New York, NY 10022, (212)407-8000

Natl. Basketball Athletic Trainers Assn. **[3265]**, 400 Colony Sq., Ste. 1750, Atlanta, GA 30361, (404)892-8919

Natl. Bench Rest Shooters Assn. **[3382]**, 2835 Guilford Ln., Oklahoma City, OK 73120-4404, (405)842-9585

Natl. Black Catholic Clergy Caucus **[2873]**, 2815 Forbes Dr., Montgomery, AL 36110, (404)226-8170

Natl. Black Caucus of State Legislators **[1375]**, 444 N Capitol St. NW, Ste. 622, Washington, DC 20001, (202)624-5457

Natl. Black McDonald's Operators Assn. **[445]**, PO Box 820668, South Florida, FL 33082-0668, (954)389-4487

Natl. Black Public Relations Soc. **[717]**, 14636 Runnymede St., Van Nuys, CA 91405, (888)976-0005

Natl. Bd. for Certification in Dental Lab. Tech. **[2384]**, 325 John Knox Rd., No. L103, Tallahassee, FL 32303, (850)205-5627

Natl. Boating Fed. **[3281]**, PO Box 4111, Annapolis, MD 21403-4111

Natl. Brotherhood of Skiers **[3388]**, 1525 E 53rd St., Ste. 418, Chicago, IL 60615, (773)955-4100

Natl. Brownfield Assn. **[716]**, 1250 S Grove Ave., Ste. 200, Barrington, IL 60010, (224)567-6790

National Burglar and Fire Alarm Assn. **[★802]**

Natl. Bus. and Disability Coun. **[2075]**, 201 I.U. Willets Rd., Albertson, NY 11507, (516)465-1516

Natl. Bus. Travel Assn. **[884]**, 110 N Royal St., 4th Fl., Alexandria, VA 22314, (703)684-0836

Natl. Candle Assn. **[511]**, 529 14th St. NW, Ste. 750, Washington, DC 20045, (202)393-2210

Natl. Career Development Assn. **[2076]**, 305 N Beech Cir., Broken Arrow, OK 74012, (918)663-7060

Natl. Cartoonists Soc. **[1718]**, 341 N Maitland Ave., Ste. 130, Maitland, FL 32751, (407)647-8839

Natl. Catholic Off. for the Deaf **[2874]**, 7202 Buchanan St., Landover Hills, MD 20784, (301)577-1684

Natl. Caucus and Center on Black Aged **[1882]**, 1220 L St. NW, Ste. 800, Washington, DC 20005, (202)637-8400

Natl. Center for Employee Ownership **[295]**, 1736 Franklin St., 8th Fl., Oakland, CA 94612, (510)208-1300

Natl. Center for Fathering **[2712]**, PO Box 413888, Kansas City, MO 64141, (800)593-DADS

National Center for Food Safety and Tech. **[★363]**

Natl. Center for Housing Mgt. **[2103]**, 12021 Sunset Hills Rd., Ste. 210, Reston, VA 20190, (703)435-9393

Natl. Center for Learning Disabilities **[2131]**, 381 Park Ave. S, Ste. 1401, New York, NY 10016, (212)545-7510

Natl. Center for Missing and Exploited Children **[1976]**, Charles B. Wang Intl. Children's Bldg., 699 Prince St., Alexandria, VA 22314-3175, (703)224-2150

Natl. Center on Poverty Law **[1342]**, 50 E Washington St., Ste. 500, Chicago, IL 60602, (312)263-3830

Natl. Center for Prosecution of Child Abuse **[1977]**, 44 Canal Center Plz., Ste. 110, Alexandria, VA 22314, (703)549-9222

National Certification Commn. in Chemistry and Chem. Engg. **[★1436]**

Natl. Cherry Growers and Indus. Found. **[1098]**, 2667 Reed Rd., Hood River, OR 97031, (541)386-5761

Natl. Chicken Coun. **[1185]**, 1015 15th St. NW, Ste. 930, Washington, DC 20005-2622, (202)296-2622

Natl. Christ Child Soc. **[2875]**, 4340 E West Hwy., Ste. 202, Bethesda, MD 20814, (301)718-0220

National CH for Professions in Special Education **[★1687]**

Natl. Coalition Against Censorship **[2618]**, 19 Fulton St., Ste. 407, New York, NY 10038, (212)807-6222

Natl. Coalition Against Violent Athletes **[3252]**, PO Box 620453, Littleton, CO 80162, (303)524-9853

Natl. Coalition of Black Meeting Planners **[613]**, 4401 Huntchase Dr., Bowie, MD 20720, (301)860-0200

Natl. Coalition for Campus Children's Centers **[1914]**, 950 Glenn Dr., Ste. 150, Folsom, CA 95630, (877)736-6222

Natl. Collegiate Athletic Assn. **[3404]**, PO Box 6222, Indianapolis, IN 46206-6222, (317)917-6222

Natl. Community Educ. Assn. **[1592]**, 3929 Old Lee Hwy., No. 91-A, Fairfax, VA 22030-2401, (703)359-8973

Natl. Community for Latino Leadership **[2800]**, 1701 K St. NW, Ste. 301, Washington, DC 20006, (202)257-4419

Natl. Community Pharmacists Assn. **[2578]**, 100 Daingerfield Rd., Alexandria, VA 22314, (703)683-8200

National Community Pharmacists Assn. Foundation **[★2578]**

Natl. Concrete Masonry Assn. **[199]**, 13750 Sunrise Valley Dr., Herndon, VA 20171-4662, (703)713-1900

A star before a book entry number signifies that the name is not listed separately, but is mentioned within the entry.

Natl. Conf. of Editorial Writers **[698]**, 3899 N Front St., Harrisburg, PA 17110, (717)703-3015

Natl. Conf. of Executives of the Arc **[567]**, 1660 L St. NW, Ste. 301, Washington, DC 20036, (225)927-0855

Natl. Cong. of Vietnamese Americans **[2831]**, 6433 Northanna Dr., Springfield, VA 22150, (703)971-9178

Natl. Cooperative Bus. Assn. **[234]**, 1401 New York Ave. NW, Ste. 1100, Washington, DC 20005, (202)638-6222

Natl. Cooperative Grocers Assn. **[235]**, 14 S Linn St., Iowa City, IA 52240, (319)466-9029

National Corporate Leadership Program **[★2091]**

Natl. Corrugated Steel Pipe Assn. **[672]**, 14070 Proton Rd., Ste. 100, LB 9, Dallas, TX 75244, (972)850-1907

Natl. Cotton Coun. of Am. **[244]**, PO Box 2995, Cordova, TN 38088-2995, (901)274-9030

Natl. Coun. of Acoustical Consultants **[154]**, 9100 Purdue Rd., Ste. 200, Indianapolis, IN 46268, (317)328-0642

Natl. Coun. for Adoption **[1873]**, 225 N Washington St., Alexandria, VA 22314, (703)299-6633

Natl. Coun. of Agricultural Employers **[927]**, 8233 Old Courthouse Rd., Ste. 200, Vienna, VA 22182, (703)790-9039

Natl. Coun. of Architectural Registration Boards **[1268]**, 1801 K St. NW, Ste. 700-K, Washington, DC 20006-1310, (202)783-6500

Natl. Coun. of Chain Restaurants **[446]**, 325 7th St. NW, Ste. 1100, Washington, DC 20004, (202)783-7971

Natl. Coun. of Churches of Christ in the U.S.A. **[2910]**, 475 Riverside Dr., Ste. 880, New York, NY 10115, (212)870-2228

Natl. Coun. of Churches, Educ. and Leadership Ministries Commn. **[2913]**, 475 Riverside Dr., 8th Fl., New York, NY 10115-0500, (212)870-2267

Natl. Coun. of Corvette Clubs **[3123]**, c/o Larry Morrison, VP of Membership, 492 Meadowlark Way, Clifton, CO 81520-8811

Natl. Coun. on Family Relations **[2087]**, 1201 W River Pkwy., Ste. 200, Minneapolis, MN 55454-1115, (763)781-9331

Natl. Coun. of Field Labor Locals **[3446]**, 8 N 3rd St., Rm. 207, Lafayette, IN 47901, (765)423-2152

Natl. Coun. for Intl. Visitors **[2683]**, 1420 K St. NW, Ste. 800, Washington, DC 20005, (202)842-1414

Natl. Coun. on Interpreting in Hea. Care **[418]**, 5505 Connecticut Ave. NW, No. 119, Washington, DC 20015-2601, (202)596-2436

Natl. Coun. of Jewish Women **[2961]**, 475 Riverside Dr., Ste. 250, New York, NY 10115, (212)645-4048

Natl. Coun. of Juvenile and Family Court Judges **[1319]**, PO Box 8970, Reno, NV 89507, (775)784-6012

National Coun. of Nonprofit Associations **[★63]**

Natl. Coun. of Nonprofits **[63]**, 1101 Vermont Ave. NW, Ste. 1002, Washington, DC 20005, (202)962-0322

Natl. Coun. of Real Estate Investment Fiduciaries **[528]**, 2 Prudential Plz., 180 N Stetson Ave., Ste. 2515, Chicago, IL 60601, (312)819-5890

Natl. Coun. of Self-Insurers **[498]**, 1253 Springfield Ave., PMB 345, New Providence, NJ 07974, (908)665-2152

Natl. Coun. of Social Security Mgt. Associations **[1374]**, 418 C St. NE, Washington, DC 20002, (202)547-8530

Natl. Coun. of State Directors of Community Colleges **[1590]**, 1 Dupont Cir. NW, Ste. 410, Washington, DC 20036, (202)728-0200

Natl. Coun. of State Tourism Directors **[3503]**, 1100 New York Ave. NW, Ste. 450, Washington, DC 20005-3934, (202)408-8422

Natl. Coun. on Teacher Retirement **[3444]**, 7600 Greenhaven Dr., Ste. 302, Sacramento, CA 95831, (916)394-2075

Natl. Coun. of Teachers of English | Conf. on English Educ. **[1616]**, 1111 W Kenyon Rd., Urbana, IL 61801-1096, (217)328-3870

Natl. Crime Prevention Coun. **[2048]**, 2001 Jefferson Davis Hwy., Ste. 901, Arlington, VA 22202-4801, (202)466-6272

Natl. Cutting Horse Assn. **[1138]**, 260 Bailey Ave., Fort Worth, TX 76107-1862, (817)244-6188

Natl. Dairy Shrine **[1050]**, PO Box 725, Denmark, WI 54208, (920)863-6333

Natl. Demolition Assn. **[225]**, 16 N Franklin St., Ste. 203, Doylestown, PA 18901-3536, (215)348-4949

Natl. Dental Assn. **[2385]**, 3517 16th St. NW, Washington, DC 20010, (202)588-1697

Natl. Dental Hygienists' Assn. **[2386]**, PO Box 22463, Tampa, FL 33622, (800)234-1096

Natl. Denturist Assn. **[2387]**, PO Box 308, Towanda, PA 18848, (888)599-7958

Natl. Derby Rallies **[3392]**, 6644 Switzer Ln., Shawnee, KS 66203, (913)962-6360

Natl. Duck Stamp Collectors Soc. **[3229]**, PO Box 43, Harleysville, PA 19438-0043

Natl. Duckpin Bowling Cong. **[3294]**, c/o Sue Burucker, Exec. Dir./Sec., 4991 Fairview Ave., Linthicum, MD 21090, (410)636-2695

Natl. Eagle Scout Assn. **[2219]**, c/o Boy Scouts of Am., 1325 W Walnut Hill Ln., PO Box 152079, Irving, TX 75015-2079, (972)580-2183

Natl. Economic Assn. **[1450]**, Spelman Coll., 350 Spelman Ln., Box 167, Atlanta, GA 30314

Natl. Electronics Ser. Dealers Assn. **[285]**, 3608 Pershing Ave., Fort Worth, TX 76107-4527, (817)921-9061

Natl. Emergency Mgt. Assn. **[1290]**, PO Box 11910, Lexington, KY 40578, (859)244-8000

Natl. Employment Counseling Assn. **[2077]**, 6836 Bee Cave Rd., Ste. 260, Austin, TX 78746, (800)347-6647

National Fantasy Fan Club for Disneyana Enthusiasts **[★3567]**

Natl. Farm-City Coun. **[1084]**, PO Box 6825, Reading, PA 19610, (877)611-8161

Natl. Farm and Ranch Bus. Mgt. Educ. Assn. **[1085]**, 1123 S Main St., Rugby, ND 58368, (701)776-5095

Natl. Farmers Union **[1086]**, 200 F St. NW, Ste. 300, Washington, DC 20001, (202)554-1600

Natl. Fed. of Paralegal Associations **[1354]**, PO Box 2016, Edmonds, WA 98020, (425)967-0045

National FFA Alumni Assn. **[★1566]**

Natl. FFA Org. **[1566]**, PO Box 68960, Indianapolis, IN 46268-0960, (317)802-6060

Natl. Fireproofing Contractors Assn. **[352]**, PO Box 1571, Westford, MA 01886, (866)250-4111

Natl. Football Found. and Coll. Hall of Fame **[3329]**, 433 E Las Colinas Blvd., Ste. 1130, Irving, TX 75039, (972)556-1000

Natl. Football League Alumni **[3330]**, 1 Washington Park, 1 Washington St., 14th Fl., Newark, NJ 07102, (973)718-7350

Natl. Foster Parent Assn. **[2152]**, 2021 E Hennepin Ave., Ste. 320, Minneapolis, MN 55413-1865, (253)853-4000

Natl. Found. for Cancer Res. **[2571]**, 4600 E West Hwy., Ste. 525, Bethesda, MD 20814, (301)654-1250

Natl. Found. for Credit Counseling **[543]**, 2000 M St. NW, Ste. 505, Washington, DC 20036, (800)388-2227

Natl. Found. for Infectious Diseases **[2474]**, 4733 Bethesda Ave., Ste. 750, Bethesda, MD 20814-5278, (301)656-0003

Natl. Frame Builders Assn. **[226]**, 4700 W Lake Ave., Glenview, IL 60025, (800)557-6957

Natl. Franchisee Assn. **[390]**, 1701 Barrett Lakes Blvd. NW, Ste. 180, Kennesaw, GA 30144, (678)797-5160

Natl. Freedom of Info. Coalition **[2731]**, Univ. of Missouri-Columbia, Journalism Inst., 101 Reynolds, Columbia, MO 65211, (573)882-4856

Natl. Frozen Pizza Inst. **[367]**, 2000 Corporate Ridge, Ste. 1000, McLean, VA 22102, (703)821-0770

Natl. Frozen and Refrigerated Foods Assn. **[368]**, PO Box 6069, Harrisburg, PA 17112, (717)657-8601

Natl. Funeral Directors and Morticians Assn. **[622]**, 6290 Shannon Pkwy., Union City, GA 30291, (404)286-6740

Natl. Gay and Lesbian Chamber of Commerce **[3493]**, 729 15th St. NW, 9th Fl., Washington, DC 20005, (202)234-9181

Natl. Glass Assn. **[400]**, 1945 Old Gallows Rd., Ste. 750, Vienna, VA 22182, (703)442-4890

Natl. Grocers Assn. **[773]**, 1005 N Glebe Rd., Ste. 250, Arlington, VA 22201-5758, (703)516-0700

Natl. Hardwood Lumber Assn. **[388]**, PO Box 34518, Memphis, TN 38184-0518, (901)377-1818

Natl. High School Athletic Coaches Assn. **[3306]**, c/o Jerome Garry, PO Box 5921, Rochester, MN 55903

Natl. Hockey League Booster Clubs **[3592]**, PO Box 805, St. Louis, MO 63188

Natl. Housing Conf. **[2104]**, 1900 M St. NW, Ste. 200, Washington, DC 20036, (202)466-2121

Natl. Housing and Rehabilitation Assn. **[2105]**, 1400 16th St. NW, Ste. 420, Washington, DC 20036-2244, (202)939-1750

Natl. Human Resources Assn. **[635]**, PO Box 7326, Nashua, NH 03060-7326, (866)523-4417

Natl. Humane Educ. Soc. **[1897]**, PO Box 340, Charles Town, WV 25414-0340, (304)725-0506

Natl. Image **[2789]**, PO Box 1368, Bonita, CA 91908, (858)495-7407

Natl. Independent Concessionaires Assn. **[376]**, PO Box 89429, Tampa, FL 33689, (727)346-9302

Natl. Indian Educ. Assn. **[1669]**, 110 Maryland Ave. NE, Ste. 104, Washington, DC 20002, (202)544-7290

Natl. Indus. for the Blind **[2605]**, 1310 Braddock Pl., Alexandria, VA 22314-1691, (703)310-0500

Natl. Inst. of Amer. Doll Artists **[3190]**, 109 Ladder Hill North, Weston, CT 06883, (203)557-3169

Natl. Inst. for Leadership Development **[538]**, 1202 W Thomas Rd., Phoenix, AZ 85013, (602)285-7495

Natl. Inst. for Trial Advocacy **[1385]**, 1685 38th St., Ste. 200, Boulder, CO 80301, (800)225-6482

Natl. Insulator Assn. **[3191]**, PO Box 188, Providence, UT 84332

Natl. InterCollegiate Flying Assn. **[3087]**, PO Box 15081, Monroe, LA 71207, (318)325-6156

Natl. Intercollegiate Soccer Officials Assn. **[3394]**, 1030 Ohio Ave., Cape May, NJ 08204

Natl. InterScholastic Swimming Coaches Assn. of Am. **[3416]**, 29 Fairview Ave., Great Neck, NY 11023-1206

Natl. - Interstate Coun. of State Boards of Cosmetology **[240]**, 7622 Briarwood Cir., Little Rock, AR 72205, (501)227-8262

Natl. Intramural-Recreational Sports Assn. **[3405]**, 4185 SW Res. Way, Corvallis, OR 97333-1067, (541)766-8211

Natl. Investigations Comm. on Unidentified Flying Objects **[1518]**, 9101 Topanga Canyon Blvd., No. 209, Chatsworth, CA 91311-5763, (818)882-0039

Natl. Investment Banking Assn. **[114]**, PO Box 6625, Athens, GA 30604, (706)208-9620

Natl. Jersey Wooly Rabbit Club **[1190]**, 309 S St. Paul, Sioux Falls, SD 57103, (810)637-1537

Natl. Jewish Center for Learning and Leadership; CLAL - The **[2950]**

Natl. Junior Coll. Athletic Assn. **[3406]**, 1631 Mesa Ave., Ste. B, Colorado Springs, CO 80906, (719)590-9788

Natl. Kappa Kappa Iota **[3519]**, 1875 E 15th St., Tulsa, OK 74104-4610, (918)744-0389

Natl. Kidney Found. **[2560]**, 30 E 33rd St., New York, NY 10016-5337, (212)889-2210

Natl. Kitchen and Bath Assn. **[512]**, 687 Willow Grove St., Hackettstown, NJ 07840, (908)852-0033

Natl. Latina Bus. Women Assn. **[534]**, 1740 W Katella Ave., Ste. Q, Orange, CA 92867, (714)724-7762

Natl. Latino Officers Assn. **[1326]**, PO Box 02-0120, Brooklyn, NY 11201, (866)579-5809

Natl. Lawyers Guild **[1275]**, 132 Nassau St., Rm. 922, New York, NY 10038, (212)679-5100

Natl. League of Families of Amer. Prisoners and Missing in Southeast Asia **[2705]**, 5673 Columbia Pike, Ste. 100, Falls Church, VA 22041, (703)465-7432

Natl. Legal Sanctuary for Community Advancement **[1339]**, 444 DeHaro St., Ste. 205, San Francisco, CA 94107, (415)553-7100

Natl. Liquor Law Enforcement Assn. **[1333]**, 11720 Beltsville Dr., Ste. 900, Calverton, MD 20705-3111, (301)755-2795

Natl. Marine Educators Assn. **[1658]**, PO Box 1470, Ocean Springs, MS 39566-1470, (228)896-9182

Natl. Marine Representatives Assn. **[587]**, PO Box 360, Gurnee, IL 60031, (847)662-3167

National Materials Properties Data Network **[★1498]**

Natl. Meat Assn. **[608]**, 1970 Broadway, Ste. 825, Oakland, CA 94612, (510)763-1533

Natl. Medical Assn. **[2549]**, 8403 Colesville Rd., Ste. 920, Silver Spring, MD 20910, (202)347-1895

Natl. Middle School Assn. **[1664]**, 4151 Executive Pkwy., Ste. 300, Westerville, OH 43081, (614)895-4730

Natl. Mitigation Banking Assn. **[1030]**, 1155 15th St. NW, Ste. 500, Washington, DC 20005, (202)457-8409

Natl. MultiCultural Inst. **[2045]**, 1666 K St. NW, Ste. 440, Washington, DC 20006-1242, (202)483-0700

Natl. Museum of Racing and Hall of Fame **[3347]**, 191 Union Ave., Saratoga Springs, NY 12866-3566, (518)584-0400

Natl. Narcotic Detector Dog Assn. **[1334]**, 379 CR 105, Carthage, TX 75633, (888)289-0070

Natl. Native Amer. AIDS Prevention Center **[1886]**, 720 S Colorado Blvd., Ste. 650-S, Denver, CO 80246, (720)382-2244

Natl. Native Amer. Law Enforcement Assn. **[1335]**, PO Box 171, Washington, DC 20044, (202)204-3065

The Natl. Needle Arts Assn. **[857]**, 1100-H Brandywine Blvd., Zanesville, OH 43701-7303, (740)455-6773

Natl. Network of Abortion Funds **[1870]**, PO Box 170280, Boston, MA 02117, (800)772-9100

Natl. Network of Episcopal Clergy Associations **[2920]**, c/o Rev. Michael R. Link, 11844 Orense Dr., Las Vegas, NV 89138

Natl. Network for Youth **[2207]**, 741 8th St. SE, Washington, DC 20003, (202)783-7949

Natl. Newspaper Assn. **[699]**, PO Box 7540, Columbia, MO 65205-7540, (573)777-4980

Natl. Oceanic Soc. **[1031]**, 17300 Red Hill Ave., Ste. 280, Irvine, CA 92614, (949)500-5451

Natl. Onsite Wastewater Recycling Assn. **[1223]**, 601 Wythe St., Alexandria, VA 22314, (800)966-2942

Natl. Org. of Bar Counsel **[1327]**, 110 E Main St., Madison, WI 53703, (608)267-8915

Natl. Org. of Blacks in Govt. **[1278]**, 3005 Georgia Ave. NW, Washington, DC 20001-3807, (202)667-3280

Natl. Org. for Human Services **[1685]**, 5341 Old Hwy. 5, Ste. 206, No. 214, Woodstock, GA 30188, (770)924-8899

Natl. Org. of Life and Hea. Insurance Guaranty Associations **[419]**, 13873 Park Center Rd., Ste. 329, Herndon, VA 20171, (703)481-5206

Natl. Org. of Minority Architects **[1410]**, Howard Univ., Coll. of Engg., Architecture and Cmpt. Sciences, School of Architecture and Design, 2366 Sixth St. NW, Rm. 100, Washington, DC 20059, (202)686-2780

Natl. Org. for the Reform of Marijuana Laws **[2624]**, 1600 K St. NW, Ste. 501, Washington, DC 20006-2832, (202)483-5500

Natl. Orientation Directors Assn. **[1562]**, Univ. of Minnesota, 1313 5th St. SE, Mail Unit 72, Minneapolis, MN 55414, (612)627-0150

Natl. Panhellenic Conf. **[3525]**, 3901 W 86th St., Ste. 398, Indianapolis, IN 46268, (317)872-3185

Natl. Panhellenic Conf. I Natl. Panhellenic Editors Conf. **[3516]**, 3901 W 86th St., Ste. 398, Indianapolis, IN 46268, (317)872-3185

Natl. Park Found. **[1357]**, 1201 Eye St. NW, Ste. 550B, Washington, DC 20005, (202)354-6460

Natl. Parks Conservation Assn. **[1358]**, 1300 19th St. NW, Ste. 300, Washington, DC 20036, (202)223-6722

Natl. Peanut Festival Assn. **[1172]**, 5622 Hwy. 231 S, Dothan, AL 36301, (334)793-4323

Natl. Pharmaceutical Coun. **[660]**, 1894 Preston White Dr., Reston, VA 20191-5433, (703)620-6390

Natl. Plant Bd. **[1266]**, c/o Aurelio Posadas, Exec. Sec., PO Box 847, Elk Grove, CA 95759, (916)709-3484

Natl. Police Canine Assn. **[1336]**, PO Box 538, Waddell, AZ 85355, (713)562-7371

Natl. Pollution Prevention Roundtable **[1182]**, 50 F St. NW, Ste. 350, Washington, DC 20001, (202)299-9701

Natl. Potato Coun. **[1099]**, 1300 L St. NW, No. 910, Washington, DC 20005, (202)682-9456

Natl. Precast Concrete Assn. **[200]**, 1320 City Center Dr., Ste. 200, Carmel, IN 46032, (317)571-9500

Natl. Press Club **[700]**, Natl. Press Bldg., 529 14th St. NW, 13th Fl., Washington, DC 20045, (202)662-7500

Natl. Public Records Res. Assn. **[472]**, 2501 Aerial Center Pkwy., Ste. 103, Morrisville, NC 27560, (919)459-2078

Natl. Quarter Horse Registry **[1139]**, 1497 S Staghorn, Toquerville, UT 84774, (435)559-2069

Natl. Ramah Commn. **[1650]**, 3080 Broadway, New York, NY 10027, (212)678-8881

Natl. Registration Center for Stud. Abroad **[1640]**, PO Box 1393, Milwaukee, WI 53201, (414)278-0631

National Registry of Microbiologists **[★1419]**

Natl. Reining Horse Assn. **[1140]**, 3000 NW 10th St., Oklahoma City, OK 73107-5302, (405)946-7400

Natl. Renal Administrators Assn. **[2542]**, 100 N 20th St., 4th Fl., Philadelphia, PA 19103, (215)320-4655

Natl. Restaurant Assn. **[447]**, 1200 17th St. NW, Washington, DC 20036, (202)331-5900

Natl. Restaurant Assn. Educational Found. **[448]**, 175 W Jackson Blvd., Ste. 1500, Chicago, IL 60604-2702, (312)715-1010

Natl. Rifle Assn. of Am. **[3383]**, 11250 Waples Mill Rd., Fairfax, VA 22030, (703)267-1600

Natl. Right to Life Comm. **[2206]**, 512 10th St. NW, Washington, DC 20004, (202)626-8800

Natl. Risk Retention Assn. **[499]**, 2214 Rock Hill Rd., Ste. 315, Herndon, VA 20170, (703)297-0059

Natl. Roof Certification and Inspection Assn. **[155]**, 2232 E Wilson Ave., Orange, CA 92867, (888)687-7663

Natl. Rural Elec. Cooperative Assn. **[272]**, 4301 Wilson Blvd., Arlington, VA 22203, (703)907-5500

Natl. Rural Housing Coalition **[2106]**, 1331 G St. NW, 10th Fl., Washington, DC 20005, (202)393-5229

Natl. Rural Utilities Cooperative Finance Corp. **[340]**, 2201 Cooperative Way, Herndon, VA 20171, (703)709-6700

Natl. School Boards Assn. **[1682]**, 1680 Duke St., Alexandria, VA 22314-3493, (703)838-6722

Natl. School Supply and Equip. Assn. **[788]**, 8380 Colesville Rd., Ste. 250, Silver Spring, MD 20910, (301)495-0240

Natl. Sci. Educ. Leadership Assn. **[1683]**, 1219 N 54 St., Omaha, NE 68132, (402)561-0176

Natl. Sci. and Tech. Educ. Partnership **[2226]**, 2500 Wilson Blvd., Ste. 210, Arlington, VA 22201-3834, (703)907-7400

Natl. Shoe Retailers Assn. **[380]**, 3037 W Ina Rd., Tucson, AZ 85741, (800)673-8446

Natl. Show Horse Registry **[1141]**, PO Box 862, Lewisburg, OH 45338, (937)962-4336

Natl. Soc. of Accountants for Cooperatives **[9]**, 136 S Keowee St., Dayton, OH 45402, (937)222-6707

Natl. Soc. of Black Engineers **[1469]**, 205 Daingerfield Rd., Alexandria, VA 22314, (703)549-2207

Natl. Soc., Daughters of the Amer. Revolution **[3049]**, 1776 D St. NW, Washington, DC 20006-5303, (202)628-1776

Natl. Soc. of Genetic Counselors **[2419]**, 401 N Michigan Ave., Chicago, IL 60611, (312)321-6834

Natl. Soc. of Hispanic MBAs **[173]**, 1303 Walnut Hill Ln., Ste. 100, Irving, TX 75038, (214)596-9338

Natl. Soc. of Insurance Premium Auditors **[500]**, PO Box 936, Columbus, OH 43216-0936, (888)846-7472

Natl. Soc. of Pershing Rifles **[3540]**, PO Box 25057, Baton Rouge, LA 70894

Natl. Soc. of Professional Insurance Investigators **[501]**, PO Box 88, Delaware, OH 43015, (888)677-4498

Natl. Soc., Sons of the Amer. Revolution **[3050]**, 1000 S 4th St., Louisville, KY 40203, (502)589-1776

Natl. Soc. of the Sons of Utah Pioneers **[3078]**, 3301 E 2920 S, Salt Lake City, UT 84109, (801)484-4441

Natl. Specialty Gift Assn. **[398]**, 7238 Bucks Ford Dr., Riverview, FL 33578, (813)374-1777

Natl. Staff Development and Training Assn. **[2235]**, PO Box 112, Merced, CA 95341-0112, (209)385-3000

Natl. Stone, Sand and Gravel Assn. **[841]**, 1605 King St., Alexandria, VA 22314-2726, (703)525-8788

Natl. Student Campaign Against Hunger and Homelessness **[2117]**, 328 S Jefferson St., Ste. 620, Chicago, IL 60661, (312)544-4436

Natl. Sunroom Assn. **[156]**, 1300 Sumner Ave., Cleveland, OH 44115-2851, (216)241-7333

Natl. Sweet Sorghum Producers and Processors Assn. **[997]**, PO Box 1356, Cookeville, TN 38503-1356, (931)644-7764

Natl. Swimming Pool Found. **[763]**, 4775 Granby Cir., Colorado Springs, CO 80919-3131, (719)540-9119

Natl. Swine Registry **[1220]**, 2639 Yeager Rd., West Lafayette, IN 47906, (765)463-3594

Natl. Systems Contractors Assn. **[286]**, 3950 River Ridge Dr. NE, Cedar Rapids, IA 52402, (319)366-6722

Natl. Tactical Officers Assn. **[1337]**, PO Box 797, Doylestown, PA 18901, (215)230-7616

Natl. Tank Truck Carriers **[817]**, 950 N Glebe Rd., Ste. 520, Arlington, VA 22203, (703)838-1960

Natl. Taxidermists Assn. **[845]**, 108 Br. Dr., Slidell, LA 70461-1912, (985)641-4682

Natl. Telecommunications Cooperative Assn. **[896]**, 4121 Wilson Blvd., Ste. 1000, Arlington, VA 22203, (703)351-2000

Natl. Translator Assn. **[130]**, 5611 Kendall Ct., Ste. 2, Arvada, CO 80002, (303)465-5742

Natl. Truck Equip. Assn. **[89]**, 37400 Hills Tech Dr., Farmington Hills, MI 48331-3414, (248)489-7090

Natl. Union of Law Enforcement Associations **[3452]**, 7700 Authur Dr., McCalla, AL 35111, (757)630-0202

Natl. Utility Contractors Assn. **[227]**, 11350 Random Hills Rd., Arlington, VA 22203-1627, (703)358-9300

Natl. Utility Contractors Assn. I Clean Water Coun. **[1225]**, 3925 Chain Bridge Rd., Ste. 301, Fairfax, VA 22030, (703)358-9300

Natl. Utility Locating Contractors Assn. **[228]**, 1501 Shirkey Ave., Richmond, MO 64085

Natl. Utility Training and Safety Educ. Assn. **[897]**, c/o Melissa Wolf, 1024 Steamboat Run, Newburgh, IN 47630, (812)508-1305

Natl. Versatility Ranch Horse Assn. **[3352]**, 590 Hwy. 105, Box 150, Monument, CO 80132, (719)487-9014

Natl. Watermelon Assn. **[1100]**, 5129 S Lakeland Dr. Ste. 1, Lakeland, FL 33813, (813)619-7575

Natl. Wheelchair Basketball Assn. **[3317]**, 1130 Elkton St., Ste. C, Colorado Springs, CO 80907, (719)266-4082

Natl. Wild Turkey Fed. **[1246]**, PO Box 530, Edgefield, SC 29824-0530, (803)637-3106

Natl. Wildlife Rehabilitators Assn. **[1247]**, 2625 Clearwater Rd., Ste. 110, St. Cloud, MN 56301, (320)230-9920

Natl. Women in Agriculture Assn. **[937]**, 1701 N Martin Luther King Ave., Oklahoma City, OK 73119, (405)424-4623

Natl. Women's Bus. Coun. **[917]**, 409 3rd St. SW, Ste. 210, Washington, DC 20024, (202)205-3850

Natl. Wood Flooring Assn. **[157]**, 111 Chesterfield Indus. Blvd., Chesterfield, MO 63005, (800)422-4556

Natl. Yogurt Assn. **[252]**, 2000 Corporate Ridge, Ste. 1000, McLean, VA 22102, (703)821-0770

Native American

First Nations Development Inst. **[2146]**

Indian Arts and Crafts Assn. **[1830]**

Inst. for Tribal Environmental Professionals **[2808]**

Natl. Indian Educ. Assn. **[1669]**

Red Earth **[2809]**

United Indians of All Tribes Found. **[2707]**

United Indian Missions Intl. **[3014]**

Native Amer. Finance Officers Assn. **[341]**, PO Box 50637, Phoenix, AZ 85076-0637, (602)330-9208

Native Amer. Fish and Wildlife Soc. **[1068]**, 8333 Greenwood Blvd., Ste. 260, Denver, CO 80221, (303)466-1725

NATSO Found. **[774]**, 1737 King St., Ste. 200, Alexandria, VA 22314, (703)549-2100

Natural Colored Wool Growers Assn. **[1209]**, PO Box 406, New Palestine, IN 46163, (317)681-4765

A star before a book entry number signifies that the name is not listed separately, but is mentioned within the entry.

Natural Disasters

World Assn. of Natural Disaster Awareness and Assistance **[2147]**

Natural Products Assn. **[775]**, 1773 T St. NW, Washington, DC 20009, (202)223-0101

Natural Resources

Intl. Assn. for Soc. and Natural Resources **[1167]**

Intl. Joint Commn. **[1168]**

Interstate Coun. on Water Policy **[1353]**

Rocky Mountain Inst. **[1169]**

Africa Environmental Watch **[1001]**

Alliance for Green Heat **[1451]**

Alliance for Renewable Energy **[1452]**

Alliance for Tompotika Conservation **[1003]**

Alternative Medicine Intl. **[2289]**

Amer. Biogas Coun. **[1390]**

Anglers for Conservation **[1005]**

BlueVoice.org **[1010]**

Citizens for Affordable Energy **[1453]**

Citizens' Alliance for Responsible Energy **[1454]**

Coalition of Natl. Park Ser. Retirees **[1176]**

Cork Forest Conservation Alliance **[1015]**

Ecological Res. and Development Gp. **[1017]**

Energy Conservation Org. **[1612]**

Energy Extraction Technologies **[1458]**

Experience Intl. **[1021]**

Focus the Nation **[2642]**

Friends of the Osa **[1025]**

Global Parks **[1026]**

GreenMotion **[1057]**

Iemanya Oceanica **[1240]**

Intl. Green Energy Coun. **[1395]**

Journey Toward Sustainability **[1622]**

Kids Ecology Corps **[1076]**

Natl. Oceanic Soc. **[1031]**

Nature Abounds **[1069]**

New Energy Indus. Assn. for Asia and the Pacific **[1460]**

Ocean Champions **[2630]**

Oceanic Preservation Soc. **[1034]**

Pacific Islands Conservation Res. Assn. **[1035]**

Paso Pacifico **[1036]**

Rainforest Partnership **[1193]**

Rights and Resources Initiative **[1095]**

Solar for Peace **[1537]**

Tropical Forest Gp. **[1043]**

Turtle Island Restoration Network **[1044]**

U.S. Offshore Wind Collaborative **[1556]**

U.S. Water and Power **[1399]**

US-China Green Energy Coun. **[1464]**

Wild Gift **[1259]**

Wilderness Intl. **[1045]**

Wind Energy Mfrs. Assn. **[913]**

Women Organizing for Change in Agriculture and NRM **[938]**

Wonderful World of Wildlife **[1260]**

World Fed. for Coral Reef Conservation **[1049]**

Natural Sciences

Acad. of Natural Sciences **[1502]**

Amer. Quaternary Assn. **[1503]**

Western Soc. of Naturalists **[1504]**

Fed. of Earth Sci. Info. Partners **[1449]**

The Intl. Lepidoptera Survey **[1472]**

Radiochemistry Soc. **[1438]**

Nature Abounds **[1069]**, PO Box 241, Clearfield, PA 16830

Naturopathic Medical Student Assn. **[2554]**, 2828 Naito Pkwy., Ste. 401, Portland, OR 97201, (503)334-4153

Naturopathic Medicine for Global Hea. **[2555]**, 37 Mulberry Row, Princeton, NJ 08540, (609)310-1340

Naturopathy

Amer. Assn. of Naturopathic Midwives **[2553]**

Naturopathic Medical Student Assn. **[2554]**

Naturopathic Medicine for Global Hea. **[2555]**

Oncology Assn. of Naturopathic Physicians **[2556]**

Pediatric Assn. of Naturopathic Physicians **[1670]**

Navigation

Intl. Loran Assn. **[1505]**

Nazarene Compassionate Ministries Intl. **[2898]**, 17001 Prairie Star Pkwy., Lenexa, KS 66220, (913)768-4808

Needlework

Spinning and Weaving Assn. **[858]**

Neighbor to Neighbor **[2619]**, 1550 Blue Spruce Dr., Fort Collins, CO 80524, (970)484-7498

Nepal SEEDS: Social Educational Environmental Development Services in Nepal **[2028]**, 800 Kansas St., San Francisco, CA 94107, (415)813-3331

NepalAama **[1584]**, PO Box 1565, Simi Valley, CA 93062

Nepalese

Assn. of Nepal and Himalayan Stud. **[1671]**

NepalAama **[1584]**

Nephrology

Amer. Assn. of Kidney Patients **[2557]**

Amer. Nephrology Nurses' Assn. **[2558]**

Children's Dialysis Intl. **[2559]**

Natl. Kidney Found. **[2560]**

Network Branded Prepaid Card Assn. **[342]**, 110 Chestnut Ridge Rd., Ste. 111, Montvale, NJ 07645-1706, (201)746-0725

Network of Conservation Educators and Practitioners **[1032]**, Amer. Museum of Natural History, Center for Biodiversity and Conservation, Central Park West, 79th St., New York, NY 10024, (212)769-5742

Network Ethiopia **[2511]**, 2401 Virginia Ave. NW, Washington, DC 20037, (202)835-8383

Network of Indian Professionals **[2792]**, PO Box 06362, Chicago, IL 60606, (312)952-0254

Networking

CEO Netweavers **[236]**

Clean Tech. and Sustainable Indus. Org. **[964]**

Global Sourcing Coun. **[631]**

Intl. Assn. of Space Entrepreneurs **[30]**

Rising Tide Capital **[265]**

Neurological Disorders

Amer. Acad. for Cerebral Palsy and Developmental Medicine **[2561]**

Amer. Asperger's Assn. **[2562]**

Autism Allies **[2308]**

Autism Care and Treatment Today! **[2309]**

Autism Ser. Dogs of Am. **[2310]**

Families with Autism Spectrum Disorders **[2313]**

Generation Rescue **[2315]**

Global Autism Collaboration **[2316]**

Intl. Coalition for Autism and All Abilities **[2318]**

Stop Calling It Autism! **[2320]**

Stories of Autism **[2321]**

S.U.C.C.E.S.S. for Autism **[2322]**

Neurosurgery

Soc. for Neuroscience in Anesthesiology and Critical Care **[2563]**

New Am. Alliance **[264]**, 8150 N Central Expy., Ste. 1625, Dallas, TX 75206, (214)466-6410

New Art Dealers Alliance **[1711]**, 55 Chrystie St. Ste. 310, New York, NY 10002, (212)594-0883

New Energy Indus. Assn. for Asia and the Pacific **[1460]**, 2055 Junction Ave., Ste. 225, San Jose, CA 95131, (408)434-1993

New England Theatre Conf. **[1859]**, 215 Knob Hill Dr., Hamden, CT 06518, (617)851-8535

New England Trails Conf. **[3428]**, PO Box 550, Charlestown, NH 03603, (603)543-1700

New Forests Proj. **[2122]**, 737 8th St. SE, Ste. 202, Washington, DC 20003, (202)464-9386

New Horizons Intl. Music Assn. **[1826]**, c/o Shirley Michaels, Ed., 1975 28th Ave., No. 18, Greeley, CO 80634, (970)301-4585

New Road Map Found. **[2110]**, PO Box 1363, Langley, WA 98260

New Tribes Mission **[3006]**, 1000 E 1st St., Sanford, FL 32771-1441, (407)323-3430

New Violin Family Assn. **[1827]**, 701 3rd St., Encinitas, CA 92024, (760)632-0554

New York Financial Writers' Assn. **[701]**, PO Box 338, Ridgewood, NJ 07451-0338, (201)612-0100

New York Genealogical and Biographical Soc. **[3067]**, 36 W 44th St., 7th Fl., New York, NY 10036-8105, (212)755-8532

New York Soc. of Security Analysts **[799]**, 1540 Broadway, Ste. 1010, New York, NY 10036-2714, (212)541-4530

New Zealand

Soc. of Australasian Specialists/Oceania **[3232]**

Newspaper Target Marketing Coalition **[626]**, 2969 Blackwood Rd., Decatur, GA 30033, (202)386-6357

Newspapers

Newspaper Target Marketing Coalition **[626]**

NGO Comm. on Disarmament, Peace and Security **[2640]**, 777 UN Plz., Ste. 3-B, New York, NY 10017, (212)687-5340

Nicaragua

Bikes Not Bombs **[2708]**

Nigerian

Egbe Omo Yoruba: Natl. Assn. of Yoruba Descendants in North America **[2810]**

Friends of Nigeria **[2811]**

Idoma Assn. USA **[2812]**

Nigerian Assn. of Pharmacists and Pharmaceutical Scientists in the Americas **[662]**, 1761 Tennessee Ave., Cincinnati, OH 45229, (513)641-3300

Nigerian Lawyers Assn. **[1276]**, 321 Broadway, 3rd Fl., New York, NY 10007, (212)566-9926

Non-Profit Chiropractic Org. **[2345]**, 601 Brady St., Ste. 201, Davenport, IA 52803, (708)459-8080

Nonviolence

Intl. Coun. for Middle East Stud. **[2701]**

Ishmael and Isaac **[2702]**

Monks Without Borders **[2946]**

One Voice of Peace **[1672]**

Student Peace Alliance **[2720]**

Sudan Sunrise **[2154]**

Voters for Peace **[2722]**

Norrie Disease Assn. **[2399]**, PO Box 3244, Munster, IN 46321

North Am. Chinese Clean-tech and Semiconductor Assn. **[287]**, PO Box 61086, Sunnyvale, CA 94088-1086

North Am. Indigenous Ministries **[3007]**, PO Box 499, Sumas, WA 98295, (604)850-3052

North America-Mongolia Bus. Coun. **[519]**, 1015 Duke St., Alexandria, VA 22314, (703)549-8444

North Amer. Assn. for the Catechumenate **[2876]**, 2915 NE Flanders, Portland, OR 97232, (503)502-6251

North Amer. Assn. for Environmental Educ. **[1619]**, 2000 P St. NW, Ste. 540, Washington, DC 20036, (202)419-0412

North Amer. Assn. of State and Provincial Lotteries **[1345]**, 1 S Broadway, Geneva, OH 44041, (440)466-5630

North Amer. Babydoll Southdown Sheep Assn. and Registry **[1210]**, PO Box 146, Wellsville, KS 66092, (785)883-4811

North Amer. Building Material Distribution Assn. **[158]**, 401 N Michigan Ave., Chicago, IL 60611, (312)321-6845

North Amer. Case Res. Assn. **[921]**, c/o Robert C. Crowner, Sec.-Treas., 3719 Meadow Ln., Saline, MI 48176, (734)429-5032

North Amer. Celtic Buyers Assn. **[180]**, 27 Addison Ave., Rutherford, NJ 07070, (201)842-9922

North Amer. Conf. on British Stud. **[1741]**, Univ. of Texas at Austin, Harry Ransom Center, PO Box 7219, Austin, TX 78712-7219, (512)232-1236

North Amer. Conf. on Ethiopian Jewry **[2691]**, 255 W 36th St., Ste. 701, New York, NY 10018, (212)233-5200

North Amer. Conf. of Separated and Divorced Catholics **[2070]**, PO Box 10, Hancock, MI 49930-0010, (906)482-0494

North Amer. Danish Warmblood Assn. **[1142]**, 32781 Chadlyn Ct., Wildomar, CA 92595-9310, (951)609-3787

North Amer. Elec. Reliability Corp. **[273]**, 116-390 Village Blvd., Princeton, NJ 08540-5721, (609)452-8060

North Amer. Equip. Dealers Assn. **[41]**, 1195 Smizer Mill Rd., Fenton, MO 63026-3480, (636)349-5000

North Amer. Family Campers Assn. **[3303]**, PO Box 318, Lunenburg, MA 01462, (401)828-0579

North Amer. Farmers' Direct Marketing Assn. **[1163]**, 62 White Loaf Rd., Southampton, MA 01073, (413)529-0386

North Amer. Football League **[3331]**, 5775 Glenridge Dr. NE, Ste. 100B, Atlanta, GA 30328, (404)475-1803

North Amer. Gun Dog Assn. **[3181]**, 17850 County Rd. 54, Burlington, CO 80807, (719)342-0776

North Amer. Limousin Found. **[988]**, 7383 S Alton Way, Ste. 100, Centennial, CO 80112-2339, (303)220-1693

North Amer. Lionhead Rabbit Club **[1191]**, c/o Jennifer Hack, Sec., 4098 N Hwy. 67, Sedalia, CO 80135, (765)346-7604

North Amer. Nietzsche Soc. **[1839]**, Univ. of Illinois, Dept. of Philosophy, 105 Gregory Hall, 810 S Wright St., Urbana, IL 61801, (217)333-1939

North Amer. Packgoat Assn. **[1109]**, PO Box 170166, Boise, ID 83717, (435)764-1111

North Amer. Performing Arts Managers and Agents **[39]**, 459 Columbus Ave., No. 133, New York, NY 10024, (718)797-4577

North Amer. Peruvian Horse Assn. **[1143]**, PO Box 2187, Santa Rosa, CA 95405, (707)544-5807

North Amer. Potbellied Pig Assn. **[946]**, 15525 E Via Del Palo, Gilbert, AZ 85298, (480)899-8941

North Amer. Professors of Christian Educ. **[1587]**, Biola Univ., 13800 Biola Ave., La Mirada, CA 90639

North Amer. Retail Dealers Assn. **[288]**, 222 S Riverside Plz., Ste. 2100, Chicago, IL 60606, (312)648-0649

North Amer. Retail Hardware Assn. **[415]**, 6325 Digital Way, No. 300, Indianapolis, IN 46278-1787, (317)290-0338

North Amer. Ring Assn. **[3182]**, PO Box 146, Gig Harbor, WA 98335, (206)219-9072

North Amer. Security Products Org. **[807]**, 1425 K St. NW, Ste. 350, Washington, DC 20005, (202)587-5743

North Amer. Shetland Sheepbreeders Assn. **[1211]**, NASSA Registry, 15603 173rd Ave., Milo, IA 50166, (641)942-6402

North Amer. Soc. for Oceanic History **[1807]**, Dept. of History, Texas Christian Univ., Box 297260, Fort Worth, TX 76129

North Amer. Soc. for the Psychology of Sport and Physical Activity **[3372]**, 1607 N Market St., Champaign, IL 61820

North Amer. South Devon Assn. **[989]**, 19590 E Main St., Ste. 202, Parker, CO 80138, (303)770-3130

North Amer. Technician Excellence **[436]**, 2111 Wilson Blvd., No. 510, Arlington, VA 22201, (703)276-7247

North Amer. Thermal Anal. Soc. **[1549]**, c/o Lois Hall, Staff Mgt. Dir., Western Kentucky Univ., Center for Res. and Development, Thermal Anal. Lab., 2413 Nashville Rd., Bowling Green, KY 42101-4101, (270)901-3490

North Amer. Truck Camper Owners Assn. **[3248]**, PO Box 30408, Bellingham, WA 98228

North Amer. Weed Mgt. Assn. **[934]**, PO Box 687, Meade, KS 67864, (620)873-8730

North Amer. Wensleydale Sheep Assn. **[1212]**, 4589 Fruitland Rd., Loma Rica, CA 95901, (530)745-5262

North Dakota State Univ. Alumni Assn. **[2761]**, 1241 N Univ. Dr., Fargo, ND 58102-2524, (701)231-6800

North-South Skirmish Assn. **[3384]**, PO Box 218, Crozet, VA 22932-0218

Northeast-Midwest Inst. **[2734]**, 50 F St. NW, Ste. 950, Washington, DC 20001, (202)464-4014

Northeastern Weed Sci. Soc. **[1154]**, PO Box 307, Fredericksburg, PA 17026, (717)787-7204

Northern Nut Growers Assn. **[1173]**, c/o William Sachs, Treas., PO Box 6216, Hamden, CT 06517-0216

Northwest Energy Efficiency Alliance **[1058]**, 421 SW 6th Ave., Ste. 600, Portland, OR 97204, (503)688-5400

Northwest Fisheries Assn. **[793]**, 2208 NW Market St., Ste. 318, Seattle, WA 98107, (206)789-6197

Northwest Regional Spinners' Assn. **[3171]**, c/o Diane Du Bray, Membership Chair, 22440 SE, 419th St., Enumclaw, WA 98022, (360)825-1634

Northwest Steam Soc. **[3242]**, PO Box 73, Hansville, WA 98340-0073, (206)310-4565

Norwegian
Innovation Norway - U.S. **[3482]**

Norwegian-American Chamber of Commerce **[3485]**, 655 3rd Ave., Ste. 1810, New York, NY 10017, (212)885-9737

Norwegian Fjord Horse Registry **[1144]**, 1801 W County Rd. 4, Berthoud, CO 80513, (303)684-6466

NOVA Hope for Haiti **[2139]**, 176 Palisade Ave., Emerson, NJ 07630, (201)675-9413

NPES: Assn. for Suppliers of Printing, Publishing and Converting Technologies **[410]**, 1899 Preston White Dr., Reston, VA 20191, (703)264-7200

Nuclear
Inst. of Nuclear Materials Mgt. **[1506]**

Nuclear Info. and Records Mgt. Assn. **[1507]**

Nuclear Info. Tech. Strategic Leadership **[1508]**

Amer. Coun. on Global Nuclear Competitiveness **[1509]**

Radiochemistry Soc. **[1438]**

United Against Nuclear Iran **[2711]**

Nuclear Energy
Amer. Coun. on Global Nuclear Competitiveness **[1509]**

Nuclear Info. Tech. Strategic Leadership **[1508]**

Nuclear Info. and Records Mgt. Assn. **[1507]**, 10 Almas Rd., Windham, NH 03087-1105, (603)432-6476

Nuclear Info. Tech. Strategic Leadership **[1508]**, PO Box 262, Mohnton, PA 19540, (610)880-0055

Nuclear Medicine
Amer. Coll. of Nuclear Medicine **[2564]**

Nuclear Steam Sys. Supply **[★1507]**

Nuclear War and Weapons
Global Security Inst. **[2709]**

Psychologists for Social Responsibility **[2710]**

United Against Nuclear Iran **[2711]**

Nudism
Amer. Assn. for Nude Recreation **[1831]**

Numismatic
Challenge Coin Assn. **[3221]**

Colonial Coin Collectors Club **[3222]**

Professional Currency Dealers Assn. **[3223]**

Professional Numismatists Guild **[3224]**

Nurseries
Horticultural Res. Inst. **[1170]**

Nursery and Landscape Assn. Executives of North Am. **[1171]**

Nursery and Landscape Assn. Executives of North Am. **[1171]**, 2130 Stella Ct., Columbus, OH 43215, (614)487-1117

Nursing
Amer. Assn. of Critical-Care Nurses **[2565]**

Vietnamese-American Nurses Assn. **[2566]**

Nutrition
Global FoodBanking Network **[2116]**

Nuts
Natl. Peanut Festival Assn. **[1172]**

Northern Nut Growers Assn. **[1173]**

O

Obesity
Natl. Assn. to Advance Fat Acceptance **[2148]**

Obstetrics and Gynecology
Endometriosis Assn. **[2567]**

Soc. for Gynecologic Investigation **[2568]**

Soc. for Menstrual Cycle Res. **[2569]**

Amer. Assn. of Naturopathic Midwives **[2553]**

Intl. Partnership for Reproductive Hea. **[2593]**

O.C. Intl. **[3008]**, PO Box 36900, Colorado Springs, CO 80936, (719)592-9292

Ocean Champions **[2630]**, PO Box 381596, Cambridge, MA 02238, (617)661-6647

Ocean Res. and Conservation Assn. **[1033]**, Duerr Lab. for Marine Conservation, 1420 Seaway Dr., 2nd Fl., Fort Pierce, FL 34949, (772)467-1600

Oceanic Preservation Soc. **[1034]**, 3063 Sterling Cir. E, No. 7, Boulder, CO 80301

Oceanography
MarineBio Conservation Soc. **[1162]**

Natl. Oceanic Soc. **[1031]**

Oceanic Preservation Soc. **[1034]**

Off. Bus. Center Assn. Intl. **[16]**, 2030 Main St., Ste. 1300, Irvine, CA 92614, (949)260-9023

Office Equipment
Bus. Solutions Assn. **[836]**

Off. and Professional Employees Intl. Union **[3435]**, c/o Mary Mahoney, Sec.-Treas., 80 Eighth Ave., Ste. 610, New York, NY 10011, (212)367-0902

Officers
CEO Netweavers **[236]**

Corporate Responsibility Officers Assn. **[237]**

Official Fan Club of the Grand Ole Opry **[3586]**, 2804 Opryland Dr., Nashville, TN 37214, (615)871-OPRY

Offshore Marine Ser. Assn. **[588]**, 990 N Corporate Dr., Ste. 210, Harahan, LA 70123, (504)734-7622

Ohio Genealogical Soc. **[3068]**, 611 State Rte. 97 W, Bellville, OH 44813-8813, (419)886-1903

Oil
Citizens for Energy Freedom **[1455]**

Crude Oil Quality Assn. **[640]**

Domestic Energy Producers Alliance **[300]**

Securing America's Future Energy **[1463]**

Oils and Fats
Inst. of Shortening and Edible Oils **[627]**

Older Women's League **[★2271]**

Olympic Educ. Center **[★3368]**

Olympic Games
U.S. Olympic Comm. **[3368]**

Virgin Islands Olympic Comm. **[3369]**

U.S. Bobsled and Skeleton Fed. **[3390]**

OMF Intl. U.S.A. **[3009]**, 10 W Dry Creek Cir., Littleton, CO 80120-4413, (303)730-4160

Omicron Delta Kappa Foundation **[★3528]**

Omicron Delta Kappa Soc. **[3528]**, 224 McLaughlin St., Lexington, VA 24450-2002, (540)458-5336

OMS Intl. **[3010]**, PO Box A, Greenwood, IN 46142, (317)888-3333

OmSpring **[2296]**, 550 Wisconsin St., San Francisco, CA 94107, (415)206-9920

On the Lighter Side, Intl. Lighter Collectors **[3160]**, PO Box 1733, Quitman, TX 75783-2733, (903)763-2795

Oncology
Amer. Coll. of Mohs Surgery **[2570]**

Natl. Found. for Cancer Res. **[2571]**

Oncology Assn. of Naturopathic Physicians **[2556]**

Oncology; Amer. Soc. of Pediatric Hematology/ **[2458]**

Oncology Assn. of Naturopathic Physicians **[2556]**, 216 NE Fremont St., Portland, OR 97212, (800)490-8509

Oncology Social Work; Assn. of **[2236]**

One Hen **[1580]**, PO Box 990781, Boston, MA 02199

One Love Worldwide **[2194]**, 1223 El Caminito Dr., Hobbs, NM 88240

One Vision Intl. **[2029]**, PO Box 20608, Knoxville, TN 37940, (865)579-3353

One Voice of Peace **[1672]**, 522 S Sunrise Way, Ste. 32, Palm Springs, CA 92264, (760)202-2330

Onomatology
Amer. Name Soc. **[1832]**

The Open Gp. **[473]**, 44 Montgomery St., Ste. 960, San Francisco, CA 94104-4704, (415)374-8280

Open Space Inst. **[1070]**, 1350 Broadway, Ste. 201, New York, NY 10018-7799, (212)290-8200

Opera Guild; Metropolitan **[1823]**

Oper. Crossroads Africa **[2608]**, PO Box 5570, New York, NY 10027, (212)289-1949

Oper. HOPE, Inc. **[2030]**, 707 Wilshire Blvd., 30th Fl., Los Angeles, CA 90017, (213)891-2900

Oper. Identity **[1874]**, 1818 Somervell St. NE, Albuquerque, NM 87112-2836, (505)293-3144

Operative Dentistry; Acad. of **[2360]**

Ophthalmology
Global Vision 2020 **[2601]**

Opportunity Finance Network **[2628]**, Public Ledger Bldg., 620 Chestnut St., Ste. 572, Philadelphia, PA 19106, (215)923-4754

OPSEC Professionals Soc. **[2743]**, PO Box 150515, Alexandria, VA 22315-0515

Optical Equipment
Optoelectronics Indus. Development Assn. **[628]**

Global Vision 2020 **[2601]**

Optical Imaging Assn. **[1166]**, PO Box 428, Fairfax, VA 22038, (703)836-1360

Options for Children in Zambia **[1978]**, 8 Stonegate Ln., Bedford, MA 01730

Optoelectronics Indus. Development Assn. **[628]**, 2010 Massachusetts Ave. NW, Washington, DC 20036, (202)416-1449

Optometry
Global Vision 2020 **[2601]**

Oral and Maxillofacial Surgery
Amer. Soc. of Maxillofacial Surgeons **[2572]**

Amer. Acad. of Restorative Dentistry **[2370]**

Amer. Assn. of Endodontists I Amer. Bd. of Endodontics **[2372]**

Oral Medicine; Amer. Acad. of **[2368]**

Orangutan Conservancy **[1248]**, PO Box 513, Los Angeles, CA 90036

Orchids
Intl. Phalaenopsis Alliance **[1153]**

A star before a book entry number signifies that the name is not listed separately, but is mentioned within the entry.

Order Fulfillment Coun. I Material Handling Indus. of Am. **[903]**, 8720 Red Oak Blvd., Ste. 201, Charlotte, NC 28217-3992, (704)676-1190

Orders and Medals Soc. of Am. **[3213]**, PO Box 198, San Ramon, CA 94583

Organic Crop Improvement Assn. **[1087]**, 1340 N Cotner Blvd., Lincoln, NE 68505, (402)477-2323

Organic Farming
   Independent Organic Inspectors Assn. **[1174]**
   Textile Exchange **[1175]**
   Food Trade Sustainability Leadership Assn. **[362]**

Organic Textile **[★1175]**

Organic Trade Assn. **[1164]**, 28 Vernon St., Ste. 413, Brattleboro, VT 05301, (802)275-3800

Org. of Amer. Historians **[1773]**, 112 N Bryan Ave., Bloomington, IN 47408-4141, (812)855-7311

Org. for Bat Conservation **[1249]**, PO Box 801, Bloomfield Hills, MI 48303, (248)645-3232

Org. of Black Airline Pilots **[34]**, 1 Westbrook Corporate Center, Westchester, IL 60154, (703)753-2047

Org. of Black Screenwriters **[314]**, 3010 Wilshire Blvd., No. 269, Los Angeles, CA 90010, (323)735-2050

Organization Development
   Org. Development Network **[629]**

Org. Development Network **[629]**, 401 N Michigan Ave., Ste. 2200, Chicago, IL 60611, (312)321-5136

Org. of News Ombudsmen **[702]**, c/o Debbie Kornmiller, Treas., The Arizona Daily Star, 4850 S Park Ave., Tucson, AZ 85714

Org. of Regulatory and Clinical Associates **[117]**, PO Box 3490, Redmond, WA 98073, (206)464-0825

Org. for Tropical Stud., North Amer. Off. **[1553]**, Duke Univ., PO Box 90630, Durham, NC 27708-0630, (919)684-5774

Organizations
   BoardSource **[2149]**
   Found. Center **[2150]**
   Mgt. Assistance Gp. **[2151]**
   Corporate Social Responsibility Assn. **[238]**
   United Way of Am. **[2091]**

Orienteering
   Natl. Assn. of Competitive Mounted Orienteering **[3370]**
   U.S. Orienteering Fed. **[3371]**

Ornithology
   Amer. Birding Assn. **[1510]**
   Amer. Ornithologists' Union **[1511]**
   Avicultural Soc. of Am. **[1512]**
   Inland Bird Banding Assn. **[1513]**

Orphan Found. of Am. **[1999]**, 21351 Gentry Dr., Ste. 130, Sterling, VA 20166, (571)203-0270

Orphan Support Africa **[1979]**, 2424 York St., Ste. 248, Philadelphia, PA 19125, (215)454-2832

Orphans Africa **[2031]**, 2610 N 8th St., Tacoma, WA 98406-7207, (253)549-0089

Orphans Against AIDS **[1980]**, 1110 Knollwood Dr., Buffalo Grove, IL 60089

Orthodontic Soc; Amer. **[2377]**

Orthodontics; Amer. Bd. of **[2374]**

Orthopedic Surgical Mfrs. Assn. **[425]**, PO Box 38805, Germantown, TN 38183-0805, (901)758-0806

Orthopedics
   Chiropractic Orthopedists of North Am. **[2341]**

Orthopedists; Amer. Coll. of Chiropractic **[2339]**

Otolaryngology Administrators; Assn. of **[2540]**

Otorhinolaryngology
   Amer. Head and Neck Soc. **[2573]**
   Amer. Laryngological, Rhinological and Otological Soc. **[2574]**

Ouachita Baptist Univ. Alumni Assn. **[2762]**, 410 Ouachita St., Arkadelphia, AR 71998, (870)245-5506

Out of Poverty thru Educ. **[1568]**, 2128 William St., No. 107, Cape Girardeau, MO 63703, (573)334-0930

Outdoor Amusement Bus. Assn. **[315]**, 1035 S Semoran Blvd., Ste. 1045A, Winter Park, FL 32792, (407)681-9444

Outdoor Indus. Assn. **[630]**, 4909 Pearl East Cir., Ste. 200, Boulder, CO 80301, (303)444-3353

Outdoor Power Equip. Aftermarket Assn. **[307]**, 341 S Patrick St., Alexandria, VA 22314, (703)549-7608

Outdoor Recreation
   Outdoor Indus. Assn. **[630]**

Antique Motorcycle Club of Am. **[3217]**

Bass Anglers Sportsman Soc. **[3326]**

Camping Women **[3301]**

Christian Camp and Conf. Assn. **[3302]**

Intl. Scale Soaring Assn. **[3216]**

Natl. Versatility Ranch Horse Assn. **[3352]**

New England Trails Conf. **[3428]**

North Amer. Family Campers Assn. **[3303]**

U.S. Lawn Bowls Assn. **[3295]**

Outdoor Writers Assn. of Am. **[703]**, 615 Oak St., Ste. 201, Missoula, MT 59801, (406)728-7434

Outreach Africa **[1981]**, PO Box 361, Union, IA 50258, (641)486-2550

Outsourcing
   Global Sourcing Coun. **[631]**

Overseas Automotive Coun. **[79]**, PO Box 13966, Research Triangle Park, NC 27709-3966, (919)406-8846

Overseas Press Club of Am. **[704]**, 40 W 45 St., New York, NY 10036, (212)626-9220

OWL - The Voice of Midlife and Older Women **[2271]**, 1025 Connecticut Ave. NW Ste. 701, Washington, DC 20036, (877)653-7966

P

Pacific 10 Conf. **[3407]**, 1350 Treat Blvd., Ste. 500, Walnut Creek, CA 94597-8853, (925)932-4411

Pacific Asia Travel Assn. **[885]**, 164 Loop Pl., Trinidad, CA 95570, (707)232-2102

Pacific Basin (Honolulu) **[★2622]**

Pacific Coast Rugby Union **[★3378]**

Pacific Coast Shellfish Growers Assn. **[794]**, 120 State Ave. NE, PMB No. 142, Olympia, WA 98501, (360)754-2744

Pacific Dermatologic Assn. **[2396]**, 575 Market St., Ste. 2125, San Francisco, CA 94105, (415)927-5729

Pacific Islands Conservation Res. Assn. **[1035]**, PO Box 302, South Beach, OR 97366

Pacific Lumber Exporters Assn. **[385]**, 2633 NW Raleigh St., No. 39, Portland, OR 97210, (503)598-3325

Pacific Maritime Assn. **[818]**, 555 Market St., San Francisco, CA 94105-2800, (415)576-3200

Pacific Seabird Gp. **[1250]**, c/o Ron LeValley, Treas., PO Box 324, Little River, CA 95456, (707)442-4302

Pacific Seafood Processors Assn. **[795]**, 1900 W Emerson Pl., No. 205, Seattle, WA 98119, (206)281-1667

Pacific Southwest Railway Museum **[1849]**, 4695 Nebo Dr., La Mesa, CA 91941-5259, (619)465-7776

Packaging
   Inst. of Packaging Professionals **[1514]**
   Petroleum Packaging Coun. **[632]**
   Women in Packaging **[633]**
   Reusable Packaging Assn. **[764]**

Packard Auto. Classics **[3124]**, PO Box 360806, Columbus, OH 43236-0806, (614)478-4946

PACON Intl. **[1160]**, 2525 Correa Rd., HIG 407A, Honolulu, HI 96822, (808)956-6163

PADI Travel Network **[★3431]**

Paint and Decorating Retailers Assn. **[513]**, 1401 Triad Center Dr., St. Peters, MO 63376-7353, (636)326-2636

Paints and Finishes
   Intl. Union of Painters and Allied Trades **[3454]**

Pakistan
   Pakistan Chamber of Commerce USA **[3502]**
   Eco Energy Finance **[1457]**

Pakistan Chamber of Commerce USA **[3502]**, 11110 Bellaire Blvd., Ste. 202, Houston, TX 77072-2600, (832)877-1234

Pakistani
   Pakistan Chamber of Commerce USA **[3502]**

Palatines to Am.: Researching German-Speaking Ancestry **[3069]**, PO Box 141260, Columbus, OH 43214, (614)267-4700

Palestine
   Middle East Investment Initiative **[336]**

Pan Amer. Hea. and Educ. Found. **[2140]**, PO Box 27733, Washington, DC 20038-7733, (202)974-3416

Panthera **[1251]**, 8 W 40th St., 18th Fl., New York, NY 10018, (646)786-0400

Paper Stock Indus. Chap. of ISRI **[908]**, PO Box 64999, Fayetteville, NC 28306, (910)426-7400

Para Sa Bata **[1982]**, 11331 Cedar Springs Dr., Frisco, TX 75035, (469)579-4544

Paralegal Educ; Amer. Assn. for **[1655]**

Paralegals
   Natl. Fed. of Paralegal Associations **[1354]**
   Alliance of Legal Document Asst. Professionals **[1340]**

Paraprofessional Healthcare Inst. **[★420]**

Parapsychological Assn. **[1516]**, PO Box 24173, Columbus, OH 43224, (202)318-2364

Parapsychology
   Acad. of Spirituality and Paranormal Stud., Inc. **[1515]**
   Parapsychological Assn. **[1516]**

Parents
   Natl. Center for Fathering **[2712]**
   Natl. Foster Parent Assn. **[2152]**
   Parents Without Partners **[2153]**

Parents, Families, and Friends of Lesbians and Gays **[2096]**, 1828 L St. NW, Ste. 660, Washington, DC 20036, (202)467-8180

Parents Without Partners **[2153]**, 1100-H Brandywine Blvd., Zanesville, OH 43701-7303, (800)637-7974

Parker Gun Collectors Assn. **[3193]**, PO Box 115, Mayodan, NC 27027

Parks and Recreation
   Assn. of Natl. Park Rangers **[1355]**
   Coalition of Natl. Park Ser. Retirees **[1176]**
   Natl. Assn. of State Park Directors **[1356]**
   Natl. Park Found. **[1357]**
   Natl. Parks Conservation Assn. **[1358]**
   Global Parks **[1026]**

Parliaments
   Amer. Inst. of Parliamentarians **[1833]**

Parole
   Assn. of State Correctional Administrators **[2049]**
   Intl. Assn. for Correctional and Forensic Psychology **[2050]**

Partners of the Americas **[2611]**, 1424 K St. NW, Ste. 700, Washington, DC 20005, (202)628-3300

Partners in Sustainable Development Intl. **[2171]**, 9005 Greenridge Dr., St. Louis, MO 63117, (314)993-5599

Partners for World Hea. **[2512]**, 7 Glasgow Rd., Scarborough, ME 04074, (207)885-1011

Partnership for a Drug-Free Am. **[★2246]**

Partnership at Drugfree.org **[2246]**, 352 Park Ave. S 9th Fl., New York, NY 10010, (212)922-1560

Paso Pacifico **[1036]**, PO Box 1244, Ventura, CA 93002-1244, (805)643-7044

Passenger Vessel Assn. **[589]**, 103 Oronoco St., Ste. 200, Alexandria, VA 22314, (703)518-5005

Pathology
   Renal Pathology Soc. **[2575]**

PCIA - The Wireless Infrastructure Assn. **[850]**, 901 N Washington St., Ste. 600, Alexandria, VA 22314-1535, (703)836-1608

Peace
   The Children of War **[2713]**
   Fellowship of Reconciliation - USA **[2714]**
   Global Ambassadors for Children **[2715]**
   Jane Addams Peace Assn. **[2716]**
   Kids for Peace **[2717]**
   One Voice of Peace **[1672]**
   Peace and Justice Stud. Assn. **[2718]**
   Peaceworkers Nonviolent Peaceforce **[2719]**
   Student Peace Alliance **[2720]**
   Sudan Sunrise **[2154]**
   Veterans for Peace **[2721]**
   Voters for Peace **[2722]**
   World Sound Healing Org. **[2155]**
   Abrahamic Alliance Intl. **[2945]**
   Americans for Peace Now **[2689]**
   Center on Conscience and War **[2641]**
   Intl. Coun. for Middle East Stud. **[2701]**
   Irish Amer. Unity Conf. **[2688]**
   Ishmael and Isaac **[2702]**
   Monks Without Borders **[2946]**

Peace House Africa **[1983]**, 6581 City W Pkwy., Eden Prairie, MN 55344, (952)465-0050

Peace and Justice Stud. Assn. **[2718]**, Prescott Coll., 220 Grove Ave., Prescott, AZ 86301, (928)350-2008

Peace Now **[★2689]**

Peaceworkers Nonviolent Peaceforce **[2719]**, 425 Oak Grove St., Minneapolis, MN 55403, (612)871-0005

Peanut and Tree Nut Processors Assn. **[369]**, PO Box 2660, Alexandria, VA 22301, (301)365-2521

Pediatric Assn. of Naturopathic Physicians **[1670]**, 216 NE Fremont St., Portland, OR 97212

Pediatric Hematology/Oncology; Amer. Soc. of **[2458]**

Pediatrics
Pediatric Assn. of Naturopathic Physicians **[1670]**

Pedorthic Footwear Assn. **[381]**, 2025 M St. NW, Ste. 800, Washington, DC 20036, (202)367-1145

Pension Real Estate Assn. **[754]**, 100 Pearl St., 13th Fl., Hartford, CT 06103, (860)692-6341

Pensions
Assn. of Public Pension Fund Auditors **[3455]**
Retirement Indus. Trust Assn. **[115]**

Pentecostal
Soc. for Pentecostal Stud. **[3024]**

People 4 Earth **[1071]**, 1612 K St. NW, Ste. 600, Washington, DC 20006, (484)919-1488

People for Haiti **[2195]**, 2132 Flameflower Ct., Trinity, FL 34655, (727)457-7272

Performing Arts
Amer. Fed. of Musicians of the U.S. and Canada **[3456]**
Intl. Performing Arts for Youth **[1834]**
Screen Actors Guild **[3457]**
Stage Directors and Choreographers Soc. **[3458]**
Voices Breaking Boundaries **[1835]**
Amer. Dance Guild **[1749]**
Independent Arts and Media **[1709]**

Performing Arts Alliance **[1727]**, 1211 Connecticut Ave. NW, Ste. 200, Washington, DC 20036, (202)207-3850

Perhaps Kids Meeting Kids Can Make a Difference **[2684]**, 380 Riverside Dr., Box 8H, New York, NY 10025

Perlite Inst. **[618]**, 4305 N 6th St., Ste. A, Harrisburg, PA 17110, (717)238-9723

Personnel
Natl. Assn. for Govt. Training and Development **[634]**
Natl. Human Resources Assn. **[635]**
Soc. for Human Rsrc. Mgt. **[636]**

Pest Control
Amer. Mosquito Control Assn. **[1177]**
Assn. of Natural Biocontrol Producers **[1178]**
Natl. Assn. of Exotic Pest Plant Councils **[1179]**
Responsible Indus. for a Sound Env. **[637]**

Pet Indus. Joint Advisory Coun. **[655]**, 1140 19th St. NW, Ste. 300, Washington, DC 20036, (202)452-1525

Petroleum
Amer. Oil and Gas Historical Soc. **[638]**
America's Natural Gas Alliance **[639]**
Crude Oil Quality Assn. **[640]**
Distribution Contractors Assn. **[3459]**
Energy Traffic Assn. **[641]**
Gas Processors Assn. **[642]**
Gas Processors Suppliers Assn. **[643]**
Independent Lubricant Mfrs. Assn. **[644]**
Intl. Assn. of Geophysical Contractors **[645]**
Intl. Oil Scouts Assn. **[646]**
Natl. Assn. of Div. Order Analysts **[647]**
Petroleum Equip. Inst. **[648]**
Ser. Sta. Dealers of America/National Coalition of Petroleum Retailers and Allied Trades **[649]**
Soc. of Professional Women in Petroleum **[650]**
Western States Petroleum Assn. **[651]**
Citizens for Affordable Energy **[1453]**
Citizens for Energy Freedom **[1455]**
Citizens Energy Plan **[1456]**
Domestic Energy Producers Alliance **[300]**
Leadership for Energy Automated Processing **[303]**
Res. Partnership to Secure Energy for Am. **[1461]**
Securing America's Future Energy **[1463]**
Set Am. Free **[2643]**

Petroleum Equip. Inst. **[648]**, PO Box 2380, Tulsa, OK 74101-2380, (918)494-9696

Petroleum Packaging Coun. **[632]**, 1519 via Tulipan, San Clemente, CA 92673, (949)369-7102

Pets
Amer. Pet Products Assn. **[652]**

Independent Pet and Animal Trans. Assn. Intl. **[653]**
Intl. Professional Groomers **[654]**
Pet Indus. Joint Advisory Coun. **[655]**
World Pet Assn. **[656]**
Animal Welfare Advocacy **[1889]**
Havana Silk Dog Assn. of Am. **[3176]**
SPCA Intl. **[1900]**
U.S.A. Coton de Tulear Club **[3186]**
U.S. Complete Shooting Dog Assn. **[3187]**

PGI **[90]**, The Terminus Bldg., 3280 Peachtree Rd. NW, Atlanta, GA 30305, (866)548-3203

Pharmaceutical Care Mgt. Assn. **[2579]**, 601 Pennsylvania Ave. NW, Ste. 740 S, Washington, DC 20004, (202)207-3610

Pharmaceutical Res. and Mfrs. of Am. **[661]**, 950 F St. NW, Ste. 300, Washington, DC 20004, (202)835-3400

Pharmaceuticals
Chain Drug Marketing Assn. **[657]**
Consumer Healthcare Products Assn. **[658]**
Intl. Pharmaceutical Excipients Coun. of the Americas **[659]**
Natl. Pharmaceutical Coun. **[660]**
Pharmaceutical Res. and Mfrs. of Am. **[661]**

Pharmacy
Alpha Zeta Omega **[3542]**
Healthcare Distribution Mgt. Assn. **[2576]**
Natl. Assn. of Chain Drug Stores **[2577]**
Natl. Community Pharmacists Assn. **[2578]**
Nigerian Assn. of Pharmacists and Pharmaceutical Scientists in the Americas **[662]**
Pharmaceutical Care Mgt. Assn. **[2579]**
Phi Delta Chi **[3543]**

Phenomena
Amer. Soc. of Dowsers **[1517]**
Natl. Investigations Comm. on Unidentified Flying Objects **[1518]**

PHI **[420]**, 349 E 149th St., 10th Fl., Bronx, NY 10451, (718)402-7766

Phi Beta Delta **[3529]**, 1630 Connecticut Ave. NW, 3rd Fl., Washington, DC 20009, (202)518-2052

Phi Chi Medical Fraternity **[3539]**, 2039 Ridgeview Dr., Floyds Knobs, IN 47119, (812)923-7270

Phi Chi Welfare Association **[★3539]**

Phi Delta Chi **[3543]**, 116 N Lafayette, Ste. B, South Lyon, MI 48178, (800)PDC-1883

Phi Epsilon Kappa **[3544]**, 901 W New York St., Indianapolis, IN 46202, (317)627-8745

Phi Kappa Phi **[3530]**, 7576 Goodwood Blvd., Baton Rouge, LA 70806, (225)388-4917

Phi Sigma **[3510]**, Quinnipiac Univ., Dept. of Biological Sciences, 275 Mt. Carmel Ave., Hamden, CT 06518-1905

Philadelphia Flyers Fan Club **[3593]**, PO Box 610, Plymouth Meeting, PA 19462

Philalethes Soc. **[2806]**, c/o John C. Householder, Jr., Bus. Mgr., 800 S 15th St., No. 1803, Sebring, OH 44672, (330)938-7582

Philanthropy
Bread for the Journey Intl. **[2156]**
Giving U.S.A. Found. **[2157]**
Good360 **[2158]**
Philanthropy Roundtable **[2159]**
Twenty-First Century Found. **[2160]**
Funders' Network for Smart Growth and Livable Communities **[2018]**
United Way of Am. **[2091]**

Philanthropy Roundtable **[2159]**, 1730 M St. NW, Ste. 601, Washington, DC 20036, (202)822-8333

Philatelic
Amer. Revenue Assn. **[3225]**
First Issues Collectors Club **[3226]**
Intl. Soc. of Worldwide Stamp Collectors **[3227]**
Korea Stamp Soc. **[3228]**
Natl. Duck Stamp Collectors Soc. **[3229]**
Rotary on Stamps Fellowship **[3230]**
Scandinavian Collectors Club **[3231]**
Soc. of Australasian Specialists/Oceania **[3232]**
Soc. for Hungarian Philately **[3233]**
Space Topic Stud. Unit **[3234]**
Sports Philatelists Intl. **[3235]**

Philately
First Issues Collectors Club **[3226]**
Intl. Soc. of Worldwide Stamp Collectors **[3227]**

Korea Stamp Soc. **[3228]**
Soc. of Australasian Specialists/Oceania **[3232]**
Space Topic Stud. Unit **[3234]**

Philippines
Mamburao-U.S.A. Assn. **[1836]**
Intl. Soc. of Filipinos in Finance and Accounting **[8]**

Philosophy
Assn. for Feminist Ethics and Social Theory **[1837]**
Intl. Soc. for Neoplatonic Stud. **[1838]**
North Amer. Nietzsche Soc. **[1839]**
Soc. for Utopian Stud. **[1840]**
Philosophy; Soc. for Natural **[1496]**

Phobias
Anxiety Disorders Assn. of Am. **[2161]**

Photographic Soc. of Am. **[3236]**, 3000 United Founders Blvd., Ste. 103, Oklahoma City, OK 73112-3940, (405)843-1437

Photography
Amer. Photographic Artists Guild **[663]**
Amer. Soc. of Photographers **[1841]**
Amer. Soc. of Picture Professionals **[664]**
Antique and Amusement Photographers Intl. **[665]**
Blue Earth Alliance **[1842]**
Independent Photo Imagers **[666]**
Photographic Soc. of Am. **[3236]**
Professional Photographers of Am. **[667]**
Professional Women Photographers **[668]**
White House News Photographers Assn. **[669]**

Physical Education
Amer. Alliance for Hea., Physical Educ., Recreation and Dance **[1673]**
Phi Epsilon Kappa **[3544]**

Physical Fitness
Fed. of Intl. Lacrosse **[3357]**
Girls on the Run Intl. **[3379]**
Intl. Assn. of Gay and Lesbian Martial Artists **[3360]**
Intl. Female Boxers Assn. **[3298]**
Intl. Natural Bodybuilding and Fitness Fed. **[3293]**
Maccabi USA/Sports for Israel **[3402]**
New England Trails Conf. **[3428]**
Professional Baseball Athletic Trainers Soc. **[3261]**
U.S. Bobsled and Skeleton Fed. **[3390]**
USA Diving **[3321]**
The World Kuoshu Fed. **[3363]**

Physically Impaired
BlazeSports Am. **[3316]**

Physicians
Catholic Medical Assn. **[2580]**
Amer. Osteopathic Coll. of Anesthesiologists **[2301]**
Global Physicians Corps **[2495]**
Heart Rhythm Soc. **[2332]**
Oncology Assn. of Naturopathic Physicians **[2556]**
Pediatric Assn. of Naturopathic Physicians **[1670]**

Physicians for Human Rights **[2668]**, 2 Arrow St., Ste. 301, Cambridge, MA 02138, (617)301-4200

Physics
Amer. Assn. of Physicists in Medicine **[2581]**
Amer. Assn. of Physics Teachers **[1674]**

Pi Beta Phi **[3553]**, 1154 Town and Country Commons Dr., Town and Country, MO 63017-8200, (636)256-0680

Pi Delta Psi Fraternity **[3554]**, PO Box 520269, Flushing, NY 11352-0269

Pi Kappa Alpha **[3555]**, 8347 W Range Cove, Memphis, TN 38125, (901)748-1868

Pi Lambda Phi Fraternity **[3556]**, 60 Newtown Rd., No. 118, Danbury, CT 06810, (203)740-1044

Pi Lambda Theta **[3520]**, 408 N Union St., PO Box 7888, Bloomington, IN 47407-7888, (812)339-1156

Pi Mu Epsilon **[3537]**, Hendrix Coll., Dept. of Mathematics and Cmpt. Sci., Conway, AR 72032, (501)450-1253

Pickle Packers Intl. **[370]**, 1620 I St. NW, Ste. 925, Washington, DC 20006, (202)331-2456

Pierre Fauchard Acad. **[2388]**, PO Box 3718, Mesquite, NV 89024-3718, (702)345-2950

Pilatus Owners and Pilots Assn. **[35]**, 6890 E Sunrise Dr., Ste. 120-114, Tucson, AZ 85702, (520)299-7485

Pilgrims
Gen. Soc. of Mayflower Descendants **[3077]**

A star before a book entry number signifies that the name is not listed separately, but is mentioned within the entry.

Pine Chemicals Assn. **[187]**, 3350 Riverwood Pkwy. SE, Ste. 1900, Atlanta, GA 30339, (770)984-5340

Pioneers **[2090]**, 930 15th St., 12th Fl., Denver, CO 80202, (303)571-1200

Pioneers
Natl. Soc. of the Sons of Utah Pioneers **[3078]**

Pipe Fabrication Inst. **[673]**, 511 Avenue of the Americas, No. 601, New York, NY 10011, (514)634-3434

Pipes
Amer. Concrete Pressure Pipe Assn. **[670]**
Natl. Assn. of Steel Pipe Distributors **[671]**
Natl. Corrugated Steel Pipe Assn. **[672]**
Pipe Fabrication Inst. **[673]**
Plastics Pipe Inst. **[674]**

Pittsburgh Penguins Booster Club **[3594]**, PO Box 903, Pittsburgh, PA 15230

Planetary Soc. **[1388]**, 85 S Grand Ave., Pasadena, CA 91106-2301, (626)793-5100

Planetwork **[1055]**, 1230 Market St., No. 517, San Francisco, CA 94102, (415)721-1591

Planning
Assn. of Divorce Financial Planners **[347]**
Building Commissioning Assn. **[141]**
Ministry Architecture **[1409]**
Natl. Assn. of Financial and Estate Planning **[338]**
Wedding Indus. Professionals Assn. **[124]**

Plant Growth Regulation Soc. of Am. **[1432]**, 1018 Duke St., Alexandria, VA 22314, (703)836-4606

Planting Empowerment **[1094]**, 1348 Euclid St. NW, No. 305, Washington, DC 20009, (202)470-2432

Plastic Loose Fill Coun. **[1180]**, 1298 Cronson Blvd., Ste. 201, Crofton, MD 21114, (510)654-0756

Plastics
Assn. of Rotational Molders Intl. **[675]**
Center for the Polyurethanes Indus. **[676]**
Plastic Loose Fill Coun. **[1180]**
Plasticville Collectors Assn. **[3237]**
Soc. of the Plastics Indus. **[677]**

Plastics Pipe Inst. **[674]**, 105 Decker Ct., Ste. 825, Irving, TX 75062, (469)499-1044

Plasticville Collectors Assn. **[3237]**, c/o John Niehaus, Sec.-Treas., 601 SE Second St., Ankeny, IA 50021-3207

Play
The Assn. for the Stud. of Play **[1843]**

Plug In Am. **[1396]**, 2370 Market St., No. 419, San Francisco, CA 94114, (415)323-3329

Plumbing
Decorative Plumbing and Hardware Assn. **[678]**
Plumbing and Drainage Inst. **[679]**
Plumbing Mfrs. Inst. **[680]**

Plumbing and Drainage Inst. **[679]**, 800 Turnpike St., Ste. 300, North Andover, MA 01845, (978)557-0720

Plumbing Mfrs. Inst. **[680]**, 1921 Rohlwing Rd., Unit G, Rolling Meadows, IL 60008, (847)481-5500

Plymouth Barracuda/Cuda Owners Club **[3125]**, c/o Ann M. Curman, Sec., 36 Woodland Rd., East Greenwich, RI 02818-3430, (401)884-4449

Pocketful of Joy **[1984]**, 24 Goose Ln., Tolland, CT 06084

Poetry
Acad. of Amer. Poets **[1844]**
Tanka Soc. of Am. **[1845]**

Point-of-Purchase Advt. Intl. **[22]**, 1600 Duke St., Ste. 610, Alexandria, VA 22314, (703)373-8800

Polar Studies
Amer. Polar Soc. **[1519]**

Policy
Citizens Energy Plan **[1456]**
Iran Policy Comm. **[2687]**

Polish
Jozef Pilsudski Inst. of Am. for Res. in the Modern History of Poland **[1846]**
Polish Amer. Cong. **[2813]**
Polish Amer. Historical Assn. **[1847]**
Polish Arts and Culture Found. **[2814]**
Polish Assistance, Inc. **[2815]**
Polish Beneficial Assn. **[2816]**
Polish Falcons of Am. **[2817]**
Union of Poles in Am. **[2818]**

Polish Amer. Cong. **[2813]**, 5711 N Milwaukee Ave., Chicago, IL 60646-6215, (773)763-9944

Polish Amer. Historical Assn. **[1847]**, Central Connecticut State Univ., 1615 Stanley St., New Britain, CT 06050, (860)832-3010

Polish Arts and Culture Found. **[2814]**, 4077 Waterhouse Rd., Oakland, CA 94602, (510)599-2244

Polish Assistance, Inc. **[2815]**, 15 E 65th St., New York, NY 10065-6501, (212)570-5560

Polish Beneficial Assn. **[2816]**, 2595 Orthodox St., Philadelphia, PA 19137, (215)535-2626

Polish Falcons of Am. **[2817]**, 381 Mansfield Ave., Pittsburgh, PA 15220-2751, (412)922-2244

Polish Tatra Sheepdog Club of Am. **[3183]**, c/o Anita Liebl, Sec., 7119 W Lakefield Dr., Milwaukee, WI 53219, (414)329-1373

Political Parties
Working Families Party **[2723]**

Politics
Amer. Assn. of Political Consultants **[2724]**
Amer. League of Lobbyists **[2725]**
Arab Amer. Inst. **[2726]**
Scientists and Engineers for Am. **[1279]**

Pollock-Krasner Found. **[1719]**, 863 Park Ave., New York, NY 10075, (212)517-5400

Polls
Amer. Assn. for Public Opinion Res. **[2727]**
Voters for Peace **[2722]**

Pollution Control
Climate Registry **[1181]**
Mfrs. of Emission Controls Assn. **[681]**
Natl. Pollution Prevention Roundtable **[1182]**
Solar Cookers Intl. **[1183]**
Spill Control Assn. of Am. **[682]**
Water Env. Fed. **[1184]**
Worldwide Pollution Control Assn. **[683]**
Responsible Purchasing Network **[316]**

Polyacrylate Absorbents; Inst. for **[185]**

Pontifical Mission Societies in the U.S. **[2877]**, 70 W 36th St., 8th Fl., New York, NY 10018, (212)563-8700

Pony of the Americas Club **[1145]**, 3828 S Emerson Ave., Indianapolis, IN 46203, (317)788-0107

Population
Population-Environment Balance **[2162]**
Soc. of Family Planning **[2413]**

Population-Environment Balance **[2162]**, PO Box 1059, Anaheim, CA 92815, (714)204-3466

Porsche Club of Am. **[3126]**, PO Box 6400, Columbia, MD 21045, (410)381-0911

Portuguese Podengo Club of Am. **[3184]**, c/o Becky Berkley, Membership Chair, 11655 Vaca Pl., San Diego, CA 92124

Postal Service
Amer. Postal Workers Union **[3460]**
Carriers and Locals Soc. **[3238]**
Natl. Assn. of Coll. and Univ. Mail Services **[684]**
Natl. Assn. of Postal Supervisors **[3461]**
Korea Stamp Soc. **[3228]**
Soc. of Australasian Specialists/Oceania **[3232]**
Space Topic Stud. Unit **[3234]**

Postal Workers
Korea Stamp Soc. **[3228]**
Soc. of Australasian Specialists/Oceania **[3232]**
Space Topic Stud. Unit **[3234]**

Postcards
Intl. Fed. of Postcard Dealers **[3239]**

Potato Assn. of Am. **[1101]**, Univ. of Maine, 5719 Crossland Hall, Rm. 220, Orono, ME 04469-5719, (207)581-3042

Poultry
Natl. Chicken Coun. **[1185]**

Poverty
Aid for the World **[2163]**
Center for Community Change **[2164]**
Community Action Partnership **[2165]**
Helping Hearts Helping Hands **[2166]**
Inter-Faith Community Services **[2167]**
MDRC **[2168]**
Mercy Beyond Borders **[2169]**
Miracles in Action **[2170]**
Partners in Sustainable Development Intl. **[2171]**
Reach Out to Romania **[2172]**
Tusubira - We Have Hope **[2173]**
Union Settlement Assn. **[2174]**
Amer. Bar Assn. Commn. on Homelessness and Poverty **[2099]**
Amer. Outreach to Ethiopia **[2114]**
Bridges to Prosperity **[2210]**
Child Empowerment Intl. **[1934]**
Chris Cares Intl. **[2013]**
Christ for the Poor **[1681]**

Eliminate Poverty Now **[1904]**
Global FoodBanking Network **[2116]**
Global Partnership for Afghanistan **[925]**
Green for All **[2612]**
HANDS for Cambodia **[2021]**
Hearts for Kenya **[1907]**
Helping Hand for Nepal **[2189]**
Innovations for Poverty Action **[2613]**
Intl. Agro Alliance **[1217]**
Millennium Campus Network **[2614]**
Natl. Student Campaign Against Hunger and Homelessness **[2117]**
Nepal SEEDS: Social Educational Environmental Development Services in Nepal **[2028]**
Restoring Institutions Services and Empowering Liberia **[2033]**
Rights and Resources Initiative **[1095]**
Rising Intl. **[1908]**
Simple Hope **[2200]**
Sky of Love **[1986]**
Vietnam Relief Effort **[2201]**
Well Done Org. **[2039]**

Poverty, Anti-
Inter-Faith Community Services **[2167]**

Power
GridWise Architecture Coun. **[1520]**
Natl. Assn. of Power Engineers **[1521]**
Amer. Coun. on Global Nuclear Competitiveness **[1509]**
America's Natural Gas Alliance **[639]**
Citizens' Alliance for Responsible Energy **[1454]**
Citizens for Energy Freedom **[1455]**
Eco Energy Finance **[1457]**
Energy Efficiency Bus. Coalition **[301]**
Energy Info. Standards Alliance **[302]**
FutureGen Alliance **[1393]**
Natl. Alliance for Advanced Tech. Batteries **[116]**
New Energy Indus. Assn. for Asia and the Pacific **[1460]**
Nuclear Info. Tech. Strategic Leadership **[1508]**
Res. Partnership to Secure Energy for Am. **[1461]**
Securing America's Future Energy **[1463]**
U.S. Water and Power **[1399]**

Power and Commun. Contractors Assn. **[229]**, 1908 Mt. Vernon Ave., Alexandria, VA 22314, (703)212-7734

Power-Motion Tech. Representatives Assn. **[467]**, 16A Journey, Ste. 200, Aliso Viejo, CA 92656, (949)859-2885

POWER: People Organized to Win Employment Rights **[2078]**, 335 S Van Nes Ave., 2nd Fl., San Francisco, CA 94103, (415)864-8372

Prairie Club **[2176]**, 12 E Willow St., Unit A, Lombard, IL 60148, (630)620-9334

Precast/Prestressed Concrete Inst. **[201]**, 200 W Adams St., No. 2100, Chicago, IL 60606, (312)786-0300

Premedical Summer Institute **[★1624]**

Presbyterian
Independent Bd. for Presbyterian Foreign Missions **[3025]**

Preschool Education
Brick by Brick for Tanzania! **[1675]**

Preservation Trades Network **[159]**, PO Box 151, Burbank, OH 44214-0151, (330)465-1504

Press
Amer. Jewish Press Assn. **[685]**
Amer. News Women's Club **[686]**
Amer. Soc. of News Editors **[687]**
Asian Amer. Journalists Assn. **[688]**
Assoc. Press Managing Editors **[689]**
Assn. of Alternative Newsweeklies **[690]**
Assn. of Amer. Editorial Cartoonists **[691]**
Assn. of Hea. Care Journalists **[692]**
Assn. for Women in Sports Media **[693]**
Automotive Aftermarket Indus. Assn. I Natl. Catalog Managers Assn. **[694]**
Intl. Center for Journalists **[695]**
Intl. Motor Press Assn. **[696]**
Natl. Assn. of Black Journalists **[697]**
Natl. Conf. of Editorial Writers **[698]**
Natl. Newspaper Assn. **[699]**
Natl. Press Club **[700]**
New York Financial Writers' Assn. **[701]**
Org. of News Ombudsmen **[702]**
Outdoor Writers Assn. of Am. **[703]**
Overseas Press Club of Am. **[704]**

Regional Reporters Assn. [705]
Soc. for Features Journalism [706]
Soc. of Professional Journalists [707]
Soc. of the Silurians [708]
Travel Journalists Guild [709]
United Nations Correspondents Assn. [710]
Newspaper Target Marketing Coalition [626]
Prevent a Litter Coalition [1898], PO Box 688, Great
Falls, VA 22066, (703)818-8009
Preventive Medicine
Soft Power Hea. [2518]
Primarily Primates, Inc. [1899], 26099 Dull Knife
Trail, San Antonio, TX 78255, (830)755-4616
Primates
Ape Action Africa [1231]
Ape Conservation Effort [1232]
Primero Agua [2267], 2675 Stonecrest Dr.,
Washington, MO 63090, (636)239-1573
Princess Kitty Fan Club [3566], PO Box 430784,
Miami, FL 33243-0784, (305)661-0528
Print Services and Distribution Assn. [838], 401 N
Michigan Ave., Ste. 2200, Chicago, IL 60611,
(800)230-0175
Printing Indus. Credit Executives [246], 1100 Main
St., Buffalo, NY 14209, (800)226-0722
Prisoners
Assn. of State Correctional Administrators [2049]
Hea. through Walls [2501]
Intl. Assn. for Correctional and Forensic Psychol-
ogy [2050]
Intl. Network of Prison Ministries [2984]
Private Art Dealers Assn. [60], PO Box 872, Lenox
Hill Sta., New York, NY 10021, (212)572-0772
Private Enterprise Res. Center [2654], Texas A&M
Univ., 4231 TAMU, College Station, TX 77843-
4231, (979)845-7722
Private Schools
The Assn. of Boarding Schools [1676]
Coun. for Amer. Private Educ. [1677]
Pro Athletes Outreach [2934], PO Box 801, Palo
Alto, CA 94302, (650)206-2962
Pro Legends [★3330]
Pro-Life Action League [2739], 6160 N Cicero Ave.,
Ste. 600, Chicago, IL 60646, (773)777-2900
Pro vs. GI Joe [3200], 4 Montage, Irvine, CA 92614-
8112, (818)371-1283
Prdt. Development and Mgt. Assn. [568], 401 N
Michigan Ave., Chicago, IL 60611, (856)439-9052
Product Testing
Intl. Air Filtration Certifiers Assn. [432]
ProEnglish [1753], 1601 N Kent St., Ste. 1100,
Arlington, VA 22209, (703)816-8821
Professional Armed Forces Rodeo Assn. [3374], c/o
Val Baker, Sec., 1985 1st St. W, No. 2523, Ran-
dolph, TX 78150-4312
Professional Assn. of Diving Instructors [3431],
30151 Tomas St., Rancho Santa Margarita, CA
92688-2125, (949)858-7234
Professional Assn. of Innkeepers Intl. [449], 207
White Horse Pike, Haddon Heights, NJ 08035,
(856)310-1102
Professional Assn. for Investment Communications
Resources [529], 12100 Sunset Hills Rd., Ste.
130, Reston, VA 20190, (866)993-0999
Professional Assn. of Small Bus. Accountants [10],
6405 Metcalf Ave., Ste. 503, Shawnee Mission, KS
66202, (866)296-0001
Professional Audio Mfrs. Alliance [289], 11242
Waples Mill Rd., Ste. 200, Fairfax, VA 22030,
(703)279-9938
Professional Aviation Maintenance Assn. [36], 400 N
Washington St., Ste. 300, Alexandria, VA 22314,
(703)778-4647
Professional Baseball Athletic Trainers Soc. [3261],
PO Box 386, Atlanta, GA 30361
Professional Beauty Assn. | Nail Mfrs. Coun. [241],
15825 N 71st St., Ste. 100, Scottsdale, AZ 85254,
(480)281-0424
Professional Coaches, Mentors and Advisors [3307],
PO Box 265, Palos Verdes Estates, CA 90274-
0265, (800)768-6017
Professional Constr. Estimators Assn. of Am. [230],
PO Box 680336, Charlotte, NC 28216, (704)489-
1494
Professional Currency Dealers Assn. [3223], c/o
James A. Simek, Sec., PO Box 7157, Westchester,
IL 60154

Professional Elecl. Apparatus Recyclers League
[274], 4255 S Buckley Rd., No. 118, Aurora, CO
80013, (877)AT-PEARL
Professional Figure Skaters Cooperative [3386], PO
Box 893, Park Forest, IL 60466, (312)296-7864
Professional Football Writers of Am. [3332], 12030
Cedar Lake Ct., Maryland Heights, MO 63043
Professional Fraternity Assn. [3526], 1011 San Ja-
cinto, Ste. 205, Austin, TX 78701, (512)789-9530
Professional Golfers' Assn. of Am. [3337], 100 Ave.
of the Champions, Palm Beach Gardens, FL
33418, (561)624-8400
Professional Landcare Network [532], 950 Herndon
Pkwy., Ste. 450, Herndon, VA 20170, (703)736-
9666
Professional Lighting and Sign Mgt. Companies of
Am. [546], 1100-H Brandywine Blvd., Zanesville,
OH 43701-7303, (740)452-4541
Professional Loadmaster Assn. [1350], PO Box
4351, Tacoma, WA 98438, (253)215-0118
Professional Numismatists Guild [3224], 28441 Ran-
cho California Rd., Ste. 106, Temecula, CA 92590,
(951)587-8300
Professional and Organizational Development
Network in Higher Educ. [1628], PO Box 3318,
Nederland, CO 80466, (303)258-9521
Professional Photographers of Am. [667], 229
Peachtree St. NE, Ste. 2200, Atlanta, GA 30303-
1608, (404)522-8600
Professional Picture Framers Assn. [1712], 3000
Picture Pl., Jackson, MI 49201, (517)788-8100
Professional Putters Assn. [3338], 28 Sioux Trail,
Ransom Canyon, TX 79366, (434)237-7888
Professional Risk Managers' Intl. Assn. [502], 400
Washington St., Northfield, MN 55057
Professional Rodeo Cowboys Assn. [3375], 101 Pro
Rodeo Dr., Colorado Springs, CO 80919-2301,
(719)593-8840
Professional Services Coun. [2655], 4401 Wilson
Blvd., Ste. 1110, Arlington, VA 22203, (703)875-
8059
Professional Ski Instructors of Am. [3389], 133 S
Van Gordon St., Ste. 200, Lakewood, CO 80228,
(303)987-9390
Professional Ski Instructors of Am. Educational
Foundation [★3389]
Professional Soc. for Sales and Marketing Training
[786], 113 McHenry Rd., No. 141, Buffalo Grove,
IL 60089, (973)882-3931
Professional and Tech. Consultants Assn. [212], PO
Box 2261, Santa Clara, CA 95055, (408)971-5902
Professional Women in Constr. [231], 315 E 56th
St., New York, NY 10022-3730, (212)486-4712
Professional Women Photographers [668], 119 W
72nd St., No. 223, New York, NY 10023
Professionals
Amer. Assn. of Electronic Reporters and
Transcribers [711]
Upwardly Global [712]
Agricultural Commodities Certification Assn. [935]
Alliance of Legal Document Asst. Professionals
[1340]
Alliance of Supplier Diversity Professionals [727]
Arab Amer. Women's Coun. [2767]
ArchVoices [1407]
Assn. of Appraiser Regulatory Officials [50]
Assn. of Biblical Counselors [2901]
Assn. of Divorce Financial Planners [347]
Coalition of Organic Landscapers [531]
Corporate Responsibility Officers Assn. [237]
Creativity Coaching Assn. [3305]
Global Sourcing Coun. [631]
Gp. Underwriters Assn. of Am. [486]
Interior Redesign Indus. Specialists [507]
Intl. Amusement and Leisure Defense Assn. [761]
Intl. Assn. of Certified Surveillance Professionals
[803]
Intl. Soc. of Filipinos in Finance and Accounting
[8]
Intl. Soc. of Sustainability Professionals [1080]
Natl. Assn. of Mortgage Processors [113]
Natl. Assn. of Professional Baseball Leagues
[3260]
Natl. Latina Bus. Women Assn. [534]
North Am. Chinese Clean-tech and Semiconduc-
tor Assn. [287]

North Amer. Football League [3331]
Professional Lighting and Sign Mgt. Companies of
Am. [546]
Professionals in Workers' Compensation [920]
Scientists and Engineers for Am. [1279]
Wedding Indus. Professionals Assn. [124]
Young Professionals in Energy [1465]
Professionals in Workers' Compensation [920], PO
Box 4435, Federal Way, WA 98063, (206)824-2899
Professions
Black Career Women [2819]
ArchVoices [1407]
Community Managers Intl. Assn. [559]
Interior Redesign Indus. Specialists [507]
Young Professionals in Energy [1465]
Professors
Assn. of Professors and Scholars of Iranian
Heritage [1646]
Program for New Americans [★2622]
Progressive Hea. Partnership [2513], PO Box
98025, Durham, NC 27708, (708)365-9564
Proj. Concern Intl. [2514], 5151 Murphy Canyon Rd.,
Ste. 320, San Diego, CA 92123-4339, (858)279-
9690
Proj. EverGreen [1155], PO Box 156, New Prague,
MN 56071, (952)758-9135
Proj. Mgt. Inst. [569], 14 Campus Blvd., Newtown
Square, PA 19073-3299, (610)356-4600
Proj. Renewal [2247], 200 Varick St., New York, NY
10014, (212)620-0340
A Promise of Hea. [2441], 419 E Fraser Dr., Pueblo
West, CO 81007, (719)547-1995
Propeller Club of the U.S. [819], 3927 Old Lee Hwy.,
Ste. 101A, Fairfax, VA 22030, (703)691-2777
Property
Unclaimed Property Professionals Org. [1359]
Assn. of Appraiser Regulatory Officials [50]
Assn. of Green Property Owners and Managers
[713]
Indus. Asset Mgt. Coun. [744]
Property Management
Assn. of Green Property Owners and Managers
[713]
Intl. Fac. Mgt. Assn. [714]
Natl. Assn. of Residential Property Managers
[715]
Property Mgt. Assn. [755], 7508 Wisconsin Ave., 4th
Fl., Bethesda, MD 20814, (301)657-9200
Prosthodontic Soc; Amer. [2378]
Prostitution
Forever Found [1951]
Protestant Church-Owned Publishers Assn. [725],
6631 Westbury Oaks Ct., Springfield, VA 22152,
(703)220-5989
Psychiatry
Intl. Assn. for Women's Mental Hea. [2551]
Psychologists for Social Responsibility [2710], 258
Harvard St., PMB 282, Brookline, MA 02446,
(202)543-5347
Psychology
Amer. Psychological Assn. | Division of Family
Psychology [2582]
Assn. of Black Psychologists [2583]
Assn. for Humanistic Psychology [2584]
Assn. for Psychological Type Intl. [2585]
North Am. Soc. for the Psychology of Sport and
Physical Activity [3372]
Psychonomic Soc. [2586]
Soc. for Personality Assessment [2587]
Intl. Assn. for Correctional and Forensic Psychol-
ogy [2050]
Psychology; Intl. Assn. for Correctional and Forensic
[2050]
Psychonomic Soc. [2586], 2424 Amer. Ln., Madison,
WI 53704-3102, (608)441-1070
Psychotherapy
Angel Harps [2588]
Kate's Voice [1678]
Music Therapy for Healing [2589]
Intl. Assn. for Women's Mental Hea. [2551]
Public Administration
Natl. Acad. of Public Admin. [1360]
Sect. for Women in Public Admin. [1361]
Public Affairs
Air Force Public Affairs Alumni Assn. [1362]

A star before a book entry number signifies that the name is not listed separately, but is mentioned within the entry.

The Asia Found. **[2728]**
Ford Found. **[2729]**
Advancing Human Rights **[2658]**
Amer. Libyan Freedom Alliance **[2636]**
Dalit Freedom Network **[2661]**
Dalit Solidarity **[2662]**
Focus the Nation **[2642]**
Fuel for Truth **[2745]**
Girls for a Change **[1956]**
Global Youth Action Network **[2756]**
Intl. Professional Partnerships for Sierra Leone **[2675]**
Iran Policy Comm. **[2687]**
Mainstream Media Proj. **[2735]**
Vote Hemp **[2746]**
Public Agency Risk Managers Assn. **[1311]**, PO Box 6810, San Jose, CA 95150, (530)823-4957
Public Finance
Assn. of Public Treasurers of the U.S. and Canada **[1363]**
Bus. Roundtable **[2730]**
Natl. Assn. of State Treasurers **[1364]**
Public Health
Assn. of State and Territorial Local Hea. Liaison Officials **[1365]**
Caribbean Public Hea. Coalition **[2590]**
Natl. Assn. for Public Hea. Statistics and Info. Systems **[1366]**
South Asian Public Hea. Assn. **[2591]**
Clinic at a Time **[2483]**
A Cup of Water Intl. **[3039]**
Env. and Human Hea., Inc. **[2410]**
Environmental Outreach and Stewardship Alliance **[1062]**
Global Network for Neglected Tropical Diseases **[2398]**
Global Solutions for Infectious Diseases **[2472]**
mHealth Alliance **[2510]**
Norrie Disease Assn. **[2399]**
Universities Allied for Essential Medicines **[1641]**
Public Information
Natl. Freedom of Info. Coalition **[2731]**
Public Interest Law
Equal Rights Advocates **[1367]**
Public Justice **[1368]**
Public Justice **[1368]**, 1825 K St. NW, Ste. 200, Washington, DC 20006-1220, (202)797-8600
Public Lands
Natl. Brownfield Assn. **[716]**
Public Policy
Economic Policy Inst. **[2732]**
Inst. for Policy Stud. **[2733]**
Northeast-Midwest Inst. **[2734]**
Intl. Professional Partnerships for Sierra Leone **[2675]**
Public Radio Prog. Directors Assn. **[730]**, 38 Milford St., Hamilton, NY 13346, (315)824-8226
Public Relations
Natl. Black Public Relations Soc. **[717]**
Public Speaking
Toastmasters Intl. **[1848]**
Public Welfare
Amer. Public Human Services Assn. | Natl. Coun. of State Human Ser. Administrators **[2231]**
Public Works
Amer. Public Works Assn. **[1369]**
Natl. Alliance of Highway Beautification Agencies **[1370]**
Publishers Info. Bur. **[24]**, 810 7th Ave., 24th Fl., New York, NY 10019, (212)872-3700
Publishing
Amer. Book Producers Assn. **[718]**
Assoc. Church Press **[719]**
Custom Content Coun. **[720]**
Great Lakes Independent Booksellers Assn. **[721]**
The Intl. Publication Planning Assn. **[722]**
Livestock Publications Coun. **[723]**
Natl. Assn. of Independent Publishers Representatives **[724]**
Protestant Church-Owned Publishers Assn. **[725]**
Small Publishers Assn. of North Am. **[726]**
Newspaper Target Marketing Coalition **[626]**
Puerto Rican Stud. Assn. **[2820]**, Cornell Univ., Latino Studies Program, 434 Rockefeller Hall, Ithaca, NY 14853-2502, (607)255-3197
Puerto Rico
Puerto Rican Stud. Assn. **[2820]**

Puerto Rico Water and Env. Assn. **[1227]**
Puerto Rico Water and Env. Assn. **[1227]**, PO Box 13702, San Juan, PR 00908-3702, (787)478-3716
Purchasing
Alliance of Supplier Diversity Professionals **[727]**
Inst. for Supply Mgt. **[728]**
Natl. Assn. of State Procurement Officials **[1371]**
Responsible Purchasing Network **[316]**

Q

Qigong Alliance Intl. **[2297]**, PO Box 750, Ely, MN 55731, (800)341-8895
Quail Unlimited **[1252]**, PO Box 70518, Albany, GA 31708, (803)637-5731
Quality Assurance
Soc. of Quality Assurance **[729]**
Intl. Air Filtration Certifiers Assn. **[432]**
Quantal Energy **[1613]**, 97 Mt. Warner Rd., Hadley, MA 01035
Quartzite Rock Assn. **[207]**, PO Box 661, Sioux Falls, SD 57101, (605)339-1520
Quaternary Assn; Amer. **[1503]**
Queen Isabella Foundation **[★2773]**
Queen Sofia Spanish Inst. **[1855]**, 684 Park Ave., New York, NY 10065, (212)628-0420
The Questers **[3091]**, 210 S Quince St., Philadelphia, PA 19107-5534, (215)923-5183

R

Rabbinical Assembly **[2962]**, 3080 Broadway, New York, NY 10027, (212)280-6000
Rabbinical Coun. of Am. **[2963]**, 305 7th Ave., 12th Fl., New York, NY 10001, (212)807-9000
Rabbits
Amer. Belgian Hare Club **[1186]**
Amer. Fed. of New Zealand Rabbit Breeders **[1187]**
Amer. Satin Rabbit Breeders' Assn. **[1188]**
Havana Rabbit Breeders Assn. **[1189]**
Natl. Jersey Wooly Rabbit Club **[1190]**
North Amer. Lionhead Rabbit Club **[1191]**
Rhinelander Rabbit Club of Am. **[1192]**
Race Track Chaplaincy of Am. **[2890]**, 2365 Harrodsburg Rd., Ste. A120, Lexington, KY 40504, (859)410-7822
Racing
Highlander Class Intl. Assn. **[3273]**
Intl. Trotting and Pacing Assn. **[3345]**
Thoroughbred Club of Am. **[3348]**
U.S. Albacore Assn. **[3286]**
U.S. Power Squadrons **[3290]**
Racism
Facing History and Ourselves Natl. Found. **[1770]**
Radiant Panel Assn. **[★437]**
Radiant Professionals Alliance **[437]**, 8512 Oswego Rd., Ste. 180, Baldwinsville, NY 13027, (315)303-4735
Radiation
Radiation Res. Soc. **[1522]**
Radiation Res. Soc. **[1522]**, PO Box 7050, Lawrence, KS 66044, (800)627-0326
Radio
Mainstream Media Proj. **[2735]**
Public Radio Prog. Directors Assn. **[730]**
ARRL Found. **[3090]**
Radiochemistry Soc. **[1438]**, PO Box 3091, Richland, WA 99354, (800)371-0542
Radiology; Amer. Acad. of Oral and Maxillofacial **[2367]**
Radiology Bus. Mgt. Assn. **[2543]**, 10300 Eaton Pl., Ste. 460, Fairfax, VA 22030, (703)621-3355
Railroads
Amer. Assn. of Private Railroad Car Owners **[731]**
Brotherhood of Locomotive Engineers and Trainmen **[3462]**
Natl. Assn. of Railway Bus. Women **[732]**
Pacific Southwest Railway Museum **[1849]**
Railway Supply Inst. **[733]**
Tourist Railway Assn. **[734]**
Trans. Communications Union | Brotherhood Railway Carmen Div. **[3463]**
Toy Train Collectors Soc. **[3214]**
Youth in Model Railroading **[3215]**
Railway Supply Inst. **[733]**, 425 3rd St. SW, Ste. 920, Washington, DC 20024-3229, (202)347-4664

Rain Forests
Rainforest Partnership **[1193]**
Tropical Forest and Climate Coalition **[1194]**
RAINBOWS **[2000]**, 1360 Hamilton Pkwy., Itasca, IL 60143, (847)952-1770
Rainforest Partnership **[1193]**, PO Box 49268, Austin, TX 78765, (512)420-0101
Randolph-Sheppard Vendors of Am. **[901]**, 940 Parc Helene Dr., Marrero, LA 70072-2421, (504)328-6373
Rangeland
Soc. for Range Mgt. **[1195]**
Raskob Found. for Catholic Activities **[2878]**, PO Box 4019, Wilmington, DE 19807-0019, (302)655-4440
Reach Across **[3011]**, PO Box 2047, Lexington, SC 29071-2047, (803)358-2330
Reach Intl. Healthcare and Training **[2515]**, PO Box 152, Caulfield, MO 65626
Reach Out to Romania **[2172]**, PO Box 18016, Anaheim, CA 92817-8016
REACT Intl. **[1373]**, 12114 Boydton Plank Rd., Dinwiddie, VA 23841, (301)316-2900
Reading
Coll. Reading and Learning Assn. **[1679]**
Real Estate
Amer. Real Estate and Urban Economics Assn. **[1680]**
Assn. of Real Estate Women **[735]**
CCIM Inst. **[736]**
CoreNet Global **[737]**
Coun. of Real Estate Brokerage Managers **[738]**
Coun. of Residential Specialists **[739]**
CRE Finance Coun. **[740]**
CREW Network **[741]**
FIABCI-U.S.A. **[742]**
Hotel Brokers Intl. **[743]**
Indus. Asset Mgt. Coun. **[744]**
Inst. of Real Estate Mgt. **[745]**
Intl. Bus. Brokers Assn. **[746]**
Intl. Real Estate Inst. **[747]**
Natl. Assn. of Hispanic Real Estate Professionals **[748]**
Natl. Assn. of Media Brokers **[749]**
Natl. Assn. of Real Estate Brokers **[750]**
Natl. Assn. of Real Estate Investment Managers **[751]**
Natl. Assn. of Real Estate Investment Trusts **[752]**
Natl. Assn. of Realtors **[753]**
Pension Real Estate Assn. **[754]**
Property Mgt. Assn. **[755]**
Real Estate Educators Assn. **[756]**
Realtors Land Inst. **[757]**
Vacation Rental Managers Assn. **[758]**
Assn. of Appraiser Regulatory Officials **[50]**
Assn. of Green Property Owners and Managers **[713]**
Real Estate Educators Assn. **[756]**, 2000 Interstate Park Dr., Ste. 306, Montgomery, AL 36109-5420, (334)625-8650
Reality Relief **[2196]**, 834 Ave. F, Billings, MT 59102, (706)201-8520
Realtors Land Inst. **[757]**, 430 N Michigan Ave., Chicago, IL 60611, (312)329-8446
Reasoning Mind **[1660]**, 3050 Post Oak Blvd., Ste. 1200, Houston, TX 77056, (281)579-1110
Rebuilding Alliance **[2107]**, 178 South Blvd., San Mateo, CA 94402, (650)325-4663
Rebuilding Haiti Now **[2197]**, 2314 Alamance Dr., West Chicago, IL 60185
Reconstruction Efforts Aiding Children without Homes **[2032]**, PO Box 4141, Winchester, VA 22604
Recording Artists, Actors and Athletes Against Drunk Driving **[2217]**, 4370 Tujunga Ave., Ste. 212, Studio City, CA 91604, (818)752-7799
Recordings
Audio Publishers Assn. **[759]**
Music Video Production Assn. **[760]**
Recovered Alcoholic Clergy Assn. **[2248]**, 127 Inverness Rd., Athens, GA 30606, (706)546-5281
Recreation
Employee Services Mgt. Found. **[2175]**
Intl. Amusement and Leisure Defense Assn. **[761]**
Intl. Assn. of Skateboard Companies **[3373]**
Natl. Assn. of RV Parks and Campgrounds **[762]**
Natl. Swimming Pool Found. **[763]**

Prairie Club [2176]
Antique Motorcycle Club of Am. [3217]
Bass Anglers Sportsman Soc. [3326]
Camping Women [3301]
Christian Camp and Conf. Assn. [3302]
Intl. Scale Soaring Assn. [3216]
Natl. 42 Players Assn. [3198]
Natl. Amateur Dodgeball Assn. [3253]
Natl. Versatility Ranch Horse Assn. [3352]
North Amer. Family Campers Assn. [3303]
Pro vs. GI Joe [3200]
U.S. Bridge Fed. [3143]
U.S. Lawn Bowls Assn. [3295]
Recreational Vehicles
SunnyTravelers [3240]
North Amer. Family Campers Assn. [3303]
Recycled Paperboard Tech. Assn. [213], PO Box 5774, Elgin, IL 60121-5774, (847)622-2544
Recycling
Cement Kiln Recycling Coalition [1196]
Clean the World [1197]
Freecycle Network [1198]
Reusable Packaging Assn. [764]
CHWMEG [906]
Sustainable Biomaterials Collaborative [1397]
Red Earth [2809], 6 Santa Fe Plz., Oklahoma City, OK 73102, (405)427-5228
RedLight Children [1912], 75 Rockefeller Plz., 17th Fl., New York, NY 10019
Reef Relief [1161], PO Box 430, Key West, FL 33041, (305)294-3100
Reformation
Soc. for Reformation Res. [1850]
Refrigeration Ser. Engineers Soc. [438], 1666 Rand Rd., Des Plaines, IL 60016-3552, (847)297-6464
Refugee Coun. U.S.A. [2737], 1628 16th St. NW, Washington, DC 20009, (202)319-2102
Refugees
Amer. Refugee Comm. [2177]
Church World Ser., Immigration and Refugee Prog. [2736]
Intl. Rescue Comm. l Spanish Refugee Aid [2178]
Intl. Rescue Comm. USA [2179]
Lutheran Immigration and Refugee Ser. [2180]
Refugee Coun. U.S.A. [2737]
Shelter for Life Intl. [2821]
Regional Airline Assn. [37], 2025 M St. NW, Ste. 800, Washington, DC 20036-3309, (202)367-1170
Regional Reporters Assn. [705], Cincinnati Enquirer, 1100 New York Ave. NW, Ste. 2005, Washington, DC 20005
Registry of Interpreters for the Deaf [2456], 333 Commerce St., Alexandria, VA 22314, (703)838-0030
Regulatory Assistance Proj. [1386], PO Box 507, Hallowell, ME 04347, (207)319-6000
Rehabilitation
Intl. Assn. of Addictions and Offender Counselors [2044]
Salute Military Golf Assn. [3339]
Rehabilitation Engg. Center [★2226]
Reiki Rays of Hope for Caregivers [2298], 9592 Dublin Ln., Mentor, OH 44060, (440)357-6517
Reinsurance Assn. of Am. [503], 1445 New York Ave., 7th Fl., Washington, DC 20005, (202)638-3690
Relief
Alliance For Relief Mission in Haiti [2181]
Americans Care and Share [2182]
Baitulmaal [2183]
Baptist Global Response [2184]
Christ for the Poor [1681]
Covenant World Relief [2185]
Global Action Intl. [2186]
Hannah's Promise Intl. Aid [2187]
Help Brings Hope for Haiti [2188]
Helping Hand for Nepal [2189]
Humanitarian African Relief Org. [2190]
Intl. Aid [2191]
Islamic Relief U.S.A. [2192]
Korean Amer. Sharing Movement [2193]
One Love Worldwide [2194]
People for Haiti [2195]
Reality Relief [2196]
Rebuilding Haiti Now [2197]

Relief Liberia Intl. [2198]
River Intl. [2199]
Simple Hope [2200]
Vietnam Relief Effort [2201]
World Emergency Relief [2202]
World Vision Intl. [3026]
Adopt-a-Village Intl. [2007]
Aid Still Required [2066]
Aid for the World [2163]
Aiding Romania's Children [1918]
Amer. Outreach to Ethiopia [2114]
Bridges Cambodia Intl. [1929]
Burundi Friends Intl. [2012]
Child Empowerment Intl. [1934]
Children's Relief Mission [1942]
Compassion into Action Network - Direct Outcome Org. [2067]
Connecting Congo [2016]
Doctors in Christ [2544]
Ethiopian Orphan Relief [1948]
Ghana Relief Org. [1955]
Global Partners Running Waters [2020]
Great Commn. Alliance [2068]
Hea. For All Missions [2134]
Heart for Africa [1959]
Help Aid Africa [2022]
Hope and Future for Children in Bolivia [1965]
Hope for Haiti's Children [1966]
Jamaica Unite [2025]
Kenya Medical Outreach [2135]
Khadarlis for Sierra Leone [2026]
Mobile Medical Disaster Relief [2138]
Nepal SEEDS: Social Educational Environmental Development Services in Nepal [2028]
Para Sa Bata [1982]
Reach Out to Romania [2172]
Restoring Institutions Services and Empowering Liberia [2033]
To Love a Child [1988]
Well Done Org. [2039]
World Assn. of Natural Disaster Awareness and Assistance [2147]
Relief Liberia Intl. [2198], 10186 Lancaster Ln. N, Maple Grove, MN 55369, (763)607-4233
Religion
Church Universal and Triumphant [3027]
Hea. Ministries Assn. [3028]
Intl. Order of Saint Luke the Physician [3029]
Maclellan Found. [3030]
Abrahamic Alliance Intl. [2945]
Assn. of Biblical Counselors [2901]
BCM Intl. [2849]
Catholic War Veterans of the U.S.A. [3080]
Center on Conscience and War [2641]
Christian Camp and Conf. Assn. [3302]
Episcopalians for Global Reconciliation [2917]
Intl. Catholic Deaf Assn. U.S. Sect. [2868]
Monks Without Borders [2946]
Natl. Alliance Against Christian Discrimination [2897]
Reach Across [3011]
Seventh Day Baptist World Fed. [2847]
United Indian Missions Intl. [3014]
Religion in an Age of Sci; Inst. on [3034]
Religious Administration
Intl. Catholic Deaf Assn. U.S. Sect. [2868]
Seventh Day Baptist World Fed. [2847]
Religious Commun. Assn. [1588], Univ. of Texas at Tyler, Dept. of Commun., 3900 Univ. Blvd., Tyler, TX 75799, (903)566-7093
Religious Educ. Assn.: An Assn. of Professors, Practitioners, and Researchers in Religious Educ. [2914], PO Box 200392, Evans, CO 80620-0392, (765)225-8836
Religious Freedom
Natl. Alliance Against Christian Discrimination [2897]
Religious Res. Assn. [3031], 618 SW 2nd Ave., Galva, IL 61434-1912, (309)932-2727
Religious Studies
Reach Across [3011]
Religious Understanding
Reach Across [3011]
Renal Administrators Assn; Natl. [2542]
Renal Pathology Soc. [2575], UNC Division of Nephropathology, 409 Brinkhous-Bullitt Bldg., CB No. 7525, Chapel Hill, NC 27599, (919)966-2421

Renewable Natural Resources Found. [1037], 5430 Grosvenor Ln., Bethesda, MD 20814-2142, (301)493-9101
Renting and Leasing
Amer. Car Rental Assn. [765]
Representative of German Indus. and Trade [174], 1776 I St. NW, Ste. 1000, Washington, DC 20006, (202)659-4777
Reproductive Health
Family Hea. Alliance [2592]
Intl. Partnership for Reproductive Hea. [2593]
Soc. of Family Planning [2413]
World Hea. Partners [2525]
Reproductive Rights
Center for Reproductive Rights [2738]
Family Hea. Alliance [2592]
Republican Governors Assn. [1376], 1747 Pennsylvania Ave. NW, Ste. 250, Washington, DC 20006, (202)662-4140
Research
Inst. of Environmental Sciences and Tech. [1523]
Religious Res. Assn. [3031]
Soc. of Res. Administrators [1524]
Universities Res. Assn. [1525]
Drilling, Observation and Sampling of the Earth's Continental Crust [1448]
Elliot Inst. [1869]
Fed. of Earth Sci. Info. Partners [1449]
Quantal Energy [1613]
Res. Partnership to Secure Energy for Am. [1461], 1650 Hwy. 6, Ste. 325, Sugar Land, TX 77478, (281)313-9555
Res. Soc. for Victorian Periodicals [1865], 939 Ridge Court, No. 2, Evanston, IL 60202
Responsible Indus. for a Sound Env. [637], 1156 15th St. NW, Ste. 400, Washington, DC 20005, (202)872-3860
Responsible Purchasing Network [316], 1201 Martin Luther King Jr. Way, Oakland, CA 94612, (866)776-1330
Restaurant Marketing and Delivery Assn. [377], 4921 Boone Ave. N, New Hope, MN 55428
Restoration Indus. Assn. [555], 9810 Patuxent Woods Dr., Ste. K, Columbia, MD 21046-1595, (443)878-1000
Restoring Institutions Services and Empowering Liberia [2033], 1250 4th St. SW, Washington, DC 20024
Retail Advt. and Marketing Assn. [23], 325 7th St. NW, Ste. 1100, Washington, DC 20004-2818, (202)661-3052
Retail Bakers of Am. [107], 202 Village Cir., Ste. 1, Slidell, LA 70458, (985)643-6504
Retail Confectioners Intl. [371], 2053 S Waverly, Ste. C, Springfield, MO 65804, (417)883-2775
Retail Design Inst. [776], 25 N Broadway, Tarrytown, NY 10591-3221, (800)379-9912
Retail Energy Supply Assn. [304], PO Box 6089, Harrisburg, PA 17112, (717)566-5405
Retail, Wholesale and Dept. Store Union [3464], 30 E 29th St., New York, NY 10016, (212)684-5300
Retailing
Assn. for Retail Tech. Standards [766]
Consumer Electronics Retailers Coalition [767]
Consumer Goods Forum [768]
Direct Gardening Assn. [769]
Intl. League of Antiquarian Booksellers [770]
Intl. Mystery Shopping Alliance [771]
Natl. Assn. for Retail Marketing Services [772]
Natl. Grocers Assn. [773]
NATSO Found. [774]
Natural Products Assn. [775]
Retail Design Inst. [776]
Retail, Wholesale and Dept. Store Union [3464]
Shop Am. Alliance [777]
Women Grocers of Am. [778]
Gift and Home Trade Assn. [784]
Retail Energy Supply Assn. [304]
Retirement
Inst. for Retired Professionals [2203]
Coalition of Natl. Park Ser. Retirees [1176]
Retirement Indus. Trust Assn. [115], 820 Jorie Blvd., Ste. 420, Oak Brook, IL 60523-2284, (941)724-0900
Reusable Packaging Assn. [764], 1100 N Glebe Rd., Ste. 1010, Arlington, VA 22201, (703)224-8284

A star before a book entry number signifies that the name is not listed separately, but is mentioned within the entry.

Rhetoric
Rhetoric Soc. of Am. **[1851]**
Rhetoric Soc. of Am. **[1851]**, c/o Cara A. Finnegan, Comm. Chair, Univ. of Illinois, 103 Commun. Bldg. MC-456, 1207 W Oregon Ave., Urbana, IL 61801
Rhinelander Rabbit Club of Am. **[1192]**, 11237 Summit School Rd., Huntingdon, PA 16652, (814)667-2406
Rifles
North-South Skirmish Assn. **[3384]**
Right to Life
Baptists for Life **[2204]**
Liberty Godparent Home **[2205]**
Natl. Right to Life Comm. **[2206]**
Pro-Life Action League **[2739]**
Rights and Resources Initiative **[1095]**, 1238 Wisconsin Ave. NW, Ste. 204, Washington, DC 20007, (202)470-3900
Rin Tin Tin Fan Club **[3598]**, PO Box 27, Crockett, TX 75835, (936)545-0471
Rising Intl. **[1908]**, 300 Potrero St., Santa Cruz, CA 95060, (831)429-7473
Rising Tide Capital **[265]**, 348 Martin Luther King Dr., Jersey City, NJ 07305, (201)432-4316
Rising Tide North Am. **[1038]**, PO Box 3928, Oakland, CA 94609, (503)438-4697
River Intl. **[2199]**, 2380 W Monte Vista Ave., Turlock, CA 95382
River Mgt. Soc. **[1039]**, PO Box 5750, Takoma Park, MD 20913-5750, (301)585-4677
River Network **[1040]**, 520 SW 6th Ave., Ste. 1130, Portland, OR 97204, (503)241-3506
River of Words **[960]**, PO Box 4000-J, Berkeley, CA 94704, (510)548-7636
Robert F. Kennedy Center for Justice and Human Rights **[2280]**, 1367 Connecticut Ave. NW, Ste. 200, Washington, DC 20036, (202)463-7575
Robotics
Assn. for Unmanned Vehicle Systems Intl. **[1526]**
Automated Imaging Assn. **[1527]**
Rock Detective Geoscience Educ. **[1601]**, 14655 Betz Ln., Red Bluff, CA 96080, (530)529-4890
Rock the Earth **[1072]**, 1536 Wynkoop St., Ste. B200, Denver, CO 80202, (303)454-3304
Rock Music
KISS Rocks Fan Club **[3584]**
Rocky Mountain Horse Assn. **[1146]**, 4037 Iron Works Pkwy., Ste. 160, Lexington, KY 40511, (859)243-0260
Rocky Mountain Inst. **[1169]**, 2317 Snowmass Creek Rd., Snowmass, CO 81654-9199, (970)927-3851
Rodeo
Professional Armed Forces Rodeo Assn. **[3374]**
Professional Rodeo Cowboys Assn. **[3375]**
RollerSoccer Intl. Fed. **[3408]**, PO Box 423318, San Francisco, CA 94142-3318, (415)864-6879
Rolls-Royce Owners' Club **[3127]**, 191 Hempt Rd., Mechanicsburg, PA 17050, (717)697-4671
Romania
Reach Out to Romania **[2172]**
Roots of Development **[2212]**, 1325 18th St. NW, Ste. 303, Washington, DC 20036, (202)466-0805
Rosicrucian
Rosicrucian Fellowship **[3032]**
Rosicrucian Fellowship **[3032]**, 2222 Mission Ave., Oceanside, CA 92058-2329, (760)757-6600
Rotary on Stamps Fellowship **[3230]**, 1327 Prince Albert Dr., St. Louis, MO 63146
Rowing
Eastern Assn. of Rowing Colleges **[3376]**
Intercollegiate Rowing Assn. **[3377]**
Roy Rogers - Dale Evans Collectors Assn. **[3587]**, PO Box 1166, Portsmouth, OH 45662, (740)353-0900
Rubber
Amer. Chem. Soc., Rubber Div. **[779]**
Natl. Assn. of Hose and Accessories Distribution **[466]**
Rugby
U.S. Rugby Football Union **[3378]**
Runaways
Natl. Network for Youth **[2207]**
Running
Girls on the Run Intl. **[3379]**
Rural Development
Abriendo Mentes **[2208]**
Act for Africa Intl. **[2209]**

Bridges to Prosperity **[2210]**
Community Empowerment Network **[2211]**
Inter-American Found. **[2740]**
Roots of Development **[2212]**
Union MicroFinanza **[2213]**
Building Community Bridges **[2011]**
Chris Cares Intl. **[2013]**
Community Development Intl. **[2014]**
Computers for Africa **[1597]**
Connecting Congo **[2016]**
Drinking Water for India **[2262]**
Fields of Growth Intl. **[2129]**
Global Partners Running Waters **[2020]**
Haiti Convention Assn. **[2214]**
HELPSudan **[1994]**
Intl. Agro Alliance **[1217]**
Into Your Hands **[2215]**
Miracles in Action **[2170]**
Natl. Women in Agriculture Assn. **[937]**
Partners in Sustainable Development Intl. **[2171]**
Reconstruction Efforts Aiding Children without Homes **[2032]**
Sustainable Biomaterials Collaborative **[1397]**
Under The Baobab Tree **[1593]**
Well Done Org. **[2039]**
Rural Education
Haiti Convention Assn. **[2214]**
Into Your Hands **[2215]**
Agami **[1581]**
HELPSudan **[1994]**
Under The Baobab Tree **[1593]**
Rural Renewable Energy Alliance **[1462]**, 2330 Dancing Wind Rd. SW, Pine River, MN 56474, (218)587-4753

S

Sabbath
Lord's Day Alliance of the U.S. **[3033]**
Seventh Day Baptist World Fed. **[2847]**
Sacred Heart League **[2879]**, PO Box 300, Walls, MS 38680-0300, (800)232-9079
Sacred Passage and the Way of Nature Fellowship **[2111]**, PO Box 3388, Tucson, AZ 85722-3388, (520)623-3588
Sacro Occipital Res. Soc. Intl. **[2346]**, PO Box 24361, Overland Park, KS 66283, (239)513-9800
SAE Intl. **[1414]**, 400 Commonwealth Dr., Warrendale, PA 15096-0001, (724)776-4841
Safe and Vault Technicians Assn. **[808]**, 3500 Easy St., Dallas, TX 75247, (214)819-9771
Safety
Amer. Biological Safety Assn. **[780]**
Assn. for the Advancement of Automotive Medicine **[2216]**
Assn. of Public-Safety Communications Officials Intl. **[1372]**
Intl. Sys. Safety Soc. **[781]**
REACT Intl. **[1373]**
Recording Artists, Actors and Athletes Against Drunk Driving **[2217]**
Trans. Safety Equip. Inst. **[782]**
United Lightning Protection Assn. **[783]**
Veterans of Safety **[2218]**
Building Security Coun. **[801]**
Intl. Assn. of Certified Surveillance Professionals **[803]**
Sailors for the Sea **[1041]**, 18 Market Sq., Newport, RI 02840, (401)846-8900
Saint Andrew's Soc. of the State of New York **[2823]**, 150 E 55th St., Ste. 3, New York, NY 10022, (212)223-4248
Saint Andrew's Ukrainian Orthodox Soc. **[2752]**, c/o Vitali Vizir, 1023 Yorkshire Dr., Los Altos, CA 94024, (440)582-1051
Saint Nicholas Soc. of the City of New York **[3070]**, c/o Jill Spiller, Exec. Dir., 20 W 44th St., Rm. 508, New York, NY 10036-6603, (212)991-9944
Saleen Club of Am. **[3128]**, 6181 Linden Dr. E, West Bend, WI 53095, (414)234-7472
Sales
Gift and Home Trade Assn. **[784]**
Natl. Assn. of Sales Professionals **[785]**
Professional Soc. for Sales and Marketing Training **[786]**
Sales and Marketing Executives Intl. **[787]**
Sales and Marketing Executives Intl. **[787]**, PO Box 1390, Sumas, WA 98295-1390, (312)893-0751

Salute Military Golf Assn. **[3339]**, PO Box 83893, Gaithersburg, MD 20883, (301)500-7449
SAMA Gp. of Associations **[792]**, PO Box 428, Fairfax, VA 22038, (703)836-1360
Samaritans Intl. **[3012]**, 370 E Cedar St., Mooresville, NC 28115-2806, (704)663-7951
Sanitation
Amer. Soc. of Sanitary Engg. **[1528]**
Clean the World **[1197]**
In Our Own Quiet Way **[2265]**
Primero Agua **[2267]**
Santa Gertrudis Breeders Intl. **[990]**, PO Box 1257, Kingsville, TX 78364, (361)592-9357
Santana 20 Class Assn. **[3282]**, 1266 Napa Creek Dr., Eugene, OR 97404, (541)517-8690
Save the Children **[2001]**, 54 Wilton Rd., Westport, CT 06880, (203)221-4030
Save the Waves Coalition **[1228]**, PO Box 183, Davenport, CA 95017, (831)426-6169
SB Latex Coun. **[188]**, 1250 Connecticut Ave. NW, Ste. 700, Washington, DC 20036, (202)419-1500
Scaffold Indus. Assn. **[160]**, 400 Admiral Blvd., Kansas City, MO 64106, (816)595-4860
Scandinavian
Independent Order of Svithiod **[2822]**
Scandinavian Collectors Club **[3231]**, c/o Donald Brent, Exec. Sec., PO Box 13196, El Cajon, CA 92020
Scholarship
Phi Chi Medical Fraternity **[3539]**
School Boards
Natl. School Boards Assn. **[1682]**
School Services
Natl. School Supply and Equip. Assn. **[788]**
Schools
Assn. for the Advancement of Intl. Educ. **[1644]**
Brick by Brick for Tanzania! **[1675]**
Haiti Convention Assn. **[2214]**
Out of Poverty thru Educ. **[1568]**
Science
Amer. Assn. for the Advancement of Sci. **[1529]**
Amer. Philosophical Soc. **[1530]**
Inst. on Religion in an Age of Sci. **[3034]**
Natl. Assn. of Academies of Sci. **[1531]**
Natl. Sci. Educ. Leadership Assn. **[1683]**
Sigma Delta Epsilon, Graduate Women in Sci. **[3545]**
Soc. of Automotive Engineers **[1532]**
Triangle Coalition for Sci. and Tech. Educ. **[1684]**
Drilling, Observation and Sampling of the Earth's Continental Crust **[1448]**
Fed. of Earth Sci. Info. Partners **[1449]**
Global Wildlife Conservation **[1238]**
The Intl. Lepidoptera Survey **[1472]**
Radiochemistry Soc. **[1438]**
Rock Detective Geoscience Educ. **[1601]**
Scientists and Engineers for Am. **[1279]**
Soc. of Turkish Amer. Architects, Engineers and Scientists **[1471]**
Sci. Commun. Network **[1165]**, 2000 P St. NW, No. 740, Washington, DC 20036, (202)463-6670
Scientific Products
Amer. Sci. Glassblowers Soc. **[789]**
Assn. of Medical Diagnostics Mfrs. **[790]**
Independent Lab. Distributors Assn. **[791]**
SAMA Gp. of Associations **[792]**
Scientists and Engineers for Am. **[1279]**, 1850 M St. NW, Ste. 1100, Washington, DC 20036, (202)223-6444
SCORE **[824]**, 1175 Herndon Pkwy., Ste. 900, Herndon, VA 20170, (703)487-3612
Scottish
Saint Andrew's Soc. of the State of New York **[2823]**
Scouting
Natl. Eagle Scout Assn. **[2219]**
Screen Actors Guild **[3457]**, 5757 Wilshire Blvd., 7th Fl., Los Angeles, CA 90036-3600, (323)954-1600
Scribes - The Amer. Soc. of Legal Writers **[1281]**, PO Box 13038, Lansing, MI 48901, (517)371-5140
Sculptors Guild **[1852]**, 55 Washington St., Ste. 256, Brooklyn, NY 11201, (718)422-0555
Sculpture
Sculptors Guild **[1852]**
Fed. of Modern Painters and Sculptors **[1716]**
Sea Turtle Conservancy **[1253]**, 4424 NW 13th St., Ste. B-11, Gainesville, FL 32609, (352)373-6441

Seafood
Northwest Fisheries Assn. **[793]**
Pacific Coast Shellfish Growers Assn. **[794]**
Pacific Seafood Processors Assn. **[795]**
Intl. Seafood Sustainability Assn. **[355]**
Sustainable Fisheries Partnership **[959]**
Secondary Education
Amer. Legion Auxiliary Girls Nation **[2621]**
Sect. for Women in Public Admin. **[1361]**, 1301 Pennsylvania Ave. NW, Ste. 840, Washington, DC 20004-1735, (202)393-7878
Securing America's Future Energy **[1463]**, 1111 19th St. NW, Ste. 406, Washington, DC 20036, (202)461-2360
Securities
Financial Indus. Regulatory Authority **[796]**
Mutual Fund Educ. Alliance **[797]**
Natl. Assn. of Securities Professionals **[798]**
New York Soc. of Security Analysts **[799]**
Security Traders Assn. **[800]**
Amer. Assn. of Professional Tech. Analysts **[847]**
Security
Building Security Coun. **[801]**
Bus. Executives for Natl. Security **[2741]**
Defense Orientation Conf. Assn. **[2742]**
Electronic Security Assn. **[802]**
Intl. Assn. of Certified Surveillance Professionals **[803]**
Intl. Assn. of Professional Security Consultants **[804]**
Intl. Org. of Black Security Executives **[805]**
Natl. Assn. of Security Companies **[806]**
North Amer. Security Products Org. **[807]**
OPSEC Professionals Soc. **[2743]**
Safe and Vault Technicians Assn. **[808]**
Security Indus. Assn. **[809]**
Women in Intl. Security **[2744]**
Assn. of Governmental Risk Pools **[1307]**
Fuel for Truth **[2745]**
Set Am. Free **[2643]**
Security Indus. Assn. **[809]**, 635 Slaters Ln., Ste. 110, Alexandria, VA 22314, (703)683-2075
Security Traders Assn. **[800]**, 80 Broad St., 5th Fl., New York, NY 10004, (203)202-7680
Security Training
Intl. Assn. of Certified Surveillance Professionals **[803]**
Seeds of HOPE Intl. **[1985]**, PO Box 49458, Colorado Springs, CO 80949, (719)473-8494
Seismology
Intl. Tsunami Info. Center **[1533]**
Self-Realization Fellowship **[3043]**, 3880 San Rafael Ave., Dept. 9W, Los Angeles, CA 90065-3298, (818)549-5151
Self Storage Assn. **[904]**, 1901 N Beauregard St., Ste. 450, Alexandria, VA 22311, (703)575-8000
Self Defense
Assn. for Women's Self Defense Advancement **[2220]**
All Japan Ju-Jitsu Intl. Fed. **[3359]**
Alliance of Guardian Angels **[2046]**
Intl. Chinese Boxing Assn. **[3297]**
Martial Arts Intl. Fed. **[3361]**
The World Kuoshu Fed. **[3363]**
World Martial Arts Assn. **[3364]**
Selfhelp
Messies Anonymous **[2221]**
Semantics
Inst. of Gen. Semantics **[1853]**
Senior Corps **[2259]**, 1201 New York Ave. NW, Washington, DC 20525, (202)606-5000
SER - Jobs for Progress Natl. **[2079]**, 100 E Royal Ln., Ste. 130, Irving, TX 75039, (469)549-3600
Serbian Bar Assn. of Am. **[1277]**, 20 S Clark, Ste. 700, Chicago, IL 60603, (312)782-8500
Service
Coalition of Ser. Indus. **[810]**
Custom Electronic Design Installation Assn. **[811]**
Equip. Ser. Assn. **[812]**
Intl. Customer Ser. Assn. **[813]**
Natl. Assn. of Ser. Managers **[814]**
Ser. Employees Intl. Union **[3465]**
Junior Optimist Octagon Intl. **[2222]**
Service Clubs
Junior Optimist Octagon Intl. **[2222]**

Links Found. **[2223]**
Ser. Employees Intl. Union **[3465]**, 1800 Massachusetts Ave. NW, Washington, DC 20036, (202)730-7000
Service Fraternities
Alpha Phi Omega Natl. Ser. Fraternity **[3546]**
Ser. for the Love of God **[2034]**, 291 Dutch Ln., Pittsburgh, PA 15236, (412)650-6292
Service Sororities
Beta Sigma Phi **[3547]**
Gamma Alpha Omega Sorority **[3548]**
Gamma Sigma Sigma **[3549]**
Ser. Specialists Assn. **[98]**, 160 Symphony Way, Ste. 2, Elgin, IL 60120, (847)760-0067
Ser. Sta. Dealers of America/National Coalition of Petroleum Retailers and Allied Trades **[649]**, 1532 Pointer Ridge Pl., Ste. E, Bowie, MD 20716, (301)390-4405
Set Am. Free **[2643]**, 7811 Montrose Rd., Ste. 505, Potomac, MD 20854-3368
Seventh Day Baptist Gen. Conf. **[2845]**, PO Box 1678, Janesville, WI 53547-1678, (608)752-5055
Seventh Day Baptist Gen. Conf. of the U.S. and Canada **[2846]**, PO Box 1678, Janesville, WI 53547-1678, (608)752-5055
Seventh Day Baptist World Fed. **[2847]**, 88 Terrace Ave., Salem, WV 26426, (304)782-1727
Seventh Generation Advisors **[1073]**, 2601 Ocean Park Blvd., Ste. 311, Santa Monica, CA 90405, (310)664-0300
Sewing
Spinning and Weaving Assn. **[858]**
Sex Addiction
Sex Addicts Anonymous **[2224]**
Sex Addicts Anonymous **[2224]**, PO Box 70949, Houston, TX 77270, (713)869-4902
Sexual Abuse
Global Centurion **[1957]**
RedLight Children **[1912]**
Shakespeare Oxford Soc. **[1735]**, PO Box 808, Yorktown Heights, NY 10598, (914)962-1717
Shalom Achshav **[★2689]**
Sharing Resources Worldwide **[2516]**, 4417 Robertson Rd., Madison, WI 53714
Shark Alliance **[1254]**, 901 E St. NW, 10th Fl., Washington, DC 20004, (202)552-2000
Sheep
Amer. Border Leicester Assn. **[1199]**
Amer. Cheviot Sheep Soc. **[1200]**
Amer. Delaine and Merino Record Assn. **[1201]**
Amer. Dorper Sheep Breeders' Soc. **[1202]**
Amer. Karakul Sheep Registry **[1203]**
Amer. North Country Cheviot Sheep Assn. **[1204]**
Amer. Oxford Sheep Assn. **[1205]**
Amer. Rambouillet Sheep Breeders' Assn. **[1206]**
Amer. Southdown Breeders' Assn. **[1207]**
Barbados Blackbelly Sheep Assn. Intl. **[1208]**
Natural Colored Wool Growers Assn. **[1209]**
North Amer. Babydoll Southdown Sheep Assn. and Registry **[1210]**
North Amer. Shetland Sheepbreeders Assn. **[1211]**
North Amer. Wensleydale Sheep Assn. **[1212]**
United Suffolk Sheep Assn. **[1213]**
Shelby Amer. Auto. Club **[3129]**, PO Box 788, Sharon, CT 06069
Shelter for Life Intl. **[2821]**, 10201 Wayzata Blvd., Ste. 230, Hopkins, MN 55305, (763)253-4082
Shields Natl. Class Assn. **[3283]**, 3225 W St. Joseph, Lansing, MI 48917, (517)372-9207
Shining Hope for Communities **[2035]**, 14 Red Glen Rd., Middletown, CT 06457, (860)218-9854
Shipping
Independent Armored Car Operators Assn. **[815]**
Intl. Furniture Trans. and Logistics Coun. **[816]**
Natl. Tank Truck Carriers **[817]**
Pacific Maritime Assn. **[818]**
Propeller Club of the U.S. **[819]**
Trans. and Logistics Coun. **[820]**
Shoe Ser. Inst. of Am. **[382]**, 305 Huntsman Ct., Bel Air, MD 21015, (410)569-3425
Shomrim Soc. **[2128]**, c/o Murry Ellman, Financial Sec., PO Box 598, Knickerbocker, NY 10002, (718)543-4825
Shooting
Cast Bullet Assn. **[3380]**

Fifty Caliber Shooters Assn. **[3241]**
Intl. Handgun Metallic Silhouette Assn. **[3381]**
Natl. Bench Rest Shooters Assn. **[3382]**
Natl. Rifle Assn. of Am. **[3383]**
North-South Skirmish Assn. **[3384]**
U.S. Revolver Assn. **[3385]**
U.S. Complete Shooting Dog Assn. **[3187]**
Shop Am. Alliance **[777]**, 1308 Westhampton Woods Ct., Chesterfield, MO 63005, (707)224-3795
Short Span Steel Bridge Alliance **[1434]**, 1140 Connecticut Ave., Ste. 705 NW, Washington, DC 20036, (301)367-6179
Shout Global Hea. **[2517]**, 103 Azalea Ct., No. 18-2, Largo, MD 20774, (240)293-3652
Sigma Alpha Lambda **[3531]**, 501 Village Green Pkwy., Ste. 1, Bradenton, FL 34209, (941)866-5614
Sigma Beta Rho Fraternity **[3557]**, PO Box 4668, New York, NY 10163, (888)333-1449
Sigma Delta Epsilon, Graduate Women in Sci. **[3545]**, PO Box 240607, St. Paul, MN 55124, (952)236-9112
Sigma Delta Pi **[3509]**, Coll. of Charleston, 66 George St., Charleston, SC 29424-0001, (843)953-5253
Sigma Gamma Epsilon **[3527]**, Univ. of Norther Iowa, Dept. of Earth Sci., Cedar Falls, IA 50614-0335, (319)273-2707
Sigma Iota Epsilon **[3535]**, Colorado State Univ., 312 Rockwell Hall, Fort Collins, CO 80521, (970)491-6265
Sigma Lambda Gamma Natl. Sorority **[3563]**, 125 E Zeller St., Suites D & E, North Liberty, IA 52317, (319)626-7679
Sigma Phi Alpha **[3515]**, Northern Arizona Univ., PO Box 15065, Flagstaff, AZ 86011-5065, (928)523-0520
Sigma Phi Epsilon **[3558]**, 310 S Blvd., PO Box 1901, Richmond, VA 23218, (804)353-1901
Sigma Phi Epsilon Educational Found. **[★3558]**
Silk Painters Intl. **[1720]**, PO Box 1074, East Point, FL 32328, (850)670-8323
Silver Age Yoga **[2606]**, 7968 Arjons Dr., Ste. 213, San Diego, CA 92126, (858)693-3110
Simple Hope **[2200]**, PO Box 4, Menomonee Falls, WI 53052, (262)569-9919
Singapore Am. Bus. Assn. **[175]**, 3 Twin Dolphin Dr., Ste. 150, Redwood City, CA 94065, (650)260-3388
Sino-American Bridge for Educ. and Hea. **[1784]**, c/o Anne S. Watt, EdD, Vice Chair, 15R Sargent St., Cambridge, MA 02140
Sister Cities Intl. **[2685]**, 915 15th St. NW, 4th Fl., Washington, DC 20005, (202)347-8630
Sisters in Crime **[922]**, PO Box 442124, Lawrence, KS 66044, (785)842-1325
Six of One Club: The Prisoner Appreciation Soc. **[3599]**, 871 Clover Dr., North Wales, PA 19454-2749, (215)699-2527
Skating
Professional Figure Skaters Cooperative **[3386]**
U.S. Speedskating **[3387]**
Skeleton Fed; U.S. Bobsled and **[3390]**
Ski and Snowboard Assn; U.S. Deaf **[3318]**
Skiing
Natl. Brotherhood of Skiers **[3388]**
Professional Ski Instructors of Am. **[3389]**
Camping Women **[3301]**
Sky of Love **[1986]**, PO Box 170241, Brooklyn, NY 11217
SkyTruth **[1081]**, PO Box 3283, Shepherdstown, WV 25443-3283, (304)885-4581
Slavic
Assn. for Slavic, East European and Eurasian Stud. **[1854]**
Slovak
Slovak Catholic Sokol **[2824]**
Slovak Catholic Sokol **[2824]**, 205 Madison St., PO Box 899, Passaic, NJ 07055, (800)886-7656
Small Business
Assn. for Enterprise Opportunity **[821]**
BEST Employers Assn. **[822]**
Intl. Coun. for Small Bus. **[823]**
SCORE **[824]**
Small Bus. Ser. Bur. **[825]**
Natl. Assn. of Small Bus. Contractors **[222]**

A star before a book entry number signifies that the name is not listed separately, but is mentioned within the entry.

Small Bus. Ser. Bur. [825], 554 Main St., PO Box
15014, Worcester, MA 01615-0014, (800)343-0939
Small Publishers Assn. of North Am. [726], PO Box
9725, Colorado Springs, CO 80932-0725,
(719)924-5534
Smile Network Intl. [2355], 211 N First St., Ste. 150,
Minneapolis, MN 55401, (612)377-1800

Snow Sports
U.S. Bobsled and Skeleton Fed. [3390]
U.S. Snowshoe Assn. [3391]
Professional Figure Skaters Cooperative [3386]

Soap Box Derby
Natl. Derby Rallies [3392]
Soap and Detergent Assn. [★183]

Soccer
Amer. Youth Soccer Org. [3393]
Natl. Intercollegiate Soccer Officials Assn. [3394]

Social Action
Fuel for Truth [2745]
Vote Hemp [2746]
World Action for Humanity [2225]
Alliance of Jamaican and Amer. Humanitarians
[2008]
Kids for Peace [2717]
Reality Relief [2196]
RedLight Children [1912]
Seventh Generation Advisors [1073]

Social Change
Graduation Pledge Alliance [2747]
Social Enterprise Alliance [826]
Girls for a Change [1956]
One Voice of Peace [1672]
Village Focus Intl. [2037]

Social Clubs
Chemists' Club [2825]
Jim Smith Soc. [2826]
The Moles [2827]
Stunts Unlimited [2828]
Social Enterprise Alliance [826], 11525 Springridge
Rd., Potomac, MD 20854, (202)758-0194

Social Fraternities
Alpha Psi Lambda Natl. [3550]
Delta Lambda Phi Natl. Social Fraternity [3551]
Kappa Delta Rho [3552]
Pi Beta Phi [3553]
Pi Delta Psi Fraternity [3554]
Pi Kappa Alpha [3555]
Pi Lambda Phi Fraternity [3556]
Sigma Beta Rho Fraternity [3557]
Sigma Phi Epsilon [3558]
Tau Kappa Epsilon [3559]

Social Issues
Natl. Sci. and Tech. Educ. Partnership [2226]
Soc. for the Stud. of Social Problems [2227]
Global Centurion [1957]
Millennium Campus Network [2614]

Social Justice
Ensaaf [2748]
Dalit Freedom Network [2661]
Dalit Solidarity [2662]

Social Problems
Eliminate Poverty Now [1904]

Social Responsibility
Corporate Social Responsibility Assn. [238]
Global Brigades [2019]
Junior Optimist Octagon Intl. [2222]

Social Security
Natl. Coun. of Social Security Mgt. Associations
[1374]

Social Service
Healing Hands Intl. [2228]
Act for Africa Intl. [2209]
Adopt-a-Village Intl. [2007]
Africa Hope [1916]
AHOPE for Children [1917]
Aid Still Required [2066]
All the Children are Children [1919]
All Our Children Intl. Outreach [1920]
Alliance For Relief Mission in Haiti [2181]
Alliance of Jamaican and Amer. Humanitarians
[2008]
Amer. Bar Assn. Commn. on Homelessness and
Poverty [2099]
Amman Imman: Water is Life [2260]
Ark Mission [1922]
Artfully AWARE [1724]
Baitulmaal [2183]

Baptist Global Response [2184]
Benefit4Kids [1924]
Breaking Ground [2009]
Bridges Cambodia Intl. [1929]
Building Community Bridges [2011]
Burundi Friends Intl. [2012]
Camp To Belong [1930]
ChangeALife Uganda [1932]
Children of Grace [1938]
Chosen Children Intl. [1944]
Clinic at a Time [2483]
Compassion into Action Network - Direct Outcome
Org. [2067]
Connecting Congo [2016]
Coun. on Accreditation [2233]
Damien Ministries [2902]
Drinking Water for India [2262]
Fields of Growth Intl. [2129]
Friends of the Children of Angola [1952]
Funders' Network for Smart Growth and Livable
Communities [2018]
Gift of Water [2263]
Global FoodBanking Network [2116]
Global Partners Running Waters [2020]
Glocal Ventures [2119]
Great Commn. Alliance [2068]
Haiti Works! [2120]
HANDS for Cambodia [2021]
Hannah's Promise Intl. Aid [2187]
Help Aid Africa [2022]
Helping Hands [1962]
Helping Hearts Helping Hands [2166]
Helping Honduras Kids [1963]
Hope and Future for Children in Bolivia [1965]
Hope for Haiti's Children [1966]
Humanitarian African Relief Org. [2190]
In Our Own Quiet Way [2265]
Indigo Threads [2024]
Intl. Action [2266]
Junior Optimist Octagon Intl. [2222]
Kenya Medical Outreach [2135]
Kids Home Intl. [1969]
Korean Amer. Sharing Movement [2193]
Loving Hands for the Needy [1971]
Malawi Children's Mission [1972]
Mama Hope [2027]
Mercy Beyond Borders [2169]
Miracles in Action [2170]
Nepal SEEDS: Social Educational Environmental
Development Services in Nepal [2028]
One Love Worldwide [2194]
One Vision Intl. [2029]
Options for Children in Zambia [1978]
Para Sa Bata [1982]
People for Haiti [2195]
Reach Out to Romania [2172]
Rebuilding Haiti Now [2197]
Reconstruction Efforts Aiding Children without
Homes [2032]
Relief Liberia Intl. [2198]
Restoring Institutions Services and Empowering
Liberia [2033]
River Intl. [2199]
Seeds of HOPE Intl. [1985]
Ser. for the Love of God [2034]
Shining Hope for Communities [2035]
Simple Hope [2200]
Sudan Sunrise [2154]
Sweet Sleep [1987]
Together for Tanzania [2036]
Two Hearts for Hope [1989]
Vietnam Relief Effort [2201]
Water Alliance for Africa [2268]
Water for Sudan [2269]
Well Done Org. [2039]
World Action for Humanity [2225]
WorldHope Corps [2040]

Social Sororities
Alpha Sigma Tau [3560]
Gamma Phi Beta [3561]
Kappa Kappa Gamma [3562]

Social Welfare
Amer. Humane Assn. [2229]
Amer. Public Human Services Assn. [2230]
Amer. Public Human Services Assn. I Natl. Coun.
of State Human Ser. Administrators [2231]
Amer. Rescue Workers [2232]

Coun. on Accreditation [2233]
Emergency Relief Response Fund [2234]
Natl. Org. for Human Services [1685]
Natl. Staff Development and Training Assn. [2235]
Abriendo Mentes [2208]
Aid Still Required [2066]
Aid for the World [2163]
Alliance of Jamaican and Amer. Humanitarians
[2008]
Amer. Bar Assn. Commn. on Homelessness and
Poverty [2099]
Amman Imman: Water is Life [2260]
Animals Deserve Absolute Protection Today and
Tomorrow [1890]
Baitulmaal [2183]
BLOOM Africa [1925]
A Bridge for Children [1927]
Bridge of Love [1928]
Bridges Cambodia Intl. [1929]
Building Bridges Worldwide [2010]
Camp To Belong [1930]
Child Literacy [1935]
Clean the World [1197]
Connecting Congo [2016]
Crutches 4 Kids [1946]
Educ. for Prosperity [2017]
Empower Orphans [1947]
Global FoodBanking Network [2116]
Goods for Good [1958]
Haiti Works! [2120]
HavServe Volunteer Ser. Network [1906]
Helping Hearts Helping Hands [2166]
Hero Initiative [1745]
Hope for Haiti [2023]
Humanitarian African Relief Org. [2190]
In Our Own Quiet Way [2265]
Indigo Threads [2024]
Junior Optimist Octagon Intl. [2222]
Korean Amer. Sharing Movement [2193]
Malawi Children's Mission [1972]
Meds and Food for Kids [1973]
Mike's Angels [1974]
One Love Worldwide [2194]
One Vision Intl. [2029]
Options for Children in Zambia [1978]
Para Sa Bata [1982]
People for Haiti [2195]
Reality Relief [2196]
Reconstruction Efforts Aiding Children without
Homes [2032]
Relief Liberia Intl. [2198]
Rising Intl. [1908]
River Intl. [2199]
Ser. for the Love of God [2034]
Simple Hope [2200]
To Love a Child [1988]
Together for Tanzania [2036]
Tusubira - We Have Hope [2173]
Village Focus Intl. [2037]
World Action for Humanity [2225]
World Spark [1990]
WorldHope Corps [2040]
Zambia Hope Intl. [1991]

Social Work
Assn. of Oncology Social Work [2236]
Clinical Social Work Assn. [2237]
Employee Assistance Professionals Assn. [2238]
Aid Still Required [2066]
Amer. Bar Assn. Commn. on Homelessness and
Poverty [2099]
Artfully AWARE [1724]
Bridge of Love [1928]
Bridges to Prosperity [2210]
Building Bridges Worldwide [2010]
Great Commn. Alliance [2068]
Hannah's Promise Intl. Aid [2187]
Hearts for Kenya [1907]
Hero Initiative [1745]
Humanitarian African Relief Org. [2190]
Meds and Food for Kids [1973]
One Love Worldwide [2194]
People for Haiti [2195]
Reality Relief [2196]
Ser. for the Love of God [2034]
Sudan Sunrise [2154]
To Love a Child [1988]
Water for Sudan [2269]

Zambia Hope Intl. **[1991]**
Social Workers
Amer. Bar Assn. Commn. on Homelessness and Poverty **[2099]**
Societas Liturgica **[2911]**, c/o Alan Barthel, Sec., 100 Witherspoon St., Louisville, KY 40202, (502)569-5759
Societe de Chimie Industrielle, Amer. Sect. **[1439]**, c/o Danielle Fraser, Admin., 80 Hathaway Dr., Stratford, CT 06615, (212)725-9539
Soc. for Adolescent Hea. and Medicine **[2338]**, 111 Deer lake Rd., Ste. 100, Deerfield, IL 60015, (847)753-5226
Society for Adolescent Medicine **[★2338]**
Soc. of African Missions **[2880]**, 23 Bliss Ave., Tenafly, NJ 07670-3001, (201)567-0450
Soc. for Amer. Baseball Res. **[3262]**, 4455 E Camelback Rd., Ste. D-140, Phoenix, AZ 85018, (602)343-6455
Soc. of Amer. Gastrointestinal and Endoscopic Surgeons **[2417]**, 11300 W Olympic Blvd., Ste. 600, Los Angeles, CA 90064, (310)437-0544
Soc. of Amer. Magicians **[3212]**, PO Box 505, Parker, CO 80134, (303)362-0575
Soc. of Amer. Registered Architects **[1411]**, PO Box 280, Newport, TN 37822, (423)721-0129
Soc. of Amer. Silversmiths **[844]**, PO Box 786, West Warwick, RI 02893, (401)461-6840
Soc. of Antique Modelers **[3088]**, 3379 Crystal Ct., Napa, CA 94558, (707)255-3547
Soc. for Applied Spectroscopy **[1539]**, 5320 Spectrum Dr., Ste. C, Frederick, MD 21703, (301)694-8122
Soc. for Asian Art **[1713]**, Asian Art Museum, 200 Larkin St., San Francisco, CA 94102, (415)581-3701
Soc. of Australasian Specialists/Oceania **[3232]**, PO Box 24764, San Jose, CA 95154-4764, (408)978-0193
Soc. of Automotive Engineers **[1532]**, 400 Commonwealth Dr., Warrendale, PA 15096-0001, (724)776-4970
Soc. of Automotive Historians **[3130]**, c/o Patrick D. Bisson, Treas., 8537 Tim Tam Trail, Flushing, MI 48433
Soc. of Cardiovascular Anesthesiologists **[2305]**, 2209 Dickens Rd., Richmond, VA 23230-2005, (804)282-0084
Soc. for Chem. Hazard Commun. **[189]**, PO Box 1392, Annandale, VA 22003-9392, (703)658-9246
Soc. for Clinical and Medical Hair Removal **[2402]**, 2424 Amer. Ln., Madison, WI 53704-3102, (608)443-2470
Soc. for Clinical Trials **[2349]**, 100 N 20th St., 4th Fl., Philadelphia, PA 19103, (215)564-3484
Soc. of Corporate Secretaries and Governance Professionals **[17]**, 521 5th Ave., New York, NY 10175, (212)681-2000
Soc. of Cost Estimating and Anal. **[343]**, 527 Maple Ave. E, Ste. 301, Vienna, VA 22180, (703)938-5090
Soc. of Critical Care Medicine **[2356]**, 500 Midway Dr., Mount Prospect, IL 60056, (847)827-6869
Soc. of Depreciation Professionals **[11]**, 347 5th Ave., Ste. 703, New York, NY 10016, (646)417-6378
Soc. for Developmental Biology **[1423]**, 9650 Rockville Pike, Bethesda, MD 20814-3998, (301)634-7815
Soc. for Disability Stud. **[2062]**, Soc. for Disability Stud., 107 Commerce Center Dr., Ste. 204, Huntersville, NC 28078, (704)274-9240
Soc. for Ecological Restoration Intl. **[1056]**, 1017 O St. NW, Washington, DC 20001, (202)299-9518
Soc. for Economic Botany **[1433]**, PO Box 299, St. Louis, MO 63166-0299
Soc. of Educators and Scholars **[1782]**, Inter Amer. Univ. of Puerto Rico, Metropolitan Campus, PO Box 191293, San Juan, PR 00919-1293
Soc. of Engg. Sci. **[1470]**, c/o S. White, Univ. of Illinois at Urbana-Champaign, Beckman Inst. for Advanced Sci. and Tech., 405 N Mathews Ave., Rm. 3361, Urbana, IL 61801
Soc. for Epidemiologic Res. **[2411]**, PO Box 990, Clearfield, UT 84089, (801)525-0231

Soc. for Ethnomusicology **[1828]**, The Musical Instrument Museum, 8550 S Priest Dr., Tempe, AZ 85284, (480)309-4077
Soc. of Exploration Geophysicists **[1484]**, PO Box 702740, Tulsa, OK 74170-2740, (918)497-5500
Soc. of Family Planning **[2413]**, 255 S 17th St., Ste. 1102, Philadelphia, PA 19103, (866)584-6758
Soc. for Features Journalism **[706]**, 200 E Las Olas Blvd., 9th Fl., Fort Lauderdale, FL 33301, (954)356-4718
Soc. for Foodservice Mgt. **[378]**, 15000 Commerce Pkwy., Ste. C, Mount Laurel, NJ 08054, (856)380-6829
Soc. of Forensic Toxicologists **[1302]**, One Mac-Donald Center, 1 N MacDonald St., Ste. 15, Mesa, AZ 85201, (480)839-9106
Soc. of Former Special Agents of the Fed. Bur. of Investigation **[2799]**, 3717 Fettler Park Dr., Dumfries, VA 22025, (703)445-0026
Soc. for French Historical Stud. **[1774]**, 551-101 Milton Ct., Long Beach, CA 90803, (562)494-6764
Soc. of Gastroenterology Nurses and Associates **[2418]**, 401 N Michigan Ave., Chicago, IL 60611, (312)321-5165
Soc. of Govt. Economists **[1289]**, PO Box 77082, Washington, DC 20013, (202)643-1743
Soc. of Govt. Travel Professionals **[886]**, PO Box 158, Glyndon, MD 21071-0158, (202)363-7487
Soc. for Gynecologic Investigation **[2568]**, 888 Bestgate Rd., Ste. 420, Annapolis, MD 21401, (404)727-8600
Soc. for Heart Valve Disease **[2457]**, 900 Cummings Ctr., Ste. 221-U, Beverly, MA 01915, (978)927-8330
Soc. for Historians of Amer. Foreign Relations **[1775]**, Dept. of History, Ohio State Univ., 106 Dulles Hall, 230 W 17th Ave., Columbus, OH 43210, (614)292-1951
Soc. for Historians of the Early Amer. Republic **[1776]**, 3355 Woodland Walk, Philadelphia, PA 19104-4531, (215)746-5393
Soc. for Historical Archaeology **[1405]**, 9707 Key West Ave., Ste. 100, Rockville, MD 20850, (301)990-2454
Soc. for History Educ. **[1629]**, California State Univ., Long Beach, 1250 Bellflower Blvd., Long Beach, CA 90840, (562)985-2573
Soc. for History in the Fed. Govt. **[1777]**, Box 14139, Benjamin Franklin Sta., Washington, DC 20044, (301)279-9697
Soc. for Human Rsrc. Mgt. **[636]**, 1800 Duke St., Alexandria, VA 22314-3499, (703)548-3440
Soc. for Hungarian Philately **[3233]**, c/o Jim Gaul, Auction Chm., 1920 Fawn Ln., Hellertown, PA 18055-2117, (610)838-8162
Soc. of Illustrators **[1721]**, 128 E 63rd St., New York, NY 10021-7303, (212)838-2560
Soc. for In Vitro Biology **[1424]**, 514 Daniels St., Ste. 411, Raleigh, NC 27605-1317, (919)562-0600
Soc. of Inkwell Collectors **[3161]**, 2203 39th St. SE, Puyallup, WA 98372, (301)919-6322
Soc. of Insurance Financial Mgt. **[344]**, PO Box 9001, Mount Vernon, NY 10552, (914)966-3180
Soc. of Insurance Trainers and Educators **[1635]**, 1821 Univ. Ave. W, Ste. S256, St. Paul, MN 55104, (651)999-5354
Soc. of Jewish Ethics **[2964]**, 1531 Dickey Dr., Atlanta, GA 30322, (404)712-8550
Soc. of Mfg. Engineers I North Amer. Mfg. Res. Institution **[1493]**, 1 SME Dr., Dearborn, MI 48121, (313)425-3000
Soc. for Menstrual Cycle Res. **[2569]**, Eastern Washington Univ., 229 Communications Bldg., Cheney, WA 99004
Soc. for Mining, Metallurgy, and Exploration **[1501]**, 12999 E Adam Aircraft Cir., Englewood, CO 80112, (303)948-4200
Soc. of Missionaries of Africa **[2881]**, 1624 21st St. NW, Washington, DC 20009-1003, (202)232-5154
Soc. for Music Perception and Cognition **[1829]**, c/o Scott Lipscomb, Treas., Univ. of Minnesota School of Music, 148 Ferguson Hall, 2106 4th St. S, Minneapolis, MN 55455, (612)624-2843
Soc. for Natural Philosophy **[1496]**, c/o Thomas J. Pence, Treas., Michigan Sta. Univ., Dept. of Mech. Engg., 2452 Engg. Bldg., East Lansing, MI 48824-1226

Soc. for Neuroscience in Anesthesiology and Critical Care **[2563]**, 520 N Northwest Hwy., Park Ridge, IL 60068-2573, (847)825-5586
Society of Neurosurgical Anesthesia and Critical Care **[★2563]**
Soc. of Our Lady of the Most Holy Trinity **[2882]**, PO Box 152, 3816 County Rd. 61, Robstown, TX 78380, (361)387-2754
Soc. for Pacific Coast Native Iris **[3207]**, 7417 92nd Pl. SE, Mercer Island, WA 98040, (206)232-7745
Soc. for Pentecostal Stud. **[3024]**, 1435 N Glenstone Ave., Springfield, MO 65802, (417)268-1084
Soc. of Permanent Cosmetic Professionals **[242]**, 69 N Broadway, Des Plaines, IL 60016, (847)635-1330
Soc. for Personality Assessment **[2587]**, 6109H Arlington Blvd., Falls Church, VA 22044, (703)534-4772
Soc. of Pi Kappa Lambda **[3541]**, Capital Univ., Conservatory of Music, 1 Coll. and Main, Columbus, OH 43209, (614)236-7211
Soc. of the Plastics Indus. **[677]**, 1667 K St. NW, Ste. 1000, Washington, DC 20006, (202)974-5200
Soc. for Prevention Res. **[2597]**, 11240 Waples Mill Rd., Ste. 200, Fairfax, VA 22030, (703)934-4850
Soc. of Professional Journalists **[707]**, Eugene S. Pulliam Natl. Journalism Center, 3909 N Meridian St., Indianapolis, IN 46208, (317)927-8000
Soc. of Professional Rope Access Technicians **[468]**, 994 Old Eagle School Rd., Ste. 1019, Wayne, PA 19087-1866, (610)971-4850
Soc. of Professional Women in Petroleum **[650]**, PO Box 420957, Houston, TX 77242
Soc. of Publication Designers **[412]**, 27 Union Sq. W, Ste. 207, New York, NY 10003, (212)223-3332
Soc. of Quality Assurance **[729]**, 154 Hansen Rd., Ste. 201, Charlottesville, VA 22911, (434)297-4772
Soc. for Range Mgt. **[1195]**, 10030 W 27th Ave., Wheat Ridge, CO 80215-6601, (303)986-3309
Soc. for Reformation Res. **[1850]**, Luther Coll., Dept. of History, 700 Coll. Dr., Decorah, IA 52101-1045
Soc. of Res. Administrators **[1524]**, 1901 N Moore St., Ste. 1004, Arlington, VA 22209, (703)741-0140
Soc. of the Silurians **[708]**, PO Box 1195, Madison Square Sta., New York, NY 10159, (212)532-0887
Soc. for the Stud. of Evolution **[1473]**, c/o Judy Stone, Sec., Colby Coll., 5720 Mayflower Hill Dr., Waterville, ME 04901, (207)859-5736
Soc. for the Stud. of Social Problems **[2227]**, 901 McClung Tower, Univ. of Tennessee, Knoxville, TN 37996-0490, (865)689-1531
Soc. for Tech. Commun. **[197]**, 9401 Lee Hwy., Ste. 300, Fairfax, VA 22031, (703)522-4114
Soc. of Toxicology **[1550]**, 1821 Michael Faraday Dr., Ste. 300, Reston, VA 20190-5348, (703)438-3115
Soc. of Turkish Amer. Architects, Engineers and Scientists **[1471]**, 821 United Nations Plz., Turkish Ctr., 2nd Fl., New York, NY 10017, (646)312-3366
Soc. for Utopian Stud. **[1840]**, Univ. of Florida, PO Box 117310, Gainesville, FL 32611-7310, (352)392-6650
Soc. for Visual Anthropology **[1402]**, Reading Area Community Coll., Soc. Sciences Div., 10 S 2nd St., Reading, PA 19603
Sociologists Without Borders **[2749]**, c/o David Brunsma, Treas., Univ. of Missouri, 312 Middlebush Hall, Columbia, MO 65211, (537)882-1067
Sociology
Sociologists Without Borders **[2749]**
Soft Power Hea. **[2518]**, 2887 Purchase St., Purchase, NY 10577, (914)694-2442
Softball
Amateur Softball Assn. of Am. **[3395]**
Intl. Senior Softball Assn. **[3396]**
Soil
Soil Sci. Soc. of Am. **[1534]**
Soil Sci. Soc. of Am. **[1534]**, 677 S Segoe Rd., Madison, WI 53711, (608)273-8080
Solar Cookers Intl. **[1183]**, 1919 21st St., Ste. 101, Sacramento, CA 95811, (916)455-4499
Solar Energy
Amer. Solar Energy Soc. **[1535]**
Global Possibilities **[1214]**
Solar Energy Indus. Assn. **[1536]**

A star before a book entry number signifies that the name is not listed separately, but is mentioned within the entry.

Solar for Peace [1537]
Eco Energy Finance [1457]
Innovation: Africa [1394]
Rural Renewable Energy Alliance [1462]
Solar Energy Indus. Assn. [1536], 575 7th St. NW, Ste. 400, Washington, DC 20004, (202)682-0556
Solar Energy Res. and Educ. Foundation [★1536]
Solar for Peace [1537], PO Box 764, Danville, CA 94526-0764, (925)208-4989
SOLE - The Intl. Soc. of Logistics [1489], 8100 Professional Pl., Ste. 111, Hyattsville, MD 20785-2229, (301)459-8446
Sons of the Amer. Legion [3075], PO Box 1055, Indianapolis, IN 46206, (317)630-1200

Sororities
Sigma Lambda Gamma Natl. Sorority [3563]
Theta Nu Xi Multicultural Sorority [3564]

SoundExchange [625], 1121 Fourteenth St. NW, Ste. 700, Washington, DC 20005, (202)640-5858
South Asian Public Hea. Assn. [2591], c/o Mayur A. Patel, MS, Treas., 1105 Grant St., Evanston, IL 60201
South Rugby Union [★3378]
Southern Early Childhood Assn. [2002], PO Box 55930, Little Rock, AR 72215-5930, (501)221-1648
Southern Historical Assn. [1704], Univ. of Georgia, Dept. of History, Rm. 111A, LeConte Hall, Athens, GA 30602-1602, (706)542-8848
Soyfoods Assn. of North Am. [998], 1050 17th St. NW, Ste. 600, Washington, DC 20036, (202)659-3520

Space
Space Stud. Inst. [1389]
Space Topic Stud. Unit [3234]

Space Stud. Inst. [1389], 1434 Flightline St., Mojave, CA 93501, (661)750-2774
Space Topic Stud. Unit [3234], c/o Carmine Torrisi, Sec., PO Box 780241, Maspeth, NY 11378
Spain-United States Chamber of Commerce [3486], Empire State Bldg., 350 5th Ave., Ste. 2600, New York, NY 10118, (212)967-2170

Spanish
Queen Sofia Spanish Inst. [1855]

Spanish-Barb Breeders Assn. [1147], PO Box 1628, Silver City, NM 88062
Spanish Mustang Registry [1148], 323 County Rd. 419, Chilton, TX 76632, (254)546-2177
Spanish World Ministries [3013], PO Box 542, Winona Lake, IN 46590-0542, (574)267-8821
SPCA Intl. [1900], PO Box 8682, New York, NY 10001
Special Care Dentistry Assn. [2389], 401 N Michigan Ave., Ste. 2200, Chicago, IL 60611, (312)527-6764

Special Education
Coun. for Children with Behavioral Disorders [1686]
Coun. for Exceptional Children [1687]
Kate's Voice [1678]

Special Interest Gp. on Accessible Computing [1443], 2 Penn Plz., Ste. 701, New York, NY 10121-0701, (212)626-0500
Special Interest Gp. for Design Automation [1442], PO Box 6000, Binghamton, NY 13902, (607)777-2943
Special Interest Gp. on Info. Retrieval [1491], 140 Governors Dr., Amherst, MA 01003-9264, (413)545-3240
Special Military Active Retired Travel Club [3073], 600 Univ. Off. Blvd., Ste. 1A, Pensacola, FL 32504, (850)478-1986
Specialty Equip. Market Assn. [91], 1575 S Valley Vista Dr., Diamond Bar, CA 91765, (909)396-0289
Species Alliance [1255], 5200 San Pablo Ave., Emeryville, CA 94608, (510)594-8355

Spectroscopy
Coblentz Soc. [1538]
Soc. for Applied Spectroscopy [1539]

Speech
Amer. Forensic Assn. [1688]
Acad. of Rehabilitative Audiology [2449]
Rhetoric Soc. of Am. [1851]

Speech and Hearing
Acad. of Rehabilitative Audiology [2449]
Intl. Catholic Deaf Assn. U.S. Sect. [2868]

Speedskating; U.S. [3387]
Spellbinders [1856], PO Box 1986, Basalt, CO 81621, (970)544-2389

Spill Control Assn. of Am. [682], 2105 Laurel Bush Rd., Ste. 200, Bel Air, MD 21015, (443)640-1085
Spinal Hea. Intl. [2594], 2221 NW 3rd Pl., Gainesville, FL 32603

Spinal Injury
Spinal Hea. Intl. [2594]
World Spine Care [2595]

Spinning and Weaving Assn. [858], PO Box 7506, Loveland, CO 80537, (970)613-4629

Spiritual Understanding
Thanks-Giving Square [3035]
Monks Without Borders [2946]
World Sound Healing Org. [2155]

Sponge and Chamois Inst. [540], 10024 Off. Center Ave., Ste. 203, St. Louis, MO 63128, (314)842-2230
Sport Marketing Assn. [835], Univ. of Memphis, 204B Fieldhouse, Memphis, TN 38152

Sporting Goods
Amer. Fly-Fishing Trade Assn. [827]
Assn. of Golf Merchandisers [828]
Billiard and Bowling Inst. of Am. [829]
Intl. Clubmakers' Guild [830]
Natl. Assn. of Sporting Goods Wholesalers [831]

Sports
Athletic Equip. Managers Assn. [3397]
Atlantic Coast Conf. [3398]
Big East Conf. [3399]
Cleveland Hockey Booster Club [3588]
Coll. Athletic Bus. Mgt. Assn. [3400]
Dale Jarrett Fan Club [3589]
Fantasy Sports Trade Assn. [832]
Golf Course Builders Assn. of Am. [833]
Golf Course Superintendents Assn. of Am. [834]
Hartford Whalers Booster Club [3590]
Intercollegiate Assn. of Amateur Athletes of Am. [3401]
Los Angeles Kings Booster Club [3591]
Maccabi USA/Sports for Israel [3402]
Natl. Assn. of Collegiate Directors of Athletics [3403]
Natl. Collegiate Athletic Assn. [3404]
Natl. Hockey League Booster Clubs [3592]
Natl. Intramural-Recreational Sports Assn. [3405]
Natl. Junior Coll. Athletic Assn. [3406]
Pacific 10 Conf. [3407]
Philadelphia Flyers Fan Club [3593]
Pittsburgh Penguins Booster Club [3594]
RollerSoccer Intl. Fed. [3408]
Sport Marketing Assn. [835]
U.S. Collegiate Athletic Assn. [3409]
U.S. Sports Acad. [3410]
Washington Capitals Fan Club [3595]
Western Athletic Conf. [3411]
World Sport Stacking Assn. [3412]
All Japan Ju-Jitsu Intl. Fed. [3359]
Amer. Coon Hunters Assn. [3355]
Amer. Legion Baseball [3257]
Bass Anglers Sportsman Soc. [3326]
BlazeSports Am. [3316]
Christian Cheerleaders of Am. [3304]
Eastern Coll. Athletic Conf. [3342]
Fed. of Intl. Lacrosse [3357]
Golf Coaches Assn. of Am. [3335]
Highlander Class Intl. Assn. [3273]
Intl. Assn. of Gay and Lesbian Martial Artists [3360]
Intl. Chinese Boxing Assn. [3297]
Intl. Female Boxers Assn. [3298]
Intl. Natural Bodybuilding and Fitness Fed. [3293]
Intl. Trotting and Pacing Assn. [3345]
Martial Arts Intl. Fed. [3361]
Natl. Assn. of Professional Baseball Leagues [3260]
Natl. Coalition Against Violent Athletes [3252]
Natl. Versatility Ranch Horse Assn. [3352]
New England Trails Conf. [3428]
North Amer. Football League [3331]
North-South Skirmish Assn. [3384]
Professional Baseball Athletic Trainers Soc. [3261]
Professional Figure Skaters Cooperative [3386]
Professional Putters Assn. [3338]
Salute Military Golf Assn. [3339]
Thoroughbred Club of Am. [3348]
U.S. Albacore Assn. [3286]
U.S. Bobsled and Skeleton Fed. [3390]

U.S. Flag Football League [3333]
U.S. Lawn Bowls Assn. [3295]
U.S. Olympic Comm. [3368]
U.S. Power Squadrons [3290]
U.S. Twirling Assn. [3267]
U.S. Women's Curling Assn. [3310]
USA Diving [3321]
The World Kuoshu Fed. [3363]
World Martial Arts Assn. [3364]

Sports Facilities
Fed. of Intl. Lacrosse [3357]
Intl. Assn. of Gay and Lesbian Martial Artists [3360]
Maccabi USA/Sports for Israel [3402]
New England Trails Conf. [3428]
Professional Baseball Athletic Trainers Soc. [3261]
U.S. Bobsled and Skeleton Fed. [3390]
USA Diving [3321]

Sports Officials
Natl. Assn. of Sports Officials [3413]
Fed. of Intl. Lacrosse [3357]
Intl. Assn. of Gay and Lesbian Martial Artists [3360]
Maccabi USA/Sports for Israel [3402]
Natl. Coalition Against Violent Athletes [3252]
New England Trails Conf. [3428]
Professional Baseball Athletic Trainers Soc. [3261]
U.S. Bobsled and Skeleton Fed. [3390]
USA Diving [3321]

Sports Officials' Development Prog. and Media Center [★3405]
Sports Philatelists Intl. [3235], c/o Norman Jacobs, Advt., 2712 N Decatur Rd., Decatur, GA 30033
Sports Turf Managers Assn. [533], 805 New Hampshire St., Ste. E, Lawrence, KS 66044, (800)323-3875
Spotted Saddle Horse Breeders' and Exhibitors' Assn. [1149], PO Box 1046, Shelbyville, TN 37162, (931)684-7496
Spring Res. Inst. [92], 422 Kings Way, Naples, FL 34104, (317)439-4811
Stage Directors and Choreographers Soc. [3458], 1501 Broadway, Ste. 1701, New York, NY 10036, (212)391-1070

Standards
Alliance for Building Regulatory Reform in the Digital Age [1435]
Building Commissioning Assn. [141]
Healthcare Laundry Accreditation Coun. [537]
Intl. Air Filtration Certifiers Assn. [432]

Standing Conf. of the Canonical Orthodox Bishops in the Americas [2905], 10 E 79th St., New York, NY 10075, (212)774-0526

Star Trek
STARFLEET [3596]
Starfleet Command [3597]

STARFLEET [3596], PO Box 8213, Bangor, ME 04402, (888)734-8735
Starfleet Command [3597], PO Box 33565, Indianapolis, IN 46203-0565, (317)508-9351
Starlight Children's Found. [2003], 2049 Century Plz. E Ste. 4320, Los Angeles, CA 90067, (310)479-1212
Stars of David Intl. [1875], 3175 Commercial Ave., Ste. 100, Northbrook, IL 60062-1915, (800)STAR-349

State Government
Natl. Black Caucus of State Legislators [1375]
Republican Governors Assn. [1376]

States Org. for Boating Access [120], 231 S LaSalle St., Ste. 2050, Chicago, IL 60604, (312)946-6283

Stationery
Bus. Solutions Assn. [836]
Greeting Card Assn. [837]
Print Services and Distribution Assn. [838]

Statistics
Caucus for Women in Statistics [1540]
Inst. of Mathematical Statistics [1541]
Intl. Biometric Soc. [1542]
Intl. Biometric Soc., Western North Amer. Region [1543]

Steam Engines
Northwest Steam Soc. [3242]

Steel Recycling Inst. [909], 680 Andersen Dr., Pittsburgh, PA 15220-2700, (412)922-2772

Stone
Allied Stone Indus. **[839]**
Indiana Limestone Inst. of Am. **[840]**
Natl. Stone, Sand and Gravel Assn. **[841]**
Stop Calling It Autism! **[2320]**, PO Box 155728, Fort Worth, TX 76155, (888)SCIA-123
Stories of Autism **[2321]**, 13110 NE 177th Pl., No. 237, Woodinville, WA 98072, (425)485-9919
Storytelling
Spellbinders **[1856]**
Strategic Account Mgt. Assn. **[606]**, 33 N LaSalle St., Ste. 3700, Chicago, IL 60602, (312)251-3131
Strategic Energy, Environmental and Trans. Alternatives **[1614]**, 18340 Yorba Linda Blvd., Ste. 107-509, Yorba Linda, CA 92886-4058, (714)777-7729
Structural Insulated Panel Assn. **[161]**, PO Box 1699, Gig Harbor, WA 98335, (253)858-7472
Student Peace Alliance **[2720]**, PO Box 27601, Washington, DC 20038, (202)684-2553
Student and Youth Travel Assn. **[887]**, 8400 Westpark Dr., 2nd Fl., McLean, VA 22102, (703)610-1263
Students
InterVarsity Link **[1689]**
Amer. Assn. of Human Design Practitioners **[253]**
Battelle for Kids **[1582]**
Close Up Found. **[2622]**
Coun. for Children with Behavioral Disorders **[1686]**
Global Brigades **[2019]**
Journey Toward Sustainability **[1622]**
Millennium Campus Network **[2614]**
Naturopathic Medical Student Assn. **[2554]**
Rock Detective Geoscience Educ. **[1601]**
Student Peace Alliance **[2720]**
Union of North Amer. Vietnamese Students Assn. **[2832]**
Stunts Unlimited **[2828]**, 15233 Ventura Blvd., Ste. 425, Sherman Oaks, CA 91403, (818)501-1970
Subaru 360 Drivers' Club **[3131]**, 23251 Hansen Rd., Tracy, CA 95304
Substance Abuse
Amer. Soc. of Addiction Medicine **[2596]**
Assn. of Halfway House Alcoholism Programs of North Am. **[2239]**
Center on Addiction and the Family **[2240]**
Informed Families Educ. Center I Natl. Family Partnership **[2241]**
Intl. Lawyers in Alcoholics Anonymous **[2242]**
NALGAP: The Assn. of Lesbian, Gay, Bisexual, and Transgender Addiction Professionals and Their Allies **[2243]**
Natl. Assn. of Addiction Treatment Providers **[2244]**
Natl. Assn. for Children of Alcoholics **[2245]**
Partnership at Drugfree.org **[2246]**
Proj. Renewal **[2247]**
Recovered Alcoholic Clergy Assn. **[2248]**
Soc. for Prevention Res. **[2597]**
Triangle Club **[2249]**
Women for Sobriety **[2250]**
Intl. Assn. of Addictions and Offender Counselors **[2044]**
Substance Abuse; Assn. for Medical Educ. and Res. in **[1661]**
S.U.C.C.E.S.S. for Autism **[2322]**, 28700 Euclid Ave., Mailbox No. 120, Wickliffe, OH 44092
Sudan Sunrise **[2154]**, 8643 Hauser Ct., Ste. 240, Lenexa, KS 66215, (913)599-0800
Sugar
Amer. Soc. of Sugar Cane Technologists **[1215]**
Sugar Indus. Technologists **[1478]**, 201 Cypress Ave., Clewiston, FL 33440, (863)983-3637
Suicide
Amer. Assn. of Suicidology **[2251]**
SunnyTravelers **[3240]**, 58800 Executive Dr., Mishawaka, IN 46544, (574)258-0571
Supply-Chain Coun. **[474]**, 12320 Barker Cypress Rd., Ste. 600, PMB 321, Cypress, TX 77429-8329, (202)962-0440
Surface Design Assn. **[859]**, PO Box 360, Sebastopol, CA 95473-0360, (707)829-3110
Surfing
Eastern Surfing Assn. **[3414]**
Surfing Medicine Intl. **[2299]**, PO Box 548, Waialua, HI 96791, (518)635-0899

Surgeons; Amer. Soc. of Maxillofacial **[2572]**
Surgeons of the U.S; Assn. of Military **[2552]**
Surgery
Amer. Soc. of Abdominal Surgeons **[2598]**
Smile Network Intl. **[2355]**
Surgery; Amer. Assn. for Hand **[2422]**
Surplus
Investment Recovery Assn. **[842]**
Surveying
Amer. Assn. for Geodetic Surveying **[1544]**
Amer. Coun. of Engg. Companies I Coun. of Professional Surveyors **[843]**
Susan Glaspell Soc. **[1736]**, 555 Jefferson St., Northumberland, PA 17857
Sustainable Agriculture
Community Agroecology Network **[1216]**
Intl. Agro Alliance **[1217]**
Multinational Exchange for Sustainable Agriculture **[1218]**
Agricultural Commodities Certification Assn. **[935]**
Natl. Women in Agriculture Assn. **[937]**
Sustainable Biomaterials Collaborative **[1397]**
Sustainable Biomaterials Collaborative **[1397]**, c/o Heeral Bhalala, Inst. for Local Self-Reliance, 2001 S St. NW, Ste. 570, Washington, DC 20009, (202)898-1610
Sustainable Fisheries Partnership **[959]**, 4348 Waialae Ave., No. 692, Honolulu, HI 96816, (202)580-8187
Sustainable Furnishings Coun. **[397]**, PO Box 205, Chapel Hill, NC 27514, (919)967-1137
Sustainable World Coalition **[1042]**, Earth Island Inst., 2150 Allston Way. No. 460, Berkeley, CA 94704, (415)737-0235
Swedish
Swedish Colonial Soc. **[1857]**
Swedish-American Chambers of Commerce, U.S.A. **[3487]**, 2900 K St. NW, Ste. 403, Washington, DC 20007, (202)536-1520
Swedish Colonial Soc. **[1857]**, 916 S Swanson St., Philadelphia, PA 19147-4332
Sweet Sleep **[1987]**, PO Box 40486, Nashville, TN 37204-9998, (615)730-7671
Sweet Sorghum Ethanol Assn. **[1398]**, 8912 Brandon Sta. Rd., Raleigh, NC 27613, (919)870-0782
Swimming
Coll. Swimming Coaches Assn. of Am. **[3415]**
Natl. InterScholastic Swimming Coaches Assn. of Am. **[3416]**
U.S. Aquatic Sports **[3417]**
U.S. Swim School Assn. **[3418]**
U.S. Synchronized Swimming **[3419]**
Swine
Amer. Guinea Hog Assn. **[1219]**
Natl. Swine Registry **[1220]**
System Safety Soc. **[★781]**
Systems Integrators
Clean Tech. and Sustainable Indus. Org. **[964]**

T

Tableware
Soc. of Amer. Silversmiths **[844]**
Taiwan
Friends of Taiwan Intl. **[2679]**
Talk About Curing Autism **[2323]**, 3070 Bristol St., Ste. 340, Costa Mesa, CA 92626, (949)640-4401
Tall Bearded Iris Soc. **[3208]**, PO Box 6991, Lubbock, TX 79493, (806)792-1878
Tall Cedar Foundation **[★2807]**
Tall Cedars of Lebanon of North Am. **[2807]**, 2609 N Front St., Harrisburg, PA 17110, (717)232-5991
Tanka Soc. of Am. **[1845]**, PO Box 521084, Tulsa, OK 74152
TASH **[2063]**, 1001 Connecticut Ave. NW, Ste. 235, Washington, DC 20036, (202)540-9020
Tau Kappa Epsilon **[3559]**, 7439 Woodland Dr., Indianapolis, IN 46268, (317)872-6533
Taxation
Amer. Taxation Assn. **[1377]**
Natl. Assn. of Enrolled Agents **[1378]**
Natl. Assn. of Tax Consultants **[1379]**
Taxidermy
Natl. Taxidermists Assn. **[845]**

Teacher Education
Assn. for the Advancement of Intl. Educ. **[1644]**
Teachers
Assn. of Teacher Educators **[1690]**
Assn. for the Advancement of Intl. Educ. **[1644]**
Rock Detective Geoscience Educ. **[1601]**
Sino-American Bridge for Educ. and Hea. **[1784]**
Teachers of English to Speakers of Other Languages **[1617]**, 1925 Ballenger Ave., Ste. 550, Alexandria, VA 22314-6820, (703)836-0774
Tech. Assn. of the Graphic Arts **[1487]**, 200 Deer Run Rd., Sewickley, PA 15143, (412)259-1706
Technical Education
Gen. Soc. of Mechanics and Tradesmen of the City of New York **[1691]**
Technology
1394 High Performance Serial Bus Trade Assn. **[846]**
Amer. Assn. of Professional Tech. Analysts **[847]**
Global Tech. Distribution Coun. **[848]**
911 Indus. Alliance **[195]**
Advanced Biofuels Assn. **[391]**
Alliance for Building Regulatory Reform in the Digital Age **[1435]**
Alliance for Renewable Energy **[1452]**
Assn. of Tech., Mgt. and Applied Engg. **[1632]**
Clean Tech. and Sustainable Indus. Org. **[964]**
Clean Tech. Trade Alliance **[1391]**
Drilling, Observation and Sampling of the Earth's Continental Crust **[1448]**
Electrification Coalition **[871]**
Electronic Indus. Citizenship Coalition **[280]**
Energy Efficiency Bus. Coalition **[301]**
Energy Extraction Technologies **[1458]**
Energy Farm **[1459]**
Energy Info. Standards Alliance **[302]**
Enterprise for a Sustainable World **[263]**
FutureGen Alliance **[1393]**
Innovation: Africa **[1394]**
Intl. Assn. of Space Entrepreneurs **[30]**
Intl. Coun. on Nanotechnology **[1440]**
North Am. Chinese Clean-tech and Semiconductor Assn. **[287]**
North Amer. Security Products Org. **[807]**
Plug In Am. **[1396]**
Rural Renewable Energy Alliance **[1462]**
Sweet Sorghum Ethanol Assn. **[1398]**
The Wind Alliance **[1557]**
TechnoServe **[2676]**, 1120 19th St. NW, 8th Fl., South Tower, Washington, DC 20036, (202)785-4515
Telecommunications
Assn. of Fed. Communications Consulting Engineers **[1545]**
Intl. Telecommunications Satellite Org. **[1546]**
Land Mobile Communications Coun. **[849]**
Natl. Assn. of Telecommunications Officers and Advisors **[1380]**
PCIA - The Wireless Infrastructure Assn. **[850]**
Telework Coalition **[851]**
Wireless Communications Assn. Intl. **[852]**
ZigBee Alliance **[853]**
1-800 Amer. Free Trade Assn. **[891]**
911 Indus. Alliance **[195]**
mHealth Alliance **[2510]**
TelecomPioneers **[★2090]**
Telemetry
Intl. Found. for Telemetering **[1547]**
Telephone Collectors Intl. **[3243]**, 3805 Spurr Cir., Brea, CA 92823, (714)528-3561
Telephone Service
1-800 Amer. Free Trade Assn. **[891]**
Telephones
Telephone Collectors Intl. **[3243]**
1-800 Amer. Free Trade Assn. **[891]**
Television
Rin Tin Tin Fan Club **[3598]**
Six of One Club: The Prisoner Appreciation Soc. **[3599]**
Telework Coalition **[851]**, 204 E St. NE, Washington, DC 20002, (202)266-0046
Tennessee Walking Horse Breeders' and Exhibitors' Assn. **[1150]**, PO Box 286, Lewisburg, TN 37091, (931)359-1574
Tennis
Amer. Medical Tennis Assn. **[3420]**

A star before a book entry number signifies that the name is not listed separately, but is mentioned within the entry.

Amer. Tennis Assn. [3421]
U.S. Natl. Tennis Acad. [3422]
Teratology Soc. [1425], 1821 Michael Faraday Dr., Ste. 300, Reston, VA 20190, (703)438-3104
Terrorism
Intl. Counter-Terrorism Officers Assn. [2750]
Fuel for Truth [2745]
United Against Nuclear Iran [2711]
Testing
ASTM Intl. [1548]
Educational Records Bur. [1692]
Intl. Air Filtration Certifiers Assn. [432]
Texas Longhorn Breeders Assn. of Am. [991], 2315 N Main St., Ste. 402, PO Box 4430, Fort Worth, TX 76164, (817)625-6241
Textile Exchange [1175], 822 Baldridge St., O'Donnell, TX 79351, (806)428-3411
Textiles
Amer. Flock Assn. [854]
Intl. Textile Market Assn. [855]
Natl. Assn. of Decorative Fabric Distributors [856]
The Natl. Needle Arts Assn. [857]
Spinning and Weaving Assn. [858]
Surface Design Assn. [859]
U.S. Assn. of Importers of Textiles and Apparel [860]
Healthcare Laundry Accreditation Coun. [537]
Thanks-Giving Square [3035], PO Box 131770, Dallas, TX 75313-1770, (214)969-1977
Theatre
Alliance of Resident Theatres/New York [1858]
New England Theatre Conf. [1859]
Theology
Natl. Assn. of Baptist Professors of Religion [1693]
Therapy
Alliance for Massage Therapy Educ. [1659]
Amer. Commn. for Accreditation of Reflexology Educ. and Training [1567]
Aromatherapy Registration Coun. [2292]
Emergency Response Massage Intl. [2537]
Intl. Soc. for Ayurveda and Hea. [2295]
Kate's Voice [1678]
Music Therapy for Healing [2589]
OmSpring [2296]
Thermal Analysis
North Amer. Thermal Anal. Soc. [1549]
Theta Nu Xi Multicultural Sorority [3564], c/o Rashida Rawls, Dir. of Communications, PO Box 32987, Phoenix, AZ 85064
Thistle Class Assn. [3284], c/o Patty Lawrence, Sec.-Treas., 6758 Little River Ln., Loveland, OH 45140, (513)583-5080
Thompson Collectors Assn. [3194], PO Box 1675, Ellicott City, MD 21041-1675
Thoroughbred Club of Am. [3348], PO Box 8098, Lexington, KY 40533-8098, (859)254-4282
Three Stooges Fan Club [3568], PO Box 747, Gwynedd Valley, PA 19437, (267)468-0810
Thunderbird and Cougar Club of Am. [3132], 422 Cooper St., Mountain Home, AR 72653
Tibet
Tibet Justice Center [2751]
Tibet Justice Center [2751], 440 Grand Ave., Ste. 425, Oakland, CA 94610, (510)486-0588
Tilt-Up Concrete Assn. [232], PO Box 204, Mount Vernon, IA 52314, (319)895-6911
Time
Intl. Soc. for the Stud. of Time [1860]
Timepieces
Independent Time and Labor Mgt. Assn. [861]
Intl. Watch Fob Assn. [3244]
Tire Indus. Assn. [862], 1532 Pointer Ridge Pl., Ste. G, Bowie, MD 20716-1883, (301)430-7280
Tire Retread and Repair Info. Bur. [863], 1013 Birch St., Falls Church, VA 22046, (703)533-7677
Tires
Tire Indus. Assn. [862]
Tire Retread and Repair Info. Bur. [863]
Titanic Historical Soc. [1808], PO Box 51053, Indian Orchard, MA 01151-0053, (413)543-4770
To Love a Child [1988], PO Box 165, Clifton Park, NY 12065, (518)859-4424
Toastmasters Intl. [1848], PO Box 9052, Mission Viejo, CA 92690-9052, (949)858-8255
Tobacco
Burley Stabilization Corp. [1221]

Together for Tanzania [2036], PO Box 395, Powhatan, VA 23139
Tooling and Mfg. Assn. [585], 1177 S Dee Rd., Park Ridge, IL 60068, (847)825-1120
TopTen USA [305], 1620 St. NW, Ste. 210, Washington, DC 20006
Torah Fund - a Campaign [★2967]
Tourism
Convention Indus. Coun. [864]
Natl. Coun. of State Tourism Directors [3503]
Tourist Railway Assn. [734], 1016 Rosser St., Conyers, GA 30012, (770)278-0088
Toxic Exposure
Beyond Pesticides [2252]
Toxicology
Soc. of Toxicology [1550]
Toy
Toy Train Collectors Soc. [3214]
Youth in Model Railroading [3215]
Toy Australian Shepherd Assn. of Am. [3185], 557 Forest Way Dr., Fort Mill, SC 29715, (803)548-7048
Toy Train Collectors Soc. [3214], c/o Louis A. Bohn, Membership Chm., 109 Howedale Dr., Rochester, NY 14616-1534, (585)663-4188
Toys
Toy Train Collectors Soc. [3214]
Youth in Model Railroading [3215]
Track and Field
Lifelong Fitness Alliance [3423]
Tractor Pulling
Professional Putters Assn. [3338]
Tractors
Gravely Tractor Club of Am. [3245]
Vintage Garden Tractor Club of Am. [3246]
Trade
Amer. Chamber of Commerce Executives [3504]
Fair Trade USA [865]
1-800 Amer. Free Trade Assn. [891]
Alliance for Amer. Mfg. [579]
Amer. Assn. of Professional Tech. Analysts [847]
Brazil-U.S. Bus. Coun. [3475]
Bridal Show Producers Intl. [123]
Efficiency First [1018]
Gift and Home Trade Assn. [784]
Global Sourcing Coun. [631]
Innovation Norway - U.S. [3482]
Intl. Air Filtration Certifiers Assn. [432]
Iraqi Amer. Chamber of Commerce and Indus. [3483]
Leadership for Energy Automated Processing [303]
Natl. Roof Certification and Inspection Assn. [155]
Reusable Packaging Assn. [764]
U.S. Indian Amer. Chamber of Commerce [3496]
U.S.-Ukraine Bus. Coun. [178]
Traditional Cowboy Arts Assn. [1705], c/o Don Bellamy, PO Box 2002, Salmon, ID 83467, (208)865-2006
Traditional Small Craft Assn. [3285], PO Box 350, Mystic, CT 06355, (425)361-7758
Traffic
Trans. Safety Equip. Inst. [782]
Trail Riders of Today [3353], c/o Margaret Scarff, Membership Comm., 4406 Carico Ln., White Hall, MD 21161, (301)622-4157
Trails
Adirondack Trail Improvement Soc. [3424]
Amer. Hiking Soc. [3425]
InterCollegiate Outing Club Assn. [3426]
IOCALUM [3427]
New England Trails Conf. [3428]
Trainers
Professional Baseball Athletic Trainers Soc. [3261]
Thoroughbred Club of Am. [3348]
Walking Horse Trainers Assn. [1151]
TransFair USA [★865]
Transition U.S. [1082], PO Box 917, Sebastopol, CA 95473, (707)763-1100
Translation
Amer. Literary Translators Assn. [1861]
Transport Workers Union of Am. [3467], 501 3rd St. NW, 9th Fl., Washington, DC 20001, (202)719-3900
Transportation
Amalgamated Transit Union [3466]

Amer. Bus Assn. [866]
Amer. Public Trans. Assn. [867]
Amer. Road and Trans. Builders Assn. [1381]
Chinese Overseas Trans. Assn. [868]
Conf. of Minority Trans. Officials [869]
Driver Employment Coun. of Am. [870]
Electrification Coalition [871]
Inst. of Trans. Engineers [1551]
Intelligent Trans. Soc. of Am. [872]
Intl. Trans. Mgt. Assn. [1382]
Light Elec. Vehicle Assn. [873]
Natl. Assn. of Publicly Funded Truck Driving Schools [874]
Natl. Assn. of Show Trucks [875]
Transport Workers Union of Am. [3467]
Trans. Clubs Intl. [876]
Trans. Lawyers Assn. [1383]
Trans. Res. Forum [1552]
Trucking Indus. Defense Assn. [877]
Trucking Mgt., Inc. [878]
Truckload Carriers Assn. [879]
Elevator U [145]
Equip. Managers Coun. of Am. [204]
Natl. Alliance of Highway Beautification Agencies [1370]
Plug In Am. [1396]
Trans. Communications Union I Brotherhood Railway Carmen Div. [3463]
Trans. Safety Equip. Inst. [782]
Trans. Assn. of Am; Community [2015]
Trans. Clubs Intl. [876], PO Box 2223, Ocean Shores, WA 98569, (877)858-8627
Trans. Communications Union I Brotherhood Railway Carmen Div. [3463], 3 Res. Pl., Rockville, MD 20850, (301)948-4910
Trans., Elevator and Grain Merchants Assn. [403], PO Box 26426, Kansas City, MO 64196, (816)569-4020
Trans. Lawyers Assn. [1383], PO Box 15122, Lenexa, KS 66285-5122, (913)895-4615
Trans. and Logistics Coun. [820], 120 Main St., Huntington, NY 11743, (631)549-8988
Trans. Res. Forum [1552], NDSU Dept. 2880, PO Box 6050, Fargo, ND 58108-6050, (701)231-7766
Trans. Safety Equip. Inst. [782], PO Box 13966, Research Triangle Park, NC 27709, (919)406-8823
Travel
Amer. Small Bus. Travelers Alliance [880]
Assn. of Corporate Travel Executives [881]
Assn. of Retail Travel Agents [882]
Cruise Lines Intl. Assn. [883]
Intl. Galapagos Tour Operators Assn. [3505]
Natl. Bus. Travel Assn. [884]
Pacific Asia Travel Assn. [885]
Soc. of Govt. Travel Professionals [886]
Student and Youth Travel Assn. [887]
The Travel Inst. [888]
Travel and Tourism Res. Assn. [889]
U.S. Travel Insurance Assn. [890]
Travel Goods Assn. [547], 301 N Harrison St., No. 412, Princeton, NJ 08540-3512, (877)TGA-1938
The Travel Inst. [888], 148 Linden St., Ste. 305, Wellesley, MA 02482, (781)237-0280
Travel Journalists Guild [709], PO Box 10643, Chicago, IL 60610-4952, (312)664-9279
Travel and Tourism Res. Assn. [889], 3048 W Clarkston Rd., Lake Orion, MI 48362, (248)708-8872
Trees
Intl. Wood Collectors Soc. [3249]
Trees and Shrubs
Amer. Soc. of Consulting Arborists [1222]
Intl. Wood Collectors Soc. [3249]
Trial Advocacy
Amer. Coll. of Trial Lawyers [1384]
Natl. Inst. for Trial Advocacy [1385]
Triangle Club [2249], PO Box 65458, Washington, DC 20035, (202)659-8641
Triangle Coalition for Sci. and Tech. Educ. [1684], 1840 Wilson Blvd., Ste. 201, Arlington, VA 22201, (703)516-5960
Triathlon
U.S.A. Triathlon [3429]
Triathlon; U.S.A. [3429]
Triumph Register of Am. [3133], 934 Coachway, Annapolis, MD 21401, (410)974-6707
Tropical Forest and Climate Coalition [1194], 1616 P St. NW, Ste. 403, Washington, DC 20036, (202)552-1828

Tropical Forest Gp. **[1043]**, 1125 Ft. Stockton Dr., San Diego, CA 92103

Tropical Studies
Org. for Tropical Stud., North Amer. Off. **[1553]**

Truck-Frame and Axle Repair Assn. **[99]**, c/o Ken Dias, 364 W 12th St., Erie, PA 16501, (877)735-1687

Truck Trailer Mfrs. Assn. **[93]**, 1020 Princess St., Alexandria, VA 22314-2247, (703)549-3010

Trucking Indus. Defense Assn. **[877]**, 6311 W Gross Point Rd., Niles, IL 60714, (847)647-7226

Trucking Mgt., Inc. **[878]**, PO Box 860725, Shawnee, KS 66286, (913)568-5873

Truckload Carriers Assn. **[879]**, 555 E Braddock Rd., Alexandria, VA 22314-2182, (703)838-1950

Trucks
Dodge Pilothouse Era Truck Club of Am. **[3247]**
North Amer. Truck Camper Owners Assn. **[3248]**
Vintage Garden Tractor Club of Am. **[3246]**

Tucker Auto. Club of Am. **[3134]**, 9509 Hinton Dr., Santee, CA 92071-2760

Tug of War
U.S. Amateur Tug of War Assn. **[3430]**

Turkey Vulture Soc. **[1256]**, 2327 Polksville Rd., Oakland, KY 42159

Turkish
Amer. Assn. of Teachers of Turkic Languages **[1694]**
Turkish Stud. Assn. **[1862]**
Amer. Turkish Friendship Coun. **[2678]**
Soc. of Turkish Amer. Architects, Engineers and Scientists **[1471]**

Turkish Stud. Assn. **[1862]**, Princeton Univ., 110 Jones Hall, Princeton, NJ 08544, (609)258-4280

Turnaround Mgt. Assn. **[570]**, 150 S Wacker Dr., Ste. 900, Chicago, IL 60606, (312)578-6900

Turtle Island Restoration Network **[1044]**, PO Box 370, Forest Knolls, CA 94933, (415)663-8590

Tuskegee Airmen, Inc. **[3047]**, PO Box 830060, Tuskegee, AL 36083, (334)421-0198

Tusubira - We Have Hope **[2173]**, PO Box 482, Mercer Island, WA 98040

Twenty-First Century Found. **[2160]**, 132 W 112th St., Lower Level, No. 1, New York, NY 10026, (212)662-3700

Two Hearts for Hope **[1989]**, PO Box 1928, Lebanon, MO 65536

Two/Ten Footwear Found. **[383]**, 1466 Main St., Waltham, MA 02451-1623, (781)736-1522

U

UHAI for Hea. **[2519]**, 37 Sophia Dr., Worcester, MA 01607

Ukrainian
Saint Andrew's Ukrainian Orthodox Soc. **[2752]**
Ukrainian Acad. of Arts and Sciences in the U.S. **[1863]**
Ukrainian Inst. of Am. **[1864]**
Ukrainian Natl. Assn. **[2829]**
U.S. Ukraine Found. **[2753]**
The Washington Gp. **[2830]**
U.S.-Ukraine Bus. Coun. **[178]**

Ukrainian Acad. of Arts and Sciences in the U.S. **[1863]**, 206 W 100 St., New York, NY 10021-1018, (212)222-1866

Ukrainian Inst. of Am. **[1864]**, 2 E 79th St., New York, NY 10021, (212)288-8660

Ukrainian Natl. Assn. **[2829]**, 2200 Rte. 10 W, Parsippany, NJ 07054, (973)292-9800

Ukrainian Res. and Documentation Center **[★1864]**

Ultra Marathon Cycling Assn. **[3312]**, PO Box 18028, Boulder, CO 80308-1028, (303)545-9566

Unclaimed Property Professionals Org. **[1359]**, 110 Wall St., 11th Fl., No. 0080, New York, NY 10005-3111, (508)883-9065

Under The Baobab Tree **[1593]**, 1725 E Bayshore Rd., Ste. 103, Redwood City, CA 94063

Underground Utility and Leak Locators Assn. **[898]**, US Sewer and Drain, 210 Field End St., Sarasota, FL 34240, (800)977-5325

Underwater Sports
Professional Assn. of Diving Instructors **[3431]**

Underwriters
Gp. Underwriters Assn. of Am. **[486]**

Unico Natl. **[2797]**, 271 U.S. Hwy. 46 W, Ste. A-108, Fairfield, NJ 07004, (973)808-0035

Unicycling Soc. of Am. **[3313]**, PO Box 21487, Minneapolis, MN 55421-0487

Unified for Global Healing **[2520]**, 487 Myrtle Ave., Unit B-7, Brooklyn, NY 11205

Union MicroFinanza **[2213]**, 1485 Getty St., Muskegon, MI 49442

Union of North Amer. Vietnamese Students Assn. **[2832]**, PO Box 433, Westminster, CA 92684

Union of Poles in Am. **[2818]**, 9999 Granger Rd., Garfield Heights, OH 44125, (216)478-0120

Union Settlement Assn. **[2174]**, 237 E 104th St., New York, NY 10029, (212)828-6000

Union for Traditional Judaism **[2965]**, 668 Amer. Legion Dr., Ste. B, Teaneck, NJ 07666, (201)801-0707

Unions
Coalition of Labor Union Women **[3468]**
Coalition of Labor Union Women Center for Educ. and Res. **[3469]**
Trans. Communications Union I Brotherhood Railway Carmen Div. **[3463]**

UniPro Foodservice **[372]**, 2500 Cumberland Pkwy., Ste. 600, Atlanta, GA 30339, (770)952-0871

Unitarian Universalist
Unitarian Universalist Historical Soc. **[3036]**
Unitarian Universalist Ministers Assn. **[3037]**

Unitarian Universalist Historical Soc. **[3036]**, 27 Grove St., Scituate, MA 02066

Unitarian Universalist Ministers Assn. **[3037]**, 25 Beacon St., Boston, MA 02108, (617)848-0498

United Against Nuclear Iran **[2711]**, PO Box 1028, New York, NY 10008-1021, (212)554-3296

United Agribusiness League **[928]**, 54 Corporate Park, Irvine, CA 92606-5105, (949)975-1424

United Assn. of Mobile Contract Cleaners **[556]**, 314 Marlow Ct., Chesapeake, VA 23322, (800)816-3240

United Bd. for Christian Higher Educ. in Asia **[1645]**, 475 Riverside Dr., Ste. 1221, New York, NY 10115, (212)870-2600

United Braford Breeders **[992]**, 422 E Main, No. 218, Nacogdoches, TX 75961, (936)569-8200

United Burundian-American Community Assn. **[2680]**, 14339 Rosetree Ct., Silver Spring, MD 20906, (240)669-6305

United Church of Christ Coalition for Lesbian, Gay, Bisexual and Transgender Concerns **[2940]**, 2592 W 14th St., Cleveland, OH 44113, (216)861-0799

United Four-Wheel Drive Associations **[3135]**, PO Box 316, Swartz Creek, MI 48473, (800)448-3932

United Indian Missions Intl. **[3014]**, PO Box 336010, Greeley, CO 80633-0601, (970)785-1176

United Indians of All Tribes Found. **[2707]**, Discovery Park, PO Box 99100, Seattle, WA 98199, (206)285-4425

United Lightning Protection Assn. **[783]**, 426 North Ave., Libertyville, IL 60048, (800)668-8572

United Methodist Assn. of Hea. and Welfare Ministries **[2427]**, 407-B Corporate Center Dr., Ste. B, Vandalia, OH 45377, (937)415-3624

United Nations Correspondents Assn. **[710]**, United Nations, 405 E 42nd St., Rm. L-213, New York, NY 10017, (212)963-7137

United Negro Coll. Fund **[1624]**, 8260 Willow Oaks Corporate Dr., PO Box 10444, Fairfax, VA 22031-8044, (703)205-3400

United Order True Sisters **[2835]**, Linton Intl. Plaza, 660 Linton Blvd., Ste. 6, Delray Beach, FL 33444, (561)265-1557

United Soybean Bd. **[1102]**, 16305 Swingley Ridge Rd., Ste. 150, Chesterfield, MO 63017, (636)530-1777

United States
Building Bridges: Middle East-US **[1642]**
Close Up Found. **[2622]**
Sino-American Bridge for Educ. and Hea. **[1784]**

U.S. Aikido Fed. **[3251]**, New York Aikikai, 142 W 18th St., New York, NY 10011, (212)242-6246

U.S. Albacore Assn. **[3286]**, 1031 Graham St., Bethlehem, PA 18015-2520

U.S. Amateur Tug of War Assn. **[3430]**, c/o Amy Breuscher, Sec., PO Box 68, Hollandale, WI 53544, (800)TUGOWAR

U.S.A. Coton de Tulear Club **[3186]**, c/o J.J. Walker, Sec., PO Box 3792, Pikeville, KY 41502, (606)639-0364

U.S.-Angola Chamber of Commerce **[3488]**, 1100 17th St. NW, Ste. 1000, Washington, DC 20036, (202)857-0789

U.S. Animal Hea. Assn. **[2599]**, 4221 Mitchell Ave., St. Joseph, MO 64507, (816)671-1144

U.S. Apple Assn. **[1103]**, 8233 Old Courthouse Rd., Ste. 200, Vienna, VA 22182, (703)442-8850

U.S. Aquatic Sports **[3417]**, c/o Debra Turner, Coor., 325 Rolling Trails Rd., Greenwood, IN 46142, (317)223-0702

U.S. Assn. of Importers of Textiles and Apparel **[860]**, 1140 Connecticut Ave., Ste. 950, Washington, DC 20036, (202)419-0444

U.S.-Bahrain Bus. Coun. **[520]**, 1615 H St. NW, Washington, DC 20062, (202)463-5628

U.S. Beet Sugar Assn. **[373]**, 1156 15th St. NW, Ste. 1019, Washington, DC 20005, (202)296-4820

U.S. Billiard Assn. **[3268]**, c/o Jim Shovak, Sec.-Treas., 58 Hawthorne Ave., East Islip, NY 11730, (516)238-6193

U.S. Bobsled and Skeleton Fed. **[3390]**, 196 Old Military Rd., Lake Placid, NY 12946, (518)523-1842

U.S. Bridge Fed. **[3143]**, 2990 Airways Blvd., Memphis, TN 38116-3828

U.S. Canoe Assn. **[3433]**, c/o Paula Thiel, Membership Chair, 487 Wylie School Rd., Voluntown, CT 06384, (860)564-2443

U.S.-China Peoples Friendship Assn. **[2620]**, 402 E 43rd St., Indianapolis, IN 46205, (317)283-7735

U.S. Collegiate Athletic Assn. **[3409]**, 4101 Washington Ave., Bldg. 601, Newport News, VA 23607, (757)706-3756

U.S. Complete Shooting Dog Assn. **[3187]**, 3329 Redlawn Rd., Boydton, VA 23917, (434)738-9757

U.S. Conf. of Catholic Bishops **[2883]**, 3211 4th St. NE, Washington, DC 20017-1104, (202)541-3000

U.S. Conf. of Catholic Bishops I Secretariat for Hispanic Affairs **[2097]**, 3211 4th St. NE, Washington, DC 20017, (202)541-3150

U.S. Coun. for Intl. Bus. **[176]**, 1212 Avenue of the Americas, New York, NY 10036, (212)354-4480

U.S. Court Reporters Assn. **[1285]**, 8430 Gross Point Rd., Ste. 115, Skokie, IL 60077, (847)470-9500

U.S. Croquet Assn. **[3309]**, 700 Florida Mango Rd., West Palm Beach, FL 33406-4461, (561)478-0760

U.S. Deaf Ski and Snowboard Assn. **[3318]**, PO Box 4, Cambridge, VT 05444

U.S. Fencing Assn. **[3325]**, 1 Olympic Plz., Colorado Springs, CO 80909-5780, (719)866-4511

U.S. Flag Football League **[3333]**, 763 Ridge Rd., Angier, NC 27501, (919)894-7976

U.S. Handball Assn. **[3341]**, 2333 N Tucson Blvd., Tucson, AZ 85716, (520)795-0434

U.S. Hang Gliding and Paragliding Assn. **[3250]**, PO Box 1330, Colorado Springs, CO 80901-1330, (719)632-8300

U.S. Hispanic Chamber of Commerce **[3495]**, 1424 K St. NW, Ste. 401, Washington, DC 20005, (202)842-1212

U.S. Indian Amer. Chamber of Commerce **[3496]**, 6030 Daybreak Cir., Ste. A150/164, Clarksville, MD 21029, (240)393-2945

United States-Indonesia Soc. **[177]**, 1625 Massachusetts Ave. NW, Ste. 550, Washington, DC 20036-2260, (202)232-1400

U.S. J/24 Class Assn. **[3287]**, 900 Old Koenig Ln., Ste. 114, Austin, TX 78756, (512)266-0033

U.S.-Japan Bus. Coun. **[3499]**, 2101 L St. NW, Ste. 1000, Washington, DC 20037, (202)728-0068

U.S.-Japan Coun. **[2681]**, 1225 Nineteenth St. NW, Ste. 700, Washington, DC 20036, (202)223-6840

U.S. Junior Chamber of Commerce **[3506]**, 7447 S Lewis Ave., Tulsa, OK 74136-6808, (918)584-2481

U.S. Lawn Bowls Assn. **[3295]**, 10639 Lindamere Dr., Los Angeles, CA 90077, (310)440-9400

U.S. Luge Assn. **[3358]**, 57 Church St., Lake Placid, NY 12946, (518)523-2071

U.S. Mariner Class Assn. **[3288]**, PO Box 273, Ship Bottom, NJ 08008

U.S. Natl. Tennis Acad. **[3422]**, 3523 McKinney Ave., No. 208, Dallas, TX 75204, (800)452-8519

A star before a book entry number signifies that the name is not listed separately, but is mentioned within the entry.

U.S. New Zealand Coun. **[521]**, DACOR Bacon House, 1801 F St. NW, Washington, DC 20006, (202)842-0772

U.S. Offshore Wind Collaborative **[1556]**, 1 Broadway, 14th Fl., Cambridge, MA 02142, (617)401-3145

U.S. Olympic Comm. **[3368]**, 27 S Tejon, Colorado Springs, CO 80903, (719)866-4529

U.S. Optimist Dinghy Assn. **[3289]**, PO Box 311, North Kingstown, RI 02852, (609)510-0798

U.S. Orienteering Fed. **[3371]**, PO Box 505, Riderwood, MD 21139, (410)802-1125

U.S. Personal Chef Assn. **[181]**, 5728 Major Blvd., Ste. 750, Orlando, FL 32819, (505)994-6372

U.S. Pilots Assn. **[38]**, 1652 Indian Point Rd., Branson, MO 65616, (417)338-2225

U.S. Police Canine Assn. **[1338]**, PO Box 80, Springboro, OH 45066-0080, (937)751-6469

U.S. Power Squadrons **[3290]**, 1504 Blue Ridge Rd., Raleigh, NC 27607, (888)367-8777

U.S. Qatar Bus. Coun. **[3489]**, 1341 Connecticut Ave. NW, Ste. 4A, Washington, DC 20036, (202)457-8555

U.S. Revolver Assn. **[3385]**, RR 1 Box 548, Scotrun, PA 18355

U.S. Rugby Football Union **[3378]**, 2500 Arapahoe Ave., Ste. 200, Boulder, CO 80302, (303)539-0300

U.S. Sailing Assn. I Coun. of Sailing Associations **[3291]**, 15 Maritime Dr., PO Box 1260, Portsmouth, RI 02871-0907, (401)683-0800

U.S. Snowshoe Assn. **[3391]**, 678 County Rte. 25, Corinth, NY 12822, (518)654-7648

U.S. Sommelier Assn. **[43]**, 1111 Lincoln Rd., Ste. 400-9, Miami Beach, FL 33139, (954)437-0449

U.S. Speedskating **[3387]**, PO Box 18370, Kearns, UT 84118, (801)417-5360

U.S. Sports Acad. **[3410]**, One Acad. Dr., Daphne, AL 36526-7055, (251)626-3303

U.S. Swim School Assn. **[3418]**, PO Box 17208, Fountain Hills, AZ 85269, (480)837-5525

U.S. Synchronized Swimming **[3419]**, 132 E Washington St., Ste. 820, Indianapolis, IN 46204, (317)237-5700

U.S. Team Penning Assn. **[3349]**, 3609 Acton Hwy., Ste. 21, Granbury, TX 76049, (817)326-4444

U.S. Travel Insurance Assn. **[890]**, 1333 H St. NW, Ste. 820, Washington, DC 20005, (800)224-6164

U.S. Twirling Assn. **[3267]**, 1608 Wortell Dr., Lincoln, CA 95648, (916)343-0062

U.S.-Ukraine Bus. Coun. **[178]**, 1300 I St. NW, Ste. 720 W, Washington, DC 20005, (202)429-0551

U.S. Ukraine Found. **[2753]**, 1 Thomas Cir. NW, Ste. 900-B, Washington, DC 20005, (202)223-2228

U.S.-Vietnam Trade Coun. **[2616]**, 1025 Vermont Ave. NW, Ste. 300, Washington, DC 20005, (202)580-6950

U.S. Water Polo **[3432]**, 2124 Maine St., Ste. 240, Huntington Beach, CA 92648, (714)500-5445

U.S. Water and Power **[1399]**, 1179 Nelrose Ave., Venice, CA 90291

U.S. Wheat Associates **[999]**, 3103 10th St. N, Ste. 300, Arlington, VA 22201, (202)463-0999

U.S. Women's Curling Assn. **[3310]**, Cleveland Skating Club, Shaker Heights, OH 44120

United Suffolk Sheep Assn. **[1213]**, PO Box 995, Ottumwa, IA 52501-0995, (641)684-5291

United Way of Am. **[2091]**, 701 N Fairfax St., Alexandria, VA 22314, (703)683-7800

Universal Design Alliance **[254]**, 3651-E Peachtree Pkwy., Ste. 311, Suwanee, GA 30024, (813)368-7420

Universal Martial Arts Brotherhood **[3362]**, 2427 Buckingham Rd., Ann Arbor, MI 48104, (734)971-7040

Universities Allied for Essential Medicines **[1641]**, 2625 Alcatraz Ave., No. 180, Berkeley, CA 94705, (510)868-1159

Universities Res. Assn. **[1525]**, 1111 19th St. NW, Ste. 400, Washington, DC 20036, (202)293-1382

Univ. Film and Video Assn. **[1623]**, 3800 Barham Blvd., Ste. 103, Los Angeles, CA 90068, (866)647-8382

Univ. of Texas at Brownsville and Texas Southmost Coll. Alumni Assn. **[2763]**, 80 Ft. Brown, Brownsville, TX 78520-4956, (956)882-4327

Univ. of Texas I Pan-American Alumni Assn. **[2764]**, 1201 W Univ. Dr., UC108, Edinburg, TX 78541, (956)381-2500

Univ. of Wisconsin I Eau Claire Alumni Assn. **[2765]**, PO Box 4004, Eau Claire, WI 54702-4004, (715)836-3266

Upenyu **[2521]**, 1 Mary Ct., Cranbury, NJ 08512, (317)460-6792

Uplift Intl. **[2522]**, PO Box 27696, Seattle, WA 98165, (206)455-0916

Upsilon Pi Epsilon Assn. **[3513]**, 158 Wetlands Edge Rd., American Canyon, CA 94503, (530)518-8488

Upwardly Global **[712]**, San Francisco Off., 582 Market St., Ste. 1207, San Francisco, CA 94104, (415)834-9901

US-China Green Energy Coun. **[1464]**, 1964 Deodara Dr., Los Altos, CA 94024-7054

US-Ireland Alliance **[179]**, 2800 Clarendon Blvd., Ste. 502 W, Arlington, VA 22201, (202)643-8742

U.S.A. Baseball **[3263]**, 403 Blackwell St., Durham, NC 27701, (919)474-8721

U.S.A. Boxing **[3299]**, 30 Cimino Dr., Colorado Springs, CO 80903, (719)866-2300

U.S.A. Defenders of Greyhounds **[1901]**, PO Box 1256, Carmel, IN 46082, (317)244-0113

USA Diving **[3321]**, 132 E Washington St., Ste. 850, Indianapolis, IN 46204, (317)237-5252

U.S.A. Rice Coun. **[1000]**, 4301 N Fairfax Dr., Ste. 425, Arlington, VA 22203, (703)236-2300

U.S.A Team Handball **[3254]**, 2330 W California Ave., Salt Lake City, UT 84104, (801)463-2000

U.S.A. Triathlon **[3429]**, 5825 Delmonico Dr., Colorado Springs, CO 80919, (719)597-9090

Used Truck Assn. **[100]**, 325 Country Club Dr., Ste. A, Stockbridge, GA 30281, (877)438-7882

USO World HQ **[2769]**, PO Box 96322, Washington, DC 20090, (703)908-6400

Utilimetrics - The Utility Tech. Assn. **[899]**, 1400 E Touhy Ave., Ste. 258, Des Plaines, IL 60018-3345, (847)480-9628

Utilities

1-800 Amer. Free Trade Assn. **[891]**

Assn. of Edison Illuminating Companies **[892]**

Edison Elec. Inst. **[893]**

Elec. Utility Indus. Sustainable Supply Chain Alliance **[894]**

NASSCO **[895]**

Natl. Telecommunications Cooperative Assn. **[896]**

Natl. Utility Training and Safety Educ. Assn. **[897]**

Regulatory Assistance Proj. **[1386]**

Underground Utility and Leak Locators Assn. **[898]**

Utilimetrics - The Utility Tech. Assn. **[899]**

Equip. Managers Coun. of Am. **[204]**

GridWise Architecture Coun. **[1520]**

Large Public Power Coun. **[1292]**

Uttaranchal Assn. of North Am. **[1781]**, 10560 Main St., Ste. LL-1, Fairfax, VA 22030, (703)273-7982

V

Vacation Rental Housekeeping Professionals **[258]**, 5380 Gulf of Mexico Dr., Ste. 105, Longboat Key, FL 34228, (850)303-1358

Vacation Rental Managers Assn. **[758]**, 9100 Purdue Rd., Ste. 200, Indianapolis, IN 46268, (317)454-8315

Vacuum Technology

AVS Sci. and Tech. Soc. **[1554]**

Valley Intl. Foosball Assn. **[3199]**, PO Box 656, Bay City, MI 48707, (800)544-1346

Valve Repair Coun. **[416]**, 1050 17th St. NW, Ste. 280, Washington, DC 20036, (202)331-8105

Variable Electronic Components Inst. **[290]**, PO Box 1070, Vista, CA 92085-1070, (760)631-0178

Vending

Intl. Assn. of Ice Cream Distributors and Vendors **[900]**

Randolph-Sheppard Vendors of Am. **[901]**

Venezuelan-American Chamber of Commerce **[3490]**, 1600 Ponce de Leon, Ste. 1004, Coral Gables, FL 33134, (786)350-1190

Veteran Motor Car Club of Am. **[3136]**, c/o Mike Welsh, Sec., 7501 Manchester Ave., Kansas City, MO 64138, (816)298-6412

Veterans

Amer. GI Forum of U.S. **[3079]**

Catholic War Veterans of the U.S.A. **[3080]**

Natl. Assn. of Atomic Veterans **[2253]**

Natl. Assn. of State Veterans Homes **[2254]**

Natl. Assn. of Veterans Prog. Administrators **[3081]**

Homosexual Info. Center **[2095]**

Military Order of the Stars and Bars **[3056]**

Salute Military Golf Assn. **[3339]**

Veterans of the Civil War; Auxiliary to Sons of Union **[3054]**

Veterans of Foreign Wars

Salute Military Golf Assn. **[3339]**

Veterans for Peace **[2721]**, 216 S Meramec Ave., St. Louis, MO 63105, (314)725-6005

Veterans of Safety **[2218]**, Univ. of Central Missouri, Humphreys 304, Warrensburg, MO 64093, (660)543-4971

Veterinary Medicine

Assn. of Amer. Veterinary Medical Colleges **[1695]**

U.S. Animal Hea. Assn. **[2599]**

Amer. Assn. of Traditional Chinese Veterinary Medicine **[2290]**

Darwin Animal Doctors **[950]**

World Vets **[1902]**

Victims

Natl. Assn. of Crime Victim Compensation Boards **[2255]**

Victims of Crime and Leniency **[2256]**

Victims of Crime and Leniency **[2256]**, PO Box 4449, Montgomery, AL 36103, (334)262-7197

Victorian

Res. Soc. for Victorian Periodicals **[1865]**

Vietnam

Glocal Ventures **[2119]**

Hannah's Promise Intl. Aid **[2187]**

Vietnam Relief Effort **[2201]**, 845 United Nations Plz., 90A, New York, NY 10017, (917)668-2600

Vietnamese

Natl. Cong. of Vietnamese Americans **[2831]**

Union of North Amer. Vietnamese Students Assn. **[2832]**

Vietnamese-American Nurses Assn. **[2566]**, PO Box 691994, Houston, TX 77269-1994

Village Focus Intl. **[2037]**, 14 Wall St., 20th Fl., New York, NY 10005, (917)621-7167

Vintage BMW Motorcycle Owners **[3220]**, c/o Roland Slabon, PO Box 599, Troy, OH 45373-0599, (770)235-5281

Vintage Chevrolet Club of Am. **[3137]**, c/o Mike McGowan, Membership Sec., PO Box 609, Lemont, IL 60439-0609, (708)455-8222

Vintage Garden Tractor Club of Am. **[3246]**, 412 W Chestnut, Pardeeville, WI 53954, (608)429-4520

Violence

Natl. Coalition Against Violent Athletes **[3252]**

Virgin Islands Olympic Comm. **[3369]**, PO Box 366, Frederiksted, VI 00841, (340)719-8462

Vision Coun. of Am. **[426]**, 225 Reinekers Ln., Ste. 700, Alexandria, VA 22314, (703)548-4560

Vision Intl; Coun. of Citizens With Low **[2056]**

Visionary Alternatives **[2300]**, 7725 Kenway Pl. E, Boca Raton, FL 33433, (561)750-4551

Visually Impaired

Assn. for Educ. and Rehabilitation of the Blind and Visually Impaired **[2600]**

Global Vision 2020 **[2601]**

Guiding Eyes for the Blind **[2602]**

Lutheran Braille Evangelism Assn. **[2603]**

Lutheran Braille Workers **[2604]**

Natl. Indus. for the Blind **[2605]**

Vocational Education

Assn. of Private Sector Colleges and Universities **[1696]**

Natl. Assn. of State Directors of Career Tech. Educ. Consortium **[1697]**

Voices Breaking Boundaries **[1835]**, PO Box 541247, Houston, TX 77254-1247, (713)524-7821

Voluntarism

AmeriCorps VISTA **[2257]**

Assn. for Healthcare Volunteer Rsrc. Professionals **[2258]**

Senior Corps **[2259]**

HavServe Volunteer Ser. Network **[1906]**

Volunteer Missionary Movement - U.S. Off. **[2884]**, 5980 W Loomis Rd., Greendale, WI 53129-1824, (414)423-8660

Volunteers for Peace **[2686]**, 7 Kilburn St., Ste. 316, Burlington, VT 05401, (802)540-3060

Von Braun Astronomical Soc. **[1413]**, PO Box 1142, Huntsville, AL 35807

Vote Hemp **[2746]**, PO Box 1571, Brattleboro, VT 05302, (202)318-8999

Voters for Peace **[2722]**, 2842 N Calvert St., Baltimore, MD 21218, (443)708-8360

VSA arts **[★2064]**

VSA - The Intl. Org. on Arts and Disability **[2064]**, 818 Connecticut Ave. NW, Ste. 600, Washington, DC 20006, (202)628-2800

W

W. E. Upjohn Inst. for Employment Res. **[2080]**, 300 S Westnedge Ave., Kalamazoo, MI 49007-4686, (269)343-5541

Waldensian
Amer. Waldensian Soc. **[3038]**

Walking Horse Trainers Assn. **[1151]**, 1101 N Main St., PO Box 61, Shelbyville, TN 37162, (931)684-5866

Wallcoverings Assn. **[514]**, 401 N Michigan Ave., Ste. 2200, Chicago, IL 60611, (312)321-5166

War Resistance
Center on Conscience and War **[2641]**
Voters for Peace **[2722]**

Warehousing
Intl. Liquid Terminals Assn. **[902]**
Order Fulfillment Coun. Material Handling Indus. of Am. **[903]**
Self Storage Assn. **[904]**

Washington Capitals Fan Club **[3595]**, PO Box 2802, Springfield, VA 22152-0802

The Washington Gp. **[2830]**, PO Box 11248, Washington, DC 20008, (202)586-7227

Washington Off. on Latin Am. **[2696]**, 1666 Connecticut Ave. NW, Ste. 400, Washington, DC 20009, (202)797-2171

Waste
Assn. of Professional Animal Waste Specialists **[905]**
Basel Action Network **[2754]**
CHWMEG **[906]**
Environmental Indus. Associations **[907]**
Natl. Onsite Wastewater Recycling Assn. **[1223]**
Paper Stock Indus. Chap. of ISRI **[908]**
Steel Recycling Inst. **[909]**
Clean the World **[1197]**
Equip. Managers Coun. of Am. **[204]**
Freecycle Network **[1198]**

Water
Alliance for Water Efficiency **[1224]**
Amman Imman: Water is Life **[2260]**
Clean Water for the World **[2261]**
A Cup of Water Intl. **[3039]**
Drinking Water for India **[2262]**
Gift of Water **[2263]**
Healing Waters Intl. **[2264]**
In Our Own Quiet Way **[2265]**
Intl. Action **[2266]**
Natl. Utility Contractors Assn. I Clean Water Coun. **[1225]**
Primero Agua **[2267]**
Water Alliance for Africa **[2268]**
Water for Sudan **[2269]**
Water Systems Coun. **[910]**
Alliance for Water Educ. **[1620]**
Irrigation Water Mgt. Soc. **[1226]**
Solar for Peace **[1537]**
U.S. Water and Power **[1399]**

Water Alliance for Africa **[2268]**, 3267 E 3300 S, No. 535, Salt Lake City, UT 84109

Water Conservation
Alliance for Water Educ. **[1620]**
Environmental Commons **[1019]**
Irrigation Water Mgt. Soc. **[1226]**

Water Env. Fed. **[1184]**, 601 Wythe St., Alexandria, VA 22314-1994, (703)684-2400

Water Polo
U.S. Water Polo **[3432]**

Water Resources
Amer. Inst. of Hydrology **[1555]**
Irrigation Water Mgt. Soc. **[1226]**
Puerto Rico Water and Env. Assn. **[1227]**
Save the Waves Coalition **[1228]**
Alliance for Water Educ. **[1620]**
Alliance for Water Efficiency **[1224]**

Amman Imman: Water is Life **[2260]**
Clean Water for the World **[2261]**
A Cup of Water Intl. **[3039]**
Drinking Water for India **[2262]**
In Our Own Quiet Way **[2265]**
Intl. Action **[2266]**
Primero Agua **[2267]**
Water Alliance for Africa **[2268]**
Water for Sudan **[2269]**

Water Sports
U.S. Canoe Assn. **[3433]**
Highlander Class Intl. Assn. **[3273]**
U.S. Albacore Assn. **[3286]**
U.S. Power Squadrons **[3290]**
USA Diving **[3321]**

Water for Sudan **[2269]**, PO Box 25551, Rochester, NY 14625, (585)383-0410

Water Systems Coun. **[910]**, 1101 30th St. NW, Ste. 500, Washington, DC 20007, (202)625-4387

The Waterfront Center **[2038]**, PO Box 53351, Washington, DC 20009, (202)337-0356

Waves of Hea. **[2523]**, 206 Bergen Ave., Ste. 203, Kearny, NJ 07032, (201)436-8888

Weather
Weather Risk Mgt. Assn. **[911]**
Rising Tide North Am. **[1038]**
Tropical Forest and Climate Coalition **[1194]**

Weather Risk Mgt. Assn. **[911]**, 529 14th St. NW, Ste. 750, Washington, DC 20045, (202)289-3800

Weatherby Collectors Assn. **[3195]**, PO Box 1217, Washington, MO 63090, (636)239-0348

WEC Intl. **[2935]**, PO Box 1707, Fort Washington, PA 19034, (215)646-2322

WECAI Network **[262]**, PO Box 550856, Fort Lauderdale, FL 33355-0856, (954)625-6606

Wedding Indus. Professionals Assn. **[124]**, 8912 E Pinnacle Peak Rd., Ste. F9-111, Scottsdale, AZ 85255, (480)626-1657

Weighing
Intl. Soc. of Weighing and Measurement **[912]**

Weightlifting
Intl. Natural Bodybuilding and Fitness Fed. **[3293]**

Well Done Org. **[2039]**, 10813 27th St. SE, Lake Stevens, WA 98258, (206)349-1574

Welsh
Welsh Natl. Gymanfa Ganu Assn. **[2833]**

Welsh Natl. Gymanfa Ganu Assn. **[2833]**, PO Box 410, Granville, OH 43023, (740)587-3936

West Gulf Maritime Assn. **[590]**, 1717 E Loop, Portway Plz., Ste. 200, Houston, TX 77029, (713)678-7655

West Indian
Montserrat Progressive Soc. of New York **[2834]**

Western Assn. of Fish and Wildlife Agencies **[1300]**, 522 Notre Dame Ct., Cheyenne, WY 82009, (307)638-1470

Western Athletic Conf. **[3411]**, 9250 E Costilla Ave., Ste. 300, Englewood, CO 80112, (303)799-9221

Western Collegiate Hockey Assn. **[3343]**, 2211 S Josephine St., Denver, CO 80208, (303)871-4223

Western Rugby Union of the United States **[★3378]**

Western Saddle Clubs Assn. **[1152]**, c/o Teri Spence, Sec., 47009 Company Rd. 13, St. Peter, MN 56082, (507)345-5856

Western Soc. of Naturalists **[1504]**, San Diego State Univ., Dept. of Biology, 5500 Campanile Dr., San Diego, CA 92182

Western States Petroleum Assn. **[651]**, 1415 L St., Ste. 600, Sacramento, CA 95814, (916)498-7750

Wheelchair and Ambulatory Sports, USA **[3319]**, c/o Ralph Armento, Operations Mgr., PO Box 5266, Kendall Park, NJ 08824-5266, (732)266-2634

Wheelchair Sports U.S.A. **[★3319]**

The Wheelmen **[3314]**, 1552 Autumn Ridge Cir., Reston, VA 20194-1563

Wheels for the World **[2065]**, Joni and Friends Intl. Disability Center, PO Box 3333, Agoura Hills, CA 91376-3333, (818)707-5664

White House News Photographers Assn. **[669]**, 7119 Ben Franklin Sta., Washington, DC 20044-7119, (202)785-5230

Widowhood
Global Action on Widowhood **[2755]**

Wild Animals Worldwide **[1257]**, 1100 Larkspur Landing Cir., Ste. 340, Larkspur, CA 94939, (866)439-0989

Wild Canid Survival and Res. Center **[★1237]**

Wild Felid Res. and Mgt. Assn. **[1258]**, PO Box 3335, Montrose, CO 81402, (970)252-1928

Wild Gift **[1259]**, PO Box 3064, Sun Valley, ID 83353, (208)726-7475

Wildcat Ser. Corp. **[2081]**, 2 Washington St., 3rd Fl., New York, NY 10004, (212)209-6000

Wilderness Intl. **[1045]**, PO Box 491, Canby, OR 97013, (503)593-0199

The Wilderness Soc. **[1046]**, 1615 M St. NW, Washington, DC 20036, (202)833-2300

Wildlife
Amara Conservation **[1230]**
Animal World USA **[949]**
Ape Conservation Effort **[1232]**
Big Wildlife **[1233]**
BlueVoice.org **[1010]**
Born Free USA **[1894]**
Darwin Animal Doctors **[950]**
Forest Bird Soc. **[1022]**
Friends of the Osa **[1025]**
Global Wildlife Conservation **[1238]**
Hummingbird Monitoring Network **[963]**
Iemanya Oceanica **[1240]**
Shark Alliance **[1254]**
Wild Animals Worldwide **[1257]**
Wild Felid Res. and Mgt. Assn. **[1258]**
Wild Gift **[1259]**
Wilderness Intl. **[1045]**
Wonderful World of Wildlife **[1260]**
World Nature Coalition **[1262]**

Wildlife Conservation
African Wild Dog Conservancy **[1229]**
Amara Conservation **[1230]**
Ape Action Africa **[1231]**
Ape Conservation Effort **[1232]**
Big Wildlife **[1233]**
The Billfish Found. **[1234]**
Desert Tortoise Coun. **[1235]**
EcoHealth Alliance **[1236]**
Endangered Wolf Center **[1237]**
Global Wildlife Conservation **[1238]**
Human-Wildlife Conflict Collaboration **[1239]**
Iemanya Oceanica **[1240]**
Intl. Assn. for Bear Res. and Mgt. **[1241]**
Intl. Bird Rescue Res. Center **[1242]**
Intl. Snow Leopard Trust **[1243]**
Jane Goodall Inst. for Wildlife Res., Educ., and Conservation **[1244]**
Keystone Conservation **[1245]**
Natl. Wild Turkey Fed. **[1246]**
Natl. Wildlife Rehabilitators Assn. **[1247]**
Orangutan Conservancy **[1248]**
Org. for Bat Conservation **[1249]**
Pacific Seabird Gp. **[1250]**
Panthera **[1251]**
Quail Unlimited **[1252]**
Sea Turtle Conservancy **[1253]**
Shark Alliance **[1254]**
Species Alliance **[1255]**
Turkey Vulture Soc. **[1256]**
Wild Animals Worldwide **[1257]**
Wild Felid Res. and Mgt. Assn. **[1258]**
Wild Gift **[1259]**
Wonderful World of Wildlife **[1260]**
World Bird Sanctuary **[1261]**
World Nature Coalition **[1262]**
Alliance for Tompotika Conservation **[1003]**
Animal World USA **[949]**
BlueVoice.org **[1010]**
Born Free USA **[1894]**
Darwin Animal Doctors **[950]**
Env. for the Americas **[962]**
Environmental Commons **[1019]**
Forest Bird Soc. **[1022]**
Human-Wildlife Conflict Collaboration **[1239]**
Hummingbird Monitoring Network **[963]**
Kids Ecology Corps **[1076]**
Paso Pacifico **[1036]**
Wilderness Intl. **[1045]**

Wildlife Mgt. Inst. **[1047]**, c/o Richard E. McCabe, VP, 1424 NW Carlson Rd., Topeka, KS 66614, (410)562-5341

Wildlife Trust **[★1236]**

William James Soc. **[1867]**, c/o Todd Lekan, Sec.-Treas., Muskingum Univ., 163 Stormont St., New Concord, OH 43762

A star before a book entry number signifies that the name is not listed separately, but is mentioned within the entry.

The Wind Alliance **[1557]**, 1100 Louisiana St., Ste. 5005, Houston, TX 77002, (713)600-9994
Wind Energy
   U.S. Offshore Wind Collaborative **[1556]**
   The Wind Alliance **[1557]**
   Wind Energy Mfrs. Assn. **[913]**
Wind Energy Mfrs. Assn. **[913]**, 345 S High St., Muncie, IN 47305, (317)733-9797
Windmill Class Assn. **[3292]**, 1571 Quarrier St., Charleston, WV 25311
Window Coverings Assn. of Am. **[515]**, 11230 Gold Express Dr., Ste. 310-149, Gold River, CA 95670, (916)943-0979
Wine and Spirits Shippers Assn. **[44]**, 11800 Sunrise Valley Dr., Ste. 425, Reston, VA 20191, (703)860-2300
Wingate Inst. for Physical Educ. in Israel **[★3402]**
Wireless Communications Assn. Intl. **[852]**, 1333 H St. NW, Ste. 700 W, Washington, DC 20005-4754, (202)452-7823
Wolf Haven Intl. **[1048]**, 3111 Offut Lake Rd., Tenino, WA 98589, (360)264-4695
Women
   African-American Female Entrepreneurs Alliance **[914]**
   Amer. Assn. for Women in Community Colleges **[1698]**
   Assn. for Women in Aviation Maintenance **[915]**
   Center for Women's Bus. Res. **[916]**
   Finnish and Amer. Women's Network **[2270]**
   Natl. Women's Bus. Coun. **[917]**
   OWL - The Voice of Midlife and Older Women **[2271]**
   United Order True Sisters **[2835]**
   Women Church Convergence **[3040]**
   Women Contractors Assn. **[918]**
   Women Entrepreneurs in Sci. and Tech. **[919]**
   Women's Funding Network **[2272]**
   Women's Intl. Center **[2273]**
   Women's Learning Partnership for Rights, Development, and Peace **[2274]**
   Women's Missionary Soc., AME Church **[3041]**
   World Day of Prayer Intl. Comm. **[3042]**
   Amer. Legion Auxiliary Girls Nation **[2621]**
   Arab Amer. Women's Coun. **[2767]**
   Camping Women **[3301]**
   Dwa Fanm **[2663]**
   Global Action on Widowhood **[2755]**
   Intl. Assn. for Women's Mental Hea. **[2551]**
   Intl. Female Boxers Assn. **[3298]**
   Intl. Healthcare Volunteers **[2439]**
   Intl. Partnership for Reproductive Hea. **[2593]**
   Jamaica Unite **[2025]**
   Mercy Beyond Borders **[2169]**
   Natl. Assn. of Black Women in Constr. **[206]**
   Natl. Latina Bus. Women Assn. **[534]**
   Natl. Women in Agriculture Assn. **[937]**
   Orphans Africa **[2031]**
   Rising Intl. **[1908]**
   U.S. Women's Curling Assn. **[3310]**
   Women Against Prostate Cancer **[2331]**
   Women in Mgt. **[571]**
   Women Organizing for Change in Agriculture and NRM **[938]**
Women Against Prostate Cancer **[2331]**, 236 Massachusetts Ave. NE, Ste. 301, Washington, DC 20002, (202)580-5730
Women Church Convergence **[3040]**, PO Box 806, Mill Valley, CA 94942, (908)753-4636
Women Constr. Owners and Executives U.S.A. **[233]**, 1004 Duke St., Alexandria, VA 22314, (800)788-3548
Women Contractors Assn. **[918]**, 10807 Jones Rd., PMB 164, Houston, TX 77065, (713)807-9977
Women Entrepreneurs in Sci. and Tech. **[919]**, 485 Mass Ave., Ste. 300, Cambridge, MA 02139, (857)998-4040
Women in Govt. **[1352]**, 1319 F St. NW, Ste. 710, Washington, DC 20004, (202)333-0825
Women in Govt. Relations **[2656]**, 801 N Fairfax St., Ste. 211, Alexandria, VA 22314-1757, (703)299-8546
Women Grocers of Am. **[778]**, 1005 N Glebe Rd., Ste. 250, Arlington, VA 22201-5758, (703)516-0700
Women in Housing and Finance **[345]**, 400 N Washington St., Ste. 300, Alexandria, VA 22314, (703)683-4742

Women in Insurance and Financial Services **[504]**, 136 Everett Rd., Albany, NY 12205, (518)694-5506
Women in Intl. Security **[2744]**, 3600 North St. NW, Lower Level, Washington, DC 20007, (202)687-3366
Women Involved in Farm Economics **[2609]**, 8463 20th St. SW, Richardson, ND 58652, (702)938-4246
Women in Mgt. **[571]**, PO Box 1032, Dundee, IL 60118-7032, (708)386-0496
Women Nationally Active for Christ **[2848]**, PO Box 5002, Antioch, TN 37011-5002, (615)731-6812
Women Organizing for Change in Agriculture and NRM **[938]**, 1775 K St. NW, Ste. 410, Washington, DC 20006, (202)331-9099
Women in Packaging **[633]**, 4290 Bells Ferry Rd., Ste. 106-17, Kennesaw, GA 30144-1300, (678)594-6872
Women of Reform Judaism **[2966]**, 633 3rd Ave., New York, NY 10017, (212)650-4050
Women for Sobriety **[2250]**, PO Box 618, Quakertown, PA 18951-0618, (215)536-8026
Women for World Hea. **[2442]**, 16291 Fantasia Ln., Huntington Beach, CA 92649, (714)846-4524
Women Writing the West **[923]**, 8547 E Arapahoe Rd., No. J-541, Greenwood Village, CO 80112-1436
Women's Basketball Coaches Assn. **[3266]**, 4646 Lawrenceville Hwy., Lilburn, GA 30047, (770)279-8027
Women's Caucus for Art **[1722]**, Canal St. Sta., PO Box 1498, New York, NY 10013, (212)634-0007
Women's Env. and Development Org. **[2650]**, 355 Lexington Ave., 3rd Fl., New York, NY 10017, (212)973-0325
Women's Funding Network **[2272]**, 505 Sansome St., 2nd Fl., San Francisco, CA 94111, (415)441-0706
Women's Intl. Center **[2273]**, PO Box 669, Rancho Santa Fe, CA 92067-0669, (858)759-3567
Women's Intl. Network of Utility Professionals **[275]**, PO Box 817, Fergus Falls, MN 56538-0817, (218)731-1659
Women's League for Conservative Judaism **[2967]**, 475 Riverside Dr., Ste. 820, New York, NY 10115, (212)870-1260
Women's Learning Partnership for Rights, Development, and Peace **[2274]**, 4343 Montgomery Ave., Ste. 201, Bethesda, MD 20814, (301)654-2774
Women's Missionary Soc., AME Church **[3041]**, 1134 11th St. NW, Washington, DC 20001, (202)371-8886
Women's Rights
   Dwa Fanm **[2663]**
   Family Hea. Alliance **[2592]**
   Global Action on Widowhood **[2755]**
   Shining Hope for Communities **[2035]**
Women's Voices for the Earth **[1074]**, PO Box 8743, Missoula, MT 59807, (406)543-3747
Wonderful World of Wildlife **[1260]**, 88 E Main St., No. 134, Mendham, NJ 07945, (908)380-8810
Wood
   Intl. Wood Collectors Soc. **[3249]**
   Wood I-Joist Mfrs. Assn. **[389]**
Wood I-Joist Mfrs. Assn. **[389]**, PO Box 1088, Roseburg, OR 97470, (541)784-2817
Wood Machinery Mfrs. of Am. **[469]**, 500 Citadel Dr., Ste. 200, Commerce, CA 90040, (323)215-0330
Wood Moulding and Millwork Producers Assn. **[★151]**
Wood Trades
   Intl. Wood Collectors Soc. **[3249]**
   Wood I-Joist Mfrs. Assn. **[389]**
Woodcarvings
   Intl. Wood Collectors Soc. **[3249]**
Woodmen
   Intl. Wood Collectors Soc. **[3249]**
Word of Mouth Marketing Assn. **[607]**, 65 E Wacker Pl., Ste. 500, Chicago, IL 60601, (312)853-4400
Workers
   Green Collar Assn. **[296]**
   Professionals in Workers' Compensation **[920]**
Working Families Party **[2723]**, 2 Nevins St., 3rd Fl., Brooklyn, NY 11217, (718)222-3796
Working Riesenschnauzer Fed. **[3188]**, c/o Martha Galuszka, Membership Dir., 324 Oakwood Ave., West Hartford, CT 06110, (860)233-2286

Workmen's Compensation
   Professionals in Workers' Compensation **[920]**
World Action for Humanity **[2225]**, PO Box 193584, San Francisco, CA 94119-3584, (415)321-0701
World Airline Entertainment Assn. **[★101]**
World Airline Historical Soc. **[3089]**, PO Box 489, Ocoee, FL 34761
World Assn. of Natural Disaster Awareness and Assistance **[2147]**, 1865 SW 4th Ave., Ste. D5-A, Delray Beach, FL 33444, (561)450-5690
World Bird Sanctuary **[1261]**, 125 Bald Eagle Ridge Rd., Valley Park, MO 63088, (636)861-3225
World for Christ Crusade **[3015]**, 1005 Union Valley Rd., West Milford, NJ 07480, (973)728-3267
World Clown Assn. **[3148]**, PO Box 12215, Merrillville, IN 46410, (219)487-5317
World Coun. of Conservative/Masorti Synagogues **[2968]**, 3080 Broadway, New York, NY 10027, (212)280-6039
World Coun. of Credit Unions **[250]**, 5710 Mineral Point Rd., Madison, WI 53705-4454, (608)395-2000
World Day of Prayer Intl. Comm. **[3042]**, 475 Riverside Dr., Rm. 729, New York, NY 10115, (212)870-3049
A World of Difference Inst. **[2004]**, 605 3rd Ave., New York, NY 10158, (212)885-7811
World Emergency Relief **[2202]**, PO Box 1760, Temecula, CA 92593, (951)225-6700
World Fed. for Coral Reef Conservation **[1049]**, PO Box 942, Safety Harbor, FL 34695
World Gold Coun. **[616]**, 424 Madison Ave., 3rd Fl., New York, NY 10017, (212)317-3800
World Hea. Ambassador **[2443]**, 7611 Little River Tpke., Ste. 108W, Annandale, VA 22003, (703)658-7060
World Hea. Imaging, Telemedicine and Informatics Alliance **[2524]**, 47 W Polk St., Ste. 100-289, Chicago, IL 60605, (312)994-9940
World Hea. Partners **[2525]**, 2140 Shattuck Ave., Ste. 1110, Berkeley, CA 94704
World Hea. Services **[2526]**, 21122 Cabin Point Rd., Disputanta, VA 23842, (817)933-2088
World Hope Intl. **[2986]**, PO Box 17151, Baltimore, MD 21297-1151, (703)923-9414
The World Kuoshu Fed. **[3363]**, PO Box 20269, Baltimore, MD 21284-0269, (443)394-9222
World Martial Arts Assn. **[3364]**, Redeemer St. John's Church, 939 - 83rd St., Brooklyn, NY 11228, (718)833-9039
World Nature Coalition **[1262]**, 601 Pennsylvania Ave. NW, South Bldg., Ste. 900, Washington, DC 20004, (202)379-2974
World Notables
   Harry S. Truman Lib. Inst. for Natl. and Intl. Affairs **[1866]**
   William James Soc. **[1867]**
World Org. of China Painters **[3172]**, 2641 NW 10th St., Oklahoma City, OK 73107-5407, (405)521-1234
World Org. of Webmasters **[475]**, PO Box 1743, Folsom, CA 95630, (916)989-2933
World Peace One **[2112]**, 5135 Dearborn St., Pittsburgh, PA 15224, (412)363-9792
World Pet Assn. **[656]**, 135 W Lemon Ave., Monrovia, CA 91016-2809, (626)447-2222
World Relief **[2923]**, 7 E Baltimore St., Baltimore, MD 21202, (443)451-1900
World Shoe Assn. **[46]**, 15821 Ventura Blvd., Ste. 415, Encino, CA 91436-2974, (818)379-9400
World Sound Healing Org. **[2155]**, PO Box 389, Ascutney, VT 05030, (802)674-9585
World Spark **[1990]**, 1635 SE Malden St., Portland, OR 97202, (503)245-7899
World Spine Care **[2595]**, 801 N Tustin Ave., Ste. 202, Santa Ana, CA 92705, (714)547-9822
World Sport Stacking Assn. **[3412]**, 11 Inverness Way S, Englewood, CO 80112, (303)962-5672
World Team **[3016]**, 1431 Stuckert Rd., Warrington, PA 18976, (215)491-4900
World Traditional Karate Org. **[3365]**, 138 Bradley Ave., Staten Island, NY 10314
World Vets **[1902]**, 802 1st Ave. N, Fargo, ND 58102, (877)688-8387
World Vision Intl. **[3026]**, 800 W Chestnut Ave., Monrovia, CA 91016-3198, (626)303-8811
World War II War Brides Assn. **[3076]**, 1125 Pinon Oak Dr., Prescott, AZ 86305, (928)237-1581

World War II
    509th Parachute Infantry Assn. **[3082]**
World Watusi Assn. **[993]**, PO Box 2610, Glen Rose,
    TX 76043, (254)898-0157
WorldatWork **[299]**, 14040 N Northsight Blvd.,
    Scottsdale, AZ 85260, (480)951-9191
WorldHope Corps **[2040]**, 11 Ardsleigh Dr., Madison,
    NJ 07940, (973)714-0023
Worldwide Assurance for Employees of Public Agen-
    cies **[1304]**, 433 Park Ave., Falls Church, VA
    22046, (703)790-8010
Worldwide Pollution Control Assn. **[683]**, 12190 Hub-
    bard St., Livonia, MI 48150, (734)525-0300
Writers
    North Amer. Case Res. Assn. **[921]**
    Sisters in Crime **[922]**
    Women Writing the West **[923]**
    Writers Guild of Am. West **[3470]**
Writers Guild of Am. West **[3470]**, 7000 W Third St.,
    Los Angeles, CA 90048, (323)951-4000
Writers Guild Found. **[★3470]**
Writing
    Amer. Handwriting Anal. Found. **[1868]**
Wuqu' Kawoq **[2527]**, PO Box 91, Bethel, VT 05032
Wyman Worldwide Hea. Partners **[2528]**, 227
    Mechanic St., Ste. 3, Lebanon, NH 03766

Y

Yacht Brokers Assn. of Am. **[591]**, 105 Eastern Ave.,
    Ste. 104, Annapolis, MD 21403, (410)940-6345
YMCA
    Assn. of YMCA Professionals **[2275]**

Yoga
    Self-Realization Fellowship **[3043]**
    Silver Age Yoga **[2606]**
    Yoga Res. Found. **[3044]**
Yoga Res. Found. **[3044]**, 6111 SW 74th Ave.,
    Miami, FL 33143, (305)666-2006
Young Professionals in Energy **[1465]**, 600 Travis
    St., Ste. 2310, Houston, TX 77002, (832)429-6344
Young Women's Christian Association of the U.S.A.
    [2282], 2025 M St. NW, Ste. 550, Washington, DC
    20036, (202)467-0801
Youth
    Amer. Youth Found. **[3045]**
    Boys' Towns of Italy **[2276]**
    Global Youth Action Network **[2756]**
    I Have a Dream Found. **[2277]**
    Natl. 4-H Coun. **[2278]**
    Natl. Assn. of Police Athletic Leagues **[2279]**
    Robert F. Kennedy Center for Justice and Human
        Rights **[2280]**
    U.S. Junior Chamber of Commerce **[3506]**
    Youth for Christ/U.S.A. **[3046]**
    Youth Venture **[924]**
    Youth to Youth Intl. **[2281]**
    Amer. Legion Baseball **[3257]**
    EcoVentures Intl. **[1075]**
    Girls for a Change **[1956]**
    Girls on the Run Intl. **[3379]**
    Global Ambassadors for Children **[2715]**
    Intl. Performing Arts for Youth **[1834]**
    Iranian Alliances Across Borders **[2796]**
    Jamaica Unite **[2025]**

    Junior Optimist Octagon Intl. **[2222]**
    Kids Making a Difference **[952]**
    Kids for Peace **[2717]**
    Student Peace Alliance **[2720]**
    Union of North Amer. Vietnamese Students Assn.
        [2832]
    Young Professionals in Energy **[1465]**
Youth for Christ/U.S.A. **[3046]**, PO Box 4478, Engle-
    wood, CO 80155, (303)843-9000
Youth in Model Railroading **[3215]**, 12990 Prince Ct.,
    Broomfield, CO 80020-5419, (303)466-2857
Youth Venture **[924]**, 1700 N Moore Ave., Ste. 2000,
    Arlington, VA 22209, (703)527-4126
Youth With a Mission **[3017]**, PO Box 26479,
    Colorado Springs, CO 80936-6479, (719)380-0505
Youth to Youth Intl. **[2281]**, 547 E 11th Ave.,
    Columbus, OH 43221, (614)224-4506
Yugntruf - Youth for Yiddish **[1791]**, 419 Lafayette
    St., 2nd Fl., New York, NY 10003, (212)889-0381
YWCA
    Young Women's Christian Association of the
        U.S.A. **[2282]**

Z

Zambia Hope Intl. **[1991]**, Hope Mountain Found.,
    5235 Westview Dr., Ste. 100, Frederick, MD
    21703, (301)624-0061
Zeta Phi Eta **[3512]**, 95 Park Ave., Washington, NJ
    07882
ZigBee Alliance **[853]**, 2400 Camino Ramon, Ste.
    375, San Ramon, CA 94583, (925)275-6607
Zoology
    Intl. Soc. of Protistologists **[1558]**

A star before a book entry number signifies that the name is not listed separately, but is mentioned within the entry.